TENTH EDITION

Managerial Economics

Mark Hirschey

University of Kansas

THOMSON
★
SOUTH-WESTERN

Australia · Canada · Mexico · Singapore · Spain · United Kingdom · United States

Managerial Economics, 10e
Mark Hirschey

Editor-in-Chief:
Jack Calhoun

VP, Team Director:
Michael P. Roche

Sr. Acquisitions Editor:
Peter Adams

Publisher of Economics:
Michael B. Mercier

Sr. Developmental Editor:
Jan Lamar

Sr. Production Editor:
Elizabeth A. Shipp

Executive Marketing Manager:
Lisa L. Lysne

Media Technology Editor:
Vicky True

Media Developmental Editor:
Peggy Buskey

Media Production Editor:
Pam Wallace

Manufacturing Coordinator:
Sandy Milewski

Internal Designer:
Rik Moore

Cover Designer:
Rik Moore

Cover Photograph:
© Photo Disc, Inc.

Production House:
Rebecca Gray Design

Printer:
Quebecor World Versailles

Library of Congress Control Number: 2002021600

For Christine—I still do.

Preface

Over the past 30 years, managerial economics has grown from a core course requirement in MBA and advanced undergraduate programs to emerge as an important branch of applied economics. The role of managers in corporations, not-for-profit institutions, and government agencies has become even more important, and the need to improve resource use in all types of organizations has become much more visible. The information age of the new millennium has put so much more data at the disposal of managers that "information overload" and the "paralysis of analysis" have become common complaints. Widespread volatility in input prices and availability, the rapid pace of technical change, plus ongoing globalization of the marketplace all combine to make difficult the efficient use of economic resources and information. Dynamic change in the economic environment also makes it difficult to accurately assess demand and supply conditions, as it increases the need for timely and effective managerial decision making. Sound economic analysis has never been more important—regardless of whether the decision-making unit is an individual, household, firm, nonprofit organization, or government agency.

A key feature of this text is its depiction of the firm as a cohesive, unified organization. The basic valuation model is constructed and used as the underlying economic model of the firm. Each topic in the text is then related to an element of the value maximization model. In this manner, effective management is seen to involve an integration of the accounting, finance, marketing, personnel, and production functions. This integrative approach demonstrates that important managerial decisions are *interdisciplinary* in the truest sense of the word. Over the years, I have come to appreciate that students find the presentation of the business firm as a unified whole, rather than a series of discrete, unrelated parts, as one of the most valuable lessons of managerial economics.

Although both microeconomic and macroeconomic relations have implications for managerial decision making, this text concentrates on microeconomic topics of particular importance. Following the development of the economic model of the firm, the vital role of profits is examined. Because the decision-making process often requires an elementary understanding of economic and statistical relations, a number of basic economic relations, statistical concepts, and optimization techniques are described early in the text. Because the demand for a firm's products plays a major role in determining its profitability and ongoing success, demand analysis and estimation is an essential area of study. An important part of this investigation is a study of the basic forces of demand and supply. This naturally leads to a discussion of economic forecasting and methods for assessing forecast reliability. Production theory, cost analysis, and linear programming techniques are then explored as means for understanding the economics of resource allocation and employment.

Another important topic is market structure analysis, which provides a foundation for studying the external economic environment and for examining the pricing practices needed for successful management. The role of government in the market economy, including the constraints it imposes on business, requires a careful examination of regulation and antitrust law. Given the government's increasing role in the demand and supply for basic services, such as education and health care, a careful consideration of the use of economic principles in public management is also provided. Finally, risk analysis and capital budgeting are shown as methods for introducing marginal analysis into the long-range strategic planning and control process. The risk analysis and capital budgeting process is not only important within firms, hospitals, and other economic organizations; it is also vital to society as a whole because it pertains to the allocation of scarce capital resources.

Managerial Economics, Tenth Edition, takes a practical problem-solving approach to the study of managerial economics. The text focuses on the economics—not the mathematics—of the managerial decision process. When appropriate, quantitative methods and tools are introduced to give greater insight into the technique of economic analysis and to facilitate the practical use of economics in decision situations. However, the emphasis throughout the text is clearly on economic intuition as a practical tool for problem solving.

CHANGES IN THE TENTH EDITION

For 30 years, *Managerial Economics* and *Fundamentals of Managerial Economics* have played an important role in shaping the teaching of managerial economics. Both were published to achieve a simple objective: to help students understand how fundamental economic concepts can be used to understand and improve the managerial decision-making process. Despite sharing this common objective, *Managerial Economics* and *Fundamentals of Managerial Economics* use slightly different methods. *Managerial Economics* features an intuitive *calculus-based* treatment of economic theory and analysis, whereas *Fundamentals of Managerial Economics* uses an intuitive *noncalculus-based* approach.

Students and instructors will find that *Managerial Economics*, Tenth Edition, provides an efficient calculus-based introduction and guide to the optimization process. Chapter 2, "Economic Optimization," illustrates how the concept of a derivative can be used as a practical tool to understand and apply marginal analysis. "Multivariate Optimization and the Lagrangian Technique," Appendix 2A at the end of Chapter 2, examines the process of optimization for equations with three or more variables. Such techniques are especially helpful when managers face constrained optimization problems, or decision situations with limited alternatives. Throughout the text, a wide variety of problems describing real-world decisions can be solved using such techniques.

Like *Fundamentals of Managerial Economics*, students and instructors will find that *Managerial Economics*, Tenth Edition, provides an intuitive guide to marginal analysis and basic economic relations. Although differential calculus is an obviously helpful tool for understanding the process of economic optimization, it is important that students not let mathematical manipulation get in the way of their basic grasp of economic concepts. The concept of a marginal can also be described graphically in an intuitive noncalculus-based approach. Once students learn to grasp the importance of marginal revenue and marginal cost concepts, the process of economic optimization becomes intuitively obvious. Although those using a noncalculus-based approach can safely skip parts of Chapter 2 and Appendix 2A, all other material is fully and completely assessable. With repeat practice using a wide variety of problems and examples throughout the text, all students are able to gain a simple, practical understanding of how economics can be used to improve managerial decisions.

Students and instructors will find that *Managerial Economics*, Tenth Edition, uses a wide variety of examples and simple numerical problems to illustrate the application of managerial economics in practical situations. The nature of the decision process and the role that economic analysis plays are emphasized throughout. This is no "cut and paste" job. *Managerial Economics*,

Tenth Edition, has been thoroughly rewritten to give students and their instructors the option to adopt a calculus-based approach for learning how to apply economic reasoning to understand and improve managerial decisions. In preparation for *Managerial Economics*, Tenth Edition, I've used both calculus-based and noncalculus-based approaches in my own MBA classes. Both work.

Of course, the environment in which managerial decisions are made is constantly changing. To maintain its value as an educational resource, a textbook must be modified and updated. This revision of *Managerial Economics* contains a number of important additions and refinements. Every chapter has been updated in response to valuable suggestions provided by students and instructors and to reflect recent developments in the field. The following section highlights some of most important changes.

Content

- Chapter 2, "Economic Optimization," illustrates how the concept of a derivative can be used as a practical tool to understand and apply marginal analysis. A new Appendix 2A, "Multivariate Optimization and the Lagrangian Technique," examines the process of optimization for equations with three or more variables.

- Chapter 4, "Demand Analysis," has been expanded to include a discussion of utility theory as a basis for demand analysis, including income and substitution effects.

- Chapter 5, "Demand Estimation," has been greatly simplified to focus on the intuitive appeal of elasticity analysis and to better illustrate the use of real-world data in the regression-based approach to demand estimation.

- Chapter 6, "Forecasting," has been simplified to bring focus on the comparative strengths and weaknesses of alternative forecasting techniques. Important strengths and limitations of macroeconomic and microeconomic forecasting techniques are stressed.

- Chapter 7, "Production Analysis and Compensation Policy," has been revised and expanded to clarify how marginal analysis forms the basis for human resource management.

- Chapter 10, "Perfect Competition and Monopoly," and Chapter 11, "Monopolistic Competition and Oligopoly," have been extensively revised to better illustrate the use of economic methodology and game theory to devise and execute an effective competitive strategy in light of market structure considerations. Recent changes in economic census information and market structure measurement are also emphasized.

- Chapter 12, "Pricing Practices," has been revised to improve upon the explanation of essential elements of markup pricing policies and transfer pricing principles.

- Chapter 13, "Regulation of the Market Economy," has undergone comprehensive revision to offer perspective on recent moves to deregulate and re-regulate various types of private-market activity. Added perspective on the size-efficiency issue is provided by considering the link between firm size and profitability for both U.S. and global competitors.

- Chapter 14, "Risk Analysis," has been revised to better explain the wide variety of business risks and the special risks borne by firms with multinational operations. The use of game theory to aid in decision making under uncertainty is also more fully examined.

- Chapter 16, "Organization Structure and Corporate Governance," has been expanded to further document the importance of organizational architecture to managerial economics.

- Chapter 17, "Public Management," has been revised and simplified to show how economic principles can be used to understand and improve the allocation of public-sector resources.

Learning Aids

- Each chapter incorporates a wide variety of simple numerical examples and detailed practical illustrations of chapter concepts. These features portray the valuable use and real-world implications of covered material.

- Each chapter now includes *four* "Managerial Applications" boxes to show current examples of how the concepts introduced in managerial economics are actually used in real-world situations. New managerial applications based on articles from the Internet or *The Wall Street Journal* are provided. This feature stimulates student interest and offers a popular basis for classroom discussion.

- The text incorporates several new regression-based illustrations of chapter concepts using actual company data or data adapted from real-world situations. Like all aspects of the text, this material is self-contained and intuitive.

- Effective managers in the new millennium must be sensitive to the special challenges posed by an increasingly global marketplace. To increase student awareness of such issues, the text also features a number of examples, managerial applications, and case studies that relate to global business topics.

- Each chapter has a case study that provides in-depth treatment of chapter concepts. To meet the needs of all instructors and students, many of these case studies are written to allow, but do not require, a computer-based approach. The case study data and detailed solutions are provided to adopters on the textbook support Web site—**http://hirschey.swcollege.com**. (Students can also access the data at the same Web site.) These case studies are especially helpful to instructors who wish to more fully incorporate the use of basic spreadsheet and statistical software in their courses.

- After having been subject to necessary revision and class testing, fully 340 new end-of-chapter questions and problems are provided. Questions are designed to give students the opportunity to grasp basic concepts on an intuitive level and express their understanding in a nonquantitative fashion. Problems cover a wide variety of decision situations and illustrate the role of economic analysis from within a simple numerical framework.

- Each chapter includes *two* self-test problems to show students how economic tools and techniques can be used to solve practical business problems. These self-test problems are a proven study aid that greatly enhances the learning value of end-of-chapter questions and problems.

Ancillary Package

Managerial Economics, Tenth Edition, is supported by the most comprehensive ancillary package available in managerial economics to make teaching and learning the material both easy and enjoyable.

Instructor's Manual The *Instructor's Manual* offers learning suggestions and detailed answers and solutions for all chapter questions and problems. As mentioned previously, the case study data and detailed solutions are provided to adopters on the textbook support Web site—**http://hirschey.swcollege.com**.

Study Guide The *Study Guide* furnishes a detailed line summary of major concepts for each chapter, a brief discussion of important economic relations as they are covered in the text, and an expanded set of 160 solved problems. This completely new edition has undergone extensive class testing and analysis. Based on the comments of students and instructors alike, this new study guide is highly recommended as a valuable learning resource. If you cannot find the study guide at your bookstore, you can also purchase it by going to the student resource section of the text Web site (**http://hirschey.swcollege.com**). The ISBN for the study guide is 0-324-17158-7.

Test Bank A comprehensive *Test Bank* offers a variety of multiple-choice questions and one-step and multistep problems for every chapter. Full solutions are included, of course. With a selection of over 500 questions and problems, the *Test Bank* is a valuable tool for exam preparation.

ExamView Computerized testing software contains all of the questions in the printed test bank. This program is an easy-to-use test creation software compatible with Microsoft Windows. Instructors can add or edit questions, instructions, and answers, and select questions by previewing them on the screen, selecting them randomly, or selecting them by number. Instructors can also create and administer quizzes online, whether over the Internet, a local area network (LAN), or a wide area network (WAN).

PowerPoint PowerPoint slides are available for use by students as an aid to note-taking and by instructors for enhancing their lectures. They can be downloaded from the text Web site—**http://hirschey.swcollege.com**.

Excel for Economics New to this edition is an interactive software program prepared by Dr. Thomas Palm, Emeritus, Portland State University. This powerful software package is a student's interactive introduction to a revolutionary approach to learning microeconomics. The power of the Excel spreadsheet, on either the PC or the Macintosh platform, is used to present economic models in a live, interactive context. This software is only available for download at the Hirschey Web site—**http://hirschey.swcollege.com**.

IRCD The IRCD (Instructor's Resource CD-ROM) includes an electronic version of the *Instructor's Manual*, *Test Bank*, *ExamView*, and PowerPoint slides.

WebTutor WebTutor is an interactive, Web-based student supplement on BlackBoard or WebCT that harnesses the power of the Internet to deliver innovative learning aids that actively engage students. The instructor can incorporate WebTutor as an integral part of the course, or the students can use it on their own as a study guide. Benefits to students include automatic and immediate feedback from quizzes and exams; interactive, multimedia-rich explanation of concepts; online exercises that reinforce what students have learned; flashcards that include audio support; and greater interaction and involvement through online discussion forums.

InfoTrac *InfoTrac College Edition* is packaged with every new copy of the textbook. It is a fully searchable online university library containing complete articles and their images. This database provides instructors and their students with four months' access to hundreds of scholarly and popular publications—all reliable sources, including magazines, journals, encyclopedias, and newsletters.

Textbook Support Web Site The data and detailed solutions for the case studies included in the textbook are available to adopters at **http://hirschey.swcollege.com**. The data for the case studies is available to students at the same Web site. Instructor and student supplements are also available for download at the Hirschey Web site.

For the latest information about the ancillary package, please contact your local representative and visit the South-Western Web site at **http://www.swcollege.com**.

Acknowledgments

A number of people have aided in the preparation of *Managerial Economics*, Tenth Edition. Helpful suggestions and constructive comments have been received from many instructors and students who have used previous editions. Numerous reviewers have also provided insights and assistance in clarifying difficult material.

The University of Kansas, students, and colleagues have provided a stimulating environment and general intellectual support. I am grateful for their efforts. I am also indebted to the South-Western staff and would like to thank Peter Adams, senior acquisitions editor; Jan Lamar, senior developmental editor; Libby Shipp; senior production editor; Rik Moore, design project manager; and Lisa Lysne, executive marketing manager, for their special efforts. Finally, I want to thank my wife Chris for her encouragement, support, and assistance.

Every effort has been made to minimize errors in the text. However, errors do occasionally slip through despite diligent efforts to provide an error-free package of text and ancillary materials. Readers are invited to correspond with me directly concerning any corrections or other suggestions.

Finally, more than ever before, it is obvious that economic efficiency is an essential ingredient in the successful management of both private-sector and public-sector organizations. Like any dynamic area of study, the field of managerial economics continues to undergo profound change in response to the challenges imposed by a rapidly evolving environment. It is exciting to participate in these developments. I sincerely hope that *Managerial Economics*, Tenth Edition, contributes to a better understanding of the usefulness of economic theory and methodology to managerial practice.

Mark Hirschey
mhirschey@ku.edu
July 2002

MARK HIRSCHEY

Mark Hirschey, Ph.D. (University of Wisconsin-Madison), is Professor and Stockton Research Fellow in the School of Business at the University of Kansas, where he teaches undergraduate and graduate courses in managerial economics and finance. Professor Hirschey is president of the Association of Financial Economists and member of several professional organizations. He has published articles in the *American Economic Review, Journal of Accounting Research, Journal of Business, Journal of Business and Economic Statistics, Journal of Finance, Journal of Financial Economics, Journal of Industrial Economics, Review of Economics and Statistics,* and other leading academic journals. He is editor of *Advances in Financial Economics* and past editor of *Managerial and Decision Economics.* Professor Hirschey is also author of *Fundamentals of Managerial Economics* and *Investments: Theory and Applications.*

Contents in Brief

Contents

Overview of Managerial Economics

CHAPTER ONE

Nature and Scope of Managerial Economics

Warren E. Buffett, the celebrated chairman and chief executive officer of Omaha, Nebraska–based Berkshire Hathaway, Inc., started an investment partnership with $100 in 1956 and has gone on to accumulate a personal net worth in excess of $30 billion. As both a manager and an investor, Buffett is renowned for focusing on the economics of businesses.

Berkshire's collection of operating businesses, including the GEICO Insurance Company, International Dairy Queen, Inc., the Nebraska Furniture Mart, and See's Candies, commonly earn 30 percent to 50 percent per year on invested capital. This is astonishingly good performance in light of the 10 percent to 12 percent return typical of industry in general. A second and equally important contributor to Berkshire's outstanding performance is a handful of substantial holdings in publicly traded common stocks, such as The American Express Company, The Coca-Cola Company, and The Washington Post Company, among others. As both manager and investor, Buffett looks for "wonderful businesses" with outstanding economic characteristics: high rates of return on invested capital, substantial profit margins on sales, and consistent earnings growth. Complicated businesses that face fierce competition or require large capital investment are shunned.[1]

Buffett's success is powerful testimony to the practical usefulness of managerial economics. Managerial economics answers fundamental questions. When is the market for a product so attractive that entry or expansion becomes appealing? When is exit preferable to continued operation? Why do some professions pay well, while others offer only meager pay? Successful managers make good decisions, and one of their most useful tools is the methodology of managerial economics.

---

1   Information about Warren Buffett's investment philosophy and Berkshire Hathaway, Inc., can be found on the Internet (http://www.berkshirehathaway.com).

HOW IS MANAGERIAL ECONOMICS USEFUL?

managerial economics

Applies economic tools and techniques to business and administrative decision making

Managerial economics applies economic theory and methods to business and administrative decision making. Managerial economics prescribes rules for improving managerial decisions. Managerial economics also helps managers recognize how economic forces affect organizations and describes the economic consequences of managerial behavior. It links economic concepts with quantitative methods to develop vital tools for managerial decision making. This process is illustrated in Figure 1.1.

Evaluating Choice Alternatives

Managerial economics identifies ways to efficiently achieve goals. For example, suppose a small business seeks rapid growth to reach a size that permits efficient use of national media advertising. Managerial economics can be used to identify pricing and production strategies to help meet this short-run objective quickly and effectively. Similarly, managerial economics provides production and marketing rules that permit the company to maximize net profits once it has achieved growth or market share objectives.

FIGURE 1.1

Managerial Economics Is a Tool for Improving Management Decision Making

Managerial economics uses economic concepts and quantitative methods to solve managerial problems.

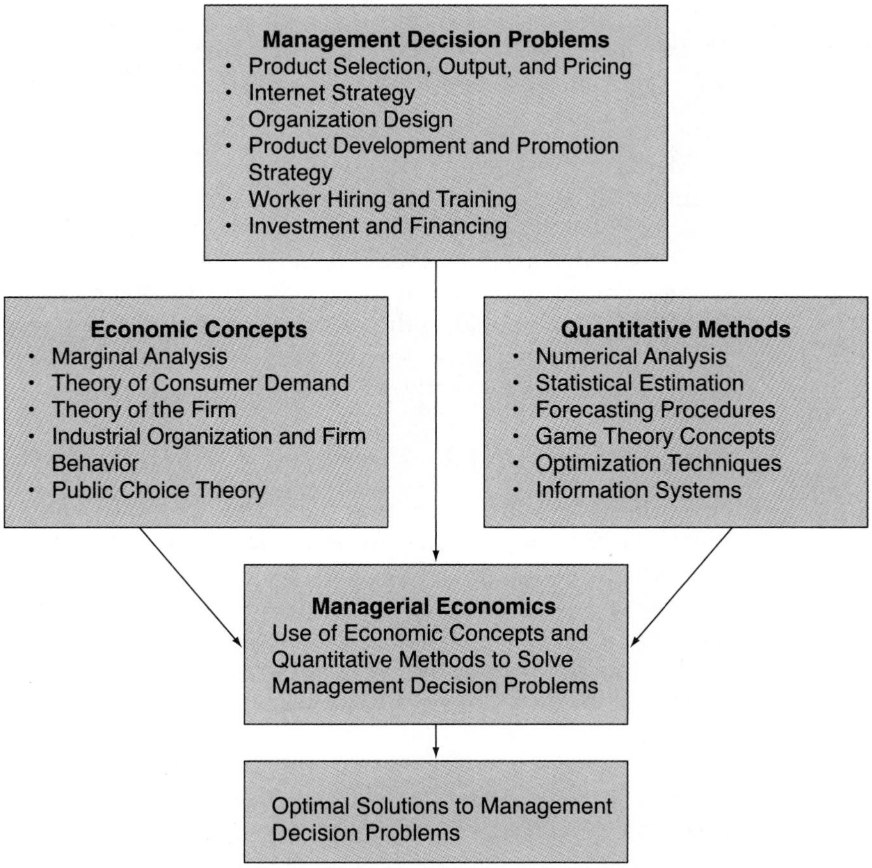

Management Decision Problems
- Product Selection, Output, and Pricing
- Internet Strategy
- Organization Design
- Product Development and Promotion Strategy
- Worker Hiring and Training
- Investment and Financing

Economic Concepts
- Marginal Analysis
- Theory of Consumer Demand
- Theory of the Firm
- Industrial Organization and Firm Behavior
- Public Choice Theory

Quantitative Methods
- Numerical Analysis
- Statistical Estimation
- Forecasting Procedures
- Game Theory Concepts
- Optimization Techniques
- Information Systems

Managerial Economics
Use of Economic Concepts and Quantitative Methods to Solve Management Decision Problems

Optimal Solutions to Management Decision Problems

MANAGERIAL APPLICATION   1.1

Managerial Ethics

In *The Wall Street Journal*, it is not hard to find evidence of unscrupulous business behavior. However, unethical conduct is neither consistent with value maximization nor with the enlightened self-interest of management and other employees. If honesty did not pervade corporate America, the ability to conduct business would collapse. Eventually, the truth always comes out, and when it does the unscrupulous lose out. For better or worse, we are known by the standards we adopt.

To become successful in business, everyone must adopt a set of principles. Ethical rules to keep in mind when conducting business include the following:

- Above all else, keep your word. Say what you mean, and mean what you say.

- Do the right thing. A handshake with an honorable person is worth more than a ton of legal documents from a corrupt individual.

- Accept responsibility for your mistakes, and fix them. Be quick to share credit for success.

- Leave something on the table. Profit *with* your customer, not *off* your customer.

- Stick by your principles. Principles are not for sale at any price.

Does the "high road" lead to corporate success? Consider the experience of one of America's most famous winners—Omaha billionaire Warren E. Buffett, chairman of Berkshire Hathaway, Inc. Buffett and Charlie Munger, the number-two man at Berkshire, are famous for doing multimillion-dollar deals on the basis of a simple handshake. At Berkshire, management relies upon the character of the people that they are dealing with rather than expensive accounting audits, detailed legal opinions, or liability insurance coverage. Buffett says that after some early mistakes, he learned to go into business only with people whom he likes, trusts, and admires. Although a company will not necessarily prosper because its managers display admirable qualities, Buffett says he has never made a good deal with a bad person.

Doing the right thing not only makes sense from an ethical perspective, but it makes business $ense, too!

See: Emelie Rutherford, "Lawmakers Involved with Enron Probe Had Personal Stake in the Company," *The Wall Street Journal Online*, March 4, 2002 (http://online.wsj.com).

Managerial economics has applications in both profit and not-for-profit sectors. For example, an administrator of a nonprofit hospital strives to provide the best medical care possible given limited medical staff, equipment, and related resources. Using the tools and concepts of managerial economics, the administrator can determine the optimal allocation of these limited resources. In short, managerial economics helps managers arrive at a set of operating rules that aid in the efficient use of scarce human and capital resources. By following these rules, businesses, nonprofit organizations, and government agencies are able to meet objectives efficiently.

Making the Best Decision

To establish appropriate decision rules, managers must understand the economic environment in which they operate. For example, a grocery retailer may offer consumers a highly price-sensitive product, such as milk, at an extremely low markup over cost—say, 1 percent to 2 percent—while offering less price-sensitive products, such as nonprescription drugs, at markups of as high as 40 percent over cost. Managerial economics describes the logic of this pricing practice with respect to the goal of profit maximization. Similarly, managerial economics reveals that auto import quotas reduce the availability of substitutes for domestically produced cars, raise auto prices, and create the possibility of monopoly profits for domestic manufacturers. It does not explain whether imposing quotas is good public policy; that is a decision involving broader political considerations. Managerial economics only describes the predictable economic consequences of such actions.

Managerial economics offers a comprehensive application of economic theory and methodology to management decision making. It is as relevant to the management of government agencies, cooperatives, schools, hospitals, museums, and similar not-for-profit institutions as it is to the management of profit-oriented businesses. Although this text focuses primarily on business applications, it also includes examples and problems from the government and non-profit sectors to illustrate the broad relevance of managerial economics.

THEORY OF THE FIRM

At its simplest level, a business enterprise represents a series of contractual relationships that specify the rights and responsibilities of various parties (see Figure 1.2). People directly involved include customers, stockholders, management, employees, and suppliers. Society is also involved because businesses use scarce resources, pay taxes, provide employment opportunities, and produce much of society's material and services output. Firms are a useful device for producing and distributing goods and services. They are economic entities and are best analyzed in the context of an economic model.

Expected Value Maximization

theory of the firm
Basic model of business

expected value maximization
Optimization of profits in light of uncertainty and the time value of money

value of the firm
Present value of the firm's expected future net cash flows

present value
Worth in current dollars

The model of business is called the **theory of the firm**. In its simplest version, the firm is thought to have profit maximization as its primary goal. The firm's owner-manager is assumed to be working to maximize the firm's short-run profits. Today, the emphasis on profits has been broadened to encompass uncertainty and the time value of money. In this more complete model, the primary goal of the firm is long-term **expected value maximization**.

The **value of the firm** is the present value of the firm's expected future net cash flows. If cash flows are equated to profits for simplicity, the value of the firm today, or its **present value**,

FIGURE 1.2

The Corporation Is a Legal Device

The firm can be viewed as a confluence of contractual relationships that connect suppliers, investors, workers, and management in a joint effort to serve customers.

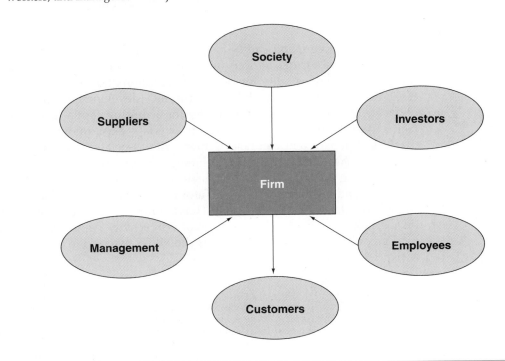

is the value of expected profits or cash flows, discounted back to the present at an appropriate interest rate.[2]

This model can be expressed as follows:

$$\text{Value of the Firm} = \text{Present Value of Expected Future Profits}$$

(1.1)

$$= \frac{\pi_1}{(1 + i)^1} + \frac{\pi_2}{(1 + i)^2} + \cdots + \frac{\pi_n}{(1 + i)^n}$$

$$= \sum_{t=1}^{n} \frac{\pi_t}{(1 + i)^t}$$

Here, $\pi_1, \pi_2, \ldots \pi_n$ represent expected profits in each year, t, and i is the appropriate interest, or discount, rate. The final form for Equation 1.1 is simply a shorthand expression in which sigma (Σ) stands for "sum up" or "add together." The term

$$\sum_{t=1}^{n}$$

means, "Add together as t goes from 1 to n the values of the term on the right." For Equation 1.1, the process is as follows: Let $t = 1$ and find the value of the term $\pi_1/(1 + i)^1$, the present value of year 1 profit; then let $t = 2$ and calculate $\pi_2/(1 + i)^2$, the present value of year 2 profit; continue until $t = n$, the last year included in the analysis; then add up these present-value equivalents of yearly profits to find the current or present value of the firm.

Because profits (π) are equal to total revenues (TR) minus total costs (TC), Equation 1.1 can be rewritten as

(1.2)

$$\text{Value} = \sum_{t=1}^{n} \frac{TR_t - TC_t}{(1 + i)^t}$$

This expanded equation can be used to examine how the expected value maximization model relates to a firm's various functional departments. The marketing department often has primary responsibility for product promotion and sales (TR); the production department has primary responsibility for product development costs (TC); and the finance department has primary responsibility for acquiring capital and, hence, for the discount factor (i) in the denominator. Important overlaps exist among these functional areas. The marketing department can help reduce costs associated with a given level of output by influencing customer order size and timing. The production department can stimulate sales by improving quality. Other departments, for example, accounting, human resources, transportation, and engineering, provide information and services vital to sales growth and cost control. The determination of TR and TC is a complex task that requires recognizing important interrelations among the various areas of firm activity. An important concept in managerial economics is that managerial decisions should be analyzed in terms of their effects on value, as expressed in Equations 1.1 and 1.2.

---

2 Discounting is required because profits obtained in the future are less valuable than profits earned presently. To understand this concept, one needs to recognize that $1 in hand today is worth more than $1 to be received a year from now, because $1 today can be invested and, with interest, grow to a larger amount by the end of the year. If we had $1 and invested it at 10 percent interest, it would grow to $1.10 in one year. Thus, $1 is defined as the present value of $1.10 due in one year when the appropriate interest rate is 10 percent.

Constraints and the Theory of the Firm

Managerial decisions are often made in light of constraints imposed by technology, resource scarcity, contractual obligations, laws, and regulations. To make decisions that maximize value, managers must consider how external constraints affect their ability to achieve organization objectives.

Organizations frequently face limited availability of essential inputs, such as skilled labor, raw materials, energy, specialized machinery, and warehouse space. Managers often face limitations on the amount of investment funds available for a particular project or activity. Decisions can also be constrained by contractual requirements. For example, labor contracts limit flexibility in worker scheduling and job assignments. Contracts sometimes require that a minimum level of output be produced to meet delivery requirements. In most instances, output must also meet quality requirements. Some common examples of output quality constraints are nutritional requirements for feed mixtures, audience exposure requirements for marketing promotions, reliability requirements for electronic products, and customer service requirements for minimum satisfaction levels.

Legal restrictions, which affect both production and marketing activities, can also play an important role in managerial decisions. Laws that define minimum wages, health and safety standards, pollution emission standards, fuel efficiency requirements, and fair pricing and marketing practices all limit managerial flexibility.

The role that constraints play in managerial decisions makes the topic of constrained optimization a basic element of managerial economics. Later chapters consider important economic implications of self-imposed and social constraints. This analysis is important because value maximization and allocative efficiency in society depend on the efficient use of scarce economic resources.

Limitations of the Theory of the Firm

optimize
Seek the best solution

satisfice
Seek satisfactory rather than optimal results

Some critics question why the value maximization criterion is used as a foundation for studying firm behavior. Do managers try to **optimize** (seek the best result) or merely **satisfice** (seek satisfactory rather than optimal results)? Do managers seek the sharpest needle in a haystack (optimize), or do they stop after finding one sharp enough for sewing (satisfice)? How can one tell whether company support of the United Way, for example, leads to long-run value maximization? Are generous salaries and stock options necessary to attract and retain managers who can keep the firm ahead of the competition? When a risky venture is turned down, is this inefficient risk avoidance? Or does it reflect an appropriate decision from the standpoint of value maximization?

It is impossible to give definitive answers to questions like these, and this dilemma has led to the development of alternative theories of firm behavior. Some of the more prominent alternatives are models in which size or growth maximization is the assumed primary objective of management, models that argue that managers are most concerned with their own personal utility or welfare maximization, and models that treat the firm as a collection of individuals with widely divergent goals rather than as a single, identifiable unit. These alternative theories, or models, of managerial behavior have added to our understanding of the firm. Still, none can supplant the basic value maximization model as a foundation for analyzing managerial decisions. Examining why provides additional insight into the value of studying managerial economics.

Research shows that vigorous competition in markets for most goods and services typically forces managers to seek value maximization in their operating decisions. Competition in the capital markets forces managers to seek value maximization in their financing decisions as well. Stockholders are, of course, interested in value maximization because it affects their rates of return on common stock investments. Managers who pursue their own interests instead of stockholders' interests run the risk of losing their jobs. Buyout pressure from unfriendly firms

MANAGERIAL APPLICATION   1.2

The World Is Turning to Capitalism and Democracy

Capitalism and democracy are mutually reinforcing. Some philosophers have gone so far as to say that capitalism and democracy are intertwined. Without capitalism, democracy may be impossible. Without democracy, capitalism may fail. At a minimum, freely competitive markets give consumers broad choices and reinforce the individual freedoms protected in a democratic society. In democracy, government does not grant individual freedom. Instead, the political power of government emanates from the people. Similarly, the flow of economic resources originates with the individual customer in a capitalistic system. It is not centrally directed by government.

Capitalism is socially desirable because of its decentralized and customer-oriented nature. The menu of products to be produced is derived from market price and output signals originating in competitive markets, not from the output schedules of a centralized planning agency. Resources and products are also allocated through market forces. They are not earmarked on the basis of favoritism or social status. Through their purchase decisions, customers dictate the quantity and quality of products brought to market.

Competition is a fundamentally attractive feature of the capitalistic system because it keeps costs and prices as low as possible. By operating efficiently, firms are able to produce the maximum quantity and quality of goods and services possible. Mass production is, by definition, production for the masses. Competition also limits concentration of economic and political power. Similarly, the democratic form of government is inconsistent with consolidated economic influence and decision making.

Totalitarian forms of government are in retreat. China has experienced violent upheaval as the country embarks on much-needed economic and political reforms. In the former Soviet Union, Eastern Europe, India, and Latin America, years of economic failure forced governments to dismantle entrenched bureaucracy and install economic incentives. Rising living standards and political freedom have made life in the West the envy of the world. Against this backdrop, the future is bright for capitalism and democracy!

See: Karen Richardson, "China and India Could Lead Asia in Technology Spending," *The Wall Street Journal Online*, March 4, 2002 (http://online.wsj.com).

("raiders") has been considerable during recent years. Unfriendly takeovers are especially hostile to inefficient management that is replaced. Further, because recent studies show a strong correlation between firm profits and managerial compensation, managers have strong economic incentives to pursue value maximization through their decisions.

It is also sometimes overlooked that managers must fully consider costs and benefits before they can make reasoned decisions. Would it be wise to seek the best technical solution to a problem if the costs of finding this solution greatly exceed resulting benefits? Of course not. What often appears to be satisficing on the part of management can be interpreted as value-maximizing behavior once the costs of information gathering and analysis are considered. Similarly, short-run growth maximization strategies are often consistent with long-run value maximization when the production, distribution, or promotional advantages of large firm size are better understood.

Finally, the value maximization model also offers insight into a firm's voluntary "socially responsible" behavior. The criticism that the traditional theory of the firm emphasizes profits and value maximization while ignoring the issue of social responsibility is important and will be discussed later in the chapter. For now, it will prove useful to examine the concept of profits, which is central to the theory of the firm.

PROFIT MEASUREMENT

The free enterprise system would fail without profits and the profit motive. Even in planned economies, where state ownership rather than private enterprise is typical, the profit motive is increasingly used to spur efficient resource use. In the former Eastern Bloc countries, the former Soviet Union, China, and other nations, new profit incentives for managers and employees have led to higher product quality and cost efficiency. Thus, profits and the profit motive play a growing role in the efficient allocation of economic resources worldwide.

Business Versus Economic Profit

business profit
Residual of sales revenue minus the explicit accounting costs of doing business

The general public and the business community typically define profit as the residual of sales revenue minus the explicit costs of doing business. It is the amount available to fund equity capital after payment for all other resources used by the firm. This definition of profit is accounting profit, or **business profit**.

The economist also defines profit as the excess of revenues over costs. However, inputs provided by owners, including entrepreneurial effort and capital, are resources that must be compensated. The economist includes a normal rate of return on equity capital plus an opportunity cost for the effort of the owner-entrepreneur as costs of doing business, just as the interest paid on debt and the wages are costs in calculating business profit. The risk-adjusted **normal rate of return** on capital is the minimum return necessary to attract and retain investment. Similarly, the opportunity cost of owner effort is determined by the value that could be received in alternative employment. In economic terms, profit is business profit minus the implicit (noncash) costs of capital and other owner-provided inputs, used by the firm. This profit concept is frequently referred to as **economic profit**.

normal rate of return
Average profit necessary to attract and retain investment

economic profit
Business profit minus the implicit costs of capital and any other owner-provided inputs

The concepts of business profit and economic profit can be used to explain the role of profits in a free enterprise economy. A normal rate of return, or profit, is necessary to induce individuals to invest funds rather than spend them for current consumption. Normal profit is simply a cost for capital; it is no different from the cost of other resources, such as labor, materials, and energy. A similar price exists for the entrepreneurial effort of a firm's owner-manager and for other resources that owners bring to the firm. These opportunity costs for owner-provided inputs offer a primary explanation for the existence of business profits, especially among small businesses.

Variability of Business Profits

profit margin
Business profit expressed as a percentage of sales

return on stockholders' equity
Accounting net income divided by the book value of total assets minus total liabilities

In practice, reported profits fluctuate widely. Table 1.1 shows business profits for a well-known sample of 30 industrial giants: those companies that comprise the Dow Jones Industrial Average. Business profit is often measured in dollar terms or as a percentage of sales revenue, called **profit margin**, as in Table 1.1. The economist's concept of a normal rate of profit is typically assessed in terms of the realized rate of **return on stockholders' equity** (ROE). Return on stockholders' equity is defined as accounting net income divided by the book value of the firm. As seen in Table 1.1, the average ROE for industrial giants found in the Dow Jones Industrial Average falls in a broad range of around 15 percent to 25 percent per year. Although an average annual ROE of roughly 10 percent can be regarded as a typical or normal rate of return in the United States and Canada, this standard is routinely exceeded by companies such as Coca-Cola, which has consistently earned a ROE in excess of 35 percent per year. It is a standard seldom met by International Paper, a company that has suffered massive losses in an attempt to cut costs and increase product quality in the face of tough environmental regulations and foreign competition.

Some of the variation in ROE depicted in Table 1.1 represents the influence of differential risk premiums. In the pharmaceuticals industry, for example, hoped-for discoveries of effective therapies for important diseases are often a long shot at best. Thus, profit rates reported by Merck and other leading pharmaceutical companies overstate the relative profitability of the drug industry; it could be cut by one-half with proper risk adjustment. Similarly, reported profit rates can overstate differences in economic profits if accounting error or bias causes

TABLE 1.1

The Profitability of Industrial Giants Included in the Dow Jones Industrial Average

Company Name	Industry	Net Income ($ Millions)	Sales ($ Millions)	Net Worth ($ Millions)	Return on Sales (Margin)	Return on Equity (ROE)
Alcoa Inc.	Metals and Mining (Div.)	1,489	22,936	11,422	6.5%	13.0%
American Express	Financial Services (Div.)	2,810	23,675	11,684	11.9%	24.0%
AT&T Corp.	Telecom. Services	6,630	65,981	107,908	10.0%	6.1%
Boeing	Aerospace/Defense	2,511	51,321	11,020	4.9%	22.8%
Caterpillar Inc.	Machinery	1,053	20,175	5,600	5.2%	18.8%
Citigroup Inc.	Financial Services (Div.)	13,519	n.a.	66,206	n.a.	20.4%
Coca-Cola	Beverage (Soft Drink)	3,669	20,458	9,316	17.9%	39.4%
Disney (Walt)	Entertainment	1,892	25,020	24,100	7.6%	7.8%
DuPont	Chemical (Basic)	2,884	28,268	13,299	10.2%	21.7%
Eastman Kodak	Precision Instrument	1,441	13,994	3,428	10.3%	42.0%
Exxon Mobil Corp.	Petroleum (Integrated)	16,910	206,083	70,757	8.2%	23.9%
General Electric	Electrical Equipment	12,735	63,807	50,492	20.0%	25.2%
General Motors	Auto and Truck	5,472	184,632	30,175	3.0%	18.1%
Hewlett-Packard	Computer and Peripherals	3,561	48,782	14,209	7.3%	25.1%
Home Depot	Retail Building Supply	2,581	45,738	15,004	5.6%	17.2%
Honeywell International	Diversified Co.	2,293	25,023	9,707	9.2%	23.6%
Intel Corp.	Semiconductor	10,669	33,726	37,322	31.6%	28.6%
International Business Machine	Computer and Peripherals	8,093	88,396	20,624	9.2%	39.2%
International Paper	Paper and Forest Products	969	28,180	12,034	3.4%	8.1%
Johnson & Johnson	Medical Supplies	4,800	29,139	18,808	16.5%	25.5%
McDonald's Corp.	Restaurant	1,977	14,243	9,204	13.9%	21.5%
Merck & Co.	Drug	6,822	40,363	14,832	16.9%	46.0%
Microsoft Corp.	Computer Software and Services	10,003	25,296	47,289	39.5%	21.2%
Minnesota Mining	Chemical (Diversified)	1,857	16,724	6,531	11.1%	28.4%
Morgan (J.P.) Chase	Bank	5,727	n.a.	42,338	n.a.	13.5%
Philip Morris	Tobacco	8,510	80,356	15,005	10.6%	56.7%
Procter & Gamble	Household Products	4,397	39,244	12,010	11.2%	36.6%
SBC Communications	Telecom. Services	7,746	53,313	31,463	14.5%	24.6%
United Technologies	Diversified Co.	1,808	26,583	8,094	6.8%	22.3%
Wal-Mart Stores	Retail Store	6,295	191,329	31,343	3.3%	20.1%
Averages		**5,371**	**54,028**	**25,374**	**9.9%**	**21.2%**

n.a. means "not applicable."

Data source: *Value Line Investment Survey*, March 4, 2002 (http://www.valueline.com). Reproduced with the permission of Value Line Publishing, Inc.

investments with long-term benefits to be omitted from the balance sheet. For example, current accounting practice often fails to consider advertising or research and development expenditures as intangible investments with long-term benefits. Because advertising and research and development expenditures are immediately expensed rather than capitalized and written off over their useful lives, intangible assets can be grossly understated for certain companies. The balance sheet of Coca-Cola does not reflect the hundreds of millions of dollars spent to establish and maintain the brand-name recognition of *Coca-Cola*, just as Merck's balance sheet fails to reflect research dollars spent to develop important product names like *Vasotec* (for the treatment of high blood pressure), *Zocor* (an antiarthritic drug), and *Singulair* (asthma medication). As a result, business profit rates for both Coca-Cola and Merck overstate each company's true economic performance.

WHY DO PROFITS VARY AMONG FIRMS?

However, even after risk adjustment and modification to account for the effects of accounting error and bias, ROE numbers reflect significant variation in economic profits. Many firms earn significant economic profits or experience meaningful economic losses at any given point. To better understand real-world differences in profit rates, it is necessary to examine theories used to explain profit variations.

Frictional Theory of Economic Profits

frictional profit theory
Abnormal profits observed following unanticipated changes in demand or cost conditions

One explanation of economic profits or losses is **frictional profit theory**. It states that markets are sometimes in disequilibrium because of unanticipated changes in demand or cost conditions. Unanticipated shocks produce positive or negative economic profits for some firms.

For example, automated teller machines (ATMs) make it possible for customers of financial institutions to easily obtain cash, enter deposits, and make loan payments. ATMs render obsolete many of the functions that used to be carried out at branch offices and foster ongoing consolidation in the industry. Similarly, new user-friendly software increases demand for high-powered personal computers (PCs) and boosts returns for efficient PC manufacturers. Alternatively, a rise in the use of plastics and aluminum in automobiles drives down the profits of steel manufacturers. Over time, barring impassable barriers to entry and exit, resources flow into or out of financial institutions, computer manufacturers, and steel manufacturers, thus driving rates of return back to normal levels. During interim periods, profits might be above or below normal because of frictional factors that prevent instantaneous adjustment to new market conditions.

Monopoly Theory of Economic Profits

monopoly profit theory
Above-normal profits caused by barriers to entry that limit competition

A further explanation of above-normal profits, **monopoly profit theory**, is an extension of frictional profit theory. This theory asserts that some firms are sheltered from competition by high barriers to entry. Economies of scale, high capital requirements, patents, or import protection enable some firms to build monopoly positions that allow above-normal profits for extended periods. Monopoly profits can even arise because of luck or happenstance (being in the right industry at the right time) or from anticompetitive behavior. Unlike other potential sources of above-normal profits, monopoly profits are often seen as unwarranted. Thus, monopoly profits are usually taxed or otherwise regulated. Chapters 10, 11, and 13 consider the causes and consequences of monopoly and how society attempts to mitigate its potential costs.

Innovation Theory of Economic Profits

innovation profit theory
Above-normal profits that follow successful invention or modernization

An additional theory of economic profits, **innovation profit theory**, describes the above-normal profits that arise following successful invention or modernization. For example, innovation profit theory suggests that Microsoft Corporation has earned superior rates of return because it successfully developed, introduced, and marketed the Graphical User Interface, a superior image-based rather than command-based approach to computer software instructions. Microsoft has continued to earn above-normal returns as other firms scramble to offer a wide variety of "user friendly" software for personal and business applications. Only after competitors have introduced and successfully saturated the market for user-friendly software will Microsoft profits be driven down to normal levels. Similarly, McDonald's Corporation earned above-normal rates of return as an early innovator in the fast-food business. With increased competition from Burger King, Wendy's, and a host of national and regional competitors,

McDonald's, like Apple, IBM, Xerox, and other early innovators, has seen its above-normal returns decline. As in the case of frictional or disequilibrium profits, profits that are due to innovation are susceptible to the onslaught of competition from new and established competitors.

Compensatory Theory of Economic Profits

compensatory profit theory
Above-normal rates of return that reward efficiency

Compensatory profit theory describes above-normal rates of return that reward firms for extraordinary success in meeting customer needs, maintaining efficient operations, and so forth. If firms that operate at the industry's average level of efficiency receive normal rates of return, it is reasonable to expect firms operating at above-average levels of efficiency to earn above-normal rates of return. Inefficient firms can be expected to earn unsatisfactory, below-normal rates of return.

Compensatory profit theory also recognizes economic profit as an important reward to the entrepreneurial function of owners and managers. Every firm and product starts as an idea for better serving some established or perceived need of existing or potential customers. This need remains unmet until an individual takes the initiative to design, plan, and implement a solution. The opportunity for economic profits is an important motivation for such entrepreneurial activity.

Role of Profits in the Economy

Each of the preceding theories describes economic profits obtained for different reasons. In some cases, several reasons might apply. For example, an efficient manufacturer may earn an above-normal rate of return in accordance with compensatory theory, but, during a strike by a competitor's employees, these above-average profits may be augmented by frictional profits. Similarly, Microsoft's profit position might be partly explained by all four theories: The company has earned high frictional profits while Adobe Systems, Computer Associates, Oracle, Veritas, and a host of other software companies tool up in response to the rapid growth in demand for user-friendly software; it has earned monopoly profits because it has some patent protection; it has certainly benefited from successful innovation; and it is well managed and thus has earned compensatory profits.

Economic profits play an important role in a market-based economy. Above-normal profits serve as a valuable signal that firm or industry output should be increased. Expansion by established firms or entry by new competitors often occurs quickly during high profit periods. Just as above-normal profits provide a signal for expansion and entry, below-normal profits provide a signal for contraction and exit. Economic profits are one of the most important factors affecting the allocation of scarce economic resources. Above-normal profits can also constitute an important reward for innovation and efficiency, just as below-normal profits can serve as a penalty for stagnation and inefficiency. Profits play a vital role in providing incentives for innovation and productive efficiency and in allocating scarce resources.

ROLE OF BUSINESS IN SOCIETY

Business contributes significantly to social welfare. The economy in the United States and several other countries has sustained notable growth over many decades. Benefits of that growth have also been widely distributed. Suppliers of capital, labor, and other resources all receive substantial returns for their contributions. Consumers benefit from an increasing quantity and quality of goods and services available for consumption. Taxes on the business profits of firms, as well as on the payments made to suppliers of labor, materials, capital, and other inputs, provide revenues needed to increase government services. All of these contributions to social welfare stem from the efficiency of business in serving economic needs.

MANAGERIAL APPLICATION   1.3

The "Tobacco" Issue

The "tobacco" issue is charged with emotion. From the standpoint of a business manager or individual investor, there is the economic question of whether or not it is *possible* to earn above-normal returns by investing in a product known for killing its customers. From a philosophical standpoint, there is also the ethical question of whether or not it is *desirable* to earn such returns, if available.

Among the well-known *gloomy* particulars are

- Medical studies suggest that breaking the tobacco habit may be as difficult as curing heroin addiction. This fuels the fire of those who seek to restrict smoking opportunities among children and "addicted" consumers.

- With the declining popularity of smoking, there are fewer smokers among potential jurors. This may increase the potential for adverse jury decisions in civil litigation against the tobacco industry.

- Prospects for additional "sin" and "health care" taxes on smoking appear high.

Some underappreciated *positive* counterpoints to consider are

- Although smoking is most common in the most price-sensitive sector of our society, profit margins remain sky high.

- Tax revenues from smokers give the government an incentive to keep smoking legal.

- High excise taxes kill price competition in the tobacco industry. Huge changes in manufacturer prices barely budge retail prices.

Although many suggest that above-average returns can be derived from investing in the tobacco business, a "greater fool" theory may be at work here. Tobacco companies and their investors only profit by finding "greater fools" to pay high prices for products that many would not buy for themselves. This is risky business, and a business plan that seldom works out in the long run.

See: Ann Zimmerman, "Wal-Mart Rejects Shareholder Call to Explain Policies on Tobacco Ads," *The Wall Street Journal Online*, March 1, 2002 (http://online.wsj.com).

Why Firms Exist

Firms exist by public consent to serve social needs. If social welfare could be measured, business firms might be expected to operate in a manner that would maximize some index of social well-being. Maximization of social welfare requires answering the following important questions: What combination of goods and services (including negative by-products, such as pollution) should be produced? How should goods and services be provided? How should goods and services be distributed? These are the most vital questions faced in a free enterprise system, and they are key issues in managerial economics.

In a free market economy, the economic system produces and allocates goods and services according to the forces of demand and supply. Firms must determine what products customers want, bid for necessary resources, and then offer products for sale. In this process, each firm actively competes for a share of the customer's dollar. Suppliers of capital, labor, and raw materials must then be compensated out of sales proceeds. The share of revenues paid to each supplier depends on relative productivity, resource scarcity, and the degree of competition in each input market.

Role of Social Constraints

Although the process of market-determined production and allocation of goods and services is highly efficient, there are potential difficulties in an unconstrained market economy. Society has developed a variety of methods for alleviating these problems through the political system. One possible difficulty with an unconstrained market economy is that certain groups could gain excessive economic power. To illustrate, the economics of producing and distributing electric power are such that only one firm can efficiently serve a given community. Furthermore, there

The Internet Revolution

In the fifteenth century, the printing press made widespread dissemination of written information easy and inexpensive. The printing press sends information from the printer to the general public. It is a one-way method of communication. In the new millennium, we have the Internet. Not only is transmitting information via the Internet cheaper and faster than in the printed form, but it also is a two-way method of communication. The Internet is a revolutionary communications tool because it has the potential for feedback from one consumer to another, or from one company to another.

For the first time, the Internet gives firms and their customers in New York City, in Jackson Hole, Wyoming, and in the wilds of Africa the same timely access to widely publicized economic news and information. With the Internet, up-to-the-minute global news and analysis are just mouse clicks away. The Internet also gives global consumers and businesses the opportunity to communicate with one another and thereby *create* fresh news and information. Over the Internet, customers can communicate about pricing or product quality concerns. Businesses can communicate about the threat posed by potential competitors. The Internet makes the production of economic news and information democratic by reducing the information-gathering advantages of very large corporations and the traditional print and broadcast media.

With the Internet, the ability to communicate economic news and information around the globe is just a mouse click away. With the Internet, companies are able to keep in touch with suppliers on a continuous basis. Internet technology makes "just in time" production possible, if not mandatory. It also puts companies in touch with their customers 24 hours a day, 7 days a week. 24/7 is more than a way of doing business; it has become the battle cry of the customer-focused organization.

Internet technology is a blessing for efficient companies with products customers crave. It is a curse for the inefficient and slow to adapt.

See: Thomas E. Webber, "Political Meddling in the Internet Is on the Rise and Needs to End," *The Wall Street Journal Online*, March 4, 2002 (http://online.wsj.com).

are no good substitutes for electric lighting. As a result, electric companies are in a position to exploit consumers; they could charge high prices and earn excessive profits. Society's solution to this potential exploitation is regulation. Prices charged by electric companies and other utilities are held to a level that is thought to be just sufficient to provide a fair rate of return on investment. In theory, the regulatory process is simple; in practice, it is costly, difficult to implement, and in many ways arbitrary. It is a poor, but sometimes necessary, substitute for competition.

An additional problem can occur when, because of economies of scale or other barriers to entry, a limited number of firms serve a given market. If firms compete fairly with each other, no difficulty arises. However, if they conspire with one another in setting prices, they may be able to restrict output, obtain excessive profits, and reduce social welfare. Antitrust laws are designed to prevent such collusion. Like direct regulation, antitrust laws contain arbitrary elements and are costly to administer, but they too are necessary if economic justice, as defined by society, is to be served.

To avoid the potential for worker exploitation, laws have been developed to equalize bargaining power of employers and employees. These labor laws require firms to allow collective bargaining and to refrain from unfair practices. The question of whether labor's bargaining position is too strong in some instances also has been raised. For example, can powerful national unions such as the Teamsters use the threat of a strike to obtain excessive increases in wages? Those who believe this to be the case have suggested that the antitrust laws should be applied to labor unions, especially those that bargain with numerous small employers.

A market economy also faces difficulty when firms impose costs on others by dumping wastes into the air or water. If a factory pollutes the air, causing nearby residents to suffer lung ailments, a meaningful cost is imposed on these people and society in general. Failure to shift these costs back onto the firm and, ultimately, to the consumers of its products means that the firm and its customers benefit unfairly by not having to pay the full costs of production. Pollution and other externalities may result in an inefficient and inequitable allocation of resources. In both government and business, considerable attention is being directed to the problem of internalizing these costs. Some of the practices used to internalize social costs include setting health and safety standards for products and work conditions, establishing emissions limits on manufacturing processes and products, and imposing fines or closing firms that do not meet established standards.

Social Responsibility of Business

What does all this mean with respect to the value maximization theory of the firm? Is the model adequate for examining issues of social responsibility and for developing rules that reflect the role of business in society?

As seen in Figure 1.3, firms are primarily economic entities and can be expected to analyze social responsibility from within the context of the economic model of the firm. This is an important consideration when examining inducements used to channel the efforts of business

FIGURE 1.3

Value Maximization Is a Complex Process

Value maximization is a complex process that involves an ongoing sequence of successful management decisions.

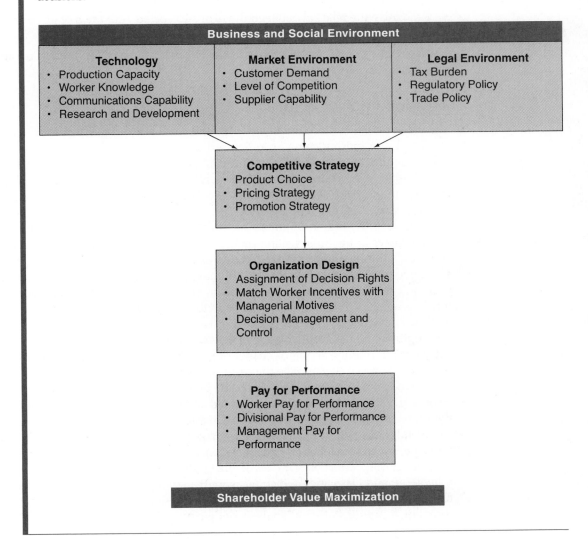

in directions that society desires. Similar considerations should also be taken into account before applying political pressure or regulations to constrain firm operations. For example, from the consumer's standpoint it is desirable to pay low rates for gas, electricity, and telecom services. If public pressures drive rates down too low, however, utility profits could fall below the level necessary to provide an adequate return to investors. In that event, capital would flow out of regulated industries, innovation would cease, and service would deteriorate. When such issues are considered, the economic model of the firm provides useful insight. This model emphasizes the close relation between the firm and society, and indicates the importance of business participation in the development and achievement of social objectives.

STRUCTURE OF THIS TEXT

Objectives

This text should help you accomplish the following objectives:

- Develop a clear understanding of the economic method in managerial decision making;
- Acquire a framework for understanding the nature of the firm as an integrated whole as opposed to a loosely connected set of functional departments; and
- Recognize the relation between the firm and society and the role of business as a tool for social betterment.

Throughout the text, the emphasis is on the *practical* application of economic analysis to managerial decision problems.

Development of Topics

The value maximization framework is useful for characterizing actual managerial decisions and for developing rules that can be used to improve those decisions. The basic test of the value maximization model, or any model, is its ability to explain real-world behavior. This text highlights the complementary relation between theory and practice. Theory is used to improve managerial decision making, and practical experience leads to the development of better theory.

Chapter 2, "Economic Optimization," begins by examining the important role that marginal analysis plays in the optimization process. The balancing of marginal revenues and marginal costs to determine the profit-maximizing output level is explored, as are other fundamental economic relations that help organizations efficiently employ scarce resources. All of these economic relations are considered based on the simplifying assumption that cost and revenue relations are known with certainty. Later in the book, this assumption is relaxed, and the more realistic circumstance of decision making with uncertainty is examined. This material shows how optimization concepts can be effectively employed in situations when managers have extensive information about the chance or probability of certain outcomes, but the end result of managerial decisions cannot be forecast precisely.

The concepts of demand and supply are basic to understanding the effective use of economic resources. The general overview of demand and supply in Chapter 3 provides a framework for the more detailed inquiry that follows. Chapter 4, "Demand Analysis," emphasizes that the successful management of any organization requires a complete understanding of the demand for its products. The demand function relates the sales of a product to such important factors as the price of the product itself, prices of other goods, income, advertising, and even weather. The role of demand elasticities, which measure the strength of relations expressed in the demand function, is also emphasized. Given the challenges posed by a rapidly changing global environment, a careful statistical analysis of demand relations is often conducted to provide the information necessary for effective decision making. Tools used by managers in the statistical analysis of demand relations are the subject of Chapter 5, "Demand Estimation." Issues addressed in the prediction of demand and cost conditions are explored more fully in Chapter 6, "Forecasting." Material in this chapter provides a useful framework for the estimation of demand and cost relations.

Chapters 7, 8, and 9 examine production and cost concepts. The economics of resource employment in the manufacture and distribution of goods and services is the focus of this material. These chapters present economic analysis as a context for understanding the logic of managerial decisions and as a means for developing improved practices. Chapter 7, "Production Analysis and Compensation Policy," develops rules for optimal employment and demonstrates how labor and other resources can be used in a profit-maximizing manner. Chapter 8, "Cost Analysis and Estimation," focuses on the identification of cost-output relations so that appropriate decisions regarding product pricing, plant size and location, and so on can be made. Chapter 9, "Linear Programming," introduces a tool from the decision sciences that can be used to solve a variety of optimization problems. This technique offers managers input for short-run operating decisions and information helpful in the long-run planning process.

The remainder of the book builds on the foundation provided in Chapters 1 through 9 to examine a variety of topics in the theory and practice of managerial economics. Chapters 10 and 11 explore market structures and their implications for the development and implementation of effective competitive strategy. Demand and supply relations are integrated to examine the dynamics of economic markets. Chapter 10, "Perfect Competition and Monopoly," offers perspective on how product differentiation, barriers to entry, and the availability of information interact to determine the vigor of competition. Chapter 11, "Monopolistic Competition and Oligopoly," considers "competition among the few" for industries in which interactions among competitors are normal. Chapter 12, "Pricing Practices," shows how the forces of supply and demand interact under a variety of market settings to signal appropriate pricing policies. Importantly, this chapter analyzes pricing practices commonly observed in business and shows how they reflect the predictions of economic theory.

Chapter 13, "Regulation of the Market Economy," focuses on the role of government by considering how the external economic environment affects the managerial decision-making process. This chapter investigates how interactions among business, government, and the public result in antitrust and regulatory policies with direct implications for the efficiency and fairness of the economic system. Chapter 14, "Risk Analysis," illustrates how the predictions of economic theory can be applied in the real-world setting of uncertainty. Chapter 15, "Capital Budgeting," examines the key elements necessary for an effective planning framework for managerial decision making. It investigates the capital budgeting process and how firms combine demand, production, cost, and risk analyses to effectively make strategic long-run investment decisions. Chapter 16, "Organization Structure and Corporate Governance," is a new chapter that offers insight concerning the value-maximizing design of the firm. Finally, Chapter 17, "Public Management," studies how the tools and techniques of managerial economics can be used to analyze decisions in the public and not-for-profit sectors and how that decision-making process can be improved.

SUMMARY

Managerial economics links economics and the decision sciences to develop tools for managerial decision making. This approach is successful because it focuses on the application of economic analysis to practical business problem solving.

- **Managerial economics** applies economic theory and methods to business and administrative decision making.

- The basic model of the business enterprise is called the **theory of the firm**. The primary goal is seen as long-term **expected value maximization**. The **value of the firm** is the present value of the firm's expected future net cash flows, whereas **present value** is the value of expected cash flows discounted back to the present at an appropriate interest rate.

- Valid questions are sometimes raised about whether managers really **optimize** (seek the best solution) or merely **satisfice** (seek satisfactory rather than optimal results). Most often, especially when information costs are considered, managers can be seen as optimizing.

- **Business profit**, or accounting profit, is the residual of sales revenue minus the explicit accounting costs of doing business. Business profit often incorporates a **normal rate of return** on capital, or the minimum return necessary to attract and retain investment for a particular use. **Economic profit** is business profit minus the implicit costs of equity and other owner-provided inputs used by the firm. **Profit margin**, or net income divided by sales, and the **return on stockholders' equity**, or accounting net income divided by the book value of total assets minus total liabilities, are useful indicators of firm performance.

- **Frictional profit theory** describes abnormal profits observed following unanticipated changes in product demand or cost conditions. **Monopoly profit theory** asserts that above-normal profits are sometimes caused by barriers to entry that limit competition. **Innovation profit theory** describes above-normal profits that arise as a result of successful invention or modernization. **Compensatory profit theory** holds that above-normal rates of return can sometimes be seen as a reward to firms that are extraordinarily successful in meeting customer needs, maintaining efficient operations, and so forth.

The use of economic methodology to analyze and improve the managerial decision-making process combines the study of theory and practice. Although the logic of managerial economics is intuitively appealing, the primary virtue of managerial economics lies in its usefulness. It works!

QUESTIONS

Q1.1   Why is it appropriate to view firms primarily as economic entities?

Q1.2   Explain how the valuation model given in Equation 1.2 could be used to describe the integrated nature of managerial decision making across the functional areas of business.

Q1.3   Describe the effects of each of the following managerial decisions or economic influences on the value of the firm:

    A. The firm is required to install new equipment to reduce air pollution.

    B. Through heavy expenditures on advertising, the firm's marketing department increases sales substantially.

    C. The production department purchases new equipment that lowers manufacturing costs.

    D. The firm raises prices. Quantity demanded in the short run is unaffected, but in the longer run, unit sales are expected to decline.

    E. The Federal Reserve System takes actions that lower interest rates dramatically.

    F. An expected increase in inflation causes generally higher interest rates, and, hence, the discount rate increases.

Q1.4   It is sometimes argued that managers of large, publicly owned firms make decisions to maximize their own welfare as opposed to that of stockholders. Would such behavior create problems in using value maximization as a basis for examining managerial decision making?

Q1.5   How is the popular notion of business profit different from the economic profit concept described in the chapter? What role does the idea of normal profits play in this difference?

Q1.6   Which concept—the business profit concept or the economic profit concept—provides the more appropriate basis for evaluating business operations? Why?

Q1.7   What factors should be considered in examining the adequacy of profits for a firm or industry?

Q1.8   Why is the concept of self-interest important in economics?

Q1.9   "In the long run, a profit-maximizing firm would never knowingly market unsafe products. However, in the short run, unsafe products can do a lot of damage." Discuss this statement.

Q1.10 Is it reasonable to expect firms to take actions that are in the public interest but are detrimental to stockholders? Is regulation always necessary and appropriate to induce firms to act in the public interest?

CASE STUDY

Is Coca-Cola the "Perfect" Business?[3]

What does a perfect business look like? For Warren Buffett and his partner Charlie Munger, vice-chairman of Berkshire Hathaway, Inc., it looks a lot like Coca-Cola. To see why, imagine going back in time to 1885, to Atlanta, Georgia, and trying to invent from scratch a nonalcoholic beverage that would make you, your family, and all of your friends rich.

Your beverage would be nonalcoholic to ensure widespread appeal among both young and old alike. It would be cold rather than hot so as to provide relief from climatic effects. It must be ordered by name—a trademarked name. Nobody gets rich selling easy-to-imitate generic products. It must generate a lot of repeat business through what psychologists call conditioned reflexes. To get the desired positive conditioned reflex, you will want to make it sweet, rather than bitter, with no after-taste. Without any after-taste, consumers will be able to drink as much of your product as they like. By adding sugar to make your beverage sweet, it gains food value in addition to a positive stimulant. To get extra-powerful combinatorial effects, you may want to add caffeine as an additional stimulant. Both sugar and caffeine work; by combining them, you get more than a double effect—you get what Munger calls a "lollapalooza" effect. Additional combinatorial effects could be realized if you design the product to appear exotic. Coffee is another popular product, so making your beverage dark in color seems like a safe bet. By adding carbonation, a little fizz can be added to your beverage's appearance and its appeal.

To keep the lollapalooza effects coming, you will want to advertise. If people associate your beverage with happy times, they will tend to reach for it whenever they are happy, or want to be happy. (Isn't that always, as in "Always Coca-Cola"?) Make it available at sporting events, concerts, the beach, and at theme parks—wherever and whenever people have fun. Enclose your product in bright, upbeat colors that customers tend to associate with festive occasions (another combinatorial effect). Red and white packaging would be a good choice. Also make sure that customers associate your beverage with festive occasions. Well-timed advertising and price promotions can help in this regard—annual price promotions tied to the Fourth of July holiday, for example, would be a good idea.

To ensure enormous profits, profit margins and the rate of return on invested capital must both be high. To ensure a high rate of return on sales, the price charged must be substantially above unit costs. Because consumers tend to be least price sensitive for moderately priced items, you would like to have a modest "price point," say roughly \$1–\$2 per serving. This is a big problem for most beverages because water is a key ingredient, and water is very expensive to ship long distances. To get around this cost-of-delivery difficulty, you will not want to

---

3   See Charles T. Munger, "How Do You Get Worldly Wisdom?" *Outstanding Investor Digest*, December 29, 1997, 24–31.

CASE STUDY (continued)

FIGURE 1.4

Is Coca-Cola the "Perfect" Business?

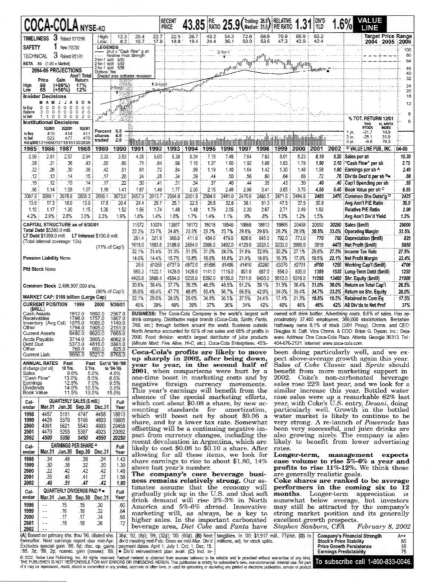

Reproduced with the permission of Value Line Publishing, Inc.

sell the beverage itself, but a key ingredient, like syrup, to local bottlers. By selling syrup to independent bottlers, your company can also better safeguard its "secret ingredients." This also avoids the problem of having to invest a substantial amount in bottling plants, machinery, delivery trucks, and so on. This minimizes capital requirements and boosts the rate of return on invested capital. Moreover, if you correctly price the key syrup ingredient, you can ensure that the enormous profits generated by carefully developed lollapalooza effects accrue to your company, and not to the bottlers. Of course, you want to offer independent bottlers the potential for highly satisfactory profits in order to provide the necessary incentive for them to push your product. You not only want to "leave something on the table" for the bottlers in terms of the bottlers' profit potential, but they in turn must also be encouraged to "leave something on the table" for restaurant and other customers. This means that you must demand that bottlers deliver a consistently high-quality product at carefully specified prices if they are to maintain their valuable franchise to sell your beverage in the local area.

If you had indeed gone back to 1885, to Atlanta, Georgia, and followed all of these suggestions, you would have created what you and I know as The Coca-Cola Company. To be sure, there would have been surprises along the way. Take widespread refrigeration, for example. Early on, Coca-Cola management saw the fountain business as the primary driver in cold carbonated beverage sales. They did not foretell that widespread refrigeration would make grocery store sales and in-home consumption popular. Still, much of Coca-Cola's success has been achieved because its management had, and still has, a good grasp of both the economics and the psychology of the beverage business. By getting into rapidly growing foreign markets with a winning formula, they hope to create local brand-name recognition, scale economies in distribution, and achieve other "first mover" advantages like the ones they have nurtured in the United States for more than 100 years.

As shown in Figure 1.4, in a world where the typical company earns 10 percent rates of return on invested capital, Coca-Cola earns three and four times as much. Typical profit rates, let alone operating losses, are unheard of at Coca-Cola. It enjoys large and growing profits, and requires practically no tangible capital investment. Almost its entire value is derived from brand equity derived from generations of advertising and carefully nurtured positive lollapalooza effects. On an overall basis, it is easy to see why Buffett and Munger regard Coca-Cola as a "perfect" business.

A. One of the most important skills to learn in managerial economics is the ability to identify a good business. Discuss at least four characteristics of a good business.

B. Identify and talk about at least four companies that you regard as having the characteristics listed here.

C. Suppose you bought common stock in each of the four companies identified here. Three years from now, how would you know if your analysis was correct? What would convince you that your analysis was wrong?

SELECTED REFERENCES

Addleson, Mark. "Stories About Firms: Boundaries, Structures, Strategies, and Processes." *Managerial & Decision Economics* 22 (June/August 2001): 169–182.

Austen-Smith, David. "Charity and the Bequest Motive: Evidence from Seventeenth-Century Wills." *Journal of Political Economy* 108 (December 2000): 1270–1291.

Baltagi, Badi H., and James M. Griffin. "The Econometrics of Rational Addiction: The Case of Cigarettes." *Journal of Business & Economic Statistics* 19 (October 2001): 449–454.

Block, Walter. "Cyberslacking, Business Ethics and Managerial Economics." *Journal of Business Ethics* 33 (October 2001): 225–231.

Demsetz, Harold, and Belén Villalonga. "Ownership Structure and Corporate Performance." *Journal of Corporate Finance* 7 (September 2001): 209–233.

Fourer, Robert, and Jean-Pierre Goux. "Optimization as an Internet Resource." *Interfaces* 31 (March 2001): 130–150.

Furubotn, Eirik G. "The New Institutional Economics and the Theory of the Firm." *Journal of Economic Behavior & Organization* 45 (June 2001): 133–153.

Grinols, Earl L., and David B. Mustard. "Business Profitability Versus Social Profitability: Evaluating Industries with Externalities—The Case of Casinos." *Managerial & Decision Economics* 22 (January–May 2001): 143–162.

Gruber, Jonathan, and Botond Köszegi. "Is Addiction 'Rational'? Theory and Evidence." *Quarterly Journal of Economics* 116 (November 2001): 1261–1303.

Harbaugh, William T., Kate Krause, and Timothy R. Berry. "Garp for Kids: On the Development of Rational Choice Behavior." *American Economic Review* 91 (December 2001): 1539–1545.

Karahan, R. Sitki. "Towards an Eclectic Theory of Firm Globalization." *International Journal of Management* 18 (December 2001): 523–532.

McWilliams, Abagail, and Donald Siegel. "Corporate Social Responsibility: A Theory of the Firm Perspective." *Academy of Management Review* 26 (January 2001): 117–127.

Muller, Holger M., and Karl Warneryd. "Inside Versus Outside Ownership: A Political Theory of the Firm." *Rand Journal of Economics* 32 (Autumn 2001): 527–541.

Subrahmanyam, Avanidhar, and Sheridan Titman. "Feedback from Stock Prices to Cash Flows." *Journal of Finance* 56 (December 2001): 2389–2414.

Woidtke, Tracie. "Agents Watching Agents? Evidence from Pension Fund Ownership and Firm Value." *Journal of Financial Economics* 63 (January 2002): 99–131.

CHAPTER TWO

Economic Optimization

Managers have to make tough choices that involve benefits and costs. Until recently, however, it was simply impractical to compare the relative pluses and minuses of a large number of managerial decisions under a wide variety of operating conditions. For many large and small organizations, economic optimization remained an elusive goal. It is easy to understand why early users of personal computers were delighted when they learned how easy it was to enter and manipulate operating information within spreadsheets. Spreadsheets were a pivotal innovation because they put the tools for insightful demand, cost, and profit analysis at the fingertips of managers and other decision makers. Today's low-cost but powerful PCs and user-friendly software make it possible to efficiently analyze company-specific data and broader industry and macroeconomic information from the Internet. It has never been easier nor more vital for managers to consider the implications of various managerial decisions under an assortment of operating scenarios.

Effective managers in the twenty-first century must be able to collect, organize, and process a vast assortment of relevant operating information. However, efficient information processing requires more than electronic computing capability; it requires a fundamental understanding of basic economic relations. Within such a framework, powerful PCs and a wealth of operating and market information become an awesome aid to effective managerial decision making.[1]

This chapter introduces a number of fundamental principles of economic analysis. These ideas form the basis for describing all demand, cost, and profit relations. Once the basics of economic relations are understood, the tools and techniques of optimization can be applied to find the best course of action.

---

1   See Kevin Voigt and William Fraser, "Are You a Bad Boss?" *The Wall Street Journal Online*, March 15, 2002 (http://www.online.wsj.com).

ECONOMIC OPTIMIZATION PROCESS

Effective managerial decision making is the process of arriving at the best solution to a problem. If only one solution is possible, then no decision problem exists. When alternative courses of action are available, the best decision is the one that produces a result most consistent with managerial objectives. The process of arriving at the best managerial decision is the goal of economic optimization and the focus of managerial economics.

Optimal Decisions

Should the quality of inputs be enhanced to better meet low-cost import competition? Is a necessary reduction in labor costs efficiently achieved through an across-the-board decrease in staffing, or is it better to make targeted cutbacks? Following an increase in product demand, is it preferable to increase managerial staff, line personnel, or both? These are the types of questions facing managers on a regular basis that require a careful consideration of basic economic relations. Answers to these questions depend on the objectives and preferences of management. Just as there is no single "best" purchase decision for all customers at all times, there is no single "best" investment decision for all managers at all times. When alternative courses of action are available, the decision that produces a result most consistent with managerial objectives is the **optimal decision**.

optimal decision
Choice alternative that produces a result most consistent with managerial objectives

A challenge that must be met in the decision-making process is characterizing the desirability of decision alternatives in terms of the objectives of the organization. Decision makers must recognize all available choices and portray them in terms of appropriate costs and benefits. The description of decision alternatives is greatly enhanced through application of the principles of managerial economics. Managerial economics also provides tools for analyzing and evaluating decision alternatives. Economic concepts and methodology are used to select the optimal course of action in light of available options and objectives.

Principles of economic analysis form the basis for describing demand, cost, and profit relations. Once basic economic relations are understood, the tools and techniques of optimization can be applied to find the best course of action. Most important, the theory and process of optimization gives practical insight concerning the value maximization theory of the firm. Optimization techniques are helpful because they offer a realistic means for dealing with the complexities of goal-oriented managerial activities.

Maximizing the Value of the Firm

In managerial economics, the primary objective of management is assumed to be maximization of the value of the firm. This *value maximization* objective was introduced in Chapter 1 and is again expressed in Equation 2.1:

(2.1)

$$\text{Value} = \sum_{t=1}^{n} \frac{\text{Profit}_t}{(1+i)^t} = \sum_{t=1}^{n} \frac{\text{Total Revenue}_t - \text{Total Cost}_t}{(1+i)^t}$$

Maximizing Equation 2.1 is a complex task that involves consideration of future revenues, costs, and discount rates. Total revenues are directly determined by the quantity sold and the prices received. Factors that affect prices and the quantity sold include the choice of products made available for sale, marketing strategies, pricing and distribution policies, competition, and the general state of the economy. Cost analysis includes a detailed examination of the prices and availability of various input factors, alternative production schedules, production methods, and so on. Finally, the relation between an appropriate discount rate and the company's mix of products and both operating and financial leverage must be determined. All these factors affect the value of the firm as described in Equation 2.1.

Greed Versus Self-Interest

Capitalism is based on voluntary exchange between self-interested parties. Given that the exchange is voluntary, both parties must perceive benefits, or profit, for market transactions to take place. If only one party were to benefit from a given transaction, there would be no incentive for the other party to cooperate, and no voluntary exchange would take place. A self-interested capitalist must also have in mind the interest of others. In contrast, a truly selfish individual is only concerned with himself or herself, without regard for the well-being of others. Self-interested behavior leads to profits and success under capitalism; selfish behavior does not.

Management guru Peter Drucker has written that the purpose of business is to create a customer—someone that will want to do business with you and your company on a regular basis. In a business deal, both parties must benefit. If not, there will be no ongoing business relationship.

The only way this can be done is to make sure that you continually take the customer's perspective. How can customer needs be met better, cheaper, or faster?

Don't wait for customers to complain or seek alternate suppliers: Seek out ways of helping before they become obvious. When customers benefit, so do you and your company. Take the customer's perspective, always. Similarly, it is best to see every business transaction from the standpoint of the person on the other side of the table.

In dealing with employees, it is best to be honest and forthright. If you make a mistake, admit it and go on. When management accepts responsibility for its failures, they gain the trust of employees and their help in finding solutions for the inevitable problems that always arise. In a job interview, for example, strive to see how you can create value for a potential employer. It is natural to see things from one's own viewpoint; it is typically much more beneficial to see things from the perspective of the person sitting on the other side of the table.

See: Ianthe Jeanne Dugan, "Before Enron, Greed Helped Sink the Respectability of Accounting," *The Wall Street Journal Online*, March 14, 2002 (http://online.wsj.com).

To determine the optimal course of action, marketing, production, and financial decisions must be integrated within a decision analysis framework. Similarly, decisions related to personnel retention and development, organization structure, and long-term business strategy must be combined into a single integrated system that shows how managerial initiatives affect all parts of the firm. The value maximization model provides an attractive basis for such an integration. Using the principles of economic analysis, it is also possible to analyze and compare the higher costs or lower benefits of alternative, suboptimal courses of action.

The complexity of completely integrated decision analysis—or global optimization—confines its use to major planning decisions. For many day-to-day operating decisions, managers typically use less complicated, partial optimization techniques. For example, the marketing department is usually required to determine the price and advertising strategy that achieves some sales goal given the firm's current product line and marketing budget. Alternatively, a production department might minimize the cost of output at a stated quality level.

The decision process, whether it is applied to fully integrated or partial optimization problems, involves two steps. First, important economic relations must be expressed in analytical terms. Second, various optimization techniques must be applied to determine the best, or optimal, solution in the light of managerial objectives. The following material introduces a number of concepts that are useful for expressing decision problems in an economic framework.

BASIC ECONOMIC RELATIONS

table
List of economic data

spreadsheet
Table of electronically stored data

Tables are the simplest and most direct form for presenting economic data. When these data are displayed electronically in the format of an accounting income statement or balance sheet, the tables are referred to as **spreadsheets**. When the underlying relation between economic data is simple, tables and spreadsheets may be sufficient for analytical purposes. In such

graph
Visual representation of data

equation
Analytical expression of functional relationships

instances, a simple **graph** or visual representation of the data can provide valuable insight. Complex economic relations require more sophisticated methods of expression. An **equation** is an expression of the functional relationship or connection among economic variables. When the underlying relation among economic variables is uncomplicated, equations offer a compact means for data description; when underlying relations are complex, equations are helpful because they permit the powerful tools of mathematical and statistical analysis to be used.

Functional Relations: Equations

The easiest way to examine basic economic concepts is to consider the functional relations incorporated in the basic valuation model. Consider the relation between output, Q, and total revenue, TR. Using functional notation, total revenue is

(2.2)
$$TR = f(Q)$$

Equation 2.2 is read, "Total revenue is a function of output." The value of the dependent variable (total revenue) is determined by the independent variable (output). The variable to the left of the equal sign is called the **dependent variable**. Its value depends on the size of the variable or variables to the right of the equal sign. Variables on the right-hand side of the equal sign are called **independent variables**. Their values are determined independently of the functional relation expressed by the equation.

dependent variable
Y variable determined by X values

independent variable
X variable determined separately from the Y variable

Equation 2.2 does not indicate the specific relation between output and total revenue; it merely states that some relation exists. Equation 2.3 provides a more precise expression of this functional relation:

(2.3)
$$TR = P \times Q$$

where P represents the price at which each unit of Q is sold. Total revenue is equal to price times the quantity sold. If price is constant at $1.50 regardless of the quantity sold, the relation between quantity sold and total revenue is

(2.4)
$$TR = \$1.50 \times Q$$

Data in Table 2.1 are specified by Equation 2.4 and graphically illustrated in Figure 2.1.

Total, Average, and Marginal Relations

Total, average, and marginal relations are very useful in optimization analysis. Whereas the definitions of totals and averages are well known, the meaning of marginals needs further

TABLE 2.1

Relation Between Total Revenue and Output; Total Revenue = $1.50 × Output

Total Revenue	Output	
$1.50	1	
3.00	2	
4.50	3	
6.00	4	
7.50	5	
9.00	6	

FIGURE 2.1

Relation Between Total Revenue and Output

When $P = \$1.50$, a one-unit increase in the quantity sold will increase total revenue by $1.50.

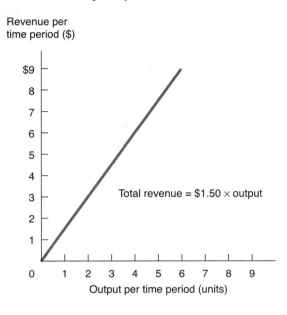

Revenue per time period ($)

Total revenue = $1.50 × output

Output per time period (units)

marginal
Change in the dependent variable caused by a one-unit change in an independent variable

marginal revenue
Change in total revenue associated with a one-unit change in output

marginal cost
Change in total cost following a one-unit change in output

marginal profit
Change in total profit due to a one-unit change in output

explanation. A **marginal** relation is the change in the dependent variable caused by a one-unit change in an independent variable. For example, **marginal revenue** is the change in total revenue associated with a one-unit change in output; **marginal cost** is the change in total cost following a one-unit change in output; and **marginal profit** is the change in total profit due to a one-unit change in output.

Table 2.2 shows the relation among totals, marginals, and averages for a simple profit function. Columns 1 and 2 display output and total profits. Column 3 shows the marginal profit earned for a one-unit change in output, whereas column 4 gives the average profit per unit at each level of output. The marginal profit earned on the first unit of output is $19. This is the change from $0 profits earned when zero units of output are sold to the $19 profit earned when one unit is produced and sold. The $33 marginal profit associated with the second unit of output is the increase in total profits (= $52 – $19) that results when output is increased from one to two units. When marginal profit is positive, total profit is increasing; when marginal profit is negative, total profit is decreasing. Table 2.2 illustrates this point. The marginal profit associated with each of the first seven units of output is positive, and total profits increase with output over this range. Because marginal profit of the eighth unit is negative, profits are reduced if output is raised to that level. Maximization of the profit function—or any function, for that matter—occurs at the point where the marginal switches from positive to negative.

When the marginal is greater than the average, the average must be increasing. For example, if a firm operates five retail stores with average annual sales of $350,000 per store and it opens a sixth store (the marginal store) that generates sales of $400,000, average sales per store will increase. If sales at the new (marginal) store are less than $350,000, average sales per store will decrease. Table 2.2 also illustrates the relation between marginal and average values. In going from four units of output to five, the marginal profit of $39 is greater than the $34 average profit at four units; therefore, average profit increases to $35. The $35 marginal profit of the sixth unit is the same as the average profit for the first five units, so average profit remains identical between five and six units. Finally, the marginal profit of the seventh unit is below the average profit at six units, causing average profit to fall.

TABLE 2.2

Total, Marginal, and Average Relations for a Hypothetical Profit Function

Units of Output Q (1)	Total Profits π^a (2)	Marginal Profits $\Delta\pi^b$ (3)	Average Profits $\overline{\pi}^c$ (4)
0	$ 0	$ 0	—
1	19	19	$19
2	52	33	26
3	93	41	31
4	136	43	34
5	175	39	35
6	210	35	35
7	217	7	31
8	208	−9	26

a   The Greek letter π (pi) is frequently used in economics and business to denote profits.
b   The symbol Δ (delta) denotes difference or change. Thus, marginal profit is expressed as $\Delta\pi = \pi_Q - \pi_{Q-1}$.
c   Average profit ($\overline{\pi}$) equals total profit (π) divided by total output (Q): $\overline{\pi} = \pi/Q$.

Graphing Total, Marginal, and Average Relations

Knowledge of the geometric relations among totals, marginals, and averages can prove useful in managerial decision making. Figure 2.2(a) presents a graph of the profit-to-output relation given in Table 2.2. Each point on the curve represents a combination of output and total profit, as do columns 1 and 2 of Table 2.2. The marginal and average profit figures from Table 2.2 have been plotted in Figure 2.2(b).

Just as there is an arithmetic relation among totals, marginals, and averages in the table, so too there is a corresponding geometric relation. To see this relation, consider the average profit per unit of output at any point along the total profit curve. The average profit figure is equal to total profit divided by the corresponding number of units of output. Geometrically, this relation is represented by the slope of a line from the origin to any point on the total profit curve. For example, consider the slope of the line from the origin to point B in Figure 2.2(a). **Slope** is a measure of the steepness of a line, and is defined as the increase (or decrease) in height per unit of movement along the horizontal axis. The slope of a straight line passing through the origin is determined by dividing the Y coordinate at any point on the line by the corresponding X coordinate. Using Δ (read *delta*) to designate change, slope $= \Delta Y/\Delta X = (Y_2 - Y_1)/(X_2 - X_1)$. Because X_1 and Y_1 are zero for any line going through the origin, slope $= Y_2/X_2$ or, more generally, slope $= Y/X$. Thus, the slope of the line $0B$ can be calculated by dividing $93, the Y coordinate at point B, by 3, the X coordinate at point B. This process involves dividing total profit by the corresponding units of output. *At any point along a total curve, the corresponding average figure is given by the slope of a straight line from the origin to that point.* Average figures can also be graphed directly, as in Figure 2.2(b), where each point on the average profit curve is the corresponding total profit divided by quantity.

The marginal relation has a similar geometric association with the total curve. In Table 2.2, each marginal figure is the change in total profit associated with a one-unit increase in output. The rise (or fall) in total profit associated with a one-unit increase in output is the slope of the total profit curve at that point.

Slopes of nonlinear curves are typically found geometrically by drawing a line tangent to the curve at the point of interest and determining the slope of the tangent. A **tangent** is a line that touches but does not intersect a given curve. In Figure 2.2(a), the marginal profit at point A is

slope
Measure of the steepness of a line

tangent
A straight line that touches a curve at only one point

FIGURE 2.2

Geometric Representation of Total, Marginal, and Average Relations:
(A) Total Profits; (B) Marginal and Average Profits

(a) Marginal profit is the slope of the total profit curve; it is maximized at point C. More important, total profit is maximized at point E, where marginal profit equals zero. (b) Average profit rises (falls) when marginal profit is greater (less) than average profit.

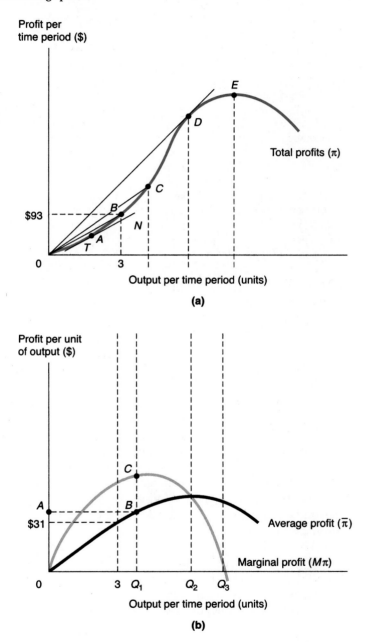

(a)

(b)

equal to the slope of the total profit curve at that point, which is equal to the slope of the tangent labeled *TAN*. *At any point along a total curve, the corresponding marginal figure is given by the slope of a line drawn tangent to the total curve at that point.* Slope or marginal figures can also be graphed directly as shown by the marginal profit curve in Figure 2.2(b).

Does Good Theory Always Work in Practice?

Have you ever been at a sporting event when a particular athlete's play became the center of attention and wondered "Where did that woman study physics?" or "Wow, who taught that guy physiology?" No, of course not. Instead, the discussion probably centered on the player's skill, finesse, or tenacity. Natural talent developed through long hours of dedicated training and intense competition are chief prerequisites for becoming an accomplished amateur or professional athlete. But if you think about it, successful athletes must also know a great deal about angles, speed, and acceleration.

Although success in sports requires that one understands the basic principles of physics and physiology, most athletes develop their "feel" for their sports on the tennis court, golf course, baseball diamond, or gridiron. Similarly, some very successful businesses are run by people with little or no formal training in accounting, finance, management, or marketing. These executives' successes testify to their ability to develop a feel for business in much the same way that the successful athlete develops a feel for his or her sport. Although the term *optimization* may be foreign to such individuals, the methodology of opti-

mization is familiar to each of them in terms of their everyday business practice. Adjusting prices to avoid stockout situations, increasing product quality to "meet the competition," and raising salaries to retain valued employees all involve a basic, practical understanding of optimization concepts.

The behavior of both the successful athlete and the successful executive can be described, or modeled, as consistent with a process of optimization. The fact that some practitioners learn their "lessons" through hands-on experience rather than in the classroom does not diminish the value of the formal educational experience. Useful theory describes and predicts actual business decisions. The old saw "That may be okay in theory, but it doesn't work in practice" is plainly incorrect. Economic theory is useful for studying managerial decision making for one simple reason—it works.

See: Peter Wonacott, "Searching for Profits, Finding Trouble," *The Wall Street Journal Online*, March 19, 2002 (http://online.wsj.com).

Several important relations among totals, marginals, and averages become apparent when considering Figure 2.2(a). First, note that the slope of the total profit curve is increasing from the origin to point *C*. Lines drawn tangent to the total profit curve become steeper as the point of tangency approaches point *C*, so marginal profit is increasing up to this point. This is also illustrated in Figure 2.2(b), where the marginal profit curve increases up to output Q_1, corresponding to point *C* on the total profit curve. At point *C*, called an **inflection point**, the slope of the total profit curve is maximized; marginal, but not average or total, profits are maximized at that output. Between points *C* and *E*, total profit continues to increase because marginal profit is still positive even though it is declining. At point *E*, the total profit curve has a slope of zero and thus is neither rising nor falling. Marginal profit at this point is zero, and total profit is maximized. Beyond *E* [output Q_3 in Figure 2.2(b)], the total profit curve has a negative slope and marginal profit is negative.

Figure 2.2(b) also shows the relation between marginals and averages. At low output levels, where the marginal profit curve lies above the average, the average is rising. Although marginal profit reaches a maximum at output Q_1 and declines thereafter, the average curve continues to rise so long as the marginal lies above it. At output Q_2, marginal and average profits are equal, and the average profit curve reaches its maximum value. Beyond Q_2, the marginal curve lies below the average, which is falling.

inflection point
Point of maximum or minimum slope

Deriving Totals from Marginal and Average Curves

Just as marginal and average profit figures can be derived from the total profit curve in Figure 2.2(a), total profits can be determined from the marginal or average profit curves of Figure 2.2(b). Total profit is average profit times the corresponding number of units of output. The total profit associated with Q_1 units of output, for example, is average profit, *A*, times output,

Q_1. Total profit is equal to the area of the rectangle $0ABQ_1$. This relation holds for all points along the average profit curve.

A similar relation exists between marginal and total profits. Total profit for any output is equal to the sum of the marginal profits up to that output quantity. Geometrically, this is the area under the marginal curve from the Y-axis to the output quantity under consideration. At output Q_1, total profit is equal to the area under the marginal profit curve, or the area $0CQ_1$.

Because average, marginal, and total relations underlie several basic principles of managerial economics, they should be thoroughly understood. Marginal cost and marginal revenue curves are derived from average or total figures. Because marginal profit equals marginal revenue minus marginal cost, profit is maximized where marginal revenue is equal to marginal cost and marginal profit is zero.

It is often worth considering the use of elementary calculus to find optimal solutions for economic problems. Calculus concepts help clarify the relations among marginals, averages, and totals and the importance of these relations in the optimization process.

MARGINALS AS THE DERIVATIVES OF FUNCTIONS[2]

Tables and graphs are useful for explaining concepts. Equations are frequently better suited for problem solving. One reason is that the powerful technique of differential calculus can be used to locate maximum or minimum values of an objective function. In addition, calculus concepts are easily extended to decision problems in which decision options are limited by one or more constraints.

Concept of a Derivative

A marginal value is the change in a dependent variable associated with a one-unit change in an independent variable. Consider the general function $Y = f(X)$. Using Δ to denote change, it is possible to express the change in the value of the independent variable, X, by the notation ΔX and the change in the dependent variable, Y, by ΔY.

The ratio $\Delta Y / \Delta X$ is a general specification of the marginal concept:

$$\text{Marginal } Y = \frac{\Delta Y}{\Delta X}$$

The change in Y, ΔY, divided by the change in X, ΔX, indicates the change in the dependent variable associated with a one-unit change in the value of X.

Figure 2.3 is a graph of a function relating Y to X that illustrates this relation. For values of X close to the origin, a relatively small change in X provides a large change in Y. Thus, the value of $\Delta Y / \Delta X = (Y_2 - Y_1)/(X_2 - X_1)$ is relatively large, showing that a small increase in X induces a large increase in Y. The situation is reversed farther out along the X-axis. A large increase in X, say from X_3 to X_4, produces only a small increase in Y, from Y_3 to Y_4, so $\Delta Y / \Delta X$ is small. The marginal relation between X and Y, as shown in Figure 2.3, changes at different points on the curve. When the curve is relatively steep, the dependent variable Y is highly responsive to changes in the independent variable; when the curve is relatively flat, Y does not respond as notably to changes in X.

derivative
Precise specification of the marginal relation

A **derivative** is a precise specification of the marginal relation. Finding a derivative involves finding the value of the ratio $\Delta Y / \Delta X$ for extremely small changes in X. The mathematical notation for a derivative is

2 This section can be skipped without loss of continuity. However, before skipping this material, students should keep in mind that a little bit of calculus goes a long way in the study of managerial economics.

FIGURE 2.3

Changing $\Delta Y/\Delta X$ over the Range of a Curve

The ratio $\Delta Y/\Delta X$ changes continuously along a curved line.

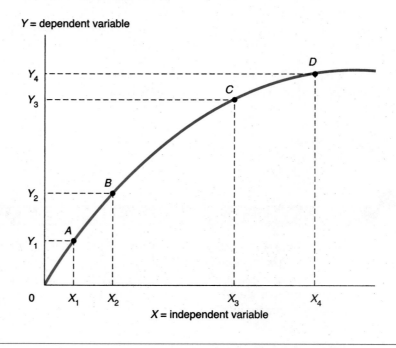

$$\frac{dY}{dX} \;=\; \frac{\text{limit}}{\Delta X \to 0}\;\; \frac{\Delta Y}{\Delta X}$$

which is read: "The derivative of Y with respect to X equals the limit of the ratio $\Delta Y/\Delta X$, as ΔX approaches zero."[3] This concept of the derivative as the limit of a ratio is precisely equivalent to the slope of a curve at a point. Figure 2.4 presents this idea, using the same curve relating Y to X as shown in Figure 2.3. Notice that in Figure 2.4 the average slope of the curve between points A and D is measured as

$$\frac{\Delta Y}{\Delta X} \;=\; \frac{Y_4 - Y_1}{X_4 - X_1}$$

and is the slope of the chord connecting the two points. Similarly, the average slope of the curve can be measured over smaller and smaller intervals of X, such as those connecting points B and C with D. At the limit, as ΔX approaches zero, the ratio $\Delta Y/\Delta X$ is equal to the

---

3   A limit can be explained briefly. If the value of a function $Y = f(X)$ approaches a constant Y^* as the value of the independent variable X approaches X^*, then Y^* is called the limit of the function as X approaches X^*. This is written as follows:

$$\frac{\text{limit}}{X \to X^*}\; f(X) \;=\; Y^*$$

For example, if $Y = X - 4$, then the limit of this function as X approaches 5 is 1; that is,

$$\frac{\text{limit}}{X \to 5}\; (X - 4) = 1$$

This says that the value of X approaches but does not quite reach 5; the value of the function $Y = X - 4$ comes closer and closer to 1.

MANAGERIAL APPLICATION **2.3**

How Entrepreneurs Shape the Economy

Firms often are started by a single individual with no more than an idea for a better product or service—the entrepreneur. Taken from the Old French word *entreprendre*, meaning "to undertake," the term *entrepreneur* refers to one who organizes, operates, and assumes the risk of a business venture. Until recently, there was little academic or public policy interest in this key function. The entrepreneur's skill was simply considered part of the labor input in production. Now, both academicians and practitioners are beginning to better understand the critical role of the entrepreneur, partly because entrepreneurship has become a formal field of study at many leading business schools.

As a catalyst, the entrepreneur brings economic resources together in the risky attempt to meet customer needs and desires. This process often leads to failure—in fact, the odds against success are long. Seldom do more than one in ten start-up businesses enjoy even minimal economic success. Even those select few that see their product or service reach a national market find stable long-term success elusive. Once established, they in turn become targets for future entrepreneurs. As

entrepreneurs create new opportunities, they destroy the old way of doing things. Entrepreneurship plays an important role in what economist Joseph Schumpeter called the "creative destruction of capitalism"—the process of replacing the old with the new and the inefficient with the efficient.

Given the long odds against success, one might wonder why so many willingly embark on ventures (adventures?) that appear doomed to fail. One reason is that one-in-a-million chance of developing "the" truly revolutionary product or service that will fundamentally change how people live, work, play, or shop. Even though the opportunity for wealth is surely an important motivation, the impact and recognition that come with creating a truly unique good or service often are equally important to entrepreneurs. Many simply want to "make a difference." Whatever the motivation, entrepreneurs play a key role in our economy.

See: Gordon G. Chang, "Eager Entrepreneurs, Far from Silicon Valley," *The Wall Street Journal Online*, March 12, 2002 (http://online.wsj.com).

FIGURE 2.4

A Derivative as the Slope of a Curve

The derivative of Y with respect to X identifies the slope of a curve.

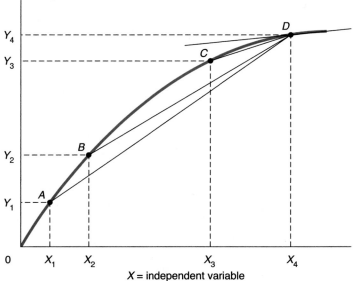

slope of a line drawn tangent to the curve—for example, at point D. The slope of this tangent is defined as the derivative, dY/dX, of the function at point D; it measures the marginal change in Y associated with a very small change in X at that point.

For example, the dependent variable Y might be total revenue, and the independent variable might be output. The derivative dY/dX shows precisely how revenue and output are related at a specific output level. Because the change in revenue associated with a change in output is defined as marginal revenue, the derivative of total revenue is a precise measure of marginal revenue at any specific output level. A similar situation exists for total cost: The derivative of the total cost function at any output level indicates marginal cost at that output.

MARGINAL ANALYSIS IN DECISION MAKING[4]

Managerial decision making frequently requires one to find the maximum or minimum value of a function. For a function to be at a maximum or minimum, its slope or marginal value must be zero.

Finding Maximums or Minimums

The *derivative* of a function is a very precise measure of its slope or marginal value at a particular point. The terms *derivative* and *marginal* are interchangeable. Thus, maximization or minimization of a function occurs where its derivative or marginal value is equal to zero. To illustrate, consider the following profit function:

(2.6)
$$\pi = -\$10,000 + \$400Q - \$2Q^2$$

Here, π is total profit and Q is output in units. As shown in Figure 2.5, if output is zero, the firm incurs a $10,000 loss (fixed costs are $10,000); but as output rises, profit also rises. Breakeven points are output levels where profit is zero and are reached at 29 and 171 units of output. Profit rises as output expands to 100 units of output, where profit is maximized at $10,000, and declines thereafter.

The profit-maximizing output is found by calculating the value of the function at a number of outputs, then plotting these as in Figure 2.5. The maximum can also be located by finding the derivative, or marginal, of the function, then determining the value of Q at which the derivative (marginal) is equal to zero.[5]

$$\text{Marginal Profit } (M\pi) = \frac{d\pi}{dQ} = \$400 - \$4Q$$

Setting marginal profit equal to zero results in

$$\begin{aligned} \$400 - \$4Q &= 0 \\ \$4Q &= \$400 \\ Q &= 100 \text{ units} \end{aligned}$$

Therefore, when $Q = 100$, marginal profit is zero and total profit is at a maximum. Beyond $Q = 100$, marginal profit is negative and total profit is decreasing. In this simple illustration, it is easy to locate the profit-maximizing value through graphic analysis, or by setting marginal profit

---

4   This section can be skipped without loss of continuity.

5   Basic rules for finding the derivative of a function are found in the appendix to this chapter.

FIGURE 2.5

Profit as a Function of Output

Total profit is maximized at 100 units, where marginal profit equals zero. Beyond that point, marginal profit is negative and total profit decreases.

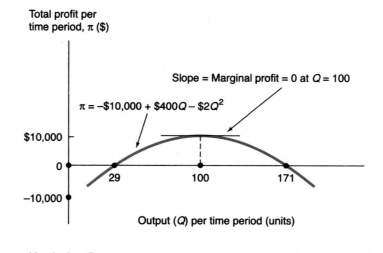

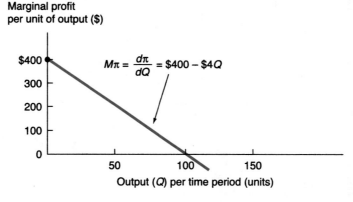

equal to zero, and then solving for Q. Had the profit function been complex, use of the marginal profit function might have been the only efficient means of determining the profit-maximizing output level.

Distinguishing Maximums from Minimums

A problem can arise when marginal relations (derivatives) are used to locate maximums or minimums. The marginal of a total function indicates whether the function is rising or falling at any point. To be maximized or minimized, the function must be neither rising nor falling; slope as measured by the marginal must be zero. Setting the marginal relation equal to zero indicates inflection points, or points of maximum or minimum slope. Because the marginal value (or derivative) is zero for both maximum and minimum values of a function, further analysis is necessary to determine whether a maximum or a minimum has been located.

This point is illustrated in Figure 2.6, where the slope of the total profit curve is zero at both points A and B. Point A is a point of minimum profits; B is the profit-maximizing output.

FIGURE 2.6

Locating Maximum and Minimum Values of a Function

The second derivative of a function is always negative when evaluated at a point of maximization and positive at a point of minimization.

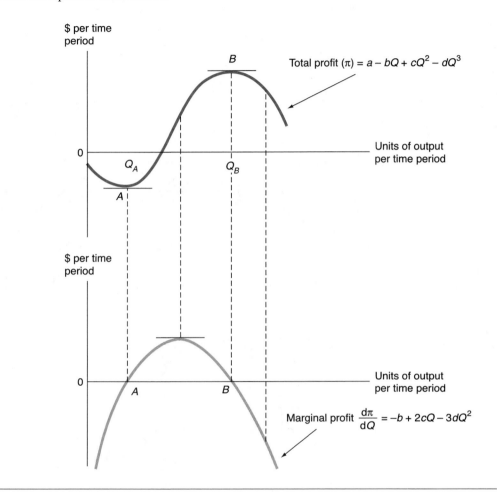

The concept of a **second derivative** is used to distinguish maximums from minimums along a function. The second derivative is simply the derivative of a marginal relations. If total profit is given by the equation $\pi = a - bQ + cQ^2 - dQ^3$, as in Figure 2.6, then the first derivative defines the marginal profit function as

second derivative
Derivative of a derivative

(2.7)
$$\frac{d\pi}{dQ} = M\pi = -b + 2cQ - 3dQ^2$$

The second derivative of the total profit function is the derivative of the marginal profit function, Equation 2.7:

$$\frac{d^2\pi}{dQ^2} = \frac{dM\pi}{dQ} = 2c - 6dQ$$

Just as the first derivative measures the slope of the total profit function, the second derivative measures the slope of the first derivative or, in this case, the slope of the marginal profit curve. The second derivative is used to distinguish between points of maximization and minimization; it is always *negative* when evaluated at a point of *maximization* and *positive* at a point of *minimization*.

The reason for this inverse relation can be seen in Figure 2.6. Note that profits reach a local minimum at point *A* because marginal profits that have been negative suddenly become positive. Marginal profits pass through the zero level from below at point *A*. The reverse holds at a point of local maximization; the marginal value is positive but declining up to the point where the total function is maximized, and it is negative thereafter. The marginal function is negatively sloped and has a negative derivative at the point of maximization for the total function.

Another example should clarify this concept. Assume the total profit function illustrated in Figure 2.6 is

(2.8) $$\text{Total Profit} = \pi = -\$3,000 - \$2,400Q + \$350Q^2 - \$8.33Q^3$$

Marginal profit is the first derivative of the total profit function:

(2.9) $$\text{Marginal Profit} = M\pi = \frac{d\pi}{dQ} = -\$2,400 + \$700Q - \$25Q^2$$

Total profit is either maximized or minimized at the points where the first derivative or marginal profit is zero:

(2.10) $$M\pi = \frac{d\pi}{dQ} = -\$2,400 + \$700Q - \$25Q^2 = 0$$

Output quantities of 4 and 24 units satisfy Equation 2.10 and are therefore points of either maximum or minimum profits.

Any equation of the form $Y = aX^2 + bX + c$ is a quadratic, and its two roots are found using the general quadratic equation:

$$X = \frac{-b \pm \sqrt{b^2 - 4ac}}{2a}$$

Substituting the values from Equation 2.10 into the quadratic equation gives

$$X = \frac{-700 \pm \sqrt{700^2 - 4(-25)(-2,400)}}{2(-25)} = \frac{-700 \pm \sqrt{490,000 - 240,000}}{-50}$$

$$= \frac{-700 \pm \sqrt{250,000}}{-50} = \frac{-700 \pm 500}{-50}$$

The plus root is

$$X_1 = \frac{-700 + 500}{-50} = \frac{-200}{-50} = 4 \text{ units}$$

and the minus root is

$$X_2 = \frac{-700 - 500}{-50} = \frac{-1,200}{-50} = 24 \text{ units}$$

Evaluation of the second derivative of the total profit function at each of these output levels indicates whether they are minimums or maximums. The second derivative of the total profit function is found by taking the derivative of the marginal profit function, Equation 2.9:

$$\frac{d^2\pi}{dQ^2} = \frac{dM\pi}{dQ} = \$700 - \$50Q$$

For example, at output quantity $Q = 4$,

$$\frac{d^2\pi}{dQ^2} = \$700 - \$50(4) = \$500$$

Because the second derivative is positive, indicating that marginal profits are increasing, **total profit is *minimized* at four units of output.** Total profit at four units of output corresponds to point A in Figure 2.6.

Evaluating the second derivative at 24 units of output gives

$$\frac{d^2\pi}{dQ^2} = \$700 - \$50(24) = -\$500$$

Because the second derivative is negative at 24 units, indicating that marginal profit is decreasing, the total profit function reaches a *maximum* at that point. This output level corresponds to point B in Figure 2.6.

Use of Marginals to Maximize the Difference Between Two Functions

profit maximization
Activity level that generates the highest profit, $MR = MC$ and $M\pi = 0$

Another example of the importance of the marginal concept in managerial economics is provided by the fundamental proposition that marginal revenue equals marginal cost at the point of **profit maximization**. It stems from the fact that the distance between revenue and cost functions is maximized at the point where their slopes are the same. Figure 2.7, where hypothetical revenue and cost functions are shown, illustrates this point. Total profit is equal to total revenue minus total cost and equals the vertical distance between the two curves at any output level. This distance is maximized at output level Q_B, where the slopes of revenue and cost curves are equal. Slopes of total revenue and total cost curves measure marginal revenues (MR) and marginal costs (MC). Where these slopes are equal, $MR = MC$.

breakeven point
Output level at which total profit is zero

That Q_B is the profit-maximizing output level can be seen by considering points to the right of Q_A. At Q_A, total revenue equals total cost: A **breakeven point** where profit equals zero is indicated. At output quantities just beyond Q_A, total revenue is rising faster than total cost, profits are increasing, and the curves are spreading farther apart. This divergence of the curves continues as long as total revenue is rising faster than total cost or, in other words, as long as $MR > MC$. Once the slope of the total revenue curve is exactly equal to the slope of the total cost curve—in other words, where marginal revenue equals marginal cost—the two curves are parallel and no longer diverging. This occurs at Q_B. Beyond Q_B, the slope of the cost curve is greater than that of the revenue curve (marginal cost is greater than marginal revenue), so the distance between them is decreasing and total profits decline. Marginal revenue equals zero at the point of **revenue maximization**, as long as total revenue is falling beyond that point. **Average cost minimization** occurs when marginal and average costs are equal and average cost is increasing as output expands.

revenue maximization
Activity level that generates the highest revenue, $MR = 0$

An example should clarify the use of marginal relations. Consider the following revenue, cost, and profit functions:

average cost minimization
Activity level that generates the lowest average cost, $MC = AC$

$$\text{Total Revenue} = TR = \$41.5Q - \$1.1Q^2$$
$$\text{Total Cost} = TC = \$150 + \$10Q - \$0.5Q^2 + \$0.02Q^3$$
$$\text{Total Profit} = \pi = TR - TC$$

FIGURE 2.7

Total Revenue, Total Cost, and Profit Maximization

The difference between the total revenue and total cost curves is greatest when their slopes are equal. At that point, marginal revenue equals marginal cost, marginal profit equals zero, and profit is maximized.

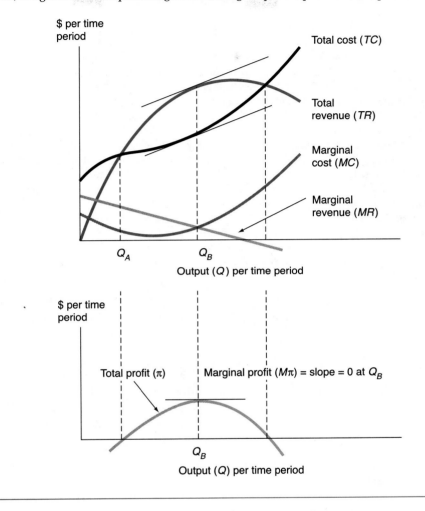

The profit-maximizing output is found by substituting total revenue and total cost functions into the profit function and then analyzing marginal profits:

$$\begin{aligned} \pi &= \text{TR} - \text{TC} \\ &= \$41.5Q - \$1.1Q^2 - (\$150 + \$10Q - \$0.5Q^2 + \$0.02Q^3) \\ &= \$41.5Q - \$1.1Q^2 - \$150 - \$10Q + \$0.5Q^2 - \$0.02Q^3 \\ &= -\$150 + \$31.5Q - \$0.6Q^2 - \$0.02Q^3 \end{aligned}$$

In this case, marginal profit is

$$M\pi = \frac{d\pi}{dQ} = \$31.5 - \$1.2Q - \$0.06Q^2$$

Setting marginal profit equal to zero and using the quadratic equation to solve for the two roots gives the solutions $Q_1 = -35$ and $Q_2 = +15$. Because negative output quantities are not possible, Q_1 is infeasible and can be rejected.

Information Brought Down the Berlin Wall

The most important ingredient for a well-functioning company, and a free market economy, is information that is accurate, timely, and inexpensive. In November 1989, the world got a renewed sense of how powerful economic information can be when the Berlin Wall, which kept East Berliners captive and barred them from the West, came tumbling down.

Obviously, the communist system was flawed as an economic and political model. It placed an extraordinary burden on the citizens of the former Soviet Union and Eastern Bloc countries. The economic inefficiency of communism resulted in an extremely low standard of living for millions of hardworking and talented people. However, economic inefficiency does not explain why the downfall of communism, punctuated by the fall of the Berlin Wall in November 1989, took place at a specific point in history. Why didn't the Berlin Wall come down during 1961 and the Berlin Blockade, or in the 1950s when Hungary and Yugoslavia were in ferment?

During 1990, while in Berlin, I heard a startling answer to a simple, but important, question: "Why did the Berlin Wall come down in November 1989?" "It's CNN," was the common refrain. "CNN?" I asked. "You mean the news on CNN couldn't be kept from the people anymore?" "Oh no, it wasn't the news on CNN. It was the commercials." I was dumbfounded. "The commercials on CNN brought down the Berlin Wall?" I asked. For many Berliners, that is indeed the case.

Before CNN became widely popular around the globe, millions of people under communist rule had no idea of the quality of life enjoyed by people in the West. Once CNN broadcast advertisements showing the wonderful variety of consumer goods and services available in the West, the secret was out and communism was doomed. Of course, the prominent role played by political and religious leaders in the fall of communism should not be minimized. Still, it is worth noting the important role played by communications technology.

See: David Bank, "Soros Insists Government Funding Must Raise Philanthropy for Gains," *The Wall Street Journal Online*, March 14, 2002 (http://online.wsj.com).

An evaluation of the second derivative of the profit function at $Q = 15$ indicates whether this is a point of profit maximization or profit minimization. The second derivative is

$$\frac{d^2\pi}{dQ^2} = \frac{dM\pi}{dQ} = -\$1.2 - \$0.12Q$$

Evaluating this derivative at $Q = 15$ indicates a value of –$3; therefore, $Q = 15$ is a point of profit maximization.

The relevance of marginal revenue and marginal cost relations to profit maximization can be demonstrated by considering the general profit expression $\pi = TR - TC$. Marginal profit is

$$M\pi = \frac{d\pi}{dQ} = \frac{dTR}{dQ} - \frac{dTC}{dQ}$$

Given that dTR/dQ is marginal revenue, MR, and dTC/dQ represents marginal cost, MC, it follows that

$$M\pi = MR - MC$$

Because maximization of any function requires that the first derivative equal zero, profit maximization occurs where

$$M\pi = MR - MC = 0$$

or where

$$MR = MC$$

In the numerical example described previously, marginal revenue and marginal cost are found by finding marginal revenue and marginal cost:

$$MR = \frac{dTR}{dQ} = \$41.5 - \$2.0Q$$

$$MC = \frac{dTC}{dQ} = \$10 - Q + \$0.06Q^2$$

At the profit-maximizing output level, $MR = MC$; thus,

$$MR = \$41.5 - \$2.2Q = \$10 - Q + \$0.06Q^2 = MC$$

Combining terms gives

$$\$31.5 - \$1.2Q - \$0.06Q^2 = 0$$

which is the same expression obtained when the marginal profit function is set equal to zero. Solving for the roots of this equation (again using the quadratic formula) results in $Q_1 = -35$ and $Q_2 = 15$, the same values found previously. This confirms that marginal revenue equals marginal cost at the output level where profit is maximized. This example also illustrates that although MR must equal MC at the profit-maximizing activity level, the converse does not hold. Profits are not necessarily maximized at any point where $MR = MC$, as for example at $Q = -35$ in the current problem.

To conclude the example, Figure 2.8 presents a graph of the revenue, cost, and profit functions. The upper section of the graph shows the revenue and cost functions. At 15 units of output, the slopes of the two curves are equal, and $MR = MC$. The lower section of the graph shows the profit function, and the profit-maximizing output is shown to be 15 units, at which output $d\pi/dQ = 0$ and $d^2\pi/dQ^2 < 0$.

INCREMENTAL CONCEPT IN ECONOMIC ANALYSIS

The marginal concept is a key component of the economic decision-making process. It is important to recognize, however, that marginal relations measure only the effect associated with unitary changes in output or some other important decision variable. Many managerial decisions involve a consideration of changes that are broader in scope. For example, a manager might be interested in analyzing the potential effects on revenues, costs, and profits of a 25 percent increase in the firm's production level. Alternatively, a manager might want to analyze the profit impact of introducing an entirely new product line, or assess the cost impact of changing the entire production system. In all managerial decisions, the study of *differences* or *changes* is the key element in the selection of an optimal course of action. The marginal concept, although correct for analyzing unitary changes, is too narrow to provide a general methodology for evaluating alternative courses of action.

The incremental concept is the economist's generalization of the marginal concept. Incremental analysis involves examining the impact of alternative managerial decisions or courses of action on revenues, costs, and profit. It focuses on changes or differences between the available alternatives. The **incremental change** is the change resulting from a given managerial decision. For example, the incremental revenue of a new item in a firm's product line is measured as the difference between the firm's total revenue before and after the new product is introduced.

incremental change
Total difference resulting from a decision

FIGURE 2.8

Profit-Maximizing Output Conditions

Profit is maximized at $Q = 15$, where $MR = MC = \$8.50$, and $M\pi = 0$.

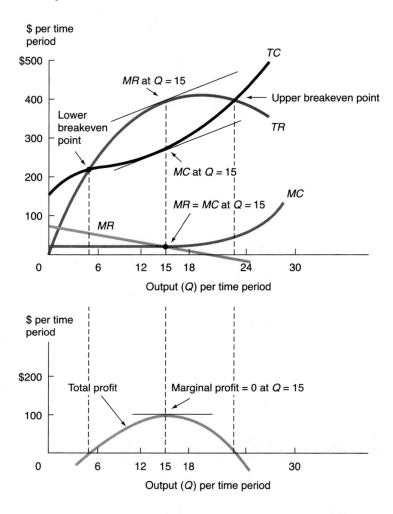

Incremental Profits

Fundamental relations of incremental analysis are essentially the same as those of marginal analy-

incremental profit
Gain or loss associated with a given managerial decision

sis. **Incremental profit** is the profit gain or loss associated with a given managerial decision. Total profit increases so long as incremental profit is positive. When incremental profit is negative, total profit declines. Similarly, incremental profit is positive (and total profit increases) if the incremental revenue associated with a decision exceeds the incremental cost. The incremental concept is so intuitively obvious that it is easy to overlook both its significance in managerial decision making and the potential for difficulty in correctly applying it.

For this reason, the incremental concept is often violated in practice. For example, a firm may refuse to sublet excess warehouse space for $5,000 per month because it figures its cost as $7,500 per month—a price paid for a long-term lease on the facility. However, if the warehouse space represents excess capacity with no current value to the company, its historical cost of $7,500 per month is irrelevant and should be disregarded. The firm would forego $5,000 in profits by turning down the offer to sublet the excess warehouse space. Similarly, any firm that adds a standard allocated charge for fixed costs and overhead to the true incremental cost of production runs the risk of turning down profitable sales.

Care must also be exercised to ensure against incorrectly assigning overly low incremental costs to a decision. Incremental decisions involve a time dimension that simply cannot be ignored. Not only must all current revenues and costs associated with a given decision be considered, but any likely future revenues and costs also must be incorporated in the analysis. For example, assume that the excess warehouse space described earlier came about following a downturn in the overall economy. Also, assume that the excess warehouse space was sublet for 1 year at a price of $5,000 per month, or a total of $60,000. An incremental loss might be experienced if the firm later had to lease additional, more costly space to accommodate an unexpected increase in production. If $75,000 had to be spent to replace the sublet warehouse facility, the decision to sublet would involve an incremental loss of $15,000. To be sure, making accurate projections concerning the future pattern of revenues and costs is risky and subject to error. Nevertheless, they cannot be ignored in incremental analysis.

Another example of the incremental concept involves measurement of the incremental revenue resulting from a new product line. Incremental revenue in this case includes not only the revenue received from sale of the new product but also any change in the revenues generated by the remainder of the firm's product line. Incremental revenues include any revenue resulting from increased sales of another product, where that increase was the result of adding the new product to the firm's line. Similarly, if the new item took sales away from another of the firm's products, this loss in revenue would be accounted for in measuring the incremental revenue of the new product.

Incremental Concept Example

To further illustrate the incremental concept, consider the financing decision typically associated with business plant and equipment financing. Consider a business whose $100,000 purchase offer was accepted by the seller of a small retail facility. The firm must obtain financing to complete the transaction. The best rates it has found are at a local financial institution that offers a renewable 5-year mortgage at 9 percent interest with a down payment of 20 percent, or 9.5 percent interest on a loan with only 10 percent down. In the first case, the borrower is able to finance 80 percent of the purchase price; in the second case, the borrower is able to finance 90 percent. For simplicity, assume that both loans require interest payments only during the first 5 years. After 5 years, either note would be renewable at then-current interest rates and would be restructured with monthly payments designed to amortize the loan over 20 years. An important question facing the firm is: What is the incremental cost of additional funds borrowed when 90 percent versus 80 percent of the purchase price is financed?

Because no principal payments are required, the annual financing cost under each loan alternative can be calculated easily. For the 80 percent loan, the annual financing cost in dollar terms is

(2.11)
$$\text{Financing Cost} = \text{Interest Rate} \times \text{Loan Percentage} \times \text{Purchase Price}$$
$$= (0.09)(0.8)(\$100,000)$$
$$= \$7,200$$

For a 90 percent loan, the corresponding annual financing cost is

$$\text{Financing Cost} = (0.095)(0.9)(\$100,000)$$
$$= \$8,550$$

To calculate the incremental cost of added funds borrowed under the 90 percent financing alternative, the firm must compare the additional financing costs incurred with the additional funds borrowed. In dollar terms, the incremental annual financing cost is

(2.12)
$$\text{Incremental Cost} = 90\% \text{ Loan Financing Cost} - 80\% \text{ Loan Financing Cost}$$
$$= \$8,550 - \$7,200$$
$$= \$1,350$$

In percentage terms, the incremental cost of the additional funds borrowed under the 90 percent financing alternative is

$$\begin{array}{ll}\text{Incremental Cost} & = \dfrac{\text{Incremental Financing Costs}}{\text{Incremental Funds Borrowed}} \\ \text{in Percentage Terms} & \end{array}$$

$$= \frac{\$8,550 - \$7,200}{\$90,000 - \$80,000}$$

$$= \frac{\$1,350}{\$10,000}$$

$$= 0.135, \text{ or } 13.5\%$$

The true incremental cost of funds for the last $10,000 borrowed under the 90 percent financing alternative is 13.5 percent, not the 9.5 percent interest rate quoted for the loan. Although this high incremental cost of funds is perhaps surprising, it is not unusual. It results because with a 90 percent loan the higher 9.5 percent interest rate is charged on the entire balance of the loan, not just on the incremental $10,000 in borrowed funds.

The incremental concept is important for managerial decision making because it focuses attention on changes or differences between available alternatives. Revenues and costs unaffected by the decision are irrelevant and should be ignored in the analysis.

SUMMARY

Effective managerial decision making is the process of finding the best solution to a given problem. Both the methodology and tools of managerial economics play an important role in this process.

- The decision alternative that produces a result most consistent with managerial objectives is the **optimal decision**.

- **Tables** are the simplest and most direct form for listing economic data. When these data are displayed electronically in the format of an accounting income statement or balance sheet, the tables are referred to as **spreadsheets**. In many instances, a simple **graph** or visual representation of the data can provide valuable insight. In other instances, complex economic relations are written using an **equation**, or an analytical expression of functional relationships.

- The value of a **dependent variable** in an equation depends on the size of the variable(s) to the right of the equal sign, which is called an **independent variable**. Values of independent variables are determined outside or independently of the functional relation expressed by the equation.

- A **marginal** relation is the change in the dependent variable caused by a one-unit change in an independent variable. **Marginal revenue** is the change in total revenue associated with a one-unit change in output; **marginal cost** is the change in total cost following a one-unit change in output; and **marginal profit** is the change in total profit due to a one-unit change in output.

- A **derivative** is a precise specification of the marginal relation. A **tangent** is a line that touches a curve at only one point.

- In graphic analysis, **slope** is a measure of the steepness of a line and is defined as the increase (or decrease) in height per unit of movement along the horizontal axis. An **inflection point** reveals a point of maximum or minimum slope. A **second derivative** is the derivative of a derivative, and is positive when an inflection point indicates a relative minimum and negative when an inflection point reveals a relative maximum.

- Marginal revenue equals marginal cost at the point of **profit maximization**, as long as total profit is falling as output expands from that point. The **breakeven point** identifies an output quantity at which total profit is zero. Marginal revenue equals zero at the point of **revenue maximization**, as long as total revenue is falling beyond that point. **Average cost minimization** occurs when marginal and average costs are equal and average cost is increasing as output expands.

- **Multivariate optimization** is the process of optimization for equations with three or more variables. Managers in several functional areas frequently face **constrained optimization** problems: decision situations that involve limited choice alternatives.

- The incremental concept is often used as the practical equivalent of marginal analysis. **Incremental change** is the total change resulting from a decision. **Incremental profit** is the profit gain or loss associated with a given managerial decision.

Each of these concepts is fruitfully applied in the practical analysis of managerial decision problems. As seen in later chapters, basic economic relations provide the underlying framework for the analysis of all profit, revenue, and cost relations.

QUESTIONS

Q2.1 What is the difference between global and partial optimization?

Q2.2 Why are computer spreadsheets a popular means for expressing economic relations?

Q2.3 Describe the relation between totals and marginals, and explain why the total is maximized when the marginal is set equal to zero.

Q2.4 Why must a marginal curve always intersect the related average curve at either a maximum or a minimum point?

Q2.5 Would you expect total revenue to be maximized at an output level that is typically greater or less than the profit-maximizing output level? Why?

Q2.6 Does the point of minimum long-run average costs always represent the optimal activity level?

Q2.7 Distinguish the incremental concept from the marginal concept.

Q2.8 Economists have long argued that if you want to tax away excess profits without affecting allocative efficiency, you should use a lump-sum tax instead of an excise or sales tax. Use the concepts developed in the chapter to support this position.

Q2.9 "It is often impossible to obtain precise information about the pattern of future revenues, costs, and interest rates. Therefore, the process of economic optimization is futile." Discuss this statement.

Q2.10 In estimating regulatory benefits, the Environmental Protection Agency (EPA) assigns a value of $4.8 million to each life saved. What factors might the EPA consider in arriving at such a valuation? How would you respond to criticism directed at the EPA that life is precious and cannot be valued in dollar terms?

SELF-TEST PROBLEMS AND SOLUTIONS

ST2.1   Profit Versus Revenue Maximization. Presto Products, Inc., manufactures small electrical appliances and has recently introduced an innovative new dessert maker for frozen yogurt and tofu that has the clear potential to offset the weak pricing and sluggish volume growth experienced during recent periods.

Monthly demand and cost relations for Presto's frozen dessert maker are as follows:

$$P = \$60 - \$0.005Q \qquad\qquad TC = \$100,000 + \$5Q + \$0.0005Q^2$$
$$MR = \partial TR/\partial Q = \$60 - \$0.01Q \qquad MC = \partial TC/\partial Q = \$5 + \$0.001Q$$

A. Set up a table or spreadsheet for Presto output (Q), price (P), total revenue (TR), marginal revenue (MR), total cost (TC), marginal cost (MC), total profit (π), and marginal profit ($M\pi$). Establish a range for Q from 0 to 10,000 in increments of 1,000 (i.e., 0, 1,000, 2,000, . . . , 10,000).

B. Using the Presto table or spreadsheet, create a graph with TR, TC, and π as dependent variables, and units of output (Q) as the independent variable. At what price/output combination is total profit maximized? Why? At what price/output combination is total revenue maximized? Why?

C. Determine these profit-maximizing and revenue-maximizing price/output combinations analytically. In other words, use Presto's profit and revenue equations to confirm your answers to part B.

D. Compare the profit-maximizing and revenue-maximizing price/output combinations, and discuss any differences. When will short-run revenue maximization lead to long-run profit maximization?

ST2.1   Solution

A. A table or spreadsheet for Presto output (Q), price (P), total revenue (TR), marginal revenue (MR), total cost (TC), marginal cost (MC), total profit (π), and marginal profit ($M\pi$) appears as follows:

Units	Price	Total Revenue	Marginal Revenue	Total Cost	Marginal Cost	Total Profit	Marginal Profit
0	$60	$ 0	$60	$100,000	$ 5	($100,000)	$55
1,000	55	55,000	50	105,500	6	(50,500)	44
2,000	50	100,000	40	112,000	7	(12,000)	33
3,000	45	135,000	30	119,500	8	15,500	22
4,000	40	160,000	20	128,000	9	32,000	11
5,000	35	175,000	10	137,500	10	37,500	0
6,000	30	180,000	0	148,000	11	32,000	(11)
7,000	25	175,000	(10)	159,500	12	15,500	(22)
8,000	20	160,000	(20)	172,000	13	(12,000)	(33)
9,000	15	135,000	(30)	185,500	14	(50,500)	(44)
10,000	10	100,000	(40)	200,000	15	(100,000)	(55)

B. Using the Presto table or spreadsheet, a graph with TR, TC, and π as dependent variables, and units of output (Q) as the independent variable appears as follows:

Presto Products, Inc.
Profit Vs. Revenue Maximization

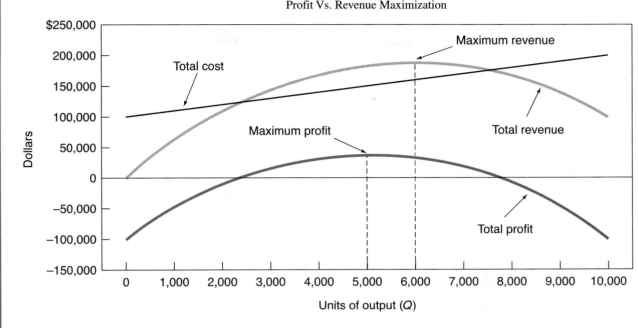

The price/output combination at which total profit is maximized is $P = \$35$ and $Q = 5{,}000$ units. At that point, $MR = MC$ and total profit is maximized at $37,500.

The price/output combination at which total revenue is maximized is $P = \$30$ and $Q = 6{,}000$ units. At that point, $MR = 0$ and total revenue is maximized at $180,000.

C. To find the profit-maximizing output level analytically, set $MR = MC$, or set $M\pi = 0$, and solve for Q. Because

$$
\begin{aligned}
MR &= MC \\
\$60 - \$0.01Q &= \$5 + \$0.001Q \\
0.011Q &= 55 \\
Q &= 5{,}000
\end{aligned}
$$

At $Q = 5{,}000$,

$$
\begin{aligned}
P &= \$60 - \$0.005(5{,}000) \\
&= \$35 \\
\pi &= -\$100{,}000 + \$55(5{,}000) - \$0.0055(5{,}000^2) \\
&= \$37{,}500
\end{aligned}
$$

(*Note*: This is a maximum because total profit is falling for $Q > 5{,}000$.)

To find the revenue-maximizing output level, set $MR = 0$, and solve for Q. Thus,

$$
\begin{aligned}
MR = \$60 - \$0.01Q &= 0 \\
0.01Q &= 60 \\
Q &= 6{,}000
\end{aligned}
$$

At $Q = 6,000$,

$$P = \$60 - \$0.005(6,000)$$
$$= \$30$$
$$\pi = TR - TC$$
$$= (\$60 - \$0.005Q)Q - \$100,000 - \$5Q - \$0.0005Q^2$$
$$= -\$100,000 + \$55Q - \$0.0055Q^2$$
$$= -\$100,000 + \$55(6,000) - \$0.0055(6,000^2)$$
$$= \$32,000$$

(*Note*: This is a revenue maximum because total revenue is decreasing for output beyond $Q > 6,000$.)

D. Given downward-sloping demand and marginal revenue curves, and positive marginal costs, the profit-maximizing price/output combination is *always* at a higher price and lower production level than the revenue-maximizing price/output combination. This stems from the fact that profit is maximized when $MR = MC$, whereas revenue is maximized when $MR = 0$. It follows that profits and revenue are only maximized at the same price/output combination in the unlikely event that $MC = 0$.

In pursuing a short-run revenue rather than profit-maximizing strategy, Presto can expect to gain a number of important advantages, including enhanced product awareness among consumers, increased customer loyalty, potential economies of scale in marketing and promotion, and possible limitations in competitor entry and growth. To be consistent with long-run profit maximization, these advantages of short-run revenue maximization must be at least worth Presto's short-run sacrifice of $5,500 (= \$37,500 - \$32,000)$ in monthly profits.

ST2.2   **Average Cost Minimization.** Pharmed Caplets, Inc., is an international manufacturer of bulk antibiotics for the animal feed market. Dr. Indiana Jones, head of marketing and research, seeks your advice on an appropriate pricing strategy for Pharmed Caplets, an antibiotic for sale to the veterinarian and feedlot-operator market. This product has been successfully launched during the past few months in a number of test markets, and reliable data are now available for the first time.

The marketing and accounting departments have provided you with the following monthly total revenue and total cost information:

$$TR = \$900Q - \$0.1Q^2 \qquad\qquad TC = \$36,000 + \$200Q + \$0.4Q^2$$
$$MR = \partial TR/\partial Q = \$900 - \$0.2Q \qquad MC = \partial TC/\partial Q = \$200 + \$0.8Q$$

A. Set up a table or spreadsheet for Pharmed Caplets output (Q), price (P), total revenue (TR), marginal revenue (MR), total cost (TC), marginal cost (MC), average cost (AC), total profit (π), and marginal profit ($M\pi$). Establish a range for Q from 0 to 1,000 in increments of 100 (i.e., 0, 100, 200, . . . , 1,000).

B. Using the Pharmed Caplets table or spreadsheet, create a graph with AC and MC as dependent variables and units of output (Q) as the independent variable. At what price/output combination is total profit maximized? Why? At what price/output combination is average cost minimized? Why?

C. Determine these profit-maximizing and average-cost minimizing price/output combinations analytically. In other words, use Pharmed Caplets' revenue and cost equations to confirm your answers to part B.

D. Compare the profit-maximizing and average-cost minimizing price/output combinations, and discuss any differences. When will average-cost minimization lead to long-run profit maximization?

ST2.2 Solution

A. A table or spreadsheet for Pharmed Caplets output (Q), price (P), total revenue (TR), marginal revenue (MR), total cost (TC), marginal cost (MC), average cost (AC), total profit (π), and marginal profit ($M\pi$) appears as follows:

Units	Price	Total Revenue	Marginal Revenue	Total Cost	Marginal Cost	Average Cost	Total Profit	Marginal Profit
0	$900	$ 0	$900	$ 36,000	$ 200	—	($ 36,000)	$ 700
100	890	89,000	880	$60,000	280	$600.00	29,000	600
200	880	176,000	860	$92,000	360	460.00	84,000	500
300	870	261,000	840	132,000	440	440.00	129,000	400
400	860	344,000	820	180,000	520	450.00	164,000	300
500	850	425,000	800	236,000	600	472.00	189,000	200
600	840	504,000	780	300,000	680	500.00	204,000	100
700	830	581,000	760	372,000	760	531.43	209,000	0
800	820	656,000	740	452,000	840	565.00	204,000	(100)
900	810	729,000	720	540,000	920	600.00	189,000	(200)
1,000	800	800,000	700	636,000	1,000	636.00	164,000	(300)

B. Using the Pharmed Caplets table or spreadsheet, a graph with AC and MC as dependent variables and units of output (Q) as the independent variable appears as follows:

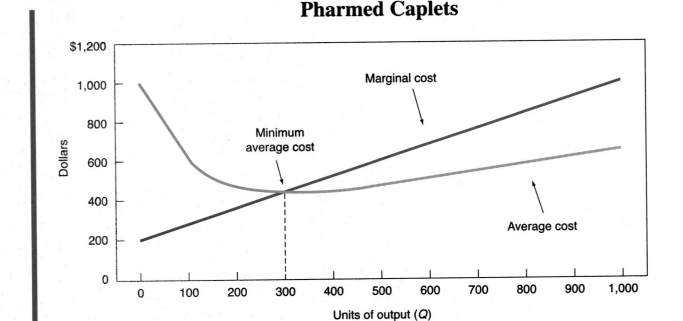

Pharmed Caplets

The price/output combination at which total profit is maximized is $P = \$830$ and $Q = 700$ units. At that point, $MR = MC$ and total profit is maximized at $209{,}000$.

The price/output combination at which average cost is minimized is $P = \$870$ and $Q = 300$ units. At that point, $MC = AC = \$440$.

C. To find the profit-maximizing output level analytically, set $MR = MC$, or set $M\pi = 0$, and solve for Q. Because

$$MR = MC$$
$$\$900 - \$0.2Q = \$200 + \$0.8Q$$
$$Q = 700$$

At $Q = 700$,

$$
\begin{aligned}
P &= TR/Q \\
&= (\$900Q - \$0.1Q^2)/Q \\
&= \$900 - \$0.1(700) \\
&= \$830 \\
\pi &= TR - TC \\
&= \$900Q - \$0.1Q^2 - \$36,000 - \$200Q - \$0.4Q^2 \\
&= -\$36,000 + \$700(700) - \$0.5(700^2) \\
&= \$209,000
\end{aligned}
$$

(*Note*: This is a profit maximum because profits are falling for $Q > 700$.)

To find the average-cost minimizing output level, set $MC = AC$, and solve for Q. Because

$$
\begin{aligned}
AC &= TC/Q \\
&= (\$36,000 + \$200Q + \$0.4Q^2)/Q \\
&= \$36,000Q^{-1} + \$200 + \$0.4Q
\end{aligned}
$$

it follows that

$$
\begin{aligned}
MC &= AC \\
\$200 + \$0.8Q &= \$36,000Q^{-1} + \$200 + \$0.4Q \\
0.4Q &= 36,000Q^{-1} \\
0.4Q^2 &= 36,000 \\
Q^2 &= 36,000/0.4 \\
Q^2 &= 90,000 \\
Q &= 300
\end{aligned}
$$

At $Q = 300$,

$$
\begin{aligned}
P &= \$900 - \$0.1(300) \\
&= \$870 \\
\pi &= -\$36,000 + \$700(300) - \$0.5(300^2) \\
&= \$129,000
\end{aligned}
$$

(*Note*: This is an average-cost minimum because average cost is rising for $Q > 300$.)

D. Given downward-sloping demand and marginal revenue curves, and a U-shaped or quadratic AC function, the profit-maximizing price/output combination will often be at a different price and production level than the average-cost minimizing price/output combination. This stems from the fact that profit is maximized when $MR = MC$, whereas average cost is minimized when $MC = AC$. Profits are maximized at the same price/output combination as where average costs are minimized in the unlikely event that $MR = MC$ and $MC = AC$ and, therefore, $MR = MC = AC$.

It is often true that the profit-maximizing output level differs from the average-cost minimizing activity level. In this instance, expansion beyond $Q = 300$, the average-cost minimizing activity level, can be justified because the added gain in revenue more than compensates for the added costs. Note that total costs rise by $240,000, from $132,000 to $372,000 as output expands from $Q = 300$ to $Q = 700$, as average cost rises from $440 to $531.43. Nevertheless, profits rise by $80,000, from $129,000 to $209,000, because total revenue rises by $320,000, from $261,000 to $581,000. The profit-maximizing activity level can be less than, greater than, or equal to the average-cost minimizing activity level depending on the shape of relevant demand and cost relations.

PROBLEMS

P2.1 **Graph Analysis**

A. Given the output (Q) and price (P) data in the following table, calculate the related total revenue (TR), marginal revenue (MR), and average revenue (AR) figures:

Q	P	TR	MR	AR
0	$10			
1	9			
2	8			
3	7			
4	6			
5	5			
6	4			
7	3			
8	2			
9	1			
10	0			

B. Graph these data using "dollars" on the vertical axis and "quantity" on the horizontal axis. At what output level is revenue maximized?

C. Why is marginal revenue less than average revenue at each price level?

P2.2 **A.** Fill in the missing data for price (P), total revenue (TR), marginal revenue (MR), total cost (TC), marginal cost (MC), profit (π), and marginal profit ($M\pi$) in the following table:

Q	P	TR	MR	TC	MC	π	$M\pi$
0	$160	$ 0	$ —	$ 0	$—	$ 0	$ —
1	150	150	150	25	25	125	125
2	140			55	30		100
3		390			35	300	75
4			90	130		350	
5	110	550		175			
6		600	50		55	370	
7		630		290	60		–30
8	80	640		355		285	
9					75		–85
10		600		525			

B. At what output level is profit maximized?

C. At what output level is revenue maximized?

D. Discuss any differences in your answers to parts B and C.

P2.3 **Marginal Analysis.** Characterize each of the following statements as true or false, and explain your answer.

A. If marginal revenue is less than average revenue, the demand curve will be downward sloping.

B. Profits will be maximized when total revenue equals total cost.

C. Given a downward-sloping demand curve and positive marginal costs, profit-maximizing firms will always sell less output at higher prices than will revenue-maximizing firms.

D. Marginal cost must be falling for average cost to decline as output expands.

E. Marginal profit is the difference between marginal revenue and marginal cost and will always equal zero at the profit-maximizing activity level.

P2.4 **Marginal Analysis: Tables.** Sarah Berra is a regional sales representative for Dental Laboratories, Inc. Berra sells alloy products created from gold, silver, platinum, and other precious metals to several dental laboratories in Maine, New Hampshire, and Vermont. Berra's goal is to maximize her total monthly commission income, which is figured at 10% of gross sales. In reviewing her monthly experience over the past year, Berra found the following relations between days spent in each state and monthly sales generated:

Maine		New Hampshire		Vermont	
Days	**Gross Sales**	**Days**	**Gross Sales**	**Days**	**Gross Sales**
0	$ 4,000	0	$ 0	0	$ 2,500
1	10,000	1	3,500	1	5,000
2	15,000	2	6,500	2	7,000
3	19,000	3	9,000	3	8,500
4	22,000	4	10,500	4	9,500
5	24,000	5	11,500	5	10,000
6	25,000	6	12,000	6	10,000
7	25,000	7	12,500	7	10,000

A. Construct a table showing Berra's marginal sales per day in each state.

B. If administrative duties limit Berra to only 10 selling days per month, how should she spend them?

C. Calculate Berra's maximum monthly commission income.

P2.5 **Marginal Analysis: Tables.** Climate Control Devices, Inc., estimates that sales of defective thermostats cost the firm an average of $25 each for replacement or repair. An independent engineering consultant has recommended hiring quality control inspectors so that defective thermostats can be identified and corrected before shipping. The following schedule shows the expected relation between the number of quality control inspectors and the thermostat failure rate, defined in terms of the percentage of total shipments that prove to be defective.

The firm expects to ship 250,000 thermostats during the coming year, and quality control inspectors each command a salary of $30,000 per year.

Number of Quality Control Inspectors	Thermostat Failure Rate (percent)
0	5.0
1	4.0
2	3.2
3	2.6
4	2.2
5	2.0

A. Construct a table showing the marginal failure reduction (in units) and the dollar value of these reductions for each inspector hired.

B. How many inspectors should the firm hire?

C. How many inspectors would be hired if additional indirect costs (lost customer goodwill and so on) were to average 30% of direct replacement or repair costs?

P2.6 **Profit Maximization: Equations.** Rochester Instruments, Inc., operates in the highly competitive electronics industry. Prices for its RII-X control switches are stable at $50 each. This means that $P = MR = \$50$ in this market. Engineering estimates indicate that relevant total and marginal cost relations for the RII-X model are

$$TC = \$78{,}000 + \$18Q + \$0.002Q^2$$
$$MC = \partial TC/\partial Q = \$18 + \$0.004Q$$

A. Calculate the output level that will maximize RII-X profit.

B. Calculate this maximum profit.

P2.7 **Profit Maximization: Equations.** 21st Century Insurance offers mail-order automobile insurance to preferred-risk drivers in the Los Angeles area. The company is the low-cost provider of insurance in this market but does not believe its $750 annual premium can be raised for competitive reasons. Its rates are expected to remain stable during coming periods; hence, $P = MR = \$750$. Total and marginal cost relations for the company are as follows:

$$TC = \$2{,}500{,}000 + \$500Q + \$0.005Q^2$$
$$MC = \partial TC/\partial Q = \$500 + \$0.01Q$$

A. Calculate the profit-maximizing activity level.

B. Calculate the company's optimal profit and return-on-sales levels.

P2.8 **Not-for-Profit Analysis.** The Denver Athlete's Club (DAC) is a private, not-for-profit athletic club located in Denver, Colorado. DAC currently has 3,500 members but is planning on a membership drive to increase this number significantly. An important issue facing Jessica Nicholson, DAC's administrative director, is the determination of an appropriate membership level. To efficiently use scarce DAC resources, the board of directors has instructed Nicholson to maximize DAC's operating surplus, defined as revenues minus operating costs. They have also asked Nicholson to determine the effects of a proposed agreement between DAC and a neighboring club with outdoor recreation and swimming pool facilities. Plan A involves paying the neighboring club $100 per DAC member. Plan B involves payment of a fixed fee of $400,000 per year. Finally, the board has determined that the membership fee for the coming year will remain constant at $2,500 per member irrespective of the number of new members added and whether Plan A or Plan B is adopted.

In the calculations for determining an optimal membership level, Nicholson regards price as fixed; therefore, $P = MR = \$2,500$. Before considering the effects of any agreement with the neighboring club, Nicholson projects total and marginal cost relations during the coming year to be as follows:

$$TC = \$3,500,000 + \$500Q + \$0.25Q^2$$
$$MC = \partial TC/\partial Q = \$500 + \$0.5Q$$

where Q is the number of DAC members.

A. Before considering the effects of the proposed agreement with the neighboring club, calculate DAC's optimal membership and operating surplus levels.

B. Calculate these levels under Plan A.

C. Calculate these levels under Plan B.

P2.9 **Revenue Maximization.** Desktop Publishing Software, Inc., develops and markets software packages for business computers. Although sales have grown rapidly during recent years, the company's management fears that a recent onslaught of new competitors may severely retard future growth opportunities. Therefore, it believes that the time has come to "get big or get out."

The marketing and accounting departments have provided management with the following monthly demand and cost information:

$$P = \$1,000 - \$1Q \qquad\qquad TC = \$50,000 + \$100Q$$
$$MR = \partial TR/\partial Q = \$1,000 - \$2Q \qquad MC = \partial TC/\partial Q = \$100$$

A. Calculate monthly quantity, price, and profit at the short-run revenue-maximizing output level.

B. Calculate these same values for the short-run profit-maximizing level of output.

C. When would short-run revenue maximization lead to long-run profit maximization?

P2.10 **Average Cost Minimization.** Giant Screen TV, Inc., is a San Diego–based importer and distributor of 60-inch screen, high-resolution televisions for individual and commercial customers. Revenue and cost relations are as follows:

$$TR = \$1,800Q - \$0.006Q^2$$
$$MR = \partial TR/\partial Q = \$1,800 - \$0.012Q$$
$$TC = \$12,100,000 + \$800Q + \$0.004Q^2$$
$$MC = \partial TC/\partial Q = \$800 + \$0.008Q$$

A. Calculate output, marginal cost, average cost, price, and profit at the average-cost minimizing activity level.

B. Calculate these values at the profit-maximizing activity level.

C. Compare and discuss your answers to parts A and B.

CASE STUDY

A Spreadsheet Approach to Finding the Economic Order Quantity

A spreadsheet is a table of data that is organized in a logical framework similar to an accounting income statement or balance sheet. At first, this marriage of computers and accounting information might seem like a minor innovation. However, it is not. For example, with computerized spreadsheets it becomes possible to easily reflect the effects on revenue, cost, and

CASE STUDY (continued)

profit of a slight change in demand conditions. Similarly, the effects on the profit-maximizing or breakeven activity levels can be easily determined. Various "what if?" scenarios can also be tested to determine the optimal or profit-maximizing activity level under a wide variety of operating conditions. Thus, it becomes easy to quantify in dollar terms the pluses and minuses (revenues and costs) of alternate decisions. Each operating and planning decision can be easily evaluated in light of available alternatives. Through the use of spreadsheet formulas and so-called "macros," managers are able to locate maximum or minimum values for any objective function based on the relevant marginal relations. Therefore, spreadsheets are a very useful tool that can be used to analyze a variety of typical optimization problems.

To illustrate the use of spreadsheets in economic analysis, consider the case of The Neighborhood Pharmacy, Inc. (NPI), a small but rapidly growing operator of a number of large-scale discount pharmacies in the greater Boston, Massachusetts, metropolitan area. A key contributor to the overall success of the company is a system of tight controls over inventory acquisition and carrying costs. The company's total annual costs for acquisition and inventory of pharmaceutical items are composed of the purchase cost of individual products supplied by wholesalers (purchase costs); the clerical, transportation, and other costs associated with placing each individual order (order costs); and the interest, insurance, and other expenses involved with carrying inventory (carrying costs). The company's total inventory-related costs are given by the expression:

$$TC = P \times X + \Theta \times X/Q + C \times Q/2$$

where TC is inventory-related total costs during the planning period, P is the purchase price of the inventory item, X is the total quantity of the inventory item that is to be ordered (used) during the planning period (use requirement), Θ is the cost of placing an individual order for the inventory item (order cost), C is inventory carrying costs expressed on a per unit of inventory basis (carrying cost), and Q is the quantity of inventory ordered at any one point in time (order quantity). Here Q is NPI's decision variable, whereas each other variable contained in the total cost function is beyond control of the firm (exogenous). In analyzing this total cost relation, NPI is concerned with picking the order quantity that will minimize total inventory-related costs. The optimal or total-cost minimizing order quantity is typically referred to as the "economic order quantity."

During the relevant planning period, the per unit purchase cost for an important prescribed (ethical) drug is $P = \$4$, the total estimated use for the planning period is $X = 5,000$, the cost of placing an order is $\Theta = \$50$; and the per unit carrying cost is $C = \$0.50$, calculated as the current interest rate of 12.5% multiplied by the per unit purchase cost of the item.

A. Set up a table or spreadsheet for NPI's order quantity (Q), inventory-related total cost (TC), purchase price (P), use requirement (X), order cost (Θ), and carrying cost (C). Establish a range for Q from 0 to 2,000 in increments of 100 (i.e., 0, 100, 200, . . . , 2,000).

B. Based on the NPI table or spreadsheet, determine the order quantity that will minimize the company's inventory-related total costs during the planning period.

C. Placing inventory-related total costs, TC, on the vertical or Y-axis and the order quantity, Q, on the horizontal or X-axis, plot the relation between inventory-related total costs and the order quantity.

D. Based on the same data as previously, set up a table or spreadsheet for NPI's order quantity (Q), inventory-related total cost (TC), and each component part of total costs, including inventory purchase (acquisition) costs, $P \times X$; total order costs, $\Theta \times X/Q$; and total carrying costs, $C \times Q/2$. Placing inventory-related total costs, TC, and each component cost category as dependent variables on the vertical or Y-axis and the order quantity, Q, as the independent variable on the horizontal or X-axis, plot the relation between inventory-related cost categories and the order quantity.

Multivariate Optimization and the Lagrangian Technique

multivariate optimization
Process of optimization for equations with three or more variables

Because many economic relations involve more than two variables, it is useful to examine the concept of **multivariate optimization**, the process of optimization for equations with three or more variables. Demand is often a function of the product's own price, the price of other goods, advertising, income, and other factors. Similarly, cost is determined by output, input prices, the nature of technology, and so on. As a result, multivariate optimization is often used in the process of optimization.

Partial Derivative Concept

Consider the demand function for a product where the quantity demanded, Q, is determined by the price charged, P, and the level of advertising, A:

(2A.1)
$$Q = f(P,A)$$

When analyzing multivariate relations, such as Equation 2A.1, one is interested in the marginal effect of each independent variable on the dependent variable. Optimization requires an analysis of how change in each independent variable affects the dependent variable, *holding constant the effect of all other independent variables*. The partial derivative is the concept used for this type of marginal analysis.

Based on the demand function of Equation 2A.1, it is possible to examine two partial derivatives:[6]

1. The partial of Q with respect to price is $\partial Q/\partial P$.
2. The partial of Q with respect to advertising expenditure is $\partial Q/\partial A$.

Rules for determining partial derivatives are essentially the same as those for simple derivatives. The concept of a partial derivative involves an assumption that all variables except the one with respect to which the derivative is being taken remain unchanged. Other variables are treated as constants. For example, consider the demand function facing MacGyver, Inc.:

(2A.2)
$$Q = 5{,}000 - 10P + 40A + PA - 0.8A^2 - 0.5P^2$$

where Q is quantity, P is price (in dollars), and A is advertising expenditures (in hundreds of dollars).

---

6 The symbol ∂, the Greek letter *delta*, is used to denote a partial derivative. In oral and written expression, the word *derivative* is frequently omitted. Reference is typically made to the *partial of Q* rather than the *partial derivative of Q*.

In this function there are two independent variables, P and A, so two partial derivatives can be evaluated. Because A is treated as a constant, the partial derivative of Q with respect to P is

$$\frac{\partial Q}{\partial P} = 0 - 10 + 0 + A - 0 - P$$

$$= -10 + A - P$$

In determining the partial of Q with respect to A, P is treated as a constant. The partial with respect to A is

$$\frac{\partial Q}{\partial A} = 0 - 0 + 40 + P - 1.6A - 0$$

$$= 40 + P - 1.6A$$

Maximizing Multivariate Functions

The maximization or minimization of multivariate functions is similar to that for single variable functions. All first-order partial derivatives must equal zero.[7] Thus, maximization of the function $Q = f(P,A)$ requires

$$\frac{\partial Q}{\partial P} = 0$$

and

$$\frac{\partial Q}{\partial A} = 0$$

To illustrate this procedure, reconsider the MacGyver demand function, Equation 2A.2, given previously:

$$Q = 5,000 - 10P + 40A + PA - 0.8A^2 - 0.5P^2$$

To maximize the value of this function, each partial must equal zero:

$$\frac{\partial Q}{\partial P} = -10 + A - P = 0$$

and

$$\frac{\partial Q}{\partial A} = 40 + P - 1.6A = 0$$

Solving these two equations simultaneously yields the values $P = \$40$ and $A = \$5,000$.[8] Inserting these numbers for P and A into Equation 2A.2 results in a value for Q of 5,800. Therefore, the maximum value of Q is 5,800.

---

7   Second-order requirements for determining maxima and minima are complex and are not necessary for the types of managerial problems considered in this text. A full discussion of these requirements can be found in any elementary calculus text.

8   Because $-10 + A - P = 0$, $P = A - 10$. Substituting this value for P into $40 + P - 1.6A = 0$ gives $40 + (A - 10) - 1.6A = 0$, which implies that $0.6A = 30$ and $A = 50$ (in 00s), or $\$5,000$. Given this value, $P = A - 10 = 50 - 10 = \$40$.

This process can be visualized by referring to Figure 2A.1, a three-dimensional graph of Equation 2A.2. For positive values of P and A, Equation 2A.2 maps out a surface with a peak at point X^*. At the peak, the surface of the figure is level. Alternatively stated, a plane that is tangent to the surface at point X^* is parallel to the PA plane. This means that the slope of the figure with respect to either P or A is zero, as is required for locating the maximum of a multivariate function.

CONSTRAINED OPTIMIZATION

In many decision problems faced by managers, there are constraints that limit options available to the decision maker. For example, a production manager may be charged with minimizing total cost, subject to the requirement that specified quantities of each of the firm's products be produced. At other times, the production manager may be concerned with maximizing output, subject to limitations on the quantities of various resources (labor, materials, or equipment) available for use.

Role of Constraints

constrained optimization
Decision situations that involve limited choice alternatives

Managers frequently face **constrained optimization** problems, decision situations with limited alternatives. Marketing managers are often charged with the task of maximizing sales, subject to the constraint that they not exceed a fixed advertising budget. Financial officers typically work within constraints imposed by financing requirements and creditor restrictions.

FIGURE 2A.1

Finding the Maximum of a Function of Two Variables: $Q = 5{,}000 - 10P + 40A + PA - 0.8A^2 - 0.5P^2$
All first-order partial derivatives are set equal to zero to find the maximum of a multivariate function.

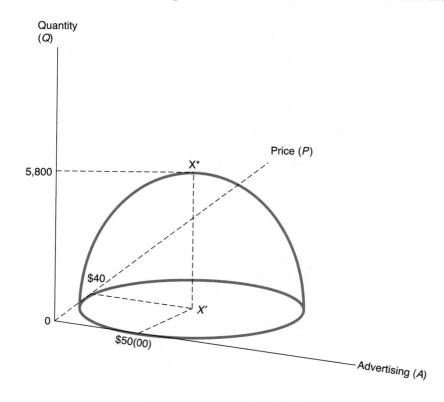

Constrained optimization problems can be solved in several ways. Where the constraint equation is not overly complex, it can be solved for in terms of one decision variable, and then that variable can be substituted for in the objective function that the firm wishes to maximize or minimize.[9] This approach converts the problem to one of unconstrained maximization or minimization, which can be solved using methods outlined previously.

This procedure can be clarified by examining its use in a constrained minimization problem. Suppose a firm produces its product on two assembly lines and operates with the following total cost function:

$$TC = \$3X^2 + \$6Y^2 - \$1XY$$

where X represents the output produced on one assembly line and Y the production from the second. Management seeks to determine the least-cost combination of X and Y, subject to the constraint that total output of the product is 20 units. The constrained optimization problem is Minimize

$$TC = \$3X^2 + \$6Y^2 - \$1XY$$

subject to

$$X + Y = 20$$

Solving the constraint for X and substituting this value into the objective function results in

$$X = 20 - Y$$

and

(2A.3)
$$
\begin{aligned}
TC &= \$3(20 - Y)^2 + \$6Y^2 - \$1(20 - Y)Y \\
&= \$3(400 - 40Y + Y^2) + \$6Y^2 - \$1(20Y - Y^2) \\
&= \$1,200 - \$120Y + \$3Y^2 + \$6Y^2 - \$20Y + Y^2 \\
&= \$1,200 - \$140Y + \$10Y^2
\end{aligned}
$$

Now it is possible to treat Equation 2A.3 as an unconstrained minimization problem. Solving it requires taking the derivative of the total cost function, setting that derivative equal to zero, and solving for the value of Y:

$$
\begin{aligned}
\frac{dTC}{dY} &= -\$140 + \$20Y = 0 \\
20Y &= 140 \\
Y &= 7
\end{aligned}
$$

A check of the sign of the second derivative evaluated at that point ensures that a minimum has been located:

$$\frac{dTC}{dY} = -\$140 + \$20Y$$

---

9 This section examines techniques for solving constrained optimization problems in which the constraints can be expressed as equations. Some constraints impose only upper or lower limits on the decision maker and, therefore, may not be "binding" at the optimal solution. Constraints of this second, more general, type are properly expressed as inequality relations. In such instances another optimizing technique, linear programming, is used to analyze the problem. Linear programming is the subject of Chapter 9.

$$\frac{d^2TC}{dY^2} = 20$$

Because the second derivative is positive, $Y = 7$ is indeed a minimum.

Substituting 7 for Y in the constraint equation allows one to determine the optimal quantity to be produced on assembly line X:

$$X + 7 = 20$$
$$X = 13$$

Thus, production of 13 units of output on assembly line X and seven units on line Y is the least-cost combination for manufacturing a total of 20 units of the firm's product. The total cost of producing that combination is

$$TC = \$3(13^2) + \$6(7^2) - \$1(13 \times 7)$$
$$= \$507 + \$294 - \$91$$
$$= \$710$$

Lagrangian Multipliers

Unfortunately, the substitution technique used in the preceding section is not always feasible. Constraint conditions are sometimes too numerous or complex for substitution to be used. In these cases, the technique of *Lagrangian multipliers* can be used.

Lagrangian technique

Method for solving constrained optimization problems

The **Lagrangian technique** for solving constrained optimization problems is a method that calls for optimizing a function that incorporates the original objective function and the constraint conditions. This combined equation, called the Lagrangian function, is created in such a way that when it is maximized or minimized the original objective function is also maximized or minimized, and all constraints are satisfied.

A reexamination of the constrained minimization problem shown previously illustrates this technique. Recall that the firm sought to minimize the function $TC = \$3X^2 + \$6Y^2 - \$1XY$, subject to the constraint that $X + Y = 20$. Rearrange the constraint to bring all terms to the right of the equal sign:

$$0 = 20 - X - Y$$

This is always the first step in forming a Lagrangian expression.

Multiplying this form of the constraint by the unknown factor λ and adding the result to the original objective function creates the Lagrangian expression:[10]

(2A.4)
$$L_{TC} = \$3X^2 + \$6Y^2 - \$1XY + \lambda(20 - X - Y)$$

L_{TC} is defined as the Lagrangian function for the constrained optimization problem under consideration.

Because it incorporates the constraint into the objective function, the Lagrangian function can be treated as an unconstrained optimization problem. The solution to the unconstrained Lagrangian problem is *always* identical to the solution of the original constrained optimization problem. To illustrate, consider the problem of minimizing the Lagrangian function constructed in Equation 2A.4. At a minimum point on a multivariate function, all partial derivatives must equal zero. The partials of Equation 2A.4 can be taken with respect to the three unknown variables, X, Y, and λ, as follows:

---

10 The Greek letter *lambda*, λ, is typically used in formulating Lagrangian expressions.

$$\frac{\partial L_{TC}}{\partial X} = 6X - Y - \lambda$$

$$\frac{\partial L_{TC}}{\partial Y} = 12Y - X - \lambda$$

and

$$\frac{\partial L_{TC}}{\partial \lambda} = 20 - X - Y$$

Setting these three partials equal to zero results in a system of three equations and three unknowns:

(2A.5) $$6X - Y - \lambda = 0$$

(2A.6) $$-X + 12Y - \lambda = 0$$

and

(2A.7) $$20 - X - Y = 0$$

Notice that Equation 2A.7, the partial of the Lagrangian function with respect to λ, is the constraint condition imposed on the original optimization problem. The Lagrangian function is constructed so that the derivative of the function taken with respect to the Lagrangian multiplier, λ, always gives the original constraint. So long as this derivative is zero, as it must be at a local extreme (maximum or minimum), the constraint conditions imposed on the original problem are met. Further, because the last term in the Lagrangian expression must equal zero ($0 = 20 - X - Y$), the Lagrangian function reduces to the original objective function, and the solution to the unconstrained Lagrangian problem is always the solution to the original constrained optimization problem.

Completing the analysis for the example illuminates these relations. To begin, it is necessary to solve the system of equations to obtain optimal values of X and Y. Subtracting Equation 2A.6 from Equation 2A.5 gives

(2A.8) $$7X - 13Y = 0$$

Multiplying Equation 2A.7 by 7 and adding Equation 2A.8 to this product gives the solution for Y:

$$
\begin{aligned}
140 - 7X - 7Y &= 0 \\
7X - 13Y &= 0 \\
\hline
140 - 20Y &= 0 \\
140 &= 20Y \\
Y &= 7
\end{aligned}
$$

Substituting 7 for Y in Equation 2A.7 yields $X = 13$, the value of X at the point where the Lagrangian function is minimized.

Because the solution of the Lagrangian function is also the solution to the firm's constrained optimization problem, 13 units from assembly line X and seven units from line Y is the least-cost combination of output that can be produced subject to the constraint that total output must be 20 units. This is the same answer obtained previously, using the substitution method.

The Lagrangian technique is a more powerful technique for solving constrained optimization problems than the substitution method; it is easier to apply with multiple constraints, and it provides valuable supplementary information. This is because the Lagrangian multiplier itself has an important economic interpretation. Substituting the values of X and Y into Equation 2A.5 gives the value of λ:

$$6 \times 13 - 7 - \lambda = 0$$
$$\lambda = \$71$$

Here, λ is interpreted as the marginal cost of production at 20 units of output. It means that if the firm were allowed to produce only 19 instead of 20 units of output, total costs would fall by approximately \$71. If the output requirement were 21 instead of 20 units, costs would increase by roughly that amount.[11]

Because $\lambda = \$71$ can be interpreted as the marginal cost of production, an offer to purchase another unit of output for \$100 is acceptable because it results in a \$29 marginal profit. Conversely, an offer to purchase an additional unit for \$50 would be rejected because a marginal loss of \$21 would be incurred. λ can be thought of as a planning variable, because it provides valuable information concerning the effects of altering current activity levels.

Another example provides additional perspective on the Lagrangian method. Recall from the discussion of Equation 2.6 and Figure 2.5 that the profit function,

$$\pi = -\$10,000 + \$400Q - \$2Q^2$$

where π is total profit and Q is output in units, is maximized at $Q = 100$ with $\pi = \$10,000$. The impact of constraints in the production process, and the value of the Lagrangian method, can be portrayed by considering the situation in which each unit of output requires 4 hours of skilled labor, and a total of only 300 hours of skilled labor is currently available to the firm. In this instance, the firm seeks to maximize the function $\pi = -\$10,000 + \$400Q - \$2Q^2$, subject to the constraint $4Q = 300$ (because $L = 4Q$). Rearrange the constraint to bring all terms to the right of the equal sign:

$$0 = 300 - 4Q$$

Multiplying this form of the constraint by λ and adding the result to the original objective function creates the Lagrangian expression:

(2A.9) $$\qquad L\pi = -\$10,000 + \$400Q - \$2Q^2 + \lambda(300 - 4Q)$$

with the following partials:

$$\frac{\partial L_\pi}{\partial Q} = 400 - 4Q - 4\lambda$$

and

$$\frac{\partial L_\pi}{\partial \lambda} = 300 - 4Q$$

---

11 Technically, λ indicates the marginal change in the objective function solution associated with an infinitesimally small change in the constraint. It only approximates the change in total cost that would take place if one more (or less) unit of output were produced.

Setting these two partials equal to zero results in a system of two equations and two unknowns. Solving provides the values $Q = 75$, $\lambda = \$25$, and, from the objective function, $\pi = \$8,750$. The constraint on skilled labor has reduced output from 100 to 75 units and has reduced total profits from $10,000 to $8,750. The value $\lambda = \$25$ indicates that should a one-unit expansion in output become possible, total profits would rise by $25. This information indicates that the maximum value of additional skilled labor is $6.25 per hour, because each unit of output requires 4 hours of labor. Assuming there are no other costs involved, $6.25 per hour is the most the firm would pay to expand employment.

The effects of relaxing the constraint as progressively more skilled labor becomes available are illustrated in Figure 2A.2. If an additional 100 hours of skilled labor, or 400 hours in total, is available, the output constraint would become $0 = 400 - 4Q$, and solved values $Q = 100$, $\lambda = \$0$, and $\pi = \$10,000$ would result. The value $\lambda = \$0$ indicates that skilled labor no longer constrains profits when 400 hours are available. Profits are maximized at $Q = 100$, which is the same result obtained in the earlier unconstrained solution to this profit maximization problem.

In this instance, the output constraint becomes nonbinding because it does not limit the profit-making ability of the firm. Indeed, the firm is not willing to employ more than 400 hours of skilled labor. To illustrate this point, consider the use of 500 hours of skilled labor and the resulting constraint $0 = 500 - 4Q$. Solved values are $Q = 125$, $\lambda = -\$25$, and $\pi = \$8,750$. The value $\lambda = -\$25$ indicates that one additional unit of output, and the expansion in employment that results, would reduce profits by $25. Conversely, a one-unit reduction in the level of output would increase profits by $25. Clearly, the situation in which $\lambda < 0$ gives the firm an incentive to reduce input usage and output, just as $\lambda > 0$ provides an incentive for growth.

Lagrangian multiplier, λ
Marginal effect on the objective function of decreasing or increasing the constraint requirement by one unit

To generalize, a **Lagrangian multiplier**, λ, indicates the marginal effect on the objective function of decreasing or increasing the constraint requirement by one unit. Often, as in the previous examples, the marginal relation described by the Lagrangian multiplier provides economic data that help managers evaluate the potential benefits or costs of relaxing constraints.

FIGURE 2A.2

The Role of Constraints in Profit Maximization
When profit is maximized, $\lambda = \$0$.

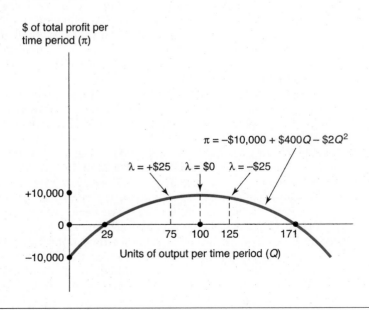

PROBLEM

2A.1   **Lagrangian Multipliers.** Amos Jones and Andrew Brown own and operate Amos & Andy, Inc., a Minneapolis–based installer of conversion packages for vans manufactured by the major auto companies. Amos & Andy has fixed capital and labor expenses of $1.2 million per year, and variable materials expenses average $2,000 per van conversion. Recent operating experience suggests the following annual demand relation for Amos & Andy products:

$$Q = 1,000 - 0.1P$$

where Q is the number of van conversions (output) and P is price.

A. Calculate Amos & Andy's profit-maximizing output, price, and profit levels.

B. Using the Lagrangian multiplier method, calculate profit-maximizing output, price, and profit levels in light of a parts shortage that limits Amos & Andy's output to 300 conversions during the coming year.

C. Calculate and interpret λ, the Lagrangian multiplier.

D. Calculate the value to Amos & Andy of having the parts shortage eliminated.

SELECTED REFERENCES

Bascha, Andreas, and Uwe Walz. "Convertible Securities and Optimal Exit Decisions in Venture Capital Finance." *Journal of Corporate Finance* 7 (September 2001): 285–306.

Epstein, Larry G. "Sharing Ambiguity." *American Economic Review* 91 (May 2001): 45–50.

French, Nick. "Decision Theory and Real Estate Investment: An Analysis of the Decision-Making Processes of Real Estate Investment Fund Managers." *Managerial & Decision Economics* 22 (October/November 2001): 399–410.

Genesove, David, and Christopher Mayer. "Loss Aversion and Seller Behavior: Evidence from the Housing Market." *Quarterly Journal of Economics* 116 (November 2001): 1233–1260.

Hansen, Lars Peter, and Thomas J. Sargent. "Robust Control and Model Uncertainty." *American Economic Review* 91 (May 2001): 60–66.

Hobijn, Bart, and Boyan Jovanovic. "The Information-Technology Revolution and the Stock Market: Evidence." *American Economic Review* 91 (December 2001): 1203–1220.

Lamont, Owen A., and Christopher Polk. "Does Diversification Destroy Value? Evidence from the Industry Shocks." *Journal of Financial Economics* 63 (January 2002): 51–77.

Loasby, Brian L. "An Entrepreneurial Theory of the Firm: Foreword by Israel M. Kirzner." *Economic Journal* 111 (June 2001): F537–F538.

Madrian, Brigitte C., and Dennis F. Shea. "The Power of Suggestion: Inertia in 401(K) Participation and Savings Behavior." *Quarterly Journal of Economics* 116 (November 2001): 1149–1187.

Nissim, Doron, and Amir Ziv. "Dividend Changes and Future Profitability." *Journal of Finance* 56 (December 2001): 2211–2134.

Persson, Torsten, Géérard Roland, and Guido Tabellini. "Disability Insurance Benefits and Labor Supply." *Journal of Political Economy* 108 (December 2000): 1162–1184.

Rajan, Raghuram G., and Luigi Zingales. "The Firm as a Dedicated Hierarchy: A Theory of the Origins and Growth of Firms." *Quarterly Journal of Economics* 116 (August 2001): 805–851.

Roberts, Peter W. "Innovation and Firm-Level Persistent Profitability: A Schumpeterian Framework." *Managerial & Decision Economics* 22 (June/August 2001): 239–250.

Rogers, Edward W. "A Theoretical Look at Firm Performance in High-Tech Organizations: What Does Existing Theory Tell Us?" *Journal of High Technology Management Research* 12 (Spring 2001): 39–61.

Wakely, Tim. "Economic Organization and Economic Knowledge, and Contingency, Complexity and the Theory of the Firm: Essays in Honour of Brian J. Loasby, Vols. I and II." *Information Economics & Policy* 13 (March 2001): 117–125.

CHAPTER THREE

Demand and Supply

Around the globe, 24 hours per day, impossible-to-regulate currency markets set prices for the U.S. dollar, Japanese yen, and the European Economic and Monetary Union's euro. Much to the chagrin of sovereign governments and their official representatives, minute-by-minute variations in currency prices are wholly determined by the converging forces of supply and demand.

For example, U.S. stock markets plunged an unprecedented 684.81 points on Monday, September 17, 2001, following the resumption of trading after terrorist attacks in New York City and Washington, DC. Those attacks left thousands dead and millions of investors understandably nervous about the economy and a potential meltdown in investor confidence. Securities markets fell sharply as investors worried that the attacks could chill consumer sentiment and throw the world economy into recession. In the currency market, the dollar plunged more than three yen, from roughly 120 yen per dollar to 117 yen per dollar, to its lowest level in nearly seven months.

When the number of yen that can be bought for a dollar falls, the dollar price of Japanese–made goods rises in the United States. This hurts both U.S. consumers and Japanese exporters. To stem the slide in the dollar, Japanese monetary authorities intervened in the currency market to buy dollars and sell yen. This had the temporary effect of increasing the supply of yen relative to dollars, and the dollar quickly jumped from just below 117 yen to nearly 118.50 yen. However, both currencies quickly slipped back to preintervention levels when it became clear that it was the Japanese central bank, and not market forces, that had caused the dollar to rise and the yen to fall. The upshot is simple: The laws of demand and supply are so powerful that they dictate the value of money itself![1]

---

[1] See Dow Jones Newswires, "Dollar Steadies vs. Euro, Yen As Bank of Japan Intervenes," *The Wall Street Journal Online*, September 17, 2001 (http://online.wsj.com).

BASIS FOR DEMAND

demand
Total quantity customers are willing and able to purchase

Demand is the quantity of a good or service that customers are willing and able to purchase during a specified period under a given set of economic conditions. The time frame might be an hour, a day, a month, or a year. Conditions to be considered include the price of the good in question, prices and availability of related goods, expectations of price changes, consumer incomes, consumer tastes and preferences, advertising expenditures, and so on. The amount of the product that consumers are prepared to purchase, its demand, depends on all these factors.

For managerial decision making, a prime focus is on market demand. Market demand is the aggregate of individual, or personal, demand. Insight into market demand relations requires an understanding of the nature of individual demand. Individual demand is determined by the value associated with acquiring and using any good or service and the ability to acquire it. Both are necessary for effective individual demand. Desire without purchasing power may lead to want, but not to demand.

Direct Demand

direct demand
Demand for consumption products

utility
Value

There are two basic models of individual demand. One, known as the theory of consumer behavior, relates to the **direct demand** for personal consumption products. This model is appropriate for analyzing individual demand for goods and services that directly satisfy consumer desires. The value or worth of a good or service, its **utility**, is the prime determinant of direct demand. Individuals are viewed as attempting to maximize the total utility or satisfaction provided by the goods and services they acquire and consume. This optimization process requires that consumers focus on the marginal utility (gain in satisfaction) of acquiring additional units of a given product. Product characteristics, individual preferences (tastes), and the ability to pay are all important determinants of direct demand.

Derived Demand

derived demand
Demand for inputs used in production

Goods and services are sometimes acquired because they are important inputs in the manufacture and distribution of other products. The outputs of engineers, production workers, sales staff, managers, lawyers, consultants, office business machines, production facilities and equipment, natural resources, and commercial airplanes are all examples of goods and services demanded not for direct consumption but rather for their use in providing other goods and services. Their demand is derived from the demand for the products they are used to provide. Input demand is called **derived demand**.

The demand for mortgage money is an example. The quantity of mortgage credit demanded is not determined directly; it is derived from the more fundamental demand for housing. The demand for air transportation to resort areas is not a direct demand but is derived from the demand for recreation. Similarly, the demand for producers' goods and services used to manufacture products for final consumption is derived. Aggregate demand for consumption goods and services determines demand for the capital equipment, materials, labor, and energy used to manufacture them. For example, the demands for steel, aluminum, and plastics are all derived demands, as are the demands for machine tools and labor. None of these producers' goods are demanded because of their direct value to consumers but because of the role they play in production.

Demand for producers' goods and services is closely related to final products demand. An examination of final product demand is an important part of demand analysis for intermediate, or producers', goods. For products whose demand is derived rather than direct, demand stems from their value in the manufacture and sale of other products. They have value because their

How the Internet Affects Demand and Supply

From an economic perspective, the Internet is the enemy of high prices and high profit margins. By greatly expanding the scope of the market, the Internet effectively eliminates geographic boundaries, especially for easily transported goods and services. This greatly increases the elasticity of demand and supply.

For example, in the pre-Internet era, anyone looking for a good deal on a high-quality vacuum cleaner might have gone to the local Wal-Mart, Target, or a specialty shop to look for the best bargain available. With the Internet, consumers can log onto Google.com, or your favorite Internet search engine; do a search on vacuum cleaners; and get data on hundreds of high-quality vacuums at extremely attractive prices. For example, with $15 to $20 for shipping via Federal Express or UPS, it is possible to have vacuums delivered in Lawrence, Kansas, from http://www.vacdepot.com/ in Houston, Texas, at prices far below those offered by the local vacuum cleaner shop.

Successful Internet retailers offer bargain prices, a broad assortment of attractive products, and speedy delivery. They also effectively handle returns and basic customer service. Of course, traditional retailers cannot stand idly by as Internet-based retailers drive them out of business. They must fight back with competitive prices, high-quality products, and an enticing in-store shopping experience. Borders is a good example of a bookseller that has effectively distinguished itself from Amazon.com and other Internet retailers by offering an appealing in-store shopping experience.

When considering the economic potential of Internet-based commerce, it is important to keep in mind that successful firms use Internet technology to maintain significant competitive advantages. The Internet, by itself, seldom confers long-lasting competitive advantages. The Internet is a marvelous communications device that greatly improves access to information about product quality, prices, and performance. The Internet broadens the market, and makes demand and supply much more sensitive to changing economic conditions.

See: Kristi Essick, "Young Guns Get Creative in Life After Venture Capital," *The Wall Street Journal Online*, December 7, 2001 (http://online.wsj.com).

employment has the potential to generate profits. Key components in the determination of derived demand are the marginal benefits and marginal costs associated with using a given input or factor of production. The amount of any good or service used rises when its marginal benefit, measured in terms of the value of resulting output, is greater than the marginal costs of using the input, measured in terms of wages, interest, raw material costs, or related expenses. Conversely, the amount of any input used in production falls when resulting marginal benefits are less than the marginal cost of employment. In short, derived demand is related to the profitability of using a good or service.

Regardless of whether a good or service is demanded by individuals for final consumption (direct demand) or as an input used in providing other goods and services (derived demand), the fundamentals of economic analysis offer a basis for investigating demand characteristics. For final consumption products, utility maximization as described by the theory of consumer behavior explains the basis for direct demand. For inputs used in the production of other products, profit maximization provides the underlying rationale for derived demand. Because both demand models are based on the optimization concept, fundamental direct and derived demand relations are essentially the same.

MARKET DEMAND FUNCTION

demand function
Relation between demand and factors influencing its level

The market **demand function** for a product is a statement of the relation between the aggregate quantity demanded and all factors that affect this quantity. In functional form, a demand function may be expressed as

(3.1) Quantity of Product X Demanded $= Q_x =$ f(Price of X, Prices of Related Goods, Expectations of Price Changes, Consumer Incomes, Tastes and Preferences, Advertising Expenditures, and so on)

The generalized demand function expressed in Equation 3.1 lists variables that commonly influence demand. For use in managerial decision making, the relation between quantity and each demand-determining variable must be specified. To illustrate what is involved, assume that the demand function for the automobile industry is

(3.2)
$$Q = a_1 P + a_2 PI + a_3 I + a_4 Pop + a_5 i + a_6 A$$

This equation states that the number of new domestic automobiles demanded during a given year (in millions), Q, is a linear function of the average price of new domestic cars (in \$), P; the average price for new import cars (in \$), PI; disposable income per household (in \$), I; population (in millions), Pop; average interest rate on car loans (in percent), i; and industry advertising expenditures (in \$ millions), A. The terms $a_1, a_2, \ldots, a_6$ are called the parameters of the demand function. Assume that the parameters of this demand function are known with certainty, as shown in the following equation:

(3.3)
$$Q = -500P + 210P_X + 200I + 20{,}000Pop - 1{,}000{,}000i + 600A$$

Equation 3.3 states that automobile demand falls by 500 for each \$1 increase in the average price charged by domestic manufacturers; it rises by 210 with every \$1 increase in the average price of new luxury cars (P_X), a prime substitute; it increases by 200 for each \$1 increase in disposable income per household (I); it increases by 20,000 with each additional million persons in the population (Pop); it decreases by 1 million for every 1 percent rise in interest rates (i); and it increases by 600 with each unit (\$1 million) spent on advertising (A).

To derive an estimate of industry demand in any given year, each parameter in Equation 3.3 is multiplied by the value of the related variable and then summed. Table 3.1 illustrates this process, showing that the estimated annual demand for new domestic automobiles is 8 million cars, assuming the stated values of each independent variable.

Industry Demand Versus Firm Demand

Market demand functions can be specified for an entire industry or for an individual firm, though somewhat different variables would typically be used in each case. Variables representing competitors' actions would be stressed in firm demand functions. For example, a firm's demand function would typically include competitors' prices and advertising expenditures. Demand for the firm's product line is negatively related to its own prices but positively related to the prices charged by competing firms. Demand for the firm's products would typically increase with its own advertising expenditures, but it could increase or decrease with additional advertising by other firms.

The parameters for specific variables ordinarily differ in industry versus firm demand functions. Consider the positive influence of population on the demand for Ford automobiles as opposed to automobiles in general. Although the effect is positive in each instance, the parameter value in the Ford demand function would be much smaller than that in the industry demand function. Only if Ford had 100 percent of the market—that is, if Ford were the industry—would the parameters for firm and industry demand be identical.

Because firm and industry demand functions differ, different models or equations must be estimated for analyzing these two levels of demand. However, demand concepts developed in this chapter apply to both firm and industry demand functions.

TABLE 3.1

Estimating Industry Demand for New Automobiles

Independent Variable (1)	Parameter Estimate (2)	Estimated Value for Independent Variable During the Coming Year (3)	Estimated Demand (4) = (2) × (3)
Average Price for New Cars (P) ($)	–500	$25,000	–12,500,000
Average Price for New Luxury Cars (P_X) ($)	210	$50,000	10,500,000
Disposable Income, per Household (I) ($)	200	$45,000	9,000,000
Population (*Pop*) (millions)	20,000	300	6,000,000
Average Interest Rate (i) (percent)	–1,000,000	8%	–8,000,000
Industry Advertising Expenditures (A) ($million)	600	$5,000	3,000,000
Total Demand (cars)			8,000,000

 ## DEMAND CURVE

demand curve
Relation between price and the quantity demanded, holding all else constant

The demand function specifies the relation between the quantity demanded and all variables that determine demand. The **demand curve** expresses the relation between the price charged for a product and the quantity demanded, holding constant the effects of all other variables. Frequently, a demand curve is shown in the form of a graph, and all variables in the demand function except the price and quantity of the product itself are held fixed. In the automobile demand function given in Equation 3.3, for example, one must hold income, population, interest rates, and advertising expenditures constant to identify the demand curve relation between new domestic automobile prices and quantity demanded.

Demand Curve Determination

To illustrate, consider the relation depicted in Equation 3.3 and Table 3.1. Assuming that import car prices, income, population, interest rates, and advertising expenditures are all held constant at their Table 3.1 values, the relation between the quantity demanded of new domestic cars and price is expressed as[2]

(3.4)
$$Q = -500P + 210(\$50,000) + 200(\$45,000) + 20,000(300)$$
$$- 1,000,000(8) + 600(\$5,000)$$
$$= 20,500,000 - 500P$$

Alternatively, when price is expressed as a function of output, the industry demand curve (Equation 3.4) can be written:

(3.5)
$$P = \$41,000 - \$0.002Q$$

---

2   At first blush, an 8 percent interest rate assumption might seem quite high by today's standards when 2.9 percent financing or $2,500 rebates are sometimes offered to boost new car sales during slow periods. However, so-called "teaser" rates of 2.9 percent are subsidized by the manufacturer; that is why promotions feature 2.9 percent financing *or* (rather than *and*) $2,500 rebates. In such instances, the alternative $2,500 rebate is a good estimate of the amount of interest rate subsidy offered by the manufacturer.

Equations 3.4 and 3.5 both represent the demand curve for automobiles given specified values for all other variables in the demand function. Equation 3.5 is shown graphically in Figure 3.1 because it is common to show price as a function of quantity in demand analysis. As is typical, a reduction in price increases the quantity demanded; an increase in price decreases the quantity demanded. The –500 slope coefficient for the price variable in Equation 3.4 means that a $1 increase in the average price of new domestic automobiles would reduce the quantity demanded by 500 cars. Similarly, a $1 decrease in the average price of new domestic automobiles would increase quantity demanded by 500 cars. When price is expressed as a function of quantity, as in Equation 3.5, a one-unit increase in Q would lead to a $0.002 reduction in the average price of new domestic cars. A 1-million car decrease in Q would lead to a $2,000 increase in average prices.

Relation Between the Demand Curve and Demand Function

The relation between the demand curve and the demand function is important and worth considering in somewhat greater detail. Figure 3.2 shows three demand curves for automobiles. Each curve is constructed in the same manner as that depicted in Equations 3.4 and 3.5 and then portrayed in Figure 3.1. In fact, $D_{8\%}$ is the same automobile demand curve characterized by

FIGURE 3.1

Hypothetical Industry Demand Curve for New Domestic Automobiles

The parameter estimate (slope coefficient) for the automobile demand curve reveals that a $1 increase in the price of new automobiles will decrease the quantity demanded by 500 units. Thus, a decline in quantity demanded of 500 autos follows a $1 increase in price.

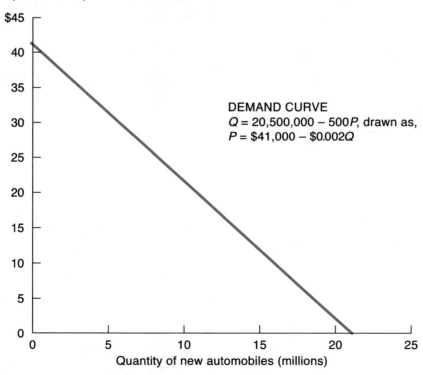

Average price per auto ($ thousands)

DEMAND CURVE
$Q = 20,500,000 - 500P$, drawn as,
$P = \$41,000 - \$0.002Q$

Quantity of new automobiles (millions)

Equation 3.5 and Figure 3.1. If $D_{8\%}$ is the appropriate demand curve, then 8 million new domestic automobiles can be sold at an average price of $25,000, whereas 10 million automobiles could be sold at an average price of $16,000, but only 6 million automobiles can be sold at an average price of $29,000 This variation is described as a **change in the quantity demanded**, defined as a movement along a single given demand curve. As average price drops from $29,000 to $25,000 to $2,100 along $D_{8\%}$, the quantity demanded rises from 6 million to 8 million to 10 million automobiles. A change in the quantity demanded refers to the effect on sales of a change in price, holding constant the effects of all other demand-determining factors.

change in the quantity demanded Movement along a given demand curve reflecting a change in price and quantity

A **shift in demand**, or switch from one demand curve to another, reflects a change in one or more nonprice variables in the product demand function. In the automobile demand-function example, a decrease in interest rates causes an increase in automobile demand, because the interest rate parameter of –1 million indicates that demand and interest rates are inversely related— that is, they change in opposite directions. When demand is inversely related to a factor such as interest rates, a reduction in the factor leads to rising demand and an increase in the factor leads to falling demand.

shift in demand Switch from one demand curve to another following a change in a nonprice determinant of demand

FIGURE 3.2

Hypothetical Industry Demand Curves for New Domestic Automobiles at Interest Rates of 6%, 8%, and 10%

A shift in the original demand curve from $D_{8\%}$ to $D_{6\%}$ follows a 2% fall in interest rates from 8% to 6%; a shift from $D_{8\%}$ to $D_{10\%}$ reflects a 2% rise in interest rates from 8% to 10%.

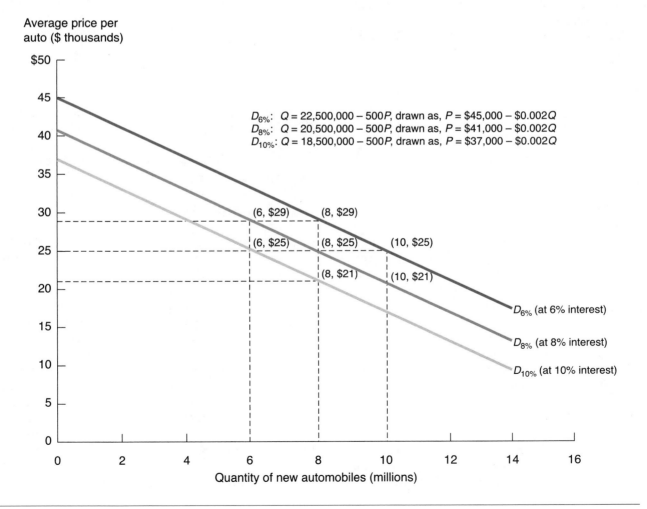

$D_{6\%}$: $Q = 22,500,000 - 500P$, drawn as, $P = \$45,000 - \$0.002Q$
$D_{8\%}$: $Q = 20,500,000 - 500P$, drawn as, $P = \$41,000 - \$0.002Q$
$D_{10\%}$: $Q = 18,500,000 - 500P$, drawn as, $P = \$37,000 - \$0.002Q$

ISP Customers Learn About Demand and Supply

In 1996, America Online, Inc. (AOL), the leader in the burgeoning Internet service provider (ISP) industry, succumbed to pressure from competitors and cut its price for unlimited access to the Internet to $19.95 per month. Usage skyrocketed. Because flat-rate pricing does not penalize unlimited usage, many subscribers simply decided to leave their connection running all day and night. Because of surging popularity among novice users, long-time subscribers found themselves locked out of the AOL system. Dedicated users became especially irate when AOL kept running TV commercials and offering promotional rates to new subscribers when it was clearly unable to handle the traffic such promotions generated. Subscriber frustration turned to litigation, and AOL was hit with lawsuits charging the company with negligence and consumer fraud.

Overloaded, facing lawsuits and the potential of massive defections from dissatisfied customers, AOL made a radical decision. AOL slashed marketing efforts aimed at recruiting new subscribers and stepped up investment in network capacity. By 1998, continuing growth in the popularity of the Internet allowed AOL to boost spending on infrastructure and even raise its fixed-rate monthly charge for unlimited access to $21.95 per month. Still, AOL suffers from having to employ a fixed-rate pricing structure that is incapable of balancing demand and supply. Like all ISPs, AOL suffers from a business plan featuring fixed-rate pricing that encourages unlimited demand and time-dependent supply costs that are variable with usage. Unlike local phone service, where fixed costs predominate and marginal usage costs are near zero, ISPs closely resemble long-distance telephone service providers. ISP costs are closely tied to time of usage, and efficient pricing must be on a per unit basis.

With time-based pricing, ISP demand will be curtailed during peak hours, and the practice of novice users logging on for days at a time will end. In the meantime, frustrated ISP customers will suffer from demand/supply imbalances created by the industry's fixed-rate pricing model.

See: Julia Angwin, Martin Peers, and Matthew Rose, "Parsons's Ascendance Sends AOL a Message from Time Warner: We're in Charge Here," *The Wall Street Journal Online*, December 6, 2001 (http://online.wsj.com).

$D_{6\%}$ is another automobile demand curve. The sole difference between $D_{8\%}$ and $D_{6\%}$ is that $D_{8\%}$ assumes an interest rate of 8 percent rather than the 6 percent interest rate used to construct $D_{6\%}$. Because the interest rate parameter is negative, a decrease in interest rates causes an increase in automobile demand. Holding all else equal, a 2 percent reduction in interest rates leads to a 2-million-unit [= –1 million × (–2)] increase in automobile demand. A 2 percent decrease in average interest rates leads to an upward or rightward shift in the original demand curve $D_{8\%}$ to the new demand curve $D_{6\%}$. This also means that a 2 percent interest rate reduction will increase automobile demand by 2 million units at each price level. At an average price of $25,000, for example, a 2 percent reduction in interest rates increases automobile demand from 8 million to 10 million units per year, as shown on $D_{6\%}$. Also as shown on $D_{6\%}$, after a 2 percent decrease in interest rates, the original quantity of 8 million automobiles could be sold at a higher average price of $29,000. Notice that demand curve $D_{8\%}$ indicates that only 8 million units could be sold at an average industry price of $25,000, when interest rates average 8 percent per year.

However, a 2 percent increase in interest rates, from 8 percent to 10 percent, causes an inward or leftward shift in the original demand curve $D_{8\%}$ to the new demand curve $D_{10\%}$. A 2 percent increase in interest rates reduces automobile demand by 2 million cars at each price level. At a price of $25,000, a 2 percent increase in interest rates reduces demand for new domestic cars from 8 million cars, the $D_{8\%}$ level, to only 6 million units, the $D_{6\%}$ level. With interest rates at 10 percent, demand for 8 million cars would only arise at the lower average price of $21,000, the $D_{10\%}$ level, again holding all other demand-determining factors constant.

From the advertising parameter of 600, it is possible to infer that demand and advertising are positively related. Rising demand follows increases in advertising, and falling demand follows reductions in advertising. The shift from $D_{8\%}$ to $D_{6\%}$ in Figure 3.2, for example, could also have resulted from a $2.5 billion increase in industry advertising rather than a 2 percent reduction in interest rates, or it could be the result of a $1.25 billion increase in industry advertising coupled with a 1 percent reduction in interest rates. In each case, the resulting demand curve is given by the equation $Q = 20,000,000 - 500P$, or $P = \$40,000 - \$0.002Q$. However, the downward shift from $D_{8\%}$ to $D_{10\%}$ in Figure 3.2 could have resulted from a $3.3 billion decrease in industry advertising rather than a 2 percent increase in interest rates, or it could be the result of a $1.67 billion decrease in industry advertising coupled with a 1 percent increase in interest rates. In each case, the resulting demand curve is given by the equation $Q = 22,500,000 - 500P$, or $P = \$45,000 - \$0.002Q$.

The distinction between changes in the quantity demanded, which reflect movements along a given demand curve, and changes in demand, which reflect shifts from one demand curve to another, is extremely important. Failure to understand the causes of changes in demand for a company's products can lead to costly, even disastrous, mistakes in managerial decision making. The task of demand analysis is made especially difficult by the fact that under normal circumstances, not only prices but also prices of other goods, income, population, interest rates, advertising, and most other demand-related factors vary from period to period. Sorting out the impact of each factor makes demand analysis one of the most challenging aspects of managerial economics.

BASIS FOR SUPPLY

supply
Total quantity offered for sale

The term **supply** refers to the quantity of a good or service that producers are willing and able to sell during a certain period under a given set of conditions. Factors that must be specified include the price of the good in question, prices of related goods, the current state of technology, levels of input prices, weather, and so on. The amount of product that producers bring to the market—the supply of the product—depends on all these influences.

Factors That Influence Supply

The supply of a product in the market is the aggregate amount supplied by individual firms. The supply of products arises from their ability to enhance the firm's value-maximization objective. The amount of any good or service supplied will rise when the marginal benefit to producers, measured in terms of the value of output, is greater than the marginal cost of production. The amount of any good or service supplied will fall when the marginal benefit to producers is less than the marginal costs of production. Thus, individual firms will expand or reduce supply based on the expected impact on profits.

Among the factors influencing the supply of a product, the price of the product itself is often the most important. Higher prices increase the quantity of output producers want to bring to market. When marginal revenue exceeds marginal cost, firms increase supply to earn the greater profits associated with expanded output. Higher prices allow firms to pay the higher production costs that are sometimes associated with expansions in output. Conversely, lower prices typically cause producers to supply a lower quantity of output. At the margin, lower prices can have the effect of making previous levels of production unprofitable.

The prices of related goods and services can also play an important role in determining supply of a product. If a firm uses resources that can be used to produce several different products, it may switch production from one product to another depending on market conditions. For example, the supply of gasoline typically declines in autumn when the price of heating oil rises. Gasoline supply typically increases during the spring and summer months with the seasonal decline in heating oil prices. Whereas the substitution of one output for another can cause an inverse relation between the supply of one product and the price of a second, complementary production relationships result in a positive relation between supply and the price of a related product. For example, ore deposits containing lead often also contain silver. An increase in the price of lead can therefore lead to an expansion in both lead and silver production.

Technology is a key determinant of product supply. The current state of technology refers to the manner in which inputs are transformed into output. An improvement in the state of technology, including any product invention or process innovation that reduces production costs, increases the quantity and/or quality of products offered for sale at a given price.

Changes in input prices also affect supply in that an increase in input prices will raise costs and reduce the quantity that can be supplied profitably at a given market price. Alternatively, a decrease in input prices increases profitability and the quantity supplied at a given price.

For some products, especially agricultural products, weather can play an important role in determining supply. Temperature, rainfall, and wind all influence the quantity that can be supplied. Heavy rainfall in early spring, for example, can delay or prevent the planting of crops, significantly limiting supply. Abundant rain during the growing season can greatly increase the available supply at harvest time. An early freeze that prevents full maturation or heavy snow that limits harvesting activity both reduce the supply of agricultural products.

Managerial decision making requires understanding both individual firm supply and market supply conditions. Market supply is the aggregate of individual firm supply, so it is ultimately determined by factors affecting firm supply. Firm supply is examined in greater detail in Chapters 7 and 8. For now, meaningful insight can be gained by understanding the nature of market supply.

MARKET SUPPLY FUNCTION

supply function
Relation between supply and all factors influencing its level

The market **supply function** for a product is a statement of the relation between the quantity supplied and all factors affecting that quantity. In functional form, a supply function can be expressed as

(3.6)
$$\begin{matrix} \text{Quantity of} \\ \text{Product } X \\ \text{Supplied} \end{matrix} = Q = \begin{matrix} f(\text{Price of } X, \text{ Prices of Related Goods,} \\ \text{Current State of Technology, Input} \\ \text{Prices, Weather, and so on}) \end{matrix}$$

The generalized supply function expressed in Equation 3.6 lists variables that influence supply. As is true with the demand function, the supply function must be made explicit to be useful for managerial decision making.

Determinants of Supply

To illustrate, consider the automobile industry example discussed previously and assume that the supply function has been specified as follows:

(3.7)
$$Q = b_1 P + b_2 P_{SUV} + b_3 W + b_4 S + b_5 E + b_6 i$$

This equation states that the number of new domestic automobiles supplied during a given period (in millions), Q, is a linear function of the average price of new domestic cars (in \$), P; average price of new sport utility vehicles (SUVs) (in \$), P_{SUV}; average hourly price of labor (wages in \$ per hour), W; average cost of steel (\$ per ton), S; average cost of energy (\$ per mcf natural gas), E; and average interest rate (cost of capital in percent), i. The terms $b_1, b_2, \ldots, b_6$ are the parameters of the supply function. Note that no explicit term describes technology, or the method by which inputs are combined to produce output. The current state of technology is an underlying or implicit factor in the industry supply function.

Substituting a set of assumed parameter values into Equation 3.7 gives the following supply function for the automobile industry:

(3.8) $Q = 2{,}000P - 400P_{SUV} - 100{,}000W - 13{,}750S - 125{,}000E - 1{,}000{,}000i$

Equation 3.8 indicates that automobile supply increases by 2,000 units for each $1 increase in the average price charged; it decreases by 400 units for each $1 increase in the average price of new sport utility vehicles; it decreases by 100,000 units for each $1 increase in wage rates, including fringes; it decreases by 13,750 units with each $1 increase in the average cost of steel; it decreases by 125,000 units with each $1 increase in the average cost of energy; and it decreases by 1 million units if interest rates rise 1 percent. Thus, each parameter indicates the effect of the related factor on supply from domestic manufacturers.

To estimate the supply of automobiles during the coming period, each parameter in Equation 3.8 is multiplied by the value of its respective variable and these products are then summed. Table 3.2 illustrates this process, showing that the supply of autos, assuming the stated values of the independent variables, is 8 million units.

Industry Supply Versus Firm Supply

Just as in the case of demand, supply functions can be specified for an entire industry or an individual firm. Even though factors affecting supply are highly similar in industry versus firm supply functions, the relative importance of such influences can differ dramatically. At one extreme, if all firms used identical production methods and identical equipment, had salaried and hourly employees who were equally capable and identically paid, and had equally skilled management, then individual firm and industry supply functions would be closely related. Each firm would be similarly affected by changes in supply conditions. Each parameter in the individual firm supply functions would be smaller than in the industry supply function, however, and would reflect each firm's relative share of the market.

More typically, firms within a given industry adopt somewhat different production methods, use equipment of different vintage, and employ labor of varying skill and compensation levels. In such cases, individual firm supply levels can be affected quite differently by various factors. Korean automakers, for example, may be able to offer subcompacts profitably at average industry prices as low as, say, $15,000 per automobile. On the other hand, U.S. auto manufacturers, who have historically operated with a labor cost disadvantage, may only be able to offer a supply of

TABLE 3.2

Estimating Industry Supply for New Automobiles

Independent Variable (1)	Parameter Estimate (2)	Estimated Value for Independent Variable During the Coming Year (3)	Estimated Supply (4) = (2) × (3)
Average Price for New Cars (P) ($)	2,000	$25,000	50,000,000
Average Price for Sport Utility Vehicles (P_{SUV}) ($)	−400	$35,000	−14,000,000
Average Hourly Wage Rate, Including Fringe Benefits (W) ($)	−100,000	$85	−8,500,000
Average Cost of Steel, per Ton (S) ($)	−13,750	$800	−11,000,000
Average Cost of Energy Input, per mcf Natural Gas (E) ($)	−125,000	$4	−500,000
Average Interest Rate (i) (in percent)	−1,000,000	8%	−8,000,000
Total Supply (cars)			8,000,000

The Import Supply Battle in the U.S. Auto Industry

The "Big Three" U.S. manufacturers typically account for 60 percent to 65 percent of the U.S. market. Japanese name plates account for roughly 25 percent; European makes are responsible for the remainder. Despite a continuing erosion in market share during the 1980s and 1990s, General Motors (GM) remains by far the largest company in the U.S. auto market. GM's current market share is in the 30 percent to 35 percent range, followed by the Ford Motor Company with roughly 25 percent; DaimlerChrysler and Toyota with 10 percent to 15 percent each; Honda, roughly 6 percent; and Nissan, roughly 4 percent. Other companies, like Hyundai (Kia), Mazda, Mitsubishi, Subaru, and Volkswagen, account for the rest.

As companies fight for market share, many new products are aimed at market niches. Chrysler, for example, returned from the brink of bankruptcy in the 1980s to record profits in the 1990s on the basis of its astonishing success with minivans. At the same time, Ford took aim at Chrysler's lucrative Jeep franchise with the Ford Explorer and outran both Jeep and Chevrolet to take first place in the sport-utility vehicle (SUV) segment.

Meanwhile, Mercedes has made significant inroads in the luxury segment of the SUV market; Honda has successfully launched "economy" SUVs.

To gain entry into important market niches, everyone seems to be merging or working together. During recent years, GM bought Saab; Ford bought Jaguar, Land Rover, and Volvo; and Chrysler hooked up with Mercedes. The three largest U.S. manufacturers all enjoy important links with foreign producers, thus blurring the distinction between foreign and domestic vehicles. From a consumer's standpoint, import competition has been a beneficial spur to innovation and quality improvement, as it keeps the lid on auto industry prices and profits. The active interplay of demand and supply through stiff global competition seems to be the industry's—and the consumer's—best bet for an efficiently functioning auto market.

See: Sholnn Freeman, "GM, Ford Report Higher U.S. Sales, But Demand Is Beginning to Slow," *The Wall Street Journal Online*, December 4, 2001 (http://online.wsj.com).

subcompacts at average industry prices in excess of, say, $21,000. This means that at relatively high average prices for the industry above $21,000 per unit, both foreign and domestic auto manufacturers would be actively engaged in car production. At relatively low average prices below $21,000, only foreign producers would offer cars. This would be reflected by different parameters describing the relation between price and quantity supplied in the individual firm supply functions for Korean and U.S. automobile manufacturers.

Individual firms supply output only when doing so is profitable. When industry prices are high enough to cover the marginal costs of increased production, individual firms expand output, thereby increasing total profits and the value of the firm. To the extent that the economic capabilities of industry participants vary, so too does the scale of output supplied by individual firms at various prices.

Similarly, supply is affected by production technology. Firms operating with highly automated facilities incur large fixed costs and relatively small variable costs. The supply of product from such firms is likely to be relatively insensitive to price changes when compared to less automated firms, for which variable production costs are higher and thus more closely affected by production levels. Relatively low-cost producers can and do supply output at relatively low market prices. Of course, both relatively low-cost and high-cost producers are able to supply output profitably when market prices are high.

SUPPLY CURVE

supply curve
Relation between price and the quantity supplied, holding all else constant

The supply function specifies the relation between the quantity supplied and all variables that determine supply. The **supply curve** expresses the relation between the price charged and the quantity supplied, holding constant the effects of all other variables. As is true with demand curves, supply curves are often shown graphically, and all independent variables in the supply function except the price of the product itself are fixed at specified levels. In the automobile supply function given in Equation 3.8, for example, it is important to hold constant the price of SUVs and the prices of labor, steel, energy, and other inputs to examine the relation between automobile price and the quantity supplied.

Supply Curve Determination

To illustrate the supply determination process, consider the relation depicted in Equation 3.8. Assuming that the price of trucks, the prices of labor, steel, energy, and interest rates are all held constant at their Table 3.2 values, the relation between the quantity supplied and price is

(3.9)
$$Q = 2,000P - 400(\$35,000) - 100,000(\$85) - 13,750(\$800)$$
$$-125,000(\$4) - 1,000,000(8)$$
$$= -42,000,000 + 2,000P$$

Alternatively, when price is expressed as a function of output, the industry supply curve (Equation 3.9) can be written

(3.10)
$$P = \$21,000 + \$0.0005Q$$

Equations 3.9 and 3.10, which represent the supply curve for automobiles given the specified values of all other variables in the supply function, are shown graphically in Figure 3.3. When the supply function is pictured with price as a function of quantity, or as $P = \$21,000 + \$0.0005Q$, industry supply will rise by 1 million new domestic cars if average price rises by \$2,000, or 1/0.0005. Industry supply increases by 0.0005 units with each \$1 increase in average price above the \$21,000 level. The \$21,000 intercept in this supply equation implies that the domestic car industry would not supply any new cars at all if the industry average price fell below \$21,000. At average prices below that level, low-cost imports would supply the entire industry demand.

Relation Between Supply Curve and Supply Function

Like the relation between the demand curve and the demand function, the relation between the supply curve and the supply function is very important in managerial decision making. Figure 3.4 shows three supply curves for automobiles: $S_{6\%}$, $S_{8\%}$, and $S_{10\%}$. $S_{8\%}$ is the same automobile supply curve determined by Equations 3.9 and 3.10 and shown in Figure 3.3. If $S_{8\%}$ is the appropriate supply curve, then 8 million automobiles would be offered for sale at an industry average price of \$25,000. Only 4 million automobiles would be offered for sale at an average price of \$23,000; but industry supply would total 12 million automobiles at an average price of \$27,000. Such movements along a given supply curve reflect a **change in the quantity supplied**. As average price rises from \$23,000 to \$25,000 to \$27,000 along $S_{8\%}$, the quantity supplied increases from 4 million to 8 million to 12 million automobiles.

change in the quantity supplied Movement along a given supply curve reflecting a change in price and quantity

Supply curves $S_{6\%}$ and $S_{10\%}$ are similar to $S_{8\%}$. The differences are that $S_{6\%}$ is based on a 6 percent interest rate, whereas $S_{10\%}$ assumes a 10 percent interest rate. Recall that $S_{8\%}$ is based on an interest rate assumption of 8 percent. Because the supply function interest rate parameter is −1,000,000, a 2 percent fall in interest rates leads to a 2-million-unit increase in automobile supply at each automobile price level. This increase is described as a downward or rightward shift in the original supply curve $S_{8\%}$ to the new supply curve $S_{6\%}$. Conversely, a 2 percent rise in interest rates leads to a 2-million-unit decrease in automobile supply at each automobile price level. This reduction is described as an upward or leftward shift in the original supply curve $S_{8\%}$ to the new supply curve $S_{10\%}$.

To avoid confusion, remember that $S_{10\%}$ lies *above* $S_{8\%}$ in Figure 3.4, whereas $D_{10\%}$ lies *below* $D_{8\%}$ in Figure 3.2. Similarly, it is important to keep in mind that $S_{6\%}$ lies *below* $S_{8\%}$ in Figure 3.4, but $D_{6\%}$ lies *above* $D_{8\%}$ in Figure 3.2. These differences stem from the fact that a rise in

FIGURE 3.3

Hypothetical Industry Supply Curve for New Domestic Automobiles

For industry prices above $21,000, the supply curve parameter estimate (slope coefficient) shows that a $1 increase in the average price of new automobiles will increase the quantity supplied by 2,000 units.

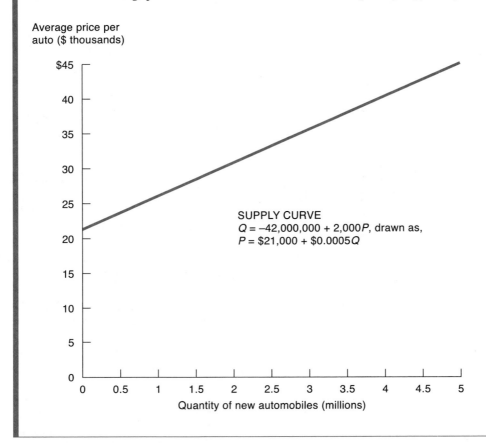

Average price per auto ($ thousands)

SUPPLY CURVE
$Q = -42{,}000{,}000 + 2{,}000P$, drawn as,
$P = \$21{,}000 + \$0.0005Q$

Quantity of new automobiles (millions)

demand involves an *upward* shift in the demand curve, whereas a fall in demand involves a *downward* shift in the demand curve. Conversely, a rise in supply involves a *downward* shift in the supply curve; a fall in supply involves an *upward* shift in the supply curve.

At a price of $25,000, for example, a 2 percent rise in interest rates reduces automobile supply from 8 million units, the $S_{8\%}$ level, to 6 million units, the $S_{10\%}$ level. This reduction in supply reflects the fact that previously profitable production no longer generates a profit because of the increase in capital costs. At a price of $25,000, a 2 percent reduction in interest rates increases automobile supply from 8 million units, the $S_{8\%}$ level, to 10 million units, the $S_{6\%}$ level. Supply rises following this decline in interest rates because, given a decline in capital costs, producers find that they can profitably expand output at the $25,000 price level from 8 million to 10 million units.

shift in supply
Movement from one supply curve to another following a change in a nonprice determinant of supply

A **shift in supply**, or a switch from one supply curve to another, indicates a change in one or more of the nonprice variables in the product supply function. In the automobile supply-function example, an increase in truck prices leads to a decrease in automobile supply, because the SUV price parameter of −400 indicates that automobile supply and truck prices are inversely related. This reflects the fact that as SUV prices rise, holding all else constant, auto manufacturers have an incentive to shift from automobile to SUV production. When automobile supply is inversely related to a factor such as SUV prices, rising SUV prices lead to falling automobile supply, and falling SUV prices lead to rising automobile supply. From the negative parameters for the price of labor, steel, energy, and interest rates, it is also possible to infer that automobile supply is inversely related to each of these factors.

FIGURE 3.4

Hypothetical Industry Supply Curves for New Domestic Automobiles at Interest Rates of 6%, 8%, and 10%

A shift in the original supply curve from $S_{8\%}$ to $S_{10\%}$ follows a 2% rise in interest rates from 8% to 10%; a shift from $S_{8\%}$ to $S_{6\%}$ reflects a 2% fall in interest rates from 8% to 6%.

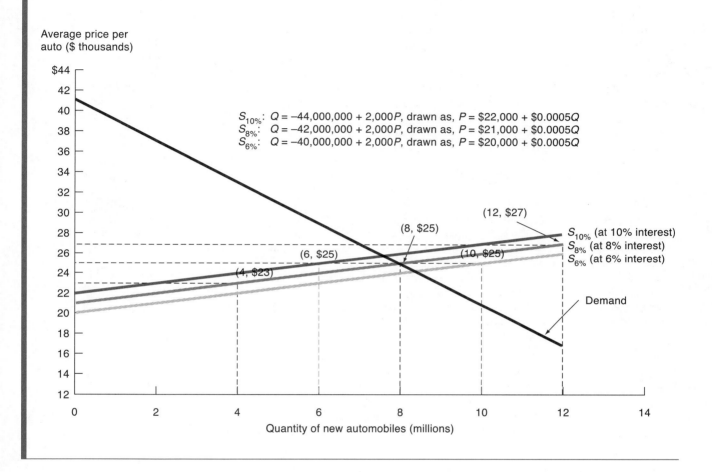

A change in interest rates is not the only factor that might be responsible for a change in the supply curve from $S_{8\%}$ to $S_{6\%}$ or $S_{10\%}$. From the energy cost parameter of –13,750, it is possible to infer that supply and steel costs are inversely related. Falling supply follows an increase in steel costs, and rising supply follows a decrease in steel costs. The shift from $S_{8\%}$ to $S_{10\%}$ in Figure 3.4, which reflects a decrease in supply, could have resulted from a $145.45 per ton increase in steel costs rather than a 2 percent increase in interest rates. Alternatively, this change could result from a $72.73 per ton increase in steel costs plus a 1 percent increase in interest rates. In each case, the resulting supply curve is given by the equation $Q = -44,000,000 + 2,000P$, or $P = \$22,000 + \$0.0005Q$. Similarly, the shift from $S_{8\%}$ to $S_{6\%}$ in Figure 3.4, which reflects an increase in supply, could have resulted from a $145.45 per ton decrease in steel costs rather than a 2 percent decrease in interest rates from 8 percent to 6 percent. This change could also result from a $72.73 per ton decrease in steel costs plus a 1 percent decrease in interest rates. In each case, the resulting supply curve is given by the equation $Q = -40,000,000 + \$2,000P$, or $P = \$20,000 + \$0.0005Q$.

For some products, a positive relation between supply and other factors such as weather is often evident. This is especially true for agricultural products. If supply were positively related to weather, perhaps measured in terms of average temperature, then rising supply would follow rising average temperature and falling supply would accompany falling average

Demand and Supply Conditions for Economists

The forces of demand and supply exert a powerful influence on the market for goods and services, and for labor and other inputs. An interesting case in point is the economics industry itself. The demand for economists originates in the private sector, where they are employed in business—usually in staff rather than line positions—as consultants and commentators; in government, where economic analysis often guides public policy; and in academia, where economists are employed in teaching capacities, primarily at the college and university levels.

Financial economists on Wall Street help price and market complex financial instruments. Although no more than 500 to 1,000 financial economists are employed in this capacity, lucrative bonus-based compensation plans make them highly visible. The National Association of Business Economists counts roughly 3,000 members. However, the employment of business economists is cyclical. During recessions, brokerages, banks, and other financial institutions trim their economics staff considerably. Consulting and speech making is the glamour end of the business. Stars can earn hundreds of thousands of

dollars per year, but the supply of such "superstars" is severely limited.

An overwhelming majority of the 20,000 members of the American Economic Association (AEA) hold academic jobs. According to *Job Openings for Economists*, an AEA publication, 80 percent to 90 percent of all job opportunities for Ph.D. economists are in four-year colleges and universities. Since the mid-1970s, the number of new Ph.D.s in economics has held steady at 750 to 800 per year, or roughly equivalent to the number of Ph.D.s granted in all areas of business administration combined. With relatively scarce supply, new Ph.D.s in accounting and finance enjoy much higher starting salaries than new Ph.D.s in economics. Good business opportunities explain the lack of Ph.D. candidates from undergraduate programs in accounting and finance, but why don't economics Ph.D. students switch to accounting or finance?

See: Dow Jones Newswires, "Economists See Short, Mild Recession, Subject to Terrorism," *The Wall Street Journal Online*, December 3, 2001 (http://online.wsj.com).

temperature. Weather is not included in the automobile supply function because there is no close relation between automobile supply and weather.

The distinction between changes in the quantity supplied, which reflect movements along a given supply curve, and a shift in supply, which reflects movement from one supply curve to another, is important, as was the distinction between changes in the quantity demanded and a shift in demand. Because the prices of related products, input prices, taxes, weather, and other factors affecting supply can be expected to vary from one period to the next, assessing the individual importance of each factor becomes a challenging aspect of managerial economics.

MARKET EQUILIBRIUM

equilibrium
Perfect balance in demand and supply

Integrating the concepts of demand and supply establishes a framework for understanding how they interact to determine market prices and quantities for all goods and services. When quantity demanded and quantity supplied are in perfect balance at a given price, the product market is said to be in **equilibrium**. An equilibrium is stable when underlying demand and supply conditions are expected to remain stationary in the foreseeable future. When underlying demand and supply are dynamic rather than constant, a change in current market prices and quantities is likely. A temporary market equilibrium of this type is often referred to as an unstable equilibrium. To understand the forces that drive market prices and quantities either up or down to achieve equilibrium, the concepts of surplus and shortage must be introduced.

Surplus and Shortage

surplus
Excess supply

shortage
Excess demand

A **surplus** is created when producers supply more of a product at a given price than buyers demand. Surplus describes a condition of excess supply. Conversely, a **shortage** is created when buyers demand more of a product at a given price than producers are willing to supply. Shortage describes a condition of excess demand. Neither surplus nor shortage will occur when a market is in equilibrium, because equilibrium is defined as a condition in which the quantities demanded and supplied are exactly in balance at the current market price. Surplus and shortage describe situations of market disequilibrium because either will result in powerful market forces being exerted to change the prices and quantities offered in the market.

To illustrate the concepts of surplus and shortage and, in the process, the concept of market equilibrium, consider the demand and supply curves for the automobile industry example depicted in Figure 3.5. Note that the demand curve is the same hypothetical demand curve shown in Figure 3.1, and it is also $D_{8\%}$ in Figure 3.2. The supply curve shown is the same one illustrated in Figure 3.3 and shown as $S_{8\%}$ in Figure 3.4. To clarify the concepts of surplus, shortage, and market equilibrium, it becomes useful to focus on the relation of the quantity supplied and the quantity demanded at each of three different hypothetical market prices.

At a market price of $27,000, the quantity demanded is 7 million units. This is easily derived from Equation 3.4, the market demand curve; $Q_D = 20{,}500{,}000 - 500(\$27{,}000) = 7$ million cars.

FIGURE 3.5

Surplus, Shortage, and Market Equilibrium

At an industry average price of $27,000, excess supply creates a surplus of 5 million units exerting downward pressure on both price and output levels. Similarly, excess demand at a price of $23,000 creates a shortage of 5 million units and upward pressure on both prices and output. Market equilibrium is achieved when demand equals supply at a price of $25,000 and quantity of 8 million units.

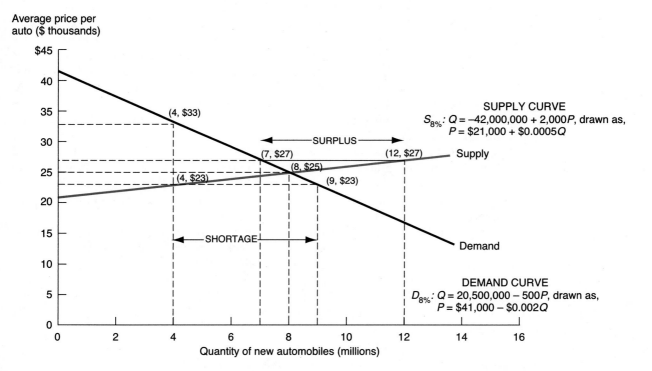

The quantity supplied at an industry average price of $27,000 is derived from the market supply curve, Equation 3.9, which indicates that $Q_S = -42,000,000 + 2,000(\$27,000) = 12$ million cars. At an average automobile price of $27,000, the quantity supplied greatly exceeds the quantity demanded. This difference of 5 million cars per year (= 12 − 7) constitutes a surplus.

An automobile surplus results in a near-term buildup in inventories and downward pressure on market prices and production. This is typical for a market with a surplus of product. Prices tend to decline as firms recognize that consumers are unwilling to purchase the quantity of product available at prevailing prices. Similarly, producers cut back on production as inventories build up and prices soften, reducing the quantity of product supplied in future periods. The automobile industry uses rebate programs and dealer-subsidized low-interest-rate financing on new cars to effectively combat the problem of periodic surplus automobile production.

A different type of market imbalance is also illustrated in Figure 3.5. At an average price for new domestic cars of $23,000, the quantity demanded rises to 9 million cars, $Q_D = 20,500,000 - 500(\$23,000) = 9$ million. At the same time, the quantity supplied falls to 4 million units, $Q_S = -42,000,000 + 2,000(\$23,000) = 4$ million. This difference of 5 million cars per year (= 9 − 4) constitutes a shortage. Shortage, or excess demand, reflects the fact that, given the current productive capability of the industry (including technology, input prices, and so on), producers cannot profitably supply more than 4 million units of output per year at an average price of $23,000, despite buyer demand for more output.

Shortages exert a powerful upward force on both market prices and output levels. In this example, the demand curve indicates that with only 4 million automobiles supplied, buyers would be willing to pay an industry average price of $33,000 [= $41,000 − $0.002(4,000,000)]. Consumers would bid against one another for the limited supply of automobiles and cause prices to rise. The resulting increase in price would motivate manufacturers to increase production while reducing the number of buyers willing and able to purchase cars. The resulting increase in the quantity supplied and reduction in quantity demanded work together to eventually eliminate the shortage.

The market situation at a price of $25,000 and a quantity of 8 million automobiles per year is displayed graphically as a balance between the quantity demanded and the quantity supplied. This is a condition of market equilibrium. There is no tendency for change in either price or quantity at a price of $25,000 and a quantity of 8 million units. The graph shows that any price above $25,000 results in surplus production. Prices in this range create excess supply, a buildup in inventories, and pressure for an eventual decline in prices to the $25,000 equilibrium level. At prices below $25,000, shortage occurs, which creates pressure for price increases. With prices moving up, producers are willing to supply more product and the quantity demanded declines, thus reducing the shortage.

market equilibrium price
Market clearing price
Only a market price of $25,000 brings the quantity demanded and the quantity supplied into perfect balance. This price is referred to as the **market equilibrium price**, or the market clearing price, because it just clears the market of all supplied product. Table 3.3 shows the surplus of quantity supplied at prices above the market equilibrium price and the shortage that results at prices below the market equilibrium price.

In short, surplus describes an excess in the quantity supplied over the quantity demanded at a given market price. A surplus results in downward pressure on both market prices and industry output. Shortage describes an excess in the quantity demanded over the quantity supplied at a given market price. A shortage results in upward pressure on both market prices and industry output. Market equilibrium describes a condition of perfect balance in the quantity demanded and the quantity supplied at a given price. In equilibrium, there is no tendency for change in either price or quantity.

Comparative Statics: Changing Demand

Managers typically control a number of the factors that affect product demand or supply. To make appropriate decisions concerning those variables, it is often useful to know how altering

TABLE 3.3

Surplus, Shortage, and Market Equilibrium in the New Car Market with 8% Interest Rates

Average Price for Domestic Automobiles ($) (1)	Quantity Supplied $(S_{8\%})$ (2)	Quantity Demanded $(D_{8\%})$ (3)	Surplus (+) or Shortage (−) (4) = (2) − (3)
$45,000	48,000,000	0	48,000,000
42,500	43,000,000	0	43,000,000
40,000	38,000,000	500,000	37,500,000
37,500	33,000,000	1,750,000	31,250,000
35,000	28,000,000	3,000,000	25,000,000
32,500	23,000,000	4,250,000	18,750,000
30,000	18,000,000	5,500,000	12,500,000
27,500	13,000,000	6,750,000	6,250,000
25,000	8,000,000	8,000,000	0
22,500	3,000,000	9,250,000	−6,250,000
20,000	0	10,500,000	−10,500,000
17,500	0	11,750,000	−11,750,000
15,000	0	13,000,000	−13,000,000
12,500	0	14,250,000	−14,250,000
10,000	0	15,500,000	−15,500,000
7,500	0	16,750,000	−16,750,000
5,000	0	18,000,000	−18,000,000
2,500	0	19,250,000	−19,250,000
0	0	20,500,000	−20,500,000

them changes market conditions. Similarly, the direction and magnitude of changes in demand and supply that are due to uncontrollable external factors, such as income or interest rate changes, need to be understood so that managers can develop strategies and make decisions that are consistent with market conditions.

comparative statics analysis
Study of changing demand and supply conditions

One relatively simple but useful analytical technique is to examine the effects on market equilibrium of changes in economic factors underlying product demand and supply. This is called **comparative statics analysis**. In comparative statics analysis, the role of factors influencing demand is often analyzed while holding supply conditions constant. Similarly, the role of factors influencing supply can be analyzed by studying changes in supply while holding demand conditions constant. Comparing market equilibrium price and output levels before and after various hypothetical changes in demand and supply conditions has the potential to yield useful predictions of expected changes.

Figures 3.6 and 3.7 illustrate the comparative statics of changing demand and supply conditions. Figure 3.6(a) combines the three automobile demand curves shown in Figure 3.2 with the automobile supply curve $S_{8\%}$ of Figure 3.4. The demand-related effects of changes in interest rates on the market price and quantity of automobiles are illustrated. Given the supply curve *S, and assuming for the moment that supply does not change in response to changes in interest rates*, the intersections of the three demand curves with the supply curve indicate the market price and quantity combinations expected at different interest rates.

At the intersection of $D_{6\%}$, which corresponds to a 6 percent interest rate, and the supply curve $S_{8\%}$, supply and demand are equal at a price of $25,800 and quantity of 9.6 million units. This result is obtained by simultaneously solving the equations for $D_{6\%}$ and $S_{8\%}$ to find the single price and quantity that satisfies both:

FIGURE 3.6(a)

Comparative Statics of (A) Changing Demand or (B) Changing Supply

(a) Holding supply conditions constant, demand will vary with changing interest rates. Demand increases with a fall in interest rates; demand falls as interest rates rise.

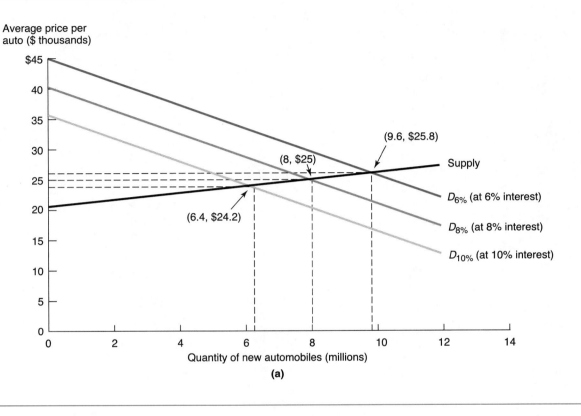

(a)

$$D_{6\%}: Q_D = 22{,}500{,}000 - 500P$$
$$S_{8\%}: Q_S = -42{,}000{,}000 + 2{,}000P$$

Demand and supply are equal at a price of $25,800 because

$$Q_D = Q_S$$
$$22{,}500{,}000 - 500P = -42{,}000{,}000 + 2{,}000P$$
$$2{,}500P = 64{,}500{,}000$$
$$P = \$25{,}800$$

The related quantity is found by substituting this $25,800 price into either the demand curve $D_{6\%}$ or the supply curve $S_{8\%}$:

$$D_{6\%}: Q_D = 22{,}500{,}000 - 500(\$25{,}800)$$
$$= 9.6 \text{ million}$$
$$S_{8\%}: Q_S = -42{,}000{,}000 + 2{,}000(\$25{,}800)$$
$$= 9.6 \text{ million}$$

Using the same procedure to find the market clearing price-quantity combination for the intersection of $D_{8\%}$ (the demand curve for an 8 percent interest rate), with $S_{8\%}$ an equilibrium price of $25,000 and quantity of 8 million units is found. With interest rates at 10 percent (curve $D_{10\%}$), the market clearing price and quantity is $24,200 and 6.4 million units. Clearly, the level

FIGURE 3.6(b)

Continued

(b) Holding demand conditions constant, supply will vary with changing interest rates. Supply falls with a rise in interest rates; supply rises as interest rates decline.

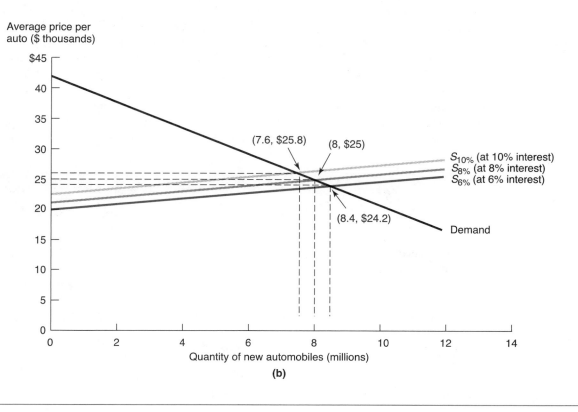

of interest rates plays an important role in the buyer's purchase decision. With higher interest rates, car buyers purchase fewer automobiles and only at progressively lower prices. In part, this reflects the fact that most car purchases are financed, and at higher interest rates, the total cost of buying an automobile is greater.

Comparative Statics: Changing Supply

Figure 3.6(b) combines the three automobile supply curves shown in Figure 3.4 with the automobile demand curve $D_{8\%}$ of Figure 3.2. The market equilibrium price and quantity effects of changing interest rates are illustrated, holding demand conditions constant *and, in particular, assuming that demand does not change in response to changes in interest rates.* Given the market demand curve $D_{8\%}$, a 2 percent fall in interest rates from 10 percent to 8 percent causes the equilibrium quantity supplied to rise from 7.6 million units on $S_{10\%}$ to 8 million units on S; a further 2 percent drop in interest rates from 8 percent to 6 percent causes the equilibrium quantity supplied to rise from 8 million units on $S_{8\%}$ to 8.4 million units on $S_{6\%}$. Similarly, in light of the market demand curve $D_{8\%}$, a 2 percent fall in interest rates from 10 percent to 8 percent causes the equilibrium price to fall from $25,800 to $25,000; a further 2 percent drop in interest rates from 8 percent to 6 percent causes the equilibrium price to fall from $25,000 to $24,200. As interest rates fall, producers find that they can profitably supply more output, even as average price falls, given the capital cost savings that would accompany lower interest rates. The effects of lower interest rates on supply are dramatic and reflect the highly capital-intensive nature of the automobile industry.

Comparative Statics: Changing Demand *and* Supply

From this analysis of hypothetical automobile demand and supply relations, it is clear that interest rates are an important factor influencing demand and supply. Factors related to overall economic activity often have important influences on both demand and supply. Figure 3.7 illustrates the comparative statics of changing demand and changing supply conditions by showing the net effects of changing interest rates. Here $S_{6\%}$ and $D_{6\%}$, both of which assume a 6 percent interest rate, yield an equilibrium price/output combination of $25,000 and 10 million cars; $S_{8\%}$ and $D_{8\%}$, which assume an 8 percent interest rate, yield an equilibrium price/output combination of $25,000 and 8 million units; $S_{10\%}$ and $D_{10\%}$, which assume a 10 percent interest rate, result in a price/output equilibrium of $25,000 and 6 million units. These price/output combinations reflect the combined effects of changing interest rates on demand and supply. The comparative statics of changes in any of the other factors that influence demand and supply can be analyzed in a similar fashion.

SUMMARY

This chapter illustrates how the forces of supply and demand establish the prices and quantities observed in the markets for all goods and services.

- **Demand** is the quantity of a good or service that customers are willing and able to purchase under a given set of economic conditions. **Direct demand** is the demand for products that directly satisfy consumer desires. The value or worth of a good or service, its **utility**, is the prime determinant of direct demand. The demand for all inputs is **derived demand** and determined by the profitability of using various inputs to produce output.

FIGURE 3.7

Comparative Statics of Changing Demand and Changing Supply Conditions

The market equilibrium price/output combination reflects the combined effects of changing demand *and* changing supply conditions.

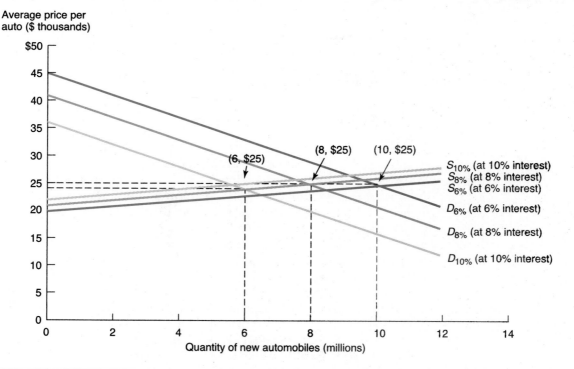

- The market **demand function** for a product is a statement of the relation between the aggregate quantity demanded and all factors that affect this quantity. The **demand curve** expresses the relation between the price charged for a product and the quantity demanded, holding constant the effects of all other variables.

- A **change in the quantity demanded** is a movement along a single demand curve. A **shift in demand**, or shift from one demand curve to another, reflects a change in one or more of the nonprice variables in the product demand function.

- The term **supply** refers to the quantity of a good or service that producers are willing and able to sell under a given set of conditions. The market **supply function** for a product is a statement of the relation between the quantity supplied and all factors affecting that quantity. A **supply curve** expresses the relation between the price charged and the quantity supplied, holding constant the effects of all other variables.

- Movements along a supply curve reflect **change in the quantity supplied**. A **shift in supply,** or a switch from one supply curve to another, indicates a change in one or more of the nonprice variables in the product supply function.

- A market is in **equilibrium** when the quantity demanded and the quantity supplied are in perfect balance at a given price. **Surplus** describes a condition of excess supply. **Shortage** is created when buyers demand more of a product at a given price than producers are willing to supply. The **market equilibrium price** just clears the market of all supplied product.

- In **comparative statics analysis**, the role of factors influencing demand or supply is analyzed while holding all else equal.

A fundamental understanding of demand and supply concepts is essential to the successful operation of any economic organization. The concepts introduced in this chapter provide the structure for the more detailed analysis of demand and supply in subsequent chapters.

QUESTIONS

Q3.1 What key ingredients are necessary for the creation of economic demand?

Q3.2 Describe the difference between direct demand and derived demand.

Q3.3 Explain the rationale for each of the demand variables in Equation 3.1.

Q3.4 Distinguish between a demand function and a demand curve. What is the difference between a change in the quantity demanded and a shift in the demand curve?

Q3.5 What key ingredients are necessary for the creation of economic supply?

Q3.6 Explain the rationale for each of the supply variables in Equation 3.5.

Q3.7 Distinguish between a supply function and a supply curve. What is the difference between a change in the quantity supplied and a shift in the supply curve?

Q3.8 "Dynamic rather than static demand and supply conditions are typically observed in real-world markets. Therefore, comparative statics analysis has only limited value." Discuss this statement.

Q3.9 Contrast the supply and demand conditions for new Ph.D.s in economics and accounting. Why do such large differences in starting salaries seem to persist over time?

Q3.10 Suppose the personal income tax was replaced with a national sales tax. How would this affect aggregate supply, aggregate demand, and interest rates?

SELF-TEST PROBLEMS AND SOLUTIONS

ST3.1 **Demand and Supply Curves.** The following relations describe demand and supply conditions in the lumber/forest products industry:

$$Q_D = 80{,}000 - 20{,}000P \qquad \text{(Demand)}$$
$$Q_S = -20{,}000 + 20{,}000P \qquad \text{(Supply)}$$

where Q is quantity measured in thousands of board feet (one square foot of lumber, one inch thick) and P is price in dollars.

A. Set up a table or spreadsheet to illustrate the effect of price (P), on the quantity supplied (Q_S), quantity demanded (Q_D), and the resulting surplus (+) or shortage (−) as represented by the difference between the quantity demanded and the quantity supplied at various price levels. Calculate the value for each respective variable based on a range for P from $1.00 to $3.50 in increments of 10¢ (i.e., $1.00, $1.10, $1.20, . . . $3.50).

B. Using price (P) on the vertical or Y-axis and quantity (Q) on the horizontal or X-axis, plot the demand and supply curves for the lumber/forest products industry over the range of prices indicated previously.

ST3.1 Solution

A. A table or spreadsheet that illustrates the effect of price (P) on the quantity supplied (Q_S), quantity demanded (Q_D), and the resulting surplus (+) or shortage (−) as represented by the difference between the quantity demanded and the quantity supplied at various price levels is as follows:

Lumber and Forest Industry Supply and Demand Relationships

Price	Quantity Demanded	Quantity Supplied	Surplus (+) or Shortage (−)
$1.00	60,000	0	−60,000
1.10	58,000	2,000	−56,000
1.20	56,000	4,000	−52,000
1.30	54,000	6,000	−48,000
1.40	52,000	8,000	−44,000
1.50	50,000	10,000	−40,000
1.60	48,000	12,000	−36,000
1.70	46,000	14,000	−32,000
1.80	44,000	16,000	−28,000
1.90	42,000	18,000	−24,000
2.00	40,000	20,000	−20,000
2.10	38,000	22,000	−16,000
2.20	36,000	24,000	−12,000
2.30	34,000	26,000	−8,000
2.40	32,000	28,000	−4,000
2.50	30,000	30,000	0
2.60	28,000	32,000	4,000
2.70	26,000	34,000	8,000
2.80	24,000	36,000	12,000
2.90	22,000	38,000	16,000
3.00	20,000	40,000	20,000
3.10	18,000	42,000	24,000
3.20	16,000	44,000	28,000
3.30	14,000	46,000	32,000
3.40	12,000	48,000	36,000
3.50	10,000	50,000	40,000

B. Using price (P) on the vertical or Y-axis and quantity (Q) on the horizontal or X-axis, a plot of the demand and supply curves for the lumber/forest products industry is as follows:

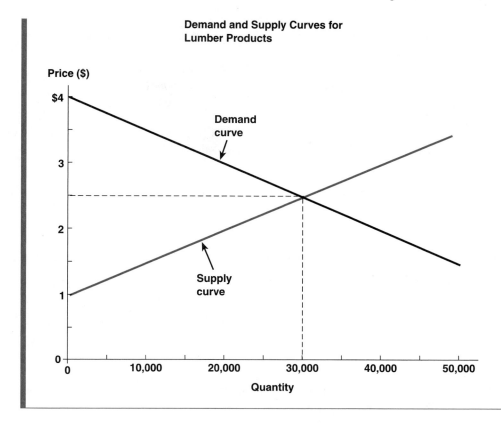

Demand and Supply Curves for Lumber Products

ST3.2   Supply Curve Determination. Information Technology, Inc., is a supplier of math coprocessors (computer chips) used to speed the processing of data for analysis on personal computers. Based on an analysis of monthly cost and output data, the company has estimated the following relation between the marginal cost of production and monthly output:

$$MC = \$100 + \$0.004Q$$

A. Calculate the marginal cost of production at 2,500, 5,000, and 7,500 units of output.

B. Express output as a function of marginal cost. Calculate the level of output when $MC = \$100$, $125, and $150.

C. Calculate the profit-maximizing level of output if wholesale prices are stable in the industry at $150 per chip and, therefore, $P = MR = \$150$.

D. Derive the company's supply curve for chips assuming $P = MR$. Express price as a function of quantity and quantity as a function of price.

ST3.2   Solution

A. Marginal production costs at each level of output are

$$
\begin{aligned}
Q &= 2{,}500: MC = \$100 + \$0.004(2{,}500) = \$110 \\
Q &= 5{,}000: MC = \$100 + \$0.004(5{,}000) = \$120 \\
Q &= 7{,}500: MC = \$100 + \$0.004(7{,}500) = \$130
\end{aligned}
$$

B. When output is expressed as a function of marginal cost

$$
\begin{aligned}
MC &= \$100 + \$0.004Q \\
0.004Q &= -100 + MC \\
Q &= -25{,}000 + 250MC
\end{aligned}
$$

The level of output at each respective level of marginal cost is

$$
\begin{aligned}
MC &= \$100: Q = -25{,}000 + 250(\$100) = 0 \\
MC &= \$125: Q = -25{,}000 + 250(\$125) = 6{,}250 \\
MC &= \$150: Q = -25{,}000 + 250(\$150) = 12{,}500
\end{aligned}
$$

C. Note from part B that $MC = \$150$ when $Q = 12{,}500$. Therefore, when $MR = \$150$, $Q = 12{,}500$ will be the profit-maximizing level of output. More formally,

$$
\begin{aligned}
MR &= MC \\
\$150 &= \$100 + \$0.004Q \\
0.004Q &= 50 \\
Q &= 12{,}500
\end{aligned}
$$

D. Because prices are stable in the industry, $P = MR$, this means that the company will supply chips at the level of output where

$$MR = MC$$

and, therefore, that

$$P = \$100 + \$0.004Q$$

This is the supply curve for math chips, where price is expressed as a function of quantity. When quantity is expressed as a function of price

$$
\begin{aligned}
P &= \$100 + \$0.004Q \\
0.004Q &= -100 + P \\
Q &= -25{,}000 + 250P
\end{aligned}
$$

PROBLEMS

P3.1 **Demand and Supply Curves.** The following relations describe monthly demand and supply conditions in the metropolitan area for recyclable aluminum:

$$
\begin{aligned}
Q_D &= 317{,}500 - 10{,}000P \qquad &\text{(Demand)} \\
Q_S &= 2{,}500 + 7{,}500P \qquad &\text{(Supply)}
\end{aligned}
$$

where Q is quantity measured in pounds of scrap aluminum and P is price in cents. Complete the following table:

Price (1)	Quantity Supplied (2)	Quantity Demanded (3)	Surplus (+) or Shortage (−) (4) = (2) − (3)
15¢			
16			
17			
18			
19			
20			

P3.2 **Demand and Supply Curves.** The following relations describe monthly demand and supply relations for dry cleaning services in the metropolitan area:

$$Q_D = 500,000 - 50,000P \qquad \text{(Demand)}$$
$$Q_S = -100,000 + 100,000P \qquad \text{(Supply)}$$

where Q is quantity measured by the number of items dry cleaned per month and P is average price in dollars.

A. At what average price level would demand equal zero?

B. At what average price level would supply equal zero?

C. Calculate the equilibrium price/output combination.

P3.3 **Demand Analysis.** The demand for housing is often described as being highly cyclical and very sensitive to housing prices and interest rates. Given these characteristics, describe the effect of each of the following in terms of whether it would increase or decrease the quantity demanded or the demand for housing. Moreover, when price is expressed as a function of quantity, indicate whether the effect of each of the following is an upward or downward movement along a given demand curve or involves an outward or inward shift in the relevant demand curve for housing. Explain your answers.

A. An increase in housing prices

B. A fall in interest rates

C. A rise in interest rates

D. A severe economic recession

E. A robust economic expansion

P3.4 **Demand and Supply Curves.** Demand and supply conditions in the market for unskilled labor are important concerns to business and government decision makers. Consider the case of a federally mandated minimum wage set above the equilibrium, or market clearing, wage level. Some of the following factors have the potential to influence the demand or quantity demanded of unskilled labor. Influences on the supply or quantity supplied may also result. Holding all else equal, describe these influences as increasing or decreasing, and indicate the direction of the resulting movement along or shift in the relevant curve(s).

A. An increase in the quality of secondary education

B. A rise in welfare benefits

C. An increase in the popularity of self-service gas stations, car washes, and so on

D. A fall in interest rates

E. An increase in the minimum wage

P3.5 **Demand Function.** The Creative Publishing Company (CPC) is a coupon book publisher with markets in several southeastern states. CPC coupon books are either sold directly to the public, sold through religious and other charitable organizations, or given away as promotional items. Operating experience during the past year suggests the following demand function for CPC's coupon books:

$$Q = 5,000 - 4,000P + 0.02Pop + 0.5I + 1.5A$$

where Q is quantity, P is price ($), Pop is population, I is disposable income per household ($), and A is advertising expenditures ($).

A. Determine the demand faced by CPC in a typical market in which $P = \$10$, $Pop = 1,000,000$ persons, $I = \$30,000$, and $A = \$10,000$.

B. Calculate the level of demand if CPC increases annual advertising expenditures from $10,000 to $15,000.

C. Calculate the demand curves faced by CPC in parts A and B.

P3.6 **Demand Curves.** The Eastern Shuttle, Inc., is a regional airline providing shuttle service between New York and Washington, DC. An analysis of the monthly demand for service has revealed the following demand relation:

$$Q = 26,000 - 500P - 250P_{OG} + 200I_B - 5,000S$$

where Q is quantity measured by the number of passengers per month, P is price ($), P_{OG} is a regional price index for other consumer goods (1967 = 1.00), I_B is an index of business activity, and S, a binary or dummy variable, equals 1 in summer months and 0 otherwise.

A. Determine the demand curve facing the airline during the winter month of January if $P_{OG} = 4$ and $I_B = 250$.

B. Determine the demand curve facing the airline, quantity demanded, and total revenues during the summer month of July if $P = \$100$ and all other price-related and business activity variables are as specified previously.

P3.7 **Supply Function.** A review of industrywide data for the jelly and jam manufacturing industry suggests the following industry supply function:

$$Q = -59,000,000 + 500,000P - 125,000P_L \\ - 500,000P_K + 2,000,000W$$

where Q is cases supplied per year, P is the wholesale price per case ($), P_L is the average price paid for unskilled labor ($), P_K is the average price of capital (in percent), and W is weather measured by the average seasonal rainfall in growing areas (in inches).

A. Determine the industry supply curve for a recent year when $P_L = \$8$, $P_K = 10$ percent, and $W = 20$ inches of rainfall. Show the industry supply curve with quantity expressed as a function of price and price expressed as a function of quantity.

B. Calculate the quantity supplied by the industry at prices of $50, $60, and $70 per case.

C. Calculate the prices necessary to generate a supply of 4 million, 6 million, and 8 million cases.

P3.8 **Supply Curve Determination.** Olympia Natural Resources, Inc., and Yakima Lumber, Ltd., supply cut logs (raw lumber) to lumber and paper mills located in the Cascade Mountain region in the state of Washington. Each company has a different marginal cost of production depending on its own cost of landowner access, labor and other cutting costs, the distance cut logs must be shipped, and so on. The marginal cost of producing one unit of output, measured as 1,000 board feet of lumber (where 1 board foot is 1 square foot of lumber, 1-inch thick), is

$$MC_O = \$350 + \$0.00005Q_O \qquad \text{(Olympia)}$$
$$MC_Y = \$150 + \$0.0002Q_Y \qquad \text{(Yakima)}$$

The wholesale market for cut logs is vigorously price competitive, and neither firm is able to charge a premium for its products. Thus, $P = MR$ in this market.

A. Determine the supply curve for each firm. Express price as a function of quantity and quantity as a function of price. (Hint: Set $P = MR = MC$ to find each firm's supply curve.)

B. Calculate the quantity supplied by each firm at prices of $325, $350, and $375. What is the minimum price necessary for each individual firm to supply output?

C. Assuming these two firms make up the entire industry in the local area, determine the industry supply curve when $P < \$350$.

D. Determine the industry supply curve when $P > \$350$. To check your answer, calculate quantity at an industry price of $375 and compare your result with part B.

P3.9 **Supply Curve Determination.** Cornell Pharmaceutical, Inc., and Penn Medical, Ltd., supply generic drugs to treat a variety of illnesses. A major product for each company is a generic equivalent of an antibiotic used to treat postoperative infections. Proprietary cost and output information for each company reveal the following relations between marginal cost and output:

$$MC_C = \$10 + \$0.004Q_C \qquad \text{(Cornell)}$$
$$MC_P = \$8 + \$0.008QP \qquad \text{(Penn)}$$

The wholesale market for generic drugs is vigorously price competitive, and neither firm is able to charge a premium for its products. Thus, $P = MR$ in this market.

A. Determine the supply curve for each firm. Express price as a function of quantity and quantity as a function of price. (Hint: Set $P = MR = MC$ to find each firm's supply curve.)

B. Calculate the quantity supplied by each firm at prices of $8, $10, and $12. What is the minimum price necessary for each individual firm to supply output?

C. Assuming these two firms make up the entire industry, determine the industry supply curve when $P < \$10$.

D. Determine the industry supply curve when $P > \$10$. To check your answer, calculate quantity at an industry price of $12 and compare your answer with part B.

P3.10 **Market Equilibrium.** Eye-de-ho Potatoes is a product of the Coeur d'Alene Growers' Association. Producers in the area are able to switch back and forth between potato and wheat production depending on market conditions. Similarly, consumers tend to regard potatoes and wheat (bread and bakery products) as substitutes. As a result, the demand and supply of Eye-de-ho Potatoes are highly sensitive to changes in both potato and wheat prices.

Demand and supply functions for Eye-de-ho Potatoes are as follows:

$$Q_D = -1,450 - 25P + 12.5P_W + 0.2Y \qquad \text{(Demand)}$$
$$Q_S = -100 + 75P - 25P_W - 12.5P_L + 10R \qquad \text{(Supply)}$$

where P is the average wholesale price of Eye-de-ho Potatoes ($ per bushel), P_W is the average wholesale price of wheat ($ per bushel), Y is income (GNP in $ billions), P_L is the average price of unskilled labor ($ per hour), and R is the average annual rainfall (in inches). Both Q_D and Q_S are in millions of bushels of potatoes.

A. When quantity is expressed as a function of price, what are the Eye-de-ho Potatoes demand and supply curves if $P = \$2$, $P_W = \$4$, $Y = \$7,500$ billion, $P_L = \$8$, and $R = 20$ inches?

B. Calculate the surplus or shortage of Eye-de-ho Potatoes when $P = \$1.50$, $2, and $2.50.

C. Calculate the market equilibrium price/output combination.

CASE STUDY

A Spreadsheet Analysis of Product Demand and Supply Conditions

Spreadsheet analysis is an appropriate means for studying the demand and supply effects of possible changes in various exogenous and endogenous variables. Endogenous variables include all important demand- and supply-related factors that are within the control of the firm. Examples include product pricing, advertising, product design, and so on. Exogenous variables consist of all significant demand- and supply-related influences that are beyond the control of the firm. Examples include competitor pricing, competitor advertising, weather, general economic conditions, and related factors.

In comparative statics analysis, the marginal influence on demand and supply of a change in any one factor can be isolated and studied in depth. The advantage of this approach is that causal relationships can be identified and responded to, if appropriate. The disadvantage of this marginal approach is that it becomes rather tedious to investigate the marginal effects of a wide range of demand and supply influences. It is here that spreadsheet analysis of demand and supply conditions becomes useful. Using spreadsheet analysis, it is possible to learn the demand and supply implications of an almost limitless range of operating scenarios. Rather than calculating the effects of only a few possibilities, it is feasible to consider even rather unlikely outcomes. A complete picture can be drawn of the firm's operating environment, and strategies for responding to a host of operating conditions can be drawn up.

To illustrate this process, consider the case of Sunbest Orange Juice, a product of California's Orange County Growers' Association. Both demand and supply of the product are highly sensitive to changes in the weather. During hot summer months, demand for Sunbest and other beverages grows rapidly. However, hot, dry weather has an adverse effect on supply by reducing the size of the orange crop.

Demand and supply functions for Sunbest are as follows:

$$Q_D = 12,275,000 - 2,500,000P + 200,000P_S + 75Y + 5,000T \text{ (Demand)}$$
$$Q_S = -27,450 + 6,000,000P - 240,000P_L - 220,000P_K - 200,000T \text{ (Supply)}$$

where P is the average wholesale price of Sunbest ($ per case), P_S is the average wholesale price of canned soda ($ per case), Y is disposable income per household ($), T is the average daily high temperature (degrees), P_L is the average price of unskilled labor ($ per hour), and P_K is the risk-adjusted cost of capital (in percent).

During the coming planning period, a wide variety of operating conditions are possible. To gauge the sensitivity of demand and supply to changes in these operating conditions, a number of scenarios that employ a range from optimistic to relatively pessimistic assumptions have been drawn up:

Operating Environment for Demand		Price of Sunbest (P)	Price of Soda (P_S)	Disposable Income (I)	Temperature (T)
Optimistic Scenario	1	$5.00	$4.00	$39,500	78.75
	2	4.80	4.10	39,400	79.00
	3	4.60	4.20	39,300	79.25
	4	4.40	4.30	39,200	79.50
	5	4.20	4.40	39,100	79.75
	6	4.00	4.50	39,000	80.00
	7	3.80	4.60	38,900	80.25
	8	3.60	4.70	38,800	80.50
	9	3.40	4.80	38,700	80.75
Pessimistic Scenario	10	3.20	4.90	38,600	81.00

CASE STUDY (continued)

Operating Environment for Supply		Price of Sunbest (P)	Price of Labor (P_L)	Cost of Capital (P_K)	Temperature (T)
Optimistic Scenario	1	$5.00	$8.00	9.00%	78.00
	2	4.80	8.15	9.25%	77.75
	3	4.60	8.30	9.50%	77.50
	4	4.40	8.45	9.75%	77.25
	5	4.20	8.60	10.00%	77.00
	6	4.00	8.75	10.25%	76.75
	7	3.80	8.90	10.50%	76.50
	8	3.60	9.05	10.75%	76.25
	9	3.40	9.20	11.00%	76.00
Pessimistic Scenario	10	3.20	9.35	11.25%	75.75

Demand and supply functions for Sunbest orange juice can be combined with data on the operating environment to construct estimates of demand, supply, and the amount of surplus or shortage under each operating scenario.

A. Set up a table or spreadsheet to illustrate the effects of changing economic assumptions on the demand for Sunbest orange juice. Use the demand function to calculate demand based on three different underlying assumptions concerning changes in the operating environment. First, assume that all demand factors change in unison from levels indicated in the Optimistic Scenario #1 to the levels indicated in Pessimistic Scenario #10. Second, fix all demand factors except the price of Sunbest at Scenario #6 levels, and then calculate the quantity demanded at each scenario price level. Finally, fix all demand factors except temperature at Scenario #6 levels, and then calculate demand at each scenario temperature level.

B. Set up a table or spreadsheet to illustrate the effects of changing economic assumptions on the supply of Sunbest orange juice. Use the supply function to calculate supply based on three different underlying assumptions concerning changes in the operating environment. First, assume that all supply factors change in unison from levels indicated in the Optimistic Scenario #1 to the levels indicated in Pessimistic Scenario #10. Second, fix all supply factors except the price of Sunbest at Scenario #6 levels, and then calculate the quantity supplied at each scenario price level. Finally, fix all supply factors except temperature at Scenario #6 levels, and then calculate supply at each scenario temperature level.

C. Set up a table or spreadsheet to illustrate the effect of changing economic assumptions on the surplus or shortage of Sunbest orange juice that results from each scenario detailed in part A and part B. Which operating scenario results in market equilibrium?

D. Are demand and supply more sensitive to changes in the price of Sunbest or to changes in temperature?

SELECTED REFERENCES

Argon, Nilay Tanik, Refik Gullu, and Nesim Erkip. "Analysis of an Inventory System Under Backorder Correlated Deterministic Demand and Geometric Supply Process." *International Journal of Production Economics* 71 (May 2001): 247–254.

Bianchi, Marco, Bjöörn R. Gudmundsson, and Gylfi Zoega. "Iceland's Natural Experiment in Supply-Side Economics." *American Economic Review* 91 (December 2001): 1564–1579.

Bolle, Friedel. "Competition with Supply and Demand Functions." *Energy Economics* 23 (May 2001): 253–277.

Cachon, Gerard P., and Martin A. Lariviere. "Contracting to Assure Supply: How to Share Demand Forecasts in a Supply Chain." *Management Science* 47 (May 2001): 629–646.

Canzoneri, Matthew B., Robert E. Cumby, and Behzad T. Diba. "Is the Price Level Determined by the Needs of Fiscal Solvency?" *American Economic Review* 91 (December 2001): 1221–1238.

Colander, David. "Effective Supply and Effective Demand." *Journal of Post Keynesian Economics* 23 (Spring 2001): 375–381.

Corbett, Charles J., and Uday S. Karmarkar. "Competition and Structure in Serial Supply Chains with Deterministic Demand." *Management Science* 47 (July 2001): 966–978.

Friedberg, Rachel M. "The Impact of Mass Migration on the Israeli Labor Market." *Quarterly Journal of Economics* 116 (November 2001): 1373–1408.

Grahovac, Jovan, and Amiya Chakravarty. "Sharing and Lateral Transshipment of Inventory in a Supply Chain with Expensive Low-Demand Items." *Management Science* 47 (April 2001): 579–594.

Kemp, Alexander G., and Linda Stephen. "Prospects for Gas Supply and Demand and Their Implications with Special Reference to the U.K." *Oxford Review of Economic Policy* 17 (Autumn 2001): 346–364.

Keskinocak, Pinar, and Sridhar Tayur. "Quantitative Analysis for Internet-Enabled Supply Chains." *Interfaces* 31 (March 2001): 70–109.

Milner, Josheph M., and Edieal J. Pinker. "Contingent Labor Contracting Under Demand and Supply Uncertainty." *Management Science* 47 (August 2001): 1046–1062.

Prencipe, Loretta W. "Relief Is Here: Demand For IT Talent Remains High, But Supply Is Greatly Improved." *Infoworld* 23 (April 2001): 49.

Reeder, George, and Tim Rowell. "Integration of Supply Chain with Demand Planning—Tropicana's Journey." *Journal of Business Forecasting Methods & Systems* 20 (Fall 2001): 3–8.

Van Donselaar, Karel, Kopczak, Laura Rock, and Marc Wouters. "The Use of Advance Demand Information in a Project-Based Supply Chain." *European Journal of Operational Research* 130 (May 2001): 519–538.

Demand Analysis

CHAPTER FOUR

Demand Analysis

Easy-to-use Web browsers have brought Internet services to millions of people, and Internet usage has boomed since the mid-1990s. However, today's Internet is still quite primitive. Much of the information accessed on today's Web is in text format only. It is flat, grey, and boring. Shopping information, economic news, stock quotes, and weather forecasts are imparted on motionless Web pages that offer the same content presented in leading newspapers like *The Wall Street Journal*, *The New York Times*, or *USA Today*. What companies and shoppers find attractive about Web-based information is its timeliness. What they don't like is that most Web-based information has yet to take advantage of this awesome new media.

To imagine the unmet potential of the Internet, consider what has happened to TV. In the early days of television, TV broadcasts were essentially radio programs with pictures. However, "talking heads" in black and white didn't really grab consumers. TV didn't mature as a medium until viewers could tune into color programs featuring sophisticated action dramas, audience-participation game shows, and live sports entertainment. With a dozen camera angles, slow motion replays, and on-screen diagrams, the NFL on television is often better than spending $100 to see the game in person.

Companies will soon communicate with their customers and suppliers using real-time interactive experiences 24 hours per day, 7 days per week (24/7). An extended Internet is also emerging through PCs and handheld devices that sense, analyze, and control the real world. Savvy firms used to struggle to understand and act upon what was happening to customer demand. Going forward, canny competitors will employ extended Internet devices that provide real-time information about both met and unmet customer demand. This allows perceptive companies to weave together Internet commerce initiatives with e-business technology to satisfy and anticipate changes in customer demand.[1]

---

1 For interesting insight on Internet trends, see Cambridge, Massachusetts–based Forrester Research at http://www.forrester.com.

BASIS FOR CONSUMER DEMAND

The ability of goods and services to satisfy consumer wants is the basis for consumer demand. This is an important topic in managerial economics because managers must know why consumers demand their products before demand can be created or met.

Utility Functions

utility function
Descriptive statement that relates satisfaction or well-being to the consumption of goods and services

A **utility function** is a descriptive statement that relates satisfaction or well-being to the consumption of goods and services. The concept of a utility function can be illustrated by using a simple two-product example. These two products can be closely related, such as basketball and football tickets, or unrelated, such as clothing and medical care. The only requirement is that each can satisfy consumer wants—that is, each provides utility. This utility function can be written in the following general form:

$$\text{(4.1)} \qquad \text{Utility} = f(\text{Goods, Services})$$

Table 4.1 charts a two-product utility function. Each element in the table shows the amount of utility derived from the consumption of each respective combination of goods (Y) and services (X). For example, consumption of three units of X and three units of Y provides 68 utils (units of satisfaction), consumption of one X and 10 Y provides 80 utils, and so on. Each product is measured in terms of the *number* of dresses, *hours* of financial planning services, *days* of vacation, and so on.

The utility derived from consumption is intangible. However, consumers reveal their preferences through purchase decisions and thereby provide tangible evidence of utility.

The utility function depicted in Table 4.1 can also be displayed graphically, as in Figure 4.1. The height of the bar associated with each combination of goods and services indicates the level of utility provided through the consumption of those items.

Marginal Utility

marginal utility
Added utility derived from increasing consumption of a particular product by one unit

Whereas total utility measures the consumer's overall level of satisfaction derived from consumption activities, **marginal utility** measures the added satisfaction derived from a one-unit increase

TABLE 4.1

Utility Derived from Consumption of Various Combinations of Goods and Services

Goods (Y)	Services (X)									
	1	**2**	**3**	**4**	**5**	**6**	**7**	**8**	**9**	**10**
1	25	36	46	55	63	70	76	81	85	88
2	37	48	58	67	75	82	88	93	97	100
3	47	58	68	77	85	92	98	103	107	110
4	55	66	76	85	93	100	106	111	115	118
5	62	73	83	92	100	107	113	118	122	125
6	68	79	89	98	106	113	119	124	128	131
7	73	84	94	103	111	118	124	129	133	136
8	77	88	98	107	115	122	128	133	137	140
9	79	90	100	109	117	124	130	135	139	142
10	80	91	101	110	118	125	131	136	140	143

FIGURE 4.1

Representative Utility Function for the Consumption of Goods and Services

Total utility increases with a rise in the consumption of goods and services.

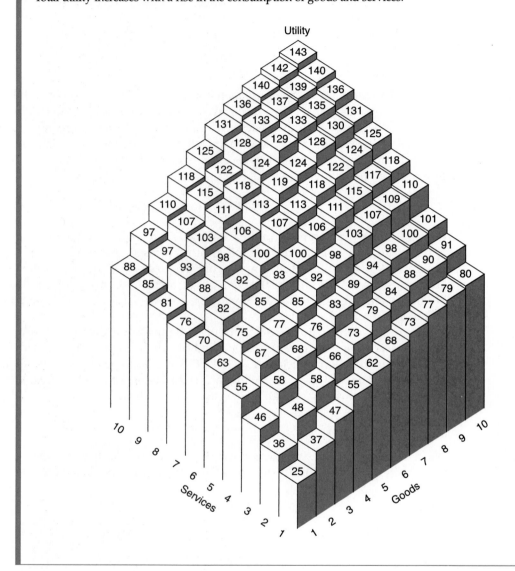

in consumption of a particular good or service, *holding consumption of other goods and services constant.* Marginal utility tends to diminish as consumption increases within a given time interval.

For example, suppose Table 4.2 illustrates the utility that a typical college-age customer of the Hamburger Stand derives from hamburger consumption during a single meal. According to the table, the marginal utility from consuming an initial hamburger is five units ($MU_{H=1} = 5$). Marginal utility is four units for a second hamburger, three units for a third, and so on.

If each hamburger costs $1, the cost per unit (util) of satisfaction derived from consuming the first hamburger is 20¢ (= $1/5 utils). A second hamburger costing $1 produces 4 utils of additional satisfaction at a cost of 25¢ per util. Note that a diminishing marginal utility for hamburgers increases the cost of each marginal unit of satisfaction. Consequently, if the typical Hamburger Stand customer had alternative consumption opportunities providing one additional unit of utility for 20¢ each, customers would be willing to increase the quantity of hamburgers purchased only if hamburger prices fell. If the required price/marginal utility trade-off

TABLE 4.2

Total and Marginal Utility Derived from Hamburger Consumption

Hamburgers per Meal, H	Total Utility, U	Marginal Utility $MU_H = \Delta U / \Delta H$	Maximum Acceptable Hamburger Price at 20¢ per MU_H
0	0	—	—
1	5	5	$1.00
2	9	4	0.80
3	12	3	0.60
4	14	2	0.40
5	15	1	0.20
6	15	0	0.00

FIGURE 4.2

Downward-Sloping Demand Curve for Hamburgers
The demand curve for hamburgers is downward sloping.

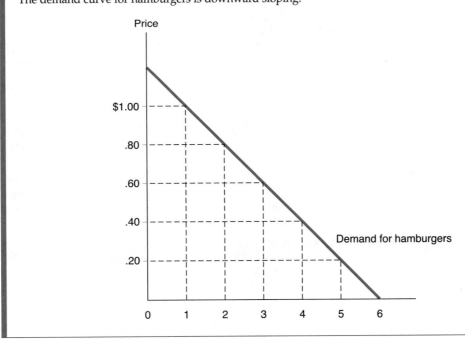

for hamburgers is 20¢ per util, then the typical Hamburger Stand customer would pay $1 for a single hamburger. However, a hamburger price of 80¢ (= 20¢ × 4 utils) would be necessary to induce the typical customer to buy a second hamburger, 60¢ would be needed for a third, 40¢ for a fourth, and so on. This gives rise to the downward-sloping demand curve shown in Figure 4.2.

law of diminishing marginal utility
As consumption of a given product increases, the added benefit derived diminishes

Law of Diminishing Marginal Utility

In general, the **law of diminishing marginal utility** states that as an individual increases consumption of a given product within a set period of time, the marginal utility gained from consumption eventually declines. This law gives rise to a downward-sloping demand curve for hamburgers and all goods and services. The law of diminishing marginal utility is illustrated in

Dell's Price War with Itself

Dell Computer Corp. is fighting a price war with itself. On any given business day, the company may offer different prices for the same personal computer (PC) sold to small businesses, large companies, or state and local governments. These price differences are no mistake. In the viciously price-competitive PC industry, the company must respond flexibly to the purchase plans of various customer groups. The company's salespeople constantly quiz customers on purchase plans, and on deals with Dell rivals. In a sense, Dell negotiates with its customers much like an auto dealer negotiates with car buyers to get the right price and financing package to close the deal.

To maintain profit margins, Dell demands flexible pricing in its contracts with suppliers. In fact, many suppliers continually update Dell on their own costs. This lets Dell adjust prices and incentives immediately in response to changes in its own costs. Dell's dynamic pricing policy lets prices adjust almost continuously. At times, Dell's PC price quote over the phone or on the company Web page can be up to $50 less than the price touted in print advertisements on the very same day!

Dell's "price war" strategy is aimed at aggressively collapsing profit margins throughout the PC market. With the lowest costs in the industry, constantly falling prices and razor-thin profit margins work to Dell's advantage. Rising sales volumes and increasing market share compensate for thinner margins and allow Dell to rapidly grow profits. Dell's "price war" policy is squarely aimed at forcing slower-moving and less efficient rivals to retrench or exit the business.

Dell's price war strategy is clearly paying off. Dell's shipments continue to grow much faster than the PC industry. In the United States, Dell accounts for more than a quarter of PC sales, compared with 6.8 percent in 1996. As rivals cut back and retrench, Dell continues to power ahead in hand-to-hand combat with its toughest competitor—itself.

See: Gary McWilliams, "Dell Will Move Its Senior Executives From Austin to Suburban Campus," *The Wall Street Journal Online*, March 11, 2002 (http://online.wsj.com).

Table 4.3, which is derived from the data in Table 4.1. When service is held constant at 4 units, the marginal utility derived from consuming goods falls with each successive unit of consumption. Similarly, the consumption of services is subject to diminishing marginal utility. Holding goods consumption constant at 1 unit, the marginal utility derived from consuming services falls continuously. The added benefit derived through consumption of each product grows progressively smaller as consumption increases, holding the other constant.

CONSUMER CHOICE

Products are typically consumed as parts of a "market basket" of goods and services. To a greater or lesser degree, goods and services can be substituted for one another. For example, an executive may own many suits and dry clean each suit only occasionally. Alternatively, an executive may own only a few suits but dry clean each one frequently. In the first instance, the executive has bought a market basket with a high proportion of total expenditures devoted to suits (goods) and relatively little devoted to dry cleaning services. The latter market basket is weighted less toward goods and more toward services.

Indifference Curves

indifference curve
Curve that identifies all combinations of goods and services that provide the same utility

With a wide variety of alternative combinations of goods and services, a large number of market baskets can be created that provide the same level of utility. An **indifference curve** represents all market baskets that provide a given consumer the same utility.

To illustrate, Figure 4.3 shows two indifference curves based on the data contained in Table 4.1. Note that 100 units of satisfaction can be derived from the consumption of three X and nine Y (point A), five X and five Y (point B), six X and four Y (point C), and 10 X and two Y (point D). Therefore, each of these points lies on the $U_1 = 100$ indifference curve. Similarly, 118 units

TABLE 4.3

Total and Marginal Utility of Goods and Services

Quantity	Goods (Y)		Services (X)	
	Total Utility	**Marginal Utility** $(MU_Y \mid X = 4)$	**Total Utility**	**Marginal Utility** $(MU_X \mid Y = 1)$
1	55	—	25	—
2	67	12	36	11
3	77	10	46	10
4	85	8	55	9
5	92	7	63	8
6	98	6	70	7
7	103	5	76	6
8	107	4	81	5
9	109	2	85	4
10	110	1	88	3

FIGURE 4.3

Representative Indifference Curves Based on Table 4.1 Data

Indifference curves show market baskets of goods and services that provide the same utility.

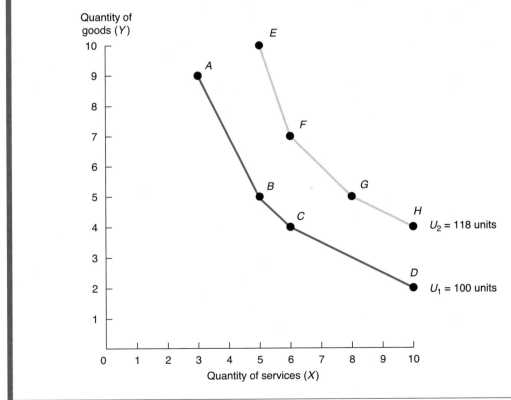

of satisfaction are derived from consumption of five X and 10 Y (point E), six X and seven Y (point F), eight X and five Y (point G), and 10 X and four Y (point H). Therefore, all these points lie on the $U_2 = 118$ indifference curve.

An indifference curve is constructed by connecting all the points representing market baskets that provide the same utility. This construction assumes that consumption can be split between market baskets. For example, the line segment between points A and B on the $U_1 = 100$ indifference curve represents a combination of market baskets A and B. The midpoint of this line segment represents consumption of one-half of market basket A plus one-half of market basket B. Similarly, the midpoint of the GH line segment represents a 50/50 combination of the G and H market baskets.

The discrete utility-function data used to derive the indifference curves shown in Figure 4.3 (see Table 4.1 and Figure 4.1) can be generalized by assuming that the consumption of goods and services can be varied continuously rather than incrementally. In the resulting utility function, indifference curves have the smooth shapes shown in Figure 4.4. The slope at each point along such indifference curves measures the consumer's rate of substitution among products.

Marginal Rate of Substitution

marginal rate of substitution
Amount of one product that must be substituted for another if utility is to remain unchanged

In Figure 4.4, the slope of each indifference curve equals the change in goods (∂Y) divided by the change in services (∂X). This relation, called the **marginal rate of substitution**, is simply the change in consumption of Y (goods) necessary to offset a given change in the consumption of X (services) if the consumer's overall level of utility is to remain constant. This can be stated algebraically:

(4.2)
$$MRS = \frac{\partial Y}{\partial X} = \text{Slope of an Indifference Curve}$$

FIGURE 4.4

Indifference Curves with Continuous Substitution of X and Y

Indifference curves have smooth U shapes when X and Y can be continuously substituted for each other.

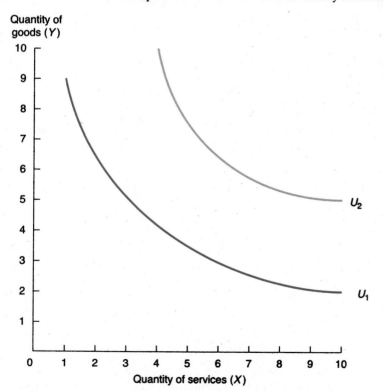

The marginal rate of substitution (*MRS*) is usually not constant but diminishes as the amount of substitution increases. For example, in Figure 4.3, as more goods are substituted for services, the amount of services necessary to compensate for a given loss of goods will continue to fall. Alternatively, as more services are substituted for goods, the amount of goods necessary to compensate for a given loss of services will continue to fall. This pattern means that the negative slope of each indifference curve tends to approach zero as one moves along from left to right.

The slope of an indifference curve is directly related to the concept of diminishing marginal utility. The marginal rate of substitution is equal to –1 times the ratio of the marginal utility derived from the consumption of each product ($MRS = -1(MU_X/MU_Y)$). Remember that the loss in utility associated with a small reduction in Y is equal to the marginal utility of Y, MU_Y, multiplied by the change in Y, ∂Y. Algebraically, this is shown as follows:

(4.3)
$$\partial U = MU_Y \times \partial Y$$

Similarly, the change in utility associated with a change in the consumption of X is

(4.4)
$$\partial U = MU_X \times \partial X$$

Along an indifference curve, the absolute value of ∂U must be equal for a given substitution of Y for X. In other words, because utility is held constant along an indifference curve, the loss in utility following a reduction in Y must be fully offset by the gain in utility associated with an increase in X. Thus, ∂U in both Equations 4.3 and 4.4 must be equal in size and have an opposite sign from a given ∂Y and ∂X. Therefore, along an indifference curve,

(4.5)
$$-(MU_X \times \partial X) = MU_Y \times \partial Y$$

Transposing the variables in Equation 4.5 produces

(4.6)
$$-\frac{MU_X}{MU_Y} = \frac{\partial Y}{\partial X}$$

$$MRS_{XY} = \text{Slope of an Indifference Curve}$$

Thus, the slope of an indifference curve (shown in Equation 4.2 to be equal to $\partial Y/\partial X$) is determined by the ratio of marginal utilities derived from each product. As one moves from left to right in Figure 4.4, the slope of each indifference curve goes from a large negative number toward zero. As seen in Equation 4.6, this implies that MU_X decreases relative to MU_Y as the relative consumption of X progressively increases.

Budget Lines

budget line
All combinations of products that can be purchased for a fixed dollar amount

To fully understand consumer decisions, the concept of a budget line must be introduced. A **budget line** represents all combinations of products that can be purchased for a fixed dollar amount. To derive a budget line, add up the amount of spending on goods and services that is feasible with a given budget. The amount of spending on goods is equal to the product of P_Y, the price of goods, times Y, the quantity purchased. Similarly, total spending on services is $P_X \times X$. When these amounts are added together, the budget line formula is derived:

$$\text{Total Budget} = \text{Spending on Goods} + \text{Spending on Services}$$
$$B = P_Y Y + P_X X$$

Solving this expression for Y so that it can be graphed as in Figure 4.5(a) results in

(4.7)
$$Y = \frac{B}{P_Y} - \frac{P_X}{P_Y} X$$

The first term in Equation 4.7 is the Y-axis intercept of the budget line. This Y-axis intercept indicates the quantity of product Y that can be purchased with a given budget, *assuming that zero units of product X are purchased*. The slope of the budget line is equal to $-P_X/P_Y$ and, therefore, is a measure of the relative prices of the products being purchased. It follows that a change in the budget level B leads to a parallel shift in the budget line, whereas a change in the relative prices of items being purchased causes the slope of the budget line to rotate.

For example, if the price for goods is $250 per unit and $100 per unit for services, the relevant budget line can be written as follows:

$$B = \$250Y + \$100X$$

or

$$Y = \frac{B}{\$250} - \frac{\$100}{\$250} X$$

FIGURE 4.5

Consumption Effects of Changes in Budget and Relative Prices

(a) An increase in budget results in a parallel outward shift in the budget line. (b) A price cut allows purchase of a greater quantity with a given budget.

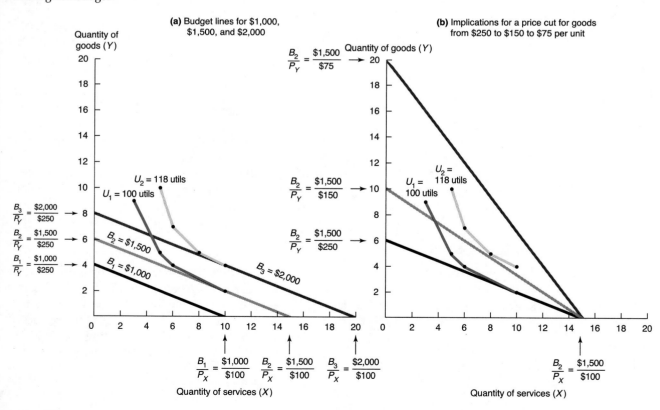

Due Diligence in E-Commerce

In the Internet environment, the authenticity of people and products being represented are often called into question. To successfully match qualified buyers and sellers, and to complete e-commerce transactions, companies need information about trading partners in a trusted, secure environment. This is especially true in business-to-business transactions where the stakes are high, and misjudgments can impact the public reputation of a brand. From a financial management standpoint, electronic transactions with unknown parties can have important implications for the efficient operation of a company's purchasing and receivables functions.

As electronic networks rush to bring millions of potential buyers and sellers together, sellers must answer a host of important questions: Is the buyer who it claims to be? Does the buyer have authority to transact for the stated business entity? Is the buyer eligible for special promotional offers? Should goods get shipped? From the buyer's perspective, similar questions must get answered: Is the seller in fact who it claims to be? Is the seller authorized to sell/service the goods being represented? Is the seller likely to be in business long enough

to honor any service agreements? How well does the seller rate in terms of on-time delivery, product satisfaction, or customer service?

Although businesses have been answering such questions for centuries, the anonymous Internet environment affords little time for face-to-face interaction or trust building. As a result, e-commerce opens the door to new customers, global reach, and exponential growth, but it also increases business risk. Effective e-commerce companies now rely upon "smart transactions" monitored by Dun & Bradstreet and other third-party guarantors that "know" automatically when to approve, deny, or seek further review of a transaction. Electronic "client certificates" ensure authenticity, confidentiality, integrity, and nonrepudiation. Using such innovations, Dun & Bradstreet, among others, is working to bring safety and confidence to e-commerce.

See: Julia Angwin, "Barry Diller Bets Big: Seeks $9 Billion in Acquisitions of E-Commerce Firms," *The Wall Street Journal Online*, March 1, 2002 (http://online.wsj.com).

Given a $1,000 budget, a maximum of 4 units of goods ($Y = \$1,000/\$250$) could be purchased. This assumes, of course, that the entire $1,000 is spent on goods and not on services. If all $1,000 is devoted to the purchase of services, a maximum of 10 units of services ($X = \$1,000/\$100$) could be purchased. These market baskets ($0X$, $4Y$ and $10X$, $0Y$) represent the endpoints of the $B_1 = \$1,000$ budget line shown in Figure 4.5(a). This budget line identifies all combinations of goods and services that can be purchased for $1,000. Notice that $1,000 is insufficient to purchase any market basket lying on the $U_1 = 100$ or $U_2 = 118$ indifference curves. A minimum expenditure of $1,500 is necessary before the $U_1 = 100$ level of satisfaction can be achieved, and a minimum of $2,000 is necessary before the $U = 118$ level can be reached.

Remember, the effect of a budget increase is to shift a budget line outward and to the right. The effect of a budget decrease is to shift a budget line inward and to the left. So long as the relative prices of goods and services remain constant, budget lines remain parallel, as is shown in Figure 4.5(a). This follows because so long as relative prices remain constant, the slope of the budget line also remains constant.

The effect of a change in relative prices is shown in Figure 4.5(b). Here the budget of $1,500 and the $100-per-unit price of services remain constant, whereas the price of goods falls progressively from $250 to $150 to $75 per unit. As the price of goods falls, a given budget will purchase more goods. Thus, a maximum of six units of goods can be purchased at a price of $250 per unit, 10 units can be purchased at a price of $150, and 20 units at a price of $75.

In general, a fall in the price of goods or services permits an increase in consumption and consumer welfare. If both prices fall by a given percentage, a parallel rightward shift in the budget line occurs that is identical to the effect of an increase in budget. For example, the increase in consumption made possible by an increase in budget from $B_2 = \$1,500$ to $B_3 = \$2,000$ as shown in Figure 4.5(a) could also be realized following a decrease in the price of goods from $250 to $187.50 and of services from $100 to $75.

Income and Substitution Effects

When product prices change, the consumer is affected in two ways. The **income effect** of a price change is the increase in overall consumption made possible by a price cut, or decrease in overall consumption that follows a price increase. The income effect shifts buyers to a higher indifference curve following a price cut or shifts them to a lower indifference curve following a price increase. The **substitution effect** of a price change describes the change in relative consumption that occurs as consumers substitute cheaper products for more expensive products. The substitution effect results in an upward or downward movement along a given indifference curve. The total effect of a price change on consumption is the sum of income and substitution effects.

Using the previous example, the total effect of a change in the price of goods is shown in Figure 4.6. When $P_Y = \$250$ and $P_X = \$100$, $U_1 = 100$ is the highest level of satisfaction that can be achieved with a $1,500 budget. This involves consumption of 10 units of service and two units of goods. Following a cut in the price of goods from $P_Y = \$250$ to $P_Y = \$140$, consumption of the $X = 8$ and $Y = 5$ market basket becomes possible, and consumer welfare rises from $U = 100$ to $U = 118$. This change in consumption involves two components. The leftward movement along the $U_1 = 100$ indifference curve to point B, a tangency with the dashed hypothetical budget line representing the new relative prices for goods and services but *no income gain*, is the substitution

FIGURE 4.6

Income and Substitution Effects Following a Reduction in the Price of Goods

A price change will result in both income and substitution effects.

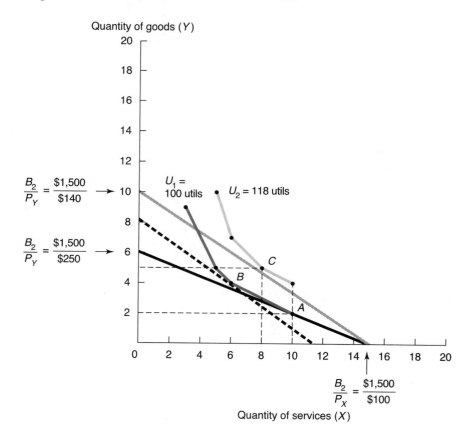

effect. It reflects the substitution of lower-priced goods for the relatively more expensive services. The upward shift from point B on the $U_1 = 100$ indifference curve to point C on the $U_2 = 118$ indifference curve is made possible by the income effect of the price reduction for goods.

OPTIMAL CONSUMPTION

It is now possible to integrate analysis of the marginal rate of substitution, prices, and budget considerations to determine optimal consumption. This involves combining the consumer preference information provided by indifference curves with the cost considerations incorporated in budget lines.

Utility Maximization

The optimal market basket maximizes a consumer's utility for a given budget expenditure. To allocate expenditures efficiently among various products, one must consider both the marginal utility derived from consumption and the prices for each product. Utility is maximized when the marginal utility derived from each individual product is proportional to the price paid. This is illustrated graphically in Figure 4.7, which shows multiple indifference curves and multiple budget lines. Optimal market baskets of goods and services are indicated by points of tangency between respective indifference curves and budget lines. To see

FIGURE 4.7

Optimal Market Baskets for Consumption
The optimal path for consumption is found when $P_X/P_Y = MU_X/MU_Y$.

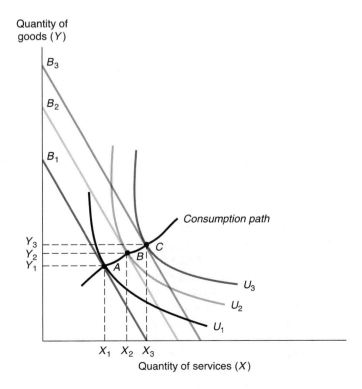

why, assume that an individual has the funds indicated by budget line B_1. In this case, the optimal consumption combination occurs at point A, the point of tangency between the budget line and indifference curve U_1. At that point, goods (Y) and services (X) are combined in proportions that maximize the utility attainable with budget expenditure B_1. No other combination of X and Y that can be purchased along budget line B_1 provides as much satisfaction, or utility. All other (X,Y) combinations along the budget line B_1 must intersect indifference curves representing lower levels of utility. Alternatively, the combination (X_1, Y_1) is the lowest-cost market basket that provides the U_1 level of utility. All other (X,Y) combinations on the U_1 indifference curve lie on higher budget lines. Similarly, (X_2, Y_2) is the lowest-cost combination of goods and services that provides utility at the U_2 level, (X_3, Y_3) is the lowest-cost market basket that provides a U_3 level of utility, and so on. All other market baskets providing U_1, U_2, and U_3 levels of utility are intersected by higher budget lines and, therefore, require a higher level of expenditure.

That optimal consumption combinations occur at points of tangency between budget lines and indifference curves leads to a very important economic principle. The slope of a budget line was shown to be -1 times the ratio of the product prices, or $-P_X/P_Y$. Recall also that the slope of an indifference curve was shown to be equal to the marginal rate of substitution of one consumption item for another when utility is held constant. The marginal rate of substitution is shown in Equation 4.6 as -1 times the ratio of the marginal utilities for each product. Thus, the slope of an indifference curve equals $-MU_X/MU_Y$.

At each point where goods and services are combined optimally, there is a tangency between the budget line and the indifference curve; hence, their slopes are equal. For optimal consumption combinations, the price ratios for goods and services must equal the ratio of their marginal utilities:

$$\text{Slope of an Indifference Curve} = \text{Slope of a Budget Line}$$

(4.8)
$$-\frac{MU_X}{MU_Y} = -\frac{P_X}{P_Y}$$

and

$$\frac{MU_X}{MU_Y} = \frac{P_X}{P_Y}$$

Alternatively,

(4.8a)
$$\frac{MU_X}{P_X} = \frac{MU_Y}{P_Y}$$

Utility is maximized when products are purchased at relative prices that equal the relative marginal utility derived from consumption. As given by Equation 4.8a, with optimal consumption proportions, an additional dollar spent on a given consumption item adds as much to total utility as would a dollar spent on any other item. Any combination of goods and services violating this rule is suboptimal because a change in the consumer's market basket could result in greater utility for the same expenditure.

In Figure 4.7, point A represents an optimal allocation, because X_1 and Y_1 provide the highest possible utility for the B_1 expenditure level. Similarly, points B and C represent efficient allocations for the B_2 and B_3 expenditure levels. By connecting all points of tangency between indifference curves and budget lines (such as points A, B, and C), a **consumption path** is identified that depicts optimal market baskets as the budget level grows.

consumption path
Optimal combinations of products as consumption increases

DEMAND SENSITIVITY ANALYSIS: ELASTICITY

For constructive managerial decision making, the firm must know the sensitivity or responsiveness of demand to changes in factors that make up the underlying demand function.

Elasticity Concept

elasticity
Percentage change in a dependent variable resulting from a 1 percent change in an independent variable

A measure of responsiveness used in demand analysis is **elasticity**, defined as the percentage change in a dependent variable, Y, resulting from a 1 percent change in the value of an independent variable, X. The equation for calculating elasticity is

(4.9)

$$\text{Elasticity} = \frac{\text{Percentage Change in } Y}{\text{Percentage Change in } X}$$

The concept of elasticity simply involves the percentage change in one variable associated with a given percentage change in another variable. The elasticity concept is also used in finance, where the impact of changes in sales on earnings under different production levels (operating leverage) and different financial structures (financial leverage) are measured by an elasticity factor. Elasticities are also used in production and cost analysis to evaluate the effect of changes in input on output, and the effect of output changes on costs.

endogenous variables
Factors controlled by the firm

exogenous variables
Factors outside the control of the firm

Factors such as price and advertising that are within the control of the firm are called **endogenous variables**. Factors outside the control of the firm, such as consumer incomes, competitor prices, and the weather, are called **exogenous variables**. The effects of changes in both types of influences must be understood if the firm is to respond effectively to changes in the economic environment. For example, a firm must understand the effects on demand of changes in both prices and consumer incomes to determine the price cut necessary to offset a decline in sales caused by a business recession. Similarly, the sensitivity of demand to changes in advertising must be quantified if the firm is to respond appropriately with price or advertising changes to an increase in competitor advertising. Determining the effects of changes in both controllable and uncontrollable influences on demand is the focus of demand analysis.

Point Elasticity and Arc Elasticity

point elasticity
Elasticity at a given point on a function

Elasticity is measured in two ways, point elasticity and arc elasticity. **Point elasticity** measures elasticity at a given point on a function. The point elasticity concept is used to measure the effect on a dependent variable Y of a very small or marginal change in an independent variable X. Although the point elasticity concept can often give accurate estimates of the effect on Y of very small (less than 5 percent) changes in X, it is not used to measure the effect on Y of large-scale changes. Elasticity typically varies at different points along a function. To assess the effects of large-scale changes in X, the arc elasticity concept is used. **Arc elasticity** measures average elasticity over a given range of a function.

arc elasticity
Average elasticity over a given range of a function

Using the lowercase epsilon as the symbol for point elasticity, the point elasticity formula is written

$$\text{Point Elasticity} = \epsilon_X = \frac{\text{Percentage Change in } Y}{\text{Percentage Change in } X}$$

(4.10)

$$= \frac{\partial Y/Y}{\partial X/X}$$

$$= \frac{\partial Y}{\partial X} \times \frac{X}{Y}$$

The $\partial Y/\partial X$ term in the point elasticity formula is the marginal relation between Y and X, and it shows the effect on Y of a one-unit change in X. Point elasticity is determined by multiplying this marginal relation by the relative size of X to Y, or the X/Y ratio at the point being analyzed.

Point elasticity measures the percentage effect on Y of a percentage change in X at a given point on a function. If $\epsilon_X = 5$, a 1 percent increase in X will lead to a 5 percent increase in Y, and a 1 percent decrease in X will lead to a 5 percent decrease in Y. Thus, when $\epsilon_X > 0$, Y changes in the same positive or negative direction as X. Conversely, when $\epsilon_X < 0$, Y changes in the opposite direction of changes in X. For example, if $\epsilon_X = -3$, a 1 percent increase in X will lead to a 3 percent decrease in Y, and a 1 percent decrease in X will lead to a 3 percent increase in Y.

Advertising Elasticity Example

An example can be used to illustrate the calculation and use of a point elasticity estimate. Assume that management of a movie theater is interested in analyzing the responsiveness of movie ticket demand to changes in advertising. Also assume that analysis of monthly data for the past year suggests the following demand function:

(4.11)
$$Q = 8{,}500 - 5{,}000P + 3{,}500P_V + 150I + 1{,}000A$$

where Q is the quantity of movie tickets, P is average ticket price (in dollars), P_V is the 1-day movie rental price at video outlets in the area (in dollars), I is average disposable income per household (in thousands of dollars), and A is monthly advertising expenditures (in thousands of dollars). (Note that I and A are expressed in thousands of dollars in this demand function.) For a typical theater, $P = \$7$, $P_V = \$3$, and income and advertising are $\$40{,}000$ and $\$20{,}000$, respectively. The demand for movie tickets at a typical theater can be estimated as

$$Q = 8{,}500 - 5{,}000(7) + 3{,}500(3) + 150(40) + 1{,}000(20)$$
$$= 10{,}000$$

Numbers that appear before each variable in Equation 4.11 are called coefficients or parameter estimates. They indicate the expected change in movie ticket sales associated with a one-unit change in each relevant variable. For example, the number 5,000 indicates that the quantity of movie tickets demanded falls by 5,000 units with every $1 increase in the price of movie tickets, or $\partial Q/\partial P = -5{,}000$. Similarly, a $1 increase in the price of videocassette rentals causes a 3,500-unit increase in movie ticket demand, or $\partial Q/\partial P_V = 3{,}500$; a $1,000 (one-unit) increase in disposable income per household leads to a 150-unit increase in demand. In terms of advertising, the expected change in demand following a one-unit ($1,000) change in advertising, or $\partial Q/\partial A$, is 1,000. With advertising expenditures of $20,000, the point advertising elasticity at the 10,000-unit demand level is

(4.12)
$$\epsilon_A = \text{Point Advertising Elasticity}$$
$$= \frac{\text{Percentage Change in Quantity } (Q)}{\text{Percent Change in Advertising } (A)}$$
$$= \frac{\partial Q/Q}{\partial A/A}$$
$$= \frac{\partial Q}{\partial A} \times \frac{A}{Q}$$
$$= 1{,}000 \times \frac{\$20}{10{,}000}$$
$$= 2$$

Thus, a 1 percent change in advertising expenditures results in a 2 percent change in movie ticket demand. This elasticity is positive, indicating a direct relation between advertising outlays and movie ticket demand. An increase in advertising expenditures leads to higher demand; a decrease in advertising leads to lower demand.

For many business decisions, managers are concerned with the impact of substantial changes in a demand-determining factor, such as advertising, rather than with the impact of very small (marginal) changes. In these instances, the point elasticity concept suffers a conceptual shortcoming.

To see the nature of the problem, consider the calculation of the advertising elasticity of demand for movie tickets as advertising increases from $20,000 to $50,000. Assume that all other demand-influencing variables retain their previous values. With advertising at $20,000, demand is 10,000 units. Changing advertising to $50,000 ($\partial A = 30$) results in a 30,000-unit increase in movie ticket demand, so total demand at that level is 40,000 tickets. Using Equation 4.10 to calculate the advertising point elasticity for the change in advertising from $20,000 to $50,000 indicates that

$$\text{Advertising Elasticity} = \frac{\partial Q}{\partial A} \times \frac{A}{Q} = \frac{30,000}{\$30} \times \frac{\$20}{10,000} = 2$$

The advertising point elasticity is $\epsilon_A = 2$, just as that found previously. Consider, however, the indicated elasticity if one moves in the opposite direction—that is, if advertising is decreased from $50,000 to $20,000. The indicated point elasticity is

$$\text{Advertising Elasticity} = \frac{\partial Q}{\partial A} \times \frac{A}{Q} = \frac{-30,000}{-\$30} \times \frac{\$50}{40,000} = 1.25$$

The indicated elasticity $\epsilon_A = 1.25$ is now different. This problem occurs because elasticities are not typically constant but vary at different points along a given demand function. The advertising elasticity of 1.25 is the advertising point elasticity when advertising expenditures are $50,000 and the quantity demanded is 40,000 tickets.

To overcome the problem of changing elasticities along a demand function, the arc elasticity formula was developed to calculate an average elasticity for incremental as opposed to marginal changes. The arc elasticity formula is

(4.13)

$$E = \text{Arc Elasticity} = \frac{\dfrac{\text{Change in } Q}{\text{Average } Q}}{\dfrac{\text{Change in } X}{\text{Average } X}} = \frac{\dfrac{Q_2 - Q_1}{(Q_2 + Q_1)/2}}{\dfrac{X_2 - X_1}{(X_2 + X_1)/2}}$$

$$= \frac{\dfrac{\Delta Q}{(Q_2 + Q_1)}}{\dfrac{\Delta X}{(X_2 + X_1)}} = \frac{\Delta Q}{\Delta X} \times \frac{X_2 + X_1}{Q_2 + Q_1}$$

The percentage change in quantity demanded is divided by the percentage change in a demand-determining variable, but the bases used to calculate percentage changes are averages of the two data endpoints rather than the initially observed value. The arc elasticity equation eliminates the problem of the elasticity measure depending on which end of the range is viewed as the initial point. This yields a more accurate measure of the relative relation between the two variables over the *range* indicated by the data. The advertising arc elasticity over the $20,000 to $50,000 range of advertising expenditures can be calculated as

$$\text{Advertising Arc Elasticity} = \frac{\text{Percentage Change in Quantity } (Q)}{\text{Percent Change in Advertising } (A)}$$

$$= \frac{(Q_2 - Q_1)/(Q_2 + Q_1)}{(A_2 - A_1)/(A_2 + A_1)}$$

$$= \frac{\Delta Q}{\Delta A} \times \frac{A_2 + A_1}{Q_2 + Q_1}$$

Relationship Marketing

Saturn prides itself on the notion that it manufactures a superior automotive product and provides superior service. Part of this superior service involves better listening to its customers and responding to their suggestions. During early summer, for example, thousands of Saturn owners typically respond to the company's invitation to attend a 3-day picnic at company headquarters in Spring Hill, Tennessee. Not only is it a way to thank owners for their business, but it also is a proven means of building customer loyalty. Mail-order merchants Cabela's, L.L. Bean, and Lands' End, among others, deploy impressive computer capabilities to better track and anticipate customer needs. At Cabela's, for example, customers that order camping equipment and hiking boots are good candidates for the company's camping and outdoor gear catalog. Lands' End customers who order chinos and other casual attire also receive specialized catalogs. At L.L. Bean, the company's unconditional 100 percent satisfaction guarantee keeps valued customers coming back. At FedEx, highly profitable customers get special attention.

Car companies, mail-order merchants, airlines (with frequent flyer programs), and hotels with repeat business customers are obvious candidates for effective relationship marketing. The untapped potential for relationship marketing lies in new and innovative applications. For example, if a company wants to sell detergent, it might obtain a database of large families and offer them a bargain price. While a typical product promotion effort would stop there, relationship marketing goes further. Relationship marketing would suggest that the firm offer such families a free washer or dryer if they remained a loyal customer for, say, 5 years. Because the markup on detergent is substantial, such a long-term promotion could be highly beneficial for both the customer and the company.

The logic behind relationship marketing is simple. It costs much more to get a new customer than it does to keep a current one, so the retention of valued customers is key to long-term success.

See: Dow Jones Newswires, "Expedia, Delta Set Marketing Deal," *The Wall Street Journal Online*, March 20, 2002 (http://online.wsj.com).

$$= \frac{30,000}{\$30} \times \frac{\$50 + \$20}{40,000 + 10,000}$$

$$= 1.4$$

Thus, a 1 percent change in the level of advertising expenditures in the range of $20,000 to $50,000 results, on average, in a 1.4 percent change in movie ticket demand.

To summarize, it is important to remember that point elasticity is a marginal concept. It measures the elasticity at a specific point on a function. Proper use of point elasticity is limited to analysis of very small changes, say 0 percent to 5 percent, in the relevant independent variable. Arc elasticity is a better concept for measuring the average elasticity over an extended range when the change in a relevant independent variable is 5 percent or more. It is the appropriate tool for incremental analysis.

PRICE ELASTICITY OF DEMAND

price elasticity of demand
Responsiveness of the quantity demanded to changes in the price of the product, holding constant the values of all other variables in the demand function

The most widely used elasticity measure is the **price elasticity of demand**, which measures the responsiveness of the quantity demanded to changes in the price of the product, holding constant the values of all other variables in the demand function.

Price Elasticity Formula

Using the formula for point elasticity, price elasticity of demand is found as

$$\epsilon_P = \text{Point Price Elasticity} = \frac{\text{Percentage Change in Quantity } (Q)}{\text{Percentage Change in Price } (P)}$$

$$(4.14) \qquad = \frac{\partial Q/Q}{\partial P/P}$$

$$= \frac{\partial Q}{\partial P} \times \frac{P}{Q}$$

where $\partial Q/\partial P$ is the marginal change in quantity following a one-unit change in price, and P and Q are price and quantity, respectively, at a given point on the demand curve.

The concept of point price elasticity can be illustrated by referring to Equation 4.11:

$$Q = 8{,}500 - 5{,}000P + 3{,}500P_V + 150I + 1{,}000A$$

The coefficient for the price variable indicates the effect on quantity demanded of a one-unit change in price:

$$\frac{\partial Q}{\partial P} = -5{,}000, \text{ a constant}$$

At the typical values of $P_V = \$3$, $I = \$40{,}000$, and $A = \$20{,}000$, the demand curve is calculated as

$$Q = 8{,}500 - 5{,}000(P) + 3{,}500(3) + 150(40) + 1{,}000(20)$$
$$= 45{,}000 - 5{,}000P$$

This demand curve relation can be used to calculate ϵ_P at two points: (1) where $P_1 = \$7$ and $Q_1 = 10{,}000$ and (2) where $P_2 = \$8$ and $Q_2 = 5{,}000$. This implies $\epsilon_{P1} = -3.5$ and $\epsilon_{P2} = -8$ because

$$(1) \quad \epsilon_{P_1} = -5{,}000 \times \left(\frac{\$7}{10{,}000}\right) = -3.5$$

$$(2) \quad \epsilon_{P_2} = -5{,}000 \times \left(\frac{\$8}{5{,}000}\right) = -8$$

Therefore, a 1 percent increase in price from the $7 movie ticket price level results in a 3.5 percent reduction in the quantity demanded. At the $8 price level, a 1 percent increase results in an 8 percent reduction in the quantity demanded. This indicates that movie ticket buyers, like most consumers, become increasingly price sensitive as average price increases. This example illustrates how price elasticity tends to vary along a linear demand curve, with ϵ_P increasing in absolute value at higher prices and lower quantities. Although price elasticity always varies along a linear demand curve, under certain conditions it can be constant along a curvilinear demand curve. This point will be illustrated in a later section.

When evaluating price elasticity estimates, recognize that price elasticities are uniformly negative. This is because the quantity demanded for all goods and services is inversely related to price. In the previous example, at a $7 price, a 1 percent *increase* in price leads to a 3.5 percent *decrease* in the quantity of movie tickets demanded. Conversely, a 1 percent decrease in price leads to a 3.5 percent increase in the quantity demanded. For convenience, the equation for price elasticity is sometimes multiplied by –1 to change price elasticities to positive numbers. When price elasticities are reported as positive numbers, or in absolute value terms, it is important to remember the underlying inverse relation between price and quantity.

Using the arc elasticity concept, the equation for price elasticity is

$$\epsilon_P = \text{Arc Price Elasticity} = \frac{\text{Percentage Change in Quantity } (Q)}{\text{Percentage Change in Price } (P)}$$

$$(4.15) \qquad = \frac{(Q_2 - Q_1)/[(Q_2 + Q_1)/2]}{(P_2 - P_1)/[(P_2 + P_1)/2]}$$

$$= \frac{\Delta Q}{\Delta P} \times \frac{P_2 + P_1}{Q_2 + Q_1}$$

This form is especially useful for analyzing the average sensitivity of demand to price changes over an extended range of prices. For example, the average price elasticity over the price range from $7 to $8 is

$$E_P = \frac{\Delta Q}{\Delta P} \times \frac{P_2 + P_1}{Q_2 + Q_1}$$

$$= \frac{-5,000}{1} \times \frac{\$8 + \$7}{5,000 + 10,000}$$

$$= -5$$

This means that, on average, a 1 percent change in price leads to a 5 percent change in quantity demanded when price is between $7 and $8 per ticket.

Price Elasticity and Total Revenue

Depending on the degree of price elasticity, a reduction in price can increase, decrease, or leave total revenue unchanged. A good estimate of price elasticity makes it possible to accurately estimate the effect of price changes on total revenue.

For decision-making purposes, three specific ranges of price elasticity have been identified. Using $|\epsilon_P|$ to denote the absolute value of the price elasticity, three ranges for price elasticity are

1. $|\epsilon_P| > 1.0$, defined as elastic demand

   Example: $\epsilon_P = -3.2$ and $|\epsilon_P| = 3.2$

2. $|\epsilon_P| = 1.0$, defined as unitary elasticity

   Example: $\epsilon_P = -1.0$ and $|\epsilon_P| = 1.0$

3. $|\epsilon_P| < 1.0$, defined as inelastic demand

   Example: $\epsilon_P = -0.5$ and $|\epsilon_P| = 0.5$

elastic demand
Situation in which a price change leads to a more than proportionate change in quantity demanded

unitary elasticity
Situation in which price and quantity changes exactly offset each other

inelastic demand
Situation in which a price change leads to a less than proportionate change in quantity demanded

With **elastic demand**, $|\epsilon_P| > 1$ and the relative change in quantity is larger than the relative change in price. A given percentage increase in price causes quantity to decrease by a larger percentage. If demand is elastic, a price increase lowers total revenue and a decrease in price raises total revenue. **Unitary elasticity** is a situation in which the percentage change in quantity divided by the percentage change in price equals –1. Since price and quantity are inversely related, a price elasticity of –1 means that the effect of a price change is *exactly* offset by the effect of a change in quantity demanded. The result is that total revenue, the product of price times quantity, remains constant. With **inelastic demand**, a price increase produces less than a proportionate decline in the quantity demanded, so total revenues rise. Conversely, when demand is inelastic, a price decrease generates a less than proportionate increase in quantity demanded, so total revenues falls. These relations are summarized in Table 4.4.

TABLE 4.4

Relationship Between Price Elasticity and Total Revenue

Elasticity	Implies	Following a Price Increase:	Following a Price Decrease:
Elastic demand, $|\epsilon_P| > 1$.	$\%\Delta Q > \%\Delta P$	Revenue decreases.	Revenue increases.
Unitary elasticity, $|\epsilon_P| = 1$.	$\%\Delta Q = \%\Delta P$	Revenue unchanged.	Revenue unchanged.
Inelastic demand $|\epsilon_P| < 1$.	$\%\Delta Q < \%\Delta P$	Revenue increases.	Revenue decreases.

Price elasticity can range from completely inelastic, where $\epsilon_P = 0$, to perfectly elastic, where $\epsilon_P = -\infty$. To illustrate, consider first an extreme case in which the quantity demanded is independent of price so that some fixed amount, Q^*, is demanded regardless of price. When the quantity demanded of a product is completely insensitive to price, $\partial Q/\partial P = 0$, and price elasticity will equal zero, irrespective of the value of P/Q. The demand curve for such a good or service is perfectly vertical, as shown in Figure 4.8.

The other limiting case, that of infinite price elasticity, describes a product that is completely sensitive to price. The demand curve for such a good or service is perfectly horizontal, as shown in Figure 4.9. Here the ratio $\partial Q/\partial P = -\infty$ and $\epsilon_P = -\infty$, regardless of the value of P/Q.

The economic properties of these limiting cases should be understood. A firm faced with a vertical or perfectly inelastic demand curve could charge any price and still sell Q^* units. Theoretically, such a firm could appropriate all of its customers' income or wealth. Conversely, a firm facing a horizontal or perfectly elastic demand curve could sell an unlimited quantity of output at the price P^*, but it would lose all sales if it raised prices by even a small amount. Such extreme cases are rare in the real world, but monopolies that sell necessities such as pharmaceuticals enjoy relatively inelastic demand. Firms in highly competitive industries, like grocery retailing, face extremely elastic demand curves.

Uses of Price Elasticity Information

Price elasticity information is useful for a number of purposes. For example, a profit-maximizing firm would never choose to lower its prices in the inelastic range of the demand curve. Such a price decrease would decrease total revenue and at the same time increase costs, because the quantity demanded would rise. A dramatic decrease in profits could result. The profitability of a price cut in the elastic range of the demand curve depends on whether the marginal revenues generated exceed the marginal cost of added production. Price elasticity information can be used to answer questions such as

FIGURE 4.8

Completely Inelastic Demand Curve: $\epsilon_P = 0$

With perfectly inelastic demand, a fixed level of output is demanded irrespective of price.

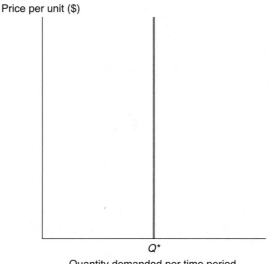

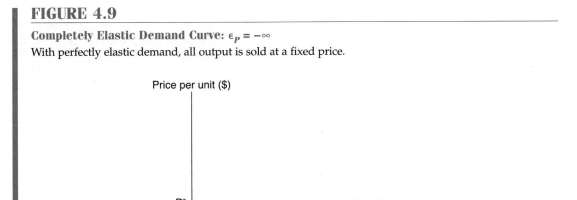

FIGURE 4.9

Completely Elastic Demand Curve: $\epsilon_P = -\infty$
With perfectly elastic demand, all output is sold at a fixed price.

- What is the expected impact on sales of a 5 percent price increase?
- How great a price reduction is necessary to increase sales by 10 percent?
- Given marginal cost and price elasticity data, what is the profit-maximizing price?

Price elasticity information plays a major role in the debate over national energy policy. Some industry and government economists argue that the price elasticity of demand for energy is sufficiently high that demand and supply fall into balance following only modest price changes. Others argue that energy price elasticities are so low that enormous price increases are necessary to reduce the quantity demanded to meet energy conservation objectives. Meanwhile, bouts of falling oil prices raise fears that low oil prices may increase Western reliance on imported oil. These issues have also risen in controversies surrounding nuclear energy, natural gas price deregulation, and alternative renewable energy sources. In the energy policy debate, the relation between price and quantity supplied—the price elasticity of supply—is also an important component. As with most economic issues, both demand and supply conditions must be analyzed to arrive at a rational decision.

Another example of the importance of price elasticity information relates to discounts sometimes offered different customer groups. *The Wall Street Journal* offers students bargain rates; airlines, restaurants, and most hotel chains offer discounts to vacation travelers and senior citizens; large corporate customers get discounts or rebates on desktop computers and auto leases. Many such discounts are substantial, sometimes in the range of 30 percent to 40 percent off standard prices. The question of whether reduced prices attract sufficient additional customers to offset lower revenues per unit is directly related to the price elasticity of demand.

PRICE ELASTICITY AND MARGINAL REVENUE

There are simple, direct relations between price elasticity, marginal revenue, and total revenue. It is worth examining such relations in detail given their importance for pricing policy.

Varying Elasticity at Different Points on a Demand Curve

All linear demand curves, except perfectly elastic or perfectly inelastic ones, are subject to varying elasticities at different points on the curve. In other words, any linear demand curve is price elastic at some output levels but inelastic at others. To see this, recall again the definition of point price elasticity expressed in Equation 4.14:

$$\epsilon_P = \frac{\partial Q}{\partial P} \times \frac{P}{Q}$$

The slope of a linear demand curve, $\partial P / \partial Q$, is constant; thus, so is its reciprocal, $1/(\partial P/\partial Q) = \partial Q/\partial P$. However, the ratio P/Q varies from 0 at the point where the demand curve intersects the horizontal axis and price equals zero, to $+\infty$ at the vertical price axis intercept where quantity equals zero. Because the price elasticity formula for a linear curve involves multiplying a negative constant by a ratio that varies between zero and $+\infty$, the price elasticity of a linear curve must range from zero to $-\infty$.

Figure 4.10 illustrates this relation. As the demand curve approaches the vertical axis, the ratio P/Q approaches infinity and ϵ_P approaches minus infinity. As the demand curve approaches the horizontal axis, the ratio P/Q approaches zero, causing ϵ_P also to approach zero. At the midpoint of the demand curve $(\partial Q/\partial P) \times (P/Q) = -1$; this is the point of unitary elasticity.

Price Elasticity and Price Changes

The relation between price elasticity and total revenue can be clarified by examining Figure 4.11 and Table 4.5. Figure 4.11(a) reproduces the demand curve shown in Figure 4.10 along

FIGURE 4.10

Price Elasticity of Demand Varies Along a Linear Demand Curve

The price elasticity of demand will vary from 0 to -∞ along a linear demand curve.

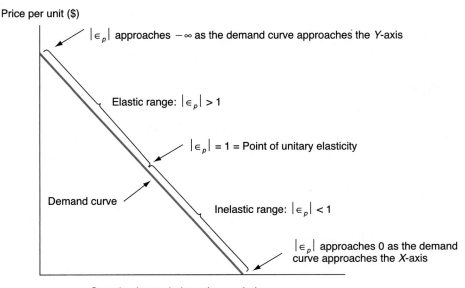

TABLE 4.5

Price Elasticity and Revenue Relations: A Numerical Example

Price P	Quantity Q	Total Revenue $TR = P \times Q$	Marginal Revenue $MR = \Delta TR$	Arc Elasticity[a] E_P
$100	1	$100	—	—
90	2	180	$80	−6.33
80	3	240	60	−3.40
70	4	280	40	−2.14
60	5	300	20	−1.44
50	6	300	0	−1.00
40	7	280	−20	−0.69
30	8	240	−40	−0.47
20	9	180	−60	−0.29
10	10	100	−80	−0.16

a   Because the price and quantity data in the table are discrete numbers, the price elasticities have been calculated by using the arc elasticity equation

$$E_P = \frac{\Delta Q}{\Delta P} \times \frac{P_2 + P_1}{Q_2 + Q_1}$$

with the associated marginal revenue curve. The demand curve shown in Figure 4.11(a) is of the general linear form

(4.16)
$$P = a - bQ$$

where a is the intercept and b is the slope coefficient. It follows that total revenue (*TR*) can be expressed as

$$TR = P \times Q$$
$$= (a - bQ) \times Q$$
$$= aQ - bQ^2$$

By definition, marginal revenue (*MR*) is the change in revenue following a one-unit expansion in output, $\partial TR / \partial Q$, and can be written

(4.17)
$$MR = \partial TR / \partial Q = a - 2bQ$$

The relation between the demand (average revenue) and marginal revenue curves becomes clear when one compares Equations 4.16 and 4.17. Each equation has the same intercept a. Both curves begin at the same point along the vertical price axis. However, the marginal revenue curve has twice the negative slope of the demand curve. This means that the marginal revenue curve intersects the horizontal axis at $\frac{1}{2} Q_X$, given that the demand curve intersects at Q_X. Figure 4.11(a) shows that marginal revenue is positive in the range where demand is price elastic, zero where $\epsilon_P = -1$, and negative in the inelastic range. Thus, there is an obvious relation between price elasticity and both average and marginal revenue.

As shown in Figure 4.11(b), price elasticity is also closely related to total revenue. Total revenue increases with price reductions in the elastic range (where $MR > 0$) because the increase in quantity demanded at the new lower price more than offsets the lower revenue per unit received at that reduced price. Total revenue peaks at the point of unitary elasticity (where $MR = 0$), since the increase in quantity associated with the price reduction exactly offsets the lower revenue received per unit. Finally, total revenue declines when price is reduced in the inelastic range (where $MR < 0$). Here, the quantity demanded continues to increase with

FIGURE 4.11

Relations Among Price Elasticity and Marginal, Average, and Total Revenue:
(a) Demand (Average Revenue) and Marginal Revenue Curves; (b) Total Revenue

In the range in which demand is elastic with respect to price, marginal revenue is positive and total revenue increases with a reduction in price. In the inelastic range, marginal revenue is negative and total revenue decreases with price reductions.

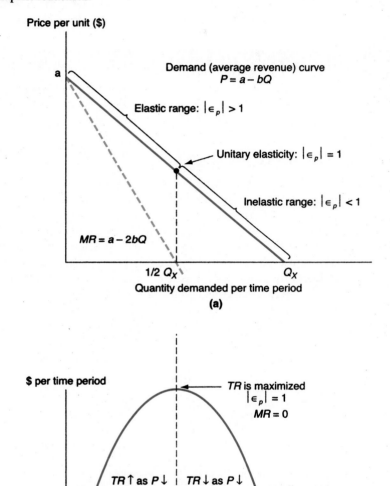

(a)

(b)

reductions in price, but the relative increase in quantity is less than the percentage decrease in price, and thus is not large enough to offset the reduction in revenue per unit sold.

The numerical example in Table 4.5 illustrates these relations. It shows that from 1 to 5 units of output, demand is elastic, $|\epsilon_P| > 1$, and a reduction in price increases total revenue. For example, decreasing price from $80 to $70 increases output from 3 to 4 units. Marginal revenue is positive over this range of output, and total revenue increases from $240 to $280. For output greater than 6 units and prices less than $50, demand is inelastic, $|\epsilon_P| < 1$. Here price reductions result in lower total revenue, because the increase in quantity demanded is not large enough to offset the lower price per unit. With total revenue decreasing as output expands, marginal revenue must be negative. For example, reducing price from $30 to $20 results in revenue declining from $240 to $180 even though output increases from eight to nine units; marginal revenue in this case is –$60.

PRICE ELASTICITY AND OPTIMAL PRICING POLICY

Firms use price discounts, specials, coupons, and rebate programs to measure the price sensitivity of demand for their products. Armed with such knowledge, and detailed unit cost information, firms have all the tools necessary for setting optimal prices.

Optimal Price Formula

As a practical matter, firms devote enormous resources to obtain current and detailed information concerning the price elasticity of demand for their products. Price elasticity estimates represent vital information because these data, along with relevant unit cost information, are essential inputs for setting a pricing policy that is consistent with value maximization. This stems from the fact that there is a relatively simple mathematical relation between marginal revenue, price, and the point price elasticity of demand.

Given any point price elasticity estimate, relevant marginal revenues can be determined easily. When this marginal revenue information is combined with pertinent marginal cost data, the basis for an optimal pricing policy is created.

The relation between marginal revenue, price, and the point price elasticity of demand follows directly from the mathematical definition of a marginal relation.[2] In equation form, the link between marginal revenue, price, and the point price elasticity of demand is

---

2   In calculus notation, marginal revenue is the derivative of the total revenue function. That is, $MR = dTR/dQ$. Because total revenue equals price times quantity ($TR = P \times Q$), marginal revenue is found by taking the derivative of the function $P \times Q$ with respect to Q:

$$MR = \frac{d(P \times Q)}{dQ}$$

Because price and quantity are interdependent in the typical demand situation, the rule for differentiating a product must be used in taking the preceding derivative:

$$MR = \frac{dTR}{dQ} = \frac{d(P \times Q)}{dQ} = P \times \frac{dQ}{dQ} + Q \times \frac{dP}{dQ}$$

$$= P \times 1 + Q \times \frac{dP}{dQ}$$

$$= P + Q \times \frac{dP}{dQ}$$

This relation is a completely general specification of marginal revenue, which, if P is factored out from the right-hand side, can be rewritten as

$$MR = P\left(1 + \frac{Q}{P} \times \frac{dP}{dQ}\right)$$

Note that the term $Q/P \times dP/dQ$ in the preceding expression is the reciprocal of the definition for point price elasticity, $\epsilon_P = dQ/dP \times (P/Q)$:

$$\frac{Q}{P} \times \frac{dP}{dQ} = \frac{1}{\frac{dQ}{dP} \times \frac{P}{Q}} = \frac{1}{\epsilon_P}$$

Thus, marginal revenue can be rewritten as

$$MR = P\left(1 + \frac{1}{\epsilon_P}\right)$$

(4.18)
$$MR = P \left(1 + \frac{1}{\epsilon_P} \right)$$

Since $\epsilon_P < 0$, the number contained within brackets in Equation 4.18 is always less than one. This means that $MR < P$, and the gap between MR and P will fall as the price elasticity of demand increases (in absolute value terms). For example, when $P = \$8$ and $\epsilon_P = -1.5$, $MR = \$2.67$. Thus, when price elasticity is relatively low, the optimal price is much greater than marginal revenue. Conversely, when $P = \$8$ and $\epsilon_P = -10$, $MR = \$7.20$. When the quantity demanded is highly elastic with respect to price, the optimal price is close to marginal revenue.

Optimal Pricing Policy Example

The simple relation between marginal revenue, price, and the point price elasticity is very useful in the setting of pricing policy. To see the usefulness of Equation 4.18 in practical pricing policy, consider the pricing problem faced by a profit-maximizing firm. Recall that profit maximization requires operating at the activity level where marginal cost equals marginal revenue. Most firms have extensive cost information and can estimate marginal cost reasonably well. By equating marginal costs with marginal revenue as identified by Equation 4.18, the profit-maximizing price level can be easily determined. Using Equation 4.18, set marginal cost equal to marginal revenue, where

$$MC = MR$$

and, therefore,

$$MR = P \left(1 + \frac{1}{\epsilon_P} \right)$$

which implies that the optimal or profit-maximizing price, P^*, equals

(4.19)
$$P^* = \frac{MC}{\left(1 + \frac{1}{\epsilon_P} \right)}$$

This simple relation between price, marginal cost, and the point price elasticity of demand may well be one of the most useful pricing tools offered by managerial economics.

To illustrate the usefulness of Equation 4.19, suppose that manager George Stevens notes a 2 percent increase in weekly sales following a 1 percent price discount on *The Kingfish* fishing reels. The point price elasticity of demand for *The Kingfish* fishing reels is

$$\epsilon_P = \frac{\text{Percentage Change in } Q}{\text{Percentage Change in } P}$$

$$= \frac{2}{-1}$$

$$= -2$$

What is the optimal retail price for *The Kingfish* fishing reels if the company's relevant marginal costs total \$25 per unit? With marginal costs of \$25 and $\epsilon_P = -2$, the profit-maximizing price is

$$P = \frac{\$25}{\left(1 + \frac{1}{-2} \right)}$$

$$= \$50$$

Therefore, the profit-maximizing price on *The Kingfish* fishing reels is $50.

To see how Equation 4.19 can be used for planning purposes, suppose Stevens can order reels through a different distributor and reduce marginal costs by $1 to $24 per unit. Under these circumstances, the new optimal retail price is

$$P = \frac{\$24}{\left(1 + \dfrac{1}{-2}\right)}$$

$$= \$48$$

Thus, the optimal retail price would fall by $2 following a $1 reduction in *The Kingfish's* relevant marginal costs.

Equation 4.19 can serve as the basis for calculating profit-maximizing prices under current cost and market-demand conditions, as well as under a variety of potential circumstances. Table 4.6 shows how profit-maximizing prices vary for a product with a $25 marginal cost as the point price elasticity of demand varies. Note that the less elastic the demand, the greater the difference between price and marginal cost. Conversely, as the absolute value of the price elasticity of demand increases (i.e., as demand becomes more price elastic), the profit-maximizing price gets closer and closer to marginal cost.

Determinants of Price Elasticity

There are three major influences on price elasticities: (1) the extent to which a good is considered a necessity; (2) the availability of substitute goods; and (3) the proportion of income spent on the product. A relatively constant quantity of electricity for residential lighting will be purchased almost irrespective of price, at least in the short run. There is no close substitute for electric service. However, goods such as men's and women's clothing face considerably more competition, and their demand depends more on price.

Demand for "big ticket" items such as automobiles, homes, and vacation travel accounts for a large share of consumer income and is relatively sensitive to price. Demand for less expensive products, such as soft drinks, candy, and cigarettes, can be relatively insensitive to price. Given the low percentage of income spent on "small ticket" items, consumers often find that searching for the best deal available is not worth the time and effort. Accordingly, the elasticity of demand is typically higher for major purchases than for small ones.

Price elasticity for an individual firm is seldom the same as that for the entire industry. In pure monopoly, the firm demand curve is also the industry demand curve, so the elasticity of demand faced by the firm at any output level is the same as that faced by the industry. Consider the other extreme—pure competition, as approximated by wheat farming. The

TABLE 4.6

Price Elasticity and Optimal Pricing Policy

Point Price Elasticity	Marginal Cost	Profit-Maximizing Price
−1.25	$25	$125.00
−1.50	25	75.00
−2.50	25	41.67
−5.00	25	31.25
−10.00	25	27.78
−25.00	25	26.04

industry demand curve for wheat is downward sloping: the lower its price, the greater the quantity of wheat that will be demanded. However, the demand curve facing any individual wheat farmer is essentially horizontal. A farmer can sell any amount of wheat at the going price, but if the farmer raises price by the smallest fraction of a cent, sales collapse to zero. The wheat farmer's demand curve—or that of any firm operating under pure competition—is perfectly elastic. Figure 4.9 illustrates such a demand curve.

The demand for producer goods and services is indirect, or derived from their value in use. Because the demand for all inputs is derived from their usefulness in producing other products, their demand is derived from the demand for final products. In contrast to the terms *final product* or *consumer demand*, the term *derived demand* describes the demand for all producer goods and services. Although the demand for producer goods and services is related to the demand for the final products that they are used to make, this relation is not always as close as one might suspect.

In some instances, the demand for intermediate goods is less price sensitive than demand for the resulting final product. This is because intermediate goods sometimes represent only a small portion of the cost of producing the final product. For example, suppose the total cost to build a small manufacturing plant is $1 million, and $25,000 of this cost represents the cost of electrical fixtures and wiring. Even a doubling in electrical costs from $25,000 to $50,000 would have only a modest effect on the overall costs of the plant—which would increase by only 2.5 percent from $1 million to $1,025,000. Rather than being highly price sensitive, the firm might select its electrical contractor based on timeliness and the quality of service provided. In such an instance, the firm's price elasticity of demand for electrical fixtures and wiring is quite low, even if its price elasticity of demand for the overall project is high.

In other situations the reverse might hold. Continuing with our previous example, suppose that steel costs represent $250,000 of the total $1 million cost of building the plant. Because of its relative importance, a substantial increase in steel costs has a significant influence on the total costs of the overall project. As a result, the price sensitivity of the demand for steel will be close to that for the overall plant. If the firm's demand for plant construction is highly price elastic, the demand for steel is also likely to be highly price elastic.

Price Elasticity of Demand for Airline Passenger Service

Southwest Airlines likes to call itself the Texas state bird. It must be some bird, because the U.S. Transportation Department regards Southwest as our dominant carrier. Fares are cut in half and traffic doubles, triples, or even quadruples whenever Southwest enters a new market. Airport authorities rake in millions of extra dollars in landing fees, parking and concession fees soar, and added business is attracted to the local area—all because Southwest has arrived! Could it be that Southwest has discovered what many airline passengers already know? Customers absolutely crave cut-rate prices that are combined with friendly service, plus arrival and departure times that are convenient and reliable. The once-little upstart airline from Texas is growing by leaps and bounds because nobody knows how to meet the demand for regional airline service like Southwest Airlines.

Table 4.7 shows information that can be used to infer the industry arc price elasticity of demand in selected regional markets served by Southwest. In the early 1990s, Southwest saw an opportunity because airfares out of San Francisco were high, and the nearby Oakland airport was underused. By offering cut-rate fares out of Oakland to Burbank, a similarly underused airport in southern California, Southwest was able to spur dramatic traffic gains and revenue growth. During the first 12 months of operation, Southwest induced a growth in airport traffic on the Oakland–Burbank route from 246,555 to 1,053,139 passengers, an increase of 806,584 passengers, following an average one-way fare cut from $86.50 to $44.69. Using the arc price elasticity formula, an arc price elasticity of demand of $E_P = -1.95$ for the Oakland–Burbank market is suggested. Given elastic demand in the Oakland–Burbank market, city-pair annual revenue grew from $21.3 to $47.1 million over this period.

TABLE 4.7

How Prices Plunge and Traffic Soars When Southwest Airlines Enters a Market

Burbank–Oakland

Passengers in 12 months before Southwest	246,555
Passengers in 12 months after Southwest	1,053,139
Increase in passengers	806,584
Average one-way fare before Southwest	$86.50
Average one-way fare after Southwest	$44.69
Decrease in one-way fares	–$41.81
Market revenue in 12 months before Southwest	$21,327,008
Market revenue in 12 months after Southwest	$47,064,782
Increase in market revenue	$25,737,774
Implied arc price elasticity of demand (E_P)	–1.95

Kansas City–St. Louis

Passengers in 12 months before Southwest	428,711
Passengers in 12 months after Southwest	722,425
Increase in passengers	293,714
Average one-way fare before Southwest	$154.42
Average one-way fare after Southwest	$45.82
Decrease in one-way fares	–$108.60
Market revenue in 12 months before Southwest	$66,201,553
Market revenue in 12 months after Southwest	$33,101,514
Decrease in market revenue	–$33,100,039
Implied arc price elasticity of demand (E_P)	–0.47

Data Source: Del Jones, "Business Soars Where Airline Flies," *USA Today*, 9/17/93, 1B–2B.

A very different picture of the price elasticity of demand for regional airline passenger service is portrayed by Southwest's experience on the Kansas City–St. Louis route. In 1992, Southwest began offering cut-rate fares between Kansas City and St. Louis and was, once again, able to spur dramatic traffic growth. However, in the Kansas City–St. Louis market, traffic growth was not sufficient to generate added revenue. During the first 12 months of Southwest's operation in this market, traffic growth in the Kansas City–St. Louis route was from 428,711 to 722,425 passengers, an increase of 293,714 passengers, following an average one-way fare cut from $154.42 to $45.82. Again using the arc price elasticity formula, a market arc price elasticity of demand of only $E_P = -0.47$ is suggested. With inelastic demand, Kansas City–St. Louis market revenue fell from $66.2 to $33.1 million over this period.

In considering these arc price elasticity estimates, remember that they correspond to each market rather than to Southwest Airlines itself. If Southwest were the single carrier or monopolist in the Kansas City–St. Louis market, it could gain revenues and cut variable costs by raising fares and reducing the number of daily departures. As a monopolist, such a fare increase would lead to higher revenues and profits. However, given the fact that other airlines operate in each market, Southwest's own demand is likely to be much more price elastic than the market demand elasticity estimates shown in Table 4.7. To judge the profitability of any fare, it is necessary to consider Southwest's revenue *and* cost structure in each market. For example, service in the Kansas City–St. Louis market might allow Southwest to more efficiently use aircraft and personnel used to serve the Dallas–Chicago market, and thus be highly profitable even when bargain-basement fares are charged.

What's in a Name?

When it comes to financial information, privately-held Mars Incorporated, in MacLean, Virginia, is secretive. With annual sales of $15 billion in pet foods, candies, and other food products, the company is also immensely profitable. According to *Forbes'* annual survey, Forrest Edward Mars, Sr., Edward Mars, Jr., Jacqueline Mars Vogel, John Mars, and the rest of the clan are worth more than *$16 billion*—one of the richest families in the world. How does Mars do it? That's simple: brand-name advertising.

Like top rivals Hershey's, Nestle, and Ralston Purina, Mars advertises like mad to create durable brand names. Since 1954, *M&M's Peanut* and *M&M's Chocolate Candies* have been known by the slogan "Melts in your mouth—not in your hand." With constant reminders, the message has not been lost on consumers who also flock to other Mars candies like *Royals Mint Chocolate, Kudos Granola Bars, Skittles Fruit Chews, Snickers Candy & Ice Cream Bars*, and *Starburst Fruit Chews*. Brand-name advertising is also a cornerstone of Mars' marketing of *Kal-Kan* petfoods; *Expert*, a superpremium dog and cat food line; and *Sheba* and *Whiskas* cat foods.

Mars is like many top-tier consumer products companies; their good name is their most valuable asset. For example, although Coca-Cola enjoys undeniable economies of scale in distribution, nothing is more valuable than its telltale moniker in white on red background. For Philip Morris, the *Marlboro* brand is the source of a large and growing river of cash flow. In the United States, more than one-half of all cigarettes are sold on the basis of a red and white box and the rugged image of a weather-beaten and sun-dried cowboy. Owners of trademarks such as *Astroturf, Coke, Frisbee, Kleenex, Kitty Litter, Styrofoam, Walkman*, and *Xerox* employ a veritable army of lawyers in an endless struggle against "generic" treatment. They know that well-established brand-name products enjoy enormous profits.

See: Suzanne Vranica, "American Express Launches Ads to Boost Brand Hurt by Travel," *The Wall Street Journal Online*, March 15, 2002 (http://online.wsj.com).

The importance of price elasticity information is examined further in later chapters. At this point, it becomes useful to consider other important demand elasticities.

CROSS-PRICE ELASTICITY OF DEMAND

Demand for most products is influenced by prices for other products. Such demand interrelationships are an important consideration in demand analysis and estimation.

Substitutes and Complements

substitutes
Related products for which a price increase for one leads to an increase in demand for the other

complements
Related products for which a price increase for one leads to a reduction in demand for the other

cross-price elasticity
Responsiveness of demand for one product to changes in the price of another

The demand for beef is related to the price of chicken. As the price of chicken increases, so does the demand for beef; consumers substitute beef for the now relatively more expensive chicken. On the other hand, a price decrease for chicken leads to a decrease in the demand for beef as consumers substitute chicken for the now relatively more expensive beef. In general, a direct relation between the price of one product and the demand for a second product holds for all **substitutes**. A price increase for a given product will increase demand for substitutes; a price decrease for a given product will decrease demand for substitutes.

Some goods and services—for example, cameras and film—exhibit a completely different relation. Here price increases in one product typically lead to a reduction in demand for the other. Goods that are inversely related in this manner are known as **complements**; they are used together rather than in place of each other.

The concept of **cross-price elasticity** is used to examine the responsiveness of demand for one product to changes in the price of another. Point cross-price elasticity is given by the following equation:

$$\epsilon_{PX} = \frac{\text{Percentage Change in Quantity of } Y}{\text{Percentage Change in Price of } X}$$

(4.20)

$$= \frac{\partial Q_Y / Q_Y}{\partial P_X / P_X}$$

$$= \frac{\partial Q_Y}{\partial P_X} \times \frac{P_X}{Q_Y}$$

where Y and X are two different products. The arc cross-price elasticity relationship is constructed in the same manner as was previously described for price elasticity:

$$E_{PX} = \frac{\text{Percentage Change in Quantity of } Y}{\text{Percentage Change in Price of } X}$$

(4.21)

$$= \frac{(Q_{Y2} - Q_{Y1})/[(Q_{Y2} + Q_{Y1})/2]}{(P_{X2} - P_{X1})/[(P_{X2} + P_{X1})/2]}$$

$$= \frac{\Delta Q_Y}{\Delta P_X} \times \frac{P_{X2} + P_{X1}}{Q_{Y2} + Q_{Y1}}$$

The cross-price elasticity for substitutes is always positive; the price of one good and the demand for the other always move in the same direction. Cross-price elasticity is negative for complements; price and quantity move in opposite directions for complementary goods and services. Finally, cross-price elasticity is zero, or nearly zero, for unrelated goods in which variations in the price of one good have no effect on demand for the second.

Cross-Price Elasticity Example

The cross-price elasticity concept can be illustrated by considering the demand function for monitored in-home health-care services provided by Home Medical Support (HMS), Inc.:

$$Q_Y = f(P_Y, P_D, P_H, P_T, i, I)$$

Here, Q_Y is the number of patient days of service per year; P_Y is the average price of HMS service; P_D is an industry price index for prescription drugs; P_H is an index of the average price of hospital service, a primary competitor; P_T is a price index for the travel industry; i is the interest rate; and I is disposable income per capita. Assume that the parameters of the HMS demand function have been estimated as follows:

$$Q_Y = 25,000 - 5P_Y - 3P_D + 10P_H + 0.0001P_T - 0.02i + 2.5I$$

The effects on Q_Y caused by a one-unit change in the prices of other goods are

$$\frac{\partial Q_Y}{\partial P_D} = -3$$

$$\frac{\partial Q_Y}{\partial P_H} = +10$$

$$\frac{\partial Q_Y}{\partial P_T} = 0.0001 \approx 0$$

Because both prices and quantities are always positive, the ratios P_D/Q_Y, P_H/Q_Y, and P_T/Q_Y are also positive. Therefore, the signs of the three cross-price elasticities in this example are determined by the sign of each relevant parameter estimate in the HMS demand function:

$$\epsilon_{PD} = (-3)(P_D/Q_Y) < 0$$

HMS service and prescription drugs are complements.

$$\epsilon_{PH} = (+10)(P_H/Q_Y) > 0$$

HMS service and hospital service are substitutes.

$$\epsilon_{PT} = (+0.0001)(P_T/Q_Y) \approx 0, \text{ so long as the ratio } P_T/Q_Y \text{ is not extremely large}$$

Demand for travel and HMS service are independent.

The concept of cross-price elasticity serves two main purposes. First, it is important for the firm to be aware of how demand for its products is likely to respond to changes in the prices of other goods. This is particularly true for firms with a wide variety of products, in which meaningful substitute or complementary relations exist within the firm's own product line. Second, cross-price elasticity information allows managers to measure the degree of competition in the marketplace. For example, a firm might appear to dominate a particular market or market segment, especially if it is the only supplier of a particular product. However, if the cross-price elasticity between a firm's output and products produced in related industries is large and positive, the firm is not immune to the threat of competitor encroachment. In the banking industry, for example, commercial banks clearly compete with money market mutual funds, savings and loan associations, credit unions, and finance companies. The extent of competition is measured in terms of cross-price elasticities of demand.

INCOME ELASTICITY OF DEMAND

For many goods, income is an important determinant of demand. Income is frequently as important as price, advertising expenditures, or credit terms. This is particularly true of luxury items such as big-screen televisions, country club memberships, elegant homes, and so on. Demand for basic commodities such as salt, bread, and milk is not very responsive to income changes. These goods are bought in fairly constant amounts regardless of changes in income.

Normal Versus Inferior Goods

income elasticity
Responsiveness of demand to changes in income, holding constant the effect of all other variables

The **income elasticity** of demand measures the responsiveness of demand to changes in income, holding constant the effect of all other variables that influence demand. Letting I represent income, point income elasticity is defined as

(4.22)

$$\epsilon_I = \frac{\text{Percentage Change in Quantity } (Q)}{\text{Percentage Change in Income } (I)}$$

$$= \frac{\partial Q/Q}{\partial I/I}$$

$$= \frac{\partial Q}{\partial I} \times \frac{I}{Q}$$

inferior goods
Products for which consumer demand declines as income rises

Income and the quantity purchased typically move in the same direction; that is, income and sales are directly rather than inversely related. Therefore, $\partial Q/\partial I$ and hence ϵ_I are positive. This does not hold for a limited number of products termed **inferior goods**. Individual consumer demand for such products as beans and potatoes, for example, is sometimes thought to decline as income increases, because consumers replace them with more desirable alternatives. More

normal goods
Products for which demand is positively related to income

typical products, whose individual and aggregate demand is positively related to income, are defined as **normal goods**.

To examine income elasticity over a range of incomes rather than at a single level, the arc elasticity relation is used:

(4.23)

$$E_I = \frac{\text{Percentage Change in Quantity } (Q)}{\text{Percentage Change in Income } (I)}$$

$$= \frac{(Q_2 - Q_1)/[(Q_2 + Q_1)/2]}{(I_2 - I_1)/[(I_2 + I_1)/2]}$$

$$= \frac{\Delta Q}{\Delta I} \times \frac{I_2 + I_1}{Q_2 + Q_1}$$

Arc income elasticity provides a measure of the average responsiveness of demand for a given product to a relative change in income over the range from I_1 to I_2.

In the case of inferior goods, individual demand actually rises during an economic downturn. As workers get laid off from their jobs, for example, they might tend to substitute potatoes for meat, hamburgers for steak, bus rides for automobile trips, and so on. As a result, demand for potatoes, hamburgers, bus rides, and other inferior goods may rise during recessions. Their demand is **countercyclical**.

countercyclical
Inferior goods whose demand falls with rising income, and rises with falling income

Types of Normal Goods

For most products, income elasticity is positive, indicating that demand rises as the economy expands and national income increases. The actual size of the income elasticity coefficient is very important. Suppose, for example, that $\epsilon_I = 0.3$. This means that a 1 percent increase in income causes demand for the product to increase by only .3 percent. Given growing national income over time, such a product would not maintain its relative importance in the economy. Another product might have $\epsilon_I = 2.5$; its demand increases 2.5 times as fast as income. If, $\epsilon_I < 1.0$ for a particular product, its producers will not share proportionately in increases in national income. However, if $\epsilon_I > 1.0$, the industry will gain more than a proportionate share of increases in income.

noncyclical normal goods
Products for which demand is relatively unaffected by changing income

Goods for which $0 < \epsilon_I < 1$ are referred to as **noncyclical normal goods**, because demand is relatively unaffected by changing income. Sales of most convenience goods, such as toothpaste, candy, soda, and movie tickets, account for only a small share of the consumer's overall budget, and spending on such items tends to be relatively unaffected by changing economic conditions. For goods having $\epsilon_I > 1$, referred to as **cyclical normal goods**, demand is strongly affected by changing economic conditions. Purchase of "big ticket" items such as homes, automobiles, boats, and recreational vehicles can be postponed and tend to be put off by consumers during economic downturns. Housing demand, for example, can collapse during recessions and skyrocket during economic expansions. These relations between income and product demand are summarized in Table 4.8.

cyclical normal goods
Products for which demand is strongly affected by changing income

TABLE 4.8

Relationship Between Income and Product Demand

Inferior goods (countercyclical)	$\epsilon_I < 0$	Basic foodstuffs, generic products, bus rides
Noncyclical normal goods	$0 < \epsilon_I < 1$	Toiletries, movies, liquor, cigarettes
Cyclical normal goods	$\epsilon_I > 1$	Automobiles, housing, vacation travel, capital equipment

Firms whose demand functions indicate high income elasticities enjoy good growth opportunities in expanding economies. Forecasts of aggregate economic activity figure importantly in their plans. Companies faced with low income elasticities are relatively unaffected by the level of overall business activity. This is desirable from the standpoint that such a business is harmed relatively little by economic downturns. Nevertheless, such a company cannot expect to share fully in a growing economy and might seek to enter industries that provide better growth opportunities.

Income elasticity figures importantly in several key national debates. Agriculture is often depressed because of the low income elasticity for most food products. This has made it difficult for farmers' incomes to keep up with those of urban workers. A somewhat similar problem arises in housing. Improving the housing stock is a primary national goal. If the income elasticity for housing is high and $\epsilon_I > 1$, an improvement in the housing stock will be a natural by-product of a prosperous economy. However, if the housing income elasticity $\epsilon_I < 1$, a relatively small percentage of additional income will be spent on houses. As a result, housing stock would not improve much over time despite a growing economy and increasing incomes. In the event that $\epsilon_I < 1$, direct government investment in public housing or rent and interest subsidies might be necessary to bring about a dramatic increase in the housing stock over time.

SUMMARY

Product demand is a critical determinant of profitability, and demand estimates are key considerations in virtually all managerial decisions. This chapter introduces a number of factors that underlie the demand for all goods and services, and methods for quantifying and interpreting demand relations.

- A **utility function** is a descriptive statement that relates satisfaction or well-being to the consumption of goods and services. **Marginal utility** measures the added satisfaction derived from a one-unit increase in consumption of a particular good or service, holding consumption of all other goods and services constant. The **law of diminishing marginal utility** states that as an individual increases consumption of a given product, the marginal utility gained from consumption eventually declines.

- An **indifference curve** represents all market baskets among which the consumer is indifferent. The **marginal rate of substitution** is simply the change in consumption of Y necessary to offset a given change in the consumption of X if the consumer's overall level of utility is to remain constant.

- A **budget line** represents all combinations of products that can be purchased for a fixed dollar amount. The **income effect** of a price change is the increase in overall consumption made possible by a price cut or the decrease in overall consumption made necessary by a price increase. The income effect results in a shift to a higher indifference curve following a price cut or a shift to a lower indifference curve following a price increase. The **substitution effect** of a price change describes the change in relative consumption that occurs as consumers substitute cheaper products for more expensive products. A **consumption path** depicts optimal market baskets for consumption as the budget expenditure level grows.

- **Elasticity** is the percentage change in a dependent variable, Y, resulting from a one-percent change in the value of an independent variable, X. **Point elasticity** measures elasticity at a point on a function. **Arc elasticity** measures the average elasticity over a given range of a function.

- Factors such as price and advertising that are within the control of the firm are called **endogenous variables**; factors outside the control of the firm such as consumer incomes, competitor prices, and the weather are called **exogenous variables**.

- The **price elasticity of demand** measures the responsiveness of the quantity demanded to changes in the price of the product, holding constant the values of all other variables in the demand function. With **elastic demand**, a price increase will lower total revenue and a decrease in price will raise total revenue. **Unitary elasticity** describes a situation in which the effect of a price change is exactly offset by the effect of a change in quantity demanded. Total revenue, the product of price times quantity, remains constant. With **inelastic demand** a price increase produces a less than proportionate decline in quantity demanded, so total revenues rises. Conversely a price decrease produces less than a proportionate increase in quantity demanded, so total revenue falls.

- A direct relation between the price of one product and the demand for another holds for all **substitutes**. A price increase for a given product will increase demand for substitutes; a price decrease for a given product will decrease demand for substitutes. Goods that are inversely related in terms of price and quantity are known as **complements**; they are used together rather than in place of each other. The concept of **cross-price elasticity** is used to examine the responsiveness of demand for one product to changes in the price of another.

- The **income elasticity** of demand measures the responsiveness of demand to changes in income, holding constant the effect of all other variables. For a limited number of **inferior goods**, individual consumer demand is thought to decline as income increases, because consumers replace them with more desirable alternatives. Demand for such products is **countercyclical**, actually rising during recessions and falling during economic booms. More typical products, whose individual and aggregate demand is positively related to income, are defined as **normal** or **superior goods**. Goods for which $0 < \epsilon_I < 1$ are often referred to as **noncyclical normal goods**, because demand is relatively unaffected by changing income. For goods having $\epsilon_I > 1$, referred to as **cyclical normal goods**, demand is strongly affected by changing economic conditions.

Demand analysis and estimation is one of the most interesting and challenging topics in managerial economics. This chapter provides a valuable, albeit brief, introduction to several key concepts that are useful in the practical analysis and estimation of demand.

QUESTIONS

Q4.1 Is the economic demand for a product determined solely by its usefulness?

Q4.2 "The utility derived from consumption is intangible and thus unobservable. Therefore, the utility concept has no practical value." Discuss this statement.

Q4.3 Is an increase in total utility or satisfaction following an increase in income inconsistent with the law of diminishing marginal utility?

Q4.4 What would an upward-sloping demand curve imply about the marginal utility derived from consumption? Why are upward-sloping demand curves not observed in the real world?

Q4.5 Describe the income, substitution, and total effects on consumption following a price increase.

Q4.6 When is use of the arc elasticity concept valid as compared with the use of the point elasticity concept?

Q4.7 Is the price elasticity of demand typically greater if computed for an industry or for a single firm in the industry? Why?

Q4.8 Is the cross-price elasticity concept useful for identifying the boundaries of an industry or market?

Q4.9 Individual consumer demand declines for inferior goods as personal income increases because consumers replace them with more desirable alternatives. Is an inverse relation between demand and national income likely for such products?

Q4.10 An estimated 80% increase in the retail price of cigarettes is necessary to cause a 30% drop in the number of cigarettes sold. Would such a price increase help or hurt tobacco industry profits?

What would be the likely effect on industry profits if this price boost was simply caused by a $1.50 per pack increase in cigarette excise taxes?

SELF-TEST PROBLEMS AND SOLUTIONS

ST4.1 **Elasticity Estimation.** Distinctive Designs, Inc., imports and distributes dress and sports watches. At the end of the company's fiscal year, brand manager J. Peterman has asked you to evaluate sales of the sports watch line by using the following data:

Month	Number of Sports Watches Sold	Sports Watch Advertising Expenditures	Sports Watch Price, P	Dress Watch Price, P_D
July	4,500	$10,000	26	50
August	5,500	10,000	24	50
September	4,500	9,200	24	50
October	3,500	9,200	24	46
November	5,000	9,750	25	50
December	15,000	9,750	20	50
January	5,000	8,350	25	50
February	4,000	7,850	25	50
March	5,500	9,500	25	55
April	6,000	8,500	24	51
May	4,000	8,500	26	51
June	5,000	8,500	26	57

In particular, Peterman has asked you to estimate relevant demand elasticities. Remember that to estimate the required elasticities, you should consider months only when the other important factors considered in the preceding table have not changed. Also note that by restricting your analysis to consecutive months, changes in any additional factors not explicitly included in the analysis are less likely to affect estimated elasticities. Finally, the average arc elasticity of demand for each factor is simply the average of monthly elasticities calculated during the past year.

A. Indicate whether there was or was not a change in each respective independent variable for each month pair during the past year.

Month–Pair	Sports Watch Advertising Expenditures, A	Sports Watch Price, P	Dress Watch Price, P_D
July–August	_____	_____	_____
August–September	_____	_____	_____
September–October	_____	_____	_____
October–November	_____	_____	_____
November–December	_____	_____	_____
December–January	_____	_____	_____
January–February	_____	_____	_____
February–March	_____	_____	_____
March–April	_____	_____	_____
April–May	_____	_____	_____
May–June	_____	_____	_____

B. Calculate and interpret the average advertising arc elasticity of demand for sports watches.

C. Calculate and interpret the average arc price elasticity of demand for sports watches.

D. Calculate and interpret the average arc cross-price elasticity of demand between sports and dress watches.

ST4.1   Solution

A.

Month–Pair	Sports Watch Advertising Expenditures, A	Sports Watch Price, P	Dress Watch Price, P_D
July–August	No change	Change	No change
August–September	Change	No change	No change
September–October	No change	No change	Change
October–November	Change	Change	Change
November–December	No change	Change	No change
December–January	Change	Change	No change
January–February	Change	No change	No change
February–March	Change	No change	Change
March–April	Change	Change	Change
April–May	No change	Change	No change
May–June	No change	No change	Change

B. In calculating the arc advertising elasticity of demand, only consider consecutive months when there was a change in advertising but no change in the prices of sports and dress watches:

August–September

$$E_A = \frac{\Delta Q}{\Delta A} \times \frac{A_2 + A_1}{Q_2 + Q_1}$$

$$= \frac{4,500 - 5,500}{\$9,200 - \$10,000} \times \frac{\$9,200 + \$10,000}{4,500 + 5,500}$$

$$= 2.4$$

January–February

$$E_A = \frac{\Delta Q}{\Delta A} \times \frac{A_2 + A_1}{Q_2 + Q_1}$$

$$= \frac{4,000 - 5,000}{\$7,850 - \$8,350} \times \frac{\$7,850 + \$8,350}{4,000 + 5,000}$$

$$= 3.6$$

On average, $E_A = (2.4 + 3.6)/2 = 3$ and demand will rise 3%, with a 1% increase in advertising. Thus, demand appears quite sensitive to advertising.

C. In calculating the arc price elasticity of demand, only consider consecutive months when there was a change in the price of sports watches, but no change in advertising nor the price of dress watches:

July–August

$$E_P = \frac{\Delta Q}{\Delta P} \times \frac{P_2 + P_1}{Q_2 + Q_1}$$

$$= \frac{5{,}500 - 4{,}500}{\$24 - \$26} \times \frac{\$24 + \$26}{5{,}500 + 4{,}500}$$

$$= -2.5$$

November–December

$$E_P = \frac{\Delta Q}{\Delta P} \times \frac{P_2 + P_1}{Q_2 + Q_1}$$

$$= \frac{15{,}000 - 5{,}000}{\$20 - \$25} \times \frac{\$20 + \$25}{15{,}000 + 5{,}000}$$

$$= -4.5$$

April–May

$$E_P = \frac{\Delta Q}{\Delta P} \times \frac{P_2 + P_1}{Q_2 + Q_1}$$

$$= \frac{4{,}000 - 6{,}000}{\$26 - \$24} \times \frac{\$26 + \$24}{4{,}000 + 6{,}000}$$

$$= -5$$

On average, $E_P = [(-2.5) + (-4.5) + (-5)]/3 = -4$. A 1% increase (decrease) in price will lead to a 4% decrease (increase) in the quantity demanded. The demand for sports watches is, therefore, elastic with respect to price.

D. In calculating the arc cross-price elasticity of demand, we only consider consecutive months when there was a change in the price of dress watches, but no change in advertising nor the price of sports watches:

September–October

$$E_{PX} = \frac{\Delta Q}{\Delta P_X} \times \frac{P_{X2} + P_{X1}}{Q_2 + Q_1}$$

$$= \frac{3{,}500 - 4{,}500}{\$46 - \$50} \times \frac{\$46 + \$50}{3{,}500 + 4{,}500}$$

$$= 3$$

May–June

$$E_{PX} = \frac{\Delta Q}{\Delta P_X} \times \frac{P_{X2} + P_{X1}}{Q_2 + Q_1}$$

$$= \frac{5{,}000 - 4{,}000}{\$57 - \$51} \times \frac{\$57 + \$51}{5{,}000 + 4{,}000}$$

$$= 2$$

On average, $E_{PX} = (3 + 2)/2 = 2.5$. Because $E_{PX} > 0$, sports and dress watches are substitutes.

ST4.2   Cross-Price Elasticity. Surgical Systems, Inc., makes a proprietary line of disposable surgical stapling instruments. The company grew rapidly during the 1990s as surgical stapling procedures continued to gain wider hospital acceptance as an alternative to manual suturing. However, price competition in the medical supplies industry is growing rapidly in the increasingly price-conscious new millennium. During the past year, Surgical Systems sold 6 million units at a price of $14.50, for total revenues of $87 million. During the current year, Surgical Systems' unit sales have fallen from 6 million units to 3.6 million units following a competitor price cut from $13.95 to $10.85 per unit.

A. Calculate the arc cross-price elasticity of demand for Surgical Systems' products.

B. Surgical Systems' director of marketing projects that unit sales will recover from 3.6 million units to 4.8 million units if Surgical Systems reduces its own price from $14.50 to $13.50 per unit. Calculate Surgical Systems' implied arc price elasticity of demand.

C. Assuming the same implied arc price elasticity of demand calculated in part B, determine the further price reduction necessary for Surgical Systems to fully recover lost sales (i.e., regain a volume of 6 million units).

ST4.2   Solution

A.

$$E_{PX} = \frac{Q_{Y2} - Q_{Y1}}{P_{X2} - P_{X1}} \times \frac{P_{X2} + P_{X1}}{Q_{Y2} + Q_{Y1}}$$

$$= \frac{3{,}600{,}000 - 6{,}000{,}000}{\$10.85 - \$13.95} \times \frac{\$10.85 + \$13.95}{3{,}600{,}000 + 6{,}000{,}000}$$

$$= 2 \text{ (Substitutes)}$$

B.

$$E_P = \frac{Q_2 - Q_1}{P_2 - P_1} \times \frac{P_2 + P_1}{Q_2 + Q_1}$$

$$= \frac{4{,}800{,}000 - 3{,}600{,}000}{\$13.50 - \$14.50} \times \frac{\$13.50 + \$14.50}{4{,}800{,}000 + 3{,}600{,}000}$$

$$= -4 \text{ (Elastic)}$$

C.

$$E_P = \frac{Q_2 - Q_1}{P_2 - P_1} \times \frac{P_2 + P_1}{Q_2 + Q_1}$$

$$-4 = \frac{6{,}000{,}000 - 4{,}800{,}000}{P_2 - \$13.50} \times \frac{P_2 + \$13.50}{6{,}000{,}000 + 4{,}800{,}000}$$

$$-4 = \frac{P_2 + \$13.50}{9(P_2 - \$13.50)}$$

$$-36P_2 + \$486 = P_2 + \$13.50$$

$$37P_2 = \$472.50$$

$$P_2 = \$12.77$$

This implies a further price reduction of 73¢:

$$\Delta P = \$12.77 - \$13.50 = -\$0.73$$

PROBLEMS

P4.1 **A. Marginal Utility.** Complete the following table, which describes the demand for goods:

Price	Units	Total Utility	Marginal Utility	Price/Marginal Utility
$11	0	0	—	—
10	1	25		
9	2	45		
8	3	60		
7	4	70		
6	5	75		

B. How does an increase in consumption affect marginal utility and the price/marginal utility ratio?

C. What is the optimal level of goods consumption if the marginal utility derived from the consumption of services costs 50¢ per util?

P4.2 **Marginal Utility.** Consider the following data:

Goods (G)		Services (S)	
Units	Total Utility	Units	Total Utility
0	0	0	0
1	100	1	70
2	160	2	124
3	210	3	175
4	250	4	220
5	275	5	250

A. Construct a table showing the marginal utility derived from the consumption of goods and services. Also show the trend in marginal utility per dollar spent (the MU/P ratio) if $P_G =$ $20 and $P_S =$ $15.

B. If consumption of two units of goods is optimal, what level of services consumption could also be justified?

C. If consumption of five units of services is optimal, what level of goods consumption could also be justified?

D. What is the optimal allocation of a $100 budget? Explain.

P4.3 **Optimal Consumption.** Alex P. Keaton is an ardent baseball fan. The following table shows the relation between the number of games he attends per month and the total utility he derives from baseball game consumption:

Number of Baseball Games per Month	Total Utility
0	0
1	50
2	90
3	120
4	140
5	150

A. Construct a table showing Keaton's marginal utility derived from baseball game consumption.

B. At an average ticket price of $10, Keaton is able to justify attending only one game per month. Calculate his cost per unit of marginal utility derived from baseball game consumption at this activity level.

C. If the cost/marginal utility trade-off found in part B represents the most Keaton is willing to pay for baseball game consumption, calculate the prices at which he would attend two, three, four, and five games per month.

D. Plot Keaton's baseball game demand curve.

P4.4   **Elasticity.** The demand for personal computers can be characterized by the following point elasticities: price elasticity = –5, cross-price elasticity with software = –4, and income elasticity = 2.5. Indicate whether each of the following statements is true or false, and explain your answer.

A. A price reduction for personal computers will increase both the number of units demanded and the total revenue of sellers.

B. The cross-price elasticity indicates that a 5% reduction in the price of personal computers will cause a 20% increase in software demand.

C. Demand for personal computers is price elastic and computers are cyclical normal goods.

D. Falling software prices will increase revenues received by sellers of both computers and software.

E. A 2% price reduction would be necessary to overcome the effects of a 1% decline in income.

P4.5   **Demand Curves.** KRMY-TV is contemplating a T-shirt advertising promotion. Monthly sales data from T-shirt shops marketing the "Eye Watch KRMY-TV" design indicate that

$$Q = 1,500 - 200P$$

where Q is T-shirt sales and P is price.

A. How many T-shirts could KRMY-TV sell at $4.50 each?

B. What price would KRMY-TV have to charge to sell 900 T-shirts?

C. At what price would T-shirt sales equal zero?

D. How many T-shirts could be given away?

E. Calculate the point price elasticity of demand at a price of $5.

P4.6   **Optimal Pricing.** In an effort to reduce excess end-of-the-model-year inventory, Harrison Ford offered a 2.5% discount off the average price of Focus SE sedans sold during the month of August. Customer response was enthusiastic, with unit sales rising by 10% over the previous month's level.

A. Calculate the point price elasticity of demand for Harrison Ford Focus SE sedans.

B. Calculate the profit-maximizing price per unit if Harrison Ford has an average wholesale cost of $10,000 and incurs marginal selling costs of $875 per unit.

P4.7   **Cross-Price Elasticity.** Kitty Russell's Longbranch Cafe in Sausalito recently reduced Nachos Supreme appetizer prices from $5 to $3 for afternoon "early bird" customers and enjoyed a resulting increase in sales from 60 to 180 orders per day. Beverage sales also increased from 30 to 150 units per day.

A. Calculate the arc price elasticity of demand for Nachos Supreme appetizers.

B. Calculate the arc cross-price elasticity of demand between beverage sales and appetizer prices.

C. Holding all else equal, would you expect an additional appetizer price decrease to $2.50 to cause both appetizer and beverage revenues to rise? Explain.

P4.8 **Income Elasticity.** Ironside Industries, Inc., is a leading manufacturer of tufted carpeting under the Ironside brand. Demand for Ironside's products is closely tied to the overall pace of building and remodeling activity and, therefore, is highly sensitive to changes in national income. The carpet manufacturing industry is highly competitive, so Ironside's demand is also very price-sensitive.

During the past year, Ironside sold 15 million square yards (units) of carpeting at an average wholesale price of $7.75 per unit. This year, disposable income per capita is expected to surge from $25,760 to $28,000 in a booming economic recovery. Without any price change, Ironside's marketing director expects current-year sales to rise to 25 million units.

A. Calculate the implied income arc elasticity of demand.

B. Given the projected rise in income, the marketing director believes that current volume of 15 million units could be maintained despite an increase in price of 50¢ per unit. On this basis, calculate the implied arc price elasticity of demand.

C. Holding all else equal, would a further increase in price result in higher or lower total revenue?

P4.9 **Cross-Price Elasticity.** B. B. Lean is a catalog retailer of a wide variety of sporting goods and recreational products. Although the market response to the company's spring catalog was generally good, sales of B. B. Lean's $140 deluxe garment bag declined from 10,000 to 4,800 units. During this period, a competitor offered a whopping $52 off their regular $137 price on deluxe garment bags.

A. Calculate the arc cross-price elasticity of demand for B. B. Lean's deluxe garment bag.

B. B. B. Lean's deluxe garment bag sales recovered from 4,800 units to 6,000 units following a price reduction to $130 per unit. Calculate B. B. Lean's arc price elasticity of demand for this product.

C. Assuming the same arc price elasticity of demand calculated in part B, determine the further price reduction necessary for B. B. Lean to fully recover lost sales (i.e., regain a volume of 10,000 units).

P4.10 **Advertising Elasticity.** Enchantment Cosmetics, Inc., offers a line of cosmetic and perfume products marketed through leading department stores. Product manager Erica Kane recently raised the suggested retail price on a popular line of mascara products from $9 to $12 following increases in the costs of labor and materials. Unfortunately, sales dropped sharply from 16,200 to 9,000 units per month. In an effort to regain lost sales, Enchantment ran a coupon promotion featuring $5 off the new regular price. Coupon printing and distribution costs totaled $500 per month and represented a substantial increase over the typical advertising budget of $3,250 per month. Despite these added costs, the promotion was judged to be a success, as it proved to be highly popular with consumers. In the period prior to expiration, coupons were used on 40% of all purchases and monthly sales rose to 15,000 units.

A. Calculate the arc price elasticity implied by the initial response to the Enchantment price increase.

B. Calculate the effective price reduction resulting from the coupon promotion.

C. In light of the price reduction associated with the coupon promotion and assuming no change in the price elasticity of demand, calculate Enchantment's arc advertising elasticity.

D. Why might the true arc advertising elasticity differ from that calculated in part C?

CASE STUDY

Optimal Level of Advertising

The concept of multivariate optimization is important in managerial economics because many demand and supply relations involve more than two variables. In demand analysis, the concept is particularly important in markets where firms face the difficult question of how to set both prices and advertising at profit-maximizing levels. In demand analysis, it is often typical to consider the quantity sold as a function of the price of the product itself, the price of other goods, advertising, income, and other factors. In cost analysis, cost is determined by output, input prices, the nature of technology, and so on. As a result, the process of multivariate optimization is often employed in the process of optimization.

To further explore the concepts of multivariate optimization and the optimal level of advertising, consider the multivariate product demand function for MacGyver, Inc., where the demand for product Q is determined by the price charged, P, and the level of advertising, A:

$$Q = 5,000 - 10P + 40A + PA - 0.8A^2 - 0.5P^2$$

When analyzing multivariate relations such as these, one is interested in the marginal effect of each independent variable on the quantity sold, the dependent variable. Optimization requires an analysis of how a change in each independent variable affects the dependent variable, holding constant the effect of all other independent variables. The partial derivative concept is used in this type of marginal analysis.

In light of the fact that the MacGyver, Inc., demand function includes two independent variables, the price of the product itself and advertising, it is possible to examine two partial derivatives: the partial of Q with respect to price, or $\partial Q/\partial P$, and the partial of Q with respect to advertising expenditures, or $\partial Q/\partial A$.

In determining partial derivatives, all variables except the one with respect to which the derivative is being taken remain unchanged. In this instance, A is treated as a constant when the partial derivative of Q with respect to P is analyzed; P is treated as a constant when the partial derivative of Q with respect to A is evaluated. Therefore, the partial derivative of Q with respect to P is

$$\frac{\partial Q}{\partial P} = 0 - 10P + 0 + A - 0 - P$$
$$= -10 + A - P$$

The partial with respect to A is

$$\frac{\partial Q}{\partial A} = 0 - 0 + 40 + P - 1.6A - 0$$
$$= 40 + P - 1.6A$$

The maximization or minimization of multivariate functions is similar to that for single variable functions. All first-order partial derivatives must equal zero. Thus, maximization of the function $Q = f(P,A)$ requires:

$$\frac{\partial Q}{\partial P} = 0$$

and

$$\frac{\partial Q}{\partial A} = 0$$

CASE STUDY (continued)

To maximize the value of the MacGyver, Inc., demand function, each partial must equal zero:

$$\frac{\partial Q}{\partial P} = -10 + A - P = 0$$

and

$$\frac{\partial Q}{\partial A} = 40 + P - 1.6A = 0$$

Solving these two equations simultaneously yields the optimal price-output-advertising combination. Because $-10 + A - P = 0$, $P = A - 10$. Substituting this value for P into $40 + P - 1.6A = 0$, gives $40 + (A - 10) - 1.6A = 0$, which implies that $0.6A = 30$ and $A = 50(00)$ or $5,000. Given this value, $P = A - 10 = 50 - 10 = \$40$.

   Inserting these numbers for P and A into the MacGyver demand function results in a value for Q of 5,800. Therefore, the maximum value of Q is 5,800 reflects an optimal price of $40 and optimal advertising of $5,000.

   The process of simultaneously determining optimal levels of price and advertising can be visualized by referring to Figure 2.9, a three-dimensional graph of the MacGyver demand function. For positive values of P and A, this demand function maps out a surface with a peak at point X^*. At the peak, the surface of the figure is level. Alternatively stated, a plane that is tangent to the surface at point X^* is parallel to the PA plane. This means that the slope of the figure with respect to either P or A is zero; as is required for locating the maximum of a multivariate function.

   Unfortunately, on the basis of Figure 2.9 it is not possible to conclusively determine whether point X^* locates an optimal point for price and advertising that will result in maximum profits, or an inflection point that indicates only a local maximum for profits. On the basis of Figure 2.9, it does not appear that point X^* is a local or global point for minimum profits, but in the absence of further analysis, the process described here can lead to mistakes in identifying minimums versus maximums, and vice versa. Absent a check of second-order conditions, the possibility of misidentifying inflection points and points of maxima and minima is always present.

   One attractive use of computer spreadsheet analysis is to create simple numerical examples that can be used to conclusively show the change in sales, profits, and other variables that occur as one moves beyond points such as point X^* identified for MacGyver, Inc.

A. Set up a table or spreadsheet for MacGyver, Inc., that illustrates the relationships among quantity (Q), price (P), the optimal level of advertising (A), the advertising-sales ratio (A/S) and sales revenue (S). In this spreadsheet, use the relations developed in the case study to define appropriate values for each of these items. Importantly,

$$\begin{aligned} Q &= 5,000 - 10P + 40A + PA - 0.8A^2 - 0.5P^2 \\ A &= \$25 + \$0.625P \\ A/S &= (1,000 \times A)/S \\ S &= P \times Q \end{aligned}$$

Establish a range for P from 0 to $125 in increments of $5 (i.e., $0, $5, $10, ... , $125). To test the sensitivity of all other variables to extreme bounds for the price variable, also set price equal to $1,000, $2,500, $10,000.

B. Based on the MacGyver table or spreadsheet, determine the price-advertising combination that will maximize the number of units sold.

C. Give an analytical explanation of the negative quantity and sales revenue levels observed at very high price-advertising combinations. Do these negative values have an economic interpretation as well?

SELECTED REFERENCES

Berndt, Ernst R., and Neal J. Rappaport. "Price and Quality of Desktop and Mobile Personal Computers: A Quarter-Century Historical Overview." *American Economic Review* 91 (May 2001): 268–273.

Bils, Mark, and Peter J. Klenow. "The Acceleration in Variety Growth." *American Economic Review* 91 (May 2001): 274–280.

Dur, Robert A. J. "Wage-Setting Institutions, Unemployment, and Voters' Demand for Redistribution Policy." *Scottish Journal of Political Economy* 48 (November 2001): 517–531.

Fehr, Ernst, and Jean-Robert Tyran. "Does Money Illusion Matter?" *American Economic Review* 91 (December 2001): 1239–1262.

Goodman, Jack. "The Latest on Demand for In-Town Real Estate." *Real Estate Finance* 17 (Winter 2001): 41–48.

Hausman, Jerry A., J. Gregory Sidak, and Hal J. Singer. "Residential Demand for Broadband Telecommunications and Consumer Access to Unaffiliated Internet Content Providers." *Yale Journal on Regulation* 18 (Winter 2001): 129–173.

Jesswein, Wayne, Kjell Knudsen, Richard Lichty, et al. "Regional Competitiveness: Determining Demand for Skilled Workers in Northeast Minnesota." *Economic Development Review* 17 (Winter 2001): 70–75.

Krishna, Pravin, Devashish Mitra, and Sajjid Chinoy. "Trade Liberalization and Labor Demand Elasticities: Evidence from Turkey." *Journal of International Economics* 55 (December 2001): 391–409.

Montgomery, Alan L. "Applying Quantitative Marketing Techniques to the Internet." *Interfaces* 31 (March 2001): 90–108.

Nijs, Vincent R., Marnik G. Dekimpe, and Jan-Benedict E. M. Steenkamp, et al. "The Category-Demand Effects of Price Promotions." *Marketing Science* 20 (Winter 2001): 1–22.

Pedroni, Peter. "Purchasing Power Parity Tests in Cointegrated Panels." *Review of Economics and Statistics* 83 (November 2001): 727–731.

Staunton, Robert H., John D. Kueck, Brendan J. Kirby, et al. "Demand Response: An Overview of Enabling Technologies." *Public Utilities Fortnightly* 139 (Nov 2001): 32–39.

Wagner, Todd H., Teh-Wei Hu, and Judith H. Hibbard. "The Demand for Consumer Health Information." *Journal of Health Economics* 20 (November 2001): 1059–1075.

Wiser, Ryan H., Meredith Fowlie, and Edward A. Holt. "Public Goods and Private Interests: Understanding Non-Residential Demand for Green Power." *Energy Policy* 29 (November 2001): 1085–1097.

Yatchew, Adonis, and Joungyeo Angela No. "Household Gasoline Demand in Canada." *Econometrica* 69 (November 2001): 1697–1709.

CHAPTER FIVE

Demand Estimation

Procter & Gamble Co. (P&G) helps consumers clean up. Households around the world rely on "new and improved" Tide to clean their clothes, Ivory and Ariel detergents to wash dishes, and Pantene Pro-V to shampoo and condition hair. Other P&G products dominate a wide range of lucrative, but slow-growing, product lines, including disposable diapers (Pampers), feminine hygiene (Always), and facial moisturizers (Oil of Olay). P&G's ongoing challenge is to figure out ways of continuing to grow aggressively outside the United States while it cultivates the profitability of dominant consumer franchises here at home. P&G's challenge is made difficult by the fact that the company already enjoys a dominant market position in many of its slow-growing domestic markets. Worse yet, most of its brand names are aging, albeit gracefully. Tide, for example, has been "new and improved" almost continuously over its 70-year history. Ivory virtually introduced the concept of bar soap nearly 100 years ago; Jif peanut butter and Pampers disposable diapers are more than 40 years old.

How does P&G succeed in businesses where others routinely fail? Quite simply, P&G is a marketing juggernaut. Although P&G's vigilant cost-cutting is legendary, its marketing expertise is without peer. Nobody does a better job at finding out what consumers want. At P&G, demand estimation is the lynchpin of its "getting close to the customer" operating philosophy.[1]

This chapter considers consumer interviews, surveys, market experiments, and regression analysis as effective means for finding out what customers want. Inexpensive PCs and user-friendly software make these both practical and extraordinarily effective demand estimation techniques.

---

1   See Cressida Connolly, "Procter & Gamble Expands Mr. Clean to Europe," *The Wall Street Journal Online*, January 10, 2002 (http://online.wsj.com).

IDENTIFICATION PROBLEM

When algebra is used to solve a system of equations, the number of unknown variables must not exceed the number of known equations. There must be at least as much known information (equations) as unknown variables. In demand estimation, there must be sufficient information to allow precise identification of all unknown variables.

Changing Nature of Demand Relations

Demand estimation is sometimes relatively simple, especially in the case of stable short-run demand relations. If a manufacturer has a substantial backlog of purchase orders, the pace of future sales can sometimes be estimated precisely. For example, aerospace manufacturer Boeing sells options for the future delivery of airplanes to major airlines such as United, American, and Delta. This allows Boeing to accurately predict the pace of future sales and adjust production schedules accordingly. Still, demand estimation involves error, even when a large and growing backlog of customer orders is evident. During the aftermath of terrorist attacks on New York City and Washington, DC, in 2001, for example, airlines canceled orders for hundreds of millions of dollars of aircraft following an unexpected downturn in passenger and freight traffic. Delivery options were canceled at a cost of millions of dollars; production schedules had to be reworked at great expense.

The dynamic nature of demand relations makes it tough to accurately estimate demand, and even tougher to determine the effect on demand of modest changes in prices, advertising, credit terms, prices of competing products, and so on. The unpredictable nature of the overall economy is another factor that makes demand estimation difficult. When the income elasticity of demand is high, demand tends to vary more than changes in economic activity. This is especially true for cyclical goods such as household appliances, machine tools, and raw materials. Demand for most goods and services is also sensitive to changes in competitor prices, competitor advertising, interest rates, and the weather. Unexpected changes in such uncontrollable variables constitute a considerable challenge to accurate short-run demand estimation.

Long-run demand estimation involves all of the difficulties encountered in short-run demand estimation, and more. When competitors have years to develop effective pricing, promotion, and product-development strategies, the sensitivity of demand to changes in any of these factors is increased. Unanticipated changes in technology, foreign competition, and government regulation also influence demand, especially in the long run.

Interplay of Demand and Supply

It is sometimes difficult to obtain accurate estimates of demand relations because linkages exist among most economic variables. Consider the difficulty of estimating the demand curve for a given product X. If data are available on the price charged and the quantity purchased at several points in time, a logical first step is to plot this information as in Figure 5.1. Can the line AB be interpreted as a demand curve? The curve connecting points 1, 2, and 3 is negatively sloped, indicating the typical inverse relation between the price charged for a product and the quantity demanded. Moreover, each data point represents the quantity of X purchased at a particular price. Nevertheless, these data offer an insufficient basis to draw the conclusion that AB is in fact the demand curve for X.

A demand curve shows the relation between the price charged and the quantity demanded, *holding constant the effects of all other variables in the demand function*. To plot a demand curve, it is necessary to obtain data on the price/quantity relation, while keeping fixed all other factors in the demand function.

The price/quantity data used to construct Figure 5.1 are insufficient to produce a demand curve because the effects of all other demand-related variables may or may not have changed.

Consider Figure 5.2, in which price/quantity data are plotted along with hypothetical supply and demand curves for product X. These data points indicate the simultaneous solution of supply and demand relations at three points in time. The intersection of the supply curve and demand curves at each point in time results in the plotted price/quantity points, but the line

FIGURE 5.1

Price/Quantity Plot for Product *X*

Price/quantity data may not plot out a demand curve.

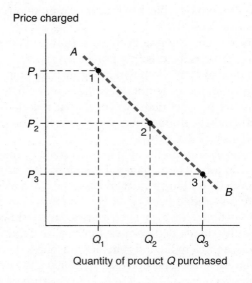

Quantity of product *Q* purchased

FIGURE 5.2

Supply and Demand Curves

Price/quantity data sometimes reflect the intersection of several different demand and supply curves.

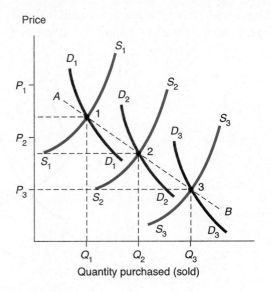

Quantity purchased (sold)

AB is *not* a demand curve. In Figure 5.2, nonprice variables in the supply and demand functions have changed between each data point.

Shifts in Demand and Supply

Suppose, for example, that new and more efficient facilities for producing *X* are completed between observation dates. This would cause a shift of the supply curve from S_1 to S_2 to S_3. Similarly, the price of a complementary product may have fallen or consumer incomes may have risen, so at any given price, larger quantities of *X* are demanded in later periods. Such influences result in a shift of the demand curve from D_1 to D_2 to D_3. When supply and/or demand curves shift over time, as is typical, the accurate estimation of demand/supply relations at any one point in time is difficult.

In the current example, both the supply and demand curves shift over time. This results in a declining price as the quantity purchased grows. The three intersection points of supply curves and the demand curves shown in Figure 5.2—points 1, 2, and 3—are the same points plotted in Figure 5.1. But these are not three points on a single demand curve for product *X*. Each point is on a *distinct* product demand curve that reflects different economic conditions. The relevant demand curve is shifting over time, so connecting each data point does not trace out a single demand curve for *X*.

Incorrectly interpreting the line *AB* (which connects points 1, 2, and 3) as a demand curve can lead to incorrect managerial decisions. If a firm makes this mistake, it might infer a high price elasticity for the product and assume that a reduction in price from P_1 to P_2 would increase quantity demanded from Q_1 to Q_2. An expansion of this magnitude might well justify such a price reduction. However, such a price cut would actually result in a much smaller increase in the quantity demanded because the true demand curve, D_1, is much less elastic than the line *AB*. Thus, a price reduction is in fact much less desirable than implied by the line *AB*.

Given the close link between demand and supply curves, data on prices and quantities must be used carefully in demand curve estimation. If the demand curve has not shifted but the supply curve *has* shifted, price/quantity data can be used to estimate demand relations. Alternatively, if there exists sufficient information to determine how each curve has shifted between data observations, demand curve estimation is possible. For example, if a technical

FIGURE 5.3

Shifting Supply Curve Tracing Out Stable Demand Curve

A demand curve is revealed if prices fall while demand conditions are held constant.

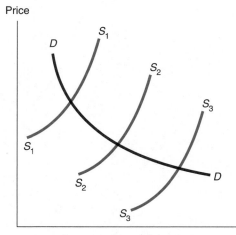

Quantity purchased (sold)

Sampling Technology for TV Advertising

Nielsen Media Research estimates the popularity of TV shows using a random sample of more than 5,000 households, containing over 13,000 people. This number fluctuates daily as about 300 households come in and out of the sample every month. Nielsen is careful to ensure that various ethnic and income groups are represented in proportion to the overall population, as measured by U.S. census data. For example, 11 to 12 percent of Nielsen TV samples are African-American, and this matches the percentage of all TV households in the United States classified as African-American.

Detailed information is collected using a "People Meter," or box about the size of a paperback book, which Nielsen installs on or near each TV set. For national programs, People Meters record what is being watched and by whom it is being watched. Each night, this information is relayed to Nielsen computers. To measure local TV audiences, Nielsen gathers information using viewer diaries four times per year, during February, May, July, and November "sweep" months. Information about which programs are airing for each

station or cable channel comes from a coded ID number that is part of almost every TV picture. Keeping track of what is on TV is also done with the help of program listings provided by networks, stations, and cable systems, as well as published TV listings for more than 1,700 TV stations and 11,000 cable systems. Nielsen's signal identification technology converts TV commercials into digital "fingerprints" that can be automatically identified.

All of this information is combined to produce the famous Nielsen ratings, which measure TV program popularity. Nielsen ratings are not just a vital indication of audience size. The more audience a program delivers, the more commercial time is worth to advertisers. Given the high cost of programming, it may take 10 million viewers for a nationally syndicated program to generate the advertising dollars necessary for business success. Against this backdrop, it comes as no surprise to learn that viewers, advertisers, TV executives, and Hollywood are all interested in Nielsen ratings!

See: Nielsen Media Research (http://www.nielsenmedia.com).

breakthrough occurs in the manufacture of a product so that industry costs fall while demand conditions are stable, the situation depicted in Figure 5.3 may arise. The demand curve, which initially was unknown, is assumed to be stable. The supply curve shifts from S_1 to S_2 to S_3. Each price/quantity point represents the intersection of the supply curves and the demand curves. Because demand-determining factors other than price are assumed to be stable, points 1, 2, and 3 all lie on the same demand curve. The demand curve *DD* is estimated by connecting the three data points. Such a situation can occur with computers and electronics. Rapid innovation often allows prices for watches, calculators, personal computers, and related products to fall markedly within a very short period of time.

Simultaneous Relations

simultaneous relation
Concurrent association

identification problem
Difficulty of estimating an economic relation in the presence of simultaneous relations

Because the market price/output equilibrium at any point in time is determined by the forces of demand and supply, a **simultaneous relation**, or concurrent association, exists between demand and supply. Shifts in demand and supply curves must be distinguished from movements along individual supply and demand curves. The problem of estimating any given economic relation in the presence of important simultaneous relations is known as the **identification problem**. To separate shifts in demand or supply from changes or movements along a single curve, information about changes in demand and supply conditions is necessary to identify and estimate demand and supply relations. Sometimes, this information is hard to find. In such instances, standard statistical techniques, such as ordinary least squares regression analysis, do not provide reliable estimates of demand or supply functions. More advanced statistical techniques, such as two-stage least squares or seemingly unrelated regression analysis, are necessary. Fortunately, the identification problem is usually not so severe as to preclude the use of widely familiar regression techniques. Even when the identification problem is quite severe, consumer interviews and market experiments can sometimes be used to obtain relevant information.

INTERVIEW AND EXPERIMENTAL METHODS

Details about customer reactions to changes in competitor prices and the caliber of competing products play a significant part in the formation of competitive strategy. Successful companies devote considerable resources toward answering a simple question: What do customers want?

Consumer Interviews

consumer interview
Questioning customers to estimate demand relations

The **consumer interview** (or survey) method requires questioning customers or potential customers to estimate the relation between demand and a variety of underlying factors. The technique can be as naive as simply asking shoppers about the quantities they would purchase at different prices. In more sophisticated approaches, trained interviewers present detailed questions to carefully selected samples to elicit desired information. Such surveys can provide excellent information on important demand relations.

Unfortunately, the quantity and quality of information obtained through interview techniques are sometimes limited. Consumers are often unable or unwilling to provide accurate answers to hypothetical questions. If an interviewer asked how you would react to a 1, 2, or 3 percent increase in the price of a specific brand of spaghetti sauce, could you respond accurately? Could you accurately predict your reaction to shifting the emphasis of the firm's media advertising campaign from the product's natural ingredients to the fact that it is high in fiber or low in cholesterol? Because most consumers are unable to answer such questions— even for major expense categories such as apparel, food, and entertainment—it is difficult for survey techniques to accurately estimate demand relations.

This is not to imply that consumer surveys have little value. Using subtle inquiries, a trained interviewer can extract useful information from consumers. For example, an interviewer might ask questions about several competing goods and learn that most customers are unaware of existing price differentials. This is an indication that demand may not be highly sensitive to price changes, so a producer should not attempt to increase the quantity sold by reducing prices. Similar questions can be used to determine whether consumers are aware of advertising programs, what their reaction is to the ads, and so on. Such survey information can be used to make better managerial decisions.

Market Experiments

market experiments
Demand estimation in a controlled environment

An alternative technique for obtaining useful product demand information involves **market experiments**. In a popular method, firms study one or more markets with specific prices, packaging, or advertising, and then vary controllable factors over time or between markets. For example, Del Monte Corporation may have determined that uncontrollable consumer characteristics are quite similar in Denver and Salt Lake City. Del Monte could raise the relative price of sliced pineapple in Salt Lake City, and then compare pineapple sales in the two markets. Alternatively, Del Monte could initiate a series of weekly or price changes in one market and then determine how these changes affect sales. With several markets, the firm might also be able to use census or survey data to determine how demographic characteristics such as income, family size, educational level, and ethnic background affect demand.

Market experiments have several serious shortcomings, however. They are expensive and usually undertaken on a scale too small to allow high levels of confidence in the results. Market experiments are seldom run for sufficiently long periods to indicate the long-run effects of various price, advertising, or packaging strategies. Difficulties associated with uncontrolled parts of market experiments also hinder their use. Changing economic conditions during the experiment can invalidate the results, especially if the experiment includes several separate markets. A local strike, layoffs by a major employer, or a severe snowstorm can ruin a market experiment. Likewise, a change in a competing product's promotion, price, or packaging can distort the results. There is also the danger that customers lost during the experiment as a result of price manipulations may not be regained when the experiment ends.

In some controlled laboratory experiments, consumers are given funds and asked to shop in a simulated store. By varying prices, product packaging, displays, and other factors, the experimenter can learn a great deal about consumer behavior. Laboratory experiments provide information similar to that of field experiments, but they have the advantages of lower cost and greater control of extraneous factors. However, subjects invariably know that they are part of an experiment, and this can distort shopping habits. They may, for example, exhibit considerably more price consciousness than is typical in their everyday shopping. Moreover, the high cost of such experiments necessarily limits the sample size, which can make inference from the sample to the general population tenuous.

Demand for Oranges: An Illustrative Market Experiment

In a classic market experiment, researchers from the University of Florida studied the demand for oranges in Grand Rapids, Michigan.[2] The experiment was designed to provide estimates of price elasticities of demand for various oranges, and to measure the cross-price elasticities of demand among varieties.

Researchers chose Grand Rapids because its size, economic base, and demographic characteristics are representative of the midwestern market for oranges. Nine supermarkets located throughout the city cooperated in the experiment, which consisted of varying the prices charged for Florida and California oranges on a daily basis for 31 days and recording the quantities of each variety sold. Price variations for each variety of orange covered a range of 32¢ per dozen, or ±16¢ around the price per dozen that existed in the market at the time the study began. More than 9,250 dozen oranges were sold during the experiment.

Price and quantity data obtained in the study enabled researchers to examine the relation between sales of each variety of orange and its price, as well as relations between sales quantities and the price charged for competing varieties. The results of this study are summarized in Table 5.1. Numbers along the diagonal represent the price elasticities of the three varieties of oranges; off-diagonal figures estimate the cross-price elasticities of demand.

The price elasticity of demand for all three varieties of oranges is high. The price elasticity $\epsilon_P = -3.07$ for Florida Indian River oranges means that a 1 percent decrease in their price results in a 3.07 percent increase in sales. Florida Interior oranges have a similar price elasticity of $\epsilon_P = -3.01$, meaning that a 1 percent decrease in their price results in a 3.01 percent increase in sales. It is

TABLE 5.1

Demand Elasticities for California and Florida Valencia Oranges

A 1% Change in the Price of	Percentage Change in the Sales of		
	Florida Indian River	**Florida Interior**	**California**
Florida Indian River	−3.07	+1.56	+0.01
Florida Interior	+1.16	−3.01	+0.14
California	+0.18	+0.09	−2.76

2   See Marshall B. Godwin, W. Fred Chapman, Jr., and William T. Hanley, *Competition Between Florida and California Valencia Oranges in the Fruit Market*, Bulletin 704, December 1965, Agricultural Experiment Stations, Institute of Food and Agricultural Services, University of Florida, Gainesville, Florida, in cooperation with the U.S. Department of Agriculture, Florida Citrus Commission.

interesting that the price elasticity of the California orange is somewhat lower, $\epsilon_P = -2.76$, indicating that demand for California oranges is somewhat less responsive to price changes than is demand for the two varieties of Florida oranges.

Cross-price elasticities of demand also reveal some interesting insights concerning the demand for oranges. Note that cross-price elasticities of demand between the two varieties of Florida oranges are positive and relatively large. The $\epsilon_{PX} = 1.16$ means that a 1 percent increase in the price of Florida Interior oranges leads to a 1.16 percent rise in demand for Florida Indian River oranges. The $\epsilon_{PX} = 1.56$ means that a 1 percent increase in the price of Florida Indian River oranges leads to a 1.56 percent rise in demand for Florida Interior oranges. This indicates that consumers view the two varieties of Florida oranges as close substitutes for one another and are willing to switch between them when price differentials exist. Cross-price elasticities of demand between the Florida and California oranges, however, are small. These cross-price elasticities range from only $\epsilon_{PX} = 0.01$ to $\epsilon_{PX} = 0.18$. Apparently, consumers do not view Florida and California oranges as close substitutes. In Grand Rapids, the market for California oranges appears distinct from the market for Florida oranges.

Researchers were able to identify and measure these relations because the 31-day study period was brief enough to prevent changes in incomes, tastes, population, and other variables that influence the demand for oranges. At the same time, researchers were able to ensure that adequate quantities of oranges were available at each experimental price.

REGRESSION ANALYSIS

regression analysis
Statistical technique that describes relations among dependent and independent variables

Regression analysis is a powerful statistical technique that describes the way in which one important economic variable is related to one or more other economic variables. Although there are clear limitations to the technique, regression analysis is often used to provide successful managers with valuable insight concerning a variety of significant economic relations.

What Is a Statistical Relation?

deterministic relation
Association that is known with certainty

A **deterministic relation** is an association between variables that is known with certainty. For example, total revenue equals price times quantity, or $TR = P \times Q$. Once the levels of price and output are known with certainty, total revenue can be exactly determined. Total revenue is an example of a deterministic relation. Similarly, if total cost = $5 \times$ quantity, then total cost can be exactly determined once the level of output is known. If all economic relations were deterministic, managers would never be surprised by higher- or lower-than-expected profits. Total revenues and total costs could be exactly determined at the start of every planning period. However, few economic relations are deterministic in nature. Economic variables are often related in ways that cannot be predicted with absolute accuracy. Almost all economic relations must be estimated.

statistical relation
Imprecise link between two variables

A **statistical relation** exists between two economic variables if the average of one is related to another, but it is impossible to predict with certainty the value of one based on the value of another. In the earlier example, if $TR = \$5Q$ *on average*, then a one-unit increase in quantity would result in an average $5 increase in total revenue. Sometimes the actual increase in total revenue would be more than $5; sometimes, it would be less.

When a statistical relation exists, the exact relation between two economic variables is not known with certainty and must be estimated. The most common means for doing so is to gather and analyze historical data. A **time series** of data is a daily, weekly, monthly, or annual sequence of data on an economic variable such as price, income, cost, or revenue. To judge the trend in profitability over time, a firm would analyze the time series of profit numbers. A **cross section** of data is a group of observations on an important economic variable at any given point in time. If a firm were interested in learning the relative importance of market share versus advertising as determinants of profitability, it might analyze a cross section of profit, advertising, and market share data for a variety of regional or local markets.

time series
Daily, weekly, monthly, or annual sequence of economic data

cross section
Sample of firm, market, or product data taken at a given point in time

scatter diagram
Plot of XY data

The simplest and most common means for analyzing a sample of historical information is to plot and visually study the data. A **scatter diagram** is a plot of data where the *dependent* variable is plotted on the vertical axis (Y-axis), and the *independent* variable is plotted on the horizontal axis (X-axis). Figure 5.4 shows scatter diagrams that plot the relation between the quantity sold and six different factors that have the potential to influence demand. Figure 5.4(a) depicts an inverse relation between the quantity sold and price, the independent X variable. An increase in price leads to a decrease in the quantity demanded; a reduction in price leads to an increase in the quantity demanded. In Figure 5.4(b), a direct relation is illustrated between the amount of advertising and demand. This means that an increase in advertising causes an increase in the level of product demand; conversely, a decrease in advertising causes a decrease in demand. No relation is evident between demand and the price of product X, an independent good, as shown in Figure 5.4(c). In Figure 5.4(d), a positive nonlinear relation between demand and income is illustrated. This implies that product Y is a cyclical normal good.

Scatter plot diagrams can impart an instinctive "feel" for the data. However, although scatter diagrams give a useful starting point, the lack of structure can limit their value. For example, the choice of which variable to call "dependent" or "independent" is often haphazard. The fact that an expansion in advertising causes an increase in product demand may seem obvious. In some instances, however, the directional nature of the link between economic variables is not apparent. Scatter diagrams illustrate correlation between variables; they do not establish causality. To warrant the inference of cause and effect, the correlation between two series of data must be interpreted in the light of previous experience or economic theory.

Specifying the Regression Model

The first step in regression analysis is to specify variables to be included in the regression model. Product demand, measured in physical units, is the dependent variable when specifying a

FIGURE 5.4

Scatter Diagrams of Various Unit Cost/Output Relations

A scatter plot of the data can suggest an underlying relation between *X* and *Y*.

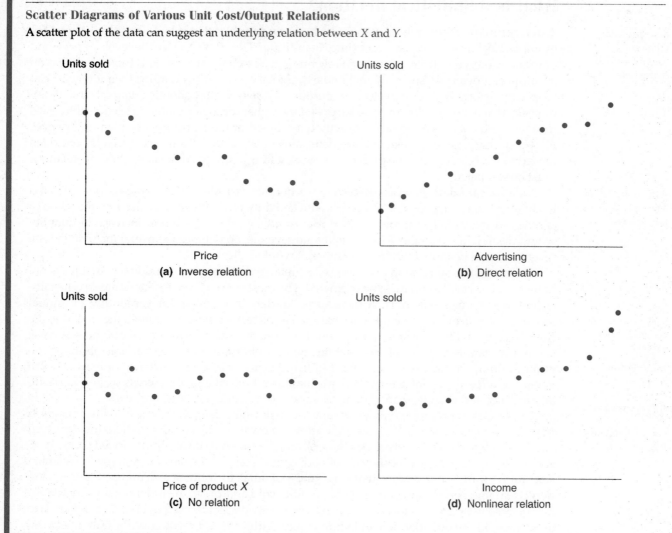

demand function. The list of independent variables, or those that influence demand, always includes the price of the product and generally includes such factors as the prices of complementary and competitive products, advertising expenditures, consumer incomes, and population of the consuming group. Demand functions for expensive durable goods, such as automobiles and houses, include interest rates and other credit terms; those for ski equipment, beverages, or air conditioners include weather conditions. Determinants of demand for capital goods, such as industrial machinery, include profit rates, capacity utilization ratios, interest rates, trends in wages, and so on.

The second step in regression analysis is to obtain reliable estimates of the variables. Data must be gathered on total output or demand, price, credit terms, capacity utilization ratios, wage rates, and the like. Obtaining accurate estimates is not always easy, especially if the study involves time series data over a number of years. Some key variables, such as consumer sentiment, may have to be estimated.

Once variables have been specified and the data have been gathered, the functional form of the regression equation must be determined. This form reflects the way in which independent variables are assumed to affect the dependent variable. The most common specification is a **linear model,** such as the following demand function:

linear model
Straight-line relation

(5.1)
$$Q = b_0 + b_P P + b_A A + b_I I$$

Q represents the unit demand for a particular product, P is the price charged, A represents advertising expenditures, and I is per capita disposable income. Unit demand is assumed to change in a linear fashion with changes in each independent variable. For example, if $b_P = -1.5$, the quantity demanded will decline by one and one-half units with each one-unit increase in price. In a linear regression model, the marginal effect of each X variable on Y is constant. The broad appeal of linear functions stems from the fact that many demand and cost relations are in fact approximately linear. Furthermore, the most popular regression technique, ordinary least squares, can be used to estimate the coefficients b_0, b_P, b_A, and b_I for linear equations.

multiplicative model
Nonlinear relation that involves X variable interactions

Another common regression model form is the **multiplicative model**:

(5.2)
$$Q = b_0 P^{b_P} A^{b_A} I^{b_I}$$

A multiplicative model is used when the marginal effect of each independent variable depends on the value of all independent variables in the regression equation. For example, the effect on quantity demanded of a price increase often depends not just on the price level but also on the amount of advertising, competitor prices, and so on. Similarly, the effect on costs of a wage hike can depend on the output levels, raw material prices, R&D expenditures, and so on. Allowing for such changes in the marginal relation is sometimes more realistic than the implicit assumption of a constant marginal in the linear model.

The benefit of added realism for the multiplicative model has no offsetting cost in terms of added complexity in estimation. Equation 5.2 can be transformed into a linear relation by using logarithms and then estimated by the least squares technique. Thus, Equation 5.2 is equivalent to

(5.3)
$$\log Q = \log b_0 + b_P \cdot \log P + b_A \cdot \log A + b_I \cdot \log I$$

When written in this form, the coefficients $\log b_0$, b_P, b_A, and b_I can be easily estimated. Given the multiplicative or log-linear form of the regression model, these coefficient estimates can also be interpreted as estimates of the constant *elasticity* of Y with respect to X, or the percentage change in Y due to a 1 percent change in X. Much more will be said about elasticity later on in the book, but for now it is worth noting that multiplicative or log-linear models imply constant elasticity.

Least Squares Method

Regression equations are typically estimated, or "fitted," by the method of ordinary least squares. This method can be illustrated by considering a simple demand estimation example. Assume that Electronic Data Processing (EDP), Inc., is a small but rapidly growing firm that provides electronic data processing services to companies, hospitals, and other organizations. EDP maintains and monitors payroll records on a contractual basis and issues payroll checks, W-2 forms, and so on, for client customers. The company has aggressively expanded its personal selling efforts and experienced a rapid expansion in the number of units sold during the past year. Table 5.2 shows EDP monthly data on contract sales (Q) and personal selling expenses (*PSE*) over the past year (12 observations).

If a linear regression model is used to describe the relation between unit sales and personal selling expenditures, the general form of the EDP regression equation is

(5.4)
$$\text{Unit Sales} = Y = b_0 + b_X X$$

TABLE 5.2

Units Sold and Personal Selling Expenditures for Electronic Data Processing, Inc.

Month	Units Sold	Personal Selling Expenditures	Fitted Value for Units Sold	Unexplained Residual
January	2,500	$43,000	2702.04	–202.04
February	2,250	39,000	2330.47	–80.47
March	1,750	35,000	1958.91	–208.91
April	1,500	34,000	1866.01	–366.01
May	1,000	26,000	1122.88	–122.88
June	2,500	41,000	2516.26	–16.26
July	2,750	40,000	2423.36	326.64
August	1,750	33,000	1773.12	–23.12
September	1,250	26,000	1122.88	127.12
October	3,000	45,000	2887.82	112.18
November	2,000	32,000	1680.23	319.77
December	2,000	34,000	1866.01	133.99
Average	2,021	$35,667	2,021	0.00

simple regression model

Relation between one dependent Y variable and one independent X variable

multiple regression model

Relation between one Y variable and two or more X variables

where unit sales is the dependent Y variable and personal selling expenditures is the independent X variable. Such a regression equation is called a **simple regression model** because it involves only one dependent Y variable and one independent X variable. A **multiple regression model** also entails one Y variable but includes two or more X variables. Other possibilities for independent X variables that might be included in a multiple regression analysis of demand include price, advertising expenditures, income, and so on.

The method of least squares estimates, or fits, the regression line that minimizes the sum of the squared deviations between the best-fitting line and the set of original data points. The technique is based on the minimization of squared deviations to avoid the problem of having positive and negative deviations cancel one another out. To illustrate, a simple regression model that relates unit sales and personal selling expenditures for EDP is written

(5.5)
$$\text{Unit Sales}_t = Y_t = b_0 + b_X X_t + u_t$$

where unit sales in month t is the dependent Y variable and the level of personal selling expenditures in month t is the independent output, or X variable; u_t is a residual or disturbance term that reflects the influences of stochastic or random elements. When time series data are examined, as they are in this example, the term t is used to signify a time period–specific subscript. If cross-section data were being examined—for example, unit sales in a number of regional markets during a given month—the various regional markets would be designated using the subscript i.

Figure 5.5 shows a plot of actual EDP unit sales and personal selling expense data from Table 5.2 along with a plot of the best-fitting line for the relevant simple regression model. The b_0 intercept marks the intersection of the regression line with the sales axis. The b_X coefficient is the slope of the regression line, and the u_t error term measures the vertical deviation of each tth data point from the fitted regression line. The least squares technique minimizes the total sum of squared u_t values by the choice of the b_0 and b_X coefficients. When b_0 and b_X coefficient estimates are combined with actual data on the independent X variable (the level of personal selling expenditures) as shown in Equation 5.5, the estimat-

FIGURE 5.5

Regression Relation Between Units Sold and Personal Selling Expenditures for Electronic Data Processing (EDP), Inc.

The regression line minimizes the sum of squared deviations.

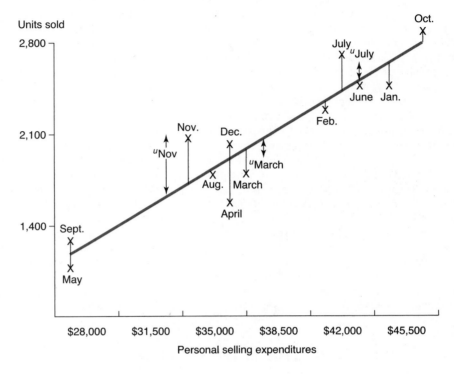

The regression equation is
UNITS = −1292 + 0.0929 *PSE*

Predictor	Coefficient	St. Dev.	*t* ratio	*p*
Constant	−1292.3	396.5	−3.26	0.009
PSE	0.09289	0.01097	8.47	0.000

SEE = 222.8 R^2 = 87.8% $\bar{R}^2$ = 86.5%
F = 85.4

ed, or fitted, total unit sales values shown in Table 5.2 can be calculated. These fitted values are connected to form the fitted regression line drawn in Figure 5.5. Fitted values for the dependent *Y* variable indicate the expected unit sales level for a given level of personal selling expenditures, or *X* variable.

MEASURES OF REGRESSION MODEL SIGNIFICANCE

Powerful desktop personal computers with sophisticated, user-friendly statistical software make the estimation of even complex demand relations quick and easy. Two leading software programs used for this purpose are *MINITAB* statistical software, published by MINITAB, Inc., and *SPSS for Windows*, published by SPSS, Inc. Both are inexpensive and easy to learn, and offer a wealth of powerful techniques for data analysis.

Lies, Damn Lies, and Government Statistics

Once a reliable source of timely and accurate statistics on the U.S. economy, the federal government's system for gathering and interpreting economic data has fallen on hard times. To illustrate, consider the tough question: How much have prices risen or fallen lately?

Think about how much more you are paying for monthly long-distance telephone service and you'll see what economists mean when they complain about adjusting for quality improvements. Chances are that your monthly long-distance bill is higher today than it was 5 years ago, but your higher bill is accounted for by more frequent and/or longer phone conversations, Internet service, and so on. The cost per minute for long-distance phone service has fallen precipitously for decades. How about the cost for a personal computer? Although the price of a PC has fallen from roughly $3,000 to less than $1,000 during the last decade, desktop computers are more powerful and easier to use than a room full of computers in the 1970s. Even when products change little, consumers adapt buying habits to moderate the effects of price increases. How do you

account for the fact that shoppers shift to apples when oranges jump from 79¢ to 89¢ per pound?

The problem is that admittedly imperfect government statistics involve errors and bias. Government statisticians are slow to recognize the effects of new technology and better products. The producer price index, which contains thousands of values for products such as bolts and valves, still has no accurate measure for semiconductors or for communications equipment, arguably the biggest category of producer durables.

What should be done? To better measure consumer prices, electronic scanning data must be utilized. Price and production indexes must also reflect quality adjustments for new products and technologies, and surveys of changes in employment must be refined. In some instances, government spending on data gathering and analysis needs to be increased. Americans and their government simply need to know what's really happening in the economy.

See: Gene Epstein, "Blame the Median When Inflation Resurges," *The Wall Street Journal Online*, February 25, 2002 (http://online.wsj.com).

Standard Error of the Estimate

standard error of the estimate (SEE)
Standard deviation of the dependent *Y* variable after controlling for the influence of all *X* variables

A useful measure for examining the accuracy of any regression model is the **standard error of the estimate (SEE)**, or the standard deviation of the dependent *Y* variable after controlling for the influence of all *X* variables. The SEE increases with the amount of scatter about the sample regression line. If each data point were to lie exactly on the regression line, then the SEE would equal zero because each $\hat{Y}_t$ (or estimated value of Y_t) would exactly equal Y_t. If there is a great deal of scatter about the regression line, then $\hat{Y}_t$ differs greatly from Y_t, and the SEE will be large.

The SEE provides a helpful means for estimating confidence intervals around any particular $\hat{Y}_t$, *given* values for the independent *X* variables. In other words, the SEE is used to determine a range within which the dependent *Y* variable can be predicted with varying degrees of statistical confidence based on the regression coefficients and values for the *X* variables. Because the best estimate of the *t*th value for the dependent variable is $\hat{Y}_t$, the SEE is used to determine just how accurate a prediction $\hat{Y}_t$ is likely to be. If the u_t error terms are normally distributed about the regression equation, as would be true when large samples of more than 30 or so observations are analyzed, there is a 95 percent probability that the dependent variable will lie within the range $\hat{Y}_t \pm (1.96 \times \text{SEE})$, or within roughly 2 SEE. The probability is 99 percent that any given $\hat{Y}_t$ will lie within the range $\hat{Y}_t \pm (2.576 \times \text{SEE})$, or within roughly 3 standard errors of its predicted value. When very small samples of data are analyzed, "critical" values slightly larger than 2 or 3 are multiplied by the SEE to obtain the 95 percent and 99 percent confidence intervals. Precise values can be obtained from a *t* table such as that found in Appendix B.

The SEE concept is portrayed graphically in Figure 5.6. The least squares regression line is illustrated as a bold straight line; the upper and lower 95 percent confidence interval limits are shown as broken curved lines. On average, 95 percent of all actual data observations will lie within roughly 2 SEE. Given a value X_t, the interval between the upper and lower confidence

FIGURE 5.6

Use of the Standard Error of the Estimate to Define Confidence Intervals

The standard error of the estimate (SEE) is used to construct a confidence interval.

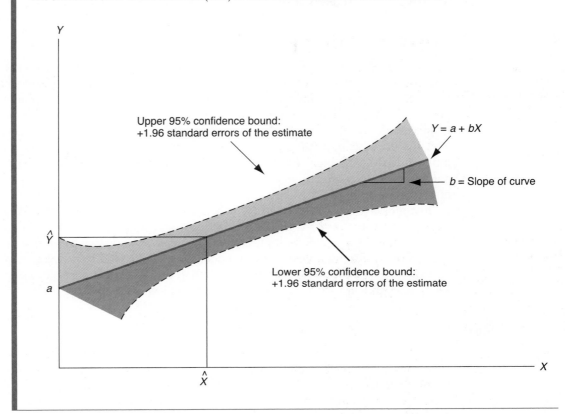

bounds can be used to predict the corresponding Y_t value with a 95 percent probability that the actual outcome will lie within that confidence interval. Notice that this confidence interval widens for sample observations that are much higher or much lower than the sample mean. Confidence bounds diverge from the regression line toward the extreme values of the sample observations. An implication worth remembering is that *relatively little confidence can be placed in the predictive value of a regression equation extended beyond the range of sample observations.*

In the EDP demand estimation example, the SEE is 222.8. This means that the standard deviation of actual Y_t values about the regression line is 222.8 sales units, since the SEE is always in the same units as the dependent Y variable. There is a 95 percent probability that any given observation Y_t will lie within roughly 2 standard errors of the relevant $\hat{Y}_t$ estimate.[3] For example, unit sales during the month of July total 2,750 units, and the expected or fitted unit sales level is 2,453.68 [= –1,292.3 + 0.09289(40,000)]. The corresponding confidence bounds for the 95 percent confidence interval are 2,453.68 ± (2 × 222.8). This means that there is roughly a 95 percent chance that actual unit sales for a month in which $40,000 is spent on personal selling will fall in a range from 2,008.08 to 2,899.28. Similarly, there is a 99 percent probability that

---

3   The precise "critical" number used in the multiplication of SEE is found in a t table such as that in Appendix C. This value is adjusted downward when sample size n is small relative to the number of coefficients k estimated in the regression model. To find the precise critical value, calculate the number of degrees of freedom, defined as $df = n - k$, and read the appropriate t value from the table. In this example, $df = n - k = 12 - 2 = 10$, and there is a 95 percent probability that any given observation Y_t will lie within precisely 2.228 standard errors of the relevant $\hat{Y}_t$ estimate. There is a 99 percent probability that actual total costs will fall within precisely 3.169 standard errors of the predicted value. Therefore, even for the very small sample size analyzed in this example, 2 standard deviations for the 95 percent confidence bounds and 3 standard deviations for the 99 percent confidence bounds work quite well.

actual unit sales will fall within roughly 3 standard errors of the predicted value, or in the range from 1,785.28 to 3,122.08. The wider the confidence interval, the higher the confidence level that actual values will be found within the predicted range.

Goodness of Fit, r, and R^2

correlation coefficient
Goodness of fit measure for a simple regression model

In a simple regression model with only one independent variable, the **correlation coefficient**, r, measures goodness of fit. The correlation coefficient falls in the range between 1 and –1. If $r = 1$, there is a perfect direct linear relation between the dependent Y variable and the independent X variable. If $r = -1$, there is a perfect inverse linear relation between Y and X. In both instances, all actual values for Y_t fall exactly on the regression line. The regression equation explains all of the underlying variation in the dependent Y variable in terms of variation in the independent X variable. If $r = 0$, zero correlation exists between the dependent and independent variables; they are autonomous. When $r = 0$, there is no relation at all between actual Y_t observations and fitted $\hat{Y}_t$ values.

coefficient of determination
Measure of the goodness of fit for a multiple regression model; the square of the coefficient of multiple correlations

In multiple regression models in which more than one independent X variable is considered, the squared value of the coefficient of multiple correlation is used in a similar manner. The square of the coefficient of multiple correlation, called the **coefficient of determination**, or R^2, shows how well a multiple regression model explains changes in the value of the dependent Y variable. R^2 is the proportion of total variation in the dependent variable explained by the full set of independent variables. In equation form, R^2 is written

(5.6)

$$R^2 = \frac{\text{Variation Explained by Regression}}{\text{Total Variation of } Y}$$

Accordingly, R^2 can take on values ranging from 0, indicating that the model provides no explanation of the variation in the dependent variable, to 1.0, indicating that all the variation is explained by the independent variables. The coefficient of determination for the regression model illustrated in Figure 5.5 is 87.8, indicating that 87.8 percent of the total variation in EDP unit sales can be explained by the underlying variation in personal selling expenditures. If R^2 is relatively high, deviations about the regression line are relatively small, as shown in Figure 5.7. In such instances, actual Y_t values are close to the regression line and values for u_t are small.

As the size of the deviations about the regression line increases, the coefficient of determination falls. At the extreme, the sum of the squared error terms equals the total variation in the dependent variable, and $R^2 = 0$. In this case, the regression model is unable to explain any variation in the dependent Y variable. A relatively low value for R^2 indicates that a given model is inadequate in terms of its overall explanatory power.

In practice, the coefficient of determination seldom equals either 0 or 100 percent. In the EDP example, $R^2 = 87.8$ percent and a relatively high level of explanatory power is realized. Fully 87.8 percent of unit sales variation is explained by the variation in the level of personal selling expenditures. For goods with stable and predictable demand patterns, demand function R^2s as high as 90 percent to 95 percent are sometimes achieved. Similarly, very high levels of R^2 can be attained in cost analysis when output is produced under controlled conditions.

Generally speaking, demand and cost analysis over time (time-series analysis) will lead to higher levels for R^2 than would a similar analysis across firms or industries at a given point in time (cross-section analysis). This is because most economic phenomena are closely related to the overall level of economic activity and thus have an important time or trend element. Such exogenous forces are held constant in cross-section analyses and therefore cannot contribute to the overall explanatory power of the regression model. In judging whether a given R^2 is sufficiently high so as to be satisfactory, the type of analysis and anticipated use of statistical results must be considered.

FIGURE 5.7

Explained and Unexplained Variations of the Dependent Variable in a Regression Model

R^2 is high when unexplained variation is low.

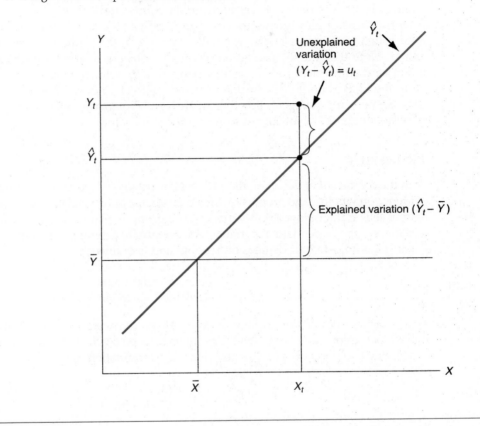

Corrected Coefficient of Determination, $\bar{R}^2$

As stated previously, $R^2 = 100$ percent results when each data point lies exactly on the regression line. Although one might think that any regression model with an $R^2 = 100$ percent would prove highly reliable, this is not always the case. The coefficient of determination for any regression equation is artificially high when too small a sample is used to estimate the model's coefficients. R^2 always equals 100 percent when the number of estimated coefficients equals or exceeds the number of observations because each data point can then be placed exactly on the regression line.

To conduct meaningful regression analysis, the sample used to estimate the regression equation must be sufficiently large so as to reflect vital characteristics of the overall population. This typically means that 30 or more data observations are needed to adequately fit a regression model. More precisely, what is usually required is 30 or more degrees of freedom (*df*). **Degrees of freedom** is the number of observations beyond the absolute minimum needed to calculate a given regression statistic. For example, to calculate an intercept term, at least one observation is needed; to calculate an intercept term plus one slope coefficient, at least two observations are required, and so on.

Because R^2 always approaches 100 percent as degrees of freedom approach zero, statisticians have developed a method for adjusting R^2 to account for the number of degrees of freedom. The **corrected coefficient of determination**, denoted by the symbol $\bar{R}^2$, is calculated by using the expression

degrees of freedom
Number of observations beyond the minimum needed to calculate a given regression statistic

corrected coefficient of determination
Downward adjustment to R^2 in light of the number of data points and estimated coefficients

(5.7)
$$\bar{R}^2 = R^2 - \left(\frac{k - 1}{n - k}\right)(1 - R^2)$$

where n is the number of observations (data points) and k is the number of estimated coefficients (intercept plus the number of slope coefficients). The downward adjustment to R^2 is large when n, the sample size, is small relative to k, the number of coefficients being estimated. Note that the $\bar{R}^2$ calculation always involves a downward adjustment to R^2. This downward adjustment to R^2 is small when n is large relative to k.

In the EDP example, $\bar{R}^2 = 86.5$ percent—a relatively modest downward adjustment from $R^2 = 87.8$ percent; it suggests that the high level of explanatory power achieved by the regression model cannot be attributed to an overly small sample size.

F Statistic

F statistic

Measure of statistical significance for the share of dependent variable variation explained by the regression model

Both the coefficient of determination R^2 and corrected coefficient of determination $\bar{R}^2$ provide evidence on whether the proportion of explained variation is relatively high or low. However, neither tells if the independent variables as a group explain a *statistically significant* share of variation in the dependent Y variable. The **F statistic** provides this information. Like $\bar{R}^2$, the F statistic is adjusted for degrees of freedom and is defined as

(5.8)
$$F_{k-1,\ n-k} = \frac{\text{Explained Variation}/(k - 1)}{\text{Unexplained Variation}/(n - k)}$$

Here, once again, n is the number of observations (data points) and k is the number of estimated coefficients (intercept plus the number of slope coefficients). Also like $\bar{R}^2$, the F statistic can be calculated in terms of the coefficient of determination, where

(5.9)
$$F_{k-1,\ n-k} = \frac{R^2/(k - 1)}{(1 - R^2)/(n - k)}$$

The F statistic is used to indicate whether a significant share of variation in the dependent variable has been explained by the regression model. The hypothesis actually tested is that the dependent Y variable is statistically *unrelated* to all the independent X variables included in the model. If this hypothesis cannot be rejected, variation explained by the regression is small. At the extreme, if $R^2 = 0$, then $F = 0$ and the regression equation provides absolutely no explanation of variation in the dependent Y variable. As the F statistic increases from zero, the hypothesis that the dependent Y variable is not statistically related to one or more of the regression's independent X variables becomes easier to reject. At some point, the F statistic becomes sufficiently large to reject the independence hypothesis and warrants the conclusion that at least some of the model's X variables explain variation in the dependent Y variable.

The F test is used to determine whether a given F statistic is statistically significant. Performing F tests involves comparing F statistics with critical values from a table of the F distribution. If a given F statistic *exceeds* the critical value from the F distribution table, the hypothesis of no relation between the dependent Y variable and the set of independent X variables can be rejected. The regression equation can then be seen as explaining significant variation in the dependent Y variable. Critical values for the F distribution are provided at the 10 percent, 5 percent, and 1 percent significance levels in Appendix C. If the F statistic for a given regression equation exceeds the F value in the table, there can be 90 percent, 95 percent, or 99 percent confidence, respectively, that the regression model explains a significant share of variation in the dependent Y variable. The 90 percent, 95 percent, and 99 percent confidence levels are popular levels for hypothesis rejection, because they imply that a true hypothesis will be rejected only one out of 10, one out of 20, or one out of 100 times, respectively.

Critical F values depend on the number degrees of freedom related to both the numerator and the denominator of Equation 5.9. In the numerator, degrees of freedom equal one less than the number of coefficients estimated in the regression equation $(k-1)$. The degrees of freedom for the denominator of the F statistic equal the number of data observations minus the number of estimated coefficients $(n-k)$. The critical value for F is denoted as F_{f_1,f_2}, where f_1, the degrees of freedom for the numerator, equals $k-1$, and f_2, the degrees of freedom for the denominator, equals $n-k$. For example, the F statistic for the EDP example involves $f_1 = k-1 = 2-1 = 1$, and $f_2 = n-k = 12-2 = 10$ degrees of freedom. Also note that the calculated $F_{1,10} = 71.73 > 10.04$, the critical F value for the $\alpha = 0.01$ or 99 percent confidence level. This means there is less than a 1 percent chance of observing such a high F statistic when there is no link between the dependent Y variable and the entire group of X variables. Given the ability to reject the hypothesis of no relation at the 99 percent confidence level, it will always be possible to reject this hypothesis at the lower, 95 percent and 90 percent, confidence levels. Because the significance with which the no-relation hypothesis can be rejected is an important indicator of overall model fit, rejection should always take place at the highest possible confidence level.

As a rule of thumb, and assuming a typical regression model including four or five independent X variables plus an intercept term, a calculated F statistic greater than 3 permits rejection of the hypothesis that there is no relation between the dependent Y variable and the X variables at the $\alpha = 0.05$ significance level (with 95 percent confidence). As seen in Figure 5.8, a calculated F statistic greater than 5 typically permits rejection of the hypothesis that there is no relation between the dependent Y variable and the X variables at the $\alpha = 0.01$ significance level (with 99 percent confidence). Critical F values are adjusted upward when sample size is small

FIGURE 5.8

F Distribution with 4 and 30 Degrees of Freedom (for a regression model with an intercept plus four X variables tested over 35 observations)

The F distribution is skewed to the right but tends toward normality as degrees of freedom become very large.

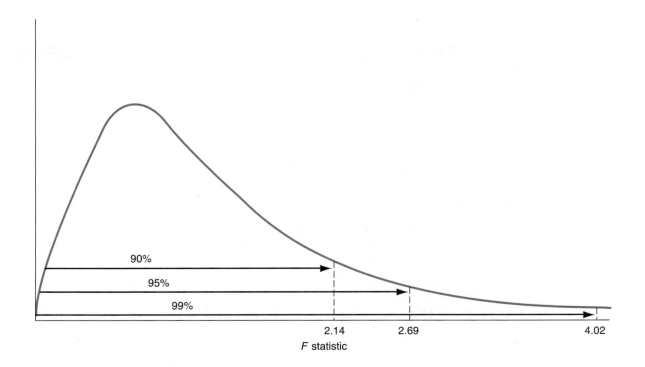

90%

95%

99%

2.14   2.69   4.02

F statistic

Spreadsheet and Statistical Software for the PC

The personal computer revolution in business really got underway in the 1980s following the publication of powerful and easy-to-use spreadsheet software. Microsoft's *Excel* has blown away the original standard, *Lotus 1-2-3*, to make income statement and balance sheet analysis quick and easy. Recent versions incorporate a broad range of tools for analysis, including net present value, internal rate of return, linear programming, and regression. Such software also allows managers to analyze and display operating data using a wide variety of charting and graphing techniques. For basic statistical analysis, *Excel* features easy-to-use statistical capabilities like regression and correlation analysis.

For more detailed analysis, thousands of successful companies worldwide, including GE, 3M, and Ford Motor Company, use *MINITAB* statistical software. The latest version, *MINITAB Release 13*, is a complete stat package that makes statistical analysis easy and fast. For example, the *Stat Guide* is extremely helpful for interpreting statistical graphs and analyses. *MINITAB Student* software is a streamlined and economical version of *Professional MINITAB*, designed specially for introductory

general and business statistics courses. The latest release of *MINITAB Student* features an intuitive and easy-to-use interface, clear manuals, and online help. *MINITAB* is a powerful programming language with sufficient documentation to help even novice users analyze data and interpret results.

For advanced statistical processing software, *SPSS® 11.0 for Windows®* embodies powerful statistical tools for in-depth analysis and modeling of business and economic data. *SPSS® 11.0 for Windows®* helps managers access data easily, quickly prepare data for analysis, analyze data thoroughly, and present results clearly. *SPSS® 11.0 for Windows®* is packed with online tutorials and plenty of examples to guide users, while interactive charts and tables help users understand and present their results effectively.

More than simply changing historical methods of data manipulation and analysis, this user-friendly software for the PC is fundamentally changing the way managers visualize and run their businesses.

See: For *MINITAB* software, see http://www.minitab.com; for SPSS products, see http://www.spss.com.

in relation to the number of coefficients included in the regression model. In such instances, precise critical *F* values must be obtained from an *F* table, such as that found in Appendix C.

MEASURES OF INDIVIDUAL VARIABLE SIGNIFICANCE

The SEE indicates the precision with which the regression model can be expected to predict the dependent *Y* variable. The standard deviation (or standard error) of each individual coefficient provides a similar measure of precision for the relation between the dependent *Y* variable and a given *X* variable. When the standard deviation of a given estimated coefficient is relatively small, a strong relation is suggested between *X* and *Y*. When the standard deviation of a coefficient estimate is relatively large, the underlying relation between *X* and *Y* is typically weak.

t Statistic

t statistic
Approximately normal test statistic with a mean of zero and a standard deviation of 1

A variety of interesting statistical tests can be conducted based on the size of an estimated coefficient and its standard deviation. These tests are based on alternate versions of the **t statistic**, or test statistic. The *t* statistic has an *approximately* normal distribution with a mean of zero and a standard deviation of 1. It describes the difference between an estimated coefficient and some hypothesized value in terms of "standardized units," or by the number of standard deviations of the coefficient estimate. The *t* statistic is normally distributed for large samples, as shown in Figure 5.9. When relatively small samples of data are considered, the *t* distribution does not display a perfectly symmetrical distribution around the mean of zero.

FIGURE 5.9

t Distribution

For large samples, the *t* statistic is normally distributed with a mean of zero and a standard deviation of 1.

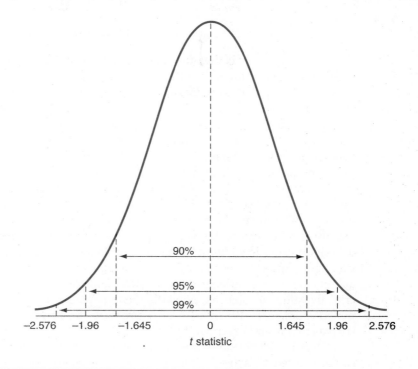

Notice that the bulk of the region under the bell-shaped curve in Figure 5.9 lies in the area around zero, the mean value of the *t* statistic. Fully 95 percent of the region under the bell-shaped curve lies within the territory between –1.96 and +1.96, or roughly ±2. For descriptive purposes, statisticians say that *t* statistics between –1.96 and +1.96 are "close" to the mean value of zero. This area is sometimes referred to as the 95 percent confidence interval, because one can be 95 percent certain that the *t* statistic is close to the mean of zero. Only 5 percent of the area under the bell-shaped curve lies in the "tails" of the distribution, or in the region below the value –1.96 or beyond the value +1.96. For descriptive purposes, statisticians say that *t* statistics outside the bounds of –1.96 and +1.96 are "not close" to, or different from, the mean value of zero. This area is sometimes referred to as the rejection region, because one can be 95 percent confident that such values are *not* typical of *t* statistics with a true mean of zero. Because 99 percent of the region under the bell-shaped curve lies within the territory between –2.576 and +2.576, or roughly ±3, only 1 percent of the area under the bell-shaped curve lies in the lower tail below –2.576, or in the upper tail beyond +2.576. Therefore, it is even more apparent that *t* values outside the bounds of –2.576 and +2.576 are "not close" to, or different from, the mean value of zero.

Two-Tail *t* Tests

In regression analysis, the most common *t* test is performed to learn if an individual slope coefficient estimate $b_X = 0$. This is known as the null hypothesis. If X and Y are indeed unrelated, then the b slope coefficient for a given X variable equals zero. If the $b_X = 0$ hypothesis can be rejected, then it is possible to infer that $b \neq 0$ and that a relation between Y and a given X variable does in fact exist.

The t statistic with $n - k$ degrees of freedom used to test the $b_X = 0$ hypothesis is given by the expression

(5.10)
$$t_{n-k} = \frac{\hat{b}_X}{\text{Standard Deviation of } \hat{b}_X}$$

where, once again, n is the number of observations (data points) and k is the number of estimated coefficients (intercept plus the number of slope coefficients). Notice that this t statistic measures the size of an individual coefficient estimate relative to the size of its underlying standard deviation.

The t statistic measures the size of the b_X coefficient relative to its standard deviation because both the size of b_X and its underlying stability are important in determining if, on average, $b_X \neq 0$. The t statistic measures the number of standard deviations between the estimated regression coefficient, $\hat{b}_X$, and zero. Because the t statistic is only approximately normal, 2 standard deviations for the 95 percent confidence interval and 3 standard deviations for the 99 percent confidence interval hold only for large samples. When $n - k$ is large, say, in excess of 30, a calculated t statistic greater than 2 usually permits rejection of the hypothesis that there is no relation between the dependent Y variable and a given X variable at the $\alpha = 0.05$ significance level (with 95 percent confidence). A calculated t statistic greater than 3 typically permits rejection of the hypothesis that there is no relation between the dependent Y variable and a given X variable at the $\alpha = 0.01$ significance level (with 95% confidence). However, critical t values are adjusted upward when sample size is small in relation to the number of estimated coefficients. When $n - k < 30$, precise critical t values can be obtained from a t table, such as that found in Appendix C.

If the calculated t statistic is greater than the relevant critical t value, the $b_X = 0$ hypothesis can be rejected. Conversely, if the calculated t statistic is not greater than the critical t value, it is not possible to reject the $b_X = 0$ hypothesis. In that case, there is no evidence of a relation between Y and a given X variable. Tests of the hypothesis $b_X = 0$ are referred to as **two-tail t tests** because either very small negative t values or very large positive t values can lead to rejection. Hypothesis tests that simply relate to matters of effect or influence are called two-tail t tests.

Returning to the EDP example, the estimated coefficient for the personal selling expenditures X variable is 0.09289. Given a standard deviation of only 0.01097, the calculated t statistic $= 8.47 > 3.169$, the critical t value for a two-tail test with $n - k = 10$ degrees of freedom at the $\alpha = 0.01$ significance level. With 99 percent confidence, the hypothesis of no effect can be rejected. Alternatively, the probability of encountering such a large t statistic is less than 1 percent [hence the probability (p) value of 0.000 in Figure 5.5] when there is in fact no relation between the total units Y variable and the personal selling expenditures X variable.

two-tail t tests
Tests of the $b = 0$ hypothesis

One-Tail t Tests

one-tail t tests
Tests of direction or comparative magnitude

Some managerial questions go beyond the simple matter of whether X influences Y. In these instances, it is interesting to determine whether a given variable, X, has a positive or a negative effect on Y or whether the effect of variable X_1 is greater or smaller than the effect of variable X_2. Tests of direction (positive or negative) or comparative magnitude are called **one-tail t tests**.

To understand the difference between one-tail and two-tail t tests, it is necessary to appreciate the nature of the t distribution. As shown in Figure 5.9, 90 percent of the area under the bell-shaped curve is between $t = -1.645$ and $t = +1.645$, 95 percent is between $t = -1.96$ and $t = +1.96$, and 99 percent is between $t = -2.576$ and $t = +2.576$. At these values, both tails of the t statistic distribution contain 10 percent, 5 percent, and 1 percent of the total area, respectively. For example, if there is in fact no relation between Y and a given X variable, the probability of a calculated t value that falls outside the bounds ± 1.645 is only 10 percent. Under these circumstances, the chance of a calculated t value that is less than -1.645 is only 5 percent; the chance of a calculated t value greater than $+1.645$ is 5 percent. If $t = 1.645$, it is possible to reject the $b_X = 0$ hypothesis with 90 percent confidence; it is possible to reject the $b_X < 0$ hypothesis with 95 percent confidence. In a two-tail t test, rejection of the null hypothesis occurs with a finding that the t statistic is not in the *region around zero*. In one-tail t tests, rejection of the null hypothesis occurs when the t statistic is in one specific tail of the distribution.

In the EDP example, the estimated coefficient for the personal selling expenditures X variable is 0.09289 with a standard deviation of 0.01097. The calculated t statistic $= 8.47 > 2.764$, the critical t value for a one-tail t test with $n - k = 10$ degrees of freedom at the $\alpha = 0.01$ significance level. With 99 percent confidence, the negative effect hypothesis can be rejected. The probability of encountering such a large positive t statistic is less than 1 percents [hence the probability (p) value of 0.000 in Figure 5.5] when there is in fact a negative relation between the total units Y variable and the personal selling expenditures X variable.

PRACTICAL SOLUTIONS TO REGRESSION PROBLEMS

Pitfalls can be encountered in regression analysis. Not the least of these is the problem that correlation by itself does not imply causality. Does advertising cause (produce) sales? Do sales cause (fund) advertising? Or does causality run in *both* directions? In light of this and other difficulties encountered in using historical data to project future relations, some caveats are in order concerning the use of regression techniques.

Choosing the Best Model

The specific form of a regression equation is typically based on a demand or cost model derived from economic theory. Nevertheless, some experimentation might sometimes prove appropriate. As a first step, it is possible to experiment with various measures of the dependent and independent variables. Often it is worthwhile to try separate output measures based upon different product classifications. The costs of producing output can and do vary depending on the types of product characteristics required by customers. Similarly, demand conditions often depend on unique product characteristics that are obscured when sales are aggregated into a product class that is too broad.

The specific functional form of the regression model is also often worthy of some experimentation. After the data on relevant dependent and independent variables have been collected, managers may have little prior reason to suspect whether the linear or log-linear (multiplicative) form of the regression equation model is most appropriate. Trying both and then relying on the form that consistently provides the best fit seems reasonable. Similarly, careful experimentation with the range of independent X variables incorporated in the regression model might be proper. Some managers use a regression method called **stepwise multiple regression**, which relies on the underlying correlation between X and Y variables to indicate the independent X variables to be included in the model. In this method, X variables are actually selected by the computer software according to their ability to reduce the overall level of unexplained variation. Using this technique, the regression analysis method has the potential to become wholly inductive in character, where the nature of the data, rather than the prior expectations of the manager, determines the specific form of the regression function.

stepwise multiple regression
Experimental method of independent variable selection based upon XY correlation

The benefit of experimentation lies in its potential for improving regression model fit. The danger of experimentation is that the resulting regression model might bear little resemblance to a robust and durable economic relation. As was described in the degrees of freedom discussion, R^2 can typically be increased by the addition of further independent variables, even if no true relation exists between the dependent Y variable and the additional X variables. An approach in which absolutely every variable is tried can lead to models that effectively pick up idiosyncratic aspects of unique samples of data but prove incapable of widespread explanation. Perhaps the safest approach to adopt when using an experimental method is to always retain a hold out, or test sample, of data in which the experimental model can be verified. If an experimental model achieves a relatively high level of explanation over samples of data that were not used in its development, then chances are improved that it offers useful insight.

Dealing with Multicollinearity

Suppose that the coefficient of determination for a regression model is near 100 percent, thus indicating that the model as a whole explains much of the variation in the dependent variable. Assume further that standard errors for the individual coefficient estimates are relatively large and that t statistics for many, if not all, independent variables are insignificant. This describes a situation in which the regression model indicates a significant relation between the dependent Y variable and the group of independent X variables, but the technique is unable to identify the

multicollinearity
Situation in which two or more independent variables are very highly correlated

various X variables as uniquely important. This problem is due to **multicollinearity**, a situation in which two or more independent variables are very highly correlated. The independent variables are not really independent of one another but have values that are jointly or simultaneously determined. Home ownership and family income are a good example. Because families who own their homes tend to have relatively high incomes, these two variables are highly correlated, and it is difficult to determine the marginal influence of each in demand analysis.

In time-series analysis, in which the pervasive influence of economic growth is at work, multicollinearity problems can be equally pervasive. In cases of perfect or near perfect collinearity between two independent variables, it becomes impossible to estimate coefficients for both variables. Even when it is possible to estimate regression coefficients for each variable, high multicollinearity reduces the reliability of coefficient estimates—particularly in relation to each coefficient estimate's standard deviation.

One practical approach for dealing with multicollinearity is to deflate or otherwise transform the independent variables. For example, to discover the independent effects of rising price levels (inflation) and rising income levels on demand, it may be appropriate to convert nominal data into real (inflation-adjusted) terms. If both age and experience contribute to employee productivity, it may be attractive to combine the two variables by multiplying them together and creating an employee "age and experience" variable. Alternatively, it is sometimes suggested to remove all but one of the correlated independent variables from the regression model. The coefficient estimate assigned to the remaining variable reflects its own influence and that of the other excluded variables. The regression model still has not identified the separate effects of the mutually correlated variables. However, so long as the relation between the correlated independent variables does not change, the resulting regression model can be used for predictive purposes.

Residual Analysis

residual
Error or unexplained variation

The least squares regression technique makes four assumptions about the distribution of the error term, or **residual**, u_t. Residuals are assumed to have a normal distribution, a random distribution, an expected value of zero, and constant (or homoskedastic) variance. A violation of any one of these assumptions impairs the validity of the technique.

Using most standard statistical software, residuals can be calculated and plotted. Plotting residuals on a linear scale provides a frequency distribution. This distribution can be examined to determine whether the residuals appear to be normally distributed and have a mean equal to zero. In most cases, frequency plots do not form a perfect bell-shaped (normal) curve, but any serious deviation will be readily indicated. A plot of the residuals in their order of occurrence provides another useful means for detecting violations of basic assumptions. For example, when plotting annual residuals in their order of occurrence, they should be randomly distributed about a mean of zero. Residuals plotted in sequence should display a horizontal band centered about the value zero, and there should also be no systematic pattern.

serial correlation
Time-related linkages in the residuals

The problem of **serial correlation** (or autocorrelation) occurs frequently in time-series analysis. When serial correlation exists, it can often be removed through data transformation, such as taking first differences. In demand analysis, serial correlation among the residuals is often caused by slowly changing prices, income, or taste. Specification of the demand model in terms of changes in each variable from one period to the next frequently overcomes this problem.

Finally, at times the variance of the residuals is not constant over the entire sample. This is especially true in cross-section studies of widely different firm or plant sizes. Common corrective action for this so-called **heteroskedasticity** problem is to transform the regression variables into logarithmic or ratio form prior to estimation or to use more sophisticated weighted least squares regression methods.

heteroskedasticity
Nonconstant variance in the disturbance term

SUMMARY

This chapter introduces methods for characterizing and estimating demand relations. An understanding of these techniques is necessary not only for the successful analysis of demand relations but also for understanding the nature of any statistical relation.

- Because the market price/output equilibrium at any point in time is determined by the forces of demand and supply, a **simultaneous relation**, or concurrent association, exists between demand and supply. The problem of estimating an economic relation in the presence of such simultaneity is the **identification problem**.

- The **consumer interview**, or survey, method involves questioning customers or potential customers to estimate demand relations. An alternative technique for obtaining useful information about product demand involves **market experiments**.

- **Regression analysis** is a powerful statistical technique that describes the way in which a dependent Y variable is related to one or more independent X variables.

- A **deterministic relation** is a relation known with certainty. A **statistical relation** exists if the average of one variable is related to another, but it is impossible to predict with certainty the value of one based on the value of another. A **time series** is a daily, a weekly, a monthly, or an annual sequence of data on an economic variable such as price, income, cost, or revenue. A **cross section** of data is a group of observations on an important economic variable at any given point in time.

- The simplest means for analyzing a sample is to plot and visually study the data. A **scatter diagram** is a data illustration in which the *dependent* variable is plotted on the vertical axis, and the *independent* variable is shown on the horizontal axis. The most common regression model specification is a **linear model** or straight-line relation. Another common regression model form is a **multiplicative model**, which involves interactions among all the X variables. A **simple regression model** involves one dependent Y variable and one independent X variable. A **multiple regression model** entails one Y variable but includes two or more X variables.

- A useful measure for examining the overall accuracy of regression models is the **standard error of the estimate (SEE)**, or the standard deviation of the dependent Y variable after controlling for the influence of all X variables. In a simple regression model with only one independent variable, the **correlation coefficient**, r, measures goodness of fit. The square of the coefficient of multiple correlation, called the **coefficient of determination**, or R^2, shows how well a multiple regression model explains changes in the value of the dependent Y variable. In statistical studies, the sample analyzed must be large enough to provide 30 or more **degrees of freedom**, or observations beyond the minimum needed to calculate a given regression statistic. The **corrected coefficient of determination**, denoted by the symbol $\bar{R}^2$, is a downward adjustment in R^2 in light of the number of data points and estimated coefficients. The *F* **statistic** offers evidence on the statistical significance of the proportion of dependent variable variation that has been explained.

- The *t* **statistic** is a test statistic that has an *approximately* normal distribution with a mean of zero and a standard deviation of 1. Hypothesis tests that simply relate to matters of effect or influence of the independent variables are called **two-tail *t* tests**. Tests of direction (positive or negative) or comparative magnitude are called **one-tail *t* tests**. Such hypothesis tests are used to evaluate demand models derived from economic theory and experimental approaches such as the **stepwise multiple regression** technique.

- A number of estimation problems are commonly encountered in regression analysis. The problem of **multicollinearity** arises when two or more independent variables are highly correlated and the regression technique is incapable of determining individual causal relations. The least squares regression technique makes four assumptions about the distribution of the error term, or **residual**, u_t. Residuals are assumed to have a normal distribution, a random distribution, an expected value of zero, and constant variance. A violation of any one of these assumptions impairs the validity of the technique. The problem of **serial correlation** (or autocorrelation) occurs frequently in time-series analysis. If the variance of the residuals is not constant over the entire sample, **heteroskedasticity** is said to exist. When residual term assumptions are violated, regression variables are sometimes transformed into logarithmic or ratio form prior to estimation, or more sophisticated weighted least squares regression methods are used.

Methods examined in this chapter are commonly used by large and small organizations in their statistical analysis of demand relations. Given the continuing rise in the diversity and complexity of the economic environment, the use of such tools is certain to grow in the years ahead.

QUESTIONS

Q5.1 What is the identification problem, and how does it make demand estimation difficult?

Q5.2 Why might customers be unwilling or unable to provide accurate demand information? When might this prove helpful?

Q5.3 How do linear and log-linear models differ in terms of their assumptions about the nature of demand elasticities?

Q5.4 If a regression model estimate of total profit is $50,000 with a standard error of the estimate of $25,000, what is the chance of an actual loss?

Q5.5 A simple regression $TR = a + bQ$ is not able to explain 19% of the variation in total revenue. What is the coefficient of correlation between TR and Q?

Q5.6 In a regression-based estimate of a demand function, the beta coefficient for advertising equals 3.75 with a standard deviation of 1.25 units. What is the range within which there can be 99% confidence that the actual parameter for advertising can be found?

Q5.7 Describe the benefits and risks entailed with the experimental stepwise regression method of analysis.

Q5.8 Describe a circumstance in which multicollinearity is likely to be a problem, and discuss a possible remedy.

Q5.9 Is serial correlation apt to be a problem in a time-series analysis of quarterly sales data over a 10-year period? Identify a possible remedy, if necessary.

Q5.10 Managers often study the profit margin-sales relation over the life cycle of individual products, rather than the more direct profit-sales relation. In addition to the economic reasons for doing so, are there statistical advantages as well? (Note: Profit margin equals profit divided by sales.)

SELF-TEST PROBLEMS AND SOLUTIONS

ST5.1 The use of regression analysis for demand estimation can be further illustrated by expanding the Electronic Data Processing (EDP), Inc., example described in the chapter. Assume that the link between units sold and personal selling expenditures described in the chapter gives only a partial view of the impact of important independent variables. Potential influences of other important independent variables can be studied in a multiple regression analysis of EDP data on contract sales (Q), personal selling expenses (PSE), advertising expenditures (AD), and average contract price (P). Because of a stagnant national economy, industry-wide growth was halted during the year, and the usually positive effect of income growth on demand was missing. Thus, the trend in national income was not relevant during this period. For simplicity, assume that relevant factors influencing EDP's monthly sales are as follows:

**Units Sold, Price, Advertising, and Personal Selling
Expenditures for Electronic Data Processing, Inc.**

Month	Units Sold	Price	Advertising Expenditures	Personal Selling Expenditures
January	2,500	$3,800	$26,800	$43,000
February	2,250	3,700	23,500	39,000
March	1,750	3,600	17,400	35,000
April	1,500	3,500	15,300	34,000
May	1,000	3,200	10,400	26,000
June	2,500	3,200	18,400	41,000
July	2,750	3,200	28,200	40,000
August	1,750	3,000	17,400	33,000
September	1,250	2,900	12,300	26,000
October	3,000	2,700	29,800	45,000
November	2,000	2,700	20,300	32,000
December	2,000	2,600	19,800	34,000
Average	2,020.83	$3,175.00	$19,966.67	$35,666.67

If a linear relation between unit sales, contract price, advertising, and personal selling expenditures is hypothesized, the EDP regression equation takes the following form:

$$\text{Sales} = Y_t = b_0 + b_P P_t + b_{AD} AD_t + b_{PSE} PSE_t + u_t$$

where Y is the number of contracts sold, P is the average contract price per month, AD is advertising expenditures, PSE is personal selling expenses, and u is a random disturbance term—all measured on a monthly basis over the past year.

When this linear regression model is estimated over the EDP data, the following regression equation is estimated (t statistics in parentheses):

$$\text{Units}_t = -117.513 - 0.296P_t + 0.036AD_t + 0.066PSE_t$$
$$(-0.35) \quad\quad (-2.91) \quad\quad (2.56) \quad\quad\quad (4.61)$$

where P_t is price, AD_t is advertising, PSE_t is selling expense, and t statistics are indicated within parentheses. The standard error of the estimate or SEE is 123.9 units, the coefficient of determination or $R^2 = 97.0\%$, the adjusted coefficient of determination is $\bar{R}^2 = 95.8\%$, and the relevant F statistic is 85.4.

A. What is the economic meaning of the $b_0 = -117.513$ intercept term? How would you interpret the value for each independent variable's coefficient estimate?

B. How is the standard error of the estimate (SEE) used in demand estimation?

C. Describe the meaning of the coefficient of determination, R^2, and the adjusted coefficient of determination, $\bar{R}^2$.

D. Use the EDP regression model to estimate fitted values for units sold and unexplained residuals for each month during the year.

ST5.1 Solution

A. The intercept term $b_0 = -117.513$ has no clear economic meaning. Caution must always be exercised when interpreting points outside the range of observed data and this intercept, like most, lies far from typical values. This intercept cannot be interpreted as the expected level of unit sales at a zero price, assuming both advertising and personal selling expenses are completely eliminated. Similarly, it would be hazardous to use this regression model to predict sales at prices, selling expenses, or advertising levels well in excess of sample norms.

Slope coefficients provide estimates of the change in sales that might be expected following a one-unit increase in price, advertising, or personal selling expenditures. In this example, sales are measured in units, and each independent variable is measured in dollars. Therefore, a $1 increase in price can be expected to lead to a 0.296-unit reduction in sales volume per month. Similarly, a $1 increase in advertising can be expected to lead to a 0.036-unit increase in sales; a $1 increase in personal selling expenditures can be expected to lead to a 0.066-unit increase in units sold. In each instance, the effect of independent X variables appears consistent over the entire sample. The t statistics for price and advertising exceed the value of 2, meaning that there can be 95% confidence that price and advertising have an effect on sales. The chance of observing such high t statistics for these two variables when in fact price and advertising have no effect on sales is less than 5%. The t statistic for the personal selling expense variable exceeds the value of 3, the critical t value for the $\alpha = 0.01$ (99% confidence level). The probability of observing such a high t statistic when in fact no relation exists between sales and personal selling expenditures is less than 1%.[4] Again, caution must be used when interpreting these individual regression coefficients. It is important not to extend the analysis beyond the range of data used to estimate the regression coefficients.

B. The standard error of the estimate, or SEE, of 123.9 units can be used to construct a confidence interval within which actual values are likely to be found based on the size of individual regression coefficients and various values for the X variables. For example, given this regression model and the values $P_t = \$3,800$, $AD_t = \$26,800$, and $PSE_t = \$43,000$ for each respective independent X variable during the month of January, the fitted value $\hat{Y}_t = 2,566.88$ can be calculated (see part D). Given these values for the independent X variables, 95% of the time actual observations for the month of January will lie within roughly 2 SEE; 99% of

---

4   The t statistic for personal selling expenses exceeds 3.355, the precise critical t value for the $\alpha = 0.01$ level and $n - k = 12 - 4 = 8$ degrees of freedom. The t statistic for price and advertising exceeds 2.306, the critical t value for the $\alpha = 0.05$ level and 8 degrees of freedom, meaning that there can be 95% confidence that price and advertising affect sales. Note also that $F_{3,8} = 85.40 > 7.58$, the precise critical F value for the $\alpha = 0.01$ significance level.

the time actual observations will lie within roughly 3 SEE. Thus, approximate bounds for the 95% confidence interval are given by the expression 2,566.88 ± (2 × 123.9), or from 2,319.08 to 2,814.68 sales units. Approximate bounds for the 99% confidence interval are given by the expression 2,566.88 ± (3 × 123.9), or from 2,195.18 to 2,938.58 sales units.

C. The coefficient of determination is $R^2 = 97.0\%$; it indicates that 97% of the variation in EDP demand is explained by the regression model. Only 3% is left unexplained. Moreover, the adjusted coefficient of determination is $\bar{R}^2 = 95.8\%$; this reflects only a modest downward adjustment to R^2 based upon the size of the sample analyzed relative to the number of estimated coefficients. This suggests that the regression model explains a significant share of demand variation—a suggestion that is supported by the F statistic. $F_{3,8} = 85.4$ and is far greater than 5, meaning that the hypothesis of no relation between sales and this group of independent X variables can be rejected with 99% confidence. There is less than a 1% chance of encountering such a large F statistic when in fact there is no relation between sales and these X variables as a group.

D. Fitted values and unexplained residuals per month are as follows:

Demand Function Regression Analysis for Electronic Data Processing, Inc.

Month	Units Sold	Price	Advertising Expenditures	Personal Selling Expenditures	Fitted Value for Units Sold	Unexplained Residuals
January	2,500	$3,800	$26,800	$43,000	2,566.88	−66.88
February	2,250	3,700	23,500	39,000	2,212.98	37.02
March	1,750	3,600	17,400	35,000	1,758.35	−8.35
April	1,500	3,500	15,300	34,000	1,646.24	−146.24
May	1,000	3,200	10,400	26,000	1,029.26	−29.26
June	2,500	3,200	18,400	41,000	2,310.16	189.84
July	2,750	3,200	28,200	40,000	2,596.51	153.49
August	1,750	3,000	17,400	33,000	1,803.83	−53.83
September	1,250	2,900	12,300	26,000	1,186.56	63.44
October	3,000	2,700	29,800	45,000	3,133.35	−133.35
November	2,000	2,700	20,300	32,000	1,930.90	69.10
December	2,000	2,600	19,800	34,000	2,074.97	−74.97
Average	2,020.83	$3,175.00	$19,966.67	$35,666.67	2,020.83	0.00

ST5.2 **Simple Regression.** The global computer software industry is dominated by Microsoft Corp. and a handful of large competitors from the United States. During the early 2000s, fallout from the government's antitrust case against Microsoft and changes tied to the Internet have caused company and industry analysts to question the profitability and long-run advantages of the industry's massive long-term investments in research and development (R&D).

The following table shows sales revenue, profit, and R&D data for a $n = 15$ sample of large firms taken from the U.S. computer software industry. Data are for the most recent fiscal year available on the academic use version of *Compustat PC+* as of September 2001. Net sales revenue, net income before extraordinary items, and research and development (R&D) expenditures are shown. R&D is the dollar amount of company-sponsored expenditures during the most recent fiscal year, as reported to the Securities and Exchange Commission on Form 10-K. Excluded from such numbers is R&D under contract to others, such as U.S. government agencies. All figures are in $ millions.

Company Name	Sales	Net Income	R&D
Microsoft Corp.	$22,956.0	$9,421.0	$3,775.0
Electronic Arts Inc.	1,420.0	116.8	267.3
Adobe Systems Inc.	1,266.4	287.8	240.7
Novell Inc.	1,161.7	49.5	234.6
Intuit Inc.	1,093.8	305.7	170.4
Siebel Systems Inc.	790.9	122.1	72.9
Symantec Corp.	745.7	170.1	112.7
Networks Associates Inc.	683.7	−159.9	148.2
Activision Inc.	583.9	−34.1	26.3
Rational Software Corp.	572.2	85.3	106.4
National Instruments Corp.	410.1	55.2	56.0
Citrix Systems Inc.	403.3	116.9	39.7
Take-two Interactive Software	387.0	25.0	5.7
Midway Games Inc.	341.0	−12.0	83.8
Eidos Plc.	311.1	40.2	75.3
Averages	2,208.5	706.0	361.0

Data source: *Compustat PC+*, September 2001.

A. A simple regression model with sales revenue as the dependent Y variable and R&D expenditures as the independent X variable yields the following results (t statistics in parentheses):

$$\text{Sales}_i = \$20.065 + \$6.062 \ \text{R\&D}_i, \ \bar{R}^2 = 99.8\%, \ \text{SEE} = 233.75, \ F = 8460.40$$
$$\quad\quad\quad (0.31) \quad\quad (91.98)$$

How would you interpret these findings?

B. A simple regression model with net income (profits) as the dependent Y variable and R&D expenditures as the independent X variable yields the following results (t statistics in parentheses):

$$\text{Profits}_i = \${-}210.31 + \$2.538 \ \text{R\&D}_i, \ \bar{R}^2 = 99.3\%, \ \text{SEE} = 201.30, \ F = 1999.90$$
$$\quad\quad\quad\quad (0.75) \quad\quad (7.03)$$

How would you interpret these findings?

C. Discuss any differences between your answers to parts A and B.

ST5.2 Solution

A. First of all, the constant in such a regression typically has no meaning. Clearly, the intercept should not be used to suggest the value of sales revenue that might occur for a firm that had zero R&D expenditures. As discussed in the problem, this sample of firms is restricted to large companies with significant R&D spending. The R&D coefficient is statistically significant at the $\alpha = 0.01$ level with a calculated t statistic value of 91.98, meaning that it is possible to be more than 99% confident that R&D expenditures affect firm sales. The probability of observing such a large t statistic when there is in fact no relation between sales revenue and R&D expenditures is less than 1%. The R&D coefficient estimate of $6.062 implies that a $1 rise in R&D expenditures leads to an average $6.062 increase in sales revenue.

The $\bar{R}^2 = 99.8\%$ indicates the share of sales variation that can be explained by the variation in R&D expenditures. Note that $F = 8460.40 > F_{1,13, \ \alpha = 0.01} = 9.07$, implying that variation in R&D spending explains a significant share of the total variation in firm sales. This suggests that R&D expenditures are a key determinant of sales in the computer software industry, as one might expect.

The standard error of the Y estimate, or SEE = $233.75 (million) is the average amount of error encountered in estimating the level of sales for any given level of R&D spending. If the u_i error terms are normally distributed about the regression equation, as would be true when large samples of more than 30 or so observations are analyzed, there is a 95% probability that observations of the dependent variable will lie within the range $\hat{Y}_i \pm (1.96 \times$ SEE), or within roughly two standard errors of the estimate. The probability is 99% that any given $\hat{Y}_i$ will lie within the range $\hat{Y}_i \pm (2.576 \times$ SEE), or within roughly *three* standard errors of its predicted value. When very small samples of data are analyzed, as is the case here, "critical" values slightly larger than two or three are multiplied by the SEE to obtain the 95% and 99% confidence intervals.

Precise critical t values obtained from a t table, such as that found in Appendix C, are $t^*_{13, \alpha=0.05} = 2.160$ (at the 95% confidence level) and $t^*_{13, \alpha=0.01} = 3.012$ (at the 99% confidence level) for $df = 15 - 2 = 13$. This means that actual sales revenue Y_i can be expected to fall in the range $\hat{Y}_i \pm (2.160 \times \$223.75)$, or $\hat{Y}_i \pm \$483.3$, with 95% confidence; and within the range $\hat{Y}_i \pm (3.012 \times \$223.75)$, or $\hat{Y}_i \pm \$673.935$, with 99% confidence.

B. As in part A, the constant in such a regression typically has no meaning. Clearly, the intercept should not be used to suggest the level of profits that might occur for a firm that had zero R&D expenditures. Again, the R&D coefficient is statistically significant at the $\alpha = 0.01$ level with a calculated t statistic value of 7.03, meaning that it is possible to be more than 99% confident that R&D expenditures affect firm profits. The probability of observing such a large t statistic when there is in fact no relation between profits and R&D expenditures is less than 1%. The R&D coefficient estimate of $2.538 suggests that a $1 rise in R&D expenditures leads to an average $2.538 increase in current-year profits.

The $\bar{R}^2 = 99.3\%$ indicates the share of profit variation that can be explained by the variation in R&D expenditures. This suggests that R&D expenditures are a key determinant of profits in the software industry. Again, notice that $F = 1999.90 > F^*_{1,13,\alpha=0.01} = 9.07$, meaning that variation in R&D spending can explain a significant share of profit variation.

The standard error of the Y estimate of SEE = $201.30 (million) is the average amount of error encountered in estimating the level of profit for any given level of R&D spending. Actual profits Y_i can be expected to fall in the range $\hat{Y}_i \pm (2.160 \times \$201.30)$, or $\hat{Y}_i \pm \$434.808$, with 95% confidence; and within the range $\hat{Y}_i \pm (3.012 \times \$201.30)$, or $\hat{Y}_i \pm \$606.3156$, with 99% confidence.

C. Clearly, a strong link between both sales revenue and profits and R&D expenditures is suggested by a regression analysis of the computer software industry. There appears to be slightly less variation in the sales-R&D relation than in the profits-R&D relation. As indicated by $\bar{R}^2$, the linkage between sales and R&D is a bit stronger than the relation between profits and R&D. At least in part, this may stem from the fact that the sample was limited to large R&D-intensive firms, whereas no such screen for profitability was included.

PROBLEMS

P5.1 **Demand Concepts.** Identify each of the following statements as true or false and explain why.

A. The effect of a $1 change in price is constant, but the elasticity of demand will vary along a linear demand curve.

B. In practice, price and quantity tend to be individually rather than simultaneously determined.

C. A demand curve is revealed if prices fall while supply conditions are held constant.

D. The effect of a $1 change in price will vary, but the elasticity of demand is constant along a log-linear demand curve.

E. Consumer interviews are a useful means for incorporating subjective information into demand estimation.

P5.2   **Regression Analysis.** Identify each of the following statements as true or false and explain why:

A. A parameter is a population characteristic that is estimated by a coefficient derived from a sample of data.

B. A one-tail t test is used to indicate whether the independent variables as a group explain a significant share of demand variation.

C. Given values for independent variables, the estimated demand relation can be used to derive a predicted value for demand.

D. A two-tail t test is an appropriate means for testing direction (positive or negative) of the influences of independent variables.

E. The coefficient of determination shows the share of total variation in demand that cannot be explained by the regression model.

P5.3   **Demand Curve Analysis.** Anathema Printers, Inc., is a leading supplier of high-speed color printers. Average price and annual unit sales data are as follows:

	1998	**1999**	**2000**	**2001**	**2002**
Price ($)	$9,000	$8,000	$6,000	$5,000	$3,000
Units sold	25,000	50,000	100,000	125,000	175,000

A. Complete the following table, and use these data to derive intercept and slope coefficients for the linear demand curve.

Year	Price	Quantity	ΔPrice	ΔQuantity	Slope = $\Delta P/\Delta Q$
1998	$9,000	25,000	—	—	—
1999	8,000	50,000			
2000	6,000	100,000			
2001	5,000	125,000			
2002	3,000	175,000			

B. Assuming that demand conditions are held constant, use the preceding data to plot a linear demand curve.

P5.4   **Identification Problem.** Business is booming for Consulting Services, Inc. (CSI), a leading supplier of data processing consulting services. The company can profitably employ technicians as quickly as they can be trained. The average hourly rate billed by CSI for trained technician services and the number of billable hours (output) per quarter over the past six quarters are as follows:

	Q–1	*Q*–2	*Q*–3	*Q*–4	*Q*–5	*Q*–6
Hourly rate ($)	$20	$25	$30	$35	$40	$45
Billable hours	2,000	3,000	4,000	5,000	6,000	7,000

Quarterly demand and supply curves for CSI services are

$$Q_D = 4{,}000 - 200P + 2{,}000T \qquad \text{(Demand)}$$
$$Q_S = -2{,}000 + 200P \qquad \text{(Supply)}$$

where Q is output, P is price, T is a trend factor, and $T = 1$ during Q–1 and increases by one unit per quarter.

A. Express each demand and supply curve in terms of price as a function of output.

B. Plot the quarterly demand curves for the last six quarterly periods. (Hint: Let $T = 1$ to find the Y intercept for Q–1, $T = 2$ for Q–2, and so on.)

C. Plot the CSI supply curve on the same graph.

D. What is this problem's relation to the identification problem?

P5.5 **Demand Estimation.** Colorful Tile, Inc., is a rapidly growing chain of ceramic tile outlets that caters to the do-it-yourself home remodeling market. In 2002, 33 stores were operated in small to medium-size metropolitan markets. An in-house study of sales by these outlets revealed the following (standard errors in parentheses):

$$Q = 5 - 5P + 2A + 0.25I + 0.2HF$$
$$ (3) \ \ (1.8) \ \ (0.7) \ \ (0.2) \ \ \ (0.1)$$
$$R^2 = 93\%, \text{Standard Error of the Estimate} = 6$$

Here, Q is tile sales (in thousands of cases), P is tile price (per case), A is advertising expenditures (in thousands of dollars), I is disposable income per capita (in thousands of dollars), and HF is household formation (in hundreds).

A. Fully evaluate and interpret these empirical results on an overall basis using R^2, $\bar{R}^2$, F statistic, and SEE information.

B. Is quantity demanded sensitive to "own" price?

C. Austin, Texas, was a typical market covered by this analysis. During 2002 in the Austin market, price was $5, advertising was $30,000, income was an average $40,000 per household, and the number of household formations was 5,000. Calculate and interpret the relevant advertising point elasticity.

D. Assume that the preceding model and data are relevant for the coming period. Estimate the probability that the Austin store will make a profit during 2003 if total costs are projected to be $300,000.

P5.6 **Elasticity Estimation.** Getaway Tours, Inc., has estimated the following multiplicative demand function for packaged holiday tours in the East Lansing, Michigan, market using quarterly data covering the past four years (16 observations):

$$Q_y = 10P_y^{-1.10}P_X^{0.5}A_y^{3.8}A_X^{2.5}I^{1.85}$$
$$R^2 = 80\%, \text{Standard Error of the Estimate} = 20$$

Here, Q_y is the quantity of tours sold, P_y is average tour price, P_x is average price for some other good, A_y is tour advertising, A_x is advertising of some other good, and I is per capita disposable income. The standard errors of the exponents in the preceding multiplicative demand function are

$$b_{P_y} = 0.04, \ b_{P_x} = 0.35, \ b_{A_y} = 0.5, \ b_{A_x} = 0.9, \text{ and } b_I = 0.45$$

A. Is tour demand elastic with respect to price?

B. Are tours a normal good?

C. Is X a complement good or substitute good?

D. Given your answer to part C, can you explain why the demand effects of A_y and A_x are both positive?

P5.7 **Correlation and Simple Regression.** Market Research, Inc., has conducted a survey to learn the relationship between income and age for a $n = 15$ sample of households in the affluent Minneapolis suburb of Eden Prarie, Minnesota. Survey results were as follows:

Age	Income	Age	Income
32	81	49	104
33	86	50	104
33	87	51	115
37	92	51	118
38	94	52	121
40	99	53	122
41	102	53	131
42	103		

A. Interpret the coefficient of correlation between the AGE and INCOME variables of 94.0%.

B. Interpret the following results for a simple regression over this sample where INCOME is the dependent Y variable and AGE is the independent X variable (t statistics in parentheses):

$$\text{INCOME}_j = \$27.377 + \$1.753 \text{ AGE}_i, \bar{R}^2 = 87.4\%, \text{SEE} = 5.261, F = 98.10$$
$$\quad\quad\quad (3.49) \quad\quad (9.90)$$

P5.8 **Simple Regression.** Ninja Pizza, Inc., is a regional franchisor of home delivery pizza outlets. To better assess the effects of price, advertising, and income on pizza demand, the company recently compiled the following survey of monthly sales and operating data at 15 of the company's outlets in southern California:

Ninja Pizza, Inc.,Operating Data at 15 Outlets

Quantity Sold	Price	Advertising Expenditures per Month	Disposable Income per Household
42,100	$11.77	$46,100	$38,000
55,500	9.96	47,200	39,100
71,100	12.36	60,900	40,100
63,200	12.49	55,600	44,200
77,200	10.68	64,400	41,800
70,900	12.07	60,700	44,800
55,600	11.97	52,100	39,900
70,700	11.23	57,900	43,600
71,400	11.26	55,600	41,700
79,400	9.79	60,100	41,200
60,600	12.29	50,700	44,000
50,800	12.70	46,500	43,300
61,800	12.33	58,600	41,000
40,500	10.88	42,800	38,300
85,300	10.14	64,800	42,100

A. As a first step in their analysis, the company ran simple regressions of pizza demand on each of the three potentially important independent variables:
The first simple regression equation is (*t* statistics in parentheses)

$$\text{QUANTITY} = 117763 - 4713 \text{ PRICE}$$
$$(2.93) \quad (-1.35)$$

$$\text{SEE} = 12800, \; R^2 = 12.3\%, \; \bar{R}^2 = 5.5\%, \; F \text{ statistic} = 1.82$$

The second simple regression equation is (*t* statistics in parentheses)

$$\text{QUANTITY} = -32655 + 1.75 \text{ ADVERTISING}$$
$$(-3.17) \quad (9.43)$$

$$\text{SEE} = 4883, \; R^2 = 87.2\%, \; \bar{R}^2 = 86.3\%, \; F \text{ statistic} = 88.84$$

The third simple regression equation is (*t* statistics in parentheses)

$$\text{QUANTITY} = -58386 + 2.94 \text{ INCOME}$$
$$(-0.95) \quad (1.99)$$

$$\text{SEE} = 11962, \; R^2 = 23.4\%, \; \bar{R}^2 = 17.5\%, \; F \text{ statistic} = 3.97$$

Based on these results, do any of the potentially important independent variables affect pizza demand?

B. What is the difference between each simple regression coefficient estimate and that which might be estimated using a multiple regression approach including all three independent variables?

P5.9 **Stepwise Regression.** As a second phase in the analysis of Ninja Pizza, Inc., survey data, the company wishes to study an experimental stepwise regression model of pizza demand. Stepwise regression model results for this sample of data are as follows (STEPWISE REGRESSION OF QUANTITY ON 3 PREDICTORS, WITH $n = 15$):

STEP	1	2	3
CONSTANT	−32655.0	817.6	−33301.7
ADVERTISING	1.75	1.69	1.45
t ratio	9.43	10.19	9.59
PRICE		−2618	−4042
t ratio		−2.20	−3.88
INCOME		1.53	
t ratio		2.98	
SEE	4883	4290	3333
R^2	87.23	90.90	94.97

A. Provide a brief evaluation of estimation results for each step in the stepwise regression model.

B. Do the step 3 estimation results differ from those obtained from a multiple regression of demand on all three independent variables?

P5.10 **Multiple Regression.** In the third phase of the Ninja Pizza, Inc., survey data analysis, the company wishes to study a multiple regression model of pizza demand. The company thinks that it is likely that the marginal influence of advertising depends upon the average price charged and income levels in the market area. Similarly, the effects of these two latter independent variables are thought to depend upon the level of advertising. Therefore, a multiplicative demand model has been estimated in log-linear form as follows:

The multiplicative regression model estimated in log-linear form is

$$LOG_e \, Q = -13.6 - 0.670 \, LOG_e \, P + 1.29 \, LOG_e \, AD + 1.15 \, LOG_e \, Y$$

Predictor	Coefficient	Standard Deviation	*t* Ratio	*p*
Constant	−13.637	3.2300	−4.22	0.001
$LOG_e \, P$	−0.6702	0.2002	−3.35	0.007
$LOG_e \, AD$	1.2944	0.1424	9.09	0.000
$LOG_e \, Y$	1.1467	0.3721	3.08	0.010

$$SEE = 0.05795, \; R^2 = 94.6\%, \; \bar{R}^2 = 93.1\%, \; F \text{ statistic} = 63.86 \; (p = 0.000)$$

A. Interpret the coefficient estimate for each respective independent variable.

B. Characterize the overall explanatory power of this log-linear regression model with that for the step 3 multiple regression model described in P5.9.

CASE STUDY

Demand Estimation for Branded Consumer Products

Demand estimation for brand-name consumer products is made difficult by the fact that managers must rely on proprietary data. There simply is not any publicly available data which can be used to estimate demand elasticities for brand-name orange juice, frozen entrees, pies, and the like—and with good reason. Competitors would be delighted to know profit margins across a broad array of competing products so that advertising, pricing policy, and product development strategy could all be targeted for maximum benefit. Product demand information is valuable and jealously guarded.

To see the process that might be undertaken to develop a better understanding of product demand conditions, consider the hypothetical example of Mrs. Smyth's Inc., a Chicago-based food company. In early 2002, Mrs. Smyth's initiated an empirical estimation of demand for its gourmet frozen fruit pies. The firm is formulating pricing and promotional plans for the coming year, and management is interested in learning how pricing and promotional decisions might affect sales. Mrs. Smyth's has been marketing frozen fruit pies for several years, and its market research department has collected quarterly data over two years for six important marketing areas, including sales quantity, the retail price charged for the pies, local advertising and promotional expenditures, and the price charged by a major competing brand of frozen pies. Statistical data published by the U.S. Census Bureau (http://www.census.gov) on population and disposable income in each of the six market areas were also available for analysis. It was therefore possible to include a wide range of hypothesized demand determinants in an empirical estimation of fruit pie demand. These data appear in Table 5.3.

The following regression equation was fit to these data:

$$Q_{it} = b_0 + b_1 P_{it} + b_2 A_{it} + b_3 PX_{it} + b_4 Y_{it} + b_5 Pop_{it} + b_6 T_{it} + u_{it}$$

Q is the quantity of pies sold during the tth quarter; P is the retail price in dollars of Mrs. Smyth's frozen pies; A represents the dollars spent for advertising; PX is the price, measured in dollars, charged for competing premium-quality frozen fuit pies; Y is dollars of disposable income per capita; Pop is the population of the market area; T is the trend factor (2000–1 = 1, . . . , 2001–4 = 8); and

CASE STUDY (continued)

TABLE 5.3

Mrs. Smyth's Gourmet Frozen Fruit Pie Regional Market Demand Data, 2000–1 to 2001–4

	Year–Quarter	Unit Sales (Q)	Price ($)	Advertising Expenditures ($)	Competitors' Price ($)	Income ($)	Population	Time Variable (T)
Atlanta, GA	2000–1	193,334	6.39	15,827	6.92	33,337	4,116,250	1
	2000–2	170,041	7.21	20,819	4.84	33,390	4,140,338	2
	2000–3	247,709	5.75	14,062	5.28	33,599	4,218,965	3
	2000–4	183,259	6.75	16,973	6.17	33,797	4,226,070	4
	2001–1	282,118	6.36	18,815	6.36	33,879	4,278,912	5
	2001–2	203,396	5.98	14,176	4.88	34,186	4,359,442	6
	2001–3	167,447	6.64	17,030	5.22	35,691	4,363,494	7
	2001–4	361,677	5.30	14,456	5.80	35,950	4,380,084	8
Chicago, IL,	2000–1	401,805	6.08	27,183	4.99	34,983	9,184,926	1
Gary, IN,	2000–2	412,312	6.13	27,572	6.13	35,804	9,237,683	2
Kenosha, WI	2000–3	321,972	7.24	34,367	5.82	35,898	9,254,182	3
	2000–4	445,236	6.08	26,895	6.05	36,113	9,272,758	4
	2001–1	479,713	6.40	30,539	5.37	36,252	9,300,401	5
	2001–2	459,379	6.00	26,679	4.86	36,449	9,322,168	6
	2001–3	444,040	5.96	26,607	5.29	37,327	9,323,331	7
	2001–4	376,046	7.21	32,760	4.89	37,841	9,348,725	8
Dallas–Fort	2000–1	255,203	6.55	19,880	6.97	34,870	5,294,645	1
Worth, TX	2000–2	270,881	6.11	19,151	6.25	35,464	5,335,816	2
	2000–3	330,271	5.62	15,743	6.03	35,972	5,386,134	3
	2000–4	313,485	6.06	17,512	5.08	36,843	5,409,350	4
	2001–1	311,500	5.83	16,984	5.29	37,573	5,409,358	5
	2001–2	370,780	5.38	15,698	6.19	37,781	5,425,001	6
	2001–3	152,338	7.41	22,057	6.94	37,854	5,429,300	7
	2001–4	320,804	6.19	17,460	6.38	39,231	5,442,595	8
Los Angeles-	2000–1	738,760	5.75	42,925	5.54	28,579	16,381,600	1
Long Beach, CA	2000–2	707,015	6.61	50,299	6.73	28,593	16,544,289	2
	2000–3	699,051	5.03	37,364	5.04	28,633	16,547,258	3
	2000–4	628,838	6.76	50,602	4.61	28,833	16,553,958	4
	2001–1	631,934	7.04	53,562	5.85	29,242	16,587,432	5
	2001–2	651,162	6.70	48,911	5.63	29,876	16,680,782	6
	2001–3	765,124	6.54	49,422	6.94	30,327	16,716,936	7
	2001–4	741,364	5.73	44,061	6.37	30,411	16,717,938	8
Minneapolis-	2000–1	291,773	5.35	13,896	5.78	29,778	2,972,443	1
St. Paul, MN	2000–2	153,018	6.33	27,429	4.73	30,079	2,974,275	2
	2000–3	574,486	5.94	31,631	6.70	30,598	2,989,720	3
	2000–4	75,396	7.00	39,176	4.58	30,718	3,020,244	4
	2001–1	590,190	5.19	33,538	5.17	30,922	3,021,618	5
	2001–2	288,112	7.02	53,643	5.15	31,199	3,025,298	6
	2001–3	276,619	7.02	60,284	5.46	31,354	3,042,834	7
	2001–4	522,446	5.23	53,595	6.06	31,422	3,063,011	8
Washington, DC,	2000–1	395,314	5.80	22,626	6.56	38,892	7,611,304	1
Baltimore, MD	2000–2	436,103	5.32	22,697	6.38	39,080	7,615,783	2
	2000–3	336,338	6.35	25,475	4.53	39,510	7,666,220	3
	2000–4	451,321	5.95	25,734	6.31	39,552	7,710,368	4
	2001–1	352,181	6.01	23,777	6.24	39,776	7,713,007	5
	2001–2	317,322	7.02	27,544	4.86	41,068	7,752,393	6
	2001–3	422,455	5.71	23,852	4.86	41,471	7,754,204	7
	2001–4	290,963	7.36	30,487	5.32	41,989	7,782,654	8
Average		391,917	6.24	29,204	5.70	34,625	7,706,365	

CASE STUDY (continued)

u_{it} is a residual (or disturbance) term. The subscript i indicates the regional market from which the observation was taken, whereas the subscript t represents the quarter during which the observation occurred. Least squares estimation of the regression equation on the basis of the 48 data observations (eight quarters of data for each of six areas) resulted in the estimated regression coefficients and other statistics given in Table 5.4.

The individual coefficients for the Mrs. Smyth's pie demand regression equation can be interpreted as follows. The intercept term, 646,958, has no economic meaning in this instance; it lies far outside the range of observed data and obviously cannot be interpreted as the demand for Mrs. Smyth's frozen fruit pies when all the independent variables take on zero values. The coefficient for each independent variable indicates the marginal relation between that variable and sales of pies, holding constant the effect of all the other variables in the demand function. For example, the –127,443 coefficient for P, the price charged for Mrs. Smyth's pies, indicates that when the effects of all other demand variables are held constant, each $1 increase in price causes quarterly sales to decline by roughly 127,443 pies. Similarly, the 5.353 coefficient for A, the advertising variable, indicates that for each $1 increase in advertising during the quarter, roughly 5.353 additional pies are sold. The 29,337 coefficient for the competitor-price variable indicates that demand for Mrs. Smyth's pies rises by roughly 29,337 pies with every $1 increase in competitor prices. The 0.344 coefficient for the Y variable indicates that, on average, a $1 increase in the average disposable income per capita for a given market leads to roughly a 0.344-unit increase in quarterly pie demand. Similarly, a one person increase in the population of a given market area leads to a small 0.024-unit increase in quarterly pie demand. Finally, the –4,406 coefficient for the trend variable indicates that pie demand is falling in a typical market by roughly 4,406 units per quarter. This means that Mrs. Smyth's is enjoying secular growth in pie demand, perhaps as a result of the growing popularity of Mrs. Smyth's products or of frozen foods in general.

Individual coefficients provide useful estimates of the expected marginal influence on demand following a one-unit change in each respective variable. However, they are only estimates. For example, it would be very unusual for a 1¢ increase in price to cause exactly a –127,443-unit change in the quantity demanded. The actual effect could be more or less. For decision-making purposes, it would be helpful to know if the marginal influences suggested by the regression model are stable or instead tend to vary widely over the sample analyzed.

TABLE 5.4

Estimated Demand Function for Mrs. Smyth's Gourmet Frozen Fruit Pies

Variable (1)	Coefficient (2)	Standard Error of Coefficient (3)	t Statistic (4) = (2) ÷ (3)
Intercept	646,958	154,147	4.20
Price (P)	–127,443	15,112	–8.43
Advertising (A)	5.353	1.114	4.81
Competitor price (PX)	29,337	12,388	2.37
Income (Y)	0.344	3.186	0.11
Population (Pop)	0.024	0.002	10.20
Time (T)	4,406	4,400	1.00

Coefficient of Determination = R^2 = 89.6%

Corrected Coefficient of Determination = $\bar{R}^2$ = 88.1%

F Statistic = 58.86

Standard error of estimate = SEE = 60,700

CASE STUDY (continued)

In general, if it is known with certainty that $Y = a + bX$, then a one-unit change in X will always lead to a b-unit change in Y. If $b > 0$, X and Y will be directly related; if $b < 0$, X and Y will be inversely related. If no relation at all holds between X and Y, then $b = 0$. Although the true parameter b is unobservable, its value is estimated by the regression coefficient $\hat{b}$. If $\hat{b} = 10$, a one-unit change in X will increase Y by 10 units. This effect may appear to be large, but it will be statistically significant only if it is stable over the entire sample. To be statistically reliable, $\hat{b}$ must be large relative to its degree of variation over the sample.

In a regression equation, there is a 68% probability that b lies in the interval $\hat{b} \pm 1$ standard error (or standard deviation) of the coefficient $\hat{b}$. There is a 95% probability that b lies in the interval $\hat{b} \pm 2$ standard errors of the coefficient. There is a 99% probability that b is in the interval $\hat{b} \pm 3$ standard errors of the coefficient. When a coefficient is at least twice as large as its standard error, one can reject at the 95% confidence level the hypothesis that the true parameter b equals zero. This leaves only a 5% chance of concluding incorrectly that $b \neq 0$ when in fact $b = 0$. When a coefficient is at least three times as large as its standard error (standard deviation), the confidence level rises to 99% and chance of error falls to 1%.

A significant relation between X and Y is typically indicated whenever a coefficient is at least twice as large as its standard error; significance is even more likely when a coefficient is at least three times as large as its standard error. The independent effect of each independent variable on sales is measured using a two-tail t statistic where:

$$t \text{ statistic} = \frac{\hat{b}}{\text{Standard error of } \hat{b}}$$

This t statistic is a measure of the number of standard errors between $\hat{b}$ and a hypothesized value of zero. If the sample used to estimate the regression parameters is large (for example, $n > 30$), the t statistic follows a normal distribution, and properties of a normal distribution can be used to make confidence statements concerning the statistical significance of $\hat{b}$. Hence $t = 1$ implies 68% confidence, $t = 2$ implies 95% confidence, $t = 3$ implies 99% confidence, and so on. For small sample sizes (for example, $df = n - k < 30$), the t distribution deviates from a normal distribution, and a t table should be used for testing the significance of estimated regression parameters.

Another regression statistic, the standard error of the estimate (SEE), is used to predict values for the dependent variable given values for the various independent variables. Thus, it is helpful in determining a range within which one can predict values for the dependent variable with varying degrees of statistical confidence. Although the best estimate of the value for the dependent variable is $\hat{Y}$, the value predicted by the regression equation, the standard error of the estimate can be used to determine just how accurate this prediction $\hat{Y}$ is likely to be. Assuming that the standard errors are normally distributed about the regression equation, there is a 68% probability that actual observations of the dependent variable Y will lie within the range $\hat{Y} \pm 1$ standard error of the estimate. The probability that an actual observation of Y will lie within two standard errors of its predicted value increases to 95%. There is a 99% chance that an actual observed value for Y will lie in the range $\hat{Y} \pm 3$ standard errors. Obviously, greater predictive accuracy is associated with smaller standard errors of the estimate.

Mrs. Smyth's could forecast the total demand for its pies by forecasting sales in each of the six market areas, then summing these area forecasts to obtain an estimate of total pie demand. Using the results from the demand estimation model and data from each individual market, it would also be possible to construct a confidence interval for total pie demand based on the standard error of the estimate.

CASE STUDY (continued)

A. Describe the statistical significance of each individual independent variable included in the Mrs. Smyth's frozen fruit pie demand equation.

B. Interpret the coefficient of determination (R^2) for the Mrs. Smyth's frozen fruit pie demand equation.

C. Use the regression model and 2001–4 data to estimate 2002–1 unit sales in the Washington, DC–Baltimore, MD, market.

D. To illustrate use of the standard error of the estimate statistic, derive the 95% confidence interval for 2002–1 actual unit sales in the Washington, DC–Baltimore, Maryland, market.

SELECTED REFERENCES

Calfee, John, Clifford Winston, and Randolph Stempski. "Econometric Issues in Estimating Consumer Preferences from Stated Preference Data: A Case Study of the Value of Automobile Travel Time." *Review of Economics and Statistics* 83 (November 2001): 699–707.

Chay, Kenneth Y., and James L. Powell. "Semiparametric Censored Regression Models." *Journal of Economic Perspectives* 15 (Fall 2001): 29–42.

Emery, Gary W. "Cyclical Demand and the Choice of Debt Maturity." *Journal of Business* 74 (October 2001): 557–590.

Fiess, Norbert, and Ronald Macdonald. "The Instability of the Money Demand Function: An I(2) Interpretation." *Oxford Bulletin of Economics & Statistics* 63 (September 2001): 475–495.

Fraumeni, Barbara M. "E-Commerce: Measurement and Measurement Issues." *American Economic Review* 91 (May 2001): 318–322.

Funke, Michael. "Money Demand in Euroland." *Journal of International Money & Finance* 20 (October 2001): 701–713.

Grytten, Jostein, Fredrik Carlsen, and Irene Skau. "The Income Effect and Supplier-Induced Demand; Evidence from Primary Physician Services in Norway." *Applied Economics* 33 (September 2001): 1455–1467.

Heiman, Amir, David R. Just, Bruce McWilliams, et al. "Incorporating Family Interactions and Socioeconomic Variables into Family Production Functions: The Case of Demand for Meats." *Agribusiness* 17 (Autumn 2001): 455–468.

Henrich, Joseph, Robert Boyd, Samuel Bowles, Colin Camerer, Ernst Fehr, Herbert Gintis, and Richard McElreath. "In Search of Homo Economicus: Behavioral Experiments in 15 Small-Scale Societies." *American Economic Review* 91 (May 2001): 73–78.

Horowitz, Joel L., and N. E. Savin. "Binary Response Models: Logits, Probits and Semiparametrics." *Journal of Economic Perspectives* 15 (Fall 2001): 43–56.

Krueger, Alan B. "Symposium on Econometric Tools." *Journal of Economic Perspectives* 15 (Fall 2001): 3–10.

Lim, Christine, and Michael Mcaleer. "Cointegration Analysis of Quarterly Tourism Demand by Hong Kong and Singapore for Australia." *Applied Economics* 33 (October 2001): 1599–1619.

Newey, Whitney K. "Flexible Simulated Moment Estimation of Nonlinear Errors-in-Variables Models." *Review of Economics and Statistics* 83 (November 2001): 616–627.

Smith, V. Kerry, Donald H. Taylor, Jr., Frank A. Sloan, F. Reed Johnson, and William H. Desvousges. "Do Smokers Respond to Health Shocks?" *Review of Economics and Statistics* 83 (November 2001): 675–687.

Sodhi, Manmohan S. "Applications and Opportunities for Operations Research in Internet-Enabled Supply Chains and Electronic Marketplaces." *Interfaces* 31 (March 2001): 56–69.

CHAPTER SIX

Forecasting

A famous economist once remarked, "We have two classes of forecasters: Those who don't know—and those who don't know that they don't know." There is more than a bit of truth to this witticism.

Experienced economists know that economic forecasting is fraught with uncertainty. To see why, consider the interrelated nature of economic forecasts. One might ask an economist, will the pace of real economic growth in the United States average an anemic 2 percent, a healthy 3 percent, or a robust 3.5 percent? What will be the rate of inflation? How will investors respond to a proposed change in the tax law, if and when such a change is passed by both Houses of Congress and signed into law by the president? Most important, how is the rate of growth in the overall economy related to inflation, and how are both apt to be affected by an important change in tax law that, at this point, is only at the proposal stage?

When chemists and physicists run experiments, they have carefully controlled laboratory environments. Economists enjoy no such luxury; they must make assumptions based on volatile economic and political conditions subject to random and violent shocks. No wonder that economic forecasters lament the difficulty of making accurate economic projections.[1]

Predicting trends in the overall economy and its impact on the cost or demand for company goods and services is one of the most difficult responsibilities facing management. However, it is a necessary task because, for better or worse, all decisions are made on the basis of future expectations. This chapter illustrates a number of forecasting techniques that have proven successful in forming accurate expectations in a wide variety of real-world applications.

---

1   See Erin Schulte, "Economists Say Fed Moves May Still Be Months Away," *The Wall Street Journal Online*, March 23, 2002 (http://online.wsj.com).

WHAT IS ECONOMIC FORECASTING?

When companies hire new workers, they must predict the relative productivity of a wide variety of individuals with diverse skills, work histories, and personalities. How much inventory should be carried? What price should be charged during the coming holiday season? Which market is the most natural path for expansion? These and a host of everyday business decisions require that managers make informed forecasts of future economic events.

Why Is Forecasting Useful?

Managers sometimes must integrate quantitative and nonquantitative information in a way not easily modeled or characterized by numbers. In such instances, there is no substitute for the extraordinary pattern recognition capabilities of the human mind. Experienced managers sometimes "know" the correct level of inventory, or right price, despite their inability to easily explain all the factors that weigh in their decisions. Although there is no good substitute for the careful intuition of an experienced manager, some firms err in their over reliance on judgmental forecasts. In some cases, the concept of forecasting is confused with goal setting. If a company asks its staff to forecast sales for the mid-Atlantic region, for example, these "forecasts" are sometimes used as yardsticks to judge sales performance. If forecast sales are exceeded, sales performance is "good"; if forecast sales are not achieved, sales performance is "poor." This sometimes leads sales staffs to underestimate future sales in a effort to boost perceived performance. Just as a successful college football coach predicts a tough year to enhance the popular perception of a winning record, sales personnel have incentives to be overly conservative in their sales projections for new or improved products. Coaches of football teams with 8-3 records sometimes lose their jobs if fans had expected a perfect 11-0 season; brand managers of even highly successful new product introductions sometimes get fired if rosy predictions are not met.

   A big advantage of the wide variety of statistical techniques commonly used in economic forecasting is that they separate the process of forecasting from the firm's goal-setting activity. When sales are forecast in an objective, systematic, and unbiased manner, the potential for accurate forecasts increases, as does the capacity for appropriate operating and planning decisions. When these forecasts involve outcomes and precipitating factors that can be quantified, it also becomes possible to access the direct ramifications of changes in controllable and uncontrollable conditions. Optimistic through pessimistic scenarios can be tested and analyzed for their performance implications and for their significance in terms of the decision-making process. Forecasting that is objective and quantitative has the potential to help almost any business; accurate business forecasting is a value-added undertaking.

COMMON TYPES OF FORECASTING PROBLEMS

Macroeconomic Forecast Problems

macroeconomic forecasting
Prediction of aggregate economic activity

Macroeconomic forecasting involves predicting aggregate measures of economic activity at the international, national, regional, or state level. Predictions of gross domestic product (GDP), unemployment, and interest rates by "blue chip" business economists capture the attention of national media, business, government, and the general public on a daily basis.[2] Other macroeconomic forecasts commonly reported in the press include predictions of consumer spending,

---

2   GDP measures aggregate business activity as described by the value at final point of sale of all goods and services produced in the domestic economy during a given period by both domestic and foreign-owned enterprises. Gross national product (GNP) is the value at final point of sale of all goods and services produced by *domestic* firms. As such, GNP does not reflect domestic production by foreign-owned firms (e.g., Toyota Camrys produced in Kentucky).

business investment, homebuilding, exports, imports, federal purchases, state and local government spending, and so on. Macroeconomic predictions are important because they are used by businesses and individuals to make day-to-day operating decisions and long-term planning decisions. If interest rates are projected to rise, homeowners may rush to refinance fixed-rate mortgages, while businesses float new bond and stock offerings to refinance existing debt or take advantage of investment opportunities. When such predictions are accurate, significant cost savings or revenue gains become possible. When such predictions are inaccurate, higher costs and lost marketing opportunities occur.

The accuracy of any forecast is subject to the influence of controllable and uncontrollable factors. In the case of macroeconomic forecasting, uncontrollable factors loom large. Take interest rate forecasting, for example. The demand for credit and short-term interest rates rises if businesses seek to build inventories or expand plant and equipment, or if consumers wish to increase installment credit. The supply of credit rises and short-term interest rates fall if the Federal Reserve System acts to increase the money supply, or if consumers cut back on spending to increase savings. Interest rate forecasting is made difficult by the fact that business decisions to build inventories, for example, are largely based on the expected pace of overall economic activity—which itself depends on interest-rate expectations. The macroeconomic environment is interrelated in ways that are unstable and cannot be easily predicted. Even policy decisions are hard to predict. For example, Federal Reserve System policy meeting minutes are confidential until months after the fact. Is it any wonder that "Fed watching" is a favorite pastime of business economists?

Microeconomic Forecast Problems

microeconomic forecasting
Prediction of partial economic data

In contrast with macroeconomic forecasting, **microeconomic forecasting** involves the prediction of disaggregate economic data at the industry, firm, plant, or product level. Unlike predictions of GDP growth, which are widely followed in the press, the general public often ignores microeconomic forecasts of scrap prices for aluminum, the demand for new cars, or production costs for Crest toothpaste. It is unlikely that the *CBS Evening News* will ever be interrupted to discuss an upward trend in used car prices, even though these data are an excellent predictor of new car demand. When used car prices surge, new car demand often grows rapidly; when used car prices sag, new car demand typically drops. The fact that used car prices and new car demand are closely related is not surprising given the strong substitute-good relation that exists between used cars and new cars.

Trained and experienced analysts often find it easier to accurately forecast microeconomic trends, such as the demand for new cars, than macroeconomic trends, such as GDP growth. This is because microeconomic forecasts abstract from the multitude of interrelationships that together determine the macroeconomy. With specialized knowledge about changes in new car prices, car import tariffs, car loan rates, and used cars prices, among other factors, it is possible to focus on the fairly narrow range of important factors that influence new car demand. In contrast, a similarly precise model of aggregate demand in the macroeconomy might involve thousands of economic variables and hundreds of functional relationships.

This is not to say that precise microeconomic forecasting is easy. For example, in August 1999, *Standard and Poor*'s DRI forecast new car and light truck sales of 15.7 million units for the 2000 model year. This was a reasonable number, and within the 15.3–16.0 million unit range of forecasts provided by the University of Michigan, Blue Chip Economic Forecasters, and others. Unfortunately, in September 2000, all such forecasts proved too conservative in light of the 17.2 million units actually sold in a robust economic environment. Undaunted, forecasters expected unit sales of 16.1 million in 2001 and 16.8 million in 2002. Those numbers looked good, until terrorist attacks in New York City and Washington, DC, on September 11, 2001, sent new car and light truck sales into a tailspin as consumer confidence plummeted. At that point, it became anybody's guess as to how long it would take for consumer confidence and new car and light truck sales to recover. Obviously, accurate auto and light truck demand forecasting is tough even for industry experts.

Problem of Changing Expectations

The subtle problem of changing expectations bedevils both macroeconomic and microeconomic forecasting. If business purchasing agents are optimistic about future trends in the economy and boost inventories in anticipation of surging customer demand, the resulting inventory buildup can itself contribute to economic growth. Conversely, if purchasing agents fear an economic downturn and cut back on orders and inventory growth, they themselves can be a main contributor to any resulting economic downturn. The expectations of purchasing agents and other managers can become a self-fulfilling prophecy because the macroeconomic environment represents the sum of the investment and spending decisions of business, government, and the public. In fact, the link between expectations and realizations has the potential to create an optimistic bias in government-reported statistics.

Government economists are sometimes criticized for being overly optimistic about the rate of growth in the overall economy, the future path of interest rates, or the magnitude of the federal deficit. As consumers of economic statistics, managers must realize that it can pay for government or politically motivated economists to be optimistic. If business leaders can be led to make appropriate decisions for a growing economy, their decisions can in fact help lead to a growing economy. Unlike many business economists from the private sector, government-employed and/or politically motivated economists often actively seek to manage the economic expectations of business leaders and the general public.

It is vital for managers to appreciate the link between economic expectations and realizations, and to be wary of the potential for forecast bias.

Data Quality Problems

Accurate forecasts require pertinent data that are current, complete, and free from error. Almost everyone has heard the familiar warning about the relation between data quality and forecast accuracy: "garbage in, garbage out." However, this statement is true in ways that are not immediately obvious. For example, if a manager wants to forecast demand for consumer or producer goods, it is often better to input incoming orders rather than shipments because shipments are sometimes subject to production delays. Similarly, the timing of order fulfillment is sometimes subject to delays in transit that are beyond the control of the shipping firm.

In addition to carefully considering the quality of data used to generate forecasts, the quantity of available data is also important. A general rule is: The more data that can be subject to analysis, the better. Some advanced forecasting software that works on desktop personal computers can function with as few as five data points. However, forecasts that result from such paltry bodies of data are often simplistic, if not trivial. Although the collection of large samples of data on market transactions can be expensive and tedious, the payoff in forecast accuracy can justify the effort.

If monthly data are seasonal in nature, it is important to have an extended time series to facilitate forecast accuracy. Most forecasting software programs used to monitor monthly activity require a minimum of 2 years of data (24 observations) to build a seasonally adjusted forecast model. Practically speaking, 2 years of monthly data are often not enough; 5 years of monthly data (60 observations) are typically necessary before a high level of monthly forecast accuracy can be achieved. Of course, most forecast software works with data of any periodicity, be it hourly, daily, weekly, monthly, or annual in nature. The ultimate consideration that must be addressed is whether the quantity and quality of data analyzed are sufficient to shed meaningful light on the forecast problem being addressed. The acid test is: Can useful forecasts be generated?

MANAGERIAL APPLICATION   **6.1**

Economic Forecasting: The Art and the Science

Many do not understand why disagreement among forecasting economists is common and why this disagreement can produce divergent economic forecasts. These concerns reflect too little appreciation of the difficulty of economic forecasting. In the real world, "all else held equal" doesn't hold very often, if ever. To forecast GDP, for example, one must be able to accurately predict the future pattern of government spending, tax and monetary policy, consumer and business spending, dollar strength against foreign currencies, weather, and so on. Although typical patterns can be inferred on the basis of past trends, an unexpected drought, winter storm, or labor strike can disrupt economic activity and upset the accuracy of economic forecasts.

In light of the uncertainties involved, it seems reasonable that different forecasting economists would accord differing importance to a wide variety of economic influences. Forecasters' judgment is reflected not only in the interpretation they give to the data generated by complex computer models but also in the models themselves. Computers may generate economic forecasts,

but they do so on the basis of programs written by economists. Computer-generated economic forecasts are only as sophisticated as the data employed, model analyzed, and the subsequent analysis.

Given the criticism often aimed at forecasters, it is ironic to note that the success of economic forecasting is responsible, at least in part, for some of its failures. Users have come to expect a nearly unattainable level of forecast accuracy. At the same time, users forget that forecasts can, by themselves, have important economic consequences. When consumers and businesses cut back on spending in reaction to the forecast of an impending mild recession, for example, they change the basis for the forecasters' initial prediction. By their behavior, they may also cause a steeper recession. This is the forecaster's dilemma: The future as we know it doesn't exist. In fact, it can't.

See: Erin Schulte, "Double Dip: Chip Faux Pas or a Real Economic Hazard," *The Wall Street Journal Online*, March 2, 2002 (http://online.wsj.com).

One of the most vexing data quality problems encountered in forecasting is the obstacle presented by government-supplied data that are often tardy and inaccurate. For example, the Commerce Department's Bureau of Economic Analysis "advanced" estimate of GDP for the fourth quarter of the year is typically published in late January of the following year. A "preliminary" revision to this estimate is then released by the Bureau of Economic Analysis on March 1; an official final revision is not made available until March 31, or until 90 days after the fact. Such delays induce uncertainty for those seeking to make projections about future trends in economic activity. Worse still, preliminary and final revisions to official GDP estimates are often large and unpredictable. Extreme variation in official estimates of key economic statistics is a primary cause of forecast error among business economists.

Finally, it is worth remembering that forecasts are, by definition, never perfect. All forecasting methods rely heavily on historical data and historical relationships. Future events are seldom, if ever, explicitly accounted for in popular forecasting techniques. Managers must combine traditional forecast methods with personal insight and knowledge of future events to create the most useful forecasts.

Common Forecast Techniques

Some forecasting techniques are basically quantitative; others are largely qualitative. The most commonly applied forecasting techniques can be divided into the following broad categories:

- Qualitative analyses
- Trend analysis and projection
- Exponential smoothing
- Econometric methods

The best forecast methodology for a particular task depends on the nature of the forecasting problem. When making a choice among forecast methodologies, a number of important factors must be considered. It is always worth considering the distance into the future that one must forecast, the lead time available for making decisions, the level of accuracy required, the quality of data available for analysis, the stochastic or deterministic nature of forecast relations, and the cost and benefits associated with the forecasting problem.

Trend analysis, market experiments, consumer surveys, and the leading indicator approach to forecasting are well suited for short-term projections. Forecasting with complex econometric models and systems of simultaneous equations have proven somewhat more useful for long-run forecasting. Typically, the greater the level of sophistication, the higher the cost. If the required level of accuracy is low, less sophisticated methods can provide adequate results at minimal cost.

QUALITATIVE ANALYSIS

qualitative analysis
An intuitive judgmental approach to forecasting based on opinion

Qualitative analysis, an intuitive judgmental approach to forecasting, can be useful if it allows for the systematic collection and organization of data derived from unbiased, informed opinion. However, qualitative methods can produce biased results when specific individuals dominate the forecasting process through reputation, force of personality, or strategic position within the organization.

Expert Opinion

personal insight
Forecast method based on personal or organizational experience

panel consensus
Forecast method based on the informed opinion of several individuals

The most basic form of qualitative analysis forecasting is **personal insight**, in which an informed individual uses personal or company experience as a basis for developing future expectations. Although this approach is subjective, the reasoned judgment of informed individuals often provides valuable insight. When the informed opinion of several individuals is relied on, the approach is called forecasting through **panel consensus**. The panel consensus method assumes that several experts can arrive at forecasts that are superior to those that individuals generate. Direct interaction among experts can help ensure that resulting forecasts embody all available objective and subjective information.

delphi method
Method that uses forecasts derived from an independent analysis of expert opinion

Although the panel consensus method often results in forecasts that embody the collective wisdom of consulted experts, it can be unfavorably affected by the forceful personality of one or a few key individuals. A related approach, the **delphi method**, has been developed to counter this disadvantage. In the delphi method, members of a panel of experts individually receive a series of questions relating to the underlying forecasting problem. Responses are analyzed by an independent party, who then tries to elicit a consensus opinion by providing feedback to panel members in a manner that prevents direct identification of individual positions. This method helps limit the steamroller or bandwagon problems of the basic panel consensus approach.

Survey Techniques

survey techniques
Interview or mailed questionnaire approach to forecasting

Survey techniques that skillfully use interviews or mailed questionnaires are an important forecasting tool, especially for short-term projection. Designing surveys that provide unbiased and reliable information is a challenging task. When properly carried out, however, survey research can provide managers with valuable information that would otherwise be unobtainable.

Surveys generally use interviews or mailed questionnaires that ask firms, government agencies, and individuals about their future plans. Businesses plan and budget virtually all their expenditures in advance of actual purchase or production decisions. Surveys asking about capital budgets, sales budgets, and operating budgets can thus provide useful forecast information. Government departments that prepare formal budgets also provide a wealth of information to the forecaster. Finally, because individual consumers routinely plan expenditures for such major items as automobiles, furniture, housing, vacations, and education, surveys of consumer intentions often accurately predict future spending on consumer goods.

Survey information may be all that is available in certain forecasting situations, as, for example, when a firm is attempting to project new product demand. Although surveys sometimes serve as an alternative to quantitative forecasting techniques, they frequently supplement rather than replace quantitative analysis. Their value stems from two influences. First, a nonquantifiable psychological element is inherent in most economic behavior; surveys and other qualitative methods are especially well suited to picking up this phenomenon. Second, quantitative models generally assume stable consumer tastes. If tastes are actually changing, survey data can suggest the nature and direction of such changes.

TREND ANALYSIS AND PROJECTION

trend analysis
Forecasting the future path of economic variables based on historical patterns

Trend analysis is based on the premise that economic performance follows an established pattern and that historical data can be used to predict future business activity. Trend analysis techniques involve characterizing the historical pattern of an economic variable and then projecting its future path based on past experience.

Trends in Economic Data

Forecasting by trend projection is predicated on the assumption that historical relationships will continue into the future. All such methods use time-series data. Weekly, monthly, or annual series of data on sales and costs, personal income, population, labor force participation rates, and GDP are all examples of economic time series.

secular trend
Long-run pattern of increase or decrease

cyclical fluctuation
Rhythmic fluctuation in an economic series due to expansion or contraction in the overall economy

seasonality
Rhythmic annual patterns in sales or profits

irregular or random influences
Unpredictable shocks to the economic system

All time series, regardless of the nature of the economic variable involved, can be described in terms of a few important underlying characteristics. A **secular trend** is the long-run pattern of increase or decrease in a series of economic data. **Cyclical fluctuation** describes the rhythmic variation in economic series that is due to a pattern of expansion or contraction in the overall economy. Seasonal variation, or **seasonality**, is a rhythmic annual pattern in sales or profits caused by weather, habit, or social custom. **Irregular or random influences** are unpredictable shocks to the economic system and the pace of economic activity caused by wars, strikes, natural catastrophes, and so on.

These four patterns are illustrated in Figure 6.1. Figure 6.1(a) shows secular and cyclical trends in sales of women's clothing. Figure 6.1(b) shows a seasonal pattern superimposed over the long-run trend (which, in this case, is a composite of the secular and cyclical trends), and random fluctuations around the seasonal curve.

Time-series analysis can be as simple as projecting or extrapolating the unadjusted trend. When one applies either simple graphic analysis or least squares regression techniques, historical data can be used to determine the average increase or decrease in the series during each period and then projected into the future. Time-series analysis can also be more sophisticated, allowing examination of seasonal and cyclical patterns in addition to the basic trend.

Because extrapolation techniques assume that a variable will follow an established path, the problem is to determine the appropriate trend curve. In theory, one could fit any mathematical function to historical data and extrapolate to estimate future values. In practice, linear, simple power, or exponential curves are typically used for economic forecasting.

Linear Trend Analysis

linear trend analysis
Assumes constant *unit* change over time

Linear trend analysis assumes a constant period-by-period *unit* change in an important economic variable over time. Such a trend is illustrated in Figure 6.2, which displays the 17 years of actual sales data for Microsoft Corp. given in Table 6.1, along with a curve representing a linear relation between sales and time over the 1984–2001 period.

A linear relation between firm sales and time, such as that illustrated in Figure 6.2, can be written as

FIGURE 6.1

Time-Series Characteristics: (A) Secular Trend and Cyclical Variation in Women's Clothing Sales; (B) Seasonal Pattern and Random Fluctuations

(a) The cyclical pattern in sales varies significantly from the normal secular trend. (b) Seasonal patterns, random fluctuations, and other influences cause deviations around the cyclical patterns of sales.

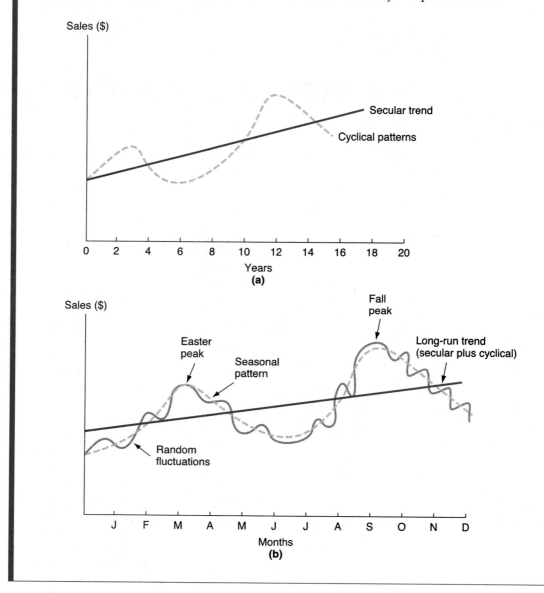

(6.1)
$$S_t = a + b \times t$$

The coefficients of this equation can be estimated by using Microsoft sales data for the 1984–2001 period and the least squares regression method as follows (*t* statistics in parentheses):

(6.2)
$$S_t = -\$6{,}440.8 + \$1{,}407.3t \qquad \bar{R}^2 = 79.7\%$$
$$(-3.47) \qquad (8.23)$$

Although a linear trend projection for firm sales is relatively naive, an important trend element is obvious in Microsoft sales data. Using the linear trend equation estimated over the 1984–2001

FIGURE 6.2

Microsoft Corp. Sales Revenue, 1984–2001

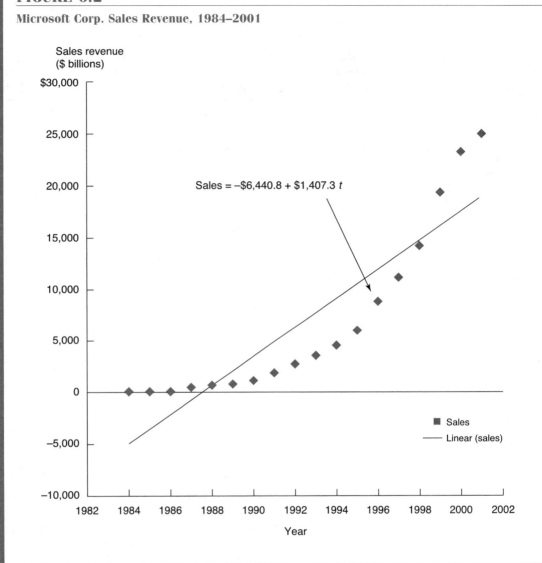

period, it is possible to forecast firm sales for future periods. To do so, it is important to realize that in this model, $t = 1$ for 1984, $t = 2$ for 1985, and so on. This means that $t = 0$ in the 1983 base period. To forecast sales in any future period, simply subtract 1983 from the year in question to determine a relevant value for t.

For example, a sales forecast for the year 2005 using Equation 6.2 is

$$
\begin{aligned}
t &= 2005 - 1983 = 22 \\
S_{2005} &= -\$6,440.8 + \$1,407.3(22) \\
&= \$24,520 \text{ million}
\end{aligned}
$$

Similarly, a sales forecast for Microsoft in the year 2010 is

$$
\begin{aligned}
t &= 2010 - 1983 = 27 \\
S_{2008} &= -\$6,440.8 + \$1,407.3(27) \\
&= \$31,556 \text{ million}
\end{aligned}
$$

TABLE 6.1

Sales Revenue for Microsoft Corp., 1984–2001

Year	Sales Revenue ($ millions)	Natural Logarithm of Sales Revenue (base *e*)	Common Logarithm of Sales Revenue (base 10)	Time Period	Fitted Sales (linear)
1984	99.5	4.600	1.998	1	−5,033.4
1985	139.5	4.938	2.145	2	−3,626.1
1986	202.1	5.309	2.306	3	−2,218.7
1987	345.9	5.846	2.539	4	−811.4
1988	590.8	6.381	2.771	5	595.9
1989	803.5	6.689	2.905	6	2,003.3
1990	1,183.4	7.076	3.073	7	3,410.6
1991	1,843.4	7.519	3.266	8	4,818.0
1992	2,758.7	7.923	3.441	9	6,225.3
1993	3,753.0	8.230	3.574	10	7,632.7
1994	4,649.0	8.444	3.667	11	9,040.0
1995	5,937.0	8.689	3.774	12	10,447.3
1996	8,671.0	9.068	3.938	13	11,854.7
1997	11,358.0	9.338	4.055	14	13,262.0
1998	14,484.0	9.581	4.161	15	14,669.4
1999	19,747.0	9.891	4.296	16	16,076.7
2000	22,956.0	10.041	4.361	17	17,484.1
2001	25,200.0	10.135	4.401	18	18,891.4

Note: 2001 data are preliminary.

Source: Company annual reports (various years).

Note that these sales projections are based on a linear trend line, which implies that sales increase by a constant dollar amount each year. In this example, Microsoft sales are projected to grow by $1,407.3 million per year. However, there are important reasons for believing that the true trend for Microsoft sales is nonlinear and that the forecasts generated by this constant change model will be relatively poor estimates of actual values. To see why a linear trend relation may be inaccurate, consider the relation between actual sales data and the linear trend shown in Figure 6.2. Remember that the least squares regression line minimizes the sum of squared residuals between actual and fitted values over the sample data. As is typical, actual data points lie above and below the fitted regression line. Note, however, that the pattern of differences between actual and fitted values varies dramatically over the sample period. Differences between actual and fitted values are generally positive in both early (1984–1987) and later (1996–2001) periods, whereas they are generally negative in the intervening 1988-1995 period. These differences suggest that the slope of the sales/time relation may not be constant but rather may be generally increasing over the 1984–2001 period. Under these circumstances, it may be more appropriate to assume that sales are changing at a constant annual *rate* rather than a constant annual amount.

Growth Trend Analysis

growth trend analysis
Assumes constant
percentage change over
time

Growth trend analysis assumes a constant period-by-period *percentage* change in an important economic variable over time. Such a forecast model has the potential to better capture the increasing annual sales pattern described by the 1984–2001 Microsoft sales data. This model is appropriate for forecasting when sales appear to change over time by a constant proportional amount rather than by the constant absolute amount assumption implicit in a simple linear model. The constant annual rate of growth model, assuming *annual* compounding, is described as follows:

(6.3)
$$\text{Sales in } t \text{ Years} = \text{Current Sales} \times (1 + \text{Growth Rate})^t$$
$$S_t = S_0(1 + g)^t$$

In words, Equation 6.3 means that sales in *t* years in the future are equal to current-period sales, S_0, compounded at a constant annual growth rate, *g*, for a period of *t* years. Use of the constant annual rate of growth model involves determining the average historical rate of growth in a variable such as sales and then using that rate of growth in a forecast equation such as Equation 6.3 to project future values. This approach is identical to the compounding value model used in finance.

Just as it is possible to estimate the constant rate of unit change in an economic time series by fitting historical data to a linear regression model of the form $Y = a + bt$, a constant annual rate of growth can be estimated using that same technique. In this case, the relevant growth rate is estimated using a linear regression model that is fit to a logarithmic transformation of the historical data. Taking common logarithms (to the base 10) of both sides of Equation 6.3 results in the expression

(6.4)
$$\log S_t = \log S_0 + \log (1 + g) \times t$$

Notice that Equation 6.4 is an expression of the form

$$Y_t = a + bt$$

where $Y_t = \log S_t$, $a = \log S_0$, $b = \log (1 + g)$, and *t* is an independent, or *X* variable. The coefficients $\log S_0$ and $\log (1 + g)$ can be estimated using the least squares regression technique.

Applying this technique to the Microsoft sales data for the 1984–2001 period results in the linear constant annual rate of growth regression model (*t* statistics in parentheses):

(6.5)
$$\log S_t = \underset{(38.39)}{1.984} + \underset{(30.57)}{0.146t} \qquad \bar{R}^2 = 98.2\%$$

Sales revenue forecasts (in millions of dollars) can be determined by transforming this estimated equation back to its original form:

(6.6)
$$S_t = (\text{Antilog } 1.984) \times (\text{Antilog } 0.146)^t$$

or

$$S_t = \$96.38(1.400)^t$$

In this model, \$96.38 million is the adjusted level of sales for $t = 0$, or 1983, because the first year of data used in the regression estimation, $t = 1$, was 1984. The number 1.400 equals 1 plus the average rate of growth using annual compounding, meaning that Microsoft sales increased at a 40.0 percent annual rate from 1984–2001.

To forecast sales in any future year by using this model, subtract 1983 from the year being forecast to determine *t*. Thus, a constant annual rate of growth model forecast for sales in 2005 is

$$t = 2005 - 1983 = 22$$
$$S_{2003} = \$96.38(1.400^{22})$$
$$= \$158,053 \text{ million}$$

Similarly, a constant growth model forecast of Microsoft sales in the year 2010 is

$$t = 2010 - 1983 = 27$$
$$S_{2008} = \$96.38(1.400^{27})$$
$$= \$850,049 \text{ million}$$

Another frequently used form of the constant growth model is based on an underlying assumption of *continuous*, as opposed to annual, compounding. The continuous growth model is expressed by the exponential equation:

(6.7)
$$Y_t = Y_0 e^{gt}$$

Taking the natural logarithm (to the base *e*) of Equation 6.7 gives:

$$\ln Y_t = \ln Y_0 + gt$$

Under an exponential rate of growth assumption, the regression model estimate of the slope coefficient, *g*, is a direct estimate of the continuous rate of growth. For example, a continuous growth model estimate for Microsoft sales is (*t* statistics in parentheses):

(6.8)
$$\ln S_t = 4.568 + 0.336_t \qquad \bar{R}^2 = 98.2\%$$
$$\quad\;\; (38.39) \;\; (30.57)$$

In this equation, the coefficient 0.336 (= 33.6 percent) is a direct estimate of the continuous compounding growth rate for Microsoft sales. Notice that *t* statistics for the intercept and slope coefficients are identical to those derived for the constant annual rate of growth regression model (Equation 6.5).

Again, sales revenue forecasts (in millions of dollars) can be derived by transforming this estimated equation back to its original form:

(6.9)
$$S_t = (\text{Exponentiate } 4.568) \times (\text{Exponentiate } 0.336)^t$$

or

$$S_t = \$96.38(1.400)^t$$

Notice that Equations 6.6 and 6.9 are identical. Subject to rounding error, identical 2005 and 2010 sales forecasts result by using either the constant annual rate of growth or the continuous compounding assumption. Either method can be relied on with an equal degree of confidence as a useful basis for a constant growth model approach to forecasting.

Linear and Growth Trend Comparison

The importance of selecting the correct structural form for a trending model can be demonstrated by comparing the sales projections that result from the two basic approaches that have been considered. Recall that with the constant change model, sales were projected to be $24.5 billion in 2005 and $31.6 billion in 2010. Compare these sales forecasts with projections of $158.1 billion in 2005 and $850.0 billion in 2010 for the constant growth rate model. Notice that the difference in the near-term forecasts (2005) is smaller than the difference between longer-term (2010) projections. This shows that if an economic time series is growing at a constant rate rather than increasing by a constant dollar amount, forecasts based on a linear trend model will tend to be less accurate the further one forecasts into the future.

The pattern of future sales for any company, and therefore the reasonableness of a linear trend projection using either a constant change model or a constant growth model, depends

The Dire Prediction Business

From time to time, the business and popular press are filled with dire predictions of pending economic doom or political collapse. The reason is quite simple: Dire predictions sell newspapers and magazines, and fill conference halls or cruise ships with seminar participants.

Economists know that most people are risk averse. People tend to worry more about the potential loss of a fixed sum, say $100,000, than they would celebrate a similar gain. This is especially true of successful retirees, who want to keep the wealth they have accumulated rather than risk an irretrievable loss. In an economic environment with rapid technical advance, well-to-do elderly become easy marks for doomsayers with dire predictions. This is despite the fact that predictions of economic collapse or political disintegration seldom prove accurate.

For example, on August 13, 1979, the Dow Jones Industrial Average (DJIA) stood at 875.30, and *Business Week* magazine ran a haunting cover story titled "The Death of Equities." To drive home the risk of imminent stock market collapse, the cover illustrated crashed paper airplanes fashioned from stock certificates. Who could

doubt its logic? During 1979, the DJIA languished between 800 and 900, levels first reached more than a decade earlier. Rising inflation, high interest rates, and a stagnant economy had taken its toll. Why not extrapolate that sorry trend and suggest that stocks would continue to fare poorly?

The answer is simple. In 1979, after more than a decade of stagnant stock prices in the face of rising business revenues and growing profits, stocks were poised for a sharp rebound, and they did. If investors had listened to the doomsayers, they would have missed the biggest bull market in history.

The U.S. economy and stock market have displayed enormous strength and resilience for more than 100 years. Before buying into a "doom and gloom" scenario, check the record.

See: Joel Baglole, "Canada's GDP Tops Forecasts As Country Dodges a Recession," *The Wall Street Journal Online*, March 1, 2002 (http://online.wsj.com).

upon firm and industry-specific considerations. Whether a firm is able to maintain a rapid pace of growth depends on a host of factors both within and beyond its own control. Successfully managing rapid growth over extended periods is extraordinarily difficult and is rarely observed in practice. To this point, Microsoft has defied conventional wisdom by maintaining rapid growth for almost 20 years. At some point, however, its massive size will limit future growth opportunities, and Microsoft's rate of growth will slow down dramatically. When applying trend projection methods, it is important to establish the degree of similarity in growth opportunities between the historical and forecast periods. Prudence also suggests that the forecast horizon be limited to a relatively short time frame (5 or 10 years, maximum).

Although trend projections provide useful results for some forecasting purposes, shortcomings can limit their usefulness. An obvious problem is that the accuracy of trend projections depends upon a continuation of historical patterns for sales, costs, and profits. Serious forecasting errors resulted when this technique was employed in the periods just prior to unanticipated economic downturns in 1982, 1991 and 2000. Trend projections cannot predict cyclical turning points and offer no help in describing *why* a particular series moves as it does. More sophisticated time-series forecasting methods, such as the Box-Jenkins technique, provide the means for analyzing trend, seasonal, cyclical, and random influences that often shape economic time series in complex business environments. For many forecasting applications, they offer a big improvement over simple extrapolation procedures.

BUSINESS CYCLE

Many important economic time series are regularly influenced by cyclical and seasonal variations. It is worth considering these influences further, because the treatment of cyclical and seasonal variations plays an important role in economic forecasting.

What Is the Business Cycle?

The profit and sales performance of all companies depends to a greater or lesser extent on the vigor of the overall economy. As shown in Figure 6.3, business activity in the United States expands at a rate of roughly 7.5 percent per year when measured in terms of GDP. With recent inflation averaging 4.5 percent per year, business activity has expanded at a rate of roughly 3 percent per year when measured in terms of inflation-adjusted, or real, dollars. During robust expansions, the pace of growth in real GDP can increase to an annual rate of 4 percent to 5 percent or more for brief periods. During especially severe economic downturns, real GDP can actually decline for an extended period. In the case of firms that use significant financial and operating leverage, a difference of a few percentage points in the pace of overall economic activity can make the difference between vigorous expansion and gut-wrenching contraction.

business cycle
Rhythmic pattern of contraction and expansion in the overall economy

One of the most important economy-wide considerations for managers is the **business cycle**, or rhythmic pattern of contraction and expansion observed in the overall economy. Table 6.2 shows the pattern of business cycle expansion and contraction that has been experienced in the United States. During the post–World War II period, between October 1945 and March 1991, there have been 9 complete business cycles. The average duration of each cyclical contraction is

FIGURE 6.3

Gross Domestic Product, 1959–Present
GDP has risen sharply.

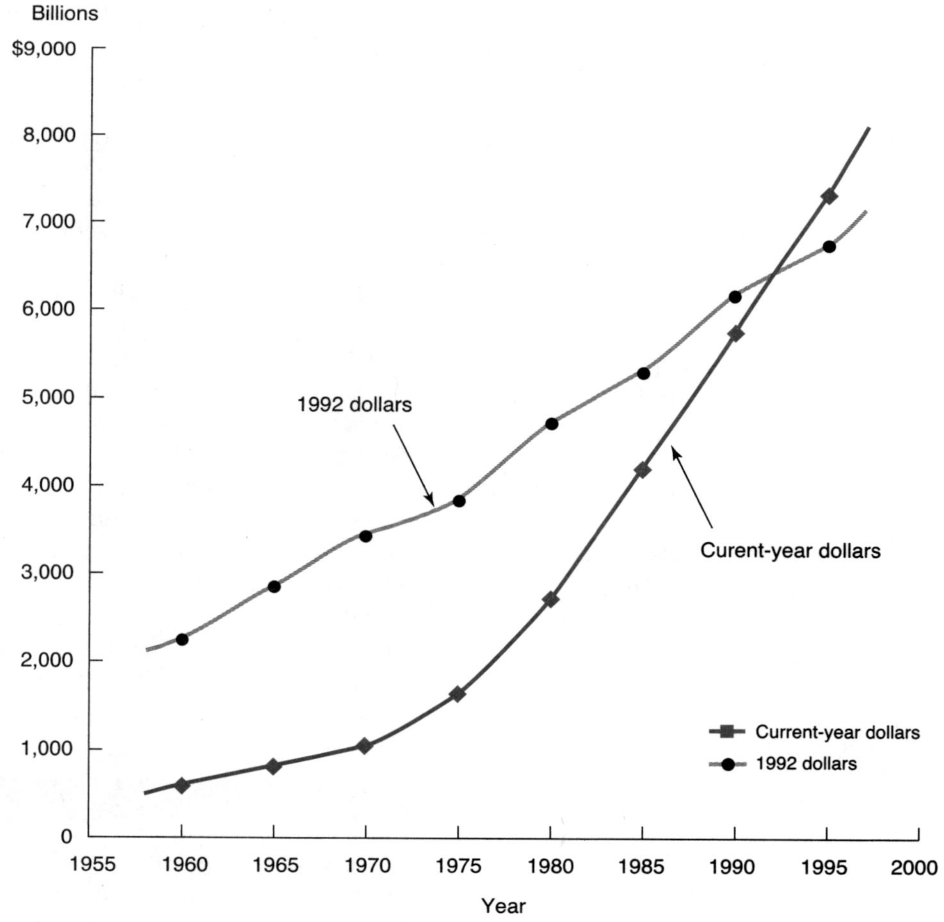

TABLE 6.2

Business Cycle Expansions and Contractions

Figures printed in **bold italic** are the wartime expansions (Civil War, World Wars I and II, Korean War, and Vietnam War); the postwar contractions; and the full cycles that include the wartime expansions.

Business Cycle Reference Dates		Duration in Months			
Trough	Peak	Contraction	Expansion	Cycle	
(Quarterly dates are in parentheses.)		(trough from previous peak)	(trough to peak)	(trough from previous trough)	(peak from previous peak)
December 1854 (IV)	June 1857 (II)	—	30	—	—
December 1858 (IV)	October 1860 (III)	18	22	48	40
June 1861 (III)	April 1865 (I)	8	*46*	30	*54*
December 1867 (I)	June 1869 (II)	*32*	18	*78*	50
December 1870 (IV)	October 1873 (III)	18	34	36	52
March 1879 (I)	March 1882 (I)	65	36	99	101
May 1885 (II)	March 1887 (II)	38	22	74	60
April 1888 (I)	July 1890 (III)	13	27	35	40
May 1891 (II)	January 1893 (I)	10	20	37	30
June 1894 (II)	December 1895 (IV)	17	18	37	35
June 1897 (II)	June 1899 (III)	18	24	36	42
December 1900 (IV)	September 1902 (IV)	18	21	42	39
August 1904 (III)	May 1907 (II)	23	33	44	56
June 1908 (II)	January 1910 (I)	13	19	46	32
January 1912 (IV)	January 1913 (I)	24	12	43	36
December 1914 (IV)	August 1918 (III)	23	*44*	35	*67*
March 1919 (I)	January 1920 (I)	*7*	10	*51*	17
July 1921 (III)	May 1923 (II)	18	22	28	40
July 1924 (III)	October 1926 (III)	14	27	36	41
November 1927 (IV)	August 1929 (III)	13	21	40	34
March 1933 (I)	May 1937 (II)	43	50	64	93
June 1938 (II)	February 1945 (I)	13	*80*	63	*93*
October 1945 (IV)	November 1948 (IV)	*8*	37	*88*	45
October 1949 (IV)	July 1953 (II)	11	*45*	48	*56*
May 1954 (II)	August 1957 (III)	*10*	39	*55*	49
April 1958 (II)	April 1960 (II)	8	24	47	32
February 1961 (I)	December 1969 (IV)	10	*106*	34	*116*
November 1970 (IV)	November 1973 (IV)	*11*	36	*117*	47
March 1975 (I)	January 1980 (I)	16	58	52	74
July 1980 (III)	July 1981 (III)	6	12	64	18
November 1982 (IV)	July 1990 (III)	16	92	28	108
March 1991 (I)	March 2001 (I)	8	120	100	128
Average all cycles:					
1854–1991 (31 cycles)		18	35	53	53*
1854–1919 (16 cycles)		22	27	48	49**
1919–1945 (6 cycles)		18	35	53	53
1945–1991 (9 cycles)		11	50	61	61
Average, peacetime cycles:					
1854–1991 (26 cycles)		19	29	48	48***
1854–1919 (14 cycles)		22	24	46	47****
1919–1945 (5 cycles)		20	26	46	45
1945–1991 (7 cycles)		11	43	53	53

* 30 cycles; ** 15 cycles; ***25 cycles; ****13 cycles.

Source: NBER at http://www.nber.org/cycles.html.

11 months, when duration is measured from the previous cyclical peak to the low point or trough of the subsequent business contraction. The average duration of each cyclical expansion is 50 months, as measured by the amount of time from the previous cyclical trough to the peak of the following business expansion. Clearly, periods of economic expansion predominate, which indicates a healthy and growing economy.

On any given business day, a wide variety of news reports, press releases, and analyst comments can be found concerning the current state and future direction of the overall economy. The reason for intense interest is obvious. Whether the current economy is in a state of boom, moderate expansion, moderate contraction, or sharp decline, there is sure to be widespread disagreement among analysts concerning current or future business prospects. This reflects the fact that, despite intense interest and widespread news coverage, the causes of economic contractions and expansions remain something of a mystery. *Why* the economy shifts from boom to bust and how such shifts might be predicted and controlled are still largely beyond our knowledge. Hopefully, the ever-increasing quality of economic data and the amazing power of computer hardware and software will unlock further mysteries of the business cycle during the next few years. In the meantime, changes in the pattern and pace of economic activity remain a matter for intense debate and conjecture.

Economic Indicators

Whereas cyclical patterns in most economic time series are erratic and make simple projection a hazardous short-term forecasting technique, a relatively consistent relation often exists among various economic variables over time. Even though many series of economic data do not exhibit a consistent pattern over time, it is often possible to find a high degree of correlation *across* these series. Should the forecaster have the good fortune to discover an economic series that leads the one being forecast, the leading series can be used as a barometer for forecasting short-term change, just as a meteorologist uses changes in a mercury barometer to forecast changes in the weather.

economic indicators
Data that describe projected, current, or past economic activity

composite index
Weighted average of leading, coincident, or lagging economic indicators

The Conference Board, a private research group, provides extensive data on a wide variety of **economic indicators** or data series that successfully describe the pattern of projected, current, or past economic activity. Table 6.3 lists 10 leading, four roughly coincident, and seven lagging economic indicators of business cycle peaks that are broadly relied upon in business cycle forecasting. Figure 6.4 shows the pattern displayed by composite indexes of these leading, coincident, and lagging indicators throughout the 1980s and 1990s. A **composite index** is a weighted average of leading, coincident, or lagging economic indicators. Keep in mind that the weights (standardization factors) used in the construction of these composite indexes will vary over time. Combining individual data into a composite index creates a forecasting series with less random fluctuation, or noise. These composite series are smoother than the underlying individual data series and less frequently produce false signals of change in economic conditions. Notice how the composite index of leading indicators consistently turns down just prior to the start of each recessionary period. Similarly, notice how this data series bottoms out and then starts to rise just prior to the start of each subsequent economic expansion. Just as leading indicators seem to earn that description based on their performance, coincident and lagging indicators perform as expected over this period.

The basis for some of these leads and lags is obvious. For example, building permits precede housing starts, and orders for plant and equipment lead production in durable goods industries. Each of these indicators directly reflects plans or commitments for the activity that follows. Other barometers are not directly related to the economic variables they forecast. An index of common stock prices is a good leading indicator of general business activity. Although the causal linkage may not be readily apparent, stock prices reflect aggregate profit expectations by investors and thus give a consensus view of the likely course of future business conditions. Thus, at any point in time, stock prices both reflect and anticipate changes in

TABLE 6.3

Leading, Coincident, and Lagging Economic Indicators

The Conference Board's Index of Leading Economic Indicators (LEI) is designed to signal peaks and troughs in the business cycle. The LEI is derived from 10 leading indicators, four coincident indicators, and seven lagging indicators. The LEI is a useful barometer of economic activity over 3 to 6 months.

Ten Leading Indicators	Average workweek of production workers in manufacturing
	Average initial weekly claims for state unemployment insurance
	New orders for consumer goods and materials, adjusted for inflation
	Vendor performance (companies receiving slower deliveries from suppliers)
	New orders for nonmilitary capital goods, adjusted for inflation
	New building permits issued
	Index of stock prices
	Money supply: M2 adjusted for inflation
	Spread between rates on 10-year Treasury bonds and federal funds
	Index of consumer expectations
Four Coincident Indicators	Manufacturing and trade sales
	Employees on nonagricultural payrolls
	Industrial production
	Personal income minus transfer payments
Seven Lagging Indicators	Average duration of unemployment
	Inventories to sales ratio, manufacturing, and trade
	Change in labor cost per unit of output, manufacturing
	Average prime rate
	Commercial and industrial loans
	Consumer installment credit to personal income ratio
	Change in consumer price index for services

Source: The Conference Board Web site at http://www.conference-board.org/economics/indicators/leading.htm.

aggregate economic conditions. All of this makes macroeconomic forecasting particularly nettlesome for investors.

Economic Recessions

economic recession
A decline in economic activity that lasts more than a few months

An **economic recession** is defined by the National Bureau of Economic Research (NBER), a private nonprofit research organization, as a significant decline in activity spread across the economy that lasts more than a few months. Recessions are visible in terms of falling industrial production, declining real income, and shrinking wholesale-retail trade. Recessions are also marked by rising unemployment. Although many economic recessions consist of two or more quarters of declining real GDP, it is most accurate to describe recession as a period of *diminishing* economic activity rather than a period of *diminished* economic activity. A recession begins just after the economy reaches a peak of output and employment and ends as the economy reaches its trough. The period between a month of peak economic activity and the subsequent economic low point defines the length of a recession. During recessions, economic growth is falling or the economy is actually contracting. As shown in Figure 6.4, recessions in the United States are rare and tend to be brief.

economic expansion
A period of rising economic activity

The period following recession is called **economic expansion**. In many cases, economic activity is below normal during both recessions and through the early part of the subsequent

FIGURE 6.4

Composite Indexes of 10 Leading, Four Coincident, and Seven Lagging Indicators (1987 + 100)

Shaded regions indicate an economic recession.

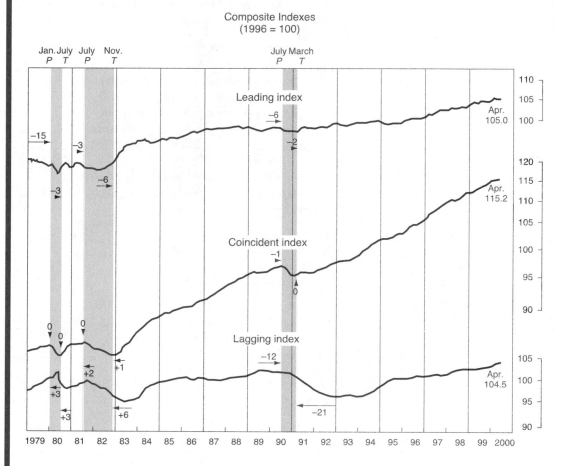

Note: *P* (peak) indicated the end of general business expansion and the beginning of recession; *T* (trough) indicates the end of general business recession and the beginning of expansion (as designated by the NBER). Thus, shaded areas represent recessions. Arrows indicate leads (–) and lags (+) in months from business cycle turning dates.

Source: The Conference Board Web site at http://www.conference-board.org.

economic expansion. Some refer to periods of less than typical economic growth as slumps, but there is no official recognition or characterization of economic slumps. In any event, expansion is the normal state of the U.S. economy.

Because economic recessions are not confined to any one sector, NBER uses economy-wide measures to assess economic activity. In principle, the best such measure is GDP, but GDP is measured only with quarterly frequency. GDP data is also notoriously prone to measurement error, and can be revised as much as a decade after its initial report. As a result, NBER maintains its own monthly chronology of economic activity to guide its description of economic activity. The broadest monthly indicator of economic activity is overall employment, and this is watched closely by the NBER as an indicator of economic vigor.

Recessions can be caused by any serious unanticipated economic or political event. For example, recessionary fears increased considerably following the tragic events of September 11, 2001. The terrorist attacks on New York City and Washington, DC, took an enormous human and economic toll. The U.S. economy is roughly 28 percent of global GDP. New York City alone contributes more than 4 percent to U.S. personal income and accounts for almost 3 percent of U.S. nonfarm employment. This awful event was a serious shock for the U.S. and global economy.

In trying to assess economic consequences from the September 11, 2001, tragedies, it is important to understand economic conditions at the time of the crisis and how the economy has responded to adverse shocks in the past. Prior to the terrorist attacks, highly stimulative monetary policy in the United States pointed to recovery. Various leading economic indicators were starting to improve, but remained below the highest values reached during January 2000. The Coincident Index of The Conference Board's Business Cycle Indicators clearly reflected tensions present in the U.S. economy when the tragedy took place. At that time, declines in U.S. industrial production and sales were almost exactly offset by rising personal income and employment. Outside the United States, only Australia displayed continuing strength in economic growth. Five important global economies—Japan, South Korea, France, Germany, and the United Kingdom—all showed economic weakness, thus placing the U.S. economy in a precarious position at a time of great national sorrow.

Table 6.4 highlights several unanticipated economic and political events that have rocked the United States since 1960. These 15 events had the potential to adversely impact the U.S. economy, but they occurred during times of varying economic prosperity. These 15 events also differed in terms of political implications. For example, in the attempted assassination of President Ronald Reagan (March 1981) and the bombing of the Alfred P. Murrah Federal Building in Oklahoma City (April 1995), those responsible were quickly apprehended, and no subsequent political events followed. The Iraqi invasion of Kuwait (August 1990), on the other hand, precipitated the Gulf War.

Notice how underlying economic conditions at the time of each crisis were important to their eventual economic impact. Although the tragic events of September 11, 2001, are unprecedented,

TABLE 6.4

Selected Critical Economic and Political Events (1960–present)

Event	Date	Economic Growth
Cuban Missile Crisis	Oct. 1, 1962	Decelerating
President John F. Kennedy assassination	Nov. 11, 1963	Decelerating
Reverend Martin Luther King, Jr., assassination	Apr. 4, 1968	Accelerating
Robert F. Kennedy assassination	June 5, 1968	Accelerating
Israeli athletes killed at Munich Olympics	Sept. 5, 1972	Accelerating
OPEC oil embargo	Oct. 25, 1973	Accelerating (followed by recession Nov. 1973)
President Ronald Reagan assassination attempt	Mar. 30, 1981	Accelerating (sandwiched between recessions)
U.S. Marine barracks bombing in Lebanon	Oct. 23, 1983	Accelerating
U.S. stock market crash	Oct. 27, 1987	Accelerating
Iraqi invasion of Kuwait	Aug. 2, 1990	Decelerating (beginning of recession July 1990)
Hurricane Andrew	Aug. 16, 1992	Accelerating
World Trade Center bombing	Feb. 26, 1993	Accelerating
Oklahoma City bombing	Apr. 19, 1995	Decelerating
U.S. Embassy bombings in Africa	Aug. 7, 1998	Accelerating
Terrorist attack on WTC and Pentagon	Sept. 11, 2001	Decelerating

Source: The Conference Board, September 2001.

it is worth noting that economic conditions on September 11, 2001, were similar to those in existence at the time of the Oklahoma City bombing (April 1995) and the Iraqi invasion of Kuwait (August 1990). In each instance, the U.S. economy was decelerating. In the case of the Oklahoma City bombing, the slowdown ended within 8 months. We now know that the U.S. economy had entered a recession (July 1990–March 1991) prior to the Iraqi invasion, so it is fair to say that neither of these comparable events caused the U.S. economy to dip into recession. Based on the information shown in Table 6.4, it is fair to say that economic trends underway before unprecedented economic and political events greatly influence their economic consequences. Obviously, the ultimate economic fallout from the terrorist attacks on New York City and Washington, DC, will not be known for quite some time.

Finally, experienced managers realize that significant time lags are often encountered between changes in the macroeconomy and their official recognition. Table 6.5 shows that NBER's Business Cycle Dating Committee usually waits 6 months to a year before officially recognizing that a major turning point in the economy has passed. This means that by the time a downturn in the economy is officially recognized, the subsequent upturn has already begun! Slow reporting, hard to decipher leads and lags in the overall economy, and unpredictable ties between economic and political events combine to make accurate macroeconomic forecasting one of the toughest challenges faced in managerial economics.

Common Sources of Forecast Information

The National Bureau of Economic Research, Inc. (NBER), founded in 1920, is a private, nonprofit, nonpartisan research organization dedicated to promoting a greater understanding of how the economy works. Their research is conducted by more than 600 university professors around the country, the leading scholars in their fields.

The NBER Web site (http://www.nber.org) is a treasure trove of forecast information and insight and offers a host of links to valuable data resources (see Figure 6.5). Consumer survey information included are the Consumer Expenditure Survey Extracts; Current Population Survey; Early Indicators of Later Work Levels, Disease, and Death; and vital statistics for births, deaths, marriage, and divorce. Links to macro data from government sources include Federal Reserve Economic Data (FRED); official business cycle dates; experimental coincident, leading, and recession indexes; and savings and investment information for 13 countries.

TABLE 6.5

Long Time Lags Are Experienced Before Turning Points in the Economy Are Documented

Official documentation of turning points in the economy is the responsibility of the Business Cycle Dating Committee of the National Bureau of Economic Research.

Recent announcement dates:

The March 2001 peak was announced November 26, 2001.
The March 1991 trough was announced December 22, 1992.
The July 1990 peak was announced April 25, 1991.
The November 1982 trough was announced July 8, 1983.
The July 1981 peak was announced January 6, 1982.
The July 1980 trough was announced July 8, 1981.
The January 1980 peak was announced June 3, 1980.

Source: National Bureau of Economic Research, September 2001 (http://www.nber.org/cycles.html).

FIGURE 6.5

The National Bureau of Economic Research Web Site
Is a Treasure Trove of Forecast Information

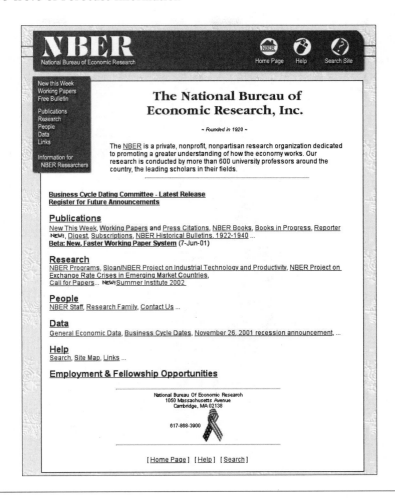

Industry data include the Manufacturing Industry Productivity Database, patent data, imports and exports by Standard Industrial Classification (SIC) category, and various IRS information.

Resources for Economists on the Internet (RFE) is another extremely valuable Web site maintained by the American Economic Association and professor Bill Goffe of the Department of Economics at the State University of New York (SUNY), Oswego campus (see Figure 6.6). The table of contents for RFE lists 1,265 resources in 74 sections and subsections of interest to academic and practicing economists, and those interested in economics. Almost all resources are also described in simple-to-understand language. RFE is a particularly good place to look for a broad array of business and economic forecasting resources on the Web. For example, under economic forecasting and consulting resources the reader will find the Conference Board's Leading Economic Indicators and various other nongovernmental data; economic commentary from Bank of America Economics and Financial Reports; macro, regional, and electrical forecasts from Foster Associates; microeconomic analysis from Glassman-Oliver Economic Consultants, Inc.; global financial market and foreign exchange analysis from *Wells Fargo Economic Reports*; and so on.

Information about economic trends is also found in leading business publications, like *The Wall Street Journal* and *Barron's*. As shown in Figure 6.7, *Barron's* survey of economic indicators

FIGURE 6.6

Resources for Economists on the Internet Is a Valuable Forecasting Resource

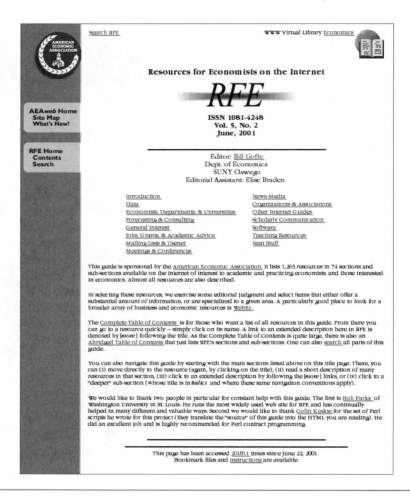

depicts the rate of change in the overall level of economic activity as indicated by GDP, durable and nondurable manufacturing, factory utilization, and other statistics. Also provided are specific data on the level of production in a wide range of basic industries such as autos, electric power, paper, petroleum, and steel. Data published weekly in *Barron's* include not only the level of production (what is made), but also distribution (what is sold), inventories (what is on hand), new orders received, unfilled orders, purchasing power, employment, and construction activity. *Forbes* magazine publishes its own biweekly index of economic activity using government data on consumer prices, manufacturer's new orders and inventories, industrial production, new housing starts, personal income, new unemployment claims, retail sales, and consumer installment credit. To measure these eight elements of the *Forbes Index*, 10 series of U.S. government data are monitored over a 14-month period.

Fortune and *Business Week* magazines also offer regular coverage of data on current and projected levels of economic activity. The quarterly *Fortune Forecast* of economic activity is based on a proprietary econometric model developed by the company's own staff economists. The forecast data and analysis published in these leading business periodicals provide managers with a useful starting point in the development of their own expectations.

FIGURE 6.7

Barron's *Publishes Timely Information on Economic Indicators*

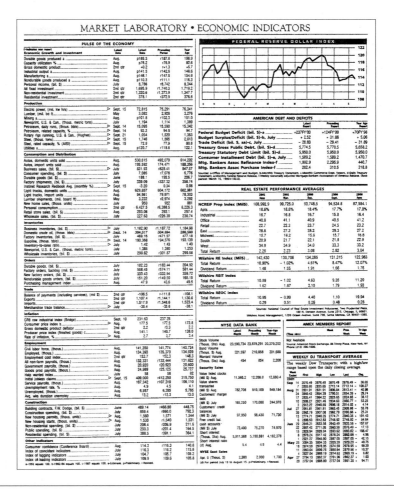

EXPONENTIAL SMOOTHING TECHNIQUES

A wide variety of statistical forecasting techniques can be used to predict unit sales growth, revenue, costs, and profit performance. These techniques range from quite simple to very sophisticated.

Exponential Smoothing Concept

exponential smoothing
Averaging method for forecasting time series of data

Exponential smoothing is a method for forecasting trends in unit sales, unit costs, wage expenses, and so on. The technique identifies historical patterns of trend or seasonality in the data and then extrapolates these patterns forward into the forecast period. Its accuracy depends on the degree to which established patterns of change are apparent and constant over time. The more regular the pattern of change in any given data series, the easier it is to forecast. Exponential smoothing (or "averaging") techniques are among the most widely used forecasting methods in business.

All leading methods of exponential smoothing involve the same essential process of data averaging. The data series to be forecast is assumed to be modeled by one, two, or three

The Stock Market and the Business Cycle

Many stock market prognosticators advise long-term investors to lighten up in advance of deteriorating economic conditions. Why buy and hold when the economic environment is worsening? Shouldn't smart investors hold cash until the economic experts know that recovery has begun? Then, business news reporters can issue the "all clear" sign, and savvy investors can reestablish long-term positions. If only life were that simple. Unfortunately, it's not.

Economic recessions are notoriously hard to identify. Typically, the National Bureau of Economic Research (NBER) is able to identify the start of an economic recession only months after the recession has begun. By the time economic recessions are identified, the economy is often already well on its way to recovery. In addition, the stock market usually starts to sag well in advance of economic downturns and rally in advance of economic recoveries. Near-term fluctuations in the stock market also give many false signals concerning economic conditions. As a famous economist once remarked, "The stock market has correctly forecast 10 of the last 6 recessions."

Look at how stock market prices change between important economic turning points and when such turns in the economy are officially recognized:

- The March 2001 peak (*S&P* 500 = 1160.33) announced November 26, 2001 (*S&P* 500 = 1157.42).
- The March 1991 trough (*S&P* 500 = 375.22) announced December 22, 1992 (*S&P* 500 = 440.31).
- The July 1990 peak (*S&P* 500 = 356.15) announced April 25, 1991 (*S&P* 500 = 379.25).
- The November 1982 trough (*S&P* 500 = 138.93) announced July 8, 1983 (*S&P* 500 = 167.08).
- The July 1981 peak (*S&P* 500 = 130.92) announced January 6, 1982 (*S&P* 500 = 119.18).
- The July 1980 trough (S&P 500 = 121.67) announced July 8, 1981 (*S&P* 500 = 132.24).
- The January 1980 peak (*S&P* 500 = 114.16) announced June 3, 1980 (*S&P* 500 = 110.51).

Upshot: Trading stocks based upon NBER announcements sure isn't a sophisticated way of market timing.

See: Michael Santoli, "Building a Better Bull," *Barron's Online*, April 8, 2002 (http://online.wsj.com).

essential components. Key components represent the level, trend, or seasonality of the data being forecast. The level of the time series to be forecast is the average about which it fluctuates. This level may be constant or slowly changing. Trend is any systematic change in the level of the time series of data. If a given forecast model includes a trend, then that trend is either projected as a straight line into the future or as a gradually diminishing amount that eventually dies out. The seasonality of a time series is a pattern of change tied to weather, custom, or tradition. Retail sales typically exhibit a strong seasonal trend over the course of the year. Many stores book 30 percent or more of annual sales during the busy Christmas selling season. Seasonal components can be additive, meaning that seasonal patterns remain constant over time, or multiplicative, meaning that seasonal patterns grow with the average level of the series.

Figure 6.8 shows nine common profiles of data that can be forecast by using popular exponential smoothing techniques. They range in complexity from the constant level of data shown in Figure 6.8(a) to the more complex dampened trend with a multiplicative seasonal influence shown in Figure 6.8(i). To ensure that the correct exponential smoothing technique is chosen, a method with sufficient flexibility to conform to the underlying data must be used. A good first step in the exponential smoothing process is to graph the data series to be forecast and then choose the exponential smoothing method that best resembles the data.

One-Parameter (Simple) Exponential Smoothing

one-parameter (simple) exponential smoothing
Method for forecasting slowly changing levels

In **one-parameter (simple) exponential smoothing**, the sole regular component is the level of the forecast data series. It is implicitly assumed that the data consist of irregular fluctuations around a constant or very slowly changing level. Simple exponential smoothing is appropriate for forecasting sales in mature markets with stable activity; it is inappropriate for forecasting in markets that are growing rapidly or are seasonal.

FIGURE 6.8

**Nine Common Trends in Economic Time Series Can Be
Forecast by Using Exponential Smoothing Methods**

Forecasting economic time series often involves a consideration of changes in the level, trend, and/or seasonality of the data.

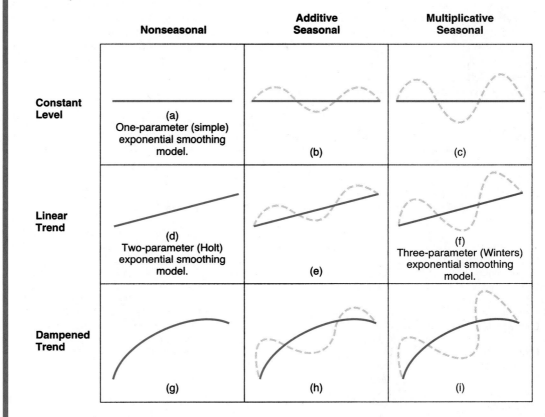

In the simple exponential smoothing model, each smoothed estimate of a given level is computed as a weighted average of the current observation and past data. Each weight decreases in an exponential pattern. The rate of decrease in the influence of past levels depends on the size of the smoothing parameter that controls the model's relative sensitivity to newer versus older data. The larger the value of the smoothing parameter, the more emphasis is placed on recent versus distant observations. However, if the smoothing parameter is very small, then a large number of data points receive nearly equal weights. In this case, the forecast model displays a long "memory" of past values.

Two-Parameter (Holt) Exponential Smoothing

**two-parameter
(Holt) exponential
smoothing**
Method for forecasting
stable growth

Simple exponential smoothing is not appropriate for forecasting data that exhibit extended trends. In **two-parameter (Holt) exponential smoothing**, the data are assumed to consist of fluctuations about a level that is changing with some constant or slowly drifting linear trend. Two-parameter exponential smoothing is often called the Holt method, after its originator C. C. Holt.[3] Two-parameter exponential smoothing is appropriate for forecasting sales in established markets with stable growth; it is inappropriate in either stable or rapidly growing markets.

---

3   C. C. Holt, *Forecasting Seasonals and Trends by Exponentially Weighted Moving Averages* (Pittsburgh, PA: Carnegie Institute of Technology, 1957).

How Good Is Your Forecasting Ability?

When making predictions of economic and social change, it is vitally important to be aware of broad trends in the overall economy. One valuable source of information on the U.S. economy is the *Statistical Abstract of the United States*. This annual publication of the U.S. Bureau of the Census offers a wealth of economic and demographic data upon which private and public sector analysts rely.

The following table offers insight concerning a number of important economic and social trends, and simple trend extrapolation estimates for the year 2010. Which forecasts will prove accurate? Which forecasts will be wide of the mark? How will these trends change over the *next* 20 years?

Category	1990	2000[1]	Percent Change	2010 (est.)	Category	1990	2000[1]	Percent Change	2010 (est.)
ACT score, comp.	20.6	21.0	1.9%	21.4	Interest rate, prime (%)	10.01	9.2	–7.8%	8.51
Births (000)	4,158	3,942	–5.2%	3,737	Marriages (000)	2,443	2,334	–4.5%	2,230
Cable TV subscribers (mil.)	50.0	66.5	33.0%	88.4	MLB attn. (000)	55,512	71,129	28.1%	91,139
Cash flow, corp. ($bil.)	$506	$943	86.4%	$1,757	MLB player salary ($000)	$598	$1,399	133.9%	$3,273
Cellular telephone subscribers (mil.)	5.3	86.0	1522.6%	1,395.5	Motion picture receipts ($mil.)	$39,982	$66,229	65.6%	$109,706
corporate deaths (000)	546.5	512.4	–6.2%	480.4	Murders	23,400	15,500	–33.8%	10,267
Corporate startups (000)	541.1	597.8	10.5%	660.4	NCAA basketball attn. (000)	28,741	28,032	–2.5%	27,340
Corporations (000)	3,717	4,710	26.7%	5,968	NCAA football attn. (000)	35,330	37,491	6.1%	39,784
Crude oil imports (mil. bbl)	2,151	3,187	48.2%	4,722	Partnerships (000)	1,554	1,759	13.2%	1,991
Crude oil production (mil. bbl)	2,685	2,147	–20.0%	1,717	Patents	99,200	163,100	64.4%	268,161
Daily newspaper circulation (mil.)	62.3	56.0	–10.1%	50.3	Pay, Annual average	$23,600	$33,300	41.1%	$46,987
Deaths (000)	2,148	2,338	8.8%	2,545	Phds granted	36,068	42,063	16.6%	49,054
Divorces (000)	1,182	1,150	–2.7%	1,119	Population, African American (mil.)	30.0	34.7	15.7%	40.0
DJLA	2,810.20	11,357.50	304.2%	45,902	Population, Total (mil.)	247.8	281.4	13.6%	319.6
Employment (mil.)	118.8	135.2	13.8%	153.9	Profit margin (mfg., %)	3.9	6.3	61.5%	10
Farms (000)	2,146	2,172	1.2%	2,198	Profit, ROE (mfg., %)	10.6	16.7	57.5%	26
Federal govt. receipts ($bil.)	$1,032	$1,956	89.5%	$3,707	Profits, corp. ($bil.)	$402	$849	111.2%	$1,793
Federal govt. spending ($bil.)	$1,253	$1,790	42.95	$2,557	Profits, corp. (after tax, $bil.)	$261	$589	125.7%	$1,329
GDP ($bil.)	$5,803	$9,963	71.7%	$17,105	R&D ($mil.)	$152,039	$257,000	69.0%	$434,421
GDP per capita	$26,834	$33,833	26.1%	$42,658	Retail store sales ($bil.)	$1,845	$3,232	75.2%	$5,662
GDP, 1996 dollars ($bil.)	$6,708	$9,319	38.9%	$12,946	SAT score, math	501	511	2.0%	521
Golfers	27,800	26,427	–4.9%	25,122	SAT score, verbal	502	505	0.6%	508
Health care spending ($bil.)	$696	$1,211	74.0%	$2,107	Scientists and engineers (000)	758.5	974.6	28.5%	1,252.3
Health care spending, Medicare ($bil.)	$110	$214	94.5%	$416	Scouts, boy (000)	4,293	4,956	15.4%	5,721
High school dropouts (000)	3,800	3,829	0.8%	3,858	Scouts, girl (000)	2,480	2,749	10.8%	3,047
High school grads (000)	8,370	6,999	–16.4%	5,853	Trade exports ($bil.)	$394	$782	98.5%	$1,552
Housing units (mil.)	94.2	105.7	12.2%	118.6	Trade imports ($bil.)	$495	$1,217	145.9%	$2,992
Housing units, owner-occupied (%)	63.9	67.4	5.5%	71.1	Travelers (Foreign to U.S.) (000)	39,363	46,395	17.9%	54,683
Induced abortions (000)	1,609	1,366	–15.1%	1,160	Travelers (U.S. to foreign) (000)	44,623	56,287	26.1%	71,000
Interest rate, mortgage (%)	10.08	7.5	–26.1%	5.51	Unemployment (mil.)	7.0	5.7	–18.6%	4.6

[1] 2000 figure or latest number available.

See: Statistical Abstract of the United States (http://www.census.gov/statab/www).

Holt's exponential smoothing model uses a smoothed estimate of the trend component as well as the level component to produce forecasts. In the two-parameter exponential smoothing forecast equation, the current smoothed level is added to a linear trend to forecast future values. The updated value of the smoothed level is computed as the weighted average of new data and the best estimate of the new level based on old data. The Holt method combines old and new estimates of the one-period change of the smoothed level, thus defining the current linear or local trend.

Three-Parameter (Winters) Exponential Smoothing

three-parameter (Winters) exponential smoothing
Method for forecasting seasonally adjusted growth

The **three-parameter (Winters) exponential smoothing** method extends the two-parameter technique by including a smoothed multiplicative index to account for the seasonal behavior of the forecast series. The three-parameter exponential smoothing technique is often called the Winters method, after its originator P. R. Winters.[4] Because much economic data involve both growth trend and seasonal considerations, three-parameter exponential smoothing is one of the most commonly used forecasting methods. It is best suited for forecasting problems that involve rapid and/or changing rates of growth combined with seasonal influences. Three-parameter exponential smoothing is suitable for forecasting sales in both rapidly growing markets and in rapidly decaying markets with seasonal influences.

Winters' three-parameter exponential smoothing model assumes that each observation is the product of a deseasonalized value and a seasonal index for that particular month or quarter. The deseasonalized values are assumed to be described by the Holt model. The Winters model involves three smoothing parameters to be used in level, trend, and seasonal index smoothing equations. The Winters model forecast is computed similarly to the Holt model forecast and then multiplied by the seasonal index for the current period. Smoothing in the Winters model is similar to the Holt model, except that in the Winters model the measurement of level is deseasonalized through dividing by the seasonal index calculated one year before. The trend smoothing equations of the two models are identical. The seasonal index is estimated as the ratio of the current observation to the current smoothed level, averaged with the previous value for that particular period.

Practical Use of Exponential Smoothing

The important point to remember about exponential smoothing, or any forecast method, is that the choice of an appropriate forecasting technique depends on the pattern data that is to be forecast.

As a case in point, Figure 6.9 shows a typical pattern of sales for the life cycle of a product. Product life cycles often progress from the introduction point, to rapid growth and market penetration, to a mature phase of sales stability, to periods of declining market share and abandonment. Over this life cycle, different methods of sales forecasting may be appropriate.

In the initial phase, and before the generation of significant market data, qualitative analyses and market experiments are highly appropriate. Once the product has been launched and is rapidly gaining market acceptance, in phase II, three-parameter exponential smoothing methods that involve level, trend, and seasonal components become relevant. In the mature phase of sales stability, phase III, two-parameter exponential smoothing models (or econometric models)

---

4   P. R. Winters, "Forecasting Sales by Exponentially Weighted Moving Averages," *Management Science 6* (April 1960), 324–342.

FIGURE 6.9

The Appropriate Forecast Technique Tends to Vary over the Life Cycle of a Product

The life cycle of a product often involves an introduction or start-up period, followed by rapid growth, maturity, decline, and abandonment. The choice of an appropriate forecast technique varies over this cycle.

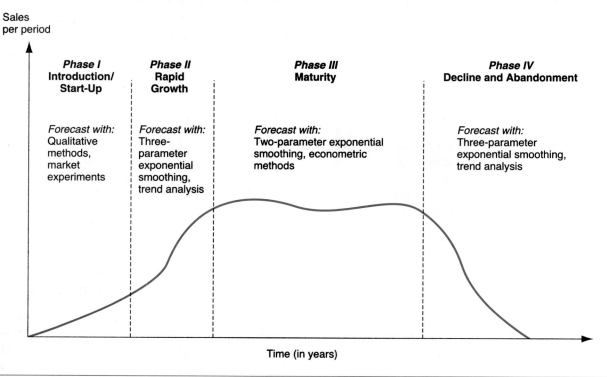

that incorporate level and seasonal components are suitable. In the fourth and final phase of declining market share and abandonment, three-parameter exponential smoothing methods that involve level, trend, and seasonal components again become relevant.

ECONOMETRIC METHODS

econometric methods
Use of economic theory and mathematical and statistical tools to forecast economic relations

Econometric methods combine economic theory with statistical tools to analyze economic relations. Econometric forecasting techniques have several advantages over alternative methods.

Advantages of Econometric Methods

Econometric methods force the forecaster to make explicit assumptions about the linkages among the variables in the economic system being examined. In other words, the forecaster must deal with causal relations. This produces logical consistency in the forecast model and increases reliability.

Another advantage of econometric methods is that the forecaster can compare forecasts with actual results and use insights gained to improve the forecast model. By feeding past forecasting errors back into the model, new parameter estimates can be generated to improve future forecasting results. The type of output provided by econometric forecasts is another major advantage. Because econometric models offer estimates of actual values for forecasted variables, these models indicate both the direction and magnitude of change. Finally, perhaps the most important advantage of econometric models relates to their ability to explain economic phenomena.

Single-Equation Models

Many managerial forecasting problems can be adequately addressed with single-equation econometric models. The first step in developing an econometric model is to express relevant economic relations in the form of an equation. When constructing a model for forecasting the regional demand for portable personal computers, one might hypothesize that computer demand (*C*) is determined by price (*P*), disposable income (*I*), population (*Pop*), interest rates (*i*), and advertising expenditures (*A*). A linear model expressing this relation is

(6.10)
$$C = a_0 + a_1P + a_2I + a_3Pop + a_4i + a_5A$$

The next step in econometric modeling is to estimate the parameters of the system, or values of the coefficients, as in Equation 6.10. The most frequently used technique for parameter estimation is the application of least squares regression analysis with either time-series or cross-section data.

Once the model coefficients have been estimated, forecasting with a single-equation model consists of evaluating the equation with specific values for the independent variables. An econometric model used for forecasting purposes must contain independent or explanatory variables whose values for the forecast period can be readily obtained.

Multiple-Equation Systems

Although forecasting problems can often be analyzed with a single-equation model, complex relations among economic variables sometimes require use of multiple-equation systems. Variables whose values are determined within such a model are *endogenous*, meaning originating from within; those determined outside, or external to, the system are referred to as *exogenous*. The values of endogenous variables are determined by the model; the values of exogenous variables are given externally. Endogenous variables are equivalent to the dependent variable in a single-equation system; exogenous and predetermined variables are equivalent to the independent variables.

identities
Economic relations that are true by definition

Multiple-equation econometric models are composed of two basic kinds of expressions, identities and behavioral equations. **Identities** express relations that are true by definition. The statement that profits (π) equal total revenue (*TR*) minus total cost (*TC*) is an example of an identity:

(6.11)
$$\pi = TR - TC$$

Profits are *defined* by the relation expressed in Equation 6.11.

behavioral equations
Economic relations that are hypothesized to be true

The second group of equations encountered in econometric models, **behavioral equations**, reflects hypotheses about how variables in a system interact with each other. Behavioral equations may indicate how individuals and institutions are expected to react to various stimuli.

Perhaps the easiest way to illustrate the use of multiple-equation systems is to examine a simple three-equation forecast model for equipment and related software sales for a personal computer retailer. As you recall, Equation 6.10 expressed a single-equation model that might be used to forecast regional demand for personal computers. However, total revenues for a typical retailer usually include not only sales of personal computers but also sales of software programs (including computer games) and sales of peripheral equipment (e.g., monitors, printers). Although actual econometric models used to forecast total sales revenue from these items might include several equations and many variables, the simple system described in this section should suffice to provide insight into the multiple-equation approach without being overly complex. The three equations are

(6.12)
$$S_t = b_0 + b_1TR_t + u_1$$

(6.13)
$$P_t = c_0 + c_1 C_{t-1} + u_2$$

(6.14)
$$TR_t = S_t + P_t + C_t$$

where S is software sales, TR is total revenue, P is peripheral sales, C is personal computer sales, t is the current time period, $t-1$ is the previous time period, and u_1 and u_2 are error, or residual, terms.

Equations 6.12 and 6.13 are behavioral hypotheses. Equation 6.12 hypothesizes that current-period software sales are a function of the current level of total revenues; Equation 6.13 hypothesizes that peripheral sales depend on previous-period personal computer sales. The last equation in the system, Equation 6.14, is an identity. It defines total revenue as being the sum of software, peripheral equipment, and personal computer sales.

Stochastic disturbance terms in the behavioral equations, u_1 and u_2, are included because hypothesized relations are not exact. Other factors that can affect software and peripheral sales are not accounted for in the system. So long as these stochastic elements are random and their expected values are zero, they do not present a barrier to empirical estimation of system parameters. If error terms are not randomly distributed, parameter estimates will be biased, and the reliability of model forecasts will be questionable. Large error terms, even if they are distributed randomly, reduce forecast accuracy.

To forecast next year's software and peripheral sales and total revenue as represented by this illustrative model, it is necessary to express S, P, and TR in terms of variables whose values are known or can be estimated at the moment the forecast is generated. In other words, each endogenous variable (S_t, P_t, and TR_t) must be expressed in terms of the exogenous and predetermined variables (C_{t-1} and C_t). Such relations are called reduced-form equations because they reduce complex simultaneous relations to their most basic and simple form. Consider the manipulations of equations in the system necessary to solve for TR via its reduced-form equation.

Substituting Equation 6.12 into 6.14—that is, replacing S_t with Equation 6.12—results in[5]

(6.15)
$$TR_t = b_0 + b_1\, TR_t + P_t + C_t$$

A similar substitution of Equation 6.13 for P_t produces

(6.16)
$$TR_t = b_0 + b_1\, TR_t + c_0 + c_1 C_{t-1} + C_t$$

Collecting terms and isolating TR in Equation 6.16 gives

$$(1 - b_1)\, TR_t = b_0 + c_0 + c_1 C_{t-1} + C_t$$

or, alternately,

(6.17)
$$TR_t = \frac{b_0 + c_0 + c_1 C_{t-1} + C_t}{(1 - b_1)}$$

$$= \frac{b_0 + c_0}{(1 - b_1)} + \frac{c_1}{(1 - b_1)} C_{t-1} + \frac{1}{(1 - b_1)} C_t$$

Equation 6.17 now relates current total revenues to previous-period and current-period personal computer sales. Assuming that data on previous-period personal computer sales can be

---

5   The stochastic disturbance terms (us) have been dropped from the illustration because their expected values are zero. The final equation for TR, however, is stochastic in nature.

obtained and that current-period personal computer sales can be estimated by using Equation 6.10, Equation 6.17 provides a forecasting model that accounts for the simultaneous relations expressed in this simplified multiple-equation system. In real-world situations, it is likely that personal computer sales depend on the price, quantity, and quality of available software and peripheral equipment. Then S, P, and C, along with other important factors, may all be endogenous, involving a number of relations in a complex multiple-equation system. Disentangling the important but often subtle relations involved makes forecasting with multiple-equation systems both intriguing and challenging.

JUDGING FORECAST RELIABILITY

forecast reliability
Predictive consistency

In comparing forecast and actual values, how close is close enough? Is **forecast reliability**, or predictive consistency, transferable to other samples and time periods? These questions must be adequately addressed prior to the implementation of any successful forecasting program.

Tests of Predictive Capability

To test predictive capability, a forecast model generated over one sample or period is used to forecast data for some alternative sample or period. The reliability of a model for predicting firm sales, such as that shown in Equation 6.2, can be tested by examining the relation between forecast and actual data for years beyond the period over which the forecast model was estimated. However, it is often desirable to test a forecast model without waiting for new data to become available. In such instances, one can divide available data into two subsamples, called a **test group** and a **forecast group**. The forecaster estimates a forecasting model using data from the test group and uses the resulting model to "forecast" the data of interest in the forecast group. A comparison of forecast and actual values can then be conducted to test the stability of the underlying cost or demand relation.

test group
Subsample of data used to generate a forecast model

forecast group
Subsample of data used to test a forecast model

Correlation Analysis

In analyzing a model's forecast capability, the correlation between forecast and actual values is of substantial interest. The formula for the simple correlation coefficient, r, for forecast and actual values, f and x, respectively, is

(6.18)
$$r = \frac{\sigma_{fx}}{\sigma_f \sigma_x}$$

where σ_{fx} is the covariance between the forecast and actual series, and σ_f and σ_x are the sample standard deviations of the forecast and actual series, respectively. Basic spreadsheet and statistical software readily provide these data, making the calculation of r a relatively simple task. Generally speaking, correlations between forecast and actual values in excess of 0.99 (99 percent) are highly desirable and indicate that the forecast model being considered constitutes an effective tool for analysis.

In cross-section analysis, in which the important trend element in most economic data is held constant, a correlation of 99 percent between forecast and actual values is rare. When unusually difficult forecasting problems are being addressed, correlations between forecast and actual data of 90 percent or 95 percent may prove satisfactory. By contrast, in critical decision situations, forecast values may have to be estimated at very precise levels. In such instances, forecast and actual data may have to exhibit an extremely high level of correlation, 99.5 percent or 99.75 percent, to generate a high level of confidence in forecast reliability.

Sample Mean Forecast Error Analysis

sample mean forecast error
Estimate of average forecast error

Further evaluation of a model's predictive capability can be made through consideration of a measure called the **sample mean forecast error**, which provides a useful estimate of the average forecast error of the model. It is sometimes called the root mean squared forecast error and is denoted by the symbol U. The sample mean forecast error is calculated as

(6.19)
$$U = \sqrt{\frac{1}{n} \sum_{i=1}^{n} (f_i - x_i)^2}$$

where n is the number of sample observations, f_i is a forecast value, and x_i is the corresponding actual value. Deviations between forecast and actual values are squared in the calculation of the mean forecast error to prevent positive and negative deviations from canceling each other out. The smaller the sample mean forecast error, the greater the accuracy associated with the forecasting model.

CHOOSING THE BEST FORECAST TECHNIQUE

To select the best technique, managers must be knowledgeable about the strengths and weaknesses of various forecast methods, the amount and quality of available data, and the human and other costs associated with generating reliable forecasts.

Data Requirements

The choice of an appropriate forecast technique often hinges on the amount of relevant historical data that is readily available and any obvious patterns in that data. For many important forecast problems, 10 years of monthly data (120 observations) are available and appropriate for forecasting future activity. In such cases, the full range of advanced forecast techniques can be considered. If only more restricted samples of data are available for analysis, then simpler forecast methods must be used.

If trend, cyclical, seasonal, or irregular patterns can be recognized, then forecast techniques that are capable of handling those patterns can be readily selected. For example, if the data are relatively stable, a simple exponential smoothing approach may be adequate. Other exponential smoothing models are appropriate for trending and seasonal data; the same model will not be applicable in all cases.

As the forecast horizon increases, the cyclical pattern of economic data may also become significant. In these cases, the need to relate the forecast variable to economic, market, and competitive factors increases, because simple trend projections may no longer be appropriate.

Time Horizon Considerations

Experience shows that sophisticated time-series models can provide accurate short-term forecasts. In the short term, the momentum of existing consumer behavior often resists dramatic change. Over a 5-year period, however, customers can find new suppliers, and needs may change. For long-range forecasts, econometric models are often appropriate. In the long term, it is essential to relate the item being forecast to its "drivers," as explanatory factors are sometimes called.

The accuracy of econometric models depends on the precision with which explanatory factors can be predicted. Although these models can also be used in the short term, they are costlier and more complex than simple exponential smoothing methods. When economic conditions are stable, econometric models are seldom more accurate than more simple trend projections and exponential smoothing methods.

As shown in Table 6.6, simple trend, econometric models, and exponential smoothing methods are all used for problems involving 3-year to 5-year forecasts. Over this intermediate term, trend projection techniques are relatively inexpensive to apply, but may produce forecasts that are not as accurate as those resulting from econometric methods. When sufficient data exist and the need for accuracy is great, the use of exponential smoothing or econometric models is often recommended. Then, the generally superior short-term forecasting abilities of smoothing models emerge. Also evident over the intermediate term are the advantages of econometric models, which are superior in relating the data to be forecast to economic conditions, price changes, competitive activities, and other explanatory variables.

When both smoothing and econometric models yield similar forecasts, managers can be reasonably certain that the forecast is consistent with underlying assumptions and has a good chance of being accurate. When forecasts produced by two or more methods are significantly different, this is a warning to exercise extreme care.

Computer and Related Costs

Computer costs are rapidly becoming an insignificant part of the forecast technique selection process. The proliferation of inexpensive and user-friendly forecast software has also lessened

TABLE 6.6

A Subjective Comparison of Alternative Forecast Techniques

		Qualitative Forecasting Methods				Quantitative Forecasting Methods						
						Statistical			Deterministic			
		Personal Insight	Delphi Method	Panel Consensus	Market Research	Summary Statistics	Trend Projections	Exponential Smoothing	Econometric Models	Market Survey	Leading Indicator	Econometric Models
Patterns of data that can be recognized and handled easily.	Trend	Not Applicable				✓	✓	✓	✓	✓	✓	✓
	Seasonal					✓		✓	✓			✓
	Cyclical					✓			✓			✓
Minimum data requirements.		Not Applicable			Low	Medium	Medium	High	Low	Medium	High	High
Time horizon for which method is appropriate.	Short term (0-3 mos.)		✓	✓	✓	✓	✓	✓	✓	✓	✓	✓
	Medium term (12-24 mos.)	✓	✓	✓	✓	✓	✓	✓	✓	✓	✓	✓
	Long term (2 yrs. or more)	✓	✓	✓	✓	✓	✓		✓			✓
Accuracy	Predicting patterns.	Medium	Medium	Medium	Medium	Low	Medium	Low	High	Low	Low	Low
	Predicting turning points.	Low	Medium	Medium	Medium	NA	Low	Low	Medium	High	Medium	Medium
Applicability	Time required to obtain forecast.	Medium	Medium	Medium	High	Low	Medium	Low	Medium	Medium	Medium	High
	Ease of understanding and interpreting the results.	High	High	High	High	High	High	Medium	High	High	High	Medium
Computer costs	Development	Not applicable				Low	Low	Low	Medium	NA	Medium	High
	Storage requirements	Not applicable				Medium	Medium	High	NA	Low	High	High
	Running	High				Low	Medium	Low	Medium	NA	NA	High

the need for sophisticated support staff. Still, other costs associated with forecast development and implementation cannot be ignored. Some major cost considerations often include data processing and storage costs, database maintenance and retrieval charges, and special hardware needs. Start-up costs to develop forecasts for new products and services, analysis, and modeling work tend to escalate over time, especially when the experience level of the forecasting staff is low. The maintenance of a complex forecasting system, on the other hand, can be relatively inexpensive if programming documentation and standards are kept current.

Role of Judgment

The most sophisticated forecast methodology provides sufficiently accurate results at minimum cost. No one flies a jet to the grocery store. Similarly, no manager would find costly and difficult methods appropriate for solving trivial forecasting problems.

To determine a suitable level of forecast accuracy, one must compare the costs and benefits of increased accuracy. When forecast accuracy is low, the probability of significant forecasting error is high, as is the chance of making suboptimal managerial decisions. Conversely, when forecast accuracy is high, the probability of substantial forecasting error is reduced and the chance of making erroneous managerial decisions is low. It is reasonable to require a relatively high level of forecast accuracy when the costs of forecast error are high. When only minor costs result from forecast error, inexpensive and less precise methods can be justified.

It is worth emphasizing that the objective of economic forecasting is to improve on the subjective judgments made by managers. All managers forecast; the goal is to make better forecasts. Nowhere in the forecasting process is the subjective judgment of managers relied on so heavily as it is in the selection of an appropriate forecast method. When it comes to the selection of the best forecast technique, there is no substitute for seasoned business judgment.

SUMMARY

Managerial decision making is often based on forecasts of future events. This chapter examines several techniques for economic forecasting, including qualitative analysis, trend analysis and projection, econometric models, and input-output methods.

- **Qualitative analysis** is an intuitive judgmental approach to forecasting that is useful when based on unbiased, informed opinion. The **personal insight** method is one in which an informed individual uses personal or organizational experience as a basis for developing future expectations. The **panel consensus** method relies on the informed opinion of several individuals. In the **delphi method**, responses from a panel of experts are analyzed by an independent party to elicit a consensus opinion.

- **Survey techniques** that skillfully use interviews or mailed questionnaires constitute another important forecasting tool, especially for short-term projections.

- **Trend analysis** involves characterizing the historical pattern of an economic variable and then projecting or forecasting its future path based on past experience. A **secular trend** is the long-run pattern of increase or decrease in economic data. **Cyclical fluctuation** describes the rhythmic variation in economic series that is due to a pattern of expansion or contraction in the overall economy. Seasonal variation, or **seasonality**, is a rhythmic annual pattern in sales or profits caused by weather, habit, or social custom. **Irregular or random influences** are unpredictable shocks to the economic system and the pace of economic activity caused by wars, strikes, natural catastrophes, and so on.

- A simple **linear trend analysis** assumes a constant period-by-period *unit* change in an important economic variable over time. **Growth trend analysis** assumes a constant period-by-period percentage change in an important economic variable over time.

- **Macroeconomic forecasting** involves predicting the pace of economic activity, employment, or interest rates at the international, national, or regional level. **Microeconomic forecasting** involves predicting economic performance, say, profitability, at the industry, firm, or plant level.

- The **business cycle** is the rhythmic pattern of contraction and expansion observed in the overall economy. **Economic indicators** are series of data that successfully describe the pattern of projected, current, or past economic activity. A **composite index** is a weighted average of leading, coincident, or lagging economic indicators. An **economic recession** is a significant decline in activity spread across the economy that lasts more than a few months. Recessions are visible in terms of falling industrial production, declining real income, shrinking wholesale-retail, and rising unemployment. An **economic expansion** exhibits rising economic activity.

- **Exponential smoothing** (or "averaging") techniques are among the most widely used forecasting methods. In **two-parameter (Holt) exponential smoothing**, the data are assumed to consist of fluctuations about a level that is changing with some constant or slowly drifting linear trend. The **three-parameter (Winters) exponential smoothing** method extends the two-parameter technique by including a smoothed multiplicative seasonal index to account for the seasonal behavior of the forecast series.

- **Econometric methods** use economic theory and mathematical and statistical tools to forecast economic relations. **Identities** are economic relations that are true by definition. **Behavioral equations** are hypothesized economic relations that are estimated by using econometric methods.

- **Forecast reliability**, or predictive consistency, must be accurately judged in order to assess the degree of confidence that should be placed in economic forecasts. A given forecast model is often estimated by using a **test group** of data and evaluated by using **forecast group** data. No forecasting assignment is complete until reliability has been quantified and evaluated. The **sample mean forecast error** is one useful measure of predictive capability.

The appropriate technique to apply in a given forecasting situation depends on such factors as the distance into the future being forecast, the lead time available, the accuracy required, the quality of data available for analysis, and the nature of the economic relations involved in the forecasting problem.

QUESTIONS

Q6.1 What is the delphi method? Describe its main advantages and limitations.

Q6.2 Describe the main advantages and limitations of survey data.

Q6.3 What is trend projection, and why is this method often used in economic forecasting?

Q6.4 What is the basic shortcoming of trend projection that barometric approaches improve on?

Q6.5 What advantage do diffusion and composite indexes provide in the barometric approach to forecasting?

Q6.6 Explain how the econometric model approach to forecasting could be used to examine various "what if" questions about the future.

Q6.7 Describe the data requirements that must be met if regression analysis is to provide a useful basis for forecasting.

Q6.8 Would a linear regression model of the advertising/sales relation be appropriate for forecasting the advertising levels at which threshold or saturation effects become prevalent?

Q6.9 Cite some examples of forecasting problems that might be addressed by using regression analysis of complex multiple-equation systems of economic relations.

Q6.10 What are the main characteristics of accurate forecasts?

SELF-TEST PROBLEMS AND SOLUTIONS

ST6.1   Gross domestic product (GDP) is a measure of overall activity in the economy. It is defined as the value at the final point of sale of all goods and services produced during a given period by both domestic and foreign-owned enterprises. GDP data for the 1966–2000 period offer the basis to test the abilities of simple constant change and constant growth models to describe the trend in GDP over time. However, regression results generated over the entire 1966–2000 period cannot be used to forecast GDP over any subpart of that period. To do so would be to overstate the forecast capability of the regression model because, by definition, the regression line minimizes the sum of squared deviations over the estimation period. To test forecast reliability, it is necessary to test the predictive capability of a given regression model over data that was not used to generate that very model. In the absence of GDP data for future periods, say 2002–2007, the reliability of alternative forecast techniques can be illustrated by arbitrarily dividing historical GDP data into two subsamples: a 1966–95 30-year test period, and a 1996–2000 5-year forecast period. Regression models estimated over the 1966–95 test period can be used to "forecast" actual GDP over the 1996–2000 period. In other words, estimation results over the 1966–95 subperiod provide a forecast model that can be used to evaluate the predictive reliability of the constant growth model over the 1996–2000 forecast period.

The accompanying table shows GDP figures for the U.S. economy for the 35-year period from 1966–2000.

Gross Domestic Product, 1966–2000 (in $ billions)

Year	GDP	*ln* GDP	Time Period
1966	$789.3	6.6711	1
1967	834.1	6.7264	2
1968	911.5	6.8151	3
1969	985.3	6.8929	4
1970	1,039.7	6.9467	5
1971	1,128.6	7.0287	6
1972	1,240.4	7.1232	7
1973	1,385.5	7.2338	8
1974	1,501.0	7.3139	9
1975	1,635.2	7.3995	10
1976	1,823.9	7.5087	11
1977	2,031.4	7.6165	12
1978	2,295.9	7.7389	13
1979	2,566.4	7.8503	14
1980	2,795.6	7.9358	15
1981	3,131.3	8.0492	16
1982	3,259.2	8.0892	17
1983	3,534.9	8.1704	18
1984	3,932.7	8.2771	19
1985	4,213.0	8.3459	20
1986	4,452.9	8.4013	21
1987	4,742.5	8.4643	22
1988	5,108.3	8.5386	23
1989	5,489.1	8.6105	24
1990	5,803.2	8.6662	25
1991	5,986.2	8.6972	26
1992	6,318.9	8.7513	27

Gross Domestic Product, 1966–2000 (in $ billions) continued

Year	GDP	*ln* GDP	Time Period
1993	6,642.3	8.8012	28
1994	7,054.3	8.8614	29
1995	7,400.5	8.9093	30
1996	7,813.2	8.9636	31
1997	8,318.4	9.0262	32
1998	8,790.2	9.0814	33
1999	9,299.2	9.1377	34
2000	9,963.1	9.2066	35

Source: http://www.bea.doc.gov.

A. Use the regression model approach to estimate the simple linear relation between the natural logarithm of GDP and time (T) over the 1966–99 subperiod, where

$$ln\ GDP_t = b_0 + b_1 T_t + u_t$$

and $ln\ GDP_t$ is the natural logarithm of GDP in year t, and T is a time trend variable (where $T_{1966} = 1$, $T_{1967} = 2$, $T_{1968} = 3, \ldots,$ and $T_{1995} = 30$); and u is a residual term. This is called a constant growth model because it is based on the assumption of a constant percentage growth in economic activity per year. How well does the constant growth model fit actual GDP data over this period?

B. Create a spreadsheet that shows constant growth model GDP forecasts over the 1996–2000 period alongside actual figures. Then, subtract forecast values from actual figures to obtain annual estimates of forecast error, and squared forecast error, for each year over the 1996–2000 period.

   Finally, compute the correlation coefficient between actual and forecast values over the 1996–2000 period. Also compute the sample average (or root mean squared) forecast error. Based upon these findings, how well does the constant growth model generated over the 1966–95 period forecast actual GDP data over the 1996–2000 period?

ST6.1 **Solution**

A. The constant growth model estimated using the simple regression model technique illustrates the linear relation between the natural logarithm of GDP and time. A constant growth regression model estimated over the 1966–95 30-year period (t statistic in parentheses), used to forecast GDP over the 1996–2000 5-year period, is

$$ln\ GDP_t = 6.609 + 0.082T_t \quad R^2 = 98.9\%$$
$$(227.74) \quad (50.19)$$

The $R^2 = 99.50\%$ and a highly significant t statistic for the time trend variable indicate that the constant growth model closely describes the change in GDP over the 1966–95 time frame. Nevertheless, even modest differences in the intercept term and slope coefficient over time can lead to large forecast errors.

B. Each constant growth GDP forecast is derived using the constant growth model coefficients estimated in part A, along with values for each respective time trend variable over the 1995–2000 period. Again, remember that $T_{1996} = 31$, $T_{1997} = 32, \ldots,$ and $T_{2000} = 35$ and that the constant growth model provides predicted, or forecast, values for $ln\ GDP_t$. To obtain forecast values for GDP_t, simply take the exponent (antilog) of each predicted $ln\ GDP_t$ variable.

   The following spreadsheet shows actual and constant growth model GDP forecasts for the 1996–2000 forecast period:

Year	GDP	*ln* GDP	Forecast *ln* GDP	Forecast GDP	Forecast Error (GDP—Forecast GDP)	Squared Forecast Error (GDP—Forecast GDP)²	Time period
1996	$7,813.2	8.9636	9.1529	$9,441.6	−$1,628.40	$2,651,677.7	31
1997	8,318.4	9.0262	9.2349	10,248.9	−1,930.5	3,726,882.3	32
1998	8,790.2	9.0814	9.3170	11,125.3	−2,335.1	5,452,506.8	33
1999	9,299.2	9.1377	9.3990	12,076.5	−2,777.3	7,713,619.7	34
2000	9,963.1	9.2066	9.4811	13,109.2	−3,146.1	9,897,699.3	35
Average	$8,836.8	9.0831	9.3170	$11,200.3	−$2,363.5	$5,888,477.2	

Correlation 99.92%   Mean squared error $2,426.62

The correlation coefficient between actual and constant growth model forecast GDP is $r_{GDP, FGDP}$ = 99.92%. The sample root mean squared forecast error is $2,426.6 billion (= $\sqrt{\$5,888,477.2}$), or 27.5% of average actual GDP over the 1996–2000 period. Thus, despite the fact that the correlation between actual and constant growth forecast model values is relatively high, forecast error is also very high. Unusually modest economic growth during the early 1990s has led to large forecast errors when data from more rapidly growing periods, like the 1980s, are used to forecast economic growth.

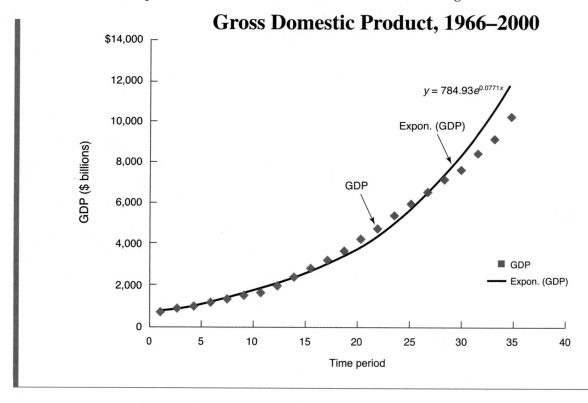

Gross Domestic Product, 1966–2000

$y = 784.93e^{0.0771x}$

ST6.2 Multiple Regression. Branded Products, Inc., based in Oakland, California, is a leading producer and marketer of household laundry detergent and bleach products. About a year ago, Branded Products rolled out its new Super Detergent in 30 regional markets following its success in test markets. This isn't just a "me too" product in a commodity market. Branded Products' detergent contains Branded 2 bleach, a successful laundry product in its own right. At the time of the introduction, management wondered whether the company could successfully crack this market dominated by Procter & Gamble and other big players.

The following spreadsheet shows weekly demand data and regression model estimation results for Super Detergent in these 30 regional markets:

Branded Products Demand Forecasting Problem

Regional Market	Demand in Cases, Q	Price per Case, P	Competitor Price, P_x	Advertising, Ad	Household Income, I	Estimated Demand, Q
1	1,290	$137	$94	$814	$53,123	1,305
2	1,177	147	81	896	51,749	1,206
3	1,155	149	89	852	49,881	1,204
4	1,299	117	92	854	43,589	1,326
5	1,166	135	86	810	42,799	1,185
6	1,186	143	79	768	55,565	1,208
7	1,293	113	91	978	37,959	1,333
8	1,322	111	82	821	47,196	1,328
9	1,338	109	81	843	50,163	1,366
10	1,160	129	82	849	39,080	1,176
11	1,293	124	91	797	43,263	1,264
12	1,413	117	76	988	51,291	1,359
13	1,299	106	90	914	38,343	1,345
14	1,238	135	88	913	39,473	1,199
15	1,467	117	99	867	51,501	1,433
16	1,089	147	76	785	37,809	1,024
17	1,203	124	83	817	41,471	1,216
18	1,474	103	98	846	46,663	1,449
19	1,235	140	78	768	55,839	1,220
20	1,367	115	83	856	47,438	1,326
21	1,310	119	76	771	54,348	1,304
22	1,331	138	100	947	45,066	1,302
23	1,293	122	90	831	44,166	1,288
24	1,437	105	86	905	55,380	1,476
25	1,165	145	96	996	38,656	1,208
26	1,328	138	97	929	46,084	1,291
27	1,515	116	97	1,000	52,249	1,478
28	1,223	148	84	951	50,855	1,226
29	1,293	134	88	848	54,546	1,314
30	1,215	127	87	891	38,085	1,215
Average	1,286	127	87	870	46,788	1,286
Minimum	1,089	103	76	768	37,809	1,024
Maximum	1,515	149	100	1,000	55,839	1,478

Regression Statistics

Multiple R	0.950792455
R Square	0.904006293
Adjusted R Square	0.8886473
Standard Error	34.97209425
Observations	30

	Coefficients	Standard Error	t Stat	P value
Intercept	807.9377685	137.8360278	5.861586274	4.09301E-06
Price, P	−5.034480186	0.456754361	−11.02229255	4.34134E-11
Competitor Price, P_x	4.860371507	1.005588065	4.833362367	5.73825E-05
Advertising, Ad	0.328043519	0.104441879	3.140919367	0.004293208
Household Income, I	0.008705656	0.001089079	7.993592833	2.38432E-08

A. Interpret the coefficient estimate for each respective independent variable.

B. Characterize the overall explanatory power of this multiple regression model in light of R^2 and the following plot of actual and estimated demand per week.

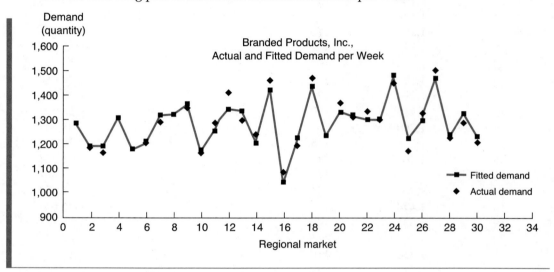

C. Use the regression model estimation results to forecast weekly demand in five new markets with the following characteristics:

Regional Forecast Market	Price per Case, P	Competitor Price, P_x	Advertising, Ad	Household Income, I
A	115	90	790	41,234
B	122	101	812	39,845
C	116	87	905	47,543
D	140	82	778	53,560
E	133	79	996	39,870
Average	125	88	856	44,410

ST6.2   Solution

A. Coefficient estimates for the P, P_x, Ad, and I independent X variables are statistically significant at the 99% confidence level. Price of the product itself (P) has the predictably negative influence on the quantity demanded, whereas the effects of competitor price (P_x), advertising (Ad) and household disposable income (I) are positive as expected. The chance of finding such large t statistics is less than 1% if, in fact, there were no relation between each variable and quantity.

B. The $R^2 = 90.4\%$ obtained by the model means that 90.4% of demand variation is explained by the underlying variation in all four independent variables. This is a relatively high level of explained variation and implies an attractive level of explanatory power. Moreover, as shown in the graph of actual and fitted (estimated) demand, the multiple regression model closely tracks week-by-week changes in demand with no worrisome divergences between actual and estimated demand over time. This means that this regression model can be used to forecast demand in similar markets under similar conditions.

C. Notice that each prospective market displays characteristics similar to those of markets used to estimate the regression model described here. Thus, the regression model estimated previously can be used to forecast demand in each regional market. Forecast results are as follows:

Regional Forecast Market	Price per Case, P	Competitor Price, P_x	Advertising, Ad	Household Income, I	Forecast Demand, Q
A	115	90	790	41,234	1,285
B	122	101	812	39,845	1,298
C	116	87	905	47,543	1,358
D	140	82	778	53,560	1,223
E	133	79	996	39,870	1,196
Average	125	88	856	44,410	1,272

PROBLEMS

P6.1 **Constant Growth Model.** The U.S. Bureau of the Census publishes employment statistics and demand forecasts for various occupations.

Occupation	Employment (1,000)	
	1998	2008
Bill collectors	311	420
Computer engineers	299	622
Physicians' assistants	66	98
Respiratory therapists	86	123
Systems analysts	617	1,194

A. Using a spreadsheet or handheld calculator, calculate the 10-year growth rate forecast using the constant growth model with annual compounding, and the constant growth model with continuous compounding for each occupation.

B. Compare your answers and discuss any differences.

P6.2 **Growth Rate Estimation.** According to the Recording Industry Association of America, 662.1 million CDs were shipped in 1994 by domestic manufacturers. Within 5 years, the number of CDs shipped rose to roughly 1 billion units.

A. Complete the following table showing annual CD shipments data for 1994–99 period.

B. Calculate the geometric average annual rate of growth for the 1994–99 period. (Hint: Calculate this growth rate using sales from 1994 and 1999.)

C. Calculate the arithmetic average annual rate of growth for the 1994–99 period. (Hint: This is the average of column 4 figures.)

D. Discuss any differences in your answers to parts B and C.

Year (1)	CD Shipments (2)	Current Shipments ÷ Previous Period Shipments (3)	Growth Rate (4) = [(3) – 1] × 100
1994	662.1	—	—
1995	722.9		
1996	778.9		
1997	753.1		
1998	847.0		
1999	938.9		

P6.3   Sales Trend Analysis. Environmental Designs, Inc., produces and installs energy-efficient window systems in commercial buildings. During the past 10 years, sales revenue has increased from $25 million to $65 million.

A. Calculate the company's growth rate in sales using the constant growth model with annual compounding.

B. Derive a 5-year and a 10-year sales forecast.

P6.4   Cost Forecasting. Dorothy Gale, a quality-control supervisor for Wizard Products, Inc., is concerned about unit labor cost increases for the assembly of electrical snap-action switches. Costs have increased from $80 to $100 per unit over the previous 3 years. Gale thinks that importing switches from foreign suppliers at a cost of $115.90 per unit may soon be desirable.

A. Calculate the company's unit labor cost growth rate using the constant rate of change model with continuous compounding.

B. Forecast when unit labor costs will equal the current cost of importing.

P6.5   Unit Sales Forecast Modeling. Boris Badenov has discovered that the change in product A demand in any given week is inversely proportional to the change in sales of product B in the previous week. That is, if sales of B rose by X% last week, sales of A can be expected to fall by X% this week.

A. Write the equation for next week's sales of A, using the variables A = sales of product A, B = sales of product B, and t = time. Assume that there will be no shortages of either product.

B. Last week, 100 units of A and 90 units of B were sold. Two weeks ago, 75 units of B were sold. What would you predict the sales of A to be this week?

P6.6   Sales Forecast Modeling. Monica Geller must generate a sales forecast to convince the loan officer at a local bank of the viability of The Iridium, a trendy restaurant on 65th and Broadway in New York City. Geller assumes that next-period sales are a function of current income, advertising, and advertising by a competing restaurant.

A. Write an equation for predicting sales if Geller assumes that the percentage change in sales is twice as large as the percentage change in income and advertising but that it is only one-half as large as, and of the opposite sign of, the percentage change in competitor advertising. Use the variables S = sales, Y = income, A = advertising, and CA = competitor advertising.

B. During the current period, sales total $500,000, median income per capita in the local market is $71,400, advertising is $20,000, and competitor advertising is $66,000. Previous period levels were $70,000 (income), $25,000 (advertising), and $60,000 (competitor advertising). Forecast next-period sales.

P6.7   Cost Forecast Modeling. Chandler Bing is product safety manager at Tribbiani-Buffay Products, Inc., a Las Vegas–based producer of data processing equipment. Bing is evaluating the cost effectiveness of a preventive maintenance program. Bing believes that monthly downtime on the packaging line caused by equipment breakdown is related to the hours spent each month on preventive maintenance.

A. Write an equation to predict next month's downtime using the variables D = downtime, M = preventive maintenance, t = time, a_0 = constant term, a_1 = regression slope coefficient, and u = random disturbance. Assume that downtime in the forecast (next) month decreases by the same percentage as preventive maintenance increased during the month preceding the current one.

B. If 40 hours were spent last month on preventive maintenance and this month's downtime was 500 hours, what should downtime be next month if preventive maintenance this month is 50 hours? Use the equation developed in part A.

P6.8 **Sales Forecast Modeling.** Toys Unlimited, Ltd., must forecast sales for a popular adult computer game to avoid stockouts or excessive inventory charges during the upcoming Christmas season. In percentage terms, the company estimates that game sales fall at double the rate of price increases and that they grow at triple the rate of customer traffic increases. Furthermore, these effects seem to be independent.

A. Write an equation for estimating the Christmas season sales, using the variables S = sales, P = price, T = traffic, and t = time.

B. Forecast this season's sales if Toys Unlimited sold 10,000 games last season at $15 each, this season's price is anticipated to be $16.50, and customer traffic is expected to rise by 15% over previous levels.

P6.9 **Simultaneous Equations.** Mid-Atlantic Cinema, Inc., runs a chain of movie theaters in the east-central states and has enjoyed great success with a Tuesday Night at the Movies promotion. By offering half off its regular $9 admission price, average nightly attendance has risen from 500 to 1,500 persons. Popcorn and other concession revenues tied to attendance have also risen dramatically. Historically, Mid-Atlantic has found that 50% of all moviegoers buy a $4 cup of buttered popcorn. Eighty percent of these popcorn buyers, plus 40% of the moviegoers that do not buy popcorn, each spend an average of $3 on soda and other concessions.

A. Write an expression describing total revenue from tickets plus popcorn plus other concessions.

B. Forecast total revenues for both regular and special Tuesday night pricing.

C. Forecast the total profit contribution earned for the regular and special Tuesday night pricing strategies if the profit contribution is 25% on movie ticket revenues and 80% on popcorn and other concession revenues.

P6.10 **Simultaneous Equations.** Supersonic Industries, based in Seattle, Washington, manufactures a wide range of parts for aircraft manufacturers. The company is currently evaluating the merits of building a new plant to fulfill a new contract with the federal government. The alternatives to expansion are to use additional overtime, to reduce other production, or both. The company will add new capacity only if the economy appears to be expanding. Therefore, forecasting the general pace of economic activity for the United States is an important input to the decision-making process. The firm has collected data and estimated the following relations for the U.S. economy:

$$
\begin{aligned}
\text{Last year's total profits (all corporations) } P_{t-1} &= \$800 \text{ billion} \\
\text{This year's government expenditures } G &= \$2,000 \text{ billion} \\
\text{Annual consumption expenditures } C &= \$600 \text{ billion} + 0.75Y + u \\
\text{Annual investment expenditures } I &= \$1,080 \text{ billion} + 0.9P_{t-1} + u \\
\text{Annual tax receipts } T &= 0.16\text{GDP} \\
\text{Net exports } X &= 0.03\text{GDP} \\
\text{National income } Y &= \text{GDP} - T \\
\text{Gross domestic product (GDP)} &= C + I + G - X
\end{aligned}
$$

Forecast each of the preceding variables through the simultaneous relations expressed in the multiple equation system. Assume that all random disturbances average out to zero.

CASE STUDY

Forecasting Global Performance for a Mickey Mouse Organization

The Walt Disney Company is one of the best known and best managed entertainment companies in the world. As the cornerstone of a carefully integrated entertainment marketing strategy, the company owns and operates the world's most acclaimed amusement parks and entertainment facilities. Some of the best known and most successful among these are Disneyland, California, and Walt Disney World, Florida—an immense entertainment center that includes the Magic Kingdom, Epcot Center, Animal Kingdom, and Disney-MGM Studios. During recent years, the company has extended its amusement park business to foreign soil with Tokyo Disneyland and Euro Disneyland, located just outside of Paris, France. Disney's foreign operations provide an interesting example of the company's shrewd combination of marketing and financial skills. To conserve scarce capital resources, Disney was able to entice foreign investors to put up 100% of the financing required for both the Tokyo and Paris facilities. In turn, Disney is responsible for the design and management of both operations, retains an important equity interest, and enjoys significant royalties on all gross revenues. Disney's innovative means for financing foreign operations has enabled the company to greatly expand its revenue and profit base without any commensurate increase in capital expenditures. As a result, the success of its foreign operations has allowed the company to increase its already enviable rate of return on stockholders' equity.

Disney is also a major force in the movie picture production business with Buena Vista, Touchstone, and Hollywood Pictures, in addition to the renowned Walt Disney Studios. The company is famous for recent hit movies such as *Beauty and the Beast*, *The Lion King*, and *Pearl Harbor*, in addition to a film library including hundreds of movie classics like *Fantasia*, *Snow White*, and *Mary Poppins*, among others. Disney employs an aggressive and highly successful video marketing strategy for new films and re-releases from the company's extensive film library. The Disney Store, a chain of retail specialty shops, profits from the sale of movie tie-in merchandise, books, and recorded music. Also making a significant contribution to the bottom line are earnings from the cable TV Disney Channel. In 1996, the Disney empire grew further with the acquisition of Capital Cities/ABC, a print and television media behemoth, for stock and cash. The company's family entertainment marketing strategy is so broad in its reach that Disney characters such as Mickey Mouse, Donald Duck, and Goofy have become an integral part of the American culture. Given its ability to turn whimsy into outstanding operating performance, the Walt Disney Company is one firm that doesn't mind being called a "Mickey Mouse Organization."

Table 6.7 shows a variety of accounting operating statistics, including revenues, cash flow, capital spending, dividends, earnings, book value, and year-end share prices for the Walt Disney Corporation during the 1980–2000 period. All data are expressed in dollars per share to illustrate how individual shareholders have benefited from the company's consistently superior rates of growth. During this time frame, for example, revenue per share grew at an annual rate of 16.3% per year, and earnings per share grew by 12.2% per year. These performance measures exceed industry and economy-wide norms by a substantial margin. Disney employees, CEO Michael D. Eisner, and all stockholders have profited greatly from the company's outstanding performance. Over the 1980–2000 period, Disney common stock exploded in price from $1.07 per share to $28.94, after adjusting for stock splits. This represents more than a 17.9% annual rate of return and makes Disney one of the truly outstanding stock-market performers during recent years.

Of course, present-day investors want to know how the company will fare during coming years. Will the company be able to continue sizzling growth, or, like many companies, will Disney find it impossible to maintain such stellar performance? On the one hand, Tokyo Disneyland and Euro Disneyland promise significant future revenues and profits

CASE STUDY (continued)

TABLE 6.7

Operating Statistics for the Walt Disney Company (all data in dollars per share)

Year	Revenues	Cash Flow	Capital Spending	Dividends	Earnings	Book Value	Year-End Stock Price[1]
1980	$0.59	$0.11	$0.10	$0.02	$0.09	$0.69	$1.07
1981	0.65	0.10	0.21	0.02	0.08	0.75	1.09
1982	0.64	0.09	0.38	0.03	0.06	0.80	1.32
1983	0.79	0.11	0.20	0.03	0.06	0.85	1.10
1984	1.02	0.13	0.12	0.03	0.06	0.71	1.25
1985	1.30	0.18	0.12	0.03	0.11	0.76	2.35
1986	1.58	0.24	0.11	0.03	0.15	0.90	3.59
1987	1.82	0.34	0.18	0.03	0.24	1.17	4.94
1988	2.15	0.42	0.37	0.03	0.32	1.48	5.48
1989	2.83	0.55	0.46	0.04	0.43	1.87	9.33
1990	3.70	0.65	0.45	0.05	0.50	2.21	8.46
1991	3.96	0.58	0.59	0.06	0.40	2.48	9.54
1992	4.77	0.72	0.35	0.07	0.51	2.99	14.33
1993	5.31	0.78	0.49	0.08	0.54	3.13	14.21
1994	6.40	0.97	0.65	0.10	0.68	3.50	15.33
1995	7.70	1.15	0.57	0.12	0.84	4.23	19.63
1996	10.50	1.32	0.86	0.14	0.74	7.96	23.25
1997	11.10	1.51	0.95	0.17	0.92	8.54	33.00
1998	11.21	1.52	1.13	0.20	0.90	9.46	30.00
1999	11.34	1.30	1.03	0.00	0.66	10.16	29.25
2000	12.09	1.58	1.02	0.21	0.90	11.65	28.94
2004-2006[2]	15.15	2.20	1.05	0.31	1.35	14.75	

1 Split-adjusted share prices.
2 Value Line estimates.

Sources: Company annual reports (various years); http://www.valueline.com.

from previously untapped global markets. Anyone with young children who has visited Disneyland or Disney World has seen their delight and fascination with Disney characters. It is also impossible not to notice how much foreign travelers to the United States seem to enjoy the Disney experience. Donald Duck and Mickey Mouse will do a lot of business abroad. Future expansion possibilities in Malaysia, China, or the former Soviet Union also hold the potential for rapid growth into the next century. On the other hand, growth of 20% per year is exceedingly hard to maintain for any length of time. At that pace, the 120,000 workers employed by Disney in 2001 would grow to over 288,000 by the year 2005, and to roughly 619,000 by the year 2010. Maintaining control with such a rapidly growing workforce would be challenging, to say the least; maintaining Disney's high level of creative energy might not be possible.

Given the many uncertainties faced by Disney and most major corporations, long-term forecasts of operating performance by industry analysts are usually restricted to a fairly short time perspective. The Value Line Investment Survey, one of the most widely respected forecast services, focuses on a 3- to 5-year time horizon. To forecast performance for any individual company, Value Line starts with an underlying forecast of the economic environment 3 to 5

CASE STUDY (continued)

years hence. During mid-2001 for example, Value Line forecast a 2004–06 economic environment in which unemployment will average 4.4% of the workforce, compared to 4.0% in 2001. Industrial production will be expanding about 3.5% per year; inflation measured by the Consumer Price Index will continue at a modest 2.5% per year. Long-term interest rates are projected to be about 6.6%, and gross domestic product will average over $11 trillion in the years 2004 through 2006, or about 15% above the 2001 total of $9.7 trillion. As Value Line states, things may turn out differently, but these plausible assumptions offer a fruitful basis for measuring the relative growth potential of various firms like Disney.[6]

The most interesting economic statistic for Disney stockholders is, of course, its stock price during some future period, say 2004–06. In economic terms, stock prices represent the net present value of future cash flows, discounted at an appropriate risk-adjusted rate of return. To forecast Disney's stock price during the 2004–06 period, one might use any or all of the data in Table 6.7. Historical numbers for a recent period, like 1980–2000, often represent a useful context for projecting future stock prices. For example, Fidelity's legendary mutual fund investor Peter Lynch argues that stock prices are largely determined by the future pattern of earnings per share. Stock prices typically rise following an increase in earnings per share and plunge when earnings per share plummet. Another renown investor, Sir John Templeton, the father of global stock market investing, focuses on book value per share. Templeton contends that future earnings are closely related to the book value of the firm, or accounting net worth. According to Templeton, "bargains" can be found when stock can be purchased in companies that sell in the marketplace at a significant discount to book value, or when book value per share is expected to rise dramatically. Both Lynch and Templeton have built a large following among investors who have profited mightily using their stock-market selection techniques.

As an experiment, it will prove interesting to employ the data provided in Table 6.7 to estimate regression models that can be used to forecast the average common stock price for The Walt Disney Company over the 2004–06 period.

A. A simple regression model over the 1980–2000 period where the Y variable is the Disney year-end stock price and the X variable is Disney's earnings per share reads as follows (t statistics in parentheses):

$$P_t = -\$2.311 + \$33.296 EPS_t \quad \bar{R}^2 = 89.2\%$$
$$(-1.68) \quad\quad (12.92)$$

Use this model to forecast Disney's average stock price for the 2004–06 period using the Value Line estimate of Disney's average earnings per share for 2004–06. Discuss this share-price forecast.

B. A simple regression model over the 1980–2000 period where the Y variable is the Disney year-end stock price and the X variable is Disney's book value per share reads as follows (t statistics in parentheses):

$$P_t = \$1.638 + \$2.924 BV_t \quad \bar{R}^2 = 90.9\%$$
$$(1.57) \quad\quad (14.15)$$

Use this model to forecast Disney's average stock price for the 2004–06 period using the Value Line estimate of Disney's average book value per share for 2004–06. Discuss this share-price forecast.

6　See "Economic Series," *The Value Line Investment Survey* (http://www.valueline.com).

CASE STUDY (continued)

C. A multiple regression model over the 1980–2000 period where the Y variable is the Disney year-end stock price and the X variables are Disney's earnings per share and book value per share reads as follows (t statistics in parentheses):

$$P_t = -\$1.181 + \$16.980 EPS_t + \$1.655 BV_t \quad \bar{R}^2 = 97.2\%$$
$$(-1.64) \quad (6.60) \quad (7.39)$$

Use this model to forecast Disney's average stock price for the 2004–06 period using the Value Line estimate of Disney's average earnings per share and book value per share for 2004–06. Discuss this share-price forecast.

D. A multiple regression model over the 1980–2000 period where the Y variable is the Disney year-end stock price and X variables include the accounting operating statistics shown in Table 6.7 reads as follows (t statistics in parentheses):

$$P_t = -\$1.052 + \$0.587 REV_t + \$19.172 CF_t + \$0.386 CAPX_t - \$12.651 DIV_t - \$5.895 EPS_t + \$0.183 BV_t \quad \bar{R}^2 = 97.3\%$$
$$(-1.22) \quad (0.30) \quad (0.60) \quad (0.09) \quad (-0.96) \quad (-0.23) \quad (0.20)$$

Use this model and Value Line estimates to forecast Disney's average stock price for the 2004-06 period. Discuss this share-price forecast.

Reproduced with the permission of Value Line Publishing, Inc.

SELECTED REFERENCES

Barro, Robert J. "Human Capital and Growth." *American Economic Review* 91 (May 2001): 12–17.

Beech, Alfred J. "Market-Based Demand Forecasting Promotes Informed Strategic Financial Planning." *Healthcare Financial Management* 55 (November 2001): 46–56.

Bertrand, Marianne, and Sendhil Mullainathan. "Do People Mean What They Say? Implications for Subjective Survey Data." *American Economic Review* 91 (May 2001): 67–72.

Bollerslev, Tim, and Jonathan H. Wright. "High-Frequency Data, Frequency Domain Inference, and Volatility Forecasting." *Review of Economics and Statistics* 83 (November 2001): 596–602.

Brownstone, David, and Robert Valletta. "The Bootstrap and Multiple Imputations: Harnessing Increased Computing Power for Improved Statistical Tests." *Journal of Economic Perspectives* 15 (Fall 2001): 129–142.

Caselli, Francesco, and Wilbur John Coleman, II. "Cross-Country Technology Diffusion: The Case of Computers." *American Economic Review* 91 (May 2001): 328–335.

Chamberlain, Gary. "Minimax Estimation and Forecasting in a Stationary Autoregression Model." *American Economic Review* 91 (May 2001): 55–59.

Cote, Murray J., and Stephen L. Tucker. "Four Methodologies to Improve Healthcare Demand Forecasting." *Healthcare Financial Management* 55 (May 2001): 54–58.

Dukart, James R. "Forecasting Demand." *Utility Business* 4 (November 2001): 33–35.

Duranton, Gilles, and Diego Puga. "Nursery Cities: Urban Diversity, Process Innovation, and the Life Cycle of Products." *American Economic Review* 91 (December 2001): 1454–1477.

Hansen, Bruce E. "The New Econometrics of Structural Change: Dating Breaks in U.S. Labor Productivity." *Journal of Economic Perspectives* 15 (Fall 2001): 117–128.

Kose, M. Ayhan, and Kei-Mu Yi. "International Trade and Business Cycles: Is Vertical Specialization the Missing Link?" *American Economic Review* 91 (May 2001): 371–375.

Langabeer, Jim, and Tim Stoughton. "Demand Planning and Forecasting in the High Technology Industry." *Journal of Business Forecasting Methods & Systems* 20 (Spring 2001): 7–10.

Toktay, L. Beril, and Lawrence M. Wein. "Analysis of a Forecasting-Production-Inventory System with Stationary Demand." *Management Science* 47 (September 2001): 1268–1281.

Production and Cost Analysis

CHAPTER SEVEN

Production Analysis and Compensation Policy

Hiring the right workers, providing proper training, and offering them an effective incentive compensation package is tough because the ongoing relationship between employers and their employees is different from any other business affiliation. If a company buys a piece of land, for example, the terms of trade can be clearly set in advance. In the case of real estate, a mutually acceptable price is determined, a deed is delivered, and the transaction is completed. However, what works for real estate transactions is far from sufficient for setting a compensation policy. "One shot" deals are fundamentally different from the typical employment relationship.

The employment relationship is never fully completed because effort is continuously renegotiable. If employees feel slighted or underpaid, they always have the option of reducing effort to the point where the resulting rate per hour or month gives an acceptable return for the amount of effort expended. However, what passes for equity in the eyes of workers creates fundamental problems for managers concerned with the health of the overall organization. As a result, managers face the continuing need to design mutually attractive compensation packages that align worker incentives and performance with organizational objectives.

Like the economic concepts to measure worker productivity, managers rely upon managerial economics to help them assess the productivity of all input factors. This makes production analysis and compensation policy one of the most interesting and fundamental challenges facing management. Production analysis is concerned with more than low-cost defect prevention. It is about producing exciting products that customers want at prices that beat the competition.[1]

---

1   T. J. Rodgers, "Options Aren't Optional in Silicon Valley," *The Wall Street Journal Online*, March 4, 2002 (http://online.wsj.com).

PRODUCTION FUNCTIONS

The production process is the creative endeavor at the heart of every successful organization. The corporate landscape is littered with examples of firms that once introduced innovative products only to see their early lead and dominant position eroded by more efficient rivals. A number of firms have also fallen prey to the mistake of succeeding at being the low-cost producer in a vanishing market. Productive efficiency is not simply about *what* or *how* to produce; it is about *both*.

Properties of Production Functions

production function
Maximum output that can be produced for a given amount of input

A **production function** specifies the maximum output that can be produced for a given amount of input. Alternatively, a production function shows the minimum quantity of input necessary to produce a given level of output. Production functions are determined by the technology available for effectively using plant, equipment, labor, materials, and so on. Any improvement in technology, such as better equipment or a training program that enhances worker productivity, results in a new production function.

Basic properties of production functions can be illustrated by examining a simple two-input, one-output system. Consider a production process in which various quantities of two inputs, X and Y, can be used to produce a product, Q. Inputs X and Y might represent resources such as labor and capital or energy and raw materials. The product Q could be physical goods such as television sets, baseball gloves, or breakfast cereal; Q could also represent services such as medical care, education, or banking.

The production function for such a system can be written

(7.1)
$$Q = f(X, Y)$$

Table 7.1 is a tabular representation of a two-input, single-output production system. Each element in the table shows the maximum quantity of Q that can be produced with a specific combination of X and Y. Table 7.1 shows, for example, that two units of X and three units of

TABLE 7.1

Representative Production Table

Units of Y Employed	Output Quantity									
10	52	71	87	101	113	122	127	129	130	131
9	56	74	89	102	111	120	125	127	128	129
8	59	75	91	99	108	117	122	124	125	126
7	61	77	87	96	104	112	117	120	121	122
6	62	72	82	91	99	107	111	114	116	117
5	55	66	75	84	92	99	104	107	109	110
4	47	58	68	77	85	91	97	100	102	103
3	35	49	59	68	76	83	89	91	90	89
2	15	31	48	59	68	72	73	72	70	67
1	5	12	35	48	56	55	53	50	46	40
	1	2	3	4	5	6	7	8	9	10

Units of *X* Employed

Y can be combined to produce 49 units of output; five units of *X* coupled with five units of *Y* results in 92 units of output; four units of *X* and 10 units of *Y* produce 101 units of *Q*, and so on. The units of input could represent *hours* of labor, *dollars* of capital, *cubic feet* of natural gas, *tons* of raw materials, and so on. Units of *Q* could be *numbers* of television sets or baseball gloves, *cases* of cereal, *patient days* of hospital care, customer *transactions* at an ATM banking facility, and so on.

The **discrete production function** described in Table 7.1 involves distinct, or "lumpy," patterns for input combination, as illustrated in Figure 7.1. The height of the bars associated with each input combination indicates the output produced. The tops of the output bars map the production surface for the system.

The discrete production data shown in Table 7.1 and Figure 7.1 can be generalized by assuming that the underlying production function is continuous. A **continuous production function** is one in which inputs can be varied in an unbroken fashion rather than incrementally, as in the preceding example.

discrete production function
Production function with distinct input patterns

continuous production function
Production function where inputs can be varied in a unbroken marginal fashion

FIGURE 7.1

Representative Production Surface

This discrete production function illustrates the output level resulting from each combination of inputs *X* and *Y*.

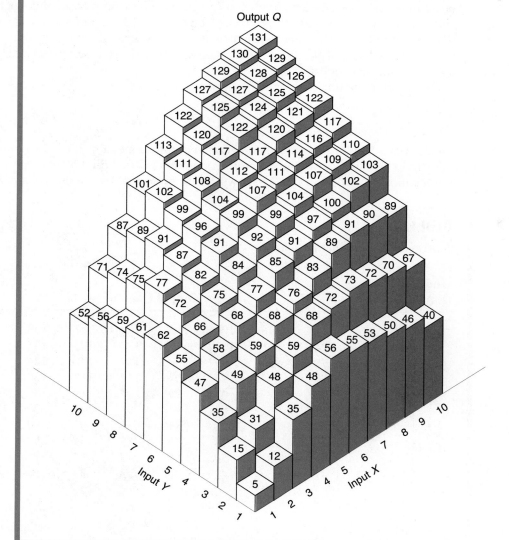

Returns to Scale and Returns to a Factor

returns to scale
Output effect of a proportional increase in all inputs

In studying production functions, two important relations between inputs and outputs are of interest. One is the relation between output and the variation in *all inputs* taken together. This is known as the **returns to scale** characteristic of a production system. Returns to scale play an important role in managerial decisions. They affect the optimal size of a firm and its production facilities. They also affect the nature of competition and thus are important in determining the profitability of investment.

returns to a factor
Relation between output and variation in only one input

A second important relation in any production system is that between output and variation in only *one of the inputs* employed. **Returns to a factor** signals the relation between the quantity of an individual input (or factor of production) employed and the level of output produced. Factor productivity is the key to determining the optimal combination of inputs that should be used to manufacture a given product. Because an understanding of factor productivity aids in the study of returns to scale, it is worth considering factor productivity concepts first.

TOTAL, MARGINAL, AND AVERAGE PRODUCT

The optimization process entails an analysis of the relation between the total and marginal values of a function. Therefore, it is useful to introduce the concepts of total, average, and marginal products for the resources employed in a production system.

Total Product

total product
Whole output from a production system

Total product is the output from a production system. It is synonymous with Q in Equation 7.1. Total product is the overall output that results from employing a specific quantity of resources in a given production system. The total product concept is used to investigate the relation between output and variation in only one input in a production function. For example, suppose that Table 7.1 represents a production system in which Y is a capital resource and X represents labor input. If a firm is operating with a given level of capital (say, $Y = 2$), then the relevant production function for the firm in the short run is represented by the row in Table 7.1 corresponding to that level of fixed capital.[2] Operating with two units of capital, output or total product depends on the quantity of labor (X) employed. This total product of X can be read from the $Y = 2$ row in Table 7.1. It is also shown in column 2 of Table 7.2 and is illustrated graphically in Figure 7.2.

TABLE 7.2

Total Product, Marginal Product, and Average Product of Factor X Holding $Y = 2$

Input Quantity (X)	Total Product of the Input (X)	Marginal Product of Input X ($MP_X = \partial Q / \partial X$)	Average Product of Input X ($AP_X = Q/X$)
1	15	+15	15.0
2	31	+16	15.5
3	48	+17	16.0
4	59	+11	14.8
5	68	+9	13.6
6	72	+4	12.0
7	73	+1	10.4
8	72	−1	9.0
9	70	−2	7.8
10	67	−3	6.7

2 The *short run* is a time period during which at least one resource in a production system is fixed. In the short run, one input is constant regardless of the quantity of output produced.

FIGURE 7.2

Total, Average, and Marginal Product for Input X, Given Y = 2

(a) Holding Y at two units, total production first rises but then falls as the amount of X employed grows.
(b) Total product rises as long as marginal product is positive.

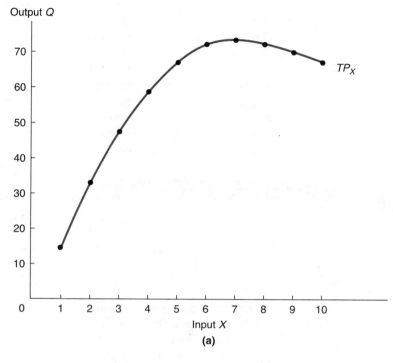

(a)

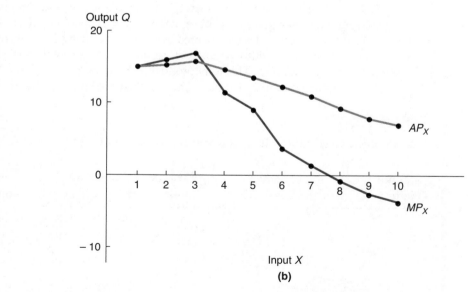

(b)

More generally, the total product for a factor of production, such as labor, can be expressed as a function relating output to the quantity of the resource employed. Continuing the example, the total product of X is given by the production function

$$Q = f(X \mid Y = 2)$$

This equation relates the output quantity Q (the total product of X) to the quantity of input X employed, fixing the quantity of Y at two units. One would, of course, obtain other total product functions for X if the factor Y were fixed at levels other than two units.

Figure 7.3(a) and 7.3(b) illustrate the more general concept of the total product of an input as the schedule of output obtained as that input increases, *holding constant the amounts of other inputs employed*. This figure depicts a continuous production function in which inputs can be varied in a marginal unbroken fashion rather than discretely. Suppose the firm wishes to fix the amount of input Y at the level Y_1. The total product curve of input X, holding input Y constant at $Y = Y_1$, rises along the production surface as the use of input X is increased.

FIGURE 7.3

Total, Marginal, and Average Product Curves: (A) Total Product Curve for X, Holding $Y = Y_1$; (B) Marginal Product Curve for X, Holding $Y = Y_1$

MP_X reaches a maximum at point A', where the slope of the TP_X curve is the greatest. AP_X is at a maximum where $MP_X = AP_X$. At point C, TP_X is at a maximum and $MP_X = 0$.

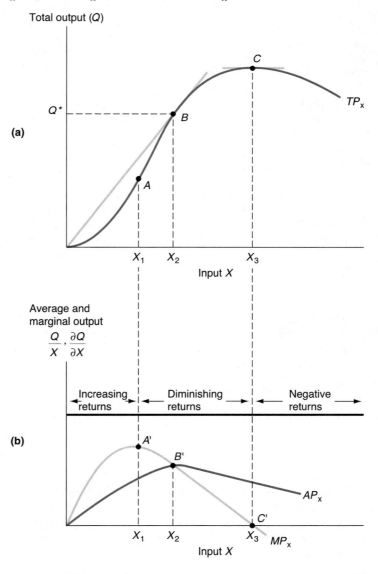

Total Quality Management

One of the hottest management concepts in recent years—the total quality management, or TQM approach—has failed to deliver promised results in many companies. However, once implementation problems are overcome, the method becomes a cornerstone of enlightened management strategy. In today's global economic environment, both large and small companies have come to recognize that improved quality is an essential ingredient for success. Still, quality management programs are not painless.

TQM requires a major commitment. In simplest terms, TQM involves a keen attention to the production process, a high level of commitment to the customer, and the involvement of employees in identifying and continuously improving upon the best production practices. TQM is not a quick fix; TQM sometimes requires basic reengineering of the firm's entire operation. TQM starts with a fundamental question—Should we be doing this at all? If affirmative, TQM then asks, "How can we do this cheaper, faster, or better?"

Analysts agree that adherence to basic concepts determines the success of any TQM effort. Among those factors thought to be most important are the following:

- The CEO must be actively and visibly behind it.
- Tunnel vision must be avoided. Ask what change does for the customer.
- Limit yourself to a few critical goals.
- Link change to a clear financial payback.
- Customize the TQM concept to meet the specific needs of customers.

Like any sound theory, these principles represent more than simply an enlightened operating philosophy; they work well in practice, too. TQM helps boost product quality, customer satisfaction, and profits. Experience shows that continuous monitoring is required to ensure that the TQM process retains an effective customer focus. TQM must be outward rather than inward looking.

See: Walter S. Mossberg, "Cheaper Office Suite Challenges Mircrosoft, But Trails on Quality," *The Wall Street Journal Online*, January 10, 2002 (http://online.wsj.com).

Marginal Product

marginal product
Change in output associated with a one-unit change in a single input

Given the total product function for an input, both marginal and average products can be easily derived. The **marginal product** of a factor, MP_X, is the change in output associated with a one-unit change in the factor input, holding all other inputs constant. For a total product function such as that shown in Table 7.2 and Figure 7.2(a), the marginal product is expressed as

$$MP_X = \frac{\partial Q}{\partial X}$$

where ∂Q is the change in output resulting from a one-unit change, ∂X, in the variable factor. This expression assumes that the quantity of the other input, Y, remains unchanged. Marginal product is shown in column 3 of Table 7.2 and in Figure 7.2(b).

Average Product

average product
Total product divided by units of input employed

(7.2)

Average product is total product divided by the number of units of input employed:

$$AP_X = \frac{Q}{X}$$

The average product for X given $Y = 2$ units is shown in column 4 of Table 7.2 and in Figure 7.2(b).

For a continuous total product function, as illustrated in Figure 7.3(a), marginal product equals the slope of the total product curve, whereas average product equals the slope of a line drawn from the origin to a point on the total product curve. The average and marginal products for input X can be determined in this manner, and these points are plotted to form the average and marginal product curves shown in Figure 7.3(b).

Three points of interest, *A*, *B*, and *C*, can be identified on the total product curve in Figure 7.3(a). Each has a corresponding location on the average or marginal curves. Point *A* is the inflection point of the total product curve. The marginal product of *X* (the slope of the total product curve) increases until this point is reached, after which it begins to decrease. This can be seen in Figure 7.3(b) where MP_X reaches its highest level at *A'*.

The second point on the total product curve, *B*, indicates the output at which the average product and marginal product are equal. The slope of a line from the origin to any point on the total product curve measures the average product of *X* at that point, whereas the slope of the total product curve equals the marginal product. At point *B*, where X_2 units of input *X* are employed, a line from the origin is tangent to the total product curve, so $MP_X = AP_X$. The slopes of successive lines drawn from the origin to the total product curve increase until point *B*, after which their slopes decline. The average product curve rises until it reaches *B*, then declines. This feature is also shown in Figure 7.3(b) as point *B'*. Here again, $MP_X = AP_X$ and AP_X is at a maximum.

The third point, *C*, indicates where the slope of the total product curve is zero and the curve is at a maximum. Beyond *C* the marginal product of *X* is negative, indicating that increased use of input *X* results in a *reduction* of total product. The corresponding point in Figure 7.3(b) is *C'*, the point where the marginal product curve intersects the *X*-axis.

LAW OF DIMINISHING RETURNS TO A FACTOR

law of diminishing returns
As the quantity of a variable input increases, the resulting rate of output increase eventually diminishes

The total and the marginal product curves in Figure 7.3 demonstrate the property known as the **law of diminishing returns**. This law states that as the quantity of a variable input increases, with the quantities of all other factors being held constant, the resulting increase in output eventually diminishes.

Diminishing Returns to a Factor Concept

The law of diminishing returns states that the marginal product of a variable factor must eventually decline as more of the variable factor is combined with other fixed resources. The law of diminishing returns is sometimes called the law of diminishing marginal returns to emphasize the fact that it deals with the diminishing marginal product of a variable input factor. The law of diminishing returns cannot be derived deductively. It is a generalization of an empirical regularity associated with every known production system.

For example, consider an assembly line for the production of refrigerators. If only one employee is put to work, that individual must perform each of the activities necessary to assemble refrigerators. Output from such a combination of labor and capital is likely to be small. In fact, it may be less than could be achieved with a smaller amount of capital, given the inefficiency of having one employee accompany a refrigerator down an assembly line rather than building it at a single station. As additional units of labor are added to this production system—holding capital input constant—output is likely to expand rapidly. The intensity with which the capital resource is used increases with additional labor, and increasingly efficient input combinations result. The improved use of capital resulting from the increase in labor could cause the marginal product, or rise in output associated with each successive employee, to actually increase over some range of additional labor. This increasing marginal productivity might reflect the benefits of worker specialization.

An example in which the marginal product of an input increases over some range is presented in Table 7.2. The first unit of labor (input *X*) results in 15 units of production. With two units of labor, 31 units can be produced. The marginal product of the second unit of labor $MP_{X=2} = 16$ exceeds that of the $MP_{X=1} = 15$. Similarly, the addition of another unit of labor results in output increasing to 48 units, indicating a marginal product of $MP_{X=3} = 17$ for the third unit of labor.

Eventually, sufficient labor is combined with the fixed capital input so that the benefits of further labor additions will not be as large as the benefits achieved earlier. When this occurs, the rate of increase in output per additional unit of labor, the marginal product of labor, will drop. Although the marginal product of labor is positive and total output increases as more units of labor are employed, the rate of increase in output eventually declines. This diminishing marginal productivity of labor is exhibited by the fourth, fifth, sixth, and seventh units of input X in Table 7.2.

Conceivably, a point might be reached where the quantity of a variable input factor is so large that total output actually begins to decline with additional employment of that factor. In the refrigerator assembly example, this might occur when the labor force became so large that additional employees actually got in each other's way and hindered the manufacturing process. This happens in Table 7.2 when more than seven units of input X are combined with two units of input Y. The eighth unit of X results in a one-unit reduction in total output, $MP_{X=8} = -1$; units 9 and 10 cause output to fall by two and three units, respectively. In Figure 7.3(b), regions where the variable input factor X exhibits increasing, diminishing, and negative returns have been labeled.

Illustration of Diminishing Returns to a Factor

Suppose Tax Advisors, Inc., has an office for processing tax returns in Scranton, Pennsylvania. Table 7.3 shows that if the office employs one certified public accountant (CPA), it can process 0.2 tax returns per hour. Adding a second CPA increases production to 1 return per hour; with a third, output jumps to 2.4 returns processed per hour. In this production system, the marginal product for the second CPA is 0.8 returns per hour as compared with 0.2 for the first CPA employed. The marginal product for the third CPA is 1.4 returns per hour. $MP_{CPA=2} = 0.8$ seems to indicate that the second CPA is four times as productive as the first, and $MP_{CPA=3} = 1.4$ says that the third CPA is more productive still. In production analysis, however, it is assumed that each unit of an input factor is like all other units of that same factor, meaning that each CPA is equally competent and efficient. If individual differences do not account for this increasing productivity, what does?

Typically, increased specialization and better utilization of other factors in the production process allow factor productivity to grow. As the number of CPAs increases, each can specialize. Also, additional CPAs may be better able to fully use computer, clerical, and other resources employed by the firm. Advantages from specialization and increased coordination cause output to rise at an increasing rate, from 0.2 to 1 return processed per hour as the second CPA is employed, and from 1 to 2.4 returns per hour as the third CPA is added.

TABLE 7.3

Production Function for Tax-Return Processing

Units of Labor Input Employed (CPAs)	Total Product of CPAs—Tax Returns Processed/Hour ($TP_{CPA} = Q$)	Marginal Product of CPAs ($MP_{CPA} = \partial Q$)	Average Product of CPAs ($AP_{CPA} = Q/X$)
1	0.2	0.2	0.20
2	1.0	0.8	0.50
3	2.4	1.4	0.80
4	2.8	0.4	0.70
5	3.0	0.2	0.60
6	2.7	−0.3	0.45

In practice, it is very rare to see input combinations that exhibit increasing returns for any factor. With increasing returns to a factor, an industry would come to be dominated by one very large producer—and this is seldom the case. Input combinations in the range of diminishing returns are commonly observed. If, for example, four CPAs could process 2.8 returns per hour, then the marginal product of the fourth CPA ($MP_{CPA=4} = 0.4$) would be less than the marginal product of the third CPA ($MP_{CPA=3} = 1.4$) and diminishing returns to the CPA labor input would be encountered.

The irrationality of employing inputs in the negative returns range, beyond X_3 in Figure 7.3, can be illustrated by noting that adding a sixth CPA would cause total output to fall from 3.0 to 2.7 returns per hour. The marginal product of the sixth CPA is –0.3 ($MP_{CPA=6} = -0.3$), perhaps because of problems with coordinating work among greater numbers of employees or limitations in other important inputs. Would the firm pay an additional employee when employing that person reduces the level of output? Obviously not: It is irrational to employ inputs in the range of negative returns.

INPUT COMBINATION CHOICE

The concept of factor productivity can be more fully explored using isoquant analysis, which explicitly recognizes the potential variability of both factors in a two-input, one-output production system. This technique is introduced to examine the role of input substitutability in determining efficient input combinations.

Production Isoquants

isoquant
Different input combinations used to efficiently produce a specified output

technical efficiency
Least-cost production of a target level of output

The term **isoquant**—derived from *iso*, meaning equal, and *quant*, from quantity—denotes a curve that represents the different combinations of inputs that can be efficiently used to produce a given level of output. Efficiency in this case refers to **technical efficiency**, meaning the least-cost production of a target level of output. If two units of X and three units of Y can be combined to produce 49 units of output, but they can also be combined less efficiently to produce only 45 units of output, the $X = 2$, $Y = 3$ input combination will lie only on the $Q = 49$ isoquant. The $X = 2$, $Y = 3$ combination resulting in $Q = 45$ is not technologically efficient, because this same input combination can produce a larger output quantity. This combination would not appear in the production function nor on the $Q = 45$ isoquant. From Table 7.1, it is clear that 91 units of output can be produced efficiently by using the input combinations $X = 3$, $Y = 8$; $X = 4$, $Y = 6$; $X = 6$, $Y = 4$; or $X = 8$, $Y = 3$. These four input combinations all lie on the $Q = 91$ isoquant. Similarly, the combinations $X = 6$, $Y = 10$; $X = 7$, $Y = 8$; $X = 10$, $Y = 7$ all result in 122 units of production and, hence, lie on the $Q = 122$ isoquant.

These two isoquants are illustrated in Figure 7.4. Each point on the $Q = 91$ isoquant indicates a different combination of X and Y that can efficiently produce 91 units of output. For example, 91 units can be produced with three units of X and eight units of Y, with four units of X and six units of Y, or with any other combination of X and Y on the isoquant $Q = 91$. A similar interpretation can be given the isoquant for $Q = 122$ units of output.

Isoquants for a continuous production function also represent different levels of output. Every point on the Q_1 isoquant in Figure 7.5(c) represents input combinations that can be used to efficiently produce an equal quantity, or isoquant, of Q_1 units of output. The isoquant curve Q_2 maps out all input combinations that result in Q_2 units of production, and so on.

Input Factor Substitution

Isoquants shapes reveal a great deal about the substitutability of input factors, as illustrated in Figure 7.5(a), (b), and (c).

FIGURE 7.4

Representative Isoquants for Table 7.1

Each point on an isoquant represents a different combination of inputs X and Y that can be used to produce the same level of output.

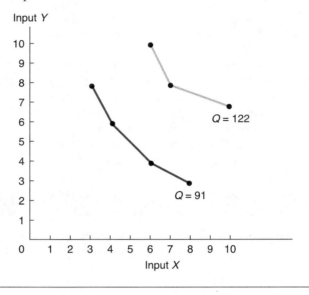

In some production systems, **input substitution** is easily accomplished. In the production of electricity, for example, fuels used to power generators often represent readily substitutable inputs. Figure 7.5(a) shows isoquants for an electric power plant with boilers equipped to burn either oil or gas. Power can be produced by burning gas only, oil only, or varying amounts of each. In this instance, gas and oil are perfect substitutes, and the electricity isoquants are straight lines. Other examples of readily substitutable inputs include fish meal and soybeans to provide protein in a feed mix, energy and time in a drying process, and United Parcel Service and the U.S. Postal Service for package delivery. In each case, production isoquants are linear.

At the other extreme of input substitutability lie production systems in which inputs are perfect complements; exact amounts of each input are required to produce a given quantity of output. Figure 7.5(b) illustrates isoquants for bicycles in which exactly two wheels and one frame are required to produce a bicycle. Wheels cannot be substituted for frames, nor vice versa. Pants and coats for men's suits, engines and bodies for trucks, and chemicals in specific compounds for prescription drugs are further examples of complementary inputs. Production isoquants for complementary inputs take the shape of right angles, as indicated in Figure 7.5(b).

Figure 7.5(c) shows a production process in which inputs can be substituted for each other within limits. A dress can be made with a relatively small amount of labor (L_1) and a large amount of cloth (C_1). The same dress can also be made with less cloth (C_2) if more labor (L_2) is used because the dress maker can cut the material more carefully and reduce waste. Finally, the dress can be made with still less cloth (C_3), but workers must be so extremely painstaking that the labor input requirement increases to L_3. Although a relatively small addition of labor, from L_1 to L_2, reduces the input of cloth from C_1 to C_2, a very large increase in labor, from L_2 to L_3, is required to obtain a similar reduction in cloth from C_2 to C_3. The substitutability of labor for cloth diminishes from L_1 to L_2 to L_3. The substitutability of cloth for labor in the manufacture of dresses also diminishes, as can be seen by considering the quantity of cloth that must be added to replace each unit of reduced labor in moving from L_3 to L_1.

Most labor-capital substitutions in production systems exhibit this diminishing substitutability. Energy and insulation used to provide home heating exhibit diminishing substitutability, as do physicians and medical technicians in providing health care services.

input substitution
Systematic replacement of productive factors

FIGURE 7.5

Isoquants for Inputs with Varying Degrees of Substitutability: (A) Electric Power Generation; (B) Bicycle Production; (C) Dress Production

(a) Straight-line isoquants indicate perfect substitution. (b) A right-angle shape for isoquants reflects inputs that are perfect complements. (c) C-shaped isoquants indicate imperfect substitutability among inputs.

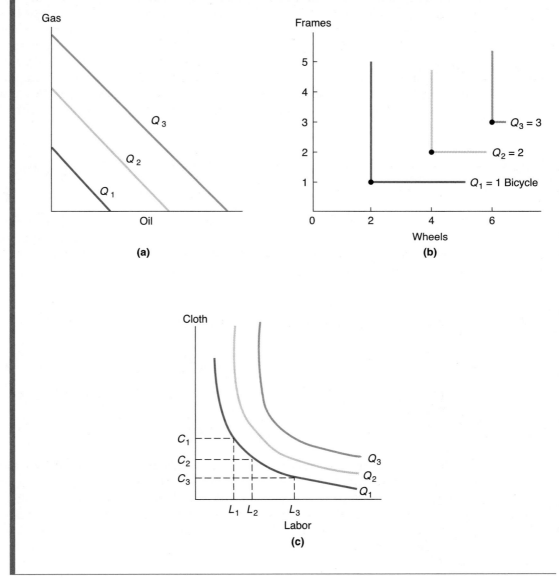

(a)

(b)

(c)

marginal rate of technical substitution (MRTS)

Amount of one input that must be substituted for another to maintain constant output

Marginal Rate of Technical Substitution

The **marginal rate of technical substitution**[3] **(MRTS)** is the amount of one input factor that must be substituted for one unit of another input factor to maintain a constant level of output. Algebraically,

(7.3)

$$MRTS = \frac{\partial Y}{\partial X} = \text{Slope of an Isoquant}$$

---

3 The term *marginal rate of technical substitution* is often shortened to *marginal rate of substitution*.

The marginal rate of technical substitution usually diminishes as the amount of substitution increases. In Figure 7.5(c), for example, as more and more labor is substituted for cloth, the increment of labor necessary to replace cloth increases. At the extremes, isoquants may even become positively sloped, indicating that the range over which input factors can be substituted for each other is limited. A classic example is the use of land and labor to produce a given output of grain. At some point, as labor is substituted for land, the farmers will trample the grain. As more labor is added, more land eventually must be added if grain output is to be maintained.

The input substitution relation indicated by the slope of a production isoquant is directly related to the concept of diminishing marginal productivity. The marginal rate of technical substitution is equal to –1 times the ratio of the marginal products of the input factors [$MRTS = -1(MP_X/MP_Y)$]. To see this, note that the loss in output resulting from a small reduction in Y equals the marginal product of Y, MP_Y, multiplied by the change in Y, ∂Y. That is,

(7.4)
$$\partial Q = MP_Y \times \partial Y$$

Similarly, the change in Q associated with the increased use of input X is given by the expression

(7.5)
$$\partial Q = MP_X \times \partial X$$

With substitution of X for Y along an isoquant, the absolute value of ∂Q in Equations 7.4 and 7.5 must be the same. The change in output associated with a reduction in input Y must be exactly offset by the change in output resulting from the increase in input X for output to remain constant—as it must along an isoquant. Therefore, along an isoquant,

(7.6)
$$-(MP_X \times \partial X) = (MP_Y \times \partial Y)$$

Transposing the variables in Equation 7.6 produces

(7.7)
$$-\frac{MP_X}{MP_Y} = \frac{\partial Y}{\partial X}$$

This means that the marginal rate of technical substitution is equal to the slope of a production isoquant:

$$MRTS_{XY} = \text{Slope of an Isoquant}^4$$

The slope of a production isoquant such as in Equation 7.3 is equal to $\partial Y/\partial X$ and is determined by the ratio of the marginal products of both inputs. In Figure 7.5(c), the isoquant Q_1 has a very steep negative slope at the point (L_1, C_1). When cloth is relatively abundant, the marginal product of labor is relatively high as compared with the marginal product of cloth. When labor is relatively abundant at, say, point (L_3, C_3), the marginal product of labor is low relative to the marginal product of cloth.

---

4 This result can also be demonstrated by using calculus notation by noting that along any isoquant the total differential of the production function must be zero (output is fixed along an isoquant). Thus, for the production function given by Equation 7.1, setting the total differential equal to zero gives

$$\frac{\partial Q}{\partial X} dX + \frac{\partial Q}{\partial Y} dY = 0$$

and, rearranging terms,

$$(-)\frac{\partial Q/\partial X}{\partial Q/\partial Y} = \frac{dY}{dX}$$

Or, because $\partial Q/\partial X = MP_X$ and $\partial Q/\partial Y = MP_Y$,

$$(-)\frac{MP_X}{MP_Y} = \frac{dY}{dX} = \text{Slope of the Isoquant}$$

Are CEOs Overpaid?

Citigroup, Inc., CEO Sanford "Sandy" Weill is a favorite target of those who believe CEOs are overpaid. Citigroup, with 2000 revenue of $64.9 billion, is the largest and most profitable financial services company in the world. It's a complex company with a wide variety of holdings. Over the 1995–2000 period, Citigroup had a 5-year growth rate of 21.3 percent, or somewhat better than average for financial service companies. Critics contend that Citigroup has done well during Weill's tenure, but not nearly so well as its CEO. Between 1995 and 2000, Weill pulled in an astonishing $785 million in total compensation. In 2000 alone, Weill cashed in stock options worth $196.2 million on top of a bonus of $18.4 million. Weill's pay is unusual, but CEOs of large U.S. corporations routinely take home total compensation that runs in excess of $5 million per year. For top CEOs with over 5 years at the helm, pay averages more than $7.5 million per year.

Proponents of modern CEO pay plans contend that companies like Citigroup have been revitalized when management focuses on bottom-line performance. Opponents argue that such plans allow CEOs to take unfair advantage of their positions. They cite examples of millions of dollars in compensation being paid to top executives in the auto, steel, and other industries following wage cuts for blue-collar workers, mass layoffs, and plant closures. Although proponents admit the need for close public scrutiny, they argue that corporate restructuring is an important requirement of a vital economy and a key task facing top executives. Proponents also note that running a large modern corporation is an exceedingly complex task and requires an individual with rare management skill.

CEOs of major U.S. corporations command billions of dollars in shareholder resources. Good decisions can mean billions of dollars in shareholder benefits; bad decisions can cost billions. In a global marketplace, it's a simple fact that good management is worth a lot.

See: Paul Beckett, "Citigroup Posts Stong Earnings Growth Despite Argentina Crisis, Enron Collapse," *The Wall Street Journal Online*, January 18, 2002 (http://online.wsj.com).

Rational Limits of Input Substitution

It is irrational for a firm to combine resources in such a way that the marginal product of any input is negative, because this implies that output could be increased by using less of that resource.[5] Note from Equation 7.6 that if the inputs X and Y are combined in proportions such that the marginal product of either factor is negative, then the slope of the production isoquant will be positive. For a production isoquant to be positively sloped, one of the input factors must have a negative marginal product. Input combinations lying along a positively sloped portion of a production isoquant are irrational and would be avoided by the firm.

In Figure 7.6, the rational limits of input substitution are where the isoquants become positively sloped. Limits to the range of substitutability of X for Y are indicated by the points of tangency between the isoquants and a set of lines drawn perpendicular to the Y-axis. Limits of economic substitutability of Y for X are shown by the tangents of lines perpendicular to the X-axis. Maximum and minimum proportions of Y and X that would be combined to produce each level of output are determined by points of tangency between these lines and the production isoquants.

ridge lines
Graphic bounds for positive marginal products

It is irrational to use any input combination outside these tangents, or **ridge lines**, as they are called. Such combinations are irrational because the marginal product of the relatively more abundant input is negative outside the ridge lines. The addition of the last unit of the excessive input factor actually reduces output. Obviously, it would be irrational for a firm to buy and employ additional units that cause production to decrease. To illustrate, suppose a firm is currently operating with a fixed quantity of input Y equal to Y_1 units, as shown in Figure 7.6. In such a situation, the firm would never employ more than X_3 units of input X, because employment of

5   This is technically correct only if the resource has a positive cost. Thus, for example, a firm might employ additional workers even though the marginal product of labor was negative if it received a government subsidy for that employment that more than offset the cost of the output reduction.

FIGURE 7.6

Maximum Variable Proportions for Inputs X and Y

The rational limits of substitution between Y and X occur where the isoquant slopes become positive.

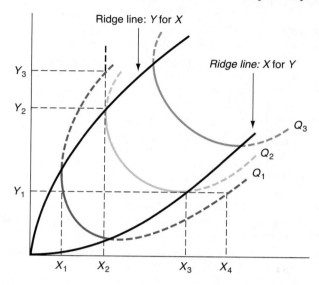

additional units of X results in production of successively lower output quantities. For example, if the firm combines Y_1 and X_4, output is equal to Q_1 units. By reducing usage of X from X_4 to X_3, output can be increased from Q_1 to Q_2. Only for input combinations lying between the ridge lines will *both* inputs have positive marginal products. It is here and along the negatively sloped portion of the isoquant that optimal input combinations are found.

MARGINAL REVENUE PRODUCT AND OPTIMAL EMPLOYMENT

To gain an understanding of how the factors of production should be combined for maximum efficiency, it is necessary to shift from the analysis of the *physical* productivity of inputs to an examination of their *economic* productivity, or net revenue-generating capability.

Marginal Revenue Product

[handwritten: This should be called marginal profit product.]

marginal revenue product
Amount of revenue generated by employing the last input unit

The economic productivity of an input is its **marginal revenue product**, or the additional net revenue generated by the last unit employed. In equation form, the marginal revenue product of input X, MRP_X, equals marginal product multiplied by the marginal revenue of output:

(7.8)

$$MRP_X = \frac{\partial TR}{\partial X}$$

$$= \frac{\partial Q}{\partial X} \times \frac{\partial TR}{\partial Q}$$

$$= MP_X \times MR_Q$$

Marginal revenue product is the economic value of a marginal unit of an input factor.[6] For example, if the addition of one more worker generates two incremental units of a product that can be

---

6   The economic value of a marginal unit of an input factor is sometimes referred to as its value of marginal product (VMP), where $VMP_X = MP_X \times P_Q$. In a perfectly competitive market, $P_Q = MR_Q$ and $VMP_X = MRP_X$.

sold for $5 each, the marginal product of labor is 2, and its marginal revenue product is $10 (= 2 × $5). Table 7.4 illustrates marginal revenue product for a simple one-factor production system. The marginal revenue product values shown in column 4 assume that each unit of output can be sold for $5. The marginal revenue product of the first unit of X employed equals the three units of output produced times the $5 revenue received per unit, or $MRP_{X=1} = \$15$. The second unit of X adds four units of production so $MRP_{X=2} = 4$. For the second unit of input, $MRP_{X=2} = \$20$. Marginal revenue products for each additional unit of X are all determined in this manner.

Optimal Level of a Single Input

To illustrate how the marginal revenue product (economic productivity) is related to input use, consider the following question: If the price of input X in the production system depicted in Table 7.4 is $12, how many units will the firm use? Clearly, the firm will employ three units of X because the value gained by adding the first three units exceeds marginal cost. When three units of X are employed, the third unit causes total revenues to rise by $15 while costing only $12. At the margin, employing the third unit of X increases total profit by $3 (= $15 − $12). A fourth unit of X would not be employed because the value of its marginal product ($10) is less than the cost of employment ($12); profit would decline by $2.

So long as marginal revenue exceeds marginal cost, profits must increase. In the context of production decisions, this means that profit will increase so long as the marginal revenue generated by an input, or its marginal revenue product, exceeds the marginal cost of employment. Conversely, when marginal revenue product is less than the cost of employment, marginal profit is negative, and the firm would reduce usage.

The concept of optimal resource use can be clarified by examining a simple production system in which a single variable labor input, L, is used to produce a single product, Q. Profit maximization requires production in which marginal revenue equals marginal cost. Because the only variable factor in the system is input L, the marginal cost of production is

$$MC_Q = \frac{\partial \text{ Total Cost}}{\partial \text{ Output}}$$

(7.9)

$$= \frac{P_L}{MP_L}$$

Dividing P_L, the price of L, by MP_L, the units of output gained by the employment of an added unit of L, provides a measure of the marginal cost of output.

Marginal revenue must equal marginal cost at the profit-maximizing output level. Therefore, MR_Q can be substituted for MC_Q in Equation 7.9, resulting in the expression

(7.10)

$$MR_Q = \frac{P_L}{MP_L}$$

TABLE 7.4

Marginal Revenue Product for a Single Input

Units of Input (X)	Total Product of X (Q)	Marginal Product of X ($MP_X = \Delta Q$)	Marginal Revenue Product of X ($MP_X \times \$5$)
1	3	3	$15
2	7	4	20
3	10	3	15
4	12	2	10
5	13	1	5

Equation 7.10 must hold for profit maximization because its right-hand side is just another expression for marginal cost. Solving Equation 7.10 for P_L results in

$$P_L = MR_Q \times MP_L$$

or, because $MR_Q \times MP_L$ is defined as the marginal revenue product of L,

(7.11)
$$P_L = MRP_L$$

A profit-maximizing firm will always set marginal revenue product equal to price (marginal cost) for every input. If marginal revenue product exceeds the cost of an input, profits could be increased by employing additional units. When the marginal cost of an input factor is greater than its marginal revenue product, profit would increase by reducing employment. Only when $MRP = P$ is profit maximized. Optimal employment and **economic efficiency** is achieved in the overall economy when all firms employ resources so as to equate each input's marginal revenue product and marginal cost.

economic efficiency
Achieved when all firms equate input marginal revenue product and marginal cost (maximize profits)

An Illustration of Optimal Employment

Determination of the optimal input level can be clarified by reconsidering the Tax Advisors, Inc., example, illustrated in Table 7.3. If three CPAs can process 2.4 returns per hour and employing a fourth CPA increases total output per hour to 2.8, then employing a fourth CPA reduces marginal product from $MP_{CPA=3} = 1.4$ to $MP_{CPA=4} = 0.4$. Employment is in a range of diminishing returns. Nevertheless, a fourth CPA should be hired if expanding employment will increase profits.

For simplicity, assume that CPA time is the only input required to process additional tax returns and that CPAs earn $35 per hour, or roughly $70,000 per year including fringe benefits. If Tax Advisors, Inc., receives $100 in revenue for each tax return prepared by the fourth CPA, a comparison of the price of labor and marginal revenue product for the fourth CPA reveals

$$P_{CPA} < MRP_{CPA=4} = MR_Q \times MP_{CPA=4}$$

because

$$\$35 < \$40 = \$100 \times 0.4$$

If a fourth CPA is hired, total profits will rise by $5 per hour (= $40 − $35). The additional CPA should be employed.

Because the marginal product for the fifth CPA equals 0.2, $MP_{CPA=5} = 0.2$, the marginal revenue product falls to only $20 per hour, or less than the $35-per-hour cost of hiring that person. The firm would incur a $15-per-hour loss by expanding hiring to that level and would, therefore, stop with employment of four CPAs.

This example assumes that CPA time is the only variable input involved in tax-return preparation. In reality, other inputs are apt to be necessary. Additional computer time, office supplies, and clerical support may also be required to increase output. If such were the case, determining the independent contribution or value of CPA input would be more complex. If *variable* overhead for CPA support staff and supplies equals 50 percent of sales revenue, then the **net marginal revenue**, or marginal revenue after all variable costs, for CPA time would be only $50 per unit (= $0.5 \times MR_Q$). In this instance, Tax Advisors, Inc., would find that the $20 (= $0.4 \times (0.5)(\$100)$) net marginal revenue product generated by the fourth CPA would not offset the necessary $35 per hour cost (wage rate). It would, therefore, employ no more than three CPAs, a level at which $MRP = 1.4 \times (0.5)(\$100) = \$70 > \$35 = P_{CPA}$. The firm will employ additional CPAs only so long as their net marginal revenue product equals or exceeds their marginal cost (price of labor).

net marginal revenue
Marginal revenue after all variable costs

This explains why, for example, a law firm might hire new associates at annual salaries of $80,000 when it expects them to generate $150,000 per year in gross billings, or 1,500 billable hours at a rate of $100 per hour. If variable costs are $70,000 per associate, only $80,000 is available to cover associate salary expenses. When customers pay $100 per hour for legal services, they are paying for attorney time and expertise plus the support of legal secretaries, law clerks, office staff, supplies, facilities, and so on. By itself, new associate time is worth much less than $100 per hour. The net marginal revenue of new associate attorney time, or CPA time in the preceding Tax Advisors, Inc., example, is the *marginal* value created after allowing for the variable costs of all other inputs that must be increased to provide service.

INPUT DEMAND FUNCTION

Data on the marginal revenue product of labor and wage rates present firms with clear incentives regarding the level of employment. If $MRP_L > P_L$, it pays to expand labor usage; when $MRP_L < P_L$, it pays to cut back. When $MRP_L = P_L$, the level of employment is optimal. When an unlimited supply of labor can be employed at a given wage rate, determining the optimal level of employment involves a simple comparison of MRP_L and P_L. However, when higher wages are necessary to expand the level of employment, this fact must be taken into account in the determination of an optimal level of employment.

Input Demand Illustration

To illustrate, consider the case of Micromachines, Inc., in Chapel Hill, North Carolina. Micromachines assembles and markets Lilliputian-size machines: tiny gears and cranks the size of large specks of dust. The firm plans to introduce a new microscopic motor with the following demand conditions:

$$Q = 300,000 - 2,500P$$

or

$$P = \$120 - \$0.0004Q$$

Motor parts are purchased from a number of independent subcontractors and put together at Micromachines' assembly plant. Each unit of output is expected to require 2 hours of labor. Total costs for parts acquisition *before* assembly labor costs are as follows:

$$TC = \$1,810,000 + \$24Q$$

To assemble this product, the firm will need to hire and train new staff. Given tight labor market conditions, Micromachines expects that an increase in employment will be possible only at higher wage rates. The firm projects the following labor supply curve in the highly competitive local labor market:

$$L_S = 10,000P_L$$

Based on this information, it is possible to derive Micromachines' demand curve for labor. Because 2 hours of labor are required for each unit of output, the company's profit function is

$$\begin{aligned} \pi &= TR - TC_{PARTS} - TC_{ASSEMBLY} \\ &= (\$120 - \$0.0004Q)Q - \$1,810,000 - \$24Q - 2P_LQ \\ &= -\$0.0004Q^2 + \$96Q - 2P_LQ - \$1,810,000 \end{aligned}$$

and $2P_LQ$ is the total cost of assembly.

To find Micromachines' labor demand curve, it is necessary to determine the firm's optimal level of output. The profit-maximizing level of output is found by setting marginal profit equal to zero ($M\pi = \partial\pi/\partial Q = 0$), where

$$M\pi = -\$0.0008Q + \$96 - 2P_L = 0$$

This implies a direct relation between the price of labor, P_L, and the firm's optimal level of output:

$$2P_L = \$96 - \$0.0008Q$$
$$P_L = \$48 - \$0.0004Q$$

This expression can be used to indicate the optimal employment level. In setting $M\pi = MR - MC = 0$, the firm has also implicitly set $MR = MC$. In terms of employment, this means that $MRP_L = P_L$ for each and every input at the profit-maximizing activity level. Therefore, Micromachines' marginal revenue product of labor is $MRP_L = \$48 - \$0.0004Q$.

To identify Micromachines' optimal level of employment at any given price of labor, simply determine the amount of labor required to produce the profit-maximizing level of output. Because each unit of output requires *two* units of labor, $L = 2Q$ and $Q = 0.5L$. By substitution, the firm's demand curve for labor is

$$P_L = MRP_L$$
$$= \$48 - \$0.0004(0.5L)$$
$$= \$48 - \$0.0002L$$

or

$$L_D = 240,000 - 5,000P_L$$

At any given wage rate, this expression indicates Micromachines' optimal level of employment. At any given employment level, this expression also indicates Micromachines' optimal wage rate. The equilibrium wage rate and employment level are determined by setting the demand for labor equal to the supply of labor:

$$\text{Labor Demand} = \text{Labor Supply}$$
$$240,000 - 5,000P_L = 10,000P_L$$
$$15,000P_L = 240,000$$
$$P_L = \$16 \text{ (wage rate)}$$

To calculate the equilibrium employment level, set labor demand equal to labor supply at a wage rate of $16:

$$\text{Labor Demand} = \text{Labor Supply}$$
$$240,000 - 5,000(\$16) = 10,000(\$16)$$
$$160,000 = 160,000 \text{ (worker hours)}$$

Individual workers are typically employed 2,000 hours per year. This implies Micromachines should hire 80 full-time workers. This also implies that Micromachines has a profit-maximizing activity level of 80,000 micromotors (units of output) because $Q = 0.5L = 0.5(160,000) = 80,000$ units.

Input Demand and Optimal Output

Using the firm's demand curve for micromotors and total profit function, it is now possible to calculate the optimal output price and profit levels:

$$P = \$120 - \$0.0004(80{,}000)$$
$$= \$88$$
$$\pi = -\$0.0004(80{,}000^2) + \$96(80{,}000) - 2(\$16)(80{,}000) - \$1{,}810{,}000$$
$$= \$750{,}000$$

From this example, it becomes clear that the optimal level of employment can be derived by calculating the profit-maximizing level of output and then determining the amount of labor required to produce that output level. In the earlier Tax Advisors, Inc., example, the point where $MRP_L = P_L$ indicates the optimal employment level. This is similar to setting $MR = MC$ for each input. In the Micromachines, Inc., example, labor costs are directly incorporated into the profit function and the point where $M\pi = 0$ is found. Both approaches yield the same profit-maximizing result because if $M\pi = MR - MC = 0$, then $MR = MC$ and $P_L = MRP_L$.

Figure 7.7 shows the marginal revenue product for an input, L, along with its market price, P_L^*. Over the range OL^*, expanding L usage increases total profits, because the marginal revenue product gained from employing each unit of L exceeds its price. Beyond L^*, increased usage of L reduces profits, because the benefits gained (MRP_L) are less than the costs incurred (P_L). Only at L^*, where $P_L^* = MRP_L$, is total profit maximized.

OPTIMAL COMBINATION OF MULTIPLE INPUTS

isocost curve or budget line
Line of constant costs

Optimal input proportions can be found graphically for a two-input, single-output system by adding an **isocost curve or budget line**, a line of constant costs, to the diagram of production isoquants. Each point on the isocost curve represents a combination of inputs, say, X and Y, whose cost equals a constant expenditure.

FIGURE 7.7

MRP Curve Is an Input Demand Curve
Profits are maximized at L^*, where $P_L^* = MRP_L$.

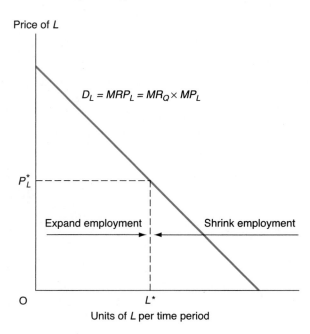

Budget Lines

Budget lines illustrated in Figure 7.8 are constructed in the following manner: Let $P_X = \$500$ and $P_Y = \$250$, the prices of X and Y. For a given budget, say, $B_1 = \$1,000$, the firm can purchase four units of Y (= $\$1,000/\$250$) and no units of X, or two units of X (= $\$1,000/\$500$) and none of Y. These two quantities represent the X and Y intercepts of a budget line, and a straight line connecting them identifies all combinations of X and Y that $\$1,000$ can purchase.

A budget line is merely a statement of the various combinations of inputs that can be purchased for a given dollar amount. For example, the various combinations of X and Y that can be purchased for a fixed budget, B, are given by the expression

$$B = P_X \times X + P_Y \times Y$$

Solving this expression for Y so that it can be graphed, as in Figure 7.8, results in

(7.12)
$$Y = \frac{B}{P_Y} - \frac{P_X}{P_Y} X \qquad P_X X + P_Y Y = B$$

The first term in Equation 7.12 is the Y-axis intercept of the isocost curve. It indicates the quantity of input Y that can be purchased with a given expenditure, *assuming zero units of input X are bought*. The slope of a budget line $\partial Y/\partial X = -P_X/P_Y$ and measures relative input prices. A change in the budget level, B, leads to a parallel shift in the budget line; changes in input prices alter the slope of the budget line.

These relations can be clarified by considering further the example illustrated in Figure 7.8. With a $\$1,000$ budget, the Y-axis intercept of the budget line has already been shown to be four units. Relative prices determine the slope of the budget line. Thus, in Figure 7.8 the slope of the isocost curves is given by the expression

$$\text{Slope} = \frac{-P_X}{P_Y} = \frac{-\$500}{\$250} = -2$$

FIGURE 7.8

Isocost Curves

Each point on an isocost line represents a different combination of inputs that can be purchased at a given expenditure level.

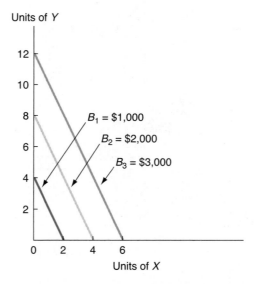

Suppose that a firm has only $1,000 to spend on inputs for the production of Q. Combining a set of production isoquants with the budget lines of Figure 7.8 to form Figure 7.9 indicates that the optimal input combination occurs at point A, the point of tangency between the budget line and a production isoquant. At that point, X and Y are combined in proportions that maximize the output attainable for an expenditure B_1. No other combination of X and Y that can be purchased for $1,000 will produce as much output. All other (X, Y) combinations along the budget line through (X_1, Y_1) must intersect isoquants representing lower output quantities. The combination (X_1, Y_1) is the least-cost input combination that can produce output Q_1. All other (X, Y) combinations on the Q_1 isoquant lie on higher budget lines. Similarly, X_2, Y_2 is the least-cost input combination for producing Q_2, and so on. All other possible combinations for producing Q_1, Q_2, and Q_3 are intersected by higher budget lines.

Expansion Path

By connecting points of tangency between isoquants and budget lines (points A, B, and C), an **expansion path** is identified that depicts optimal input combinations as the scale of production expands.

expansion path
Optimal input combinations as the scale of production expands

At the point of optimal input combination, isocost and the isoquant curves are tangent and have equal slope. The slope of an isocost curve equals $-P_X/P_Y$. The slope of an isoquant curve equals the marginal rate of technical substitution of one input factor for another when the quantity of production is held constant. Therefore, for optimal input combinations, the ratio of input prices must equal the ratio of input marginal products, as is shown in Equation 7.13:

(7.13)

$$\frac{P_X}{P_Y} = \frac{MP_X}{MP_Y}$$

FIGURE 7.9

Optimal Input Combinations

The points of tangency between the isoquant and isocost curves depict optimal input combinations at different activity levels.

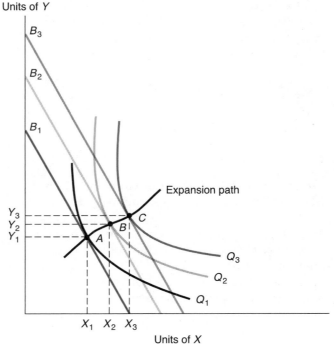

Alternatively, marginal product-to-price ratio must be equal for each input:

(7.14)
$$\frac{MP_X}{P_X} = \frac{MP_Y}{P_Y}$$

Optimal input proportions are employed when an additional dollar spent on any input yields the same increase in output. Any input combination violating this rule is suboptimal because a change in input proportions could result in the same quantity of output at lower cost.

Illustration of Optimal Input Proportions

The Tax Advisors, Inc., example can further illustrate these relations. Assume that in addition to three CPAs, four bookkeepers are employed at a wage (including fringes) of $15 per hour and that $MP_{B=4} = 0.3$. This compares with a CPA wage of $35 per hour and $MP_{CPA=3} = 1.4$. Based on these assumptions, the marginal product per dollar spent on each input is

$$\frac{MP_{B=4}}{P_B} = \frac{0.3}{\$15} = 0.02 \text{ Units per Dollar (for bookkeepers)}$$

and

$$\frac{MP_{CPA=3}}{P_{CPA}} = \frac{1.4}{\$35} = 0.04 \text{ Units per Dollar (for CPAs)}$$

Such an input combination violates the optimal proportions rule because the ratios of marginal products to input prices are not equal. The last dollar spent on bookkeeper labor input produces ("buys") 0.02 units of output (tax-return preparations), whereas the last dollar spent on CPA time produces twice as much, 0.04 units. By transferring $1 of cost from bookkeeper time to CPA time, the firm could increase total output by 0.02 tax-return preparations per hour without increasing total cost. Expenditures on the CPA input represent a better use of firm resources, and the company should reallocate resources to employ relatively more CPAs and relatively fewer bookkeepers.

In Equation 7.9, it was shown that the marginal product-to-price ratio indicates the marginal cost of output from a marginal unit of input X or Y. In terms of this example, this implies that

$$MC_Q = \frac{P_B}{MP_{B=4}} = \frac{\$15}{0.3} = \$50 \text{ per Unit (using bookkeepers)}$$

and

$$MC_Q = \frac{P_{CPA}}{MP_{CPA=3}} = \frac{\$35}{1.4} = \$25 \text{ per Unit (using CPAs)}$$

Again, the superior economic productivity of CPAs is indicated; they are able to produce output at one-half the marginal cost of output produced by bookkeepers.

It is important to recognize that the preceding analysis for determining optimal proportions of multiple inputs considers input price and input marginal product (productivity) relations only. Because the economic value of output is not considered, these data are insufficient to allow calculation of optimal employment *levels*. Notice in the Tax Advisors, Inc., example that the marginal cost of output using either input is much less than the $100 marginal revenue per tax return. It is quite possible that more CPAs *and* more bookkeepers should be hired. The next section introduces output value to determine the optimal level of resource employment.

MANAGERIAL APPLICATION   **7.3**

Should We Raise the Minimum Wage?

Congress raised the minimum wage to $4.75 per hour on October 1, 1996, and to $5.15 per hour on September 1, 1997. At that time, a youth subminimum wage of $4.25 per hour was also established for newly-hired employees under the age of 20 during their first 90 consecutive calendar days of employment. President Clinton argued that a boost, offered as a well-deserved raise for hardworking Americans, was the right thing to do because the minimum wage had been relatively stagnant during recent years. Indeed, after adjusting for inflation, the minimum wage has fallen sharply. In 1960, when the minimum wage was $1.60 per hour, it was equivalent to $7.92 per hour in current, or 2000, dollars.

When workers retain their jobs after the minimum wage has been boosted, it's mainly teenagers in part-time service occupations, like fast-food restaurants, who benefit. The potential benefits of an increase in the minimum wage, namely higher incomes for teenagers and the working poor, are obvious. What is less obvious is the cost in terms of lost employment opportunities. Whenever the decision to add or subtract workers is faced, an employer compares the marginal revenue product of the last worker hired to the marginal cost of employment. At the margin, each worker's job must be justified by bringing to the employer at least as much in added revenue as is necessary to pay the marginal cost of employment. When the minimum wage is increased from $5.15 to $6.50 or higher, low-skill workers unable to produce more than $5.15 per hour in employer benefits get laid off.

The bottom line is simple: Worker productivity must be enhanced if you want to increase incomes among the working poor. Raising the minimum wage while holding job skills constant will *reduce* not enhance income opportunities for minimum-wage workers.

See: A Wall Street Journal News Roundup, "Brazil Raises Minimum Wage 11.1%, Posts Trade Surplus of $594 Million," *The Wall Street Journal Online*, April 2, 2002 (http://online.wsj.com).

OPTIMAL LEVELS OF MULTIPLE INPUTS

Cost minimization requires only that the ratios of marginal product to price be equal for all inputs. Alternatively, cost minimization dictates that inputs be combined in optimal proportions for a given or target level of output.

Optimal Employment and Profit Maximization

Profit maximization requires that a firm employ optimal input proportions *and* produce an optimal quantity of output. *Cost minimization and optimal input proportions are necessary but not sufficient conditions for profit maximization.*

Profit maximization dictates that the firm employ all inputs up to the point where $MC_Q = MR_Q$. Profit maximization requires for each and every input that

(7.15)
$$\frac{P_X}{MP_X} = MR_Q$$

and

(7.16)
$$\frac{P_Y}{MP_Y} = MR_Q$$

Rearranging produces

(7.17)
$$P_X = MP_X \times MR_Q = MRP_X$$

and

(7.18)
$$P_Y = MP_Y \times MR_Q = MRP_Y$$

Profits are maximized when inputs are employed so that price equals marginal revenue product for each input.

The difference between cost minimization and profit maximization is simple. Cost minimization requires efficient resource use, as reflected by optimal input proportions. Profit maximization requires efficient resource use *and* production of an optimal level of output, as made possible by the optimal employment of all inputs.

Illustration of Optimal Levels of Multiple Inputs

A final look at the Tax Advisors, Inc., example illustrates these relations. Recall that with three CPAs and four bookkeepers, the ratio of marginal products to price for each input indicates a need to employ more CPAs relative to the number of bookkeepers. Assume that hiring one more bookkeeper leaves unchanged their marginal product of 0.3 tax returns processed per hour ($MP_{B=5} = 0.3$). In addition, assume that with this increased employment of bookkeepers the marginal product of the fourth CPA increases from 0.4 to 0.7 tax returns processed per hour. This assumption reflects the fact that the marginal productivity of an input factor (CPAs) is typically enhanced when used in conjunction with more of a complementary input, bookkeepers in this case. Now $MP_{B=5} = 0.3$ and $MP_{CPA=4} = 0.7$. With the costs of each input remaining constant at $P_B = \$15$ and $P_{CPA} = \$35$, the marginal product-to-price ratios are now equal:

$$\frac{MP_{B=5}}{P_B} = \frac{0.3}{\$15} = 0.02 \text{ Units per Dollar (for bookkeepers)}$$

and

$$\frac{MP_{CPA=4}}{P_{CPA}} = \frac{0.7}{\$35} = 0.02 \text{ Units per Dollar (for CPAs)}$$

The combination of four CPAs and five bookkeepers is now optimal from a cost-minimizing standpoint, and input *proportions* are optimal. However, it is unclear whether an optimal *level* of input has been employed. Does the resulting output level maximize profit? To answer this question, it becomes necessary to determine if marginal revenue product equals the marginal cost of each input. If net marginal revenue (*NMR*) per return remains at $\$50 = (\$100 \times 0.5)$, then

$$\begin{aligned} MRP_B &= MP_B \times NMR_Q \\ &= 0.3 \times \$50 = \$15 \\ MRP_B &= \$15 = P_B \end{aligned}$$

and

$$\begin{aligned} MRP_{CPA} &= MP_{CPA} \times NMR_Q \\ &= 0.7 \times \$50 = \$35 \\ MRP_{CPA} &= \$35 = P_{CPA} \end{aligned}$$

Marginal revenue product equals marginal cost for each input. The combination of four CPAs and five bookkeepers is an optimal *level* of employment because the resulting output quantity maximizes profit.

RETURNS TO SCALE

constant returns to scale
When a given percentage increase in all inputs leads to an identical percentage increase in output

increasing returns to scale
When the proportional increase in output is larger than an underlying proportional increase in input

decreasing returns to scale
When output increases at a rate less than the proportionate increase in inputs

Closely related to the productivity of individual inputs is the question of how a proportionate increase in all inputs will affect total production. **Constant returns to scale** exist when a given percentage increase in all inputs leads to that same percentage increase in output. **Increasing returns to scale** are prevalent if the proportional increase in output is larger than the underlying proportional increase in inputs. If output increases at a rate less than the proportionate increase in inputs, **decreasing returns to scale** are present.

Evaluating Returns to Scale

The returns-to-scale concept can be clarified by reexamining the production data in Table 7.1. Assume that the production system represented by those data is currently operating with one unit of input X and three units of input Y. Production from such an input combination would be 35 units. Doubling X and Y results in an input combination of $X = 2$ and $Y = 6$. Output from this input combination would be 72 units. A 100 percent increase in both X and Y increases output by 37 units ($= 72 - 35$), a 106 percent increase ($= 37/35 = 1.06$). Over this range, output increases more than proportionately to the increase in the productive factors. The production system exhibits increasing returns to scale over this range of input use.

The returns to scale of a production system can vary over different levels of input usage. Consider, for example, the effect of a 50 percent increase in X and Y from the input combination $X = 2$, $Y = 6$. Increasing X by 50 percent results in employment of three units of that factor ($= 2 \times 1.5$), whereas a 50 percent increase in Y leads to nine units ($= 6 \times 1.5$) of that input being used. The new input combination results in 89 units of production. Therefore, a 50 percent increase in input employment generates only a 24 percent [$= (89 - 72)/72$] increase in output. Because the increase in output is less than proportionate to the underlying increase in input, the production system exhibits decreasing returns to scale over this range.

Isoquant analysis can be used to examine returns to scale for a two-input, single-output production system. Consider the production of Q_1 units of output by using the input combination of (X_1, Y_1). If doubling both inputs shifts production to Q_2, and if Q_2 is precisely twice as large as Q_1, the system is said to exhibit constant returns to scale over the range (X_1, Y_1) to $(2X_1, 2Y_1)$. If Q_2 is greater than twice Q_1, returns to scale are increasing; if Q_2 is less than double Q_1, the system exhibits decreasing returns to scale.

Returns to scale can also be examined graphically, as in Figure 7.10. In this graph, the slope of a curve drawn from the origin up the production surface indicates whether returns to scale are constant, increasing, or decreasing.[7] A curve drawn from the origin with a constant slope indicates that returns to scale are constant. If a curve from the origin exhibits a constantly increasing slope, increasing returns to scale are indicated. If a production function increases at a decreasing rate, decreasing returns to scale are indicated.

A more general condition is a production function with first increasing, then decreasing, returns to scale. The region of increasing returns is attributable to specialization. As output increases, specialized labor can be used and efficient, large-scale machinery can be used in the production process. Beyond some scale of operation, however, further gains from specialization are limited, and coordination problems may begin to increase costs substantially. When coordination expenses more than offset additional benefits of specialization, decreasing returns to scale set in.

---

7   Both inputs X and Y can be plotted on the horizontal axis of Figure 7.10 because they bear constant proportions to one another. What is actually being plotted on the horizontal axis is the number of units of some fixed input combination.

FIGURE 7.10

Returns to Scale May Be Constant, Decreasing, or Increasing

A straight-line production function indicates constant returns to scale, and a given percentage change in all inputs will cause the same percentage change in output. When the slope of such a line from the origin is falling, decreasing returns to scale are indicated. If the slope of such a line from the origin is rising, increasing returns to scale are revealed. If decreasing returns to scale are present, total output grows slower than input use; when increasing returns to scale are present, total output grows faster than input use.

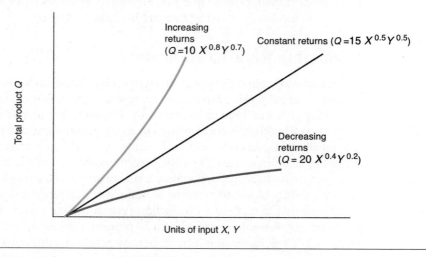

Output Elasticity and Returns to Scale

Even though graphic representations of returns to scale such as Figure 7.10 are intuitively appealing, returns to scale can be accurately determined for any production function through analysis of output elasticities. **Output elasticity**, ε_Q, is the percentage change in output associated with a 1 percent change in all inputs and a practical means for returns to scale estimation. Letting $\underline{X}$ represent all input factors,

output elasticity
Percentage change in output associated with a 1 percent change in all inputs

(7.19)

$$\varepsilon_Q = \frac{\text{Percentage Change in Output } (Q)}{\text{Percentage Change in All Inputs } (\underline{X})}$$

$$= \frac{\partial Q/Q}{\partial \underline{X}/\underline{X}} = \frac{\partial Q}{\partial \underline{X}} \times \frac{\underline{X}}{Q}$$

where $\underline{X}$ refers to capital, labor, energy, and so on, then the following relations hold:

If	Then	Returns to Scale Are:
Percentage change in Q > Percentage change in $\underline{X}$	$\varepsilon_Q > 1$	Increasing
Percentage change in Q = Percentage change in $\underline{X}$	$\varepsilon_Q = 1$	Constant
Percentage change in Q < Percentage change in $\underline{X}$	$\varepsilon_Q < 1$	Diminishing

Thus, returns to scale can be analyzed by examining the relationship between the rate of increase in inputs and the quantity of output produced.

Returns to Scale Estimation

In most instances, returns to scale can be easily estimated. For example, assume that all inputs in the unspecified production function $Q = f(X, Y, Z)$ are increased by using the constant factor k, where $k = 1.01$ for a 1 percent increase, $k = 1.02$ for a 2 percent increase, and so on. Then, the production is

(7.20) $$hQ = f(kX, kY, kZ)$$

where h is the proportional increase in Q resulting from a k-fold increase in each input factor. From Equation 7.20, it is evident that the following relationships hold:

- If $h > k$, then the percentage change in Q is greater than the percentage change in the inputs, $\epsilon_Q > 1$, and the production function exhibits increasing returns to scale.
- If $h = k$, then the percentage change in Q equals the percentage change in the inputs, $\epsilon_Q = 1$, and the production function exhibits constant returns to scale.
- If $h < k$, then the percentage change in Q is less than the percentage change in the inputs, $\epsilon_Q < 1$, and the production function exhibits decreasing returns to scale.

For certain production functions, called homogeneous production functions, when each input factor is multiplied by a constant k, the constant can be completely factored out of the production function expression. Following a k-fold increase in all inputs, the production function takes the form $hQ = k^n f(X,Y,Z)$. The exponent n provides the key to returns-to-scale estimation. If $n = 1$, then $h = k$ and the function exhibits constant returns to scale. If $n > 1$, then $h > k$, indicating increasing returns to scale, whereas $n < 1$ indicates $h < k$ and decreasing returns to scale. In all other instances, the easiest means for determining the nature of returns to scale is through numerical example.

To illustrate, consider the production function $Q = 2X + 3Y + 1.5Z$. Returns to scale can be determined by learning how an arbitrary, say 2 percent, increase in all inputs affects output. If, initially, $X = 100$, $Y = 200$, and $Z = 200$, output is found to be

$$\begin{aligned} Q_1 &= 2(100) + 3(200) + 1.5(200) \\ &= 200 + 600 + 300 = 1{,}100 \text{ units} \end{aligned}$$

Increasing all inputs by 2 percent (letting $k = 1.02$) leads to the input quantities $X = 102$, $Y = 204$, and $Z = 204$, and

$$\begin{aligned} Q_2 &= 2(102) + 3(204) + 1.5(204) \\ &= 204 + 612 + 306 = 1{,}122 \text{ units} \end{aligned}$$

Because a 2 percent increase in all inputs has led to a 2 percent increase in output ($1.02 = 1{,}122/1{,}100$), this production system exhibits constant returns to scale.

PRODUCTION FUNCTION ESTIMATION

Given enough input/output observations, either over time for a single firm or at a single point in time for a number of firms in an industry, regression techniques can be used to estimate the parameters of production functions.

Cubic Production Functions

From a theoretical standpoint, the most appealing functional form for production function estimation might be cubic, such as the equation

(7.21) $$Q = a + bXY + cX^2Y + dXY^2 - eX^3Y - fXY^3$$

This form is general in that it exhibits stages of first increasing and then decreasing returns to scale. The marginal products of the input factors exhibit a pattern of first increasing and then decreasing returns, as was illustrated in Figure 7.3.

MANAGERIAL APPLICATION   7.4

The Most Productive Companies in America

The table below depicts sales per employee and net income per employee for a sample of 10 of the most productive companies in America. Freddie Mac (Federal Home Loan Mortgage Corporation) purchases single-family and multifamily residential mortgages and mortgage-related securities, which it finances primarily by issuing debt instruments in the capital markets. It's a capital-intensive business, and highly lucrative. Freddie Mac generates an astonishing $8.6 million in sales per employee, and net income of $727,714 per employee. Similarly, Burlington Resources, Inc., a prosperous oil and natural gas producer, requires few employees to efficiently conduct its business. Others that generate enormous profits per employee include software juggernaut Microsoft Corp., financial services powerhouse Stilwell Financial (purveyor of Janus mutual funds), and biopharmaceutical leader Biogen.

The amazing productivity of such companies puts into sharp focus the performance of another corporate icon, McDonald's Corp. Although the "golden arches" are familiar to hamburger lovers everywhere, it's a labor-intensive business that generates meager profits per employee. Data on company productivity, like profits per employee, are worth considering because low-profit companies tend to pay substandard wages and offer limited investment potential. Over the long run, capable employees and long-term investors succeed when their companies prosper.

See: Aaron Lucchetti, "Stilwell to Give Janus Employees Larger Stake in Fund Company," *The Wall Street Journal Online*, February 19, 2002 (http://online.wsj.com).

Company	Sales ($mil.)	Net Income ($ mil.)	Employees (000)	Sales per Employee	Net Income per Employee
Federal Home Loan Mortgage ("Freddie Mac")	$29,969	$2,547	3.5	$8,562,571	$727,714
Burlington Resources, Inc.	3,147	675	1.8	1,765,003	378,575
Microsoft Corp.	22,956	9,421	39.1	587,110	240,946
Biogen, Inc.	926	334	1.5	628,103	226,154
Stilwell Financial, Inc.	2,248	664	3.5	647,494	191,158
Bristol Myers Squibb	18,216	4,711	44.0	414,000	107,068
Qualcomm Inc.	3,197	670	6.3	507,425	106,383
AOL Time Warner Inc.	6,886	1,232	15.0	459,067	82,133
Coca-Cola Co.	20,458	2,177	36.9	554,417	58,997
McDonald's Corp.	14,243	1,977	364.0	39,129	5,432

Frequently, however, real-world data do not exhibit enough dispersion to indicate the full range of increasing and then decreasing returns. In these cases, simpler functional specifications can be used to estimate production functions. The full generality of a cubic function may be unnecessary, and an alternative linear or log-linear model specification can be usefully applied in empirical estimation. The multiplicative production function described in the next section is one such approximation that has proven extremely useful in empirical studies of production relationships.

power production function
Multiplicative relation between input and output

Power Production Functions

One function commonly used in production studies is the **power production function**, a multiplicative relation between output and input that takes the form

(7.22)
$$Q = b_0 X^{b_1} Y^{b_2}$$

Power functions have properties that are useful in empirical research. Power functions allow the marginal productivity of a given input to depend on the levels of *all* inputs used, a condition that often holds in actual production systems. Power functions are also easy to estimate in log-linear form using least squares regression analysis because Equation 7.22 is mathematically equivalent to

(7.23)
$$\log Q = \log b_0 + b_1 \log X + b_2 \log Y$$

Returns to scale are also easily calculated by summing the exponents of the power function or, alternatively, by summing the log-linear model coefficient estimates. As seen in Figure 7.10, if the sum of power function exponents is less than 1, diminishing returns are indicated. A sum greater than 1 indicates increasing returns. If the sum of exponents is exactly 1, returns to scale are constant, and the powerful tool of linear programming, described in Chapter 9, can be used to determine optimal input-output relations for the firm.

Power functions have been successfully used in a large number of empirical production studies since Charles W. Cobb and Paul H. Douglas's pioneering work in the late 1920s. The impact of their work is so great that power production functions are frequently referred to as Cobb-Douglas production functions.

The primary determinant of the functional form used to estimate any model of production depends on the relation hypothesized by the researcher. A simple linear approach will be adequate in many instances. In others, a power function or log-linear approach can be justified. When specification uncertainty is high, a number of plausible alternative model specifications can be fitted to the data to determine which form seems most representative of actual conditions.

PRODUCTIVITY MEASUREMENT

Productivity analysis and measurement is important at the company, industry, and economy-wide levels. For the overall economy, growing economic productivity makes possible improvements in the economic welfare of the general population. From the company's perspective, productivity betterment holds the key to growing profits and employee compensation.

How Is Productivity Measured?

Studies of output per hour in individual industries and the overall economy have been a responsibility of the Bureau of Labor Statistics (BLS) since the 1800s. A study of 60 manufacturing industries, prompted by congressional concern that human labor was being displaced by machinery, was released as *Hand and Machine Labor* in 1898. This report provided striking evidence of the savings in labor resulting from mechanization in the last half of the nineteenth century. The effects of advances in productivity on employment remained an important focus of the BLS throughout the 1920s and 1930s. During this period, the Bureau began preparation and publication of industry productivity indexes based upon production data from the periodic *Census of Manufactures* and employment statistics collected by BLS. In 1940, Congress authorized the BLS to undertake continuing studies of productivity and technological change. The onset of World War II caused a change in emphasis from apprehension of unemployment to concern with making the most efficient use of scarce labor resources. In recent years, public interest in productivity measurement and enhancement has grown as expanding worker productivity has been recognized as an important indicator of economic progress.

productivity growth
Rate of increase in output per unit of input

labor productivity
Output per worker hour

multifactor productivity
Output relative to the combined inputs of labor, capital, and intermediate purchases

One of the most prominent uses of economic survey information is to track the pace of economic betterment, or **productivity growth**, in the overall economy. Productivity growth is the rate of increase in output per unit of input. **Labor productivity** refers to the relationship between output and the worker time used to generate that output. It is the ratio of output per worker hour. In **multifactor productivity** measures, output is related to combined inputs of labor, capital, and intermediate purchases. Worker input is measured by the number of hours of labor expended in the production of output. Capital includes expenditures for equipment, structures, land, and inventories. Intermediate purchases are composed of expenditures for materials, fuels, electricity, and purchased services.

Advances in productivity reflect the ability to produce more output per unit of input. Such advances are a significant source of growing national income and rising economic betterment. Over time, the U.S. economy has been able to produce more goods and services, not just by employing more labor and other inputs, but by making production more efficient. Production is becoming more efficient in a number of ways. Increased training and education make workers increasingly productive. Invention and innovation lead to improved capital equipment; advances in management techniques lead to better organization design and improvements in worker incentives.

Improvements in worker productivity are measured by taking an index series for output and dividing it by an index series for employee hours. Both "factory floor" or production workers and office workers are included in employee hours. Although separate data are collected for production workers and nonproduction workers, only the sum of the two is used in productivity measurement because it is impossible to determine what share of output is attributable to production versus nonproduction workers.

Increases in multifactor productivity are evaluated by dividing an index series for output by an index series for the combined inputs of labor, capital, and intermediate purchases. Each index series is simply a way of expressing, in percentage terms, the change in some variable from a given point in time to another point in time. For example, let's say that output increased by 10 percent from an initial year (2001) to a subsequent year (2002). The index for our arbitrarily chosen base year of 2001 would be 100; the index for 2002 would be 110. Conversely, if output had declined in 2002 by 10 percent, the 2002 index value would be 90. If an industry produced only one product, calculating an output index series would be simple. However, that is seldom true. Most often, it is necessary to account for productivity changes among industries that produce many different products, and products that change dramatically over time.

Figure 7.11 illustrates how productivity, measured as output per hour in the private nonfarm sector, accelerated during the late 1990s. Productivity growth more than doubled from an annual rate of 1.4 percent per year before 1995 to an annual rate of 3 percent from 1995 through 2000. Without a doubt, some of this increase can be described as the typical change in productivity growth that occurs over the business cycle. During economic booms, like that enjoyed during the late 1990s, productivity growth tends to rise as factories move towards full utilization. During recessions, productivity growth lags with worker layoffs and plant closings. However, even if as much as 0.5 percent of the late 1990s boost in productivity growth can be attributed to business cycle effects, a structural acceleration in productivity growth of at least 1 percent has taken place. Although economists are yet uncertain about the relative magnitude of cyclical versus structural influences, all agree that productivity growth has been helped by an increase in the amount of capital per worker hour (capital deepening) and by improvements in the measurable skills of the work force (labor quality).

A significant share of the recent boost in productivity growth is attributable to broader economic forces. Specifically, more effective use of worker skills has become possible through recent improvements in communications technology. Increasingly, companies have been eager to buy powerful computers and computer software at relatively low prices. Rapid advances in computer hardware and software technology, combined with the widespread adoption of the Internet, have led to an unprecedented boom in communications technology. Benefits from the recent boom in communications technology are evident in every home and workplace, and are broadly reflected in the late 1990s burst in productivity growth.

Trends in Industry Productivity

Industry productivity measures describe the relationship between output and the labor time involved in its production. They show the changes from period to period in the amount of

FIGURE 7.11

Productivity Growth Jumped in the Late 1990s

The rate of productivity growth increased after 1995.

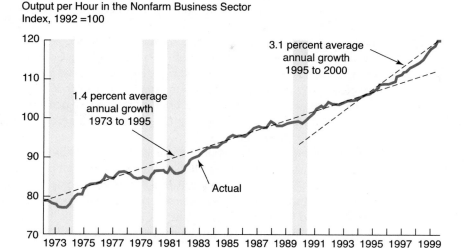

Output per Hour in the Nonfarm Business Sector
Index, 1992 =100

3.1 percent average annual growth 1995 to 2000

1.4 percent average annual growth 1973 to 1995

Actual

Note: Productivity is the average of income- and product-side measures. Productivity for 2000 is inferred from the first three quarters. Shading indicates recessions.

Source: *Economic Report of the President*, U.S. Government Printing Office, Washington, DC, 2001, p. 27.

goods and services produced per hour. Although these measures relate output to hours of employees or all persons engaged in an industry, they do not measure the specific contribution of labor, capital, or any other factor of production. Rather, they reflect the joint effects of many influences, including changes in technology; capital investment; level of output; utilization of capacity, energy, and materials; the organization of production; managerial skill; and the characteristics and effort of the workforce.

To calculate productivity measures for industries with diverse and changing output, different products are aggregated into one output measure by weighting (multiplying) the relative change in output of each product by its share in the total value of output. In this way, higher value products that require more resources to produce are given higher weight. For tangible products, such as tons of steel, developing an output index series and productivity measures can be fairly straightforward. In other industries, particularly in the services sector, developing output indexes and productivity measures is more challenging. In many instances, data for the quantities of output produced or the number of times a service has been performed are not available. However, changes in revenue are typically available, and changes in revenue reflect changes in both the quantity of output and its price. Price changes can be accounted for by dividing an index of revenue by a price index. This leaves an index of quantity that can be used to measure productivity.

Industry studies cover a variety of manufacturing and nonmanufacturing industries at the sector, industry group, and industry-level classifications. Measures for over 175 industries are published on an annual basis, beginning as early as 1947. Coverage includes industries in the manufacturing, mining, trade, transportation, communication, public utilities, finance, and business and personal services sectors. In addition to measures of industry worker productivity, BLS publishes multifactor productivity statistics for certain industries. First released in 1987, industry multifactor productivity measures relate output to the combined inputs of labor, capital, and intermediate purchases. Unlike worker productivity measures, multifactor productivity measures are free from the effects of changes in the ratio of capital to labor and alterations in the ratio of intermediate purchases to labor. Because of the enormous data requirements for the measurement of capital and intermediate purchases, only a limited number of industry multifactor productivity measures has been published.

As shown in Figure 7.12, almost all manufacturing industries posted productivity gains from 1990 to 1999. Output per hour increased in 111 of the 119 industries. Productivity advanced an amazing 5 percent per year in 12 industries. Another 49 industries experienced exceptional annual productivity growth in the 2.5–4.9 percent range. Computer and office equipment posted the largest average annual gain, 33.3 percent. The five largest manufacturing industries all registered growth in output per hour from 1990 to 1999. Worker productivity rose a stunning 26 percent in electronic components and accessories; 3.3 percent in miscellaneous plastics products; 3.2 percent in motor vehicles and equipment; 1.3 percent in commercial printing; and 0.6 percent in meat products.

From 1990 to 1999, unit labor costs fell in 34 of the 119 industries in the manufacturing sector. Of the 34 industries, only pulp mills had decreasing worker productivity (–3 percent). The largest declines in unit labor costs were computer and office equipment (–22.3 percent) and electronic components and accessories (–17.6 percent). In the early years of the period, 1990–95, output per hour increased in 106 of the 119 industries. In 20 industries, productivity advanced 5 percent per year or more. An additional 36 industries experienced annual productivity growth in the 2.5–4.9 percent range.

Comparing the 1990–95 period with the 1995–99 period, productivity growth rates increased in 72 of 119 manufacturing industries. In 14 industries, annual output per hour grew at least 5 percentage points faster in 1995–99 than in 1990-95. Another 24 industries posted annual productivity growth rates 2.0–4.9 percentage points above their 1990–95 rates. All 13 of the

FIGURE 7.12

Manufacturing Productivity Growth Has Been Impressive

The number of manufacturing industries with annual productivity growth of 3.0 percent or more increased after 1995.

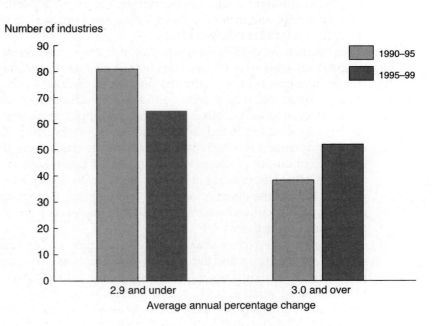

Source: Bureau of Labor Statistics, News, May 15, 2001; http://www.bls.gov/lpc/.

industries that experienced productivity declines in the earlier period registered productivity improvements in the later period. Seven of these 13 industries experienced positive productivity growth in the 1995–99 period.

Uses and Limitations of Productivity Data

Measures of output per hour are useful for analyzing trends in labor costs across industries, comparing productivity progress among countries, examining the effects of technological improvements, and analyzing related economic and industrial activities. Such analyses usually require that indexes of output per hour be used in conjunction with other data. Related data on production and employment are useful in studying technological effects. To study trends in labor costs, data on earnings and other labor expenditures must be compiled.

It is important to recognize that productivity measures of output per hour are subject to certain qualifications. Among these is the fact that existing techniques may not fully take into account changes in the quality of goods and services produced. Although efforts have been made to maintain consistency of coverage between the output and labor input estimates, some statistical differences remain that can confound intertemporal comparisons. Estimates of influences tied to nonproduction worker hours, unpaid family workers, the self-employed, and paid managers are also subject to a wide margin of error. Finally, year-to-year changes in output per hour are sometimes irregular and, therefore, are not necessarily indicative of basic changes in long-term trends. Because of these statistical limitations, productivity measures cannot be considered precise. Instead, they should be interpreted as useful indicators subject to measurement error.

Unfortunately, industry productivity measures are not available at the county, state, or regional level. They are nationwide averages that can sometimes vary from one locale to another. BLS worker productivity and multifactor productivity indexes are published annually in the bulletin, *Productivity Measures for Selected Industries*. Indexes of output per hour also are published in the *Statistical Abstract of the United States* and are available in the Bureau's LABSTAT database, on BLS data diskettes, or on the Internet at the BLS Web site (http://stats.bls.gov). A limited amount of the most current data is provided in annual news releases. Technical notes describing the methodology used to develop the indexes are available on request.

SUMMARY

This chapter introduces and analyzes the creative process of production. Several important properties of production systems are examined.

- A **production function** specifies the maximum output that can be produced for a given amount of inputs. A **discrete production function** involves distinct, or "lumpy," patterns for input combinations. In a **continuous production function**, inputs can be varied in a unbroken marginal fashion.

- The **returns to scale** characteristic of a production system describes the output effect of a proportional increase in all inputs. The relation between output and variation in only one of the inputs used is described as the **returns to a factor**.

- The **total product** indicates the total output from a production system. The **marginal product** of a factor, MP_X, is the change in output associated with a one-unit change in the factor input, holding all other inputs constant. A factor's **average product** is the total product divided by the number of units of that input employed.

- The **law of diminishing returns** states that as the quantity of a variable input increases, with the quantities of all other factors being held constant, and the resulting rate of increase in output eventually diminishes.

- An **isoquant** represents the different combinations of inputs that can be used efficiently to produce a specified quantity of output. Efficiency in this case refers to **technical efficiency**, meaning the least-cost production of a target level of output.

- **Input substitution**, or the systematic replacement of productive factors, is an important consideration when judging the efficiency of any production system. The **marginal rate of technical substitution** measures the amount of one input that must be substituted for another to maintain a constant level of output. It is irrational for a firm to use any input combination outside the **ridge lines** that indicate the bounds of positive marginal products.

- The **marginal revenue product** is the amount of revenue generated by employing the last input unit. Profit maximization requires that marginal revenue product and marginal cost be set equal for each input. **Economic efficiency** is achieved in the overall economy when all firms employ resources to equate each input's marginal revenue product and marginal cost. In all instances, it is important to consider the **net marginal revenue** of each input, or marginal revenue after all variable costs. Similarly important is the firm's **isocost curve** (or **budget line**), or line of constant costs. An **expansion path** depicts optimal input combinations as the scale of production expands.

- **Constant returns to scale** exist when a given percentage increase in all inputs leads to that same percentage increase in output. **Increasing returns to scale** are prevalent if the proportional increase in output is larger than the underlying proportional increase in inputs. If output increases at a rate less than the proportionate increase in inputs, **decreasing returns to scale** are present.

- **Output elasticity**, ϵ_Q, is the percentage change in output associated with a 1 percent change in all inputs, and it is a practical means for returns-to-scale estimation. **Power production functions** indicate a multiplicative relation between input and output and are often used in production function estimation.

- One of the most prominent uses of economic survey information is to track the pace of economic betterment, or **productivity growth**, in the overall economy. Productivity growth is the rate of increase in output per unit of input. **Labor productivity** refers to the relationship between output and the worker time used to generate that output. It is the ratio of output per worker hour. In **multifactor productivity** measures, output is related to combined inputs of labor, capital, and intermediate purchases.

The successful analysis and estimation of production relations is fundamental to the ongoing success of any organization. Concepts developed in this chapter can be used to understand, refine, and improve the policies of successful companies.

QUESTIONS

Q7.1 Is use of the least-cost input combinations a necessary condition for profit maximization? Is it a sufficient condition? Explain.

Q7.2 "Output per worker is expected to increase by 10% during the next year. Therefore, wages can also increase by 10% with no harmful effects on employment, output prices, or employer profits." Discuss this statement.

Q7.3 Commission-based and piece-rate–based compensation plans are commonly employed by businesses. Use the concepts developed in the chapter to explain these phenomena.

Q7.4 "Hourly wage rates are an anachronism. Efficiency requires incentive-based pay tied to performance." Discuss this statement.

Q7.5 Explain why the MP/P relation is deficient as the sole mechanism for determining the optimal level of resource employment.

Q7.6   Develop the appropriate relations for determining the optimal quantities of all inputs to employ in a production system, and explain the underlying rationale.

Q7.7   Suppose that labor, capital, and energy inputs must be combined in fixed proportions. Does this mean that returns to scale will be constant?

Q7.8   What is meant by the "pace" of economic productivity growth, and why is it important to economic welfare?

Q7.9   Cite some potential causes and possible cures for increasing productivity growth in the United States.

Q7.10   Explain why company productivity is important to managers, employees, and investors. Is superior worker productivity a necessary and sufficient condition for above-average compensation?

SELF-TEST PROBLEMS AND SOLUTIONS

ST7.1   **Optimal Input Usage.** Medical Testing Labs, Inc., provides routine testing services for blood banks in the Los Angeles area. Tests are supervised by skilled technicians using equipment produced by two leading competitors in the medical equipment industry. Records for the current year show an average of 27 tests per hour being performed on the Testlogic-1 and 48 tests per hour on a new machine, the Accutest-3. The Testlogic-1 is leased for $18,000 per month, and the Accutest-3 is leased at $32,000 per month. On average, each machine is operated 25 8-hour days per month.

A. Describe the logic of the rule used to determine an optimal mix of input usage.

B. Does Medical Testing Lab usage reflect an optimal mix of testing equipment?

C. Describe the logic of the rule used to determine an optimal level of input usage.

D. If tests are conducted at a price of $6 each while labor and all other costs are fixed, should the company lease more machines?

ST7.1   **Solution**

A. The rule for an optimal combination of Testlogic-1 (*T*) and Accutest-3 (*A*) equipment is

$$\frac{MP_T}{P_T} = \frac{MP_A}{P_A}$$

This rule means that an identical amount of additional output would be produced with an additional dollar expenditure on each input. Alternatively, an equal marginal cost of output is incurred irrespective of which input is used to expand output. Of course, marginal products and equipment prices must both reflect the same relevant time frame, either hours or months.

B. On a per-hour basis, the relevant question is

$$\frac{27}{\$18,000/(25 \times 8)} \overset{?}{=} \frac{48}{\$32,000/(25 \times 8)}$$

$$0.3 \overset{\checkmark}{=} 0.3$$

On a per-month basis, the relevant question is

$$\frac{27 \times (25 \times 8)}{\$18,000} \overset{?}{=} \frac{48 \times (25 \times 8)}{\$32,000}$$

$$0.3 \overset{\checkmark}{=} 0.3$$

In both instances, the last dollar spent on each machine increased output by the same 0.3 units, indicating an *optimal mix* of testing machines.

C. The rule for optimal input employment is

$$MRP = MP \times MR_Q = \text{Input Price}$$

This means that the level of input employment is optimal when the marginal sales revenue derived from added input usage is just equal to input price, or the marginal cost of employment.

D. For each machine hour, the relevant question is

<u>Testlogic-1</u>

$$MRP_T = MP_T \times MR_Q \overset{?}{=} P_T$$

$$27 \times \$6 \overset{?}{=} \$18{,}000/(25 \times 8)$$

$$\$162 > \$90$$

<u>Accutest-3</u>

$$MRP_A = MP_A \times MR_Q \overset{?}{=} P_A$$

$$48 \times \$6 \overset{?}{=} \$32{,}000/(25 \times 8)$$

$$\$288 > \$160$$

Or, in per-month terms (assuming 25 8-hour workdays per month):

<u>Testlogic-1</u>

$$MRP_T = MP_T \times MR_Q \overset{?}{=} P_T$$

$$27 \times (25 \times 8) \times \$6 \overset{?}{=} \$18{,}000$$

$$\$32{,}400 > \$18{,}000$$

<u>Accutest-3</u>

$$MRP_A = MP_A \times MR_Q \overset{?}{=} P_A$$

$$48 \times (25 \times 8) \times \$6 \overset{?}{=} \$32{,}000$$

$$\$57{,}600 > \$32{,}000$$

In both cases, each machine returns more than its marginal cost (price) of employment, and expansion would be profitable.

ST7.2   **Production Function Estimation.** Washington-Pacific, Inc., manufactures and sells lumber, plywood, veneer, particle board, medium-density fiberboard, and laminated beams. The company has estimated the following multiplicative production function for basic lumber products in the Pacific Northwest market using monthly production data over the past 2½ years (30 observations):

$$Q = b_0 L^{b_1} K^{b_2} E^{b_3}$$

where

Q = output

L = labor input in worker hours

K = capital input in machine hours

E = energy input in BTUs

Each of the parameters of this model was estimated by regression analysis using monthly data over a recent 3-year period. Coefficient estimation results were as follows:

$$\hat{b}_0 = 0.9; \ \hat{b}_1 = 0.4; \ \hat{b}_2 = 0.4; \ \hat{b}_3 = 0.2$$

The standard error estimates for each coefficient are

$$\sigma_{\hat{b}_0} = 0.6; \quad \sigma_{\hat{b}_1} = 0.1; \quad \sigma_{\hat{b}_2} = 0.2; \quad \sigma_{\hat{b}_3} = 0.1$$

A. Estimate the effect on output of a 1% decline in worker hours (holding K and E constant).

B. Estimate the effect on output of a 5% reduction in machine hours availability accompanied by a 5% decline in energy input (holding L constant).

C. Estimate the returns to scale for this production system.

ST7.2   Solution

A. For Cobb-Douglas production functions, calculations of the elasticity of output with respect to individual inputs can be made by simply referring to the exponents of the production relation. Here a 1% decline in L, holding all else equal, will lead to a 0.4% decline in output. Notice that

$$\frac{\partial Q/Q}{\partial L/L} = \frac{\partial Q}{\partial L} \times \frac{L}{Q}$$

$$= \frac{(b_0 b_1 L^{b_1-1} K^{b_2} E^{b_3}) \times L}{Q}$$

$$= \frac{b_0 b_1 L^{b_1-1+1} K^{b_2} E^{b_3}}{b_0 L^{b_1} K^{b_2} E^{b_3}}$$

$$= b_1$$

Because $(\partial Q/Q)/(\partial L/L)$ is the percent change in Q due to a 1% change in L,

$$\frac{\partial Q/Q}{\partial L/L} = b_1$$

$$\partial Q/Q = b_1 \times \partial L/L$$

$$= 0.4(-0.01)$$

$$= -0.004 \text{ or } -0.4\%$$

B. From part A it is obvious that

$$\partial Q/Q = b_2(\partial K/K) + b_3(\partial E/E)$$

$$= 0.4(-0.05) + 0.2(-0.05)$$

$$= -0.03 \text{ or } -3\%$$

C. In the case of Cobb-Douglas production functions, returns to scale are determined by simply summing exponents because

$$Q = b_0 L^{b_1} K^{b_2} E^{b_3}$$
$$hQ = b_0(kL)^{b_1}(kK)^{b_2}(kE)^{b_3}$$
$$k^{b_1+b_2+b_3}b_0 L^{b_1}K^{b_2}E^{b_3}$$
$$k^{b_1+b_2+b_3}Q$$

Here $b_1 + b_2 + b_3 = 0.4 + 0.4 + 0.2 = 1$ indicating constant returns to scale. This means that a 1% increase in all inputs will lead to a 1% increase in output, and average costs will remain constant as output increases.

PROBLEMS

P7.1 **Marginal Rate of Technical Substitution.** The following production table provides estimates of the maximum amounts of output possible with different combinations of two input factors, X and Y. (Assume that these are just illustrative points on a spectrum of continuous input combinations.)

Units of Y Used	Estimated Output per Day				
5	210	305	360	421	470
4	188	272	324	376	421
3	162	234	282	324	360
2	130	188	234	272	305
1	94	130	162	188	210
	1	2	3	4	5
	Units of X used				

A. Do the two inputs exhibit the characteristics of constant, increasing, or decreasing marginal rates of technical substitution? How do you know?

B. Assuming that output sells for $3 per unit, complete the following tables:

X Fixed at 2 Units

Units of Y Used	Total Product of Y	Marginal Product of Y	Average Product of Y	Marginal Revenue Product of Y
1				
2				
3				
4				
5				

Y Fixed at 3 Units

Units of X Used	Total Product of X	Marginal Product of X	Average Product of X	Marginal Revenue Product of X
1				
2				
3				
4				
5				

C. Assume that the quantity of X is fixed at 2 units. If output sells for $3 and the cost of Y is $120 per day, how many units of Y will be employed?

D. Assume that the company is currently producing 162 units of output per day using 1 unit of X and 3 units of Y. The daily cost per unit of X is $120 and that of Y is also $120. Would you recommend a change in the present input combination? Why or why not?

E. What is the nature of the returns to scale for this production system if the optimal input combination requires that X = Y?

P7.2 Production Function Concepts. Indicate whether each of the following statements is true or false. Explain your answers.

A. Decreasing returns to scale and increasing average costs are indicated when $\epsilon_Q < 1$.

B. If the marginal product of capital falls as capital usage grows, the returns to capital are decreasing.

C. L-shaped isoquants describe production systems in which inputs are perfect substitutes.

D. Marginal revenue product measures the profit earned through expanding input usage.

E. The marginal rate of technical substitution will be affected by a given percentage increase in the marginal productivity of all inputs.

P7.3 Compensation Policy. "Pay for performance" means that employee compensation closely reflects the amount of value derived from each employee's effort. In economic terms, the value derived from employee effort is measured by net marginal revenue product. It is the amount of profit generated by the employee, before accounting for employment costs. Holding all else equal, indicate whether each of the following factors would be responsible for increasing or decreasing the amount of money available for employee merit-based pay.

A. Government mandates for employer-provided health insurance

B. Rising productivity due to better worker training

C. Rising employer sales due to falling imports

D. Falling prices for industry output

E. Rising prevalence of uniform employee stock options

P7.4 Returns to Scale. Determine whether the following production functions exhibit constant, increasing, or decreasing returns to scale.

A. $Q = 0.5X + 2Y + 40Z$

B. $Q = 3L + 10K + 500$

C. $Q = 4A + 6B + 8AB$

D. $Q = 7L^2 + 5LK + 2K^2$

E. $Q = 10L^{0.5}K^{0.3}$

P7.5 Optimal Compensation Policy. Café-Nervosa.com, based in Seattle, Washington, is a rapidly growing family business that offers a line of distinctive coffee products to local and regional coffee shops. Founder and president Frasier Crane is reviewing the company's sales force compensation plan. Currently, the company pays its three experienced sales staff members a salary based on years of service, past contributions to the company, and so on. Niles Crane, a new sales trainee and brother of Fraiser Crane, is paid a more modest salary. Monthly sales and salary data for each employee are as follows:

Sales Staff	Average Monthly Sales	Monthly Salary
Roz Doyle	$160,000	$6,000
Daphne Moon	100,000	4,500
Martin Crane	90,000	3,600
Niles Crane	75,000	2,500

Niles Crane has shown great promise during the past year, and Fraiser Crane believes that a substantial raise is clearly justified. At the same time, some adjustment to the compensation paid to other sales personnel also seems appropriate. Fraiser Crane is considering changing from the current compensation plan to one based on a 5% commission. He sees such a plan as being more fair to the parties involved and believes it would also provide strong incentives for needed market expansion.

A. Calculate Café-Nervosa.com's salary expense for each employee expressed as a percentage of the monthly sales generated by that individual.

B. Calculate monthly income for each employee under a 5% of monthly sales commission-based system.

C. Will a commission-based plan result in efficient relative salaries, efficient salary levels, or both?

P7.6 **Optimal Input Mix.** The First National Bank received 3,000 inquiries following the latest advertisement describing its 30-month IRA accounts in the *Boston World*, a local newspaper. The most recent ad in a similar advertising campaign in *Massachusetts Business*, a regional business magazine, generated 1,000 inquiries. Each newspaper ad costs $500, whereas each magazine ad costs $125.

A. Assuming that additional ads would generate similar response rates, is the bank running an optimal mix of newspaper and magazine ads? Why or why not?

B. Holding all else equal, how many inquiries must a newspaper ad attract for the current advertising mix to be optimal?

P7.7 **Optimal Input Level.** The Route 66 Truck Stop, Inc., sells gasoline to both self-service and full-service customers. Those who pump their own gas benefit from the lower self-service price of $1.50 per gallon. Full-service customers enjoy the service of an attendant, but they pay a higher price of $1.60 per gallon. The company has observed the following relation between the number of attendants employed per day and full-service output:

Route 66 Truck Stop, Inc.

Number of Attendants per Day	Full-Service Output (gallons)
0	0
1	2,000
2	3,800
3	5,400
4	6,800
5	8,000

A. Construct a table showing the net marginal revenue product derived from attendant employment.

B. How many attendants would Route 66 employ at a daily wage rate of $160 (including wages and benefits)?

C. What is the highest daily wage rate Route 66 would pay to hire four attendants per day?

P7.8 **Optimal Input Level.** Ticket Services, Inc., offers ticket promotion and handling services for concerts and sporting events. The Sherman Oaks, California, branch office makes heavy use of spot radio advertising on WHAM-AM, with each 30-second ad costing $100. During the past year, the following relation between advertising and ticket sales per event has been observed:

$$\text{Sales (units)} = 5,000 + 100A - 0.5A^2$$
$$\partial\text{Sales (units)}/\partial\text{Advertising} = 100 - A$$

Here, A represents a 30-second radio spot ad, and sales are measured in numbers of tickets.

Rachel Green, manager for the Sherman Oaks office, has been asked to recommend an appropriate level of advertising. In thinking about this problem, Green noted its resemblance to the optimal resource employment problem she had studied in a managerial economics course that was part of her M.B.A. program. The advertising/sales relation could be thought of as a production function, with advertising as an input and sales as the output. The problem is to determine the profit-maximizing level of employment for the input, advertising, in this "production" system. Green recognized that to solve the problem, she needed a measure of output value. After reflection, she determined that the value of output is $2 per ticket, the net marginal revenue earned by Ticket Services (price minus all marginal costs except advertising).

A. Continuing with Green's production analogy, what is the marginal product of advertising?

B. What is the rule for determining the optimal amount of a resource to employ in a production system? Explain the logic underlying this rule.

C. Using the rule for optimal resource employment, determine the profit-maximizing number of radio ads.

P7.9 **Net Marginal Revenue.** Will Truman & Associates, LLC, is a successful Manhattan–based law firm. Worker productivity at the firm is measured in billable hours, which vary between partners and associates.

Partner time is billed to clients at a rate of $250 per hour, whereas associate time is billed at a rate of $125 per hour. On average, each partner generates 25 billable hours per 40-hour work week, with 15 hours spent on promotion, administrative, and supervisory responsibilities. Associates generate an average of 35 billable hours per 40-hour work week and spend 5 hours per week in administrative and training meetings. Variable overhead costs average 50% of revenues generated by partners and, given supervisory requirements, 60% of revenues generated by associates.

A. Calculate the annual (50 work weeks) net marginal revenue product of partners and associates.

B. If partners earn $175,000 and associates earn $70,000 per year, does the company have an optimal combination of partners and associates? If not, why not? Make your answer explicit and support any recommendations for change.

P7.10 **Production Function Estimation.** Consider the following Cobb-Douglas production function for bus service in a typical metropolitan area:

$$Q = b_0 L^{b_1} K^{b_2} F^{b_3}$$

where

Q = output in millions of passenger miles

L = labor input in worker hours

K = capital input in bus transit hours

F = fuel input in gallons

Each of the parameters of this model was estimated by regression analysis using monthly data over a recent 3-year period. Results obtained were as follows (standard errors in parentheses):

$$\hat{b}_0 = 1.2; \quad \hat{b}_1 = 0.28; \quad \hat{b}_2 = 0.63; \quad \hat{b}_3 = 0.12$$

The standard error estimates for each coefficient are

$$\sigma_{\hat{b}_0} = 0.4; \quad \sigma_{\hat{b}_1} = 0.15; \quad \sigma_{\hat{b}_2} = 0.12; \quad \sigma_{\hat{b}_3} = 0.07$$

A. Estimate the effect on output of a 4% decline in worker hours (holding K and F constant).

B. Estimate the effect on output of a 3% reduction in fuel availability accompanied by a 4% decline in bus transit hours (holding L constant).

C. Estimate the returns to scale for this production system.

CASE STUDY

Productivity Measurement and Enhancement in the Services Sector

The measurement and enhancement of worker productivity is an important challenge facing all managers. Productivity enhancement is vital given the role of labor as a key input in the production of goods and services and in light of the generally increasing vigor of domestic and import competition. Of course, before incentives to enhance worker productivity can be introduced, the multiple dimensions of worker productivity must be made explicit and accurately measured. Management must be able to clearly articulate the many important dimensions of worker output and communicate this information effectively to workers.

The business and popular press is replete with examples of firms and industries that have foundered because of problems tied to the inaccurate measurement of "blue-collar" worker productivity. When worker incentives are carelessly tied to piece-rate production, mass quantities of low-quality output sometimes result. Similarly, worker incentive pay plans that emphasize high-quality output can fail to provide necessary incentives for timely delivery. What is often overlooked in the discussion of workers' efficiency and labor productivity is that the definition and measurement of productivity is perhaps even more difficult in the case of managers and other "white-collar" workers. Problems encountered in the definition and measurement of white-collar worker productivity can be illustrated by considering the productivity of college and university professors.

For most 2-year and 4-year college and university professors, teaching is a primary component of their work assignment. Faculty members have a standard teaching load, defined by the number of class hours per term, number of students taught, or a multiple of the two, called "student contact hours." However, not all student contact hours are alike. For example, it is possible to generate large numbers of student contact hours per faculty member simply by offering courses in a mass lecture setting with hundreds of students per class. In other cases, a faculty member might work with a very small number of students in an advanced seminar or laboratory course, generating relatively few student credit hours. The teaching "product" in each of these course settings is fundamentally similar, and few would argue that the number of students taught is an irrelevant basis for comparing the productivity of professors teaching these different types of classes.

On the other hand, few would suggest defining teaching productivity solely in terms of the sheer quantity of students taught. Student course evaluations are typically required to provide evidence from student "customers" concerning the quality of instruction. Many schools rely on such data as an exclusive measure of teaching quality. At other schools, student course-evaluation data are supplemented by peer review of teaching methods and materials, interviews of former students, and so on. Measures of both the quantity and quality of instruction must be employed in the measurement of teaching productivity.

In addition to their important teaching role, faculty members are expected to play an active role in the ongoing administration of their academic institution. At a minimum, they participate in the peer review of faculty, in student and faculty recruiting, and in curriculum and program development. Faculty often play an active role on committees that conduct the everyday management of the institution. This faculty governance system is an important organizational difference between most academic and nonacademic institutions. Faculty members are both workers and management. Measuring "output" as related to these activities, and hence productivity, is very difficult.

At many schools, faculty members also play an important liaison role with external constituents. Alumni provide important financial resources to colleges and universities and appreciate programs designed for their benefit. Nondegree "short courses" are often offered on topical subjects at nominal charge for the benefit of alumni and the community at large. Similarly, faculty are asked to give lectures to local groups, interviews for local media, and informal consulting services to local firms and organizations. Often these services are provided for free or at nominal charge as part of the faculty member's "service" function. Similarly, faculty are sometimes called on to provide service to external academic and professional organizations. Participation at national and regional academic conventions, editing academic journals, and helping design and write professional exams are typical examples of expected but unpaid services.

The preceding duties are supplemented by faculty research requirements at most 4-year colleges and universities and at all graduate institutions. This requirement is fundamental to the growth and development of colleges and universities but is often misunderstood by those outside of academia. To be granted the doctoral degree, doctoral candidates must complete a rigorous series of courses and exams and meet a dissertation requirement. A doctoral dissertation is a book-length independent study that makes an important contribution to knowledge in a scholarly discipline. In fulfilling this requirement, doctoral students demonstrate their capacity to participate in the discovery of new knowledge. A key difference between the role of university professors and that of other teachers is that professors must be intimately involved with the creation and dissemination of new knowledge. Thus, the research component is a key ingredient of professorial output.

Research output is extremely varied. In the physical sciences, new compounds or other physical products may result. Similarly, such research may lead to new process techniques. In most academic fields, the primary research product is new knowledge communicated in the form of research reports or other scholarly publications. As with teaching, measuring the quantity and quality of research output proves to be most challenging. Judging the value of a research product is often quite subjective, and its worth may not be recognized for years.

Given the difficulties involved with evaluating highly specialized and detailed research, many institutions consider the dollar amount of research funds awarded to an individual to be a useful indicator of the quantity and quality of research output. It is anomalous that a school's best researchers and highest-paid faculty members may be the least expensive in terms of their net costs to the institution. When established researchers are able to consistently obtain external funding in excess of incremental costs, their net employment costs can be nil. In such instances, the disadvantages to an institution of losing a star researcher are obvious.

Of course, just as in the case of measuring teaching quality, difficulties are encountered in measuring the quality of published research output. In most instances, the quality of published articles and books is judged in terms of the reputation of the publisher or editor, the level of readership enjoyed, and so on. Over time, the number of new research outlets has grown to keep pace with the growing level of specialization in the various disciplines. In economics, for example, there are as many as 200 possible research outlets. However, only a relative handful are widely read in any given subdiscipline. Competition for scarce journal space in such outlets is fierce. Acceptance rates at leading journals often average no more than 5% to 10% of those articles submitted. When one considers that a productive scholar is typically able to complete no more than one or two substantial research projects per year, the odds are very much against achieving publication of one or two first-rate journal articles per year. Thus, research productivity is usually measured in terms of both the quantity and quality of published research.

CASE STUDY (continued)

In sum, defining the role of professors at colleges and universities provides an interesting example of the difficulties involved in measuring worker productivity. Each individual academic institution must define on an ongoing basis the relative importance of the teaching, research, and service components of faculty output. Once this has been determined, the difficult task of defining and measuring faculty-member productivity on each dimension must begin.

Based on the preceding information and in light of the focus of your academic institution, answer the following questions:

A. How would you define faculty-member productivity?

B. Do you agree with the view that many elements of professorial output do not easily lend themselves to quantitative evaluation? How might you measure such productivity?

C. Would productivity clauses for professors' contracts make sense economically? What problems do you see in implementing such clauses in actual practice?

D. Reconsider your answers to parts A through C for other service-industry occupations (for example, doctors, lawyers, and legislators). Are the issues discussed unique to academia?

A Constrained Optimization Approach to Developing the Optimal Input Combination Relationships

I t was noted in Chapter 7 that the determination of optimal input proportions could be viewed either as a problem of maximizing output for a given expenditure level or, alternatively, as a problem of minimizing the cost of producing a specified level of output. This appendix shows how the Lagrangian technique for constrained optimization can be used to develop the optimal input proportion rule.

Constrained Production Maximization

Consider the problem of maximizing output from a production system described by the general equation

(7A.1)
$$Q = f(X, Y)$$

subject to a budget constraint. The expenditure limitation can be expressed as

(7A.2)
$$E^* = P_X \times X + P_Y \times Y$$

which states that the total expenditure on inputs, E^*, is equal to the price of input X, P_X, times the quantity of X employed, plus the price of Y, P_Y, times the quantity of that resource used in the production system. Equation 7A.2 can be written in the form of a Lagrangian constraint, as developed in Chapter 2, as

(7A.3)
$$0 = E^* - P_X \times X - P_Y \times Y$$

The Lagrangian function for the maximization of the production function, Equation 7A.1, subject to the budget constraint expressed by Equation 7A.3, can then be written as

(7A.4)
$$\text{Max } L_Q = f(X, Y) + \lambda(E^* - P_X \times X - P_Y \times Y)$$

Maximization of the constrained production function is accomplished by setting the partial derivatives of the Lagrangian expression taken with respect to X, Y, and λ equal to zero, and then solving the resultant system of equations. The partials of Equation 7A.4 are

(7A.5)
$$\frac{\partial L_Q}{\partial X} = \frac{\partial f(X, Y)}{\partial X} - \lambda P_X = 0$$

(7A.6)
$$\frac{\partial L_Q}{\partial Y} = \frac{\partial f(X, Y)}{\partial Y} - \lambda P_X = 0$$

and

(7A.7)
$$\frac{\partial L_Q}{\partial \lambda} = E^* - P_X \times X - P_Y \times Y = 0$$

Equating these three partial derivatives to zero results in a set of conditions that must be met for output maximization subject to the budget limit.

Note that the first terms in Equations 7A.5 and 7A.6 are the marginal products of X and Y respectively. In other words, $\partial f(X, Y)/\partial X$ equals $\partial Q/\partial X$, which by definition is the marginal product of X; and the same is true for $\partial f(X, Y)/\partial Y$. Thus, those two expressions can be rewritten as

$$MP_X - \lambda P_X = 0$$

and

$$MP_Y - \lambda P_Y = 0$$

or, alternatively, as

(7A.8)
$$MP_X = \lambda P_X$$

and

(7A.9)
$$MP_Y = \lambda P_Y$$

The conditions required for constrained output maximization, expressed by Equations 7A.8 and 7A.9, can also expressed by the ratio of equations. Thus,

(7A.10)
$$\frac{MP_X}{MP_Y} = \frac{\lambda P_X}{\lambda P_Y}$$

Canceling the lambdas in Equation 7A.10 results in the condition required for optimal input use developed in the chapter.

(7A.11)
$$\frac{MP_X}{MP_Y} = \frac{P_X}{P_Y}$$

For maximum production, given a fixed expenditure level, the input factors must be combined in such a way that the ratio of their marginal products is equal to the ratio of their prices. Alternatively, transposing Equation 7A.11 derives the expression

$$\frac{MP_X}{P_X} = \frac{MP_Y}{P_Y}$$

Optimal input proportions require that the ratio of marginal product to price must be equal for all input factors.

Constrained Cost Minimization

The relationship developed here can also be derived from the problem of minimizing the cost of producing a given quantity of output. In this case, the constraint states that some level of output, Q^*, must be produced from the production system described by the function $Q = f(X, Y)$. Written in the standard Lagrangian format, the constraint is $0 = Q^* - f(X, Y)$. The cost, or expenditure, function is given as $E = P_X \times x + P_Y \times Y$. The Lagrangian function for the constrained cost minimization problem, then, is

(7A.12) $$L_E = P_X \times X + P_Y \times Y + \lambda[Q^* - f(X, Y)]$$

As shown here, the conditions for constrained cost minimization are provided by the partial derivatives of Equation 7A.12:

(7A.13) $$\frac{\partial L_E}{\partial X} = P_X - \lambda \frac{\partial (fX, Y)}{\partial X} = 0$$

(7A.14) $$\frac{\partial L_E}{\partial Y} = P_Y - \lambda \frac{\partial (fX, Y)}{\partial Y} = 0$$

and

(7A.15) $$\frac{\partial L_E}{\partial \lambda} = Q^* - f(X, Y) = 0$$

Notice that the terms on the left-hand side in Equations 7A.13 and 7A.14 are the marginal products of X and Y respectively, so each of these expressions can be rewritten as

$$P_X - \lambda MP_X = 0$$

and

$$P_Y - \lambda MP_Y = 0$$

or, alternatively, as

(7A.16) $$P_X = \lambda MP_X$$

and

(7A.17) $$P_Y = \lambda MP_Y$$

Taking the ratio of Equation 7A.16 to Equation 7A.17 and canceling the lambdas again produces the basic input optimality relation

$$\frac{P_X}{P_Y} = \frac{MP_X}{MP_Y}$$

PROBLEM

7A.1 Assume that a firm produces its product in a system described in the following production function and price data:

$$Q = 3X + 5Y + XY$$
$$P_X = \$3$$
$$P_Y = \$6$$

Here, X and Y are two variable input factors employed in the production of Q.

A. What are the optimal input proportions for X and Y in this production system? Is this combination rate constant regardless of the output level?

B. It is possible to express the cost function associated with the use of X and Y in the production of Q as Cost $= P_X X + P_Y Y$ or Cost $= \$3X + \$6Y$? Use the Lagrangian technique to determine the maximum output that the firm can produce operating under a \$1,000 budget constraint for X and Y. Show that the inputs used to produce that level of output meet the optimality conditions derived in part A.

C. What is the additional output that could be obtained from a marginal increase in the budget?

D. Assume that the firm is interested in minimizing the cost of producing 14,777 units of output. Use the Lagrangian method to determine what optimal quantities of X and Y to employ. What will be the cost of producing that output level? How would you interpret λ, the Lagrangian multiplier, in this problem?

SELECTED REFERENCES

Autor, David H. "Why Do Temporary Help Firms Provide Free General Skills Training?" *Quarterly Journal of Economics* 116 (November 2001): 1409–1448.

Bowles, Samuel, Herbert Gintis, and Melissa Osborne. "Incentive-Enhancing Preferences: Personality, Behavior, and Earnings." *American Economic Review* 91 (May 2001): 155–158.

Brickley, James A., and Jerold L. Zimmerman. "Changing Incentives in a Multitask Environment: Evidence from a Top-Tier Business School." *Journal of Corporate Finance* 7 (December 2001): 367–396.

Cutler, David M., and Mark Mcclellan. "Productivity Change in Health Care." *American Economic Review* 91 (May 2001): 281–286.

Datta, Sudip, Mai Iskandar-Datta, and Kartik Raman. "Executive Compensations and Corporate Acquisition Decisions." *Journal of Finance* 56 (December 2001): 2299–2336.

Deli, Daniel N., and Raj Varma. "Contracting in the Investment Management Industry." *Journal of Financial Economics* 63 (January 2002): 79–98.

Dhawan, Rajeev. "Firm Size and Productivity Differential: Theory and Evidence from a Panel of U.S. Firms." *Journal of Economic Behavior & Organization* 44 (March 2001): 269–293.

Findlay, Ronald, and Ronald W. Jones. "Input Trade and the Location of Production." *American Economic Review* 91 (May 2001): 29–33.

Geoffrion, Arthur M., and Ramayya Krishnan. "Prospects for Operations Research in the E-Business Era." *Interfaces* 31 (March 2001): 6–36.

Hermalin, Benjamin, and Nancy Wallace. "Firm Performance and Executive Compensation in the Savings and Loan Industry." *Journal of Financial Economics* 61 (July 2001): 139–170.

Matolcsy, Zoltan P. "Executive Cash Compensation and Corporate Performance During Different Economic Cycles." *Contemporary Accounting Research* 17 (Winter 2000): 671–692.

Meulbroek, Lisa K. "The Efficiency of Equity-Linked Compensation: Understanding the Full Cost of Awarding Executive Stock Options." *Financial Management* 30 (Summer 2001): 5–44.

Morgan, Angela G., and Annette B. Poulsen. "Linking Pay to Performance—Compensation Proposals in the *S&P* 500." *Journal of Business* 62 (December 2001): 489–523.

Ohanian, Lee E. "Why Did Productivity Fall So Much During the Great Depression?" *American Economic Review* 91 (May 2001): 34–38.

Perry, Tod, and Marc Zenner. "Pay for Performance? Government Regulation and the Structure of Compensation Contracts." *Journal of Business* 62 (December 2001): 453–488.

CHAPTER EIGHT

Cost Analysis and Estimation

Fans of the Chevrolet Camaro and Pontiac Firebird mourned when General Motors (GM) announced that these classic muscle cars were headed for that big parking lot in the sky at the end of the 2001 model year. GM management said the Camaro and Firebird had become victims of America's obsession with sport utility vehicles and light trucks. Management would have us believe that the kids who used to crave inexpensive but fun-to-drive muscle cars were now driving $35,000 Ford Explorers.

The truth is that poor product quality, outdated design, lackluster marketing, and tough competition from foreign rivals killed the Camaro and Firebird. It's simply not true that young people, and the young at heart, no longer want cars that are fast, loud, and cheap. To convince yourself of this, simply go downtown in almost any city or suburb in America on Friday or Saturday night. It won't be long before you get nearly blown off the sidewalk by some kid slouched behind the wheel of a "low-rider" with windows vibrating to the thump of ultra-amplified bass. In the 1970s or 1980s, that kid was in a Camaro or Firebird. Today, they probably drive a Honda Civic or Acura Integra. Both are relatively cheap, stylish, and easy to customize. If you're not into customizing, try a Toyota Celica GT-S 2133 Liftback 2D (6-Spd.). It's more than a stylish, dependable bargain priced at about $23,000. It's fun to drive. A high-quality car is more than neat looking and dependable; it's a blast to get behind the wheel of a high-quality car.

Cost estimation and control is part of the continual process of making products that exceed customer expectations. Quick fixes don't work. This chapter shows how making things faster, cheaper, and better requires a fundamental appreciation of cost concepts.[1]

---

1 Karen Lundegaard, "Big Three Trail Their Rivals in Consumer Reports Survey," *The Wall Street Journal Online*, March 13, 2002 (http://online.wsj.com).

WHAT MAKES COST ANALYSIS DIFFICULT?

Cost analysis is made difficult by the effects of unforeseen inflation, unpredictable changes in technology, and the dynamic nature of input and output markets. Wide divergences between economic costs and accounting valuations are common. This makes it extremely important to adjust accounting data to create an appropriate basis for managerial decisions.

The Link Between Accounting and Economic Valuations

Accurate cost analysis involves careful consideration of relevant decision alternatives. In many instances, the total costs of making a given decision are clear only when viewed in light of what is done *and* what is not done. Careful decision analysis includes comparing the relative costs and benefits of each decision alternative. No option can be viewed in isolation; each choice plays an important role in shaping the relevant costs and benefits of *all* decision alternatives.

Evaluation of a proposal to expand output requires that revenues gained from added sales be compared with the higher production costs incurred. In weighing a recommendation to expand, managers must compare the revenues derived from investment and the cost of needed funds. Expected benefits from an advertising promotion must be measured in relation to the costs of personal selling, media promotion, and direct marketing. Even a decision to pave the employees' parking lot or to refurbish the company lunchroom involves a comparison between projected costs and the expected benefits derived from improved morale and worker productivity. In every case, the decision-making process involves a comparison between the costs and the benefits resulting from various decision alternatives.

Corporate restructuring often involves eliminating nonstrategic operations to redeploy assets and strengthen core lines of business. When nonessential assets are disposed of in a depressed market, there is typically no relation between low "fire sale" proceeds and book value, historical cost, or replacement cost. Conversely, when assets are sold to others who can more effectively use such resources, sale proceeds can approximate replacement value and greatly exceed historical costs and book values. Even under normal circumstances, the link between economic and accounting values can be tenuous. Economic worth as determined by profit-generating capability, rather than accounting value, is always the most vital consideration when determining the cost and use of specific assets.

Historical Versus Current Costs

The term *cost* can be defined in a number of ways. The correct definition varies from situation to situation. In popular terminology, cost generally refers to the price that must be paid for an item. If a firm buys an input for cash and uses it immediately, few problems arise in defining and measuring its cost. However, if an input is purchased, stored for a time, and then used, complications can arise. The problem can be acute if the item is a long-lived asset like a building that will be used at varying rates for an indeterminate period.

When costs are calculated for a firm's income tax returns, the law requires use of the actual dollar amount spent to purchase the labor, raw materials, and capital equipment used in production. For tax purposes, **historical cost**, or actual cash outlay, is the relevant cost. This is also generally true for annual 10-K reports to the Securities and Exchange Commission and for reports to stockholders.

Despite their usefulness, historical costs are not appropriate as a sole basis for many managerial decisions. Current costs are typically much more relevant. **Current cost** is the amount that must be paid under prevailing market conditions. Current cost is influenced by market conditions measured by the number of buyers and sellers, the present state of technology, inflation, and so on. For assets purchased recently, historical cost and current cost are typically the same.

historical cost
Actual cash outlay

current cost
Amount paid under prevailing market conditions

For assets purchased several years ago, historical cost and current cost are often quite different. Since World War II, inflation has been an obvious source of large differences between current and historical costs throughout most of the world. With an inflation rate of roughly 5 percent per year, prices double in less than 15 years and triple in roughly 22 years. Land purchased for $50,000 in 1970 often has a current cost in excess of $200,000. In California, Florida, Texas, and other rapidly growing areas, current costs run much higher. Just as no homeowner would sell his or her home for a lower price based on lower historical costs, no manager can afford to sell assets or products for less than current costs.

A firm also cannot assume that the accounting historical cost is the same as the relevant economic cost of using a given piece of equipment. For example, it is not always appropriate to assume that use costs equal zero just because a machine has been fully depreciated using appropriate accounting methods. If a machine could be sold for $10,000 now, but its market value is expected to be only $2,000 1 year from now, the relevant cost of using the machine for one additional year is $8,000.[2] Again, there is little relation between the $8,000 relevant cost of using the machine and the zero cost reported on the firm's income statement.

Historical costs provide a measure of the market value of an asset at the time of purchase. Current costs are a measure of the market value of an asset at the present time. Traditional accounting methods and the IRS rely heavily on the historical cost concept because it can be applied consistently across firms and is easily verifiable. However, when historical and current costs differ markedly, reliance on historical costs sometimes leads to operating decisions with disastrous consequences. The savings and loan (S&L) industry debacle in the United States during the late 1980s is a clear case in point. On a historical cost basis, almost all thrifts appeared to have solid assets to back up liabilities. On a current cost basis, however, many S&Ls proved insolvent because assets had a current market value below the current market value of liabilities. The move by federal and state bank regulators toward market-value-based accounting methods is motivated by a desire to avoid S&L-type disasters in the future.

Replacement Cost

replacement cost
The cost of duplicating productive capability using current technology

Although it is typical for current costs to exceed historical costs, this is not always the case. Computers and many types of electronic equipment cost much less today than they did just a few years ago. In many high-tech industries, the rapid advance of technology has overcome the general rate of inflation. As a result, current costs are falling. Current costs for computers and electronic equipment are determined by what is referred to as **replacement cost**, or the cost of duplicating productive capability using current technology. For example, the value of used personal computers tends to fall by 30 to 40 percent per year. In valuing such assets, the appropriate measure is the much lower replacement cost—not the historical cost. Similarly, if a company holds electronic components in inventory, the relevant cost for pricing purposes is replacement costs.

In a more typical example, consider a construction company that has an inventory of 1,000,000 board feet of lumber, purchased at a historical cost of $200,000, or $200 per 1,000 board feet (a board foot of lumber is 1 square foot of lumber, 1 inch thick). Assume that lumber prices rise by 50 percent, and the company is asked to bid on a construction project that would require lumber. What cost should the construction company assign to the lumber—the $200,000 historical cost or the $300,000 replacement cost? The answer is the replacement cost of $300,000. The company will have to pay $300,000 to replace the lumber it uses on the new construction project. In fact, the construction company could sell its current inventory of lumber to others for the

---

2   This statement involves a slight oversimplification. The economic cost of using a machine for 1 year is its current market value minus the discounted present value of its worth 1 year from now. This adjustment is necessary to account for the fact that future dollars have a lower *present* value than dollars received today.

prevailing market price of $300,000. Under current market conditions, the lumber has a worth of $300,000. The amount of $300,000 is the relevant economic cost for purposes of bidding on the new construction project. For income tax purposes, however, the appropriate cost basis for the lumber inventory is still the $200,000 historical cost.

OPPORTUNITY COSTS

When a firm uses resources, it bids against alternative users. To be efficient, a resource's value in use must be at least as much as its value in alternative opportunities. The role played by choice alternatives in cost analysis is formalized by the opportunity cost concept.

Opportunity Cost Concept

opportunity cost
Foregone value associated with current rather than next-best use of an asset

Opportunity cost is the foregone value associated with the current rather than next-best use of an asset. In other words, cost is determined by the highest-valued *opportunity* that must be foregone to allow current use. The cost of aluminum used in the manufacture of soft drink containers, for example, is determined by its value in alternative uses. Soft drink bottlers must pay an aluminum price equal to this value, or the aluminum will be used in the production of alternative goods, such as airplanes, building materials, cookware, and so on. Similarly, if a firm owns capital equipment that can be used to produce either product A or product B, the relevant cost of product A includes the profit of the alternative product B that cannot be produced because the equipment is tied up in manufacturing product A.

The opportunity cost concept explains asset use in a wide variety of circumstances. Gold and silver are pliable yet strong precious metals. As such, they make excellent material for dental fillings. However, when speculation drove precious metals prices skyrocketing during the 1970s, plastic and ceramic materials became a common substitute for dental gold and silver. More recently, lower market prices have again allowed widespread dental use of both metals. Still, dental customers must be willing to pay a price for dental gold and silver that is competitive with the price paid by jewelry customers and industrial users.

Explicit and Implicit Costs

explicit cost
Out-of-pocket expenditures

implicit cost
Noncash costs

Typically, the costs of using resources in production involve both out-of-pocket costs, or **explicit costs**, and other noncash costs, called **implicit costs**. Wages, utility expenses, payment for raw materials, interest paid to the holders of the firm's bonds, and rent on a building are all examples of explicit expenses. The implicit costs associated with any decision are much more difficult to compute. These costs do not involve cash expenditures and are therefore often overlooked in decision analysis. Because cash payments are not made for implicit costs, the opportunity cost concept must be used to measure them. The rent that a shop owner could receive on buildings and equipment if they were not used in the business is an implicit cost of the owner's own retailing activity, as is the salary that an individual could receive by working for someone else instead of operating his or her own establishment.

An example should clarify these cost distinctions. Consider the costs associated with the purchase and operation of a law practice. Assume that the minority partners in an established practice, Donnell, Young, Doyle & Frutt, can be bought for $225,000, with an additional $25,000 needed for initial working capital. Lindsay Doyle has personal savings of $250,000 to invest in such an enterprise; Bobby Donnell, another possible buyer, must borrow the entire $250,000 at a cost of 15 percent, or $37,500 per year. Assume that operating costs are the same no matter who owns the practice and that Doyle and Donnell are equally capable of completing the purchase. Does the $37,500 in annual interest expenses make Donnell's potential operating cost

GE's "20-70-10" Plan

The General Electric Co. (GE) routinely identifies the top 20 percent, the middle 70 percent, and the bottom 10 percent of its 100,000 managerial and professional employees. According to Jack Welch, legendary former chairman of GE, the top 20 percent and middle 70 percent often trade places, but the bottom 10 percent tend to remain there. At GE, those employees found in the bottom 10 percent are given a chance to improve. However, if performance doesn't improve quickly, they had better find another job.

Among its managers and professionals, GE loses about 8,000 per year through turnover and attrition. Of those, about 60 percent, or 4,800, are forced out—both in good times and bad. Even among the highest-ranking 600 GE executives, about 60 leave each year. Fewer than 20 are due to retirement or opportunities elsewhere. There just isn't much empathy for underperformance at GE. Welch was famous for arguing that underperforming managers and professionals will eventually be fired anyway, and delaying the inevitable is a form of "corporate cruelty."

Welch retired at the end of 2001, but GE has no plans to retire its 20-70-10 plan. Not only is the plan embraced by new CEO Jeffrey Immelt, but other top corporations are also seeking to emulate GE's success. Although employee performance reviews have long been an important part of effective management, it's new for bosses to rank every employee in each department. Newer still is the practice of asking those at the bottom to leave. The rationale for tough performance reviews is that companies want to make way for promising new hires. Similarly, if downsizing becomes necessary, is it fair to throw out solid performers and keep weaker employees?

To be sure, GE's tough 20-70-10 plan has its detractors. Critics argue that top-to-bottom rankings are sometimes arbitrary. In some instances, discharged workers have filed lawsuits charging discrimination. Unfazed, GE and its imitators are going forward with their top-to-bottom rankings.

See: Dow Jones Newswires," GE's Immelt: Willing to Cooperate with US's EPA on Hudson," *The Wall Street Journal Online*, January 18, 2002 (http://online.wsj.com).

greater than that of Doyle? For managerial decision purposes, the answer is no. Even though Donnell has higher explicit interest costs, true financing costs may well be the same for both individuals. Doyle has an implicit interest cost equal to the amount that could be earned on an alternative $250,000 investment. If a 15 percent return can be earned by investing in other assets of equal risk, then Doyle's implicit investment opportunity cost is also $37,500 per year. In this case, Doyle and Donnell each have a financing cost of $37,500 per year. Doyle's cost is implicit and Donnell's is explicit.

Will total operating costs be identical for both individuals? Not necessarily. Just as the implicit cost of Doyle's capital must be included in the analysis, so too must implicit labor costs be included for each individual. If Doyle is a senior partner earning $250,000 a year and Donnell is a junior partner earning $150,000 annually, implicit labor costs will be different. When both individuals have ready employment alternatives, the implicit labor expense for each potential buyer is the amount of income forfeited by foregoing such alternative employment. Thus, implicit labor costs are $250,000 for Doyle and $150,000 for Donnell. On an annual basis, Doyle's total capital plus labor costs are $287,500, all of which are implicit. Donnell's total annual costs are $187,500, including explicit capital costs of $37,500 plus implicit labor costs of $150,000.

INCREMENTAL AND SUNK COSTS IN DECISION ANALYSIS

Relevant costs and benefits for any decision are limited to those that are affected by it. To limit the confounding influence of irrelevant cost information, it is helpful to focus on the causal relation between costs and a given managerial decision, as well as on the reversible or nonreversible nature of some cost categories.

Incremental Cost

incremental cost
Change in cost caused by a given managerial decision

Incremental cost is the change in cost caused by a given managerial decision. Whereas marginal cost is the change in cost following a one-unit change in output, incremental costs typically involve multiple units of output. For example, incremental costs are the relevant consideration when an air carrier considers the cost of adding an additional departure from New York's La Guardia Airport to upstate New York. When all current departures are full, it is impractical to consider adding a single passenger-mile unit of output. Similarly, the incremental cost concept comes into play when judging the costs of adding a new product line, advertising campaign, production shift, or organization structure.

Inappropriate managerial decisions can result when the incremental concept is ignored or applied incorrectly. Consider, for example, a commercial real estate firm that refuses to rent excess office space for $750 per month because it figures cost as $1,000 per month—or incremental operating costs of $150 plus interest and overhead charges of $850. If the relevant incremental cost is indeed only $150 per month, turning away the prospective renter causes a $600 (= $750 – $150) per month loss in **profit contribution**, or profit before fixed charges. Interest and overhead charges will be incurred irrespective of whether the excess space is rented. By adding the prospective renter, the landlord has the same interest and overhead expenses as before, *plus* $600 in added revenues after incremental operating expenses. The net effect of rejecting such a renter would be to reduce profit contribution and net profits by $600.

profit contribution
Profit before fixed charges

Care must be exercised to ensure against incorrectly assigning a lower than appropriate incremental cost. If excess capacity results from a temporary reduction in demand, this must be taken into account. Accepting the $750 per month renter in the previous example is a mistake if doing so causes more profitable renters to be turned away. When excess capacity is caused by a temporary drop in demand, only short-term or month-to-month leases should be offered at the bargain price of $750 per month. In this way, pricing flexibility can be maintained while the net cost of temporary excess capacity is minimized. In any event, all incremental costs, including those that might be incurred in the future, must be considered.

Sunk Costs

Inherent in the incremental cost concept is the principle that any cost not affected by a decision is irrelevant to that decision. A cost that does not vary across decision alternatives is called a **sunk cost**; such costs do not play a role in determining the optimal course of action.

sunk cost
Cost that does not vary across decision alternatives

For example, suppose a firm has spent $5,000 on an option to purchase land for a new factory at a price of $100,000. Also assume that it is later offered an equally attractive site for $90,000. What should the firm do? The first thing to recognize is that the $5,000 spent on the purchase option is a sunk cost that must be ignored. If the firm purchases the first property, it must pay a price of $100,000. The newly offered property requires an expenditure of only $90,000 and results in a $10,000 savings. In retrospect, purchase of the $5,000 option was a mistake. It would be a compounding of this initial error to follow through with the purchase of the first property and lose an additional $10,000.

In managerial decision making, care must be taken to ensure that only those costs actually affected by a decision are considered. These incremental costs can include both implicit and explicit costs. If long-term commitments are involved, both current and future incremental costs must also be accounted for. Any costs not affected by available decision alternatives are sunk and irrelevant.

SHORT-RUN AND LONG-RUN COSTS

cost function
The cost-output relation

Proper use of relevant cost concepts requires an understanding of the relation between cost and output, or the **cost function**. Two basic cost functions are used in managerial decision making: **short-run cost functions**, used for day-to-day operating decisions, and **long-run cost functions**, used for long-range planning.

How Is the Operating Period Defined?

The **short run** is the operating period during which the availability of at least one input is fixed. In the **long run**, the firm has complete flexibility with respect to input use. In the short run, operating decisions are typically constrained by prior capital expenditures. In the long run, no such restrictions exist. For example, a management consulting firm operating out of rented office space might have a short-run period as brief as several weeks, the time remaining on the office lease. A firm in the hazardous waste disposal business with 25- to 30-year leases on disposal sights has significant long-lived assets and faces a lengthy period of operating constraints.

The economic life of an asset and the degree of specialization affect the time length of operating period constraints. Consider, for example, a health maintenance organization's (HMO) automobile purchase for delivering home-based health care. If the car is a standard model without modification, it represents an unspecialized input factor with a resale value based on the used car market in general. However, if the car has been modified by adding refrigeration equipment for transporting perishable medicines, it becomes a more specialized input with full value only for those who need a vehicle with refrigeration equipment. In this case, the market price of the car might not equal its value in use to the HMO. To the extent that specialized input factors are employed, the short run is lengthened. When only unspecialized factors are used, the short run is condensed.

The amount of time required to order, receive, and install new assets also influences the duration of the short run. Many manufacturers face delays of several months when ordering new plant and equipment. Air carriers must place their equipment orders 5 or more years in advance of delivery. Electric utilities frequently require 8 or more years to bring new generating plants on line. For all such firms, the short-run operating period is an extended period of time.

Long-run cost curves are called *planning curves*; short-run cost curves are called *operating curves*. In the long run, plant and equipment are variable, so management can plan the most efficient physical plant, given an estimate of the firm's demand function. Once the optimal plant has been determined and the resulting investment in equipment has been made, short-run operating decisions are constrained by these prior decisions.

Fixed and Variable Costs

Fixed costs do not vary with output. These costs include interest expenses, rent on leased plant and equipment, depreciation charges associated with the passage of time, property taxes, and salaries for employees not laid off during periods of reduced activity. Because all costs are variable in the long run, long-run fixed costs always equal zero. **Variable costs** fluctuate with output. Expenses for raw materials, depreciation associated with the use of equipment, the variable portion of utility charges, some labor costs, and sales commissions are all examples of variable expenses. In the short run, both variable and fixed costs are often incurred. In the long run, all costs are variable.

A sharp distinction between fixed and variable costs is not always possible nor realistic. For example, CEO and staff salaries may be largely fixed, but during severe business downturns, even CEOs take a pay cut. Similarly, salaries for line managers and supervisors are fixed only within certain output ranges. Below a lower limit, supervisors and managers get laid off. Above an upper limit, additional supervisors and managers get hired. The longer the duration of abnormal demand, the greater the likelihood that some fixed costs will actually vary. In recognition of this, such costs are sometimes referred to as *semivariable*.

SHORT-RUN COST CURVES

short-run cost curve
Cost-output relation for a specific plant and operating environment

A **short-run cost curve** shows the minimum cost impact of output changes for a specific plant size and in a given operating environment. Such curves reflect the optimal or least-cost input combination for producing output under fixed circumstances. Wage rates, interest rates, plant configuration, and all other operating conditions are held constant.

Any change in the operating environment leads to a *shift* in short-run cost curves. For example, a general rise in wage rates leads to an upward shift; a fall in wage rates leads to a downward shift. Such changes must not be confused with *movements along* a given short-run cost curve caused by a change in production levels. For an existing plant, the short-run cost curve illustrates the minimum cost of production at various output levels under current operating conditions. Short-run cost curves are a useful guide to operating decisions.

Short-Run Cost Categories

Both fixed and variable costs affect short-run costs. Total cost at each output level is the sum of total fixed cost (a constant) and total variable cost. Using TC to represent total cost, TFC for total fixed cost, TVC for total variable cost, and Q for the quantity of output produced, various unit costs are calculated as follows:

$$\text{(8.1)} \qquad \text{Total Cost} = TC = TFC + TVC$$

$$\text{(8.2)} \qquad \text{Average Fixed Cost} = AFC = \frac{TFC}{Q}$$

$$\text{(8.3)} \qquad \text{Average Variable Cost} = AVC = \frac{TVC}{Q}$$

$$\text{(8.4)} \qquad \text{Average Cost} = AC = \frac{TC}{Q} = AFC + AVC$$

$$\text{(8.5)} \qquad \text{Marginal Cost} = MC = \frac{\partial TC}{\partial Q}$$

These cost categories are portrayed in Table 8.1. Using these data, it is possible to identify the various cost relations as well as to examine cost behavior. Table 8.1 shows that *AFC* declines

TABLE 8.1

Short-Run Cost Relations

Quantity Q	Total Cost $TC = TFC + TVC$	Marginal Cost $MC = \partial TC/\partial Q$	Total Fixed Cost TFC	Total Variable Cost TVC	Average Cost $AC = TC/Q$	Average Fixed Cost $AFC = TFC/Q$	Average Variable Cost $AVC = TVC/Q$
1	$120	—	$100	$ 20		100.00	20.00
2	138	18	100	38	69.00	50.00	19.00
3	151	13	100	51	50.33	33.33	17.00
4	162	11	100	62	40.50	25.00	15.50
5	175	13	100	75	35.00	20.00	15.00
6	190	15	100	90	31.67	16.67	15.00
7	210	20	100	110	30.00	14.29	15.71
8	234	24	100	134	29.25	12.50	16.75
9	263	29	100	163	29.22	11.11	18.11
10	300	37	100	200	30.00	10.00	20.00

Gaps in GAAP?

Generally accepted accounting principles (GAAP) offer companies and their auditors a consistent set of rules to follow in their reporting of company income statement and balance sheet information. GAAP also offers a measure of "quality control" that assures investors that reported numbers have been consistently derived from a set of uniform principles applied to all companies. This makes it possible for investors to compare reported results over time and across firms and industries. At least, this is how GAAP works in theory. Sometimes, accounting practice falls far short of the ideal. In some instances, it seems as if companies and their auditors come up with the numbers the companies want, irrespective of actual economic performance.

Common accounting tricks that managers and investors must be on the lookout for include

- Misleading focus on pro-forma results. Some firms seek to minimize poor operating performance by encouraging investors to overlook standard accounting charges.

- Excessive one-time R&D charges. These one-time charges are taken at the time of an acquisition to cover expenses for research and development that is "in process" but not yet commercially viable. By separating these expenses from revenues that might be gained in the future, future earnings can be overstated.

- Extravagant one-time "restructuring reserves." When normal expenses are written off ahead of time, future earnings are overstated.

- Aggressive revenue recognition. When service contracts stretch out for years, booking revenue too early inflates sales and earnings.

The Securities and Exchange Commission (SEC) has become concerned that the quality of financial reporting is eroding. It should be. If basic accounting practices ever lose credibility with investors and the general public, financial markets and economic performance would suffer greatly.

See: Alen Mattich, "Accountants Under the Microscope Post Enron," *The Wall Street Journal Online*, January 18, 2002 (http://online.wsj.com).

---

continuously with increases in output. *AC* and *AVC* also decline as long as they exceed *MC*, but increase when they are less than *MC*. Alternatively, so long as *MC* is less than *AC* and *AVC*, both average cost categories will decline. When *MC* is greater than *AC* and *AVC*, both average cost categories will rise. Also note that *TFC* is invariant with increases in output and that *TVC* at each level of output equals the sum of *MC* up to that output.

Marginal cost is the change in cost associated with a one-unit change in output. Because fixed costs do not vary with output, fixed costs do not affect marginal costs. Only variable costs affect marginal costs. Therefore, marginal costs equal the change in total costs *or* the change in total variable costs following a one-unit change in output:

$$MC = \frac{\partial TC}{\partial Q} = \frac{\partial TVC}{\partial Q}$$

Short-Run Cost Relations

Relations among short-run cost categories are shown in Figure 8.1. Figure 8.1(a) illustrates total cost and total variable cost curves. The shape of the total cost curve is determined entirely by the total variable cost curve. The slope of the total cost curve at each output level is identical to the slope of the total variable cost curve. Fixed costs merely shift the total cost curve to a higher level. This means that marginal costs are independent of fixed cost.

The shape of the total variable cost curve, and hence the shape of the total cost curve, is determined by the productivity of variable input factors employed. The variable cost curve in Figure 8.1 increases at a decreasing rate up to output level Q_1, then at an increasing rate. Assuming constant input prices, this implies that the marginal productivity of variable inputs first increases, then decreases. Variable input factors exhibit increasing returns in the range from 0 to Q_1 units and show diminishing returns thereafter. This is a typical finding. Fixed

FIGURE 8.1

Short-Run Cost Curves

(a) The productivity of variable input factors determines the slope of both the total and variable cost curves. An increase (decrease) in fixed costs shifts the total cost curve upward (downward), but it has no effect on variable cost curves. (b) Marginal cost declines to Q_1. Both average total cost and average variable costs fall (rise) when marginal cost is lower (higher).

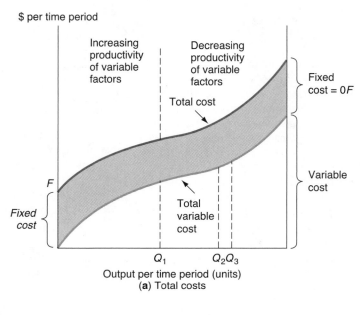

(a) Total costs

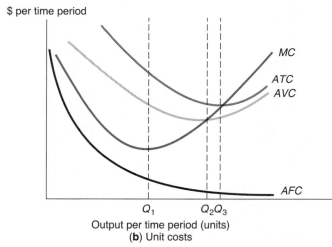

(b) Unit costs

plant and equipment are usually designed to operate at a target production level. Operating below the target output level results in some excess capacity. In the below-target output range, production can be increased more than proportionately to increases in variable inputs. At above-target output levels, fixed factors are intensively used, and the law of diminishing returns takes over. There, a given percentage increase in variable inputs results in a smaller relative increase in output.

The relation between short-run costs and the productivity of variable input factors is also reflected by short-run unit cost curves, as shown in Figure 8.1(b). Marginal cost declines over the range of increasing productivity and rises thereafter. This imparts the familiar U-shape to average variable cost and average total cost curves. At first, marginal cost curves also typically decline rapidly in relation to the average variable cost curve and the average total cost curve. Near the target output level, the marginal cost curve turns up and intersects each of the *AVC* and *AC* short-run curves at their respective minimum points.[3]

LONG-RUN COST CURVES

long-run cost curve
Cost-output relation for the optimal plant in the present operating environment

In the long run, the firm has complete input flexibility. All long-run costs are variable. A **long-run cost curve** shows the minimum cost impact of output changes for the optimal plant size in the present operating environment.

Long-Run Total Costs

Long-run cost curves show the least-cost input combination for producing output assuming an *ideal* input selection. As in the case of short-run cost curves, wage rates, interest rates, plant configuration, and all other operating conditions are held constant. Any change in the operating environment leads to a shift in long-run cost curves. For example, product inventions and process improvements that occur over time cause a downward *shift* in long-run cost curves. Such changes must not be confused with *movements along* a given long-run cost curve caused by changes in the output level. Long-run cost curves reveal the nature of economies or diseconomies of scale and optimal plant sizes. They are a helpful guide to planning decisions.

If input prices are not affected by the amount purchased, a *direct* relation exists between long-run total cost and production functions. A production function that exhibits constant returns to scale is linear, and doubling inputs leads to doubled output. With constant input prices, doubling inputs doubles total cost and results in a linear total cost function. If increasing returns to scale are present, output doubles with less than a doubling of inputs and total cost. If production is subject to decreasing returns to scale, inputs and total cost must more than double to cause a twofold increase in output. A production function exhibiting first increasing and then decreasing returns to scale is illustrated, along with its implied cubic cost function, in Figure 8.2. Here, costs increase less than proportionately with output over the range in which returns to scale are increasing but at more than a proportionate rate after decreasing returns set in.

A direct relation between production and cost functions requires constant input prices. If input prices are a function of output, cost functions will reflect this relationship. Large-volume discounts can lower unit costs as output rises, just as costs can rise with the need to pay higher wages to attract additional workers at high output levels. The cost function for a firm facing constant returns to scale but rising input prices as output expands takes the shape shown in Figure 8.2. Costs rise more than proportionately as output increases. Quantity discounts produce a cost function that increases at a decreasing rate, as in the increasing returns section of Figure 8.2.

Economies of Scale

economies of scale
Decreasing long-run average costs

Economies of scale exist when long-run average costs decline as output expands. Labor specialization often gives rise to economies of scale. In small firms, workers generally do several jobs, and proficiency sometimes suffers from a lack of specialization. Labor productivity can be higher in large firms, where individuals are hired to perform specific tasks. This can reduce unit costs for large-scale operations.

Technical factors can also lead to economies of scale. Large-scale operation permits the use of highly specialized equipment, as opposed to the more versatile but less efficient machines

---

3   Relations among total, average, and marginal curves are discussed in greater detail in Chapter 2.

FIGURE 8.2

Total Cost Function for a Production System Exhibiting Increasing, Then Decreasing, Returns to Scale

With increasing returns to scale, total cost rises slower than total output. With decreasing returns to scale, total cost rises faster than total output. Total cost functions often display an S-shape, reflecting varying returns to scale at various activity levels.

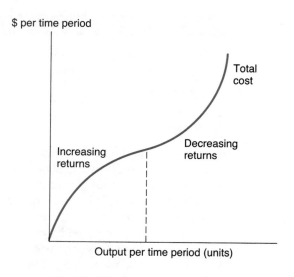

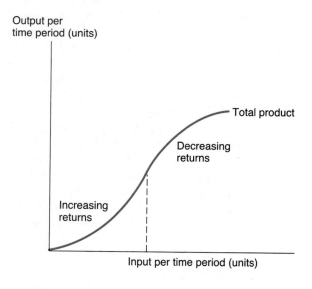

used in smaller firms. Also, the productivity of equipment frequently increases with size much faster than its cost. A 500,000-kilowatt electricity generator costs considerably less than two 250,000-kilowatt generators, and it also requires less fuel and labor when operated at capacity. Quantity discounts give rise to money-related pecuniary economies through large-scale purchasing of raw materials, supplies, and other inputs. These economies extend to the cost of capital when large firms have easy access to capital markets and can acquire funds at lower rates.

At some output level, economies of scale are typically exhausted, and average costs level out and begin to rise. Increasing average costs at high output levels are often attributed to limitations in the ability of management to coordinate large-scale organizations. Staff overhead also tends to grow more than proportionately with output, again raising unit costs. The current trend toward small to medium-sized businesses indicates that diseconomies limit firm sizes in many industries.

Cost Elasticities and Economies of Scale

cost elasticity
Percentage change in total cost associated with a 1 percent change in output

It is often easy to calculate scale economies by considering cost elasticities. **Cost elasticity**, ϵ_C, measures the percentage change in total cost associated with a 1 percent change in output.

Algebraically, the elasticity of cost with respect to output is

$$\epsilon_C = \frac{\text{Percentage Change in Total Cost } (TC)}{\text{Percentage Change in Output } (Q)}$$

$$= \frac{\partial TC/TC}{\partial Q/Q}$$

$$= \frac{\partial TC}{\partial Q} \times \frac{Q}{TC}$$

Cost elasticity is related to economies of scale as follows:

If	Then	Which Implies
Percentage change in TC < Percentage change in Q	$\epsilon_C < 1$	Economies of scale (decreasing AC)
Percentage change in TC = Percentage change in Q	$\epsilon_C = 1$	No economies of scale (constant AC)
Percentage change in TC > Percentage change in Q	$\epsilon_C > 1$	Diseconomies of scale (increasing AC)

With a cost elasticity of less than one ($\epsilon_C < 1$), costs increase at a slower rate than output. Given constant input prices, this implies higher output-to-input ratios and economies of scale. If $\epsilon_C = 1$, output and costs increase proportionately, implying no economies of scale. Finally, if $\epsilon_C > 1$, for any increase in output, costs increase by a greater relative amount, implying decreasing returns to scale. To prevent confusion concerning cost elasticity and returns to scale, remember that an inverse relation holds between average costs and scale economies but that a direct relation holds between resource usage and returns to scale. Thus, although $\epsilon_C < 1$ implies falling AC and economies of scale, because costs are increasing more slowly than output, recall from Chapter 7 that an output elasticity greater than 1 ($\epsilon_Q > 1$) implies increasing returns to scale, because output is increasing faster than input usage. Similarly, diseconomies of scale are implied by $\epsilon_C > 1$, diminishing returns are indicated when $\epsilon_Q < 1$.

Long-Run Average Costs

Short-run cost curves relate costs and output for a specific scale of plant. Long-run cost curves identify the optimal scale of plant for each production level. Long-run average cost (*LRAC*) curves can be thought of as an envelope of short-run average cost (*SRAC*) curves.

This concept is illustrated in Figure 8.3, which shows four short-run average cost curves representing four different scales of plant. Each of the four plants has a range of output over which it is most efficient. Plant A, for example, provides the least-cost production system for output in the range 0 to Q_1 units; plant B provides the least-cost system for output in the range

FIGURE 8.3

Short-Run Cost Curves for Four Scales of Plant

Short-run cost curves represent the most efficient range of output for a given plant size. The solid portion of each *SRAC* curve indicates the minimum long-run average cost for each level of output.

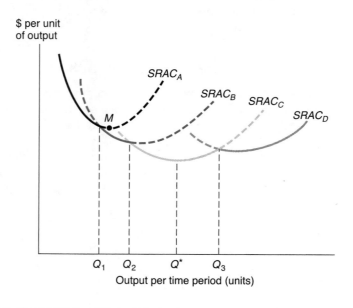

FIGURE 8.4

Long-Run Average Cost Curve as the Envelope of Short-Run Average Cost Curves

The long-run average cost curve is the envelope of short-run average cost curves. The optimal scale for a plant is found at the point of minimum long-run average costs.

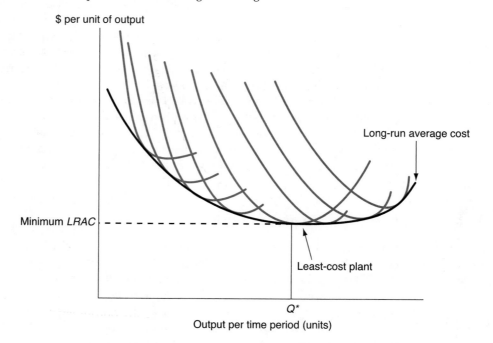

What'n Heck Is a FASB?

The Financial Accounting Standards Board (FASB) is a nongovernmental body empowered by the Securities and Exchange Commission with responsibility for determining the nature and scope of accounting information. Started in 1973 as the logical successor to the accounting profession's Accounting Principles Board, FASB develops new accounting standards in an elaborate process that reflects the views of accountants, business executives, security analysts, and the public. As a result, FASB plays a key role in defining the specific information that must be incorporated in published corporate financial statements. FASB provides essential input concerning the framework for accounting balance sheets that define the current financial status of a company ("where it is") and for accounting income statements that show changes in a company's financial performance ("where it is going"). By standardizing the content and format of such reports, FASB helps managers run their businesses better and helps investors better monitor their investments.

FASB is also instrumental in the resolution of a broad range of important and controversial accounting issues. For example, FASB plays a key role in the debate over accounting policy issues, including the controversy on whether to require firms to use current market values rather than historical-cost book values for accounts receivables, bonds, and intangible assets like brand names and patents. This is a highly controversial issue, because the market-value approach would lead to a much different picture of corporate assets and liabilities for many companies.

Given the wide range of important accounting issues being addressed, the role played by FASB has grown steadily. At times, the public perception of FASB has failed to match this pace. This is changing as FASB's public visibility increases. FASB-inspired guidelines allow companies to report assets and incomes that are closer to real economic values. For investors, more detailed disclosure of income, assets, and liabilities are an important benefit of standardized accounting rules.

See: Steve Liesman, Jonathan Weil, and Scott Paltrow, "FASB Is Criticized for Inaction on Off-Balance-Sheet Debt Issue," *The Wall Street Journal Online*, January 18, 2002 (http://online.wsj.com).

Q_1 to Q_2; plant C is most efficient for output quantities Q_2 to Q_3; and plant D provides the least-cost production process for output above Q_3.

The solid portion of each curve in Figure 8.3 indicates the minimum long-run average cost for producing each level of output, assuming only four possible scales of plant. This can be generalized by assuming that plants of many sizes are possible, each only slightly larger than the preceding one. As shown in Figure 8.4, the long-run average cost curve is then constructed tangent to each short-run average cost curve. At each point of tangency, the related scale of plant is optimal; no other plant can produce that particular level of output at so low a total cost. Cost systems illustrated in Figures 8.3 and 8.4 display first economies of scale, then diseconomies of scale. Over the range of output produced by plants A, B, and C in Figure 8.3, average costs are declining; these declining costs mean that total costs are increasing less than proportionately with output. Because plant D's minimum cost is greater than that for plant C, the system exhibits diseconomies of scale at this higher output level.

Production systems that reflect first increasing, then constant, then diminishing returns to scale result in U-shaped long-run average cost curves such as the one illustrated in Figure 8.4. With a U-shaped long-run average cost curve, the most efficient plant for each output level is typically not operating at the point where short-run average costs are minimized, as can be seen in Figure 8.3. Plant A's short-run average cost curve is minimized at point M, but at that output level, plant B is more efficient; B's short-run average costs are lower. In general, when economies of scale are present, the least-cost plant will operate at less than full capacity. Here, **capacity** refers not to a physical limitation on output but rather to the point at which short-run average costs are minimized. Only for that single output level at which long-run average cost is minimized (output Q^* in Figures 8.3 and 8.4) is the optimal plant operating at the minimum point on its short-run average cost curve. At any output level greater than Q^*, diseconomies of scale prevail, and the most efficient plant is operating at an output level slightly greater than capacity.

capacity
Output level at which short-run average costs are minimized

MINIMUM EFFICIENT SCALE

The number of competitors and ease of entry is typically greater in industries with U-shaped long-run average cost curves than in those with L-shaped or downward-sloping long-run average cost curves. Insight on the competitive implications of cost/output relations can be gained by considering the minimum efficient scale concept.

Competitive Implications of Minimum Efficient Scale

minimum efficient scale
Output level at which long-run average costs are minimized

Minimum efficient scale (MES) is the output level at which long-run average costs are minimized. MES is at the minimum point on a U-shaped long-run average cost curve (output Q^* in Figures 8.3 and 8.4) and at the corner of an L-shaped long-run average cost curve.

Generally speaking, competition is vigorous when MES is low relative to total industry demand. This fact follows from the correspondingly low barriers to entry from capital investment and skilled labor requirements. Competition can be less vigorous when MES is large relative to total industry output because barriers to entry tend to be correspondingly high and can limit the number of potential competitors. When considering the competitive impact of MES, industry size must always be considered. Some industries are large enough to accommodate many effective competitors. In such instances, even though MES is large in an absolute sense, it can be relatively small and allow vigorous competition.

When the cost disadvantage of operating plants that are of less than MES size is modest, there will seldom be serious anticompetitive consequences. The somewhat higher production costs of small producers can be overcome by superior customer service and regional location to cut transport costs and delivery lags. In such instances, significant advantages to large-scale operation have little economic impact. Therefore, the barrier-to-entry effects of MES depend on the size of MES relative to industry demand *and* the slope of the long-run average cost curve at points of less-than-MES-size operations. Both must be considered.

Transportation Costs and MES

Transportation costs include terminal, line-haul, and inventory charges associated with moving output from production facilities to customers. Terminal charges consist of handling expenses necessary for loading and unloading shipped materials. Because terminal charges do not vary with the distance of shipment, they are as high for short hauls as for long hauls.

Line-haul expenses include equipment, labor, and fuel costs associated with moving products a specified distance. They vary directly with the distance shipped. Although line-haul expenses are relatively constant on a per-mile basis, they vary widely from one commodity to another. It costs more to ship a ton of fresh fruit 500 miles than to ship a ton of coal a similar distance. Fresh fruit comes in odd shapes and sizes and requires more container space per pound than a product like coal. Any product that is perishable, fragile, or particularly susceptible to theft (e.g., consumer electronics, cigarettes, liquor) has high line-haul expenses because of greater equipment, insurance, and handling costs.

Finally, there is an inventory cost component to transportation costs related to the time element involved in shipping goods. The time required in transit is extremely important because slower modes such as railroads and barges delay the receipt of sale proceeds from customers. Even though out-of-pocket expenses are greater, air cargo or motor carrier shipments speed delivery and can reduce the total economic costs of transporting goods to market.

As more output is produced at a given plant, it becomes necessary to reach out to more distant customers. This can lead to increased transportation costs per unit sold. Figure 8.5 illustrates an L-shaped long-run average cost curve reflecting average production costs that first decline and then become nearly constant. Assuming relatively modest terminal and inventory costs, greater line-haul expenses cause transportation costs per unit to increase at a relatively constant

FIGURE 8.5

Effect of Transportation Costs on Optimal Plant Size

High transportation costs reduce the MES plant size from Q_A^* to Q_B^*. As transportation costs rise relative to production costs, MES plant size will fall.

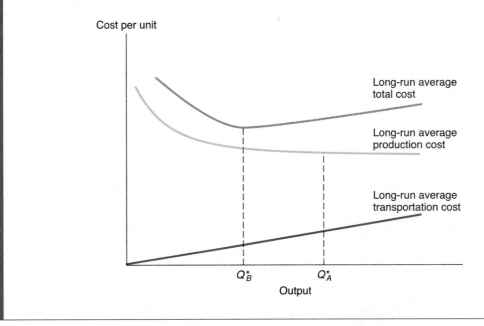

rate. Before transportation costs, Q_A^* represents the MES plant size. Including transportation expenses, the MES plant size falls to Q_B^*. In general, as transportation costs become increasingly important, MES will fall. When transportation costs are large in relation to production costs—as is the case with milk, bottled soft drinks, gravel, and cement—even small, relatively inefficient production facilities can be profitable when located near important markets. When transportation costs are relatively insignificant—as is the case of aluminum, electronic components, personal computers, and medical instruments—markets are national or international in scope, and economies of scale cause output to be produced at only a few large plants.

FIRM SIZE AND PLANT SIZE

The cost function for a multiplant firm can be the sum of the cost functions for individual plants. It can also be greater or less than this figure. For this reason, it is important to examine the relative importance of economies of scale that arise within production facilities, intraplant economies, and those that arise between and among plants, or multiplant economies of scale.

Multiplant Economies and Diseconomies of Scale

multiplant economies of scale
Cost advantages from operating multiple facilities in the same line of business or industry

multiplant diseconomies of scale
Cost disadvantages from managing multiple facilities in the same line of business or industry

Multiplant economies of scale are cost advantages that arise from operating multiple facilities in the same line of business or industry. **Multiplant diseconomies of scale** are cost disadvantages that arise from managing multiple facilities in the same line of business or industry.

To illustrate, assume a U-shaped long-run average cost curve for a given plant, as shown in Figure 8.4. If demand is sufficiently large, the firm will employ n plants, each of optimal size and producing Q^* units of output. In this case, what is the shape of the firm's long-run average cost curve? Figure 8.6 shows three possibilities. Each possible long-run average cost curve has important implications for the minimum efficient firm size, Q_F^*. First, the long-run average cost

FIGURE 8.6

Three Possible Long-Run Average Cost Curves for a Multiplant Firm

(a) Constant costs characterize a multiplant facility that has neither economies nor diseconomies of scale.
(b) Average costs decline if a multiplant firm is more efficient than a single-plant firm. (c) The average costs
of operating several plants can eventually rise when coordinating costs overcome multiplant economies.

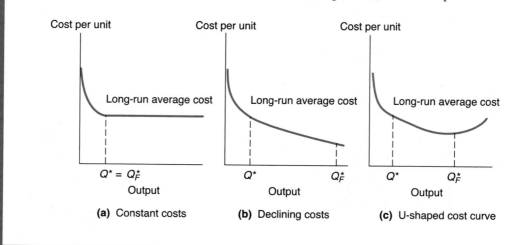

curve can be L-shaped, as in Figure 8.6(a), if no economies or diseconomies result from combining plants. Second, costs could decline throughout the entire range of output, as in Figure
8.6(b), if multiplant firms are more efficient than single-plant firms. When they exist, such cases
are caused by economies of multiplant operation. For example, all plants may use a central
billing service, a common purchasing or distribution network, centralized management, and so
on. The third possibility, shown in Figure 8.6(c), is that costs first decline beyond Q^*, the output
of the most efficient plant, and then begin to rise. In this case, multiplant economies of scale
dominate initially, but they are later overwhelmed by the higher costs of coordinating many
operating units.

All three shapes of cost curves shown in Figure 8.6 are found in the U.S. economy. Because
optimal plant and firm sizes are identical only when multiplant economies are negligible, the
magnitude of both influences must be carefully considered in evaluating the effect of scale
economies. Both intraplant and multiplant economies can have an important impact on minimum efficient firm size.

Economics of Multiplant Operation: An Example

An example can help clarify the relation between firm size and plant size. Consider Plainfield
Electronics, a New Jersey–based company that manufactures industrial control panels. The
firm's production is consolidated at a single Eastern-seaboard facility, but a multiplant alternative to centralized production is being considered. Estimated demand, marginal revenue,
and *single-plant* production plus transportation cost curves for the firm are as follows:

$$P = \$940 - \$0.02Q$$

$$MR = \frac{\partial TR}{\partial Q} = \$940 - \$0.04Q$$

$$TC = \$250,000 + \$40Q + \$0.01Q^2$$

$$MC = \frac{\partial TC}{\partial Q} = \$40 + \$0.02Q$$

Plainfield's total profit function is

$$\begin{aligned}
\pi &= TR - TC \\
&= P \times Q - TC \\
&= (\$940 - \$0.02Q)Q - \$250{,}000 - \$40Q - \$0.01Q^2 \\
&= -\$0.03Q^2 + \$900Q - \$250{,}000
\end{aligned}$$

The profit-maximizing activity level with centralized production is the output level at which $M\pi = MR - MC = 0$ and, therefore, $MR = MC$.

Setting marginal revenue equal to marginal cost and solving for the related output quantity gives

$$\begin{aligned}
MR &= MC \\
\$940 - \$0.04Q &= \$40Q + \$0.02Q \\
\$0.06Q &= \$900 \\
Q &= 15{,}000
\end{aligned}$$

At $Q = 15{,}000$,

$$\begin{aligned}
P &= \$940 - \$0.02Q \\
&= \$940 - \$0.02(15{,}000) \\
&= \$640
\end{aligned}$$

and

$$\begin{aligned}
\pi &= -\$0.03(15{,}000)^2 + \$900(15{,}000) - \$250{,}000 \\
&= \$6{,}500{,}000
\end{aligned}$$

Therefore, profits are maximized at the $Q = 15{,}000$ output level under the assumption of centralized production. At that activity level, $MC = MR = \$640$, and $M\pi = 0$.

To gain insight regarding the possible advantages of operating multiple smaller plants, the average cost function for a single plant must be examined. To simplify matters, assume that multiplant production is possible under the same cost conditions described previously. Also assume that there are no other multiplant economies or diseconomies of scale.

The activity level at which average cost is minimized is found by setting marginal cost equal to average cost and solving for Q:

$$\begin{aligned}
AC &= TC/Q \\
&= (\$250{,}000 + \$40Q + \$0.01Q^2)/Q \\
&= \$250{,}000Q^{-1} + \$40 + \$0.01Q
\end{aligned}$$

and

$$\begin{aligned}
MC &= AC \\
\$40 + \$0.02Q &= \$250{,}000Q^{-1} + \$40 + \$0.01Q \\
250{,}000Q^{-1} &= 0.01Q \\
Q^2 &= \frac{250{,}000}{0.01} \\
Q &= \sqrt{25{,}000{,}000} \\
&= 5{,}000
\end{aligned}$$

Average cost is minimized at an output level of 5,000. This output level is the minimum efficient plant scale. Because the average cost-minimizing output level of 5,000 is far less than the single-plant profit-maximizing activity level of 15,000 units, the profit-maximizing level of total output occurs at a point of rising average costs. Assuming centralized production, Plainfield would maximize profits at an activity level of Q = 15,000 rather than Q = 5,000 because market-demand conditions are such that, despite the higher costs experienced at Q = 15,000, the firm can profitably supply output up to that level.

Because centralized production maximized profits at an activity level well beyond that at which average cost is minimized, Plainfield has an opportunity to reduce costs and increase profits by adopting the multiplant alternative. Although the single-plant Q = 15,000 profit-maximizing activity level and the Q = 5,000 average cost-minimizing activity level might suggest that multiplant production at three facilities is optimal, this is incorrect. Profits were maximized at Q = 15,000 under the assumption that both marginal revenue and marginal cost equal $640. However, with multiplant production and each plant operating at the Q = 5,000 activity level, marginal cost will be lowered and multiplant production will entail a new, higher profit-maximizing activity level. Notice that when Q = 5,000,

$$
\begin{aligned}
MC &= \$40 + \$0.02Q \\
&= \$40 + \$0.02(5,000) \\
&= \$140
\end{aligned}
$$

With multiple plants all operating at 5,000 units per year, MC = $140. Therefore, it is profitable to expand production as long as the marginal revenue obtained exceeds this minimum MC = $140. This assumes, of course, that each production facility is operating at the optimal activity level of Q = 5,000.

The optimal multiplant activity level for the firm, assuming optimal production levels of Q = 5,000 at multiple plants, can be calculated by equating MR to the multiplant MC = $140:

$$
\begin{aligned}
MR &= \$140 = MC \\
\$940 - \$0.04Q &= \$140 \\
\$0.04Q &= \$800 \\
Q &= 20,000
\end{aligned}
$$

Given optimal multiplant production of 20,000 units and average cost-minimizing activity levels of 5,000 units for each plant, multiplant production at four facilities is suggested:

$$
\begin{aligned}
\text{Optimal Number of Plants} &= \frac{\text{Optimal Multiplant Activity Level}}{\text{Optimal Production per Plant}} \\
&= \frac{20,000}{5,000} \\
&= 4
\end{aligned}
$$

At Q = 20,000,

$$
\begin{aligned}
P &= \$940 - \$0.02(20,000) \\
&= \$540
\end{aligned}
$$

and

$$
\begin{aligned}
\pi &= TR - TC \\
&= P \times Q - 4 \times TC \text{ per plant} \\
&= \$540(20,000) - 4[\$250,000 + \$40(5,000) + \$0.01(5,000^2)] \\
&= \$8,000,000
\end{aligned}
$$

Given these cost relations, multiplant production is preferable to the centralized production alternative because it results in maximum profits that are $1.5 million larger. As shown in Figure 8.7, this follows from the firm's ability to concentrate production at the minimum point on the single-plant U-shaped average cost curve.

Finally, it is important to recognize that the optimal multiplant activity level of 20,000 units described in this example is based on the assumption that each production facility produces exactly 5,000 units of output and, therefore, $MC = \$140$. Marginal cost will only equal $140 with production of $Q = 5,000$, or some round multiple thereof (e.g., $Q = 10,000$ from two plants, $Q = 15,000$ from three plants, and so on). The optimal multiplant activity-level calculation is more complicated when this assumption is not met. Plainfield could not produce $Q = 21,000$ at $MC = \$140$. For an output level in the 20,000 to 25,000 range, it is necessary to equate marginal revenue with the marginal cost of each plant at its optimal activity level.

Plant Size and Flexibility

The plant that can produce an expected output level at the lowest possible cost is not always the optimal plant size. Consider the following situation. Although actual demand for a product is uncertain, it is expected to be 5,000 units per year. Two possible probability distributions for this demand are given in Figure 8.8. Distribution L exhibits a low degree of variability in demand, and distribution H indicates substantially higher variation in possible demand levels.

Now suppose that two plants can be employed to produce the required output. Plant A is quite specialized and is geared to produce a specified output at a low cost per unit. If more or

FIGURE 8.7

Plainfield Electronics: Single Versus Multiplant Operation

In this example, profit is maximized at a production level well beyond that at which average cost is minimized for a single plant. Profits are greater with four plants because output can then be produced at minimum cost.

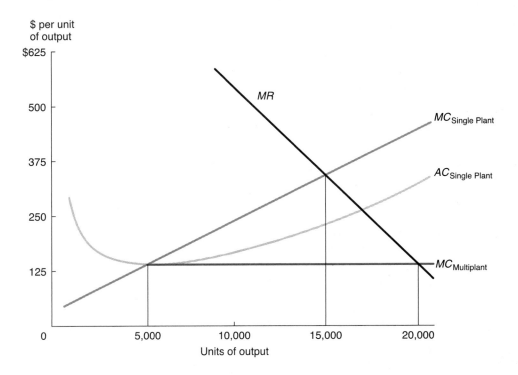

less than the specified output is produced (in this case 5,000 units), unit production costs rise rapidly. Plant *B*, on the other hand, is more flexible. Output can be expanded or contracted without excessive cost penalties, but unit costs are not as low as those of plant *A* at the optimal output level. These two cases are shown in Figure 8.9.

Plant *A* is more efficient than plant *B* between 4,500 and 5,500 units of output; outside this range, *B* has lower costs. Which plant should be selected? The answer depends on the level and

FIGURE 8.8

Probability Distributions of Demand

Distribution *L* has a low degree of variability from the expected demand level. Distribution *H* varies substantially from the expected demand level.

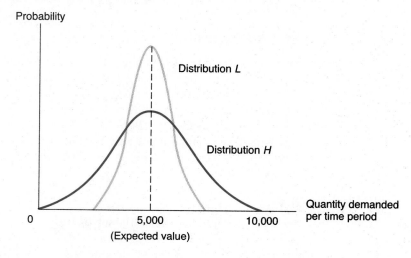

FIGURE 8.9

Alternative Plants for Production of Expected 5,000 Units of Output

Unit costs are lower for plant *A* than for plant *B* between 4,500 and 5,500 units of output. Outside this range, plant *B* has lower unit costs.

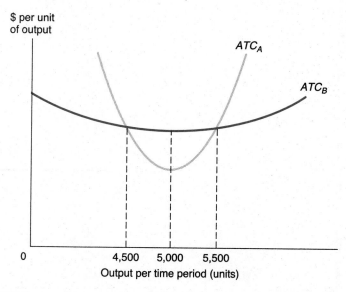

MANAGERIAL APPLICATION   8.4

Bigger Isn't Always Better

When economies of scale are substantial, larger firms are able to achieve lower costs of production or distribution than their smaller rivals. These cost advantages translate into higher and more stable profits and a permanent competitive advantage for larger firms in some industries. When diseconomies of scale are operative, larger firms suffer a cost disadvantage when compared to their smaller rivals. Smaller firms are then able to translate the benefits of small size into a distinct competitive advantage.

In general, industries dominated by large firms tend to be those in which there are significant economies of scale, important advantages to vertical integration, and a prevalence of mass marketing. As a result, large organizations with sprawling plants emphasize large quantities of output at low production costs. Use of national media, especially TV advertising, is common. In contrast, industries in which "small is beautiful" tend to be those characterized by diseconomies of scale, considerable advantages to subcontracting for "just in time" assembly and manufacturing, and niche marketing that emphasizes the use of highly skilled individuals adept at personal selling. Small factories with flexible production schedules are common.

Rather than mass quantity, many smaller companies emphasize quality. Instead of the sometimes slow-to-respond hierarchical organizations of large companies, smaller companies feature "flat" organizations with decentralized decision making and authority.

Even though the concept of diseconomies of large size is well known, it is sometimes not appreciated how common the phenomenon is in actual practice. Many sectors of industrial manufacturing have found that the highly flexible and customer-sensitive nature of smaller companies can lead to distinct competitive advantages. The villain sometimes encountered by large-scale firms is not any diseconomy of scale in the production process itself, but rather the burden that size places on effective management. Big often means complex, and complexity results in inefficiencies and bureaucratic snarls that can strangle effective communication.

See: Dow Jones Newswires, "Arbitrage Spreads on Pending Mergers and Acquisitions," *The Wall Street Journal Online*, January 18, 2002 (http://online.wsj.com).

variability of expected average total costs. If the demand probability distribution with low variation, distribution *L*, is correct, the more specialized facility is optimal. If probability distribution *H* more correctly describes the demand situation, the lower minimum cost of more specialized facilities is more than offset by the possibility of very high costs of producing outside the 4,500- to 5,500-unit range. Plant *B* could then have lower expected costs or a more attractive combination of expected costs and potential variation.

LEARNING CURVES

For many manufacturing processes, average costs decline substantially as *cumulative* total output increases. Improvements in the use of production equipment and procedures are important in this process, as are reduced waste from defects and decreased labor requirements as workers become more proficient in their jobs.

Learning Curve Concept

learning curve
Average cost reduction over time due to production experience

When knowledge gained from manufacturing experience is used to improve production methods, the resulting decline in average costs is said to reflect the effects of the firm's **learning curve**. The learning curve or experience curve phenomenon affects average costs in a way similar to that for any technical advance that improves productive efficiency. Both involve a downward shift in the long-run average cost curve at all levels of output. Learning through production experience permits the firm to produce output more efficiently at each and every output level.

To illustrate, consider Figure 8.10, which shows hypothetical long-run average cost curves for periods *t* and *t* + 1. With increased knowledge about production methods gained through the experience of producing Q_t units in period *t*, long-run average costs have declined for

FIGURE 8.10

Long-Run Average Cost Curve Effects of Learning

Learning will cause a downward shift from $LRAC_t$ to $LRAC_{t+1}$. An average cost decline from C to A reflects the effects of both learning and economies of scale.

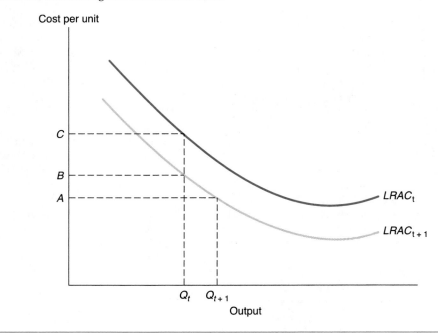

every output level in period $t + 1$, which means that Q_t units could be produced during period $t + 1$ at an average cost of B rather than the earlier cost of C. The learning curve cost savings is BC. If output were expanded from Q_t to Q_{t+1} between these periods, average costs would fall from C to A. This decline in average costs reflects both the learning curve effect, BC, and the effect of economies of scale, AB.

To isolate the effect of learning or experience on average cost, it is necessary to identify carefully that portion of average-cost changes over time that is due to other factors. One of the most important of these changes is the effect of economies of scale. As seen before, the change in average costs experienced between periods t and $t + 1$ can reflect the effects of both learning and economies of scale. Similarly, the effects of important technical breakthroughs, causing a downward shift in $LRAC$ curves, and input-cost inflation, causing an upward shift in $LRAC$ curves, must be constrained to examine learning curve characteristics. Only when output scale, technology, and input prices are all held constant can the learning curve relation be accurately represented.

Figure 8.11 depicts the learning curve relation suggested by Figure 8.10. Note that learning results in dramatic average cost reductions at low total production levels, but it generates increasingly modest savings at higher cumulative production levels. This reflects the fact that many improvements in production methods become quickly obvious and are readily adopted. Later gains often come more slowly and are less substantial.

Learning Curve Example

The learning curve phenomenon is often characterized as a constant percentage decline in average costs as cumulative output increases. This percentage represents the proportion by which unit costs decline as the cumulative quantity of total output doubles. Suppose, for example, that average costs per unit for a new product were $100 during 2001 but fell to $90 during 2002.

FIGURE 8.11

Learning Curve on an Arithmetic Scale

The learning curve reflects the percentage decline in average cost as total cumulative output doubles from Q_t to $2Q_t$.

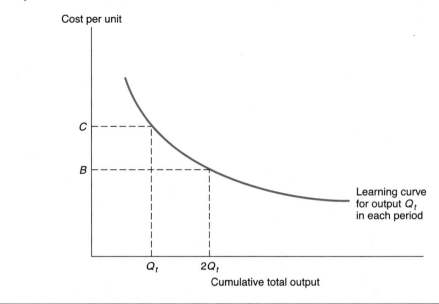

Furthermore, assume that average costs are in constant dollars, reflecting an accurate adjustment for input/price inflation and an identical basic technology being used in production. Given equal output in each period to ensure that the effects of economies of scale are not incorporated in the data, the learning or experience rate, defined as the percentage by which average cost falls as output doubles, is the following:

$$\text{Learning Rate} = \left(1 - \frac{AC_2}{AC_1}\right) \times 100$$

$$= \left(1 - \frac{\$90}{\$100}\right) \times 100$$

$$= 10\%$$

Thus, as *cumulative* total output doubles, average cost is expected to fall by 10 percent. If annual production is projected to remain constant, it will take 2 additional years for cumulative output to double again. One would project that average unit costs will decline to $81 (90 percent of $90) in 2004. Because cumulative total output at that time will equal 4 years' production, at a constant annual rate, output will again double by 2008. At that time, the learning curve will have reduced average costs to $72.90 (90 percent of $81).

Because the learning curve concept is often improperly described as a cause of economies of scale, it is worth repeating that the two are distinct concepts. Scale economies relate to cost differences associated with different output levels *along* a single *LRAC* curve. Learning curves relate cost differences to total cumulative output. They are measured by *shifts* in *LRAC* curves over time. These shifts result from improved production efficiencies stemming from knowledge gained through production experience. Care must be exercised to separate learning and scale effects in cost analysis.

Research in a number of industries, ranging from aircraft manufacturing to semiconductor memory-chip production, has shown that learning or experience can be very important in some production systems. Learning or experience rates of 20 percent to 30 percent are sometimes reported. These high learning rates imply rapidly declining manufacturing costs as cumulative total output increases. It should be noted, however, that many learning curve studies fail to account adequately for the expansion of production. Therefore, reported learning or experience rates sometimes include the effects of both learning and economies of scale. Nevertheless, managers in a wide variety of industries have found that the learning curve concept has considerable strategic implications.

Strategic Implications of the Learning Curve Concept

What makes the learning curve phenomenon important for competitive strategy is its possible contribution to achieving and maintaining a dominant position in a given market. By virtue of their large relative volume, dominant firms have greater opportunity for learning than do smaller, nonleading firms. In some instances, the market share leader is able to drive down its average cost curve faster than its competitors, underprice them, and permanently maintain a leadership position. Nonleading firms face an important and perhaps insurmountable barrier to relative improvement in performance. Where the learning curve advantages of leading firms are important, it may be prudent to relinquish nonleading positions and redeploy assets to markets in which a dominant position can be achieved or maintained.

A classic example illustrating the successful use of the learning curve concept is Dallas–based Texas Instruments (TI). TI's main business is producing semiconductor chips, which are key components used to store information in computers and a wide array of electronic products. With growing applications for computers and "intelligent" electronics, the demand for semiconductors is expanding rapidly. Some years ago, TI was one of a number of leading semiconductor manufacturers. At this early stage in the development of the industry, TI made the decision to price its semiconductors well below then-current production costs, given expected learning curve advantages in the 20 percent range. TI's learning curve strategy proved spectacularly successful. With low prices, volume increased dramatically. Because TI was making so many chips, average costs were even lower than anticipated; it could price below the competition; and dozens of competitors were knocked out of the world market. Given a relative cost advantage and strict quality controls, TI rapidly achieved a position of dominant leadership in a market that became a source of large and rapidly growing profits.

To play an important role in competitive strategy, learning must be significant. Cost savings of 20 percent to 30 percent as cumulative output doubles must be possible. If only modest effects of learning are present, product quality or customer service often plays a greater role in determining firm success. Learning is also apt to be more important in industries with an abundance of new products or new production techniques rather than in mature industries with well-known production methods. Similarly, learning tends to be important in industries with standardized products and competition based on price rather than product variety or service. Finally, the beneficial effects of learning are realized only when management systems tightly control costs and monitor potential sources of increased efficiency. Continuous feedback of information between production and management personnel is essential.

ECONOMIES OF SCOPE

Cost analysis focuses not just on how much to produce but also on what combination of products to offer. By virtue of their efficiency in the production of a given product, firms often enjoy cost advantages in the production of related products.

economies of scope
Cost reduction from producing complementary products

Economies of Scope Concept

Economies of scope exist when the cost of joint production is less than the cost of producing multiple outputs separately. A firm will produce products that are complementary in the sense that producing them together costs less than producing them individually. Suppose that a regional airline offers regularly scheduled passenger service between midsize city pairs and that it expects some excess capacity. Also assume that there is a modest local demand for air parcel and small-package delivery service. Given current airplane sizes and configurations, it is often less costly for a single carrier to provide both passenger and cargo services in small regional markets than to specialize in one or the other. Regional air carriers often provide both services. This is an example of economies of scope. Other examples of scope economies abound in the provision of both goods and services. In fact, the economies of scope concept explains why firms typically produce multiple products.

Studying economies of scope forces management to consider both direct and indirect benefits associated with individual lines of business. For example, some financial services firms regard checking accounts and money market mutual funds as "loss leaders." When one considers just the revenues and costs associated with marketing and offering checking services or running a money market mutual fund, they may just break even or yield only a marginal profit. However, successful firms like Dreyfus, Fidelity, and Merrill Lynch correctly evaluate the profitability of their money market mutual funds within the context of overall operations. These funds are a valuable delivery vehicle for a vast array of financial products and services. By offering money market funds on an attractive basis, financial services companies establish a working relation with an ideal group of prospective customers for stocks, bonds, and other investments. When viewed as a delivery vehicle or marketing device, money market mutual funds may be one of the industry's most profitable financial product lines.

Exploiting Scope Economies

Economies of scope are important because they permit a firm to translate superior skill in a given product line into unique advantages in the production of complementary products. Effective competitive strategy often emphasizes the development or extension of product lines related to a firm's current stars, or areas of recognized strength.

For example, PepsiCo, Inc., has long been a leader in the soft drink market. Over time, the company has gradually broadened its product line to include various brands of regular and diet soft drinks, Gatorade, Tropicana, Fritos and Doritos chips, Grandma's Cookies, and other snack foods. PepsiCo can no longer be considered just a soft drink manufacturer. It is a widely diversified beverages and snack foods company for whom well over one-half of total current profits come from non–soft drink lines. PepsiCo's snack foods and sport drink product line extension strategy was effective because it capitalized on the distribution network and marketing expertise developed in the firm's soft drink business. In the case of PepsiCo, soft drinks, snack foods and sports beverages are a natural fit and a good example of how a firm has been able to take the skills gained in developing one star (soft drinks) and use them to develop others (snack foods, sport drinks).

The economies of scope concept offers a useful means for evaluating the potential of current and prospective lines of business. It naturally leads to definition of those areas in which the firm has a comparative advantage and its greatest profit potential.

COST-VOLUME-PROFIT ANALYSIS

cost-volume-profit analysis
Analytical technique used to study relations among costs, revenues, and profits

Cost-volume-profit analysis, sometimes called breakeven analysis, is an important analytical technique used to study relations among costs, revenues, and profits. Both graphic and algebraic methods are employed. For simple problems, simple graphic methods work best. In more complex situations, analytic methods, possibly involving spreadsheet software programs, are preferable.

Cost-Volume-Profit Charts

A basic cost-volume-profit chart composed of a firm's total cost and total revenue curves is depicted in Figure 8.12. Volume of output is measured on the horizontal axis; revenue and cost are shown on the vertical axis. Fixed costs are constant regardless of the output produced and are indicated by a horizontal line. Variable costs at each output level are measured by the distance between the total cost curve and the constant fixed costs. The total revenue curve indicates the price/demand relation for the firm's product; profits or losses at each output are shown by the distance between total revenue and total cost curves.

In the example depicted in Figure 8.12, fixed costs of $60,000 are represented by a horizontal line. Variable costs for labor and materials are $1.80 per unit, so total costs rise by that amount for each additional unit of output. Total revenue based on a price of $3 per unit is a straight line through the origin. The slope of the total revenue line is steeper than that of the total cost line.

Below the breakeven point, found at the intersection of the total revenue and total cost lines, the firm suffers losses. Beyond that point, it begins to make profits. Figure 8.12 indicates a breakeven point at a sales and cost level of $150,000, which occurs at a production level of 50,000 units.

Algebraic Cost-Volume-Profit Analysis

Although cost-volume-profit charts can be used to portray profit/output relations, algebraic techniques are typically more efficient for analyzing decision problems. The algebra of cost-volume-profit analysis can be illustrated as follows. Let

$$P = \text{Price per unit sold}$$

FIGURE 8.12

Linear Cost-Volume-Profit Chart

Output levels below the breakeven point produce losses. As output grows beyond the breakeven point, increasingly higher profits result.

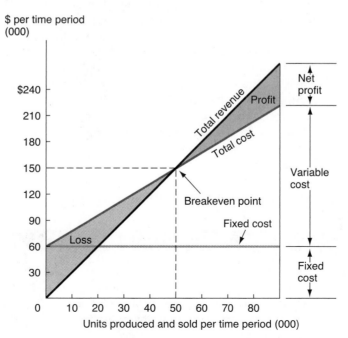

$$Q \;=\; \text{Quantity produced and sold}$$
$$TFC \;=\; \text{Total fixed costs}$$
$$AVC \;=\; \text{Average variable cost}$$
$$\pi_C \;=\; \text{Profit contribution}$$

On a per-unit basis, profit contribution equals price minus average variable cost ($\pi_C = P - AVC$). Profit contribution can be applied to cover fixed costs and then to provide profits. It is the foundation of cost-volume-profit analysis.

One useful application of cost-volume-profit analysis lies in the determination of breakeven activity levels. A **breakeven quantity** is a zero profit activity level. At breakeven quantity levels, total revenue ($P \times Q$) exactly equals total costs ($TFC + AVC \times Q$):

breakeven quantity
A zero profit activity level

$$\text{Total Revenue} \;=\; \text{Total Cost}$$
$$P \times Q \;=\; TFC + AVC \times Q$$
$$(P - AVC)Q \;=\; TFC$$

It follows that breakeven quantity levels occur where

(8.6)

$$Q_{BE} \;=\; \frac{TFC}{P - AVC}$$
$$=\; \frac{TFC}{\pi_C}$$

Thus, breakeven quantity levels are found by dividing the per-unit profit contribution into total fixed costs. In the example illustrated in Figure 8.12, $P = \$3$, $AVC = \$1.80$, and $TFC = \$60,000$. Profit contribution is $\$1.20$ (= $\$3.00 - \$1.80$), and the breakeven quantity is

$$Q \;=\; \frac{\$60,000}{\$1.20}$$
$$=\; 50,000 \text{ units}$$

Textbook Publishing: A Cost-Volume-Profit Example

The textbook publishing business provides a good illustration of the effective use of cost-volume-profit analysis for new product decisions. Consider the hypothetical cost-volume-profit analysis data shown in Table 8.2. Fixed costs of $100,000 can be estimated quite accurately. Variable costs are linear and set by contract. List prices are variable, but competition keeps prices within a sufficiently narrow range to make a linear total revenue curve reasonable. Variable costs for the proposed book are $92 a copy, and the price is $100. This means that each copy sold provides $8 in profit contribution. Applying the breakeven formula from Equation 8.6, the breakeven sales volume is 12,500 units, calculated as

$$Q \;=\; \frac{\$100,000}{\$8}$$
$$=\; 12,500 \text{ units}$$

Publishers evaluate the size of the total market for a given book, competition, and other factors. With these data in mind, they estimate the probability that a given book will reach or exceed the breakeven point. If the publisher estimates that the book will neither meet nor exceed the breakeven point, they may consider cutting production costs by reducing the

TABLE 8.2

Cost-Volume-Profit Analysis for Textbook Publishing

Cost Category	Dollar Amount
Fixed Costs	
Copyediting and other editorial costs	$ 15,750
Illustrations	32,750
Typesetting	51,500
Total fixed costs	$100,000
Variable Costs	
Printing, binding, and paper	$ 22.50
Bookstore discounts	25.00
Sales staff commissions	8.25
Author royalties	10.00
General and administrative costs	26.25
Total variable costs per copy	$92.00
List price per copy	$100.00

number of illustrations, doing only light copyediting, using a lower grade of paper, negotiating with the author to reduce the royalty rate, and so on.

Assume now that the publisher is interested in determining how many copies must sell to earn a $20,000 profit. Because profit contribution is the amount available to cover fixed costs and provide profit, the answer is found by adding the profit requirement to the book's fixed costs and then dividing by the per-unit profit contribution. The sales volume required in this case is 15,000 books, found as follows:

$$Q = \frac{\text{Fixed Costs} + \text{Profit Requirement}}{\text{Profit Contribution}}$$

$$= \frac{\$100,000 + \$20,000}{\$8}$$

$$= 15,000 \text{ units}$$

Consider yet another decision problem that might confront the publisher. Assume that a book club has offered to buy 3,000 copies at a price of $77 per copy. Cost-volume-profit analysis can be used to determine the incremental effect of such a sale on the publisher's profits.

Because fixed costs do not vary with respect to changes in the number of textbooks sold, they should be ignored. Variable costs per copy are $92, but note that $25 of this cost represents bookstore discounts. Because the 3,000 copies are being sold directly to the club, this cost will not be incurred. Hence, the relevant variable cost is only $67 (= $92 − $25). Profit contribution per book sold to the book club is $10 (= $77 − $67), and $10 times the 3,000 copies sold indicates that the order will result in a total profit contribution of $30,000. Assuming that these 3,000 copies would not have been sold through normal sales channels, the $30,000 profit contribution indicates the increase in profits to the publisher from accepting this order.

Degree of Operating Leverage

Cost-volume-profit analysis is also a useful tool for analyzing the financial characteristics of alternative production systems. This analysis focuses on how total costs and profits vary with operating leverage or the extent to which fixed production facilities versus variable production facilities are employed.

The relation between operating leverage and profits is shown in Figure 8.13, which contrasts the experience of three firms, *A, B,* and *C,* with differing degrees of leverage. The fixed costs of firm *B* are typical. Firm *A* uses relatively less capital equipment and has lower fixed costs, but it has a steeper rate of increase in variable costs. Firm *A* breaks even at a lower activity level than

FIGURE 8.13

Breakeven and Operating Leverage

The breakeven point for firm *C* occurs at the highest output level. Once this level is reached, profits rise at a faster rate than for firm *A* or *B*.

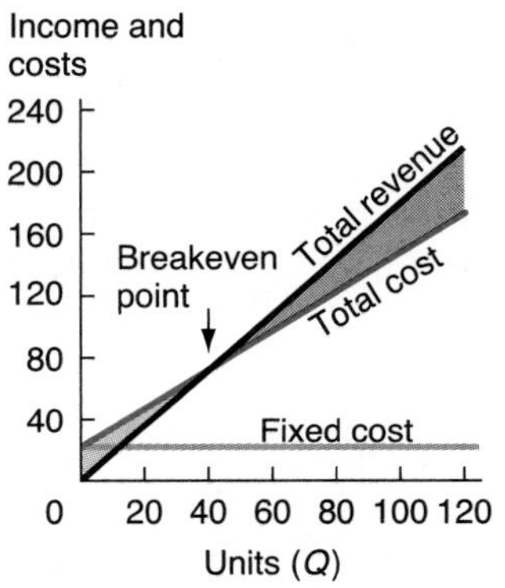

Firm A

Selling price = $2.00
Fixed cost = $20,000
Variable cost = $1.50Q

Units sold (Q)	Sales	Cost	Profit
20,000	$ 40,000	$ 50,000	– $10,000
40,000	80,000	80,000	0
60,000	120,000	110,000	10,000
80,000	160,000	140,000	20,000
100,000	200,000	170,000	30,000
120,000	240,000	200,000	40,000

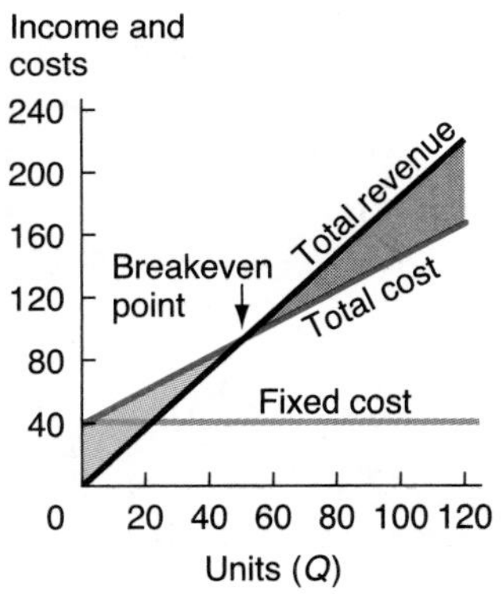

Firm B

Selling price = $2.00
Fixed cost = $40,000
Variable cost = $1.20Q

Units sold (Q)	Sales	Cost	Profit
20,000	$ 40,000	$ 64,000	– $24,000
40,000	80,000	88,000	– 8,000
60,000	120,000	112,000	8,000
80,000	160,000	136,000	24,000
100,000	200,000	160,000	40,000
120,000	240,000	184,000	56,000

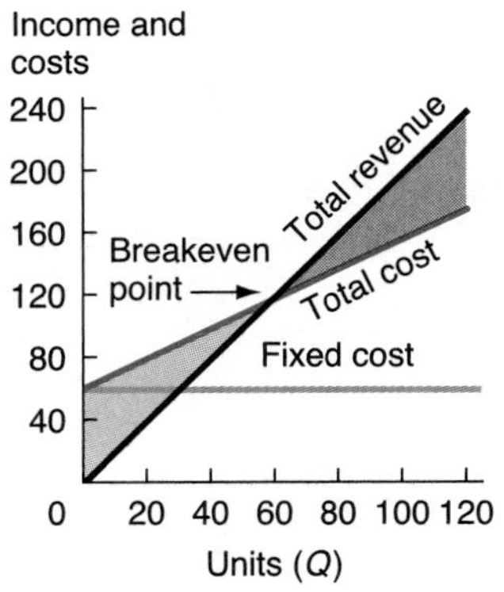

Firm C

Selling price = $2.00
Fixed cost = $60,000
Variable cost = $1.00Q

Units sold (Q)	Sales	Cost	Profit
20,000	$ 40,000	$ 80,000	– $40,000
40,000	80,000	100,000	– 20,000
60,000	120,000	120,000	0
80,000	160,000	140,000	20,000
100,000	200,000	160,000	40,000
120,000	240,000	180,000	60,000

does firm *B*. For example, at a production level of 40,000 units, *B* is losing $8,000, but *A* breaks even. Firm *C* is highly automated and has the highest fixed costs, but its variable costs rise slowly. Firm *C* has a higher breakeven point than either *A* or *B*, but once *C* passes the breakeven point, profits rise faster than those of the other two firms.

degree of operating leverage
Percentage change in profit from a 1% change in output

The **degree of operating leverage** is the percentage change in profit that results from a 1 percent change in units sold:

(8.7)

$$\text{Degree of Operating Leverage} = \frac{\text{Percentage Change in Profit}}{\text{Percentage Change in Sales}}$$

$$= \frac{\partial \pi / \pi}{\partial Q / Q}$$

$$= \frac{\partial \pi}{\partial Q} \times \frac{Q}{\pi}$$

The degree of operating leverage is an elasticity concept. It is the elasticity of profits with respect to output. When based on linear cost and revenue curves, this elasticity will vary. The degree of operating leverage is always greatest close to the breakeven point.

For firm *B* in Figure 8.13, the degree of operating leverage at 100,000 units of output is 2.0, calculated as follows:[4]

$$DOL_B = \frac{\partial \pi / \pi}{\partial Q / Q}$$

$$= \frac{(\$41,600 - \$40,000)/\$40,000}{(102,000 - 100,000)/100,000} = \frac{\$1,600/\$40,000}{2,000/100,000}$$

$$= \frac{4\%}{2\%} = 2$$

Here, π is profit and Q is the quantity of output in units.

For linear revenue and cost relations, the degree of operating leverage can be calculated at any level of output. The change in output is ∂Q. Fixed costs are constant, so the change in profit $\partial \pi = \partial Q(P - AVC)$, where P is price per unit and AVC is average variable cost.

Any initial profit level $\pi = Q(P - AVC) - TFC$, so the percentage change in profit is

$$\frac{\partial \pi}{\pi} = \frac{\partial Q(P - AVC)}{Q(P - AVC) - TFC}$$

The percentage change in output is $\partial Q/Q$, so the ratio of the percentage change in profits to the percentage change in output, or profit elasticity, is

$$\frac{\partial \pi / \pi}{\partial Q / Q} = \frac{\partial Q(P - AVC)/[Q(P - AVC) - TFC]}{\partial Q / Q}$$

$$= \frac{\partial Q(P - AVC)}{Q(P - AVC) - TFC} \times \frac{Q}{\partial Q}$$

After simplifying, the degree of operating leverage formula at any given level of output is[5]

---

4   This calculation arbitrarily assumes that $\partial Q = 2,000$. If $\partial Q = 1,000$ or $\partial Q = 4,000$, the degree of operating leverage still equals 2, because these calculations are based on linear cost and revenue curves. However, if a base other than 100,000 units is chosen, the degree of operating leverage will vary.

5   Because $TFC = Q(AFC)$ and $AC = AVC + AFC$, where AFC is average fixed cost, Equation 8.8 can be reduced further to a form that is useful in some situations:

$$DOL = \frac{Q(P - AVC)}{Q(P - AVC) - Q(AFC)}$$

$$= \frac{P - AVC}{P - AC}$$

(8.8)   Degree of Operating Leverage at Point $Q = \dfrac{Q(P - AVC)}{Q(P - AVC) - TFC}$

Using Equation 8.8, firm *B*'s degree of operating leverage at 100,000 units of output is calculated as

$$DOL_B \text{ at } 100,000 \text{ units } = \frac{100,000(\$2.00 - \$1.20)}{100,000(\$2.00 - \$1.20) - \$40,000}$$

$$= \frac{\$80,000}{\$40,000} = 2$$

Equation 8.8 can also be applied to firms *A* and *C*. When this is done, firm *A*'s degree of operating leverage at 100,000 units equals 1.67 and firm *C*'s equals 2.5. With a 2 percent increase in volume, firm *C*, the firm with the most operating leverage, will experience a profit increase of 5 percent. For the same 2 percent gain in volume, the firm with the least leverage, firm *A*, will have only a 3.3 percent profit gain. As seen in Figure 8.13, the profits of firm *C* are most sensitive to changes in sales volume, whereas firm *A*'s profits are relatively insensitive to volume changes. Firm *B*, with an intermediate degree of leverage, lies between these two extremes.

Limitations of Linear Cost-Volume-Profit Analysis

Cost-volume-profit analysis helps explain relations among volume, prices, and costs. It is also useful for pricing, cost control, and other financial decisions. However, linear cost-volume-profit analysis has its limitations.

Linear cost-volume-profit analysis has a weakness in what it implies about sales possibilities for the firm. Linear cost-volume-profit charts are based on constant selling prices. To study profit possibilities with different prices, a whole series of charts is necessary, with one chart for each price. With sophisticated spreadsheet software, the creation of a wide variety of cost-volume-profit charts is relatively easy. Using such software, profit possibilities for different pricing strategies can be quickly determined. Alternatively, nonlinear cost-volume-profit analysis can be used to show the effects of changing prices.

Linear cost-volume-profit analysis can be hampered by the underlying assumption of constant average costs. As unit sales increase, existing plant and equipment can be worked beyond capacity, thus reducing efficiency. The need for additional workers, longer work periods, and overtime wages can also cause variable costs to rise sharply. If additional plant and equipment is required, fixed costs will also rise. Such changes influence both the level and the slope of cost functions.

Although linear cost-volume-profit analysis has proven useful for managerial decision making, care must be taken to ensure that it is not applied when underlying assumptions are violated. Like any decision tool, cost-volume-profit analysis must be used with discretion.

SUMMARY

Cost analysis plays a key role in most managerial decisions. This chapter introduces a number of cost concepts, shows the relation between cost functions and production functions, and examines several cost analysis issues.

- For tax purposes, **historical cost**, or historical cash outlay, is the relevant cost. This is also generally true for annual 10-K reports to the Securities and Exchange Commission and for reports to stockholders. **Current cost**, the amount that must be paid under prevailing market conditions, is typically more relevant for decision-making purposes.

- Current costs are often determined by **replacement costs**, or the cost of duplicating productive capability using present technology. Another prime determinant of current cost is **opportunity cost**, or the foregone value associated with the current rather than the next-best use of a given asset. Both of these cost categories typically involve out-of-pocket costs, or **explicit costs**, and noncash costs, called **implicit costs**.

- **Incremental cost** is the change in cost caused by a given managerial decision and often involves multiple units of output. Incremental costs are a prime determinant of **profit contribution**, or profit before fixed charges. Neither are affected by **sunk costs**, which do not vary across decision alternatives.

- Proper use of relevant cost concepts requires an understanding of the cost/output relation, or **cost function**. **Short-run cost functions** are used for day-to-day operating decisions; **long-run cost functions** are employed in the long-range planning process. The **short run** is the operating period during which the availability of at least one input is fixed. In the **long run**, the firm has complete flexibility. **Fixed costs** do not vary with output and are incurred only in the short run. **Variable costs** fluctuate with output in both the short and the long run.

- A **short-run cost curve** shows the minimum cost impact of output changes for a specific plant size and in a given operating environment. A **long-run cost curve** shows the minimum cost impact of output changes for the optimal plant size using current technology in the present operating environment.

- **Economies of scale** originate from production and market-related sources and cause long-run average costs to decline. **Cost elasticity**, ϵ_C, measures the percentage change in total cost associated with a 1 percent change in output.

- **Capacity** refers to the output level at which short-run average costs are minimized. **Minimum efficient scale** (MES) is the output level at which long-run average costs are minimized.

- **Multiplant economies of scale** are cost advantages that arise from operating multiple facilities in the same line of business or industry. Conversely, **multiplant diseconomies of scale** are cost disadvantages that arise from managing multiple facilities in the same line of business or industry.

- When knowledge gained from manufacturing experience is used to improve production methods, the resulting decline in average cost reflects the effects of the firm's **learning curve**. **Economies of scope** exist when the cost of joint production is less than the cost of producing multiple outputs separately.

- **Cost-volume-profit analysis**, sometimes called breakeven analysis, is used to study relations among costs, revenues, and profits. A **breakeven quantity** is a zero profit activity level. The **degree of operating leverage** is the percentage change in profit that results from a 1 percent change in units sold; it can be understood as the elasticity of profits with respect to output.

Cost analysis poses a continuing challenge to management in all types of organizations. Using the concepts and tools discussed in this chapter, successful managers are able to manage costs effectively.

QUESTIONS

Q8.1   The relevant cost for most managerial decisions is the current cost of an input. The relevant cost for computing income for taxes and stockholder reporting is the historical cost. What advantages or disadvantages do you see in using current costs for tax and stockholder reporting purposes?

Q8.2   What are the relations among historical costs, current costs, and opportunity costs?

Q8.3 What is the difference between marginal and incremental cost?

Q8.4 What is a sunk cost, and how is it related to a decision problem?

Q8.5 What is the relation between production functions and cost functions? Be sure to include in your discussion the effect of conditions in input factor markets.

Q8.6 Explain why $\epsilon_Q > 1$ indicates increasing returns to scale, where $\epsilon_C < 1$ indicates economies of scale. (See Chapter 7 for the definition of output elasticity.)

Q8.7 The president of a small firm has been complaining to his controller about rising labor and material costs. However, the controller notes that average costs have not increased during the past year. Is this possible?

Q8.8 Given the short-run total cost curve in Figure 8.1(b), explain why (a) Q_1 is the minimum of the MC curve, (b) Q_2 is the minimum of the AVC curve, (c) Q_3 is the minimum of the ATC curve, and (d) the MC curve cuts the AVC and ATC curves at their minimum points.

Q8.9 Will firms in industries in which high levels of output are necessary for minimum efficient scale tend to have substantial degrees of operating leverage?

Q8.10 Do operating strategies of average cost minimization and profit maximization always lead to identical levels of output?

SELF-TEST PROBLEMS AND SOLUTIONS

ST8.1 Learning Curves. Modern Merchandise, Inc., makes and markets do-it-yourself hardware, housewares, and industrial products. The company's new Aperture Miniblind is winning customers by virtue of its high quality and quick order turnaround time. The product also benefits because its price point bridges the gap between ready-made vinyl blinds and their high-priced custom counterpart. In addition, the company's expanding product line is sure to benefit from cross-selling across different lines. Given the success of the Aperture Miniblind product, Modern Merchandise plans to open a new production facility near Beaufort, South Carolina. Based on information provided by its chief financial officer, the company estimates fixed costs for this product of $50,000 per year and average variable costs of

$$AVC = \$0.5 + \$0.0025Q$$

where AVC is average variable cost (in dollars) and Q is output.

A. Estimate total cost and average total cost for the projected first-year volume of 20,000 units.

B. An increase in worker productivity because of greater experience or learning during the course of the year resulted in a substantial cost saving for the company. Estimate the effect of learning on average total cost if actual second-year total cost was $848,000 at an actual volume of 20,000 units.

ST8.1 Solution

A. The total variable cost function for the first year is

$$\begin{aligned} TVC &= AVC \times Q \\ &= (\$0.5 + \$0.0025Q)Q \\ &= \$0.5Q + \$0.0025Q^2 \end{aligned}$$

At a volume of 20,000 units, estimated total cost is

$$TC = TFC + TVC$$
$$= \$50,000 + \$0.5Q + \$0.0025Q^2$$
$$= \$50,000 + \$0.5(20,000) + \$0.0025(20,000^2)$$
$$= \$1,060,000$$

Estimated average cost is

$$AC = TC/Q$$
$$= \$1,060,000/20,000$$
$$= \$53 \text{ per case}$$

B. If actual total costs were $848,000 at a volume of 20,000 units, actual average total costs were

$$AC = TC/Q$$
$$= \$848,000/20,000$$
$$= \$42.40 \text{ per case}$$

Therefore, greater experience or learning has resulted in an average cost saving of $10.60 per case because

$$\text{Learning Effect} = \text{Actual } AC - \text{Estimated } AC$$
$$= \$42.40 - \$53$$
$$= -\$10.60 \text{ per case}$$

Alternatively,

$$\text{Learning Rate} = \left(1 - \frac{AC_2}{AC_1}\right) \times 100$$

$$= \left(1 - \frac{\$42.40}{\$53}\right) \times 100$$

$$= 20\%$$

ST8.2 Minimum Efficient Scale Estimation. Kanata Corporation is a leading manufacturer of telecommunications equipment based in Ontario, Canada. Its main product is microprocessor-controlled telephone switching equipment, called automatic private branch exchanges (PABXs), capable of handling 8 to 3,000 telephone extensions. Severe price cutting throughout the PABX industry continues to put pressure on sales and margins. To better compete against increasingly aggressive rivals, the company is contemplating the construction of a new production facility capable of producing 1.5 million units per year. Kanata's in-house engineering estimate of the total cost function for the new facility is

$$TC = \$3,000 + \$1,000Q + \$0.003Q^2$$
$$MC = \$1,000 + \$0.006Q$$

where TC = total costs in thousands of dollars, Q = output in thousands of units, and MC = marginal costs in thousands of dollars.

A. Estimate minimum efficient scale in this industry.

B. In light of current PABX demand of 30 million units per year, how would you evaluate the future potential for competition in the industry?

ST8.2   Solution

A. Minimum efficient scale is reached when average costs are first minimized. This occurs at the point where $MC = AC$.

$$
\begin{aligned}
\text{Average Costs} \;=\; AC \;&=\; TC/Q \\
&=\; (\$3{,}000 + \$1{,}000Q + \$0.003Q^2)/Q \\
&=\; \frac{\$3{,}000}{Q} + \$1{,}000 + \$0.003Q
\end{aligned}
$$

Therefore,

$$
\begin{aligned}
MC \;&=\; AC \\
\$1{,}000 + \$0.006Q \;&=\; \frac{\$3{,}000}{Q} + \$1{,}000 + \$0.003Q \\
0.003Q \;&=\; \frac{3{,}000}{Q} \\
\frac{3{,}000}{Q^2} \;&=\; 0.003 \\
Q^2 \;&=\; 1{,}000{,}000 \\
Q \;&=\; 1{,}000(000) \text{ or 1 million}
\end{aligned}
$$

(*Note: AC* is rising for $Q > 1{,}000(000)$.)

Alternatively, MES can be calculated using the point cost elasticity formula, because MES is reached when $\epsilon_C = 1$.

$$
\begin{aligned}
\epsilon_C \;&=\; \frac{\partial TC}{\partial Q} \times \frac{Q}{TC} \\
\frac{(\$1{,}000 + \$0.006Q)Q}{(\$3{,}000 + \$1{,}000Q + \$0.003Q^2)} \;&=\; 1 \\
1{,}000Q + 0.006Q^2 \;&=\; 3{,}000 + 1{,}000Q + 0.003Q^2 \\
0.003Q^2 \;&=\; 3{,}000 \\
Q^2 \;&=\; 1{,}000{,}000 \\
Q_{MES} \;&=\; 1{,}000(000) \text{ or 1 million}
\end{aligned}
$$

B. With a minimum efficient scale of 1 million units and total industry sales of 30 million units, up to 30 efficiently sized competitors are possible in Kanata's market.

$$
\begin{aligned}
\text{Potential Number of Efficient Competitors} \;&=\; \frac{\text{Market Size}}{\text{MES Size}} \\
&=\; \frac{30{,}000{,}000}{1{,}000{,}000} \\
&=\; 30
\end{aligned}
$$

Thus, there is the potential for $n = 30$ efficiently sized competitors and, therefore, vigorous competition in Kanata's industry.

PROBLEMS

P8.1 **Cost and Production Functions.** The total product curve shown here describes a production system in which X is the only variable input. Answer the following questions relating production to costs:

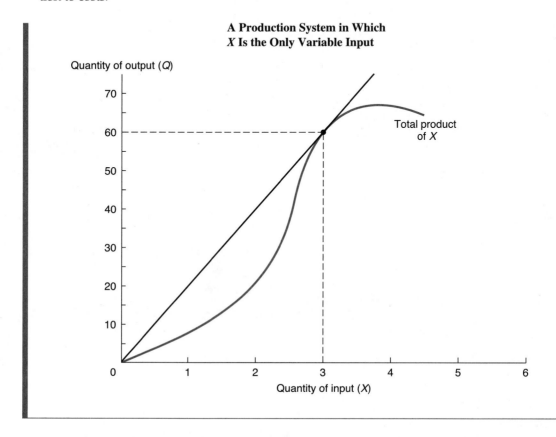

A Production System in Which
X Is the Only Variable Input

A. Over approximately what range of input X will marginal costs be falling if P_X is not affected by the amount purchased?

B. At approximately what level of employment of input X will average variable costs be minimized?

C. If P_X = $25, what is the minimum average variable cost in this production system?

D. What is the marginal cost of production at 60 units of output?

E. If the price of output is $2 per unit, is employment of 3 units of X optimal for a profit-maximizing firm (assuming again that X costs $25 per unit)? Explain.

P8.2 **Cost Relations.** Determine whether each of the following is true or false. Explain why.

A. Average cost equals marginal cost at the minimum efficient scale of plant.

B. When total fixed cost and price are held constant, an increase in average variable cost will typically cause a reduction in the breakeven activity level.

C. If $\epsilon_C > 1$, diseconomies of scale and increasing average costs are indicated.

D. When long-run average cost is decreasing, it can pay to operate larger plants with some excess capacity rather than smaller plants at their peak efficiency.

E. An increase in average variable cost always increases the degree of operating leverage for firms making a positive net profit.

P8.3 **Cost Curves.** Indicate whether each of the following involves an upward or downward shift in the long-run average cost curve or, instead, involves a leftward or rightward movement along a given curve. Also indicate whether each will have an increasing, decreasing, or uncertain effect on the level of average cost.

    A. A rise in wage rates

    B. A decline in output

    C. An energy-saving technical change

    D. A fall in interest rates

    E. An increase in learning or experience

P8.4 **Incremental Cost.** McFarland-Adler, Inc., produces innovative interior decorating software that it sells to design studios, home furnishing stores, and so on. The yearly volume of output is 15,000 units. Selling price and costs per unit are as follows:

Selling Price		$250
Costs:		
Direct material	$40	
Direct labor	60	
Variable overhead	30	
Variable selling expenses	25	
Fixed selling expenses	20	– $175
Unit profit before tax		$ 75

Management is evaluating the possibility of using the Internet to sell its software directly to consumers at a price of $300 per unit. Although no added capital investment is required, additional shipping and handling costs are estimated as follows:

Direct labor	$30 per unit
Variable overhead	$5 per unit
Variable selling expenses	$2 per unit
Fixed selling expenses	$20,000 per year

    A. Calculate the incremental profit that McFarland-Adler would earn by customizing its instruments and marketing them directly to end users.

P8.5 **Accounting and Economic Costs.** Three graduate business students are considering operating a fruit smoothie stand in the Harbor Springs, Michigan, resort area during their summer break. This is an alternative to summer employment with a local firm, where they would each earn $6,000 over the 3-month summer period. A fully equipped facility can be leased at a cost of $8,000 for the summer. Additional projected costs are $1,000 for insurance and $1.20 per unit for materials and supplies. Their fruit smoothies would be priced at $3 per unit.

    A. What is the accounting cost function for this business?

    B. What is the economic cost function for this business?

    C. What is the economic breakeven number of units for this operation? (Assume a $3 price and ignore interest costs associated with the timing of lease payments.)

P8.6 **Profit Contribution.** Angelica Pickles is manager of a Quick Copy franchise in White Plains, New York. Pickles projects that by reducing copy charges from 5¢ to 4¢ each, Quick Copy's $600-per-week profit contribution will increase by one-third.

    A. If average variable costs are 2¢ per copy, calculate Quick Copy's projected increase in volume.

    B. What is Pickles' estimate of the arc price elasticity of demand for copies?

P8.7   **Cost Elasticity.** Power Brokers, Inc. (PBI), a discount brokerage firm, is contemplating open-ing a new regional office in Providence, Rhode Island. An accounting cost analysis of monthly operating costs at a dozen of its regional outlets reveals average fixed costs of $4,500 per month and average variable costs of

$$AVC = \$59 - \$0.006Q$$

where AVC is average variable costs (in dollars) and Q is output measured by number of stock and bond trades.

A typical stock or bond trade results in $100 gross commission income, with PBI paying 35% of this amount to its sales representatives.

A. Estimate the trade volume necessary for PBI to reach a target return of $7,500 per month for a typical office.

B. Estimate and interpret the elasticity of cost with respect to output at the trade volume found in part A.

P8.8   **Multiplant Operation.** Appalachia Beverage Company, Inc., is considering alternative pro-posals for expansion into the Midwest. Alternative 1: Construct a single plant in Indianapolis, Indiana, with a monthly production capacity of 300,000 cases, a monthly fixed cost of $262,500, and a variable cost of $3.25 per case. Alternative 2: Construct three plants, one each in Muncie, Indiana; Normal, Illinois; and Dayton, Ohio, with capacities of 120,000, 100,000, and 80,000, respectively, and monthly fixed costs of $120,000, $110,000, and $95,000 each. Variable costs would be only $3 per case because of lower distribution costs. To achieve these cost savings, sales from each smaller plant would be limited to demand within its home state. The total estimated monthly sales volume of 200,000 cases in these three Midwestern states is distributed as follows: 80,000 cases in Indiana, 70,000 cases in Illinois, and 50,000 cases in Ohio.

A. Assuming a wholesale price of $5 per case, calculate the breakeven output quantities for each alternative.

B. At a wholesale price of $5 per case in all states, and assuming sales at the projected levels, which alternative expansion scheme provides Appalachia with the highest profit per month?

C. If sales increase to production capacities, which alternative would prove to be more prof-itable?

P8.9   **Learning Curves.** The St. Thomas Winery plans to open a new production facility in the Napa Valley of California. Based on information provided by the accounting department, the company estimates fixed costs of $250,000 per year and average variable costs of

$$AVC = \$10 + \$0.01Q$$

where AVC is average variable cost (in dollars) and Q is output measured in cases of output per year.

A. Estimate total cost and average total cost for the coming year at a projected volume of 4,000 cases.

B. An increase in worker productivity because of greater experience or learning during the course of the year resulted in a substantial cost saving for the company. Estimate the effect of learning on average total cost if actual total cost was $522,500 at an actual volume of 5,000 cases.

P8.10   **Cost-Volume-Profit Analysis.** Untouchable Package Service (UPS) offers overnight pack-age delivery to Canadian business customers. UPS has recently decided to expand its facilities to better satisfy current and projected demand. Current volume totals 2 million packages per week at a price of $12 each, and average variable costs are constant at all output levels. Fixed costs are $3 million per week, and profit contribution averages one-third of revenues on each delivery. After completion of the expansion project, fixed costs will double, but variable costs will decline by 25%.

A. Calculate the change in UPS's weekly breakeven output level that is due to expansion.

B. Assuming that volume remains at 2 million packages per week, calculate the change in the degree of operating leverage that is due to expansion.

C. Again assuming that volume remains at 2 million packages per week, what is the effect of expansion on weekly profit?

CASE STUDY

Estimating the Costs of Nursing Care

Cost estimation and cost containment are an important concern for a wide range of for-profit and not-for-profit organizations offering health care services. For such organizations, the accurate measurement of nursing costs per patient day (a measure of output) is necessary for effective management. Similarly, such cost estimates are of significant interest to public officials at the federal, state, and local government levels. For example, many state Medicaid reimbursement programs base their payment rates on historical accounting measures of average costs per unit of service. However, these historical average costs may or may not be relevant for hospital management decisions. During periods of substantial excess capacity, the overhead component of average costs may become irrelevant. When the facilities of providers are fully used and facility expansion becomes necessary to increase services, then all costs, including overhead, are relevant. As a result, historical average costs provide a useful basis for planning purposes only if appropriate assumptions can be made about the relative length of periods of peak versus off-peak facility usage. From a public-policy perspective, a further potential problem arises when hospital expense reimbursement programs are based on historical average costs per day, because the care needs and nursing costs of various patient groups can vary widely. For example, if the care received by the average publicly supported Medicaid patient actually costs more than that received by non-Medicaid patients, Medicaid reimbursement based on average costs for the entire facility would be inequitable to providers and could create access barriers for some Medicaid patients.

As an alternative to traditional cost estimation methods, one might consider using the engineering technique to estimate nursing costs. For example, the labor cost of each type of service could be estimated as the product of an estimate of the time required to perform each service times the estimated wage rate per unit of time. Multiplying this figure by an estimate of the frequency of service provides an estimate of the aggregate cost of the service. A possible limitation to the accuracy of this engineering cost-estimation method is that treatment of a variety of illnesses often requires a combination of nursing services. To the extent that multiple services can be provided simultaneously, the engineering technique will tend to overstate actual costs unless the effect on costs of service "packaging" is allowed for.

Nursing cost estimation is also possible by means of a carefully designed regression-based approach using variable cost and service data collected at the ward, unit, or facility level. Weekly labor costs for registered nurses (RNs), licensed practical nurses (LPNs), and nursing aides might be related to a variety of patient services performed during a given measurement period. With sufficient variability in cost and service levels over time, useful estimates of variable labor costs become possible for each type of service and for each patient category (e.g., Medicaid, non-Medicaid). An important advantage of a regression-based approach is that it explicitly allows for the effect of service packaging on variable costs. For example, if shots and wound-dressing services are typically provided together, this will be reflected in the regression-based estimates of variable costs per unit.

CASE STUDY (continued)

TABLE 8.3

Nursing Costs per Patient Day, Nursing Services, and Profit Status for 40 Hospitals in Southeastern States

Hospital	Nursing Costs per Patient Day	Shots	IV Therapy	Pulse Taking	Wound Dressing	Profit Status (1= for-profit, 0=not-for-profit)
1	125.00	1.50	0.75	2.25	0.75	0
2	125.00	1.50	0.75	2.25	0.75	0
3	115.00	1.50	0.50	2.00	0.50	1
4	125.00	2.00	0.75	2.25	0.75	0
5	122.50	1.50	0.50	2.25	0.75	0
6	120.00	1.50	0.75	2.25	0.75	1
7	125.00	1.75	0.75	2.00	0.50	0
8	130.00	1.75	0.75	2.25	0.75	0
9	117.50	1.50	0.50	2.25	0.50	0
10	130.00	1.75	0.75	3.25	0.75	0
11	125.00	1.50	0.75	3.00	0.50	0
12	127.50	1.50	0.75	2.50	0.75	0
13	125.00	1.75	0.75	2.50	0.50	0
14	125.00	1.50	0.50	2.50	0.75	0
15	120.00	1.50	0.75	2.25	0.50	0
16	125.00	1.50	0.50	2.25	0.75	0
17	130.00	1.75	0.75	2.50	0.75	0
18	120.00	1.50	0.50	2.25	0.50	0
19	125.00	1.50	0.75	2.25	0.75	0
20	122.50	1.50	0.50	2.50	0.75	0
21	117.50	1.75	0.50	2.00	0.50	1
22	120.00	1.50	0.50	2.50	0.50	0
23	122.50	1.50	0.75	2.50	0.75	1
24	117.50	1.50	0.50	2.50	0.50	0
25	132.50	1.75	0.75	2.50	0.75	0
26	120.00	1.75	0.50	2.25	0.50	1
27	122.50	1.75	0.50	2.50	0.50	0
28	125.00	1.50	0.75	2.50	0.75	0
29	125.00	1.50	0.50	2.00	0.75	0
30	130.00	1.75	0.75	2.25	0.75	0
31	115.00	1.50	0.50	2.00	0.50	0
32	115.00	1.50	0.50	2.25	0.50	0
33	130.00	1.75	0.75	2.50	0.75	0
34	132.50	1.75	0.75	3.00	0.75	0
35	117.50	1.50	0.50	2.00	0.50	1
36	122.50	1.50	0.50	2.50	0.75	0
37	112.50	1.50	0.50	2.00	0.50	0
38	130.00	1.50	0.75	3.25	0.75	0
39	130.00	1.50	0.75	3.25	0.75	1
40	125.00	1.50	0.75	3.00	0.75	1

CASE STUDY (continued)

Long-run costs per nursing facility can be estimated using either cross-section or time-series methods. By relating total facility costs to the service levels provided by a number of hospitals, nursing homes, or out-patient care facilities during a specific period, useful cross-section estimates of total service costs are possible. If case mixes were to vary dramatically according to type of facility, then the type of facility would have to be explicitly accounted for in the regression model analyzed. Similarly, if patient mix or service-provider efficiency is expected to depend, at least in part, on the for-profit or not-for-profit organization status of the care facility, the regression model must also recognize this factor. These factors plus price-level adjustments for inflation would be accounted for in a time-series approach to nursing cost estimation.

To illustrate a regression-based approach to nursing cost estimation, consider the following cross-section analysis of variable nursing costs conducted by the Southeast Association of Hospital Administrators (SAHA). Using confidential data provided by 40 regional hospitals, SAHA studied the relation between nursing costs per patient day and four typical categories of nursing services. These annual data appear in Table 8.3 The four categories of nursing services studied include shots, intravenous (IV) therapy, pulse taking and monitoring, and wound dressing. Each service is measured in terms of frequency per patient day. An output of 1.50 in the shots service category means that, on average, patients received one and one-half shots per day. Similarly, an output of 0.75 in the IV service category means that IV services were provided daily to 75% of a given hospital's patients, and so on. In addition to four categories of nursing services, the not-for-profit or for-profit status of each hospital is also indicated. Using a "dummy" (or binary) variable approach, the profit status variable equals 1 for the eight for-profit hospitals included in the study and zero for the remaining 32 not-for-profit hospitals.

Cost estimation results for nursing costs per patient day derived using a regression-based approach are shown in Table 8.4.

A. Interpret the coefficient of determination (R^2) estimated for the nursing cost function.

B. Describe the economic and statistical significance of each estimated coefficient in the nursing cost function.

C. Average nursing costs for the eight for-profit hospitals in the sample are only $120.94 per patient day, or $3.28 per patient day less than the $124.22 average cost experienced by the 32 not-for-profit hospitals. How can this fact be reconciled with the estimated coefficient of –2.105 for the for-profit status variable?

D. Would such an approach for nursing cost estimation have practical relevance for publicly funded nursing cost reimbursement systems?

TABLE 8.4

Nursing Costs per Patient Day: Cost Estimation Results

Variable Name	Coefficient (1)	Standard Error of Coefficient (2)	*t* Statistic (1)÷(2)=(3)
Intercept	76.182	5.086	14.98
Shots	11.418	2.851	4.00
IV	10.052	3.646	2.76
Pulse	4.532	1.153	3.93
Wound dressing	18.932	3.370	5.62
For-profit status	–2.105	0.883	–2.38

Coefficient of determination = R^2 = 84.1%
Standard error of estimate = SEE = $2.21

SELECTED REFERENCES

Achee, Rebecca, Thornton and Peter Thompson. "Learning from Experience and Learning from Others: An Exploration of Learning and Spillovers in Wartime Shipbuilding." *American Economic Review* 91 (December 2001): 1350–1368.

Angrist, Joshua D., and Alan B. Krueger. "Instrumental Variables and the Search for Identification: From Supply and Demand to Natural Experiments." *Journal of Economic Perspectives* 15 (Fall 2001): 69–87.

Baily, Martin Neal, and Robert Z. Lawrence. "Do We Have a New E-Conomy?" *American Economic Review* 91 (May 2001): 308–312.

Chan, Louis K. C., Josef Lakonishok, and Theodore Sougiannis. "The Stock Market Valuation of Research and Development Expenditures." *Journal of Finance* 56 (December 2001): 2431–2456.

Gul, Ferdinand A. "Free Cash Flow, Debt-Monitoring and Managers' Lifo/Fifo Policy Choice." *Journal of Corporate Finance* 7 (December 2001): 475–492.

Hausman, Jerry. "Mismeasured Variables in Econometric Analysis: Problems from the Right and Problems from the Left." *Journal of Economic Perspectives* 15 (Fall 2001): 57–68.

Ittner, Christopher D., and David F. Larcker. "Assessing Empirical Research in Managerial Accounting: A Value-Based Management Perspective." *Journal of Accounting and Economics* 32 (December 2001): 349–410.

Lambert, Richard A. "Contracting Theory and Accounting." *Journal of Accounting and Economics* 32 (December 2001): 3–87.

Levitt, Steven D., and Jack Porter. "Sample Selection in the Estimation of Air Bag and Seat Belt Effectiveness." *Review of Economics and Statistics* 83 (November 2001): 603–615.

Litan, Robert E., and Alice M. Rivlin. "Projecting the Economic Impact of the Internet." *American Economic Review* 91 (May 2001): 313–317.

Morgenstern, Richard D., William A. Pizer, and Jhih-Shyang Shih. "The Cost of Environmental Protection." *Review of Economics and Statistics* 83 (November 2001): 732–738.

Verrecchia, Robert E. "Essays on Disclosure." *Journal of Accounting and Economics* 32 (December 2001): 97–180.

Wooldridge, Jeffrey M. "Applications of Generalized Method of Moments Estimation." *Journal of Economic Perspectives* 15 (Fall 2001): 87–100.

Worthington, Andres C. "Efficiency in Pre-Merger and Post-Merger Non-Bank Financial Institutions." *Managerial & Decision Economics* 22 (December 2001): 439–452.

Zimmerman, Jerold L. "Conjectures Regarding Empirical Managerial Accounting Research." *Journal of Accounting and Economics* 32 (December 2001): 411–427.

CHAPTER NINE

Linear Programming

Linear programming, or so-called "solver" PC software, can be used to figure out the best answer to an assortment of questions expressed in terms of functional relationships. In a fundamental sense, linear programming is a straightforward development from the more basic "what if" approach to problem solving. In a traditional "what-if" approach, one simply enters data or a change in input values in a computer spreadsheet and uses spreadsheet formulas and macros to calculate resulting output values. A prime advantage of the "what if" approach is that it allows managers to consider the cost, revenue, and profit implications of changes in a wide variety of operating conditions. An important limitation of the "what if" method is that it can become a tedious means of searching for the best answer to planning and operating decisions.

Linear programming can be thought of as performing "what-if in reverse." All you do is specify appropriate objectives and a series of constraint conditions, and the software will determine the appropriate input values. When production goals are specified in light of operating constraints, linear programming can be used to identify the cost-minimizing operating plan. Alternatively, using linear programming techniques, a manager might find the profit-maximizing activity level by specifying production relationships and the amount of available resources.

Linear programming has proven to be an adept tool for solving problems encountered in a number of business, engineering, financial, and scientific applications. In a practical sense, typically encountered constrained optimization problems seldom have a simple rule-of-thumb solution. This chapter illustrates how linear programming can be used to quickly and easily solve real-world decision problems.[1]

---

1 Kornelia Heusener and Gesa Von Wichert, "Profit Pressure in the Cargo Industry," *The Wall Street Journal Online*, March 18, 2002 (http://online.wsj.com).

BASIC ASSUMPTIONS

linear programming
A solution method for maximization or minimization decision problems subject to underlying constraints

Linear programming is a useful method for analyzing and solving certain types of management decision problems. To know when linear programming techniques can be applied, it is necessary to understand basic underlying assumptions.

Inequality Constraints

Many production or resource constraints faced by managers are inequalities. Constraints often limit the resource employed to less than or equal to (≤) some fixed amount available. In other instances, constraints specify that the quantity or quality of output must be greater than or equal to (≥) some minimum requirement. Linear programming handles such constraint inequalities easily, making it a useful technique for finding the **optimal solution** to many management decision problems.

optimal solution
Best answer

A typical linear programming problem might be to maximize output subject to the constraint that no more than 40 hours of skilled labor per week be used. This labor constraint is expressed as an inequality where skilled labor ≤ 40 hours per week. Such an operating constraint means that no more than 40 hours of skilled labor can be used, but some excess capacity is permissible, at least in the short run. If 36 hours of skilled labor were fruitfully employed during a given week, the 4 hours per week of unused labor is called excess capacity.

Linearity Assumption

As its name implies, linear programming can be applied only in situations in which the relevant objective function and constraint conditions are linear. Typical managerial decision problems that can be solved using the linear programming method involve revenue and cost functions and their composite, the profit function. Each must be linear; as output increases, revenues, costs, and profits must increase in a linear fashion. For revenues to be a linear function of output, product prices must be constant. For costs to be a linear function of output, both returns to scale and input prices must be constant. Constant input prices, when combined with constant returns to scale, result in a linear total cost function. If both output prices and unit costs are constant, then profit contribution and profits also rise in a linear fashion with output.

Product and input prices are relatively constant when a typical firm can buy unlimited quantities of input and sell an unlimited amount of output without changing prices. This occurs under conditions of pure competition. Therefore, linear programming methods are clearly applicable for firms in perfectly competitive industries with constant returns to scale. However, linear programming is also applicable in many other instances. Because linear programming is used for marginal analysis, it focuses on the effects of fairly modest output, price, and input changes. For moderate changes in current operating conditions, a constant-returns-to-scale assumption is often valid. Similarly, input and output prices are typically unaffected by modest changes from current levels. As a result, sales revenue, cost, and profit functions are often linear when only moderate changes in operations are contemplated and use of linear programming methods is valid.

To illustrate, suppose that an oil company must choose the optimal output mix for a refinery with a capacity of 150,000 barrels of oil per day. The oil company is justified in basing its analysis on the $25-per-barrel prevailing market price for crude oil, regardless of how much is purchased or sold. This assumption might not be valid if the company were to quickly expand refinery output by a factor of 10, but within the 150,000 barrels per day range of feasible output, prices will be approximately constant. Up to capacity limits, it is also reasonable to expect that a doubling of crude oil input would lead to a doubling of refined output, and that returns to scale are constant.

LP: More Than a Visual Approach

LP is often portrayed as a visual means of characterizing management problems. It is—at least when a limited number of products or product dimensions are being analyzed. When the optimal level of production for two products is sought, for example, a simple graph of the appropriate LP problem gives managers a useful intuitive basis for considering the best means of meeting a variety of production criteria. When a multitude of products are offered, or when a large number of production characteristics must be considered, the typical LP problem becomes too complex to be visualized graphically. In such instances, computer-based solutions using spreadsheets offer a tractable alternative for analyzing and solving LP problems.

LP techniques are commonly used to solve problems in transportation routing, staff scheduling, and financial planning. Whenever a company needs to move a quantity of goods from and to multiple locations, such as plants, regional warehouses, or retail stores, it faces a practical LP problem. By minimizing route mileage, operating costs can also be minimized, and outlays for capital investment can be kept at a minimum. Many companies routinely save thousands of dollars per year on shipping costs by solving LP problems of this type. Businesses and government agencies use LP methods to solve the problem of scheduling employees' working hours to meet customer service demands, which might vary by the hour or the day, in light of employee availability and preferences. Other examples of practical applications include models to help investors decide on the optimal allocation of a stock and bond portfolio.

Detailed user tips on successful LP applications, often with free follow-up from the author, can be found in an almost limitless number on the Internet. One of the best sites for getting started is sponsored by Lindo Systems, Inc. There you can find LP case studies for telecommunications network design, supply chain management, and so on. These examples provide the best reason to become familiar with the technique. LP works!

See: Lindo Systems, Inc. (http://www.lindo.com).

In many instances, the underlying assumption of linearity is entirely valid. In other instances in which the objective function and constraint conditions can be usefully approximated by linear relations, the linear programming technique can also be fruitfully applied. Only when objective functions and constraint conditions are inherently nonlinear must more complicated *mathematical programming* techniques be applied. In most managerial applications, even when the assumption of linearity does not hold precisely, linear approximations seldom distort the analysis.

PRODUCTION PLANNING FOR A SINGLE PRODUCT

Although linear programming has been widely applied in managerial decision making, it has been used most frequently in production decisions. To illustrate the method, a simple two-input/one-output problem is examined. Later sections consider more realistic and complex problems.

Production Processes

Assume that a firm produces a single product, Q, using two inputs, L and K, which might represent labor and capital. Instead of assuming continuous substitution between L and K, as in Chapter 7, assume that Q can be produced using only four input combinations. In other words, four different production processes are available for making Q, each of which uses a different fixed combination of inputs L and K. The production processes might represent four different plants, each with its own fixed asset configuration and labor requirements. Alternatively, they could be four different assembly lines, each using a different combination of capital equipment and labor.

The four production processes are illustrated as rays in Figure 9.1. Process A requires the combination of 15 units of L and 1 unit of K for each unit of Q produced. Process B uses 10 units of L and 2 units of K for each unit of output. Processes C and D use 7.5 units of L and 3 units of K, and 5 units of L with 5 units of K, respectively, for each unit of Q produced. Each point along the production ray for process A combines L and K in the ratio 15 to 1; process rays B, C, and D are developed in the same way. Each point along a single production ray combines the two inputs in a fixed ratio, with the ratios differing from one production process to another. If L and K represent labor and capital inputs, the four production processes might be different plants employing different production techniques. Process A is very labor intensive in comparison with the other production systems, whereas B, C, and D are based on increasingly capital-intensive technologies.

Point A_1 indicates the combination of L and K required to produce one unit of output using the A process. Doubling both L and K doubles the quantity of Q produced; this is indicated by the distance moved along ray A from A_1 to A_2. Line segment $0A_2$ is exactly twice the length of

FIGURE 9.1

Production Process Rays in Linear Programming

Points along each process ray represent combinations of inputs L and K required for that production process to produce output.

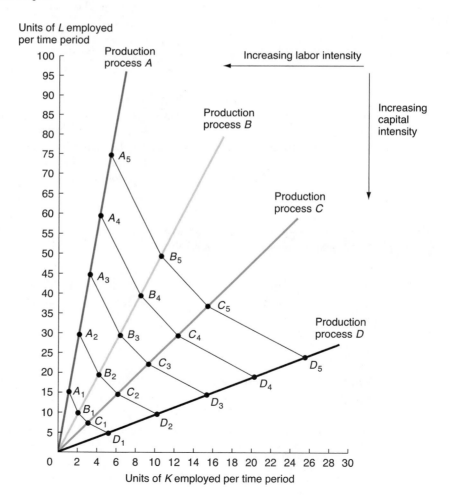

line segment $0A_1$ and thus represents twice as much output. Along production process ray A, the distance $0A_1 = A_1A_2 = A_2A_3 = A_3A_4 = A_4A_5$. Each of these line segments indicates the addition of one unit of output using increased quantities of L and K in the fixed ratio of 15 to 1.

Output along the ray increases proportionately with increases in the input factors. If each input is doubled, output is doubled; if inputs increase by a factor of 10 percent, output increases by 10 percent. This follows from the linearity assumption noted previously: Each production process must exhibit constant returns to scale.

Output is measured in the same way along the three other production process rays in Figure 9.1. Point C_1 indicates the combination of L and K required to produce 1 unit of Q using process C. The production of 2 units of Q using that process requires the combination of L and K indicated at point C_2; the same is true for points C_3, C_4, and C_5. Although production of additional units using process C is indicated by line segments of equal length, just as for process A, these line segments are of different lengths between the various production systems. Whereas each production process exhibits constant returns to scale, equal distances along *different* process rays do not ordinarily indicate equal output quantities.

Production Isoquants

Joining points of equal output on the four production process rays creates a set of isoquant curves. Figure 9.2 illustrates isoquants for $Q = 1, 2, 3, 4,$ and 5. These isoquants have the same interpretation as those developed in Chapter 8. Each isoquant represents combinations of input factors L and K that can be used to produce a given quantity of output. Production isoquants in linear programming are composed of linear segments connecting the various production process rays. Each of these isoquant segments is parallel to one another. For example, line segment A_1B_1 is parallel to segment A_2B_2; isoquant segment B_3C_3 is parallel to B_2C_2.

Points along each segment of an isoquant between two process rays represent a combination of output from each of the two adjoining production processes. Consider point X in Figure 9.2, which represents production of 4 units of Q using 25 units of L and 16 units of K. None of the available production processes can manufacture Q using L and K in the ratio of 25 to 16, but that combination is possible by producing part of the output with process C and part with process D. In this case, 2 units of Q can be produced using process C and 2 units using process D. Production of 2 units of Q with process C uses 15 units of L and 6 units of K. For the production of 2 units of Q with process D, 10 units each of L and K are necessary. Although no single production system is available that can produce 4 units of Q using 25 units of L and 16 units of K, processes C and D together can produce that combination.

All points lying along production isoquant segments can be interpreted in a similar manner. Each point represents a linear combination of output using the production process systems that bound the particular segment. Point Y in Figure 9.2 provides another illustration. At Y, 3 units of Q are produced, using a total of 38.5 units of L and 4.3 units of K.[2] This input/output combination is possible through a combination of processes A and B. This can be analyzed algebraically. To produce 1 unit of Q by process A requires 15 units of L and 1 unit of K. Therefore, to produce 1.7 units of Q requires 25.5 (1.7×15) units of L and 1.7 (1.7×1) units of K. To produce a single unit of Q by process B requires 10 units of L and 2 units of K, so 1.3 units of Q requires 13 (10×1.3) units of L and 2.6 (2×1.3) units of K. Thus, point Y calls for the production of 3 units of Q in total, 1.7 units by process A and 1.3 units by process B, using a total of 38.5 units of L and 4.3 units of K.

---

2   Another assumption of linear programming is that fractional variables are permissible. In many applications, this assumption is not important. For example, in the present illustration, we might be talking about labor hours and machine hours for the inputs. The solution value calling for $L = 38.5$ merely means that 38.5 hours of labor are required.

   In some cases, however, inputs are large (whole plants, for example), and the fact that linear programming assumes divisible variables is important. In such cases, linear programming as described here may be inappropriate, and a more complex technique, integer programming, may be required.

FIGURE 9.2

Production Isoquants in Linear Programming

Each point along an isoquant represents the output level resulting from a given combination of inputs. For example, point X depicts the production of four units of Q by using 25 units of L and 16 units of K.

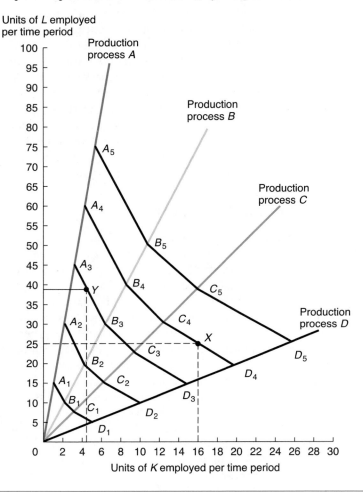

One method of determining the quantity to be produced by each production process at varying points along the isoquant is called the relative distance method. The **relative distance method** is based on the fact that the location of a point along an isoquant determines the relative shares of production for the adjacent processes. If point X in Figure 9.2 were on process ray C, all output would be produced using process C. Similarly, if X were on process ray D, all output would be produced using process D. Because point X lies between process rays C and D, both processes C and D will be used to produce this output. Process C will be used relatively more than process D if X is closer to process ray C than to process ray D. Similarly, process D will be used relatively more than process C if X is closer to process ray D than to process ray C. Because point X in Figure 9.2 lies at the midpoint of the Q = 4 isoquant segment between C_4 and D_4, it implies production using processes C and D in equal proportions. Thus, at point X, Q = 4, Q_C = 2, and Q_D = 2.

The relative proportions of process A and process B used to produce Q = 3 at Point Y can be determined in a similar manner. Because Y lies closer to process ray A than to process ray B, point Y entails relatively more output from process A than from process B. The share of total output produced using process A is calculated by considering the distance B_3Y relative

relative distance method
Graphic technique used to solve linear programming problems

to B_3A_3. The share of total output produced using process B is calculated by considering the distance A_3Y relative to A_3B_3. Starting from point B_3, the segment B_3Y covers 56.6 percent of the total distance B_3A_3. This means that at point Y, about 56.6 percent of total output is produced using process A ($Q_A = 0.566 \times 3 = 1.7$) and 43.4 percent (= $1.0 - 0.566$) using process B ($Q_B = 0.434 \times 3 = 1.3$). Alternatively, starting from point A_3, note that the segment A_3Y covers 43.4 percent of the total distance A_3B_3. At point Y, 43.4 percent of total output is produced using process B and 56.6 percent using process A. Extreme accuracy would require painstaking graphic detail, but in many instances the relative distance method can adequately approximate production intensities along isoquants.

Least-Cost Input Combinations

Adding isocost curves to a set of isoquants permits one to determine least-cost input combinations for the production of product Q. This is shown in Figure 9.3 under the assumption that each unit of L costs \$3 and each unit of K costs \$10. The isocost curve illustrated indicates a total expenditure of \$150.

FIGURE 9.3

Determination of the Least-Cost Production Process

The tangency between the isoquant and isocost lines at point B_3 reveals the least-cost combination of inputs.

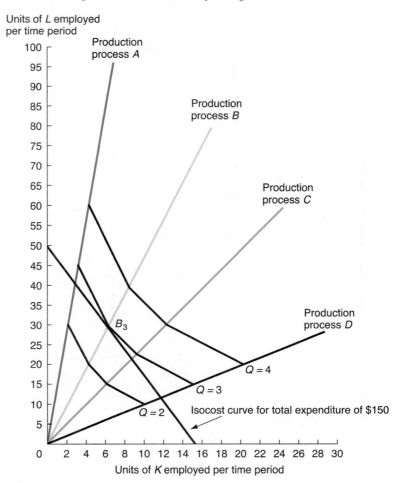

The tangency between the isocost curve and the isoquant curve for $Q = 3$ at point B_3 indicates that process B, which combines inputs L and K in the ratio 5 to 1, is the least-cost method of producing Q. For any expenditure level, production is maximized by using process B. Alternatively, process B is the least-cost method for producing any quantity of Q, given the assumed prices for L and K.

Optimal Input Combinations with Limited Resources

Frequently, firms faced with limited inputs during a production period find it optimal to use inputs in proportions other than the least-cost combination. To illustrate, consider the effect of limits on the quantities of L and K available in our example. Assume that only 20 units of L and 11 units of K are available during the current production period and that the firm seeks to maximize output of Q. These constraints are shown in Figure 9.4. The horizontal line drawn at $L = 20$ indicates the upper limit on the quantity of L that can be employed during the production period; the vertical line at $K = 11$ indicates a similar limit on the quantity of K.

FIGURE 9.4

Optimal Input Combination with Limited Resources

Given limited resources, output is maximized at point R because this point lies on the higher isoquant that intersects the feasible space.

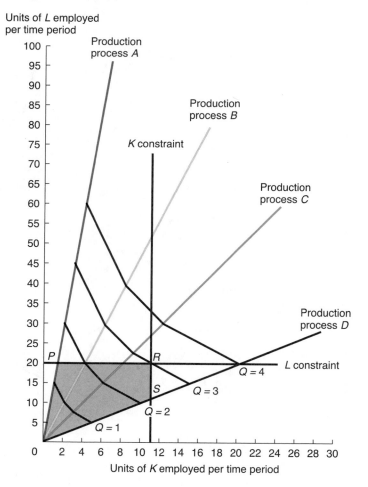

Production possibilities for this problem are determined by noting that, in addition to limitations on inputs L and K, the firm must operate within the area bounded by production process rays A and D. Combining production possibilities with input constraints restricts the firm to operation within the shaded area on $0PRS$ in Figure 9.4. This area is known as the **feasible space** in the programming problem. Any point within this space combines L and K in a technically feasible ratio without exceeding availability limits on L and K. Because the firm is trying to maximize production of Q subject to constraints on the use of L and K, it should operate at the feasible space point that touches the highest possible isoquant. This is point R in Figure 9.4, where $Q = 3$.

feasible space

Graphical region that is both technically and economically feasible and includes the optimal solution

Although it is possible to solve the foregoing problem by using carefully drawn graphs, it is typically easier to combine graphic analysis with analytical techniques to obtain accurate solutions efficiently. For example, consider Figure 9.4 again. Even if the isoquant for $Q = 3$ were not drawn, it would be apparent from the slopes of the isoquants for 2 or 4 units of output that the optimal solution to the problem must be at point R. It is obvious from the graph that maximum production is obtained by operating at the point where both inputs are fully employed. Because R lies between production processes C and D, the output-maximizing input combination uses only those two production processes. All 20 units of L and 11 units of K will be employed, because point R lies at the intersection of these two input constraints.

Using this information from the graph, it is possible to quickly and easily solve for the optimal quantities to be produced using processes C and D. Recall that each unit of output produced using process C requires 7.5 units of L. Thus, the total L required in process C equals $7.5 \times Q_C$. Similarly, each unit produced using process D requires 5 units of L, so the total L used in process D equals $5 \times Q_D$. At point R, 20 units of L are being used in processes C and D together, and the following must hold:

(9.1)
$$7.5Q_C + 5Q_D = 20$$

A similar relation can be developed for the use of K. Each unit of output produced from process C requires 3 units of K, whereas process D uses 5 units of K to produce each unit of output. The total use of K in processes C and D equals 11 units at point R, so

(9.2)
$$3Q_C + 5Q_D = 11$$

Equations 9.1 and 9.2 both must hold at point R. Output quantities from processes C and D at that location are determined by solving these equations simultaneously. Subtracting Equation 9.2 from Equation 9.1 to eliminate the variable Q_D isolates the solution for Q_C:

$$
\begin{array}{rcl}
7.5Q_C + 5Q_D &=& 20 \\
\text{minus}\quad 3.0Q_C + 5Q_D &=& 11 \\
\hline
4.5Q_C &=& 9 \\
Q_C &=& 2
\end{array}
$$

Substituting 2 for Q_C in Equation 9.2 determines output from process D:

$$
\begin{array}{rcl}
3(2) + 5Q_D &=& 11 \\
5Q_D &=& 5 \\
Q_D &=& 1
\end{array}
$$

Total output at point R is 3 units, composed of 2 units from process C and 1 unit from process D.

The combination of graphic and analytic techniques allows one to obtain precise linear programming solutions with relative ease.

LP on the PC!

Managers of small to medium-sized companies often plug hypothetical financial and operating data into spreadsheet software programs and then recalculate profit figures to see how various changes might affect the bottom line. A major problem with this popular "What if?" approach to decision analysis is the haphazard way in which various alternatives are considered. Dozens of time-consuming recalculations are often necessary before suggestions emerge that lead to a clear improvement in operating efficiency. Even then, managers have no assurance that more profitable or cost-efficient decision alternatives are not available.

The frustrations of "What if?" analysis are sure to become a thing of the past with the increasing popularity of new *Solver* LP programs, included as a basic feature of spreadsheet software, like *Microsoft Excel*. *Solver* LP tools are capable of solving all but the toughest problems and are extremely user-friendly for those with little LP training or computer experience. More powerful, but still easy to use, LP software is provided by Lindo Systems,

Inc. Lindo is the leading supplier of LP optimization software to business, government, and academia. Lindo software is used to provide critical answers to thousands of businesses, including over one-half of the *Fortune* 500. *What'sBest!* is an innovative LP program and a popular modeling tool for business problems. First released in 1985, *What'sBest!* soon became the industry leader, specializing in tackling large-scale, real-world problems. Like more basic *Solver* LP programs, *What'sBest!* software is designed for the PC environment.

It is stunning to note how quickly inexpensive, powerful, and easy-to-use LP software for the PC has come forth. As new generations of user-friendly LP software emerge, appreciation of the value of the LP technique as a practical and powerful tool for decision analysis will continue to flourish as a powerful and practical tool for managerial decision making.

See: Home page information for *Lindo*, *Lingo*, and *What'sBest!* software can be found on the Internet (http://www.lindo.com).

PRODUCTION PLANNING FOR MULTIPLE PRODUCTS

Many production decisions are more complex than the preceding example. Consider the problem of finding the optimal output mix for a multiproduct firm facing restrictions on productive facilities and other inputs. This problem, which is faced by a host of companies producing consumer and producer goods alike, is readily solved with linear programming techniques.

Objective Function Specification

Consider a firm that produces products X and Y and uses inputs A, B, and C. To maximize total profit, the firm must determine optimal quantities of each product subject to constraints imposed on input availability. It is often useful to structure such a linear programming problem in terms of the maximization of profit contribution, or total revenue minus variable costs, rather than to explicitly maximize profits. Of course, fixed costs must be subtracted from profit contribution to determine net profits. However, because fixed costs are constant, maximizing profit contribution is tantamount to maximizing profit. The output mix that maximizes profit contribution also maximizes net profit.

objective function
Equation that expresses the goal of a linear programming problem

An equation that expresses the goal of a linear programming problem is called the **objective function**. Assume that the firm wishes to maximize total profits from the two products, X and Y, during each period. If per-unit profit contribution (the excess of price over average variable costs) is \$12 for product X and \$9 for product Y, the objective function is

(9.3)
$$\text{Maximize } \pi = \$12Q_X + \$9Q_Y$$

Q_X and Q_Y represent the quantities of each product produced. The total profit contribution, π, earned by the firm equals the per-unit profit contribution of X times the units of X produced and sold, plus the profit contribution of Y times Q_Y.

Constraint Equation Specification

Table 9.1 specifies the available quantities of each input and their usage in the production of X and Y. This information is all that is needed to form the constraint equations.

The table shows that 32 units of input A are available in each period. Four units of A are required to produce each unit of X, whereas 2 units of A are necessary to produce 1 unit of Y. Because 4 units of A are required to produce a single unit of X, the total amount of A used to manufacture X can be written as $4Q_X$. Similarly, 2 units of A are required to produce each unit of Y, so $2Q_Y$ represents the total quantity of A used to produce product Y. Summing the quantities of A used to produce X and Y provides an expression for the total usage of A. Because this total cannot exceed the 32 units available, the constraint condition for input A is

(9.4)
$$4Q_X + 2Q_Y \leq 32$$

The constraint for input B is determined in a similar manner. One unit of input B is necessary to produce each unit of either X or Y, so the total amount of B employed is $1Q_X + 1Q_Y$. The maximum quantity of B available in each period is 10 units; thus, the constraint requirement associated with input B is

(9.5)
$$1Q_X + 1Q_Y \leq 10$$

Finally, the constraint relation for input C affects only the production of Y. Each unit of Y requires an input of 3 units of C, and 21 units of input C are available. Usage of C is given by the expression $3Q_Y$, and the relevant constraint equation is

(9.6)
$$3Q_Y \leq 21$$

Constraint equations play a major role in solving linear programming problems. One further concept must be introduced, however, before the linear programming problem is completely specified and ready for solution.

Nonnegativity Requirement

Because linear programming is merely a mathematical tool for solving constrained optimization problems, nothing in the technique itself ensures that an answer makes economic sense. In a production problem for a relatively unprofitable product, the mathematically optimal output level might be a *negative* quantity, clearly an impossible solution. In a distribution problem, an optimal solution might indicate negative shipments from one point to another, which again is impossible.

TABLE 9.1

Inputs Available for Production of X and Y

Input	Quantity Available per Time Period	Quantity Required per Unit of Output	
		X	Y
A	32	4	2
B	10	1	1
C	21	0	3

To prevent economically meaningless results, a nonnegativity requirement must be introduced. This is merely a statement that all variables in the problem must be equal to or greater than zero. For the present production problem, the following expressions must be added:

$$Q_X \geq 0$$

and

$$Q_Y \geq 0$$

GRAPHIC SPECIFICATION AND SOLUTION

Having specified all the component parts of the firm's linear programming problem, the problem can now be illustrated graphically and analyzed algebraically.

Analytic Expression

The decision problem is to maximize total profit contribution, π, subject to resource constraints. This is expressed as

(9.3)
$$\text{Maximize } \pi = \$12Q_X + \$9Q_Y$$

subject to the following constraints:

(9.4)   Input A: $4Q_X + 2Q_Y \leq 32$
(9.5)   Input B: $1Q_X + 1Q_Y \leq 10$
(9.6)   Input C: $3Q_Y \leq 21$

where

$$Q_X \geq 0 \text{ and } Q_Y \geq 0$$

Each variable and coefficient is exactly as specified previously.

Graphing the Feasible Space

In Figure 9.5, the graph of the constraint equation for input A, $4Q_X + 2Q_Y = 32$, indicates the maximum quantities of X and Y that can be produced given the limitation on the availability of input A. A maximum of 16 units of Y can be produced if no X is manufactured; 8 units of X can be produced if the output of Y is zero. Any point along the line connecting these two outputs represents the maximum combination of X and Y that can be produced with no more than 32 units of A.

This constraint equation divides the XY plane into two half spaces. Every point lying on the line or to the left of the line satisfies the constraint expressed by the equation $4Q_X + 2Q_Y \leq 32$; every point to the right of the line violates that expression. Only points on the constraint line or to the left of it are in the feasible space. The shaded area of Figure 9.5 represents the feasible area limited by the constraint on input A.

In Figure 9.6, the feasible space is limited further by adding constraints for inputs B and C. The constraint on input B is expressed as $Q_X + Q_Y = 10$. If no Y is produced, a maximum of 10 units of X can be produced; if output of X is zero, 10 units of Y can be manufactured. All combinations of X and Y lying on or to the left of the line connecting these two points are feasible with respect to utilization of input B.

FIGURE 9.5

Constraint Imposed by Limitations on Input *A*

The constraint equation for input *A* represents the maximum combination of *X* and *Y* that can be produced with 32 units of *A*.

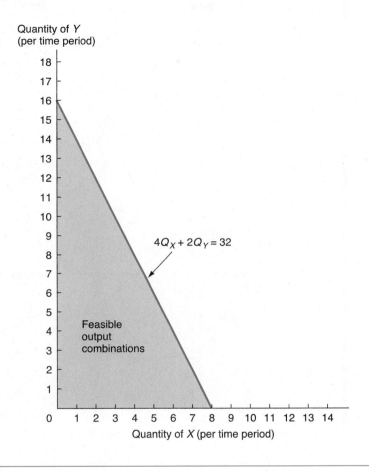

The horizontal line at $Q_Y = 7$ in Figure 9.6 represents the constraint imposed by input *C*. Because *C* is used only in the production of *Y*, it does not constrain the production of *X*. Seven units are the maximum quantity of *Y* that can be produced with 21 units of *C* available.

These three input constraints, together with the nonnegativity requirement, completely define the feasible space shown as the shaded area of Figure 9.6. Only points within this area meet all constraints.

Graphing the Objective Function

The objective function, $\pi = \$12Q_X + \$9Q_Y$, can be graphed in $Q_X Q_Y$ space as a series of isoprofit curves. This is illustrated in Figure 9.7, where isoprofit curves for $36, $72, $108, and $144 are shown. Each isoprofit curve illustrates all possible combinations of *X* and *Y* that result in a constant total profit contribution. For example, the isoprofit curve labeled $\pi = \$36$ identifies each combination of *X* and *Y* that results in a total profit contribution of $36; all output combinations along the $\pi = \$72$ curve provide a total profit contribution of $72; and so on. It is clear from Figure 9.7 that isoprofit curves are a series of parallel lines that take on higher values as one moves upward and to the right.

FIGURE 9.6

Feasible Space

The feasible space is reduced further by the addition of constraints on inputs *B* and *C*. Only points within the shaded region meet all constraints.

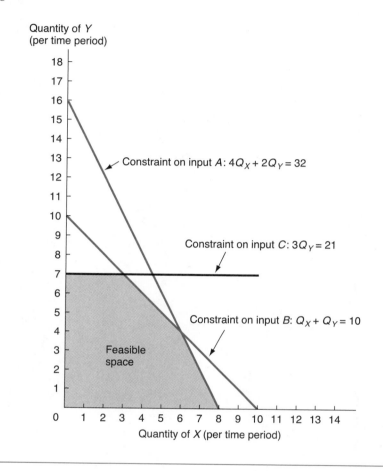

The general formula for isoprofit curves can be developed by considering the profit function $\pi = aQ_X + bQ_Y$, where *a* and *b* are the profit contributions of products *X* and *Y*, respectively. Solving the isoprofit function for Q_Y creates an equation of the following form:

$$Q_Y = \frac{\pi}{b} - \frac{a}{b} \, Q_X$$

Given the individual profit contributions, *a* and *b*, the Q_Y intercept equals the profit level of the isoprofit curve divided by the profit per unit earned on Q_Y, π/b. Slope of the objective function is given by the relative profitability of the two products, $-a/b$. Because the relative profitability of the products is not affected by the output level, the isoprofit curves consist of a series of parallel lines. In this example, all isoprofit curves have a slope of –12/9, or –1.33.

Graphic Solution

Because the firm's objective is to maximize total profit, it should operate on the highest isoprofit curve obtainable. To see this point graphically, Figure 9.7 combines the feasible space limitations shown in Figure 9.6 with the family of isoprofit curves discussed here. Using this

FIGURE 9.7

Graphic Solution of the Linear Programming Problem

Points along the isoprofit line represent all possible combinations of X and Y that result in the same profit level. Point M is on the highest isoprofit curve that intersects the feasible space. Thus, it represents the output combination that will maximize total profit given input constraints.

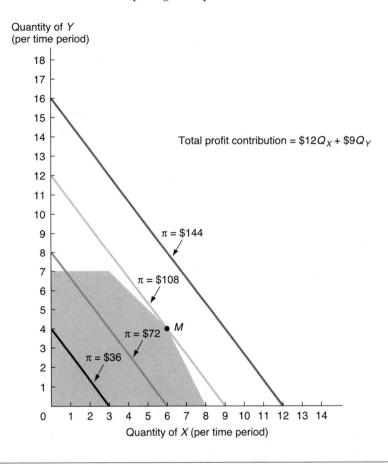

approach, point M in the figure is indicated as the optimal solution. At point M, the firm produces 6 units of X and 4 units of Y, and the total profit is \$108 [=(\$12 × 6) + (\$9 × 4)], which is the maximum available under the conditions stated in the problem. No other point within the feasible spaces touches so high an isoprofit curve.

Using the combined graphic and analytical method introduced in the preceding section, M can be identified as the point where $Q_X = 6$ and $Q_Y = 4$. At M, constraints on inputs A and B are binding. At M, 32 units of input A and 10 units of input B are being completely used to produce X and Y. Thus, Equations 9.4 and 9.5 can be written as equalities and solved simultaneously for Q_X and Q_Y. Subtracting two times Equation 9.5 from Equation 9.4 gives

$$4Q_X + 2Q_Y = 32$$
$$\text{minus } \underline{2Q_X + 2Q_Y = 20}$$
$$2Q_X = 12$$
$$Q_X = 6$$

Substituting 6 for Q_X in Equation 9.5 results in

$$6 + Q_Y = 10$$
$$Q_Y = 4$$

corner point
Spot in the feasible space where the X-axis, Y-axis, or constraint conditions intersect

Notice that the optimal solution to the linear programming problem occurs at a **corner point** of the feasible space. A corner point is a spot in the feasible space where the X-axis, Y-axis, or constraint conditions intersect. The optimal solution to any linear programming problem always lies at a corner point. Because all of the relations in a linear programming problem must be linear by definition, every boundary of the feasible space is linear. Furthermore, the objective function is linear. Thus, the constrained optimization of the objective function takes place either at a corner of the feasible space or at one boundary face, as is illustrated by Figure 9.8.

In Figure 9.8, the linear programming example has been modified by assuming that each unit of either X or Y yields a profit of $5. In this case, the optimal solution to the problem includes any of the combinations of X and Y found along line LM. All of these combinations are feasible and result in a total profit of $50. If all points along line LM provide optimal combinations of output, the combinations found at corners L and M are also optimal. Because the firm is indifferent about producing at point L or at point M, or at any point in between, any such location provides an optimal solution to the production problem.

The search for an optimal solution can be limited to just the corners of each linear programming problem's feasible space. This greatly reduces the number of necessary computations.

ALGEBRAIC SPECIFICATION AND SOLUTION

Many linear programming problems contain too many variables and constraints to allow solution by graphic analysis. Algebraic methods often must be employed. Algebraic techniques are

FIGURE 9.8

Graphic Solution of a Linear Programming Problem When the Objective Function Coincides with a Boundary of the Feasible Space

When the objective function coincides with the boundary of the feasible space, several different output combinations will produce maximum profits.

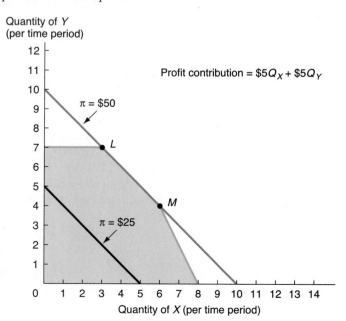

of great practical relevance because they can be used to solve complex linear programming problems with user-friendly computer software.

Slack Variables

The concept of **slack variables** must be introduced to solve linear programming problems algebraically. In the case of less-than-or-equal-to constraints, slack variables are used to *increase* the left side to equal the right side limits of the constraint conditions. In the illustrative problem, one slack variable is added to each constraint to account for excess capacity. The firm is faced with capacity constraints on input factors A, B, and C, so the algebraic specification of the problem contains three slack variables: S_A, indicating the units of A that are not used in any given solution; S_B, representing unused units of B; and S_C, which measures the unused units of C.

With slack variables, each constraint equation becomes an equality rather than an inequality. After adding the relevant slack variable, the constraint on input A, $4Q_X + 2Q_Y \leq 32$, is

(9.7)
$$4Q_X + 2Q_Y + S_A = 32$$

$S_A = 32 - 4Q_X - 2Q_Y$ is the amount of input A not used to produce X or Y. Similar equality constraints can be specified for inputs B and C. The equality form of the constraint on input B is

(9.8)
$$1Q_X + 1Q_Y + S_B = 10$$

The constraint equation for input C is

(9.9)
$$3Q_Y + S_C = 21$$

The introduction of slack variables not only simplifies algebraic analysis, but slack variables' solution values also provide useful information. In a production problem, for example, slack variables with *zero* values at the optimal solution indicate inputs that are limiting factors and cause bottlenecks. Slack variables with *positive* values at the optimal solution indicate excess capacity in the related input factor. Slack variables cannot take on negative values, because this would imply that the amount of resource use exceeds available supply. The information provided by slack variable solution values is important in long-range planning and is a key benefit derived from algebraic solution methods.

Algebraic Solution

The complete specification of the illustrative programming problem is as follows:

(9.3)
$$\text{Maximize } \pi = \$12Q_X + \$9Q_Y$$

subject to these constraints:

(9.7)
(9.8)
(9.9)
$$4Q_X + 2Q_Y + S_A = 32$$
$$1Q_X + 1Q_Y + S_B = 10$$
$$3Q_Y + S_C = 21$$

where

$$Q_X \geq 0, Q_Y \geq 0, S_A \geq 0, S_B \geq 0, S_C \geq 0$$

The problem is to find the set of values for variables Q_X, Q_Y, S_A, S_B, and S_C that maximizes Equation 9.3 and at the same time satisfies the constraints imposed by Equations 9.7, 9.8, and 9.9.

As shown previously, a single exact solution to a system of three constraint equations with five unknown variables cannot be determined without further information. A simultaneous solution to the constraint equations must be found, but there are more unknowns (five) than constraint equations (three). Here, a unique solution does not exist; multiple solutions are possible. However, because the solution to any linear programming problem occurs at a corner of the feasible space, values can be determined for some of the unknown variables in Equations 9.7, 9.8, and 9.9. At each corner point, the number of known constraint conditions is exactly equal to the number of unknown variables. In such circumstances, a single unique solution can be found for each variable at each corner point of the feasible space. The optimal solution is that corner point solution with the most desirable value for the objective function.[3]

Consider Figure 9.9, in which the feasible space for the illustrative problem has been graphed once again. At the origin, where neither X nor Y is produced, Q_X and Q_Y both equal zero. Slack exists in all inputs, however, so S_A, S_B, and S_C are all greater than zero. Now move up the vertical axis to point K. Here Q_X and S_C both equal zero, because no X is being produced and input C is being used to the fullest extent possible. However, Q_Y, S_A, and S_B all exceed zero. At point L, Q_X, Q_Y, and S_A are all positive, but S_B and S_C equal zero. The remaining corners, M and n, can be examined similarly, and at each of them the number of nonzero-valued variables exactly equals the number of constraints. At each corner point, the constraints can be expressed as a system with three equations and three unknowns that can be solved algebraically.

Solving the constraint equations at each corner point provides values for Q_X and Q_Y, as well as for S_A, S_B, and S_C. The total profit contribution at each corner is likewise determined by inserting relevant values for Q_X and Q_Y into the objective function (Equation 9.3). The corner solution that produces the maximum profit is the optimal solution to the linear programming problem.

This iterative process is followed in what is called the **simplex solution method**. Computer programs find solution values for all variables at each corner point, then isolate that corner point with the optimal solution to the objective function. Highly complex linear programming problems can be solved in only a few seconds when using the simplex method and high-speed desktop computers. They are long and tedious when done by hand. Although it is perhaps not worth delving into the simplex procedure in great detail, the method can be illustrated for the present example.

Although a unique solution for this problem is obtained when any two variables are set equal to zero, it is convenient to begin by setting Q_X and Q_Y equal to zero and examining the origin solution. Substituting zero values for Q_X and Q_Y into the constraint Equations 9.7, 9.8, and 9.9 results in a value for each slack variable that equals the total units available: $S_A = 32$, $S_B = 10$, and $S_C = 21$. At the origin, neither X nor Y is produced and no input is used in production. Total profit contribution at the origin corner of the feasible space is zero.

Similarly, it is possible to examine the solution at a second corner point, n in Figure 9.9, where Q_Y and S_A equal zero. After making the appropriate substitution into constraint Equation 9.7, the value for Q_X is

(9.7)

$$4Q_X + 2Q_Y + S_A = 32$$
$$(4 \times Q_X) + (2 \times 0) + 0 = 32$$
$$4Q_X = 32$$
$$Q_X = 8$$

With the value of Q_X determined, it is possible to substitute into Equations 9.8 and 9.9 and determine values for S_B and S_C:

simplex solution method
Iterative technique used to provide algebraic solutions for linear programming problems

---

3 In almost all linear programming problems, the number of nonzero-valued variables in all corner solutions exactly equals the number of constraints in the problem. Only under a particular condition known as *degeneracy*, when more than two constraints coincide at a single corner of the feasible space, are there fewer nonzero-valued variables. This condition does not hinder the technique of solution considered in this chapter.

FIGURE 9.9

Determination of Zero-Valued Variables at Corners of the Feasible Space

At all corner points of the feasible space, the number of nonzero-valued variables equals the number of constraint equations.

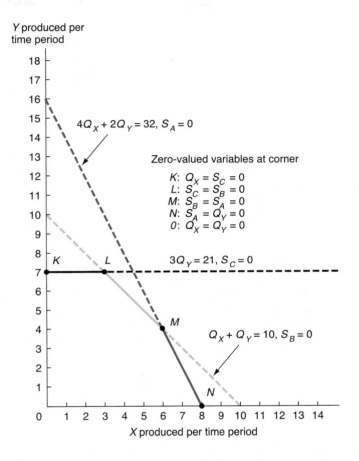

Y produced per time period

$4Q_X + 2Q_Y = 32$, $S_A = 0$

Zero-valued variables at corner

K: $Q_X = S_C = 0$
L: $S_C = S_B = 0$
M: $S_B = S_A = 0$
N: $S_A = Q_Y = 0$
0: $Q_X = Q_Y = 0$

$3Q_Y = 21$, $S_C = 0$

$Q_X + Q_Y = 10$, $S_B = 0$

X produced per time period

$$Q_X + Q_Y + S_B = 10$$

(9.8)
$$8 + 0 + S_B = 10$$
$$S_B = 2$$

and

(9.9)
$$3Q_Y + S_C = 21$$
$$(3 \times 0) + S_C = 21$$
$$S_C = 21$$

Total profit contribution at this point is

(9.3)
$$\pi = \$12Q_X + \$9Q_Y$$
$$= (\$12 \times 8) + (\$9 \times 0)$$
$$= \$96$$

Next, assign zero values to S_B and S_A to reach solution values for point M. Substituting zero values for S_A and S_B in Equations 9.7 and 9.8 results in two equations with two unknowns:

(9.7)
$$4Q_X + 2Q_Y + 0 = 32$$
(9.8)
$$Q_X + Q_Y + 0 = 10$$

Multiplying Equation 9.8 by two and subtracting this result from Equation 9.7 provides the solution value for Q_X:

(9.7)
$$4Q_X + 2Q_Y = 32$$
$$\text{minus } 2Q_X + 2Q_Y = 20$$
$$2Q_X = 12$$
$$Q_X = 6$$

Then, substituting 6 for Q_X in Equation 9.8 finds $Q_Y = 4$. Total profit contribution in this case is $108 [= (\$12 \times 6) + (\$9 \times 4)]$.

Similar algebraic analysis provides the solution for each remaining corner of the feasible space. However, rather than work through those corner solutions, the results are shown in Table 9.2. It is apparent, just as illustrated in the earlier graphic analysis, that the optimal solution occurs at point M, where 6 units of X and 4 units of Y are produced. Total profit is $108, which exceeds the profit at any other corner of the feasible space.

Slack Variables at the Solution Point

At each corner point solution, values for each slack variable are also determined. For example, at the optimal solution (corner M) reached in the preceding section, S_A and S_B both equal zero, meaning that inputs A and B are used to the fullest extent possible. S_C is not equal to zero and must be solved for. To find the solution for S_C, $Q_Y = 4$ is substituted into Constraint Equation 9.9:

(9.9)
$$3 \times Q_Y + S_C = 21$$
$$3 \times 4 + S_C = 21$$
$$S_C = 9$$

The optimal combination of X and Y completely exhausts available quantities of inputs A and B, but 9 units of input C remain unused. Because inputs A and B impose effective constraints on the firm's profits, more of each must be acquired to expand output. Input C is in excess supply, so the firm would certainly not want more capacity of C; it might even attempt to reduce its purchases of C during future periods. If C is a fixed facility, such as a machine tool, the firm might offer some of that excess capacity to other companies.

TABLE 9.2

Algebraic Solution to a Linear Programming Problem

Solution at Corner	Value of Variable					Total Profit Contribution
	Q_Y	Q_Y	S_A	S_B	S_C	
O	0	0	32	10	21	$ 0
N	8	0	0	2	21	$ 96
M	6	4	0	0	9	$108
L	3	7	6	0	0	$ 99
K	0	7	18	3	0	$ 63

Internet Message Boards

Message boards are online "communities" that allow people to communicate about common interests on the Internet. Common interests might include business topics, like linear programming and long-term investing, or nonbusiness interests, like gardening. On message boards, the communication is ongoing and broad-based. Hundreds of individuals may contribute to an especially active message board during the course of a few days. This is different from online "chat," where conversations are brief and visible only to a small handful of current participants. Although chat dialogue disappears after only a few moments, message board posts are longer and remain visible for extended periods. Message board dialogue is typically linked, so that interested parties can go back and forth about a given topic. Message board dialogue is also searchable, thus allowing for detailed exchanges to take place. Lively message board communities can be a productive and entertaining way of gathering useful business and economic information.

Message board categories contain different boards with a common theme. For example, there are 16 categories or broad grouping of interests listed on the Yahoo! Message Boards. The "Business & Finance" category, for example, has individual boards for discussing "Investments," "Services," "Communications Services," and Level 3 Communications, along with several hundred other individual companies in this field.

When using message boards, it's important to remember to

- **Be careful what you believe.** Message board information is no substitute for independent research. Don't rely on it for business or investment decisions.
- **Be skeptical of other posters.** Never assume people are who they say they are, know what they say they know, or are affiliated with whom they say they are affiliated.
- **Be careful what you post.** Never assume that you are anonymous and cannot be identified by your messages.

With these caveats in mind, by all means log on and check it out. You'll be amazed at what people are talking about on the Internet!

See: Nicholas Kulish, "SBC Official Says Microsoft's Power Could Limit New Messaging Service," *The Wall Street Journal Online*, April 9, 2002 (http://online.wsj.com).

Computer-Based Solution Methods

The linear programming problem illustrated thus far is simple by design. It can be solved graphically and algebraically to illustrate the linear programming technique using both methods. However, linear programming problems encountered in the real world are often quite complex and frequently involve a large number of constraints and output variables. Such problems are too complicated to solve graphically. The geometry is messy for three outputs and impossible for four or more. In real-world applications, computer software programs use algebraic techniques to handle large numbers of variables and constraints.

THE DUAL IN LINEAR PROGRAMMING

For every maximization problem in linear programming, there exists a symmetrical minimization problem; for every minimization problem, there exists a symmetrical maximization problem.

The Duality Concept

primal
Original problem statement (symmetrical to dual)

dual
Secondary problem statement (symmetrical to primal)

Pairs of related maximization and minimization problems are known as **primal** and **dual** linear programming problems. The concept of duality demonstrates the symmetry between the value of a firm's products and the value of resources used in production. With the duality concept, it is possible to show that value maximization can be attained by focusing on either resource requirements and the revenue-generating capability of a firm's products or on the cost of resources and their productivity.

In addition to providing valuable insight into the economics of optimal resource employment, duality provides the key to solving difficult constrained optimization problems. Because of the symmetry between primal and dual problem specifications, either one can be construct-ed from the other and the solution to either problem can be used to solve both. This is helpful because it is sometimes easier to obtain the solution to the dual problem than to the original or primal problem.

Finally, the duality concept also allows one to evaluate the solution to a constrained decision problem in terms of the activity required for optimization and in terms of the economic impact of constraint conditions. Analysis of the constraint conditions and slack variable solutions fre-quently provides important information for long-range planning. In fact, the **primal solution** is often described as a tool for short-run operating decisions, whereas the **dual solution** is often seen as a tool for long-range planning. The duality concept shows how operating decisions and long-range planning are related.

primal solution
Input for short-run operating decisions

dual solution
Input for long-range planning

Shadow Prices

shadow prices
Implicit values associ-ated with linear-programming-problem decision variables

To examine the duality concept, the idea of implicit values or **shadow prices** must be intro-duced. In the primal linear programming problem discussed previously, the values Q_X and Q_Y maximize the firm's profit subject to constraints imposed by limitations of input factors A, B, and C. Duality theory indicates that an identical operating decision would result if one had instead chosen to minimize the costs of resources employed in producing Q_X and Q_Y, subject to an output constraint.

The key to this duality is that relevant costs are not the acquisition costs of inputs but, rather, the economic costs of using them. For a resource that is available in a fixed amount, this cost is not acquisition cost but opportunity cost. Consider, for example, a skilled labor force employed by a firm. If workers are fully utilized producing valuable products, a reduction in skilled labor will reduce valuable output, and an increase in skilled labor will increase the production of valuable output. If some labor is shifted from the production of one product to another, the cost of using skilled labor in this new activity is the value of the original product that can no longer be produced. The marginal cost of a constrained resource that is fully utilized is its opportunity cost as measured by the value of foregone production. If a limited resource such as skilled labor is not fully utilized, then at least the last unit of that resource is not productive and its marginal value is zero. Acquiring additional excess resources does not increase valuable output. The firm would incur a zero opportunity cost if it applied currently unused resources in some different activity.

The economic value, or opportunity cost, of a constrained resource depends on the extent to which it is utilized. When a limited resource is fully utilized, its marginal value in use is positive. When a constrained resource is not fully utilized, its marginal value in use is zero. Minimizing the value of limited resources used to produce valuable output is nothing more than minimiz-ing the opportunity cost of employing those resources. Minimization of opportunity costs is equivalent to maximizing the value of output produced with those resources.

Because the economic value of constrained resources is determined by their value in use rather than by historical acquisition costs, such amounts are called implicit values or shadow prices. The term *shadow price* is used because it represents the price that a manager would be willing to pay for additional units of a constrained resource. Comparing the shadow price of a resource with its acquisition price indicates whether the firm has an incentive to increase or decrease the amount acquired during future production periods. If shadow prices exceed acquisition prices, the resource's marginal value exceeds marginal cost and the firm has an incentive to expand employment. If acquisition cost exceeds the shadow price, there is an incentive to reduce employment. These relations and the importance of duality can be clari-fied by relating the dual to the linear programming problem discussed previously.

Dual Objective Function[4]

In the original or primal problem statement, the goal is to maximize profits, and the (primal) objective function is

(9.3)
$$\text{Maximize } \pi = \$12Q_X + \$9Q_Y$$

The dual problem goal is to minimize implicit values or shadow prices for the firm's resources. Defining V_A, V_B, and V_C as the shadow prices for inputs A, B, and C, respectively, and π^* as the total implicit value of the firm's fixed resources, the dual objective function (the dual) is

(9.10)
$$\text{Minimize } \pi^* = 32V_A + 10V_B + 21V_C$$

Because the firm has 32 units of A, the total implicit value of input A is 32 times A's shadow price, or $32V_A$. If V_A, or input A's shadow price, is found to be \$1.50 when the dual equations are solved, the implicit value of A is \$48 (= 32 × \$1.50). Inputs B and C are handled in the same way.

Dual Constraints

In the primal problem, the constraints stated that the total units of each input used to produce X and Y must be equal to or less than the available quantity of input. In the dual, the constraints state that the total value of inputs used to produce one unit of X or one unit of Y must not be less than the profit contribution provided by a unit of these products. In other words, the shadow prices of A, B, and C times the amount of each of the inputs needed to produce a unit of X or Y must be equal to or greater than the unit profit contribution of X or of Y. Because resources have value only when used to produce output, they can never have an implicit value, or opportunity cost, that is less than the value of output.

In the example, unit profit is defined as the excess of price over variable cost, price and variable cost are both constant, and profit per unit for X is \$12 and for Y is \$9. As shown in Table 9.1, each unit of X requires 4 units of A, 1 unit of B, and 0 units of C. The total implicit value of resources used to produce X is $4V_A + 1V_B$. The constraint requiring that the implicit cost of producing X be equal to or greater than the profit contribution of X is

(9.11)
$$4V_A + 1V_B \geq 12$$

Because 2 units of A, 1 unit of B, and 3 units of C are required to produce each unit of Y, the second dual constraint is

(9.12)
$$2V_A + 1V_B + 3V_C \geq 9$$

Because the firm produces only two products, the dual problem has only two constraint equations.

Dual Slack Variables

Dual slack variables can be incorporated into the problem, thus allowing the constraint conditions to be expressed as equalities. Letting L_X and L_Y represent the two slack variables, constraint Equations 9.11 and 9.12 become

---

4 Rules for constructing the dual linear programming problem from its related primal are provided in Appendix 9A, at the end of this chapter.

(9.13)
$$4V_A + 1V_B - L_X = 12$$

and

(9.14)
$$2V_A + 1V_B + 3V_C - L_Y = 9$$

These slack variables are *subtracted* from the constraint equations, because greater-than-or-equal-to inequalities are involved. Using slack variables, the left-hand sides of the constraint conditions are thus *decreased* to equal the right-hand sides' profit contributions. Dual slack variables measure the *excess* of input value over output value for each product. Alternatively, dual slack variables measure the opportunity cost associated with producing X and Y. This can be seen by examining the two constraint equations. Solving constraint Equation 9.13 for L_X, for example, provides

$$L_X = 4V_A + 1V_B - 12$$

This expression states that L_X is equal to the implicit cost of producing 1 unit of X minus the profit contribution provided by that product. The dual slack variable L_X is a measure of the opportunity cost of producing product X. It compares the profit contribution of product X, \$12, with the value to the firm of the resources necessary to produce it.

A zero value for L_X indicates that the marginal value of resources required to produce 1 unit of X is exactly equal to the profit contribution received. This is similar to marginal cost being equal to marginal revenue at the profit-maximizing output level. A positive value for L_X indicates that the resources used to produce X are more valuable, in terms of the profit contribution they can generate, when used to produce the other product Y. A positive value for L_X measures the firm's opportunity cost (profit loss) associated with production of product X. The slack variable L_Y is the opportunity cost of producing product Y. It will have a value of zero if the implicit value of resources used to produce 1 unit of Y exactly equals the \$9 profit contribution provided by that product. A positive value for L_Y measures the opportunity loss in terms of the foregone profit contribution associated with product Y.

A firm would not choose to produce if the value of resources required were greater than the value of resulting output. It follows that a product with a positive slack variable (opportunity cost) is not included in the optimal production combination.

Solving the Dual Problem

The dual programming problem can be solved with the same algebraic technique that was employed to obtain the primal solution. In this case, the dual problem is

(9.10)
$$\text{Minimize } \pi^* = 34V_A + 10V_B + 21V_C$$

subject to

(9.13)
$$4V_A + 1V_B - L_X = 12$$

and

(9.14)
$$2V_A + 1V_B + 3V_C - L_Y = 9$$

where

$$V_A, V_B, V_C, L_X, \text{ and } L_Y \text{ all} \geq 0$$

Because there are only two constraints in this programming problem, the maximum number of nonzero-valued variables at any corner solution is two. One can proceed with the solution by setting three of the variables equal to zero and solving the constraint equations for the values of the remaining two. By comparing the value of the objective function at each feasible solution, the point at which the function is minimized can be determined. This is the dual solution.

To illustrate the process, first set $V_A = V_B = V_C = 0$, and solve for L_X and L_Y:

(9.13)
$$(4 \times 0) + (1 \times 0) - L_X = 12$$
$$L_X = -12$$

(9.14)
$$(2 \times 0) + (1 \times 0) + 0 + (3 \times 0) - L_Y = 9$$
$$L_Y = -9$$

Because L_X and L_Y cannot be negative, this solution is outside the feasible set.

The values just obtained are inserted into Table 9.3 as solution 1. All other solution values can be calculated in a similar manner and used to complete Table 9.3. It is apparent from the table that not all solutions lie within the feasible space. Only solutions 5, 7, 9, and 10 meet the nonnegativity requirement while also providing a number of nonzero-valued variables that are exactly equal to the number of constraints. These four solutions coincide with the corners of the dual problem's feasible space.

At solution 10, the total implicit value of inputs A, B, and C is minimized. Solution 10 is the optimum solution, where the total implicit value of employed resources exactly equals the $108 maximum profit primal solution. Thus, optimal solutions to primal and dual objective functions are identical.

At the optimal solution, the shadow price for input C is zero, $V_C = 0$. Because shadow price measures the marginal value of an input, a zero shadow price implies that the resource in question has a zero marginal value to the firm. Adding another unit of this input adds nothing to the firm's maximum obtainable profit. A zero shadow price for input C is consistent with the primal solution that input C is not a binding constraint. Excess capacity exists in C, so additional units of C would not increase production of either X or Y. The shadow price for input A of $1.50 implies that this fixed resource imposes a binding constraint. If an additional unit of

TABLE 9.3

Solutions for the Dual Programming Problem

Solution Number	V_A	V_B	V_C	L_X	L_Y	Total Value Imputed to the Firm's Resources
1	0	0	0	-12	-9	a
2	0	0	3	-12	0	a
3	0	0	b	0	b	a
4	0	9	0	-3	0	a
5	0	12	0	0	3	$120
6	0	12	-1	0	0	a
7	4.5	0	0	6	0	$144
8	3	0	0	0	-3	a
9	3	0	1	0	0	$117
10	1.5	6	0	0	0	$108

a   Outside the feasible space.
b   No solution.

A is added, the firm can increase total profit by $1.50. It would increase profits to buy additional units of input *A* at any price less than $1.50 per unit, at least up until the point at which *A* is no longer a binding constraint. This assumes that the cost of input *A* is currently fixed. If those costs are variable, the firm would be willing to pay $1.50 *above* the current price of input *A* to eliminate this constraint. Because availability of *B* also imposes an effective constraint, the firm can also afford to pay up to $6 for a marginal unit of *B*.

Finally, both dual slack variables equal zero at the optimal solution. This means that the implicit value of resources required to produce a single unit of *X* or *Y* is exactly equal to the profit contribution provided. The opportunity cost of producing *X* and *Y* is zero, meaning that the resources required for their production are not more valuable in some alternative use. This is consistent with the primal solution, because both *X* and *Y* are produced at the optimal solution. Any product with a positive opportunity cost is suboptimal and would not be produced.

Using the Dual Solution to Solve the Primal

The dual solution does not indicate optimal amounts of *X* and *Y*. It does, however, provide all the information necessary to determine the optimum output mix. The dual solution shows that input *C* does not impose a binding constraint on output of *X* and *Y*. Further, it demonstrates that $\pi = \pi^*$ = $108 at the optimum output of *X* and *Y*. The dual solution also offers evidence on the value of primal constraint slack variables. To see this, recall the three constraints in the primal problem:

$$\text{Constraint on } A: \quad 4Q_X + 2Q_Y + S_A = 32$$
$$\text{Constraint on } B: \quad 1Q_X + 1Q_Y + S_B = 10$$
$$\text{Constraint on } C: \quad 3Q_Y + S_C = 21$$

The dual solution indicates that the constraints on *A* and *B* are binding, because both inputs have positive shadow prices, and only resources that are fully utilized have a nonzero marginal value. Accordingly, the slack variables S_A and S_B equal zero, and the binding primal constraints can be rewritten as

$$4Q_X + 2Q_Y = 32$$

and

$$1Q_X + 1Q_Y = 10$$

With two equations and only two unknowns, this system can be solved for Q_X and Q_Y. Multiplying the second constraint by two and subtracting from the first provides

$$4Q_X + 2Q_Y = 32$$
$$\text{minus } 2Q_X + 2Q_Y = 20$$
$$2Q_X = 12$$
$$Q_X = 6$$

and

$$6 + Q_Y = 10$$
$$Q_Y = 4$$

These values of Q_X and Q_Y, found after learning from the dual which constraints were binding, are identical to the values found by solving the primal problem directly. Having obtained the value for Q_Y, it is possible to substitute value for Q_Y in constraint *C* and solve for the amount of slack in that resource:

It's a RIOT on the Internet!

Here's an idea for you. How would you like access to a Remote Interactive Optimization Testbed (RIOT) on the Internet? It's a simple concept, as in simply amazing.

RIOT creates an interface between the Web and linear programming solver programs that allows anyone with access to the Web to submit a linear program and have it solved. There has been a proliferation of linear programming solver software since 1980, like *Cplex, Lingo, Minos,* and so on. However, each of these solver programs implements different algorithms, like the simplex method, and offers different solution options, like sensitivity analysis. Depending on the problem to be solved, some solvers can be more or less efficient than others in terms of speed, accuracy, number of iterations, and available options.

LP applications on RIOT range from the serious, like a planar robot simulator with obstacle avoidance and open-pit mining problems, to the whimsical, like major league baseball and basketball elimination problems. Over time, continuing improvements promise users the opportunity to find the optimal value (maximum or minimum) for any linear function of a certain number of variables given a set of m linear constraints on these variables (equalities or inequalities).

Like everything on the Web, RIOT is still relatively new and bound to evolve rapidly over time. At this point, it is a free offering designed to achieve four main objectives:.

- **Educational.** RIOT provides educational information via HTML and interactive problems presented through an easy-to-use interface.

- **Research.** RIOT showcases state-of-the-art algorithms developed locally by UC Berkeley engineering faculty and others.

- **Comparative research.** RIOT provides efficiency information for different algorithms that solve similar problems.

- **Showcase applications.** RIOT provides a forum to showcase new and innovative applications of linear programming techniques.

RIOT is an enormously practical tool. It's on the Internet. It's free. What a RIOT!

See: Home page for RIOT can be found on the Internet (http://riot.ieor.berkeley.edu/riot/index.html).

$$3Q_Y + S_C = 21$$
$$S_C = 21 - 3 \times 4 = 9$$

These relations, which allow one to solve either the primal or the dual specification of a linear programming problem and then quickly obtain the solution to the other, can be generalized by the two following expressions:

(9.15)   Primal Objective Variable$_i$ × Dual Slack Variable$_i$ ≡ 0

(9.16)   Primal Slack Variable$_j$ × Dual Objective Variable$_j$ ≡ 0

Equation 9.15 states that if an ordinary variable in the primal problem takes on a nonzero value in the optimal solution to that problem, its related dual slack variable must be zero. Only if a particular Q_i is zero valued in the solution to the primal can its related dual slack variable, L_i, take on a nonzero value. A similar relation exists between the slack variables in the primal problem and their related ordinary variables in the dual, as indicated by Equation 9.16. If the primal slack variable is nonzero valued, then the related dual variable will be zero valued, and vice versa.

CONSTRAINED COST MINIMIZATION: ANOTHER LP EXAMPLE

Constrained cost-minimization problems are frequently encountered in managerial decision making. One such example is the problem of minimizing advertising expenditures subject to certain audience exposure requirements.

Background Information

Consider a firm that is planning an advertising campaign for a new product. Goals set for the campaign include exposure to at least 100,000 individuals, no fewer than 80,000 of whom have an annual income of at least $50,000 and no fewer than 40,000 of whom are single. For simplicity, assume that the firm has only radio and television media available for this campaign. One television advertisement costs $10,000 and is expected to reach an average audience of 20,000 persons. Ten thousand of these individuals will have an income of $50,000 or more, and 4,000 will be single. A radio advertisement costs $6,000 and reaches a total audience of 10,000, all of whom have at least $50,000 in income. Eight thousand of those exposed to a radio advertisement are single. Table 9.4 summarizes these data.

Primal Problem

The objective is to minimize the cost of the advertising campaign. Because total cost is merely the sum of the amounts spent on radio and television advertisements, the objective function is

$$\text{Minimize Cost} = \$6,000R + \$10,000TV$$

where R and TV represent the number of radio and television ads, respectively, that are employed in the advertising campaign.

This linear programming problem has three constraint equations, including the minimum audience exposure requirement, the audience income requirement, and the marital status requirement. The minimum audience exposure requirement states that the number of persons exposed to radio ads plus the number exposed to television ads must be equal to or greater than 100,000 persons. Algebraically, 10,000 times the number of radio ads plus 20,000 times the number of television advertisements must be equal to or greater than 100,000:

$$10,000R + 20,000TV \geq 100,000$$

The two remaining constraints can be constructed in a similar fashion from the data in Table 9.4. The audience income constraint is written

$$10,000R + 10,000TV \geq 80,000$$

and the marital status constraint is given by

$$8,000R + 4,000TV \geq 40,000$$

Combining the cost-minimization objective function with these three constraint conditions written in equality form using slack variables gives the complete linear programming problem:

TABLE 9.4

Advertising Media Relations

	Radio	Television
Cost per ad	$ 6,000	$10,000
Total audience per ad	10,000	20,000
Audience per ad with income ≥$50,000	10,000	10,000
Unmarried audience per ad	8,000	4,000

$$\text{Minimize Cost} = \$6{,}000R + \$10{,}000TV$$

subject to

$$10{,}000R + 20{,}000TV - S_A = 100{,}000$$
$$10{,}000R + 10{,}000TV - S_I = 80{,}000$$
$$8{,}000R + 4{,}000TV - S_S = 40{,}000$$

and

$$R, TV, S_A, S_I, \text{ and } S_S \geq 0$$

S_A, S_I, and S_S are slack variables indicating the extent to which minimums on total audience exposure, exposure to individuals with incomes of at least \$50,000, and exposure to single individuals, respectively, have been exceeded. Note that each slack variable is *subtracted* from the relevant constraint equation because greater-than-or-equal-to inequalities are involved. Excess capacity or nonzero slack variables for any of the constraints mean that audience exposure minimums have been exceeded.

The solution to this linear programming problem is easily obtained using a combination of graphic and analytical methods. Figure 9.10 illustrates this solution. The feasible space problem

FIGURE 9.10

Advertising Cost-Minimization Linear Programming Problem

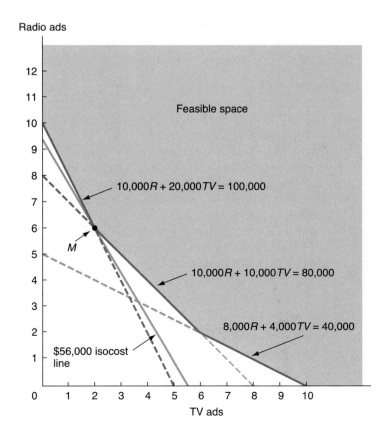

is bordered by the three constraint equations and the nonnegativity requirements. An isocost curve shows that costs are minimized at point M, where the total audience exposure and income constraints are binding. With these constraints binding, slack variables $S_A = S_I = 0$. Thus,

$$
\begin{aligned}
10,000R + 20,000TV &= 100,000 \\
\text{minus } 10,000R + 10,000TV &= 80,000 \\
\hline
10,000TV &= 20,000 \\
TV &= 2
\end{aligned}
$$

and

$$
\begin{aligned}
10,000R + 20,000(2) &= 100,000 \\
10,000R &= 60,000 \\
R &= 6
\end{aligned}
$$

The firm should employ six radio advertisements and two television advertisements to minimize costs while still meeting audience exposure requirements. Total cost for such a campaign is $56,000.

Dual Problem

The dual to the advertising-mix problem is a constrained-maximization problem, because the primal is a minimization problem. The objective function of the dual is expressed in terms of shadow prices or implicit values for the primal constraint conditions. The dual objective function includes an implicit value, or shadow price, for the minimum audience exposure requirement, the audience income requirement, and the marital status requirement. Because constraint limits in the primal problem become the dual objective function coefficients, the dual objective function is

$$
\text{Maximize } C^* = 100,000V_A + 80,000V_I + 40,000V_S
$$

where V_A, V_I, and V_S are shadow prices for the minimum audience exposure, audience income, and marital status requirements.

Dual constraints are based on the two variables from the primal objective function. Thus, there are two constraint conditions in the dual, the first associated with radio advertisements and the second with television advertisements. Both constraints are of the less-than-or-equal-to type, because primal constraints are of the greater-than-or-equal-to type.

The radio advertising constraint limit is the $6,000 radio advertisements coefficient from the primal objective function. Coefficients for each shadow price in this constraint equation are given by the advertising effectiveness measures for a single radio advertisement. The coefficient for the audience exposure shadow price, V_A, is 10,000, the number of individuals reached by a single radio advertisement. Similarly, the coefficient for V_I is 10,000 and that for V_S is 8,000. Thus, the dual radio advertisements constraint is

$$
10,000V_A + 10,000V_I + 8,000V_S \leq \$6,000
$$

The dual television advertising constraint is developed in the same fashion. Because each TV advertisement reaches a total audience of 20,000, this is the coefficient for the V_A variable in the second dual constraint equation. Coefficients for V_I and V_S are 10,000 and 4,000, respectively, because these are the numbers of high-income and single persons reached by one TV advertisement. The $10,000 cost of a television advertisement is the limit to the second dual constraint, which can be written

$$20{,}000V_A + 10{,}000V_I + 4{,}000V_S \leq \$10{,}000$$

Following the introduction of constraint slack variables, the dual programming problem is

$$\text{Maximize } C^* = 100{,}000V_A + 80{,}000V_I + 40{,}000V_S$$

subject to

$$10{,}000V_A + 10{,}000V_I + 8{,}000V_S + L_R = \$\,6{,}000$$
$$20{,}000V_A + 10{,}000V_I + 4{,}000V_S + L_{TV} = \$10{,}000$$

and

$$V_A, V_I, V_S, L_R, \text{ and } L_{TV} \geq 0$$

Solving the Dual

It is possible but difficult to solve this dual problem using a three-dimensional graph or the simplex method. However, because the primal problem has been solved already, information from this solution can be used to easily solve the dual. Remember that the solutions to the primal and dual of a single linear programming problem are complementary, and the following must hold:

$$\text{Primal Objective Variable}_i \times \text{Dual Slack Variable}_i = 0$$
$$\text{Primal Slack Variable}_j \times \text{Dual Objective Variable}_j = 0$$

In this linear programming problem,

$$R \times L_R = 0 \text{ and } TV \times L_{TV} = 0$$

and

$$S_A \times V_A = 0, S_I \times V_I = 0, \text{ and } S_S \times V_S = 0$$

Because both R and TV have nonzero solutions in the primal, the dual slack variables L_R and L_{TV} must equal zero at the optimal solution. Furthermore, because there is excess audience exposure to the single marital status category in the primal solution, $S_S \neq 0$, the related dual shadow price variable V_S must also equal zero in the optimal solution. This leaves only V_A and V_I as two unknowns in the two-equation system of dual constraints:

$$10{,}000V_A + 10{,}000V_I = \$\,6{,}000$$
$$20{,}000V_A + 10{,}000V_I = \$10{,}000$$

Subtracting the second constraint equation from the first gives

$$-10{,}000V_A = -\$4{,}000$$
$$V_A = \$0.40$$

Substituting the value $0.40 for VA in either constraint equation produces a value of $0.20 for V_I. Finally, substituting the appropriate values for V_A, V_I, and V_S into the dual objective function gives a value of $C^* = \$56{,}000$ [= ($0.40 × 100,000) + ($0.20 × 80,000) + ($0 × 40,000)]. This is the same figure as the $56,000 minimum cost solution to the primal.

Interpreting the Dual Solution

The primal solution tells management the minimum-cost advertising mix. The dual problem results are equally valuable. Each dual shadow price indicates the change in cost that would accompany a one-unit change in the various audience exposure requirements. These prices show the marginal costs of increasing each audience exposure requirement by one unit. For example, V_A is the marginal cost of reaching the last individual in the overall audience. If there were a one-person reduction in the total audience exposure requirement, a cost saving of $V_A = \$0.40$ would be realized. The marginal cost of increasing total audience exposure from 100,000 to 100,001 individuals would also be 40¢.

Shadow prices for the remaining constraint conditions are interpreted in a similar manner. The shadow price for reaching individuals with incomes of at least $50,000 is $V_I = \$0.20$, or 20¢. It would cost an extra 20¢ per person to reach more high-income individuals. A zero value for V_S, the marital status shadow price, means that the proposed advertising campaign already reaches more than the 40,000 minimum required number of single persons. Thus, a small change in the marital status constraint has no effect on total costs.

By comparing these marginal costs with the benefits derived from additional exposure, management is able to judge the effectiveness of its media advertising campaign. If the expected profit per exposure exceeds 40¢, it would prove profitable to design an advertising campaign for a larger audience. Likewise, if the expected return per exposure to high-income individuals is greater than 20¢, promotion to this category of potential customers should be increased. Conversely, if marginal profitability is less than marginal cost, audience size and/or income requirements should be reduced.

Dual slack variables also have an interesting interpretation. They represent opportunity costs of using each advertising medium. L_R measures the excess of cost over benefit associated with using radio, whereas L_{TV} indicates the excess of cost over benefit for television. Since $L_R = L_{TV} = 0$, the marginal benefit derived just equals the marginal cost incurred for both media. Both radio and TV are included in the optimal media mix, as was indicated in the primal solution.

This example again demonstrates the symmetry of the primal and dual specifications of linear programming problems. Either specification can be used to describe and solve the same basic problem. Both primal and dual problem statements and solutions offer valuable insight for decision making.

SUMMARY

Linear programming is a valuable technique for solving maximization or minimization problems in which inequality constraints are imposed on the decision maker. This chapter introduces graphic and analytic approaches for setting up, solving, and interpreting the solutions to such problems.

- **Linear programming** is a proven tool used to isolate the best solution, or **optimal solution**, to decision problems. The technique is ideally suited to solving decision problems that involve an objective function to be maximized or minimized, where the relevant objective function is subject to inequality constraints.

- Simple linear programming problems can be solved graphically using the **relative distance method**. The **feasible space** is the graphical region showing the linear programming problem solution space that is both technically and economically feasible.

- An equation that expresses the goal of a linear programming problem is called the **objective function**.

- The optimal solution to a linear programming problem occurs at the intersection of the objective function and a **corner point** of the feasible space. A corner point is a spot in the feasible space where the *X*-axis, *Y*-axis, or constraint conditions intersect.

- **Slack variables** indicate the amount by which constraint conditions are exceeded. In the case of less-than-or-equal-to constraints, slack variables are used to *increase* the left side to equal the right side limits of the constraint conditions. In the case of greater-than-or-equal-to constraints, slack variables are used to *decrease* the left side to equal the right side limits of the constraint conditions.
- The **simplex solution method** is an iterative method used to solve linear programming problems. In this procedure, computer programs find solution values for all variables at each corner point, then isolate that corner point with the optimal solution to the objective function.
- For every maximization problem in linear programming, there exists a symmetrical minimization problem; for every minimization problem, there exists a symmetrical maximization problem. These pairs of related maximization and minimization problems are known as the **primal** and **dual** linear programming problems.
- The **primal solution** is often described as a tool for short-run operating decisions, whereas the **dual solution** is often seen as a tool for long-range planning. Both provide management with valuable insight for the decision-making process.
- **Shadow prices** are implicit values or opportunity costs associated with linear programming problem decision variables. In the case of output, shadow prices indicate the marginal cost of a one-unit increase in output. In the case of the constraints, shadow prices indicate the marginal cost of a one-unit relaxation in the constraint condition.

During recent years, rapid advances in user-friendly computer software have allowed the widespread application of linear programming techniques to a broad range of complex managerial decision problems. With the background provided in this chapter, it is possible to apply this powerful technique to a wide array of problems in business, government, and the not-for-profit sector.

QUESTIONS

Q9.1 Give some illustrations of managerial decision situations in which you think the linear programming technique would be useful.

Q9.2 Why can't linear programming be used in each of the following circumstances

A. Strong economies of scale exist.

B. As the firm expands output, the prices of variable factors of production increase.

C. As output increases, product prices decline.

Q9.3 Do equal distances along a given production process ray in a linear programming problem always represent an identical level of output?

Q9.4 Assume that output can be produced only using processes A and B. Process A requires inputs L and K to be combined in the fixed ratio $2L{:}4K$, and process B requires $4L{:}2K$. Is it possible to produce output efficiently using $3L$ and $3K$? Why or why not?

Q9.5 Describe the relative distance method used in graphic linear programming analysis.

Q9.6 Is the number of isocost, isorevenue, or isoprofit lines in a typical two-input bounded feasible space limited?

Q9.7 In linear programming, why is it so critical that the number of nonzero-valued variables exactly equals the number of constraints at corners of the feasible space?

Q9.8 Will maximizing a profit contribution objective function always result in also maximizing total net profits?

Q9.9 The primal problem calls for determining the set of outputs that will maximize profit, subject to input constraints.

A. What is the dual objective function?

B. What interpretation can be given to the dual variables called the shadow prices or implicit values?

C. What does it mean if a dual variable or shadow price equals zero?

Q9.10 How are the solution values for primal and dual linear programming problems actually employed in practice?

SELF-TEST PROBLEMS AND SOLUTIONS

ST9.1 **Cost Minimization.** Idaho Natural Resources (INR) has two mines with different production capabilities for producing the same type of ore. After mining and crushing, the ore is graded into three classes: high, medium, and low. The company has contracted to provide local smelters with 24 tons of high-grade ore, 16 tons of medium-grade ore, and 48 tons of low-grade ore each week. It costs INR $10,000 per day to operate mine A and $5,000 per day to run mine B. In a day's time, mine A produces 6 tons of high-grade ore, 2 tons of medium-grade ore, and 4 tons of low-grade ore. Mine B produces 2, 2, and 12 tons per day of each grade, respectively. Management's short-run problem is to determine how many days per week to operate each mine under current conditions. In the long run, management wishes to know how sensitive these decisions will be to changing economic conditions.

A report prepared for the company by an independent management consultant addressed the company's short-run operating concerns. The consultant claimed that the operating problem could be solved using linear programming techniques by which the firm would seek to minimize the total cost of meeting contractual requirements. Specifically, the consultant recommended that INR do the following:

$$\text{Minimize Total Cost} = \$10,000A + \$5,000B$$

subject to

$6A + 2B \geq 24$	(high-grade ore constraint)
$2A + 2B \geq 16$	(medium-grade ore constraint)
$4A + 12B \geq 48$	(low-grade ore constraint)
$A \leq 7$	(mine A operating days in a week constraint)
$B \leq 7$	(mine B operating days in a week constraint)

or, in their equality form,

$$6A + 2B - S_H = 24$$
$$2A + 2B - S_M = 16$$
$$4A + 12B - S_L = 48$$
$$A + S_A = 7$$
$$B + S_B = 7$$

where

$$A, B, S_H, S_M, S_L, S_A, \text{ and } S_B \geq 0$$

Here, A and B represent the days of operation per week for each mine; S_H, S_M, and S_L represent excess production of high-, medium-, and low-grade ore, respectively; and S_A and S_B are days per week that each mine is not operated.

A graphic representation of the linear programming problem was also provided. The graph suggests an optimal solution at point X, where constraints 1 and 2 are binding. Thus, $S_H = S_M = 0$ and

$$
\begin{array}{rcl}
6A + 2B - 0 & = & 24 \\
\text{minus } \underline{2A + 2B - 0} & = & \underline{16} \\
4A & = & 8 \\
A & = & 2 \text{ days per week}
\end{array}
$$

Substitute $A = 2$ into the high-grade ore constraint:

$$
\begin{array}{rcl}
6(2) + 2B & = & 24 \\
12 + 2B & = & 24 \\
2B & = & 12 \\
B & = & 6 \text{ days per week}
\end{array}
$$

A minimum total operating cost per week of $50,000 is suggested, because

$$
\begin{array}{rcl}
\text{Total Cost} & = & \$10,000A + \$5,000B \\
& = & \$10,000(2) + \$5,000(6) \\
& = & \$50,000
\end{array}
$$

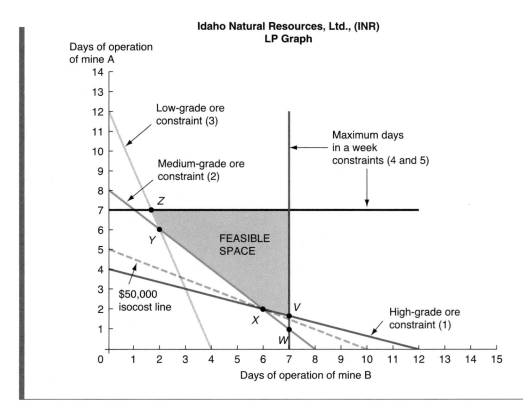

**Idaho Natural Resources, Ltd., (INR)
LP Graph**

The consultant's report did not discuss a variety of important long-run planning issues. Specifically, INR wishes to know the following, holding all else equal:

A. How much, if any, excess production would result if the consultant's operating recommendation were followed?

B. What would be the cost effect of increasing low-grade ore sales by 50%?

C. What is INR's minimum acceptable price per ton if it is to renew a current contract to provide one of its customers with 6 tons of high-grade ore per week?

D. With current output requirements, how much would the cost of operating mine A have to rise before INR would change its operating decision?

E. What increase in the cost of operating mine B would cause INR to change its current operating decision?

ST9.1 Solution

A. If the consultant's operating recommendation of $A = 2$ and $B = 6$ were followed, 32 tons of excess low-grade ore production would result. No excess production of high- or medium-grade ore would occur. This can be shown by solving for S_H, S_M, and S_L at the recommended activity level.

From the constraint equations, we find the following:

$$(1) \qquad 6(2) + 2(6) - S_H = 24$$
$$S_H = 0$$
$$(2) \qquad 2(2) + 2(6) - S_M = 16$$
$$S_M = 0$$
$$(3) \qquad 4(2) + 12(6) - S_L = 48$$
$$S_L = 32$$

B. There would be a *zero cost impact* of an increase in low-grade ore sales from 48 to 72 tons (= 1.5×48). With $A = 2$ and $B = 6$, 80 tons of low-grade ore are produced. A 50% increase in low-grade ore sales would simply reduce excess production from $S_L = 32$ to $S_L = 8$, because

$$(3') \qquad 4(2) + 12(6) - S_L = 72$$
$$S_L = 8$$

Graphically, the effect of a 50% increase in low-grade ore sales would be to cause a rightward shift in the low-grade ore constraint to a new constraint line with endpoints $(0B, 18A)$ and $(6B, 0A)$. Although such a shift would reduce the feasible space, it would not affect the optimal operating decision of $A = 2$ and $B = 6$ (at point X).

C. If INR did not renew a contract to provide one of its current customers with 6 tons of high-grade ore per week, the high-grade ore constraint would fall from 24 to 18 tons per week. The new high-grade ore constraint, reflecting a parallel leftward shift, is written

$$(1') \qquad 6A + 2B - S_H = 18$$

and has endpoints $(0B, 3A)$ and $(9B, 0A)$. With such a reduction in required high-grade ore sales, the high-grade ore constraint would no longer be binding and the optimal production point would shift to point W, and $A = 1$ and $B = 7$ (because $S_M = S_B = 0$). At this point, high-grade ore production would equal 20 tons, or 2 tons more than the new high-grade ore requirement:

$$6(1) + 2(7) - S_H = 18$$
$$S_H = 2$$

with operating costs of

$$\text{Total Cost} = \$10{,}000A + \$5{,}000B$$
$$= \$10{,}000(1) + \$5{,}000(7)$$
$$= \$45{,}000$$

Therefore, renewing a contract to provide one of its current customers with 6 tons of high-grade ore per week would result in our earlier operating decision of $A = 2$ and $B = 6$ and total costs of $50,000, rather than the $A = 1$ and $B = 7$ and total costs of $45,000 that would otherwise be possible. The marginal cost of renewing the 6-ton contract is $5,000, or $833 per ton.

$$\text{Marginal Cost} = \frac{\text{Change in Operating Costs}}{\text{Number of Tons}}$$
$$= \frac{\$50{,}000 - \$45{,}000}{6}$$
$$= \$833 \text{ per ton}$$

D. In general, the isocost relation for this problem is

$$C_0 = C_A A + C_B B$$

where C_0 is any weekly cost level, and C_A and C_B are the daily operating costs for mines A and B, respectively. In terms of the graph, A is on the vertical axis and B is on the horizontal axis. From the isocost formula we find the following:

$$A = C_0/C_A - (C_B/C_A)B$$

with an intercept of C_0/C_A and a slope equal to $-(C_B/C_A)$. The isocost line will become steeper as C_B increases relative to C_A. The isocost line will become flatter (slope will approach zero) as C_B falls relative to C_A.

   If C_A increases to slightly more than $15,000, the optimal feasible point will shift from point X ($6B$, $2A$) to point V ($7B$, $1.67A$), because the isocost line slope will then be less than $-1/3$, the slope of the high-grade ore constraint ($A = 4 - (1/3)B$). Thus, an increase in C_A from $10,000 to at least $15,000, or an increase of *at least $5,000*, is necessary before the optimal operating decision will change.

E. An increase in C_B of *at least $5,000* to slightly more than $10,000 will shift the optimal point from point X to point Y ($2B$, $6A$), because the isocost line slope will then be steeper than -1, the slope of the medium-grade ore constraint ($A = 8 - B$).

   An increase in C_B to slightly more than $30,000 will be necessary before point Z ($1.67B$, $7A$) becomes optimal. With $C_B \geq \$30{,}000$ and $C_A = \$10{,}000$, the isocost line slope will be steeper than -3, the slope of the low-grade ore constraint, $A = 12 - 3B$.

   As seems reasonable, the greater C_B is relative to C_A, the more mine A will tend to be employed. The greater C_A is relative to C_B, the more mine B will tend to be employed.

ST9.2 **Profit Maximization.** Interstate Bakeries, Inc., is an Atlanta-based manufacturer and distributor of branded bread products. Two leading products, Low Calorie, Q_A, and High Fiber, Q_B, bread, are produced using the same baking facility and staff. Low Calorie bread requires 0.3 hours of worker time per case, whereas High Fiber bread requires 0.4 hours of worker time per case. During any given week, a maximum of 15,000 worker hours are available for these two products. To meet grocery retailer demands for a full product line of branded bread products, Interstate must produce a minimum of 25,000 cases of Low Calorie bread and 7,500 cases of High Fiber bread per week. Given the popularity of low-calorie products in general, Interstate must also ensure that weekly production of Low Calorie bread is at least twice that of High Fiber bread.

Low Calorie bread is sold to groceries at a price of $42 per case; the price of High Fiber bread is $40 per case. Despite its lower price, the markup on High Fiber bread substantially exceeds that on Low Calorie bread. Variable costs are $30.50 per case for Low Calorie bread, but only $17 per case for High Fiber bread.

A. Set up the linear programming problem that the firm would use to determine the profit-maximizing output levels for Low Calorie and High Fiber bread. Show both the inequality and equality forms of the constraint conditions.

B. Completely solve the linear programming problem.

C. Interpret the solution values for the linear programming problem.

D. Holding all else equal, how much would variable costs per unit on High Fiber bread have to fall before the production level indicated in part B would change?

ST9.2 Solution

A. First, the profit contribution for Low Calorie bread, Q_A, and High Fiber bread, Q_B, must be calculated.

$$\frac{\text{Profit contribution}}{\text{per unit}} = \text{Price} - \frac{\text{Variable costs}}{\text{per unit}}$$

Thus,

$$\pi_A = \$42 - \$30.50 = \$11.50 \text{ per case of } Q_A$$
$$\pi_B = \$40 - \$17 = \$23 \text{ per case of } Q_B$$

This problem requires maximization of profits, subject to limitations on the amount of each product produced, the acceptable ratio of production, and available worker hours. The linear programming problem is

$$
\begin{array}{lr}
\text{Maximize} & \pi = \$11.50Q_A + \$23Q_B \\
\text{Subject to} & Q_A \geq 25{,}000 \\
& Q_B \geq 7{,}500 \\
& Q_A - 2Q_B \geq 0 \\
& 0.3Q_A + 0.4Q_B \leq 15{,}000
\end{array}
$$

In equality form, the constraint conditions are

(1)	$Q_A - S_A = 25{,}000$	(Low Calorie constraint)
(2)	$Q_B - S_B = 7{,}500$	(High Fiber constraint)
(3)	$Q_A - 2Q_B - S_R = 0$	(Acceptable ratio constraint)
(4)	$0.3Q_A + 0.4Q_B + S_W = 15{,}000$	(Worker hours constraint)
	$Q_A, Q_B, S_A, S_B, S_R, S_W \geq 0$	

Here, Q_A and Q_B are cases of Low Calorie and High Fiber bread, respectively. S_A, S_B, are variables representing excess production of Low Calorie and High Fiber bread, respectively. S_R is the amount by which the production of Low Calorie bread exceeds the minimally acceptable amount, given High Fiber production. S_W is excess worker capacity.

B. By graphing the constraints and the highest possible isoprofit line, the optimal point X occurs where $S_R = S_W = 0$.

Thus,

$$(1) \qquad Q_A - S_A = 25{,}000$$
$$(2) \qquad Q_B - S_B = 0$$
$$(3) \qquad Q_A - 2Q_B - 0 = 0$$
$$(4) \qquad 0.3Q_A + 0.4Q_B + 0 = 15{,}000$$

From (3), $Q_A = 2Q_B$. Substituting this value into (4) yields

$$0.3(2Q_B) + 0.4Q_B = 15{,}000$$
$$Q_B = 15{,}000$$

From (3),

$$Q_A - 2(15{,}000) = 0$$
$$Q_A = 30{,}000$$

From (1),

$$30{,}000 - S_A = 25{,}000$$
$$S_A = 5{,}000$$

From (2),

$$15{,}000 - S_B = 7{,}500$$
$$S_B = 7{,}500$$

And the total profit contribution per week is

$$\pi = \$11.50(30{,}000) + \$23(15{,}000)$$
$$= \$690{,}000$$

C. Solution values can be interpreted as follows:

$Q_A = 30{,}000$ — Optimal production of Low Calorie bread is 30,000 cases per week.

$Q_B = 15{,}000$ — Optimal production of High Fiber bread is 15,000 cases per week.

$S_A = 5{,}000$ — The production of Low Calorie bread exceeds the 25,000 case minimum by 5,000 units.

$S_B = 7{,}500$ — The production of High Fiber bread exceeds the 7,500 case minimum by 7,500 units.

$S_R = 0$ — The minimally acceptable 2:1 ratio of Low Calorie:High Fiber bread is produced.

$S_W = 0$ — All worker hours are utilized; no excess worker capacity exists.

$\pi = \$690{,}000$ — Maximum weekly profit contribution given constraints

D. $7.67 per case. In the initial problem, there are two feasible solutions that are at the corners of the feasible space that is furthest away from the origin. The optimal solution point X entails production of $Q_A = 30{,}000$, $Q_B = 15{,}000$ and $\pi = \$690{,}000$. An inferior cornerpoint solution is at point Y where $Q_A = 40{,}000$, $Q_B = 7{,}500$ and $\pi = \$632{,}500$.

Analytically, point X is preferred to point Y because it emphasizes production of the higher-margin High Fiber bread. Graphically, point X is preferred to point Y because the slope of the isoprofit line (equal to -2) is "steeper" than the slope of the worker hours constraint (4) (equal to -1.33). If the slope of the isoprofit line became slightly less negative than the worker hours constraint, then the optimal production level would shift from point X to point Y.

In general, the isoprofit line formula is

$$\pi = \pi_A Q_A + \pi_B Q_B$$

or

$$Q_A = (\pi/\pi_A) - (\pi_B/\pi_A)Q_B$$

In this specific case, the isoprofit line is

$$Q_A = (\pi/\$11.50) - (\$23/\$11.50)Q_B$$

To intersect the feasible space at point Y rather than point X, the slope of this line would have to become slightly less negative than -1.33. To solve for the required level for π_B, note that if

$$\frac{\pi_B}{\$11.50} < 1.33$$

then

$$\pi_B < \$15.33$$

Given a price of High Fiber bread of $40 per unit, a profit contribution of $15.33 implies variable costs per unit of $24.67 because

$$
\begin{aligned}
\pi_B &= \text{Price} - \text{Variable costs per unit} \\
&= \$40 - \$24.67 \\
&= \$15.33
\end{aligned}
$$

Therefore, to change the optimal production point from point X to point Y, variable costs per unit on High Fiber bread would have to rise by at least $7.67 per unit:

$$
\begin{aligned}
\text{Change in variable costs} &= \text{New level} - \text{Initial level} \\
&= \$24.67 - \$17 \\
&= \$7.67
\end{aligned}
$$

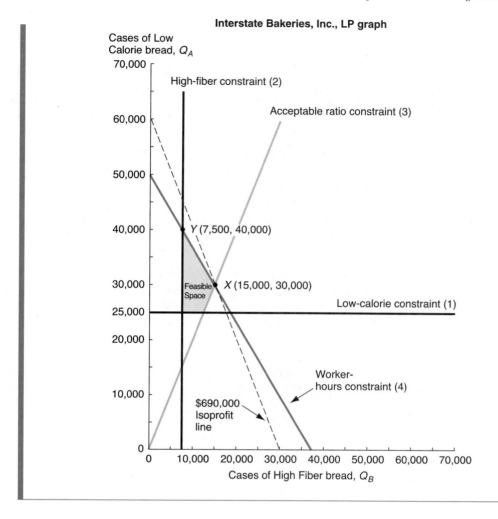

Interstate Bakeries, Inc., LP graph

PROBLEMS

P9.1   **LP Basics.** Indicate whether each of the following statements is true or false and explain why.

    A. Constant returns to scale and constant input prices are the only requirements for a total cost function to be linear.

    B. Changing input prices will always alter the slope of a given isocost line.

    C. In profit-maximization linear programming problems, negative values for slack variables imply that the amount of an input resource employed exceeds the amount available.

    D. Equal distances along a given process ray indicate equal output quantities.

    E. Nonbinding constraints are constraints that intersect at the optimum solution.

P9.2   **Fixed Input Combinations.** Cherry Devices, Inc., assembles connectors and terminals for electronic products at a plant in New Haven, Connecticut. The plant uses labor (L) and capital (K) in an assembly line process to produce output (Q), where

$$Q = 0.025L^{0.5}K^{0.5}$$
$$MP_L = 0.0025(0.5)L^{-0.5}K^{0.5}$$
$$= \frac{0.0125K^{0.5}}{L^{0.5}}$$

$$MP_K = 0.025(0.5)L^{0.5}K^{-0.5}$$
$$= \frac{0.0125L^{0.5}}{K^{0.5}}$$

A. Calculate how many units of output can be produced with 4 units of labor and 400 units of capital and with 16 units of labor and 1,600 units of capital. Are returns to scale increasing, constant, or diminishing?

B. Calculate the change in the marginal product of labor as labor grows from 4 to 16 units, holding capital constant at 400 units. Similarly, calculate the change in the marginal product of capital as capital grows from 400 to 1,600 units, holding labor constant at 4 units. Are returns to each factor increasing, constant, or diminishing?

C. Assume now and throughout the remainder of the problem that labor and capital must be combined in the ratio 4L:400K. How much output could be produced if Cherry has a constraint of $L = 4,000$ and $K = 480,000$ during the coming production period?

D. What are the marginal products of each factor under the conditions described in part C?

P9.3 **LP Setup and Interpretation.** The Syflansyd Nut Company has enjoyed booming sales following the success of its "Sometimes You Feel Like a Nut, Sometimes You Don't" advertising campaign. Syflansyd packages and sells four types of nuts in four different types of mixed-nut packages. These products include bulk (B), economy (E), fancy (F), and regular (R) mixed-nut packages. Each of these packages contains a different mixture of almonds (A), cashews (C), filberts (F), and peanuts (P). Based on its contracts with current suppliers, the company has the following daily inventory of each of the following nuts: almonds, 8,000 ounces; cashews, 7,000 ounces; filberts, 7,500 ounces; and peanuts, 10,000 ounces.

Given available inventory, it is management's goal to maximize profits by offering the optimum mix of the four package types. Profit earned per package type is as follows:

Bulk	$0.50
Economy	$0.25
Fancy	$1.25
Regular	$0.75

The composition of each of the four package types can be summarized as follows:

	Ounces per Package			
	Bulk	**Economy**	**Fancy**	**Regular**
Almonds	35	2	3	2
Cashews	35	1	4	2
Filberts	35	1	3	2
Peanuts	35	8	2	6
Total	140	12	12	12

Solution values for the optimal number of packages to produce (decision variables) and excess capacity (slack variables) are the following:

$$B = 0$$
$$E = 0$$
$$F = 1,100$$
$$R = 1,300$$
$$S_A = 2,100$$

$$S_C = 0$$
$$S_F = 1,600$$
$$S_P = 0$$

A. Identify and interpret the appropriate Syflansyd objective function.

B. Using both inequality and equality forms, set up and interpret the resource constraints facing the Syflansyd Company.

C. Calculate optimal daily profit, and provide a complete interpretation of the full solution to this linear programming problem.

P9.4 **Cost Minimization.** Ray Barone is sole proprietor of Delmar Custom Homes (DCH), a family-run construction company. The company uses two types of crews on its Long Island, New York, home construction projects. Type A crews consist of master carpenters and skilled carpenters, whereas B crews include skilled carpenters and unskilled labor. Each home involves framing (F), roofing (R), and finish carpentry (FC). During recent months, A crews have demonstrated a capability of framing one home, roofing two, and doing finish carpentry for no more than four homes per month. Capabilities for B crews are framing three homes, roofing two, and completing finish carpentry for one during a month. DCH has agreed to build 10 homes during the month of July but has subcontracted 10% of framing and 20% of finish carpentry requirements. Labor costs are $60,000 per month for A crews and $45,000 per month for B crews.

A. Formulate the linear programming problem that DCH would use to minimize its total labor costs per month, showing both the inequality and equality forms of the constraint conditions.

B. Solve the linear programming problem and interpret your solution values.

C. Assuming that DCH can both buy and sell subcontracting services at prevailing prices of $8,000 per unit for framing and $14,000 per unit for finish carpentry, would you recommend that the company alter its subcontracting policy? If so, how much could the company save through such a change?

D. Calculate the minimum increase in A-crew costs necessary to cause DCH to change its optimal employment combination for July.

P9.5 **Optimal Credit Policy.** Mimi Bobeck is a senior loan officer with Citybank in Cleveland, Ohio. Bobeck has both corporate and personal lending customers. On average, the profit contribution margin or interest rate spread is 1.5% on corporate loans and 2% on personal loans. This return difference reflects the fact that personal loans tend to be riskier than corporate loans. Bobeck seeks to maximize the total dollar profit contribution earned, subject to a variety of restrictions on her lending practices. To limit default risk, Bobeck must restrict personal loans to no more than 50% of the total loans outstanding. Similarly, to ensure adequate diversification against business-cycle risk, corporate lending cannot exceed 75% of loaned funds. To maintain good customer relations by serving the basic needs of the local business community, Bobeck has decided to extend at least 25% of her total credit authorization to corporate customers on an ongoing basis. Finally, Bobeck cannot exceed her current total credit authorization of $100 million.

A. Using the inequality form of the constraint conditions, set up and interpret the linear programming problem that Bobeck would use to determine the optimal dollar amount of credit to extend to corporate (C) and personal (P) lending customers. Also formulate the LP problem using the equality form of the constraint conditions.

B. Use a graph to determine the optimal solution, and check your solution algebraically. Fully interpret solution values.

P9.6 **Optimal Portfolio Decisions.** The James Bond Fund is a mutual fund (open-end investment company) with an objective of maximizing income from a widely diversified corporate bond portfolio. The fund has a policy of remaining invested largely in a diversified portfolio of investment-grade bonds. Investment-grade bonds have high investment quality and receive a rating of Baa or better by Moody's, a bond-rating service. The fund's investment policy states that investment-grade bonds are to be emphasized, representing at least three times the amount of junk bond holdings. Junk bonds pay high nominal returns but have low investment quality, and they receive a rating of less than Baa from Moody's. To maintain the potential for high investor income, at least 20% of the fund's total portfolio must be invested in junk bonds. Like many funds, the James Bond Fund cannot use leverage (or borrowing) to enhance investor returns. As a result, total bond investments cannot total more than 100% of the portfolio. Finally, the current expected return for investment-grade (I) bonds is 9%, and it is 12% for junk (J) bonds.

A. Using the inequality form of the constraint conditions, set up and interpret the linear programming problem that the James Bond Fund would use to determine the optimal portfolio percentage holdings of investment-grade (I) and junk (J) bonds. Also formulate the problem using the equality form of the constraint conditions. (Assume that the fund managers have decided to remain fully invested and therefore hold no cash at this time.)

B. Use a graph to determine the optimal solution, and check your solution algebraically. Fully interpret solution values.

C. Holding all else equal, how much would the expected return on junk bonds have to fall to alter the optimal investment policy determined in part B? Alternatively, how much would the return on investment-grade bonds have to rise before a change in investment policy would be warranted?

D. In anticipation of a rapid increase in interest rates and a subsequent economic downturn, the investment committee has decided to minimize the fund's exposure to bond price fluctuations. In adopting a defensive position, what is the maximum share of the portfolio that can be held in cash given the investment policies stated in the problem?

P9.7 **Cost Minimization.** Carolina Power and Light (CP&L) is a small electric utility located in the Southeast. CP&L currently uses coal-fired capacity to satisfy its base load electricity demand, which is the minimum level of electricity demanded 24 hours per day, 365 days per year.

CP&L currently burns both high-sulfur eastern coal and low-sulfur western coal. Each type of coal has its advantages. Eastern coal is more expensive ($50 per ton) but has higher heat-generating capabilities. Although western coal does not generate as much heat as eastern coal, western coal is less expensive ($25 per ton) and does not cause as much sulfur dioxide pollution. CP&L's base load requirements are such that at least 2,400 million BTUs must be generated per hour. Each ton of eastern coal burned generates 40 million BTUs, and each ton of western coal burned generates 30 million BTUs. To limit sulfur dioxide emissions, the state's Environmental Protection Agency (EPA) requires CP&L to limit its total burning of sulfur to no more than 1.5 tons per hour. This affects CP&L's coal usage, because eastern coal contains 2.5% sulfur and western coal contains 1.5% sulfur. The EPA also limits CP&L particulate emissions to no more than 900 pounds per hour. CP&L emits 10 pounds of particulates per ton of eastern coal burned and 15 pounds of particulates per ton of western coal burned.

A. Set up and interpret the linear program that CP&L would use to minimize hourly coal usage costs in light of its constraints.

B. Calculate and interpret all relevant solution values.

C. Holding all else equal, how much would the price of western coal have to rise before only eastern coal would be used? Explain.

P9.8 **Profit Maximization.** Creative Accountants, Ltd., is a small San Francisco–based accounting partnership specializing in the preparation of individual (I) and corporate (C) income tax returns. Prevailing prices in the local market are $125 for individual tax return preparation and $250 for corporate tax return preparation.

Five accountants run the firm and are assisted by four bookkeepers and four secretaries, all of whom work a typical 40-hour workweek. The firm must decide how to target its promotional efforts to best use its resources during the coming tax preparation season. Based on previous experience, the firm expects that an average of 1 hour of accountant time will be required for each individual return prepared. Corporate return preparation will require an average of 2 accountant-hours and 2 bookkeeper-hours. One hour of secretarial time will also be required for typing each individual or corporate return. In addition, variable computer and other processing costs are expected to average $25 per individual return and $100 per corporate return.

A. Set up the linear programming problem that the firm would use to determine the profit-maximizing output levels for preparing individual and corporate returns. Show both the inequality and equality forms of the constraint conditions.

B. Completely solve and interpret the solution values for the linear programming problem.

C. Calculate maximum possible net profits per week for the firm, assuming that the accountants earn $1,500 per week, bookkeepers earn $500 per week, secretaries earn $10 per hour, and fixed overhead (including promotion and other expenses) averages $5,000 per week.

D. After considering the preceding data, one senior accountant recommended letting two bookkeepers go while retaining the rest of the current staff. Another accountant suggested that if any bookkeepers were let go, an increase in secretarial staff would be warranted. Which is the more profitable suggestion? Why?

E. Using the equality form of the constraint conditions, set up, solve, and interpret solution values for the dual linear programming problem.

F. Does the dual solution provide information useful for planning purposes? Explain.

P9.9 **Revenue Maximization.** Architect Elaine Benes is managing director of Designed for Sales (DFS), Inc., an Evanston, Illinois–based designer of single-family and multifamily housing units for real estate developers, building contractors, and so on. Benes' challenge is to determine an optimal mix of output during the current planning period. DFS offers custom designs for single-family units, Q_1, for $3,000 and custom designs for multifamily units (e.g., duplexes, fourplexes), Q_2, for $2,000 each. Both types of output make use of scarce drafting, artwork, and architectural resources. Each custom design for single-family units requires 12 hours of drafting, 2 hours of artwork, and 6 hours of architectural input. Each custom design for multifamily units requires 4 hours of drafting, 5 hours of artwork, and 6 hours of architectural input. Currently, DFS has 72 hours of drafting, 30 hours of artwork, and 48 hours of architectural services available on a weekly basis.

A. Using the equality form of the constraint conditions, set up the primal linear program that Benes would use to determine the sales revenue-maximizing product mix. Also set up the dual.

B. Solve for and interpret all solution values.

C. Would DFS's optimal product mix be different with a profit-maximization goal rather than a sales revenue-maximization goal? Why or why not?

P9.10 **Optimal Output.** Omaha Meat Products (OMP) produces and markets Cornhusker Plumpers, an extra-large frankfurter product being introduced on a test market basis into the St. Louis, Missouri, area. This product is similar to several others offered by OMP, and it can be produced with currently available equipment and personnel using any of three alternative production methods. Method A requires 1 hour of labor and 4 processing-facility hours to produce 100 packages of plumpers, one unit of Q_A. Method B requires 2 labor hours and 2 processing-facility hours for each unit of Q_B, and method C requires 5 labor hours and 1 processing-facility hour for each unit of Q_C. Because of slack demand for other products, OMP currently has 14 labor hours and 6 processing-facility hours available per week for producing Cornhusker Plumpers. Cornhusker Plumpers are currently being marketed to grocery retailers at a wholesale price of $1.50 per package, and demand exceeds current supply.

A. Using the equality form of the constraint conditions, set up the primal and dual linear programs that OMP would use to maximize production of Cornhusker Plumpers given currently available resources.

B. Calculate and interpret all solution values.

C. Should OMP expand its processing-facility capacity if it can do so at a cost of $40 per hour?

D. Discuss the implications of a new union scale calling for a wage rate of $20 per hour.

CASE STUDY

LP Pension Funding Model

Several companies have learned that a well-funded and comprehensive employee benefits package constitutes an important part of the compensation plan needed to attract and retain key personnel. An employee stock ownership plan, profit-sharing arrangements, and deferred compensation to fund employee retirement are all used to allow productive employees to share in the firm's growth and development. Among the fringe benefits offered under the cafeteria-style benefits plans is comprehensive medical and dental care furnished through local health maintenance organizations, on-site daycare centers for employee children, and "eldercare" support for the aging parents and other dependents of workers.

Many companies also provide their employees with so-called "defined benefit" pension plans. Under defined benefit plans, employers usually offer workers a fixed percentage of their final salary as a retirement annuity. In a typical arrangement, a company might offer employees a retirement annuity of 1.5% of their final salary for each year employed. A 10-year veteran would earn a retirement annuity of 15% of final salary, a 20-year veteran would earn a retirement annuity of 30% of final salary, and so on. Because each employee's retirement benefits are defined by the company, the company itself is obligated to pay for promised benefits.

Over time, numerous firms have found it increasingly difficult to forecast the future rate of return on invested assets, the future rate of inflation, and the morbidity (death rate) of young, healthy, active retirees. As a result, several organizations have discontinued traditional defined benefit pension plans and instead have begun to offer new "defined contribution" plans. A defined contribution plan features a matching of company plus employee retirement contributions, with no prescribed set of retirement income benefits defined beforehand. Each employee is typically eligible to contribute up to 10% of their pre-tax income into the plan, with the company matching the first 5% or so of such contributions. Both company and employee contributions compound on a tax-deferred basis until the point of retirement. At that time, employees can use their pension funds to purchase an annuity, or draw a pension income from earned interest, plus dividends and capital gains.

Defined contribution plans have some obvious advantages over traditional defined benefit pension plans. From the company's perspective, defined benefit pension plans became much less attractive when accounting rule changes during the late 1980s required them to record as a liability any earned but not funded pension obligations. Unfunded pension liabilities caused gigantic one-time charges against operating income during the early 1990s for AT&T, General Motors, IBM, and a host of other large corporations. Faced with enormous one-time charges during an initial catch-up phase, plus the prospect of massive and rapidly growing retirement expenses over time, many large and small firms have simply elected to discontinue their defined contribution plan altogether. From the employee's perspective, defined contribution plans are attractive because they are portable from one employer to another. Rather than face the prospect of losing pension benefits after changing from one employer to another, employees appreciate the advantage of being able to take their pension plans with them as they switch jobs. Defined contribution plans are also attractive because they allow employees to tailor retirement funding contributions to fit individual needs. Younger employees faced with the necessity of buying a home or paying for children's educational expenses can limit pension contributions to minimal levels; older workers with greater discretionary income and a more imminent retirement can provide the maximum pension contribution allowed by law. An added benefit of defined contribution compensation plans is that individual workers can allocate pension investments according to individual risk preferences. Older workers who are extremely risk averse can focus their investments on short-term government securities; younger and more venturesome employees can devote a larger share of their retirement investment portfolio to common stocks.

Workers appreciate companies that offer flexible defined contribution pension plans and closely related profit-sharing and deferred compensation arrangements. To maximize plan benefits, firms must make modest efforts to educate and inform employees about retirement income needs and objectives. Until recently, compensation consultants suggested that employees could retire comfortably on a retirement income that totaled 80% of their final salary. However, concerns about the underfunding of federal Social Security and Medicaid programs and apprehension about the rapid escalation of medical care costs make retirement with sufficient assets to fund a pension income equal to 100% of final salary a worthy goal. To fund such a nest egg requires substantial regular savings and an impressive rate of return on pension plan assets. Workers who save 10% of income for an extended period, say, 30 years, have historically been able to fund a retirement income equal to 100% of final salary. This assumes, of course, that the pension plan portfolio is able to earn significant returns over time. Investing in a broadly diversified portfolio of common stocks has historically provided the best returns. Since 1926, the real (after-inflation) rate of return on NYSE stocks is 6.4% per year; the real return on bonds is only 0.5% per year. Indeed, over every 30-year investment horizon during that time interval, stocks have beat short-term bonds (money market instruments) and long-term bonds. The added return from common stocks is the predictable reward for assuming the greater risks of stock-market investing. However, to be sure of earning the market risk premium on stocks, one must invest in several different companies (at least 30) for several years (at least 30). For most pension plans, investments in no-load low-expense common stock index funds work best in the long run. However, bond market funds have a place in some pension portfolios, especially for those at or near the retirement age.

To illustrate the type of retirement income funding model that a company might make available to employees, consider the following scenario. Suppose that an individual employee has accumulated a pension portfolio worth $250,000 and hopes to receive initial post-retirement income of $500 per month, or $6,000 per year. To provide a total return from current income (yield) plus growth (capital gains) of at least 7%, a minimum of 25% of the portfolio should be invested in common stocks. To limit risk, stocks should total no more than 50% of the overall portfolio, and a minimum of 5% should be invested in long-term taxable bonds, 5% in medium-term tax-exempt bonds, and 5% in a short-term money-market mutual fund. Moreover, not more than 75% of the overall portfolio should be invested in stocks plus long-term taxable bonds, and at least $30,000 should be available in money markets plus medium-term tax-exempt bonds to provide sufficient liquidity to fund emergencies. Assume that common stocks have a before-tax dividend yield of 3.5%, with expected growth from capital appreciation of 6.5% per year. Similar figures for long-term taxable bonds are 6% plus 1.5%, 4% plus 1% for medium-term tax-exempt bonds, and 4.5% plus 0% for money market instruments. Also assume that the effective marginal tax rate is 30%.

A. Set up the linear programming problem that a benefits officer might use to determine the total-return maximizing allocation of the employee's pension portfolio. Use the inequality forms of the constraint conditions.

CASE STUDY (continued)

B. Solve this linear programming problem and interpret all solution values. Also determine the employee's expected before-tax and after-tax income levels.

C. Calculate the amount of unrealized capital gain earned per year on this investment portfolio.

D. What is the total return opportunity cost of the $6,000 after-tax income constraint?

Rules for Forming the Dual Linear Programming Problem

Given the importance of duality, a list of simple rules that can be used to form the dual program to any given primal program would be useful. Four such rules exist. They are as follows:

1. Change a maximize objective to minimize, and vice versa.
2. Reverse primal constraint inequality signs in dual constraints (i.e., change $\geq$ to $\leq$, and $\leq$ to $\geq$).
3. Transpose primal constraint coefficients to get dual constraint coefficients.
4. Transpose objective function coefficients to get limits in dual constraints, and vice versa.

(The word *transpose* is a matrix algebra term that simply means that each row of coefficients is rearranged into columns so that row 1 becomes column 1, row 2 becomes column 2, and so on.)

To illustrate the rules for transformation from primal and dual, consider the following simple example.

Primal Problem

$$\text{Maximize} \quad \pi = \pi_1 Q_1 + \pi_2 Q_2 + \pi_3 Q_3$$

$$\text{subject to} \quad a_{11}Q_1 + a_{12}Q_2 + a_{13}Q_3 \leq r_1$$

$$a_{21}Q_1 + a_{22}Q_2 + a_{23}Q_3 \leq r_2$$

$$Q_1, Q_2, Q_3 \geq 0$$

where π is profits and Q is output. Thus, π_1, π_2 and π_3 are unit profits for Q_1, Q_2 and Q_3, respectively. The resource constraints are given by r_1 and r_2. The constants in the primal constraints reflect the input requirements for each type of output. For example, a_{11} is the amount of resource r_1 in one unit of output Q_1. Similarly, a_{12} is the amount of resource r_1 in one unit of output Q_2, and a_{13} is the amount of resource r_1 in one unit of output Q_3. Thus, $a_{11}Q_1 + a_{12}Q_2 + a_{13}Q_3$ is the total amount of resource r_1 used in production. The remaining input requirements, a_{21}, a_{22} and a_{23}, have a similar interpretation. For convenience, this primal problem statement can be rewritten in matrix notation as follows:

Primal Problem

Maximize $\quad \pi = \pi_1 Q_1 + \pi_2 Q_2 + \pi_3 Q_3$

subject to $\quad \begin{bmatrix} a_{11} & a_{12} & a_{13} \\ a_{21} & a_{22} & a_{23} \end{bmatrix} \times \begin{bmatrix} Q_1 \\ Q_2 \\ Q_3 \end{bmatrix} \le \begin{bmatrix} r_1 \\ r_2 \end{bmatrix}$

$$Q_1, Q_2, Q_3 \ge 0$$

Matrix notation is just a convenient means for writing large systems of equations. In going from matrix form back to equation form, one just multiplies each row element by each column element. For example, the left side of the first constraint equation is $a_{11} \times Q_1$ plus $a_{12} \times Q_2$ plus $a_{13} \times Q_3$, or $a_{11}Q_1 + a_{12}Q_2 + a_{13}Q_3$, and this sum must be less than or equal to r_1.

Given the expression of the primal program in matrix notation, the four rules for transformation given previously can be used to convert from the primal to the dual. Following these rules, the dual is written as follows:

Dual Problem

Minimize $\quad \pi^* = r_1 V_1 + r_2 V_2$

subject to $\quad \begin{bmatrix} a_{11} & a_{21} \\ a_{12} & a_{22} \\ a_{13} & a_{23} \end{bmatrix} \times \begin{bmatrix} V_1 \\ V_2 \end{bmatrix} \ge \begin{bmatrix} \pi_1 \\ \pi_2 \\ \pi_3 \end{bmatrix}$

$$V_1, V_2 \ge 0$$

Then, converting from matrix back to equation form gives the following:

Dual Problem

Minimize $\quad \pi^* = r_1 V_1 + r_2 V_2$

subject to $\quad a_{11} V_1 + a_{21} V_2 \ge \pi_1$

$\qquad\qquad a_{12} V_1 + a_{22} V_2 \ge \pi_2$

$\qquad\qquad a_{13} V_1 + a_{23} V_2 \ge \pi_3$

$\qquad\qquad V_1, V_2 \ge 0$

Here, V_1 and V_2 are the shadow prices for resources r_1 and r_2, respectively. Because r_1 and r_2 represent the quantities of the two resources available, the objective function measures the total implicit value of the resources available. Recalling the interpretation of a_{11} and a_{21} from the primal, it is obvious that $a_{11}V_1 + a_{21}V_2$ is the total value of inputs used to produce one unit of output Q_1. Similarly, $a_{12}V_1 + a_{22}V_2$ is the total value of inputs used in production of a unit of output Q_2, and $a_{13}V_1 + a_{23}V_2$ is the total value of inputs used in production of a unit of output Q_3.

Finally, the primal and dual linear programming problems can be fully specified through the introduction of slack variables. Remember that with less-than-or-equal-to constraints, the left side of the constraint equation must be brought up to equal the right side. Thus, slack variables must be added to the left side of such constraint equations. With greater-than-or-equal-to constraints, the left side of the constraint equation must be brought down to equal the right side. Thus, slack variables must be *subtracted from* the left side of such constraint equations. With this, the full specification of the preceding primal and dual linear programs can be written as follows:

Primal Problem	**Dual Problem**

$$\text{Maximize} \quad \pi = \pi_1 Q_1 + \pi_2 Q_2 + \pi_3 Q_3$$

$$\text{Minimize} \quad \pi^* = r_1 V_1 + r_2 V_2$$

$$\text{subject to} \quad a_{11}Q_1 + a_{12}Q_2 + a_{13}Q_3 + S_1 = r_1$$
$$a_{21}Q_1 + a_{22}Q_2 + a_{23}Q_3 + S_2 = r_2$$

$$\text{subject to} \quad a_{11}V_1 + a_{21}V_2 - L_1 = \pi_1$$
$$a_{12}V_1 + a_{22}V_2 - L_2 = \pi_2$$
$$a_{13}V_1 + a_{23}V_2 - L_3 = \pi_3$$

$$Q_1, Q_2, Q_3, S_1, S_2 \geq 0$$

$$V_1, V_2, L_1, L_2, L_3 \geq 0$$

where S_1 and S_2 are slack variables representing excess capacity of resources r_1 and r_2, respectively. L_1, L_2 and L_3 are also slack variables; they represent the amount by which the value of resources used in the production of Q_1, Q_2, and Q_3 exceeds the value of output as measured by π_1, π_2 and π_3, respectively. Thus, L_1, L_2 and L_3 measure the opportunity cost, or foregone profit, as a result of producing the last unit of Q_1, Q_2 and Q_3.

Understanding these basic rules simplifies construction of the dual, given a primal program, and facilitates understanding and interpretation of the constraints and coefficients found in both primal and dual linear programming problems.

SELECTED REFERENCES

Allen, David E., Lyn C. Thomas, and Harry Zheng. "Stripping Coupons with Linear Programming." *Journal of Fixed Income* 10 (September 2000): 80–87.

Arbel, Ami, and Pekka Korhonen. "Using Objective Values to Start Multiple Objective Linear Programming Algorithms." *European Journal of Operational Research* 128 (February 2001): 587–596.

Atamturk, A., E. L. Johnson, and J. T. Linderoth, et al. "A Relational Modeling System for Linear and Integer Programming." *Operations Research* 48 (November/December 2000): 846–857.

Brucker, Peter, and Sigrid Knust. "A Linear Programming and Constraint Propagation-Based Lower Bound for the RCPSP." *European Journal of Operational Research* 127 (December 2000): 355–362.

Carlier, Jacques, and Emmanuel Neron. "A New LP-Based Lower Bound for the Cumulative Scheduling Problem." *European Journal of Operational Research* 127 (December 2000): 363–382.

Cavichia, Mario Conrado, and Marcos Nereu. "Piecewise Linear Programming via Interior Points." *Computers & Operations Research* 27 (November 2000): 1303–1324.

Chiang, Jershan. "Fuzzy Linear Programming Based on Statistical Confidence Interval and Interval-Valued Fuzzy Set." *European Journal of Operational Research* 129 (February 2001): 65–86.

Gautier, Antoine, Bernard F. Lamond, Daniel Pare, et al. "The Quebec Ministry of Natural Resources Uses Linear Programming to Understand the Wood-Fiber Market." *Interfaces* 30 (November/Deccember 2000): 32–48.

Helmes, Kurt, Stefan Rohl, and Richard H. Stockbridge. "Computing Moments of the Exit Time Distribution for Markov Processes by Linear Programming." *Operations Research* 49 (July/August 2001): 516–530.

Jung, Ho-Won. "A Linear Programming Model Dealing with Ordinal Ratings in Policy Capturing of Performance Appraisal." *European Journal of Operational Research* 134 (November, 2001): 493–497.

Krcmar, Emina, Brad Stennes, G. Cornelis Van Kooten, et al. "Carbon Sequestration and Land Management Under Uncertainty." *European Journal of Operational Research* 135 (December 2001): 616–629.

Little, J. "Enhancing the Performance of Constraint Programming Through the Introduction of Linear Programming." *Journal of the Operational Research Society* 52 (January 2001): 82–92.

Makowski, David, Eligius M. T. Hendrix, Martin K. Van Ittersum, et al. "Generation and Presentation of Nearly Optimal Solutions for Mixed-Integer Linear Programming, Applied to a Case in Farming System Design." *European Journal of Operational Research* 132 (July 2001): 425–438.

Nishizaki, Ichiro, and Masatoshi Sakawa. "On Computational Methods for Solutions of Multiobjective Linear Production Programming Games." *European Journal of Operational Research* 129 (March 2001): 386–413.

Patterson, Mike C., and Bob Harmel. "Using Microsoft Excel Solver for Linear Programming Assignment Problems." *International Journal of Management* 18 (September 2001): 308–313.

Market Structure Analysis and Estimation

CHAPTER TEN

Perfect Competition and Monopoly

irms operating in perfectly competitive industries find it very difficult to sustain attractive rates of return on investment. Take newsprint production, for example. When the economy is booming, newspapers are able to attract lots of advertisers and the demand for newsprint soars. During recessions, advertising falls as does the demand for newsprint. As the demand for newsprint rises and falls with trends in the overall economy, newsprint prices oscillate wildly. Because newsprint is a commodity-like product, Abitibi Consolidated, the leading newsprint manufacturer in North America, and Bowater, Inc., the second-largest newsprint manufacturer, struggle to earn nominal rates of return of 8 percent on stockholders' equity. Much higher profit rates are earned by their customers, newspaper companies like Dow Jones & Co., publisher of *The Wall Street Journal* and *Barron's*, and Gannett Co., publisher of *USA Today* and a host of local papers. Local newspapers in one-newspaper towns have a limited monopoly on the provision of want-ad advertising, regional news, and sports reporting. Monopoly power allows distinctive newspapers to consistently earn 15 percent to 20 percent and more on stockholders' equity.[1]

This chapter shows why producers of commodity-like products earn only meager rates of return, while monopoly producers of distinctive goods and services have the potential for significant above-normal profits. Taken together, these market structures can be viewed as the endpoints along a continuum of decreasing competition, moving from perfect competition to monopolistic competition to oligopoly to monopoly. Monopolistic competition and oligopoly are the subjects of Chapter 11.

1   David Dakshaw, "The Competition Prevention Center," *The Wall Street Journal Online*, January 29, 2002 (http://online.wsj.com).

CONTRAST BETWEEN PERFECT COMPETITION AND MONOPOLY

Stark differences between buyer and seller behavior in perfectly competitive and monopoly markets are evident. These dissimilarities are characterized briefly in this section and then discussed more fully in the rest of the chapter.

What Is Market Structure?

market
Firms and individuals willing and able to buy or sell a given product

market structure
The competitive environment

A **market** consists of all firms and individuals willing and able to buy or sell a particular product. This includes firms and individuals currently engaged in buying and selling a particular product, as well as potential entrants. **Market structure** describes the competitive environment in the market for any good or service. Market structure is typically characterized on the basis of four important industry characteristics: the number and size distribution of active buyers and sellers and potential entrants, the degree of product differentiation, the amount and cost of information about product price and quality, and conditions of entry and exit.

Effects of market structure are measured in terms of the prices paid by consumers, availability and quality of output, employment and career advancement opportunities, and the pace of product innovation, among other factors. Generally speaking, the greater the number of market participants, the more vigorous is price and product quality competition. The more even the balance of power between sellers and buyers, the more likely it is that the competitive process will yield maximum benefits. However, a close link between the numbers of market participants and the vigor of price competition does not always hold true. For example, there are literally thousands of producers in most major milk markets. Price competition is nonexistent, however, given an industry cartel that is sustained by a federal program of milk price supports. Nevertheless, there are few barriers to entry, and individual milk producers struggle to earn a normal return. In contrast, price competition can be spirited in aircraft manufacturing, newspaper, cable television, long-distance telephone service, and other markets with as few as two competitors. This is particularly true when market participants are constrained by the viable threat of potential entrants.

potential entrants
Firms and individuals with the economic resources to enter a particular market, given sufficient economic incentives

A **potential entrant** is an individual or firm posing a sufficiently credible threat of market entry to affect the price/output decisions of incumbent firms. Potential entrants play extremely important roles in many industries. Some industries with only a few active participants might at first appear to hold the potential for substantial economic profits. However, a number of potential entrants can have a substantial effect on the price/output decisions of incumbent firms. For example, Dell, Gateway, Hewlett-Packard, IBM, and other leading computer manufacturers are viable potential entrants into the computer component manufacturing industry. These companies use their threat of potential entry to obtain favorable prices from suppliers of microprocessors, monitors, and peripheral equipment. Despite having only a relative handful of active foreign and domestic participants, computer components manufacturing is both highly innovative and vigorously price competitive. The mere threat of entry by potential entrants is sometimes enough to keep industry prices and profits in check and to maintain a high level of productive efficiency.

Perfect Competition

perfect competition
A market structure characterized by a large number of buyers and sellers of an identical product

price takers
Buyers and sellers whose individual transactions are so small that they do not affect market prices

Perfect competition is a market structure characterized by a large number of buyers and sellers of essentially the same product. Each market participant is too small to influence market prices. Individual buyers and sellers are **price takers**. Firms take market prices as given and devise their production strategies accordingly. Free and complete demand and supply information is available in a perfectly competitive market, and there are no meaningful barriers to entry and exit. As a result, vigorous price competition prevails. Only a normal rate of return on investment is possible in the long run. Economic profits are possible only during periods of short-run disequilibrium before rivals mount an effective competitive response.

Is the Stock Market Perfectly Competitive?

The New York Stock Exchange (NYSE) is the largest organized U.S. securities market. Established in 1817, the NYSE is the primary marketplace for the common and preferred stocks of roughly 3,400 large and medium-size companies. The NYSE enjoys near-monopoly status by virtue of the fact that NYSE trading accounts for roughly 80 percent of the composite volume in listed company shares. The remainder is off-the-floor electronic trading by institutions and trading on eight smaller regional exchanges.

The National Association of Securities Dealers Automated Quotations service, or Nasdaq for short, is an electronic trading system for thousands of unlisted companies whose shares are traded on a negotiated basis among hundreds of brokers and dealers. Nasdaq's National Market System covers roughly 6,000 common stocks; Nasdaq Small Cap Issues include another 3,000 smaller companies. (More than 10,000 inactively traded stocks are listed in the "pink sheets.")

The Nasdaq multiple dealer market is designed to produce narrow bid-ask spreads through dealer competi-

tion. However, a lack of competition was suggested in a *Journal of Finance* article titled "Why Do Nasdaq Market Makers Avoid Odd Eighth Quotes?" by professors William G. Christie and Paul Schultz. They found that dealer bid-ask spreads for a large number of Nasdaq stocks were often at least 25¢, or twice the 1/8 (12.5¢) minimum, and raised the question of whether Nasdaq dealers implicitly colluded to maintain wide spreads. A federal lawsuit was brought alleging that 37 securities firms had indeed conspired to fix prices on the Nasdaq stock market by setting inside spreads. In December 1997, a settlement was reached in the Nasdaq price-fixing law-suit, with Wall Street firms including Merrill Lynch & Co. and Citigroup's Salomon Smith Barney paying a record $1.03 billion settlement.

Thus, even in markets widely recognized as almost perfectly competitive, elements of inefficiency and monopoly pricing are sometimes present. *Caveat emptor!*

See: Erin Schulte, "Tech Upgrades, Earnings Reports Spur Stocks Higher," *The Wall Street Journal Online*, January 23, 2002 (http://online.wsj.com).

Monopoly

monopoly
A market structure characterized by a single seller of a highly differentiated product

price makers
Buyers and sellers whose large transactions affect market prices

Monopoly is a market structure characterized by a single seller of a product with no good substitutes. Because a monopolist is the sole provider of a desired commodity, the monopolist is the industry. Producers must compete for a share of the consumer's overall market basket of goods, but monopolists face no effective competition for specific products from either established or potential rivals. As such, monopolists are **price makers** that exercise significant control over market prices. This allows the monopolist to simultaneously determine price and output for the firm (and the industry). Substantial barriers to entry or exit deter potential entrants and offer both efficient and inefficient monopolists the opportunity for economic profits, even in the long run.

 FACTORS THAT DETERMINE THE LEVEL OF COMPETITION

Two key conditions determine the level of competition in a given market: the number and relative size of buyers and sellers, and the extent to which the product is standardized. These factors, in turn, are influenced by the nature of the product and production systems, the scope of potential entry, and buyer characteristics.

Effect of Product Characteristics on Market Structure

Good substitutes increase competition. To illustrate, rail freight and passenger service between two points is typically supplied by only one railroad. Transportation service is available from several sources, however, and railroads compete with bus lines, truck companies, barges, air-lines, and private autos. The substitutability of these other modes of transportation for rail service increases the degree of competition in the transportation service market.

It is important to realize that market structures are not static. In the 1800s and early 1900s—before the introduction of trucks, buses, automobiles, and airplanes—railroads faced very little competition. Railroads could charge excessive prices and earn monopoly profits. Because of this exploitation, laws were passed giving public authorities permission to regulate railroad prices. Over the years, such regulation became superfluous given intermodal competition. Other firms were enticed by railroad profits to develop competing transportation service systems, which ultimately led to a much more competitive market structure. Today, few would argue that railroads retain significant monopoly power, and public regulation of the railroads has been greatly reduced in recognition of this fact.

Physical characteristics of a product can also influence the degree of competition. A low ratio of distribution cost to total cost, for example, tends to increase competition by widening the geographic area over which any particular producer can compete. Rapid perishability of a product yields the opposite effect. In considering the level of competition for a product, the national, regional, or local nature of the market must be considered.

Effect of Production Characteristics on Competition

When minimum efficient scale is large in relation to overall industry output, only a few firms are able to attain the output size necessary for productive efficiency. In such instances, competitive pressures may allow only a few firms to survive. On the other hand, when minimum efficient scale is small in relation to overall industry output, many firms are able to attain the size necessary for efficient operation. Holding all else equal, competition tends to be most vigorous when many efficient competitors are present in the market. This is especially true when firms of smaller-than-minimum-efficient scale face considerably higher production costs, and when the construction of minimum-efficient–scale plants involves the commitment of substantial capital, skilled labor, and material resources. When construction of minimum-efficient–scale plants requires the commitment of only modest resources or when smaller firms face no important production cost disadvantages, economies of scale have little or no effect on the competitive potential of new or entrant firms.

Effect of Entry and Exit Conditions on Competition

barrier to entry
Any advantage for industry incumbents over new arrivals

barrier to mobility
Any advantage for large leading firms over small nonleading rivals

Maintaining above-normal profits or inefficient operations over the long run requires substantial barriers to entry, mobility, or exit. A **barrier to entry** is any factor or industry characteristic that creates an advantage for incumbents over new arrivals. Legal rights such as patents and local, state, or federal licenses can present formidable barriers to entry in pharmaceuticals, cable television, television and radio broadcasting, and other industries. A **barrier to mobility** is any factor or industry characteristic that creates an advantage for large leading firms over smaller nonleading rivals. Factors that sometimes create barriers to entry and/or mobility include substantial economies of scale, scope economies, large capital or skilled-labor requirements, and ties of customer loyalty created through advertising and other means.

It is worth keeping in mind that barriers to entry and mobility can sometimes result in compensating advantages for consumers. Even though patents can lead to monopoly profits for inventing firms, they also spur valuable new product and process development. Although efficient and innovative leading firms make life difficult for smaller rivals, they can have the favorable effect of lowering prices and increasing product quality. Therefore, a complete evaluation of the economic effects of entry barriers involves a consideration of both costs and benefits realized by suppliers and customers.

barrier to exit
Any limit on asset redeployment from one line of business or industry to another

Whereas barriers to entry can impede competition by making entry or nonleading firm growth difficult, competitive forces can also be diminished through barriers to exit. A **barrier to exit** is any restriction on the ability of incumbents to redeploy assets from one industry or line of business to another. During the late 1980s, for example, several state governments initiated legal proceedings to impede plant closures by large employers in the steel, glass, automobile, and other industries. By imposing large fines or severance taxes or requiring substantial expenditures for worker retraining, they created significant barriers to exit.

By impeding the asset redeployment that is typical of any vigorous competitive environment, barriers to exit can dramatically increase both the costs and risks of doing business. Even though one can certainly sympathize with the difficult adjustments faced by both individuals and firms affected by plant closures, government actions that create barriers to exit can have the unintended effect of retarding industrial development and market competition.

Effect of Buyers on Competition

monopsony
A market with one buyer

Generally speaking, if there are only a few buyers in a given market, there will be less competition than if there are many buyers. **Monopsony** exists when a single firm is the sole buyer of a desired product or input. Monopsony characterizes local labor markets with a single major employer, as well as many local agricultural markets with a single feed mill or livestock buyer. Similarly, the federal government is a monopsony buyer of military weapons and equipment. Major retailers such as Wal-Mart, Target, and Sears all enjoy monopsony power in the purchase of apparel, appliances, auto parts, and other consumer products. Such buyer power is especially strong in the purchase of "house brand" goods, where suppliers sell much if not all of their production to a single retailer. Monopsony is more common in factor input markets than in markets for final demand.

In terms of economic efficiency, monopsony is least harmful, and can sometimes even be beneficial, in those markets in which a monopsony buyer faces a monopoly seller. For example, consider the case of the town in which one mill is the sole employer of unskilled labor. The mill is a monopsony because it is a single buyer of labor, and it may be able to use its power to reduce wage rates below competitive levels. If workers organize a union to bargain collectively with their employer, a single monopoly seller of labor is created that could offset the employer's monopsony power and increase wages toward competitive market norms. Not only is monopsony accepted in such situations, but it is sometimes encouraged by public policy.

Effect of Product Differentiation on Competition

In addition to the number and size distribution of actual and potential competitors, market structure is also described by the degree of product differentiation. Product differentiation includes any real or perceived differences in the quality of goods and services offered to consumers. Sources of product differentiation include all of the various forms of advertising promotion, plus new products and processes made possible by effective programs of research and development.

The availability and cost of information about prices and output quality is a similarly important determinant of market structure. Competition is always most vigorous when buyers and sellers have ready access to detailed price/performance information.

Finally, market structure is broadly determined by entry and exit conditions. Low regulatory barriers, modest capital requirements, and nominal standards for skilled labor and other inputs all increase the likelihood that competition will be vigorous. Because all of these elements of market structure have important consequences for the price/output decisions made by firms, the study of market structure is an important ingredient of managerial economics

PERFECT COMPETITION

Market characteristics described in the preceding section determine the level of competition in the market for any good or service. This section focuses on the special features of perfectly competitive markets and illustrates why perfect competition is desirable from a social perspective.

Characteristics of Perfectly Competitive Markets

Perfect competition exists when individual producers have no influence on market prices; they are price takers as opposed to price makers. This lack of influence on price typically requires

- *Large numbers of buyers and sellers.* Each firm produces a small portion of industry output, and each customer buys only a small part of the total.
- *Product homogeneity.* The output of each firm is essentially the same as the output of any other firm in the industry.
- *Free entry and exit.* Firms are not restricted from entering or leaving the industry.
- *Perfect dissemination of information.* Cost, price, and product quality information is known by all buyers and all sellers.

These basic conditions are too restrictive for perfect competition to be commonplace. Although the stock market approaches the perfectly competitive ideal, imperfections occur even there. For example, the acquisition or sale of large blocks of securities by institutional investors clearly affects prices, at least in the short run. Nevertheless, because up to 1,000 shares of any stock can be bought or sold at the current market price, the stock market approaches the ideal of a perfectly competitive market. Similarly, many industrial firms must make output decisions without any control over price, and examination of a perfectly competitive market structure provides insights into these operating decisions. A clear understanding of perfect competition also provides a reference point from which to analyze monopolistic competition and oligopoly, as described in Chapter 11.

Market Price Determination

Market prices in competitive industries are determined by aggregate supply and demand; individual firms have no control over price. Total industry demand reflects an aggregation of the quantities that individual firms will buy at each price. Industry supply reflects a summation of the quantities that individual firms are willing to supply at different prices. The intersection of industry demand and supply curves determines market price.

Data in Table 10.1 illustrate the process by which an industry supply curve is constructed. First, suppose that each of five firms in an industry is willing to supply varying quantities at different prices. Summing the individual supply quantities of these five firms at each price determines their combined supply schedule, shown in the Partial Market Supply column. For example, at a price of $2, the output supplied by the five firms are 15, 0, 5, 25, and 45 (thousand) units, respectively, resulting in a combined supply of 90 (000) units at that price. With a product price of $8, supply quantities become 45, 115, 40, 55, and 75, for a total supply by the five firms of 330 (000) units.

Now assume that there are actually 5,000 firms in the industry, each with an individual supply schedule identical to one of the five firms illustrated in the table. There are 1,000 firms just like each one illustrated in Table 10.1; the total quantity supplied at each price is 1,000 times that shown under the Partial Market Supply schedule. This supply schedule is illustrated in Figure 10.1. Adding the market demand curve to the industry supply curve, as in Figure 10.2, allows one to determine the equilibrium market price.

Market price is found by equating market supply and market demand to find the equilibrium price/output level. Using the curves illustrated in Figure 10.2, we have

$$\text{Demand} = \text{Supply}$$
$$\$40 - \$0.0001Q = -\$0.254 + \$0.000025Q$$
$$\$0.000125Q = \$40.254$$
$$Q = 322{,}032$$

TABLE 10.1

Market Supply Schedule Determination

Price ($)	Quantity Supplied by Firm (000)					Partial Market Supply × 1,000	Total Market = Supply
	1 +	2 +	3 +	4 +	5 =		
1	5	0	5	10	30	50	50,000
2	15	0	5	25	45	90	90,000
3	20	20	10	30	50	130	130,000
4	25	35	20	35	55	170	170,000
5	30	55	25	40	60	210	210,000
6	35	75	30	45	65	250	250,000
7	40	95	35	50	70	290	290,000
8	45	115	40	55	75	330	330,000
9	50	130	45	65	80	370	370,000
10	55	145	50	75	85	410	410,000

$$P = \$40 - \$0.0001(322{,}032)$$
$$= \$40 - \$32.20$$
$$= \$7.80$$

Although both the quantity demanded and supplied depend on price, a simple example demonstrates the inability of individual firms to affect price. The total demand function in Figure 10.2 is described by the equation

(10.1) $$\text{Quantity Demanded} = Q = 400{,}000 - 10{,}000P$$

or, solving for price,

(10.1a)
$$\$10{,}000P = \$400{,}000 - Q$$
$$P = \$40 - \$0.0001Q$$

According to Equation 10.1a, a 100-unit change in Q would cause only a $0.01 change in price. A $0.0001 price increase would lead to a one-unit decrease in total market demand; a $0.0001 price reduction would lead to a one-unit increase in total market demand.

The demand curve shown in Figure 10.2 is redrawn for an individual firm in Figure 10.3. The slope of the curve is –0.0001, the same as in Figure 10.2; only the scales have been changed. The $7.80 intercept is the going market price as determined by the intersection of the market supply and demand curves in Figure 10.2.

At the scale shown in Figure 10.3, the firm's demand curve is seen to be, for all practical purposes, a horizontal line. Thus, it is clear that under perfect competition, the individual firm's output decisions do not affect price in any meaningful way. Price can be assumed constant irrespective of the output level at which the firm chooses to operate.

Firm Price/Output Decision

Profit maximization requires that a firm operate at the output level at which marginal revenue and marginal cost are equal. With price constant, average revenue equals marginal revenue. Therefore, maximum profits result when market price is set equal to marginal cost for firms in a perfectly competitive industry. In the example shown in Figure 10.4, the firm chooses to operate

FIGURE 10.1

Hypothetical Industry Supply Curve

Industry supply is the sum of the quantities that individual firms supply at each price.

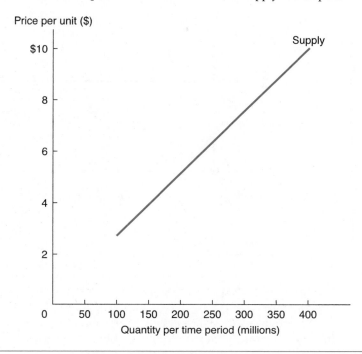

FIGURE 10.2

Market Price Determination in Perfect Competition

The perfectly competitive market-equilibrium price/output combination can be determined by equating the market demand and supply curves.

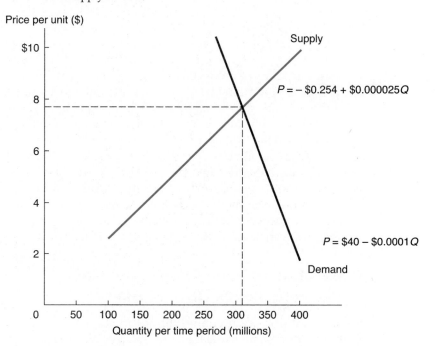

FIGURE 10.3

Demand Curve for a Single Firm in Perfect Competition

Firms face horizontal demand curves in perfectly competitive markets.

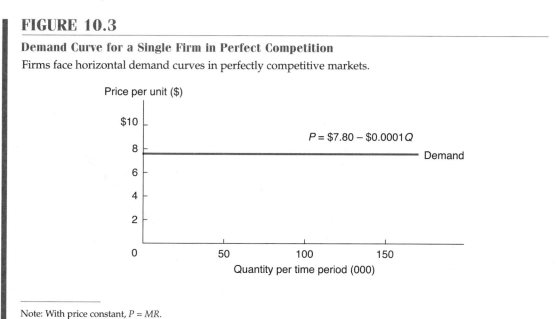

Note: With price constant, $P = MR$.

at output level Q^*, where price (and hence marginal revenue) equals marginal cost, and profits are maximized.

A normal profit, defined as the rate of return necessary to attract capital investment, is included as part of economic costs. Therefore, any profit shown in a graph such as Figure 10.4 is defined as economic profit and represents an above-normal rate of return. The firm incurs economic losses whenever it fails to earn a normal profit. A firm might show a small accounting profit but be suffering economic losses because these profits are insufficient to provide an adequate return to the firm's stockholders. In such instances, firms are unable to replace plant and equipment and will exit the industry in the long run.

In Figure 10.4 the firm produces and sells Q^* units of output at an average cost of C dollars; with a market price P, the firm earns economic profits of $P - C$ dollars per unit. Total economic profit, $(P - C)Q^*$, is shown by the shaded rectangle *PMNC*.

Over the long run, positive economic profits attract competitors. Expanding industry supply puts downward pressure on market prices and pushes cost upward because of increased demand for factors of production. Long-run equilibrium is reached when all economic profits and losses have been eliminated and each firm in the industry is operating at an output that minimizes long-run average cost (*LRAC*). Long-run equilibrium for a firm under perfect competition is graphed in Figure 10.5. At the profit-maximizing output, price (or average revenue) equals average cost, so the firm neither earns economic profits nor incurs economic losses. When this condition exists for all firms in the industry, new firms are not encouraged to enter the industry nor are existing ones pressured into leaving it. Prices are stable, and each firm is operating at the minimum point on its short-run average cost curve. All firms must also be operating at the minimum cost point on the long-run average cost curve; otherwise, they will make production changes, decrease costs, and affect industry output and prices. Accordingly, a stable equilibrium requires that firms operate with optimally sized plants.

Illustration of Price/Output Decisions in Perfectly Competitive Markets

The optimal price/output level for a firm in a perfectly competitive market can be further illustrated using a more detailed example. Assume that you are interested in determining the

FIGURE 10.4

Competitive Firm's Optional Price/Output Combination

Given a horizontal demand curve, $P = MR$. Thus, short-run equilibrium occurs when $P = MR = MC$.

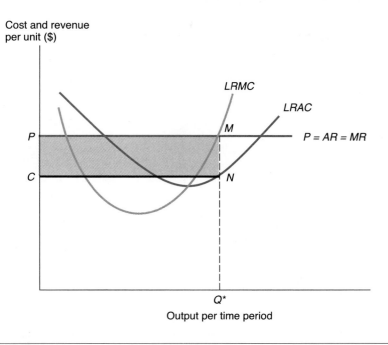

FIGURE 10.5

Long-Run Equilibrium in a Competitive Market

Long-run equilibrium is reached when Q^* units of output are produced at minimum $LRAC$. Thus, $P = MR = MC = AC$, and economic (excess) profits equal zero.

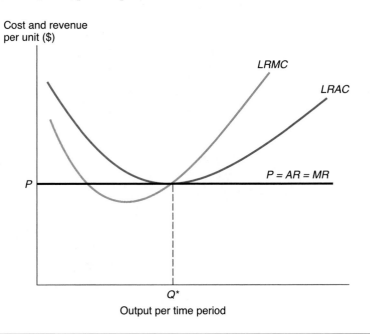

Is Ticketmaster a Monopoly?

In the 1980s, a small upstart named Ticketmaster decided to pay arenas millions of dollars for the right to sell their tickets and helped them develop effective marketing tactics. With Ticketmaster's help, selling tickets went from being a costly headache to a care-free and revenue-maximizing endeavor. As part of the bargain, Ticketmaster gained exclusive marketing rights for initial ticket sales. Because on-site box offices open later, and only when tickets are left over, Ticketmaster often accounts for 85 to 90 percent of sales for hundreds of on-site facilities.

Most people concede that Ticketmaster provides valuable services for venue operators and their customers. However, few would describe Ticketmaster service charges as modest. Long ago, Ticketmaster recognized that customers would pay a lot for ticket-buying services. Ticketmaster levels convenience fees, building facility charges, and order handling charges. For example, on April 14, 2002, Crosby, Stills, Nash & Young gave a concert at the Ice Palace Arena in Tampa, Florida. A first-level seat cost $125. The Ticketmaster convenience charge was $11.75, the building facility charge was $2.75, and the order handling charge was $3.30 (see table below). That's $167.80 for a single ticket, provided standard mail delivery was okay; UPS delivery cost more. That's a price that might bring tears to *Suite Judy Blue Eyes*.

In defense of such high fees, Ticketmaster argues that venue promotion services do not come cheap. As the sole ticket vendor, Ticketmaster can also assure venue operators that tickets will be priced properly in light of booking alternatives. However, it is Ticketmaster's marketing savvy and choke-hold on information concerning the ticket-buying habits of the general public that has trustbusters worried about monopoly power in the computerized ticketing services industry.

At what point is it reasonable for society to limit the success of dominant, innovative companies like Ticketmaster? Are such limits ever reasonable?

The Cost of Being a Fan: Selected Prices for Tickets Sold Through Ticketmaster

Venue	Primary Act	Location	Ticket Price	Convenience Charge + Building Facility Charge[1]	Handling Fee[2]
Philips Arena	Creed	Atlanta, GA	$40.50	$6.00	$1.65
Pantages Theatre	Walt Disney's *The Lion King*	Los Angeles, CA	15.00–125.00	7.50 + 2.00	3.05
Fleet Center	Elton John & Billy Joel	Boston, MA	45.00–175.00	9.00	3.00
D.A.R. Constitution Hall	Alicia Keys	Washington, DC	40.00	7.70 + 0.50	3.50
Nassau Coliseum	Janet Jackson	Uniondale, NY	32.50–92.50	7.90 + 2.50	3.00
Pebble Beach Golf Links	AT&T Pebble Beach National Pro-Am	Monterey, CA	40.00	4.50	2.00
Ice Palace Arena	Crosby, Stills, Nash & Young	Tampa, FL	39.50–150.00	11.75+2.75	3.30
Freeman Coliseum	San Antonio Stock Show	San Antonio, TX	12.00–22.00	3.75 + 1.50	3.10
Sovereign Bank Arena	World Wrestling Federation	Trenton, NJ	18.00–40.00	6.20 + 0.50	2.50
Nationwide Arena	Ringling Bros. and Barnum & Bailey Circus	Columbus, OH	10.00–35.00	3.50 + 1.00	2.00

1   Each ticket purchased through ticket centers, over the telephone, or on Ticketmaster Online is subject to a per ticket convenience charge. Telephone and online orders require use of a major credit card.

2   Orders processed over the telephone or on Ticketmaster Online are also subject to a per order handling charge. With standard mail delivery, tickets will be received at least 48 hours prior to the event (no additional charge). UPS delivery by 5:00 P.M. in 2 business days ($19.50), or by noon on Sat., if order placed by Wed. prior ($25.00).

Source: Web survey by the author, December 14, 2001 (http://www.ticketmaster.com).

See: Julia Angwin, "Ticketmaster's Online Resell System to Compete with Scalpers and eBay," *The Wall Street Journal Online*, April 5, 2002 (http://online.wsj.com).

profit-maximizing activity level for the Hair Stylist, Ltd., a hairstyling salon in College Park, Maryland. Given the large number of competitors, the fact that stylists routinely tailor services to meet customer needs, and the lack of entry barriers, it is reasonable to assume that the market is perfectly competitive and that the average $20 price equals marginal revenue, $P = MR = \$20$. Furthermore, assume that the firm's operating expenses are typical of the 100 firms in the local market and can be expressed by the following total and marginal cost functions:

$$TC = \$5,625 + \$5Q + \$0.01Q^2$$
$$MC = \$5 + \$0.02Q$$

where TC is total cost per month including capital costs, MC is marginal cost, and Q is the number of hairstylings provided.

The optimal price/output combination can be determined by setting marginal revenue equal to marginal cost and solving for Q:

$$
\begin{aligned}
MR &= MC \\
\$20 &= \$5 + \$0.02Q \\
\$0.02Q &= \$15 \\
Q &= 750 \text{ hairstylings per month}
\end{aligned}
$$

At this output level, maximum economic profits are

$$
\begin{aligned}
\pi &= TR - TC \\
&= \$20Q - \$5,625 - \$5Q - \$0.01Q^2 \\
&= \$20(750) - \$5,625 - \$5(750) - \$0.01(750^2) \\
&= \$0
\end{aligned}
$$

The $Q = 750$ activity level results in zero economic profits. This means that the Hair Stylist is just able to obtain a normal or risk-adjusted rate of return on investment because capital costs are already included in the cost function. The $Q = 750$ output level is also the point of minimum average production costs ($AC = MC = \$20$). Finally, with 100 identical firms in the industry, industry output totals 75,000 hairstylings per month.

Firm Supply Curve

Market supply curves are the sum of supply for individual firms at various prices. The perfectly competitive firm's short-run supply curve corresponds to that portion of the marginal cost curve that lies above the average variable cost curve. Because $P = MR$ under perfect competition, the quantity supplied by the perfectly competitive firm is found at the point where $P = MC$, so long as price exceeds average variable cost.

To clarify this point, consider the options available to the firm. Profit maximization always requires that the firm operate at the output level at which marginal revenue equals marginal cost. Under perfect competition, the firm will either produce nothing and incur a loss equal to its fixed costs, or it will produce an output determined by the intersection of the horizontal demand curve and the marginal cost curve. If price is less than average variable costs, the firm should produce nothing and incur a loss equal to total fixed cost. Losses will increase if any output is produced and sold when $P < AVC$. If price exceeds average variable cost, then each unit of output provides at least some profit contribution to help cover fixed costs and provide profit. The minimum point on the firm's average variable cost curve determines the lower limit, or cutoff point, of its supply schedule.

This is illustrated in Figure 10.6. At a very low price such as $1, $MR = MC$ at 100 units of output. The firm has a total cost per unit of $2 and a price of only $1, so it is incurring a loss of

FIGURE 10.6

Price, Cost, and Optimal Supply Decisions for a Firm Under Pure Competition

The minimum point of $1.25 on the *AVC* curve is the lowest price level at which the firm will supply output.

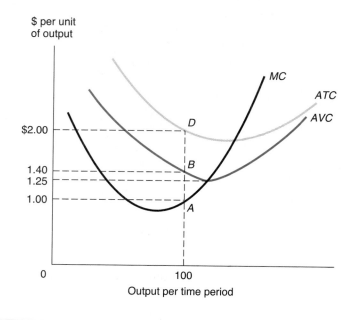

$1 per unit. This loss consists of a fixed cost component ($2.00 − $1.40 = $0.60) and a variable cost component ($1.40 − $1.00 = $0.40). Thus, the total loss is

$$\text{Total Loss} = (100 \text{ Units}) \times (\$0.60 \text{ Fixed Cost Loss} + \$0.40 \text{ Variable Cost Loss})$$
$$= \$100$$

If the firm simply shut down and terminated production, it would not incur variable costs, and its loss would be reduced to the level of fixed costs, or 100($0.60) = $60.

Price fails to cover variable costs at prices below $1.25, the minimum point on the *AVC* curve, so this is the lowest price at which the firm will operate. Above $1.25, price more than covers variable costs. Even though total costs are not covered at prices less than $2, it is preferable to operate when $1.25 < P < $2 and earn at least some profit contribution to cover a portion of total fixed costs rather than to shut down and incur losses equal to total fixed costs.

MONOPOLY

Perfect monopoly lies at the opposite extreme from perfect competition on the market structure continuum. Monopoly exists when a single firm is the sole producer of a good that has no close substitutes; in other words, there is a single firm in the industry. Perfect monopoly, like perfect competition, is seldom observed.

Characteristics of Monopoly Markets

Monopoly exists when an individual producer has the ability to set market prices. Monopoly firms are price makers as opposed to price takers. Their control over price typically requires

- *A single seller.* A single firm produces all industry output. The monopoly is the industry.
- *Unique product.* Monopoly output is perceived by customers to be distinctive and preferable to its imperfect substitutes.
- *Blockaded entry and exit.* Firms are heavily restricted from entering or leaving the industry.
- *Imperfect dissemination of information.* Cost, price, and product quality information is withheld from uninformed buyers.

As in the case of perfect competition, these basic conditions are too restrictive for monopoly to be commonplace in actual markets. Few goods are produced by single producers, and fewer still are free from competition of close substitutes. Even public utilities are imperfect monopolies in most of their markets. Electric companies approach a perfect monopoly in the residential lighting market but face strong competition from gas and oil suppliers in the heating market. In all industrial and commercial power markets, electric utilities face competition from gas- and oil-powered private generators. Even though perfect monopoly rarely exists, it is still worthy of careful examination. Many of the economic relations found under monopoly can be used to estimate optimal firm behavior in the less precise, but more prevalent, partly competitive and partly monopolistic market structures that dominate the real world.

Price/Output Decision Under Monopoly

Under monopoly, the industry demand curve is identical to the firm demand curve. Because industry demand curves slope downward, monopolists also face a downward-sloping demand curve. In Figure 10.7, for example, 100 units can be sold at a price of $10 a unit. At an $8 price, quantity demanded rises to 150 units. If the firm decides to sell 100 units, it will receive $10 a unit; if it wishes to sell 150 units, it must accept an $8 price. The monopolist can set either price or quantity, but not both. Given one, the value of the other is determined along the demand curve.

A monopoly uses the same profit-maximization rule as does any other firm: It operates at the output level at which marginal revenue equals marginal cost. The monopoly demand curve

FIGURE 10.7

Firm's Demand Curve Under Monopoly

The demand curve for a monopolist is the industry demand curve.

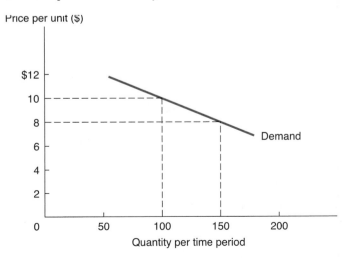

is not horizontal, however, so marginal revenue does not coincide with price at any but the first unit of output. Marginal revenue is always less than price for output quantities greater than one because of the negatively sloped demand curve. Because the demand (average revenue) curve is negatively sloped and hence declining, the marginal revenue curve must lie below it.

When a monopoly equates marginal revenue and marginal cost, it simultaneously determines the output level and the market price for its product. This decision is illustrated in Figure 10.8. The firm produces Q units of output at a cost of C per unit and sells this output at price P. Profits, which equal $(P - C)$ times Q, are represented by the area $PP'C'C$ and are at a maximum. Remember, Q is an optimal short-run output level only because average revenue, or price, is greater than average variable cost, as shown in Figure 10.8. If price is below average variable cost, losses are minimized by shutting down. Thus, if $P < AVC$, optimal $Q = 0$.

Illustration of Price/Output Decisions in Monopoly Markets

To further illustrate price/output decisions under monopoly, the previous Hair Stylist, Ltd., example can be modified to reflect an assumption that the firm has a monopoly in the College Park market, perhaps because of restrictive licensing requirements. In the earlier example, each of 100 perfectly competitive firms had a profit-maximizing activity level of 750 hairstylings per month, for a total industry output of 75,000 hairstylings per month.

FIGURE 10.8

Price/Output Decision Under Monopoly

Monopoly equilibrium occurs where $MR = MC$. However, $P > ATC$, and the firm earns economic (excess) profits.

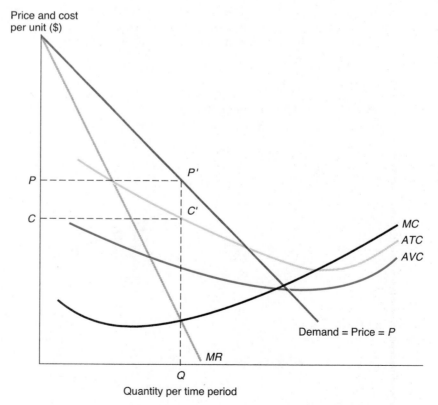

As a monopoly, the Hair Stylist provides all industry output. For simplicity, assume that the Hair Stylist operates a chain of salons and that the cost function for each shop is the same as in the previous example. By operating each shop at its average cost-minimizing activity level of 750 hairstylings per month, the Hair Stylist can operate with Marginal Cost = Average Cost = $20.

Assume that industry demand and marginal revenue curves for hair stylings in the College Park market are

$$P = \$80 - \$0.0008Q$$
$$MR = \$80 - \$0.0016Q$$

The monopoly profit-maximizing activity level is obtained by setting marginal revenue equal to marginal cost, or marginal profit equal to zero ($M\pi = 0$), and solving for Q:

$$MR = MC$$
$$\$80 - \$0.0016Q = \$20$$
$$\$0.0016Q = \$60$$
$$Q = 37{,}500 \text{ hairstylings per month}$$

The optimal market price is

$$P = \$80 - \$0.0008(37{,}500)$$
$$= \$50$$

At the $Q = 37{,}500$ activity level, the Hair Stylist will operate a chain of 50 salons (= 37,500/750). Although each outlet produces $Q = 750$ hairstylings per month, a point of optimum efficiency, the benefits of this efficiency accrue to the company in the form of economic profits rather than to consumers in the form of lower prices. Economic profits from each shop are

$$\pi = TR - TC$$
$$= P \times Q - AC \times Q$$
$$= \$50(750) - \$20(750)$$
$$= \$22{,}500 \text{ per month}$$

With 50 shops, the Hair Stylist earns total economic profits of $1,125,000 per month. As a monopoly, the industry provides only 37,500 units of output, down from the 75,000 units provided in the case of a perfectly competitive industry. The new price of $50 per hairstyling is up substantially from the perfectly competitive price of $20. The effects of monopoly power are reflected in terms of higher consumer prices, reduced levels of output, and substantial economic profits for the Hair Stylist, Inc.

Long-Run Equilibrium Under Monopoly

In general, any industry characterized by monopoly *sells less* output at *higher prices* than would the same industry if it were perfectly competitive. From the perspective of the firm and its stockholders, the benefits of monopoly are measured in terms of the economic profits that are possible when competition is reduced or eliminated. From a broader social perspective, these private benefits must be weighed against the costs borne by consumers in the forms of higher prices and reduced availability of desired products. Employees and suppliers also suffer from the reduced employment opportunities associated with lower production in monopoly markets.

Is This Why They Call It "Hardball"?

In late 2001, commissioner Bud Selig broke open the books to show that major league baseball (MLB) had lost $1.4 billion during the previous 5 years. Worse yet, operating losses of more than $500 million per year on stagnant revenues of $3.5 billion are threatening to kill the game, according to Selig. Obviously, Congress and the players' union need to rally around Selig's plan to reduce player salaries and allow him to get rid of the Montreal Expos and the Minnesota Twins. Local governments also need to pony up for new and more elaborate stadiums.

Selig's ploy may be nothing more than public posturing ahead of what promises to be tough labor negotiations. MLB operates much like a corporation with 30 different regional offices (local franchises). Although individual clubs compete on the playing field, they aren't economic competitors. In a competitive market, one competitor's gain comes at the expense of others. In baseball, the success of one franchise brings increased prosperity for all. Through revenue sharing, all clubs prospered when Barry Bonds broke Mark McGwire's

home run record. When the Giants or the Yankees come to town, home team ticket sales soar. Ineptitude at one franchise weakens the profit picture for everyone.

MLB is clearly concerned about its poisoned collective bargaining environment. On the other side of the table is the Major League Players' Association. The players' association is a monopoly seller of baseball player talent, and the owners are a monopsony employer. The labor-market standoff in major league baseball is a classic confrontation between a powerful monopsony employer (the owners) and a powerful monopoly employee group (the players' association). It will indeed be interesting to see if Selig and the player's association are successful in getting the general public to pay part of the tab for escalating player salaries and ever more elaborate stadiums.

See: Dow Jones Newswires, "Minnesota Court Upholds Injunction Forcing Twins to Play in '02," *The Wall Street Journal Online*, January 22, 2002 (http://online.wsj.com).

underproduction
A situation that occurs when a monopolist curtails production to a level at which marginal cost is less than price

Monopolies have an incentive to underproduce and earn economic profits. **Underproduction** results when a monopoly curtails output to a level at which the value of resources employed, as measured by the marginal cost of production, is less than the social benefit derived, where social benefit is measured by the price that customers are willing to pay for additional output. Under monopoly, marginal cost is less than price at the profit-maximizing output level. Although resulting economic profits serve the useful functions of providing incentives and helping allocate resources, it is difficult to justify above-normal profits that result from market power rather than from exceptional performance.

As shown earlier, in equilibrium, perfectly competitive firms must operate at the minimum point on the *LRAC* curve. This requirement does not hold under monopoly. For example, again consider Figure 10.8 and assume that the *ATC* curve represents the long-run average cost curve for the firm. The monopolist will produce *Q* units of output at an average cost of *C* per unit, somewhat above the minimum point on the *ATC* curve.

natural monopoly
An industry in which the market-clearing price occurs at a point at which the monopolist's long-run average costs are still declining

In this case, the firm is called a **natural monopoly**, because the market-clearing price, where $P = MC$, occurs at a point at which *long-run* average costs are still declining. In other words, market demand is insufficient to justify full utilization of even one minimum efficient–scale plant. A single monopolist can produce the total market supply at a lower total cost than could any number of smaller firms, and competition naturally reduces the number of competitors until only a single monopoly supplier remains. Electric and local telephone utilities are classic examples of natural monopoly, because any duplication in production and distribution facilities would increase consumer costs.

Is Monopoly Always Bad?

Natural monopoly presents something of a dilemma. On the one hand, economic efficiency could be enhanced by restricting the number of producers to a single firm. On the other hand, monopolies have an incentive to underproduce and can generate unwarranted economic profits.

Nevertheless, it is important to recognize that monopoly is not always as socially harmful as sometimes indicated. In the case of Microsoft Corp., for example, the genius of Bill Gates and a multitude of research associates has created a dynamic computer software juggernaut. The tremendous stockholder value created through their efforts, including billions of dollars in personal wealth for Gates and his associates, can be viewed only as a partial index of their contribution to society in general. Other similar examples include the DeKalb Corporation (hybrid seeds), Kellogg Company (ready-to-eat cereal), Lotus Corporation (spreadsheet software), and the Reserve Fund (money market mutual funds), among others. In instances such as these, monopoly profits are the just rewards flowing from truly important contributions of unique firms and individuals.

It is also important to recognize that monopoly profits are often fleeting. Early profits earned by each of the firms mentioned previously attracted a host of competitors. For example, note the tremendous growth in the money market mutual fund business since the November 1971 birth of the Reserve Fund. Today the Reserve Fund is only one of roughly 500 money market mutual funds available, and it accounts for only a small fraction of the roughly $1 trillion in industry assets. Similarly, Lotus Corporation is now a footnote in the computer software industry. The tremendous social value of invention and innovation often remains long after early monopoly profits have dissipated.

COUNTERVAILING POWER: THE MONOPOLY/MONOPSONY CONFRONTATION

Unregulated monopoly sellers typically limit production and offer their products at high prices. The private and social costs of this behavior are often measured by above-normal profits, inefficient production methods, and lagging rates of innovation. How is this inefficiency reduced, if not eliminated, in unregulated markets? Sometimes the answer lies in the development of countervailing forces within markets.

Seller Versus Buyer Power

countervailing power
Buyer market power that offsets seller market power, and vice versa

Countervailing power is an economic influence that creates a closer balance between previously unequal sellers and buyers. The classic example is a single employer in a small town that might take advantage of the local labor force by offering less-than-competitive wages. As the single employer, the company has a monopsony in the local labor market. Workers might decide to band together and form a union, a monopoly seller in the local labor market, to offset the monopsony power of the employer.

To illustrate this classic confrontation, consider Figure 10.9, which shows demand and supply relations in a local labor market. The downward-sloping demand for labor is simply the marginal revenue product of labor (MRP_L) curve and shows the amount of net revenue generated through employment of an additional unit of labor ($\partial TR/\partial L$). It is the product of the marginal product of labor (MP_L) and the marginal revenue of output (MR_Q). Thus, $MRP_L = \partial TR/\partial L = MP_L \times MR_Q$. MRP_L falls as employment expands because of the labor factor's diminishing returns. An upward-sloping supply curve reflects that higher wages are typically necessary to expand the amount of labor offered. Perfectly competitive demand and supply conditions create an exact balance between demand and supply, and the competitive equilibrium wage, W_C, and employment level, E_C, are observed.

A monopsony employer facing a perfectly competitive supply of labor sets its marginal cost of labor, MC_L, equal to the marginal benefit derived from employment. Because the employer's marginal benefit is measured in terms of the marginal revenue product of labor, an unchecked monopsonist sets $MC_L = MRP_L$. Notice that the MC_L curve exceeds the labor supply curve at each point, based on the assumption that wages must be increased for all workers in order to

FIGURE 10.9

Monopoly Union and Monopsony Employer Confrontation in the Labor Market

In a perfectly competitive labor market, the equilibrium wage is at W_C. A monopoly union facing competitive labor demand will seek a higher wage of W_U. A monopsony employer facing a competitive labor supply will offer a lower wage of W_M.

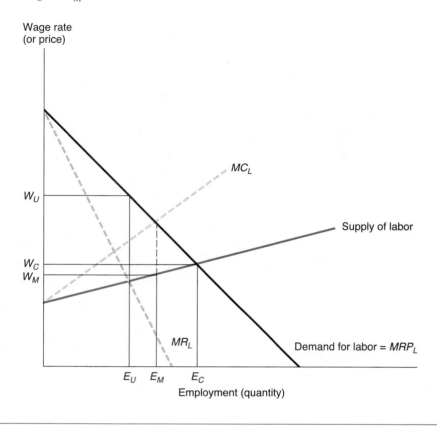

hire additional employees. This is analogous to cutting prices for all customers in order to expand sales, causing the *MR* curve to lie below the demand curve. Because workers need to be paid only the wage rate indicated along the labor supply curve for a given level of employment, the monopsonist employer offers employees a wage of W_M and a less than competitive level of employment opportunities, E_M.

An unchecked union, or monopoly seller of labor, could command a wage of W_U if demand for labor were competitive. This solution is found by setting the marginal revenue of labor (MR_L) equal to the labor supply curve, which represents the marginal cost of labor to the union. Like any monopoly seller, the union can obtain higher wages (prices) only by restricting employment opportunities (output) for union members. A union is able to offer its members only the less than competitive employment opportunities, E_U, if it attempts to maximize labor income.

Compromise Solution

What is likely to occur in the case of the monopoly union/monopsony employer confrontation? Typically, wage/employment bargaining produces a compromise wage/employment outcome. Compromise achieved through countervailing power has the beneficial effect of moving the labor market away from the inefficient unchecked monopoly or monopsony solutions toward a more efficient labor market equilibrium. However, only in the unlikely event of perfectly matched monopoly/monopsony protagonists will the perfectly competitive outcome occur. Depending on the relative power of the union and the employer, either an above-market or a below-market wage outcome typically results, and employment opportunities are often below competitive employment levels. Nevertheless, monopoly/monopsony confrontations can have the beneficial effect of improving economic efficiency from that experienced under either unchecked monopoly or monopsony.

MEASUREMENT OF BUSINESS PROFIT RATES

In long-run equilibrium, profits in perfectly competitive industries are usually just sufficient to provide a normal risk-adjusted rate of return. In monopoly markets, barriers to entry or exit can allow above-normal profits, even over the long run. Nevertheless, high profits are sometimes observed in vigorously competitive markets, while some monopolies stumble from one year to the next without realizing superior rates of return. To appreciate the sources of profit differences, it is first necessary to understand conventional measures of business profits.

Rate of Return on Stockholders' Equity

return on stockholders' equity (ROE)
Business profits expressed as a percentage of owner-supplied capital

Business profit rates are best evaluated using the accounting rate of **return on stockholders' equity (ROE)**. ROE is net income divided by the book value of stockholders' equity, where stockholders' equity is total assets minus total liabilities. As seen in Table 10.2, ROE can also be described as the product of three common accounting ratios. ROE equals the firm's profit margin multiplied by the total asset turnover ratio, all times the firm's leverage ratio:

(10.2)

$$
\begin{aligned}
\text{ROE} &= \frac{\text{Net Income}}{\text{Equity}} \\[6pt]
&= \frac{\text{Net Income}}{\text{Sales}} \times \frac{\text{Sales}}{\text{Total Assets}} \times \frac{\text{Total Assets}}{\text{Equity}} \\[6pt]
&= \text{Profit Margin} \times \frac{\text{Total Asset}}{\text{Turnover}} \times \text{Leverage}
\end{aligned}
$$

profit margin
Net income expressed as a percentage of sales revenue

Profit margin is accounting net income expressed as a percentage of sales revenue and shows the amount of profit earned per dollar of sales. When profit margins are high, robust demand or stringent cost controls, or both, allow the firm to earn a significant profit contribution. Holding capital requirements constant, profit margin is a useful indicator of managerial efficiency in responding to rapidly growing demand and/or effective measures of cost containment. Table 10.2 shows the outstanding profit margins reported by smokeless tobacco producer UST, Inc.; diversified financial services provider Stilwell Financial, Inc., growth stock manager of the Janus Group of mutual funds; and Internet portal Yahoo! However, rich profit margins do not necessarily guarantee a high rate of return on stockholders' equity. Despite high profit margins, firms in mining, construction, heavy equipment manufacturing, cable TV, and motion picture production often earn only modest rates of return because significant capital expenditures are required before meaningful sales revenues can be generated. Thus, it is vitally important to consider the magnitude of capital requirements when interpreting the size of profit margins for a firm or an industry.

total asset turnover
Sales revenue divided by the book value of total assets

Total asset turnover is sales revenue divided by the book value of total assets. When total asset turnover is high, the firm makes its investments work hard in the sense of generating a large amount of sales volume. A broad range of business and consumer service business enjoys high rates of total asset turnover that allow efficient firms to earn attractive rates of return on stockholders' equity despite modest profit margins. For example, consider environmental services juggernaut Waste Management, Inc. Despite modest profit margins and a conservative financial structure, Waste Management reports a sterling ROE by virtue of the

TABLE 10.2

Operating Statistics for a Sample of 50 Large Firms Taken from the *Standard & Poor's* 500

Company Name	Industry Name	Return on Stockholders' Equity (ROE) (%)	Profit Margin (%)	Total Asset Turnover Ratio	Leverage Ratio
Alberto Culver 'B'	Toiletries/cosmetics	15.3%	4.3%	0.62	2.18
Albertson's, Inc.	Grocery	16.7%	2.5%	0.42	2.75
Anheuser-Busch	Beverage (alcoholic)	35.8%	12.0%	1.08	3.22
AOL-Time Warner	Entertainment	5.6%	2.0%	1.87	5.28
Apple Computer	Computer and peripherals	14.9%	7.7%	0.85	1.66
Bank of America	Bank	18.5%	n.a.	n.a.	14.24
Bed Bath & Beyond	Retail (special lines)	23.5%	7.0%	0.46	1.55
Bristol-Myers Squibb	Drug	48.2%	20.6%	0.85	1.98
Deere & Co.	Machinery	5.8%	2.5%	1.06	2.51
Dell Computer	Computer and peripherals	35.0%	7.4%	0.45	2.16
Delta Air Lines	Air transport	20.0%	6.4%	1.29	4.04
Dillard's, Inc.	Retail store	7.7%	2.5%	0.91	2.80
Dow Jones & Co.	Newspaper	40.2%	11.1%	0.76	2.77
EMC Corp.	Computer and peripherals	23.5%	17.4%	1.07	1.45
Fannie Mae	Financial svcs. (div.)	22.2%	n.a.	n.a.	32.63
Ford Motor	Auto and truck	26.3%	4.5%	1.70	10.03
Freddie Mac	Financial svcs. (div.)	19.0%	n.a.	n.a.	33.18
Gannett Co.	Newspaper	19.9%	17.5%	1.71	1.95
Gateway Inc.	Computer and peripherals	22.0%	5.1%	0.46	1.96
Harley-Davidson	Recreation	23.0%	10.9%	0.86	1.82
Hershey Foods	Food processing	26.9%	7.4%	0.84	3.05
Hilton Hotels	Hotel/gaming	12.4%	8.2%	4.30	6.54
Home Depot	Retail building supply	18.8%	6.0%	0.44	1.38
Limited Inc.	Retail (special lines)	20.4%	4.5%	0.42	1.90
Mattel, Inc.	Recreation	9.3%	3.3%	0.93	2.61
Merck & Co.	Drug	44.5%	18.0%	1.09	2.69
Merrill Lynch & Co.	Securities brokerage	20.4%	7.5%	9.41	25.63
N.Y. Times	Newspaper	21.4%	9.9%	1.12	2.41
NIKE, Inc. 'B'	Shoe	18.5%	6.4%	0.65	1.87
Nordstrom, Inc.	Retail store	17.1%	4.0%	0.60	2.58
Nortel Networks	Foreign telecom.	10.5%	6.7%	1.13	1.75
Palm, Inc.	Wireless networking	5.6%	5.4%	1.21	1.25
Quaker Oats	Food processing	180.6%	8.4%	0.51	10.90
Schwab (Charles)	Securities brokerage	25.9%	12.5%	6.22	12.88
Southwest Airlines	Air transport	16.7%	10.0%	1.19	1.99
Sprint Corp.	Telecom. services	16.5%	10.2%	1.28	2.07
St. Jude Medical	Medical supplies	18.1%	12.9%	1.39	1.96
Starbucks Corp.	Restaurant	10.6%	6.1%	0.75	1.30
Stilwell Fin'l	Financial svcs. (div.)	38.4%	25.8%	1.02	1.51
SunTrust Banks	Bank	14.7%	n.a.	n.a.	12.51
Target Corp.	Retail store	20.2%	3.5%	0.51	2.92
Texas Instruments	Semiconductor	16.6%	16.2%	1.59	1.62
UST, Inc.	Tobacco	233.7%	31.0%	0.67	5.06
Wal-Mart Stores	Retail store	22.1%	3.5%	0.43	2.72
Waste Management	Environmental	25.2%	8.5%	1.73	5.15
Wells Fargo	Bank	16.9%	n.a.	n.a.	9.86
Wendy's Int'l	Restaurant	15.6%	8.0%	0.91	1.77
WorldCom Inc.	Telecom. Services	7.7%	10.8%	2.45	1.75
Wrigley (Wm.) Jr.	Food processing	27.1%	14.9%	0.75	1.36
Yahoo! Inc.	Internet	10.7%	22.9%	2.50	1.17
Averages		**27.7%**	**9.6%**	**1.39**	**5.25**

Source: *Value Line Investment Survey for Windows*, July 1, 2001.
Reproduced with permission of Value Line Publishing, Inc.

fact that it reports a total asset turnover rate that is well in excess of industry and corporate norms. Waste Management has learned that the wise use of assets is a key ingredient of success in the often cutthroat environmental services business.

leverage
The ratio of the book value of assets divided by stockholders' equity

Leverage is often defined as the ratio of total assets divided by stockholders' equity. It reflects the extent to which debt and preferred stock are used in addition to common stock financing. Leverage is used to amplify firm profit rates over the business cycle. During economic booms, leverage can dramatically increase the firm's profit rate; during recessions and other economic contractions, leverage can just as dramatically decrease realized rates of return, if not lead to losses. Despite ordinary profit margins and modest rates total asset turnover, ROE in the securities brokerage, hotel, and gaming industries can sometimes benefit through use of a risky financial strategy that employs significant leverage. However, it is worth remembering that a risky financial structure can lead to awe-inspiring profit rates during economic expansions, such as that experienced during the late 1990s; it can also lead to huge losses during economic downturns, such as that in 2001.

Typical Business Profit Rates

For successful large and small firms in the United States and Canada, ROE averages roughly 12 percent during a typical year. This average ROE is comprised of a typical profit margin on sales revenue of roughly 4 percent, a standard total asset turnover ratio of 1.0 times, and a common leverage ratio of roughly 3:1:

(10.2a)

$$\frac{\text{Typical}}{\text{ROE}} = \text{Profit Margin} \times \frac{\text{Total Asset}}{\text{Turnover}} \times \text{Leverage}$$

$$= 4\% \times 1.0 \times 3$$

$$= 12\%$$

ROE is an attractive measure of firm performance because it shows the rate of profit earned on funds committed to the enterprise by its owners, the stockholders. When ROE is at or above 12 percent per year, the rate of profit is generally sufficient to compensate investors for the risk involved with a typical business enterprise. When ROE consistently falls far below 12 percent per year, profit rates are generally insufficient to compensate investors for the risks undertaken. Of course, when business risk is substantially higher than average, a commensurately higher rate of return is required. When business risk is somewhat lower than average, a somewhat lower than average profit rate is adequate.

This naturally suggests an important question: How is it possible to know if business profit rates in any given circumstance are sufficient to compensate investors for the risks undertaken? The answer to this difficult question turns out to be rather simple: just ask current and potential shareholders and bondholders. Shareholders and bondholders implicitly inform management of their risk/return assessment of the firm's performance on a daily basis. If performance is above the minimum required, the firm's bond and stock prices rise; if performance is below the minimum required, bond and stock prices fall. For privately held companies, the market's risk/return assessment comes at less frequent intervals, such as when new bank financing is required. If performance is above the minimum required, bank financing is easy to obtain; if performance is below the minimum required, bank financing is difficult or impossible to procure. As a practical matter, firms must consistently earn a business profit rate or ROE of at least 12 percent per year in order to grow and prosper. If ROE consistently falls below this level, sources of financing tend to dry up and the firm withers and dies. If ROE consistently exceeds this level, new debt and equity financing are easy to obtain, and growth by new and established competitors is rapid.

Although ROE is perhaps the most useful available indicator of business profits, other accounting measures can also be used to compare profit rates across different lines of business.

Wrigley's Success Formula

People have enjoyed chewing gum–like substances for a long time. From the Native Americans of New England, the early colonists learned to chew the gum-like resin that formed on spruce trees when the bark was cut. Lumps of spruce gum were sold in the eastern United States during the early 1800s, making it the first commercial chewing gum in the United States. Modern chewing gum began in the late 1860s when chicle was brought to this country and tried as a chewing gum ingredient. Chicle comes from the latex of the sapodilla tree, which grows in the tropical rain forests of Central America. It made possible a smooth, springy, satisfying chew and holds flavors longer and better. By the start of the twentieth century, modern chewing gum was well on its way to popularity.

This is when William Wrigley, Jr., came to Chicago from Philadelphia. His father sold Wrigley's Scouring Soap. As an extra incentive to merchants, Wrigley offered premiums. One of these premiums was baking powder. When baking powder proved to be more popular than soap, Wrigley switched to the baking powder business. In 1892, Wrigley got the idea of offering two packages of chewing gum with each can of baking powder. Once again the premium—chewing gum—seemed more promising than the product it was supposed to promote. Wrigley began marketing that chewing gum under his own name. His first two brands were *Lotta* and *Vassar*. *Juicy Fruit* and *Spearmint* came in 1893

Getting a foothold in the chewing gum business was not easy. Wrigley built a loyal following as he stuck to a basic principle: "Even in a little thing like a stick of gum, quality is important." Wrigley was also a pioneer in the use of advertising to promote the sale of branded merchandise. He saw that consumer acceptance of Wrigley's gum could be built faster by telling people about the product through newspaper and magazine ads, outdoor posters, and other forms of advertising.

For more than 100 years, quality products and relentless brand-name advertising has been Wrigley's success formula. It's a formula that works.

See: Home page information for Wrigley's can be found on the Internet (http://www.wrigley.com).

---

return on assets (ROA)
Net income divided by the book value of total assets

The accounting **return on assets (ROA)**, defined as net income divided by total assets, is also a useful indicator of the business profit rate. Like ROE, ROA captures the effects of managerial operating decisions; unlike ROE, ROA is unaffected by the amount of leverage. Therefore, although ROA is a useful alternative indicator of the basic profitability of a business, it fails to account for the effects of financial leverage decisions on firm performance. As such, ROE has some advantages over ROA as a fundamental measure of business profits. Irrespective of whether ROE, ROA, or some other measure of business profits is employed, consistency requires that comparisons be made using a common basis.

LINK BETWEEN MARKET STRUCTURE AND BUSINESS PROFIT RATES

High business profit rates are derived from some combination of high profit margins, quick total asset turnover, and a high rate of total assets to stockholders' equity. High business profits generally indicate superior efficiency, modest competition, a wise use of assets, and/or use of a risky financial structure.

Business Profit Rates by Industry Group

In a perfectly competitive market, profit margins are low. This stems from the fact that in a perfectly competitive market, theory suggests that $P = MC$ and $MC = AC$. As a result, when average cost includes a risk-adjusted normal rate of return on investment, $P = AC$. This means that when profit margin is measured as $(P - AC)/P$, profit margins will tend to be low and reflect only a normal rate of return in perfectly competitive markets. On the other hand, theory asserts that $P > MC$ in monopoly markets. When profit margin is measured as $(P - AC)/P$, profit margins will tend to be high and reflect above-normal rates of return in monopoly markets. However, a problem is encountered when profit margins earned in the business world are used as indicators of the level of competition in the marketplace. Without detailed firm-specific data, how is it possible to know if higher profit margins are due to higher prices, and perhaps monopoly power, or instead due to lower costs and, therefore, superior efficiency?

The short answer is simple. It is impossible to know the source of above-normal profit margins without direct access to detailed price and cost data. Unfortunately, this information is seldom available. For example, McDonald's discloses company-wide profit rates to conform with Securities and Exchange Commission reporting requirements but jealously guards secret information for individual restaurants. McDonald's would never voluntarily disclose profit rates by restaurant location or menu item for fear that such disclosures would intensify unwanted competition. By simply building new restaurants, McDonald's already sends out a signal that acts as a beacon to Burger King, Pizza Hut, Subway, and a host of other competitors. Why make it easier for competitors by telling them exactly where the "gold" is buried?

Table 10.3 shows business profit rates for a sample of industry groups obtained from corporate income tax data. Although such industry groups correspond only loosely with economic markets, these data offer useful perspective on profit differences across a variety of important lines of business. As shown in Table 10.3, historical profit rates tend to be high in professional services such as legal services, dentists, and physicians. In these professions, capital requirements tend to be low, and profit rates are high. Capital-intensive business such as coal mining, paper, railroads, and hospitals routinely earn sub-par rates of return on invested capital. An interesting feature of Table 10.3 and Figure 10.10 is that they illustrate a phenomenon known as the **reversion to the mean**.

reversion to the mean
Over time, the tendency for business profit rates to revert toward a risk-adjusted normal rate of return

Over time, entry into highly profitable industries and nonleading firm growth causes above-normal profits to regress toward the mean. Conversely, bankruptcy and exit allow the below-normal profits of depressed industries to rise toward the mean. For example, drugs, health-care services, and medical supplies were among our most profitable industries during the late 1980s as an aging population and government-sponsored health programs have caused the demand for health care to skyrocket. In the late 1990s, however, a proliferation of new drug therapies, cost-containment measures, and government regulations conspired to limit profit-making opportunities in health care. As a result, profits and sales growth in the industry turned downward. Over the next decade, it is not likely that health-care industry profits will dramatically exceed all-industry averages; they will have regressed towards the mean profit level. At the same time, major air carriers such as United, American, and Delta typically earn meager profits, at best, because they operate in an industry with a homogenous product (safe air travel) and huge fixed costs. As a result, price competition is vicious. Still, profit rates for the airlines and other travel industries are bound to rise over the next few years because the industry cannot continue to sustain the enormous losses incurred during the early part of this decade. Bankruptcy and exit will allow prices and profits to rise toward a risk-adjusted normal rate of return for survivors.

On an overall basis, the degree of competition is an important contributor to the level of profitability that can be achieved by efficient firms. The level of profitability actually achieved is a function of both market structure and firm performance. To see the role played by firm-specific factors, it is informative to examine profit rates for top performers.

Business Profit Rates for Top-Performing Large Firms

ROE is high to the extent that the firm enjoys a high profit margin on sales, a high rate of total asset turnover, or benefits from financial leverage. To see the relative importance of firm-specific

TABLE 10.3

Corporate Profitability in 50 Large Industry Groups

Industry Group	Total Active Corporations	Gross Profit (% of sales)	Net Profit Margin (% of sales)	Return on Equity (ROE)
Agricultural production	91,164	47.20%	2.50%	6.50%
Alcoholic beverages	4,615	25.30%	3.10%	22.30%
Auto repair and services	98,333	55.70%	1.30%	9.40%
Banks	3,820	99.60%	21.90%	11.20%
Bottled soft drinks and flavorings	653	47.50%	9.80%	21.20%
Chemicals and allied products	9,079	22.30%	1.90%	11.90%
Coal mining	1,521	31.10%	3.90%	3.80%
Computers and office machines	3,782	37.80%	8.20%	26.40%
Crude petroleum and natural gas	13,772	41.70%	6.30%	4.10%
Drugs	2,536	56.80%	15.40%	22.80%
Eating and drinking places	215,393	56.70%	2.50%	15.00%
Electrical goods	30,004	18.90%	1.00%	8.20%
Farm machinery	1,984	37.10%	8.80%	27.70%
Footwear, except rubber	191	36.00%	4.00%	14.20%
Furniture and home furnishings stores	48,678	35.30%	1.60%	9.50%
Gasoline service stations	31,376	15.50%	0.70%	11.70%
Grocery stores	45,534	24.40%	1.40%	18.40%
Hardware stores	10,677	32.60%	0.60%	4.10%
Heavy construction contractors	23,071	22.20%	3.20%	11.10%
Hospitals	1,493	90.10%	1.50%	1.40%
Hotels and other lodging places	30,636	58.70%	4.40%	9.80%
Industrial chemicals, plastics, and synthetics	4,219	32.20%	7.40%	12.50%
Knitting mills	552	25.70%	3.00%	11.00%
Legal services	72,848	98.40%	4.80%	101.50%
Life insurance companies	1,685	25.90%	7.00%	8.50%
Liquor stores	14,407	20.00%	1.00%	11.50%
Local and interurban passenger transit	18,155	80.40%	2.00%	10.80%
Logging, sawmills, and planing mills	11,694	22.60%	1.10%	2.90%
Metals and minerals	6,377	10.50%	1.60%	9.00%
Motion picture production and distribution	20,925	53.50%	2.70%	2.60%
Motion picture theaters	1,711	71.20%	2.50%	5.70%
Motor vehicle dealers	42,289	11.70%	0.80%	17.50%
Motor vehicles and automotive equipment	27,667	22.20%	1.30%	9.50%
Newspapers	5,936	68.30%	14.90%	25.20%
Nursing and personal care facilities	15,303	88.00%	1.10%	5.10%
Offices of dentists	47,344	96.40%	3.60%	77.10%
Offices of physicians	127,872	95.50%	1.20%	38.70%
Paper and paper products	11,362	24.00%	1.40%	5.50%
Petroleum and petroleum products	13,828	11.10%	1.10%	7.80%
Petroleum refining	224	21.20%	6.60%	10.70%
Plumbing and heating, except electric	995	34.90%	7.50%	15.40%
Pulp, paper, and board mills	293	28.40%	1.90%	3.20%
Radio, TV, and communication equipment	3,182	36.70%	4.60%	14.90%
Railroad transportation	780	71.90%	3.10%	2.10%
Security brokers and services	10,468	97.80%	21.80%	17.80%
Soaps, cleaners, and toilet goods	3,056	38.10%	11.50%	33.70%
Telephone and other communication services	17,302	73.50%	7.30%	9.20%
Toys, sporting, and photographic goods	12,537	28.00%	2.60%	26.80%
Trucking and warehousing	82,313	70.60%	2.60%	14.40%
Water supply and other sanitary services	13,661	72.20%	5.60%	9.90%
Averages	**25,146**	**46.47%**	**4.75%**	**15.82%**

Source: U.S. corporate federal income tax data, 2001 (http://www.bizstats.com).

FIGURE 10.10

Profit Rates Display Mean Reversion over Time

Entry into high-profit industries drives down both prices and profits. Over time, entry causes above-normal profits to regress toward normal profit rate, whereas exit allows the below-normal profits of depressed industries to rise toward the mean.

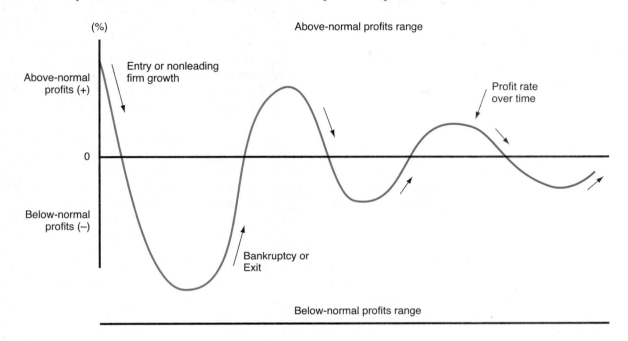

factors as contributors to high rates of business profits, it is interesting to analyze the components of ROE for top-performing large firms shown in Table 10.2. Many such companies earn a ROE of 20 to 35 percent per year on a regular basis. Drug companies such as Bristol-Myers Squibb and Merck display the lofty profit margins associated with the marketing of innovative patent-protected pharmaceuticals. Other firms with special characteristics are also found among high-profit margin firms. For example, the William Wrigley Jr. Co. and Hershey Foods Corp. enjoy dominant market positions in the chewing gum and candy industries, respectively. Dow Jones & Co., publishers of *The Wall Street Journal* and *Barron's* financial weekly, produces information that is a must read for Wall Street professionals and thereby enjoys enviable brand-name recognition in the financial news and reporting business.

It is interesting to note that the top-performing firms displayed in Table 10.2 exemplify wide variety in terms of industry and in terms of the relative importance of profit margins, total asset turnover, and leverage as contributors to ROE. This diversity suggests that firm-specific factors, such as superior efficiency, and industry-related factors, such as market power, both contribute to the realization of above-normal rates of return.

COMPETITIVE STRATEGY IN PERFECTLY COMPETITIVE AND MONOPOLY MARKETS

In perfectly competitive markets, the ready imitation of rivals makes ongoing success a constant struggle. In monopoly markets, entry and growth by nonleading firms often eat away at proprietary advantages. In both instances, development of an effective competitive strategy is vital to long-run success.

Competitive Strategy in Perfectly Competitive Markets

competitive strategy
The search for a favorable competitive position in an industry or line of business

Competitive strategy is the search for a favorable competitive position and durable above-normal profits in an industry or line of business.

In perfectly competitive industries, above-normal returns sometimes reflect **economic luck**, or temporary good fortune due to unexpected changes in industry demand or cost conditions. For example, during 2001 many small to mid-size oil refineries and gasoline retailers benefited greatly when oil prices unexpectedly shot up following temporary oil shortages. At the same time, many other firms experienced economic losses following the unanticipated rise in energy costs. Both sets of companies experienced a reversal of fortune when energy prices plummeted. Grain farmers also benefit mightily when export demand for agricultural products skyrockets and suffer when export demand withers.

economic luck
Temporary good fortune due to unexpected changes in industry demand or cost conditions

In other instances, above-normal returns in perfectly competitive industries reflect what is known as **economic rents**, or profits due to uniquely productive inputs. An exceptionally well-trained workforce, talented management, or superior land and raw materials can all lead to above-normal profits. In parts of the country where school systems provide outstanding primary and secondary education, firms are able to hire a basic workforce with a high rate of literacy and strong basic skills. Businesses that are able to employ such workers at a typical wage are able to earn superior profits when compared with the average rate of return for all competitors in the United States and Canada. Local tax subsidies designed to attract investment and job opportunities can also lower the cost of capital and create economic rents for affected firms. In many parts of the country, government initiatives often lead to economic rents for affected firms. On the other hand, if local taxes or government regulations prove to be especially onerous, economic losses can result for affected companies.

economic rents
Profits due to uniquely productive inputs

Another important source of above-normal profits in perfectly competitive industries is **disequilibrium profits**. Disequilibrium profits are above-normal returns that can be earned in the time interval that often exists between when a favorable influence on industry demand or cost conditions first transpires and the time when competitor entry or growth finally develops.

disequilibrium profits
Above-normal returns that can be earned in the time interval between when a favorable influence on industry demand or cost conditions first transpires and the time when competitor entry or growth finally develops

Disequilibrium losses are below-normal returns suffered in the time interval that can arise between when an unfavorable influence on industry demand or cost conditions first transpires and the time when exit or downsizing finally occurs. When barriers to entry and exit are minimal, competitor reactions tend to be quick and disequilibrium profits are fleeting. When barriers to entry and exit are significant, competitor reactions tend to be slow and disequilibrium profits can persist for extended periods. In the quintessential perfectly competitive industry, disequilibrium profits are quickly dissipated. In real-world markets, disequilibrium profits can persist over an entire business cycle even in the most competitive industries. In retailing, for example, labor and inventory costs have been cut dramatically following the introduction of computerized price scanners. Despite the vigorously price-competitive nature of the retailing business, early innovators who first adopted the bar code technology have been able to earn above-normal profits for a number of years. Innovative grocery retailers have enjoyed dramatically lower costs and profit margins on sales of 2 percent to 3.5 percent, versus a more typical 1 percent, over a decade and more.

disequilibrium losses
Below-normal returns that can be suffered in the time interval that often exists between when an unfavorable influence on industry demand or cost conditions first transpires and the time when exit or downsizing finally occurs

In equilibrium, perfectly competitive markets only offer the potential for a normal rate of return on investment. If many capable competitors offer identical products, vigorous price competition tends to eliminate disequilibrium profits. The only exception to this rule is that superior efficiency can sometimes lead to superior profits, even in perfectly competitive markets. Above-normal profits in perfectly competitive industries are usually transitory and reflect the influences of economic rents, luck, or disequilibrium conditions. If above-normal returns persist for extended periods in a given industry or line of business, then elements of uniqueness are probably at work.

Competitive Strategy in Monopoly Markets

Above-normal returns tend to be fleeting in perfectly competitive industries but can be durable for efficient firms that benefit from meaningful monopoly advantages. As in any perfectly competitive industry, above-normal profit rates can be observed if monopoly firms temporarily benefit from some unanticipated increase in demand or decrease in costs. Similarly, monopolists can benefit from temporary affluence due to unexpected changes in industry demand or cost conditions or uniquely productive inputs. What is unique about monopoly is the potential for long-lasting above-normal rates of return.

In this age of instant global communication and rapid technical advance, no monopoly is permanently secure from the threat of current or potential competitors. Product characteristics, the local or regional limits of the market, the time necessary for reactions by established or new competitors, the pace of innovation, unanticipated changes in government regulation and tax policy, and a host of additional considerations all play an important role in defining the scope and durability of monopoly power. When attempting to describe monopoly advantages, it is always helpful to consider the number and size of potential competitors, degree of product differentiation, level of information available in the marketplace, and conditions of entry.

Table 10.4 summarizes major characteristics typical of perfectly competitive and monopolistic markets. To develop an effective competitive strategy, it is necessary to assess the degree to which the characteristics of an individual market embody elements of each. Although the probability of successful entry is greater in perfectly competitive markets, monopoly markets lure new and established competitors with the promise of long-lasting, above-normal returns. Because the decision to enter any new market or line of business involves a careful balancing

TABLE 10.4

Summary of Perfect Competition and Monopoly (Monopsony) Market-Structure Characteristics

	Perfect Competition	**Monopoly (Monopsony)**
Number of actual or potential competitors	Many small buyers and sellers	A single seller (buyer) of a valued product
Product differentiation	None—each buyer and seller deals in an identical product	Very high—no close substitutes available
Information	Complete and free information on price and product quality	Highly restricted access to price and product-quality information
Conditions of entry and exit	Complete freedom of entry and exit	Very high barriers caused by economies of scale (natural monopoly), patents, copyrights, government franchises, or other factors
Profit potential	Normal profit in long run; economic profits (losses) in short run only	Potential for economic profits in both short and long run
Examples	Some agricultural markets (grain); commodity, stock, and bond markets; some nonspecialized input markets (unskilled labor)	Monopoly (sellers): Local telephone service (basic hook-up); municipal bus companies; gas, water, and electric utilities. Monopsony (buyers): state and local governments (roads): U.S. government (defense electronics)

of expected costs and expected benefits, the monopoly advantages can act as a powerful induce-ment to competitors. Preservation of monopoly advantages is only likely when firms maintain the distinctive and valuable characteristics sought by customers. Similarly, the search for above-normal profits is only likely to be successful when firms create products that are faster, cheaper, or better than those offered by rivals.

Why Market Niches Are Attractive

Entry into a perfectly competitive industry is not apt to result in long-lasting, above-normal rates of return under even the best of circumstances. For example, a grain producer located along a river or on exceptionally fertile soil would enjoy lower-than-average irrigation costs and fertilizer expenses, and higher profits could result. However, potential buyers would have to pay a price premium for such productive land, and subsequent investors would earn only a normal rate of return on their investment. No landowner is going to sell highly productive or well-situated land at a bargain-basement price. Similarly, purchase of a business that enjoys recognized monopoly power seldom leads to economic profits because anticipated abnormal returns on plant and equipment are reflected in purchase prices. Much like fertile land brings a price premium in the real estate market, monopoly franchises bring a premium price in the stock market. As a result, the purchase of a recognized monopoly leads to only a risk-adjusted normal rate of return for subsequent investors. Monopolists make money; investors in fully appreciated monopoly do not.

Only new and unique products or services have the potential to create monopoly profits. Imitation of such products may be protected by patents, copyrights, or other means. In many instances, these above-normal profits reflect the successful exploitation of a market niche. A **market niche** is a segment of a market that can be successfully exploited through the special capabilities of a given firm or individual. To be durable, above-normal profits derived from a market niche must not be vulnerable to imitation by competitors.

market niche
A segment of a market that can be successfully exploited through the special capabilities of a given firm or individual

For example, Avon Products, Inc., is rightly famous for its entrepreneurial army of inde-pendent sales representatives. "Avon Calling!" is a greeting that has long generated huge cash returns for the company in the United States and abroad. In Japan, for example, Avon's profit rate and popularity is even greater than that enjoyed in the United States. Avon has succeeded where others have failed because it has developed and nurtured the direct selling market for cosmetics. Better than anyone else, Avon knows cosmetics, toiletries, costume jewelry, and other products that many women want and knows how much they are willing to pay for them. Avon keeps on growing despite numerous assaults from would-be competitors and regular predic-tions that its primary market is a sure-fire casualty of dual-income households. Indeed, its domestic and foreign business is so profitable that Avon has been the subject of repeated takeover speculation. To thwart such advances, the company has initiated a dramatic program to streamline operations in an effort to enhance already high profits. In the meantime, Avon keeps on dominating its market niche.

Another interesting example of a firm that successfully exploits a profitable market niche is provided by Stilwell Financial, Inc., a diversified financial services firm best known for its Janus Group of mutual funds. Janus has a dominant and extraordinarily profitable market niche in the worldwide mutual fund business. Founder Tom Bailey was an early advocate of growth stock investing in the technology sector. Not only has the idea proved popular to U.S. investors, but Japanese and European investors have jumped on the Janus bandwagon as well. As a result, Stilwell enjoys double-digit growth, net profit margins that average in excess of 25 percent of sales, and a rate of return on assets of roughly 40 percent per year.

Avon Products and Stilwell Financial are only two examples of the many firms that enjoy tremendous success through market niche dominance. To attain similar success, a firm must first recognize the attractiveness of the market niche and then successfully apply the concept to its own business. Few firms achieve any great measure of success in trying to be all things to all customers. Lasting success requires exploitation of those segments of the market that can be best served using the special capabilities of a given firm or individual.

Information Barriers to Competitive Strategy

Any use of market structure information as a guide to competitive strategy must address the challenge posed by measurement problems encountered in defining the magnitude and root cause of above-normal rates of return. To be sure, accounting profit data derived from a historical perspective give much useful information for operating decisions and tax purposes. However, these data sometimes measure economic profits only imperfectly. For example, advertising and research and development (R&D) expenditures are expensed for both reporting and tax purposes, even though each can give rise to long-term economic benefits. An expense-as-incurred treatment of advertising and R&D expenditures can lead to errors in profit measurement. Although current net income is depressed when advertising and R&D are written off before the end of their useful lives, intangible assets can be understated when they fail to reflect the value of brand names and other innovative products. Depending on the true rate of economic amortization for advertising and R&D and the rate of growth in expenditures for each, business profit rates can be either understated or overstated. In either event, reported business profit rates, such as ROE, can substantially misstate economic profits. At the same time, other imperfections in accrual accounting methods lead to imperfectly matched revenues and costs and, therefore, to some misstatement of economic profits over time.

Beyond these and other obvious limitations of accounting data, business practices are often expressly intended to limit the loss of valuable trade secret information. Why would anyone give competitors any more than the bare minimum of information? It is well-known, for example, that firms patent only what they cannot otherwise keep secret. Combined with the limitations of publicly available data on profitability, business practices create an information barrier that hides the true details about economic profit rates. At the same time, such obfuscation makes defining the scope of monopoly power difficult, as it hides the costs and benefits of entry into monopoly markets from both private and public decision makers.

SUMMARY

Market structure analysis begins with the study of perfect competition and monopoly. Competition is said to be perfect when producers offer what buyers want at prices just sufficient to cover the marginal cost of output. Monopoly is socially less desirable given its tendency for underproduction, high prices, and excess profits.

- **Market structure** describes the competitive environment in the market for any good or service. A **market** consists of all firms and individuals willing and able to buy or sell a particular product. This includes firms and individuals currently engaged in buying and selling a particular product, as well as potential entrants. A **potential entrant** is an individual or firm posing a sufficiently credible threat of market entry to affect the price/output decisions of incumbent firms.

- **Perfect competition** is a market structure characterized by a large number of buyers and sellers of essentially the same product, where each market participant's transactions are so small that they have no influence on the market price of the product. Individual buyers and sellers are **price takers**. Such firms take market prices as given and devise their production strategies accordingly.

- **Monopoly** is a market structure characterized by a single seller of a highly differentiated product. Monopoly firms are price makers that exercise significant control over market prices.

- A **barrier to entry** is any factor or industry characteristic that creates an advantage for incumbents over new arrivals. A **barrier to mobility** is any factor or industry characteristic that creates an advantage for large leading firms over smaller nonleading rivals. A **barrier to exit** is any restriction on the ability of incumbents to redeploy assets from one industry or line of business to another.
- **Monopsony** exists when a single firm is the sole buyer of a desired product or input.
- A **natural monopoly** occurs when the market-clearing price, where $P = MC$, occurs at a point at which *long-run* average costs are still declining.
- **Underproduction** results when a monopoly curtails output to a level at which the value of resources employed, as measured by the marginal cost of production, is less than the social benefit derived, where social benefit is measured by the price customers are willing to pay for additional output.
- **Countervailing power** is an economic influence that creates a closer balance between previously unequal sellers and buyers.
- Business profit rates are best measured by the accounting rate of **return on stockholders' equity** measure. ROE is defined as net income divided by the book value of stockholders' equity, where stockholders' equity is the book value of total assets minus total liabilities. High ROE is derived from some combination of high **profit margins**, quick **total asset turnover**, and high **leverage** or a high rate of total assets to stockholders' equity. Business profits are also sometimes measured by the **return on assets**, defined as net income divided by the book value of total assets. Although ROA is a useful alternative indicator of the basic profitability of a business, it fails to account for the effects of financial leverage decisions on firm performance.
- Business profit rates often display a phenomenon known as **reversion to the mean**. Over time, entry into highly profitable industries tends to cause above-normal profits to regress toward the mean, just as bankruptcy and exit allow the below-normal profits of depressed industries to rise toward the mean.
- The nature of competition determines the suitability of managerial decisions and the speed with which they must be made. Survival of the fittest translates into success for the most able, and extinction of the least capable. **Competitive strategy** is the search for a favorable competitive position in an industry or line of business.
- In perfectly competitive industries, above-normal returns sometimes reflect **economic luck**, or temporary good fortune due to unexpected changes in industry demand or cost conditions. In other instances, above-normal returns in perfectly competitive industries reflect **economic rents**, or profits due to uniquely productive inputs. Another important source of above-normal profits in perfectly competitive industries is **disequilibrium profits**. Disequilibrium profits are above-normal returns that can be earned in the time interval between when a favorable influence on industry demand or cost conditions first transpires and the time when competitor reactions finally develop. **Disequilibrium losses** are below-normal returns that can be suffered in the time interval that often exists between when an unfavorable influence on industry demand or cost conditions first transpires and the time when exit or downsizing finally occurs.
- Only new and unique products or services have the potential to create monopoly profits. In many instances, these above-normal profits reflect the successful exploitation of a market niche. A **market niche** is a segment of a market that can be successfully exploited through the special capabilities of a given firm or individual.

Many real-world markets do in fact closely approximate the perfectly competitive ideal, but elements of monopoly are often encountered. As a result, these market structure concepts often provide a valuable guide to managerial decision making.

QUESTIONS

Q10.1 What are the primary elements of market structure?

Q10.2 Describe the perfectly competitive market structure and provide some examples.

Q10.3 Describe the monopoly market structure and provide some examples.

Q10.4 How are barriers to entry and exit similar? How are they different?

Q10.5 Why is the firm demand curve horizontal in perfectly competitive markets? Does this mean that the perfectly competitive industry demand curve is also horizontal?

Q10.6 Why are the perfectly competitive firm and the perfectly competitive industry supply curves upward sloping?

Q10.7 From a social standpoint, what is the problem with monopoly?

Q10.8 Why are both industry and firm demand curves downward sloping in monopoly market structure?

Q10.9 Give an example of monopoly in the labor market. Discuss such a monopoly's effect on wage rates and on inflation.

Q10.10 Describe the economic effects of countervailing power, and cite examples of markets in which countervailing power is observed.

SELF-TEST PROBLEMS AND SOLUTIONS

ST10.1 Market Value and Profitability. The paper and forest products industry is dominated by large integrated manufacturers. According to data from the Census of Manufacturers, roughly 50% of industry output comes from giant plants with more than 500 employees. This is despite the fact that specialized minimills with as few as 20 to 49 employees have recently emerged in the industry to take advantage of market niches. On an overall basis, this major industry group is one of the largest and most important in our economy in terms of sales, profits, and employment. Low prices combined with innovative new products, such as recycled newspaper products, have swept the industry and given innovative competitors the means to earn above-average rates of return. In this highly competitive environment, the way to survive and prosper is to reduce operating expenses, increase product quality, and improve customer service. As much as any other single industry, paper and forest products companies have taken advantage of advances in computer-based methods of data collection and analysis to improve their relation with suppliers, keep inventories lean, and boost sales by better serving customer demands.

To assess the effect of firm size on the business success of these companies, the table shows the rate of return on stockholders' equity (%), firm size as measured by the book value of stockholders' equity (in $ millions), rate of growth in book value (%), and leverage as captured by the ratio of long-term debt to total capital (%) for an $n = 17$ sample of paper and forest product companies. The profitability effects of firm size indicate how economies of scale translate into higher profits, or how diseconomies of large-scale production translate into lower profits. Growth can have positive effects on profit rates because rapid growth typically reflects companies with attractive product lines and/or cost-efficient operations. Finally, leverage has the potential to contribute to higher profits during periods of robust economic conditions, but can penalize profit rates during recessions or periods of tepid demand.

Company Name	Return on Shareholders' Equity	Shareholders' Equity	Book Value Growth 1–Year	% LTD/Capital
Abitibi Consolidated	−1.63	1,850.6	−5.3	49.7
Boise Cascade	9.02	1,614.1	11.8	51.6
Bowater Inc.	5.04	1,770.8	6.2	45.1
Domtar Inc.	9.10	1,253.7	16.4	36.5
Georgia-Pacific Group	19.09	3,750.0	17.4	56.4
Glatfelter (P.H.)	11.56	358.1	3.7	45.7
Int'l Paper	5.34	10,304.0	−14.3	47.5
Longview Fibre	4.75	420.5	1.3	54.1
Louisiana-Pacific	16.31	1,360.0	13.7	42.7
Mead Corp.	6.81	2,430.8	7.2	35.4
Pope & Talbot	7.73	186.1	9.2	44.1
Potlatch Corp.	4.44	921.0	−1.3	43.3
Rayonier Inc.	10.51	652.9	3.5	63.4
Temple-Inland	9.91	1,927.0	−1.1	39.4
Wausau-Mosinee	10.77	393.8	3.5	35.9
Westvaco Corp	6.69	2,171.3	−3.3	40.9
Weyerhaeuser Co.	9.49	7,173.0	39.5	35.7
Willamette Ind.	11.82	2203.7	9.5	42.5

Sources: Company annual reports.

A. A multiple regression model with each paper and forest products company's rate of return on stockholders' equity (ROE) as the dependent Y variable and firm size (BV), growth (GR), and leverage (LTD) as independent X variables gives the following results (t statistics in parentheses):

$$ROE = 2.689 - 9.09E\text{-}05\ BV + 0.216\ GR - + 0.107\ LTD$$
$$(0.40)\quad (-0.22)\qquad\quad (2.27)\qquad\quad (0.76)$$
$$R^2 = 27.2\%,\ SEE = 4.371$$

How would you interpret these findings?

B. What suggestions might you make for a more detailed study of the determinants of profitability for paper and forest products companies versus other types of companies?

ST10.1 Solution

A. As is typically the case, the constant in such a regression has no economic meaning. Clearly, the intercept should not be used to suggest the rate of return on stockholders' equity for a paper and forest products company that has zero values for the book value of stockholders' equity, growth, and leverage. Zero values for all of these variables are not observed for any of these paper and forest products companies, and extrapolation beyond the range of actual observations is always dangerous.

    The coefficient estimate of −9.09E-05 for total assets implies that a $1 million rise in stockholders' equity would lead to an average −0.00009% decline in the ROE. However, the coefficient on this measure of firm size is *not* statistically significant at the $\alpha = 0.1$ level with a calculated t statistic value of −0.22, meaning that it is not possible to argue on the basis of these data that there is any strong link between profitability and firm size in the paper and forest products industry. Although business leaders regard the accounting book value of assets in place as a favorable indication of the firm's ability to earn attractive rates of return in the future, the downturn in industry profitability in 2001 led to especially severe profit problems for industry leaders. Controversies tied to environmental concerns, like the spotted-owl crisis, make matters even worse for large companies that are convenient targets of consumer activists and regulators.

The coefficient estimate of 0.216 for growth implies that a 1% rise in growth leads to an average 0.216% increase in ROE. The growth coefficient is statistically significant at the $\alpha = 0.05$ level with a calculated t statistic value of 2.27, meaning that it is possible to be more than 95% confident that growth has a statistically significant affect on ROE. The probability of observing such a large t statistic when there is in fact no relation between ROE and growth is less than 5%.

The coefficient estimate of 0.107 for *LTD* implies that a 1% rise in leverage leads to an average 0.107% increase in ROE. However, this effect is not significant at even the $\alpha = 0.1$ level, meaning theat there is no strong link between ROE and leverage in the sample analyzed. Given rather tepid economic growth, high financial leverage had no beneficial effect of boosting profitability during the 2001 sample period.

The $R^2 = 27.2\%$ is quite modest and indicates the share of variation in ROE that can be explained by the model as a whole. This relatively low level of explained variation must be interpreted in light of the very small sample size involved. The standard error of the Y estimate of SEE = 4.371% is the average amount of error encountered in estimating ROE using this multiple regression model. If the u_i error terms are normally distributed about the regression equation, as would be true when large samples of more than 30 or so observations are analyzed, there is a 95% probability that observations of the dependent variable will lie within the range $\hat{Y}_i \pm (1.96 \times \text{SEE})$, or within roughly two standard errors of the estimate. The probability is 99% that any given $\hat{Y}_i$ will lie within the range $\hat{Y}_i \pm (2.576 \times \text{SEE})$, or within roughly three standard errors of its predicted value. When very small samples of data are analyzed, as is the case here, "critical" t values slightly larger than two or three are multiplied by the SEE to obtain the 95% and 99% confidence intervals.

Precise critical t values obtained from a t table, such as that found in Appendix C, are $t^*_{14,\alpha=0.05} = 2.145$ (at the 95% confidence level) and $t^*_{14,\alpha=0.01} = 2.977$ (at the 99% confidence level) for $df = 18 - 4 = 14$. This means that actual ROE can be expected to fall in the range $\hat{Y}_i \pm (2.145 \times 4.371)$, or $\hat{Y}_i \pm 9.376$, with 95% confidence; and within the range $\hat{Y}_i \pm (2.977 \times 4.371)$, or $\hat{Y}_i \pm 13.012$, with 99% confidence.

B. Collection of a broader and more descriptive sample of data is a necessary first step in a more detailed study of the determinants of the return on stockholders' equity for paper and forest products companies. With only 18 observations of annual data, the regression technique is clearly handicapped in this application. Perhaps a pooled cross-section sample of annual data over the past 5 years, or $n = 90 (= 18 \times 5)$ observations, would provide a sufficiently broad sample of data to offer a meaningful perspective on the determinants of profitability for forest and paper products companies. In addition, a larger sample of data would make it possible to investigate the potential role of additional independent variables, such as the level of advertising spending, the role of regional economic growth, and so on.

ST10.2 Perfect Competition and Monopoly. The City of Columbus, Ohio, is considering two proposals to privatize municipal garbage collection. First, a leading waste disposal firm has offered to purchase the city's plant and equipment at an attractive price in return for an exclusive franchise on residential service. A second proposal would allow several individual workers and small companies to enter the business without any exclusive franchise agreement or competitive restrictions. Under this plan, individual companies would bid for the right to provide service in a given residential area. The city would then allocate business to the lowest bidder.

The city has conducted a survey of Columbus residents to estimate the amount that they would be willing to pay for various frequencies of service. The city has also estimated the total cost of service per resident. Service costs are expected to be the same whether or not an exclusive franchise is granted.

A. Complete the following table.

Trash Pickups per Month	Price per Pickup	Total Revenue	Marginal Revenue	Total Cost	Marginal Cost
0	$5.00			$0.00	
1	4.80			3.75	
2	4.60			7.45	
3	4.40			11.10	
4	4.20			14.70	
5	4.00			18.00	
6	3.80			20.90	
7	3.60			23.80	
8	3.40			27.20	
9	3.20			30.70	
10	3.00			35.00	

B. Determine price and the level of service if competitive bidding results in a perfectly competitive price/output combination.

C. Determine price and the level of service if the city grants a monopoly franchise.

ST10.2 Solution

A.

Trash Pickups per Month	Price per Pickup	Total Revenue	Marginal Revenue	Total Cost	Marginal Cost
0	$5.00	$0.00	—	$0.00	—
1	4.80	4.80	$4.80	3.75	$3.75
2	4.60	9.20	4.40	7.45	3.70
3	4.40	13.20	4.00	11.10	3.65
4	4.20	16.80	3.60	14.70	3.60
5	4.00	20.00	3.20	18.00	3.30
6	3.80	22.80	2.80	20.90	2.90
7	3.60	25.20	2.40	23.80	2.90
8	3.40	27.20	2.00	27.20	3.40
9	3.20	28.80	1.60	30.70	3.50
10	3.00	30.00	1.20	35.00	4.30

B. In a perfectly competitive industry, $P = MR$, so the optimal activity level occurs where $P = MC$. Here, $P = MC = \$3.40$ at $Q = 8$ pickups per month.

C. A monopoly maximizes profits by setting $MR = MC$. Here, $MR = MC = \$3.60$ at $Q = 4$ pickups per month and $P = \$4.20$ per pickup.

PROBLEMS

P10.1   Market Structure Concepts. Indicate whether each of the following statements is true or false, and explain why.

A. In long-run equilibrium, every firm in a perfectly competitive industry earns zero profit. Thus, if price falls, none of these firms will be able to survive.

B. Perfect competition exists in a market when all firms are price takers as opposed to price makers.

C. A natural monopoly results when the profit-maximizing output level occurs at a point where long-run average costs are declining.

D. Downward-sloping industry demand curves characterize both perfectly competitive and monopoly markets.

E. A decrease in the price elasticity of demand would follow an increase in monopoly power.

P10.2 **Perfectly Competitive Firm Supply.** Mankato Paper, Inc., produces uncoated paper used in a wide variety of industrial applications. Newsprint, a major product, is sold in a perfectly competitive market. The following relation exists between the firm's newsprint output and total production costs:

Total Output (tons)	Total Cost
0	$25
1	75
2	135
3	205
4	285
5	375
6	475
7	600

A. Construct a table showing Mankato's marginal cost of newsprint production.

B. What is the minimum price necessary for Mankato to supply one ton of newsprint?

C. How much newsprint would Mankato supply at industry prices of $75 and $100 per ton?

P10.3 **Perfectly Competitive Equilibrium.** Demand and supply conditions in the perfectly competitive market for unskilled labor are as follows:

$$Q_D = 150 - 16P \qquad \text{(Demand)}$$
$$Q_S = 8P \qquad \text{(Supply)}$$

where Q is millions of hours of unskilled labor and P is the wage rate per hour.

A. Graph the industry demand and supply curves.

B. Determine the industry equilibrium price/output combination both graphically and algebraically.

C. Calculate the level of excess supply (unemployment) if the minimum wage is set at $7 per hour.

P10.4 **Perfectly Competitive Industry Supply.** Farm Fresh, Inc., supplies sweet peas to canners located throughout the Mississippi River Valley. Like some grain and commodity markets, the market for sweet peas is perfectly competitive. The company's total and marginal costs per ton are given by the following relations:

$$TC = \$250,000 + \$200Q + \$0.02Q^2$$
$$MC = \partial TC/\partial Q = \$200 + \$0.04Q$$

A. Calculate the industry price necessary for the firm to supply 5,000, 10,000, and 15,000 tons of sweet peas.

B. Calculate the quantity supplied by Farm Fresh at industry prices of $200, $500, and $1,000 per ton.

P10.5 **Perfectly Competitive Firm and Industry Supply.** New England Textiles, Inc., is a medium-sized manufacturer of blue denim that sells in a market for which it is perfectly competitive. The total cost function for this product is described by the following relation:

$$TC = \$25,000 + \$1Q + \$0.000008Q^2$$
$$MC = \partial TC/\partial Q = \$1 + \$0.000016Q$$

where Q is square yards of blue denim produced per month.

A. Derive the firm's supply curve, expressing quantity as a function of price.

B. Derive the industry's supply curve if New England Textiles is one of 500 competitors.

C. Calculate industry supply per month at a market price of $2 per square yard.

P10.6 **Perfectly Competitive Equilibrium.** Bada Bing, Ltd., supplies standard 128 MB-RAM chips to the U.S. computer and electronics industry. Like the output of its competitors, Bada Bing's chips must meet strict size, shape, and speed specifications. As a result, the chip-supply industry can be regarded as perfectly competitive. The total cost and marginal cost functions for Bada Bing are

$$TC = \$1,000,000 + \$20Q + \$0.0001Q^2$$
$$MC = \partial TC/\partial Q = \$20 + \$0.0002Q$$

where Q is the number of chips produced.

A. Calculate Bada Bing's optimal output and profits if chip prices are stable at $60 each.

B. Calculate Bada Bing's optimal output and profits if chip prices fall to $30 each.

C. If Bada Bing is typical of firms in the industry, calculate the firm's equilibrium output, price, and profit levels.

P10.7 **Monopoly Equilibrium.** Parvati Fluid Controls, Inc., (PFC) is a major supplier of reverse osmosis and ultrafiltration equipment, which helps industrial and commercial customers achieve improved production processes and a cleaner work environment. The company has recently introduced a new line of ceramic filters that enjoy patent protection. Relevant cost and revenue relations for this product are as follows:

$$TR = \$300Q - \$0.001Q^2$$
$$MR = \partial TR/\partial Q = \$300 - \$0.002Q$$
$$TC = \$9,000,000 + \$20Q + \$0.0004Q^2$$
$$MC = \partial TC/\partial Q = \$20 + \$0.0008Q$$

where TR is total revenue, Q is output, MR is marginal revenue, TC is total cost, including a risk-adjusted normal rate of return on investment, and MC is marginal cost.

A. As a monopoly, calculate PFC's optimal price/output combination.

B. Calculate monopoly profits and the optimal profit margin at this profit-maximizing activity level.

P10.8 **Monopoly Versus Perfectly Competitive Equilibrium.** Big Apple Music, Inc., enjoys an exclusive copyright on music written and produced by the Fab Four, a legendary British rock group. Total and marginal revenues for the group's CDs are given by the following relations:

$$TR = \$15Q - \$0.000005Q^2$$
$$MR = \partial TR/\partial Q = \$15 - \$0.00001Q$$

Marginal costs for production and distribution are stable at \$5 per unit. All other costs have been fully amortized.

A. Calculate Big Apple's output, price, and profits at the profit-maximizing activity level.

B. What record price and profit levels would prevail following expiration of copyright protection based on the assumption that perfectly competitive pricing would result?

P10.9 **Monopoly Versus Perfectly Competitive Equilibrium.** During recent years, Moon Macro Systems, Inc., has enjoyed substantial economic profits derived from patents covering a wide range of inventions and innovations for high-performance workstations used in a variety of scientific applications. A recent introduction, the Ultra80, has proved especially profitable. Market demand and marginal revenue relations for the Ultra80 are as follows:

$$P = \$5,500 - \$0.005Q$$
$$MR = \partial TR/\partial Q = \$5,500 - \$0.01Q$$

Fixed costs are nil because research and development expenses have been fully amortized during previous periods. Average variable costs are constant at \$4,500 per unit.

A. Calculate the profit-maximizing price/output combination and economic profits if Moon enjoys an effective monopoly on the Ultra80 because of its patent protection.

B. Calculate the price/output combination and total economic profits that would result if competitors offer clones that make the Ultra80 market perfectly competitive.

P10.10 **Monopoly/Monopsony Confrontation.** Safecard Corporation offers a unique service. The company notifies credit card issuers after being informed that a subscriber's credit card has been lost or stolen. The Safecard service is sold to card issuers on a 1-year subscription basis. Relevant revenue and cost relations for the service are as follows:

$$TR = \$5Q - \$0.00001Q^2$$
$$MR = \partial TR/\partial Q = \$5 - \$0.00002Q$$
$$TC = \$50,000 + \$0.5Q + \$0.000005Q^2$$
$$MC = \partial TC/\partial Q = \$0.5 + \$0.00001Q$$

where *TR* is total revenue, *Q* is output measured in terms of the number of subscriptions in force, *MR* is marginal revenue, *TC* is total cost, including a risk-adjusted normal rate of return on investment, and *MC* is marginal cost.

A. If Safecard has a monopoly in this market, calculate the profit-maximizing price/output combination and optimal total profit.

B. Calculate Safecard's optimal price, output, and profits if credit card issuers effectively exert monopsony power and force a perfectly competitive equilibrium in this market.

CASE STUDY

The Profitability Effects of Large Firm Size

Does large firm size, pure and simple, give rise to monopoly profits? This question has been a source of great interest in both business and government, and the basis for lively debate over the years. Monopoly theory states that large relative firm size within a given economic market gives rise to the potential for above-normal profits. However, monopoly theory makes no prediction at all about a link between large firm size and the potential for above-normal profits. By itself, it is not clear what economic advantages are gained from large firm size. Pecuniary or money-related economies of large size in the purchase of labor, raw materials, or other inputs are sometimes suggested. For example, some argue that large firms enjoy a comparative advantage in the acquisition of investment funds given their ready access to organized capital markets. Others contend that capital markets are themselves very efficient in the allocation of scarce capital resources and that all firms, both large and small, must offer investors a competitive rate of return.

Still, without a doubt, firm size is a matter of significant business and public interest. Ranking among the largest industrial corporations in the United States is a matter of significant corporate pride for employees and top executives. Sales and profit levels achieved by such firms are widely reported and commented upon in the business and popular press. At times, congressional leaders have called for legislation that would bar mergers among giant companies on the premise that such combinations create monolithic giants that impair competitive forces. Movements up and down lists of the largest corporations are chronicled, studied, and commented on. It is perhaps a little known fact that, given the dynamic nature of change in the overall economy, few companies are able to maintain, let alone enhance, their relative position among the largest corporations over a 5- to 10-year period. With an annual attrition rate of 6% to 10% among the 500 largest corporations, it indeed appears to be "slippery" at the top.

To evaluate the link, if any, between profitability and firm size, it is interesting to consider the data contained in Table 10.5. These are data on $n = 25$ of the largest companies in the world. Both industrials and nonindustrials are included, thus giving broad perspective on any possible link between firm size and profitability. Ranked by sales, this sample of giant companies reported at least $42.3 billion in annual sales revenue (all figures in $ millions).

Table 10.5 shows profitability as measured by net income, and three standard measures of firm size. Net worth, or stockholders' equity, is defined in accounting terms as total assets minus total liabilities. It is a useful measure of the total funds committed to the enterprise by stockholders through paid in capital plus retained earnings. Total assets is perhaps the most common accounting measure of firm size and indicates the book value of all tangible plant and equipment, plus the recognized intangible value of acquired assets with customer goodwill due to brand names, patents, and so on. Sales revenue is a third common measure of firm size. From an economic perspective, sales is an attractive measure of firm size because it is not susceptible to accounting manipulation or bias, nor is it influenced by the relative capital or labor intensity of the enterprise. When size is measured by sales revenue, measurement problems tied to inflation, replacement cost errors, and so on, are minimized.

The simplest means for studying the link between profitability and firm size is to regress profits on firm size, when size is measured along the different dimensions of stockholders' equity, total assets, and sales. It is also worth considering the effect of firm size on the rate of profitability. When firm size is measured using stockholders' equity, it is interesting to consider the effect of stockholders' equity on the rate of profitability as measured by the return on stockholders' equity (ROE). Similarly, when firm size is measured using the book value of total assets, it is intriguing to see if the return on assets (ROA) is affected by size (asset level); when firm size is measured by sales revenue, it is fascinating to see if profit margins (MGN) are affected by size (sales). A significant link between profitability and firm size is suggested to the extent that ROE, ROA and/or MGN tend to be higher among the very largest companies.

CASE STUDY (continued)

TABLE 10.5

Net Profit, Net Worth, Total Assets, and Sales Revenue for 25 Global Giants with Sales Revenue of More Than $42.3 Billion

Company Name	Industry	Net Income	Net Worth	Total Assets	Sales	ROE	ROA	MGN
General Motors	Auto	5,576	20,862	274,730	176,558	26.7%	2.0%	3.2%
Wal-Mart Stores	Retail	5,709	25,843	70,349	165,013	22.1%	8.1%	3.5%
Ford Motor	Auto	7,237	27,537	276,229	162,558	26.3%	2.6%	4.5%
Exxon Mobil Corp.	Oil	8,380	63,466	144,521	160,883	13.2%	5.8%	5.2%
DaimlerChrysler	Auto	5,173	36,313	175,889	151,035	14.2%	2.9%	3.4%
Toyota Motor	Auto	4,540	65,116	154,884	119,656	7.0%	2.9%	3.8%
Shell Transport	Oil	7,531	56,171	113,883	105,366	13.4%	6.6%	7.1%
Royal Dutch Petr.	Oil	7,531	56,171	113,883	105,366	13.4%	6.6%	7.1%
Int'l Business Mach.	Computer	6,962	20,511	87,495	87,548	33.9%	8.0%	8.0%
BP Amoco	Oil	6,204	43,281	89,561	83,566	14.3%	6.9%	7.4%
Philip Morris	Tobacco	7,675	15,305	61,381	78,596	50.1%	12.5%	9.8%
Total Fina Elf	Oil	3,372	27,857	81,533	75,545	12.1%	4.1%	4.5%
Hitachi, Ltd.	Electronics	160	27,134	92,804	75,483	0.6%	0.2%	0.2%
Matsushita Elec.	Electronics	950	33,021	73,208	69,500	2.9%	1.3%	1.4%
Sony Corp.	Electronics	1,149	20,593	64,219	63,082	5.6%	1.8%	1.8%
AT&T Corp.	Telecom	5,450	85,253	169,406	62,391	6.4%	3.2%	8.7%
Boeing	Defense	2,030	11,462	36,147	57,993	17.7%	5.6%	3.5%
Honda Motor	Auto	2,476	18,211	46,212	57,536	13.6%	5.4%	4.3%
Nissan Motor	Auto	−6,456	8,767	61,709	56,388	−73.6%	−10.5%	−11.4%
Gen'l Electric	Electronics	10,717	42,557	82,583	55,645	25.2%	13.0%	19.3%
SBC Communications	Telecom	7,439	27,726	83,215	48,960	26.8%	8.9%	15.2%
NEC Corp.	Electronics	99	9,303	43,895	47,538	1.1%	0.2%	0.2%
Kroger Co.	Grocery	966	2,683	17,966	45,352	36.0%	5.4%	2.1%
Unilever	Food	2,930	15,197	32,816	43,650	19.3%	8.9%	6.7%
Hewlett-Packard	Computer	3,125	18,295	35,297	42,370	17.1%	8.9%	7.4%
Averages		**4,277**	**31,145**	**99,353**	**87,903**	**13.7%**	**4.3%**	**4.9%**

Data source: *Compustat PC+*, September 2001.

Nonlinearities can be investigated through the use of second-order (quadratic) and third-order (cubic) terms for the size variable. For example, a positive and statistically significant coefficient for the sales-squared variable would indicate that profit margins increase at a pace faster than the rate of change in sales. A positive and statistically significant coefficient for the sales-cubed variable indicates a growing rate of increase in profit margins, and so on. The effects of firm size on profits and profit rates among giant corporations are shown in Table 10.6.

A. Based upon the findings reported in Table 10.6, discuss the relation between firm size and profitability. Does large firm size increase profitability?

B. Discuss any differences among alternative profit rate measures. Based upon the findings reported in Table 10.6, discuss the relation between firm size and profit rates. Does large firm size increase profit rates?

C. Does the fact that auto giant Nissan Motor reported a net loss make it more or less difficult to find a positive link between profitability and firm size for the entire sample during this period? Should this observation be dropped from the analysis? What other important determinants of profitability might be included in a more detailed study of the profitability/firm size relation?

CASE STUDY (continued)

TABLE 10.6

Profitability Effects of Firm Size (*t* statistics in parentheses)

Dependent Variable	Size Measure	Intercept	Size	Size^2	Size^3	R^2	F stat.
Profits	Net worth	−2372.400 (−0.87)	3.76E-02 (1.47)	−4.30E-06 (−0.63)	1.08E-11 (0.21)	40.3%	4.72
Profits	Total assets	−2016.240 (−0.52)	1.24E-02 (1.07)	−6.00E-07 (−0.63)	9.27E-13 (0.43)	24.5%	2.27
Profits	Sales	3392.820 (0.25)	−9.63E-02 (−0.21)	1.97E-06 (0.41)	−7.70E-12 (−0.50)	21.7%	1.94
ROE	Net worth	−0.0191 (−0.09)	1.40E-05 (0.72)	−2.90E-10 (−0.57)	1.63E-15 (0.42)	4.1%	0.30
ROA	Total assets	0.050 (0.89)	1.36E-07 (0.08)	−1.50E-12 (−0.11)	2.24E-18 (0.07)	3.6%	0.26
MGN	Sales	0.116 (0.51)	−2.40E-06 (−0.31)	2.79E-11 (0.34)	−9.70E-17 (−0.37)	1.6%	0.12

SELECTED REFERENCES

Armstrong, Mark. "Access Pricing, Bypass, and Universal Service." *American Economic Review* 91 (May 2001): 297–301.

Bacidore, Jeffrey M., and George Sofianos. "Liquidity Provision and Specialist Trading in NYSE-Listed Non-U.S. Stocks." *Journal of Financial Economics* 63 (January 2002): 133–158.

Biehl, Andrew R. "Durable-Goods Monopoly with Stochastic Values." *Rand Journal of Economics* 32 (Autumn 2001): 565–577.

Cope, Robert F., III, David E. Dismukes, and Rachelle F. Cope. "Modeling Regional Electric Power Markets and Market Power." *Managerial & Decision Economics* 22 (December 2001): 411–429.

Feinberg, Yossi, and Morton I. Kamien. "Highway Robbery: Complementary Monopoly and the Hold-Up Problem." *International Journal of Industrial Organization* 19 (December 2001): 1603–1621.

Fernandez, Raquel, and Richard Rogerson. "Sorting and Long-Run Inequality." *Quarterly Journal of Economics* 116 (November 2001): 1305–1341.

Garza-Gomez, Xavier. "The Information Content of the Book-to-Market Ratio." *Financial Analysts Journal* 57 (November/December 2001): 78–95.

Hausman, Jerry A., J. Gregory Sidak, and Hal J. Singer. "Cable Modems and DSL: Broadband Internet Access for Residential Customers." *American Economic Review* 91 (May 2001): 302–307.

Huang, S., Y. Yang, and K. Anderson. "A Theory of Finitely Durable Goods Monopoly with Used-Goods Market and Transaction Costs." *Management Science* 47 (November 2001): 1515–1532.

Jacobson, Robert, and Gary Hansen. "Modeling in the Competitive Process." *Managerial & Decision Economics* 22 (June/August 2001): 251–263.

Lamoreaux, Naomi R., and Kenneth L. Sokoloff. "Market Trade in Patents and the Rise of a Class of Specialized Inventors in the 19th Century United States." *American Economic Review* 91 (May 2001): 39–44.

Mini, Federico. "The Role of Incentives for Opening Monopoly Markets: Comparing GTE and BOC Cooperation with Local Entrants." *Journal of Industrial Economics* 49 (September 2001): 379–414.

Ottaviani, Marco, and Andrea Prat. "The Value of Public Information in Monopoly." *Econometrica* 69 (November 2001): 1673–1683.

Uri, Noel D. "Monopoly Power and the Problem of CLEC Access Charges." *Telecommunications Policy* 25 (September/October 2001): 611–623.

Weaver, Samuel C. "Measuring Economic Value Added: A Survey of the Practices of EVA Proponents." *Journal of Applied Finance* 11 (2001): 50–60.

CHAPTER ELEVEN

Monopolistic Competition and Oligopoly

O nce the seventh-highest market capitalization company in America, Houston's energy giant Enron Corp. stumbled from a stock-market valuation of $62 billion in January 2001 to penny stock status and Chapter 11 bankruptcy protection in less than a year. A similar fate befell Troy, Michigan–based discount retailer Kmart Corp., which on January 22, 2002, became the largest retailer to ever seek bankruptcy protection. With 275,000 employees and more than 2,100 stores, Kmart is trying to restructure and avoid becoming road kill for retail juggernaut Wal-Mart Stores, Inc.

The demise of corporate titans did not begin with Enron and end with Kmart. The creative destruction of capitalism is ongoing and unforgiving. From 1928–1996, Bethlehem Steel Corp. was a fixture in the Dow Jones Industrial Average. In 1972, imaging company Polaroid Corp. was the most revered member of the Nifty 50, a group of stock-market favorites. Both filed for federal bankruptcy protection in 2001. Xerox Corp., another Nifty 50 favorite, was once so dominant in the copy business that it became a verb, as in "Xerox this." Xerox hangs on, but business has dwindled in the face of growing competition from electronic media.

Despite massive financial resources and compelling brand names, corporate behemoths often stumble. Large size can breed deadly complacency. To survive and prosper in the new millennium, many large-scale organizations have cut back and refocused in order to become smaller, more nimble organizations.[1] This chapter offers perspective on how the nature of competition is affected by the number and size distribution of buyers and sellers; it examines competition in the partly competitive, partly monopolistic world of monopolistic competition and oligopoly.

---

1   See Amy Merrick, "Kmart Lays Out Plans to Trim Its Size, Boost Efficiency, in Bankruptcy Filing," *The Wall Street Journal Online*, January 22, 2002 (http://online.wsj.com).

CONTRAST BETWEEN MONOPOLISTIC COMPETITION AND OLIGOPOLY

Monopolistic competition and oligopoly provide differing perspectives on the nature of competition in imperfectly competitive markets. Attributes of the monopolistic competition and oligopoly market models are outlined in this section and then elaborated on in the rest of the chapter.

Monopolistic Competition

The economic environment faced by many firms cannot be described as perfectly competitive. Likewise, few firms enjoy clear monopoly. Real-world markets commonly embody elements of both perfect competition and monopoly. Firms often introduce valuable new products or process innovations that give rise to above-normal rates of return in the short run. In the long run, however, entry and imitation by new rivals erode the dominant market share enjoyed by early innovators, and profits eventually return to normal. Still, in sharp contrast to perfectly competitive markets, the unique product characteristics of individual firms often remain valued by consumers. Consumers often continue to prefer Campbell's Soup, Dockers, Oil of Olay, Rubbermaid, Tide, and other favorite brands after comparable products have been introduced by rivals. The partly competitive, partly monopolistic market structure encountered by firms in the apparel, food, hotel, retailing, and consumer products industries is called monopolistic competition. Given the lack of perfect substitutes, monopolistically competitive firms exercise some discretion in setting prices—they are not price takers. However, given vigorous competition from imitators offering close but not identical substitutes, such firms enjoy only a normal risk-adjusted rate of return on investment in long-run equilibrium.

monopolistic competition
A market structure characterized by a large number of sellers of differentiated products

Monopolistic competition is similar to perfect competition in that it entails vigorous price competition among a large number of firms. The major difference between these two market structure models is that consumers perceive important differences among the products offered by monopolistically competitive firms, whereas the output of perfectly competitive firms is homogeneous. This gives monopolistically competitive firms at least some discretion in setting prices. However, the availability of many close substitutes limits this price-setting ability and drives profits down to a normal risk-adjusted rate of return in the long run. As in the case of perfect competition, above-normal profits are possible only in the short run, before the monopolistically competitive firm's rivals can take effective countermeasures.

Oligopoly

oligopoly
A market structure characterized by few sellers and interdependent price/output decisions

Oligopoly is the market structure model that describes competition among a handful of competitors sheltered by significant barriers to entry. Oligopolists might produce a homogeneous product, such as aluminum, steel, or semiconductors; or differentiated products such as Cheerios, Coca-Cola, Marlboro, MTV, and Nintendo. Innovative leading firms in the ready-to-eat cereal, beverage, cigarette, entertainment, and computer software industries, among others, have the potential for economic profits even in the long run. With few competitors, economic incentives also exist for such firms to devise illegal agreements to limit competition, fix prices, or otherwise divide markets. The history of antitrust enforcement in the United States provides numerous examples of "competitors" who illegally entered into such agreements. Yet there are also examples of markets in which vigorous competition among a small number of firms generates obvious long-term benefits for consumers. It is therefore erroneous to draw a simple link between the number of competitors and the vigor of competition.

In an industry characterized by oligopoly, only a few large rivals are responsible for the bulk of industry output. As in the case of monopoly, high to very high barriers to entry are typical.

Under oligopoly, the price/output decisions of firms are interrelated in the sense that direct reactions among rivals can be expected. As a result, decisions of individual firms anticipate the likely response of competitors. This competition among the few involves a wide variety of price and nonprice methods of rivalry, as determined by the institutional characteristics of each particular market. Even though limited numbers of competitors give rise to a potential for economic profits, above-normal rates of return are far from guaranteed. Competition among the few can be vigorous.

Dynamic Nature of Competition

In characterizing the descriptive relevance of the monopolistic competition and oligopoly models of seller behavior, it is important to recognize the dynamic nature of real-world markets. For example, as late as the mid 1980s it seemed appropriate to regard the automobile and personal computer manufacturing markets as oligopolistic in nature. Today, it seems fairer to regard each industry as monopolistically competitive. In the automobile industry, GM, Ford, and Daimler Chrysler have found Toyota, Honda, Nissan, and a host of specialized competitors to be formidable foes. Aggressive competitors like Dell, Compaq, Hewlett-Packard, and Gateway first weakened, and then obliterated, IBM's early lead in the PC business. Prices and profit margins for PCs continue to fall as improving technology continues to enhance product quality.

In many formerly oligopolistic markets, the market discipline provided by a competitive fringe of smaller domestic and foreign rivals is sufficient to limit the potential abuse of a few large competitors. In the long-distance telephone service market, for example, AT&T, MCI WorldCom, and Sprint have long dominated the industry. However, emerging competition from the so-called regional Bell operating companies (REBOCs), along with a host of smaller specialized providers, cause long-distance phone service price and service quality competition to be spirited. Similarly, the competitive fringe in wireless communications and cable TV promises to force dramatic change during the years ahead.

It is unfortunate, but public perceptions and government regulatory policy sometimes lag behind economic reality. It is essential that timely and accurate market structure information be available to form the basis for managerial investment decisions that relate to entry or exit from specific lines of business. Similarly, enlightened public policy requires timely information.

MONOPOLISTIC COMPETITION

Most firms are subject to rivalry, though perhaps not as vigorous as would exist under perfect competition. Even though most firms face a large number of competitors with similar products, many still have some control over the price of their product. They cannot sell all that they want at a fixed price, nor would they lose all sales if they raised prices slightly. Most firms face downward-sloping demand curves, signifying less-than-perfect competition.

Characteristics of Monopolistically Competitive Markets

Monopolistic competition exists when individual producers have moderate influence over product prices, where each product enjoys a degree of uniqueness in the perception of customers. This market structure has some important similarities and dissimilarities with perfectly competitive markets. Monopolistic competition is characterized by

- *Large numbers of buyers and sellers.* Each firm produces a small portion of industry output, and each customer buys only a small part of the total.
- *Product heterogeneity.* The output of each firm is perceived to be essentially different from, though comparable with, the output of other firms in the industry.

- *Free entry and exit.* Firms are not restricted from entering or leaving the industry.
- *Perfect dissemination of information.* Cost, price, and product quality information is known by all buyers and all sellers.

These basic conditions are not as restrictive as those for perfect competition and are fairly commonplace in actual markets. Vigorous monopolistic competition is evident in the banking, container and packaging, discount and fashion retail, electronics, food manufacturing, office equipment, paper and forest products, and most personal and professional service industries. Although individual firms are able to maintain some control over pricing policy, their pricing discretion is severely limited by competition from firms offering close but not identical substitutes.

Monopolistic competition is a realistic description of competition in a wide variety of industries. As in perfectly competitive markets, a large number of competitors make independent decisions in monopolistically competitive markets. A price change by any one firm does not cause other firms to change prices. If price reactions did occur, then an oligopoly market structure would be present. The most distinctive characteristic of monopolistic competition is that each competitor offers a unique product that is an imperfect substitute for those offered by rivals. Each firm is able to differentiate its product from those of its adversaries. Nevertheless, each firm's demand function is significantly affected by the presence of numerous competitors producing goods that consumers view as reasonably close substitutes. Exogenous changes in demand and cost conditions also tend to have a similar effect on all firms and frequently lead to comparable pricing influences.

Product differentiation takes many forms. Quality differentials, packaging, credit terms, or superior maintenance service can all differentiate products, as can advertising that leads to brand-name identification. Not only is a tube of Crest toothpaste different from Colgate toothpaste, but a tube of Crest at a nearby convenience store is different from an identical tube available at a distant discount retailer. Because consumers evaluate products on the basis of their ability to satisfy specific wants, as well as when and where they have them, products involve not only quantity, quality, and price characteristics but time and place attributes as well. The important factor in all of these forms of product differentiation is that some consumers prefer the product of one seller to those of others.

The effect of product differentiation is to create downward-sloping firm demand curves in monopolistically competitive markets. Unlike a price taker facing a perfectly horizontal demand curve, the firm is able to independently determine an optimal price/output combination. The degree of price flexibility enjoyed depends on the strength of product differentiation. The more differentiated a firm's product, the lower the substitutability of other products for it. Strong differentiation results in greater consumer loyalty and greater control over price. This is illustrated in Figure 11.1, which shows the demand curves of firms A and B. Consumers view firm A's product as being only slightly differentiated from the bulk of industry output. Because many other firms offer acceptable substitutes, firm A is close to being a price taker. Conversely, firm B has successfully differentiated its product, and consumers are therefore less willing to accept substitutes for B's output. Firm B's demand is relatively less sensitive to price changes.

Price/Output Decisions Under Monopolistic Competition

As its name suggests, monopolistic competition embodies elements of both monopoly and perfect competition. The monopoly aspect is most forcefully observed in the short run. For example, consider Figure 11.2. With the demand curve, D_1, and its related marginal revenue curve, MR_1, the optimum output, Q_1, is found at the point where $MR_1 = MC$. Short-run monopoly profits equal to the area P_1LMAC_1 are earned. Such profits can be derived from new product introductions, product and process improvements, creative packaging and marketing, or other factors such as an unexpected rise in demand.

FIGURE 11.1

Relation Between Product Differentiation and Elasticity of Demand

Firm B's steeper demand curve relative to firm A's reflects stronger product differentiation and hence less sensitivity to price changes.

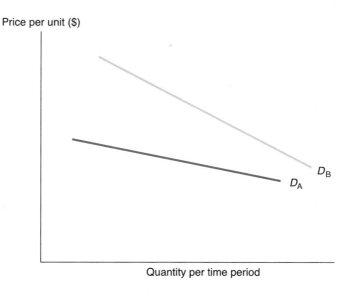

Over time, short-run monopoly profits attract competition, and other firms enter the industry. This competitive aspect of monopolistic competition is seen most forcefully in the long run. As competitors emerge to offer close but imperfect substitutes, the market share and profits of the initial innovating firm diminish. Firm demand and marginal revenue curves shift to the left as, for example, from D_1 to D_2 and from MR_1 to MR_2 in Figure 11.2. Optimal long-run output occurs at Q_2, the point where $MR_2 = MC$. Because the optimal price P_2 equals ATC_2, where cost includes a normal profit just sufficient to maintain capital investment, economic profits are zero.

The price/output combination (P_2Q_2) describes a monopolistically competitive market equilibrium characterized by a high degree of product differentiation. If new entrants offered perfect rather than close substitutes, each firm's long-run demand curve would become more nearly horizontal, and the perfectly competitive equilibrium, D_3 with P_3 and Q_3, would be approached. Like the (P_2Q_2) high-differentiation equilibrium, the (P_3Q_3) no-differentiation equilibrium is something of an extreme case. In most instances, competitor entry reduces but does not eliminate product differentiation. An intermediate price/output solution, one between (P_2Q_2) and (P_3Q_3), is often achieved in long-run equilibrium. Indeed, it is the retention of at least some degree of product differentiation that distinguishes the monopolistically competitive equilibrium from that achieved in perfectly competitive markets.

A firm will never operate at the minimum point on its average cost curve in monopolistically competitive equilibrium. Each firm's demand curve is downward sloping and is tangent to the ATC curve at some point above minimum ATC. However, this does not mean that a monopolistically competitive industry is inefficient. The very existence of a downward-sloping demand curve implies that consumers value an individual firm's products more highly than they do products of other producers. The higher prices and costs of monopolistically competitive industries, as opposed to perfectly competitive industries, reflect the economic cost of product variety. If consumers are willing to bear such costs, then such costs must not be excessive. The success of branded products in the face of generic competition, for example, is powerful evidence of consumer preferences for product variety.

FIGURE 11.2

Price/Output Combinations Under Monopolistic Competition

Long-run equilibrium under monopolistic competition occurs when $MR = MC$ and $P = AC$. This typically occurs between (P_2, Q_2) (the high-price/low-output equilibrium) and (P_3, Q_3) (the low-price/high-output equilibrium).

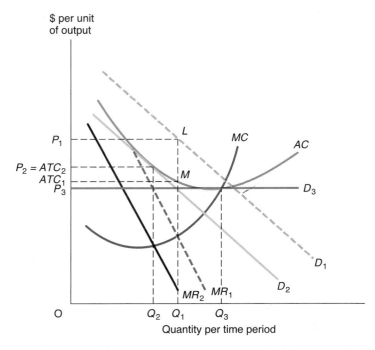

Although perfect competition and monopoly are somewhat rare in real-world markets, monopolistic competition is frequently observed. For example, in 1960 a small ($37 million in sales) office-machine company, Haloid Xerox, Inc., revolutionized the copy industry with the introduction of the Xerox 914 copier. Xerography was a tremendous improvement over electrofax and other coated-paper copiers. It permitted the use of untreated paper, which produced clearer and less expensive copies. Invention of the dry copier established what is now Xerox Corporation at the forefront of a rapidly growing office-copier industry and propelled the firm to a position of virtual monopoly by 1970. Between 1970 and 1980, the industry's market structure changed dramatically because of an influx of competition as many of Xerox's original patents expired. IBM entered the copier market in April 1970 with its Copier I model and expanded its participation in November 1972 with Copier II. Eastman Kodak made its entry into the market in 1975 with its Ektaprint model. Of course, Minnesota Mining and Manufacturing (3M) had long been a factor in the electrofax copier segment of the market. A more complete list of Xerox's recent domestic and international competitors would include at least 30 firms. The effect of this entry on Xerox's market share and profitability was dramatic. Between 1970 and 1978, for example, Xerox's share of the domestic copier market fell from 98 percent to 56 percent, and its return on stockholders' equity fell from 23.6 percent to 18.2 percent.

More recently, Xerox's leadership position has been squandered and its profitability has collapsed in the face of vicious price and product quality competition. Because Canon, Kodak, 3M, Panasonic, Ricoh, Savin, and Sharp copiers are only close rather than perfect substitutes for Xerox machines, the industry is commonly described as monopolistically competitive. Effective (but imperfect) competition for paper copies also comes from low-cost printers tied to PCs and from electronic communications, which obviate the need for paper copies. Make no mistake about it, monopolistic competition can be tough on industry leaders that fail to keep up—just ask Xerox.

Intel: Running Fast to Stay in Place

Intel is the dominant and most profitable maker of integrated circuits, the microscopic pieces of silicon chips used to power electronic computers, calculators, video games, and a burgeoning array of other products. *intel inside*™ is a trademark that identifies products produced by a company whose microprocessors are the brains of more than five times as many personal computers as its nearest rival. So complete has been Intel's grip on the PC market that sales are expected to explode from $33.7 billion in 2000 to roughly $53.5 billion in 2005, while profits surge from $10.7 billion to roughly $14.5 billion.

Despite its enviable record of success, and despite obvious strengths, Intel's core business is facing its biggest challenge in a decade. Led by Advanced Micro Devices, Inc., Cyrix, Inc., International Business Machines, Inc., Texas Instruments, Inc., and a handful of foreign firms, competitors are rushing to produce alternatives to Intel chips. Imitators can quickly erode the profits of early innovators like Intel, a company that has come to count on giant-sized operating margins of over 40 percent. During recent years, investors and market analysts have

both posed an important question: Is Intel's dominance of the integrated circuits market coming to an end?

Not without a fight, it won't. Intel is led by visionary chairman Andrew S. Grove, author of the best-seller *Only the Paranoid Survive*, and his hand-picked successor CEO Craig R. Barrett. Driven by paranoia, Intel is dragging competitors into court for patent infringement, slashing prices, and boldly promoting its products. The company is strengthening its close working relationship with manufacturers of end-user products to ensure compatibility and maximize the benefits of new microprocessor innovations. Most important, Intel has launched a campaign to speed product development and expand its potential market.

Intel's speedup of microprocessor technology will affect everyone who uses electronic products. Not the least of those affected will be Intel's competitors.

See: Terho Vimonen, "Intel Clears $100 Million to Upgrade Its Philippine Chip-Making Facilities," *The Wall Street Journal Online*, January 23, 2002 (http://online.wsj.com).

ILLUSTRATION OF MONOPOLISTICALLY COMPETITIVE EQUILIBRIUM

The process of price/output adjustment and the concept of equilibrium in monopolistically competitive markets can be further illustrated by the following example. Assume that the Skyhawk Trailer Company, located in Toronto, Ontario, owns patents covering important design features of its Tomahawk II, an ultralight camping trailer that can safely be towed by high-mileage subcompact cars. Skyhawk's patent protection has made it very difficult for competitors to offer similar ultralight trailers. The Tomahawk II is highly successful, and a flood of similar products can be expected within 5 years as Skyhawk's patent protection expires.

Skyhawk has asked its financial planning committee to identify short- and long-run pricing and production strategies for the Tomahawk II. To facilitate the decision-making process, the committee has received the following revenue and cost data from Skyhawk's marketing and production departments:

$$TR = \$20,000Q - \$15.6Q^2$$
$$MR = \partial TR/\partial Q = \$20,000 - \$31.2Q$$
$$TC = \$400,000 + \$4,640Q + \$10Q^2$$
$$MC = \partial TC/\partial Q = \$4,640 + \$20Q$$

where *TR* is revenue (in dollars), *Q* is quantity (in units), *MR* is marginal revenue (in dollars), *TC* is total cost per month, including a risk-adjusted normal rate of return on investment (in dollars), and *MC* is marginal cost (in dollars).

As a first step in the analysis, one might determine the optimal price/output combination if the committee were to decide that Skyhawk should take full advantage of its current monopoly position and maximize short-run profits. To find the short-run profit-maximizing price/output combination, set Skyhawk's marginal revenue equal to marginal cost and solve for Q:

$$
\begin{aligned}
MR &= MC \\
\$20{,}000 - \$31.2Q &= \$4{,}640 + \$20Q \\
\$51.2Q &= \$15{,}360 \\
Q &= 300 \text{ units}
\end{aligned}
$$

and

$$
\begin{aligned}
P &= \$20{,}000 - \$15.6(300) \\
&= \$15{,}320 \\
\pi &= TR - TC \\
&= -\$25.6(300^2) + \$15{,}360(300) - \$400{,}000 \\
&= \$1{,}904{,}000
\end{aligned}
$$

Therefore, the financial planning committee should recommend a $15,320 price and 300-unit output level to Skyhawk management if the firm's objective is to maximize short-run profit. Such a planning decision results in roughly $1.9 million in profit during those months when Skyhawk's patent protection effectively deters competitors.

Now assume that Skyhawk can maintain a high level of brand loyalty and product differentiation in the long run, despite competitor offerings of similar trailers, but that such competition eliminates any potential for economic profits. This is consistent with a market in monopolistically competitive equilibrium, where $P = AC$ at a point above minimum long-run average costs. Skyhawk's declining market share is reflected by a leftward shift in its demand curve to a point of tangency with its average cost curve. Although precise identification of the long-run price/output combination is very difficult, the planning committee can identify the bounds within which this price/output combination can be expected to occur.

The high-price/low-output combination is identified by the point of tangency between the firm's average cost curve and a new demand curve reflecting a *parallel leftward* shift in demand (D_2 in Figure 11.2). This parallel leftward shift assumes that the firm can maintain a high degree of product differentiation in the long run. The low-price/high-output equilibrium combination assumes no residual product differentiation in the long run and it is identified by the point of tangency between the average cost curve and a new horizontal firm demand curve (D_3 in Figure 11.2). This is, of course, also the perfectly competitive equilibrium price/output combination.

The equilibrium high-price/low-output combination that follows a parallel leftward shift in Skyhawk's demand curve can be determined by equating the slopes of the firm's original demand curve and its long-run average cost curve. Because a parallel leftward shift in firm demand results in a new demand curve with an identical slope, equating the slopes of the firm's initial demand and average cost curves identifies the monopolistically competitive high-price/low-output equilibrium.

For simplicity, assume that the previous total cost curve for Skyhawk also holds in the long run. To determine the slope of this average cost curve, one must find out how average costs vary with respect to output.

$$
\begin{aligned}
AC = TC/Q &= (\$400{,}000 + \$4{,}640Q + \$10Q^2)/Q \\
&= \frac{\$400{,}000 + \$4{,}640 + \$10Q}{Q} \\
&= \$400{,}000Q^{-1} + \$4{,}640 + \$10Q
\end{aligned}
$$

The slope of this average cost curve is given by the expression

$$\partial AC / \partial Q \ = \ -400{,}000Q^{-2} \ + \ 10$$

The slope of the new demand curve is given by

$$\partial P / \partial Q \ = \ -15.6 \text{ (same as the original demand curve)}$$

In equilibrium,

$$
\begin{aligned}
\text{Slope of } AC \text{ Curve} \ &= \ \text{Slope of Demand Curve} \\
-400{,}000Q^{-2} + 10 \ &= \ -15.6 \\
Q^{-2} \ &= \ 25.6 / 400{,}000 \\
Q^{2} \ &= \ 400{,}000 / 25.6 \\
Q \ &= \ 125 \text{ Units} \\
P \ &= \ AC \\
&= \ \frac{\$400{,}000}{125} \ + \ \$4{,}640 \ + \ \$10(125) \\
&= \ \$9{,}090
\end{aligned}
$$

and

$$
\begin{aligned}
\pi \ &= \ P \ \times \ Q \ - \ TC \\
&= \ \$9{,}090(125) \ - \ \$400{,}000 \ - \ \$4{,}640(125) \ - \ \$10(125^{2}) \\
&= \ \$0
\end{aligned}
$$

This high-price/low-output monopolistically competitive equilibrium results in a decrease in price from \$15,320 to \$9,090 and a fall in output from 300 to 125 units per year. Only a risk-adjusted normal rate of return will be earned, eliminating Skyhawk's economic profits. This long-run equilibrium assumes that Skyhawk would enjoy the same low price elasticity of demand that it experienced as a monopolist. This assumption may or may not be appropriate. New entrants often have the effect of both cutting a monopolist's market share and increasing the price elasticity of demand. It is often reasonable to expect entry to cause both a leftward shift of and some flattening in Skyhawk's demand curve. To see the extreme limit of the demand curve–flattening process, the case of a perfectly horizontal demand curve can be considered.

The low-price/high-output (perfectly competitive) equilibrium combination occurs at the point where $P = MR = MC = AC$. This reflects that the firm's demand curve is perfectly horizontal, and average costs are minimized. To find the output level of minimum average costs, set $MC = AC$ and solve for Q:

$$
\begin{aligned}
\$4{,}640 \ + \ \$20Q \ &= \ \$400{,}000Q^{-1} \ + \ \$4{,}640 \ + \ \$10Q \\
\$10Q \ &= \ \$400{,}000Q^{-1} \\
Q^{2} \ &= \ 40{,}000 \\
Q^{2} \ &= \ \sqrt{40{,}000} \\
&= \ 200 \text{ units} \\
P \ &= \ AC \\
&= \ \frac{\$400{,}000}{200} \ + \ \$4{,}640 \ + \ \$10(200) \\
&= \ \$8{,}640
\end{aligned}
$$

and

$$\begin{aligned}
\pi &= P \times Q - TC \\
&= \$8,640(200) - \$400,000 - \$4,640(200) - \$10(200^2) \\
&= \$0
\end{aligned}$$

Under this low-price equilibrium scenario, Skyhawk's monopoly price falls in the long run from an original $15,320 to $8,640, and output falls from the monopoly level of 300 units to the competitive equilibrium level of 200 units per month. The company would earn only a risk-adjusted normal rate of return, and economic profits would equal zero.

Following expiration of its patent protection, management can expect that competitor entry will reduce Skyhawk's volume from 300 units per month to a level between $Q = 125$ and $Q = 200$ units per month. The short-run profit-maximizing price of $15,320 will fall to a monopolistically competitive equilibrium price between $P = \$9,090$, the high-price/low-output equilibrium, and $P = \$8,640$, the low-price/high-output equilibrium. In deciding on an optimal short-run price/output strategy, Skyhawk must weigh the benefits of high near-term profitability against the long-run cost of lost market share resulting from competitor entry. Such a decision involves consideration of current interest rates, the speed of competitor imitation, and the future pace of innovation in the industry, among other factors.

OLIGOPOLY

The theory of monopolistic competition recognizes that firms often have some control over price but that their price flexibility is limited by a large number of close substitutes. This theory assumes that in making decisions firms do not consider competitor reactions. Such a behavioral assumption is appropriate for some industries but not others. When individual firm actions cause competitors to react, oligopoly exists.

Characteristics of Oligopoly Markets

Oligopoly is present when a handful of competitors dominate the market for a good or service and each firm makes pricing and marketing decisions in light of the expected response by rivals. Individual firms have the ability to set pricing and production strategy, and they enjoy the potential for economic profits in both the short run and the long run. Oligopoly describes markets that can be characterized as follows:

- *Few sellers.* A handful of firms produces the bulk of industry output.
- *Homogeneous or unique product.* Oligopoly output can be homogeneous (e.g., aluminum) or distinctive (e.g., ready-to-eat cereal).
- *Blockaded entry and exit.* Firms are heavily restricted from entering or leaving the industry.
- *Imperfect dissemination of information.* Cost, price, and product quality information is withheld from uninformed buyers.

In the United States, aluminum, cigarettes, electrical equipment, filmed entertainment production and distribution, glass, long-distance telecommunications, and ready-to-eat cereals are all produced and sold under conditions of oligopoly. In each of these industries, a small number of firms produces a dominant percentage of all industry output. In the ready-to-eat breakfast cereal industry, for example, Kellogg, Kraft (Post cereals), General Mills, Nabisco, and Quaker Oats are responsible for almost all domestic production in the United States. Durable customer loyalty gives rise to fat profit margins and rates of return on assets that are two to three times food industry norms. Corn Flakes, Sugar Frosted Flakes, Cheerios, Raisin

Bran, Wheaties, and a handful of other brands continue to dominate the industry year after year and make successful entry extremely difficult. Even multinational food giant Nestlé sought and obtained a joint venture agreement with General Mills rather than enter the potentially lucrative European breakfast cereal market by itself. Long-distance telephone service is also highly concentrated, with AT&T, Sprint, and WorldCom providing almost all domestic wire-line service to residential customers.

Oligopoly also is present in a number of local markets. In many retail markets for gasoline and food, for example, only a few service stations and grocery stores compete within a small geographic area. Drycleaning services are also sometimes provided by a relative handful of firms in small to medium-size cities and towns.

Price/Output Decisions Under Oligopoly

Demand curves relate quantity demanded to price, holding constant the effect of all other variables. One variable that is typically assumed to remain fixed is the price charged by competing firms. In oligopoly, however, if one firm changes its price, other firms react by changing their prices. The demand curve for the initial firm shifts position so that instead of moving along a single demand curve as it changes price, the firm moves to an entirely new demand curve.

The phenomenon of shifting demand curves is illustrated in Figure 11.3(a). Firm A is initially producing Q_1 units of output and selling them at a price of P_1. Demand curve D_1 applies here, assuming that prices charged by other firms remain fixed. Under this assumption, a price cut from P_1 to P_2 would increase demand to Q_2. Assume, however, that only a few firms operate in the market and that each has a fairly large share of total sales. If one firm cuts its price and obtains a substantial increase in volume, other firms lose a large part of their business. Furthermore, they know exactly why their sales have fallen and react by cutting their own prices. This action shifts firm A down to the second demand curve, D_2, reducing its demand at P_2 from Q_2 to Q_3 units. The new curve is just as unstable as the old one, so knowledge of its shape is useless to firm A; if it tries to move along D_2, competitors will react, forcing the company to yet another demand curve.

Shifting demand curves presents no real difficulty in making price/output decisions if each firm knows how rivals will react to price changes. The reactions would just be built into the price/demand relation, and a new demand curve could be constructed to include interactions among firms. Curve D_3 in Figure 11.3(b) represents such a reaction-based demand curve; it shows how price reductions affect quantity demanded after competitive reactions have been taken into account. The problem with this approach is that different interfirm behavior leads to different pricing decision rules.

Cartel Arrangements

cartel
Firms operating with a formal agreement to fix prices and output

collusion
A covert, informal agreement among firms in an industry to fix prices and output levels

All firms in an oligopoly market benefit if they get together and set prices to maximize industry profits. A group of competitors operating under such a formal overt agreement is called a **cartel**. If an informal covert agreement is reached, the firms are said to be operating in **collusion**. Both practices are illegal in the United States. However, cartels are legal in some parts of the world, and U.S. multinational corporations sometimes become involved with them in foreign markets. Several important domestic markets are also dominated by producer associations that operate like cartels and appear to flourish without interference from the government. Agricultural commodities such as milk are prime examples of products marketed under cartel-like arrangements.

A cartel that has absolute control over all firms in an industry can operate as a monopoly. To illustrate, consider the situation shown in Figure 11.4. The marginal cost curves of each firm are summed horizontally to arrive at an industry marginal cost curve. Equating the cartel's total marginal cost with the industry marginal revenue curve determines the profit-maximizing output and the price, P^*, to be charged. Once this profit-maximizing price/output level has been

FIGURE 11.3

Shifting Demand Under Oligopoly

(a) A price reduction to P_2 by firm A temporarily increases output to Q_2. As other firms reduce prices, demand shifts back from D_1 to D_2 and firm A's output drops to Q_3. (b) In contrast to D_1 and D_2, the demand curve D_3 reflects firm A's projections of the price reactions of competitors.

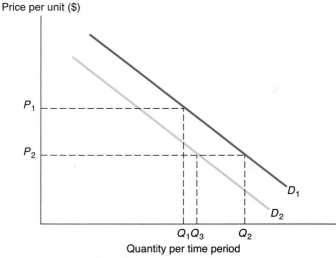

(a) Demand curves that do not explicitly recognize reactions

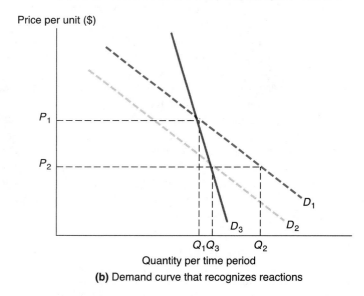

(b) Demand curve that recognizes reactions

determined, each individual firm finds its optimal output by equating its own marginal cost curve to the previously determined profit-maximizing marginal cost level for the industry.

Profits are often divided among firms on the basis of their individual level of production, but other allocation techniques can be employed. Market share, production capacity, and a bargained solution based on economic power have all been used in the past. For a number of reasons, cartels are typically rather short-lived. In addition to the long-run problems of changing products and of entry into the market by new producers, cartels are subject to disagreements among members. Although firms usually agree that maximizing joint profits is mutually benefi-

FIGURE 11.4

Price/Output Determination for a Cartel

Horizontal summation of the *MC* curves for each firm gives the cartel's *MC* curve. Output for each firm is found by equating its own *MC* to the industry profit-maximizing *MC* level.

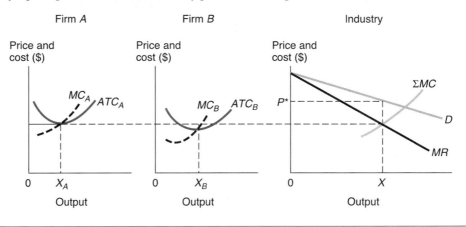

cial, they seldom agree on the equity of various profit-allocation schemes. This problem can lead to attempts to subvert the cartel agreement.

Cartel subversion can be extremely profitable. Consider a two-firm cartel in which each member serves 50 percent of the market. Cheating by either firm is very difficult, because any loss in profits or market share is readily detected. The offending party also can easily be identified and punished. Moreover, the potential profit and market share gain to successful cheating is exactly balanced by the potential profit and market share cost of detection and retribution. Conversely, a 20-member cartel promises substantial profits and market share gains to successful cheaters. At the same time, detecting the source of secret price concessions can be extremely difficult. History shows that cartels including more than a very few members have difficulty policing and maintaining member compliance. With respect to cartels, there is little honor among thieves.

Price Leadership

price leadership
A situation in which one firm establishes itself as the industry leader and all other firms in the industry accept its pricing policy

An informal but sometimes effective means for reducing oligopolistic uncertainty is through **price leadership**. Price leadership results when one firm establishes itself as the industry leader and other firms follow its pricing policy. This leadership may result from the size and strength of the leading firm, from cost efficiency, or as a result of the ability of the leader to establish prices that produce satisfactory profits throughout the industry.

A typical case is price leadership by a dominant firm, usually the largest firm in the industry. The leader faces a price/output problem similar to monopoly; other firms are price takers and face a competitive price/output problem. This is illustrated in Figure 11.5, where the total market demand curve is D_T, the marginal cost curve of the leader is MC_L, and the horizontal summation of the marginal cost curves for all of the price followers is labeled MC_f. Because price followers take prices as given, they choose to operate at the output level at which their individual marginal costs equal price, just as they would in a perfectly competitive market. Accordingly, the MC_f curve represents the supply curve for following firms. At price P_3, followers would supply the entire market, leaving nothing for the dominant firm. At all prices below P_3, the horizontal distance between the summed MC_f curve and the market demand curve represents the price leader's demand. At a price of P_1, for example, price followers provide Q_2

FIGURE 11.5

Oligopoly Pricing with Dominant-Firm Price Leadership

When the price leader has set an industry price of P_2, the price leader will maximize profits at Q_1 units of output. Price followers will supply a combined output of $Q_4 - Q_1$.

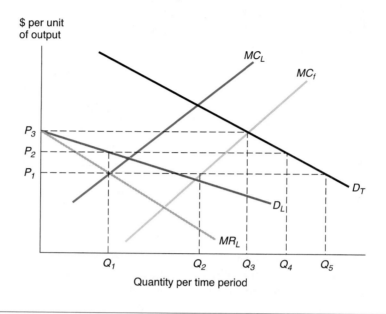

units of output, leaving demand of $Q_5 - Q_2$ for the price leader. Plotting all of the residual demand quantities for prices below P_3 produces the demand curve for the price leader, D_L in Figure 11.5, and the related marginal revenue curve, MR_L.

More generally, the leader faces a demand curve of the following form:

(11.1)
$$D_L = D_T - S_f$$

where D_L is the leader's demand, D_T is total demand, and S_f is the followers' supply curve found by setting $P = MC_f$ and solving for Q_f, the quantity that will be supplied by the price followers. Because D_T and S_f are both functions of price, D_L is likewise determined by price.

Because the price leader faces the demand curve D_L as a monopolist, it maximizes profit by operating at the point where marginal revenue equals marginal cost, $MR_L = MC_L$. At this optimal output level for the leader, Q_1, market price is established at P_2. Price followers supply a combined output of $Q_4 - Q_1$ units. A stable short-run equilibrium is reached if no one challenges the price leader.

A second type of price leadership is **barometric price leadership**. In this case, one firm announces a price change in response to what it perceives as a change in industry supply and demand conditions. This change could stem from cost increases that result from a new industry labor agreement, higher energy or material costs, higher taxes, or a substantial shift in industry demand. With barometric price leadership, the price leader is not necessarily the largest or the dominant firm in the industry. The price-leader role might even pass from one firm to another over time. To be effective, the price leader must only be accurate in reading the prevailing industry view of the need for price adjustment. If the price leader makes a mistake, other firms may not follow its price move, and the price leader may have to rescind or modify the announced price change to retain its leadership position.

barometric price leadership
A situation in which one firm in an industry announces a price change in response to what it perceives as a change in industry supply and demand conditions and other firms respond by following the price change

Kinked Demand Curve

An often-noted characteristic of oligopoly markets is "sticky" prices. Once a general price level has been established, whether through cartel agreement or some less formal arrangement, it tends to remain fixed for an extended period. Such rigid prices are sometimes explained by what is referred to as the **kinked demand curve** theory of oligopoly prices. A kinked demand curve is a firm demand curve that has different slopes for price increases as compared with price decreases. The kinked demand curve describes a behavior pattern in which rival firms follow any decrease in price to maintain their respective market shares but refrain from following price increases, allowing their market shares to grow at the expense of the competitor increasing its price. The demand curve facing individual firms is kinked at the current price/output combination, as illustrated in Figure 11.6. The firm is producing Q units of output and selling them at a price of P per unit. If the firm lowers its price, competitors retaliate by lowering their prices. The result of a price cut is a relatively small increase in sales. Price increases, on the other hand, result in significant reductions in the quantity demanded and in total revenue, because customers shift to competing firms that do not follow the price increase.

Associated with the kink in the demand curve is a point of discontinuity in the marginal revenue curve. As a result, the firm's marginal revenue curve has a gap at the current price/output level, which results in price rigidity. To see why, recall that profit-maximizing firms operate at the point where marginal cost equals marginal revenue. Typically, any change in marginal cost leads to a new point of equality between marginal costs and marginal revenues and to a new optimal price. However, with a gap in the marginal revenue curve, the price/output combination at the kink can remain optimal despite fluctuations in marginal costs. As illustrated in Figure 11.6, the firm's marginal cost curve can vacillate between MC_1 and MC_2 without causing any change in the profit-maximizing price/output combination. Small changes in marginal costs have no effect; only large changes in marginal cost lead to price changes. In perfectly competitive grain markets, prices change every day. In the oligopolistic ready-to-eat cereals market, prices change less frequently.

FIGURE 11.6

Kinked Demand Curve

When price cuts are followed but price increases are not, a kink develops in the firm's demand curve. At the kink, the optimal price remains stable despite moderate changes in marginal costs.

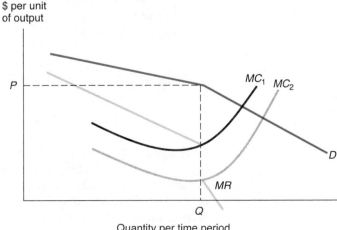

Government-Guaranteed Oligopoly

The Federal National Mortgage Association and the Federal Home Loan Mortgage Corp., or Fannie Mae and Freddie Mac, enjoy immense benefits from being government-sponsored entities that are also for-profit, publicly traded stockholder-owned corporations. Both are huge and highly profitable, despite the fact that they operate in a relatively simple and low-risk business. Fannie and Freddie purchase billions in home mortgages from thrifts and other financial institutions every year. Most of these loans are packaged and resold to investors as mortgage-backed securities, thus enabling home buyers to tap pension funds and other institutional money.

Both have implied U.S. government guarantees of their liabilities. This earns them the highest possible credit ratings on their debt securities and allows them to attract institutional investors at the lowest possible interest rate. Although the U.S. government charges nothing for its implied credit guarantee, Fannie and Freddie together reap billions of dollars per year in profits. In no small part, the amazingly good profit performance of Fannie and Freddie comes from the fact that they enjoy

much lower interest costs on borrowed funds than the amount paid by their purely private-sector competitors.

Both Fannie and Freddie make a profit by selling packages of home loans to investors at an interest rate that is roughly 1 percent per year lower than that on the underlying pool of mortgages. In so doing, they earn an annual rate of return on stockholders' equity in excess of 25 percent per year, or nearly double the profit rate earned by the average financial institution. These extraordinary profit rates are also remarkably stable. As a result, their stock-price performance has been sensational. Long-term investors saw their initial investments in Fannie and Freddie multiply more than ten-fold over the past decade and look forward to continued gains of 12 percent to 15 percent per year.

Obviously, there are tangible rewards to government-guaranteed oligopoly!

See: Janet Morrissey, "Wachovia, Fannie Mae Offer Home Loans for Nation's Finest," *The Wall Street Journal Online*, January 8, 2002 (http://online.wsj.com).

NONPRICE COMPETITION

"Meet it or beat it" is a pricing challenge that often results in quick competitor price reductions, and price wars always favor the deep pockets of established incumbents. As a result, many successful entrants find nonprice methods of competition an effective means for growing market share and profitability in the face of entrenched rivals.

Advantages of Nonprice Competition

Because rival firms are likely to retaliate against price cuts, oligopolists often emphasize nonprice competition to boost demand. To illustrate, assume that a firm demand function is given by Equation 11.2:

$$
\begin{aligned}
Q_A &= f(P_A, P_X, Ad_A, Ad_X, SQ_A, SQ_X, I, Pop, \ldots) \\
&= a - bP_A + cP_X + dAd_A - eAd_X + fSQ_A \\
&\quad - gSQ_X + hI + iPop + \ldots
\end{aligned}
$$

(11.2)

where Q_A is the quantity of output demanded from firm A, P_A is A's price, P_X is the average price charged by other firms in the industry, Ad is advertising expenditures, SQ denotes an index of styling and quality, I represents income, and Pop is population. The firm can control three variables in Equation 11.2: P_A, Ad_A, and SQ_A. If it reduces P_A in an effort to stimulate demand, it will probably cause a reduction in P_X, offsetting the hoped-for effects of the initial price cut. Rather than boosting sales, firm A may have simply started a price war.

Now consider the effects of changing Ad_A and SQ_A. Effective advertising shifts the firm's demand curve to the right, thus enabling the firm to increase sales at a given price or to sell the same quantity at a higher price. Any improvement in styling or quality would have a comparable effect, as would easier credit terms, better service, and more convenient retail locations. Although competitors react to nonprice competition, their reaction is often slower and less direct than that for price changes. Nonprice changes are generally less obvious to rivals, and the design of an effective response is often time-consuming and difficult. Advertising campaigns have to be designed; media time and space must be purchased. Styling and quality changes frequently require long lead times, as do fundamental improvements in customer service. Furthermore, nonprice competition can alter customer buying habits, and regaining lost customers can prove to be difficult. Although it may take longer to establish a reputation through nonprice competition, its advantageous effects are likely to be more persistent than the fleeting benefits of a price cut.

The optimal level of nonprice competition is defined by resulting marginal benefits and marginal costs. Any form of nonprice competition should be pursued as long as marginal benefits exceed marginal costs. For example, suppose that a product has a market price of $10 per unit and a variable cost per unit of $8. If sales can be increased at an additional cost of less than $2 per unit, these additional expenditures will increase profits and should be made.

Optimal Level of Advertising

Advertising is one of the most common methods of nonprice competition. Others include personal selling, improvements in product quality, expansions in customer service, research and development, and so on. The profit-maximizing amount of nonprice competition is found by setting the marginal cost of the activity involved equal to the marginal revenue or marginal benefit derived from it. For example, the optimal level of advertising occurs at that point where the marginal revenues derived from advertising just offset the marginal cost of advertising.

The marginal revenue derived from advertising is measured by the marginal profit contribution generated. This is the difference between marginal revenue, MR, and the marginal cost of production and distribution, MC_Q, before advertising costs:

(11.3)
$$\frac{\text{Marginal Revenue}}{\text{Derived from Advertising}} = \frac{\text{Marginal}}{\text{Revenue}} - \frac{\text{Marginal Cost}}{\text{of Output}}$$

$$MR_A = MR - MC_Q$$

The marginal cost of advertising, again expressed in terms of the marginal cost of selling one additional unit of output, can be written:

(11.4)
$$\frac{\text{Marginal Cost}}{\text{of Advertising}} = \frac{\text{Change in Advertising Expenditures}}{\text{One-Unit Change in Demand}}$$

$$MC_A = \frac{\partial\text{Advertising Expenditures}}{\partial\text{Demand}} = \frac{\partial Ad}{\partial Q}$$

The optimal level of advertising is found where

$$\frac{\text{Marginal Revenue}}{\text{Derived from Advertising}} = \text{Marginal Cost of Advertising}$$

$$MR - MC_Q = \frac{\partial\text{Advertising Expenditures}}{\partial\text{Demand}}$$

$$MR_A = MC_A$$

In general, it will pay to expand advertising expenditures so long as $MR_A > MC_A$. Because the marginal profit derived from advertising is

(11.5)
$$M\pi_A = MR_A - MC_A$$

the optimal level of advertising occurs at the point where

$$M\pi_A = 0$$

This relation is illustrated in Figure 11.7. As long as $MR_A > MC_A$, $M\pi_A > 0$, and it will pay to expand the level of advertising. Conversely, if $MR_A < MC_A$, then $M\pi_A < 0$, and it will pay to reduce the level of advertising expenditures. The optimal level of advertising is achieved when $MR_A = MC_A$, and $M\pi_A = 0$.

Example of Optimal Advertising

The effect of advertising on the optimal price/output combination can be further illustrated with a more detailed example. Suppose that Consumer Products, Inc., has a new prescription ointment called Regain that can be used to restore hair loss due to male pattern baldness in some patients. Currently, Regain is marketed through doctors without any consumer advertising. Given the newness of the product, demand for Regain is expected to increase rapidly following the initiation of consumer advertising. Samantha Stevens, an ad executive with the McMann & Tate Advertising Agency, projects that demand would double following the start of a $500,000 per month media advertising campaign developed by the agency. To illustrate the profit impact of the proposed television advertising campaign, it is necessary to identify the projected effect on demand and revenue relations.

Current monthly demand for the product is described by the following expressions:

$$Q = 25,000 - 100P$$

FIGURE 11.7

Optimal Level of Advertising

A firm will expand the level of advertising up to the point where the net marginal revenue generated just equals the marginal cost of advertising.

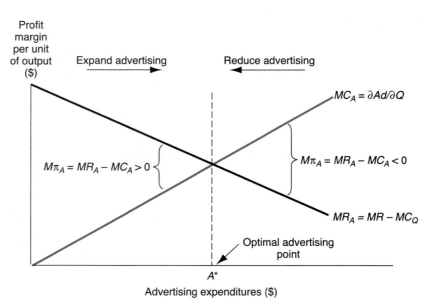

or

$$P = \$250 - \$0.01Q$$

This market demand implies total and marginal revenue functions of

$$TR = P \times Q = \$250Q - \$0.01Q^2$$
$$MR = \partial TR/\partial Q = \$250 - \$0.02Q$$

Assume total and marginal costs before advertising expenses are given by the expressions

$$TC = \$250,000 + \$50Q$$
$$MC = \partial TC/\partial Q = \$50$$

The optimal price/output combination is found by setting $MR = MC$ and solving for Q. Because marginal costs are constant at \$50 per unit, the pre-advertising optimal activity level for Regain is

$$MR = MC$$
$$\$250 - \$0.02Q = \$50$$
$$0.02Q = 200$$
$$Q = 10,000$$

and

$$P = \$250 - \$0.01Q$$
$$= \$250 - \$0.01(10,000)$$
$$= \$150$$
$$\pi = TR - TC$$
$$= \$250(10,000) - \$0.01(10,000^2) - \$250,000 - \$50(10,000)$$
$$= \$750,000 \text{ per month}$$

Following a 100 percent advertising-inspired increase in demand, the new monthly demand relations for Regain are

$$Q = 2(25,000 - 100P)$$
$$= 50,000 - 200P$$

or

$$P = \$250 - \$0.005Q$$

This new advertising-induced market demand implies new total and marginal revenue functions of

$$TR = \$250Q - \$0.005Q^2$$
$$MR = \$250 - \$0.01Q$$

The new optimal price/output combination is found by setting the new $MR = MC$ and solving for Q. Because marginal costs remain constant at \$50 per unit, the new optimal activity level for Regain is

$$MR = MC$$
$$\$250 - \$0.01Q = \$50$$
$$0.01Q = 200$$
$$Q = 20,000$$

and

$$P = \$250 - \$0.005Q$$
$$= \$250 - \$0.005(20,000)$$
$$= \$150$$
$$\pi = TR - TC$$
$$= \$250(20,000) - \$0.005(20,000^2) - \$250,000$$
$$- \$50(20,000) - \$500,000$$
$$= \$1,250,000 \text{ per month}$$

Notice that sales have doubled from 10,000 to 20,000 at the $150 price. The effect on profits is dramatic, rising from $750,000 to $1.25 million, even after accounting for the additional $500,000 in media expenditures. Therefore, the new advertising campaign appears fully warranted. In fact, given the $1.25 million in profits that are generated by a doubling in unit sales at a price of $150, Consumer Products would be willing to pay up to that full amount to double sales. From this perspective, the $500,000 price charge for the advertising campaign represents a relative bargain. The profit implications of other forms of advertising, or other types of nonprice competition, can be measured in a similar fashion.

GAME THEORY

game theory
General framework to help decision making when firm payoffs depend on actions taken by other firms

Game theory concepts are used to develop effective competitive strategies for setting prices, the level of product quality, research and development, advertising, and other forms of nonprice competition in oligopoly markets. Game theory concepts have also been used to set public policy for currency market intervention in emerging markets and auction strategies for broadcast spectrum in the telecommunications industry. This brief introduction shows how managers can use a simple understanding of game theory concepts to make better managerial decisions.

Prisoner's Dilemma

simultaneous-move game
Choices are made without specific knowledge of competitor counter moves

sequential-move game
Choices are made after observing competitor moves

one-shot game
A one-time interaction

repeat game
Ongoing interaction

Game theory is a general framework to help decision making when firm payoffs depend on actions taken by other firms. Because decision interdependence is a prime characteristic of oligopoly markets, game theory concepts have a wide variety of applications in the study of oligopoly. In a **simultaneous-move game**, each decision maker makes choices without specific knowledge of competitor counter moves. In a **sequential-move game**, decision makers make their move after observing competitor moves. If two firms set prices without knowledge of each other's decisions, it is a simultaneous-move game. If one firm sets its price only after observing its rival's price, the firm is said to be involved in a sequential-move game. In a **one-shot game**, the underlying interaction between competitors occurs only once; in a **repeat game**, there is an ongoing interaction between competitors.

A game theory strategy is a decision rule that describes the action taken by a decision maker at any point in time. A simple introduction to game theory strategy is provided by perhaps the

Prisoner's Dilemma
A classic conflict-of-interest situation

most famous of all simultaneous-move one-shot games: The so-called **Prisoner's Dilemma**. Suppose two suspects, Bonnie and Clyde, are jointly accused of committing a specific crime, say inside trading. Furthermore, assume that the conviction of either suspect cannot be secured without a signed confession by one or both suspects. As shown in Table 11.1, if neither Bonnie nor Clyde confesses, the prosecutor will be unable to obtain a conviction, and both will be set free. If only one suspect confesses, turns state's evidence and implicates the other, then the one confessing will get the relatively light penalty of a having to pay a fine and serving probation, and the implicated party will receive the harsh sentence of 5 years in prison. If both suspects confess, then each will receive a stiff 2-year sentence. If both suspects are held in isolation, neither knows what the other will do, and a classic conflict-of-interest situation is created.

dominant strategy
Decision that gives the best result for either party regardless of the action taken by the other

Although each suspect can control the range of sentencing outcomes, neither can control the ultimate outcome. In this situation, there is no **dominant strategy** that results in the best result for either suspect regardless of the action taken by the other. Both would be better off if they could be assured that the other would not confess, because if neither confesses both are set free. However, in failing to confess, each is exposed to the risk that the other will confess. By not confessing, they would then receive the harsh sentence of 5 years in prison. This uncertainty creates the Prisoner's Dilemma. To confess, or not to confess—that is the question.

secure strategy
Decision that guarantees the best possible outcome given the worst possible scenario

A **secure strategy**, sometimes called the maximin strategy, guarantees the best possible outcome given the worst possible scenario. In this case, the worst possible scenario for each suspect is that the other chooses to confess. Each suspect can avoid the worst possible outcome of receiving a harsh 5 years in prison sentence only by choosing to confess. For each suspect, the secure strategy is to confess, thereby becoming a prisoner, because neither could solve the riddle posed by the Prisoner's Dilemma.

Though the Prisoner's Dilemma is posed within the scope of a bargaining problem between two suspects, it has obvious practical applications in business. Competitors like Coca-Cola and Pepsi-Cola confront similar bargaining problems on a regular basis. Suppose each has to decide whether or not to offer a special discount to a large grocery store retailer. Table 11.2 shows that if neither offers discount pricing, a weekly profit of $12,500 will be earned by Coca-Cola, and $9,000 per week will be earned by its smaller competitor, Pepsi-Cola. This is the best possible scenario for both. However, if Coca-Cola is the only one to offer a discount, it will earn $10,000 per week, while Pepsi-Cola profits fall to $1,000 per week. If Pepsi-Cola offers a discount and Coca-Cola continues to charge the regular price, Pepsi-Cola profits will total $6,500 per week while Coca-Cola weekly profits fall to $1,500. The only secure means Coca-Cola has for avoiding the possibility of a meager $1,500 per week profit is to grant a discount price to the retailer, thereby assuring itself of a weekly profit of at least $4,000. Similarly, the only means Pepsi-Cola has of avoiding the possibility of meager profits of $1,000 per week is to also grant a discount price to the grocery retailer, thereby assuring

TABLE 11.1

The Prisoner's Dilemma Payoff Matrix

| | Confession Strategy | Suspect #2: Clyde | |
		Not Confess	Confess
Suspect #1: Bonnie	**Not Confess**	Freedom, Freedom	5-year prison term, Fine and probation
	Confess	Fine and probation, 5-year prison term	2-year prison term, 2-year prison term

TABLE 11.2

A Hypothetical Prisoner's Dilemma Faced by Coca-Cola and Pepsi-Cola

		Pepsi-Cola	
		Discount Price	**Regular Price**
Coca-Cola	**Discount Price**	$4,000, $2,000	$10,000, $1,000
	Regular Price	$1,500, $6,500	$12,500, $9,000

itself of at least $2,000 in weekly profits. For both Coca-Cola and Pepsi-Cola, the only secure strategy is to offer discount prices, thereby assuring consumers of bargain prices and themselves of modest profits of $4,000 and $2,000 per week, respectively.

Nash Equilibrium

Nash equilibrium
Set of decision strategies where no player can improve through a unilateral change in strategy

In Table 11.2, each firm's secure strategy is to offer a discount price regardless of the other firm's actions. The outcome is that both firms offer discount prices and earn relatively modest profits. This outcome is also called a **Nash equilibrium** because, given the strategy of its competitor, neither firm can improve its own payoff by unilaterally changing its own strategy. In the case of Coca-Cola, given that Pepsi-Cola has chosen a discount pricing strategy, it too would decide to offer discount prices. When Pepsi-Cola offers discount prices, Coca-Cola can earn profits of $4,000 rather than $1,500 per week by also offering a discount. Similarly, when Coca-Cola offers discount prices, Pepsi-Cola can earn maximum profits of $2,000 per week, versus $1,000 per week, by also offering a discount.

Clearly, profits are less than if they colluded and both charged regular prices. As seen in Table 11.2, Coca-Cola would earn $12,500 per week and Pepsi-Cola would earn $9,000 per week if both charged regular prices. This is a business manifestation of the Prisoner's Dilemma because the dual discount pricing Nash equilibrium is inferior from the firms' viewpoint to a collusive outcome where both competitors agree to charge regular prices.

Of course, if firms collude and agree to charge high prices, consumers are made worse off. This is why price collusion among competitors is illegal in the United States, as discussed in Chapter 13.

Nash Bargaining

Nash bargaining
Where two competitors haggle over some item of value

A **Nash bargaining** game is another application of the simultaneous-move, one-shot game. In Nash bargaining, two competitors or players "bargain" over some item of value. In a simultaneous-move, one-shot game, the players have only one chance to reach an agreement.

For example, suppose the board of directors specifies a $1 million profit-sharing pool provided that both management and workers can come to agreement concerning how such profits are to be distributed. For simplicity, assume that this pool can only be distributed in amounts of $0, $500,000, and $1 million. If the sum of the amounts requested by each party totals more than $1 million, neither party receives anything. If the sum of the amounts requested by each party totals no more than $1 million, each party receives the amount requested.

Table 11.3 shows the nine possible outcomes from such a profit-sharing bargaining game. If the workers request $1 million, the only way that they would get any money at all is if management requests nothing. Similarly, if management requests $1 million, the only way they get money is if workers request nothing. If either party requests nothing, Nash equilibrium solutions are achieved when the other party requests the full $1 million. Thus, the ($1 million, $0) and ($0, $1 million) solutions are both Nash equilibriums. However, suppose the workers

TABLE 11.3

Nash Bargaining Game over Profit-Pool Sharing

		Management		
	Request Strategy	$0	$500,000	$1,000,000
Workers	$0	$0 $0	$0, $500,000	$0, $1,000,000
	$500,000	$500,000, $0	$500,000, $500,000	$0, $0
	$1,000,000	$1,000,000, $0	$0, $0	$0, $0

request $500,000; then the Nash equilibrium response from management would be to also request $500,000. If management requests $500,000, then the Nash equilibrium response from workers would be to also request $500,000. Thus, the ($500,000, $500,000) payoff is also a Nash equilibrium. This game involves three Nash equilibriums out of nine possible solutions. In each Nash equilibrium, the entire profit-sharing pool is paid out. In the six remaining outcomes, some of the profit-sharing pool would not be distributed. Such suboptimal outcomes can and do occur in real-life situations.

However, in contemplating the bargaining process, workers are apt to note that a request for $0 is dominated by asking for either $500,000 or $1 million. If you do not ask for anything, you are sure of getting nothing. Similarly, management will never do worse, and may do better, if it asks for something. As a result, the $0 request strategy is dominated for both parties and will tend not to be followed. In addition, a request for the entire $1 million by either party will not be successful unless the other party requests nothing. Because a $0 request by either party is not likely, neither party is likely to request the full $1 million. In this case, the logical and rational request from each party is $500,000, or an equal 50/50 sharing of the profit pool.

Repeat Games

repeat games
A comprehensive statistical profile of the economy, from the national, to the state, to the local level

The study of one-shot pricing and product quality games might lead one to conclude that even tacit collusion is impossible. This is not true because competitors often interact on a continuous basis. In such circumstances, firms are said to be involved in **repeat games**.

When a competitive game is repeated over and over, firms receive sequential payoffs that shape current and future strategies. For example, in Table 11.2, both Coca-Cola and Pepsi-Cola might tacitly or secretly agree to charge regular prices so long as the other party continues to do so. If neither firm cheats on such a collusive agreement, discounts will never be offered, and maximum profits will be earned. Although there is an obvious risk involved with charging regular prices, there is also an obvious cost if either or both firms offer discount pricing. If each firm is convinced that the other will maintain regular prices, both will enjoy high profits. This resolve is increased if each firm is convinced that the other will quickly match any discount pricing strategy. In fact, it is rational for colluding firms to quickly and severely punish colluding competitors who "cheat" by lowering prices.

However, although it is important to recognize that the repeat nature of competitor interactions can sometimes harm consumers, it is equally important to recognize that repetitive interactions in the marketplace provide necessary incentives for firms to produce high-quality goods. In any one-shot game, it would pay firms with high-quality reputations to produce low-cost or shoddy goods. In the real world, the ongoing interaction between firms and their customers provides incentives for firms to maintain product consistency. For example, both

Dot.com

With all the hoopla, it is tough to sort out what's real and what's Internet hype. For companies, building a publishing-only Web site is the first step to becoming an e-business. Most businesses have already done this. That's fine as far as it goes; it's an extremely cost-efficient way to distribute basic information. However, the payoff for business starts with "self-service" Web sites where customers can do things like check the status of an account or trace a package online (like at FedEX). The real payoff begins with transaction-based Web sites that go beyond just buying and selling to create a dynamic and interactive flow of information.

An e-business is created when companies put their core processes online to improve service, cut costs, or boost revenue. For example, IBM helped Charles Schwab Web-enable their brokerage systems for online trading and customer service. Since opening, Schwab's Web service has generated over 1 million online accounts totaling over $50 billion in assets. E-business economics are compelling. According to management consultants, traditional bank transactions cost more than a dollar; the same transaction over the Web costs about 1¢. Issuing a

paper airline ticket costs about $8; an e-ticket costs just $1. Customers love the convenience; management loves the lower costs.

Although a number of companies use the Web to further exploit long-standing competitive advantages, it is not clear that companies can use the Web to create durable competitive advantages. Hoping to stand out from the crowd, some Internet merchants devote as much as 70 percent of total revenues to advertising. "Get ahead and stay ahead" is the mantra at Amazon.com, a company trying to create a durable online marketing presence in books, electronics, computers, toys and games, health and beauty aids, DVDs, and much more. To date, Amazon.com has proven adept at quickly growing online revenues. It's a widely recognized online leader. However, even for Amazon.com, building online profits has proven elusive.

See: Nick Wingfield, "Amazon Posts Surprise Profit; Sales Rose 15% in 4th Quarter," *The Wall Street Journal Online*, January 23, 2002 (http://online.wsj.com).

Coca-Cola and Pepsi-Cola have well-deserved reputations for providing uniformly high-quality soft drinks. They have both invested millions of dollars in product development and quality control to ensure that consumers can depend upon the taste, smell, and feel of Coca-Cola and Pepsi-Cola products. Moreover, because the value of millions of dollars spent on brand-name advertising would be lost if product quality were to deteriorate, that brand-name advertising is itself a type of quality assurance provided to customers of Coca-Cola and Pepsi-Cola. At Wal-Mart, *Satisfaction Guaranteed, or your money back*, is more than just a slogan. It is their business; it is what separates Wal-Mart from fly-by-night operators or low-quality discount stores. Similarly, customers of DaimlerChrysler depend upon that company's well-deserved reputation for producing high-quality cars, trucks, and minivans. Like any written guarantee or insurance policy, repeat transactions in the marketplace give consumers confidence that they will get what they pay for.

MARKET STRUCTURE MEASUREMENT

To formulate an effective competitive strategy, managers must accurately assess the current competitive environment for actual and potential products. Data gathered by the federal government, private market research firms, and trade associations are often useful for this purpose. This section shows the types of market structure data available from public sources and explains why they are important for decision-making purposes.

How Are Economic Markets Measured?

An economic market consists of all individuals and firms willing and able to buy or sell competing products during a given period. The key criterion in identifying competing products is similarity in use. Precise determination of whether a specific good is a distinct economic product involves an evaluation of cross-price elasticities for broad classes of goods. When cross-price elasticities are large and positive, goods are substitutes for each other and can be thought of as competing products in a single market. Conversely, large negative cross-price elasticities indicate complementary products. Complementary products produced by a single firm must be evaluated as a single product line serving the same market. If complementary products are produced by other companies, evaluating the potential of a given product line involves incorporating exogenous influences beyond the firm's control. When cross-price elasticities are near zero, goods are in separate economic markets and can be separately analyzed as serving distinct consumer needs. Therefore, using cross-price elasticity criteria to desegregate the firm's overall product line into its distinct economic markets is an important task confronting managers.

To identify relevant economic markets and define their characteristics, firms in the United States make extensive use of economic data collected by the Bureau of the Census of the U.S. Department of Commerce. Because these data provide valuable information on economic activity across the broad spectrum of U.S. industry, it is worthwhile to briefly consider the method and scope of the economic censuses.

Economic Census

economic census
A comprehensive statistical profile of the economy, from the national, to the state, to the local level

Once every 5 years, the **economic census** provides a comprehensive statistical profile of the economy, from the national, to the state, to the local level. Censuses are taken at 5-year intervals during years ending with the digits 2 and 7—for example, 1992, 1997, 2002, 2007, and so on. As shown in Figure 11.8, the economic census covers economic activity in important sectors such as manufacturing, retail and wholesale trade, services, minerals, and construction. Sectors covered account for roughly three-quarters of total economic activity originating in the private sector. Principal industry groups with incomplete coverage are agriculture, education, financial services, forestry, professional services, and transportation.

The economic census is the primary source of detailed public facts about the nation's economy. As such, census data are essential inputs for decisions made by managers in government, business, and the not-for-profit sector. Economic census data allows businesses to compare company sales to census totals for specific industries or areas, calculate market share, evaluate performance, and make plans for expansion or asset redeployment. Companies can use census data to lay out territories, allocate advertising, and locate new stores or offices. Firms supplying goods and services to other businesses also use census data to target industries for business-to-business marketing. Manufacturers look at statistics on materials consumed to learn more about industries that use their products and to gain insight concerning industry growth potential. All firms compare operating ratios to census averages to see how they stack up against competitive norms. Consultants, government researchers, and job seekers use census data to analyze changes in industrial structure, location, and the pace of growth in job opportunities. Both state and federal regulators use census data to monitor business activity as captured by fluctuations in monthly retail sales, gross domestic product (GDP), and other such measures. Industry trade associations and news media study census data to learn key business facts and to project trends. Legislators use census data in the preparation and evaluation of new legislation designed to spur economic development. State and local government agencies monitor census information to better understand their regional economic base and to help them better focus efforts to attract new businesses and/or retain existing firms.

The economic census covers nearly all of the U.S. economy in its establishment statistics. There also are several related programs, including the collection and publication of statistics on minority- and women-owned businesses. Separate censuses of agriculture and government are also conducted at the same time as the economic census. Results from this most recent economic census were issued on CD-ROM and on the Internet in a series of continuing reports over a period of more than 2 years, starting in early 1999. Only summary reports are issued in print.

FIGURE 11.8

Economic Census Data Are Available on the Internet

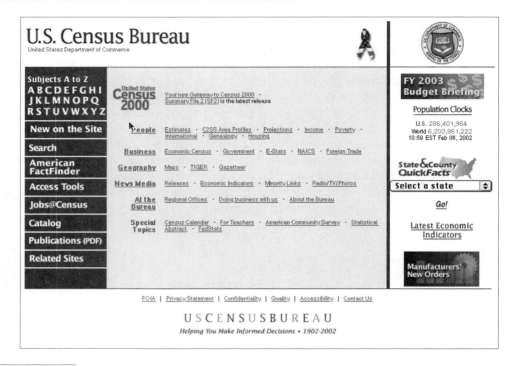

Source: U.S. Census Bureau (http://www.census.gov).

How Economic Census Data Are Collected and Published

The 1997 economic census measured economic activity during calendar year 1997. Census forms were mailed to more than 5 million companies in December 1997, with a due date of February 12, 1998. There were over 500 versions of the census form, each customized to particular industries. Some very small companies did not receive a census form. The economic census is authorized by law; compliance is mandatory. The law requires firms to respond and specifies penalties for firms that fail to report. The law also requires the Census Bureau to maintain confidentiality. Individual responses may be seen only by sworn Census Bureau employees. Moreover, precautions are taken to insure that no data are published that could reveal the identity or activity of any individual business.

Economic census statistics are collected and published primarily at the "establishment" level of aggregation. An establishment is a business or industrial unit at a single physical location that produces or distributes goods or performs services. For example, a single store or factory constitutes a single establishment under the census system. Of course, many companies own or control more than one establishment, and those establishments may be located in different geographic areas. They are often also engaged in different kinds of business activity. By collecting separate information for each establishment, the economic census is able to include detailed data for each industry group and geographic area.

North American Industry Classification System (NAICS)
A method for categorizing establishments by the principal economic activity in which they are engaged

Industry statistics contained in the economic census are largely classified using the **North American Industry Classification System (NAICS)**. To a lesser extent, the classification of some industries is based upon the old Standard Industrial Classification (SIC) system that was used in previous censuses. Both NAICS and SIC systems categorize establishments by the principal activity in which they are engaged. The NAICS, developed in cooperation with Canada and Mexico, classifies North America's economic activities at 2-, 3-, 4-, and 5-digit levels of detail. The U.S. version of NAICS further defines some industries to a more precise sixth digit of detail. The NAICS represents 96 sectors (3-digit codes), 313 industry groups (4-digit codes), and, as implemented in the United States, 1,170 industries (5 - and 6-digit codes).

The NAICS example in Table 11.4 illustrates the makeup of the broadcasting and telecommunications sector in the state of Colorado during 1997. Notice the logical progression as one moves from the 3-digit broadcasting and telecommunications sector (513), to the 4-digit telecommunications industry group (5133), to 5-digit wireless telecommunications carriers (except satellite) industry (51332), to the very narrow 6-digit paging industry (513321). Economists generally agree that 5-digit or 6-digit classifications correspond quite closely with the economic definition of a market. Establishments grouped at the 5-digit or 6-digit levels produce products that are ready substitutes for one another and thus function as competitors. Managers who analyze census data to learn about the number and size distribution of actual and potential competitors focus their attention primarily on data provided at the 5-digit or 6-digit levels. The Census Bureau also classifies products. In the case of manufacturing and mining industries, products are classified in a manner consistent with the NAICS structure. The first 6 digits of the 10-digit product code are normally the same as the NAICS code for the industry with which the product is most frequently associated. Broad product or service lines also are provided for retail and wholesale trade and other service industries.

The most detailed economic census data are provided for the United States as a whole. Key statistics, albeit progressively fewer, are available for states, metropolitan areas (MAs), counties,

TABLE 11.4

NAICS Data Is Available at the U.S., State, and Local Levels of Detail

The North American Industry Classification System (NAICS) represents 96 sectors (3-digit codes), 313 industry groups (4-digit codes), and, as implemented in the United States, 1,170 industries (5- and 6-digit codes). This example shows the makeup of the broadcasting and telecommunications sector in the state of Colorado during 1997.

NAICS Code	Description	Establishments	Revenue ($1,000)	Annual Payroll ($1,000)	Paid Employees
513	Broadcasting and telecommunications	960	8,392,739	2,062,393	43,139
5131	Radio and television broadcasting	160	508,221	140,940	4,287
51311	Radio broadcasting	119	191,315	62,803	2,666
513111	Radio networks	9	25,432	5,974	245
513112	Radio stations	110	165,883	56,829	2,421
51312	Television broadcasting	41	316,906	78,137	1,621
5132	Cable networks and program distribution	137	1,318,198	200,056	6,145
51321	Cable networks	21	140,427	22,229	424
51322	Cable and other program distribution	116	1,177,771	177,827	5,721
5133	Telecommunications	663	6,566,320	1,721,397	32,707
51331	Wired telecommunications carriers	438	5,522,088	1,430,795	26,698
51332	Wireless telecommunications carriers (except satellite)	138	589,492	78,891	1,837
513321	Paging	59	264,559	26,529	773
513322	Cellular and other wireless telecommunications	79	324,933	52,362	1,064
51333	Telecommunications resellers	55	391,664	192,891	3,653
51334	Satellite telecommunications	12	14,397	5,455	134
51339	Other telecommunications	20	48,679	13,365	385

Data source: U.S. Census Bureau (http://www.census.gov).

and other places with 2,500 or more inhabitants. Only limited data are provided for ZIP codes. Statistics for smaller areas are typically withheld to avoid disclosing information about individual firms. The level of geographic detail varies widely for major data items. Basic census content includes several key statistics such as the number of establishments (or companies), number of employees, payroll, and measures of output like sales revenue, which the economic census refers to as the value of shipments.

Because the economic census is now based on the NAICS, only limited information is published according to the old SIC system. However, a detailed "bridge table" showing the relationships between NAICS and SIC categories makes for an easier comparison between current and previous statistics. Although still very slow by private-sector standards, 2002 economic census results will become available on the Internet much faster than the results from prior censuses, which were largely distributed in printed form. Although only highlights of recent economic censuses are available in printed form, software on both CD-ROM and the Internet allows companies to print detailed data. Given a faster publication cycle, industry reports for manufacturing, mining, and construction, previously issued in both preliminary and final form, are now issued only once. In another recent change, all reports are now titled simply as economic census reports. They are no longer treated as if each sector had a separate census, e.g., the census of manufacturers.

Detailed data are issued, sector by sector, on CD-ROM and on the Internet. Geographic area series (published for all sectors) provide detail for establishments with employees, for the nation, states, and substate areas. ZIP code statistics are also published for most sectors. Industry series reports for manufacturing, mining, and construction provide national totals on groups of related industries and their products. Limited data are available for individual states. Subject series (all sectors) provide national and limited local data on special topics including merchandise line sales, concentration ratios, and both establishment and firm sizes. Summary reports by sector provide highlights of the data in print. They feature primarily national data and general statistics by state, and include illustrations of some of the more detailed data available in electronic media. Table 11.4 shows a typical example of the level of detail available in the geographic area series. This example shows the makeup of the broadcasting and telecommunications sector in the state of Colorado during 1997.

CENSUS MEASURES OF MARKET CONCENTRATION

Pricing strategies and profit rates tend to be heavily influenced by the vigor of competition. As a result, information from the economic census on the number and size distribution of competitors is a vital input into the managerial decision-making process.

Concentration Ratios

In addition to those directly engaged in business, both government and the public share an interest in the number and size distribution of competitors. A small number of competitors can sometimes have direct implications for regulation and antitrust policy. Thus, considerable public resources are devoted to monitoring both the size distribution and economic performance of firms in several important sectors of the economy. Among those sectors covered by the economic census, manufacturing is clearly the largest, accounting for approximately 20 percent of aggregate economic activity in the United States. Firm sizes in manufacturing are also much larger than in other major sectors such as retail and wholesale trade, construction, legal and medical services, and so on. Among the more than 16 million business enterprises in the United States, manufacturing is the domain of the large corporation. Thus, the manufacturing sector provides an interesting basis for considering data that are available on the size distribution of firms.

Table 11.5 shows census information on the number of competitors, industry sales, and leading-firm market share data for a small sample of industries. Industries that contain a large number of firms of roughly equal sizes are generally regarded as vigorously competitive. Questions about the intensity of competition sometimes arise when only a limited number of competitors are present, or when only a handful of large firms dominate the industry.

As shown in Table 11.5, the economic census uses two different methods to describe the degree of competitor size inequality within an industry. The most commonly used group measures of leading-firm market share data are calculated from sales information for various

TABLE 11.5

Number of Firms and Concentration Ratios for a Representative Sample of Manufacturing Industries from the U.S. Economic Census

The number of firms, concentration ratios, and the HHI give differing insight on the extent of competition as captured by the size distribution of competitors.

Industry	NACIS Code	Number of Firms	Industry Sales ($ millions)	Top 4 Firms (CR4)	Top 8 Firms (CR8)	Top 20 Firms (CR20)	Top 50 Firms (CR50)	Herfindahl Hirschmann Index (HHI) Top 50 Firms
Breakfast cereal	31123	48	9,099	82.9	93.5	99.2	100.0	2,445.9
Dairy products (except frozen)	31151	948	52,812	18.1	28.4	48.6	66.7	169.8
Bread and bakery products	31181	9,489	25,953	33.2	43.6	58.3	69.0	423.4
Coffee and tea	31192	215	3,645	57.5	70.0	87.1	95.4	1,187.2
Soft drinks	31211	1,008	13,131	44.7	55.6	70.1	83.0	663.4
Carpet and rug mills	31411	413	11,493	51	65.0	81.0	92.9	922.5
Footwear	31621	366	4,211	27.7	42.4	65.0	84.3	317.0
Luggage	316991	270	1,426	51.9	62.4	75.0	86.8	1,418.6
Printing	32311	36,617	90,565	10.1	14.8	22.4	29.7	43.3
Petroleum refineries	32411	122	158,668	28.5	48.6	81.6	97.6	422.1
Petrochemicals	32511	42	19,469	59.8	83.3	98.0	100.0	1,187.0
Soap and cleaning compounds	32561	1,583	30,928	40.7	55.1	68.1	78.0	625.9
Cement	32731	176	6,532	33.5	52.0	78.7	96.9	466.6
Primary aluminum production	331312	13	6,225	59	81.7	100.0	n.a.	1,230.6
Ferrous metal foundries	33151	986	17,428	18	30	48.4	66.3	176.4
Hardware	33251	906	11,062	17.4	27.7	47.4	68.6	154.6
Construction machinery	33312	723	22,117	49.6	59.5	72.6	84.6	1,020.3
Computer and peripheral equipment	33411	1,870	110,055	37.0	52.1	72.8	86.3	464.9
Telephones	33421	548	38,376	54.4	66.5	78.5	88.2	999.4
Semiconductors	33441	5,652	139,084	34.3	42.8	54.2	65.5	413.7
Lighting fixtures	33512	1,160	9,404	28.6	39.6	52.6	65.6	272.8
Automobiles	33611	253	205,544	88.3	97.5	99.7	99.9	2,862.8
Guided missiles and space vehicles	336414	15	16,247	89.2	99.7	100.0	n.a.	n.a.
Medical equipment	3911	12,123	44,894	16.3	24.0	37.4	54.4	137.5
Jewelry and silverware	33991	3,737	8,304	11.1	17.0	28.7	45.1	65.2

Note: n.a. means not available. Data withheld to avoid disclosing information for individual companies.
Data source: U.S. Census Bureau, 1997 census, May 24, 2001.

concentration ratios
Data that show the percentage market share held by a group of leading firms

clusters of top firms. These group market share data are called **concentration ratios** because they measure the percentage market share concentrated in (or held by) an industry's top four (CR_4), eight (CR_8), 20 (CR_{20}), or 50 (CR_{50}) firms. Thus, the concentration ratio for a group of n leading firms is defined in percentage terms as:

(11.6)
$$CR_n = \frac{\sum_{i=1}^{n} \text{Firm Sales}_i}{\text{Industry Sales}} \times 100$$

where i refers to an individual firm.

Theoretically, concentration ratios can range between $CR_n = 0$ for an industry with a massive number of small competitors, to $CR_n = 100$ for an industry represented by a single monopolist. In the manufacturing sector where concentration tends to be highest, four-firm concentration ratios tend to fall in a broad range between $CR_4 = 20$ and $CR_4 = 60$; eight-firm concentration ratios often lie in a range between $CR_8 = 30$ and $CR_8 = 70$. When concentration ratios are low, industries tend to include many firms, and competition tends to be vigorous. Industries in which the four leading firms are responsible for less than 20 percent of total industry sales (i.e., $CR_4 < 20$) are highly competitive and approximate the perfect competition model. On the other hand, when concentration ratios are high, leading firms dominate following firms in terms of size, and leading firms may have more potential for pricing flexibility and economic profits. Industries in which the four leading firms control more than 80 percent of total industry sales (i.e., $CR_4 > 80$) are often described as highly concentrated. Industries with a $CR_4 < 20$ or $CR_4 > 80$, however, are quite rare. Three-quarters of all manufacturing activity takes place in industries with concentration ratios falling in the range $20 \leq CR_4 \leq 80$. In terms of relative importance, market structures that can be described as monopolistically competitive are much more common than perfect competition or monopoly.

Herfindahl Hirschmann Index

Herfindahl Hirschmann Index (HHI)
The sum of squared market shares for all n industry competitors

By definition, concentration ratios rise with greater competitor size inequality within a given industry. Concentration ratios, however, are unaffected by the degree of size inequality within each respective group of leading firms. This can create problems because competition within industries featuring a handful of large competitors can be much more vigorous than in those where a single dominant firm faces no large adversaries. For example, although $CR_4 = 100$ would signal monopoly in the case of a single dominant firm, it might describe a vigorously competitive industry if each of the leading four firms enjoy roughly equal market shares of 25 percent. The **Herfindahl Hirschmann Index (HHI)**, named after the economists who invented it, is a popular measure of competitor size inequality that reflects size differences among large and small firms. Calculated in percentage terms, the HHI is the sum of the squared market shares for all n industry competitors:

(11.7)
$$HHI = \sum_{i=1}^{n} \left(\frac{\text{Firm Sales}_i}{\text{Industry Sales}} \times 100 \right)^2$$

For example, a monopoly industry with a single dominant firm is described by a $CR_4 = 100$ and an $HHI = 100^2 = 10,000$. A vigorously competitive industry where each of the leading four firms enjoys market shares of 25 percent is also described by a $CR_4 = 100$, but features an $HHI = 25^2 + 25^2 + 25^2 + 25^2 = 2,500$. Like concentration ratios, the HHI approaches zero for industries characterized by a large number of very small competitors.

Limitations of Concentration Ratios and HHI Information

Despite the obvious attraction of census concentration ratios and HHI data as useful information on the number and size distribution of current competitors, it is prudent to remain cautious in their use and interpretation. Important limitations must be recognized. By not appreciating these limitations, one might make fundamental errors in judging the vigor of competition within industries.

A major drawback of concentration ratio and HHI information is that they take a long time to collect and publish. Data for 1997 were not generally available on the Internet until 2000 and 2001; data for 2002 will be collected in 2003 and published in 2004 and 2005. In many fast-moving markets, these data are obsolete before they are published. Even in less dynamic markets, they provide only an imperfect guide to managerial decision making. As a result, many managers supplement census information with current data available on the Internet from market research firms.

A further important weakness of census concentration ratio and HHI information is that they ignore domestic sales by foreign competitors (imports) as well as exports by domestic firms. Only data on domestic sales from *domestic production*, not total domestic sales, are reported. This means, for example, that if foreign imports have a market share of 25 percent, the four leading domestic automobile manufacturers account for 66.2 percent (= 88.3 percent of 75 percent) of total U.S. foreign plus domestic car sales (NAICS 33611), rather than the 88.3 percent, as Table 11.5 suggests. For industries with significant import competition, concentration ratios and HHI data significantly overstate the relative importance of leading domestic firms. Concentration ratios and HHI information also overstate market power for several industries in which increasing foreign competition has been responsible for the liquidation or merger of many smaller domestic firms with older, less efficient production facilities. Despite reduced numbers of domestic firms and the consequent rise in concentration, an increase in foreign competition often makes affected industries more efficient and more competitive rather than less so. The impact of foreign competition is important in many industries, but it is particularly so in manufacturing industries such as apparel, steel, automobiles, cameras, copiers, motorcycles, and television sets.

Another limitation of concentration ratio data is that they are *national totals*, whereas a relevant economic market may be national, regional, or local in scope. If high transportation costs or other product characteristics keep markets regional or local rather than national in scope, concentration ratios can significantly understate the relative importance of leading firms. For example, the leading firm in many metropolitan newspaper markets often approaches 100 percent of classified advertising and subscription revenues. Thus, a national CR_4 for newspapers would significantly understate local market power. Although national four-firm concentration ratios of less than 25 percent usually suggest a highly competitive market, the local or regional character of some markets can make national concentration figures meaningless. Examples of other products with local or regional rather than national markets include milk, bread and bakery products, commercial printing, and ready-mix concrete.

Additional problems occur because concentration ratios and HHI information provide an imperfect view of market structure by including only firms that are *currently active* in a particular industry. Recall that an economic market includes all firms willing and able to sell an identifiable product. Besides firms currently active in an industry, this includes those that can be regarded as likely potential entrants. Often the mere presence of one or more potential entrants constitutes a sufficient threat to force competitive market behavior in industries with only a handful of established competitors. Major retailers such as Wal-Mart, Target, and Sears, for example, use their positions as potential entrants into manufacturing to obtain attractive prices on a wide range of private-label merchandise such as clothing, lawn mowers, washing machines, and so on.

Characteristics of Wonderful Businesses

Interesting perspectives on the characteristics of "wonderful businesses" are given by legendary Wall Street investors T. Rowe Price and Warren E. Buffett. The late T. Rowe Price was founder of Baltimore–based T. Rowe Price and Associates, Inc., one of the largest no-load mutual fund organizations in the United States, and the father of the "growth stock" theory of investing. According to Price, attractive growth stocks have low labor costs, superior research to develop products and new markets, a high rate of return on stockholders' equity (ROE), elevated profit margins, rapid earnings per share (EPS) growth, lack cutthroat competition, and are comparatively immune from regulation. Omaha's Warren E. Buffett, the billionaire head of Berkshire Hathaway, Inc., also looks for companies that have strong franchises and enjoy pricing flexibility, high ROE, high cash flow, owner-oriented management, and predictable earnings that are not natural targets of regulation. Like Price, Buffett has profited enormously through his investments.

The table shows Berkshire's major common stock holdings in large and highly profitable growth companies in late 2001. The Coca-Cola Company, Berkshire's biggest and most successful holding, typifies the concept of a wonderful business. Coca-Cola enjoys perhaps the world's strongest franchise, owner-oriented management, and growing profits. From the standpoint of being a wonderful business, Coca-Cola is clearly the "real thing." Berkshire also holds a large stake in The American Express Company, a premier travel and financial services firm strategically positioned to benefit from aging baby boomers. Gillette, a global leader in toiletries and a wide variety of consumer products, is another top holding.

Above-normal returns from investing in wonderful businesses are only possible if their virtues are not fully recognized by other investors. Buffett has profited by taking major positions in wonderful companies that suffer from some significant, but curable, malady. Once he buys them, Buffett is very reluctant to sell. It's a simple, but very successful, investment philosophy.

Major Holdings of Berkshire Hathaway, Inc.

Company	Ticker	Return on Equity (%)	Expected Earnings Growth (%)	Market Cap. ($ billions)
American Express	AXP	14.4	13	43.5
Coca-Cola	KO	32.6	12	115.0
Gillette	G	29.1	10	34.9
First Data	FDC	22.8	15	28.4
H&R Block	HRB	33.1	14	7.5
Moody's	MCO	47.7	15	5.3
Washington Post	WPO	16.0	10	4.8
Wells Fargo	WFC	12.6	12	72.4
Wesco Financial	WSC	5.0	15	2.2

Sources: SEC reports and http://yahoo.finance.com.

See: Judith Burns, "Buffett Tells Investors to Get Tough with Companies," *The Wall Street Journal Online*, March 5, 2002 (http://online.wsj.com).

Finally, considering concentration ratio and HHI data in isolation can lead to deceptive conclusions regarding the vigor of competition because they measure only part of market structure; other components include barriers to entry or exit, nonprice competition, vertical integration, and so on. Under certain circumstances, even a very few large competitors can compete vigorously. *Competition among the few can be spirited.* For example, the market for large commercial and military aircraft is viciously competitive despite being dominated by only two global competitors: Boeing, from the United States, and Airbus Industrie, the European multinational consortium. In addition to considering the number and size distribution of competitors, firms must judge the competitive environment in light of foreign competition, transportation costs, regional product differences, likely potential entrants, advertising, customer loyalty, research and development, demand growth, and economies of scale in production, among other factors, to make accurate pricing and output decisions. All of these features constitute important elements of market structure.

COMPETITIVE STRATEGY IN MONOPOLISTIC COMPETITION AND OLIGOPOLY MARKETS

Developing and implementing an effective competitive strategy in imperfectly competitive markets involves a never-ending search for uniquely attractive products. Not all industries offer the same potential for sustained profitability; not all firms are equally capable of exploiting the profit potential that is available.

Competitive Strategy in Imperfectly Competitive Markets

It is always helpful to consider the number and size distribution of competitors, degree of product differentiation, level of information available in the marketplace, and conditions of entry when attempting to define market structure. Unfortunately, these and other readily obtained data are seldom definitive. Conditions of entry and exit are subtle and dynamic, as is the role of unseen potential entrants. All of this contributes to the difficulty of correctly assessing the profit potential of current products or prospective lines of business.

Rather than consider simply what is, effective managers must contemplate what might be. This is especially true when seeking to develop an effective competitive strategy. An effective competitive strategy in imperfectly competitive markets must be founded on the firm's **competitive advantage**. A competitive advantage is a unique or rare ability to create, distribute, or service products valued by customers. It is the business-world analog to what economists call **comparative advantage**, or when one nation or region of the country is better suited to the production of one product than to the production of some other product. For example, when compared with the United States and Canada, Mexico enjoys a relative abundance of raw materials and cheap labor. As such, Mexico is in a relatively good position to export agricultural products, oil, and finished goods that require unskilled labor to the U.S. and Canadian market. At the same time, the United States and Canada enjoy a relative abundance of highly educated people, capital goods, and investment resources. Therefore, the United States and Canada are in a relatively good position to export machine tools, computer equipment, education, and professional services to Mexico.

An effective competitive strategy in imperfectly competitive markets grows out of a sophisticated understanding of the rules of competition in a given line of business or industry. The ultimate aim of this strategy is to cope with or, better still, change those rules in the company's favor. To do so, managers must understand and contend with the rivalry among existing competitors, entry of new rivals, threat of substitutes, bargaining power of suppliers, and the bargaining power of buyers. Just as all industries are not alike in terms of their inherent profit potential, all firms are not alike in terms of their capacity to exploit available opportunities. In the business world, long-lasting above-normal rates of return require a sustainable competitive advantage that, by definition, cannot be easily duplicated.

Nike's use of basketball superstar Michael Jordan as the focal point of its extensive media advertising and product development campaign is an interesting case in point. Like other highly successful and innovative advertising campaigns, the Nike promotion captured the imagination of consumers and put competitors like Reebok at a distinct disadvantage. After all, there is only one Michael Jordan. Nike sales surged as consumers got caught up in the enthusiasm of Jordan's amazing basketball prowess and the excitement generated as the

competitive advantage
A unique or rare ability to create, distribute, or service products valued by customers

comparative advantage
When one nation or region of the country is better suited to the production of one product than to the production of some other product

Jordan–led Chicago Bulls marched to NBA championships. However, Jordon's popularity and Nike sales plummeted following Jordan's two surprise retirements from basketball, only to surge once again upon his triumphant returns. Meanwhile, Reebok, the second largest basketball shoe manufacturer in America, seeks to capture consumers' interest with the "Shaq Attack," an extensive media promotion and product development strategy built around NBA star Shaquille O'Neal.

The risks of star-based advertising as an effective form of nonprice competition in the nondurable consumer products industries became even more readily apparent following the well-documented failure of Pepsi's sponsorship of musical legend Michael Jackson during the mid 1990s. Pepsi not only lost the millions of dollars it spent on an obviously ineffective Michael Jackson–based advertising campaign, but it also lost valuable market share to rival Coca-Cola.

This is not to suggest that advertising and other nonprice methods of competition have not been used to great advantage by many successful firms in imperfectly competitive markets. In fact, these techniques are often a primary force in developing a strong basis for product differentiation. Table 11.6 summarizes major characteristics typical of the monopolistic competition and oligopoly market structures. To develop an effective competitive strategy, it is necessary to assess the degree to which an individual industry or line of business embodies elements of each of these market structures. Although the probability of successful entry is higher in monopolis-

TABLE 11.6

Summary of Monopolistic Competition and Oligopoly (Oligopsony) Market-Structure Characteristics

	Monopolistic Competition	**Oligopoly**
Number of actual or potential competitors	Many sellers	Few sellers whose decisions are directly related to those of competitors
Product differentiation	Consumers perceive differences among the products of various competitors	High or low, depending on entry and exit conditions
Information	Low-cost information on price and product quality	Restricted access to price and product-quality information; cost and other data are often proprietary
Conditions of entry and exit	Easy entry and exit	High entry or exit barriers because of economies of scale, capital requirements, advertising, research and development costs, or other factors
Profit potential	Economic (above-normal) profits in short run only; normal profit in long run	Potential for economic (above-normal) profits in both short and long run
Examples	Clothing, consumer financial services, professional services, restaurants	Automobiles, aluminum, soft drinks, investment banking, long-distance telephone service, pharmaceuticals

tically competitive markets, only difficult-to-enter oligopoly markets hold the potential for long-lasting above-normal returns.

In sum, firms in imperfectly competitive markets have the potential to earn economic profits in the long run only to the extent that they impart a valuable degree of uniqueness to the goods or services provided. Success, measured in terms of above-normal rates of return, requires a comparative advantage in production, distribution, or marketing that cannot easily be copied. That such success is difficult to achieve and is often rather fleeting is obvious when one considers the most profitable companies in America.

The Most Profitable Companies in America

Table 11.7 shows business profit rates for a sample of top-performing large firms from the United States. Profitability is measured by the rate of return on equity, thereby including the effects of both operating and financing decisions. These data demonstrate that market leaders earn truly extraordinary profits. In industries that produce distinctive goods and services, and in others that offer fairly mundane products, the most profitable firms in America earn an average rate of return on equity (ROE) that is a whopping 310.4 percent of all-industry norms. This means that the most profitable firm in a typical industry earns roughly 42.09 percent on equity, or far in excess of the average return on equity of 14.12 percent per year for large and highly successful U.S. companies. Notice that this average profit rate is only slightly above the 12 percent long-term average ROE typical for all companies.

It is obvious that the most profitable companies in America are able to outpace industry norms by a significant margin. Some of this variation in business profits represents the influence of risk premiums necessary to compensate investors if one business is inherently riskier than another. In the prescription pharmaceuticals industry, for example, hoped-for discoveries of effective therapies for important diseases are often a long-shot at best. However, apart from such risks, the observed intraindustry variation in profitability makes it clear that many firms earn significant economic profits or experience meaningful economic losses at any given point in time. Some above-normal returns in monopolistically competitive and oligopoly markets also reflect temporary good fortune due to unexpected changes in industry demand or cost conditions and/or profits due to uniquely productive inputs. However, most superior performers clearly are doing something faster, better, or cheaper than the competition.

When Large Size Is a *Disadvantage*

If economies of scale are substantial, larger firms are able to achieve lower costs of production or distribution than their smaller rivals. These cost advantages can translate into higher and more stable profits, and a significant competitive advantage for larger firms. Diseconomies of large-scale organizations work in the opposite direction. When diseconomies of scale are operative, larger firms suffer a cost disadvantage when compared to smaller rivals. Smaller firms are then able to translate the benefits of small size into a distinct competitive advantage. Rather than losing profits and sales opportunities to larger rivals, smaller firms can enjoy higher profit rates and gain market share over time.

Industries dominated by large firms tend to be those in which there are significant economies of scale, important advantages to vertical integration, and a prevalence of mass marketing. As a result, large organizations with sprawling plants emphasize large quantities of output at low production costs. Use of national media, especially TV advertising, is common. Industries in which "small is beautiful" tend to be characterized by diseconomies of scale, "just in time" assembly and manufacturing, and niche marketing that emphasizes the use of highly skilled individuals adept at personal selling. Small factories with flexible production schedules are common. Rather than emphasize long production runs, many smaller companies focus on product quality. Instead of the sometimes slow-to-respond hierarchical organizations of large

TABLE 11.7

The Relative Profitability of Top-Performing Companies

In both dynamic and mundane industries, top-performers earn profit rates that are more than three times industry norms.

Top-Performing Company	Industry	Top-Performer ROE	Industry ROE	Relative Profitability
True North	Advertising	23.49	17.78	132.2%
Alliant Techsystems	Aerospace/defense	56.07	14.78	379.4%
Northwest Airlines	Air transport	32.14	14.18	226.7%
Oshkosh B'Gosh	Apparel	138.43	17.50	791.0%
Navistar Int'l	Auto and truck	28.35	14.24	199.1%
Delphi Automotive	Auto parts (OEM)	33.84	17.54	192.9%
Tenneco Automotive	Auto parts (replacement)	19.43	15.39	126.3%
North Fork Bancorp	Bank	35.61	18.09	196.8%
Royal Bank of Canada	Bank (Canadian)	14.72	14.72	100.0%
National City Corp.	Bank (Midwest)	24.51	19.35	126.7%
Anheuser-Busch	Beverage (alcoholic)	35.75	13.56	263.7%
Coca-Cola	Beverage (soft drink)	33.98	9.72	349.6%
USG Corp.	Building materials	50.17	16.96	295.8%
Cablevision Sys.	Cable TV	20.86	2.55	818.0%
Numac Energy	Canadian energy	13.83	7.19	192.4%
Centex Construction	Cement and aggregates	31.78	16.12	197.2%
Georgia Gulf	Chemical (basic)	75.43	13.47	560.0%
Millipore Corp.	Chemical (diversified)	34.45	15.28	225.5%
WD-40 Co.	Chemical (specialty)	38.94	15.05	258.7%
Dell Computer	Computer and peripherals	35.04	9.90	353.9%
Adobe Systems	Computer software and svcs	38.16	16.96	225.0%
Sepracor, Inc.	Drug	117.34	14.05	835.2%
IPALCO Enterprises	Electric util. (Central)	17.93	11.60	154.6%
Allegheny Energy	Electric utility (East)	17.77	11.31	157.1%
Black Hills	Electric utility (West)	16.83	10.78	156.2%
Gen'l Cable	Electrical equipment	28.26	17.03	165.9%
Plantronics Inc.	Electronics	61.22	12.80	478.3%
Imax Corp.	Entertainment	22.71	5.57	407.7%
Waste Management	Environmental	25.20	12.03	209.5%
Alliance Capital Mgmt.	Financial svcs. (div.)	83.53	20.11	415.4%
Sara Lee Corp.	Food processing	91.97	16.55	555.7%
Sysco Corp.	Food wholesalers	25.75	11.21	229.7%
Nokia Corp. ADR	Foreign telecom.	34.41	11.02	312.3%
Miller (Herman)	Furn./home furnishings	47.43	18.73	253.2%
Barrick Gold	Gold/silver mining	7.96	3.72	214.0%
Kroger Co.	Grocery	35.99	10.78	333.9%
IMS HEALTH	Healthcare info systems	48.91	12.49	391.6%
Black & Decker	Home appliance	37.48	18.13	206.8%
Newhall Land & Farming	Homebuilding	64.69	17.47	370.3%
Int'l Game Tech.	Hotel/gaming	56.02	12.72	440.4%
Ralston Purina Group	Household products	69.40	30.47	227.8%
Equifax, Inc.	Industrial services	100.11	13.99	715.6%
Protective Life	Insurance (life)	17.69	13.38	132.2%
PMI Group	Insurance (prop/casualty	15.53	10.73	144.7%
Briggs & Stratton	Machinery	30.79	14.44	213.2%
Winnebago	Manuf. housing/rec veh	27.67	14.27	193.9%
Sea Containers Ltd.	Maritime	12.69	2.76	459.8%
Apria Healthcare	Medical services	96.46	12.37	779.8%

TABLE 11.7 *(continued)*

The Relative Profitability of Top-Performing Companies

Top-Performing Company	Industry	Top-Performer ROE	Industry ROE	Relative Profitability
AmeriSource Health	Medical supplies	49.96	15.01	332.8%
Illinois Tool Works	Metal fabricating	18.93	13.95	135.7%
Freep't-McMoRan C&G	Metals and mining (div.)	19.94	6.50	307.0%
UGI Corp.	Natural gas (distrib.)	16.84	10.05	167.6%
Mitchell Energy	Natural gas (diversified	20.21	9.87	204.8%
Dow Jones & Co.	Newspaper	40.16	12.29	326.8%
Lexmark Int'l `A'	Office equip and supplies	48.32	17.13	282.1%
Diamond Offshore	Oilfield services/equip.	8.84	2.37	373.0%
Sealed Air	Packaging and container	9.15	21.30	43.0%
Georgia-Pacific Group	Paper and forest products	19.09	9.30	205.4%
Conoco Inc.	Petroleum (integrated)	17.16	9.81	174.9%
Berry Petroleum	Petroleum (producing)	15.49	5.42	286.1%
Mettler-Toledo Int'l	Precision instrument	51.71	13.13	394.0%
Deluxe Corp.	Publishing	48.65	21.30	228.4%
Burlington Northern	Railroad	13.86	9.54	145.4%
Topps Co.	Recreation	45.84	14.23	322.2%
Jack in the Box	Restaurant	35.09	14.68	239.0%
Intimate Brands	Retail (special lines)	84.24	15.44	545.6%
Fastenal Co.	Retail building supply	23.21	14.69	158.0%
Dollar General Corp.	Retail store	23.69	15.31	154.7%
Morgan S. Dean Witter	Securities brokerage	28.15	18.95	148.5%
PMC-Sierra	Semiconductor	31.04	13.66	227.2%
Lam Research	Semiconductor cap equip	27.35	17.07	160.2%
Timberland Co.	Shoe	27.62	14.06	196.4%
Worthington Inds.	Steel (general)	14.77	10.81	136.6%
Pohang Iron ADR	Steel (integrated)	15.96	12.99	122.9%
Tellabs, Inc.	Telecom. equipment	26.29	2.32	1133.2%
Polymer Group	Textile	13.80	6.05	228.1%
N.Y. Community Bancorp	Thrift	21.99	15.97	137.7%
Carlisle Cos.	Tire and rubber	19.94	13.21	150.9%
Philip Morris	Tobacco	50.14	17.62	284.6%
Chattem Inc.	Toiletries/cosmetics	46.28	18.76	246.7%
Forward Air	Trucking/transp. leasing	29.19	15.65	186.6%
Sawtek Inc.	Wireless networking	23.08	2.35	982.1%
Averages		**42.09**	**14.12**	**310.4%**

Data source: *The Value Line Investment Survey for Windows*, September, 2001.
Reproduced with the permission of Value Line Publishing, Inc.

companies, smaller companies feature "flat" organizations with quick, decentralized decision making and authority.

The villain sometimes encountered by large-scale firms is not any diseconomy of scale in the production process itself, but rather the burden that size places on effective management. Big often means complex, and complexity results in inefficiencies and bureaucratic snarls that can strangle effective communication. In the former Soviet Union, a huge, highly centralized, run-from-the-top system came crashing down as a result of its own gigantic weight. Hoping to avoid a similar fate, many large organizations are now splitting assets into smaller independent operating units that can react quickly to customer needs without the typically long delays of large organizations. IBM, for example, has split into independent operating units that compete directly with each other to provide customers with the latest in computer equipment and software. GM, seeking to become more lean and agile like Japanese competitors, established Saturn as an independent operating unit. Exxon is selling domestic exploration and production operations to smaller independents that chop overhead and earn significant profits despite low volume and depressed oil prices. These examples suggest that many large corporations are going through a metamorphosis that will favor organizations that are especially adept at reallocating capital among nimble, entrepreneurial operating units.

In the past, when foreign visitors wanted to experience firsthand the latest innovations in U.S. business and administrative practice, they found it mandatory to visit major corporations in Chicago, Detroit, New York, and Pittsburgh. Today, it is more likely that they would make stops at Boston's Route 128, California's Silicon Valley, or North Carolina's Research Triangle. From electronics instrumentation to specialized steel, smaller companies have replaced larger companies in positions of industry leadership. The trend towards a higher level of efficiency for smaller companies has become so widespread that larger companies are now finding that meeting the needs of the customer sometimes requires a dramatic downsizing of the large-scale organization.

Threat of Potential Competition

The potential for above-normal rates of return is a powerful inducement to the entry of new competitors and to the rapid growth of nonleading firms. Imitation may be the sincerest form of flattery, but it is also the most effective enemy of above-normal rates of return. Regression to the mean is the rule rather than the exception for above-normal corporate profit rates over time. During recent years, after-tax rates of return on stockholders' equity have usually been in the range of 9 percent to 10 percent per year. Just as in the stock market where investors rarely earn excess returns, individual companies rarely earn in excess of 15 percent to 20 percent for more than a decade. A consistent ROE $\geq$ 20 percent is simply unheard of for an entire industry with several competitors over a sustained period. Therefore, it seems reasonable to conclude that price and nonprice methods of competition are often vigorous, even in imperfectly competitive industries with few active or potential competitors.

SUMMARY

This chapter extends the study of market structure to monopolistic competition and oligopoly. These models describe the behavior of competitors in imperfectly competitive markets across a broad spectrum of our economy in which both price competition and a wide variety of methods of nonprice competition are observed.

- **Monopolistic competition** is similar to perfect competition in that it entails vigorous price competition among a large number of firms and individuals. The major difference is that consumers perceive important differences among the products offered by monopolistically competitive firms, whereas the output of perfectly competitive firms is homogeneous.

- In an industry characterized by **oligopoly**, only a few large rivals are responsible for the bulk of industry output. High to very high barriers to entry are typical, and the price/output decisions of firms are interrelated in the sense that direct reactions from rivals can be expected. This "competition among the few" involves a wide variety of price and nonprice methods of rivalry.

- A group of competitors operating under a formal overt agreement is called a **cartel**. If an informal covert agreement is reached, the firms are said to be operating in **collusion**. Both practices are generally illegal in the United States. However, cartels are legal in many parts of the world, and multinational corporations often become involved with them in foreign markets.

- **Price leadership** results when one firm establishes itself as the industry leader and all other firms accept its pricing policy. This leadership may result from the size and strength of the leading firm, from cost efficiency, or as a result of the recognized ability of the leader to forecast market conditions accurately and to establish prices that produce satisfactory profits for all firms in the industry. Under a second type of price leadership, **barometric price leadership**, the price leader is not necessarily the largest or dominant firm in the industry. The price leader must only be accurate in reading the prevailing industry view of the need for price adjustment.

- An often-noted characteristic of oligopoly markets is "sticky" prices. Once a general price level has been established, whether through cartel agreement or some less formal arrangement, it tends to remain fixed for an extended period. Such rigid prices are often explained by what is referred to as the **kinked demand curve** theory of oligopoly prices. A kinked demand curve is a firm demand curve that has different slopes for price increases versus price decreases.

- **Game theory** is a general framework to help decision making when firm payoffs depend on actions taken by other firms. In a **simultaneous-move game**, each decision maker makes choices without specific knowledge of competitor counter moves. In a **sequential-move game**, decision makers make their move after observing competitor moves. In a **one-shot game**, the underlying interaction between competitors occurs only once; in a **repeat game**, there is an ongoing interaction between competitors.

- The so-called **Prisoner's Dilemma** is a classic conflict-of-interest situation. A **dominant strategy** gives the best result for either party regardless of the action taken by the other. A **secure strategy** guarantees the best possible outcome given the worst possible scenario. In a **Nash equilibrium**, neither player can improve its own payoff by unilaterally changing its own strategy. In a **Nash bargaining** game, two competitors or players "bargain" over some item of value. When competitors interact on a continuous basis, they are said to be involved in **repeat games**. Like any written guarantee or insurance policy, repeat transactions in the marketplace give consumers confidence that they'll get what they pay for.

- The **economic census** provides a comprehensive statistical profile of the national economy. They are taken at 5-year intervals during years ending with the digits 2 and 7—for example, 1992, 1997, 2002, and so on. The **North American Industry Classification System (NAICS)** categorizes establishments by the principal economic activity in which they are engaged. Below the 2-digit major group or sector level, the NAICS system proceeds to desegregated levels of increasingly narrowly defined activity.

- **Concentration ratios** measure the percentage market share held by (concentrated in) a group of top firms. When concentration ratios are low, industries tend to be made up of many firms, and competition tends to be vigorous. When concentration ratios are high, leading firms dominate and sometimes have the potential for pricing flexibility and economic profits. The **Herfindahl Hirschmann Index (HHI)** is a measure of competitor size inequality that reflects size differences among both large and small firms. Calculated in percentage terms, the HHI is the sum of the squared market shares for all n industry competitors:

- An effective competitive strategy in imperfectly competitive markets must be founded on the firm's **competitive advantage**. A competitive advantage is a unique or rare ability to create, distribute, or service products valued by customers. It is the business-world analog to what economists call **comparative advantage**, or when one nation or region of the country is better suited to the production of one product than to the production of some other product.

Public and private sources offer valuable service through their regular collection and publication of market structure data on the number and size distribution of competitors, market size, growth, capital intensity, investment, and so on. All of this information is useful to the process of managerial decision making and provides a useful starting point for the development of successful competitive strategy.

QUESTIONS

Q11.1 Describe the monopolistically competitive market structure and provide some examples.

Q11.2 Describe the oligopolistic market structure and provide some examples.

Q11.3 Explain the process by which economic profits are eliminated in a monopolistically competitive industry as compared to a perfectly competitive industry.

Q11.4 Would you expect the demand curve for a firm in a monopolistically competitive industry to be more or less elastic after economic profits have been eliminated?

Q11.5 "One might expect firms in a monopolistically competitive industry to experience greater swings in the price of their products over the business cycle than those in an oligopolistic industry. However, fluctuations in profits do not necessarily follow the same pattern." Discuss this statement.

Q11.6 Will revenue-maximizing firms have short-run profits as large as or larger than profit-maximizing firms? If so, when? If not, why not?

Q11.7 Is short-run revenue maximization necessarily inconsistent with the more traditional long-run profit-maximizing model of firm behavior? Why or why not?

Q11.8 Why is the four-firm concentration ratio only an imperfect measure of market power?

Q11.9 The statement "You get what you pay for" reflects the common perception that high prices indicate high product quality and low prices indicate low quality. Irrespective of market structure considerations, is this statement always correct?

Q11.10 "Economic profits result whenever only a few large competitors are active in a given market." Discuss this statement.

SELF-TEST PROBLEMS AND SOLUTIONS

ST11.1 Game Theory. One of the most dynamic changes taking place in our economy is the evolution of the personal computer from a document preparation and computing device to a communicating device. What we used to view as stand-alone personal computers, televisions, VCRs, telephones, fax and copy machines are all converging toward nimble communications devices with the ability to fulfill a number of tasks simultaneously. Nowhere is the influence of this trend more obvious than in the communications equipment industries. This is the sector within which manufacturers produce household audio and video equipment, prerecorded records and tapes, telephone and telegraph apparatus, and radio and television communications equipment. Because many commercial users have unique needs, equipment suppliers sometimes have significant ability to influence the price charged for what is often a bundle of specialized goods and services. As a result, game theory concepts prove useful to both buyers and sellers of communications devices.

To illustrate, suppose two local suppliers are seeking to win the right to upgrade the communications capability of the internal "intranets" that link a number of customers with their suppliers. The system quality decision facing each competitor, and potential profit payoffs, are illustrated in the table. The first number listed in each cell is the profit earned by U.S. Equipment Supply; the second number indicates the profit earned by Business Systems, Inc. For example, if both competitors, U.S. Equipment Supply and Business Systems, Inc., pursue a high-quality strategy, U.S. Equipment Supply will earn $25,000 and Business Systems, Inc., will earn $50,000. If U.S. Equipment Supply pursues a high-quality strategy while Business Systems, Inc., offers low-quality goods and services, U.S. Equipment Supply will earn $40,000; Business Systems, Inc., earns $22,000. If U.S. Equipment Supply offers low-quality goods while Business Systems, Inc., offers high-quality goods, U.S. Equipment Supply will suffer a net loss of $25,000, and Business Systems, Inc., will earn $20,000. Finally, if U.S. Equipment Supply offers low-quality goods while Business Systems, Inc., offers low-quality goods, both U.S. Equipment Supply and Business Systems, Inc., will earn $25,000.

		Business Systems, Inc.	
	Quality Strategy	**High Quality**	**Low Quality**
U.S. Equipment Supply	**High Quality**	$25,000, $50,000	$40,000, $22,000
	Low Quality	−$25,000, $20,000	$25,000, $25,000

A. Does U.S. Equipment Supply and/or Business Systems, Inc., have a dominant strategy? If so, what is it?

B. Does U.S. Equipment Supply and/or Business Systems, Inc., have a secure strategy? If so, what is it?

C. What is the Nash equilibrium concept, and why is it useful? What is the Nash equilibrium for this problem?

ST11.1 Solution

A. The dominant strategy for U.S. Equipment Supply is to provide high-quality goods. Irrespective of the quality strategy chosen by Business Systems, Inc., U.S. Equipment Supply can do no better than to choose a high-quality strategy. To see this, note that if Business Systems, Inc., chooses to produce high-quality goods, the best choice for U.S. Equipment Supply is to also provide high-quality goods because the $25,000 profit then earned is better than the $25,000 loss that would be incurred if U.S. Equipment Supply chose a low-quality strategy. If Business Systems, Inc., chose a low-quality strategy, the best choice by U.S. Equipment Supply would again be to produce high-quality goods. U.S. Equipment Supply's high-quality strategy profit of $40,000 dominates the low-quality payoff for U.S. Equipment Supply of $25,000.

Business Systems, Inc., does not have a dominant strategy. To see this, note that if U.S. Equipment Supply chooses to produce high-quality goods, the best choice for Business Systems, Inc., is to also provide high-quality goods because the $50,000 profit then earned is better than the $22,000 profit if Business Systems, Inc., chose a low-quality strategy. If U.S. Equipment Supply chose a low-quality strategy, the best choice by Business Systems, Inc., would be to produce low-quality goods and earn $25,000 versus $20,000.

B. The secure strategy for U.S. Equipment Supply is to provide high-quality goods. By choosing to provide high-quality goods, U.S. Equipment Supply can be guaranteed a profit payoff of at least $25,000. By pursuing a high-quality strategy, U.S. Equipment Supply can eliminate the chance of losing $25,000, as would happen if U.S. Equipment Supply chose a low-quality strategy while Business Systems, Inc., chose to produce high-quality goods.

The secure strategy for Business Systems, Inc., is to provide low-quality goods. By choosing to provide high-quality goods, Business Systems, Inc., can guarantee a profit payoff of only $20,000. Business Systems, Inc., can be assured of earning at least $22,000 with a low-quality strategy. Thus, the secure strategy for Business Systems, Inc., is to provide low-quality goods.

C. A set of strategies constitutes a Nash equilibrium if, given the strategies of other players, no player can improve its payoff through a unilateral change in strategy. The concept of Nash equilibrium is very important because it represents a situation where every player is doing the best possible in light of what other players are doing.

Although useful, the notion of a secure strategy suffers from a serious shortcoming. In the present example, suppose Business Systems, Inc., reasoned as follows: "U.S. Equipment Supply will surely choose its high-quality dominant strategy. Therefore, I should not choose my secure low-quality strategy and earn $22,000. I should instead choose a high-quality strategy and earn $50,000." A natural way of formalizing the "end result" of such a thought process is captured in the definition of Nash equilibrium.

In the present example, if U.S. Equipment Supply chooses a high-quality strategy, the Nash equilibrium strategy is for Business Systems, Inc., to also choose a high-quality strategy. Similarly, if Business Systems, Inc., chooses a high-quality strategy, the Nash equilibrium strategy is for U.S. Equipment Supply to also choose a high-quality strategy. Thus, a Nash equilibrium is reached when both firms adopt high-quality strategies.

Although some problems have multiple Nash equilibriums, that is not true in this case. A combination of high-quality strategies for both firms is the only set of strategies where no player can improve its payoff through a unilateral change in strategy.

ST11.2   Columbia Drugstores, Inc., based in Seattle, Washington, operates a chain of 30 drugstores in the Pacific Northwest. During recent years, the company has become increasingly concerned with the long-run implications of competition from a new type of competitor, the so-called superstore.

To measure the effects of superstore competition on current profitability, Columbia asked management consultant Mindy McConnell to conduct a statistical analysis of the company's profitability in its various markets. To net out size-related influences, profitability was measured by Columbia's gross profit margin, or earnings before interest and taxes divided by sales. Columbia provided proprietary company profit, advertising, and sales data covering the last year for all 30 outlets, along with public trade association and Census Bureau data concerning the number and relative size distribution of competitors in each market, among other market characteristics.

As a first step in the study, McConnell decided to conduct a regression-based analysis of the various factors thought to affect Columbia's profitability. The first is the relative size of leading competitors in the relevant market, measured at the Standard Metropolitan Statistical Area (SMSA) level. Columbia's market share, MS, in each market area is expected to have a positive effect on profitability given the pricing, marketing, and average-cost advantages that accompany large relative size. The market concentration ratio, CR, measured as the combined market share of the four largest competitors in any given market, is expected to have a negative effect on Columbia's profitability given the stiff competition from large, well-financed rivals. Of course, the expected negative effect of high concentration on Columbia profitability contrasts with the positive influence of high concentration on industry profits that is sometimes observed.

Both capital intensity, K/S, measured by the ratio of the book value of assets to sales, and advertising intensity, A/S, measured by the advertising-to-sales ratio, are expected to exert positive influences on profitability. Given that profitability is measured by Columbia's gross profit margin, the coefficient on capital intensity measured Columbia's return on tangible investment. Similarly, the coefficient on the advertising variable measures the profit effects of advertising. Growth, GR, measured by the geometric mean rate of change in total disposable income in each market, is expected to have a positive influence on Columbia's profitability, because some disequilibrium in industry demand and supply conditions is often observed in rapidly growing areas.

Profit-Margin and Market-Structure Data for Columbia Drugstores, Inc.

Store No.	Profit Margin	Market Share	Concen-tration	Capital Intensity	Advertising Intensity	Growth	Superstore (S=1 if super-store present)
1	15.0	25.0	75.0	10.0	10.0	7.5	0
2	10.0	20.0	60.0	7.5	10.0	2.5	1
3	15.0	40.0	70.0	7.5	10.0	5.0	0
4	15.0	30.0	75.0	15.0	12.5	5.0	0
5	15.0	50.0	75.0	10.0	12.5	0.0	0
6	20.0	50.0	70.0	10.0	12.5	7.5	1
7	15.0	50.0	70.0	7.5	10.0	0.0	1
8	25.0	40.0	60.0	12.5	15.0	5.0	0
9	20.0	10.0	40.0	10.0	12.5	5.0	0
10	10.0	30.0	60.0	10.0	12.5	0.0	0
11	15.0	20.0	60.0	12.5	12.5	7.5	1
12	10.0	30.0	75.0	12.5	10.0	2.5	0
13	15.0	50.0	75.0	7.5	10.0	5.0	0
14	10.0	20.0	75.0	7.5	12.5	2.5	0
15	10.0	10.0	50.0	7.5	10.0	2.5	0
16	20.0	30.0	60.0	15.0	12.5	2.5	0
17	15.0	30.0	50.0	7.5	12.5	5.0	1
18	20.0	40.0	70.0	7.5	12.5	5.0	0
19	10.0	10.0	60.0	12.5	10.0	2.5	0
20	15.0	20.0	70.0	5.0	12.5	7.5	0
21	20.0	20.0	40.0	7.5	10.0	7.5	0
22	15.0	10.0	50.0	15.0	10.0	5.0	1
23	15.0	40.0	40.0	7.5	12.5	5.0	1
24	10.0	30.0	50.0	5.0	7.5	0.0	0
25	20.0	40.0	70.0	15.0	12.5	5.0	0
26	15.0	40.0	70.0	12.5	10.0	5.0	1
27	10.0	20.0	75.0	7.5	10.5	2.5	0
28	15.0	10.0	60.0	12.5	12.5	5.0	0
29	10.0	30.0	75.0	5.0	7.5	2.5	0
30	10.0	20.0	75.0	12.5	12.5	0.0	0

Finally, to gauge the profit implications of superstore competition, McConnell used a "dummy" (or binary) variable where $S = 1$ in each market in which Columbia faced superstore competition and $S = 0$ otherwise. The coefficient on this variable measures the average profit rate effect of superstore competition. Given the vigorous nature of superstore price competition, McConnell expects the superstore coefficient to be both negative and statistically significant, indicating a profit-limiting influence. The Columbia profit-margin data and related information used in McConnell's statistical analysis are given in the preceding table. Regression model estimates for the determinants of Columbia's profitability are as follows:

Determinants of Profitability for Columbia Drugstores, Inc.

Variable Name	Coefficient (1)	Standard Error of Coefficient (2)	t Statistic (3) = (1) ÷ (1)
Intercept	7.846	3.154	2.49
Market share	0.214	0.033	6.50
Concentration	−0.203	0.038	−5.30

Variable Name	Coefficient (1)	Standard Error of Coefficient (2)	*t* Statistic (3) = (1) ÷ (1)
Capital intensity	0.289	0.123	2.35
Advertising intensity	0.722	0.233	3.09
Growth	0.842	0.152	5.56
Superstore	–2.102	0.828	–2.54

Coefficient of determination = R^2 = 84%
Standard error of the estimate = SEE = 1.872%

A. Describe the overall explanatory power of this regression model, as well as the relative importance of each continuous variable.

B. Based on the importance of the binary or dummy variable that indicates superstore competition, do superstores pose a serious threat to Columbia's profitability?

C. What factors might Columbia consider in developing an effective competitive strategy to combat the superstore influence?

ST11.2 Solution

A. The coefficient of determination R^2 = 84% means that 84% of the total variation in Columbia's profit-rate variability is explained by the regression model. This is a relatively high level of explanation for a cross-section study such as this, suggesting that the model provides useful insight concerning the determinants of profitability. The intercept coefficient of 7.846 has no economic meaning because it lies far outside the relevant range of observed data. The 0.214 coefficient for the market-share variable means that, on average, a 1% (unit) rise in Columbia's market share leads to a 0.214% (unit) rise in Columbia's profit margin. Similarly, as expected, Columbia's profit margin is positively related to capital intensity, advertising intensity, and the rate of growth in the market area. Conversely, high concentration has the expected limiting influence. Because of the effects of leading-firm rivalry, a 1% rise in industry concentration will lead to a 0.203% decrease in Columbia's profit margin. This means that relatively large firms compete effectively with Columbia.

B. Yes, the regression model indicates that superstore competition in one of Columbia's market areas reduces Columbia's profit margin on average by 2.102%. Given that Columbia's rate of return on sales routinely falls in the 10% to 15% range, the profit-limiting effect of superstore competition is substantial. Looking more closely at the data, it appears that Columbia faces superstore competition in only one of the seven lucrative markets in which the company earns a 20% to 25% rate of return on sales. Both observations suggest that current and potential superstore competition constitutes a considerable threat to the company and one that must be addressed in an effective competitive strategy.

C. Development of an effective competitive strategy to combat the influence of superstores involves the careful consideration of a wide range of factors related to Columbia's business. It might prove fruitful to begin this analysis by more carefully considering market characteristics for Store No. 6, the one Columbia outlet able to earn a substantial 20% profit margin despite superstore competition. For example, this analysis might suggest that Columbia, like Store No. 6, should specialize in service (e.g., prescription drug delivery) or in a slightly different mix of merchandise. On the other hand, perhaps Columbia should follow the example set by Wal-Mart in its early development and focus its plans for expansion on small to medium-size markets. In the meantime, Columbia's still-profitable stores in major metropolitan areas could help fund future growth.

Although obviously only a first step, a regression-based study of market structure such as that described here can provide a very useful beginning to the development of an effective competitive strategy.

PROBLEMS

P11.1 Market Structure Concepts. Indicate whether each of the following statements is true or false and explain why.

A. Equilibrium in monopolistically competitive markets requires that firms be operating at the minimum point on the long-run average cost curve.

B. A high ratio of distribution cost to total cost tends to increase competition by widening the geographic area over which any individual producer can compete.

C. The price elasticity of demand tends to fall as new competitors introduce substitute products.

D. An efficiently functioning cartel achieves a monopoly price/output combination.

E. An increase in product differentiation tends to increase the slope of firm demand curves.

P11.2 Monopolistically Competitive Demand. Would the following factors increase or decrease the ability of domestic auto manufacturers to raise prices and profit margins? Why?

A. Decreased import quotas

B. Elimination of uniform emission standards

C. Increased automobile price advertising

D. Increased import tariffs (taxes)

E. A rising value of the dollar, which has the effect of lowering import car prices

P11.3 Monopolistically Competitive Equilibrium. Soft Lens, Inc., has enjoyed rapid growth in sales and high operating profits on its innovative extended-wear soft contact lenses. However, the company faces potentially fierce competition from a host of new competitors as some important basic patents expire during the coming year. Unless the company is able to thwart such competition, severe downward pressure on prices and profit margins is anticipated.

A. Use Soft Lens's current price, output, and total cost data to complete the table:

Price ($)	Monthly Output (million)	Total Revenue ($million)	Marginal Revenue ($million)	Total Cost ($million)	Marginal Cost ($million)	Average Cost ($million)	Total Profit ($million)
$20	0			$0			
19	1			12			
18	2			27			
17	3			42			
16	4			58			
15	5			75			
14	6			84			
13	7			92			
12	8			96			
11	9			99			
10	10			105			

(Note: Total costs include a risk-adjusted normal rate of return.)

B. If cost conditions remain constant, what is the monopolistically competitive high-price/low-output long-run equilibrium in this industry? What are industry profits?

C. Under these same cost conditions, what is the monopolistically competitive low-price/high-output equilibrium in this industry? What are industry profits?

D. Now assume that Soft Lens is able to enter into restrictive licensing agreements with potential competitors and create an effective cartel in the industry. If demand and cost conditions remain constant, what is the cartel price/output and profit equilibrium?

P11.4 Competitive Strategy. Gray Computer, Inc., located in Colorado Springs, Colorado, is a privately held producer of high-speed electronic computers with immense storage capacity and computing capability. Although Gray's market is restricted to industrial users and a few large government agencies (e.g., Department of Health, NASA, National Weather Service), the company has profitably exploited its market niche.

Glen Gray, founder and research director, has recently announced his retirement, the timing of which will unfortunately coincide with the expiration of several patents covering key aspects of the Gray computer. Your company, a potential entrant into the market for supercomputers, has asked you to evaluate the short- and long-run potential of this market. Based on data gathered from your company's engineering department, user surveys, trade associations, and other sources, the following market demand and cost information has been developed:

$$P = \$54 - \$1.5Q$$
$$MR = \partial TR/\partial Q = \$54 - \$3Q$$
$$TC = \$200 + \$6Q + \$0.5Q^2$$
$$MC = \partial TC/\partial Q = \$6 + \$1Q$$

where P is price, Q is units measured by the number of supercomputers, MR is marginal revenue, TC is total costs including a normal rate of return, MC is marginal cost, and all figures are in millions of dollars.

A. Assume that these demand and cost data are descriptive of Gray's historical experience. Calculate output, price, and economic profits earned by the Gray company as a monopolist. What is the point price elasticity of demand at this output level?

B. Calculate the range within which a long-run equilibrium price/output combination would be found for individual firms if entry eliminated Gray's economic profits. (Note: Assume that the cost function is unchanged and that the high-price/low-output solution results from a parallel shift in the demand curve while the low-price/high-output solution results from a competitive equilibrium.)

C. Assume that the point price elasticity of demand calculated in part A is a good estimate of the relevant arc price elasticity. What is the potential overall market size for supercomputers?

D. If no other near-term entrants are anticipated, should your company enter the market for supercomputers? Why or why not?

P11.5 Game Theory. Assume that IBM and Dell Computer have an inventory of personal computers that they would like to sell before a new generation of faster, cheaper machines is introduced. The question facing each competitor is whether or not they should widely advertise a "close out" sale on these discontinued items or instead let excess inventory work itself off over the next few months. If both aggressively promote their products with a nationwide advertising campaign, each will earn profits of $5 million. If one advertises while the other does not, the firm that advertises will earn $20 million, while the one that does not advertise will earn $2 million. If neither advertises, both will earn $10 million. Assume this is a one-shot game and both firms seek to maximize profits.

	Dell Computer	
Promotion Strategy	**Advertise**	**Do Not Advertise**
Advertise	$5, $5	$20, $2
Do Not Advertise	$2, $20	$10, $10

IBM

A. What is the dominant strategy for each firm? Are these also secure strategies?

B. What is the Nash equilibrium?

C. Would collusion work in this case?

P11.6 Cartel Equilibrium. The Hand Tool Manufacturing Industry Trade Association recently published the following estimates of demand and supply relations for hammers:

$$Q_D = 60,000 - 10,000P \qquad \text{(Demand)}$$
$$Q_S = 20,000P \qquad \text{(Supply)}$$

A. Calculate the perfectly competitive industry equilibrium price/output combination.

B. Now assume that the industry output is organized into a cartel. Calculate the industry price/output combination that will maximize profits for cartel members. (Hint: As a cartel, industry $MR = \$6 - \$0.0002Q$.)

C. Compare your answers to parts A and B. Calculate the price/output effects of the cartel.

P11.7 Kinked Demand Curves. Safety Service Products (SSP) faces the following segmented demand and marginal revenue curves for its new infant safety seat:

1. Over the range from 0 to 10,000 units of output,

$$P_1 = \$60 - Q$$
$$MR_1 = \partial TR_1/\partial Q = \$60 - \$2Q$$

2. When output exceeds 10,000 units,

$$P_2 = \$80 - \$3Q$$
$$MR_2 = \partial TR_2/\partial Q = \$80 - \$6Q$$

The company's total and marginal cost functions are as follows:

$$TC = \$100 + \$20Q + \$0.5Q^2$$
$$MC = \partial TC/\partial Q = \$20 + \$1Q$$

where P is price (in dollars), Q is output (in thousands), MR is marginal revenue, TC is total cost, and MC is marginal cost, all in thousands of dollars.

A. Graph the demand, marginal revenue, and marginal cost curves.

B. How would you describe the market structure of the industry in which SSP operates? Explain why the demand curve takes the shape indicated previously.

C. Calculate price, output, and profits at the profit-maximizing activity level.

D. How much could marginal costs rise before the optimal price would increase? How much could they fall before the optimal price would decrease?

P11.8 Supply Reactions. Anaheim Industries, Inc., and Binghampton Electronics, Ltd., are the only suppliers to the National Weather Service of an important electronic instrument. The Weather Service has established a fixed-price procurement policy, however, so $P = MR$ in this market. Total and marginal cost relations for each firm are as follows:

$$TC_A = \$7,000 + \$250Q_A + \$0.5Q_A^2 \quad \text{(Anaheim)}$$
$$MC_A = \partial TC_A/\partial Q_A = \$250 + \$1Q_A$$
$$TC_B = \$8,000 + \$200Q_B + \$1Q_B^2 \quad \text{(Binghampton)}$$
$$MC_B = \partial TC_B/\partial Q_B = \$200 + \$2Q_B$$

where Q is output in units, and $MC > AVC$ for each firm.

A. What is the minimum price necessary for each firm to supply output?

B. Determine the supply curve for each firm.

C. Based on the assumption that $P = P_A = P_B$, determine industry supply curves when $P < \$200$, $\$200 < P < \$250$, and $P > \$250$.

P11.9 Nonprice Competition. General Cereals, Inc. (GCI), produces and markets Sweeties!, a popular ready-to-eat breakfast cereal. In an effort to expand sales in the Secaucus, New Jersey, market, the company is considering a 1-month promotion whereby GCI would distribute a coupon for a free daily pass to a local amusement park in exchange for three box tops, as sent in by retail customers. A 25% boost in demand is anticipated, even though only 15% of all eligible customers are expected to redeem their coupons. Each redeemed coupon costs GCI $6, so the expected cost of this promotion is 30¢ (= 0.15 × $6 ÷ 3) per unit sold. Other marginal costs for cereal production and distribution are constant at $1 per unit.

Current demand and marginal revenue relations for Sweeties! are

$$Q = 16{,}000 - 2{,}000P$$
$$MR = \partial TR/\partial Q = \$8 - \$0.001Q$$

Demand and marginal revenue relations that reflect the expected 25% boost in demand for Sweeties! are the following:

$$Q = 20{,}000 - 2{,}500P$$
$$MR = \partial TR/\partial Q = \$8 - \$0.0008Q$$

A. Calculate the profit-maximizing price/output and profit levels for Sweeties! prior to the coupon promotion.

B. Calculate these same values subsequent to the Sweeties! coupon promotion and following the expected 25% boost in demand.

P11.10 Price Leadership. Louisville Communications, Inc., offers 24-hour telephone answering service for individuals and small businesses in southeastern states. Louisville is a dominant, price-leading firm in many of its markets. Recently, Memphis Answering Service, Inc., and Nashville Recording, Ltd., have begun to offer services with the same essential characteristics as Louisville's service. Total and marginal cost functions for Memphis (M) and Nashville (N) services are as follows:

$$TC_M = \$75{,}000 - \$7Q_M + \$0.0025Q^2{}_M$$
$$MC_M = \partial TC_M/\partial Q_M = -\$7 + \$0.005Q_M$$
$$TC_N = \$50{,}000 + \$3Q_N + \$0.0025Q^2{}_N$$
$$MC_N = \partial TC_N/\partial Q_N = \$3 + \$0.005Q_N$$

Louisville's total and marginal cost relations are as follows:

$$TC_L = \$300{,}000 + \$5Q_L + \$0.0002Q^2{}_L$$
$$MC_L = \partial TC_L/\partial Q_L = \$5 + \$0.0004Q_L$$

The industry demand curve for telephone answering service is

$$Q = 500{,}800 - 19{,}600P$$

Assume throughout this problem that the Memphis and Nashville services are perfect substitutes for Louisville's service.

A. Determine the supply curves for the Memphis and Nashville services, assuming that the firms operate as price takers.

B. What is the demand curve faced by Louisville?

C. Calculate Louisville's profit-maximizing price and output levels. (Hint: Louisville's total and marginal revenue relations are $TR_L = \$25Q_L - \$0.00005Q^2{}_L$, and $MR_L = \$25 - \$0.0001Q_L$.)

D. Calculate profit-maximizing output levels for the Memphis and Nashville services.

E. Is the market for service from these three firms in short-run equilibrium?

CASE STUDY

The Profitability of Multinational Operations

Like market power in domestic markets, market power in foreign markets will have positive effects on the market value of the firm when it is an important determinant of future above-normal returns. In fact, greater valuation effects may be associated with market power in foreign as opposed to domestic operations. Although substantial numbers of efficiently sized competitors are available in an overwhelming share of U.S. markets, generally smaller foreign markets tend to be dominated by few large competitors. Entry barriers due to economies of scale tend to be more onerous, and the advantages to established leading firms greater, in foreign as opposed to U.S. markets. Antitrust and other policies limiting monopoly power also tend to be more vigorously pursued in the United States than in many foreign countries. In fact, some foreign governments encourage monopoly to gain a comparative advantages in foreign trade. Thus, the valuation effects of market power in foreign operations can be interesting in isolation, as well as in contrast with perhaps smaller effects due to market power in domestic operations.

Although the effects of market power are often indirectly measured using concentration ratios in studies conducted at the industry level of aggregation, studies using firm-level data often consider profit rate data directly. Generally speaking, concentration ratios for a firm's primary product industry are only a poor measure of market power for widely diversified firms. Even weighted average concentration ratios reflecting firm involvement in a number of industries can fail to capture market power influences because the possibility of a critical concentration ratio is neglected. Both reasons help explain why concentration ratios seldom have any discernible influence on the market value of the firm.

High profit rates can show the influences of relatively higher prices, lower costs, or both. By themselves, it is impossible to determine if high profit rates reflect the exercise of market power or superior efficiency. As such, profit rate data are an imperfect proxy for market power. They remain, however, a useful index of the relative attractiveness of one line of business or industry. If profit rates for foreign operations consistently exceed profit rates for U.S. operations, one might conclude that foreign markets are generally more attractive because they entail relatively less product market competition than U.S. markets. If profit rates for foreign operations have market value effects that invariably exceed the valuation effects of profit rates for U.S. operations, one might conclude that profit rates from foreign markets tend to be both higher and more long-lasting than profit rates earned in U.S. markets.

To estimate the effects of profit rates on the market value of the firm, it is necessary to build a simple economic model. To illustrate, consider the simple accounting identity that total assets equal the value of stockholders' equity plus total liabilities:

(11.8)   Total Assets = Stockholders' Equity + Total Liabilities

This means that the total assets of any corporation are financed either through the sale of common stock and retained earnings or through debt financing. When the market value of

CASE STUDY (continued)

common stock is used as an economic measure of the value of stockholder equity, then Equation 11.6 implies:

$$\text{(11.9)} \qquad \frac{\text{Market Value of}}{\text{Common Stock}} = \frac{\text{Total}}{\text{Assets}} - \frac{\text{Total}}{\text{Liabilities}} + \epsilon$$

The error term ϵ (epsilon) allows for the fact that the market value of common stock seldom exactly equals the difference between assets and liabilities, which is defined as the book value of stockholders' equity. As such, ϵ reflects the combined influence of accounting errors and bias. For example, because the accounting profession does not typically assign a value to intangible assets like advertising and R&D, the market price of common stock is often much greater than the accountant's book value of stockholders' equity.

The effects of profit rates on the market value of the firm can be estimated by expanding the number of independent X variables in Equation 11.9 to include profit rates on domestic and foreign operations. If current profit rates are a useful indicator of the multinational firm's future profit-making potential, an impact on the current market value of the firm can be anticipated. If profit rates on foreign operations are higher and/or more stable than profit rates on domestic operations, a somewhat greater influence of foreign profit rates on the market value of the firm can also be anticipated.

To properly isolate the market value effects of profit rates in both foreign and domestic markets, it is important to control for the risk implications of multinational involvement. In many instances, multinational involvement not only allows firms to expand product markets, but also provides a "portfolio" of regulatory environments, economic conditions, and trade currencies. Although exchange risk can be limited at minimal cost through participation in highly developed currency markets, limiting risks associated with political intervention (increased taxation, expropriation) and localized economic fluctuations can be costly. Thus, a firm's degree of "multinationalism" may have important implications for its overall risk level. To the extent that conventional measures fail to reflect the greater risks associated with multinational activity, the degree of multinational involvement can convey additional risk information. If multinationals face greater than typical levels of risk, or involve substantial hedging expenses, a firm's degree of multinational involvement can have negative valuation effects. In addition, one might expect positive valuation effects to accompany high expected growth because a firm's options for future investment are largely determined by expected growth in demand.

Based on these considerations, a regression model that can be used to learn the relative market-value impacts of domestic versus foreign profit rates can be written

$$\text{(11.10)} \qquad \begin{aligned} \text{Market Value/Assets} = {} & b_0 + b_1\, 1/\text{Assets} + b_2\, \text{Debt/Assets} \\ & + b_3\, \text{ROA}_i + b_4\, \text{Growth} + b_5\, \text{Foreign/Domestic} + u \end{aligned}$$

In this equation, notice that each size-related variable has been deflated, or normalized, by the book value of total assets. Without deflation of size-related variables, the link between market value and profits could be dominated by size effects: By definition, large firms have high market values and profits. The deflation of all size-related variables makes it possible to focus on the valuation effects of profit rate differences between foreign and domestic operations. In this model, the profit rate of interest is called the return on total assets, or ROA, and defined as net income (profits) divided by the book value of total assets. Like ROE, ROA is a basic measure of the firm's rate of return on investment; unlike ROE, the ROA measure does not directly reflect the firm's use of financial leverage.

For exploratory purposes, the simple economic model described in Equation 11.10 is estimated over an $n = 25$ sample of the largest U.S. multinationals. In an annual survey, *Forbes* shows foreign sales, foreign profits, and foreign assets for top U.S. multinationals. To estimate

CASE STUDY (continued)

Equation 11.8, it is necessary to supplement Forbes data with market value, leverage, and estimated earnings per share growth information from the Value Line/Value Screen database. Table 11.8 shows the actual data used in the regression analysis.

Over this sample of large multinationals, the average ROA = 7.55% is comprised of an average profit rate for domestic operation of ROA_D = 6.72%, and an average profit rate for foreign operations of ROA_F = 9.45%.

A. A multiple regression analysis based upon the data contained in Table 11.8 revealed the following (*t* statistics in parentheses):

$$\text{Market Value/Assets} = -0.215 + 6,860 \, 1/\text{Assets} + 0.242 \, \text{Debt/Assets}$$
$$(-0.25) \quad (7,956) \qquad\qquad (0.22)$$
$$+28.109 \, \text{ROA} \, -0.043 \, \text{Growth}$$
$$(6.52) \qquad\qquad (-0.85)$$

Based on the statistical importance of the ROA variable, is it reasonable to conclude that stock-market investors believe that current rates of return will persist into future periods?

TABLE 11.8

Market Value and the Profitability of Foreign Operations for 25 Top U.S. Multinationals

Company	Industry	Market Value of Common	Total Debt	Foreign Profit	Total Profit	Foreign Assets	Total Assets	EPS Growth
American International Group	Insurance	52,397	41,582	1,746	2,897	56,343	148,431	13.5
Chevron	Petroleum	42,727	8,239	1,560	2,607	17,420	38,378	10.0
Citicorp	Bank	44,972	125,858	2,146	3,788	161,000	270,000	13.0
Coca-Cola	Soft drinks	133,057	2,557	2,366	3,492	6,090	16,161	16.5
Compaq Computer	Computer	19,958	469	679	1,313	3,306	10,526	17.5
Digital Equipment	Computer	5,870	2,217	−147	−112	5,178	10,075	0.0
Dow Chemical	Chemical	19,794	8,961	777	2,101	14,047	24,673	13.5
du Pont (E.I.) de Nemours	Chemical	53,189	14,925	1,051	3,636	15,435	37,987	11.5
Eastman Kodak	Precision instruments	27,974	1,592	236	1,011	5,740	14,438	12.0
Exxon	Petroleum	124,511	14,607	5,153	7,510	55,589	95,527	8.0
Ford	Auto	35,272	180,029	223	4,446	79,106	262,867	9.0
General Electric	Electrical equipment	169,984	3,900	1,596	7,280	82,976	272,402	14.5
General Motors	Auto	41,604	132,445	3,365	4,953	58,785	222,142	17.0
Hewlett-Packard	Computer	52,143	1,221	1,612	2,586	15,121	27,699	20.0
IBM	Computer	85,230	24,891	3,541	5,429	42,007	81,132	21.5
Intel	Semiconductor	111,246	525	1,982	5,157	4,784	23,735	19.0
Johnson & Johnson	Medical supplies	64,678	3,396	1,332	2,287	9,147	20,010	14.0
Mobil	Petroleum	49,320	8,849	2,035	3,328	31,330	46,408	11.5
Motorola	Semiconductor	35,706	3,420	1,066	1,154	8,604	24,076	12.5
PepsiCo	Soft drinks	46,098	13,733	−175	1,149	7,802	24,512	13.5
Philip Morris Cos	Tobacco	95,169	25,291	1,608	6,303	20,558	54,871	18.0
Procter & Gamble	Household products	74,816	7,764	1,125	3,046	11,222	27,730	13.0
Texaco	Petroleum	25,959	9,227	931	2,274	14,312	31,443	11.0
United Technologies	Diversified	16,541	4,309	714	1,037	6,374	16,745	16.5
Xerox	Office equipment	16,617	16,360	792	1,206	14,541	28,120	14.5
Averages		57,793	26,255	1,493	3,195	29,873	73,204	13.6

Data source: Value Line/Value Screen Data Base, January 1, 1997; Brian Zajac, "Buying American," *Forbes*, July 28, 1997, 218–220. Reproduced with the permission of Value Line Publishing, Inc.

CASE STUDY (continued)

B. A second multiple regression analysis based upon the data contained in Table 11.8 revealed the following (*t* statistics in parentheses):

$$Market\ Value/Assets\ =\ -0.016\ +\ 7{,}145\ 1/Assets\ +\ 0.660\ Debt/Assets$$
$$(-0.01)\quad (0.82)\qquad\qquad (0.52)$$
$$+13.018\ ROA_F\ +\ 6.885\ ROA_D\ -\ 0.040\ Growth\ +\ 0.150\ Foreign/Domestic$$
$$(4.52)\qquad\quad (1.30)\qquad\quad (-0.72)\qquad\qquad (0.94)$$

Based on the importance of the ROA variables for foreign versus domestic operations, is it reasonable to conclude that foreign markets may be more or less competitive than the U.S. market?

SELECTED REFERENCES

Anderson, Simon P., and Andre De Palma. "Product Diversity in Asymmetric Oligopoly: Is the Quality of Consumer Goods Too Low." *Journal of Industrial Economics* 49 (June 2001): 113–135.

Arthur, N. "Board Composition as the Outcome of an Internal Bargaining Process: Empirical Evidence." *Journal of Corporate Finance* 7 (September 2001): 307–340.

Bennett, James A., and Richard W. Sias. "Can Money Flows Predict Stock Returns?" *Financial Analysts Journal* 57 (November/December 2001): 64–77.

Coate, Malcolm B. "Market Structure and Competition Policy: Game-Theoretic Approaches." *Managerial & Decision Economics* 22 (December 2001): 465–466.

Fiegenbaum, Avi, Howard Thomas, and Ming-Je Tang. "Linking Hypercompetition and Strategic Group Theories: Strategic Maneuvering in the US Insurance Industry." *Managerial & Decision Economics* 22 (June/August 2001): 265–279.

Friedman, James. "Oligopoly Pricing: Old Ideas and New Tools." *Journal of Economic Literature* 39 (June 2001): 573–575.

Hirschey, Mark. "Cisco and the Kids." *Financial Analysts Journal* 57 (July/August 2001): 48–59.

Jacobs, Michael S. "Second Order Oligopoly Problems with International Dimensions: Sequential Mergers, Maverick Firms and Buyer Power." *Antitrust Bulletin* 46 (Fall 2001): 537–568.

Jin, Jim Y. "Monopolistic Competition and Bounded Rationality." *Journal of Economic Behavior & Organization* 45 (June 2001): 175–184.

Kramer, Jonathan K., and Jonathan R. Peters. "An Interindustry Analysis of Economic Value Added as a Proxy for Market Value Added." *Journal of Applied Finance* 11 (2001): 41–49.

Linnemann, Ludger. "The Price Index Effect, Entry, and Endogenous Markups in a Macroeconomic Model of Monopolistic Competition." *Journal of Macroeconomics* 23 (Summer 2001): 441–458.

Merlone, Ugo. "Cartelizing Effects of Horizontal Shareholding Interlocks." *Managerial & Decision Economics* 22 (September 2001): 333–337.

Pichler, Pegaret, and William Wilhelm. "A Theory of The Syndicate: Form Follows Function." *Journal of Finance* 56 (December 2001): 2237–2264.

Sims, Christopher A. "Pitfalls of a Minimax Approach to Model Uncertainty." *American Economic Review* 91 (May 2001): 51–54.

Walker, Mark, and John Wooders. "Minimax Play at Wimbledon." *American Economic Review* 91 (December 2001): 1521–1538.

CHAPTER TWELVE

Pricing Practices

Pricing practices sometimes seem peculiar. When first-class hotel rooms in London, Tokyo, or Paris go for $300 to $500 per night, Holiday Inns offers Weekend WebSavers℠ rates at Chicago's O'Hare International Airport from as low as $62.48 per night—more than 50 percent off regular prices. Not to be outdone, Howard Johnson's says vacations are more fun with family package rates up to 70 percent off regular prices. Meanwhile, Marriott offers advance purchase rates on the Internet for as low as $59 per night at the Courtyard Marriott Village at Lake Buena Vista, Florida. At the Hilton Durham, in North Carolina, weekday rates are $109.95 and $89.95 on the weekend. What is going on here?

Rather than a mad scramble to build market share at any cost, hotel-chain rates represent a shrewd use of information technology. Any night that hotel rooms stand empty represents lost revenue, and because hotel costs are largely fixed, revenue losses translate directly into lost profits. A room rate of $59 per night does not begin to cover fixed construction, maintenance, and interest costs, but it makes a nice profit contribution when the alternative is weekend vacancy. By segmenting their markets, hotels are able to charge the maximum amount the market will bear on weekdays and on weekends. Similarly, hotel marketing gets fierce for convention business, especially when conventions meet at traditionally slack periods. Is it any wonder that the American Economic Association holds annual meetings around New Year's Day in cold-weather cities?[1]

This chapter examines common pricing practices and illustrates their value as a practical means for achieving profit-maximizing prices under a wide variety of demand and cost conditions.

---

1 See Motoko Rich, "Holiday Inn Owner Will Build Hotels Even as Industry Slows," *The Wall Street Journal Online*, January 16, 2002 (http://online.wsj.com).

MARKUP PRICING

markup pricing
Setting prices to cover direct costs plus a percentage profit contribution

Markup pricing is the most commonly employed pricing method. Given the popularity of the technique, it behooves managers to fully understand the rationale for markup pricing. When this rationale is understood, markup pricing methods can be seen as the practical means for achieving optimal prices under a wide variety of demand and cost conditions.

Markup Pricing Technology

The development of pricing practices to profitably segment markets has reached a fine art with the Internet and use of high-speed computer technology. Why do *Business Week, Forbes, Fortune,* and *The Wall Street Journal* offer bargain rates to students but not to business executives? It is surely not because it costs less to deliver the *Journal* to students, and it is not out of benevolence; it is because students are not willing or able to pay the standard rate. Even at 50 percent off regular prices, student bargain rates more than cover marginal costs and make a significant profit contribution. Similarly, senior citizens who eat at Holiday Inns enjoy a 10 to 15 percent discount and make a meaningful contribution to profits. Conversely, relatively high prices for popcorn at movie theaters, peanuts at the ball park, and clothing at the height of the season reflect the fact that customers can be insensitive to price changes at different places and at different times of the year. Regular prices, discounts, rebates, and coupon promotions are all pricing mechanisms used to probe the breadth and depth of customer demand and to maximize profitability.

Although profit maximization requires that prices be set so that marginal revenues equal marginal cost, it is not necessary to calculate both to set optimal prices. Just using information on marginal costs and the point price elasticity of demand, the calculation of profit-maximizing prices is quick and easy. Many firms derive an optimal pricing policy using prices set to cover direct costs plus a percentage markup for profit contribution. Flexible markup pricing practices that reflect differences in marginal costs and demand elasticities constitute an efficient method for ensuring that $MR = MC$ for each line of products sold. Similarly, peak and off-peak pricing, price discrimination, and joint product pricing practices are efficient means for operating so that $MR = MC$ for each customer or customer group and product class.

Markup on Cost

In a conventional approach, firms estimate the average variable costs of producing and marketing a given product, add a charge for variable overhead, and then add a percentage markup, or profit margin. Variable overhead costs are usually allocated among all products according to average variable costs. For example, if total variable overhead costs are projected at $1.3 million per year and variable costs for planned production total $1 million, then variable overhead is allocated to individual products at the rate of 130 percent of variable cost. If the average variable cost of a product is estimated to be $1, the firm adds a charge of 130 percent of variable costs, or $1.30, for variable overhead, obtaining a fully allocated cost of $2.30. To this figure the firm might add a 30 percent markup for profits, or 69¢, to obtain a price of $2.99 per unit.

markup on cost
The difference between price and cost, measured relative to cost, expressed as a percentage

Markup on cost is the profit margin for an individual product or product line expressed as a percentage of unit cost. The markup-on-cost, or *cost-plus*, formula is given by the expression:

(12.1)
$$\text{Markup on Cost} = \frac{\text{Price} - \text{Cost}}{\text{Cost}}$$

profit margin
The difference between the price and cost of a product

The numerator of this expression, called the **profit margin**, is measured by the difference between price and cost. In the example cited previously, the 30 percent markup on cost is calculated as

$$\begin{aligned} \text{Markup on Cost} &= \frac{\text{Price} - \text{Cost}}{\text{Cost}} \\ &= \frac{\$2.99 - \$2.30}{\$2.30} \\ &= 0.30, \text{ or } 30\% \end{aligned}$$

Solving Equation 12.1 for price provides the expression that determines price in a cost-plus pricing system:

(12.2) $$\text{Price} = \text{Cost} (1 + \text{Markup on Cost})$$

Continuing with the previous example, the product selling price is found as

$$\begin{aligned} \text{Price} &= \text{Cost} (1 + \text{Markup on Cost}) \\ &= \$2.30(1.30) \\ &= \$2.99 \end{aligned}$$

Markup on Price

markup on price
The difference between price and cost, measured relative to price, expressed as a percentage

Profit margins, or markups, are sometimes calculated as a percentage of price instead of cost. **Markup on price** is the profit margin for an individual product or product line expressed as a percentage of price, rather than unit cost as in the markup-on-cost formula. This alternative means of expressing profit margins can be illustrated by the markup-on-price formula:

(12.3) $$\text{Markup on Price} = \frac{\text{Price} - \text{Cost}}{\text{Price}}$$

Profit margin is the numerator of the markup-on-price formula, as in the markup-on-cost formula. However, unit cost has been replaced by price in the denominator.

The markup-on-cost and markup-on-price formulas are simply alternative means for expressing the relative size of profit margins. To convert from one markup formula to the other, just use the following expressions:

(12.4) $$\text{Markup on Cost} = \frac{\text{Markup on Price}}{1 - \text{Markup on Price}}$$

(12.5) $$\text{Markup on Price} = \frac{\text{Markup on Cost}}{1 + \text{Markup on Cost}}$$

Therefore, the 30 percent markup on cost described in the previous example is equivalent to a 23 percent markup on price:

$$\text{Markup on Price} = \frac{0.3}{1 + 0.3} = 0.23 \text{ or } 23\%$$

An item with a cost of $2.30, a 69¢ markup, and a price of $2.99 has a 30 percent markup on cost and a 23 percent markup on price. This illustrates the importance of being consistent in the choice of a cost or price basis when comparing markups among products or sellers.

Markup pricing is sometimes criticized as a naive pricing method based solely on cost considerations—and the wrong costs at that. Some who employ the technique may ignore demand conditions, emphasize fully allocated accounting costs rather than marginal costs, and arrive at suboptimal price decisions. However, a categorical rejection of such a popular and successful pricing practice is clearly wrong. Although inappropriate use of markup pricing formulas will lead to suboptimal managerial decisions, successful firms typically employ the method in a way that is consistent with profit maximization. Markup pricing can be viewed as an efficient rule-of-thumb approach to setting optimal prices.

Role of Cost in Markup Pricing

Although a variety of cost concepts are employed in markup pricing, most firms use a standard, or fully allocated, cost concept. Fully allocated costs are determined by first estimating direct costs per unit, then allocating the firm's expected indirect expenses, or overhead, assuming a standard or normal output level. Price is then based on standard costs per unit, irrespective of short-term variations in actual unit costs.

Unfortunately, use of the standard cost concept can create several problems. Sometimes, firms fail to adjust historical costs to reflect recent or expected price changes. Also, accounting costs may not reflect true economic costs. For example, fully allocated costs can be appropriate when a firm is operating at full capacity. During **peak** periods, when facilities are fully utilized, expansion is required to increase production. Under such conditions, an increase in production requires an increase in all plant, equipment, labor, materials, and other expenditures. However, if a firm has excess capacity, as during **off-peak** periods, only those costs that actually rise with production—the incremental costs per unit—should form a basis for setting prices.

Successful firms that employ markup pricing use fully allocated costs under normal conditions but offer price discounts or accept lower margins during off-peak periods when excess capacity is available. In some instances, output produced during off-peak periods is much cheaper than output produced during peak periods. When fixed costs represent a substantial share of total production costs, discounts of 30 percent to 50 percent for output produced during off-peak periods can often be justified on the basis of lower costs.

"Early bird" or afternoon matinee discounts at movie theaters provide an interesting example. Except for cleaning expenses, which vary according to the number of customers, most movie theater expenses are fixed. As a result, the revenue generated by adding customers during off-peak periods can significantly increase the theater's profit contribution. When off-peak customers buy regularly priced candy, popcorn, and soda, even lower afternoon ticket prices can be justified. Conversely, on Friday and Saturday nights when movie theaters operate at peak capacity, a small increase in the number of customers would require a costly expansion of facilities. Ticket prices during these peak periods reflect fully allocated costs. Similarly, McDonald's, Burger King, Arby's, and other fast-food outlets have increased their profitability substantially by introducing breakfast menus. If fixed restaurant expenses are covered by lunch and dinner business, even promotionally priced breakfast items can make a notable contribution to profits.

Role of Demand in Markup Pricing

Successful companies differentiate markups according to variations in product demand elasticities. Foreign and domestic automobile companies regularly offer rebates or special equipment packages for slow-selling models. Similarly, airlines promote different pricing schedules for business and vacation travelers. The airline and automobile industries are only two examples of sectors in which vigorous competition requires a careful reflection of demand and supply factors in pricing practice. In the production and distribution of many goods and services, successful firms quickly adjust prices to different market conditions.

Examining the margins set by a successful regional grocery store chain provides interesting evidence that demand conditions play an important role in cost-plus pricing. Table 12.1 shows the firm's typical markup on cost and markup on price for a variety of products. A field

peak
Period of full capacity usage

off-peak
Period of excess capacity

TABLE 12.1

Markups Charged on a Variety of Grocery Items

Item	Markup on Cost (%)	Markup on Price (%)
Bread—private label	0–5	0–5
Bread—brand name	30–40	23–29
Breakfast cereals (dry)	5–15	5–13
Cake mixes	15–20	13–17
Coffee	0–10	0–9
Cold cuts (processed meats)	20–45	17–31
Cookies	20–30	17–23
Delicatessen items	35–45	26–31
Fresh fruit—in season	40–50	29–33
Fresh fruit—out of season	15–20	13–17
Fresh vegetables—in season	40–50	29–33
Fresh vegetables—out of season	15–20	13–17
Ground beef	0–10	0–9
Ice cream	15–20	13–17
Laundry detergent	5–10	5–9
Milk	0–5	0–5
Nonprescription drugs	33–55	26–35
Pastries (cakes, pies, etc.)	20–30	17–23
Pet foods	15–20	13–17
Snack foods	20–25	17–20
Soft drinks	0–10	0–9
Spices	30–60	23–38
Soup	0–15	0–13
Steak	15–35	13–26
Toilet tissue	10–15	9–13
Toothpaste	15–20	13–17

manager with over 20 years' experience in the grocery business provided the author with useful insight into the firm's pricing practices. He stated that the "price sensitivity" of an item is the primary consideration in setting margins. Staple products like bread, coffee, ground beef, milk, and soup are highly price sensitive and carry relatively low margins. Products with high margins tend to be less price sensitive.

Note the wide range of margins applied to different items. The 0 percent to 10 percent markup on cost for ground beef, for example, is substantially lower than the 15 percent to 35 percent margin on steak. Hamburger is a relatively low-priced meat with wide appeal to families, college students, and low-income groups whose price sensitivity is high. In contrast, relatively expensive sirloin, T-bone, and porterhouse steaks appeal to higher-income groups with lower price sensitivity.

It is also interesting to see how seasonal factors affect the demand for grocery items like fruits and vegetables. When a fruit or vegetable is in season, spoilage and transportation costs are at their lowest levels, and high product quality translates into enthusiastic consumer demand, which leads to high margins. Consumer demand shifts away from high-cost/low-quality fresh fruits and vegetables when they are out of season, thereby reducing margins on these items.

In addition to seasonal factors that affect margins over the course of a year, some market forces affect margins within a given product class. In breakfast cereals, for example, the markup on cost for highly popular corn flakes averages only 5 percent to 6 percent, with brands offered

10¢ for a Gallon of Gas in Dayton, Ohio

In every state, retail gasoline prices must be clearly visible to passing motorists. At the same time, octane content is regulated so that the gas available for sale meets minimum standards as a clean-burning fuel. With prominently displayed prices, and consistently high gas quality, the groundwork is in place for vicious price competition.

Price-conscious drivers commonly bypass high-price stations in the effort to save as little as 2¢ or 3¢ per gallon. As a result, profit margins on gasoline are notoriously low. Margins are typically so low that convenience stores see gasoline as a "loss leader" for other high-margin products. Although the typical driver will go out of the way to save no more than 50¢ on a tank of gas, that same driver will see nothing wrong with going inside the convenience store and paying $1.29 for a large cup of soda, 89¢ for a candy bar, or $3.49 for a pack of cigarettes. In no small way, convenience stores offer gasoline as a means of generating traffic for soda, candy, and cigarettes.

For example, in November 2001, Cincinnati–based Kroger Co., which has about 180 grocery stores with

gas stations, opened a new store and gas station in Dayton, Ohio. During a 3-day grand opening period, Kroger decided to price its gasoline 10¢ per gallon below local market norms as a means for generating favorable customer interest and publicity. Competitors took notice, too. Just down the street, the Meijer superstore/gas station, owned by closely held Meijer Inc. of Grand Rapids, Michigan, decided to cut its price. An all-out price war developed. Within hours, gasoline prices in Dayton fell from $1.08 (the Midwest market average) to 50¢ per gallon, and briefly all the way down to 10¢ per gallon! In commenting on the situation, Kroger officials said that such prices were not part of the company's "everyday price strategy," but "we intend to be competitive."

See: Maxwell Murphy, "Kroger Versus Meijer: Gasoline Price War Rages in Dayton,"*The Wall Street Journal Online*, November 30, 2001 (http://online.wsj.com).

by Post and Kellogg's competing with a variety of local store brands. Cheerios and Wheaties, both offered only by General Mills, Inc., enjoy a markup on cost of 15 percent to 20 percent. Thus, availability of substitutes directly affects the markups on various cereals. It is interesting to note that among the wide variety of items sold in a typical grocery store, the highest margins are charged on spices. Apparently, consumer demand for nutmeg, cloves, thyme, bay leaves, and other spices is quite insensitive to price. The manager interviewed said that in more than 20 years in the grocery business, he could not recall a single store coupon or special offered on spices.

This retail grocery store pricing example provides valuable insight into how markup pricing rules can be used in setting an efficient pricing policy. It is clear that the price elasticity concept plays a key role in the firm's pricing decisions. To examine those decisions further, it is necessary to develop a method for determining optimal markups in practical pricing policy.

MARKUP PRICING AND PROFIT MAXIMIZATION

There is a simple inverse relation between the optimal markup and the price sensitivity of demand. The optimal markup is large when the underlying price elasticity of demand is low; the optimal markup is small when the underlying price elasticity of demand is high.

Optimal Markup on Cost

Recall from Chapter 4 that there is a direct relation among marginal revenue, price elasticity of demand, and the profit-maximizing price for a product. This relation was expressed as

(12.6)
$$MR = P\left(1 + \frac{1}{\epsilon_P}\right)$$

To maximize profit, a firm must operate at the activity level at which marginal revenue equals marginal cost. Because marginal revenue always equals the right side of Equation 12.6, at the profit-maximizing output level, it follows that $MR = MC$ and

(12.7)
$$P\left(1 + \frac{1}{\epsilon_P}\right) = MC$$

or

(12.8)
$$P = MC\left(\frac{1}{1 + \frac{1}{\epsilon_P}}\right)$$

Equation 12.8 provides a formula for the profit-maximizing price for any product in terms of its price elasticity of demand. The equation states that the profit-maximizing price is found by multiplying marginal cost by the term

$$\left(\frac{1}{1 + \frac{1}{\epsilon_P}}\right)$$

To derive the optimal markup-on-cost formula, recall from Equation 12.2 that the price established by a cost-plus method equals cost multiplied by the expression (1 + Markup on Cost). Equation 12.7 implies that marginal cost is the appropriate cost basis for cost-plus pricing and that

$$MC(1 + \text{Markup on Cost}) = MC\left(\frac{1}{1 + \frac{1}{\epsilon_P}}\right)$$

By dividing each side of this expression by MC and subtracting 1 yields the expression

$$\text{Markup on Cost} = \left(\frac{1}{1 + \frac{1}{\epsilon_P}}\right) - 1$$

After simplifying, the optimal markup on cost, or profit-maximizing markup-on-cost, formula can be written

(12.9)
$$\frac{\text{Optimal Markup}}{\text{on Cost}} = OMC^* = \frac{-1}{\epsilon_P + 1}$$

optimal markup on cost
The profit-maximizing cost markup, equal to –1 divided by the quantity 1 plus the price elasticity of demand

The **optimal markup-on-cost** formula can be illustrated through use of a simple example. Consider the case of a leading catalog retailer of casual clothing and sporting equipment that wishes to offer a basic two-strap design of Birkenstock leather sandals for easy on-and-off casual wear. Assume the catalog retailer pays a wholesale price of $25 per pair for Birkenstock sandals and markets them at a regular catalog price of $75 per pair. This typical $50 profit margin implies a standard markup on cost of 200 percent because

$$\text{Markup on Cost} = \frac{\text{Price} - \text{Cost}}{\text{Cost}}$$
$$= \frac{\$75 - \$25}{\$25}$$
$$= 2, \text{ or } 200\%$$

In a preseason sale, the catalog retailer offered a discounted "early bird" price of $70 on Birkenstock sandals and noted a moderate increase in weekly sales from 275 to 305 pairs per week. This $5 discount from the regular price of $75 represents a modest 6.7 percent markdown. Using the arc price elasticity formula, the implied arc price elasticity of demand on Birkenstock sandals is

$$E_P = \frac{Q_2 - Q_1}{P_2 - P_1} \times \frac{P_2 + P_1}{Q_2 + Q_1}$$

$$= \frac{305 - 275}{\$70 - \$75} \times \frac{\$70 + \$75}{305 + 275}$$

$$= -1.5$$

In the absence of additional evidence, this arc price elasticity of demand $E_P = -1.5$ is the best available estimate of the current point price elasticity of demand. Using Equation 12.9, the $75 regular catalog price reflects an optimal markup on cost of 200 percent because

$$\begin{aligned}\text{Optimal Markup} \atop \text{on Cost} &= \frac{-1}{\epsilon_P + 1} \\ &= \frac{-1}{-1.5 + 1} \\ &= 2.0 \text{ or } 200\%\end{aligned}$$

Optimal Markup on Price

Just as there is a simple inverse relation between a product's price sensitivity and the optimal markup on cost, so too is there a simple inverse relation between price sensitivity and the **optimal markup on price**. The profit-maximizing markup on price is easily determined using relations derived previously. Dividing each side of Equation 12.7 by P yields the expression

optimal markup on price
The profit-maximizing price markup, equal to -1 times the inverse of the price elasticity of demand

$$\frac{MC}{P} = 1 + \frac{1}{\epsilon_P}$$

Subtracting 1 from each side of this equation and simplifying gives

$$\frac{MC - P}{P} = \frac{1}{\epsilon_P}$$

Then, multiplying each side of this expression by -1 yields

(12.10)
$$\frac{P - MC}{P} = \frac{-1}{\epsilon_P}$$

Notice that the left side of Equation 12.9 is an expression for markup on price. Thus, the optimal markup-on-price formula is

(12.11)
$$\begin{aligned}\text{Optimal Markup} \atop \text{on Price} &= \text{OMP}^* = \frac{-1}{\epsilon_P}\end{aligned}$$

The optimal markup-on-price formula can be illustrated by continuing with the previous example of a catalog retailer and its optimal pricing policy for Birkenstock leather sandals. As you may recall from that example, the catalog retailer pays a wholesale price of $25 per pair for Birkenstock sandals, markets them at a regular catalog price of $75 per pair, and the arc price elasticity of demand $E_P = -1.5$ is the best available estimate of the current point price elasticity of demand. This typical $50 profit margin implies a standard markup on price of 66.7 percent because

$$\text{Markup on Price} = \frac{\text{Price} - \text{Cost}}{\text{Price}}$$
$$= \frac{\$75 - \$25}{\$75}$$
$$= 0.667, \text{ or } 66.7\%$$

If it can again be assumed that the arc price elasticity of demand $E_P = -1.5$ is the best available estimate of the current point price elasticity of demand, the $75 regular catalog price reflects an optimal markup on price because

$$\text{Optimal Markup on Price} = \frac{-1}{\epsilon_P}$$
$$= \frac{-1}{-1.5}$$
$$= 0.667 \text{ or } 66.7\%$$

Table 12.2 shows the optimal markup on marginal cost and on price for products with varying price elasticities of demand. As the table indicates, the more elastic the demand for a product, the more price sensitive it is and the smaller the optimal margin. Products with relatively less elastic demand have higher optimal markups. In the retail grocery example, a very low markup is consistent with a high price elasticity of demand for milk. Demand for fruits and vegetables during their peak seasons is considerably less price sensitive, and correspondingly higher markups reflect this lower price elasticity of demand.

Another Optimal Markup Example

The use of the optimal markup formulas can be further illustrated by considering the case of Betty's Boutique, a small specialty retailer located in a suburban shopping mall. In setting its

TABLE 12.2

Optimal Markup on Marginal Cost and Price at Various Price Elasticity Levels

Price Elasticity of Demand ϵ_P	Optimal Markup on Marginal Cost (%), $\frac{-1}{\epsilon_P + 1}$	Optimal Markup on Price(%), $\frac{-1}{\epsilon_P}$
−1.5	200.0	66.7
−2.0	100.0	50.0
−2.5	66.7	40.0
−5.0	25.0	20.0
−10.0	11.1	10.0
−25.0	4.2	4.0

initial $36 price for a new spring line of blouses, Betty's added a 50 percent markup on cost. Costs were estimated at $24 each: the $12 purchase price of each blouse, plus $6 in allocated variable overhead costs, plus an allocated fixed overhead charge of $6. Customer response was so strong that when Betty's raised prices from $36 to $39 per blouse, sales fell only from 54 to 46 blouses per week. Was Betty's initial $36 price optimal? Is the new $39 price suboptimal? If so, what is the optimal price?

At first blush, Betty's pricing policy seems clearly inappropriate. It is always improper to consider allocated fixed costs in setting prices for any good or service; only marginal or incremental costs should be included. However, by adjusting the amount of markup on cost or markup on price employed, Betty's can implicitly compensate for the inappropriate use of fully allocated costs. It is necessary to carefully analyze both the cost categories included and the markup percentages chosen before judging a given pricing practice.

To determine Betty's optimal markup, it is necessary to calculate an estimate of the point price elasticity of demand and relevant marginal cost, and then apply the optimal markup formula. Betty's standard cost per blouse includes the $12 purchase cost, plus $6 allocated variable costs, plus $6 fixed overhead charges. However, for pricing purposes, only the $12 purchase cost plus the allocated variable overhead charge of $6 are relevant. Thus, the relevant marginal cost for pricing purposes is $18 per blouse. The allocated fixed overhead charge of $6 is irrelevant for pricing purposes because fixed overhead costs are unaffected by blouse sales.

The $3 price increase to $39 represents a moderate 7.7 percent rise in price. Using the arc price elasticity formula, the implied arc price elasticity of demand for Betty's blouses is

$$
\begin{aligned}
E_P &= \frac{Q_2 - Q_1}{P_2 - P_1} \times \frac{P_2 + P_1}{Q_2 + Q_1} \\
&= \frac{46 - 54}{\$39 - \$36} \times \frac{\$39 + \$36}{46 + 54} \\
&= -2
\end{aligned}
$$

If it can be assumed that this arc price elasticity of demand $\epsilon_P = -2$ is the best available estimate of the current point price elasticity of demand, the $36 price reflects an optimal markup of 100 percent on relevant marginal costs of $18 because

$$
\begin{aligned}
\frac{\text{Optimal Markup}}{\text{on Cost}} &= \frac{-1}{\epsilon_P + 1} \\
&= \frac{-1}{-2 + 1} \\
&= 1 \text{ or } 100\%
\end{aligned}
$$

Similarly, the $36 price reflects an optimal markup on price because

$$
\begin{aligned}
\frac{\text{Optimal Markup}}{\text{on Price}} &= \frac{-1}{\epsilon_P} \\
&= \frac{-1}{-2} \\
&= 0.5 \text{ or } 50\%
\end{aligned}
$$

Betty's actual markup on relevant marginal costs per blouse is an optimal 100 percent, because

$$
\begin{aligned}
\text{Markup on Cost} &= \frac{\$36 - \$18}{\$18} \\
&= 1 \text{ (or } 100\%)
\end{aligned}
$$

Why Do Some Price Wars Never Seem to End?

In supermarkets, permanent price wars rage for items such as coffee, cola, pet foods, paper products, and frozen foods. Top-of-the-line frozen food entré prices continue to drop as H.J. Heinz, Nestlé, ConAgra, Campbell's Soup, and Kraft battle for overcrowded freezer space. In the salty snacks business, PepsiCo and Borden continue years of price warfare that has crumbled the margins of a once highly profitable business. In consumer electronics, computer manufacturers have had to contend with a marketplace that sees declining prices on a monthly, weekly, or even daily basis.

Price wars, once a tool of limited strategic value in mature businesses, are becoming a disheartening fact of life in industries ranging from autos to credit cards to steel to computers. A growing number of companies trapped into protecting investments that are too big to write off are forced to pursue market share at all costs. Worse yet, using price wars to bump off competitors is much more difficult these days because weak competitors are often acquired by firms with deep pockets, or can file for bankruptcy protection from creditors and

keep operating. The only clear winners in this ongoing process of constant price warfare are consumers, who have come to enjoy and expect ever lower prices.

Businesses with high fixed costs are likely to display savage price competition. With commodity-like products, widely available price and product-quality information, and/or high fixed costs, competition to fill excess capacity can be fierce. Nowhere are the effects of savage price-cutting more evident than on the Internet, where marginal costs are often near zero. With negligible costs for downloading to new customers, free software, sometimes called "freeware, " is standard. Similarly, when distant suppliers are no more than a mouse click away, local and regional suppliers face unrelenting price competition. This is all bad news for companies, and good news for the consumer. More than ever, the customer is king!

See: Sholnn Freeman and Joseph B. White, "Auto Price War Persists with GM Expected to Introduce $2002 Cash-Rebate," *The Wall Street Journal Online*, January 3, 2002 (http://online.wsj.com).

Similarly, Betty's markup on price is an optimal 50 percent, because

$$\text{Markup on Price} = \frac{\$36 - \$18}{\$36}$$
$$= 0.5 \text{ (or 50\%)}$$

Therefore, Betty's initial $36 price on blouses is optimal, and the subsequent $3 price increase should be rescinded.

This simple example teaches an important lesson. Despite the improper consideration of fixed overhead costs and a markup that might at first appear unsuitable, Betty's pricing policy is entirely consistent with profit-maximizing behavior because the end result is an efficient pricing policy. Given the prevalence of markup pricing in everyday business practice, it is important that these pricing practices be carefully analyzed before they are judged suboptimal. The widespread use of markup pricing methods among highly successful firms suggests that the method is typically employed in ways that are consistent with profit maximization. Far from being a naive rule of thumb, markup pricing practices allow firms to arrive at optimal prices in an efficient manner.

PRICE DISCRIMINATION

With multiple markets or customer groups, the potential exists to enhance profits by charging different prices and markups to each relevant market segment. Market segmentation is an important fact of life for firms in the airline, entertainment, hotel, medical, legal, and professional services industries. Firms that offer goods also often segment their market between wholesale and retail buyers and between business, educational, not-for-profit, and government customers.

Requirements for Profitable Price Discrimination

price discrimination
A pricing practice that sets prices in different markets that are not related to differences in costs

Price discrimination occurs whenever different classes of customers are charged different markups for the same product. Price discrimination occurs when different customers are charged the same price despite underlying cost differences, and when price differentials fail to reflect cost discrepancies.

For price discrimination to be profitable, different price elasticities of demand must exist in the various submarkets. Unless price elasticities differ among submarkets, there is no point in segmenting the market. With identical price elasticities and identical marginal costs, profit-maximizing pricing policy calls for the same price and markup to be charged in all market segments. A **market segment** is a division or fragment of the overall market with unique demand or cost characteristics. For example, wholesale customers tend to buy in large quantities, are familiar with product costs and characteristics, and are well-informed about available alternatives. Wholesale buyers are highly price sensitive. Conversely, retail customers tend to buy in small quantities, are sometimes poorly informed about product costs and characteristics, and are often ignorant about available alternatives. As a group, retail customers are often less price sensitive than wholesale buyers. Markups charged to retail customers usually exceed those charged to wholesale buyers.

market segment
A division or fragment of the overall market with essentially unique characteristics

For price discrimination to be profitable, the firm must also be able to efficiently identify relevant submarkets and prevent transfers among affected customers. Detailed information must be obtained and monitored concerning customer buying habits, product preferences, and price sensitivity. Just as important, the price-discriminating firm must be able to monitor customer buying patterns to prevent reselling among customer subgroups. A highly profitable market segmentation between wholesale and retail customers can be effectively undermined if retail buyers are able to obtain discounts through willing wholesalers. Similarly, price discrimination among buyers in different parts of the country can be undermined if customers are able to resell in high-margin territories those products obtained in bargain locales.

Role Played by Consumers' Surplus

consumers' surplus
The value to customers of goods and services above and beyond the amount they pay sellers

The underlying motive for price discrimination can be understood using the concept of **consumers' surplus**. Consumers' surplus is the value of purchased goods and services above and beyond the amount paid to sellers. To illustrate, consider Figure 12.1, in which a market equilibrium price/output combination of P^* and Q^* is shown. The total value of output to customers is given by the area under the demand curve, or area $0ABQ^*$. Because the total revenue paid to producers is price times quantity, equal to area $0P^*BQ^*$, the area P^*AB represents the value of output above the amount paid to producers—that is, the consumers' surplus. For example, if a given customer is willing to pay $200 for a certain overcoat but is able to obtain a bargain price of $150, the buyer enjoys $50 worth of consumers' surplus. If another customer places a value of only $150 on the overcoat, he or she would enjoy no consumers' surplus following a purchase for $150.

Consumers' surplus arises because individual consumers place different values on goods and services. Customers that place a relatively high value on a product will pay high prices; customers that place a relatively low value on a product are only willing to pay low prices. As one proceeds from point A downward along the market marginal curve in Figure 12.1, customers that place a progressively lower marginal value on the product enter the market. At low prices, both high-value and low-value customers are buyers; at high prices, only customers that place a relatively high value on a given product are buyers.

When product value differs greatly among various groups of customers, a motive for price discrimination is created. By charging higher prices to customers with a high marginal value of consumption, revenues will increase without affecting costs. Sellers with the ability to vary prices according to the value placed on their products by buyers are able to capture at least

FIGURE 12.1

Consumers' Surplus

Consumers' surplus is shown by the area *P*AB* and represents the value of output to consumers above and beyond the amount they pay to producers.

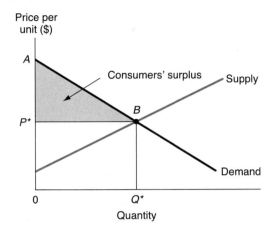

some of the value represented by consumers' surplus. Such price discrimination will always increase profits because it allows the firm to increase total revenue without affecting costs. A firm that is precise in its price discrimination always charges the maximum each market segment is willing to pay. Price discrimination is charging what the market will bear.

Finally, it is important to recognize that price discrimination does not carry any evil connotation in a moral sense. In some circumstances, price discrimination leads to lower prices for some customer groups and to a wider availability of goods and services. For example, a municipal bus company might charge lower prices for the elderly and the handicapped. In such circumstances, the bus company is price discriminating in favor of elderly and handicapped riders and against other customers. This type of price discrimination provides elderly and handicapped customers a greater opportunity to ride the bus. Because of incremental revenues provided by elderly and handicapped riders, the bus company may also be able to offer routes that could not be supported by revenues from full-fare customers alone, or it may be able to operate with a lower taxpayer subsidy.

Degrees of Price Discrimination

The extent to which a firm can engage in price discrimination is classified into three major categories. Under **first-degree price discrimination**, the firm extracts the maximum amount each customer is willing to pay for its products. Each unit is priced separately at the price indicated along each product demand curve. Such pricing precision is rare because it requires that sellers know the maximum price each buyer is willing to pay for each unit of output. Purchase decisions must also be monitored closely to prevent reselling among customers. Although first-degree price discrimination is uncommon, it has the potential to emerge in any market where discounts from posted prices are standard and effective prices are individually negotiated between buyers and sellers. When sellers possess a significant amount of market power, consumer purchases of big-ticket items such as appliances, automobiles, homes, and professional services all have the potential to involve first-degree price discrimination.

Second-degree price discrimination, a more frequently employed type of price discrimination, involves setting prices on the basis of the quantity purchased. Bulk rates are typically set with high prices and markups charged for the first unit or block of units purchased, but

first-degree price discrimination
Charging different prices to each customer

second-degree price discrimination
Charging different prices based on use rates or quantities purchased

progressively greater discounts are offered for greater quantities. Quantity discounts that lead to lower markups for large versus small customers are a common means of discriminating in price between retail and wholesale customers. Book publishers often charge full price for small purchases but offer 40 percent to 50 percent off list prices when 20 or more units are purchased. Public utilities, such as electric companies, gas companies, and water companies, also frequently charge block rates that are discriminatory. Consumers pay a relatively high markup for residential service, whereas commercial and industrial customers pay relatively low markups. Office equipment such as copy machines and servers (mainframe computers) are other examples of products for which second-degree price discrimination is practiced, especially when time sharing among customers is involved.

third-degree price discrimination
Charging different prices to each customer class

The most commonly observed form of price discrimination, **third-degree price discrimination**, results when a firm separates its customers into several classes and sets a different price for each customer class. Customer classifications can be based on for-profit or not-for-profit status, regional location, or customer age. *Barron's, Forbes, The Wall Street Journal,* and other publishers routinely offer educational discounts that can be in excess of 30 percent to 40 percent off list prices. These publishers are eager to penetrate the classroom on the assumption that student users will become loyal future customers. Auto companies, personal computer manufacturers, and others also prominently feature educational discounts as part of their marketing strategy. Many hospitals also offer price discounts to various patient groups. If unemployed and uninsured patients are routinely charged only what they can easily afford to pay for medical service, whereas employed and insured medical patients are charged maximum allowable rates, the hospital is price discriminating in favor of the unemployed and against the employed. Widespread price discounts for senior citizens represent a form of price discrimination in favor of older customers but against younger customers.

PRICE DISCRIMINATION EXAMPLE

Price discrimination is profitable because it allows the firm to enhance revenues without increasing costs. It is an effective means for increasing profits because it allows the firm to more closely match marginal revenues and marginal costs. A firm that can segment its market maximizes profits by operating at the point where marginal revenue equals marginal cost in each market segment. A detailed example is a helpful means for illustrating this process.

Price/Output Determination

Suppose that Midwest State University (MSU) wants to reduce the athletic department's operating deficit and increase student attendance at home football games. To achieve these objectives, a new two-tier pricing structure for season football tickets is being considered.

A market survey conducted by the school suggests the following market demand and marginal revenue relations:

Public Demand	**Student Demand**
$P_P = \$225 - \$0.005Q_P$	$P_S = \$125 - \$0.00125Q_S$
$MR_P = \partial TR_P/\partial Q_P = \$225 - \$0.01Q_P$	$MR_S = \partial TR_S/\partial Q_S = \$125 - \$0.0025Q_S$

From these market demand and marginal revenue curves, it is obvious that the general public is willing to pay higher prices than are students. The general public is willing to purchase tickets up to a market price of $225, above which point market demand equals zero. Students are willing to enter the market only at ticket prices below $125.

During recent years, the football program has run on an operating budget of $1.5 million per year. This budget covers fixed salary, recruiting, insurance, and facility-maintenance expenses. In addition to these fixed expenses, the university incurs variable ticket-handling, facility-cleaning, insurance, and security costs of $25 per season ticketholder. The resulting total cost and marginal cost functions are

$$TC = \$1,500,000 + \$25Q$$
$$MC = \partial TC/\partial Q = \$25$$

What are the optimal football ticket prices and quantities for each market, assuming that MSU adopts a new season ticket pricing policy featuring student discounts? To answer this question, one must realize that because $MC = \$25$, the athletic department's operating deficit is minimized by setting $MR = MC = \$25$ in each market segment and solving for Q. This is also the profit-maximizing strategy for the football program. Therefore

Public Demand

$$MR_P = MC$$
$$\$225 - \$0.01Q_P = \$25$$
$$\$0.01Q_P = \$200$$
$$Q_P = 20,000$$

and

$$P_P = \$225 - \$0.005(20,000)$$
$$= \$125$$

Student Demand

$$MR_S = MC$$
$$\$125 - \$0.0025Q_S = \$25$$
$$\$0.0025Q_S = \$100$$
$$Q_S = 40,000$$

and

$$P_S = \$125 - \$0.00125(40,000)$$
$$= \$75$$

The football program's resulting total operating surplus (profit) is

$$
\begin{aligned}
\text{Operating Surplus (Profit)} &= TR_P + TR_S - TC \\
&= \$125(20,000) + \$75(40,000) \\
&\quad - \$1,500,000 - \$25(60,000) \\
&= \$2.5 \text{ million}
\end{aligned}
$$

To summarize, the optimal price/output combination with price discrimination is 20,000 in unit sales to the general public at a price of $125 and 40,000 in unit sales to students at a price of $75. This two-tier pricing practice results in an optimal operating surplus (profit) of $2.5 million.

Comparison with the One-Price Alternative

To gauge the implications of this new two-tier ticket pricing practice, it is interesting to contrast the resulting price/output and surplus levels with those that would result if MSU maintained its current one-price ticket policy.

If tickets are offered to students and the general public at the same price, the total amount of ticket demand equals the sum of student plus general public demand. The student and general public market demand curves are

$$Q_P = 45,000 - 200P_P \text{ and } Q_S = 100,000 - 800P_S$$

Under the assumption $P_P = P_S$, total demand (Q_T) equals

$$Q_T = Q_P + Q_S$$
$$= 145,000 - 1,000P$$

and

$$P = \$145 - \$0.001Q$$

which implies that

$$MR = \partial TR/\partial Q = \$145 - \$0.002Q$$

These aggregate student-plus-general-public market demand and marginal revenue curves hold only for prices below \$125, a level at which both the general public and students purchase tickets. For prices above \$125, only nonstudent purchasers buy tickets, and the public demand curve $P_P = \$225 - \$0.005Q_P$ represents total market demand as well. This causes the actual total demand curve to be kinked at a price of \$125, as shown in Figure 12.2.

The uniform season ticket price that maximizes operating surplus (or profits) is found by setting $MR = MC$ for the total market and solving for Q:

$$MR = MC$$
$$\$145 - \$0.002Q = \$25$$
$$\$0.002Q = \$120$$
$$Q = 60,000$$
$$P = \$145 - \$0.001(60,000)$$
$$= \$85$$

and

$$Q_P = 45,000 - 200(\$85) \qquad\qquad Q_S = 100,000 - 800(\$85)$$
$$= 28,000 \qquad\qquad\qquad\qquad = 32,000$$

$$\text{Operating surplus (profit)} = TR - TC$$
$$= \$85(60,000) - \$1,500,000$$
$$- \$25(60,000)$$
$$= \$2.1 \text{ million}$$

Observe that the total number of tickets sold equals 60,000 under both the two-tier and the single-price policies. This results because the marginal cost of a ticket is the same under each scenario. Ticket-pricing policies featuring student discounts increase student attendance from

32,000 to 40,000 and maximize the football program's operating surplus at $2.5 million (rather than $2.1 million). It is the preferred pricing policy when viewed from MSU's perspective. However, such price discrimination creates both "winners" and "losers." Winners following adoption of student discounts include students and MSU. Losers include members of the general public, who pay higher football ticket prices or find themselves priced out of the market.

Graphic Illustration

The MSU pricing problem and the concept of price discrimination can be illustrated graphically. Figure 12.2 shows demand curves for the general public in part (a) and for students in part (b). The aggregate demand curve in part (c) represents the horizontal sum of the quantities demanded at each price in the public and student markets. The associated marginal revenue curve, MR_{P+S}, has a similar interpretation. For example, marginal revenue equals $25 at an attendance level of 20,000 in the public market and $25 at an attendance level of 40,000 in the student market. Accordingly, one point on the total marginal revenue curve represents output of 60,000 units and marginal revenue of $25. From a cost standpoint, it does not matter whether tickets are sold to the public or to students. The single marginal cost curve $MC = \$25$ applies to each market.

Graphically solving this pricing problem is a two-part process. The profit-maximizing total output level must first be determined, and then this output must be allocated between submarkets. Profit maximization occurs at the aggregate output level at which marginal revenue and marginal cost are equal. Figure 12.2(c) shows a profit-maximizing output of 60,000 tickets, where marginal cost and marginal revenue both equal $25. Proper allocation of total output between the two submarkets is determined graphically by drawing a horizontal line to indicate that $25 is the marginal cost in each market at the indicated aggregate output level. The intersection of this horizontal line with the marginal revenue curve in each submarket indicates the optimal distribution of sales and pricing structure. In this example, profits are maximized at an attendance (output) level of 60,000, selling 20,000 tickets to the public at a price of $125 and 40,000 tickets to students at a price of $75.

FIGURE 12.2

Price Discrimination for an Identical Product Sold in Two Markets

Price discrimination results in higher prices for market segments with low price elasticity (public) and lower prices for market segments with high price elasticity (students).

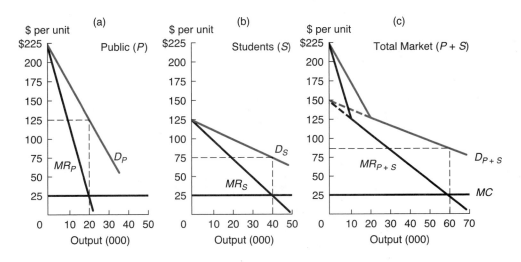

MULTIPLE-UNIT PRICING STRATEGIES

When products have different values for different customers, profits can sometimes be enhanced by using multiple-unit pricing strategies. With multiple-unit pricing, all customers typically face the same pricing schedule, but the price paid is determined by the value to consumers of the total amount purchased. Unlike single-unit pricing, where all customers are charged a unit price that sets $MR = MC$, multiple-unit pricing can result in some combination of per-unit and "lump sum" fees. Like price discrimination, multiple-unit pricing strategies have proven an effective means for extracting consumers' surplus for the benefit of producers.

Two-Part Pricing

two-part pricing
A per-unit fee equal to marginal cost, plus a fixed fee equal to the amount of consumers' surplus generated at that price

Athletic clubs, time-share vacation resorts, golf courses, and a wide variety of "membership organizations" offer goods and services using two-part pricing. A common **two-part pricing** technique is to charge all customers a fixed "membership" fee per month or per year, plus a per-unit usage charge. In general, a firm can enhance profits by charging each customer a per-unit fee equal to marginal cost, plus a fixed fee equal to the amount of consumers' surplus generated at that per-unit fee.

In the case of golf course memberships, for example, two-part pricing often consists of a large lifetime membership fee plus "greens fees" charged for each round of golf played. To illustrate how such a two-part pricing practice might prove profitable, assume that an individual avid golfer's demand and marginal revenue curves can be written

$$P = \$100 - \$1Q$$
$$MR = \partial TR / \partial Q = \$100 - \$2Q$$

where P is the price of a single round of golf, and Q is the number of rounds played during a given year. For simplicity, also assume that the marginal cost of a round of golf is $20, and that fixed costs are nil. This gives the following total and marginal cost relations:

$$TC = \$20Q$$
$$MC = \partial TC / \partial Q = \$20$$

As shown in Figure 12.3(a), the profit-maximizing single-unit price for a monopoly golf course is found by setting $MR = MC$, where

$$MR = MC$$
$$\$100 - \$2Q = \$20$$
$$2Q = 80$$
$$Q = 40$$

At the profit-maximizing quantity of 40, the optimal single-unit price is $60 and total profits equal $1,600 because

$$P = \$100 - \$1(40)$$
$$= \$60$$
$$\pi = TR - TC$$
$$= \$60(40) - \$20(40)$$
$$= \$1,600$$

Notice from Figure 12.3 (a) that the value of consumers' surplus at a standard per-unit price is equal to the region under the demand curve that lies above the profit-maximizing price of $60.

FIGURE 12.3

Monopoly Per-Unit Pricing Versus Two-Part Pricing

When product value varies according to the amount purchased, profits can be enhanced by setting price equal to marginal cost, plus a fee equal to consumers' surplus at that activity level.

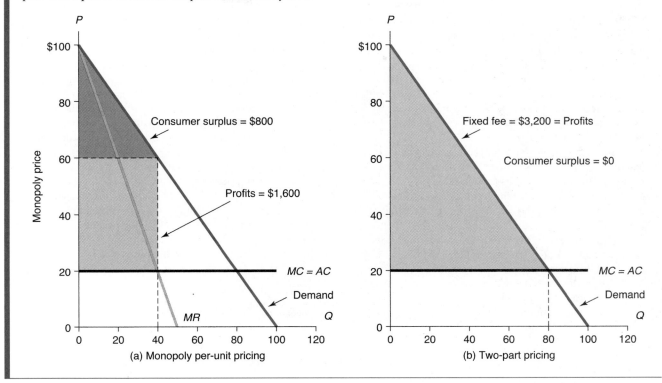

(a) Monopoly per-unit pricing

(b) Two-part pricing

Because the area of a such a triangle is one-half the value of the base times the height, the value of consumers' surplus equals

$$\text{Consumers' Surplus} = \frac{1}{2}\,[(40 \times (\$100 - \$60)]$$
$$= \$800$$

In words, this means that at a single-unit price of $60, such an individual will choose to play 40 rounds of golf, resulting in total revenues of $2,400 and total profits of $1,600 for the golf course. The fact that consumers' surplus equals $800 means that the avid golfer in question would have been willing to pay an additional $800 to play these 40 rounds of golf. This is an amount above and beyond the $2,400 paid. The avid golfer received a real bargain.

As an alternative to charging a single-unit price of $60 per round, consider the profits that could be earned using a two-part pricing scheme. To maximize profits, the golf course would choose to charge a per-unit price that equals marginal cost, plus a fixed fee equal to the amount of consumers' surplus received by each consumer at this price. Remember, in Figure 12.3, that the value of consumers' surplus is equal to the region under the demand curve that lies above the per-unit price. When the per-unit price is set equal to marginal cost, $P = \$20$ and $Q = 80$ because

$$P = MC$$
$$\$100 - \$1Q = \$20$$
$$Q = 80$$

At the per-unit price of $20 and output level of 80, the value of consumers' surplus equals

Do Colleges Price Discriminate?

Most college students receive financial aid. At many colleges, the average financial aid recipient comes from a family with annual income in excess of $50,000—and many came from families with incomes exceeding $100,000. As a result, some economists suggest that college financial aid is not about "needy students" but is instead a means of price discrimination designed to extract the largest net amount from students, their families, and the government.

Some economists argue that colleges levy a list price (tuition) set far above what most people can pay and then offer varying discounts (financial aid) so that each customer is charged what the traffic will bear. Financial aid is available when the cost of college exceeds the "expected family contribution," a measure based on family income, assets, the number of children, and so on. Even a small college could lose millions of dollars in federal aid if it kept tuition affordable. According to critics, federal subsidies and virtual exemption from antitrust laws have produced skyrocketing college costs and price discrimination. Economist Milton Friedman estimates

that colleges could operate at a profit by charging half of what the Ivy League schools charge.

In defense of current financial aid practices, school administrators point out that many would be unable to afford college without some cross-subsidization among students. Private schools also use endowment income to supplement student tuition and fees, whereas public colleges and universities enjoy substantial tax-revenue income. Even the premiums paid by out-of-state students at leading state universities fail to cover fully allocated costs per student. However, average costs may not be relevant for pricing purposes. The marginal cost per student is often nearly zero, and even very low net tuition-plus-fee income can often make a significant contribution to overhead. From an economic perspective, the pricing practices of colleges and universities may in fact be consistent with the theory of price discrimination.

See: Lynn Asinof, "Colleges Clamp Down on Financial Aid, Making Haggling a Difficult Approach," *The Wall Street Journal Online*, April 11, 2002 (http://online.wsj.com).

$$\text{Consumers' Surplus} = \frac{1}{2}\left[(80 \times (\$100 - \$20)\right]$$
$$= \$3,200$$

Thus, $3,200 is the maximum membership fee the golfer in question would pay to play 80 rounds of golf per year when modest additional "greens fees" of $20 per round are charged. It follows that the profit-maximizing two-part pricing scheme is to charge each player an annual membership fee of $3,200 per year plus "greens fees" of $20 per round played. Total golf course revenues of $4,800 represent the full value derived from playing 80 rounds of golf per year, cover marginal costs of $1,600 (= $20 × 80), and result in a $3,200 profit for the golf course.

Throughout this discussion it has implicitly been assumed that the seller must enjoy at least some market power in order to institute any two-part pricing scheme. Otherwise, competitors would undercut the amount of annual membership fees, and per-unit prices would converge on marginal costs. Therefore, it is unsurprising that high golf membership fees tend to be most common in urban areas where conveniently located golf courses are in short supply. In outlying or rural areas, where restrictions on the location of new golf courses are less stringent, large membership fees tend to be relatively rare.

Bundle Pricing

bundle pricing
A lump sum amount equal to the total area under the demand curve when $P = MC$

Another way firms with market power enhance profits is by a variant of two-part pricing called **bundle pricing**. If you've ever purchased a 12-pack of soft drinks, a year's supply of tax preparation services, or bought a "two-for-the-price-of-one" special, you have firsthand experience with the bundle pricing concept. When significant consumers' surplus exists, profits can be enhanced if products are purchased together as a single package or bundle of goods or services. Bundles can be of a single product, like soft drinks or legal services, or they can be comprised of closely related goods and services. For example, car manufacturers often bundle "luxury packages" comprised of new car options like power steering, power brakes, automatic transmissions, tinted glass, and so on. Similarly, car dealers often bundle services, like oil changes, transmission fluid changes, radiator flushes, and tune-ups at a "special package price."

In the case of a single product sold in multiple-unit bundles, the optimal bundle price is derived in a manner similar to the optimal two-part price calculation described in Figure 12.3. As in the case of two-part pricing, the optimal level of output is determined by setting price equal to marginal cost and solving for quantity. Then, the optimal bundle price is a single lump sum amount equal to the total area under the demand curve at that point. In Figure 12.3(b), for example, the optimal bundle price of $4,800 would include the total value of consumers' surplus generated with a single per-unit price (or $3,200), plus total cost (or $1,600).

Optimal pricing for bundles of related but not identical products is figured in an analogous manner. Again, the total amount charged equals the value of the total area under the demand curve at the optimal output level, where output is defined as a bundle of related goods or services. As in the case of two-part pricing, the optimal level of output is determined by setting price equal to marginal cost and solving for quantity. Then, the optimal bundle price is simply a lump sum amount equal to the total area under the demand curve at that activity level. In the case of related but not identical products, bundle pricing is sometimes used because firms are not able to precisely determine the amounts different consumers are willing to pay for different products. If managers had precise information about the value of each individual product for each individual consumer, the firm could earn even higher profits by precisely tying the price charged to the value derived by each customer.

MULTIPLE-PRODUCT PRICING

It is difficult to think of a firm that does not produce a variety of products. Almost all companies produce multiple models, styles, or sizes of output, and each of these variations can represent a separate product for pricing purposes. Although multiple-product pricing requires the same basic analysis as for a single product, the analysis is complicated by demand and production interrelations.

Demand Interrelations

Demand interrelations arise because of competition or complementarity among various products or product lines. If products are interrelated, either as substitutes or complements, a change in the price of one affects demand for the other. Multiple-product pricing decisions must reflect such influences. In the case of a two-product firm, the marginal revenue functions for each product can be written as

(12.12)
$$MR_A = \frac{\partial TR}{\partial Q_A} = \frac{\partial TR_A}{\partial Q_A} + \frac{\partial TR_B}{\partial Q_A}$$

(12.13)
$$MR_B = \frac{\partial TR}{\partial Q_B} = \frac{\partial TR_B}{\partial Q_B} + \frac{\partial TR_A}{\partial Q_B}$$

The first term on the right side of each equation represents the marginal revenue directly associated with each product. The second term depicts the indirect marginal revenue associated with each product and indicates the change in revenues due to a change in sales of the alternative product. For example, $\partial TR_B/\partial Q_A$ in Equation 12.12 shows the effect on product B revenues of an additional unit sold of product A. Likewise, $\partial TR_A/\partial Q_B$ in Equation 12.13 represents the change in revenues received from product A when an additional unit of product B is sold.

Cross-marginal revenue terms that reflect demand interrelations can be positive or negative. For complementary products, the net effect is positive because increased sales of one product lead to increased revenues from another. For substitute products, increased sales of one product reduce demand for another, and the cross-marginal revenue term is negative. Accurate price determination in the case of multiple products requires a complete analysis of pricing decision effects. This often means that optimal pricing requires an application of incremental analysis to ensure that the total implications of pricing decisions are reflected.

Production Interrelations

by-product

Output that is customarily produced as a direct result of an increase in the production of some other output

Whereas many products are related to one another through demand relationships, others are related in terms of the production process. A **by-product** is any output that is customarily produced as a direct result of an increase in the production of some other output. Although it is common to think of by-products as resulting only from physical production processes, they are also generated in the process of providing services. One of the primary reasons why top accounting firms have become such a leading force in the management information systems (MIS) consulting business is that information generated in the auditing process has natural MIS implications, and vice versa. In this way, auditing and consulting services are joint products produced in variable proportions. The cost of providing each service depends greatly on the extent to which the other is also provided. Given the efficiencies of joint production, it is common for an accounting firm's auditing clients to also become MIS consulting clients.

Multiple products are produced in variable proportions for a wide range of goods and services. In the refining process for crude oil, gasoline, diesel fuel, heating oil, and other products are produced in variable proportions. The cost and availability of any single by-product depends on the demand for others. By-products are also sometimes the unintended or unavoidable consequence of producing certain goods. When lumber is produced, scrap bark and sawdust are also created for use in gardening and paper production. When paper is produced, residual chemicals and polluted water are created that must be treated and recycled. Indeed, pollution can be thought of as the necessary by-product of many production processes. Because pollution is, by definition, a "bad" with harmful social consequences rather than a "good" with socially redeeming value, production processes must often be altered to minimize this type of negative joint product.

Production interrelations are sometimes so strong that the degree of jointness in production is relatively constant. For example, many agricultural products are jointly produced in a fixed ratio. Wheat and straw, beef and hides, milk and butter are all produced in relatively fixed proportions. In mining, gold and copper, silver and lead, and other precious metals and minerals are often produced jointly in fixed proportions. Appropriate pricing and production decisions are possible only when such interrelations are accurately reflected.

Joint Products Produced in Variable Proportions

Firms can often vary the proportions in which joint products are created. Even the classic example of fixed proportions in the joint production of beef and hides holds only over short periods: Leaner or heavier cattle can be bred to provide differing proportions of these two products. When the proportions of joint output can be varied, it is possible to construct separate marginal cost relations for each product.

The marginal cost of either joint product produced in variable proportions equals the increase in total costs associated with a one-unit increase in that product, holding constant the quantity of the other joint product produced. Optimal price/output determination for joint products in this case requires a simultaneous solution of marginal cost and marginal revenue relations. The firm maximizes profit by operating at the output level where the marginal cost of producing each joint product just equals the marginal revenue it generates. The profit-maximizing combination of joint products A and B, for example, occurs at the output level where $MR_A = MC_B$ and $MR_B = MC_B$.

It is important to note, however, that although it is possible to determine the separate marginal costs of goods produced in variable proportions, it is impossible to determine their indi-

common costs

Expenses that are necessary for manufacture of a joint product

vidual average costs. This is because **common costs** are expenses necessary for manufacture of a joint product. Common costs of production—raw material and equipment costs, management expenses, and other overhead—cannot be allocated to each individual by-product on any economically sound basis. Only costs that can be separately identified with a specific by-product can be allocated. For example, tanning costs for hides and refrigeration costs for beef are separate identifiable costs of each by-product. Feed costs are common and cannot be allocated between hide and beef production. Any allocation of common costs is wrong and arbitrary.

Joint Products Produced in Fixed Proportions

An interesting case of joint production is that of by-products produced in fixed proportions. Products that must be produced in fixed proportions should be considered as a package or bundle of output. When by-products are jointly produced in fixed proportions, all costs are common, and there is no economically sound method of cost allocation. Optimal price/output determination for output produced in fixed proportions requires analysis of the relation between marginal revenue and marginal cost for the combined output package. As long as the sum of marginal revenues obtained from all by-products is greater than the marginal cost of production, the firm gains by expanding output.

Figure 12.4 illustrates the pricing problem for two products produced in fixed proportions. Demand and marginal revenue curves for each by-product and the single marginal cost curve for production of the combined output package are shown. Vertical summation of the two marginal revenue curves indicates the total marginal revenue generated by both by-products. Marginal revenue curves are summed vertically because each unit of output

FIGURE 12.4

Optimal Pricing for Joint Products Produced in Fixed Proportions

For joint products produced in fixed proportions, the optimal activity level occurs at the point where the marginal revenues derived from both products (MR_T) equal the marginal cost of production.

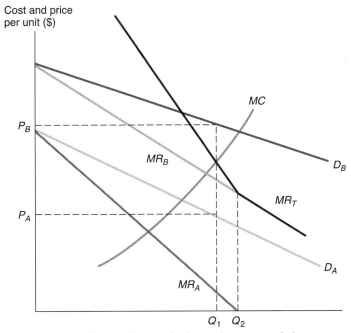

provides revenues from the sale of both by-products. The intersection of the total marginal revenue curve MR_T with the marginal cost curve identifies the profit-maximizing output level.

The optimal price for each by-product is determined by the intersection of a vertical line at the profit-maximizing output level with each by-product's demand curve. Q_1 represents the optimal quantity of the output package to be produced, and P_A and P_B are the prices to be charged for each by-product.

Notice that the MR_T curve in Figure 12.4 coincides with the marginal revenue curve for product B at all output quantities greater than Q_2. This is because MR_A becomes negative at that point, and the firm would not sell more than the quantity of product A represented by output package Q_2. The total revenue generated by product A is maximized at output Q_2; sales of any larger quantity of product A would reduce revenues and profits.

If the marginal cost curve for the output package intersects the total marginal revenue curve to the right of Q_2, profit maximization requires that the firm raise output up to this point of intersection. At that point, product B must be priced as indicated by its demand and marginal revenue curves. Because product B sales offer the sole motivation for production beyond the Q_2 level, the marginal revenue generated from product B sales must be sufficient to cover the marginal costs of producing the entire output package. In this instance, profit maximization requires that $MR_B = MC$. Beyond the Q_2 level, the marginal cost of product A is zero; product A is the unavoidable by-product of product B production. Beyond the Q_2 level, the price of product A is set in order to maximize profits in that $MR_A = MC_A = 0$. This pricing situation is illustrated in Figure 12.5, which shows the same demand and marginal revenue curves presented in Figure 12.4, along with a new marginal cost curve. The optimal output quantity is Q_3, determined by the intersection of the marginal cost curve and the total marginal revenue

FIGURE 12.5

Optimal Pricing for Joint Products Produced in Fixed Proportions with Excess Production of One Product

When all of by-product A cannot be sold at a price that generates positive marginal revenue, its sales will be limited to the point where $MR_A = 0$. Excess production, shown as $Q_3 - Q_2$, will be destroyed or otherwise held off the market.

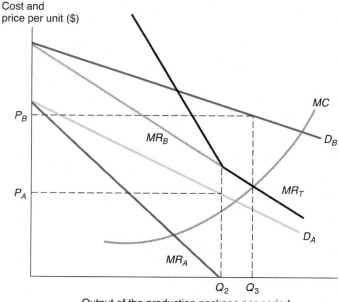

Corn Growers Discover Oil!

Sugar-rich kernels of corn can be used to produce ethanol, a clean-burning fuel used in automobiles. Although the technology for ethanol production from corn has been available since the 1980s, recent strides have made the technology much more economical. Until recently, it took 1 bushel of corn to produce 2.6 gallons of ethanol. New refining methods now allow 2.8 gallons of ethanol to be produced from a single bushel of corn.

At present, most commercial ethanol operations are located in the Midwest near major corn-growing areas. In the future, the most attractive markets for expanding ethanol production may be near important population centers where air pollution is a major concern. Federal mandates require much of California, Long Island, New York City, and the lower Hudson Valley to reduce air pollution by using reformulated gas that contains a higher oxygen level. Although the natural gas derivative MTBE is a popular additive for reformulated gasoline, MTBE is also a carcinogen found to be a serious contaminant in drinking water. The New York legislature and governor

have approved a phase-out of MTBE in New York state by 2004. California has banned MTBE as of the end of 2002, and there are similar calls to do so nationally.

With MTBE on its way out, corn growers argue that ethanol is the next best available additive. Their argument is bolstered by the fact that ethanol mixed with gasoline not only reduces air pollution by creating a cleaner burning mixture, but that ethanol production also reduces our dependence on imported oil. Ethanol production creates a market for surplus farm products and thereby helps alleviate rural poverty. Therefore, when important byproducts from ethanol production are mentioned, dried distillers grain, an excellent livestock feed, is seldom discussed. For many, ethanol production is inherently attractive because creating automobile fuel from corn creates important social and environmental byproducts.

See: Dow Jones Newswires,"New York Corn Growers Push for Ethanol Processing Plant," *The Wall Street Journal Online*, November 9, 2001 (http://online.wsj.com).

---

curve. Product *B* is sold in the amount indicated by output package Q_3 and is priced at P_B. The sales quantity of product *A* is limited to the amount in output Q_2 and is priced at P_A. The excess quantity of product *A* produced, shown as $Q_3 - Q_2$, must be destroyed or otherwise kept out of the market so that its price and total revenue is not lowered below that indicated at Q_2.

An example of joint output that is sometimes destroyed or otherwise held off the market is provided by sliced pineapple and pineapple juice; juice is produced as a by-product as pineapples are peeled and sliced. Some years ago, an excessive amount of pineapple juice was produced, and rather than put it on the market and depress prices, the excess was destroyed. Seeing a profit-making opportunity, Dole, Del Monte, and other producers advertised heavily to shift the demand curve for pineapple juice outward. New products were also created, such as pineapple-grapefruit juice, to spur demand for the waste by-product. Canning machinery was also improved to reduce the amount of juice. Today, little if any pineapple excess juice by-product is produced. Similarly, firms in many other industries have discovered new and valuable uses for previously discarded by-products.

EXAMPLE OF JOINT PRODUCT PRICING

A graphic approach offers a useful introduction to the solution of joint product pricing problems, but many real-world problems require a more detailed analytic treatment. An example of a price/output decision for two products produced in fixed proportions will help clarify the technique.

Joint Products Without Excess By-Product

The Vancouver Paper Company, located in Vancouver, British Columbia, produces newsprint and packaging materials in a fixed 1:1 ratio, or 1 ton of packaging materials per 1 ton of newsprint.

These two products, A (newsprint) and B (packaging materials), are produced in equal quantities because newsprint production leaves scrap by-product that is useful only in the production of lower-grade packaging materials. The total and marginal cost functions for Vancouver can be written

$$TC = \$2,000,000 + \$50Q + \$0.01Q^2$$
$$MC = \partial TC/\partial Q = \$50 + \$0.02Q$$

where Q is a composite package or bundle of output consisting of 1 ton of product A and 1 ton of product B. Given current market conditions, demand and marginal revenue curves for each product are as follows:

Newsprint	Packaging Materials
$P_A = \$400 - \$0.01Q_A$	$P_B = \$350 - \$0.015Q_B$
$MR_A = \partial TR_A/\partial Q_A = \$400 - \$0.02Q_A$	$MR_B = \partial TR_B/\partial Q_B = \$350 - \$0.03Q_B$

For each unit of Q produced, the firm obtains one unit of product A and one unit of product B for sale to customers. The revenue derived from the production and sale of one unit of Q is composed of revenues from the sales of one unit of product A plus one unit of product B. Therefore, the total revenue function is merely a sum of the revenue functions for products A and B:

$$TR = TR_A + TR_B$$
$$= P_AQ_A + P_BQ_B$$

Substituting for P_A and P_B results in the total revenue function

$$TR = (\$400 - \$0.01Q_A)Q_A + (\$350 - \$0.015Q_B)Q_B$$
$$= \$400Q_A - \$0.01Q_A{}^2 + \$350Q_B - \$0.015Q^2{}_B$$

Because one unit of product A and one unit of product B are contained in each unit of Q, $Q_A = Q_B = Q$. This allows substitution of Q for Q_A and Q_B to develop a total revenue function in terms of Q, the unit of production:

$$TR = \$400Q - \$0.01Q^2 + \$350Q - \$0.015Q^2$$
$$= \$750Q - \$0.025Q^2$$

This total revenue function assumes that all quantities of product A and B produced are also sold. It assumes no dumping or withholding from the market for either product. It is the appropriate total revenue function if, as in Figure 12.4, the marginal revenues of both products are positive at the profit-maximizing output level. When this occurs, revenues from each product contribute toward covering marginal costs.

The profit-maximizing output level is found by setting $MR = MC$ and solving for Q:

$$MR = MC$$
$$\$750 - \$0.05Q = \$50 + \$0.02Q$$
$$0.07Q = 700$$
$$Q = 10{,}000 \text{ units}$$

At the activity level $Q = 10,000$ units, marginal revenues for each product are positive:

$$MR_A = \$400 - \$0.02Q_A$$
$$= \$400 - \$0.02(10,000)$$
$$= \$200 \text{ (at 10,000 Units)}$$

$$MR_B = \$350 - \$0.03Q_B$$
$$= \$350 - \$0.03(10,000)$$
$$= \$50 \text{ (at 10,000 Units)}$$

Each product makes a positive contribution toward covering the marginal cost of production, where

$$MC = \$50 + \$0.02Q$$
$$= \$50 + \$0.02(10,000)$$
$$= \$250$$

There is no reason to expand or reduce production because $MR = MR_A + MR_B = MC = \$250$, and each product generates positive marginal revenues.

Prices for each product and total profits for Vancouver can be calculated from the demand and total profit functions:

$$P_A = \$400 - \$0.01Q_A$$
$$= \$400 - \$0.01(10,000)$$
$$= \$300$$

$$P_B = \$350 - \$0.015Q_B$$
$$= \$350 - \$0.015(10,000)$$
$$= \$200$$

and

$$\pi = P_A Q_A + P_B Q_B - TC$$
$$= \$300(10,000) + \$200(10,000) - \$2,000,000$$
$$- \$50(10,000) - \$0.01(10,000^2)$$
$$= \$1,500,000$$

Vancouver should produce 10,000 units of output and sell the resulting 10,000 units of product *A* at a price of \$300 per ton and 10,000 units of product *B* at a price of \$200 per ton. An optimum total profit of \$1.5 million is earned at this activity level.

Joint Production with Excess By-Product (Dumping)

The determination of a profit-maximizing activity level is only slightly more complex if a downturn in demand for either product *A* or *B* causes marginal revenue for one product to be negative when all output produced is sold to the marketplace.

Suppose that an economic recession causes the demand for product *B* (packaging materials) to fall dramatically, while the demand for product *A* (newsprint) and marginal cost conditions hold steady. Assume new demand and marginal revenue relations for product *B* of

$$P'_B = \$290 - \$0.02Q_B$$
$$MR'_B = \partial TR'_B / \partial Q_B = \$290 - \$0.04Q_B$$

A dramatically lower price of \$90 per ton [= \$290 − \$0.02(10,000)] is now required to sell 10,000 units of product *B*. However, this price and activity level is suboptimal.

To see why, the profit-maximizing activity level must again be calculated, assuming that all output is sold. The new marginal revenue curve for *Q* is

$$MR = MR_A + MR'_B$$
$$= \$400 - \$0.02Q_A + \$290 - \$0.04Q_B$$
$$= \$690 - \$0.06Q$$

If all production is sold, the profit-maximizing level for output is found by setting $MR = MC$ and solving for Q:

$$
\begin{aligned}
MR &= MC \\
\$690 - \$0.06Q &= \$50 + \$0.02Q \\
0.08Q &= 640 \\
Q &= 8,000
\end{aligned}
$$

At $Q = 8,000$, the sum of marginal revenues derived from both by-products and the marginal cost of producing the combined output package each equal $210, because

$$
\begin{aligned}
MR &= \$690 - \$0.06Q \\
&= \$690 - \$0.06(8,000) \\
&= \$210
\end{aligned}
\qquad
\begin{aligned}
MC &= \$50 + \$0.02Q \\
&= \$50 + \$0.02(8,000) \\
&= \$210
\end{aligned}
$$

However, the marginal revenue of product B is no longer positive:

$$
\begin{aligned}
MR_A &= \$400 - \$0.02Q_A \\
&= \$400 - \$0.02(8,000) \\
&= \$240
\end{aligned}
\qquad
\begin{aligned}
MR'_B &= \$290 - \$0.04Q_B \\
&= \$290 - \$0.04(8,000) \\
&= -\$30
\end{aligned}
$$

Even though $MR = MC = \$210$, the marginal revenue of product B is negative at the $Q = 8,000$ activity level. This means that the price reduction necessary to sell the last unit of product B causes Vancouver's total revenue to decline by $30. Rather than sell product B at such unfavorable terms, Vancouver would prefer to withhold some from the marketplace. In contrast, Vancouver would like to produce and sell more than 8,000 units of product A because $MR_A > MC$ at the 8,000 unit activity level. It would be profitable for the company to expand production of Q just to increase sales of product A, even if it had to destroy or otherwise withhold from the market the unavoidable added production of product B.

Under these circumstances, set the marginal revenue of product A, the only product sold at the margin, equal to the marginal cost of production to find the profit-maximizing activity level:

$$
\begin{aligned}
MR_A &= MC \\
\$400 - \$0.02Q &= \$50 + \$0.02Q \\
\$0.04Q &= \$350 \\
Q &= 8,750 \text{ units}
\end{aligned}
$$

Under these circumstances, Vancouver should produce 8,750 units of $Q = Q_A = Q_B$. Because this activity level is based on the assumption that only product A is sold at the margin and that the marginal revenue of product A covers all marginal production costs, *the effective marginal cost of product B is zero*. As long as production is sufficient to provide 8,750 units of product A, 8,750 units of product B are also produced without any additional cost.

With an effective marginal cost of zero for product B, its contribution to firm profits is maximized by setting the marginal revenue of product B equal to zero (its effective marginal cost):

$$
\begin{aligned}
MR'_B &= MC_B \\
\$290 - \$0.04Q_B &= \$0 \\
\$0.04Q_B &= \$290 \\
Q_B &= 7,250
\end{aligned}
$$

Whereas a total of 8,750 units of Q should be produced, only 7,250 units of product B will be sold. The remaining 1,500 units of Q_B must be destroyed or otherwise withheld from the market.

Optimal prices and the maximum total profit for Vancouver are as follows:

$$P_A = \$400 - \$0.01Q_A$$
$$= \$400 - \$0.01(8,750)$$
$$= \$312.50$$

$$P'_B = \$290 - \$0.02Q_B$$
$$= \$290 - \$0.02(7,250)$$
$$= \$145$$

$$\pi = P_A Q_A + P'_B Q_B - TC$$
$$= \$312.50(8,750) + \$145(7,250) - \$2,000,000$$
$$- \$50(8,750) - \$0.01(8,750^2)$$
$$= \$582,500$$

No other price/output combination has the potential to generate as large a profit for Vancouver.

TRANSFER PRICING

Expanding markets brought about by improvements in communication and transportation, as well as falling trade barriers, have led to the development of large, multidivision firms that cut across national boundaries. A vexing challenge for many large corporations surrounds the need to set an appropriate price for the transfer of goods and services among divisions.

Transfer Pricing Problem

vertical relation
When the output of one division or company is the input to another

vertical integration
When a single company controls various links in the production chain from basic inputs to final output

The transfer pricing problem results from the difficulty of establishing profitable relationships among divisions of a single company when each separate business unit stands in **vertical relation** to the other. A vertical relation is one where the output of one division or company is the input to another. **Vertical integration** occurs when a single company controls various links in the production chain from basic inputs to final output. Media powerhouse AOL-Time Warner, Inc., is vertically integrated because it owns AOL, an Internet service provider (ISP) and cable TV systems, plus a number of programming properties in filmed entertainment (e.g., Warner Bros.) and television production (e.g., HBO, CNN), commonly referred to as content providers. Vertically integrated companies in this field own and operate the distribution network and the programming that is sold over that network.

transfer pricing
The pricing of products transferred among divisions of a firm

To combat the problems of coordinating large-scale enterprises that are vertically integrated, separate profit centers are typically established for each important product or product line. Despite obvious advantages, this decentralization has the potential to create problems. The most critical of these is the problem of **transfer pricing**, or the pricing of intermediate products transferred among divisions. To maximize profits for the vertically integrated firm, it is essential that a profit margin or markup only be charged at the final stage of production. All intermediate products transferred internally must be transferred at marginal cost.

Transfer Pricing for Products Without External Markets

Think of the divisionalized firm as a type of internal market. Like external markets, the internal markets of divisionalized firms act according to the laws of supply and demand. Supply is offered by various upstream suppliers to meet the demand of downstream users. Goods and services must be transferred and priced each step along the way from basic raw materials to finished products.

For simplicity, consider the problem faced by a vertically integrated firm that has different divisions at distinct points along the various steps of the production process, and assume for the moment that no external market exists for transferred inputs. If each separate division is established as a profit center to provide employees with an efficiency incentive, a transfer pricing problem can occur. Suppose each selling division adds a markup over its marginal cost for inputs sold to other divisions. Each buying division would then set its marginal revenue from output equal to the division's marginal cost of input. This process would culminate in a marginal cost to the ultimate upstream user that exceeds the sum total of marginal costs for each transferring division. All of the markups charged by each transferring division drive a wedge between the firm's true marginal cost of production and the marginal cost to the last or ultimate upstream user. As a result, the ultimate upstream user buys less than the optimal amount of input and produces less than the profit-maximizing level of output.

For example, it would be inefficient if AOL, a major ISP, paid more than the marginal cost of programming produced by its own subsidiaries. If each subsidiary added a markup to the marginal cost of programming sold to the parent company, AOL would buy less than a profit-maximizing amount of its own programming. In fact, AOL would have an incentive to seek programming from other purveyors so long as the external market price was less than the internal transfer price. Such an incentive could create extreme inefficiencies, especially when the external market price is less than the transfer price but greater than the marginal cost of programming produced by AOL's own subsidiaries.

An effective transfer pricing system leads to activity levels in each division that are consistent with profit maximization for the overall enterprise. This observation leads to the most basic rule for optimal transfer pricing: *When transferred products cannot be sold in external markets, the marginal cost of the transferring division is the optimal transfer price.* One practical means for insuring that an optimal amount of input is transferred at an optimal transfer price is to inform buying divisions that the marginal cost curve of supplying divisions is to be treated like a supply schedule. Alternatively, supplying divisions could be informed about the buying division's marginal revenue or demand curve and told to use this information in determining the quantity supplied. In either case, each division would voluntarily choose to transfer an optimal amount of input at the optimal transfer price.

Transfer Pricing with Perfectly Competitive External Markets

The transfer pricing problem is only sightly more complicated when transferred inputs can be sold in external markets. When transferred inputs can be sold in a perfectly competitive external market, the external market price represents the firm's opportunity cost of employing such inputs internally. As such, it would never pay to use inputs internally unless their value to the firm is at least as great as their value to others in the external market. This observation leads to a second key rule for optimal transfer pricing: *When transferred products can be sold in perfectly competitive external markets, the external market price is the optimal transfer price.* If upstream suppliers wish to supply more than downstream users desire to employ at a perfectly competitive price, excess input can be sold in the external market. If downstream users wish to employ more than upstream suppliers seek to furnish at a perfectly competitive price, excess input demand can be met through purchases in the external market. In either event, an optimal amount of input is transferred internally.

Of course, it is hard to imagine why a firm would be vertically integrated in the first place if all inputs could be purchased in perfectly competitive markets. Neither Kellogg's nor McDonald's, for example, have extensive agricultural operations to ensure a steady supply of foodstuffs. Grains for cereal and beef for hamburgers can both be purchased at prices that closely approximate marginal cost in perfectly competitive input markets. On the other hand, if an input market is typically competitive but punctuated by periods of scarcity and shortage, it can pay to maintain some input producing capability. For example, ExxonMobil Corp. has considerable production facilities that supply its extensive distribution network with gasoline, oil, and petroleum products. These production facilities offer ExxonMobil some protection against the threat of supply stoppages. Similarly, Coca-Cola has long-term supply contracts with orange growers to ensure a steady supply of product for its Minute Maid juice operation. Both ExxonMobil and Coca-Cola are examples of vertically integrated firms with inputs offered in markets that are usually, but not always, perfectly competitive.

Transfer Pricing with Imperfectly Competitive External Markets

The typical case of vertical integration involves firms with inputs that can be transferred internally or sold in external markets that are not perfectly competitive. Again, it never pays to use inputs internally unless their value to the firm is at least as great as their value to others in the external market. This observation leads to a third and final fundamental rule for optimal transfer pricing: *When transferred products can be sold in imperfectly competitive external markets, the optimal transfer price equates the marginal cost of the transferring division to the marginal revenue derived from the combined internal and external markets.* In other words, when inputs can be sold in imperfectly competitive external markets, internal input demand must reflect the opportunity to supply input to the external market at a price in excess of marginal cost. If upstream suppliers wish to offer more input than downstream users desire to employ when input $MC = MR$ from the combined market, excess supply can be sold in the external market. If downstream users want to employ more than upstream suppliers seek to furnish when $MC = MR$, excess internal demand can be met through added purchases in the external market. In both cases, an optimal amount of input is transferred internally.

 GLOBAL TRANSFER PRICING EXAMPLE

Although the transfer pricing concept can be introduced conceptually through the use of graphic analysis, most real-world applications are complex and must be solved algebraically. For this reason, examination of a detailed numerical example can be fruitful.

Profit Maximization for an Integrated Firm

Josiah Bartlet & Sons, Inc., is a small integrated domestic manufacturer of material handling equipment. Demand and marginal revenue curves for the firm are

$$P = \$100 - \$0.001Q$$
$$MR = \partial TR/\partial Q = \$100 - \$0.002Q$$

Relevant total cost, marginal cost, and profit functions are

$$TC = \$312,500 + \$25Q + \$0.0015Q^2$$
$$MC = \partial TC/\partial Q = \$25 + \$0.003Q$$
$$\pi = TR - TC$$
$$= \$100Q - \$0.001Q^2 - \$312,500 - \$25Q - \$0.0015Q^2$$
$$= -\$0.0025Q^2 + \$75Q - \$312,500$$

Profit maximization occurs at the point where $MR = MC$, so the optimal output level is

$$MR = MC$$
$$\$100 - \$0.002Q = \$25 + \$0.003Q$$

$$75 = 0.005Q$$
$$Q = 15,000$$

This implies that

$$P = \$100 - \$0.001(15,000)$$
$$= \$85$$
$$\pi = TR - TC$$
$$= -\$0.0025(15,000^2) + \$75(15,000) - \$312,500$$
$$= \$250,000$$

Therefore, the optimal price/output combination is $85 and 15,000 units for this integrated firm, and profits total $250,000. To be optimal, transfer prices must ensure operation at these levels.

Transfer Pricing with No External Market

Consider how the situation changes if the firm is reorganized into separate manufacturing and distribution division profit centers, and no external market exists for the transferred product. The demand curve facing the distribution division is precisely the same as the firm's output demand curve. Although the total cost function of the firm is unchanged, it can be broken down into the costs of manufacturing and distribution.

Assume that such a breakdown results in the following divisional cost functions:

$$TC_{Mfg} = \$250,000 + \$20Q + \$0.001Q^2$$
$$MC_{Mfg} = \partial TC_{Mfg}/\partial Q = \$20 + \$0.002Q$$

and

$$TC_{Distr} = \$62,500 + \$5Q + \$0.0005Q^2$$
$$MC_{Distr} = \partial TC_{Distr}/\partial Q = \$5 + \$0.001Q$$

With divisional operation, the total and marginal cost functions for the firm are

$$TC = TC_{Mfg} + TC_{Distr}$$
$$MC = MC_{Mfg} + MC_{Distr}$$

and precisely the same as before.

To demonstrate the derivation of an appropriate activity level, the net marginal revenue for the distribution division is set equal to the marginal cost of the manufacturing division:

$$MR - MC_{Distr} = MC_{Mfg}$$
$$\$100 - \$0.002Q - \$5 - \$0.001Q = \$20 + \$0.002Q$$
$$75 = 0.005Q$$
$$Q = 15,000$$

The 15,000-unit output level remains optimal for profit maximization. If the distribution division determines the quantity it will purchase by movement along its marginal revenue curve, and the manufacturing division supplies output along its marginal cost curve, then the market-clearing transfer price is the price that results when $MR - MC_{Distr} = MC_{Mfg}$. At 15,000 units of output, the optimal transfer price is

$$P_T = MC_{Mfg}$$
$$= \$20 + \$0.002(15,000)$$
$$= \$50$$

At a transfer price of $P_T = \$50$, the quantity supplied by the manufacturing division equals 15,000. This is the same quantity demanded by the distribution division at a $P_T = \$50$, because

$$MR - MC_{Distr} = P_T$$
$$\$100 - \$0.002Q - \$5 - \$0.001Q = \$50$$
$$45 = 0.003Q$$
$$Q = 15,000$$

At a transfer price of $P_T > \$50$, the distribution division will accept fewer units of output than the manufacturing division wants to supply. If $P_T < \$50$, the distribution division will seek to purchase more units than the manufacturing division desires to produce. Only at a $50 transfer price are supply and demand in balance in the firm's internal market.

Competitive External Market with Excess Internal Demand

To consider the effects of an external market for the transferred product, assume that the company is able to *buy* an unlimited quantity of a comparable product from a foreign supplier at a price of $35. The product supplied by the foreign manufacturer meets the exact same specifications as that produced by Josiah Bartlet & Sons. Because an unlimited quantity can be purchased for $35, a perfectly competitive external market exists for the transferred product, and the optimal transfer price equals the external market price. For $P_T = \$35$, the quantity demanded by the distribution division is

$$MR - MC_{Distr} = P_T$$
$$\$100 - \$0.002Q - \$5 - \$0.001Q = \$35$$
$$60 = 0.003Q$$
$$Q = 20,000$$

whereas the quantity supplied by the manufacturing division is

$$P_T = MC_{Mfg}$$
$$\$35 = \$20 + \$0.002Q$$
$$15 = 0.002Q$$
$$Q = 7,500$$

In this case of excess internal demand, the distribution division will purchase all 7,500 units produced internally plus an additional 12,500 units from the foreign supplier. The price impact for customers and the profit impact for Josiah Bartlet & Sons are dramatic. Domestic customer prices and total profits are now calculated as

$$P = \$100 - \$0.001(20,000)$$
$$= \$80$$

and

$$\pi = TR - TC_{Mfg} - TC_{For} - TC_{Distr}$$

$$= \$100(20{,}000) - \$0.001(20{,}000^2) - \$250{,}000 - \$20(7{,}500)$$

$$- \$0.001(7{,}500^2) - \$35(12{,}500) - \$62{,}500 - \$5(20{,}000)$$

$$- \$0.0005(20{,}000^2)$$

$$= \$343{,}750$$

Josiah Bartlet & Sons' domestic customers benefit from the increased availability of goods, 20,000 versus 15,000 units, and lower prices, $80 versus $85 per unit. The opportunity to purchase goods at a price of $35 from a foreign supplier benefits the company because profits grow from $250,000 to $343,750. The firm now manufactures only 7,500 of the units sold to customers and has become much more of a distributor than an integrated manufacturer and distributor. Josiah Bartlet & Sons has been able to make its business and profits grow by focusing efforts on distribution, where it enjoys a comparative advantage.

Competitive External Market with Excess Internal Supply

It is interesting to contrast these results with those achieved under somewhat different circumstances. For example, assume that Josiah Bartlet & Sons is able to sell an unlimited quantity of its goods to a foreign distributor at a price of $80. For simplicity, also assume that sales to this new market have no impact on the firm's ability to sell to current domestic customers and that this market can be supplied under the same cost conditions as previously. If $P_T = \$80$, the quantity demanded by the distribution division is

$$MR - MC_{Dist.} = P_T$$

$$\$100 - \$0.002Q - \$5 - \$0.001Q = \$80$$

$$15 = 0.003Q$$

$$Q = 5{,}000$$

whereas the quantity supplied by the manufacturing division is

$$P_T = MC_{Mfg}$$

$$\$80 = \$20 + \$0.002Q$$

$$60 = 0.002Q$$

$$Q = 30{,}000$$

In this instance of excess internal supply, the distribution division will purchase all 5,000 units desired internally, while the manufacturing division will offer an additional 25,000 units to the new foreign distributor. Again, the price impact for customers and the profit impact for Josiah Bartlet & Sons are dramatic. Domestic customer prices and total profits are now as follows:

$$P = \$100 - \$0.001(5{,}000)$$

$$= \$95$$

and

$$\pi = TR_{Dom} + TR_{For} - TC_{Mfg} - TC_{Distr}$$

$$= \$100(5{,}000) - \$0.001(5{,}000^2) + \$80(25{,}000) - \$250{,}000$$

$$- \$20(30{,}000) - \$0.001(30{,}000^2) - \$62{,}500 - \$5(5{,}000)$$

$$- \$0.0005(5{,}000^2)$$

$$= \$625{,}000$$

Under this scenario, Josiah Bartlet & Sons' domestic market shrinks from an initial 15,000 to 5,000 units, and prices rise somewhat from $85 to $95 per unit. At the same time, foreign customers benefit from the increased availability of goods, 25,000 versus none previously, and the attractive purchase price of $80 per unit. The opportunity to sell at a price of $80 to a foreign distributor has also benefited the company, because profits grew from $250,000 to $625,000. The company now distributes only 5,000 of 30,000 units sold to customers and has become much more of a manufacturer than a distributor. By emphasizing manufacturing, Josiah Bartlet & Sons makes its business and profits grow by focusing efforts on what it does best.

RIDDLES IN PRICING PRACTICE

As this chapter illustrates, economic reasoning is a powerful tool that can be used to understand and improve pricing practices. For example, popular markup pricing methods can be interpreted as an efficient rule-of-thumb approach toward setting profit-maximizing prices. Similarly, multiple-unit pricing methods, like two-part pricing and bundle pricing, are efficient means for capturing additional profits when the value of goods and services varies from one consumer to another.

Still, it would be misleading to infer that there are no important remaining mysteries in pricing practice. In fact, significant riddles remain. For example, no doubt you have noticed the popularity of what is sometimes called "odd-number pricing." Prices like $6.99 are much more common than $7; 99¢ is much more commonly employed than $1. You and I both know that 99¢ is much more commonly employed than $1 because buyers feel they are getting a "bargain" for 99¢. A $1 price seems "significantly" more expensive. For buyers, 99¢ often "feels" more than 1¢ cheaper than $1. This we all know. What economists and marketing scholars don't know is why buyers can be lured by a 99¢ price, and be turned off by a $1 price. Is there some failure in the computational ability of buyers? Does it have something to do with the way the brain processes information? To this point, there is no conclusive answer.

One innovative explanation for the popularity of odd-number pricing is that readers of Latin-based languages like English process written material from left to right. For example, as you read this page, you are processing information from left to right. As a result, the first digit processed when a consumer notes a price of $6.99 is the number six, not the higher number seven, as would be the case with a price of $7. Thus, in the English-speaking world, a price of $6.99 often seems "significantly" less than $7.

This interpretation gains favor when one considers the fact that the popularity of odd-numbered pricing is greatest in the case of goods and services offered in vigorously price competitive environments. For example, most states have regulations governing both the octane content, or quality, of motor car gasoline and the advertising of pump prices. It is a typical requirement that gasoline prices must be prominently displayed so that drivers can easily evaluate prices from curbside as they drive down the street. This makes the retail gasoline market one of the most viciously price competitive of all consumer markets. Just think of the times you have gone out of your way to save 2¢ or 3¢ per gallon, or a total of only 30¢ or 40¢ on a tank of gas. Gasoline customers are notoriously price sensitive, and gasoline retailers know this. Perhaps that is why gasoline retailers use odd-numbered pricing to such an extreme that gas prices are typically expressed in terms of 9/10 of a cent! Can you think of another product you buy regularly where the price charged is expressed in terms of 9/10 of a cent? I can't. Of course, it is difficult to explain why such price-sensitive gasoline customers will feverishly search for the very best bargain on gasoline and then turn around and spend 99¢ at that same gasoline station on a large ice-filled cup of Coca-Cola!

In short, economic reasoning has long proved an effective means for understanding pricing practices and for designing improvements in the pricing practices of individual firms. At the same time, the relevance of input from psychology and other social and physical sciences should not be minimized. The ongoing design of effective pricing practices benefits from knowledge gained in a wide variety of areas.

SUMMARY

This chapter examines a number of popular pricing practices. It becomes apparent that, when studied in detail, the methods commonly employed by successful firms reflect a careful appreciation of the use of marginal analysis to derive profit-maximizing prices.

- Many firms derive an optimal pricing policy using a technique called **markup pricing**, whereby prices are set to cover all direct costs plus a percentage markup for profit contribution. Flexible markup pricing practices that reflect differences in marginal costs and demand elasticities constitute an efficient method for ensuring that $MR = MC$.

- **Markup on cost** is the profit margin for an individual product or product line expressed as a percentage of unit cost. The numerator of this expression, called the **profit margin**, is the difference between price and cost. **Markup on price** is the profit margin for an individual product or product line expressed as a percentage of price, rather than unit cost.

- During **peak** periods, facilities are fully utilized. A firm has excess capacity during **off-peak** periods. Successful firms that employ markup pricing typically base prices on fully allocated costs under normal conditions but offer price discounts or accept lower margins during off-peak periods when substantial excess capacity is available.

- The **optimal markup-on-cost** formula is $OMC^* = -1/(\epsilon_P + 1)$. The **optimal markup-on-price** formula is $OMP^* = -1/\epsilon_P$. Either formula can be used to derive profit-maximizing prices solely on the basis of marginal cost and price elasticity of demand information.

- **Price discrimination** occurs whenever different market segments are charged different price markups for the same product. A **market segment** is a division or fragment of the overall market with essentially different or unique demand or cost characteristics. Price discrimination is evident whenever identical customers are charged different prices, or when price differences are not proportional to cost differences. Through price discrimination, sellers are able to increase profits by appropriating the **consumers' surplus**. Consumers' surplus (or customers' surplus) is the value of purchased goods and services above and beyond the amount paid to sellers.

- The extent to which a firm can engage in price discrimination is classified into three major categories. Under **first-degree price discrimination**, the firm extracts the maximum amount each customer is willing to pay for its products. Each unit is priced separately at the price indicated along each product demand curve. **Second-degree price discrimination** involves setting prices on the basis of the quantity purchased. Quantity discounts that lead to lower markups for large versus small customers are a common means for second-degree price discrimination. The most commonly observed form of price discrimination, **third-degree price discrimination**, results when a firm separates its customers into several classes and sets a different price for each customer class.

- Multiple-unit pricing strategies have also proved an effective means for extracting consumers' surplus for the benefit of producers. In general, a firm can enhance profits by using **two-part pricing** comprised of a per-unit fee equal to marginal cost, plus a fixed fee equal to the amount of consumers' surplus generated at that per-unit fee. If you have ever purchased a 12-pack of soft drinks, a year's supply of tax preparation services, or bought a "two-for-the-price-of-one" special, you have firsthand experience with the **bundle pricing** concept. As in the case of two-part pricing, the optimal level of output is determined by setting price equal to marginal cost and solving for quantity. Then, the optimal bundle price is a single lump sum amount equal to the total area under the demand curve at that point.

- A **by-product** is any output that is customarily produced as a direct result of an increase in the production of some other output. Profit maximization requires that marginal revenue be set equal to marginal cost for each by-product. Although the marginal costs of by-products produced in variable proportions can be determined, it is impossible to do so for by-products produced in fixed proportions. **Common costs**, or expenses that are necessary for manufacture of a joint product, cannot be allocated on any economically sound basis.

- A **vertical relation** is one where the output of one division or company is the input to another. **Vertical integration** occurs when a single company controls various links in the production chain from basic inputs to final output. **Transfer pricing** deals with the problem of pricing intermediate products transferred among divisions of vertically integrated firms. When transferred products cannot be sold in competitive external markets, the marginal cost of the transferring division is the optimal transfer price. When transferred products can be sold in perfectly competitive external markets, the external market price is the optimal transfer price. When transferred products can be sold in imperfectly competitive external markets, the optimal transfer price equates the marginal cost of the transferring division to the marginal revenue derived from the combined internal and external markets.

Throughout the chapter, it has been shown that efficient pricing practices require a careful analysis of marginal revenues and marginal costs for each relevant product or product line. Rule-of-thumb pricing practices employed by successful firms can be reconciled with profit-maximizing behavior when the costs and benefits of pricing information are properly understood. These practices add tremendous value to the managerial decision-making process.

QUESTIONS

Q12.1 What is markup pricing?

Q12.2 Develop and explain the relation between the markup-on-cost and the markup-on-price formulas.

Q12.3 Identify and interpret the relation between the optimal markup on cost and the point price elasticity of demand.

Q12.4 Illustrate the relation between the optimal markup on price and the point price elasticity of demand.

Q12.5 "One of the least practical suggestions that economists have offered to managers is that they set marginal revenues equal to marginal costs." Discuss this statement.

Q12.6 "Marginal cost pricing, as well as the use of incremental analysis, is looked upon with favor by economists, especially those on the staffs of regulatory agencies. With this encouragement, regulated industries do indeed employ these rational techniques quite frequently. Unregulated firms, on the other hand, use marginal or incremental cost pricing much less frequently, sticking to cost-plus, or full-cost, pricing except under unusual circumstances. In my opinion, this goes a long way toward explaining the problems of the regulated firms vis-à-vis unregulated industry." Discuss this statement.

Q12.7 What is price discrimination?

Q12.8 What conditions are necessary before price discrimination is both possible and profitable? Why does price discrimination result in higher profits?

Q12.9 Discuss the role of common costs in pricing practice.

Q12.10 Why is it possible to determine the marginal costs of joint products produced in variable proportions but not those of joint products produced in fixed proportions?

SELF-TEST PROBLEMS AND SOLUTIONS

ST12.1 George Constanza is a project coordinator at Kramer-Seinfeld & Associates, Ltd., a large Brooklyn-based painting contractor. Constanza has asked you to complete an analysis of profit margins earned on a number of recent projects. Unfortunately, your predecessor on this project was abruptly transferred, leaving you with only sketchy information on the firm's pricing practices.

A. Use the available data to complete the following table:

Price	Marginal Cost	Markup on Cost (%)	Markup on Price (%)
$100	$25	300.0	75.0
240	72		
680	272	150.0	60.0
750		100.0	
2,800			40.0
	2,700	33.3	
	3,360		20.0
5,800			10.0
6,250		5.3	
	10,000		0.0

B. Calculate the missing data for each of the following proposed projects, based on the available estimates of the point price elasticity of demand, optimal markup on cost, and optimal markup on price:

Project	Price Elasticity	Optimal Markup on Cost (%)	Optimal Markup on Price (%)
1	−1.5	200.0	66.7
2	−2.0		
3		66.7	
4			25.0
5	−5.0	25.0	
6		11.1	10.0
7	−15.0		
8	−20.0		5.0
9			4.0
10	−50.0	2.0	

ST12.1 Solution

A.

Price	Marginal Cost	Markup on Cost (%)	Markup on Price (%)
$100	$25	300.0	75.0
240	72	233.3	70.0
680	272	150.0	60.0
750	375	100.0	50.0
2,800	1,680	66.7	40.0
3,600	2,700	33.3	25.0
4,200	3,360	25.0	20.0
5,800	5,220	11.1	10.0
6,250	5,938	5.3	5.0
10,000	10,000	0.0	0.0

B.

Project	Price Elasticity	Optimal Markup on Cost (%)	Optimal Markup on Price (%)
1	−1.5	200.0	66.7
2	−2.0	100.0	50.0
3	−2.5	66.7	40.0
4	−4.0	33.3	25.0
5	−5.0	25.0	20.0
6	−10.0	11.1	10.0
7	−15.0	7.1	6.7
8	−20.0	5.3	5.0
9	−25.0	4.2	4.0
10	−50.0	2.0	2.0

ST12.2 Optimal Markup on Price. TLC Lawncare, Inc., provides fertilizer and weed control lawn services to residential customers. Its seasonal service package, regularly priced at $250, includes several chemical spray treatments. As part of an effort to expand its customer base, TLC offered $50 off its regular price to customers in the Dallas area. Response was enthusiastic, with sales rising to 5,750 units (packages) from the 3,250 units sold in the same period last year.

A. Calculate the arc price elasticity of demand for TLC service.

B. Assume that the arc price elasticity (from part A) is the best available estimate of the point price elasticity of demand. If marginal cost is $135 per unit for labor and materials, calculate TLC's optimal markup on price and its optimal price.

ST12.2 Solution

A.

$$E_P = \frac{\Delta Q}{\Delta P} \times \frac{P_2 + P_1}{Q_2 + Q_1}$$

$$= \frac{5,750 - 3,250}{\$200 - \$250} \times \frac{\$200 + \$250}{5,750 + 3,250}$$

$$= -2.5$$

B. Given $\epsilon_P = E_P = -2.5$, the optimal TLC markup on price is

$$\begin{aligned} \text{Optimal Markup on Price} &= \frac{-1}{\epsilon_P} \\ &= \frac{-1}{-2.5} \\ &= 0.4 \text{ or } 40\% \end{aligned}$$

Given $MC = \$135$, the optimal price is

$$\begin{aligned} \text{Optimal Markup on Price} &= \frac{P - MC}{P} \\ 0.4 &= \frac{P - \$135}{P} \\ 0.4P &= P - \$135 \\ 0.6P &= \$135 \\ P &= \$225 \end{aligned}$$

PROBLEMS

P12.1   **Markup Calculation.** Controller Dana Scully has asked you to review the pricing practices of Fox Mulder, Inc., an importer and regional distributor of low-priced cosmetics products (e.g., The Black Oil). Use the following data to calculate the relevant markup on cost and markup on price for the following five items:

Product	Price	Marginal Cost	Markup on Cost (%)	Markup on Price (%)
A	$2	$0.20		
B	3	0.60		
C	4	1.20		
D	5	2.00		
E	6	3.00		

P12.2   **Optimal Markup.** Dr. Robert Romano, chief of staff at County General Hospital, has asked you to propose an appropriate markup pricing policy for various medical procedures performed in the hospital's emergency room. To help in this regard, you consult a trade industry publication that provides data about the price elasticity of demand for medical procedures. Unfortunately, the abrasive Dr. Romano failed to mention whether he wanted you to calculate the optimal markup as a percentage of price or as a percentage of cost. To be safe, calculate the optimal markup on price and optimal markup on cost for each of the following procedures:

Procedure	Price Elasticity	Optimal Markup on Cost	Optimal Markup on Price
A	−1		
B	−2		
C	−3		
D	−4		
E	−5		

P12.3   **Markup on Cost.** Brake-Checkup, Inc., offers automobile brake analysis and repair at a number of outlets in the Philadelphia area. The company recently initiated a policy of matching the lowest advertised competitor price. As a result, Brake-Checkup has been forced to reduce the average price for brake jobs by 3%, but it has enjoyed a 15% increase in customer traffic. Meanwhile, marginal costs have held steady at $120 per brake job.

A. Calculate the point price elasticity of demand for brake jobs.

B. Calculate Brake-Checkup's optimal price and markup on cost.

P12.4   **Optimal Markup on Cost.** The Bristol, Inc., is an elegant dining establishment that features French cuisine at dinner six nights per week and brunch on weekends. In an effort to boost traffic from shoppers during the Christmas season, the Bristol offered Saturday customers $4 off its $16 regular price for brunch. The promotion proved successful, with brunch sales rising from 250 to 750 units per day.

A. Calculate the arc price elasticity of demand for brunch at the Bristol.

B. Assume that the arc price elasticity (from part A) is the best available estimate of the point price elasticity of demand. If marginal cost is $8.56 per unit for labor and materials, calculate the Bristol's optimal markup on cost and its optimal price.

P12.5 **Peak/Off-Peak Pricing.** Nash Bridges Construction Company is a building contractor serving the Gulf Coast region. The company recently bid on a Gulf-front causeway improvement in Biloxi, Mississippi. Nash Bridges has incurred bid development and job cost-out expenses of $25,000 prior to submission of the bid. The bid was based on the following projected costs:

Cost Category	Amount
Bid development and job cost-out expenses	$25,000
Materials	881,000
Labor (50,000 hours @ $26)	1,300,000
Variable overhead (40% of direct labor)	520,000
Allocated fixed overhead (6% of total costs)	174,000
Total costs	$2,900,000

A. What is Nash Bridges' minimum acceptable (breakeven) contract price, assuming that the company is operating at peak capacity?

B. What is the Nash Bridges' minimum acceptable contract price if an economic downturn has left the company with substantial excess capacity?

P12.6 **Incremental Pricing Analysis.** The General Eclectic Company manufactures an electric toaster. Sales of the toaster have increased steadily during the previous 5 years, and, because of a recently completed expansion program, annual capacity is now 500,000 units. Production and sales during the upcoming year are forecast to be 400,000 units, and standard production costs are estimated as follows:

Materials	$6.00
Direct labor	4.00
Variable indirect labor	2.00
Fixed overhead	3.00
Allocated cost per unit	$15.00

In addition to production costs, General incurs fixed selling expenses of $1.50 per unit and variable warranty repair expenses of $1.20 per unit. General currently receives $20 per unit from its customers (primarily retail department stores), and it expects this price to hold during the coming year.

After making the preceding projections, General received an inquiry about the purchase of a large number of toasters by a discount department store. The inquiry contained two purchase offers:

- Offer 1: The department store would purchase 80,000 units at $14.60 per unit. These units would bear the General label and be covered by the General warranty.
- Offer 2: The department store would purchase 120,000 units at $14.00 per unit. These units would be sold under the buyer's private label, and General would not provide warranty service.

A. Evaluate the incremental net income potential of each offer.

B. What other factors should General consider when deciding which offer to accept?

C. Which offer (if either) should General accept? Why?

P12.7 **Price Discrimination.** Coach Industries, Inc., is a leading manufacturer of recreational vehicle products. Its products include travel trailers, fifth-wheel trailers (towed behind pick-up trucks), and van campers, as well as parts and accessories. Coach offers its fifth-wheel trailers to both dealers (wholesale) and retail customers. Ernie Pantusso, Coach's controller, estimates that each fifth-wheel trailer costs the company $10,000 in variable labor and material expenses. Demand and marginal revenue relations for fifth-wheel trailers are

$$P_W = \$15,000 - \$5Q_W \qquad \text{(Wholesale)}$$
$$MR_W = \partial TR_W / \partial Q_W = \$15,000 - \$10Q_W$$
$$P_R = \$50,000 - \$20Q_R \qquad \text{(Retail)}$$
$$MR_R = \partial TR_R / \partial Q_R = \$50,000 - \$40Q_R$$

A. Assuming that the company can price discriminate between its two types of customers, calculate the profit-maximizing price, output, and profit contribution levels.

B. Calculate point price elasticities for each customer type at the activity levels identified in part A. Are the differences in these elasticities consistent with your recommended price differences in part A? Why or why not?

P12.8 **Two-Part Pricing.** The San Diego Tennis & Racquette Club has asked Rachel Green to devise a profit-maximizing pricing strategy. In doing so, Green knows that a typical player will want to play 15 hours per season if court time costs $25 per hour. On average, this demand falls by $2^1/_2$ hours for each $10 increase in the price of court time. These data suggest the following demand and marginal revenue relations:

$$P = \$85 - \$4Q$$
$$MR = \partial TR / \partial Q = \$85 - \$8Q$$

where P is the price of 1-hour court time on the club's indoor tennis court, and Q is the number of hours of court time an individual player of average talent would demand during the tennis season. For simplicity, assume that the marginal cost of 1 hour of court time is $5 and that fixed costs are nil. This gives the following total and marginal cost relations:

$$TC = \$5Q$$
$$MC = \partial TC / \partial Q = \$5$$

A. Calculate the profit-maximizing price, output, profit level, and consumers' surplus assuming a per-unit price is charged each customer.

B. Calculate the profit-maximizing price, output and profit level assuming a two-part pricing strategy is adopted for each customer.

C. Now assume that fixed costs of $500,000 are incurred, and 1,000 customers are attracted when an optimal two-part pricing strategy is adopted. Calculate total profits.

P12.9 **Joint Product Pricing.** Each ton of ore mined from the Baby Doe Mine in Leadville, Colorado, produces 1 ounce of silver and 1 pound of lead in a fixed 1:1 ratio. Marginal costs are $10 per ton of ore mined.

The demand and marginal revenue curves for silver are

$$P_S = \$11 - \$0.00003Q_S$$
$$MR_S = \partial TR_S / \partial Q_S = \$11 - \$0.00006Q_S$$

and the demand and marginal revenue curve for lead are

$$P_L = \$0.4 - \$0.000005Q_L$$
$$MR_L = \partial TR_L / \partial Q_L = \$0.4 - \$0.00001Q_L$$

where Q_S is ounces of silver and Q_L is pounds of lead.

A. Calculate profit-maximizing sales quantities and prices for silver and lead.

B. Now assume that wild speculation in the silver market has created a fivefold (or 500%) increase in silver demand. Calculate optimal sales quantities and prices for both silver and lead under these conditions.

P12.10 Transfer Pricing. Simpson Flanders, Inc., is a Motor City–based manufacturer and distributor of valves used in nuclear power plants. Currently, all output is sold to North American customers. Demand and marginal revenue curves for the firm are as follows:

$$P = \$1,000 - \$0.015Q$$
$$MR = \partial TR/\partial Q = \$1,000 - \$0.03Q$$

Relevant total cost, marginal cost, and profit functions are

$$TC = \$1,500,000 + \$600Q + \$0.005Q^2$$
$$MC = \partial TC/\partial Q = \$600 + \$0.01Q$$
$$\pi = TR - TC$$
$$= -\$0.02Q^2 + \$400Q - \$1,500,000$$

A. Calculate the profit-maximizing activity level for Simpson Flanders when the firm is operated as an integrated unit.

B. Assume that the company is reorganized into two independent profit centers with the following cost conditions:

$$TC_{Mfg} = \$1,250,000 + \$500Q + \$0.005Q^2$$
$$MC_{Mfg} = \$500 + \$0.01Q$$
$$\text{and,}$$
$$TC_{Distr} = \$250,000 + \$100Q$$
$$MC_{Distr} = \$100$$

Calculate the transfer price that ensures a profit-maximizing level of profit for the firm, with divisional operation based on the assumption that all output produced is to be transferred internally.

C. Now assume that a major distributor in the European market offers to buy as many valves as Simpson Flanders wishes to offer at a price of $645. No impact on demand from the company's North American customers is expected, and current facilities can be used to supply both markets. Calculate the company's optimal price(s), output(s), and profits in this situation.

CASE STUDY

Pricing Practices in the Denver, Colorado, Newspaper Market

On May 12, 2000, the two daily newspapers in Denver, Colorado, filed an application with the U.S. Department of Justice for approval of a joint operating arrangement. The application was filed by The E.W. Scripps Company, whose subsidiary, the Denver Publishing Company, published the *Rocky Mountain News*, and the MediaNews Group, Inc., whose subsidiary, the Denver Post Corporation, published the *Denver Post*. Under the proposed joint operating agreement, printing and commercial operations of both newspapers were to be handled by a new entity, the "Denver Newspaper Agency," owned by the parties in equal shares. This type of joint operating agreement provides for the complete independence of the news and editorial departments of the two newspapers. The rationale for such an arrangement, as provided for under the Newspaper Preservation Act, is to preserve multiple independent editorial voices in towns and cities too small to support two or more newspapers. The act requires joint operating arrangements, such as that proposed by the Denver newspapers, to obtain the prior written consent of the attorney general of the United States in order to qualify for the antitrust exemption provided by the act.

CASE STUDY (continued)

Scripps initiated discussions for a joint operating agreement after determining that the *News* would probably fail without such an arrangement. In their petition to the Justice Department, the newspapers argued that the *News* had sustained $123 million in net operating losses while the financially stronger *Post* had reaped $200 million in profits during the 1990s. This was a crucial point in favor of the joint operating agreement application because the attorney general must find that one of the publications is a failing newspaper and that approval of the arrangement is necessary to maintain the independent editorial content of both newspapers. Like any business, newspapers cannot survive without a respectable bottom line. In commenting on the joint operating agreement application, Attorney General Janet Reno noted that Denver was one of only five major American cities still served by competing daily newspapers. The other four are Boston, Chicago, New York, and Washington, DC. Of course, these other four cities are not comparable in size to Denver; they are much bigger. None of those four cities can lay claim to two newspapers that are more or less equally matched and strive for the same audience. In fact, that there is not a single city in the United States that still supports two independently owned and evenly matched, high-quality newspapers that vie for the same broad base of readership.

Economies of scale in production explain why few cities can support more than one local newspaper. Almost all local newspaper production and distribution costs are fixed. Marginal production and distribution costs are almost nil. After the local news stories and local advertising copy are written, there is practically no additional cost involved with expanding production from, say, 200,000 to 300,000 newspapers per day. Once a daily edition is produced, marginal costs may be as little as 5¢ per newspaper. When marginal production costs are minimal, price competition turns vicious. Whichever competitor is out in front in terms of total circulation simply keeps prices down until the competition goes out of business or is forced into accepting a joint operating agreement. This is exactly what happened in Denver. Until recently, the cost of a daily newspaper in Denver was only 25¢ each weekday and 50¢ on Sunday at the newsstand, and even less when purchased on an annual subscription basis. The smaller *News* had much higher unit costs and simply could not afford to compete with the *Post* at such ruinously low prices. This is why the production of local newspapers is often described as a classic example of natural monopoly.

On Friday, January 5, 2001, Attorney General Reno gave the green light to a 50-year joint operating agreement between the *News* and its longtime rival, the *Post*. Starting January 22, 2001, the publishing operations of the *News* and the *Post* were consolidated. The Denver Newspaper Agency, owned 50/50 by the owners of the *News* and *Post*, is now responsible for the advertising, circulation, production, and other business departments of the newspapers. Newsrooms and editorial functions remain independent. Therefore, the owners of the *News* and *Post* are now working together to achieve financial success, but the newsroom operations remain competitors. Under terms of the agreement, E.W. Scripps Company, parent of the struggling *News*, agreed to pay owners of the *Post* $60 million. Both newspapers publish separately Monday through Friday. The *News* publishes the only Saturday paper and the *Post* the only Sunday paper.

A. Use your knowledge of monopoly pricing practices to explain why advertising rates and newspaper circulation prices were likely to increase, and jobs were likely to be lost, following adoption of this joint operating agreement. Use company information to support your argument (see http://www.denverpost.com and http://www.rockymountainnews.com).

B. In many cases, classified ads to sell real estate in a local newspaper can cost five to ten times as much as a similar ad used to announce a garage sale. Use your knowledge of price discrimination to explain how local newspaper monopolies generate enormous profits from selling classified advertising that varies in price according to the value of the item advertised.

C. Widely differing fares for business and vacation travelers on the same flight have led some to accuse the airlines of price discrimination. Do airline fare differences or local newspaper classified-ad rate differences provide stronger evidence of price discrimination?

SELECTED REFERENCES

Allen, Ralph C., and Jack H. Stone. "Rent Extraction, Principal-Agent Relationships, and Pricing Strategies: Vendor Licensing During the 1996 Olympic Games in Atlanta." *Managerial & Decision Economics* 22 (December 2001): 431–438.

Baker, George, Robert Gibbons, and Kevin J. Murphy. "Bringing the Market Inside the Firm?" *American Economic Review* 91 (May 2001): 212–218.

Bernstein, Jerry, and David Macias. "Engineering New-Product Success: The New-Product Pricing Process at Emerson." *Industrial Marketing Management* 31 (January 2002): 51–64.

Brown, Ken, Anthony Damiano, Brian Jenkins, et al. "Congestion Pricing: New Risks for Lenders." *Journal of Project Finance* 6 (Winter 2001): 21–29.

Considine, Timothy J. "Markup Pricing in Petroleum Refining: A Multiproduct Framework." *International Journal of Industrial Organization* 19 (December 2001): 1499–1526.

Cornell, Bradford, and Qaio Liu. "The Parent Company Puzzle: When Is the Whole Worth Less Than One of the Parts?" *Journal of Corporate Finance* 7 (December 2001): 341–366.

Ellig, Jerry. "Internal Markets and the Theory of the Firm." *Managerial & Decision Economics* 22 (June/ August 2001): 227–237.

Malkiel, Burton G., and Aleksander Radisich. "The Growth of Index Funds and the Pricing of Equity Securities." *Journal of Portfolio Management* 27 (Winter 2001): 9–21.

O'Connell, Paul G. J., and Shang-Jin Wei. "The Bigger They Are, the Harder They Fall: Retail Price Differences Across U.S. Cities." *Journal of International Economics* 56 (January 2002): 21–53.

Partington, Graham, and Max Stevenson. "The Probability and Timing of Price Reversals in the Property Market." *Managerial & Decision Economics* 22 (October/November 2001): 389–398.

Rogoff, Kenneth. "Why Not a Global Currency?" *American Economic Review* 91 (May 2001): 243–247.

Schill, Michael J., and Chunsheng Zhou. "Pricing and Emerging Industry: Evidence from Internet Subsidiary Carve-Outs." *Financial Management* 30 (Autumn 2001): 5–33.

Smith, Barry C., Dirk P. Gunther, B. Venkateshwara Rao, and Richard M. Ratliff. "E-Commerce and Operations Research in Airline Planning, Marketing, and Distribution." *Interfaces* 31 (March 2001): 37–55.

Sudhir, K. "Competitive Pricing Behavior in the Auto Market: A Structural Analysis." *Marketing Science* 20 (Winter 2001): 42–60.

Yamawaki, Hideki. "Price Reactions to New Competition: A Study of U.S. Luxury Car Market, 1986–1997." *International Journal of Industrial Organization* 20, (January 2002): 19–39.

Long-Term Investment Decisions

CHAPTER THIRTEEN

Regulation of the Market Economy

In the new millennium, managers must be sensitive to regulatory policies both at home and abroad. If there was ever any doubt about the far-reaching importance of foreign regulatory bodies, that doubt was eliminated on July 3, 2001, when the European Commission turned thumbs down on the proposed acquisition of Honeywell, Inc., by General Electric Co (GE).

According to the commission, GE's dominant position in the markets for jet engines, combined with its financial strength and vertical integration into aircraft leasing, gave GE significant market power. At the same time, Honeywell is a leading supplier of avionics products and jet engines for corporate aircraft. The commission found that a merged entity would be able to leverage the respective market power of each company. Market dominance would have been created or strengthened as a result of horizontal overlaps in some markets as well as through the extension of GE's financial power and vertical integration to Honeywell activities. According to the commission, a merger between GE and Honeywell would foreclose competition and adversely affect product quality, service, and consumers' prices.[1]

What is captivating about this case is that the European Commission and the U.S. Department of Justice worked together during the investigation but reached different conclusions. Ironically, the Justice Department voted to allow the GE–Honeywell merger. This chapter considers the economic and social rationale for regulation, and explains the reasons behind conflicting opinions on government regulation in the market economy. Regulators must balance efficiency and equity considerations. This is a fascinating and controversial process.

---

1   See Andy Pasztor and JoAnne Lublin, "Skeptics Wonder if Honeywell CEO Will Revive, Expand Firm's Business," *The Wall Street Journal Online*, February 21, 2002 (http://online.wsj.com).

COMPETITION AND THE ROLE OF GOVERNMENT

When considering the role of government in the market economy, it has been traditional to focus on how government influences economic activity through tax policies, law enforcement, and infrastructure investments in highways, water treatment facilities, and the like. More recently, interest has shifted to how and why the government regulates private market activity.

How Government Influences Business

Government affects what and how firms produce, influences conditions of entry and exit, dictates marketing practices, prescribes hiring and personnel policies, and imposes a host of other requirements on private enterprise. Government regulation of the market economy is a controversial topic because the power to tax or compel has direct economic consequences.

For example, local telephone service monopolies are protected by a web of local and federal regulation that gives rise to above-normal rates of return while providing access to below-market financing. Franchises that confer the right to offer cellular telephone service in a major metropolitan area are literally worth millions of dollars and can be awarded in the United States only by the Federal Communications Commission (FCC). The federal government also spends hundreds of millions of dollars per year to maintain artificially high price supports for selected agricultural products such as milk and grain, but not chicken and pork. Careful study of the motivation and methods of such regulation is essential to the study of managerial economics because of regulation's key role in shaping the managerial decision-making process.

The pervasive and expanding influence of government in the market economy can be illustrated by considering the growing role played by the FCC, a once obscure agency known only for regulation of the broadcast industry and AT&T. The FCC currently holds the keys to success for a number of emerging communications technologies. The FCC determines the fate of digital audio broadcasting, which does away with static on car radio channels; personal communication networks that make users reachable anywhere with a pocket phone; and interactive television, which lets customers order goods and communicate with others through a television set. The FCC has also taken on the daunting and controversial task of restricting indecent and obscene material broadcast over the Internet. As such, the FCC is the focus of debates over free speech and the government's role in shaping rapid advances in communications technology.

Although all sectors of the U.S. economy are regulated to some degree, the method and scope of regulation vary widely. Most companies escape price and profit restraint, except during periods of general wage-price control, but they are subject to operating regulations governing pollution emissions, product packaging and labeling, worker safety and health, and so on. Other firms, particularly in the financial and the public utility sectors, must comply with financial regulation in addition to such operating controls. Banks and savings and loan institutions, for example, are subject to state and federal regulation of interest rates, fees, lending policies, and capital requirements. Unlike firms in the electric power and telecommunications industries, banks and savings and loans face no explicit limit on profitability.

efficiency
Production of what consumers demand in a least-cost fashion

regulation
Government order having the force of law

equity
Concern for a just distribution of wealth

Economic and social considerations enter into decisions of what and how to regulate. Economic considerations relate to the cost and efficiency implications of regulatory methods. From an economic **efficiency** standpoint, a given mode of **regulation** or government control is desirable to the extent that benefits exceed costs. In terms of efficiency, the question is whether market competition by itself is sufficient, or if it needs to be supplemented with government regulation. **Equity**, or fairness, criteria must also be carefully weighed when social considerations bear on the regulatory decision-making process. Therefore, the incidence, or placement, of costs and benefits of regulatory decisions is important. If a given change in regulatory policy provides significant benefits to the poor, society may willingly bear substantial costs in terms of lost efficiency.

Economic Considerations

Economic regulation began and continues in part because of the public's perception of market imperfections. It is sometimes believed that unregulated market activity can lead to inefficiency and waste or to market failure. **Market failure** is the inability of a system of market institutions to sustain socially desirable activities or to eliminate undesirable ones.

market failure
The inability of market institutions to sustain desirable activity or eliminate undesirable activity

A first cause of market failure is **failure by market structure**. For a market to realize the beneficial effects of competition, it must have many producers (sellers) and consumers (buyers), or at least the ready potential for many to enter. Some markets do not meet this condition. Consider, for example, water, power, and some telecommunications markets. If customer service in a given market area can be most efficiently provided by a single firm (a natural monopoly situation), such providers would enjoy market power and could earn economic profits by limiting output and charging high prices. As a result, utility prices and profits were placed under regulatory control, which has continued with the goal of preserving the efficiency of large-scale production while preventing the higher prices and economic profits of monopoly. When the efficiency advantages of large size are not thought to be compelling, antitrust policy limits the market power of large firms.

failure by market structure
Insufficient market participants for active competition

A second kind of market failure is **failure by incentive**. In the production and consumption of goods and services, social values and costs often differ from the private costs and values of producers and consumers. Differences between private and social costs or benefits are called **externalities**. A negative externality is a cost of producing, marketing, or consuming a product that is not borne by the product's producers or consumers. A positive externality is a benefit of production, marketing, or consumption that is not reflected in the product pricing structure and, hence, does not accrue to the product's producers or consumers.

failure by incentive
Breakdown of the pricing mechanism as a reflection of all costs and benefits of production and consumption

externalities
Differences between private and social costs or benefits

Environmental pollution is one well-known negative externality. Negative externalities also arise when employees are exposed to hazardous working conditions for which they are not fully compensated. Similarly, a firm that dams a river to produce energy and thereby limits the access of others to hydropower creates a negative externality. Positive externalities can result if an increase in a firm's activity reduces costs for its suppliers, who pass these cost savings on to their other customers. For example, economies of scale in semiconductor production made possible by increased computer demand have lowered input costs for all users of semiconductors. As a result, prices have fallen for computers and a wide variety of "intelligent" electronic appliances, calculators, toys, and so on. Positive externalities in production can result when a firm trains employees who later apply their knowledge in work for other firms. Positive externalities also arise when an improvement in production methods is transferred from one firm to another without compensation. The dam cited previously for its potential negative externalities might also provide positive externalities by offering flood control or recreational benefits.

In short, externalities lead to a difference between private and social costs and benefits. Firms that provide substantial positive externalities without compensation are unlikely to produce at the socially optimal level. Consumption activities that confer positive externalities may not reach the socially optimal level. In contrast, negative externalities can channel too many resources to a particular activity. Producers or consumers that generate negative externalities do not pay the full costs of production or consumption and tend to overutilize social resources.

Social Considerations

Competition promotes efficiency by giving firms incentives to produce the types and quantities of products that consumers want. Competitive pressures force each firm to use resources wisely to earn at least a normal profit. The market-based resource allocation system is efficient when it responds quickly and accurately to consumer preferences. Not only are these features

MANAGERIAL APPLICATION   13.1

How Do You Regulate a Global Economy?

Pressed by the emergence of regional trading blocs in North America, Europe, and East Asia, global corporations are developing chameleon-like abilities to change quickly to fit a rapidly evolving global economic environment. Government intervention in world currency, bond, and stock markets—sometimes used to stem short-term capital flows—can have the unintended effect of choking off long-term investment and economic growth. At the same time, global manufacturers move factories and labs around the world without reference to national boundaries.

The global focus of modern corporations represents a striking evolution from the U.S. multinational alternately feared and courted by developing countries around the globe since the 1960s. These giants treated foreign operations as subsidiaries for producing products designed and engineered back home. The chain of command and nationality of the company were clear. This is not the case today. With the United States no longer dominating the world economy, new technologies, capital, and talents flow in multiple directions. The most sophisticated manufacturing companies often make breakthroughs in foreign labs, place shares with foreign investors, and put foreigners

on the fast track to the top. The recent wave of mergers, acquisitions, and strategic alliances has further clouded traditional corporate/national relations. International competitors seeking cost efficiencies and product-quality improvements now often find themselves working together to efficiently penetrate new and emerging markets. At the same time, the pro-capitalism revolution of the past decade has resulted in market-driven policies that make social, political, and cultural differences among companies less significant.

Nagging questions remain. Does corporate nationality matter? What nation, if any, controls the technology developed by global companies? What obligation do global corporations have to follow rules imposed by Washington, Ottawa, Paris, or Tokyo on their foreign operations?

Global companies clearly raise important questions for government regulations and policies designed to retain control over national identities.

See: Shirley Leving, "McDonald's Profits Sink 40%, Weakened by Global Slump," *The Wall Street Journal Online,* January 28, 2002 (http://online.wsj.com).

---

consumer sovereignty
Buyer supremacy in the marketplace

of competitive markets attractive on an economic basis, but they are also consistent with basic democratic principles. Preservation of consumer choice or **consumer sovereignty** is an important feature of competitive markets. By encouraging and rewarding individual initiative, competition greatly enhances personal freedom. For this reason, less vigorous competitive pressure indicates diminishing buyer supremacy in the marketplace. Firms with market power can limit output and raise prices to earn economic profits, whereas firms in competitive markets refer to market prices to determine optimal output quantities. Regulatory policy can be a valuable tool with which to control monopolies, restoring control over price and quantity decisions to the public.

limit concentration
Social goal of regulation is to restrict undue influence

A second social purpose of regulatory intervention is to **limit concentration** of economic and political power. It has long been recognized that economic and social relations become intertwined and that concentrated economic power is generally inconsistent with the democratic process. The laws of incorporation, first passed during the 1850s, play an important role in the U.S. economic system. These laws have allowed owners of capital (stockholders) to pool economic resources without also pooling political resources, thereby allowing big business and democracy to coexist. Of course, the large scale of modern corporations has sometimes diminished the controlling influence of individual stockholders. In these instances, regulatory and antitrust policy have limited the growth of large firms to avoid undue concentration of political power.

Important social considerations often constitute compelling justification for government intervention in the marketplace. Deciding whether a particular regulatory reform is warranted is complicated because social considerations can run counter to efficiency considerations.

REGULATORY RESPONSE TO INCENTIVE FAILURES

To help preserve the competitive environment, government regulation addresses problems created by positive and negative externalities in production, marketing, and consumption. In granting patents and operating subsidies, government provides compensation to reward activity that provides positive externalities. Local, state, and federal governments levy taxes to limit negative externalities. Property rights, grants, taxes, and operating controls are common focal points of government/business interaction.

Property Rights Regulation

property rights
The license to limit use by others

Property rights give the power to limit use by others of specific land, plant and equipment, and other assets. The deed to a piece of land, for example, explicitly defines a property right. The establishment and maintenance of private property rights is essential to the workings of a competitive market. Property rights are so fundamental to the free market economy and democratic form of government that they are protected in the United States by the Fifth Amendment to the Constitution. Although local zoning laws limit property rights by restricting the types of buildings allowed in a particular neighborhood, these laws cannot be so burdensome as to deprive owners from the rightful use of their property. Although the public interest might be served by regulations designed to preserve wetlands or endangered species, owners are entitled to compensation for any loss they might suffer as a result.

Regulation of property rights is a common, though seldom discussed, method of giving incentives to promote service in the public interest. Common examples are FCC control of local television and radio broadcasting rights; federal and state regulatory bodies that govern national or state chartering of banks and savings and loan institutions; and insurance commissions that oversee insurance company licensing at the state level. In each of these instances, firms must be able to demonstrate fiscal responsibility and evidence that they are meeting customer needs. Should firms fail to meet established criteria, public franchises can be withdrawn, or new franchises can be offered to potential competitors.

Property rights regulation can be effective, but can be frustrated by imprecise operating criteria. For example, how much poorly rated local programming should any given television station be required to produce? How progressive a stance should local banks take toward electronic funds transfer services? Without clear, consistent, and workable standards of performance, operating grant regulation is hampered by inefficiency and waste.

Patents and the Tort System

patents
Exclusive property rights to produce, use, or sell an invention or innovation for a limited period

Patents grant an exclusive right to produce, use, or sell an invention or innovation for a limited period of time. For U.S. patent applications filed on or after June 8, 1995, utility and plant patents can be granted for a term that begins with the date of the grant and usually ends 20 years from the date of the patent application. Utility patents may be granted to anyone who invents or discovers any new or improved process, machine, manufactured product, or composition of matter. Plant patents may be granted to anyone who invents or discovers and asexually reproduces any distinct and new variety of plant. Maintenance fees totaling a few thousand dollars must be paid over the life of such patents. Design patents may be granted to anyone who invents a new, original, and ornamental design for a manufactured product, and last 14 years from the grant date. Design patents do not involve maintenance fees.

Without patents, competitors could quickly develop identical substitutes for new products or processes, and inventing firms would fail to reap the full benefit of their technological breakthroughs. In granting patents, the public confers a limited opportunity for monopoly profits to stimulate research activity and economic growth. By limiting the patent monopoly, competition is encouraged to extend and develop the common body of knowledge. The patent monopoly is subject to other restrictions besides the time limit. Firms cannot use patents to unfairly monopolize or otherwise limit competition, as the Federal Trade Commission (FTC) claimed in a 1995 action against Dell Computer Corp.

At that time, Dell was a member of the Video Electronics Standards Association (VESA), a standards-setting body for the computer industry. In 1992, VESA set a new standard for the design of computer bus hardware, or the equipment that transmits information from one computer component to another. According to the FTC, before the new standard was approved, Dell certified that it did not violate any of its intellectual property rights. However, after the new VESA standard was implemented, Dell changed its mind and announced that the standard did in fact violate one of its patents. By then, over a million computers using the new VESA standard had already been sold, and other computer manufacturers could not switch to an alternate design without creating a vexing compatibility problem. This would have put Dell in a position to collect substantial royalty payments were it not for a settlement with the FTC in which Dell agreed not to enforce its patent rights against computer manufacturers using the standard.

The rules of contract law provide for the enforcement of patents and other legal agreements among firms. Because it is impossible to specify all possible outcomes in writing a legal contract, the court system provides an open forum for dispute resolution. Even if all possible outcomes could be specified beforehand, legal enforcement would still be necessary to ensure that all parties honor their agreements. If a manufacturer fails to deliver goods to a wholesaler as promised, the wholesaler can go to the courts to enforce its agreement with the manufacturer. Without such enforcement, firms would have no recourse but to depend exclusively on the goodwill of others. The legal system also includes a body of law designed to provide a mechanism for victims of accidents and injury to receive just compensation for their loss. Called the **tort system**, these laws create an incentive for firms and other parties to act responsibly in commerce. Because of the threat of being sued for their transgressions, firms are encouraged to prevent accidents and resulting economic damages.

Like patents that are difficult and costly to enforce in the courts, the tort system can itself result in significant costs. For example, both sides to a legal dispute have almost unlimited ability to take sworn depositions from witnesses and seek documents in the pretrial "discovery" process. Because discovery must be provided without payment from the requesting party, there is no incentive to limit the size of any request. Requesting parties can and have used the discovery process to impose significant litigation costs on the other side, even in lawsuits that later prove frivolous. As a result, proposals have been made to place limits on the amount of free discovery that can be requested, set caps on the amount of punitive damages, foster proper use of expert testimony, and encourage other means of dispute resolution.

Subsidy Policy

Government sometimes responds to positive externalities by providing subsidies. **Subsidy policy** can be indirect, like government construction and highway maintenance grants that benefit the trucking industry. They can be direct payments, such as agricultural payment-in-kind (PIK) programs, special tax treatments, and government-provided low-cost financing.

Tax credits on business investment and depletion allowances on natural resource extraction are examples of tax subsidies given in recognition of social benefits such as job creation and energy independence. Positive externalities associated with industrial parks induce government to provide local tax incremental financing or industrial revenue bond financing for such facilities. This low-cost financing is thought to provide compensation for the external benefits of economic development.

Tradable emissions permits are pollution licenses granted by the government to firms and individuals. Rather than spend millions of dollars on new equipment, raw materials, or production methods to meet pollution abatement regulations, firms sometimes purchase tradable emissions permits from other companies. These tradable emmissions permits are a valuable commodity that can be worth millions of dollars. Opponents of this system argue that they infringe on the public's right to a clean and safe environment. Proponents contend that the

---

tort system
A body of law that provides a means for victims of accidents and injury to receive just compensation for their loss

subsidy policy
Government grants that benefit firms and individuals

tradable emissions permits
Permits that give firms the property right to pollute and then sell that right to others

The Sotheby's Price-Fixing Scandal

The art world and social elite of New York were shocked in December 2001 when jurors found that A. Alfred Taubman, former chairman of venerable Sotheby's Holdings, Inc., had conspired with Sir Anthony Tennant, the former chairman of rival Christie's International PLC, to fix the commission rates charged its wealthy art clients. Sotheby's, like Christie's, is an auctioneer of fine arts, antiques, and collectibles. Property in a variety of collecting categories are featured, including paintings, jewelry, decorative arts, and books. The company's auction business is comprised of a number of related activities, including on-site and Internet auctions, the purchase and resale of art and other collectibles, and the brokering of art and collectibles through negotiated sales. The company also markets and brokers luxury residential real estate, conducts art-related financing activities, and provides insurance brokerage services.

A chronology of at least a dozen meetings between Taubman and Tennant convinced jurors that the two had met to set identical rates for art-selling clients. Tennant was also indicted on price-fixing charges but refused to

leave Britain to stand trial; the United States cannot extradite him under British law. The government's key witness in the case was Sotheby's former chief executive, Diana D. Brooks, who testified that Taubman instructed her to strike an agreement on commission rates with her counterpart at Christie's.

This conviction represents a spectacular downfall for Taubman, who made a fortune developing shopping malls and rose to social prominence by buying a controlling stake in Sotheby's. At the time of his price-fixing conviction, Taubman had already agreed to pay $186 million toward the settlement of civil charges stemming from the case. His holdings, including stakes in Taubman Centers Inc., are valued at $700 million to $1 billion. The 76-year-old Taubman faces a maximum of 3 years in prison and a $350,000 fine.

See: Kathryn Kranhold, "Former Sotheby's Chairman Is Found Guilty of Conspiring to Fix Client Fees," *The Wall Street Journal Online*, December 6, 2001 (http://online.wsj.com).

costs of pollution abatement make trade-offs inevitable. Moreover, they argue that the tradable emissions permits do not confer new licenses to pollute; they merely transfer licenses from one polluter to another. Nevertheless, by awarding tradable emissions permits worth millions of dollars to the worst offenders of a clean environment, environmentally sensitive firms and consumers have been hurt, at least on a relative basis.

Tax Policy

tax policy
Fines and penalties that limit undesirable performance

Whereas subsidy policy gives firms positive incentives for desirable performance, **tax policy** confers penalties designed to limit undesirable performance. Tax policy includes both regular tax payments and fines or penalties that may be assessed intermittently.

Local, state, or federal fines for exceeding specified weight limits on trucks, pollution taxes, and effluent charges are common examples of tax policies intended to limit negative externalities. The appropriate tax level is extremely difficult to determine because of problems associated with estimating the magnitude of negative externalities. For example, calculating some of the social costs of air pollution, such as more frequent house painting, is relatively straightforward. Calculating the costs of increased discomfort—even death—for emphysema patients is more difficult. Nevertheless, regulators must consider the full range of consequences of negative externalities to create appropriate and effective incentives for pollution control.

Although tax policy complements subsidy and property rights grant policies, an important distinction should not be overlooked. If society wants to limit the harmful consequences of air pollution, either subsidies for pollution reduction or taxes on pollution can provide effective incentives. Subsidies imply that firms have a right to pollute because society pays to reduce pollution. In contrast, a system of pollution tax penalties asserts society's right to a clean environment. Firms must reimburse society for the damage caused by their pollution. Many prefer tax policy as a method for pollution reduction on the grounds that it explicitly recognizes the public's right to a clean and safe environment.

Operating Controls

operating controls
Regulation by government directive

Operating controls prohibit certain actions while compelling others. Operating controls that achieve 100 percent compliance create a situation similar to that reached under a prohibitive tax policy. In each instance, undesirable activity is completely eliminated, and no tax revenues are collected. When operating controls result in less than full compliance, operating control regulation becomes like tax policy because fines and levies increase the costs to violators.

The effectiveness of operating control regulation can be limited by vague or imprecise statutory standards. If sanctions against violators are poorly defined or lenient, incentives for compliance can be weak. Beyond the difficulties created by poorly defined regulations and sanctions, problems can arise when conflicting operating controls are imposed. For example, mandatory safety standards and pollution controls have increased automobile costs by several hundred dollars per unit. Other indirect costs are also incurred. Auto safety and pollution standards have the effect of reducing fuel efficiency and thus reduce U.S. energy independence.

The clearest difference between operating control regulation and regulation via tax or subsidy policies is the reliance on nonmonetary incentives for compliance. There are no easy alternatives to operating control regulation when social costs are prohibitive (e.g., nuclear disaster, groundwater contamination, and so on). Unfortunately, many firms direct their efforts toward being exempted from operating controls rather than toward reducing the negative externalities of concern to society.

WHO PAYS THE COSTS OF REGULATION?

Regulation is expensive. The regulatory system can increase consumer prices and cut profits when dispute resolution is slow, litigation costs are high, and the outcomes of legal proceedings are risky. Socially beneficial regulatory reform involves setting rules that provide fair and efficient dispute resolution.

Demand and Supply Effects

tax incidence
Point of tax collection

tax burden
Economic cost of tax

The question of who pays for regulation can seldom be determined merely by identifying the fined, taxed, or otherwise regulated party. Although the point of tax collection, or the **tax incidence**, of pollution charges may be a given corporation, this **tax burden** may be passed on to customers or suppliers.

In general, who pays for operating control regulation depends on the elasticity of demand for the final products of affected firms. Figure 13.1 illustrates this issue by considering the theoretically polar extremes of perfectly elastic demand for final products, [Fig. 13.1(a)], and perfectly inelastic demand for final products, [Fig. 13.1(b)]. Identically upward-sloping *MC* curves are assumed in each instance. Here, as is often the case, regulation is assumed to increase marginal costs by a fixed amount per unit. This amount, *t*, can reflect pollution taxes per unit of output or regulation-induced cost increases.

Figure 13.1(a) shows that good substitutes for a firm's product and highly elastic demand prevent producers from passing taxes or regulation-induced cost increases on to customers. In this case, producers—including investors, employees, and suppliers—are forced to bear the burden of regulation. Falling rates of return on invested capital and high unemployment are symptomatic of such influences.

Figure 13.1(b) shows the effect of regulation-induced cost or tax increases in the case of perfectly inelastic final-product demand. Without substitute products, producers can pass the burden of regulation on to customers and encounter relatively few disadvantages because of regulation-induced cost increases. When demand is inelastic, the consumer pays for regulation.

Although the preceding analysis is greatly simplified, it shows that taxes or regulation-induced cost increases have differing effects when demand relationships vary. Similarly, the effect of regulation on industries with similar product-demand elasticities varies to the extent that supply characteristics differ.

FIGURE 13.1

Regulatory Burden Allocation Under Elastic and Inelastic Demand

(a) Highly elastic product demand places the burden of regulation-induced cost increases on producers, who must cut production from Q_1 to Q_2. (b) Low elasticity of product demand allows producers to raise prices from P_1 to P_2, and consumers bear the burden of regulation-induced cost increases.

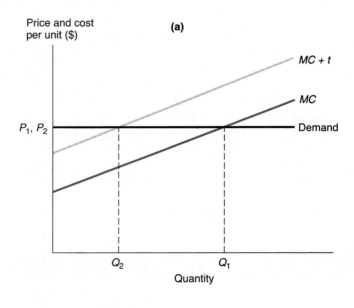

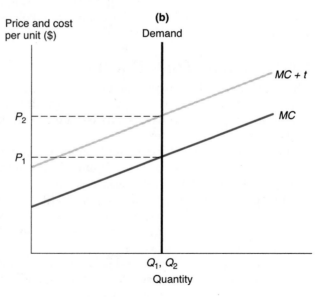

Regulation Cost Sharing Example

To illustrate the effects of regulation-induced cost increases, consider the effects of a new regulation prohibiting herbicide usage in corn production, perhaps because of fears about groundwater contamination. Assume that the industry is perfectly competitive, so the $3 market price of corn represents both average and marginal revenue per bushel ($P = MR = \$3$). The marginal cost relation for each farmer, before any new regulations are imposed, is

$$MC = \partial TC / \partial Q = \$0.6 + \$0.04Q$$

where Q is bushels of corn (in thousands). The optimal level of corn production per farm is calculated by setting $MR = MC$ and solving for Q:

$$
\begin{aligned}
MR &= MC \\
\$3 &= \$0.6 + \$0.04Q \\
\$0.04Q &= \$2.4 \\
Q &= 60(000) \text{ or } 60,000 \text{ bushels}
\end{aligned}
$$

Given a perfectly competitive market, the supply curve for each producer is given by the marginal cost curve. From the marginal cost relation, the quantity of corn supplied by each farmer is

$$
\begin{aligned}
\text{Supply Price} &= \text{Marginal Cost} \\
P &= \$0.6 + \$0.04Q
\end{aligned}
$$

or

$$Q = -15 + 25P$$

If the corn industry consists of 200,000 farmers with farms of equal size, total industry supply is

$$
\begin{aligned}
Q_S &= 200,000(-15 + 25P) \\
&= -3,000,000 + 5,000,000P \qquad \text{(Supply)}
\end{aligned}
$$

To complete the industry profile prior to the new regulation on herbicides, assume that industry demand is given by the relation

$$Q_D = 15,000,000 - 1,000,000P \qquad \text{(Demand)}$$

In equilibrium,

$$
\begin{aligned}
Q_S &= Q_D \\
-3,000,000 + 5,000,000P &= 15,000,000 - 1,000,000P \\
6,000,000P &= 18,000,000 \\
P &= \$3 \text{ per bushel}
\end{aligned}
$$

and

$$
\begin{aligned}
Q_S &= -3,000,000 + 5,000,000(3) \\
&= 12,000,000(000), \text{ or } 12 \text{ billion bushels} \\
Q_D &= 15,000,000 - 1,000,000(3) \\
&= 12,000,000(000), \text{ or } 12 \text{ billion bushels}
\end{aligned}
$$

Now assume that reducing herbicide usage increases the amount of tillage needed to keep weed growth controlled and causes the yield per acre to drop, resulting in a 25 percent increase in the marginal costs of corn production. For individual farmers, the effect on marginal costs is reflected as

$$
\begin{aligned}
MC' &= 1.25(\$0.6 + \$0.04Q) \\
&= \$0.75 + \$0.05Q
\end{aligned}
$$

If only a few farmers in a narrow region of the country are subject to the new regulation, as would be true in the case of state or local pollution regulations, then market prices would remain stable at \$3, and affected farmers would curtail production dramatically to 45,000 bushels each, because

$$MR = MC'$$
$$\$3 = \$0.75 + \$0.05Q$$
$$\$0.05Q = \$2.25$$
$$Q = 45(000), \text{ or } 45,000 \text{ bushels}$$

Given a perfectly competitive industry and, therefore, a perfectly elastic demand for corn, local pollution regulations will force producers to bear the entire burden of regulation-induced cost increases.

A different situation arises when all producers are subject to the new herbicide regulation. In this instance, the revised individual-firm supply curve is

$$\text{Supply Price} = \text{Marginal Cost}$$
$$P = \$0.75 + \$0.05Q$$

or

$$Q = -15 + 20P$$

Total industry supply, assuming that all 200,000 farmers remain in business (something that may not happen if the resulting changes in profit levels are substantial), equals

$$Q'_S = 200,000(-15 + 20P)$$
$$= -3,000,000 + 4,000,000P \qquad \text{(New Supply)}$$

The equilibrium industry price/output combination is found where

$$Q'_S = Q_D$$
$$-3,000,000 + 4,000,000P = 15,000,000 - 1,000,000P$$
$$5,000,000P = 18,000,000$$
$$P = \$3.60 \text{ per bushel}$$

and

$$Q'_S = -3,000,000 + 4,000,000(3.60)$$
$$= 11,400,000(000), \text{ or } 11.4 \text{ billion bushels}$$
$$Q_D = 15,000,000 - 1,000,000(3.60)$$
$$= 11,400,000(000), \text{ or } 11.4 \text{ billion bushels}$$

At the new market price, each individual farm produces 57,000 bushels of corn:

$$Q = -15 + 20(3.60)$$
$$= 57(000), \text{ or } 57,000 \text{ bushels}$$

Thus, industry-wide regulation of herbicides has a relatively smaller impact on producers because the effects of regulation are partially borne by consumers through the price increase from

$3 to $3.60 per bushel. This example illustrates why state and local authorities find it difficult to regulate firms that operate in highly competitive national markets. Such regulations usually are initiated at the national level.

REGULATORY RESPONSE TO STRUCTURAL FAILURES

Public utility regulation, which controls the prices and profits of established monopolies, is an attempt to enjoy the benefits of low-cost production by large firms while avoiding the social costs of unregulated monopoly. Tax and antitrust policies also address the problem of structural failures by limiting monopoly abuse.

Dilemma of Natural Monopoly

natural monopoly
The preeminence of a single efficient supplier

In some industries, average costs decline as output expands, and a single large firm has the potential to produce total industry output more efficiently than any group of smaller producers. Demand equals supply at a point where the industry long-run average cost curve is still declining. The term **natural monopoly** describes this situation, because monopoly is a direct result of the superior efficiency of a single large producer.

For example, consider Figure 13.2. Here the firm will produce Q units of output at an average cost of C per unit. Note that this cost level is above the minimum point on the long-run average cost curve, and average costs are still declining. As a monopolist, the firm can earn an economic profit equal to the rectangle $PP'C'C$, or $Q(P - C)$. Local electric, gas, and water companies are classic examples of natural monopolies, because the duplication of production and distribution facilities would greatly increase costs if more than one firm served a given area.

FIGURE 13.2

Price/Output Decisions Under Monopoly

Without regulation, monopolies would charge excessively high prices and produce too little output.

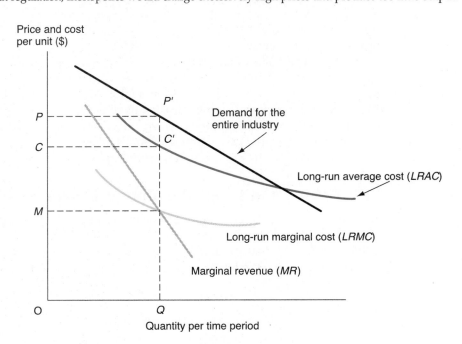

This situation presents a dilemma. Economic efficiency could be enhanced by restricting the number of producers to a single firm. However, this entails risk because monopolists tend to underproduce and earn economic profits. Although such profits give powerful incentives for efficiency, they are difficult to justify when they result from market power rather than from exceptional performance.

Underproduction occurs when the firm curtails production to a level at which the marginal value of resources needed to produce an additional unit of output (marginal cost) is less than the benefit derived from the additional unit. For example, at output levels just greater than Q in Figure 13.2, consumers are willing to pay approximately P dollars per unit, so the value of additional units is P. However, the marginal cost of producing an additional unit is slightly less than M dollars and well below P, so marginal cost does not equal marginal value. Society would find an expansion of output desirable.

Natural monopoly poses a dilemma because monopoly has the potential for greatest efficiency, but unregulated monopoly can lead to economic profits and underproduction. One possible solution is to allow natural monopoly to persist but to impose price and profit regulations.

Utility Price and Profit Regulations

The most common method of monopoly regulation is price and profit control. Such regulations result in larger output quantities and lower profits than would be the case with unrestricted monopoly. This situation is illustrated in Figure 13.3. A monopolist operating without regulation would produce Q_1 units of output and charge a price of P_1. If regulators set a ceiling on prices at P_2, the firm's effective demand curve becomes the kinked curve P_2AD. Because price is a constant from 0 to Q_2 units of output, marginal revenue equals price in this range; that is, P_2A is the marginal revenue curve over the output range $0Q_2$. For output beyond Q_2, marginal revenue is given by the original marginal revenue function. The marginal revenue curve is now discontinuous at Q_2, with a gap between points A and L. This regulated firm maximizes profits by operating at Q_2 and charging the ceiling price, P_2. Marginal revenue is greater than marginal cost up to that output but is less than marginal cost beyond it.

Profits are also reduced by this regulatory action. Without price regulation, price P_1 is charged, a cost of C_1 per unit is incurred, and Q_1 is produced. Profit is $(P_1 - C_1) \times (Q_1)$, which equals the area P_1BFC_1. With price regulation, the price is P_2, the cost is C_2, Q_2 units are sold, and profits are represented by the smaller area P_2AEC_2.

To determine a fair price, a regulatory commission must estimate a fair or normal rate of return, given the risk inherent in the enterprise. The commission then approves prices that produce the target rate of return on the required level of investment. In the case illustrated by Figure 13.3, if the profit at price P_2, when divided by the investment required to produce Q_2, were to produce more than the target rate of return, price would be reduced until actual and target rates of return became equal. This assumes, of course, that cost curves in Figure 13.3 do not include equity capital costs. The profit that the regulator allows is business profit, not economic profit.

Utility Price and Profit Regulation Example

To further illustrate the concept of public utility regulation, consider the case of the Malibu Beach Telephone Company, a small telephone utility serving urban customers in southern California. At issue is the monthly rate for local telephone service. The monthly demand for service is given by the relation

$$P = \$22.50 - \$0.00004Q$$

where P is service price in dollars and Q is the number of customers served. Annual total cost and marginal cost curves, excluding a normal rate of return, are given by the following expressions:

FIGURE 13.3

Monopoly Price Regulation: Optimal Price/Output Decision Making

Monopoly regulation imposes a price ceiling at P_2 just sufficient to provide a fair return (area P_2AEC_2) on investment. Under regulation, price falls from P_1 to P_2 and output expands from Q_1 to Q_2.

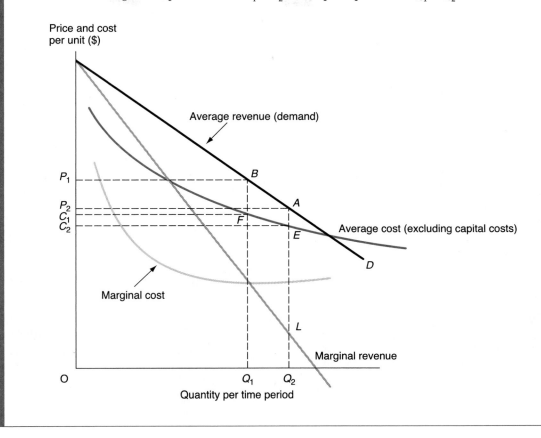

$$TC = \$3,750,000 + \$70Q + 0.00002Q^2$$
$$MC = \partial TC/\partial Q = \$70 + \$0.00004Q$$

where cost is expressed in dollars.

To find the profit-maximizing level of output, demand and marginal revenue curves for annual service must be derived. This will give all revenue and cost relations a common annual basis. The demand curve for annual service is 12 times monthly demand:

$$P = 12(\$22.5 - \$0.00004Q)$$
$$= \$270 - \$0.00048Q$$

Total and marginal revenue curves for this annual demand curve are

$$TR = \$270Q - \$0.00048Q^2$$
$$MR = \partial TR/\partial Q = \$270 - \$0.00096Q$$

The profit-maximizing level of output is found by setting $MC = MR$ (where $M\pi = 0$) and solving for Q:

$$MC = MR$$
$$\$70 + \$0.00004Q = \$270 - \$0.00096Q$$
$$\$0.001Q = \$200$$
$$Q = 200,000$$

The monthly service price is

$$P = \$22.50 - \$0.00004(200,000)$$
$$= \$14.50 \text{ per month (or } \$174 \text{ per year)}$$

This price/output combination generates annual total profits of

$$\pi = \$270Q - \$0.00048Q^2 - \$3,750,000 - \$70Q - \$0.00002Q^2$$
$$= -\$0.0005Q^2 + \$200Q - \$3,750,000$$
$$= -\$0.0005(200,000^2) + \$200(200,000) - \$3,750,000$$
$$= \$16,250,000$$

If the company has $125 million invested in plant and equipment, the annual rate of return on investment is

$$\text{Return on Investment} = \frac{\$16,250,000}{\$125,000,000} = 0.13, \text{ or } 13\%$$

Now assume that the State Public Utility Commission decides that a 12 percent rate of return is fair given the level of risk taken and conditions in the financial markets. With a 12 percent rate of return on total assets, Malibu Beach would earn business profits of

$$\pi = \text{Allowed Return} \times \text{Total Assets}$$
$$= 0.12 \times \$125,000,000$$
$$= \$15,000,000$$

To determine the level of output that would generate this level of total profits, total profit must be set equal to $15 million:

$$\pi = TR - TC$$
$$\$15,000,000 = -\$0.0005Q^2 + \$200Q - \$3,750,000$$

This implies that

$$-\$0.0005Q^2 + \$200Q - \$18,750,000 = 0$$

which is a function of the form $aQ^2 + bQ - c = 0$. Solving for the roots of this equation provides the target output level. We use the quadratic equation as follows:

$$Q = \frac{-b \pm \sqrt{b^2 - 4ac}}{2a}$$

$$= \frac{-200 \pm \sqrt{200^2 - 4(-0.0005)(18,750,000)}}{2(-0.0005)}$$

$$= \frac{-200 \pm \sqrt{2,500}}{-0.001}$$

$$= 150,000 \text{ or } 250,000$$

Microsoft's Antitrust Woes

On November 2, 2001, Microsoft Corp. announced that it had reached a settlement with the U. S. government in its 3-year antitrust case. The settlement pact imposes restrictions for a 5-year period on how the company develops and licenses software, works with independent software vendors, and communicates about the inner workings of its software with partners and competitors. Microsoft's compliance with the agreement will be verified by an independent, on-site, three-member panel of computer experts.

Under the terms of the accord, Microsoft may not enter into licensing agreements with PC manufacturers that restrict such manufacturers from working with other software developers, a practice referred to as "exclusive dealing." It also requires Microsoft to provide other software makers with access to elements of its Windows source code, called "application programming interfaces," which are necessary for them to make independent applications work under the Windows operating system.

In an important win for Microsoft, the Justice Department settlement does not impose any restrictions on features Microsoft is allowed to incorporate in newer versions of its Windows operating system. Microsoft will be able to continue to innovate and combine new Internet browser software with its basic operating system. This is important because the personal computer has been transformed from a computing device, where desktop applications like *Microsoft Word* are important, to an Internet communications device, where efficient information search and communication are key.

What remains to be seen is if Microsoft can recapture some of the excitement that made it a stock-market darling during the 1990s when investors saw the value of Microsoft stock multiply more than 100:1. Microsoft first went public in 1986, when it generated $197.5 million in revenues and $39.3 million in net income. By 2005, Microsoft revenues are expected to surge to $45 billion, while profits swell to $16.7 billion. Hitting these revenue and profit targets will be tough in an increasingly competitive market environment.

See: Mark Wigfield, "Federal Judge Says No New Hearings Are Needed to Weigh Microsoft Pact," *The Wall Street Journal Online*, March 6, 2002 (http://online.wsj.com).

Because public utility commissions generally want utilities to provide service to the greatest possible number of customers at the lowest possible price, the upper figure $Q = 250,000$ is the appropriate output level. To induce Malibu Beach Telephone to operate at this output level, regulatory authorities would determine the maximum allowable price for monthly service as

$$P = \$22.50 - \$0.00004(250,000)$$
$$= \$12.50$$

This $12.50-per-month price provides service to the broadest customer base possible, given the need to provide Malibu Beach with the opportunity to earn a 12 percent rate of return on investment.

Problems with Utility Price and Profit Regulation

Although the concept of utility price and profit regulation is simple, several practical problems arise in public utility regulation. In practice, it is impossible to exactly determine cost and demand schedules, or the minimum investment required to support a given level of output. Moreover, because utilities serve several classes of customers, many different rate schedules could produce the desired profit level. If profits for the local electric power company are too low, should rates be raised for summer (peak) or for winter (off-peak) users? Should industrial, commercial, or residential customers bear the burden of higher rates?

Regulators also make mistakes with regard to the optimal level and growth of service. For example, if a local telephone utility is permitted to charge excessive rates, the system will grow at a faster-than-optimal rate. Similarly, when the allowed rate of return exceeds the cost of capital, electric, gas, and water utilities have an incentive to overexpand fixed assets and shift to overly capital-intensive methods of production. In contrast, if prices allowed to natural gas producers are too low, consumers will be encouraged to deplete scarce gas supplies, producers will limit exploration and development, and gas shortages can occur. If gas prices are too low and offer only a below-market rate of return on capital, necessary expansion will be thwarted.

regulatory lag
The delay between when a change in regulation is appropriate and the date it becomes effective

A related problem is that of **regulatory lag**, or the delay between when a change in regulation is appropriate and the date it becomes effective. During the 1970s and 1980s, inflation exerted constant upward pressure on costs. At the same time, consumers and voters were able to reduce, delay, or deny reasonable rate increases. This caused severe financial hardship for a number of utilities and their stockholders. More recently, rapid changes in technology and competitive conditions have rendered obsolete many traditional forms of regulation in the electricity and telecommunications industries. When regulators are slow to react to such changes, both consumers and the industry suffer.

Traditional forms of regulation can also lead to inefficiency. If a utility is guaranteed a minimum return on investment, operating inefficiencies can be offset by higher prices. The process of utility regulation itself is also costly. Detailed demand and cost analyses are necessary to provide a reasonable basis for rate decisions. It is expensive to pay regulatory officials, full-time utility commission staffs, record-keeping costs, and the expense of processing rate cases. All of these expenses are ultimately borne by consumers. Although many economists can see no reasonable alternative to utility regulation for electric, gas, local telephone, and private water companies, the costs and inefficiency of such regulation are troubling.

ANTITRUST POLICY

Antitrust policy in the United States is designed to protect competition. If competitive forces are vibrant, consumer prices are and unwarranted economic profits are low. Product quality, innovation, and economic growth also tend to be high. In a vigorously competitive economic environment, there will be corporate winners and losers. This is fine so long as the game is played fairly. When unfair methods of competition emerge, antitrust policy is brought to bear.

Overview of Antitrust Law

antitrust laws
Laws that promote competition and prevent monopoly

Antitrust laws are designed to promote competition and prevent unwarranted monopoly. By itself, large firm size or market dominance is no offense; it is any *unfairly* gained competitive advantage that is against the law. The primary objection to monopolies, cartels, and other restraints of trade is that they injure consumers by increasing prices. High monopoly prices also curtail consumption and thereby reduce consumer welfare. A further objection to monopoly is that unchecked economic power stiffles innovation and often fails to provide necessary incentives for operating efficiency. As British economist John Hicks once wrote, "The best of all monopoly profits is a quiet life." Thus, complacency on the part of monopolists can impede economic progress.

The choice between pure competition and monopoly is easy. Unfortunately, that is seldom the decision facing those charged with antitrust enforcement. Antitrust concerns tend to arise in industries where firms have some market power, but also face competition. In such instances, mergers and restrictive practices that may create or enhance market power may also promote efficiency and benefit consumers. Antitrust enforcement is made difficult by the need to identify corporate conduct whose *primary* effect is to lessen competition and harm consumers.

There is no single antitrust statute in the United States. Federal antitrust law is based on two important statutes—the Sherman Act and the Clayton Act—and their amendments. An important characteristic of these laws is that they broadly ban, but never define, "restraints of trade," "monopolization," "unfair competition," and so on. By never precisely defining such key terms, the statutes left the courts to decide the specific legality or illegality of various business practices. Because of this, many principles in antitrust law rest on judicial interpretation. Individual court decisions, called *case law*, and statutory standards, called *statutory law*, must be consulted to assess the legality of business behavior.

Sherman Act

The Sherman Act of 1890 was the first federal antitrust legislation. It is brief and to the point. Section 1 forbids contracts, combinations, or conspiracies in restraint of trade. Section 2 forbids monopolizing behavior. Both sections can be enforced through the civil courts or by criminal proceedings. On conviction, corporate punishment can be in the form of fines not to exceed $10 million. Individuals face a felony conviction and may be fined up to $350,000 or imprisoned for a period of time up to 3 years. Firms and individuals violating the Sherman Act also face the possibility of paying triple damages to injured parties who bring civil suits.

The Sherman Act is often criticized as being too vague. Even with landmark decisions against the tobacco, powder, and oil trusts, enforcement has been sporadic. On the one hand, businesspeople claim not to know what is legal; on the other, the Justice Department is sometimes criticized as being ignorant of monopoly-creating practices and failing to act in a timely fashion. Despite its shortcomings, the Sherman Act remains one of the government's main weapons against anticompetitive behavior.

Clayton Act

Congress passed two laws in 1914 to overcome weaknesses in the Sherman Act. The more important of these, the Clayton Act, addresses problems of mergers, interlocking directorates, price discrimination, and tying contracts. The Federal Trade Commission Act outlaws unfair methods of competition in commerce and establishes the FTC, an agency intended to enforce the Clayton Act.

Section 2 of the Clayton Act prohibits sellers from discriminating in price among business customers, unless cost differentials or competitive pressure justifies the price differentials. As a primary goal, the act seeks to prevent a strong regional or national firm from employing selective price cuts to drive weak local firms out of business. It was thought that once competitors in one market were eliminated, national firms could then charge monopoly prices and use resulting excess profits to subsidize cutthroat competition in other areas. The Robinson-Patman Act, passed in 1936, amended the section of the Clayton Act dealing with price discrimination. It declares specific forms of price discrimination illegal, especially those related to chain-store purchasing practices.

Section 3 of the Clayton Act forbids tying contracts that reduce competition. A firm, particularly one with a patent on a vital process or a monopoly on a natural resource, could use licensing or other arrangements to restrict competition. One such method is the tying contract, whereby a firm ties the acquisition of one item to the purchase of another. For example, IBM once refused to sell its business machines. It only rented machines to customers and then required them to buy IBM punch cards, materials, and maintenance service. This had the effect of reducing competition in these related industries. The IBM lease agreement was declared illegal under the Clayton Act, and the company was forced to offer machines for sale and to separate leasing arrangements from agreements to purchase other IBM products.

Finally, although the Sherman Act prohibits voting trusts that lessened competition, interpretation of the act did not always prevent one corporation from acquiring the stock of competing firms and then merging these firms into itself. Section 7 of the Clayton Act prohibits stock mergers that reduce competition. Either the Antitrust Division of the Justice Department or the FTC can bring suit under Section 7 to prevent mergers. If mergers have been consummated prior to the suit, divestiture can be ordered. The Clayton Act also prevents individuals from serving on the boards of directors of two competing companies. So-called competitors having common directors would obviously not compete very hard. Although the Clayton Act made it illegal for firms to merge through stock transactions when the effect is to lessen competition, the law left a loophole. A firm could purchase the assets of a competing firm, integrate the operations into its own, and thus reduce competition. The Celler-Kefauver Act closed this loophole, making asset acquisitions illegal when the effect of such purchases is to reduce competition. By a slight change in wording, it made clear Congress's intent to attack all mergers that threatened competition, whether vertical mergers between buyers and sellers, horizontal and market extension mergers between actual or potential competitors, or purely conglomerate mergers between unrelated firms.

Antitrust Enforcement

The Sherman Act is brought to bear—with both criminal and civil penalties—in cases involving monopolization, price-fixing agreements, and other unreasonable restraints on trade. The Clayton Act is used to address specific problems created by mergers and certain forms of price discrimination, exclusive dealing agreements, and tie-in sales conditioned on the purchase of related products.

The Justice Department and the FTC have overlapping enforcement responsibilities. The Justice Department may bring actions under the Sherman Act, and the FTC may initiate actions under the Federal Trade Commission Act. Both may initiate proceedings under the Clayton Act. In addition, major regulatory agencies, such as the Federal Communications Commission, the Federal Energy Regulatory Commission, and the Surface Transportation Board, all review mergers under their own statutory authority.

Generally speaking, the Justice Department concerns itself with significant or flagrant offenses under the Sherman Act, as well as with mergers for monopoly covered by Section 7 of the Clayton Act. In most instances, the Justice Department brings charges under the Clayton Act only when broader Sherman Act violations are also involved. In addition to policing law violations, the Sherman Act assigns the Justice Department the duty of restraining possible future violations. Firms found to be in violation of the law often receive detailed federal court injunctions that regulate future business activity. Injunctive relief in the form of dissolution or divestiture decrees is a much more typical outcome of Justice Department suits than are criminal penalties.

Although the Justice Department can institute civil and criminal proceedings, civil proceedings are typically the responsibility of the FTC. The FTC is an administrative agency of the executive branch that has quasi-judicial powers with which it enforces compliance with the Clayton Act. Because the substantive provisions of the Clayton Act do not create criminal offenses, the FTC has no criminal jurisdiction. The FTC holds hearings about suspected violations of the law and issues cease and desist orders if violations are found. Cease and desist orders under the Clayton Act are subject to review by appellate courts.

Horizontal Merger Guidelines

Antitrust policy is applied if a specific business practice is thought to substantially lessen competition or tend to create a monopoly. Mergers and other business practices are legal so long as they do not affect the vigor of competition. A significant recent challenge for antitrust enforcement has been the dramatic increase in merger activity.

As illustrated in Figure 13.4, a skyrocketing stock market caused the merger market to come roaring back to life during the late 1990s. In evaluating such mergers, enforcement agencies must strike a fine balance between expected cost savings and any possible harm to competition. Both present-day and potential competitors must be considered. The impact on competition is particularly difficult to evaluate in industries experiencing rapid structural and technological

FIGURE 13.4

The 1990s Was a Decade of Intense Merger Activity

The number and total value of mergers and acquisitions soared during the 1990s.

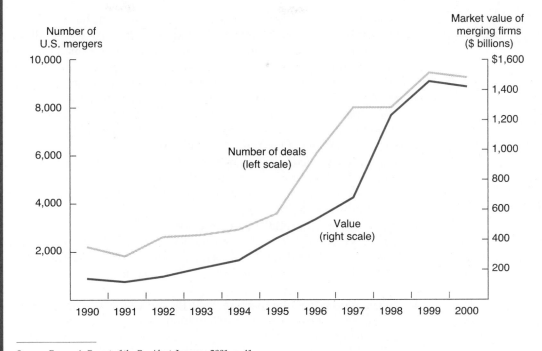

Source: *Economic Report of the President*, January 2001, p. 41.

change. Mergers do not have to create monopoly to result in higher prices and lower output. Greater industry concentration can make it easier for firms to communicate their intentions, and the interests of competitors may be less likely to diverge. For example, mergers can make price cutting less profitable by reducing customer alternatives. This is especially true when merging firms feature powerful brands that are particularly close substitutes.

Enforcement agencies must balance concerns about market power against the efficiencies mergers can make possible. There are several ways in which mergers can reduce costs. Mergers can allow one firm to take advantage of another's superior technology and allow merging firms to specialize in activities that each does best. Mergers may also increase efficiency by eliminating fixed costs or allowing longer production runs.

The challenge for effective antitrust enforcement is to prevent mergers and competitive practices that harm consumers but to allow those that create substantial benefits. To evaluate the market power and the efficiency effects of mergers, the FTC and the Department of Justice (DOJ) use a jointly derived framework called **horizontal merger guidelines**. Steps taken in merger reviews are as follows:

horizontal merger guidelines
Government approval standards for combinations among competitors

- Define the relevant market and calculate its concentration before and after the merger.
- Assess whether the merger raises concerns about adverse competitive effects.
- Determine whether entry by other firms into the market would counteract those effects.
- Consider any expected efficiency gains.

Remember from Chapter 11 that industry concentration is measured by the Herfindahl Hirschmann Index (HHI), a measure named after the economists who invented it. Calculated in percentage terms, the HHI is the sum of the squared market shares for all n industry competitors:

$$(13.1) \qquad HHI = \sum_{i=1}^{n} \left(\frac{\text{Firm Sales}_i}{\text{Industry Sales}} \times 100 \right)^2$$

For example, a market consisting of four firms with market shares of 30 percent, 30 percent, 20 percent, and 20 percent has an HHI of 2,600 (= $30^2 + 30^2 + 20^2 + 20^2$). Although it is desirable to include all firms in the calculation, lack of information about small firms is not critical because such firms do not affect the HHI significantly. A monopoly industry with a single dominant firm is described by a four-firm concentration ratio of 100 percent, or $CR_4 = 100$, and a $HHI = 100^2$ = 10,000. A vigorously competitive industry where each of the leading four firms enjoys market shares of 25 percent is also described by a $CR_4 = 100$, but features a $HHI = 25^2 + 25^2 + 25^2 + 25^2 =$ 2,500. Like the four-firm concentration ratio, the HHI approaches zero for industries characterized by a large number of very small competitors.

When a merger occurs, or a pending merger is proposed, the increase in concentration as measured by the HHI can be calculated by doubling the product of the market shares of the merging firms. For example, the merger of firms with 5 percent and 10 percent shares of the market would increase the HHI by 100 (= $2 \times 5 \times 10$). To see this is the case, simply recall that in calculating the HHI before the merger, the market shares of merging firms are squared individually, or $a^2 + b^2$. After the merger, the sum of those individual firm market shares would be squared, or $(a + b)^2$, which equals $a^2 + 2ab + b^2$. The merger-induced increase in the HHI, therefore, is represented by $2ab$, which is the product of two times the market shares of the merging firms.

In evaluating horizontal mergers, the FTC and DOJ consider both the post-merger market concentration and the increase in concentration resulting from the merger as potentially useful indicators of competitive implications. According to horizontal merger guidelines, the general standards for horizontal mergers are as follows:

1. *Unconcentrated Markets with Post-Merger HHI Below 1,000.* Mergers resulting in relatively unconcentrated markets are not likely to have adverse competitive effects and ordinarily will be approved.

2. *Moderately Concentrated Markets with Post-Merger HHI Between 1,000 and 1,800.* Mergers producing an increase in the HHI of less than 100 points in moderately concentrated markets are unlikely to have adverse competitive consequences and ordinarily will be approved. Mergers producing an increase in the HHI of more than 100 points in moderately concentrated markets have the potential to raise significant competitive concerns and would be scrutinized.

3. *Highly Concentrated Markets with Post-Merger HHI Above 1,800.* Mergers producing an increase in the HHI of less than 50 points, even in highly concentrated markets, are unlikely to have adverse competitive consequences and ordinarily will be approved. Mergers producing an increase in the HHI of more than 50 points in highly concentrated markets have the potential to raise significant competitive concerns and would be scrutinized. Where the post-merger HHI exceeds 1,800, it will be presumed that mergers producing an increase in the HHI of more than 100 points are likely to create or enhance market power and would ordinarily not be approved.

Although the FTC and DOJ realize that the post-merger level of market concentration and the change in concentration resulting from a merger affect the degree to which a merger raises competitive concerns, both recognize that market concentration data sometimes misstate the competitive significance of a given merger. For example, changes in technology can make long-entrenched rivals susceptible to innovative products produced by new foreign or domestic competitors. Changes in technology also have the potential to reshape the demand for substitutes outside historically relevant markets. Recent advances in the satellite transmission of voice and data communication have clearly reduced the market power of local telecommunications and cable television companies. Similarly, the exploding use of the Internet allows customers to compare the price and performance of goods and services offered by both local and distant providers.

It is from within this framework that recent antitrust policy initiatives can be evaluated.

Recent Antitrust Policy Initiatives

The development and adoption of new technology is essential to economic growth over time. To the extent that recent antitrust policy initiatives hinder or otherwise interfere with invention and innovation, such initiatives come at a significant social cost, irrespective of any compensating virtues. During recent years, some of the most important and controversial antitrust initiatives have come in increasingly important network industries.

Americans are intimately familiar with networks such as credit card networks, telephone networks, and computer networks. The distinguishing feature of all such networks is that their value grows as customer use becomes more widespread. New telephone subscribers increase the potential number of people that one can call; expanding use of the Internet increases the amount of information on the Web. Similarly, when more retail outlets, department stores, and restaurants adopt a given credit card, the value of that credit card grows for all its holders. The added value that new users add to network goods and services is called a **network externality**. Networks became a recent concern in antitrust policy because the Clinton Justice Department feared that if inferior networks got a decisive lead in "installed base" among consumers, switching costs might be sufficient to keep customers from switching to a superior standard. Switching costs might also constitute a barrier to entry in the industry and enable network monopolists to tie or bundle a second product in such a way as to foreclose competition in that secondary market.

network externality
Added value that new users add to network goods and services

Concern over competition and innovation among general-purpose credit cards recently prompted the Justice department to file suit against the two largest networks, Visa and MasterCard. Although Visa and MasterCard began as separate and competing networks owned and governed by their card-issuing members, substantial overlap now exists given the willingness of each network to accept new members. The Justice Department case focuses on the potential innovation-reducing effects of this overlapping ownership and governance arrangement. In particular, the Justice Department alleges that Visa and MasterCard have unnecessarily delayed implementation of "smart card" technology that has the potential to better monitor fraud and credit risk. Although the outcome of this case remains in doubt, it remains as an example of aggressive antitrust policy in this area.

Preserving competition in telecommunications networks has also been a high priority in antitrust policy. As you know, a computer network is nothing more than a means for linking computers and peripheral equipment (e.g., printers) so that they can communicate with one another. The Internet is simply a seamless connection that allows information to freely travel from one computer network to another. An Internet backbone is a powerful, high-message-capacity system that links regional or metropolitan networks to the Internet. For example, when customers use AOL as their Internet service provider (ISP), they often use a telephone modem to connect to AOL's network [sometimes called a local area network (LAN)]. In turn, AOL's network is connected to the Internet via several Internet backbones. To provide ready customer service, AOL and other ISPs must lease capacity on the Internet backbone facilities provided by major telecommunications providers. In 1998, fearing an anticompetitive increase in concentration in this "network of networks," the Justice Department required MCI Communications Corp. to divest its Internet backbone business as a precondition to its approval of MCI's merger with WorldCom, Inc. Two years later, in 2000, the proposed merger of MCI-WorldCom, Inc., and Sprint Corp., the nation's No. 2 and No. 3 long-distance companies and the top two Internet backbone providers, proved too much for antitrust authorities, who turned thumbs down on the deal.

MANAGERIAL APPLICATION   13.4

The Enron Debacle

In November 2001, Enron Corp. filed the largest voluntary Chapter 11 bankruptcy petition in U.S. history—a stunning collapse for a company worth more than $60 billion less than a year earlier. Historically, Enron's principal business was the transportation and marketing of natural gas and electricity to markets throughout the United States. More recently, the company built a large commodities trading, risk management, and financial services business that led to its eventual downfall.

Enron ran into trouble trading energy futures contracts. A futures contract is a binding legal document that commits the buyer to take delivery, and the seller to make delivery, of an underlying asset in a specified quantity and quality at a specific delivery time and place. Because futures contracts involve obligations to buy and sell a specific commodity for a preset price, both buyers and sellers of futures contracts are exposed to the potential for unlimited losses in the event of adverse market conditions. Like stock options and stock index options, futures contracts on commodities like natural gas are called "financial derivatives" because their economic value is derived from changes in the price of natural gas or some other underlying commodity.

To control risk and lend stability to futures markets, Congress enacted the Commodity Exchange Act in 1974 and established the Commodity Futures Trading Commission (CFTC), an independent federal regulatory agency with jurisdiction over futures trading. The CFTC strives to protect market participants against manipulation, abusive trade practices, and fraud. Critics contend that the Enron bankruptcy could have been averted had the company not won various regulatory exemptions in the Commodity Futures Modernization Act of 2000, a law that drastically reduced the power of government regulatory agencies overseeing futures markets. Without such exemptions, the CFTC might have regulated EnronOnline as an "organized exchange" and put controls in place to avoid financial disaster for Enron employees, investors, and trading partners.

See: Michael Schroeder and Cassell Bryan-Low, "After Enron, Congress Backs Off from Deregulation, Calls for Controls," *The Wall Street Journal Online*, January 29, 2002 (http://online.wsj.com).

Clearly the biggest and most controversial antitrust initiative undertaken in the networking area is the Justice Department's case against Microsoft Corp. The Justice Department claims that Microsoft has misused its dominance of the market for personal computer operating systems to maintain dominance of that market and to extend dominance to related markets, primarily the market for browser software. A browser is computer software that allows users to access and navigate the Internet. The Justice Department claims that Microsoft has unfairly required computer manufacturers to install the Microsoft browser as a precondition of their receiving licenses to install Windows (its dominant personal computer operating system) and that Microsoft has required computer manufacturers to display ISP icons on the main "pop-up screen" only when such ISPs agree to employ the Microsoft browser. For its part, Microsoft contends that integrating its browser with the Windows operating system enhances the functionality of both and that its contractual arrangements with computer manufacturers and ISPs are nothing more than standard cross-promotional arrangements.

The case against Microsoft, like actions against Visa and MasterCard and telecom mergers, represents historic initiatives designed to maintain vigorous competition in markets dominated by network externalities. The challenge for antitrust policy makers is to preserve competitive opportunities without punishing successful competitors. Striking the right balance between regulation and market pressure is essential for promoting innovation and protecting consumer welfare in fast-moving high-tech markets.

PROBLEMS WITH REGULATION

The need for regulation stems from economic and social factors that stimulate market failures due to incentive or structural problems. However, despite obvious benefits, there are costs to various regulatory methods. It is therefore useful to look closely at both the problems and the unfilled promise of economic regulation.

Costs of Regulation

An obvious cost of regulation is the expense to local, state, and federal governments for supervisory agencies. In 2000, federal government estimates for administrative expenditures on business regulation totaled in excess of $18.5 billion dollars per year. Billions more are spent each year by local and state agencies. It is interesting that the largest regulatory budgets at the federal level are not those of traditional regulatory agencies, such as the Securities and Exchange Commission or Federal Trade Commission but are those devoted to the broader regulatory activities of the Department of Labor for employment and job safety standards and the Department of Agriculture for food inspection.

Although the direct costs of regulation are immense, they may be less than the hidden or indirect costs borne by the private sector. For example, extensive reporting requirements of the Occupational Safety and Health Administration (OSHA) drive up administrative costs and product prices. Consumers also bear the cost of auto emission standards mandated by the Environmental Protection Agency (EPA). In the case of auto emissions, the National Academy of Sciences and the National Academy of Engineering estimate the annual benefits of the catalytic converter at only one-half the billions of dollars in annual costs. One might ask if the social advantages of this method of pollution control are sufficient to offset what appear to be significant economic disadvantages. Similarly, the economic and noneconomic benefits of regulation must be sufficient to offset considerable private costs for pollution control, OSHA-mandated noise reductions, health and safety equipment, FTC-mandated business reports, and so on.

As shown in Figure 13.5, economic costs of regulation are clearly material, and rising. In a recent study, the Small Business Administration (SBA) estimated that the total costs of regulation fell from 1977 to 1988, but rose sharply from 1988 to 2000. In 2000, SBA estimates the total costs to society from all forms of government regulation at $721 billion (in 1995 dollars).

FIGURE 13.5

Total Direct and Indirect Costs of Federal Government Regulation

The costs of regulation rose sharply during the 1990s.

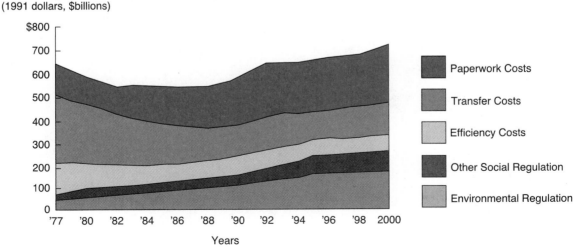

Annualized regulatory costs
(1991 dollars, $billions)

Legend:
- Paperwork Costs
- Transfer Costs
- Efficiency Costs
- Other Social Regulation
- Environmental Regulation

Years

Source: Department of Commerce data.

As shown in Figure 13.6, the costs of environmental regulation amount to 27.6 percent of the total. Clean air and water controls are especially significant and are expected to rachet upwards after 2000 when the full effects of the 1990 clean air amendments are felt. Other social regulation with important cost consequences (9.4 percent of the total) includes regulation of worker safety and health, auto safety, nuclear safety, and job security. Regulatory costs measured in terms of lost efficiency (efficiency costs, 10.7 percent) are thought to be especially important in transportation, international trade, communications, and agriculture. Indirect regulation, which transfers costs from producers to consumers, are another big regulatory cost item (19.6 percent). "Voluntary" controls over imports of autos, textiles, and agricultural products such as sugar cost billions, while entrenched pressure groups make them hard to eliminate. A final major source of regulatory costs is paperwork, now estimated to account for roughly 6 billion worker hours per year and 32.7 percent of the total cost of regulation.

With roughly 285 million Americans, SBA figures suggest that total regulatory costs average roughly $2,530 per year for each man, woman, and child in the United States. Other reasonable estimates put this per capita cost at $3,300 per year, an amount equivalent to almost $1 trillion per year, or roughly 13 percent of gross domestic product. Given this magnitude, consideration of the total costs of regulation must play a prominent role in decisions about what and how to regulate.

Size-Efficiency Problem

Any debate concerning the problems and promise of regulation must emphasize the fact that antitrust and regulatory policy are designed to protect competition. This is not the same thing as protecting competitors. In any vigorously competitive economy there will be winners and

FIGURE 13.6

The Total Cost of Regulation Includes Direct and Indirect Costs

Indirect costs, like the paperwork burden, comprise a significant share of the total costs of regulation.

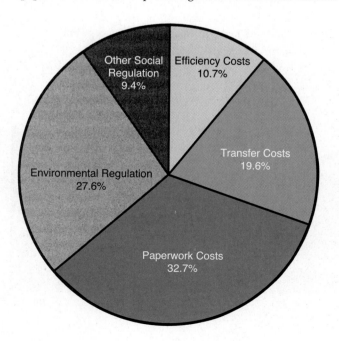

losers. In a competitive market as large as the United States, winners tend to be enormously successful; losers quickly fade or go out of business altogether. Is Microsoft Corp. enormously profitable and successful simply because it offers new and innovative products, or is it able to offer new and innovative products simply because it is large and enormously profitable? Obviously, Microsoft's ongoing battles with regulatory authorities continue because of differing views concerning the origin of the company's size-efficiency linkage. Company officials maintain that Microsoft's growth and profitability are a direct result of its ability to offer innovative computer software. Meanwhile, government regulators contend that the company has used its dominance of the marketplace to unfairly eclipse software rivals.

The size-efficiency debate between Microsoft and the federal government is the type of "chicken or the egg" argument common to high-technology industries. Mergers that seem innocuous today may eliminate future competition; others that increase concentration today pose no significant anticompetitive problem. For example, the 1997 merger between Boeing Co. and McDonnell Douglas Corp. reduced the number of sellers of large commercial aircraft worldwide from only three to two, the other being Airbus Industrie, the European multinational consortium. Nevertheless, the FTC decided that McDonnell Douglas's 5 percent market share overstated that company's future competitive significance because it only reflected the filling of old orders. Advances in aviation design had left McDonnell Douglas behind, and the vast majority of airlines no longer considered purchasing its aircraft. As a result, the Boeing-McDonnell Douglas merger did not eliminate viable future competition in the commercial aircraft market. Moreover, after consulting with the Department of Defense, the FTC concluded that there were no prospects for Boeing and McDonnell Douglas to bid on the same defense projects. Having concluded that the merger raised antitrust concerns in neither commercial nor defense markets, the FTC did not challenge the merger agreement.

Apart from such a case-by-case review, critics point to a general perception of rising monopoly profits as evidence of overly lenient antitrust policy during recent years. For example, Figure 13.7 shows the dramatic increase in **Tobin's q ratio**, defined as the ratio of market value relative to the replacement cost of tangible assets that occurred for nonfinancial firms during the 1990s. In the early 1980s, Nobel laureate James Tobin conceived of this measure as an indicator of pending capital investment. According to Tobin, when high profits cause market values to greatly exceed replacement costs, firms have powerful incentives to expand, and capital investment should boom. Conversely, when low profits cause market values to fall below replacement costs, firms will shrink, and capital investment can be expected to wither.

More recently, economists have used Tobin's q ratio as an indicator of above-normal or monopoly profits. As seen in Figure 13.7, Tobin's q ratio surged from below 100 percent in 1990 to above 200 percent by the end of the decade. However, it is difficult to make the simple conclusion that monopoly profits soared during this period. In the early 1990s, the overall economy suffered a sharp recession that dramatically reduced corporate profits and stock prices. By the end of the 1990s, the economy had logged the longest peacetime expansion in history, and both corporate profits and stock prices surged to record levels. Much of the trend in Tobin's q depicted in Figure 13.7 can be explained by the business cycle. More fundamental changes were also at work. Leading firms today are characterized by growing reliance on what economists refer to as intangible assets, like advertising capital, brand names, customer goodwill, patents, and so on. For leading firms like Coca-Cola, Intel, and Microsoft, tangible assets play a relatively small role in company valuation. Given the growing importance of intangible capital in our economy, it becomes misleading to infer a simple increase in monopoly profits following an increase in Tobin's q over time.

Tobin's q ratio
A ratio calculated as the market value of the firm divided by the replacement cost of tangible assets

Capture Problem

It is a widely held belief that regulation is in the public interest and influences firm behavior toward socially desirable ends. However, in the early 1970s, Nobel laureate George Stigler

FIGURE 13.7

Corporate Profits and Stock Prices Soared During the 1990s

Tobin's q, or the market value to replacement cost ratio, rose sharply during the 1990s.

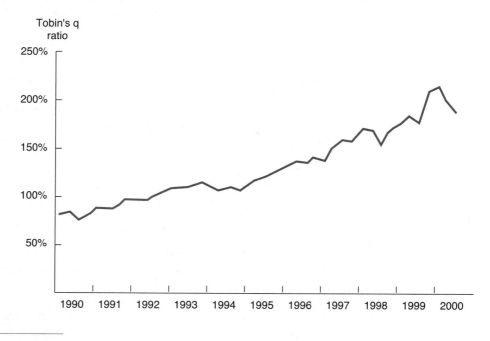

Source: *Economic Report of the President*, January 2001, p. 137.

capture theory
Economic hypothesis suggesting that regulation is sometimes sought to limit competition and obtain government subsidies

and his colleague Sam Peltzman at the University of Chicago introduced an alternative **capture theory** of economic regulation. According to Stigler and Peltzman, the machinery and power of the state are a potential resource to every industry. With its power to prohibit or compel, to take or give money, the state can and does selectively help or hurt a vast number of industries. Because of this, regulation may be actively sought by industry. They contended that regulation is typically *acquired* by industry and is designed and operated primarily for industry's benefit.

Types of state favors commonly sought by regulated industries include direct money subsidies, control over entry by new rivals, control over substitutes and complements, and price fixing. Domestic "air mail" subsidies, Federal Deposit Insurance Corporation (FDIC) regulation that reduces the rate of entry into commercial banking, suppression of margarine sales by butter producers, price fixing in motor carrier (trucking) regulation, and American Medical Association control of medical training and licensing can be interpreted as historical examples of control by regulated industries.

In summarizing their views on regulation, Stigler and Peltzman suggest that regulators should be criticized for pro-industry policies no more than politicians for seeking popular support. Current methods of enacting and carrying out regulations only make the pro-industry stance of regulatory bodies more likely. The only way to get different results from regulation is to change the political process of regulator selection and to provide economic rewards to regulators who serve the public interest effectively.

public interest theory
A view of regulation as a government-imposed means of private-market control

Capture theory is in stark contrast to more traditional **public interest theory**, which sees regulation as a government-imposed means of private-market control. Rather than viewing regulation as a "good" to be obtained, controlled, and manipulated, public interest theory views regulation as a method for improving economic performance by limiting the harmful effects of market failure. Public interest theory is silent on the need to provide regulators with economic incentives to improve regulatory performance. Unlike capture theory, a traditional view has been that the public can trust regulators to make a good-faith effort to establish regulatory policy in the public interest.

To be sure, suggestions of a capture problem are debatable. The need to provide regulators with positive economic incentives to ensure regulation in the public interest is also highly controversial. Nevertheless, growing dissatisfaction with traditional approaches to government regulation has led to a deregulation movement that continues today.

DEREGULATION MOVEMENT

deregulation
The reduction of government control of the free market

Growing concern with the costs and problems of government regulation gave birth to a **deregulation** movement that has grown to impressive dimensions. Although it is difficult to pinpoint a single catalyst for the movement, it is hard to overlook the role played by Stigler, Peltzman, and other economists (notably, Alfred E. Kahn) who illustrated that the regulatory process can sometimes harm consumer interests.

Major Steps Toward Deregulation

A recent study by the Brookings Institution documented important benefits of deregulation. In five major industries—natural gas, telecommunications, airlines, trucking, and railroads—that were deregulated, it was found that regulatory reform generated highly beneficial results.[2] Prices fell 4 percent to 15 percent within the first 2 years after deregulation. Within 10 years, prices were 25 percent to 50 percent lower. Deregulation also leads to service quality improvements. Crucial social goals like airline safety, reliability of gas service, and reliability of the telecommunications network were maintained or improved by deregulation. Regulatory reform also tends to confer benefits on most consumers. Although it is possible to find narrowly defined groups of customers in special circumstances who paid somewhat higher prices after deregulation, the gains to the vast majority of consumers far outweighed negative effects on small groups. Finally, deregulation offers benefits in the sense of permitting greater customer choice.

Table 13.1 highlights some of the major steps taken toward deregulation in the United States since 1970. Although many industries have felt the effects of changing state and local regulation, changing federal regulation has been most pronounced in the financial, telecommunications, and transportation sectors. Since 1975, for example, it has been illegal for securities dealers to fix commission rates. This broke a 182-year tradition under which the New York Stock Exchange (NYSE) set minimum rates for each 100-share ("round lot") purchase. Until 1975, everyone charged the minimum rate approved by the NYSE. Purchase of 1,000 shares cost a commission of 10 times the minimum, even though the overhead and work involved are roughly the same for small and large stock transactions. Following deregulation, commission rates tumbled, and, predictably, some of the least efficient brokerage firms merged or otherwise went out of business. Today, commission rates have fallen 70 percent to 90 percent or more, and the industry is noteworthy for increasing productivity and the variety of new product introductions. It is also worth mentioning that since brokerage rates were deregulated, the number of sales offices in the industry, trading volume, employment, and profits have skyrocketed. All of this may lead many observers to conclude that deregulation can benefit consumers without causing any lasting damage to industry. In fact, a leaner, more efficient industry may be one of the greatest benefits of deregulation.

In Canada, the deregulation movement led to privatization of government-owned Air Canada. Trucking, historically a regulated industry, also was deregulated. Specialized telecommunications services industries were deregulated and thrown open to competition. In other

---

2 See Robert Crandall and Jerry Ellig, *Economic Deregulation and Customer Choice: Lessons for the Electric Industry*, Center for Market Processes, Fairfax, VA, 1997.

TABLE 13.1

Major Steps Toward Deregulation

1970 Federal Reserve Board frees interest rates on large bank deposits with short maturities ($100,000 or more) for 6 months or less.

1971 Federal Communications Commission (FCC) allows companies to set up long-distance telephone networks and compete with AT&T by offering private-line services.

1975 Securities and Exchange Commission prohibits fixed commissions on stock and bond sales.

1978 Congress deregulates prices for airline passenger service.

1979 FCC allows AT&T to sell a limited range of unregulated services (e.g., data processing).

1980 Congress allows banks to pay interest on checking, increases competition for commercial loans. Interstate Commerce Commission begins to dismantle trucking and railroad regulation.

1981 FCC allots airwave space for two cellular phone franchises in every city—one for the local telephone company and one for a competing provider.

1982 Congress allows savings and loans to make commercial loans and related investments; Department of Justice and Federal Trade Commission relax merger guidelines.

1984 Department of Justice order splitting AT&T into seven operating subsidiaries becomes effective. Judge Harold Greene retains indefinite control of the "Baby Bells."

1986 Congress deregulates interest rates for passbook statement savings accounts.

1991 FCC caps long-distance rates and institutes limited profit-rate deregulation for the interstate services of local telephone companies; eliminates price caps for AT&T's large business customers.

1992 FCC eases caps on radio and TV station ownership; sets in motion the process to allow networks full access to syndication revenues from reruns of hit shows.

1995 Congress votes to require all regulations that cost the economy in excess of $25 million to be subject to cost-benefit analysis.

1996 The Telecommunications Act outlines the route for telecommunications deregulations; Federal Energy Regulatory Commission opens up competition in electricity generation. "Freedom to Farm" law reduces crop-production subsidies, promises market forces greater influence in the supply of agricultural products.

1999 Repeal of the Glass-Steagal Act of 1933 and the Bank Holding Company Act of 1956 removes barriers between banks, insurance companies, and insurers.

areas where the government considered continued regulation desirable and necessary, regulatory agencies were pressured to reform and improve the regulatory decision-making process to reduce inefficiencies, bureaucratic delays, and administrative red tape.

Regulation Versus Deregulation Controversy

In evaluating the effects of deregulation, and in gauging the competitive implications of market exit by previously viable firms, it is important to remember that protecting competition is not the same as protecting competitors. Without regulation, it is inevitable that some competitors will fall by the wayside and that concentration will rise in some markets. Although such trends must be watched closely for anticompetitive effects, they are characteristics of a vigorously competitive environment. Although some think that there is simply a question of regulation versus deregulation, this is seldom the case. On grounds of economic and political feasibility, it is often most fruitful to consider approaches to improving existing methods of regulation.

An important problem with regulation is that regulators seldom have the information or expertise to specify, for example, the correct level of utility investment, minimum transportation costs, or the optimum method of pollution control. Because technology changes rapidly in most regulated industries, only industry personnel working at the frontier of current technology have such specialized knowledge. One method for dealing with this technical expertise problem is to have regulators focus on the preferred outcomes of regulatory processes, rather than on the technical means that industry adopts to achieve those ends. The FCC's decision to adopt downward-adjusting price caps for long-distance telephone service is an example of this developing trend toward **incentive-based regulation**. If providers of long-distance telephone service are able to reduce costs faster than the FCC-mandated decline in prices, they will enjoy an increase in profitability. By setting price caps that fall over time, the FCC ensures that consumers share in expected cost savings while companies enjoy a positive incentive to innovate. This approach to regulation focuses on the objectives of regulation while allowing industry to meet those goals in new and unique ways. Tying regulator rewards and regulated industry profits to objective, output-oriented performance criteria has the potential to create a desirable win/win situation for regulators, utilities, and the general public. For example, the public has a real interest in safe, reliable, and low-cost electric power. State and federal regulators who oversee the operations of utilities could develop objective standards for measuring utility safety, reliability, and cost efficiency. Tying firm profit rates to such performance-oriented criteria could stimulate real improvements in utility and regulator performance.

incentive-based regulation
Rules that benefit consumers through enhanced efficiency

REGULATORY REFORM FOR THE NEW MILLENNIUM

Competitive forces provide a persistent and socially desirable constraining influence on firm behavior. When vigorous competition is absent, government regulation can be justified through both efficiency and equity criteria. When regulation is warranted, business, government, and the public must work together to ensure that regulatory processes represent the public interest. The unnecessary costs of antiquated regulations dictate that **regulatory reform** is likely to remain a significant social concern.

regulatory reform
Improvement in government control to enhance efficiency and fairness

Promoting Competition in Electric Power Generation

The electric power industry comprises three different components: the generation of electric power, the transmission of electric power from generators to local utilities, and the distribution of electricity by local utilities to commercial and residential customers. All three segments of the industry are currently subject to some state and federal regulation. Competition has generally been regarded as unlikely in the transmission and local distribution of electricity, given their natural monopoly characteristics. However, competition has emerged in the wholesale generation of electric power, and regulators now face the question of how to foster and encourage such competition.

The ability to buy and sell electric power permits utilities to efficiently employ existing capacity. By buying power from unregulated sources, utilities can meet peak-load demands on hot days or during winter storms and avoid the need to invest in additional production facilities. When utilities purchase power from others, the Federal Power Act of 1935 requires the Federal Energy Regulatory Commission (FERC) to ensure that prices charged on interstate sales are "just and reasonable" in light of necessary costs. With the emergence of competition in the electric power generation market, however, the need for FERC regulation of all interstate sales on a cost-of-service basis has diminished.

When purchasers of electric power have a number of alternative sources, a competitive market can develop, and market prices can take the place of prices based on cost-of-service regulation. Indeed, by the early 1990s, the availability of alternative power sources had encouraged more than a dozen states to use competitive procurement policies for intrastate acquisition of electric power, rather than cost-of-service regulation. Competition in the electric power generation industry can be promoted by allowing local utilities access to transmission facilities that link them with alternative energy sources, provided that the owners of transmission facilities are compensated for their use. In addition, federal legislation may be required to repeal sections of the Public Utility Holding Company Act of 1935, which creates barriers to entry and obstacles to the development of new wholesale power sources.

Fostering Competition in the Cable Television Industry

Cable television is available to more than 90 percent of U.S. households, and more than 60 percent of all such households subscribe to cable service. Services historically provided include improved reception for television programs broadcast over the air on advertiser-supported networks such as CBS, NBC, ABC, and the FOX network, and specialized programming from cable networks such as CNN, MTV, and the Disney Channel. In coming years, much of the growth in cable TV revenues will come from the provision of new shopping and data communication services. The problem is that consumers in most communities receive these services from a single monopoly provider. Regulators must decide how to encourage continued innovation in programming and in the development of new cable services, while at the same time restraining industry prices.

One possible competitor for existing cable companies is the local telephone company, although they have to install new fiber-optic cable to provide competitive services. Standing in the way, however, are regulations that prohibit competition from telephone companies. Rules that would allow telephone companies to carry television programming and other video services would clearly enhance competition in the industry. Similarly, requiring local cable companies to transmit programming provided by others would free up access to local markets. Rules would have to be put in place to guarantee open access to local cable markets and reasonable fees to the local cable companies for program transmission.

Another potential competitor for existing cable companies is provided by "sky cable" and new emerging technologies for over-the-air transmission of specialized programming and data. Such technologies are an effective competitor for local cable companies, especially in large cities and residential areas with dense population. If such forms of competition are allowed to meet their potential, the local cable monopoly problem may soon become moot.

Improving Regulation of Health and Safety

Decisions to smoke cigarettes, go scuba diving in Baja, California, or ride a roller coaster at an amusement park involve risk. Similarly, decisions to take a job as a management consultant, as an ironworker in the construction trades, or as a commodities broker involve a trade-off between the risks and perceived benefits of employment. In the United States, government seeks to control these risks by offering consumers and employees redress for wrongful injury through the tort system and by an extensive and growing policy of health and safety regulation.

Proponents of expanded government health and safety regulation assert that consumers and employees either do not have sufficient information or are incapable of making appropriate decisions in these areas. If certain risks are extremely high or prohibitively expensive, society sometimes assumes the burden of paying for them out of equity considerations. Public concern over risk has also given rise to legislation that requires risk to be eliminated. For example, the Delaney Clause of the Food, Drug, and Cosmetics Act prohibits the use in food of substances shown to cause any cancer in animals or humans.

However, just as firms and individuals must balance risk and benefits when making decisions, so too must regulators. Although regulators often target catastrophic risks that have a small probability of occurring, they can overlook modest risks that occur frequently. It may be good politics to target products with a very small chance of leading to cancer, but it may be more economic to focus on methods for increasing consumer awareness on the dangers of obesity. In regulating health and safety, government must focus on regulations with benefits that outweigh unavoidable costs.

Reforming Environmental Regulation

Environmental regulation expanded greatly during the 1970s and 1980s. By requiring firms and consumers to account for pollution costs, the Clean Air Act, the Clean Water Act, and the Resource Conservation and Recovery Act have all limited environmental waste. At the same time, each of these environmental regulations imposes significant costs on the private economy. Although the United States already spends more on pollution abatement than any other industrialized nation, this total is sure to rise sharply in the years ahead.

Significant uncertainties surround environmental issues and the costs and benefits of various means of environmental regulation. For example, in the case of acid rain, studies show that simple mitigation strategies can be much more cost effective than the types of regulatory controls favored by Congress. Similarly, there may exist more efficient alternatives for correcting externalities associated with gasoline consumption. A rise in gasoline consumption increases the nation's vulnerability to oil price shocks and pollution. The most direct way of dealing with such problems would be to impose a user fee per gallon on gasoline consumption that is commensurate with resulting externalities.

The scope and importance of environmental concerns will become more clear as better information becomes available and more effective methods of regulation begin to yield results. At this point, it seems clear that economic incentives decrease compliance costs by allowing firms the flexibility to meet environmental regulations in the most efficient manner possible. With economic incentives tied to environmental objectives, rather than to the means used to achieve them, firms and society in general benefit through a practical approach to protecting the environment.

SUMMARY

Government rules, regulations, and tax policy play a key role in shaping competitive forces. By understanding the rationale for government involvement in the market economy, a better appreciation of the part played by business is gained.

- From an economic **efficiency** standpoint, a given mode of **regulation** or government control is desirable to the extent that benefits exceed costs. In terms of efficiency, the question is whether market competition by itself is adequate or if government regulation is desirable. **Equity**, or fairness, criteria must also be carefully weighed when social considerations bear on the regulatory decision-making process.

- **Market failure** is the failure of market institutions to sustain socially desirable activities or to eliminate undesirable ones. **Failure by market structure** occurs in markets with too few buyers and sellers for effective competition. **Failure by incentive** occurs when some important benefits or costs of production and consumption are not reflected in industry prices. Differences between private and social costs or benefits are called **externalities**. For example, air pollution is a type of negative externality.

- Competitive markets are also attractive because they are consistent with basic democratic principles. Preservation of consumer choice or **consumer sovereignty** is an important feature of competitive markets. A second social purpose of regulatory intervention is to **limit concentration** of economic and political power.

- **Property rights** give firms the prerogative to limit use by others of specific land, plant and equipment, and other assets. The establishment and maintenance of private property rights are essential to the workings of a competitive market. With **patents**, government grants an exclusive property right to produce, use, or sell an invention or innovation for a limited period (20 years in the United States). These valuable grants of legal monopoly power are intended to stimulate research and development. The **tort system** includes a body of law designed to provide a mechanism for victims of accidents and injury to receive just compensation for their loss. These laws create an incentive for firms and other parties to act responsibly in commerce.

- Government also responds to positive externalities by providing subsidies to private business firms. **Subsidy policy** can be direct or indirect, like government construction and highway maintenance grants that benefit the trucking industry. **Tradable emissions permits** are a new and controversial form of government subsidy that give firms the property right to pollute and to sell that right to others if they wish. Whereas subsidy policy gives firms positive incentives for desirable performance, **tax policy** contains penalties, or negative subsidies, designed to limit undesirable performance. Tax policy includes both regular tax payments and fines or penalties that may be assessed intermittently.

- **Operating controls** are regulations or standards that limit undesirable behavior by compelling certain actions while prohibiting others. The question of who pays for such regulation is seldom answered by simply referring to the point of tax collection, or point of **tax incidence**. The economic cost of regulation, or the **tax burden**, is often passed on to customers or suppliers.

- In some industries, average costs decline as output expands. The term **natural monopoly** describes this situation, because monopoly is a direct result of the superior efficiency of a single large producer. In such circumstances, the process of regulation is expensive in terms of administrative costs, lost operating efficiency, and the misallocation of scarce resources. Contributing to these costs is the problem of **regulatory lag**, or delay between the time a change in regulation is appropriate and the date it becomes effective.

- **Antitrust laws** are designed to promote competition and prevent unwarranted monopoly. These laws seek to improve economic efficiency by enhancing consumer sovereignty and the impartiality of resource allocation while limiting concentrations in both economic and political power.

- According to **horizontal merger guidelines**, mergers resulting in relatively unconcentrated markets or that result in a modest increase in market concentration are not likely to have adverse competitive effects and ordinarily will be approved. Mergers producing a large increase in market concentration, particularly those in already highly concentrated markets, are likely to create or enhance market power and would generally not be approved.

- The added value that new users add to network goods and services is called a **network externality**. Networks became a recent concern in antitrust policy because the Clinton Justice Department feared that if inferior networks got a decisive lead in "installed base" among consumers, switching costs might be sufficient to keep customers from switching to a superior standard. Switching costs might also constitute a barrier to entry in the industry and enable network monopolists to tie or bundle a second product in such a way as to foreclose competition in that secondary market.

- **Tobin's q ratio** is defined as the ratio of the market value of the firm relative to the replacement cost of tangible assets. Nobel laureate James Tobin conceived of this measure as an indicator of pending capital investment. According to Tobin, when high profits cause market values to greatly exceed replacement costs, firms have powerful incentives to expand, and capital investment should boom. Conversely, when low profits cause market values to fall below replacement costs, firms will shrink, and capital investment can be expected to wither. More recently, economists have used Tobin's q ratio as an indicator of above-normal or monopoly profits. However, given the growing importance of intangible capital in our economy, it becomes misleading to infer a simple increase in monopoly profits following an increase in Tobin's q over time.

- The **capture theory** of economic regulation says that the power of the state to prohibit or compel and to take or give money is often manipulated to selectively help or hurt a vast number of industries. Because of this, regulation may be actively *sought* by an industry. Capture theory contrasts sharply with the more traditional **public interest theory** view of regulation as a government-imposed means of private-market control.

- State and federal regulators have begun to address the high costs of regulation through new methods of **incentive-based regulation**, whereby both companies and their customers benefit through enhanced efficiency.

- In recognition that the regulatory process can sometimes harm rather than help consumer interests, a **deregulation** movement has sprung up and has grown to impressive dimensions. Similarly, the unnecessary costs of other forms of regulation dictate that **regulatory reform** is likely to remain a significant social concern.

Government regulation of the market economy is a natural by-product of public concern that unrestricted market competition has the potential to harm economic performance. As the benefits and costs of government/business interaction become better understood, the potential grows for a more constructive approach to government regulation.

QUESTIONS

Q13.1 Define the term *market failure* and cite some causes. Also, cite some examples of market failure.

Q13.2 What role does the price elasticity of demand play in determining the short-run effects of regulations that increase fixed costs? What if they lead to increased variable costs?

Q13.3 Given the difficulties encountered with utility regulation, it has been suggested that nationalization might lead to a more socially optimal allocation of resources. Do you agree? Why or why not?

Q13.4 Antitrust statutes in the United States have been used to attack monopolization by big business. Does labor monopolization by giant unions have the same potential for the misallocation of economic resources?

Q13.5 When will an increase in the minimum wage increase employment income for unskilled laborers? When will it cause this income to fall? Based on your experience, which is more likely?

Q13.6 Explain why state tax rates on personal income vary more on a state-by-state basis than do corresponding tax rates on corporate income.

Q13.7 Do the U.S. antitrust statutes protect competition or competitors? What is the difference?

Q13.8 Define price discrimination. When is it legal? When is it illegal? Cite some common examples of price discrimination.

Q13.9 Is the deregulation movement consistent or inconsistent with the capture theory of economic regulation?

Q13.10 "Regulation is often proposed on the basis of equity considerations and opposed on the basis of efficiency considerations. As a result, the regulation versus deregulation controversy is not easily resolved." Discuss this statement.

SELF-TEST PROBLEMS AND SOLUTIONS

ST13.1 During each 24-hour period, coal-fired electricity-generating plants emit substantial amounts of sulfur dioxide and particulate pollution into the atmosphere. Concerned citizens are appalled at the aesthetic and environmental implications of such pollution, as well as the potential health hazard to the local population.

In analyzing remedies to the current situation, three general methods used to control pollution are generally considered:

- Regulations—licenses, permits, compulsory standards, and so on.
- Payments—various types of government aid to help companies install pollution-control equipment. Aid can take the form of forgiven local property taxes, income tax credits, special accelerated depreciation allowances for pollution-control equipment, low-cost government loans, and so on.
- Charges—excise taxes on polluting fuels (e.g., coal or oil), pollution discharge taxes, and other taxes.

Answer the following questions in light of these alternative methods of pollution control.

A. Pollution is a negative production externality and an example of market failure. Why do markets fail?

B. What is the incentive provided to polluters under each method of pollution control?

C. Who pays for a clean environment under each form of control?

D. On the basis of both efficiency and equity considerations, which form of pollution control is most attractive?

ST13.1 Solution

A. Market failure sometimes occurs because the number of buyers and sellers is too small to ensure vigorous competition. Small numbers of sellers are sometimes caused by economies of scale in production, distribution, or marketing; barriers to entry caused by high capital, skilled labor, or other input requirement; or government-imposed barriers due to franchise grants, rules, or regulations.

Market failure can also occur if some of the costs or benefits of production or consumption are not reflected in market prices. Air, water, and noise pollution that emits from an industrial facility represent a cost of production that is imposed on society in general. Without appropriate charges for such pollution, producers, suppliers, and customers receive an implicit subsidy from the public at large. By failing to pay such environmental costs, they avoid paying the full cost of production and consumption. In general, if some product benefit (cost) is not reflected in firm revenues (costs), then suboptimal production quantities and output prices will result and provide both firms and their customers improper economic incentives.

B. Each alternative method of pollution control provides producers with a different set of incentives. With rules and regulations, producers often have an incentive to litigate or otherwise petition to be made a "special case" and thereby avoid regulatory costs. Rules and regulations are also sometimes difficult to monitor and enforce given the problems of determining legislative intent and regulated firm compliance. With a scheme of payments to reduce the flow of pollution, polluters have positive incentives to reduce emissions and improve economic performance. A benefit of this approach is that firms often respond better to the "carrot" of promised rewards than to the "stick" of threatened penalties. Under a pollution control method of fines or dollar penalties for noncompliance, firms have an economic incentive to reduce pollution in order to avoid charges. However, this method of forcing compliance is sometimes regarded as coercive and met with resistance.

C. When polluters are forced to respond to rules and regulations, the company, customers, employees, and stockholders are all faced with the prospect of paying the costs of pollution reduction. The incidence of pollution cleanup costs depends on the elasticity of demand for the firm's products and on the elasticity of supply. When product demand is highly inelastic, customers have no good substitutes for the products of the polluting firm and therefore must ultimately pay the costs of cleanup. When product demand is highly elastic, customers are able to avoid the costs of pollution reduction by transferring their business to other providers who need not charge for such expenses. In such circumstances, the firm, suppliers, employees, and stockholders bear the costs of pollution reduction. This situation is very similar to that faced by firms subject to pollution charges. In both instances, society's right to a clean environment is implied.

A system of payments to encourage pollution reduction contrasts in fundamental ways with rules and regulations and pollution charges and taxes. This method of pollution reduction is obviously attractive to polluters in that it is free and voluntary, rather than compulsory. It even provides a profit-making opportunity in pollution reduction that increases according to the scope of pollution. Moreover, when society pays a firm to reduce the level of its own pollution, the company's right to pollute is implicitly recognized.

D. Efficiency considerations typically favor payments and charges over rules and regulations as the more efficient methods of pollution control. From an efficiency standpoint, pollution charges are especially attractive in that they recognize pollution as a sometimes necessary cost of doing business, and they force cleanup costs to be borne by those who benefit most directly.

However, equity considerations make the choice among pollution control methods less certain. The regulatory process is attractive from an equity standpoint in that it ensures due process (a day in court) for the polluter. All parties are also treated equitably in the sense that all polluters are equal before the law. Payments for pollution reduction are sometimes favored on an equity basis in that it avoids penalizing polluters with "sunk" investment costs and employees that work in older production facilities that face new domestic and foreign competitors. Pollution charges are often favored on an equity basis in that it forces a close link between prices and full economic costs. Pollution charges, like payments for pollution reduction, are sometimes criticized as favoring large companies versus their smaller competitors.

Therefore, there is no single "best" method of pollution regulation. All are employed because each has the ability to meet efficiency and equity criteria in specific circumstances.

ST13.2 Pollution Control Costs. Anthony Soprano is head of Satriale Pork Producers, Inc., a family-run pork producer with a hog-processing facility in Musconetcong, New Jersey. Each hog processed yields both pork and a render by-product in a fixed 1:1 ratio. Although the by-product is unfit for human consumption, some can be sold to a local pet food company for further processing. Relevant annual demand and cost relations are as follows:

$$P_P = \$110 - \$0.00005Q_P$$
(Demand for pork)

$$MR_P = \partial TR_P / \partial Q_P = \$110 - \$0.0001Q_P$$
(Marginal revenue from pork)

$$P_B = \$10 - \$0.0001Q_B$$
(Demand for render by-product)

$$MR_B = \partial TR_B / \partial Q_B = \$10 - \$0.0002Q_B$$
(Marginal revenue from render by-product)

$$TC = \$10,000,000 + \$60Q$$
(Total cost)

$$MC = \partial TC / \partial Q = \$60$$
(Marginal cost)

Here, P is price in dollars, Q is the number of hogs processed (with an average weight of 100 pounds), and Q_P and Q_B are pork and render by-product per hog, respectively; both total and marginal costs are in dollars. Total costs include a risk-adjusted normal return of 15% on a $50 million investment in plant and equipment.

Currently, the city allows the company to dump excess by-product into its sewage treatment facility at no charge, viewing the service as an attractive means of keeping a valued employer in the area. However, the sewage treatment facility is quickly approaching peak capacity and must be expanded at an expected operating cost of $3 million per year. This is an impossible burden on an already strained city budget.

A. Calculate the profit-maximizing price/output combination and optimal total profit level for Satriale.

B. How much by-product will the company dump into the Musconetcong sewage treatment facility at the profit-maximizing activity level?

C. Calculate output and total profits if the city imposes a $35 per unit charge on the amount of by-product Satriale dumps.

D. Calculate output and total profits if the city imposes a fixed $3-million-per-year tax on Satriale to pay for the sewage treatment facility expansion.

E. Will either tax alternative permit Satriale to survive in the long run? In your opinion, what should the city of Musconetcong do about its sewage treatment problem?

ST13.2 Solution

A. Solution to this problem requires that one look at several production and sales options available to the firm. One option is to produce and sell equal quantities of pork (P) and by-product (B). In this case, the firm sets relevant $MC = MR$.

$$MC = MR_P + MR_B = MR$$
$$\$60 = \$110 - \$0.0001Q + \$10 - \$0.0002Q$$
$$0.0003Q = 60$$
$$Q = 200,000 \text{ hogs}$$

Thus, the profit-maximizing output level for production and sale of equal quantities of P and B would be 200,000 hogs. However, the marginal revenues of both products must be positive at this sales level for this to be an optimal activity level.

Evaluated at 200,000 hogs:

$$MR_P = \$110 - \$0.0001(200,000)$$
$$= \$90$$
$$MR_B = \$10 - \$0.0002(200,000)$$
$$= -\$30$$

Because the marginal revenue for B is negative, and Satriale can costlessly dump excess production, the sale of 200,000 units of B is suboptimal. This invalidates the entire solution developed previously because output of P is being held down by the negative marginal revenue associated with B. The problem must be set up to recognize that Satriale will stop selling B at the point where its marginal revenue becomes zero because, given production for P, the marginal cost of B is zero.

Set:

$$MR_B = MC_B$$
$$\$10 - \$0.0002Q_B = \$0$$

$$0.0002Q_B = 10$$
$$Q_B = 50,000 \text{ units}$$

Thus, 50,000 units of B are the maximum that would be sold. Any excess units will be dumped into the city's sewage treatment facility. The price for B at 50,000 units is

$$P_B = \$10 - \$0.0001Q_B$$
$$= 10 - 0.0001(50,000)$$
$$= \$5$$

To determine the optimal production of P (pork), set the marginal revenue of P equal to the marginal cost of hog processing because pork production is the only motive for processing more than 50,000 units:

$$MR_P = MC_P = MC_Q$$
$$\$110 - \$0.0001Q_P = \$60$$
$$0.0001Q_P = 50$$
$$Q_P = 500,000 \text{ units}$$
$$(\text{Remember } (Q_P = Q)$$

and

$$P_P = \$110 - \$0.00005Q_P$$
$$= 110 - 0.00005(500,000)$$
$$= \$85$$

Excess profits at the optimal activity level for Satriale are

$$\text{Excess profits} = \pi = TR_P + TR_B - TC$$
$$= P_P \times Q_P + P_B \times Q_B - TC_Q$$
$$= \$85(500,000) + \$5(50,000) - \$10,000,000 - \$60(500,000)$$
$$= \$2,750,000$$

Because total costs include a normal return of 15% on $50 million in investment,

$$\text{Total profits} = \text{Required return} + \text{Excess profits}$$
$$= 0.15(\$50,000,000) + \$2,750,000$$
$$= \$10,250,000$$

B. With 500,000 hogs being processed, but only 50,000 units of B sold, dumping of B is

$$\text{Units } B \text{ dumped} = \text{Units produced} - \text{Units sold}$$
$$= 500,000 - 50,000$$
$$= 450,000 \text{ units}$$

C. In part A, it is shown that if all P and B produced is sold, an activity level of $Q = 200,000$ results in $MR_B = -\$30$. A dumping charge of $35 per unit of B will cause Satriale to prefer to sell the last unit of B produced (and lose $30) rather than pay a $35 fine. Therefore, this fine, as does any fine greater than $30, will eliminate dumping and cause Satriale to reduce processing to 200,000 hogs per year. This fine structure would undoubtedly reduce or eliminate the need for a new sewage treatment facility.

Although eliminating dumping is obviously attractive in the sense of reducing sewage treatment costs, the $35 fine has the unfortunate consequence of cutting output substantially. Pork prices rise to $P_P = \$110 - \$0.00005(200,000) = \$100$, and by-product prices fall to $P_B = \$10 - \$0.0001(200,000) = -\$10$. This means Satriale will pay the pet food company $10 per unit to accept all of its by-product sludge. Employment will undoubtedly fall as well. In addition to these obvious short-run effects, long-run implications may be especially serious. At $Q = 200,000$, Satriale's excess profits are

$$
\begin{aligned}
\text{Excess profits} &= TR_P + TR_B - TC \\
&= \$110Q - \$0.00005Q^2 + \$10Q - \$0.0001Q^2 - \$10,000,000 - \$60Q \\
&= \$110(200,000) - \$0.00005(200,000^2) + \$10(200,000) \\
&\quad - \$0.0001(200,000^2) - \$10,000,000 - \$60(200,000) \\
&= -\$4,000,000 \text{ (a loss)}
\end{aligned}
$$

This means that total profits are

$$
\begin{aligned}
\text{Total profits} &= \text{Required return} + \text{Excess profits} \\
&= 0.15(\$50,000,000) + (-\$4,000,000) \\
&= \$3,500,000
\end{aligned}
$$

This level of profit is insufficient to maintain investment. Although a $35 dumping charge will eliminate dumping, it is likely to cause the firm to close down or move to some other location. The effect on employment in Musconetcong could be disastrous.

D. In the short run, a $3 million tax on Satriale has no effect on dumping, output, or employment. At the $Q = 500,000$ activity level, a $3 million tax would reduce Satriale's total profits to $7,250,000, or $250,000 below the required return on investment. However, following imposition of a $3 million tax, the firm's survival and total employment would be imperiled in the long run.

E. No. Satriale is not able to bear the burden of either tax alternative. Obviously, there is no single best alternative here. The highest fixed tax the company can bear in the long run is $2.75 million, the full amount of excess profits. If the city places an extremely high priority on maintaining employment, perhaps a $2.75 million tax on Satriale plus $250,000 in general city tax revenues could be used to pay for the new sewage system treatment facility.

PROBLEMS

P13.1 **Costs of Regulation.** People of many different age groups and circumstances take advantage of part-time employment opportunities provided by the fast-food industry. Given the wide variety of different fast-food vendors, the industry is fiercely competitive, as is the so-called unskilled labor market. In each of the following circumstances, indicate whether the proposed changes in government policy are likely to have an increasing, a decreasing, or an uncertain effect on employment opportunities in this industry.

A. Elimination of minimum wage law coverage for those working less than 20 hours per week

B. An increase in spending for education that raises basic worker skills

C. An increase in the employer portion of federally mandated FICA insurance costs

D. A requirement that employers install expensive new worker-safety equipment

E. A state requirement that employers pay 8% of wages to fund a new national health-care program

P13.2 **Natural Monopoly.** On May 12, 2000, the two daily newspapers in Denver, Colorado, filed an application with the U.S. Department of Justice for approval of a joint operating agreement. The application was filed by The E.W. Scripps Company, whose subsidiary, the Denver Publishing Company, published the *Rocky Mountain News*, and the MediaNews Group, Inc., whose subsidiary, the Denver Post Corporation, published the *Denver Post*. Under the proposed arrangement, printing and commercial operations of both newspapers were to be handled by a new entity, the "Denver Newspaper Agency," owned by the parties in equal shares. This type of joint operating agreement provides for the complete independence of the news and editorial departments of the two newspapers. The rationale for such an arrangement, as provided for under the Newspaper Preservation Act, is to preserve multiple independent editorial voices in towns and cities too small to support two or more newspapers. The act requires joint operating arrangements, such as that proposed by the Denver newspapers, obtain the prior written consent of the Attorney General of the United States in order to qualify for the antitrust exemption provided by the act.

Scripps initiated discussions for a joint operating agreement after determining that the *News* would probably fail without such an arrangement. In their petition to the Justice Department, the newspapers argued that the *News* had sustained $123 million in net operating losses while the financially stronger *Post* had reaped $200 million in profits during the 1990s. This was a crucial point in favor of the joint operating agreement application because the attorney general must find that one of the publications is a failing newspaper and that approval of the arrangement is necessary to maintain the independent editorial content of both newspapers. Like any business, newspapers cannot survive without a respectable bottom line. In commenting on the joint operating agreement application, Attorney General Janet Reno noted that Denver was one of only five major American cities still served by competing daily newspapers. The other four are Boston, Chicago, New York, and Washington, DC. Of course these other four cities are not comparable in size to Denver; they are much bigger. None of those four cities can lay claim to two newspapers that are more or less equally matched and strive after the same audience.

A. Use the natural monopoly concept to explain why there is not a single city in the United States that still supports two independently owned and evenly matched, high-quality newspapers that vie for the same broad base of readership.

B. On Friday January 5, 2001, Attorney General Reno gave the green light to a 50-year joint operating agreement between *News* and its longtime rival, the *Post*. Starting January 22, 2001, the publishing operations of the *News* and the *Post* were consolidated. At the time the joint operating agreement was formed, neither news organization would speculate on job losses or advertising and circulation rate increases from the deal. Based upon your knowledge of natural monopoly, would you predict an increase or decrease in prices following establishment of the joint operating agreement? Would you expect newspaper production (and employment) to rise or fall? Why?

P13.3 **Price Fixing.** An antitrust case launched more than a decade ago sent tremors throughout the academic community. Over the 1989–1991 period, the Department of Justice (DOJ) investigated a number of highly selective private colleges for price fixing. The investigation focused on "overlap group" meetings comprised of about half of the most selective private colleges and universities in the United States. The group included 23 colleges, from small liberal arts schools like Colby, Vassar, and Middlebury to larger research universities like Princeton and MIT. DOJ found that when students applied to more than one of the 23 institutions, school officials met to coordinate the exact calculation of such students' financial need.

Although all of the overlap colleges attempted to use the same need formula, difficult-to-interpret information from students and parents introduced some variation into their actual need calculations. DOJ alleged that the meetings enabled the colleges to collude on higher tuition and to increase their tuition revenue. The colleges defended their meetings, saying that they needed coordination to fully cover the needs of students from low-income families. Although colleges want able, needy students to add diversity to their student body, no college can afford a disproportionate share of needy students simply because it makes relatively generous need calculations.

Although the colleges denied DOJ's price-fixing allegation, they discontinued their annual meetings in 1991.

A. How would you determine if the overlap college meetings resulted in price fixing?

B. If price fixing did indeed occur at these meetings, which laws might be violated?

P13.4 Tying Contracts. In a celebrated 4-year antitrust case, the Department of Justice charged Microsoft Corporation with a wide range of anticompetitive behavior. Among the charges leveled by the DOJ was the allegation that Microsoft illegally "bundled" the sale of its Microsoft Explorer Internet browser software with its basic Windows operating system. DOJ alleged that by offering a free browser program, Microsoft was able to extend its operating system monopoly and "substantially lessen competition and tend to create a monopoly" in the browser market by undercutting rival Netscape Communications, Inc. Microsoft retorted that it had the right to innovate and broaden the capability of its operating system software over time. Moreover, Microsoft noted that Netscape distributed its rival Internet browser software Netscape Navigator free to customers, and that it was merely meeting the competition by offering its own free browser program.

A. Explain how Microsoft's bundling of free Internet browser software with its Windows operating system could violate U.S. antitrust laws, and be sure to mention which laws in particular might be violated.

B. Who was right in this case? In other words, did Microsoft's bundling of Microsoft Explorer with Windows extend its operating system monopoly and "substantially lessen competition and tend to create a monopoly" in the browser market?

P13.5 Horizontal Merger Guidelines. The following table shows premerger market share data for four hypothetical markets. Assume that the Department of Justice has received a merger proposal from the third-largest and the fifth-largest competitors in each market. Attorneys for each firm have petitioned the government for advice as to whether or not their merger proposal would or would not be acceptable under the horizontal merger guidelines promulgated by the FTC and DOJ.

Competitor Rank	Premerger Firm Market Share Data			
	Market A	Market B	Market C	Market D
1	40%	25%	10%	50%
2	30%	25%	10%	25%
3	15%	10%	8%	10%
4	10%	10%	8%	10%
5	5%	6%	8%	2%
6		5%	8%	2%
7		5%	8%	1%
8		5%	8%	
9		5%	8%	
10		4%	8%	
11			8%	
12			8%	
Totals	100%	100%	100%	100%

A. Calculate the premerger HHI measures for each market and the change in the HHI assuming each proposed merger were approved.

B. In each market, indicate whether or not the proposed merger is apt to be approved according to the horizontal merger guidelines. Why or why not?

P13.6 **Costs of Regulation.** Hathaway-Ross Instruments, Inc., manufactures an innovative piece of diagnostic equipment used in medical laboratories and hospitals. OSHA has determined that additional safety precautions are necessary to bring radioactive leakage occurring during use of this equipment down to ascceptable levels. Total and marginal production costs, including a normal rate of return on investment but before additional safeguards are installed, are as follows:

$$TC = \$5,000,000 + \$5,000Q$$
$$MC = \partial TC/\partial Q = \$5,000$$

Market demand and marginal revenue relations are the following:

$$P_L = \$15,000 - \$12.5Q_L \qquad \text{(Medical Laboratory Demand)}$$
$$MR_L = \partial TR/\partial Q_L = \$15,000 - \$25Q_L$$
$$P_H = \$10,000 - \$1Q_H \qquad \text{(Hospital Demand)}$$
$$MR_H = \partial TR/\partial Q_H = \$10,000 - \$2Q_H$$

A. Assuming that the company faces two distinct markets, calculate the profit-maximizing price/output combination in each market and economic profits.

B. Describe the short- and long-run implications of meeting OSHA standards if doing so raises marginal cost by $1,000 per machine.

C. Calculate the point price elasticity at the initial (part A) profit-maximizing activity level in each market. Are the differential effects on sales in each market that were seen in part B typical or atypical?

P13.7 **Incidence of Regulation Costs.** The Smokey Mountain Coal Company sells coal to electric utilities in the southeast. Unfortunately, Smokey's coal has a high particulate content, and, therefore, the company is adversely affected by state and local regulations governing smoke and dust emissions at its customers' electricity-generating plants. Smokey's total and marginal cost relations are

$$TC = \$1,000,000 + \$5Q + \$0.0001Q^2$$
$$MC = \partial TC/\partial Q = \$5 + \$0.0002Q$$

where Q is tons of coal produced per month and TC includes a risk-adjusted normal rate of return on investment.

A. Calculate Smokey's profit at the profit-maximizing activity level if prices in the industry are stable at $25 per ton and therefore $P = MR = \$25$.

B. Calculate Smokey's optimal price, output, and profit levels if a new state regulation results in a $5-per-ton cost increase that can be fully passed on to customers.

C. Determine the effect on output and profit if Smokey must fully absorb the $5-per-ton cost increase.

P13.8 **Cost of Import Tariffs.** Topo Gigo Imports, Ltd., located in San Francisco, California, is an importer and distributor of a leading Japanese–made desktop dry copier. The U.S. Commerce Department recently told the company that it will be subject to a new 5.75% tariff on the import cost of copiers. Topo Gigo is concerned that the tariff will slow its sales, given the highly competitive nature of the copier market. Relevant market demand and marginal revenue relations are as follows:

$$P = \$13,800 - \$0.23Q$$
$$MR = \partial TR/\partial Q = \$13,800 - \$0.46Q$$

Topo Gigo's marginal cost per copier equals the import cost of $8,000 per unit, plus 15% to cover transportation, insurance, and related selling expenses. In addition to these costs, Topo Gigo's fixed costs, including a normal rate of return, come to $15 million per year.

A. Calculate Topo Gigo's optimal price/output combination and economic profits before imposition of the tariff.

B. Calculate Topo Gigo's optimal price/output combination and economic profits after imposition of the tariff.

C. Compare your answers to parts A and B. Who pays the economic burden of the import tariff?

P13.9 **Utility Regulation.** The Woebegone Water Company, a small water utility serving rural customers in Minnesota, is currently engaged in a rate case with the regulatory commission under whose jurisdiction it operates. At issue is the monthly rate that the company will charge for unmetered sewer and water service. The demand curve for monthly service is $P = \$40 - \$0.01Q$. This implies annual demand and marginal revenue curves of

$$P = \$480 - \$0.12Q$$
$$MR = \partial TR/\partial Q = \$480 - \$0.24Q$$

where P is service price in dollars and Q is the number of customers served. Total and marginal costs per year (before investment return) are described by the following function:

$$TC = \$70,000 + \$80Q + \$0.005Q^2$$
$$MC = \partial TC/\partial Q = \$80 + \$0.01Q$$

The company has assets of $2 million and the utility commission has authorized an 11.5% return on investment.

A. Calculate Woebegone's profit-maximizing price (monthly and annually), output, and rate-of-return levels.

B. Woebegone has requested a monthly price of $22. Calculate Woebegone's output and total return on investment if the request were to be granted. Why are these values different from those calculated in part A?

C. What monthly price should the commission grant to limit Woebegone to an 11.5% rate of return?

P13.10 **Costs of Regulation.** The Klamath Paper Company produces corrugated boxes for industrial packaging at a plant located in Klamath Falls, Oregon. For each ton of packaging materials produced, 100 gallons of waste-water pollutant is dumped into the Klamath River. Klamath's revenue and manufacturing cost relations for corrugated boxes are

$$TR = \$6,000Q - \$0.15Q^2$$
$$MR = \partial TR/\partial Q = \$6,000 - \$0.3Q$$
$$TC = \$18,000,000 + \$2,000Q + \$0.05Q^2$$
$$MC = \partial TC/\partial Q = \$2,000 + \$0.1Q$$

Both price and total manufacturing cost (which includes capital costs) are in dollars, and Q is in tons of output. The Oregon Department of Natural Resources (DNR) is considering various pollution tax schemes designed to provide funding for clean-up operations as well as reduce Klamath's waste-water pollution. The DNR has determined that discharges into the river must be cut to meet new federal water-quality guidelines. Alternatively, the Klamath Water District water-treatment facility could be expanded to deal with water-treatment needs at a public cost of $2.5 million per year—costs that must be met through pollution charges, other taxes, or both.

A. Calculate Klamath's optimal output, price, discharge, and profit levels based on the assumption of no pollution taxes nor disposal costs.

B. Calculate these same levels if a $2-per-gallon waste-water disposal charge is imposed on the company.

C. If Klamath is required to recycle all waste water, Klamath calculates total recycling costs (in dollars) as

$$TC_R = \$2W + \$0.000005W^2$$
$$= \$2(100Q) - \$0.000005(100Q)^2$$
$$= \$200Q + \$0.05Q^2$$

where W is gallons of recycled waste water. This implies a marginal recycling cost per ton of production of

$$MC_R = \partial TC_R/\partial Q = \$200 + \$0.1Q$$

Calculate optimal output, price, discharge, and profit levels in this situation.

D. Describe the advantages and disadvantages of the disposal charge and recycling alternatives.

CASE STUDY

The Network Television Fin-Syn Regulation Controversy

When viewers think of FCC regulation of network television, they often think of censorship or of the FCC controlling the renewal of local broadcast licenses. Although TV censors are the butt of frequent jokes by David Letterman on CBS's "Late Show" and Jay Leno on NBC's "The Tonight Show," TV censorship in the United States is very mild when compared to that in many foreign countries, and it has little economic or political impact. Although more important, FCC control over the renewal of local broadcast licenses also has little direct effect on the network broadcasting business.

It might come as a big surprise to many viewers that network television was historically subject to heavy economic regulation in terms of what are referred to as financial interest and network syndication rules. These so-called fin-syn rules were adopted in the early 1970s to prevent ABC, CBS, and NBC from collectively dominating the broadcast industry. The financial interest rule long prohibited networks from having an ownership interest in shows produced for them by others. The network syndication rule barred networks from selling internally produced programs into the domestic syndication or rerun market. Limits on network access to the rerun market were an important disincentive to network production of new television shows. A single half-hour episode of prime-time programming can cost several million dollars. Given tremendous costs, few television programs, even popular hit shows like "Seinfeld," "Drew Carey," and "The Simpsons," make money on their initial runs. The big profits come from subsequent syndication sales of reruns to network affiliates or independent stations in the late afternoon or early evening hours.

CASE STUDY (continued)

Fin-syn rules effectively brought about a separation between the production of television entertainment programming and broadcasting. With the exception of prime-time sports and news coverage, which they offered without restriction, the networks used to serve primarily as distributors of entertainment programs produced by independent Hollywood producers. The networks paid fees for the rights to distribute specific shows. They hoped to make enough money from selling advertising time on their initial run to more than offset fees and earn a profit. Fin-syn rules were introduced because the FCC was concerned that vertical integration (control of production, distribution, and exhibition) unfairly enhanced the power of the networks. By taking away long-term rights to programs created by the networks, and severely restricting their participation in syndication, the FCC effectively eliminated incentives for the networks to produce programs. This effectively separated production from distribution. Those in favor of fin-syn regulation hoped that the rules would benefit independent television producers by giving them more autonomy from the networks and allow the producers to benefit from the lucrative syndication market. Proponents believed the rules would cultivate more diverse and innovative television content. Another potential advantage was that independent television stations stand to benefit when networks are barred from syndication. If the networks owned the syndication rights to off-network programs, they might "warehouse" their best programs, or steer popular reruns to network owned and operated stations.

From the beginning, fin-syn regulation was controversial. Networks felt that fin-syn regulation was unfair and did not solve perceived problems. Some argued that fin-syn rules undermined the role of independent producers. Small independent producers, for example, often cannot afford to fund expensive new series that often lose money during their initial network run. Hence, fin-syn rules tend to favor large production companies tied to major movie studios, like Hollywood–based Time-Warner Television. In 1983, swayed by anti-fin-syn arguments and a political climate favoring deregulation, the FCC proposed eliminating most of the rules. At that time, a massive lobbying effort by Hollywood production companies defeated the deregulation efforts and kept the rules in place. It was only in the early 1990s, and after the combined television audience controlled by the three major networks (ABC, CBS, and NBC) had fallen from 90% to 65%, that change became imminent. An intense lobbying effort pitted major television producers (for fin-syn) against the networks (against fin-syn). In 1991, the FCC relaxed fin-syn regulation. A federal appeals court relaxed the rules even further and effectively eliminated fin-syn regulation altogether by November 1995.

The elimination of fin-syn rules has increased in-house production by the big three networks. By 1992, for example, NBC was the single largest supplier of its own prime-time programming. Production companies have also gotten more involved with distribution. Fox Broadcasting, supported by its direct relationship with a major Hollywood studio, was an early innovator in expanding from production into the distribution of television programming. Once the rules against combining production with distribution were eliminated, it also became possible for Walt Disney, a major Hollywood studio, to purchase Cap Cities/ABC, one of the three major networks. Despite obvious benefits, some worries still remain. Independent producers worry that networks will no longer require their services, or show favoritism toward in-house productions.

Briefly explain the following:

A. The causes and consequences of regulation according to the public interest theory of regulation

B. The causes and consequences of regulation according to the capture theory of regulation

C. How the network television fin-syn deregulation controversy supports or contradicts each theory

SELECTED REFERENCES

Arocena, Pablo, and Catherine Waddams Price. "Generating Efficiency: Economic and Environmental Regulation of Public and Private Electricity Generators in Spain." *International Journal of Industrial Organization* 20 (January 2002): 41–69.

Banerjee, Ajeyo, and E. Woodrow Eckard. "Why Regulate Insider Trading? Evidence from the First Great Merger Wave (1897–1903)." *American Economic Review* 91 (December 2001): 1329–1349.

Besley, Timothy, and Maitreesh Ghatak. "Government Versus Private Ownership of Public Goods." *Quarterly Journal of Economics* 116 (November 2001): 1343–1372.

Bittlingmayer, George. "Regulatory Uncertainty and Investment: Evidence from Antitrust Enforcement." *Cato Journal* 20 (Winter 2001): 295–325.

Coates, Dennis. "The Microeconomics of Market Failures." *Managerial & Decision Economics* 22 (September 2001): 339–340.

Daines, Robert. "Does Delaware Law Improve Firm Value?" *Journal of Financial Economics* 62 (December 2001): 525–558.

Evenett, Simon. "The Antitrust of Nations." *Harvard International Review* 23 (Fall 2001): 76–77.

Glaeser, Edward L., and Andrei Shleifer. "A Reason for Quantity Regulation." *American Economic Review* 91 (May 2001): 431–435.

Hirschey, Mark, Vernon J. Richardson, and Susan Scholz. "Value Relevance of Nonfinancial Information: The Case of Patent Data." *Review of Quantitative Finance & Accounting* 17 (November 2001): 223–235.

Minda, Gary. "Antitrust Regulability and the New Digital Economy: A Proposal for Integrating 'Hard' and 'Soft' Regulation." *Antitrust Bulletin* 46 (Fall 2001): 439–511.

Nakamura, Masao, Takuya Takahashi, and Ilan Vertinsky. "Why Japanese Firms Choose to Certify: A Study of Managerial Responses to Environmental Issues." *Journal of Environmental Economics & Management* 42 (July 2001): 23–52.

Peoples, Jr., James, and Wayne K. Talley. "Black–White Earnings Differentials: Privatization Versus Deregulation." *American Economic Review* 91 (May 2001): 164–168.

Sauer, Raymond D. "The Political Economy of Gambling Regulation." *Managerial & Decision Economics* 22 (January-May 2001): 5–15.

Sidak, J Gregory. "An Antitrust Rule for Software Integration." *Yale Journal on Regulation* 18 (Winter 2001): 1.

Weller, Charles D. "Can Japan Compete? Empirical Findings Just in Time for International Antitrust Policy." *Antitrust Bulletin* 46 (Fall 2001): 569–590.

CHAPTER FOURTEEN

Risk Analysis

At the dawn of the new millennium, stock-market speculators scrambled to bet their hard-earned money on Amazon.com, Cisco Systems, Yahoo!, and others poised to take advantage of the Internet. Speculators piled into a handful of stock-market favorites at unheard of valuations, only to see a significant chunk of their portfolios vanish as the Internet bubble burst. Within 18 months, the *S&P* 500 crumbled by more than 30 percent and Nasdaq crashed by more than 70 percent. Many dot.com investors lost everything as *The Wall Street Journal* mused about "the madness of crowds."

Then, to make a bad situation worse, the terrorist attacks of September 11, 2001, on New York City and Washington, DC, sent a shiver through global financial markets that caused a plunge in both consumer confidence and retail sales. Add in a currency crisis emanating from Argentina and other emerging markets, and the essential elements fell into place for a sharp economic downturn in the United States, Europe, and Asia. Against this background, managers faced a host of vital decisions necessary for shrewd risk management. Will savvy risk management by public officials and business leaders bring a quick return to prosperity, or will decision makers stumble and see economic recession spread around the globe? Time will tell, but stock-market investors were clearly hedging their bets during early 2002.[1]

This chapter introduces certainty equivalents, risk-adjusted discount rates, decision trees, simulation, and game theory techniques as practical means for dealing with such questions. They are effective tools for decision making under conditions of risk and uncertainty.

---

1 See Daniel A. Greenbaum, "401(k)s Shift Risk to Workers," *The Wall Street Journal Online*, March 6, 2002 (http://online.wsj.com).

CONCEPTS OF RISK AND UNCERTAINTY

Let's face it, risk is a four-letter word. When it comes to investing, managers and other investors often prefer not to hear much about the chance of loss. That is why billions of dollars sit in low-yielding certificates of deposit or Treasury securities "backed by the full faith and credit of the U.S. government." However, although the local bank can guarantee savers that their funds will be returned intact, it does nothing to protect them from the risk that inflation will reduce the real value of their assets. To make effective investment decisions, managers must understand the many faces of risk.

Economic Risk and Uncertainty

Managers sometimes know with certainty the outcomes that each possible course of action will produce. A firm with $100,000 in cash that can be invested in a 30-day Treasury bill yielding 6 percent ($493 interest income for 30 days) or used to prepay a 10 percent bank loan ($822 interest expense for 30 days) can determine with certainty that prepayment of the bank loan provides a $329 higher 1-month return. A retailer can just as easily predict the cost savings earned by placing a given order directly with the manufacturer versus through an independent wholesaler; manufacturers can often forecast the precise cost effect of meeting a rush order when overtime wages rather than standard labor rates are required. Order backlogs give a wide variety of consumer and producer goods manufacturers a clear indication of product demand conditions. Similarly, book, magazine, and trade journal publishers accurately judge product demand conditions on the basis of subscription revenues. Resort hotels can often foretell with a high degree of accuracy the amount of food, beverages, and linen service required to meet the daily needs of a 1,500-person convention, especially when such conventions are booked on a regular basis. Even when events cannot be predicted exactly, only a modest level of decision uncertainty is present in such situations.

Many other important managerial decisions are made under conditions of risk or uncertainty. **Economic risk** is the chance of loss because all possible outcomes and their probability of happening are unknown. Actions taken in such a decision environment are purely speculative, such as the buy and sell decisions made by traders and other speculators in commodity, futures, and options markets. All decision makers are equally likely to profit as well as to lose; luck is the sole determinant of success or failure. **Uncertainty** exists when the outcomes of managerial decisions cannot be predicted with absolute accuracy but all possibilities and their associated probabilities are known. Under conditions of uncertainty, informed managerial decisions are possible. Experience, insight, and prudence allow managers to devise strategies for minimizing the chance of failing to meet business objectives. Although luck still plays a role in determining ultimate success, managers can deal effectively with an uncertain decision environment by limiting the scope of individual projects and developing contingency plans for dealing with failure.

When the level of risk and the attitudes toward risk taking are known, the effects of uncertainty can be directly reflected in the basic valuation model of the firm. The certainty equivalent method converts expected risky profit streams to their certain sum equivalents to eliminate value differences that result from different risk levels. For risk-averse decision makers, the value of a risky stream of payments is less than the value of a certain stream, and the application of certainty equivalent adjustment factors results in a downward adjustment in the value of expected returns. For risk-seeking decision makers, the value of a risky stream of payments is greater than that of a certain stream, and application of certainty equivalent adjustment factors results in an upward adjustment in the value of expected returns. In both cases, risky dollars are converted into certain-sum equivalents. Another method used to reflect uncertainty in the basic valuation model is the risk-adjusted discount rate approach. In this technique, the interest rate used in the denominator of the basic valuation model depends on the

economic risk
Chance of loss due to the fact that all possible outcomes and their probability of occurrence are unknown

uncertainty
When the outcomes of managerial decisions cannot be predicted with absolute accuracy but all possibilities and their associated probabilities of occurrence are known

level of risk. For highly risk-averse decision makers, higher discount rates are implemented; for less risk-averse decision makers, lower discount rates are employed. Using this technique, discounted expected profit streams reflect risk differences and become directly comparable.

General Risk Categories

business risk
Chance of loss associated with a given managerial decision

market risk
Chance that a portfolio of investments can lose money because of swings in the financial markets as a whole

inflation risk
Danger that a general increase in the price level will undermine the real economic value of any legal agreement that involves a fixed promise to pay over an extended period

interest-rate risk
Market risk that stems from the fact that changing interest rates affect the value of any agreement that involves a fixed promise to pay over a specified period

credit risk
Chance that another party will fail to abide by its contractual obligations

liquidity risk
Difficulty of selling corporate assets or investments that have only a few willing buyers or are otherwise not easily transferable at favorable prices under typical market conditions

derivative risk
Chance that volatile financial derivatives such as commodities futures and index options could create losses in underlying investments by increasing rather than decreasing price volatility

cultural risk
Chance of loss because of product market differences due to distinctive social customs

currency risk
Loss due to changes in the domestic-currency value of foreign profits

Business risk is the chance of loss associated with a given managerial decision. Such losses are a normal by-product of the unpredictable variation in product demand and cost conditions. Business risk must be dealt with effectively; it seldom can be eliminated.

In a globally competitive environment with instant communication, managers face a wide variety of risks. For managers, a main worry is something called **market risk**, or the chance that a portfolio of investments can lose money because of overall swings in the financial markets. Managers must be concerned about market risk because it influences the cost and timing of selling new debt and equity securities to investors. When a bear market ensues, investors are not the only ones to lose. Companies unable to raise funds for new plant and equipment must forego profitable investment opportunities when the cost of financing escalates. **Inflation risk** is the danger that a general increase in the price level will undermine the real economic value of corporate agreements that involve a fixed promise to pay a specified amount over an extended period. Leases, rental agreements, and corporate bonds are all examples of business contracts that can be susceptible to inflation risk. **Interest-rate risk** is another type of market risk that can severely affect the value of corporate investments and obligations. This stems from the fact that a fall in interest rates will increase the value of any contract that involves a fixed promise to pay over an extended time frame. Conversely, a rise in interest rates will decrease the value of any agreement that involves fixed interest and principal payments.

Credit risk is the chance that another party will fail to abide by its contractual obligations. A number of companies have lost substantial sums because other parties were either unable or unwilling to provide raw commodities, rental space, or financing at agreed-upon prices. Like other investors, corporations must also consider the problem of **liquidity risk**, or the difficulty of selling corporate assets or investments that are not easily transferable at favorable prices under typical market conditions. Another type of risk is related to the rapidly expanding financial derivatives market. A financial derivative is a security that derives value from price movements in some other security. **Derivative risk** is the chance that volatile financial derivatives such as commodities futures and index options could create losses in underlying investments by increasing price volatility.

Special Risks of Global Operations

Cultural risk is borne by companies that pursue a global investment strategy. Product market differences due to distinctive social customs make it difficult to predict which products might do well in foreign markets. For example, breakfast cereal is extremely popular and one of the most profitable industries in the United States, Canada, and the United Kingdom. However, in France, Germany, Italy, and many other foreign countries, breakfast cereal is less popular and less profitable. In business terms, breakfast cereal doesn't "travel" as well as U.S.–made entertainment like movies and television programming.

Currency risk is another important danger facing global businesses because most companies wish to eventually repatriate foreign earnings back to the domestic parent. When the U.S. dollar rises in value against foreign currencies such as the Canadian dollar, foreign profits translate into fewer U.S. dollars. Conversely, when the U.S. dollar falls in value against the Canadian dollar, profits earned in Canada translate into more U.S. dollars. Because price swings in the relative value of currencies are unpredictable and can be significant, many multi-

Internet Fraud

The Internet allows individuals or companies to communicate with a large audience without spending a lot of time, effort, or money. Anyone can reach tens of thousands of people by building an Internet Web site, posting a message on an online bulletin board, entering a discussion in a live "chat" room, or sending mass e-mails. It is easy for fraud perpetrators to make their messages look credible; it is nearly impossible for investors to tell the difference between fact and fiction.

Investment frauds seen online mirror frauds perpetrated over the phone or by mail:

- **The "pump and dump" scam.** Paid promoters sometimes accumulate stock and then leak imaginary favorable information to pump up the stock price. After the stock price has risen, fraudulent promoters dump their shares on an unsuspecting public.

- **The pyramid.** Many Internet frauds are merely electronic versions of the classic "pyramid" scheme in which participants attempt to make money solely by recruiting new participants.

- **The "risk-free" fraud.** Be wary of opportunities that promise spectacular profits or "guaranteed" returns. If the deal sounds too good to be true, then it probably is.

- **Off-shore frauds.** Watch out for off-shore scams and investment "opportunities" in other countries. When you send your money abroad and something goes wrong, it is more difficult to find out what happened and to locate your money.

The Securities and Exchange Commission (SEC) is effectively tracking Internet investment fraud and has taken quick action to stop scams. With the cooperation of federal and state criminal authorities, the SEC has also helped put Internet fraudsters in jail. If you believe any person or entity may have violated the federal securities laws, submit a complaint at http://www.sec.gov.

See: John Hart and Michael Rothberg, "Anonymous Internet Posting Pits Free Speech Against Accountability," *The Wall Street Journal Online*, March 6, 2002 (http://online.wsj.com).

---

government policy risk
Chance of loss because foreign government grants of monopoly franchises, tax abatements, and favored trade status can be tenuous

expropriation risk
Danger that business property located abroad might be seized by host governments

national firms hedge against currency price swings using financial derivatives in the foreign currency market. This hedging is not only expensive but can be risky during volatile markets.

Global investors also experience **government policy risk** because foreign government grants of monopoly franchises, tax abatements, and favored trade status can be tenuous. In the "global friendly" 1990s, many corporate investors seem to have forgotten the widespread confiscations of private property owned by U.S. corporations in Mexico, Cuba, Libya, the former Soviet Union, and in a host of other countries. **Expropriation risk**, or the risk that business property located abroad might be seized by host governments, is a risk that global investors must not forget. During every decade of the twentieth century, U.S. and other multinational corporations have suffered from expropriation and probably will in the years ahead.

PROBABILITY CONCEPTS

A clear understanding of probability concepts provides a background for discussing various methods of effective risk analysis. Marketing directors cannot accurately assess the potential of new products or pricing strategies without data. Managers cannot make insightful investment decisions without reliable information about risk.

Probability Distribution

probability
Chance of occurrence

probability distribution
List of possible events and probabilities

The **probability** of an event is the chance, or odds, that the incident will occur. If all possible events or outcomes are listed, and if a probability is assigned to each event, the listing is called a **probability distribution**. For example, suppose a sales manager observes that there is a 70 percent chance that a given customer will place a specific order versus a 30 percent chance that the customer will not. This situation is described by the probability distribution shown in Table 14.1.

Both possible outcomes are listed in column 1, and the probabilities of each outcome, expressed as decimals and percentages, appear in column 2. Notice that the probabilities sum to 1.0, or 100 percent, as they must if the probability distribution is complete. In this simple example, risk can be read from the probability distribution as the 30 percent chance of the firm not receiving the order. For most managerial decisions, the relative desirability of alternative events or outcomes is not absolute. A more general measure of the relation between risk and the probability distribution is typically required to adequately incorporate risk considerations into the decision-making process.

Suppose a firm is able to choose only one of two investment projects, each calling for an outlay of $10,000. Assume also that profits earned from the two projects are related to the general level of economic activity during the coming year, as shown in Table 14.2. This table is known as a **payoff matrix** because it illustrates the dollar outcome associated with each possible state of nature. Both projects provide a $5,000 profit in a normal economy, higher profits in an economic boom, and lower profits if a recession occurs. However, project *B* profits vary far more according to the state of the economy than do profits from project *A*. In a normal economy, both projects return $5,000 in profit. Should the economy be in a recession next year, project *B* will produce nothing, whereas project *A* will still provide a $4,000 profit. If the economy is booming next year, project *B*'s profit will increase to $12,000, but profit for project *A* will increase only moderately, to $6,000.

Project *A* is clearly more desirable if the economy is in recession, whereas project *B* is superior in a boom. In a normal economy, the projects offer the same profit potential, and both are equally desirable. To choose the best project, one needs to know the likelihood of a boom, a recession, or normal economic conditions. If such probabilities can be estimated, the expected profits and variability of profits for each project can be determined. These measures make it possible to evaluate each project in terms of expected return and risk, where risk is measured by the deviation of profits from expected values.

payoff matrix
Table that shows outcomes associated with each possible state of nature

TABLE 14.1

Simple Probability Distribution

Event (1)	Probability of Occurrence (2)
Receive order	0.7 = 70%
Do not receive order	0.3 = 30%
Total	1.0 = 100%

TABLE 14.2

Payoff Matrix for Projects *A* and *B*

State of the Economy	Profits	
	Project *A*	Project *B*
Recession	$4,000	$ 0
Normal	5,000	5,000
Boom	6,000	12,000

Expected Value

expected value

Anticipated realization

The **expected value** is the anticipated realization from a given payoff matrix and probability distribution. It is the *weighted-average* payoff, where the weights are defined by the probability distribution.

To continue with the previous example, assume that forecasts based on the current trend in economic indicators suggest a 2 in 10 chance of recession, a 6 in 10 chance of a normal economy, and a 2 in 10 chance of a boom. As probabilities, the probability of recession is 0.2, or 20 percent; the probability of normal economic activity is 0.6, or 60 percent; and the probability of a boom is 0.2, or 20 percent. These probabilities add up to 1.0 (0.2 + 0.6 + 0.2 = 1.0), or 100 percent, and thereby form a complete probability distribution, as shown in Table 14.3.

If each possible outcome is multiplied by its probability and then summed, the weighted average outcomes is determined. In this calculation, the weights are the probabilities of occurrence, and the weighted average is called the expected outcome. Column 4 of Table 14.3 illustrates the calculation of expected profits for projects A and B. Each possible profit level in column 3 is multiplied by its probability of occurrence from column 2 to obtain weighted values of the possible profits. Summing column 4 of the table for each project gives a weighted average of profits under various states of the economy. This weighted average is the expected profit from the project.

The expected-profit calculation is expressed by the equation

(14.1)
$$\text{Expected Profit} = E(\pi) = \sum_{i=1}^{n} \pi_i \times p_i$$

Here, π_i is the profit level associated with the ith outcome, p_i is the probability that outcome i will occur, and n is the number of possible outcomes or states of nature. Thus, $E(\pi)$ is a weighted average of possible outcomes (the π_i values), with each outcome's weight equal to its probability of occurrence.

The expected profit for project A is obtained as follows:

$$E(\pi_A) = \sum_{i=1}^{3} \pi_i \times p_i$$
$$= \pi_1 \times p_1 + \pi_2 \times p_2 + \pi_3 \times p_3$$

TABLE 14.3

Calculation of Expected Values

	State of the Economy (1)	Probability of This State Occurring (2)	Profit Outcome if This State Occurs (3)	Expected Profit Outcome (4) = (2) × (3)
Project A	Recession	0.2	$4,000	$ 800
	Normal	0.6	5,000	3,000
	Boom	0.2	6,000	1,200
		1.0	Expected Profit A	$5,000
Project B	Recession	0.2	$0	$0
	Normal	0.6	5,000	3,000
	Boom	0.2	12,000	2,400
		1.0	Expected Profit B	$5,400

$$= \$4,000(.2) + \$5,000(0.6) + \$6,000(0.2)$$
$$= \$5,000$$

The results in Table 14.3 are shown as a bar chart in Figure 14.1. The height of each bar signifies the probability that a given outcome will occur. The probable outcomes for project *A* range from $4,000 to $6,000, with an average, or expected, value of $5,000. For project *B*, the expected value is $5,400, and the range of possible outcomes is from $0 to $12,000.

For simplicity, this example assumes that only three states of nature can exist in the economy: recession, normal, and boom. Actual states of the economy range from deep depression, as in the early 1930s, to tremendous booms, such as in the mid- to late 1990s, with an unlimited number of possibilities in between. Suppose sufficient information exists to assign a probability to each possible state of the economy and a monetary outcome in each circumstance for every project. A table similar to Table 14.3 could then be compiled that would include many more entries for columns 1, 2, and 3. This table could be used to calculate expected values as shown, and the probabilities and outcomes could be approximated by the continuous curves in Figure 14.2.

Figure 14.2 is a graph of the probability distribution of returns for projects *A* and *B*. In general, the tighter the probability distribution, the more likely it is that actual outcomes will be close to expected values. The more loose the probability distribution, the less likely it is that actual outcomes will be close to expected values. Because project *A* has a relatively tight

FIGURE 14.1

Relation Between State of the Economy and Project Returns

Project *B* has a greater expected return and a higher dispersion in returns (risk) than project *A*.

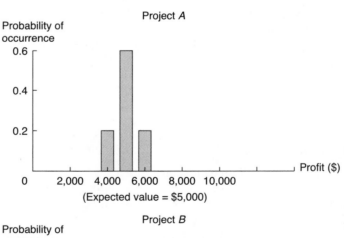

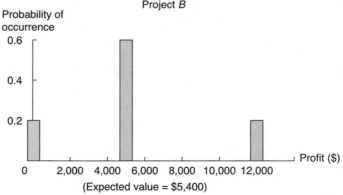

FIGURE 14.2

Probability Distributions Showing Relation Between State of the Economy and Project Returns

The actual return from project *A* is likely to be close to the expected value. It is less likely that the actual return from project *B* will be close to the expected value.

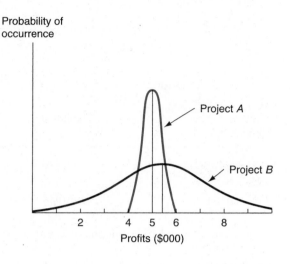

probability distribution, its actual profit is more likely to be close to its expected value than is that of project *B*.

Absolute Risk Measurement

Risk is a complex concept, and some controversy surrounds attempts to define and measure it. Common risk measures that are satisfactory for most purposes are based on the observation that tight probability distributions imply low risk because of the correspondingly small chance that actual outcomes will differ greatly from expected values. From this perspective, project *A* is less risky than project *B*.

Standard deviation, shown as σ (sigma), is a popular and useful measure of absolute risk. **absolute risk**
Overall dispersion of possible payoffs

Absolute risk is the overall dispersion of possible payoffs. The smaller the standard deviation, the tighter the probability distribution and the lower the risk in absolute terms. To calculate standard deviation using probability information, the expected value or mean of the return distribution must first be calculated as

(14.2)
$$\text{Expected Value} = E(\pi) = \sum_{i=1}^{n} (\pi_i p_i)$$

In this calculation, π_i is the profit or return associated with the *i*th outcome; p_i is the probability that the *i*th outcome will occur; and $E(\pi)$, the expected value, is a weighted average of the various possible outcomes, each weighted by the probability of its occurrence.

The deviation of possible outcomes from the expected value must then be derived:

$$\text{Deviation}_i = \pi_i - E(\pi)$$

The squared value of each deviation is then multiplied by the relevant probability and summed. This arithmetic mean of the squared deviations is the variance of the probability distribution:

(14.3)
$$\text{Variance} = \sigma^2 = \sum_{i=1}^{n} [\pi_i - E(\pi)]^2 p_i$$

The standard deviation is found by obtaining the square root of the variance:

(14.4)
$$\text{Standard Deviation} = \sigma = \sqrt{\sum_{i=1}^{n} [\pi_i - E(\pi)]^2 p_i}$$

The standard deviation of profit for project *A* can be calculated to illustrate this procedure:

Deviation $[\pi_i - E(\pi)]$	Deviation² $[\pi_i - E(\pi)]^2$	Deviation² × Probability $[\pi_i - E(\pi)]^2 \times p_i$
\$4,000 – \$5,000 = –\$1,000	\$1,000,000	\$1,000,000(0.2) = \$200,000
\$5,000 – \$5,000 = 0	0	\$0(0.6) = \$0
\$6,000 – \$5,000 = \$1,000	\$1,000,000	\$1,000,000(0.2) = \$200,000
		Variance = σ^2 = \$400,000

$$\text{Standard deviation} = \sigma = \sqrt{\sigma^2} = \sqrt{\$400,000} = \$632.46$$

Using the same procedure, the standard deviation of project *B*'s profit is \$3,826.23. Because project *B* has a larger standard deviation of profit, it is the riskier project.

Relative Risk Measurement

Problems sometimes arise when standard deviation is used to measure risk. If an investment project is relatively expensive and has large expected cash flows, it will have a large standard deviation of returns without being truly riskier than a smaller project. Suppose a project has an expected return of \$1 million and a standard deviation of only \$1,000. Some might reasonably argue that it is less risky than an alternative investment project with expected returns of \$1,000 and a standard deviation of \$900. The *absolute* risk of the first project is

relative risk
Variation in possible returns compared with the expected payoff amount

greater; the risk of the second project is much larger relative to the expected payoff. **Relative risk** is the variation in possible returns compared with the expected payoff amount.

A popular method for determining relative risk is to calculate the coefficient of variation. Using probability concepts, the coefficient of variation is

(14.5)
$$\text{Coefficient of Variation} = v = \frac{\sigma}{E(\pi)}$$

In general, when comparing decision alternatives with costs and benefits that are not of approximately equal size, the coefficient of variation measures relative risk better than does the standard deviation.

Other Risk Measures

The standard deviation and coefficient of variation risk measures are based on the *total* variability of returns. In some situations, however, a project's total variability overstates its risk. This is because projects with returns that are less than perfectly correlated can be combined, and the variability of the resulting portfolio of investment projects is less than the sum of individual project risks. Much recent work in finance is based on the idea that project risk should be measured in terms of its contribution to total return variability for the firm's asset portfolio. The contribution of a single investment project to the overall variation of the firm's asset port-

beta
Measure of the systematic variability of one asset's returns with returns on other assets

folio is measured by a concept known as *beta*. **Beta** is a measure of the systematic variability or covariance of one asset's returns with returns on other assets.

The concept of beta should be employed when the returns from potential investment projects are likely to greatly affect or be greatly affected by current projects. However, in most circumstances the standard deviation and coefficient of variation measures provide adequate assessments of risk.

STANDARD NORMAL CONCEPT

Managers often estimate the scope of investment project payoff possibilities to construct a range of optimistic to pessimistic scenarios. Once this has been done, the risk of a given course of action can be characterized in terms of the distribution of possible outcomes. The standard normal concept is an intuitive and practical means for assessing the dispersion of possible outcomes in terms of expected value and standard deviation measures.

Normal Distribution

normal distribution
Symmetrical distribution about the mean or expected value

The relation among risk, standard deviation, and the coefficient of variation can be clarified by examining the characteristics of a normal distribution, as shown in Figure 14.3. A **normal distribution** has a symmetrical dispersion about the mean or expected value. If a probability distribution is normal, the actual outcome will lie within ±1 standard deviation of the mean roughly 68 percent of the time; the probability that the actual outcome will be within ±2 standard deviations of the expected outcome is approximately 95 percent; and there is a greater than 99 percent probability that the actual outcome will occur within ±3 standard deviations of the mean. The smaller the standard deviation, the tighter the distribution about the expected value and the smaller the probability of an outcome that is very different from the expected value.

Probability distributions can be viewed as a series of *discrete values* represented by a bar chart, such as in Figure 14.1, or as a *continuous function* represented by a smooth curve, such as

FIGURE 14.3

Probability Ranges for a Normal Distribution

When returns display a normal distribution, actual outcomes will lie within ±1 standard deviation of the mean 68.26 percent of the time, within ±2 standard deviations 95.46 percent of the time, and within ±3 standard deviations 99.74 percent of the time.

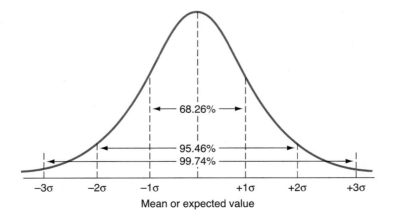

that in Figure 14.2. Probabilities associated with the outcomes in Figure 14.1 are given by the *heights* of the bars, whereas in Figure 14.2, the probabilities must be found by calculating the area under the curve between points of interest.

Standardized Variables

standardized variable
Variable with a mean of 0 and a standard deviation equal to 1

Distribution of costs or revenues can be transformed or standardized. A **standardized variable** has a mean of 0 and a standard deviation equal to 1. Any distribution of revenue, cost, or profit data can be standardized with the following formula:

(14.6)
$$z = \frac{x - \mu}{\sigma}$$

where z is the standardized variable, x is the outcome of interest, and μ and σ are the mean and standard deviation of the distribution, respectively. If the point of interest is 1σ away from the mean, then $x - \mu = \sigma$, so $z = \sigma/\sigma = 1.0$. When $z = 1.0$, the point of interest is 1σ away from the mean; when $z = 2$, the value is 2σ away from the mean; and so on. Although the standard normal distribution theoretically runs from minus infinity to plus infinity, the probability of occurrences beyond 3 standard deviations is very near zero.

Use of the Standard Normal Concept: An Example

Suppose that the Martha Stewart Realty is considering a boost in advertising to reduce a large inventory of unsold homes. Management plans to make its media decision using the data shown in Table 14.4 on the expected success of television versus newspaper promotions. For simplicity, assume that the returns from each promotion are normally distributed. If the television promotion costs $2,295 and the newspaper promotion costs $4,013, what is the probability that each will generate a profit?

To calculate the probability that each promotion will generate a profit, it is necessary to calculate the portion of the total area under the normal curve that is to the right of (greater than) each breakeven point (see Figure 14.3). Here, the breakeven point is where the profit contribution before advertising costs just equals the required advertising expenditure. Using methods described earlier, relevant expected values and standard deviations are $E(R_{TV}) = \$2,500$, $\sigma_{TV} = \$250$, $E(R_N) = \$5,000$, and $\sigma_N = \$600$. For the television promotion, the breakeven

TABLE 14.4

Return Distributions for Television and Newspaper Promotions

	Market Response	Probability of Occurring (P_i)	Return (R_i) (profit contribution before ad costs)
Television	Poor	0.125	$2,000
	Good	0.750	2,500
	Very Good	0.125	3,000
Newspaper	Poor	0.125	3,800
	Good	0.750	5,000
	Very Good	0.125	6,200

Why Lotteries Are Popular

The success of state-run lotteries is convincing evidence that many in our society display risk-seeking behavior, especially when small sums of money are involved. The popularity of lotteries stems from the fact that ticket buyers appear eager to pay $1 for a bet that has an expected return of less than $1. When only 50 percent of lottery-ticket revenues are paid out in the form of prizes, each $1 ticket has an expected return of only 50¢. In such circumstances, the "price" of $1 in expected return is $2 in certain dollars. The willingness to pay such a premium for the unlikely chance at a lottery payoff that might reach into the millions of dollars stems from the fact that such opportunities are rare and lottery-ticket buyers value them highly. Many of the poor, uneducated, or elderly have no opportunity for hitting the jackpot in their careers. The lottery is their only chance, however remote, at a substantial sum of money. It should therefore come as no surprise that lottery-ticket buyers tend to be poor, uneducated, and elderly.

The success of state-run lotteries is noteworthy because it reflects risk attitudes that are fairly unusual.

Typically, consumers and investors display risk-averse behavior, especially when substantial sums of money are involved. Still, the eagerness of consumers to take on enormous risks when small sums of money are involved has made gambling one of America's great growth industries.

If legislative agendas are any indication, Americans can expect to see even more riverboat gambling, card clubs, off-track betting parlors, and casinos in their own backyards. Indian-run casinos are also becoming increasingly popular. Americans are so eager to gamble that they are shifting long-established leisure-time expenditures. Today, U.S. consumers spend more on legal games of chance than on movie theaters, books, amusement attractions, and recorded music combined!

Pouring quarters into a slot machine is easy and apparently appealing to a growing number of Americans.

See: Dow Jones Newswires, "Gtech, Kentucky Lottery Get Deal," *The Wall Street Journal Online*, January 29, 2002 (http://online.wsj.com).

revenue level of $2,295 is 0.82 standard deviations less than (to the left of) the expected return level of $2,500 because

$$z = \frac{x_{TV} - E(R_{TV})}{\sigma_{TV}}$$

$$= \frac{\$2,295 - \$2,500}{\$250}$$

$$= -0.82$$

Table C1 in Appendix C at the back of the book shows that the standard normal distribution function value for $z = -0.82$ is 0.2939. This means that 29.39 percent of the region under the normal curve lies between $2,295 ($z = -0.82$) and the expected revenue level of $2,500. Because 29.39 percent of the total area under the normal curve lies between x_{TV} and $E(R_{TV})$, the profit probability for the television promotion is $0.2939 + 0.5 = 0.7939$ or 79.39 percent.

For the newspaper promotion, z is calculated as

$$z = \frac{x_N - E(R_N)}{\sigma_N}$$

$$= \frac{\$4,013 - \$5,000}{\$600}$$

$$= -1.645$$

After interpolating, the probability value for $z = -1.645$ is 0.45. This means that 0.45, or 45 percent, of the total area under the normal curve lies between x_N and $E(R_N)$, and it implies a profit probability for the newspaper promotion of $0.45 + 0.5 = 0.95$, or 95 percent. In terms of profit probability, the newspaper advertisement is the less risky alternative.

UTILITY THEORY AND RISK ANALYSIS

The assumption of risk aversion is basic to many decision models in managerial economics. Because this assumption is so crucial, it is appropriate to examine attitudes toward risk and discuss why risk aversion holds in general.

Possible Risk Attitudes

risk aversion
Desire to avoid or minimize uncertainty

risk neutrality
Focus on expected values, not return dispersion

risk seeking
Preference for speculation

In theory, three possible attitudes toward risk are present: aversion to risk, indifference to risk, and preference for risk. **Risk aversion** characterizes individuals who seek to avoid or minimize risk. **Risk neutrality** characterizes decision makers who focus on expected returns and disregard the dispersion of returns (risk). **Risk seeking** characterizes decision makers who prefer risk. Given a choice between more risky and less risky investments with identical expected monetary returns, a risk averter selects the less risky investment and a risk seeker selects the riskier investment. Faced with the same choice, the risk-neutral investor is indifferent between the two investment projects. Some individuals prefer high-risk projects and the corresponding potential for substantial returns, especially when relatively small sums of money are involved. Entrepreneurs, innovators, inventors, speculators, and lottery ticket buyers are all examples of individuals who sometimes display risk-seeking behavior. Risk-neutral behavior is exhibited in some business decision making. However, most managers and investors are predominantly risk averters, especially when substantial dollar amounts are involved.

Relation Between Money and Its Utility

diminishing marginal utility
When additional increments of money bring ever smaller increments of added benefit

At the heart of risk aversion is the notion of **diminishing marginal utility** for money. If someone with no money receives $5,000, it can satisfy his or her most immediate needs. If such a person then receives a second $5,000, it will obviously be useful, but the second $5,000 is not quite so necessary as the first $5,000. Thus, the value, or *utility*, of the second, or *marginal*, $5,000 is less than the utility of the first $5,000, and so on. Diminishing marginal utility of money implies that the marginal utility of money diminishes for additional increments of money. Figure 14.4 graphs the relation between money and its utility, or value. In the figure, utility is measured in units of value or satisfaction, an index that is unique to each individual.

FIGURE 14.4

Example of a Money/Utility Relation

A risk seeker's marginal utility of money increases. A risk-indifferent individual has a constant marginal utility of money. A risk averter displays a diminishing marginal utility of money.

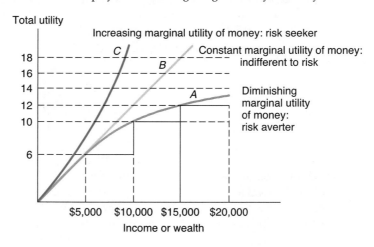

Employee Stock Options

In a conventional employee stock option plan, key employees are granted the right to buy a fixed number of shares for a predetermined period. The number of shares granted depends on the employee's level of responsibility. Usually, the number of shares granted under an employee stock option plan is commensurate with total compensation. According to current tax law, the exercise period for employee stock options cannot exceed 10 years, but may be less. Because stock prices usually rise from 12 percent to 14 percent per year, on average, from the employee's perspective, the longer the exercise period, the better.

An employee can exercise the right to buy stock covered by a stock option plan once the vesting period has been completed. The vesting period is an employment time frame after which granted options can be exercised. The length of the vesting period is designed by the employer to keep valued employees motivated. It is also designed to keep employees from bolting to the competition. Structured properly, an employee stock option plan with appropriate vesting requirements can create "golden handcuffs" that benefit both valued employees and their employers.

Once exercised, employee stock options create a taxable event for the employee. The difference between the current market price and the original exercise price, multiplied by the number of shares covered, is used to calculate the amount of employee compensation derived from the option exercise. By granting employee stock options, employers replace cash compensation that reduces operating income with contingent-based pay that never appears on the income statement. Income statements issued by companies with extensive stock option plans can dramatically understate the total amount of employee compensation. This can result in earnings statements that present too rosy a picture of corporate performance. Such problems become evident when the company's stock price falters, and employees clamor for more cash compensation.

In the long run, investors lose out unless they consider the economic cost of employee stock options.

See: T. J. Rogers, "Options Aren't Optional in Silicon Valley," *The Wall Street Journal Online*, March 4, 2002 (http://online.wsj.com).

For risk averters, money has diminishing marginal utility. If such an individual's wealth were to double suddenly, he or she would experience an increase in happiness or satisfaction, but the new level of well-being would not be twice the previous level. In cases of diminishing marginal utility, a less than proportional relation holds between total utility and money. Accordingly, the utility of a doubled quantity of money is less than twice the utility of the original level. In contrast, those who are indifferent to risk perceive a strictly proportional relationship between total utility and money. Such a relation implies a constant marginal utility of money, and the utility of a doubled quantity of money is exactly twice the utility of the original level. Risk seekers perceive a more than proportional relation between total utility and money. In this case, the marginal utility of money increases. With increasing marginal utility of money, the utility of doubled wealth is more than twice the utility of the original amount. These relations are illustrated in Figure 14.4.

Even though total utility increases with increased money for risk averters, risk seekers, and those who are indifferent to risk, the relation between total utility and money is quite different for each group. These differences lead to dissimilar risk attitudes. Because individuals with a diminishing marginal utility for money suffer more pain from a dollar lost than the pleasure derived from a dollar gained, they seek to avoid risk. Risk averters require a very high return on any investment that is subject to much risk.

In Figure 14.4, for example, a gain of $5,000 from a base of $10,000 brings 2 units of additional satisfaction, but a $5,000 loss causes a 4-unit loss in satisfaction. A person with this utility function and $10,000 would be unwilling to make an investment with a 50/50 chance of winning or losing $5,000. The 9-unit expected utility of such a gamble [$E(u) = 0.5$ times the utility of $5,000 + 0.5 times the utility of $15,000 = 0.5 \times 6 + 0.5 \times 12 = 9$] is less than the 10 units of utility obtained by forgoing the gamble and keeping $10,000 in certain wealth.

Because an individual with a constant marginal utility for money values a dollar gained just as highly as a dollar lost, the expected utility from a fair gamble always exactly equals the utility of the expected outcome. An individual indifferent to risk makes decisions on the basis of expected monetary outcomes and is not concerned with possible variation in the distribution of outcomes.

ADJUSTING THE VALUATION MODEL FOR RISK

Diminishing marginal utility leads directly to risk aversion, and risk aversion is reflected in the basic valuation model used to determine the worth of a firm. If a managerial decision affects the firm's risk level, the value of the firm is impacted. Two primary methods are used to adjust the basic valuation model to account for decision making under conditions of uncertainty.

Basic Valuation Model

The basic valuation model developed in Chapter 1 is

(14.7)
$$V = \sum_{t=1}^{n} \frac{\pi_i}{(1 + i)^t}$$

This model states that the value of the firm is equal to the discounted present worth of future profits. Under conditions of certainty, the numerator is profit, and the denominator is a time-value adjustment using the risk-free rate of return *i*. After time-value adjustment, the profits to be earned from various projects are strictly and completely comparable.

Under conditions of uncertainty, the profits shown in the numerator of the valuation model as π equal the expected value of profits during each future period. This expected value is the best available estimate of the amount to be earned during any given period. However, because profits cannot be predicted with absolute precision, some variability is to be anticipated. If the firm must choose between two alternative methods of operation, one with high expected profits and high risk and another with smaller expected profits and lower risks, some technique must be available for making the alternative investments comparable. An appropriate ranking and selection of projects is possible only if each respective investment project can be adjusted for considerations of both time value of money and risk. At least two popular methods are employed to make such adjustments. In the first, expected profits are adjusted to account for risk. In the second, the interest rate used in the denominator of the valuation model is increased to reflect risk considerations. Either method can be used to ensure that value-maximizing decisions are made.

Certainty Equivalent Adjustments

certainty equivalent
Assured sum that equals an expected risky amount in utility terms

The **certainty equivalent** method is an adjustment to the numerator of the basic valuation model to account for risk. Under the certainty equivalent approach, decision makers specify the certain sum that they regard comparable to the expected value of a risky investment alternative. The certainty equivalent of an expected risk amount typically differs in dollar terms but not in terms of the amount of utility provided. To illustrate, suppose that you face the following choices:

- Invest $100,000. From a successful project, you receive $1,000,000; if it fails, you receive nothing. If the probability of success is 0.5, or 50 percent, the investment's expected payoff is $500,000 (= 0.5 × $1,000,000 + 0.5 × $0).
- You do not make the investment; you keep the $100,000.

If you find yourself indifferent between the two alternatives, $100,000 is your certainty equivalent for the risky expected return of $500,000. In other words, a certain or riskless amount of $100,000 provides exactly the same utility as the 50/50 chance to earn $1,000,000 or $0. You are indifferent between these two alternatives.

In this example, any certainty equivalent of less than $500,000 indicates risk aversion. If the maximum amount that you are willing to invest in the project is only $100,000, you are exhibiting very risk-averse behavior. Each certain dollar is "worth" five times as much as each risky dollar of expected return. Alternatively, each risky dollar of expected return is worth only 20¢ in terms of certain dollars. In general, any risky investment with a certainty equivalent less than the expected dollar value indicates risk aversion. A certainty equivalent greater than the expected value of a risky investment indicates risk preference.

certainty equivalent adjustment factor, α
Ratio of a certain sum divided by an expected risky amount, where both dollar values provide the same level of utility

Any expected risky amount can be converted to an equivalent certain sum using the **certainty equivalent adjustment factor,** α, calculated as the ratio of a certain sum divided by an expected risky amount, where both dollar values provide the same level of utility:

(14.8)
$$\frac{\text{Certainty Equivalent}}{\text{Adjustment Factor}} = \alpha = \frac{\text{Equivalent Certain Sum}}{\text{Expected Risky Sum}}$$

The certain sum numerator and expected return denominator may vary in dollar terms, but they provide the exact same reward in terms of utility. In the previous investment problem, in which a certain sum of $100,000 provides the same utility as an expected risky return of $500,000, the certainty equivalent adjustment factor $\alpha = 0.2 = \$100,000/\$500,000$. This means that the "price" of one dollar in risky expected return is 20¢ in certain dollar terms.

The following general relations enable managers to use the certainty equivalent adjustment factor to analyze risk attitudes:

If	Then	Implies
Equivalent certain sum < Expected risky sum	$\alpha < 1$	Risk aversion
Equivalent certain sum = Expected risky sum	$\alpha = 1$	Risk indifference
Equivalent certain sum > Expected risky sum	$\alpha > 1$	Risk preference

risk-adjusted valuation model
Valuation model that reflects time-value and risk considerations

The appropriate α value for a given managerial decision varies according to the level of risk and degree of the decision maker's risk aversion.

The basic valuation model (Equation 14.7) can be converted into a **risk-adjusted valuation model**, one that explicitly accounts for risk:

(14.9)
$$V = \sum_{t=1}^{n} \frac{\alpha E(\pi_i)}{(1 + i)^t}$$

In this risk-adjusted valuation model, expected future profits, $E(\pi_t)$, are converted to their certainty equivalents, $\alpha E(\pi_t)$, and are discounted at a risk-free rate, i, to obtain the risk-adjusted present value of a firm or project. With the valuation model in this form, one can appraise the effects of different courses of action with different risks and expected returns.

To use Equation 14.9 for real-world decision making, managers must estimate appropriate αs for various investment opportunities. Deriving such estimates can prove difficult, because α varies according to the size and riskiness of investment projects as well as according to the risk attitudes of managers and investors. In many instances, however, the record of past investment decisions offers a guide that can be used to determine appropriate certainty equivalent adjustment factors. The following example illustrates how managers use certainty equivalent adjustment factors in practical decision making.

Certainty Equivalent Adjustment Example

Assume that operations at Burns & Allen Industries have been seriously disrupted by problems with a faulty boiler at its main fabrication facility. In fact, state fire marshals shut the facility down for an extended period recently following repeated overheating and minor explosions. The boiler problem was solved when it was discovered that a design flaw had made the pilot light safety switch inoperable.

Burns & Allen retained the Denver law firm of Dewey, Cheetum & Howe to recover economic damages from the boiler manufacturer. The company has filed suit in state court for $250,000 in damages. Prior to filing suit, the attorney estimated legal, expert witness, and other litigation costs to be $10,000 for a fully litigated case, for which Burns & Allen had a 10 percent chance of receiving a favorable judgment. For simplicity, assume that a favorable judgment will award Burns & Allen 100 percent of the damages sought, whereas an unfavorable judgment will result in the firm receiving zero damages. Also assume that $10,000 is the most Burns & Allen would be willing to pay to sue the boiler manufacturer.

In filing suit against the boiler manufacturer, Burns & Allen has made a risky investment decision. By its willingness to bear litigation costs of $10,000, the company has implicitly stated that it regards these out-of-pocket costs to be *at least* equivalent to the value of the risky expectation of receiving a favorable judgment against the boiler manufacturer. In other words, Burns & Allen is willing to exchange $10,000 in certain litigation costs for the possibility of receiving a $250,000 judgment against the boiler manufacturer.

Burns & Allen's investment decision can be characterized using the certainty equivalent adjustment method. To do this, it is important to realize that the $10,000 in litigation costs is incurred irrespective of the outcome of a fully litigated case. This $10,000 represents a certain sum that the company must value as highly as the expected risky outcome to be willing to file suit. The expected risky outcome, or expected return from filing suit, is

$$
\begin{aligned}
\text{Expected Return} &= \text{Favorable Judgment Payoff} \times \text{Probability} \\
&\quad + \text{Unfavorable Judgment Payoff} \times \text{Probability} \\
&= \$250{,}000(0.1) + \$0(0.9) \\
&= \$25{,}000
\end{aligned}
$$

To justify filing suit, Burns & Allen's certainty equivalent adjustment factor for investment projects of this risk class must be

$$
\begin{aligned}
\alpha &= \frac{\text{Certain Sum}}{\text{Expected Risky Sum}} \\
&= \frac{\text{Litigation Costs}}{\text{Expected Return}} \\
&= \frac{\$10{,}000}{\$25{,}000} \\
&= 0.4
\end{aligned}
$$

Therefore, each risky dollar of expected return from the litigation effort is worth, in terms of utility, *at least* 40¢ in certain dollars. Alternatively, $10,000 is the certain sum equivalent of the risky expected return of $25,000.

Now assume that after Burns & Allen goes to court, incurring $5,000 in litigation costs, especially damaging testimony by an expert witness dramatically changes the outlook of the case in Burns & Allen's favor. In response, the boiler manufacturer's attorney offers an out-of-court settlement in the amount of $30,000. However, Burns & Allen's attorney recommends that the company reject this offer, estimating that it now has a 50/50 chance of obtaining a favorable judgment in the case. Should Burns & Allen follow the attorney's advice and reject the settlement offer?

In answering this question, one must keep in mind that having already spent ("sunk") $5,000 in litigation costs, Burns & Allen must consider as relevant litigation costs only the additional $5,000 necessary to complete litigation. These $5,000 litigation costs, plus the $30,000 out-of-court settlement offer, represent the relevant certain sum, because proceeding with the suit will require an "investment" of these additional litigation plus opportunity costs. Given the revised outlook for a favorable judgment, the expected return to full litigation is

$$\text{Expected Return} = (\$250,000)(0.5) + (\$0)(0.5)$$
$$= \$125,000$$

In light of Burns & Allen's earlier decision to file suit on the basis that each dollar of expected risky return was "worth" 40¢ in certain dollars, this expected return would have a $50,000 (=$125,000 × 0.4) certainty equivalent value. Because this amount exceeds the settlement offer plus remaining litigation costs, the settlement offer seems deficient and should be rejected. On the basis of Burns & Allen's revealed risk attitude, an out-of-court settlement offer has to be at least $45,000 to receive favorable consideration. At that point, the settlement plus saved litigation costs of $5,000 would equal the certainty equivalent value of the expected return from continuing litigation.

This simple example illustrates that historical investment decisions offer a useful guide to current decisions. If a potential project's required investment and risk levels are known, the α implied by a decision to accept the investment project can be calculated. This project-specific α can then be compared with αs for prior projects with similar risks. Risk-averse individuals should invest in projects if calculated αs are *less* than or equal to those for accepted historical projects in the same risk class. Furthermore, given an estimate of expected return and risk, the maximum amount that the firm should be willing to invest in a given project can also be determined from the certainty equivalent adjustment factor. Risk-averse management will accept new projects if the level of required investment per dollar of expected return is less than or equal to that for historical projects of similar risk.

Risk-Adjusted Discount Rates

risk-adjusted discount rate
Risk-free rate of return plus the required risk premium

risk premium
Added expected return for a risky asset over that of a riskless asset

Another way to incorporate risk in managerial decision making is to adjust the discount rate or denominator of the basic valuation model (Equation 14.7). Like certainty equivalent factors, **risk-adjusted discount rates** are based on the trade-off between risk and return for individual investors. Suppose an investor is indifferent to a riskless asset with a sure 5 percent rate of return, a moderately risky asset with a 10 percent expected return, and a very risky asset with a 15 percent expected return. As risk increases, higher expected returns on investment are required to compensate for additional risk. Observe also that the required **risk premium** is directly related to the level of risk associated with a particular investment. This is a common situation.

The basic valuation model shown in Equation 14.7 can be adapted to account for risk through adjustment of the discount rate, i, where

(14.10)
$$V = \sum_{t=1}^{n} \frac{E(\pi_i)}{(1 + k)^t}$$

The risk-adjusted discount rate k is the sum of the risk-free rate of return, R_F, plus the required risk premium, R_p:

$$k = R_F + R_p$$

In Equation 14.10, value is measured by the present worth of expected future income or profits, $E(\pi_t)$, discounted at a risk-adjusted rate.

Risk-Adjusted Discount Rate Example

Suppose the Property & Casualty Insurance Company (P&C) is contemplating the purchase of one of the two database and file management software systems offered by Rockford Files, Inc. System A is specifically designed for P&C's current computer software system and cannot be used with those of other providers; system B is compatible with a broad variety of computer software systems, including P&C's and those of other software providers. The expected investment outlay is $500,000 for each alternative. Expected annual cost savings (cash inflows) over 5 years are $175,000 per year for system A and $185,000 per year for system B. The standard deviation of expected annual returns from system A is $10,000, whereas that of system B is $15,000. In view of this risk differential, P&C management has decided to evaluate system A with a 10 percent cost of capital and system B with a 15 percent cost of capital.

The risk-adjusted value for each system is as follows:[2]

$$\text{Value}_A = \sum_{t=1}^{5} \frac{\$175,000}{(1.10)^t} - \$500,000$$

$$= \$175,000 \times \left(\sum_{t=1}^{5} \frac{1}{(1.10)^t} \right) - \$500,000$$

$$= \$175,000 \times 3.7908 - \$500,000$$

$$= \$163,390$$

$$\text{Value}_B = \sum_{t=1}^{5} \frac{\$185,000}{(1.15)^t} - \$500,000$$

$$= \$185,000 \times \left(\sum_{t=1}^{5} \frac{1}{(1.15)^t} \right) - \$500,000$$

$$= \$185,000 \times 3.3522 - \$500,000$$

$$= \$120,157$$

Because the risk-adjusted value of system A is larger than that for system B, P&C should choose system A. This choice maximizes the value of the firm.

DECISION TREES AND COMPUTER SIMULATION

Decision trees that follow the sequential nature of the decision-making process provide a logical framework for decision analysis under conditions of uncertainty. When a high degree of uncertainty exists and data are not readily available, computer simulation often provides

---

2   The terms

$$\sum_{t=1}^{5} \frac{1}{(1.10)^t} = 3.7908$$

and

$$\sum_{t=1}^{5} \frac{1}{(1.15)^t} = 3.3522$$

are present-value-of-an-annuity interest factors. Tables of interest factors for various interest rates and years (*t* values) appear in Appendix B.4.

the basis for reasonable conjecture. Application of these methods was once arduous and time-consuming. Today, new computer software fully automates the process of decision tree analysis and computer simulation. More than ever before, these techniques constitute useful and practical means for risk assessment and effective managerial decision making.

Decision Trees

decision tree
Map of a sequential decision-making process

decision points
Instances when management must select among choice alternatives

chance events
Possible outcomes following each decision point

A **decision tree** is a sequential decision-making process. Decision trees are designed for analyzing decision problems that involve a series of choice alternatives that are constrained by previous decisions. They illustrate the complete range of future possibilities and their associated probabilities in terms of a logical progression from an initial **decision point**, through each subsequent constrained decision alternative, to an ultimate outcome. Decision points are instances where management must select among several choice alternatives. **Chance events** are possible outcomes following each decision point.

Decision trees are widely employed because many important decisions are made in stages. For example, a pharmaceutical company considering expansion into the generic prescription drug market might take the following steps:

- Spend $100,000 to survey supply and demand conditions in the generic drug industry.

- If survey results are favorable, spend $2 million on a pilot plant to investigate production methods.

- Depending on cost estimates and potential demand, either abandon the project, build a large plant, or build a small one.

These decisions are made in stages; subsequent determinations depend on prior judgments. The sequence of events can be mapped out to visually resemble the branches of a tree— hence the term *decision tree.*

Figure 14.5 illustrates the decision-tree method for the pharmaceutical company decision problem. Assume that the company has completed its industry supply and demand analysis and determined that it should develop a full-scale production facility. Either a large plant or a small plant can be built. The probability is 50 percent for high demand, 30 percent for medium demand, and 20 percent for low demand. Depending on actual demand, the present value of net cash flows, defined as sales revenue minus operating costs, ranges from $8.8 million to $1.4 million for a large plant and from $2.6 million to $1.4 million for a small plant.

Because demand probabilities are known, the expected value of cash flow can be determined, as in column 5 of Figure 14.5. Investment outlays are deducted from expected net cash flow to obtain the expected net present value for each decision. The expected net present value is $730,000 for the large plant and $300,000 for the small one. Notice the wide range of possible outcomes for the large plant. Actual net present values for the large plant investment equal the present value of cash flows (column 4) minus the large plant investment cost of $5 million. These values vary from $3.8 million to –$3.6 million. Actual net present values for the small plant investment range only from $600,000 to –$600,000. Clearly, the smaller plant appears less risky based on the width of the range of possible net present value outcomes. Because the investment requirement differs for each plant, the coefficient of variation for each plant's net present value can be examined to provide an alternate measure of relative risk. The coefficient of variation for the large plant's present value is 4.3, whereas that for the small plant is only 1.5.[3] Again, risk appears greater for the large plant alternative.

---

3   Using Equation 14.6 and data on possible returns in Figure 14.5, the standard deviation for the big plant is $3.155 million and for the small plant it is $458,260. Dividing these standard deviations by the appropriate expected return for each respective plant size, as in Equation 14.5, gives the coefficient of variation.

FIGURE 14.5

Illustrative Decision Tree

The expected net present value of each investment alternative (column 5) is determined by linking possible outcomes (column 2), probabilities (column 3), and monetary values (column 4).

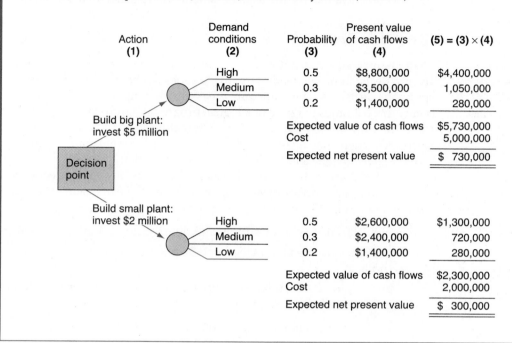

Action (1)	Demand conditions (2)	Probability (3)	Present value of cash flows (4)	(5) = (3) × (4)
	High	0.5	$8,800,000	$4,400,000
	Medium	0.3	$3,500,000	1,050,000
	Low	0.2	$1,400,000	280,000
Build big plant: invest $5 million			Expected value of cash flows Cost	$5,730,000 5,000,000
			Expected net present value	$ 730,000
	High	0.5	$2,600,000	$1,300,000
Build small plant: invest $2 million	Medium	0.3	$2,400,000	720,000
	Low	0.2	$1,400,000	280,000
			Expected value of cash flows Cost	$2,300,000 2,000,000
			Expected net present value	$ 300,000

These risk and expected return differentials can be incorporated into the decision-making process in a variety of ways. Assigning utility values to the cash flows given in column 4 of Figure 14.5 would state column 5 in terms of expected utility. The company could then choose the plant size that provided the greatest expected utility. Alternatively, present values given in column 4 could be adjusted using the certainty equivalent or risk-adjusted discount rate method. The plant that offers the largest risk-adjusted net present value is the optimal choice.

Computer Simulation

computer simulation
Use of computer software and workstations or sophisticated desktop computers to create outcome scenarios

Another technique designed to assist managers in making decisions under uncertainty is **computer simulation**. Computer simulation involves the use of computer software and sophisticated desktop computers to create a wide variety of decision outcome scenarios. These simulations illustrate a broad range of possible outcomes to help managers assess the possible and probable consequences of decision alternatives. Using the computer simulation technique, a variety of hypothetical "What if?" questions can be asked and answered on the basis of measurable differences in underlying assumptions. More than just informed conjecture, computer simulation allows managers to make precise judgments concerning the desirability of various choices on the basis of highly detailed probability information.

Computer simulations require probability distribution estimates for a number of variables, such as investment outlays, unit sales, product prices, input prices, and asset lives. In some instances, full-scale simulations are expensive and time-consuming and therefore restricted to projects such as major plant expansions or new-product decisions. When a firm is deciding whether to accept a major undertaking involving an outlay of millions of dollars, full-scale computer simulations provide valuable insights that are well worth their cost. Somewhat less expensive, limited-scale simulations are used to project outcomes for projects or strategies.

Game Theory at the FCC

One of the most successful game theory applications has been in the design of FCC auctions used to allocate electromagnetic spectrum, a highly valuable and finite public resource. In the design of the auction process, the FCC has relied on advice from top game theorists at Stanford, Yale, and other leading universities. The agency has generally adopted a standard English auction in which the winner pays what it bids, and everyone can see all bids as they are made. Game theory research shows that open auctions stimulate bidding, whereas sealed auctions foster restraint for fear of needlessly paying too much.

Although the FCC initially favored auctioning off vital spectrum licenses all at once to make it easier for bidders to assemble efficient blocs of adjoining areas, this approach entails a nightmare of complexity. Complicating the problem is the fact that bidders must be allowed some flexibility to withdraw bids when adjoining areas are sold to others. If all offers could be withdrawn easily, however, the integrity of the process would suffer. A sequential auction, where areas are put up for bid one at a time, also

involves problems because it denies participants the opportunity to bid more for economically efficient blocks of service areas. Winning bidders in a sequential auction have the potential for a snowballing effect where one success leads to another, and another, and another. After considering a wide variety of options, the FCC adopted a modified sequential bidding approach.

How does it work? Consider the PCS spectrum auction, which began on December 12, 2000, and ended on January 26, 2001. After 101 rounds of bidding, 422 licenses covering 195 markets, including New York, Los Angeles, Chicago, Boston and Washington, DC, were allocated. The FCC's competitive bidding process allowed for rapid deployment and ensured that spectrum went to the highest value use. The American taxpayer also benefited when the PCS auction raised $16,857,046,150!

See: Jacquie Jordan, "Triton PCS to Acquire Excess PCS Spectrum from Ntelos," *The Wall Street Journal Online*, December 12, 2001 (http://online.wsj.com).

Instead of using complete probability distributions for each variable included in the problem, results are simulated based on best-guess estimates for each variable. Changes in the values of each variable are then considered to see the effects of such changes on project returns. Typically, returns are highly sensitive to some variables, less so to others. Attention is then focused on the variables to which profitability is most sensitive. This technique, known as **sensitivity analysis**, is less expensive and less time-consuming than full-scale computer simulation, but it still provides valuable insight for decision-making purposes.

sensitivity analysis
Limited form of computer simulation that focuses on important decision variables

Computer Simulation Example

To illustrate the computer simulation technique, consider the evaluation of a new minimill investment project by Remington Steel, Inc. The exact cost of the plant is not known, but it is expected to be about $150 million. If no difficulties arise in construction, this cost can be as low as $125 million. An unfortunate series of events such as strikes, greater than projected increases in material costs, and/or technical problems could drive the required investment outlay as high as $225 million. Revenues from the new facility depend on the growth of regional income and construction, competition, developments in the field of metallurgy, steel import quotas and tariffs, and so on. Operating costs depend on production efficiency, the cost of raw materials, and the trend in wage rates. Because sales revenues and operating costs are uncertain, annual profits are unpredictable.

Assuming that probability distributions can be developed for each major cost and revenue category, a computer program can be constructed to simulate the pattern of future events. Computer simulation randomly selects revenue and cost levels from each relevant distribution and uses this information to estimate future profits, net present values, or the rate of return on investment. This process is repeated a large number of times to identify the central tendency of projected returns and their expected values. When the computer simulation is completed, the frequency pattern and range of future returns can be plotted and analyzed. Although the expected value of future profits is of obvious interest, the range of possible outcomes is similarly important as a useful indicator of risk.

The computer simulation technique is illustrated in Figures 14.6 and 14.7. Figure 14.6 is a flow chart that shows the information flow pattern for the simulation procedure just described. Figure 14.7 illustrates the frequency distribution of rates of return generated by such a simu-

FIGURE 14.6

Simulation for Investment Planning

Computer simulation allows detailed analysis of managerial problems involving complex cost and revenue relations.

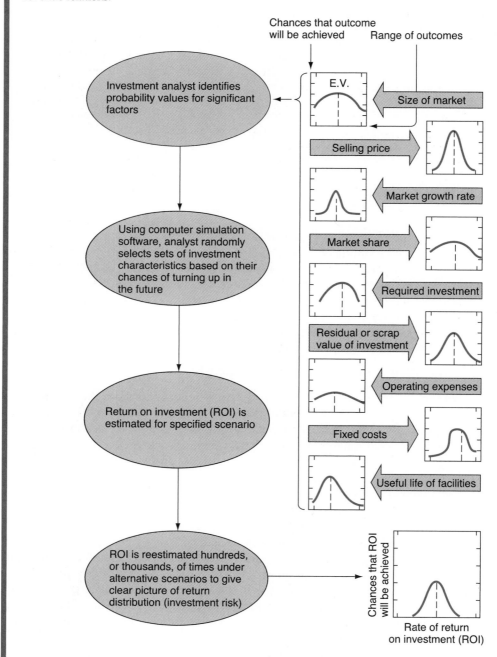

FIGURE 14.7

Expected Rates of Return on Investments *X* and *Y*

Investments *X* and *Y* both have continuous distributions of returns around their expected values.

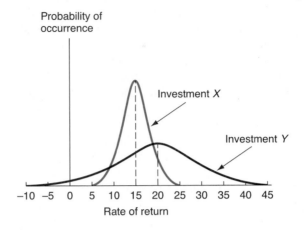

lation for two alternative projects, *X* and *Y*, each with an expected cost of $20 million. The expected rate of return on investment *X* is 15 percent, and 20 percent on investment *Y*. However, these are only average rates of return derived by the computer simulation. The range of simulated returns is from –10 percent to 45 percent for investment *Y*, and from 5 percent to 25 percent for investment *X*. The standard deviation for *X* is only 4 percent; that for *Y* is 12 percent. Based on this information, the coefficient of variation is 0.267 for investment *X* and 0.60 for investment *Y*. Investment *Y* is clearly riskier than investment *X*. A decision about which alternative to choose can be made on the basis of expected utility, or on the basis of a present value determination that incorporates either certainty equivalents or risk-adjusted discount rates.

USES OF GAME THEORY IN RISK ANALYSIS

In an uncertain economic environment, value maximization is achieved using the risk-adjusted valuation models described in this chapter. Under certain circumstances, especially when the decision environment is hostile rather than neutral and when extreme uncertainty exists, other game theory decision criteria may be appropriate.

Game Theory and Auction Strategy

Game theory dates from the 1940s, when mathematician John von Neuman and economist Oskar Morgenstern decided to turn their card-playing ability into a more general theory of decision making under uncertainty. They discovered that deciding when to bluff, fold, stand pat, or raise is not only relevant when playing cards, but also when opposed by aggressive competitors in the marketplace. Rules they developed are increasingly regarded as relevant for analyzing competitive behavior in a wide variety of settings. One of the most interesting uses of game theory is to analyze bidder strategy in auctions.

English auction
Most familiar type of auction, where an auctioneer keeps raising the price until a single highest bidder remains

The most familiar type of auction is an **English auction**, where an auctioneer keeps raising the price until a single highest bidder remains. The advantage of an English auction is that it is widely regarded as a fair and open process. It is an effective approach for obtaining high winning bid prices. Because participants can see and hear what rivals are doing, bidders often act aggressively. In fact, winners sometimes overpay for their winning bids. The so-called

winner's curse
Where overly aggressive bidders pay more than the economic value of auctioned-off items

winner's curse results when overly aggressive bidders pay more than the economic value of auctioned-off items. For example, participants in the bidding process for off-shore oil properties in the Gulf of Mexico routinely seemed to overestimate the amount of oil to be found.

Another commonly employed auction method is a **sealed-bid auction**, where all bids are secret and the highest bid wins. Local and state governments, for example, employ the sealed-bid approach to build roads, buy fuel for schools and government offices, and to procure equipment and general supplies. A compelling advantage of the sealed-bid approach is that it is relatively free from the threat of collusion because, at least ostensibly, no one knows what anyone else is doing. The downside to the approach is that it could yield less to the government when airwave space is auctioned off because the approach often encourages bidders to act cautiously.

sealed-bid auction
Auction where all bids are secret and the highest bid wins

Vickrey auction
Where the highest sealed bid wins, but the winner pays the price of the second-highest bid

A relatively rare sealed-bid auction method is a **Vickrey auction**, where the highest sealed bid wins, but the winner pays the price of the second-highest bid. The reason for this design is that the technique tends to produce high bids because participants know beforehand that they will not be forced to pay the full amount of their winning bid. A disadvantage of the technique is that it creates the perception that the buyer is taking advantage of the seller by paying only the second highest price.

Dutch auction
Winning bidder is the first participant willing to pay the auctioneer's price

Another uncommon auctioning method is the so-called reverse or **Dutch auction**. In a Dutch auction, the auctioneer keeps lowering a very high price until a winning bidder emerges. The winning bidder is the first participant willing to pay the auctioneer's price. A disadvantage of this approach is that bidders tend to act cautiously out of fear of overpaying for auctioned items. In terms of the FCC's sale of airwave space, a Dutch auction might yield less to the government than an English auction. Offsetting this disadvantage is the fact that winning bidders would then be left with greater resources to quickly build a viable service network.

In auctions of airwave space for new communications services, the FCC uses a number of auction strategies to achieve a variety of sometimes conflicting goals. To raise the most money while creating efficient service areas and encouraging competitive bidding, the FCC uses all four basic auction strategies. To better understand the motives behind these auction strategies, it is necessary to examine game theory rules for decision making under uncertainty.

Maximin Decision Rule

maximin criterion
Decision choice method that provides the best of the worst possible outcomes

One decision standard that is sometimes applicable for decision making under uncertainty is the **maximin criterion**.[4] This criterion states that the decision maker should select the alternative that provides the best of the worst possible outcomes. This is done by finding the worst possible (minimum) outcome for each decision alternative and then choosing the option whose worst outcome provides the highest (maximum) payoff. This criterion instructs one to maximize the minimum possible outcome.

To illustrate, consider Table 14.5, which shows the weekly profit contribution payoffs from alternative gasoline-pricing strategies by the self-service U-Pump gas station in Jackson, Wyoming. Assume that U-Pump has just been notified of a 3¢ reduction in the wholesale price of gas. If U-Pump reduces its current self-service price by 3¢ per gallon, its weekly profit contribution will depend on the reaction, if any, of its nearest competitor. If U-Pump's competitor matches the price reduction, a $2,500 profit contribution will result. Without any competitor reaction, U-Pump would earn $3,000. If U-Pump and its competitor both maintain current prices, U-Pump will earn $5,000, whereas if U-Pump did not match the competitor's price cut, U-Pump would earn only $1,000. The worst possible outcome following a price reduction by U-Pump is $2,500, but a $1,000 outcome is possible if U-Pump maintains its current price. The maximin criterion requires U-Pump to reduce its price, because the minimum possible out-

---

4   As seen in Chapter 11, this is equivalent to a secure strategy.

TABLE 14.5

U-Pump's Weekly Profit Contribution Payoff Matrix

		States of Nature	
	Decision Alternatives	**Competitor Reduces Prices**	**Competitor Maintains Current Price**
States of Nature	**Reduce Price**	$2,500	$3,000
	Maintain Current Price	$1,000	$5,000

U-Pump's Weekly Profit Contribution Opportunity Loss or Regret Matrix

		States of Nature	
	Decision Alternatives	**Competitor Reduces Prices**	**Competitor Maintains Current Price**
States of Nature	**Reduce Price**	$0 (= $2,500 – $2,500)	$2,000 (= $5,000 – $3,000)
	Maintain Current Price	$1,500 (= $2,500 – $1,000)	$0 (= $5,000 – $5,000)

come from this decision is greater than the minimum $1,000 payoff possible by maintaining the current price.

Although the maximin criterion suffers from the obvious shortcoming of focusing on the most pessimistic outcome for each decision alternative, it should not be dismissed as naive and unsophisticated. The maximin criterion implicitly assumes a very strong aversion to risk and is appropriate for decisions involving the possibility of catastrophic outcomes. When decision alternatives involve outcomes that endanger worker lives or the survival of the organization, for example, the maximin criterion can be an appropriate technique. Similarly, if the state of nature that prevails depends on the course of action taken by the decision maker, the maximin criterion might be appropriate. In the preceding example, one might expect that a decision by U-Pump to reduce prices would cause the competitor to follow suit, resulting in the worst possible outcome for that decision alternative.

Minimax Regret Decision Rule

minimax regret criterion
Decision choice method that minimizes the maximum possible regret (opportunity loss) associated with a wrong decision *after the fact*

opportunity loss
Difference between a given payoff and the highest possible payoff for the resulting state of nature

A second useful decision criterion focuses on the opportunity loss associated with a decision rather than on its worst possible outcome. This decision rule, known as the **minimax regret criterion**, states that the decision maker should minimize the maximum possible regret (opportunity loss) associated with a wrong decision *after the fact*. This criterion instructs one to minimize the difference between possible outcomes and the best outcome for each state of nature.

To illustrate this decision technique, the concept of opportunity loss, or regret, must be examined in greater detail. In game theory, **opportunity loss** is defined as the difference between a given payoff and the highest possible payoff for the resulting state of nature. Opportunity losses result because returns actually received under conditions of uncertainty are frequently lower than the maximum return that would have been possible had perfect knowledge been available beforehand.

Table 14.5 shows the opportunity loss or regret matrix associated with U-Pump's gasoline-pricing problem. It was constructed by finding the maximum payoff for a given state of nature and then subtracting from this amount the payoffs that would result from various decision alternatives. Opportunity loss is always a positive figure or zero, because each alternative payoff is subtracted from the largest payoff possible in a given state of nature. For example, if U-Pump's competitor reduced its price, the best possible decision for that state of nature would be for U-Pump to have also reduced prices. After the fact, U-Pump would have no regrets had it done so. Should U-Pump maintain its current price, the firm would experience a $1,500 opportunity loss, or regret. To calculate this amount, subtract the $1,000 payoff associated with U-Pump's maintaining its current price despite a competitor price reduction from the $2,500 payoff that it would have received from matching the competitor's price reduction. Similarly, if U-Pump would reduce its price while its competitor maintains the current price, U-Pump would experience a $2,000 opportunity loss or regret after the fact.

The minimax regret criterion would cause U-Pump to maintain the current retail price of gasoline because this decision alternative minimizes the maximum regret, or opportunity loss. The maximum regret in this case is limited to the $1,500 loss that would result if the competitor reduced its current price. If U-Pump were to reduce its price while the competitor maintained its current price, U-Pump's opportunity loss would be $2,000 per week, $500 more than the maximum regret from U-Pump maintaining its current price.

TABLE 14.6

U-Pump's Calculation of Expected Opportunity Loss

	From the Loss Matrix					
	Reduce Price			**Maintain Current Price**		
State of Nature	**Probability of This State of Nature (1)**	**Opportunity Loss of This Outcome (2)**	**Expected Opportunity Loss (3) = (1) × (2)**	**Probability of This State of Nature (1)**	**Opportunity Loss of This Outcome (2)**	**Expected Opportunity Loss (3) = (1) × (2)**
Competitor reduces price	0.5	$ 0	$ 0	0.5	$1,500	$750
Competitor maintains current price	0.5	$2,000	$1,000 $1,000	0.5	$0	$ 0 $750

Cost of uncertainty = Minimum expected opportunity loss = $750.

	From the Payoff Matrix					
	Reduce Price			**Maintain Current Price**		
State of Nature	**Probability (1)**	**Outcome (2)**	**(3) = (1) × (2)**	**Probability (1)**	**Outcome (2)**	**Loss (3) = (1) × (2)**
Competitor reduces price	0.5	$2,500	$1,250	0.5	$1,000	$ 500
Competitor maintains current price	0.5	$3,000	$1,500 $2,750	0.5	$5,000	$2,500 $3,000

Expected value of a correct decision after the fact = $2,500(0.5) + $5,000(0.5) = $3,750.
Cost of uncertainty = Expected value of a correct decision − Expected value of best alternative
= $3,750 − $3,000 = $750.

Cost of Uncertainty

An unavoidable opportunity loss is the cost associated with uncertainty. Therefore, the expected opportunity loss associated with a decision provides a measure of the expected monetary gain from the removal of all uncertainty about future events. From the opportunity loss or regret matrix, the **cost of uncertainty** is measured by the minimum expected opportunity loss. From the payoff matrix, the cost of uncertainty is measured by the difference between the expected payoff associated with choosing the correct alternative under each state of nature (which will be known only after the fact) and the highest expected payoff available from among the decision alternatives. The cost of uncertainty is the unavoidable economic loss that is due to chance. Using this concept, it becomes possible to judge the value of gaining additional information before choosing among decision alternatives.

cost of uncertainty
Minimum expected opportunity loss

The previous gasoline-pricing problem can illustrate this use of opportunity loss. On the basis of the data in Table 14.5, the expected opportunity loss of each decision alternative can be calculated as shown in Table 14.6. Here it is assumed that U-Pump projects a 50/50, or 50 percent, chance of a competitor price reduction. The minimum expected opportunity cost in this case is $750 and represents U-Pump's loss from not knowing its competitor's pricing reaction with certainty. This cost of uncertainty represents the $750 value to U-Pump of resolving doubt about its competitor's pricing policy. U-Pump would be better off if it could eliminate this uncertainty by making an expenditure of less than $750 on information gathering.

Firms often engage in activities aimed at reducing the uncertainty of various alternatives before making an irrevocable decision. For example, a food-manufacturing company will employ extensive marketing tests in selected areas to gain better estimates of sales potential before going ahead with the large-scale introduction of a new product. Manufacturers of consumer goods frequently install new equipment in a limited number of models to judge reliability and customer reaction before including the equipment in all models. Similarly, competitors often announce price changes well in advance of their effective date to elicit the reaction of rivals.

SUMMARY

Risk analysis plays an integral role in the decision process for most business problems. This chapter defines the concept of economic risk and illustrates how the concept can be dealt with in the managerial decision-making process.

- **Economic risk** is the chance of loss due to the fact that all possible outcomes and their probability of occurrence are unknown. **Uncertainty** exists when the outcomes of managerial decisions cannot be predicted with absolute accuracy but all possibilities and their associated probabilities of occurrence are known.

- **Business risk** is the chance of loss associated with a given managerial decision. Many different types of business risk are apparent in the globally competitive 1990s. **Market risk** is the chance that a portfolio of investments can lose money because of swings in the stock market as a whole. **Inflation risk** is the danger that a general increase in the price level will undermine real economic values. **Interest-rate risk** stems from the fact that a fall in interest rates will increase the value of any agreement that involves a fixed promise to pay interest and principal over a specified period. **Credit risk** is the chance that another party will fail to abide by its contractual obligations. Corporations must also consider the problem of **liquidity risk,** or the difficulty of selling corporate assets or investments that have only a few willing buyers or that are otherwise not easily transferable at favorable prices under typical market conditions. **Derivative risk** is the chance that volatile financial derivatives could create losses in underlying investments by increasing rather than decreasing price volatility.

- **Cultural risk** is borne by companies that pursue a global rather than a solely domestic investment strategy. Product market differences due to distinctive social customs make it difficult to predict which products might do well in foreign markets. **Currency risk** is another important danger facing global businesses because most companies wish to eventually repatriate foreign earnings back to the domestic parent. Finally, global investors also experience **government policy risk** because foreign government grants of monopoly franchises, tax abatements, and favored trade status can be tenuous. **Expropriation risk,** or the risk that business property located abroad might be seized by host governments, is another type of risk that global investors must not forget.

- The **probability** of an event is the chance, or odds, that the incident will occur. If all possible events or outcomes are listed, and if a probability of occurrence is assigned to each event, the listing is called a **probability distribution**. A **payoff matrix** illustrates the outcome associated with each possible state of nature. The **expected value** is the anticipated realization from a given payoff matrix.

- **Absolute risk** is the overall dispersion of possible payoffs. The smaller the standard deviation, the tighter the probability distribution and the lower the risk in absolute terms. **Relative risk** is the variation in possible returns compared with the expected payoff amount. **Beta** is a measure of the systematic variability or covariance of one asset's returns with returns on other assets.

- A **normal distribution** has a symmetrical distribution about the mean or expected value. If a probability distribution is normal, the actual outcome will lie within ±1 standard deviation of the mean roughly 68 percent of the time. The probability that the actual outcome will be within ±2 standard deviations of the expected outcome is approximately 95 percent; and there is a greater than 99 percent probability that the actual outcome will occur within ±3 standard deviations of the mean. A **standardized variable** has a mean of 0 and a standard deviation equal to 1.

- **Risk aversion** characterizes individuals who seek to avoid or minimize risk. **Risk neutrality** characterizes decision makers who focus on expected returns and disregard the dispersion of returns (risk). **Risk seeking** characterizes decision makers who prefer risk. At the heart of risk aversion is the notion of **diminishing marginal utility**, where additional increments of money bring ever smaller increments of marginal utility.

- Under the **certainty equivalent** approach, decision makers specify the certain sum that they regard comparable to the expected value of a risky investment alternative. Any expected risky amount can be converted to an equivalent certain sum using the **certainty equivalent adjustment factor**, α, calculated as the ratio of a certain sum divided by an expected risky amount, where both dollar values provide the same level of utility. The **risk-adjusted valuation model** reflects both time value and risk considerations.

- The **risk-adjusted discount rate** k is the sum of the risk-free rate of return, R_F, plus the required risk premium, R_p. The difference between the expected rate of return on a risky asset and the rate of return on a riskless asset is the **risk premium** on the risky asset.

- A **decision tree** is a map of a sequential decision-making process. Decision trees are designed for analyzing decision problems that involve a series of choice alternatives that are constrained by previous decisions. **Decision points** represent instances when management must select among several choice alternatives. **Chance events** are possible outcomes following each decision point.

- **Computer simulation** involves the use of computer software and workstations or sophisticated desktop computers to create a wide variety of decision outcome scenarios. **Sensitivity analysis** focuses on those variables that most directly affect decision outcomes, and it is less expensive and less time-consuming than full-scale computer simulation.

- **Game theory** is a useful decision framework employed to make choices in hostile environments and under extreme uncertainty. A variety of auction strategies are based on game theory principles.

- The most familiar type of auction is an **English auction**, where an auctioneer keeps raising the price until a single highest bidder remains. A **winner's curse** results when overly aggressive bidders pay more than the economic value of auctioned items. In a **sealed-bid auction**, all bids are secret and the highest bid wins. A relatively rare sealed-bid auction method is a **Vickrey auction**, where the highest sealed bid wins, but the winner pays the price of the second-highest bid. Another auctioning method is the so-called reverse or Dutch auction. In a **Dutch auction**, the auctioneer keeps lowering a very high price until a winning bidder emerges. The winning bidder is the first participant willing to pay the auctioneer's price.

- A game-theory decision standard that is sometimes applicable for decision making under uncertainty is the **maximin criterion**, which states that the decision maker should select the alternative that provides the best of the worst possible outcomes. The **minimax regret criterion** states that the decision maker should minimize the maximum possible regret (opportunity loss) associated with a wrong decision *after the fact*. In game theory, **opportunity loss** is defined as the difference between a given payoff and the highest possible payoff for the resulting state of nature. From the opportunity loss or regret matrix, the **cost of uncertainty** is measured by the minimum expected opportunity loss.

Decision making under conditions of uncertainty is greatly facilitated by use of the tools and techniques discussed in this chapter. Although uncertainty can never be eliminated, it can be assessed and dealt with to minimize its harmful consequences.

QUESTIONS

Q14.1 Define the following terms:
  A. Probability distribution
  B. Expected value
  C. Standard deviation
  D. Coefficient of variation
  E. Risk
  F. Diminishing marginal utility of money
  G. Certainty equivalent
  H. Risk-adjusted discount rate
  I. Decision tree
  J. Simulation

Q14.2 What is the main difficulty associated with making decisions solely on the basis of comparisons of expected returns?

Q14.3 The standard deviation measure of risk implicitly gives equal weight to variations on both sides of the expected value. Can you see any potential limitations of this treatment?

Q14.4 "Utility is a theoretical concept that cannot be observed or measured in the real world. Hence, it has no practical value in decision analysis." Discuss this statement.

Q14.5 Graph the relation between money and its utility for an individual who buys both household fire insurance and state lottery tickets.

Q14.6 When the basic valuation model is adjusted using the risk-free rate, *i*, what economic factor is being explicitly accounted for?

Q14.7 If the expected net present value of returns from an investment project is $50,000, what is the maximum price that a risk-neutral investor would pay for it? Explain.

Q14.8 "Market estimates of investors' reactions to risk cannot be measured precisely, so it is impossible to set risk-adjusted discount rates for various classes of investment with a high degree of precision." Discuss this statement.

Q14.9 What is the value of decision trees in managerial decision making?

Q14.10 When is it most useful to use game theory in decision analysis?

SELF-TEST PROBLEMS AND SOLUTIONS

ST14.1 Certainty Equivalent Method. MacKenzie-Rabb, Inc., is a Texas–based manufacturer and distributor of components and replacement parts for the auto, machinery, farm, and construction equipment industries. The company is currently funding a program of capital investment that is necessary to reduce production costs and thereby meet an onslaught of competition from low-cost suppliers located in Mexico and throughout Latin America. MacKenzie-Rabb has a limited amount of capital available and must carefully weigh both the risks and potential rewards associated with alternative investments. In particular, the company seeks to weigh the advantages and disadvantages of a new investment project, project X, in light of two other recently adopted investment projects, project Y and project Z:

Expected Cash Flows After Tax (CFAT) per Year

Year	Project X	Project Y	Project Z
2001	$10,000	$20,000	$0
2002	10,000	18,000	2,500
2003	10,000	16,000	5,000
2004	10,000	14,000	7,500
2005	10,000	12,000	10,000
2006	10,000	10,000	12,500
2007	10,000	8,000	15,000
2008	10,000	6,000	17,500
2009	10,000	4,000	20,000
2010	10,000	2,000	22,500
PV of Cash Flow @ 5%		$91,131	$79,130
Investment Outlay in 2000:	$60,000	$60,000	$50,000

A. Using a 5% risk-free rate, calculate the present value of expected cash flows after tax (CFAT) for the 10-year life of project X.

B. Calculate the minimum certainty equivalent adjustment factor for each project's CFAT that would justify investment in each project.

C. Assume that the management of MacKenzie-Rabb is risk averse and uses the certainty equivalent method in decision making. Is project X as attractive or more attractive than projects Y and Z?

D. If the company would not have been willing to invest more than $60,000 in project Y nor more than $50,000 in project Z, should project X be undertaken?

ST14.1 Solution

A. Using a 5% risk-free rate, the present value of expected cash flows after tax (CFAT) for the 10-year life of project X is $77,217, calculated as follows:

Expected Cash Flows After Tax (CFAT) per Year

Year	Project X	PV of $1 at 5%	PV of CFAT at 5%
2001	$10,000	0.9524	$9,524
2002	10,000	0.9070	9,070
2003	10,000	0.8638	8,638
2004	10,000	0.8227	8,227
2005	10,000	0.7835	7,835
2006	10,000	0.7462	7,462
2007	10,000	0.7107	7,107
2008	10,000	0.6768	6,768
2009	10,000	0.6446	6,446
2010	10,000	0.6139	6,139
PV of Cash Flow @ 5%			$77,217

B. To justify each investment alternative, the company must have a certainty equivalent adjustment factor of at least $\alpha_X = 0.777$ for project X, $\alpha_Y = 0.658$ for project Y, and $\alpha_Z = 0.632$ for project Z, because:

$$\alpha = \frac{\text{Certain Sum}}{\text{Expected Risky Sum}}$$

$$= \frac{\text{Investment Outlay (opportunity cost)}}{\text{Present Value CFAT}}$$

Project X

$$\alpha_X = \frac{\$60,000}{\$77,217} = 0.777$$

Project Y

$$\alpha_Y = \frac{\$60,000}{\$91,131} = 0.658$$

Project Z

$$\alpha_Z = \frac{\$50,000}{\$79,130} = 0.632$$

In other words, each risky dollar of expected profit contribution from project X must be "worth" at least (valued as highly as) 77.7¢ in certain dollars to justify investment. For project Y, each risky dollar must be worth at least 65.8¢ in certain dollars; each risky dollar must be worth at least 63.2¢ to justify investment in project Z.

C. Given managerial risk aversion, project X is the least attractive investment because it has the highest "price" on each risky dollar of expected CFAT. In adopting projects Y and Z, MacKenzie-Rabb implicitly asserted that it is willing to pay between 63.2¢ (project Z) and 65.8¢ (project Y) per each expected dollar of CFAT.

D. No. If the prices described previously represent the maximum price the company is willing to pay for such risky returns, then project X should not be undertaken.

ST14.2 Project Valuation. Quality Foods, Inc., is a leading grocery retailer in the greater Washington, DC, metropolitan area. The company is currently engaged in an aggressive store refurbishing program and is contemplating expansion of its in-store delicatessen department. A number of investment alternatives are being considered, including the construction of facilities for a new restaurant-quality carryout service for Chinese food. This investment project is to be evaluated using the certainty equivalent adjustment factor method and the risk-adjusted discount rate method. If the project has a positive value when both methods are employed, the project will be undertaken. The project will not be undertaken if either evaluation method suggests that the investment will fail to increase the value of the firm. Expected cash flow after tax (CFAT) values over the 5-year life of the investment project and relevant certainty equivalent adjustment factor information are as follows:

Hot Food Carryout Counter Investment Project

Time Period (years)	Alpha	Project E(CFAT)
0	1.00	($75,000)
1	0.95	22,500
2	0.90	25,000
3	0.85	27,500
4	0.75	30,000
5	0.70	32,500
Total		$62,500

At the present time, an 8% annual rate of return can be obtained on short-term U.S. government securities; the company uses this rate as an estimate of the risk-free rate of return.

A. Use the 8% risk-free rate to calculate the present value of the investment project.

B. Using this present value as a basis, utilize the certainty equivalent adjustment factor information given previously to determine the risk-adjusted present value of the project.

C. Use an alternative risk-adjusted discount rate method of project valuation on the assumption that a 15% rate of return is appropriate in light of the level of risk undertaken.

D. Compare and contrast your answers to parts B and C. Should the investment be made?

ST14.2 Solution

A. The present value of this investment project can be calculated easily using a handheld calculator with typical financial function capabilities or by using the tables found in Appendix B. Using the appropriate discount factors corresponding to an 8% risk-free rate, the present value of the investment project is calculated as follows:

Hot Food Carryout Counter Investment Project

Time Period (years)	Present Value of $1 at 8%	Project E(CFAT)	Present Value of E(CFAT) at 8%
0	1.0000	($75,000)	($75,000)
1	0.9259	22,500	20,833
2	0.8573	25,000	21,433
3	0.7938	27,500	21,830
4	0.7350	30,000	22,050
5	0.6806	32,500	22,120
Total		$62,500	$33,266

B. Using the present value given in part A as a basis, the certainty equivalent adjustment factor information given previously can be employed to determine the risk-adjusted present value of the project:

Hot Food Carryout Counter Investment Project

Time Period (years)	Present Value of $1 at 8%	Project E(CFAT)	Present Value of E(CFAT) at 8%	Alpha	Risk-Adjusted Value
0	1.0000	($75,000)	($75,000)	1.00	($75,000)
1	0.9259	22,500	20,833	0.95	19,791
2	0.8573	25,000	21,433	0.90	19,290
3	0.7938	27,500	21,830	0.85	18,556
4	0.7350	30,000	22,050	0.75	16,538
5	0.6806	32,500	22,120	0.70	15,484
Total		$62,500	$33,266		$14,659

C. An alternative risk-adjusted discount rate method of project valuation based on a 15% rate of return gives the following project valuation:

Hot Food Carryout Counter Investment Project

Time Period (years)	Present Value of $1 at 15%	Project E(CFAT)	Present Value of E(CFAT) at 15%
0	1.0000	($75,000)	($75,000)
1	0.8696	22,500	19,566
2	0.7561	25,000	18,903
3	0.6575	27,500	18,081
4	0.5718	30,000	17,154
5	0.4972	32,500	16,159
Total		$62,500	$14,863

D. The answers to parts B and C are fully compatible; both suggest a positive risk-adjusted present value for the project. In part B, the certainty equivalent adjustment factor method reduces the present value of future receipts to account for risk differences. As is typical, the example assumes that money to be received in the more distant future has a greater risk and, hence, a lesser certainty equivalent value. In the risk-adjusted discount rate approach of part C, the discount rate of 15% entails a time-factor adjustment of 8% plus a risk adjustment of 7%. Like the certainty equivalent adjustment factor approach, the risk-adjusted discount rate method gives a risk-adjusted present value for the project. Because the risk-adjusted present value of the project is positive under either approach, the investment should be made.

PROBLEMS

P14.1 **Risk Preferences.** Identify each of the following as being consistent with risk-averse, risk-neutral, or risk-seeking behavior in investment project selection. Explain your answers.

A. Larger risk premiums for riskier projects

B. Preference for smaller, as opposed to larger, coefficients of variation

C. Valuing certain sums and expected risky sums of equal dollar amounts equally

D. Having an increasing marginal utility of money

E. Ignoring the risk levels of investment alternatives

P14.2 **Certainty Equivalents.** The certainty equivalent concept can be widely employed in the analysis of personal and business decision making. Indicate whether each of the following statements is true or false and explain why:

A. The appropriate certainty equivalent adjustment factor, α, indicates the minimum price in certain dollars that an individual should be willing to pay per risky dollar of expected return.

B. An $\alpha \neq 1$ implies that a certain sum and a risky expected return of different dollar amounts provide equivalent utility to a given decision maker.

C. If previously accepted projects with similar risk have αs in a range from $\alpha = 0.4$ to $\alpha = 0.5$, an investment with an expected return of $150,000 is acceptable at a cost of $50,000.

D. A project for which $NPV > 0$ using an appropriate risk-adjusted discount rate has an implied α factor that is too large to allow project acceptance.

E. State lotteries that pay out 50% of the revenues that they generate require players who place at least a certain $2 value on each $1 of expected risky return.

P14.3 **Expected Value.** Duddy Kravitz, a broker with Caveat Emptor, Ltd., offers free investment seminars to local PTA groups. On average, Kravitz expects 1% of seminar participants to purchase $25,000 in tax-sheltered investments and 5% to purchase $5,000 in stocks and bonds. Kravitz earns a 4% net commission on tax shelters and a 1% commission on stocks and bonds. Calculate Kravitz's expected net commissions per seminar if attendance averages 10 persons.

P14.4 **Probability Concepts.** Aquarius Products, Inc., has just completed development of a new line of skin-care products. Preliminary market research indicates two feasible marketing strategies: (1) creating general consumer acceptance through media advertising or (2) creating distributor acceptance through intensive personal selling by company representatives. The marketing manager has developed the following estimates for sales under each alternative:

Media Advertising Strategy		Personal Selling Strategy	
Probability	**Sales**	**Probability**	**Sales**
0.1	$ 500,000	0.3	$1,000,000
0.4	1,500,000	0.4	1,500,000
0.4	2,500,000	0.3	2,000,000
0.1	3,500,000		

A. Assume that the company has a 50% profit margin on sales (that is, profits equal one-half of sales revenue). Calculate expected profits for each plan.

B. Construct a simple bar graph of the possible profit outcomes for each plan. Which plan appears to be riskier?

C. Assume that management's utility function resembles the one illustrated in the following figure. Which strategy should the marketing manager recommend?

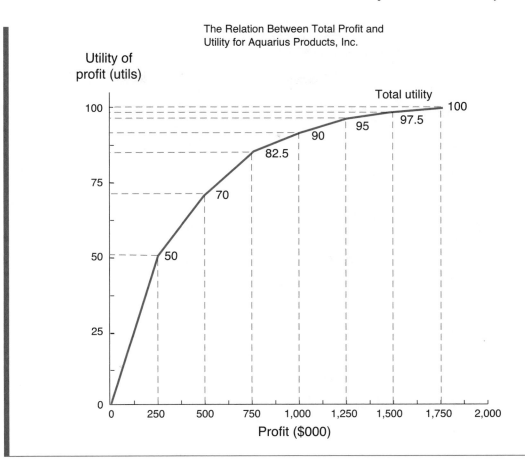

The Relation Between Total Profit and
Utility for Aquarius Products, Inc.

P14.5 **Probability Concepts.** Sam Malone, marketing director for Narcissism Records, Inc., has just completed an agreement to rerelease a recording of "The Boss's Greatest Hits." (The Boss had a number of hits on the rock and roll charts during the early 1980s.) Preliminary market research indicates two feasible marketing strategies: (1) concentration on developing general consumer acceptance by advertising on late-night television or (2) concentration on developing distributor acceptance through intensive sales calls by company representatives. Malone developed estimates for sales under each alternative plan and has constructed payoff matrices according to his assessment of the likelihood of product acceptance under each plan. These data are as follows:

Strategy 1 Consumer Television Promotion		Strategy 2 Distributor-Oriented Promotion	
Probability	**Outcome (sales)**	**Probability**	**Outcome (sales)**
0.32	$250,000	0.125	$250,000
0.36	1,000,000	0.750	750,000
0.32	1,750,000	0.125	1,250,000

A. Assuming that the company has a 50% profit margin on sales, calculate the expected profits for each plan.

B. Construct a simple bar graph of the possible profit outcomes for each plan. Which plan appears to be riskier?

C. Calculate the standard deviation of the profit distribution associated with each plan.

D. Assume that the management of Narcissism has a utility function like the one illustrated in the following figure. Which marketing strategy should Malone recommend?

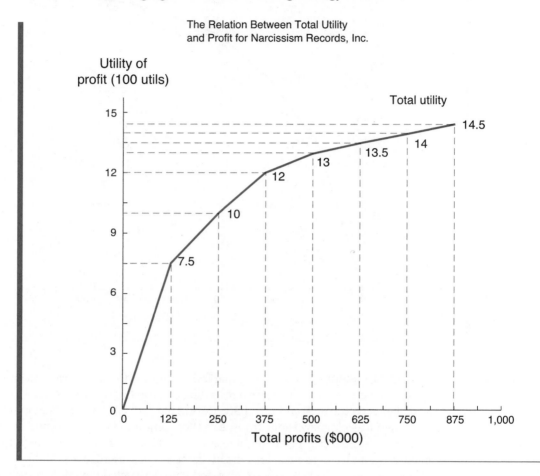

The Relation Between Total Utility and Profit for Narcissism Records, Inc.

P14.6 Risk-Adjusted Discount Rates. One-Hour Dryclean, Inc., is contemplating replacing an obsolete dry-cleaning machine with one of two innovative pieces of equipment. Alternative 1 requires a current investment outlay of $25,373, whereas alternative 2 requires an outlay of $24,199. The following cash flows (cost savings) will be generated each year over the new machines' 4-year lives:

	Probability	**Cash Flow**
Alternative 1	0.18	$ 5,000
	0.64	10,000
	0.18	15,000
Alternative 2	0.125	$ 8,000
	0.75	10,000
	0.125	12,000

A. Calculate the expected cash flow for each investment alternative.

B. Calculate the standard deviation of cash flows (risk) for each investment alternative.

C. The firm will use a discount rate of 12% for the cash flows with a higher degree of dispersion and a 10% rate for the less risky cash flows. Calculate the expected net present value for each investment. Which alternative should be chosen?

P14.7 **Certainty Equivalent Method.** Tex-Mex, Inc., is a rapidly growing chain of Mexican food restaurants. The company has a limited amount of capital for expansion and must carefully weigh available alternatives. Currently, the company is considering opening restaurants in Santa Fe or Albuquerque, New Mexico. Projections for the two potential outlets are as follows:

City	Outcome	Annual Profit Contribution	Probability
Albuquerque	Failure	$100,000	0.5
	Success	200,000	0.5
Santa Fe	Failure	$60,000	0.5
	Success	340,000	0.5

Each restaurant would require a capital expenditure of $700,000, plus land acquisition costs of $500,000 for Albuquerque and $1 million for Santa Fe. The company uses the 10% yield on riskless U.S. Treasury bills to calculate the risk-free annual opportunity cost of investment capital.

A. Calculate the expected value, standard deviation, and coefficient of variation for each outlet's profit contribution.

B. Calculate the minimum certainty equivalent adjustment factor for each restaurant's cash flows that would justify investment in each outlet.

C. Assuming that the management of Tex-Mex is risk averse and uses the certainty equivalent method in decision making, which is the more attractive outlet? Why?

P14.8 **Decision Trees.** Keystone Manufacturing, Inc., is analyzing a new bid to supply the company with electronic control systems. Alpha Corporation has been supplying the systems, and Keystone is satisfied with its performance. However, a bid has just been received from Beta Controls, Ltd., a firm that is aggressively marketing its products. Beta has offered to supply systems for a price of $120,000. The price for the Alpha system is $160,000. In addition to an attractive price, Beta offers a money-back guarantee. That is, if Beta's systems do not match Alpha's quality, Keystone can reject and return them for a full refund. However, if it must reject the machines and return them to Beta, Keystone will suffer a delay costing the firm $60,000.

A. Construct a decision tree for this problem and determine the maximum probability that Keystone could assign to rejection of the Beta system before it would reject that firm's offer, assuming that it decides on the basis of minimizing expected costs.

B. Assume that Keystone assigns a 50% probability of rejection to the Beta Controls. Would Keystone be willing to pay $15,000 for an assurance bond that would pay $60,000 in the event that the Beta Controls fail the quality check? (Use the same objective as in part A.) Explain.

P14.9 **Standard Normal Concept.** Speedy Business Cards, Inc., supplies customized business cards to commercial and individual customers. The company is preparing a bid to supply cards to the Nationwide Realty Company, a large association of independent real estate agents. Because paper, ink, and other costs cannot be determined precisely, Speedy anticipates that costs will be normally distributed around a mean of $20 per unit (each 500-card order) with a standard deviation of $2 per unit.

A. What is the probability that Speedy will make a profit at a price of $20 per unit?

B. Calculate the unit price necessary to give Speedy a 95% chance of making a profit on the order.

C. If Speedy submits a successful bid of $23 per unit, what is the probability that it will make a profit?

P14.10 Game Theory. Sierra Mountain Bike, Inc., is a producer and wholesaler of rugged bicycles designed for mountain touring. The company is considering an upgrade to its current line by making high-grade chrome alloy frames standard. Of course, the market response to this upgrade in product quality depends on the competitor's reaction, if any. The company's comptroller projects the following annual profits (payoffs) following resolution of the upgrade decision:

	States of Nature	
Sierra's Decision Alternatives	**Competitor Upgrade**	**No Competitor Upgrade**
Upgrade	$1,000,000	$1,500,000
Do not upgrade	800,000	2,000,000

A. Which decision alternative would Sierra choose given a maximin criterion? Explain.

B. Calculate the opportunity loss or regret matrix.

C. Which decision alternative would Sierra choose given a minimax regret criterion? Explain.

CASE STUDY

AOL-Time Warner Is Playing Games with Stockholders

AOL-Time Warner, Inc., the world's largest media and entertainment company, was created through the merger of America Online, Inc., with Time Warner, a company that is best known as the publisher of magazines such as *Fortune*, *Time*, *People*, and *Sports Illustrated*. The company is a media powerhouse comprised of Internet technologies and electronic commerce (America Online), cable television systems, filmed entertainment and television production, cable and broadcast television, recorded music and music publishing, magazine publishing, book publishing, and direct marketing. AOL-Time Warner has the potential to profit whether people go to theaters, buy or rent videos, watch cable or broadcast TV, or listen to records.

Just as impressive as AOL-Time Warner's commanding presence in the entertainment field is its potential for capitalizing on its recognized strengths during coming years. AOL-Time Warner is a leader in terms of embracing new entertainment-field technology. The company's state-of-the-art cable systems allow subscribers to rent movies, purchase a wide array of goods and services, and participate in game shows and consumer surveys—all from the privacy of their own homes. Wide channel flexibility also gives the company the opportunity to expand pay-per-view TV offerings to meet demand from specialized market niches. In areas where cable systems have sufficient capacity, HBO subscribers are now offered a choice of programming on different channels. AOL-Time Warner also has specialized networks, like TVKO , to offer special events on a regular pay-per-view basis.

Time Warner, AOL-Time Warner's predecessor company, is also famous for introducing common stockholders to the practical use of game theory concepts. In 1991, the company introduced a controversial plan to raise new equity capital through use of a complex "contingent" rights offering. After months of assuring Wall Street that it was close to raising new equity from other firms through strategic alliances, Time Warner instead asked its shareholders to ante up more cash. Under the plan, the company granted holders of its 57.8 million shares of common stock the rights to 34.5 million shares of new common, or 0.6 rights per share. Each right enabled a shareholder to pay Time Warner $105 for an unspecified number of new common shares. Because the number of new shares that might be purchased for $105 was unspecified, so too was the price per share. Time Warner's Wall Street advisers structured the offer so that the new stock would be offered at cheaper prices if fewer shareholders chose to exercise their rights.

In an unusual arrangement, the rights from all participating shareholders were to be placed in a pool to determine their pro rata share of the 34.45 million shares to be distributed. If 100% of Time Warner shareholders chose to exercise their rights, the price per share would be $105; the number of shares owned by each shareholder would increase by 60%; and each shareholder would retain his or her same proportionate ownership in the company. In the event that less than 100% of the shareholders chose to participate, participating shareholders would receive a discount price and increase their proportionate interest in the company. If only 80% of Time Warner shareholders chose to exercise their rights, the price per share would be $84; if 60% chose to exercise their rights, the price per share would be $63. These lower prices reflect the fact that if only 80% of Time Warner shareholders chose to exercise their rights, each $105 right would purchase 1.25 shares; if 60% chose to exercise their rights, each $105 right would purchase roughly 1.667 shares. Finally, to avoid the possibility of issuing equity at fire-sale prices, Time Warner reserved the privilege to cancel the equity offering entirely if fewer than 60% of holders chose to exercise their rights.

The terms of the offer were designed to make Time Warner shareholders feel compelled to exercise their rights in hopes of getting cheap stock and avoiding seeing their holdings diluted. Although such contingent rights offerings are a common capital-raising technique in Britain, prior to the Time Warner offering they had never been proposed on such a large scale in the United States. Wall Street traders and investment bankers lauded the Time Warner offer as a brilliant coercive device—a view that might have been colored by the huge fees they stood to make on the offering. Advisory fees for Merrill Lynch and Time Warner's seven other key advisers were projected at $41.5 million to $145 million, depending on the number of participating shareholders. An additional $20.7 million to $34.5 million was set aside to pay other investment bankers for soliciting shareholders to exercise their rights. Time Warner's advisers argued that their huge fees totaling 5.22% of the proceeds to the company were justified because the offering entered uncharted ground in terms of Wall Street experience. Disgruntled shareholders noted that a similar contingent rights offering by Bass PLC of Britain involved a fee of only 2.125% of the proceeds to the company, despite the fact that the lead underwriter, Schroders PLC, agreed to buy and resell any new stock that was not claimed by rights holders. This led to charges that Time Warner's advisers were charging underwriters' fees without risking any of their own capital.

Proceeds from the offering were earmarked to help pay down the $11.3 billion debt Time Inc. took on to buy Warner Communications Inc. 2 years previously, when Time Warner was formed. Time Warner maintained that it was in intensive talks with potential strategic partners and that the rights offering would strengthen its hand in those negotiations by improving the company's balance sheet. Time Warner said that the rights offering would enhance its ability to enter into strategic alliances or joint ventures with partners overseas. Such alliances would help the company penetrate markets in Japan, Europe, and elsewhere. Critics of the plan argued that the benefits from strategic alliances come in small increments and that Time Warner had failed to strike any such deals previously because it wants both management control and a premium price from potential partners. These critics also maintained that meaningful revenue from any such projects is probably years away.

Stockholder reaction to the Time Warner offering was immediate and overwhelmingly negative. On the day the offering was announced, Time Warner shares closed at $99.50, down $11.25, in New York Stock Exchange composite trading. This was in addition to a decline of $6 suffered the previous day on the basis of a report in *The Wall Street Journal* that some form

CASE STUDY (continued)

of equity offering was being considered. After trading above $120 per share in the days prior to the first reports of a pending offer, Time Warner shares plummeted by more than 25% to $88 per share within a matter of days. This is yet one more disappointment for the company's long-suffering common stockholders. During the summer of 1989, Time cited a wide range of synergistic benefits to be gained from a merger with Warner Communications and spurned a $200 per share buyout offer from Paramount Communications, Inc. This is despite the fact that the Paramount offer represented a fat 60% premium to the then prevailing market price of $125 for Time stock. During the succeeding 2-year period, Time Warner stock failed to rise above this $125 level and traded as low as $66 per share during the fall of 1990. Meanwhile, the hoped-for Time Warner synergy has yet to emerge.

A. Was Paramount's above-market offer for Time, Inc., consistent with the notion that the prevailing market price for common stock is an accurate reflection of the discounted net present value of future cash flows? Was management's rejection of Paramount's above-market offer for Time, Inc., consistent with the value-maximization concept?

B. Assume that a Time Warner shareholder could buy additional shares at a market price of $90 or participate in the company's rights offering. Construct the payoff and regret matrices per share that correspond to a $90 per share purchase decision versus a decision to participate in the rights offering with subsequent 100%, 80%, and 60% participation by all Time Warner shareholders.

C. Describe the relevant maximin and minimax shareholder strategies.

D. Explain why the price of Time Warner common stock fell following the announcement of the company's controversial rights offering. Is such an offering in the best interests of current shareholders?

SELECTED REFERENCES

Abel, Andrew B. "Will Bequests Attenuate the Predicted Meltdown in Stock Prices When Baby Boomers Retire?" *Review of Economics and Statistics* 83 (November 2001): 589–595.

Bell, Timothy B., Wayne R. Landsman, and Douglas A. Shackelford. "Auditors' Perceived Business Risk and Audit Fees: Analysis and Evidence." *Journal of Accounting Research* 39 (June 2001): 35–43.

Byrne, Peter J, and Stephen Lee. "Risk Reduction and Real Estate Portfolio Size." *Managerial & Decision Economics* 22 (October/November 2001): 369–379.

Cooley, Thomas F., and Vincenzo Quadrini. "Financial Markets and Firm Dynamics." *American Economic Review* 91 (December 2001): 1286–1310.

Deck, Cary A. "A Test of Game-Theoretic and Behavioral Models of Play in Exchange and Insurance Environments." *American Economic Review* 91 (December 2001): 1546–1555.

Dee, Thomas S., and William N. Evans. "Behavioral Policies and Teen Traffic Safety." *American Economic Review* 91 (May 2001): 91–96.

Docking, Dianne Scott, Mark Hirschey, and Elaine Jones. "Reaction of Bank Stock Prices to Loan-Loss Reserve Announcements." *Review of Quantitative Finance & Accounting* 15 (November 2000): 277–297.

Goeree, Jacob K., and Charles A. Holt. "Ten Little Treasures of Game Theory and Ten Intuitive Contradictions." *American Economic Review* 91 (December 2001): 1402–1422.

Hirschey, Mark, Vernon J. Richardson, and Susan Scholz. "How 'Foolish' Are Internet Investors?" *Financial Analysts Journal* 56 (January/February 2000): 62–69.

Kroszner, Randall S., and Philip E. Strahan. "Bankers on Boards: Monitoring, Conflicts of Interest, and Lender Liability." *Journal of Business* 62 (December 2001): 415–452.

Lewis, Craig M., Richard J. Rogalski, and James K. Seward. "The Long-Run Performance of Firms That Issue Convertible Debt: An Empirical Analysis of Operating Characteristics and Analyst Forecasts." *Journal of Corporate Finance* 7 (December 2001): 447–474.

Lo, Andrew W. "Risk Management for Hedge Funds: Introduction and Overview." *Financial Analysts Journal* 57 (November/December 2001): 16–33.

Mitchell, Mark, and Todd Pulvino. "Characteristics of Risk and Return in Risk Arbitrage." *Journal of Finance* 56 (December 2001): 2135–2176.

Pan, Jun. "The Jump-Risk Premia Implicit in Options: Evidence from an Integrated Time-Series Study." *Journal of Financial Economics* 63 (January 2002): 3–50.

Syau, Yu-Ru, and Hai-Teh Hsieh. "Fuzzy Numbers in the Credit Rating of Enterprise Financial Condition." *Review of Quantitative Finance and Accounting* 17 (December 2001): 351–360.

CHAPTER FIFTEEN

Capital Budgeting

Berkshire Hathaway, General Electric, and Johnson & Johnson are standout performers in terms of the amount of wealth created for shareholders. What these diverse companies share is a common devotion to the capital budgeting process. They manage capital resources using two simple concepts: (1) Funds employed in the business have a cost that must be paid, and (2) funds should be allocated where they generate the largest profit.

For example, careful asset redeployment within the General Electric empire allows GE to maintain rapid growth and an enviable rate of return on invested capital. At the cornerstone of GE's capital budgeting process is a "value added" concept that measures wealth created, or lost, for GE shareholders. To determine the value added from a given line of business or investment project, GE deducts the explicit or implicit cost of capital employed from the after-tax profit earned on operations. What's left over is the amount of value added for shareholders. GE then simply allocates its capital among those investment ideas that generate the most value added. If attractive investment opportunities are abundant, GE seeks additional debt or equity financing. If too few compelling investment projects are available, GE uses excess capital to buy back its stock or pay down debt. This simple philosophy has propelled GE, and companies like it, to stunning success.[1]

This chapter describes the mechanics of capital budgeting as an application of marginal analysis. In capital budgeting, marginal revenue is measured by the incremental cash flows derived from investment projects; marginal cost is the added expense of new investment capital. The value of the firm is maximized when these marginal revenues and marginal costs are equal.

---

1   Ben Siegel, "Filing Shows Berkshire Hathaway Paid $223.4 Million for Albecca," *The Wall Street Journal Online*, February 22, 2002 (http://online.wsj.com).

CAPITAL BUDGETING PROCESS

Management invests hundreds of billions of dollars per year in fixed assets. By their very nature, these investment decisions have the potential to affect a firm's fortunes over several years. A good decision can boost earnings sharply and dramatically increase the value of the firm. A bad decision can lead to bankruptcy. Effective planning and control is essential if the health and long-run viability of the firm is to be assured.

What Is Capital Budgeting?

capital budgeting
Long-term investment planning process

The term *capital* refers to the funds employed to finance fixed assets used in production; a budget is a detailed plan of projected inflows and outflows over future periods. **Capital budgeting** is the process of planning expenditures that generate cash flows expected to extend beyond 1 year. The choice of 1 year is arbitrary, of course, but it is a convenient cutoff for distinguishing between classes of expenditures. Examples of capital outlays are expenditures for land, buildings and equipment, and for additions to working capital (e.g., inventories and receivables) made necessary by expansion. New advertising campaigns or research and development programs are also likely to have impacts beyond 1 year and come within the classification of capital budgeting expenditures.

Capital budgeting integrates the various elements of the firm. Although the financial manager generally has administrative control of the capital budgeting process, the effectiveness of a firm's capital investments depends on input from all major departments. The marketing department makes a key contribution by providing sales forecasts. Because operating costs must be estimated, the accounting, production, engineering, and purchasing departments are also involved. The initial outlay, or investment cost, must be estimated; again, engineering and purchasing typically provide input. Obtaining funds and estimating their cost are major tasks of the financial manager. Finally, these various estimates must be drawn together in the form of a project evaluation. Although the finance department generally writes up the evaluation report, top management ultimately sets standards of acceptability.

Project Selection Process

A firm's growth and development, even its ability to remain competitive and to survive, depend on a constant flow of ideas for new products and ways to make existing products better and at lower cost. A well-managed firm goes to great lengths to develop good capital budgeting proposals. For example, a sales representative may report that customers are asking for a particular product that the company does not now produce. The sales manager then will discuss the idea with the marketing research group to determine the size of the market for the proposed product. If it appears likely that a substantial market does exist, cost accountants and engineers will be asked to estimate production costs. If it appears that the product can be produced and sold to yield a sufficient profit, the project will be undertaken.

If a firm has capable and imaginative managers and other employees, and if its incentive system is working properly, several ideas for capital investment will be advanced. Some ideas will be both practical and profitable, whereas others will not. As a result, procedures must be established for screening project alternatives.

Project Classification Types

Analyzing capital expenditure proposals is not a costless operation; benefits can be gained from careful analysis, but such investigations are costly. For certain types of projects, a relatively detailed analysis may be warranted; for others, cost/benefit studies suggest that simpler procedures should be used. Firms generally classify projects into a number of categories and analyze those projects in each category somewhat differently.

replacement projects
Maintenance of business investments

Replacement projects are expenditures necessary to replace worn-out or damaged equipment. These projects are necessary if the firm is to continue in its current businesses. The relevant issues are (a) Should the company continue to offer current products and services? and (b) Should existing plant and equipment be employed for this purpose? Usually, the answers to both questions are yes, so maintenance decisions are typically routine and made without going through an elaborate decision process.

cost reduction projects
Expenditures to replace obsolete plant and equipment

Cost reduction projects include expenditures to replace serviceable but obsolete plant and equipment. The purpose of these investment projects is to lower production costs by lowering expenses for labor, raw materials, heat, or electricity. These decisions are often discretionary, so a more detailed analysis is generally required to support the expenditure. Decision-making authority usually rests at the manager or higher level in the organization.

safety and environmental projects
Mandatory nonrevenue-producing investments

Capital expenditures made necessary by government regulation, collective bargaining agreements, or insurance policy requirements fall into a further **safety and environmental projects** category. Such capital expenditures are sometimes called "mandatory" investments because they often are nonrevenue-producing in nature. How they are handled depends on their size and complexity; most often they are quite routine, and treatment is similar to replacement and cost reduction projects.

expansion projects
Expenditures to increase availability of existing products

Expansion projects involve expenditures to increase the availability of existing products and services. For example, investment projects to expand the number of service outlets or distribution facilities are included in this category. These investment decisions are relatively complex because they require an explicit forecast of the firm's future supply and demand conditions. Detailed analysis is required, and the final decision is made at a high level within the firm, perhaps at the level of the controller or chief financial officer.

Expansion into new products or markets requires expenditures necessary to produce new products and services or to expand into new geographic areas. Strategic decisions that could change the fundamental nature of the firm's business are involved. Expenditures of large sums over extended investment horizons are often necessary. Final decisions are often made by the chief executive officer or board of directors.

STEPS IN CAPITAL BUDGETING

If an individual investor identifies and invests in a stock or bond whose expected return is greater than the cost of funds, the investor's portfolio will increase in value. Similarly, if a firm identifies or creates an investment opportunity with a present value greater than its cost, the value of the firm will increase. The more effective the firm's capital budgeting process, the higher its growth rate and the greater its future value. In theory, the capital budgeting process involves six logical steps.

Sequence of Project Valuation

First, the cost of the project must be determined. This is similar to finding the price that must be paid for a stock or bond. Next, management must estimate the expected cash flows from the project, including the value of the asset at a specified terminal date. This is similar to estimating the future dividend or interest payment stream on a stock or bond. Third, the riskiness of projected cash flows must be estimated. To do this, management needs information about the probability distributions of future cash flows. Fourth, given the riskiness of projected cash flows and the cost of funds under prevailing economic conditions as reflected by the riskless rate, the firm must determine the appropriate discount rate, or cost of capital, at which the project's cash flows are to be discounted. This is equivalent to finding the required rate of return on a stock or bond investment. Fifth, expected cash flows are converted to a present value to obtain a clear estimate of the investment project's value to the firm. This is equivalent to finding the present value of expected future dividends or interest plus principal payments. Finally, the present value of expected cash inflows is compared with the required outlay, or cost, of the project. If the present value of cash flows derived from a project exceeds the cost of the investment, the project should be accepted. Otherwise, the project should be rejected.

Cash Flow Estimation

The most important and difficult step in the analysis of a capital budgeting project is estimating its cash flows—the investment outlays and the annual net cash inflows after the project goes into operation. Many variables are involved in cash flow forecasting, and several individuals and departments participate in the process. For example, forecasts of unit sales and sales prices are normally made by the marketing department, based on its knowledge of price elasticity, advertising effects, the state of the economy, competitors' reactions, and trends in consumers' tastes. The size of necessary capital outlays associated with a new product are generally obtained from the engineering and product development staffs; operating costs are estimated by cost accountants, production experts, personnel specialists, purchasing agents, and so forth.

It is difficult to make accurate forecasts of the costs and revenues associated with a large, complex project, so forecast errors can be large. For example, when several major oil companies decided to build the Alaska pipeline, the original cost forecasts were in the neighborhood of $700 million, but the final cost was closer to $7 billion. Similar miscalculations are common in forecasts of new product design costs. As difficult as plant and equipment costs are to estimate, sales revenues and operating costs over the life of the project are generally even more uncertain.

In October 2001, for example, a slowing economy and sluggish customer acceptance finally spelled the end to one of the most expensive Internet access projects in the nation. After 3 1/2 years and $5 billion in expenses, Sprint FON Group (Sprint), a subsidiary of Sprint Corporation, pulled the plug on a project affectionately known as its integrated on-demand network, or ION. After attracting only 4,000 customers, ION proved to be an extravagant money pit. Sprint spent roughly $1.25 million per ION customer and staked ambitious growth plans on the prospect of marrying voice and data services. However, a sharp downturn in the telecom sector raised the risk of ION and other speculative spending projects aimed at connecting local telecom customers to high-speed broadband communications networks. In a company press release, Sprint CEO William T. Esrey killed the massive project with the terse comment: "We are taking significant steps to reduce our cost structure and sharpen our focus on the products and services that hold the best potential for growth and return on investment."

Unfortunately, although the Sprint ION fiasco represents a spectacular flop in corporate capital budgeting, it is not a unique example. In 1999, and only 6 months after launching the world's first global satellite phone network, Iridium LLC fell deep into the red as it failed to come close to meeting sales targets. At that time, Iridium reported a quarterly loss of $505 million on revenues of only $1.45 million. Bankruptcy followed when the company failed to find a market niche for its mobile phone handsets serviced by an expensive network of satellites. In the aftermath, investors and creditors sued Motorola, Inc., contending that Motorola had kept control of Iridium, a former subsidiary, after it went public in 1997. Creditors of Iridium contended in court filings that money lent to Iridium was actually funneled to Motorola and should be returned. At the time, creditors and investors sought more than $2 billion in damages from Motorola and another $3.5 billion for damages from Iridium. This litigation came at a bad time for Motorola, which announced its first quarterly loss in 15 years, plant closings, and worker layoffs.

Given enormous financial strength, Sprint has been able to absorb losses on the ION project, and Motorola has recovered from the Iridium debacle. Such miscues would have forced weaker firms into bankruptcy. Still, the enormous burden imposed on shareholders and creditors by such capital budgeting mistakes makes clear the importance of sound forecasting in the capital budgeting process.

The financial staff's role in the forecasting process involves coordinating the efforts of the other departments, such as engineering and marketing; ensuring that everyone involved with the forecast uses a consistent set of economic assumptions; and making sure that no biases are inherent in the forecasts. This last point is extremely important, because division managers often become emotionally involved with pet projects or develop empire-building complexes, leading to cash flow forecasting biases that make bad projects look good—on paper. For the capital budgeting process to be successful, the pattern of expected cash inflows and outflows must be established within a consistent and unbiased framework.

Incremental Cash Flow Evaluation

Accounting income statements reflect a mix of cash and noncash expenses and revenues. Accountants deduct labor costs, which are cash outflows, from revenues, which may or may not be entirely in cash because sales are often made on credit. At the same time, accountants do not deduct capital outlays, which are cash outflows, but do deduct depreciation expenses, which are not cash outflows. In capital budgeting, it is critical that decisions are based strictly on cash flows, the actual dollars that flow into and out of the company during each time period.

incremental cash flows
Change in net cash flows due to an investment project

The relevant cash flows for capital budgeting purposes are the incremental cash flows attributable to a project. **Incremental cash flows** are the period-by-period changes in net cash flows that are due to an investment project:

(15.1)
$$\text{Project } CF_t = \frac{CF_t \text{ for Corporation}}{\text{with Project}} - \frac{CF_t \text{ for Corporation}}{\text{Without Project}}$$

It is possible to construct a firm's pro forma cash flow statements with and without a project for each year of the project's life and then measure annual project cash flows as the differences in cash flows between the two sets of statements. In practice, a number of problems must be addressed successfully if the incremental cash flows from a given investment project are to be estimated successfully.

As described in Chapter 8, a sunk cost is any expenditure outlay that has already occurred or has been agreed to on a contractual basis. Sunk costs are not incremental costs, they are not relevant to subsequent investment decisions, and they should not be included in the analysis of such decisions. Suppose, for example, that Gourmet Foods, Ltd., is evaluating the possibility of opening a retail store in a newly developed section of Albuquerque. A year ago, Gourmet Foods hired a consulting firm to perform an on-site analysis at a cost of $100,000, and this $100,000 has already been paid and expensed for tax purposes. Is this expenditure a relevant cost with respect to Gourmet's still-pending capital budgeting decision? The answer is no. The $100,000 represents a sunk cost. Gourmet Foods cannot recover this amount regardless of whether the new facility is opened. This money is gone. Whether the pending investment project should be accepted or rejected depends on the incremental costs and revenues associated with the project from this point *forward*. Whether the earlier commitment of $100,000 looks good or bad in hindsight is irrelevant. It is essential that irrelevant sunk costs not confound investment decisions.

It sometimes turns out that a project looks unprofitable when all costs, including sunk costs, are considered. On an incremental basis, however, many of these same projects have the potential to generate a significant profit contribution when only incremental cash flows are included. An investment project should be undertaken only when incremental cash flows exceed the cost of investment on a present-value basis. It is essential that irrelevant sunk costs be deleted from the analysis so that correct forward-looking investment decisions can be made.

A second possible problem relates to the improper treatment of opportunity costs. All relevant opportunity costs must be included in the capital budgeting process. For example, suppose

Market-Based Capital Budgeting

The real key to creating corporate wealth is to apply a market-based approach to capital budgeting. The power of the market-based capital budgeting concept stems from the fact that managers cannot know if an operation is really creating value for the corporation until they calculate and apply the true cost of capital to all assets employed. To grow the company in a value-maximizing manner, the firm must weigh the answers to two important questions.

Question No. 1: What is the true cost of capital? The cost of borrowed capital is easy to estimate. It is the interest paid, adjusted to reflect the tax deductibility of interest payments. The cost of equity capital is more difficult to estimate. It is the return shareholders could get if they invested in a portfolio of companies about as risky as the company itself. From this perspective, the relevant cost of capital is its opportunity cost.

Question No. 2: How much capital is tied up in the operation? Capital traditionally consists of the current value of real estate, machines, vehicles, and the like, plus working capital. Proponents of market-based capital

budgeting say there is more. What about the money spent on R&D and on employee training? For decision-making purposes the return on all investments must be calculated over a reasonable life, say 3 to 5 years.

When both questions are answered, multiply the amount of capital from Question No. 2 by the rate of return from Question No. 1 to get the dollar cost of capital. The market value added by the capital budgeting process is operating earnings minus these capital costs, all on an after-tax basis. If the amount of market value added is positive, the operation is creating wealth. If market value added is negative, the operation is destroying capital.

The key is to ensure that the firm's investments generate a profit above and beyond the explicit and implicit cost of capital.

See: Dow Jones Newswires, "Kerr-McGee Announces 2002 Capital Budget," *The Wall Street Journal Online*, January 8, 2002 (http://online.wsj.com).

Gourmet Foods already owns a piece of land that is suitable for the new store. When evaluating the new retail facility, should the cost of the land be disregarded because no additional cash outlay would be required? Certainly not, because there is an opportunity cost inherent in the use of the property. Suppose that the land could be sold to net $150,000 after commissions and taxes. Use of the site for the new store would require foregoing this inflow, so the $150,000 must be charged as an opportunity cost against the project. The proper land cost is the $150,000 market-determined value, irrespective of historical acquisition costs.

A further potential problem involves the effects of the project on other parts of the firm. For example, suppose that some of the new outlet's customers are already customers at Gourmet Foods' downtown store. Revenues and profits generated by these customers would not be new to the firm but would represent transfers from one outlet to another. Cash flows produced by such customers should not be treated as incremental in the capital budgeting analysis. On the other hand, having a new suburban store might actually increase customer awareness in the local market and thereby attract additional customers to the downtown outlet. In this case, additional revenues projected to flow to the downtown store should be attributed to the new suburban facility. Although they are often difficult to identify and quantify, externalities such as these are important and must be considered.

A fourth problem can relate to the timing of cash flows. Year-end accounting income statements seldom reflect exactly when revenues or expenses occur. Because of the time value of money, capital budgeting cash flows should be analyzed according to when they occur. A time line of daily cash flows would in theory be most accurate, but it is sometimes costly to construct and unwieldy to use. In the case of Gourmet Foods, it may be appropriate to measure incremental cash flows on a quarterly or monthly basis using an electronic spreadsheet. In other cases, it may be appropriate simply to assume that all cash flows occur at the end or midpoint of every year.

Finally, tax considerations are often important because they can have a major impact on cash flows. In some cases, tax effects can make or break a project. It is critical that taxes be dealt with correctly in capital budgeting decisions. This is difficult because the tax laws are extremely complex and are subject to interpretation and change. For example, salvage value has no effect on the depreciable basis and hence on the annual depreciation expense that can be taken. Still, when performing a cash flow analysis, the market value of an asset at the end of the project represents a relevant expected cash inflow. Any difference between salvage value and depreciated book value at the end of a project is currently treated as ordinary income and is taxed at the firm's marginal tax rate. The staff in charge of evaluating capital investment projects must rely heavily on the firm's accountants and tax lawyers and also must develop a working knowledge of current tax law.

Accounting income statements provide a crucial basis for estimating the relevant cash flows from investment projects. This information must be adjusted, however, to carefully reflect the economic pattern of inflows and outflows so that value-maximizing investment decisions can be made. Though a formidable task, firms can and do overcome problems posed by sunk costs, opportunity costs, spillovers, and tax considerations. To illustrate, the following section offers a simplified example of cash flow estimation.

CASH FLOW ESTIMATION EXAMPLE

To illustrate several important aspects of cash flow analysis and see how they relate to one another, consider a capital budgeting decision that faces Silicon Valley Controls Corp. (SVCC), a California–based high-tech firm. SVCC's research and development department has been applying its expertise in microprocessor technology to develop a small computer specifically designed to control home appliances. Once programmed, the computer system automatically controls the heating and air-conditioning systems, security system, hot water heater, and even small appliances such as a coffee maker. By increasing the energy efficiency of a home, the appliance control computer can save on energy costs and hence pay for itself. The project evaluation effort has reached the stage at which a decision about whether to go forward with production must be made.

SVCC's marketing department plans to target sales of the appliance control computer to the owners of larger homes; the computer is cost-effective only for homes with 2,000 or more square feet of heated and air-conditioned space. The marketing vice president believes that annual sales would be 25,000 units if the appliance control computers were priced at $2,200 each. The engineering department has estimated that the firm would need a new manufacturing facility. Such a plant could be built and made ready for production in 2 years, once the "go ahead" decision is made. The plant would require a 25-acre site, and SVCC currently has an option to purchase a suitable tract of land for $1.2 million. If the decision is made to go ahead with the project, building construction could begin immediately and would continue for 2 years. Because the project has an estimated economic life of 6 years, the overall planning period is 8 years: 2 years for plant construction (years 1 and 2) plus 6 years for operation (years 3 through 8). The building would cost $8 million and have a 31.5-year life for tax purposes. A $4 million payment would be due the building contractor at the end of each year of construction. Manufacturing equipment, with a cost of $10 million and a 7-year life for tax purposes, is to be installed and paid for at the end of the second year of construction, just prior to the beginning of operations.

The project also requires a working capital investment equal to 12 percent of estimated sales during the coming year. The initial working capital investment is to be made at the end of year 2 and is increased at the end of each subsequent period by 12 percent of the expected increase in the following year's sales. After completion of the project's 6-year operating period, the land is expected to have a market value of $1.7 million; the building, a value of $1 million; and the equipment, a value of $2 million. The production department has estimated that variable manufacturing costs would total 65 percent of dollar sales and that fixed overhead costs, excluding depreciation, would be $8 million for the first year of operations. Sales prices and fixed overhead costs, other than depreciation, are projected to increase with inflation, which is expected to average 6 percent per year over the 6-year production period.

SVCC's marginal federal-plus-state tax rate is 40 percent, and its weighted average cost of capital is 15 percent. For capital budgeting purposes, the company's policy is to assume that cash flows occur at the end of each year. Because the plant would begin operations at the start of year 3, the first operating cash flows would be realized at the end of year 3. As one of the company's financial analysts, you have been assigned the task of supervising the capital budgeting analysis. For now, you may assume that the project has the same risk as the firm's current average project, and hence you may use the 15 percent corporate cost of capital for this project.

The first step in the analysis is to summarize the investment outlays required for the project; this is done in Table 15.1. Note that the land cannot be depreciated, and hence its depreciable basis is $0. Because the project will require an increase in net working capital during year 2, this is shown as an investment outlay for that year.

Once capital requirements have been identified, operating cash flows that will occur once production begins must be estimated; these are set forth in Table 15.2. The operating cash flow estimates are based on information provided by SVCC's various departments. Note that the sales price and fixed costs are projected to increase each year by the 6 percent inflation rate, and because variable costs are 65 percent of sales, they too will rise by 6 percent each year. The changes in net working capital (NWC) represent the additional investments required to support sales increases (12 percent of the next year's sales increase, which in this case results only from inflation) during years 3 through 7, as well as the recovery of the cumulative net working capital investment in year 8. Amounts for depreciation were obtained by multiplying the depreciable basis by the Modified Accelerated Cost Recovery System (MACRS) depreciation allowance rates set forth in footnote *c* to Table 15.2.

The analysis also requires an estimation of the cash flows generated by salvage values. Table 15.3 summarizes this analysis. First is a comparison between projected market and book values for salvageable assets. Land cannot be depreciated and has an estimated salvage value greater than the initial purchase price. Thus, SVCC would have to pay taxes on the profit. The building has an estimated salvage value less than the book value; it will be sold at a loss for tax purposes. This loss will reduce taxable income and thus will generate a tax savings; in effect, the company has been depreciating the building too slowly, so it will write off the loss against ordinary income. Equipment, however, will be sold for more than book value, so the company will have to pay ordinary taxes on the $2 million profit. In all cases, the book value is the depreciable basis minus accumulated depreciation, and the total cash flow from salvage is merely the sum of the land, building, and equipment components.

TABLE 15.1

Investment Outlay Analysis for New Plant Investment Project

Fixed Assets	Year 0	Year 1	Year 2	Total Costs	Depreciable Basis
Land	$1,200,000	$ 0	$ 0	$ 1,200,000	$ 0
Building	0	4,000,000	4,000,000	8,000,000	8,000,000
Equipment	0	0	10,000,000	10,000,000	10,000,000
Total fixed assets	$1,200,000	$4,000,000	$14,000,000	$19,200,000	
Net working capital*a*	0	0	6,600,000	6,600,000	
Total investment	$1,200,000	$4,000,000	$20,600,000	$25,800,000	

a Twelve percent of first year's sales or 0.12 ($55,000,000) = $6,600,000.

TABLE 15.2

Net Cash Flows from Operations for New Plant Investment Project

	Year					
	3	**4**	**5**	**6**	**7**	**8**
Unit sales	25,000	25,000	25,000	25,000	25,000	25,000
Sale price[a]	$ 2,200	$ 2,332	$ 2,472	$ 2,620	$ 2,777	$ 2,944
Net sales[a]	$55,000,000	$58,300,000	$61,800,000	$65,500,000	$69,425,000	$73,600,000
Variable costs[b]	35,750,000	37,895,000	40,170,000	42,575,000	45,126,250	47,840,000
Fixed costs (overhead)[a]	8,000,000	8,480,000	8,988,800	9,528,128	10,099,816	10,705,805
Depreciation (building)[c]	120,000	240,000	240,000	240,000	240,000	240,000
Depreciation (equipment)[c]	2,000,000	3,200,000	1,900,000	1,200,000	1,100,000	600,000
Earnings before taxes	$ 9,130,000	$ 8,485,000	$10,501,200	$11,956,872	$12,858,934	$14,214,195
Taxes (40%)	3,652,000	3,394,000	4,200,480	4,782,749	5,143,574	5,685,678
Projected net operating income	5,478,000	5,091,000	6,300,720	7,174,123	7,715,361	8,528,517
Add back noncash expenses[d]	$ 2,120,000	$ 3,440,000	$ 2,140,000	$ 1,440,000	$ 1,340,000	$840,000
Cash flow from operations[e]	$ 7,598,000	$ 8,531,000	$ 8,440,720	$ 8,614,123	$ 9,055,361	$ 9,368,517
Investment in net working capital (NWC)[f]	(396,000)	(420,000)	(444,000)	(471,000)	(501,000)	8,832,000
New salvage value[g]						5,972,000
Total projected cash flows	$ 7,202,000	$ 8,111,000	$ 7,996,720	$ 8,143,123	$ 8,554,361	$24,172,517

---

[a] Year 3 estimate increased by the assumed 6 percent inflation rate.
[b] Sixty-five percent of net sales.
[c] MACRS depreciation rates were estimated as follows:

	Year					
	3	**4**	**5**	**6**	**7**	**8**
Building	1.5%	3%	3%	3%	3%	3%
Equipment	20	32	19	12	11	6

These percentages are multiplied by the depreciable basis to get the depreciation expense for each year. Not that the allowances have been rounded for ease of computation.

[d] In this case, depreciation on building and equipment.
[e] Net operating income plus noncash expenses.
[f] Twelve percent of next year's increase in sales. For example, year 4 sales are $3.3 million over year 3 sales, so the addition to NWC in year 3 required to support year 4 sales is (0.12)($3,300,000) = $396,000. The cumulative working capital investment is recovered when the project ends.
[g] See Table 15.3 for the net salvage value calculation.

As illustrated by this SVCC example, cash flow estimation involves a detailed analysis of demand, cost, and tax considerations. Even for fairly simple projects, such as that described here, the analysis can become complicated. Innovative, powerful spreadsheet software makes possible the accurate estimation of cash flows under a variety of operating assumptions, for even the most complex projects. More than just allowing managers to enter and manipulate data in several useful ways, these spreadsheet programs also incorporate various effective techniques for project evaluation. Among these techniques are a number of valuable capital budgeting decision rules.

TABLE 15.3

Net Salvage Value Calculation for New Plant Investment Project

	Land	Building	Equipment
Salvage (ending market value)	$1,700,000	$ 1,000,000	$2,000,000
Initial cost	1,200,000	8,000,000	10,000,000
Depreciable basis (year 2)	0	8,000,000	10,000,000
Book value (year 8)[a]	1,200,000	6,680,000	0
Capital gains income	$ 500,000	$ 0	$ 0
Ordinary income (loss)[b]	0	(5,680,000)	2,000,000
Taxes[c]	$ 200,000	$(2,272,000)	$ 800,000
Net salvage value (salvage value—taxes)	$1,500,000	$3,272,000	$1,200,000

Total cash flow from salvage value = $1,500,000 + $3,272,000 + $1,200,000 = $5,972,000.

[a] Book value for the building in year 8 equals depreciable basis minus accumulated MACRS depreciation of $1,320,000. The accumulated depreciation on the equipment is $10,000,000. See Table15.2.

[b] Building: $1,000,000 market value - $6,680,000 book value = $5,680,000 depreciation shortfall, which is treated as an operating expense in year 8.

   Equipment: $2,000,000 market value - $0 book value = $2,000,000 depreciation recapture, which is treated as ordinary income in year 8.

[c] All taxes are based on SVCC's 40% marginal federal-plus-state rate. The table is set up to differentiate ordinary income from captial gains because different tax rates are often charged on those two income sources.

CAPITAL BUDGETING DECISION RULES

An economically sound capital budgeting decision rule must consistently lead to the acceptance of projects that will increase the value of the firm. When the discounted present value of expected future cash flows exceeds the cost of investment, a project represents a worthy use of scarce resources and should be accepted for investment. When the discounted present value of expected future cash flows is less than the cost of investment, a project represents an inappropriate use of scarce resources and should be rejected. An effective capital budgeting decision rule must also lead to a consistent ranking of projects from most to least desirable and should be easy to apply.

Net Present-Value Analysis

net present value (NPV)
Current-dollar difference between marginal revenues and marginal costs

Perhaps the most commonly employed method for long-term investment project evaluation is called **net present-value (NPV)** analysis. NPV analysis is the difference between the marginal revenues and marginal costs for individual investment projects, when both revenues and costs are expressed in present value terms. NPV analysis meets all of the criteria for an effective capital budgeting decision rule cited previously. As a result, it is the most routinely applied capital budgeting decision rule. However, the NPV method is only one of four capital budgeting decision rules that might be encountered in practice. Other techniques that are sometimes used to rank capital investment projects include the profitability index or benefit/cost ratio method, the internal rate of return approach, and the payback period. Each of these alternative capital budgeting decision rules, with the possible exception of the payback period, incorporates the essential features of NPV analysis and can be used to provide useful information on the desirability of individual projects. A comparison across methods is useful.

NPV analysis is based on the timing and magnitude of cash inflows and outflows, because traditional accounting data can obscure differences between cash and noncash expenses and revenues, tax considerations, and so on. NPV analysis is commonly used by managers to correctly employ marginal analysis in the capital budgeting process. To see NPV analysis as a reflection of marginal analysis and the value-maximization theory of the firm, recall from Chapter 2 the basic valuation model:

$$(15.2) \quad \begin{aligned} \text{Value} &= \sum_{t=1}^{n} \frac{\pi_t}{(1 + k)^t} \\ &= \sum_{t=1}^{n} \frac{\text{Total Revenue}_t - \text{Total Cost}_t}{(1 + k)^t} \\ &= \sum_{t=1}^{n} \frac{\text{Net Cash Flow}_t}{(1 + k)^t} \end{aligned}$$

In this equation, *Net Cash Flow$_t$* represents the firm's total after-tax profit plus noncash expenses such as depreciation; k, which is based on an appraisal of the firm's overall riskiness, represents the average cost of capital to the firm. The value of the firm is simply the discounted present value of the difference between total cash inflows and total cash outflows. Any investment project is desirable if it increases the firm's net present value, and it is undesirable if accepting it causes the firm's net present value to decrease.

The use of net present-value analysis in capital budgeting involves the application of the present value model described in Equation 15.2 to individual projects rather than to the firm as a whole. The procedure starts with an estimation of the expected net cash flows. Depending on the nature of the project, these estimates will have a greater or lesser degree of risk. For example, the benefits from replacing a piece of equipment used to produce a stable, established product can be estimated more accurately than those from an investment in equipment to produce a new and untried product. Next, the expected cost or investment outlay of the project must be estimated. This cost estimate will be quite accurate for purchased equipment, because cost equals the invoice price plus delivery and installation charges. Cost estimates for other kinds of projects may be highly uncertain or speculative. The next step involves the determination of an appropriate discount rate, or **cost of capital**, for the project. A high discount rate is used for high-risk projects, and a low discount rate is used for low-risk projects. The cost of capital is considered in detail later in this chapter, but for now it may be thought of as being determined by the riskiness of the project—that is, by the uncertainty of the expected cash flows and the investment outlay. Finally, the present value of expected cash outflows must be subtracted from the present value of expected cash inflows to determine the net present value of the project. If *NPV* > 0, the project should be accepted. If *NPV* < 0, the project should be rejected. In equation form, the net present value of an individual project can be written as follows:

cost of capital
Discount rate

$$(15.3) \quad NPV_i = \sum_{t=1}^{n} \frac{E(CF_{it})}{(1 + k_i)^t} - \sum_{t=1}^{n} \frac{C_{it}}{(1 + k_i)^t}$$

where NPV_i is the NPV of the *i*th project, $E(CF_{it})$ represents the expected cash inflows of the *i*th project in the *t*th year, k_i is the risk-adjusted discount rate applicable to the *i*th project, and C_i is the project's investment cost or cash outflow.

To illustrate the NPV method, consider the SVCC capital investment project discussed earlier. Table 15.4 shows net cash flows per year over the entire 8-year planning period in nominal dollars, as well as in dollars discounted using the firm's 15 percent cost of capital. Overall, the net cash flow earned on the project expressed in nominal dollars is $38,379,720.

TABLE 15.4

Consolidated End-of-Year Net Cash Flow Analysis for New Plant Investment Project Example

Year (1)	Net Nominal Cash Flows (2)	Cumulative Net Nominal Cash Flows (3)	Present-Value Interest Factor (PVIF) at 15% (4)	Net Discounted Cash Flows (5) = (2) × (4)	Cumulative Net Discounted Cash Flows (6)
0	($1,200,000)	($1,200,000)	1.0000	($1,200,000)	($1,200,000)
1	(4,000,000)	(5,200,000)	0.8696	(3,478,261)	(4,678,261)
2	(20,600,000)	(25,800,000)	0.7561	(15,576,560)	(20,254,820)
3	7,202,000	(18,598,000)	0.6575	4,735,432	(15,519,389)
4	8,111,000	(10,487,000)	0.5718	4,637,491	(10,881,898)
5	7,996,720	(2,490,280)	0.4972	3,975,783	(6,906,115)
6	8,143,123	5,652,843	0.4323	3,520,497	(3,385,618)
7	8,554,360	14,207,203	0.3759	3,215,901	(169,717)
8	24,172,517	38,379,720	0.3269	7,902,039	7,732,321
Sum	$38,379,720			$7,732,321	

Note: Negative net cash flows represent net cash outlays and are shown within parentheses.

This amount is the sum of column 2 and is equal to the last entry in column 3, which shows the culmination of net cash flows over the life of the project. Net nominal cash flow is a misleading measure of the attractiveness of the project, however, because cash outlays necessary to fund the project must be made substantially before cash inflows are realized. A much more relevant measure of the attractiveness of this project is net cash flow expressed in present-value terms, where each dollar of cash outflow and inflow is converted on a common current-dollar basis. In column 5, net nominal cash flows from column 2 are multiplied by present-value interest factors from column 4 that reflect a 15 percent cost of capital assumption. These present-value interest factors are used to convert the nominal dollar outlays and returns from various periods on a common present-value basis.

The NPV for this investment project is given by the cumulative net discounted cash flow of $7,732,321 earned over the entire life of the project. This amount is given at the base of column 5 and is the sum of net discounted cash flows over the life of the project. Note also that this amount is given as the last entry in column 6, because it reflects the cumulative net discounted cash flow earned by the end of the project, year 8. Alternatively, NPV is simply the difference between the $27,987,141 present value of cash inflows from column 5, year 3 through year 8, minus the $20,254,820 present value of cash outflows from column 5, year 0 through 2. In equation form, the NPV for this project is calculated as follows:

$$NPV = PV \text{ of Cash Inflows} - PV \text{ of Cash Outflows}$$

(15.4)

$$= \$27,987,141 - \$20,254,820$$

$$= \$7,732,321$$

Because dollar inflows received in the future are worth less than necessary dollar outlays at the beginning of the project, the NPV for the project is much less than the $38,379,720 received in net nominal cash flows (see columns 2 and 3). This divergence between nominal and discounted cash flow figures reflects the time value of money. In present-value terms, the difference between the incremental costs and incremental revenues derived from this project is \$7,732,321. This is a desirable project that if undertaken would increase the value of the firm by this amount.

Firms typically make investments in projects showing positive net present values, reject those with negative net present values, and choose between mutually exclusive investments on the basis of higher net present values. For many capital budgeting problems, the use of the NPV method is far more complex than the preceding description suggests. The capital budgeting problem may require analysis of mutually exclusive projects with different expected lives or with substantially different initial costs. A complication also arises when the size of the firm's capital budget is limited. Under these conditions, a variant of the simple NPV is used to select projects that maximize the value of the firm.

Profitability Index or Benefit/Cost Ratio Analysis

Although individual projects might promise relatively attractive yields, combining them can create unforeseen difficulties. Undertaking a large number of projects simultaneously can require a very fast rate of expansion. Additional personnel requirements and organizational problems can arise that diminish overall rates of return. At some point in the capital budgeting process, management must decide what total volume of favorable projects the firm can successfully undertake without significantly reducing projected returns. Another reason for limiting the capital budget at some firms is the reluctance or inability to obtain external financing by issuing debt or selling stock. For example, considering the plight of firms with substantial amounts of debt during economic recession, management may simply refuse to use high levels of debt financing. Such capital rationing complicates the capital budgeting process and requires more complex tools of analysis.

A variant of NPV analysis that is often used in complex capital budgeting situations is called the **profitability index (PI)**, or the benefit/cost ratio method. The profitability index is calculated as follows:

profitability index (PI)
Benefit/cost ratio

(15.5)

$$PI = \frac{PV \text{ of Cash Inflows}}{PV \text{ of Cash Outflows}} = \frac{\sum_{t=1}^{n} [E(CF_{it})/(1 + k_i)^t]}{\sum_{t=1}^{n} [C_{it}/(1 + k_i)^t]}$$

The PI shows the *relative* profitability of any project, or the present value of benefits per dollar of cost.

In the SVCC example described in Table 15.4, $NPV > 0$ implies a desirable investment project and $PI > 1$. To see that this is indeed the case, we can use the profitability index formula, given in Equation 15.5, and the present value of cash inflows and outflows from the project, given in Equation 15.4. The profitability index for the SVCC project is

$$PI = \frac{PV \text{ of Cash Inflows}}{PV \text{ of Outflows}}$$

$$= \frac{\$27,987,141}{\$20,254,820}$$

$$= 1.38$$

This means that the SVCC capital investment project returns \$1.38 in cash inflows for each dollar of cash outflow, when both figures are expressed in present-value terms.

In PI analysis, a project with $PI > 1$ should be accepted and a project with $PI < 1$ should be rejected. Projects will be accepted provided that they return more than a dollar of discounted benefits for each dollar of cost. Thus, the PI and NPV methods always indicate the same accept/reject decisions for independent projects, because $PI > 1$ implies $NPV > 0$ and $PI < 1$ implies $NPV < 0$. However, for alternative projects of unequal size, PI and NPV criteria can give different project rankings. This can sometimes cause problems when mutually exclusive projects are being evaluated. Before investigating the source of such conflicts, however, it is worthwhile to introduce two additional capital budgeting decision rules.

Internal Rate of Return Analysis

internal rate of return (IRR)
Discount rate that equates present value of cash inflows and outflows
(15.6)

The **internal rate of return (IRR)** is the interest or discount rate that equates the present value of the future receipts of a project to the initial cost or outlay. The equation for calculating the internal rate of return is simply the NPV formula set equal to zero:

$$NPV_i = 0 = \sum_{t=1}^{n} \frac{E(CF_{it})}{(1 + k_i^*)^t} - \sum_{t=1}^{n} \frac{C_{it}}{(1 + k_i^*)^t}$$

Here the equation is solved for the discount rate, k_i^*, which produces a zero net present value or causes the sum of the discounted future receipts to equal the initial cost. That discount rate is the internal rate of return earned by the project.

Because the net present-value equation is complex, it is difficult to solve for the actual internal rate of return on an investment without a computer or sophisticated calculator. For this reason, trial and error is sometimes employed. One begins by arbitrarily selecting a discount rate. If it yields a positive NPV, the internal rate of return must be greater than the discount rate used, and another higher rate is tried. If the chosen rate yields a negative NPV, the internal rate of return on the project is lower than the discount rate, and the NPV calculation must be repeated using a lower discount rate. This process of changing the discount rate and recalculating the net present value continues until the discounted present value of the future cash flows equals the initial cost. The interest rate that brings about this equality is the yield, or internal rate of return on the project.

Using trial and error, an electronic financial calculator, or a spreadsheet software program such as *Microsoft Excel*, the internal rate of return for the SVCC investment project is $IRR = 25.1$ percent. Because this IRR exceeds the 15 percent cost of capital, the project is attractive and should be undertaken. In general, internal rate of return analysis suggests that projects should be accepted when the $IRR > k$ and rejected when the $IRR < k$. When the $IRR > k$, the marginal rate of return earned on the project exceeds the marginal cost of capital. As in the case of projects with an $NPV > 0$ and $PI > 1$, the acceptance of all investment projects with $IRR > k$ will lead management to maximize the value of the firm. In instances in which capital is scarce and only a limited number of desirable projects can be undertaken at one point in time, the IRR can be used to derive a rank ordering of projects from most desirable to least desirable. Like a rank ordering of all $NPV > 0$ projects from highest to lowest PIs, a rank ordering of potential investment projects from highest to lowest IRRs allows managers to effectively employ scarce funds.

Payback Period Analysis

payback period
Number of years required to recover initial investment

The **payback period** is the expected number of years of operation required to recover an initial investment. When project cash flows are discounted using an appropriate cost of capital, the discounted payback period is the expected number of years required to recover the initial investment from discounted net cash flows. Payback period calculation is quick and easy using actual or discounted net cash flows. In equation form, the payback period is

(15.7)   Payback Period = Number of Years to Recover Investment

The payback period can be thought of as a breakeven time period. The shorter the payback period, the more desirable the investment project. The longer the payback period, the less desirable the investment project.

To illustrate, consider the SVCC capital investment project discussed earlier. Table 15.4 shows net cash flows per year over the entire 8-year planning period in nominal dollars, as well as in dollars discounted using the firm's 15 percent cost of capital. In nominal dollars, the total amount of investment is $25.8 million, which is the sum of the dollar outlays given in the first three rows of column 2. As shown in the third row of column 3, a negative $25.8 million is also the cumulative value of the nominal net cash flow as of the end of year 2, just prior to the beginning of plant operations. When the nominal cash outlay of $25.8 million is discounted using the firm's 15 percent cost of capital, the present value of the investment cash outlay is $20,254,820, the sum of discounted cash outlays given in the first three rows of column 5. As shown in the third row of column 6, a negative $20,254,820 is also the cumulative value of net discounted cash flow as of the end of year 2, just prior to the beginning of plant operations.

Based on nominal dollar cash outflows and inflows, the payback period is completed between the end of year 5, when the cumulative net nominal cash flow is a negative $2,490,280, and the end of year 6, when the cumulative net nominal cash flow is a positive $5,652,843. Using nominal dollars, the payback period in years is calculated as

$$\text{Nominal Payback Period} = 5.00 + \$2,490,280/\$8,143,123$$
$$= 5.30 \text{ years}$$

Based on cash outflows and inflows discounted using the firm's 15 percent cost of capital, the payback period is completed between the end of year 7, when the cumulative net discounted cash flow is a negative $169,717, and the end of year 8, when the cumulative net discounted cash flow is a positive $7,732,321. Using discounted net cash flows, the payback period in years is calculated as

$$\text{Discounted Payback Period} = 7.00 + \$169,717/\$7,902,039$$
$$= 7.02 \text{ years}$$

Of course, these payback period calculations are based on the typical assumption that cash inflows are received continuously throughout the operating period. If cash inflows are received only at the end of the operating period, then the nominal payback period in this example would be 6 years and the discounted payback period would be 8 years. The exact length of the payback period depends on underlying assumptions concerning the pattern of cash inflows.

Note that the payback period is a breakeven calculation in that if cash flows come in at the expected rate until the payback year, the project will break even in an accounting sense. However, the nominal payback period does not take into account the cost of capital; the cost of the debt and equity used to undertake the project is not reflected in the cash flow calculation. The discounted payback period does take account of capital costs—it shows the breakeven year after covering debt and equity costs. Both payback methods have the serious deficiency of not taking into account any cash flows beyond the payback year. Other capital budgeting decision rules are more likely to lead to better project rankings and selections. The discounted payback period, however, does provide useful information about how long funds will be tied up in a project. The shorter the discounted payback period, the greater the project's liquidity. Also, cash flows expected in the distant future are generally regarded as riskier than near-term cash flows. Therefore, the discounted payback period is a useful but rough measure of liquidity and project risk.

Is the Sun Setting on Japan's Vaunted MOF?

Long the power center of Japanese government, Japan's Ministry of Finance (MOF) is under attack for bungling economic policy and manipulating the Japanese stock market and real estate values. At risk is its bureaucratic authority and the whole concept of the managed Japanese economy. MOF officials argue that relinquishing control over the economy would imperil full employment and cause a stock-market crash in Japan. However, continued trade surpluses with Canada, the United States, and other trade partners have caused trade friction and stifled global economic growth.

The aura of infallibility that the MOF cultivated during Japan's postwar "economic miracle" has all but disappeared in the gloom of Japan's deepening economic malaise. No longer can supporters point to a continuing series of economic triumphs. Instead, the MOF has made a number of foolish public errors by failing to deal effectively with stock manipulation scandals and by botching privatization plans for government monopolies. It also alienated Japan's biggest banks and

brokerages throughout a series of embarrassing scandals. Politicians whom the MOF used to dominate now openly challenge the ministry's role in Japanese government.

It may be several years before fundamental economic reforms take hold in Japan. Many Japanese politicians and business leaders remain fervent nationalists who believe that Japan continues to work superbly as a society. It is a common view that the extent to which the country becomes less Japanese, or more integrated globally, it can no longer be Japan. In a real sense, the MOF sees itself as the guardian of Japan's conservative heritage. Thus, although there is a clear move underway in Japan to make the MOF more accountable, any severe undermining of its authority seems years away, at best. Although Japanese bureaucracy, elected officials, and industry are strongly motivated to change, they remain even more tightly bound to Japanese tradition and culture.

See: Nathan K. Lewis, "Japan Needs a Reagan Revolution," *The Wall Street Journal Online*, April 1, 2002 (http://online.wsj.com).

CHOOSING AMONG ALTERNATIVE PROJECTS

The preceding section shows how application of the net present-value method in the capital budgeting process permits a rank ordering of investment projects from most attractive to least attractive. An investment project is attractive and should be pursued as long as the discounted net present value of cash inflows is greater than the discounted net present value of the investment requirement, or net cash outlay.

Decision Rule Conflict Problem

The attractiveness of investment projects increases with the size of NPV. High NPV projects are inherently more appealing and are preferred to low NPV projects. Any investment project that is incapable of generating sufficient cash inflows to cover necessary cash outlays, when both are expressed on a present-value basis, should not be undertaken. In the case of a project with $NPV = 0$, project acceptance would neither increase nor decrease the value of the firm. Management would be indifferent to pursuing such a project. NPV analysis represents a practical application of the marginal concept, in which the marginal revenues and marginal costs of investment projects are considered on a present-value basis. Use of the NPV technique in the evaluation of alternative investment projects allows managers to apply the principles of marginal analysis in a simple and clear manner. The widespread practical use of the NPV technique lends support to the view that value maximization is the prime objective pursued by managers in the capital budgeting process.

Just as acceptance of $NPV > 0$ projects will enhance the value of the firm, so too will acceptance of projects for which the $PI > 1$ and the $IRR > k$. Acceptance of projects for which $NPV < 0$, $PI < 1$, or $IRR < k$ would be unwise and would reduce the value of the firm. Because each of these project evaluation techniques shares a common focus on the present value of net cash inflows and outflows, these techniques display a high degree of consistency in terms of the project accept/reject decision. This high degree of consistency might even lead one to question the usefulness of having these alternative ways of project evaluation when only one, the NPV method, seems sufficient for decision-making purposes.

However, even though alternative capital budgeting decision rules consistently lead to the same project accept/reject decision, they involve important differences in terms of project ranking. Projects ranked most favorably using the NPV method may appear less so when analyzed using the PI or IRR methods. Projects ranked most favorably using the PI or IRR methods may appear less so when analyzed using the NPV technique.

If the application of any capital budgeting decision rule is to consistently lead to correct investment decisions, it must consider the time value of money in the evaluation of all cash flows and must rank projects according to their ultimate impact on the value of the firm. NPV, PI, and IRR methods satisfy both criteria, and each can be used to value and rank capital budgeting projects. The payback method does not meet both of the preceding criteria and should be used only as a complement to the other techniques. However, each of the NPV, PI, and IRR methods incorporates certain assumptions that can and do affect project rankings. Understanding the sources of these differences and learning how to deal with them is an important part of knowing how to correctly evaluate alternative investment projects.

Reasons for Decision Rule Conflict

As discussed earlier, NPV is the difference between the marginal revenues and marginal costs of an individual investment project, when both revenues and costs are expressed in present-value terms. NPV measures the relative attractiveness of alternative investment projects by the discounted dollar difference between revenues and costs. NPV is an *absolute* measure of the attractiveness of a given investment project. Conversely, the PI reflects the difference between the marginal revenues and marginal costs of an individual project in ratio form. The PI is the ratio of the discounted present value of cash inflows divided by the discounted present value of cash outflows. PI is a *relative* measure of project attractiveness. It follows that application of the NPV method leads to the highest ranking for large profitable projects. Use of the PI method leads to the highest ranking for projects that return the greatest amount of cash inflow per dollar of outflow, regardless of project size. At times, application of the NPV method can create a bias for larger as opposed to smaller projects—a problem when all favorable *NPV* > 0 projects cannot be pursued. When capital is scarce, application of the PI method has the potential to create a better project mix for the firm's overall investment portfolio.

Both NPV and PI methods differ from the IRR technique in terms of their underlying assumptions regarding the reinvestment of cash flows during the life of the project. In the NPV and PI methods, excess cash flows generated over the life of the project are "reinvested" at the firm's cost of capital. In the IRR method, excess cash flows are reinvested at the IRR. For especially attractive investment projects that generate an exceptionally high rate of return, the IRR can actually overstate project attractiveness because reinvestment of excess cash flows at a similarly high IRR is not possible. When reinvestment at the project-specific IRR is not possible, the IRR method must be adapted to take into account the lower rate of return that can actually be earned on excess cash flows generated over the life of individual projects. Otherwise, use of the NPV or PI methods is preferable.

Ranking Reversal Problem

A further and more serious conflict can arise between NPV and IRR methods when projects differ significantly in terms of the magnitude and timing of cash flows. When the size or pattern of alternative project cash flows differ greatly, each project's NPV can react quite differently to changes in the discount rate. As a result, changes in the appropriate discount rate can sometimes lead to reversals in project rankings.

To illustrate the potential for conflict between NPV and IRR rankings and the possibility of ranking reversals, Table 15.5 shows a further development of the SVCC plant investment project example. Assume that the company is considering the original new plant investment project in light of an alternative proposal to buy and remodel an existing plant. Old plant and equipment can be purchased for an initial cash outlay of $11.5 million and can be remodeled at a cost of $2 million per year over the next 2 years. As before, a net working capital investment of $6.6 million will be required just prior to opening the remodeled production facility. For simplicity, assume that after year 2, all cash inflows and outflows are the same for the remodeled and new plant facilities.

Note that the new plant proposal involves an initial nominal cash outlay of $25.8 million, whereas the remodeled plant alternative involves a nominal cash outlay of $22.1 million. In addition to this difference in project size, the two investment alternatives differ in terms of the timing of cash flows. The new plant alternative involves a larger but later commitment of funds. To see the implications of these differences, notice how the "remodel old plant" alternative is preferred at and below the firm's 15 percent cost of capital using NPV and PI methods, even though the IRR of 25.06 percent for the new plant project exceeds the IRR of 23.57 percent for the "remodel old plant" alternative. Also troubling is the fact that the relative ranking of these projects according to NPV and PI methods is reversed at higher discount rates. Notice how the "build new plant" alternative is preferred using NPV and PI techniques when a 25 percent discount rate is employed.

TABLE 15.5

Comparison of the "Build New Plant" Versus "Remodel Old Plant" Investment Project Example Using Alternative Capital Budgeting Decision Rules

A. Investment Project Cash Flow Projections

Year	Build New Plant Project New Nominal Cash Flows	Remodel Old Plant Project Net Nominal Cash Flows
0	($1,200,000)	($11,500,000)
1	(4,000,000)	(2,000,000)
2	(20,600,000)	(8,600,000)
3	7,202,000	7,202,000
4	8,111,000	8,111,000
5	7,996,720	7,996,720
6	8,143,123	8,143,123
7	8,554,360	8,554,360
8	24,172,517	24,172,517
Sum	$38,379,720	$42,079,720
IRR	25.06%	23.57%

Note: Negative net cash flows represent net cash outlays and are shown within parentheses

B. Evaluation Using Alternative Capital Budgeting Decision Rules

	Build New	Remodel Old
0% Discount Rate:		
PV of cash inflows	$64,179,720	$64,179,720
PV of cash outflows	$25,800,000	$22,100,000
NPV	$38,379,720	$42,079,720
PI	2.49	2.90
Discounted payback period	5.30	4.85
15% Discount Rate:		
PV of cash inflows	$27,987,142	$27,987,142
PV of cash outflows	$20,254,820	$19,741,966
NPV	$7,732,321	$8,245,176
PI	1.38	1.42
Discounted payback period	7.02	6.89
25% Discount Rate:		
PV of cash inflows	$17,614,180	$17,614,180
PV of cash outflows	$17,584,000	($18,604,000)
NPV	$30,180	($989,820)
PI	1.00	0.95
Discounted payback period	7.99	—

Figure 15.1 displays the potential conflict between NPV, PI, and IRR project rankings at various interest rates by showing the effect of discount rate changes on the NPV of each alternative investment project. This **net present-value profile** relates the NPV for each project to the discount rate used in the NPV calculation. Using a $k = 0$ percent discount rate, the NPV for the "build new plant" investment project is $38.4 million, and it is $42.1 million for the "remodel old plant" alternative. These NPV values correspond to the difference between nominal dollar cash inflows and outflows for each project and also coincide with NPV line Y-axis intercepts of $38.4 million for the "build new plant" project and $42.1 million for the "remodel old plant" alternative. The X-axis intercept for each curve occurs at the discount rate where $NPV = 0$ for each project. Because $NPV = 0$ when the discount rate is set equal to the IRR, or when $IRR = k$, the X-axis intercept for the "build new plant" alternative is at the $IRR = 25.06$ percent level, and it is at the $IRR = 23.57$ percent level for the "remodel old plant" alternative.

Figure 15.1 illustrates how ranking reversals can occur at various NPV discount rates. Given higher nominal dollar returns and, therefore, a higher Y-axis intercept, the "remodel old plant" alternative is preferred when very low discount rates are used in the NPV calculation. Given a higher IRR and, therefore, a higher X-axis intercept, the "build new plant" alternative is preferred when very high discount rates are used in the calculation of NPV. Between very high and low discount rates is an interest rate where NPV is the same for both projects. A reversal of project rankings occurs at the **crossover discount rate**, where NPV is equal for two or more investment alternatives. In this example, the "remodel old plant" alternative is preferred when

FIGURE 15.1

NPV Profiles for the "Build New Plant" Versus "Remodel Old Plant" Investment Project Alternatives
Each profile relates project NPV to the discount rate used in the NPV calculation.

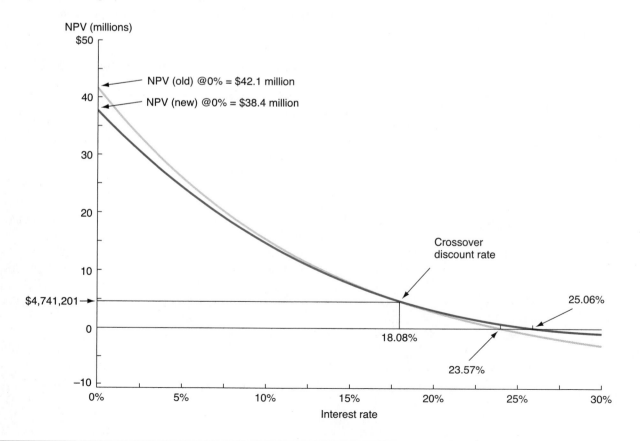

using the NPV criterion and a discount rate k that is less than the crossover discount rate. The "build new plant" alternative is preferred when using the NPV criterion and a discount rate k that is greater than the crossover discount rate. This ranking reversal problem is typical of situations in which investment projects differ greatly in terms of their underlying NPV profiles. Hence, a potentially troubling conflict exists between NPV, PI, and IRR methods.

Making the Correct Investment Decision

The ranking reversal problem and suggested conflict between NPV, PI, and IRR methods is actually much less serious than one might imagine. Many comparisons between alternative investment projects involve neither crossing NPV profiles nor crossover discount rates as shown in Figure 15.1. Some other project comparisons involve crossover discount rates that are either too low or too high to affect project rankings at the current cost of capital. As a result, there is often no meaningful conflict between NPV and IRR project rankings.

When crossover discount rates are relevant, they can be easily calculated as the IRR of the cash flow *difference* between two investment alternatives. To see that this is indeed the case, consider how cash flows differ between each of the two plant investment alternatives considered previously. The "build new plant" alternative involves a smaller initial cash outflow of $1.2 million versus $11.5 million, a $10.3 million saving, but it requires additional outlays of $2 million at the end of year 1 plus an additional $12 million at the end of year 2. Except for these differences, the timing and magnitude of cash inflows and outflows from the two projects are identical. The IRR for the cash flow difference between two investment alternatives exactly balances the present-value cost of higher cash outflows with the present-value benefit of higher cash inflows. At this IRR, the cash flow difference between the two investment alternatives has an NPV equal to zero. When k is less than this crossover IRR, the investment project with the greater nominal dollar return will have a larger NPV and will tend to be favored. In the current example, this is the "remodel old plant" alternative. When k is greater than the crossover IRR, the project with an earlier cash flow pattern will have the larger NPV and be favored. In the current example, this is the "build new plant" alternative. When k equals the crossover IRR, the cash flow difference between projects has an $NPV = 0$, and each project has exactly the same NPV.

Once an economically relevant crossover discount rate has been determined, management must decide whether to rely on NPV or IRR decision rules in the resolution of the ranking reversal problem. Logic suggests that the NPV ranking should dominate because that method will result in a value-maximizing selection of projects. In most situations, it is also more realistic to assume reinvestment of excess cash flows during the life of a project at the current cost of capital k. This again favors NPV over IRR rankings. As a result, conflicts between NPV and IRR project rankings are usually resolved in favor of the NPV rank order.

Given the size-based conflict between the NPV and PI methods, which one should be relied on in the ranking of potential investment projects? The answer depends upon the amount of available resources. For a firm with substantial investment resources and a goal of maximizing shareholder wealth, the NPV method is better. For a firm with limited resources, the PI approach allocates scarce resources to the projects with the greatest relative effect on value. Using the PI method, projects are evaluated on the basis of their NPV per dollar of investment, avoiding a possible bias toward larger projects. In some cases, this leads to a better combination of investment projects and higher firm value. The PI, or benefit/cost ratio, approach has also proved to be a useful tool in public-sector decision making, where allocating scarce public resources among competing projects is a typical problem.

As seen in the evaluation of alternative capital budgeting decision rules, the attractiveness of investment projects varies significantly depending on the interest rate used to discount future cash flows. Determination of the correct discount rate is a vitally important aspect of the capital budgeting process. This important issue is the subject of the next section.

Federal Government Support for R&D

The National Science Foundation (NSF) is an independent U.S. government agency responsible for promoting science and engineering in the United States. NSF programs invest over $3.3 billion per year in almost 20,000 research and education projects in science and engineering. NSF is also responsible for keeping track of research and development (R&D) spending and productivity in government agencies, firms, universities and colleges, or other nonprofit institutions.

At present, more than $250 billion per year is spent in the United States on R&D. Roughly 15 percent to 20 percent of this amount is spent on basic research that advances scientific knowledge but has no immediate commercial objective. Another 20 percent to 25 percent is spent on applied research that brings scientific knowledge closer to specific commercial application. The results of basic and applied research in science and engineering are ordinarily published and shared broadly within the scientific community. Such efforts can be distinguished from proprietary research and industrial development, the results of which are kept confidential for commercial reasons or for national security. Most R&D spending, roughly 60 percent to 65 percent, is devoted to industrial development.

Federal government agencies provide about 30 percent percent of all R&D funding, but as much as 60 percent of basic research funding. The National Institutes of Health (NIH), for example, are a principal source of funding for biomedical research. NIH programs provide funds for such projects as AIDS/HIV treatment, cancer research, and the Human Genome Project. The government has also taken a direct role in scientific education through the NSF and other agencies such as the Department of Energy. Federally funded research has been directly responsible for major developments in space technology, defense systems, energy, medicine, and agriculture. Federal tax incentives also encourage innovation in the private sector. Through grants, subsidies, and tax incentives, the federal government has supported basic research that underlies important applied advances in private industry. Partnerships with institutions such as universities have also proven to be an effective risk-sharing mechanism for R&D efforts that have the potential to create widespread social benefits.

This is a private-public partnership that works!

See: Home page information for the National Science Foundation can be found on the Internet (http://www.nsf.gov/start.htm).

COST OF CAPITAL

If firms typically considered projects one by one and raised investment funds for each project separately, calculation of a suitable discount rate would be easy. The correct discount rate to employ for each investment project would simply be the marginal cost of capital for that project. However, determination of the correct discount rate for individual projects is seldom that straightforward.

Component Cost of Debt Financing

Firms rarely consider individual projects in isolation but instead tend to evaluate *portfolios* of potential investment projects to be funded from an ongoing stream of new capital funds generated by retained earnings and new capital-raising efforts. New projects are funded by a mix of debt and equity financing, and each debt and equity component of new capital can be expected to have different costs. Calculation of the correct discount rate for any given potential investment project typically involves weighing the relative importance of each component cost of new financing.

component cost of debt
Interest rate investors require on debt, adjusted for taxes

The **component cost of debt** is the interest rate that investors require on debt, adjusted for taxes. If a firm borrows $100,000 for 1 year at 10 percent interest, the before-tax cost is $10,000 and the before-tax interest rate is 10 percent. However, interest payments on debt are deductible for income tax purposes. It is necessary to account for this tax deductibility by adjusting the cost of debt to an after-tax basis. The deductibility of interest payments means, in effect, that the government pays part of a firm's interest charges. This reduces the firm's cost of debt financing. The after-tax component cost of debt is given by the following expression:

(15.8)
$$k_d = (\text{Interest Rate}) \times (1.0 - \text{Tax Rate})$$

Assuming that the firm's marginal federal-plus-state tax rate is 40 percent, the after-tax cost of debt will be 60 percent (= 1.0 – 0.4) of the nominal interest rate.

component cost of equity
Rate of return stockholders require on common stock

The relevant component cost of debt applies only to *new* debt, not to the interest on old or previously outstanding debt. In other words, the cost of new debt financing is what is relevant in terms of the *marginal cost of debt*. It is irrelevant that the firm borrowed at higher or lower rates in the past.

Component Cost of Equity Financing

risk-free rate of return (R_F)
Investor reward for postponing consumption

risk premium (R_P)
Investor reward for risk taking

The **component cost of equity** is the rate of return stockholders require on common stock. This return includes a compensation to investors for postponing their consumption, plus a return to compensate for risk taking. Therefore, the component cost of equity consists of a **risk-free rate of return, R_F,** plus a **risk premium, R_P**:

(15.9)
$$k_e = R_F + R_P$$

The risk-free return is typically estimated by the interest rate on short-term U.S. government securities. On a daily basis, these rates of return can be obtained from *The Wall Street Journal* and other sources. Various methods can be used to estimate R_P for different securities. Because dividends paid to stockholders are not deductible for income tax purposes, dividend payments must be made with after-tax dollars. There is no tax adjustment for the component cost of equity capital.

A first method for estimating k_e and R_P is based on the capital asset pricing model, or CAPM. This method assumes that the risk of a stock depends on the sensitivity of its return to changes in the return on all securities. A stock that is twice as risky as the overall market would entail twice the market risk premium; a security that is one-half as risky as the overall market would earn one-half the market risk premium, and so on. In the CAPM approach, the riskiness of a given stock is measured in terms of the variability of its return relative to the variability of returns on all stocks, perhaps as represented by the volatility in the *Standard and Poor's 500 Index*. A firm's **beta coefficient**, β, is a measure of this variability. In a simple regression model, the beta coefficient for an individual firm, β_i, is estimated as

beta coefficient
Measure of relative stock-price variability

(15.10)
$$R_i = \alpha_i + \beta_i R_M + e$$

where R_i is the weekly or monthly return on a given stock and R_M is a similar return on the market as a whole (e.g., the *Standard and Poor's 500 Index*). A stock with average risk has a beta of 1.0. Low-risk stocks have betas less than 1.0; high-risk stocks have betas greater than 1.0. Although beta estimation is a relatively simple task, managers seldom need to actually run such regressions. Analysts at Merrill Lynch and other leading brokerage houses, as well as investment advisory services such as *The Value Line Investment Survey*, provide beta estimates that can be used for equity capital cost estimation for individual companies and/or operating divisions.

In addition to data on the R_F rate and β_i for a given company, the CAPM approach requires an estimate of the expected rate of return on the market as a whole. This return, k_M, is a relative benchmark for measuring the risk premium on the market. With these three inputs, R_F, β_i, and k_M, the CAPM estimate of the required rate of return on any given stock is

(15.11)
$$k_e = R_F + \beta_i(k_M - R_F)$$

where the value $(k_M - R_F)$ is the market risk premium, or risk premium on an average stock. Multiplying this market risk premium by the index of risk for a particular stock, or β_i, gives the risk premium for that stock.

To illustrate, assume that $R_F = 8$ percent, $k_M = 14$ percent, and $\beta_i = 0.5$ for a given stock. Remember, $\beta_i = 0.5$ means that a given stock is only one-half as risky as the overall market. Under such circumstances, the stock's required return is

$$k_e = 8 + 0.5(14 - 8) = 8 + 3 = 11\%$$

If $\beta_i = 1.5$, indicating that a stock is 50% riskier than the average security, then k_e is

$$k_e = 8 + 1.5(14 - 8) = 8 + 9 = 17\%$$

A second common technique adds a premium of 4 percent or 5 percent onto the risk premium paid on a firm's long-term bonds. Using this approach, the total risk premium on equity equals the difference between the yield on the firm's debt and that on risk-free government bonds, *plus* 4 percent to 5 percent. For example, if risk-free government bonds yield 8 percent, and a firm's bonds are priced to yield 10 percent, the cost of equity, k_e, is

$$k_e = \text{Firm Bond Rate} + 4\% \text{ to } 5\% \text{ Risk Premium}$$
$$= 10\% + (4\% \text{ to } 5\%) = 14\% \text{ to } 15\%$$

Given an 8 percent return on risk-free government bonds, this implies a total risk premium for equity of 6 percent to 7 percent, because

$$14\% \text{ to } 15\% = 8\% + R_p$$
$$R_p = 6\% \text{ to } 7\%$$

Managers who rely on this method often cite historical studies suggesting that the long-term annual risk premium on investments in common stocks is generally 6 percent to 7 percent over that earned on government bonds. The primary difficulty with estimating risk premiums from historical returns is that historical returns differ depending on the beginning and ending dates of the estimation period, and past differences in stock and bond returns may not precisely indicate future required risk premiums.

Yet another method for determining the cost of equity is to use a constant growth model. If earnings, dividends, and the stock price all grow at the same rate, then

(15.12)
$$\frac{\text{Required Return}}{\text{on Equity}} = \text{Dividend Yield} + \text{Capital Gains}$$
$$= \frac{\text{Expected Dividend}}{\text{Current Stock Price}} + \frac{\text{Expected}}{\text{Growth Rate}}$$
$$= \frac{\text{Dividend}}{\text{Price}} + \frac{\text{Expected}}{\text{Rate Growth}}$$
$$k_e = \frac{D_1}{P_0} + g$$

The rationale for this equation is that stockholder returns are derived from dividends and capital gains. If past growth rates in earnings and dividends have been relatively stable, and if investors expect a continuation of past trends, then g may be based on the firm's historic growth rate. However, if the company's growth has been abnormally high or low, either because of its own unique situation or because of general economic conditions, investors cannot project historical growth rate into the future. Security analyst estimates of g must then be relied on. These earnings forecasts are regularly found in *Barron's*, *The Value Line Investment Survey*, and other sources and offer a useful proxy for the growth expectations of investors in general. When security analyst growth projections are combined with the dividend yield expected during the coming period, k_e can be estimated as

$$(15.13) \qquad k_e = \frac{D_1}{P_0} + \begin{array}{l} \text{Growth Rate Projected} \\ \text{by Security Analysts} \end{array}$$

In practice, it is often best to use all of these methods and try to arrive at a consensus estimate of the component cost of equity financing.

Weighted Average Cost of Capital

Suppose that the interest rate on new debt is 7.5 percent and the firm's marginal federal-plus-state income tax rate is 40 percent. This implies a 4.5 percent after-tax component cost of debt. Also assume that the firm has decided to finance next year's projects by selling debt. Does this mean that next year's investment projects have a 4.5 percent cost of capital? The answer is no, at least not usually. In financing a particular set of projects with debt, the firm typically uses some of its potential for obtaining further low-cost debt financing. As expansion takes place, the firm typically finds it necessary to raise additional high-cost equity to avoid unacceptably high leverage. As a result, the current component cost of debt seldom measures the true long-term opportunity cost of debt financing. To illustrate, suppose that the firm has a current 4.5 percent cost of debt and a 10 percent cost of equity. In the first year it borrows heavily, using its debt capacity in the process, to finance projects yielding 6 percent. In the second year, it has projects available that yield 9 percent, or substantially above the return on first-year projects, but it cannot accept them because they would have to be financed with 10 percent equity. To avoid this problem, the firm should be viewed as an ongoing concern, and the cost of capital should be calculated as a weighted average of the various types of funds it uses.

weighted-average cost of capital
Marginal cost of a composite dollar of debt and equity financing

optimal capital structure
Combination of debt and equity that minimizes the firm's weighted-average cost of capital

The **weighted-average cost of capital** is the interest rate necessary to attract additional funds for new capital investment projects. It is the marginal cost of a composite dollar of debt and equity financing. The proper set of weights to employ in computing the weighted-average cost of capital is determined by the firm's optimal capital structure. The **optimal capital structure** is the combination of debt and equity financing that minimizes the firm's overall weighted-average cost of capital.

In general, the risk to investors is lower on debt and higher on common stock. Risk aversion among investors makes debt the lowest component-cost source of funds and equity the highest component-cost source. However, the firm's risk increases as debt financing grows, because the higher the debt level, the greater the probability that under adverse conditions the firm will not make interest and principal payments. Because interest rates on debt are lower than the expected rate of return (dividends plus capital gains) on common stock, this can cause the weighted-average cost of capital to decline with modest amounts of debt financing. More debt means higher financial risk, which offsets this effect to some extent. As a result, the weighted-average cost of capital first declines as a firm moves from zero debt to some positive amount of debt, hits a minimum (perhaps over a range rather than at some specific amount of debt), and then rises as an increasing level of debt drives the firm's risk position beyond acceptable levels. Thus, each firm has an optimal amount of debt that minimizes its cost of capital and maximizes its value.

Figure 15.2 shows how the cost of capital changes as the debt ratio increases for a hypothetical industry with about average risk. The average cost of capital figures in the graph are calculated in Table 15.6. In the figure, each dot represents one of the firms in the industry.

FIGURE 15.2

Hypothetical Cost-of-Capital Schedules for an Industry

A U-shaped weighted-average cost of capital curve reflects, first, lower capital costs because of the tax benefits of debt financing and, second, increasing capital costs as bankruptcy risk increases for highly leveraged firms.

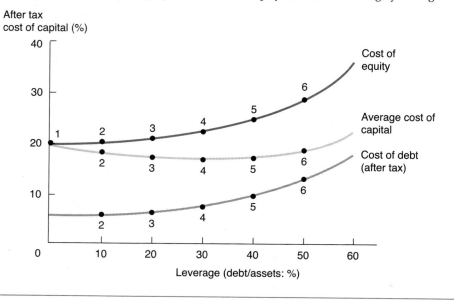

TABLE 15.6

Calculation of Average Cost of Capital for Hypothetical Firms with Different Debt Ratios

		Percentage of Total (1)	Component Cost (2)		Weighted Cost $\frac{(1) \times (2)}{100}$ (3)
Firm 1	Debt	0	6.0		0.00
	Equity	100	20.0		20.00
		100%		Average cost	20.00%
Firm 2	Debt	10	6.0		0.60
	Equity	90	20.0		18.00
		100%		Average cost	18.60%
Firm 3	Debt	20	6.0		1.20
	Equity	80	20.0		16.00
		100%		Average cost	17.20%
Firm 4	Debt	30	7.0		2.10
	Equity	70	21.0		14.70
		100%		Average cost	16.80%
Firm 5	Debt	40	9.0		3.60
	Equity	60	22.5		13.50
		100%		Average cost	17.10%
Firm 6	Debt	50	12.0		6.00
	Equity	50	24.0		12.00
		100%		Average cost	18.00%
Firm 7	Debt	60	17.0		10.20
	Equity	40	27.5		11.00
		100%		Average cost	21.20%

Capital Allocation at Berkshire Hathaway, Inc.

Warren E. Buffett, chairman and CEO of Berkshire Hathaway, Inc., has the uncommon ability to communicate management insights in a disarmingly modest and humorous fashion. Among his most important lessons are the following:

- *It is far better to buy a wonderful company at a fair price than a fair company at a wonderful price.* In a difficult business, no sooner is one problem solved than another surfaces. "There is never just one cockroach in the kitchen."

- *When a management with a reputation for brilliance tackles a business with a reputation for bad economics, it is the reputation of the business that remains intact.* According to Buffett, attractive economics include a 20 percent plus rate of return on capital without leverage or accounting gimmicks, high margins, high cash flow, low capital investment requirements, a lack of government regulation, and strong prospects for continuing growth. "Good jockeys do well on good horses," Buffett says, "but not on broken down old nags."

- *Management does better by avoiding dragons, not slaying them.* Buffett attributes his success to avoiding, rather than solving, tough business problems. As Buffett says, "We have been successful because we concentrated on identifying 1-foot hurdles that we could step over rather than because we acquired any ability to clear 7-footers."

- *It is not a sin to miss a business opportunity outside one's area of expertise.* By inference, it is a sin to miss opportunities that you are fully capable of understanding.

- *Do not join with managers who lack admirable qualities, no matter how attractive the prospects of their business.* When searching for businesses to buy, Buffett looks for first-class businesses accompanied by first-class management.

The approach seems to work. Buffett's personal stake in Berkshire is now worth $35 billion!

See: Andrew Bary, "Analysts Say Berkshire Stock Is Still a Pretty Good Bargain," *The Wall Street Journal Online*, March 17, 2002 (http://online.wsj.com).

For example, the dot labeled "one" represents firm 1, a company with no debt. Because its projects are financed entirely with 10 percent equity money, firm 1's average cost of capital is 10 percent. Firm 2 raises 10 percent of its capital as debt, and it has a 4.5 percent after-tax cost of debt and a 10 percent cost of equity. Firm 3 also has a 4.5 percent after-tax cost of debt and 10 percent cost of equity, even though it uses 20 percent debt. Firm 4 has an 11 percent cost of equity and a 4.8 percent after-tax cost of debt. Because it uses 30 percent debt, a before-tax debt risk premium of 0.5 percent and an equity risk premium of 1 percent have been added to account for the additional risk of financial leverage. Notice that the required return on both debt and equity rises with increasing leverage for firms 5, 6, and 7. Providers of debt and equity capital typically believe that because of the added risk of financial leverage, they should obtain higher yields on the firm's securities. In this particular industry, the threshold debt ratio that begins to worry creditors is about 20 percent. Below the 20 percent debt level, creditors are unconcerned about any risk induced by debt; above 20 percent, they are aware of higher risks and require compensation in the form of higher expected rates of return.

In Table 15.6, the debt and equity costs of the various firms are averaged on the basis of their respective proportions of the firm's total capital. Firm 1 has a weighted-average cost of capital equal to 10 percent, firm 2 has a weighted-average cost of 9.45 percent, firm 3 has a weighted-average cost of 8.9 percent, and firm 4 has a weighted-average cost of 9.14 percent. These weighted costs, together with those of the other firms in the industry, are plotted in Figure 15.2. Firms with approximately 20 percent debt in their capital structure have the lowest weighted-average after-tax cost of capital, equal to 8.9 percent. Accordingly, proper calculation of the cost of capital requires that the cost of equity for a firm in the industry be given a weight of 0.8 and the cost of debt be given a weight of 0.2—the firm's optimal capital structure.

OPTIMAL CAPITAL BUDGET

A profit-maximizing firm operates at the point where marginal revenue equals marginal cost. In terms of the capital budgeting process, this implies that the marginal rate of return earned on the last acceptable investment project is just equal to the firm's relevant marginal cost of capital. The **optimal capital budget** is the funding level required to underwrite a value-maximizing level of new investment.

optimal capital budget
Funding required to underwrite a value-maximizing level of new investment

investment opportunity schedule (IOS)
Pattern of returns for all potential investment projects

Investment Opportunity Schedule

The **investment opportunity schedule (IOS)** shows the pattern of returns for all of the firm's potential investment projects. Figure 15.3(a) shows an investment opportunity schedule for a hypothetical firm. The horizontal axis measures the dollar amount of investment commitments made during a given year. The vertical axis shows both the rate of return earned on each proj-

FIGURE 15.3

Illustrative Capital Budgeting Decision Process

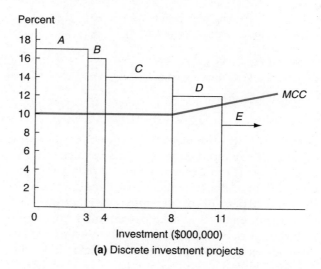

(a) Discrete investment projects

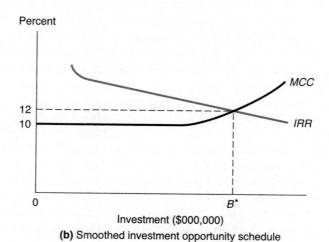

(b) Smoothed investment opportunity schedule

ect and the percentage cost of capital. Each box denotes a given project. Project *A*, for example, calls for an outlay of $3 million and promises a 17 percent rate of return; project *B* requires an outlay of $1 million and promises a 16 percent yield, and so on. The last investment, project *E*, simply involves buying 9 percent government bonds. By displaying this stepwise pattern of potential returns on a single graph, the firm's IOS is depicted. Figure 15.3(b) generalizes the IOS concept to show a smooth pattern of potential returns. The curve labeled *IRR* shows the internal rate of return potential for each project in the portfolio of investment projects available to the firm. It is important to remember that these projects are arrayed from left to right in terms of declining attractiveness as measured by the IRR criterion. Therefore, project *A* is more attractive than project *E*, and the IRR schedule is downward sloping from left to right.

Although the IOS provides important input into the capital budget decision-making process, by itself it is insufficient for determining the optimal capital budget. Both the returns and costs of potential projects must be considered. To define the optimal capital budget, a means for evaluating the marginal cost of funds must be incorporated into the process.

Marginal Cost of Capital

marginal cost of capital (MCC)
Financing cost of an additional investment project, expressed on a percentage basis

The **marginal cost of capital (MCC)** is the extra financing cost necessary to fund an additional investment project, expressed on a percentage basis. When the firm is considering an entire portfolio of potential investment projects, the marginal cost of capital is the incremental financing cost of a relevant mix of debt and equity financing. Therefore, the MCC is typically given by the firm's weighted-average cost of capital. As drawn in Figure 15.3(b), the marginal cost of capital is constant at 10 percent up until the point where the firm has raised an additional $8 million. After this point, capital costs begin to rise. Given these IOS and MCC schedules, the firm should accept projects *A* through *D*, obtaining and investing $11 million. Project *E*, the government bond investment alternative, should be rejected. The smooth curves in Figure 15.3(b) indicate that the firm should invest *B** dollars, the optimal capital budget. At this investment level, the marginal cost of capital is 12 percent, exactly the same as the IRR on the marginal investment project.

Whenever the optimal capital budget *B** is determined, the IRR always equals the MCC for the last project undertaken. The condition that must be met for any budget to be optimal is that *IRR* = *MCC*. This means that the final project accepted for investment is a breakeven project, in that it provides an IRR that is just equal to the discount rate. For this project, *NPV* = 0, *PI* = 1, and *IRR* = *k*. By accepting all earlier and more attractive projects, value maximization is assured because the firm has accepted all projects where *NPV* > 0, *PI* > 1, and *IRR* > *k*. This means that the area above the MCC schedule but below the IRR (or IOS schedule) represents the net profit earned on the firm's new investment projects. The *IRR* = *MCC* optimal capital budget condition is completely analogous to the *MR* = *MC* requirement for profit maximization. When *MR* = *MC*, all profitable units have been produced and sold. When *IRR* = *MCC*, all profitable investment projects have likewise been accepted.

Economic Value-Added Analysis

economic value added (EVA©)
Adjusted accounting profit minus the cost of capital employed

An intuitive and increasingly popular method for judging the efficiency of the firm's capital budgeting process is called **economic value-added (EVA©)** analysis. EVA© is an accounting-based estimate of the profit added through the firm's capital budgeting process. The formula for EVA© is

(15.14)

$$\text{Economic Value Added (EVA®)} = \text{Adjusted Earnings} - \text{Capital Costs}$$

$$= \text{Adjusted Earnings} - (\text{Marginal Cost of Capital} \times \text{Value of Capital Employed})$$

As shown in Equation 15.14, EVA© is an accounting-based measure of the net profit contribution earned after adjusting accounting earnings for noncash expenses and the cost of capital employed by the firm or division. Like NPV analysis, firm or divisional activity adds value when EVA© > 0; firm or divisional activity destroys value when EVA© < 0. Value maximization requires that the firm undertake all investment projects that feature positive EVA©; projects featuring negative EVA© should be rejected. For positive EVA© investment projects, the greater the EVA©, the more desirable the investment project.

When EVA© is calculated, accounting net income provides a useful starting point for analysis. However, if net income is negatively affected by the amortization of goodwill, or the failure to capitalize and amortize investments in intangible assets like research and development and brand-name advertising, net income can fail to provide an accurate indication of economic performance. In such instances, cash flow numbers may provide better insight regarding firm or divisional performance. **Earnings before interest, taxes, depreciation, and amortization (EBITDA)** is one such cash flow measure that is commonly employed. EBITDA is simply revenue minus all expenses, except interest charges, income taxes, depreciation, and amortization charges. EBITDA shows the gross amount of cash flow that the company is bringing in, and reflects the cash flow available to finance corporate acquisitions. The advantage of focusing on EBITDA rather than net income numbers is that EBITDA avoids any errors in the application of accounting accrual methodology. A disadvantage of focusing on EBITDA is that managers can sometimes overlook the need to make necessary investments in plant and equipment. To ensure that funds for necessary capital expenditures will be available, prudent managers often focus on **free cash flow**, or EBITDA minus the cost of essential new plant and equipment. Although such cash flow adjustments to accounting net income numbers can be controversial, they are sometimes necessary if the firm's capital budgeting process is to reflect economic reality.

Of course, in actual practice the estimation of an appropriate marginal cost of capital can itself be controversial. When EVA© analysis is being conducted, it is essential that managers remember that an appropriate marginal cost of capital reflects the opportunity cost of employed funds. If free cash flow derived from operations is to be retained in the organization, it must produce a return that is at least commensurate with that available on similar investment projects inside and outside the firm. As a result, a practical and typical hurdle rate is the firm's expected marginal rate of return on investment. For example, if the corporation as a whole earns an average return of 12 percent on invested capital, it is rare that investment projects promising less than that amount will be approved. Instead of adopting marginal investment projects that promise below-average returns, top management will typically use free cash flow to buy back stock or repay borrowed funds. Of course, if special financing is obtained to fund division activity, and particularly if division assets are used to secure such financing, then division-specific cost of funds can be readily calculated. Otherwise, the divisional cost of financing must be estimated based upon the firm's overall marginal cost of capital.

EVA© methodology is helpful because it forces managers at all levels in the corporation to explicitly consider the cost of capital in their planning and operating decisions. As such, it has become a vital tool in the ongoing success of such standout performers as the Coca-Cola Company, General Electric Company, Gillette Co., and Procter & Gamble Co., among others.

Postaudit

To assure that an optimal capital budget has indeed been determined, the methods and data employed must often be carefully reexamined at the end of the capital budgeting process. The **postaudit** is a careful examination of actual and predicted results, coupled with a detailed reconciliation of any differences.

One of the most important advantages of the postaudit is that managerial forecasts of revenues and costs tend to improve when decision makers systematically compare projections to actual outcomes. Conscious or subconscious biases can be observed and eliminated, and new

EBITDA
Earnings before interest, taxes, depreciation, and amortization

free cash flow
EBITDA minus the cost of essential new plant and equipment

postaudit
Careful reconciliation of actual and predicted results

forecasting methods can be sought as their need becomes apparent. People simply tend to work better if they know that their actions are being monitored. It is important to remember that businesses are run by people, and people can perform at higher or lower levels of efficiency. When a divisional team has made a forecast in a capital budgeting proposal, it is putting its reputation on the line. Because of the postaudit, these managers have every incentive to make good on their projections. If costs rise above predicted levels or sales fall below expectations, managers in production, sales, and related areas have incentives to strive to bring results into line with earlier forecasts.

Of course, it must be recognized that each element of the cash flow forecast is subject to uncertainty, so a percentage of all projects undertaken by a reasonably aggressive firm will prove to be unsuccessful. This must be considered when appraising the performances of managers who submit capital expenditure requests. Projects also sometimes fail to meet expectations for reasons that no one could realistically have anticipated. For example, wild fluctuations in both oil prices and interest rates during recent years have made long-term forecasts of any sort very difficult. It is also sometimes hard to separate the operating results of one investment from those of contemporaneous projects. If the postaudit process is not used carefully, managers may be reluctant to suggest potentially profitable but risky projects. Because of these difficulties, some firms tend to play down the importance of the postaudit. However, the best-run and most successful organizations in business and government are those that put the greatest emphasis on postaudits. Accordingly, the postaudit process is one of the most important elements in an effective capital budgeting system.

SUMMARY

Long-term investment decisions are important because substantial amounts of funds are often committed for extended periods. They are difficult because they entail forecasts of uncertain future events that must be relied on heavily.

- **Capital budgeting** is the process of planning expenditures that generate cash flows expected to extend beyond 1 year. Several different types of investment projects may be involved, including **replacement projects**, or maintenance of business projects; **cost reduction projects** to replace obsolete plant and equipment; mandatory nonrevenue-producing **safety and environmental projects**; and **expansion projects** to increase the availability of existing products and services.

- In all cases, the focus is on **incremental cash flows**, or the period-by-period changes in net cash flows that are due to the investment project. The most common tool for project valuation is **net present-value (NPV)** analysis, where NPV is the difference between project marginal revenues and marginal costs, when both are expressed in present-value terms. The conversion to present-value terms involves use of an appropriate discount rate, or **cost of capital**.

- Alternative decision rules include the **profitability index (PI)**, or benefit/cost ratio; **internal rate of return (IRR)**, or discount rate that equates the present value of receipts and outlays; and the **payback period**, or number of years required to recover the initial investment.

- Managers must be aware of the **net present-value profile** for individual projects, a graph that relates the NPV for each project to the discount rate used in the NPV calculation. A reversal of project rankings occurs at the **crossover discount rate**, where NPV is equal for two or more investment alternatives.

- To properly value cash flows over the life of a project, the cost of capital funds must be determined. The **component cost of debt** is the interest rate that investors require on debt, adjusted for taxes. The **component cost of equity** is the rate of return stockholders require on common stock. This includes a **risk-free rate of return** to compensate investors for

636

Q15.9 Recent academic studies in financial economics conclude that stockholders of target firms in takeover bids "win" (earn abnormal returns) and that stockholders of successful bidders do not lose subsequent to takeovers, even though takeovers usually occur at substantial premiums over prebid market prices. Is this observation consistent with capital market efficiency?

Q15.10 What important purposes are served by the postaudit?

SELF-TEST PROBLEMS AND SOLUTIONS

ST15.1 NPV and Payback Period Analysis. Suppose that your college roommate has approached you with an opportunity to invest $25,000 in her fledgling home health-care business. The business, called Home Health Care, Inc., plans to offer home infusion therapy and monitored in-the-home health-care services to surgery patients in the Brainerd, Minnesota, area. The funds would be used to lease a delivery vehicle, to purchase supplies, and for working capital. The terms of the proposal are that you would receive $5,000 at the end of each year in interest on a $25,000 loan to be repaid in full at the end of a 10-year period.

A. Assuming a 10% required rate of return, calculate the present value of cash flows and the net present value of the proposed investment.

B. Based on this same interest-rate assumption, calculate the cumulative cash flow of the proposed investment for each period in both nominal and present-value terms.

C. What is the payback period in both nominal and present-value terms?

D. What is the difference between the nominal and present-value payback period? Can the present-value payback period ever be shorter than the nominal payback period?

ST15.1 Solution

A. The present value of cash flows and the net present value of the proposed investment can be calculated as follows:

Year	Cash Flow	Present-Value Interest Factor	Present-Value Cash Flow
0	($25,000)	1.0000	($25,000)
1	5,000	0.9091	4,545
2	5,000	0.8264	4,132
3	5,000	0.7513	3,757
4	5,000	0.6830	3,415
5	5,000	0.6209	3,105
6	5,000	0.5645	2,822
7	5,000	0.5132	2,566
8	5,000	0.4665	2,333
9	5,000	0.4241	2,120
10	5,000	0.3855	1,928

Cost of Capital	10.0%
Present Value of Benefits	$30,723
Present Value of Cost	$25,000
Net Present Value	$5,723

B. The cumulative cash flow of the proposed investment for each period in both nominal and present-value terms is

Year	Cash Flow	Present-Value Interest Factor	Present-Value Cash Flow	Cumulative Cash Flow	Cumulative PV Cash Flow
0	($25,000)	1.0000	($25,000)	($25,000)	($25,000)
1	5,000	0.9091	4,545	(20,000)	(20,455)
2	5,000	0.8264	4,132	(15,000)	(16,322)
3	5,000	0.7513	3,757	(10,000)	(12,566)
4	5,000	0.6830	3,415	(5,000)	(9,151)
5	5,000	0.6209	3,105	0	(6,046)
6	5,000	0.5645	2,822	5,000	(3,224)
7	5,000	0.5132	2,566	10,000	(658)
8	5,000	0.4665	2,333	15,000	1,675
9	5,000	0.4241	2,120	20,000	3,795
10	5,000	0.3855	1,928	25,000	5,723

Payback Period	5 years
Present-Value Payback Period	8.28 years (= 8 + $658/$2,333)

C. Based on the information provided in part B, it is clear that the cumulative cash flow in nominal dollars reached $0 at the end of year 5. This means that the nominal payback period is 5 years. The cumulative cash flow in present-value dollars exceeds $0 when the year 8 interest payment is received. This means that the present-value payback period is roughly 8 years. If cash flows were received on a continuous basis, the present-value payback period would be 8.28 years (= $658/$2,333).

D. Assuming a positive rate of interest, the present-value payback period is always longer than the nominal payback period. This stems from the fact that present-value dollars are always less than nominal dollars, and it therefore takes longer to receive a fixed dollar amount back in terms of present-value dollars rather than in nominal terms.

ST15.2 Decision Rule Conflict. Kate O'Brien has been retained as a management consultant by Winfred-Louder, a local department store, to analyze two proposed capital investments, projects X and Y. Project X is a sophisticated working capital and inventory control system based upon a powerful personal computer, called a system server, and PC software specifically designed for inventory processing and control in the retailing business. Project Y is a similarly sophisticated working capital and inventory control system based upon a powerful personal computer and general purpose PC software. Each project has a cost of $10,000, and the cost of capital for both projects is 12%. The projects' expected net cash flows are as follows:

	Expected Net Cash Flow	
Year	Project X	Project Y
0	($10,000)	($10,000)
1	6,500	3,500
2	3,000	3,500
3	3,000	3,500
4	1,000	3,500

A. Calculate each project's nominal payback period, net present value (NPV), internal rate of return (IRR), and profitability index (PI).

B. Should both projects be accepted if they are interdependent?

C. Which projects should be accepted if they are mutually exclusive?

D. How might a change in the cost of capital produce a conflict between the NPV and IRR rankings of these two projects? At what values of k would this conflict exist? (Hint: Plot the NPV profiles for each project to find the crossover discount rate k.)

E. Why does a conflict exist between NPV and IRR rankings?

ST15.2 Solution

A. *Payback*:

To determine the nominal payback period, construct the cumulative cash flows for each project:

	Cumulative Cash Flow	
Year	**Project X**	**Project Y**
0	($10,000)	($10,000)
1	(3,500)	(6,500)
2	(500)	(3,000)
3	2,500	500
4	3,500	4,000

$$\text{Payback}_X = 2 + \frac{\$500}{\$3,000} = 2.17 \text{ years}$$

$$\text{Payback}_Y = 2 + \frac{\$3,000}{\$3,500} = 2.86 \text{ years}$$

Net Present Value (NPV):

$$NPV_X = -\$10,000 + \frac{\$6,500}{(1.12)^1} + \frac{\$3,000}{(1.12)^2} + \frac{\$3,000}{(1.12)^3} + \frac{\$1,000}{(1.12)^4}$$

$$= \$966.01$$

$$NPV_Y = -\$10,000 + \frac{\$3,500}{(1.12)^1} + \frac{\$3,500}{(1.12)^2} + \frac{\$3,500}{(1.12)^3} + \frac{\$3,500}{(1.12)^4}$$

$$= \$630.72$$

Internal Rate of Return (IRR):
To solve for each project's IRR, find the discount rates that set NPV to zero:

$$IRR_X = 18.0\%$$
$$IRR_Y = 15.0\%$$

Profitability Index (PI):

$$PI_X = \frac{PV \text{ Benefits}}{PV \text{ Costs}} = \frac{\$10,966.01}{\$10,000} = 1.10$$

$$PI_Y = \frac{\$10,630.72}{\$10,000} = 1.06$$

B. Using all methods, project X is preferred over project Y. Because both projects are acceptable under the NPV, IRR, and PI criteria, both projects should be accepted if they are interdependent.

C. Choose the project with the higher NPV at $k = 12\%$, or project X.

D. To determine the effects of changing the cost of capital, plot the NPV profiles of each project. The crossover rate occurs at about 6% to 7%. To find this rate exactly, create a project Δ, which is the difference in cash flows between projects X and Y:

Year	Project X – Project Y = Project Δ Net Cash Flow
0	$ 0
1	3,000
2	(500)
3	(500)
4	(2,500)

Then find the IRR of project Δ:

$$IRR_\Delta = \text{Crossover Rate} = 6.2\%$$

Thus, if the firm's cost of capital is less than 6.2%, a conflict exists, because $NPV_Y > NPV_X$ but $IRR_X > IRR_Y$.

Graphically, the crossover discount rate is illustrated as follows:

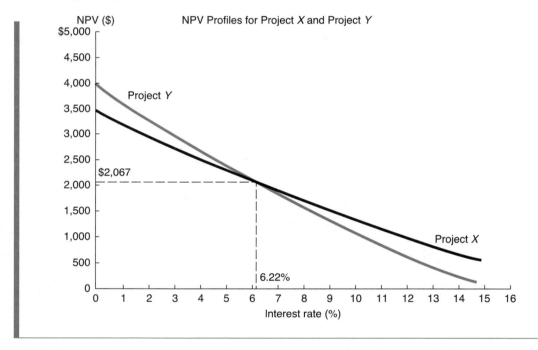

E. The basic cause of conflict is the differing reinvestment rate assumptions between NPV and IRR. The conflict occurs in this situation because the projects differ in their cash flow timing.

PROBLEMS

P15.1 Cost of Capital. Identify each of the following statements as true or false, and explain your answers.

A. Information costs both increase the marginal cost of capital and reduce the internal rate of return on investment projects.

B. Depreciation expenses involve no direct cash outlay and can be safely ignored in investment-project evaluation.

C. The marginal cost of capital will be less elastic for larger firms than for smaller firms.

D. In practice, the component costs of debt and equity are jointly rather than independently determined.

E. Investments necessary to replace worn-out or damaged equipment tend to have low levels of risk.

P15.2 **Decision Rule Criteria.** The net present value (NPV), profitability index (PI), and internal rate of return (IRR) methods are often employed in project valuation. Identify each of the following statements as true or false, and explain your answers.

A. The IRR method can tend to understate the relative attractiveness of superior investment projects when the opportunity cost of cash flows is below the IRR.

B. A $PI = 1$ describes a project with an $NPV = 0$.

C. Selection solely according to the NPV criterion will tend to favor larger rather than smaller investment projects.

D. When $NPV = 0$, the IRR exceeds the cost of capital.

E. Use of the PI criterion is especially appropriate for larger firms with easy access to capital markets.

P15.3 **Cost of Capital.** Indicate whether each of the following would increase or decrease the cost of capital that should be used by the firm in investment project evaluation. Explain.

A. Interest rates rise because the Federal Reserve System tightens the money supply.

B. The stock market suffers a sharp decline, as does the company's stock price, without (in management's opinion) any decline in the company's earnings potential.

C. The company's home state eliminates the corporate income tax in an effort to keep or attract valued employers.

D. In an effort to reduce the federal deficit, Congress raises corporate income tax rates.

E. A merger with a leading competitor increases the company's stock price substantially.

P15.4 **Present Value.** New York City licenses taxicabs in two classes: (1) for operation by companies with fleets and (2) for operation by independent driver-owners having only one cab. Strict limits are imposed on the number of taxicabs by restricting the number of licenses, or medallions, that are issued to provide service on the streets of New York City. This medallion system dates from a Depression-era city law designed to address an overabundance of taxis that depressed driver earnings and congested city streets. In 1937, the city slapped a moratorium on the issuance of new taxicab licenses. The number of cabs, which peaked at 21,000 in 1931, fell from 13,500 in 1937 to 11,787 in May 1996 when the city broke a 59-year cap and issued an additional 400 licenses. However, because the city has failed to allow sufficient expansion, taxicab medallions have developed a trading value in the open market. After decades of often-explosive medallion price increases, individually-owned licenses now trade for more than $200,000 each, and fleet licenses fetch more than $250,000 each.

A. Discuss the factors determining the value of a license. To make your answer concrete, estimate numerical values for the various components that together can be summarized in a medallion price of $200,000.

B. What factors would determine whether a change in the fare fixed by the city would raise or lower the value of a medallion?

C. Cab drivers, whether hired by companies or as owners of their own cabs, seem unanimous in opposing any increase in the number of cabs licensed. They argue that an increase in the number of cabs would increase competition for customers and drive down what they regard as an already unduly low return to drivers. Is their economic analysis correct? Who would gain and who would lose from an expansion in the number of licenses issued at a nominal fee?

P15.5 **NPV and PI.** The Pacific Princess luxury cruise line is contemplating leasing an additional cruise ship to expand service from the Hawaiian Islands to Long Beach or San Diego. A financial analysis by staff personnel resulted in the following projections for a 5-year planning horizon:

	Long Beach	San Diego
Cost	$2,000,000	$3,000,000
PV of expected cash flow @ $k = 15\%$	2,500,000	3,600,000

A. Calculate the net present value for each service. Which is more desirable according to the NPV criterion?

B. Calculate the profitability index for each service. Which is more desirable according to the PI criterion?

C. Under what conditions would either or both of the services be undertaken?

P15.6 **NPV and PI.** Louisiana Drilling and Exploration, Inc. (LD&E), has the funds necessary to complete one of two risky oil and gas drilling projects. The first, Permian Basin 1, involves the recovery of a well that was plugged and abandoned 5 years ago but that may now be profitable, given improved recovery techniques. The second, Permian Basin 2, is a new onshore exploratory well that appears to be especially promising. Based on a detailed analysis by its technical staff, LD&E projects a 10-year life for each well with annual net cash flows as follows:

Project	Probability	Annual Cash Flow
Permian Basin 1	0.08	$ 500,000
	0.84	1,000,000
	0.08	1,500,000
Permian Basin 2	0.18	300,000
	0.64	900,000
	0.18	1,500,000

In the recovery-project valuation, LD&E uses an 8% riskless rate and a standard 12% risk premium. For exploratory drilling projects, the company uses larger risk premiums proportionate to project risks as measured by the project coefficient of variation. For example, an exploratory project with a coefficient of variation one and one-half times that for recovery projects would require a risk premium of 18% (= 1.5 × 12%). Both projects involve land acquisition, as well as surface preparation and subsurface drilling costs of $3 million each.

A. Calculate the expected value, standard deviation, and coefficient of variation for annual net operating revenues from each well.

B. Calculate and evaluate the NPV for each project using the risk-adjusted discount rate method.

C. Calculate and evaluate the PI for each project.

P15.7 **Investment Project Choice.** Monk's Coffee Shop is considering investment in two alternative capital budgeting projects. Project *A* is an investment of $75,000 to replace working but obsolete refrigeration equipment. Project *B* is an investment of $150,000 to expand dining room facilities. Relevant cash flow data for the two projects over their expected 2-year lives are as follows:

Project A

Year 1		Year 2	
Probability	Cash Flow	Probability	Cash Flow
0.18	$ 0	0.08	$ 0
0.64	50,000	0.84	50,000
0.18	100,000	0.08	100,000

Project B

Year 1		Year 2	
Probability	Cash Flow	Probability	Cash Flow
0.50	$ 0	0.125	$ 0
0.50	200,000	0.75	100,000
		0.125	200,000

A. Calculate the expected value, standard deviation, and coefficient of variation of cash flows for each project.

B. Calculate the risk-adjusted NPV for each project using a 15% cost of capital for the riskier project and a 12% cost of capital for the less risky one. Which project is preferred using the NPV criterion?

C. Calculate the PI for each project, and rank the projects according to the PI criterion.

D. Calculate the IRR for each project, and rank the projects according to the IRR criterion.

E. Compare your answers to parts B, C, and D, and discuss any differences.

P15.8 **Cash Flow Estimation.** Cunningham's Drug Store, a medium-size drugstore located in Milwaukee, Wisconsin, is owned and operated by Richard Cunningham. Cunningham's sells pharmaceuticals, cosmetics, toiletries, magazines, and various novelties. Cunningham's most recent annual net income statement is as follows:

Sales revenue	$1,800,000
Total costs	
Cost of goods sold	$1,260,000
Wages and salaries	200,000
Rent	120,000
Depreciation	60,000
Utilities	40,000
Miscellaneous	30,000
Total	1,710,000
Net profit before tax	$ 90,000

Cunningham's sales and expenses have remained relatively constant over the past few years and are expected to continue unchanged in the near future. To increase sales, Cunningham is considering using some floor space for a small soda fountain. Cunningham would operate the soda fountain for an initial 3-year period and then would reevaluate its profitability. The soda fountain would require an incremental investment of $20,000 to lease furniture, equipment, utensils, and so on. This is the only capital investment required during the 3-year period. At the end of that time, additional capital would be required to continue operating the soda fountain, and no capital would be recovered if it were shut down. The soda fountain is expected to have annual sales of $100,000 and food and materials expenses of $20,000 per year. The soda fountain is also expected to increase wage and salary expenses by 8% and utility expenses by 5%. Because the soda fountain will reduce the floor space available for display of other merchandise, sales of non-soda fountain items are expected to decline by 10%.

A. Calculate net incremental cash flows for the soda fountain.

B. Assume that Cunningham has the capital necessary to install the soda fountain and that he places a 12% opportunity cost on those funds. Should the soda fountain be installed? Why or why not?

P15.9 **Cash Flow Analysis.** The Nigelwick Press, Inc. (NPI), is analyzing the potential profitability of three printing jobs put up for bid by the State Department of Revenue:

	Job *A*	Job *B*	Job *C*
Projected winning bid (per unit)	$5.00	$8.00	$7.50
Direct cost per unit	$2.00	$4.30	$3.00
Annual unit sales volume	800,000	650,000	450,000
Annual distribution costs	$90,000	$75,000	$55,000
Investment required to produce annual volume	$5,000,000	$5,200,000	$4,000,000

Assume that (1) the company's marginal city-plus-state-plus-federal tax rate is 50%; (2) each job is expected to have a 6-year life; (3) the firm uses straight-line depreciation; (4) the average cost of capital is 14%; (5) the jobs have the same risk as the firm's other business; and (6) the company has already spent $60,000 on developing the preceding data. This $60,000 has been capitalized and will be amortized over the life of the project.

A. What is the expected net cash flow each year? (Hint: Cash flow equals net profit after taxes plus depreciation and amortization charges.)

B. What is the net present value of each project? On which project, if any, should NPI bid?

C. Suppose that NPI's primary business is quite cyclical, improving and declining with the economy, but that job *A* is expected to be countercyclical. Might this have any bearing on your decision?

P15.10 **Cost of Capital.** Eureka Membership Warehouse, Inc., is a rapidly growing chain of retail outlets offering brand-name merchandise at discount prices. A security analyst's report issued by a national brokerage firm indicates that debt yielding 13% composes 25% of Eureka's overall capital structure. Furthermore, both earnings and dividends are expected to grow at a rate of 15% per year.

Currently, common stock in the company is priced at $30, and it should pay $1.50 per share in dividends during the coming year. This yield compares favorably with the 8% return currently available on risk-free securities and the 14% average for all common stocks, given the company's estimated beta of 2.

A. Calculate Eureka's component cost of equity using both the capital asset pricing model and the dividend yield plus expected growth model.

B. Assuming a 40% marginal federal-plus-state income tax rate, calculate Eureka's weighted-average cost of capital.

CASE STUDY

Investment Project Analysis at FlightSafety International, Inc.

FlightSafety International, Inc., trains more than 30,000 corporate, commercial, and military pilots per year and has found its niche business to be enormously profitable. Net profit margins have averaged roughly 30% of sales during the 1980s and mid-1990s. It is the only company to have earned a spot on *Forbes'* annual list of the best up-and-comers in every year during this period. Over this period, FlightSafety's profits rose more than fivefold, and the company racked up an average rate of return on common equity of 18% to 20% per year. Its stock was up from $7 a share (split-adjusted) in 1982 to more than $50 in 1996, at which point FlightSafety was purchased by Berkshire Hathaway, Inc., in a cash and stock transaction worth $1.5 billion. Among the 9,500 stockholders that benefited from the company's amazing success is company founder, chairman, and president Albert Ueltschi and his family, who owned roughly one-third of FlightSafety common stock prior to the Berkshire buyout.

What separates FlightSafety from other small companies that look good for a couple of years and then crash and burn is the quality of top management. Ueltschi is widely regarded as dedicated, highly intelligent, and honest. He started FlightSafety in 1951, while working as a pilot for Pan American Airways. Since 1946 he had served as the personal pilot to Pan Am's colorful founder, Juan Trippe, flying Trippe around in a converted B-23 military transport. During the early years of this association, Ueltschi noticed that other corporate CEOs were buying surplus military planes and converting them into corporate aircraft. He also noticed that many of the former military pilots who were signing on as corporate pilots had little or no training on the specific planes they were being hired to fly. Ueltschi reasoned that corporations would pay to rectify this dangerous situation.

Ueltschi opened an office next to Pan Am's LaGuardia terminal and began hiring moonlighting pilots from Pan Am and United to train corporate pilots. Actual flight instruction was done in the clients' aircraft. Additional instrument training was done on instrument trainers, rented by the hour from United Airlines. Early clients included Kodak, Burlington Industries, and National Distillers. Ueltschi poured all the profits back into the business, a practice he still abides by. During the past decade, the company has spent ever-increasing amounts on new plant and equipment; current capital expenditures total roughly $100 million per year.

Today FlightSafety is the largest independent flight trainer in the United States. So complete is its grip on the market that 20 aircraft manufacturers, among them Gulfstream, Cessna, and Learjet, include its training with the price of a new plane. The company trains pilots on sophisticated flight simulators at training centers located adjacent to manufacturers' plants, military bases, and commercial airports. Flight simulators not only recreate the look, feel, and sound of flying specific planes but also simulate emergency flight conditions—such as wind shear or the loss of a hydraulic system—that one does not want to attempt with an actual plane. Training on a simulator is also significantly cheaper than training in an actual plane. FlightSafety's simulator time for a Boeing 737, for example, costs about $550 an hour. Operating costs for an actual 737 are about $3,000 an hour. The company, which now builds most of its own simulators at a cost of $8 million to $12 million each, is putting new ones into service at a rate of three per quarter.

To illustrate the company's capital budgeting process, assume that FlightSafety had built a given simulator for $8 million 2 years ago. The company uses straight-line depreciation over the simulator's projected 12-year life. Therefore, the used flight simulator has a present depreciated book value of $6.5 million; it has a current market value of $7.5 million (before taxes). If kept, the used simulator will last 10 more years and produce an expected net cash flow before tax (CFBT) of $2.5 million per year. A new flight simulator costs $12 million to build but has greater capabilities and is expected to generate CFBT of $4 million per year over a useful life of 15 years. Assume that neither the new nor the used flight simulator has any salvage value

CASE STUDY (continued)

at the end of its projected useful life, a marginal state-plus-federal tax rate of 40%, a current after-tax discount rate of 20%, and straight-line depreciation.

A. Calculate the expected NPV for retention of the used flight simulator equipment.

B. Calculate the expected NPV for construction of the new flight simulator equipment.

C. Based on the NPV criterion, should FlightSafety retain the used flight simulator equipment, build new equipment, or both? Why?

SELECTED REFERENCES

Allen, Jeffrey W. "Private Information and Spin-Off Performance." *Journal of Business* 74 (April 2001): 281–306.

Arnold, Glen C., and Panos D. Hatzopoulos. "The Theory-Practice Gap in Capital Budgeting: Evidence from the United Kingdom." *Journal of Business Finance & Accounting* 27 (June/July 2000): 603–626.

Bernardo, Antonio, Hongbin Cai, and Jiang Luo. "Capital Budgeting and Compensation with Asymmetric Information and Moral Hazard." *Journal of Financial Economics* 61 (September 2001): 311–344.

Bhattacharya, Utpal, and B. Ravikumar. "Capital Markets and the Evolution of Family Businesses." *Journal of Business* 74 (April 2001): 187–220.

Brockman, Paul, and Dennis Chung. "Managerial Timing and Corporate Liquidity: Evidence from Actual Share Repurchases." *Journal of Financial Economics* 61 (September 2001): 417–448.

Doyle, Joanne M., and Toni M. Whited. "Fixed Costs of Adjustment, Coordination, and Industry Investment." *Review of Economics and Statistics* 83 (November 2001): 628–638.

Gelos, R. Gaston, and Alberto Isgut. "Fixed Capital Adjustment: Is Latin America Different?" *Review of Economics and Statistics* 83 (November 2001): 717–726.

Goergen, Marc, and Luc Renneboog. "Investment Policy, Internal Financing and Ownership Concentration in the U.K." *Journal of Corporate Finance* 7 (September 2001): 257–284.

Gomes, Joao F. "Financing Investment." *American Economic Review* 91 (December 2001): 1263–1285.

Hall, Robert E. "Struggling to Understand the Stock Market." *American Economic Review* 91 (May 2001): 1–11.

Hall, Robert E. "The Stock Market and Capital Accumulation." *American Economic Review* 91 (December 2001): 1185–1202.

Hirschey, Mark, and Vernon J. Richardson. "Valuation Effects of Patent Quality: A Comparison for Japanese and U.S. Firms." *Pacific Basin Finance Journal* 9 (January 2001): 65–72.

Kogan, Leonid. "An Equilibrium Model of Irreversible Investment." *Journal of Financial Economics* 62 (November 2001): 201–245

McConnell, John J., Mehmet Ozbilgin, and Sunil Wahal. "Spin-offs, Ex Ante." *Journal of Business* 74 (April 2001): 245–280.

Poterba, James M. "Demographic Structure and Asset Returns." *Review of Economics and Statistics* 83 (November 2001): 565–584.

Summary

CHAPTER SIXTEEN

Organization Structure and Corporate Governance

Conventional wisdom has it that Dell Computer Corp. manufactures and services desktop computers, notebooks, and workstations. In fact, Dell "merely" oversees the quick assembly of parts supplied by Intel and other component manufacturers into customer-ordered configurations. Dell doesn't "make" computers in the sense of manufacturing them out of parts that Dell itself develops. Although Dell is justly praised for its deft use of the Internet for communicating efficiently with customers and suppliers, it is underappreciated the extent to which the company represents a newer type of "virtual" corporation. Another example of the virtual corporation is Sara Lee Corp. Long renowned as a global manufacturer and marketer of high-quality, brand-name products, Sara Lee now contracts out much of its manufacturing work.

Although both Dell and Sara Lee might be regarded as "stealth" virtual corporations, there is nothing subtle about the importance of virtual relationships at Cendant Corp. Cendant links individuals and corporations through franchise partners and business alliances in travel (car rental giant Avis, timeshare operator Resort Condominiums International), lodging (Days Inn, Howard Johnson, Ramada, Super 8), and real estate services (Century 21, Coldwell Banker, and ERA). More than a corporate strategy, virtual relationships are the essence of Cendant.

For Dell, Sara Lee, Cendant, and many other companies, the days of trying to do everything in-house have given way to outsourcing deals, long-term contracts, strategic alliances, and joint ventures. As a result, issues of organization structure and corporate governance have reached a level of vital importance in "virtually" every corporation.[1]

---

1   See Gary McWilliams, "Dell Raises 4th-Quarter Profit Forecast As Its Share of World PC Market Grows," *The Wall Street Journal Online*, January 21, 2002 (http://online.wsj.com).

ORGANIZATION STRUCTURE

Once crucial decisions have been made regarding what to produce, equally important decisions regarding *how* to produce must be answered. In other words, managers must ask: What is the value-maximizing design of the firm? What are the logical boundaries of the firm, and how do these boundaries evolve over time? These are vitally important questions that must be addressed at all levels of the organization on an ongoing basis. The successful firm is a living organism; it must efficiently adapt to an ever-changing economic environment.

What Is Organization Structure?

The optimal design of the firm is the organization type that most successfully meets customer demands. This design composition of the firm is traditionally referred to as its structure. **Organization structure** is described by the vertical and horizontal relationships among the firm, its customers, and suppliers. A **vertical relation** is a business connection between companies at *different* points along the production-distribution chain from raw materials, to finished goods, to delivered products. An example of a vertical relation is the business linkage between Wal-Mart Stores, Inc., the giant discount retailer, and Rubbermaid, the leading manufacturer of rubberized food- and household-storage products. By way of contrast, a **horizontal relation** is a business affiliation between companies at the *same* point along the production-distribution chain. The commercial relationship between Wal-Mart Stores, Inc., and Target Corp., the parent company of Target discount stores, Marshall Field's, and Mervyn's, is an example of a horizontal relation.

In discussing organization structure, both positive (what is) and normative (what should be) issues are relevant. Years ago, the make-or-buy decision was seen as a fairly simple, yet vital determinant of the firm's ongoing success. It was then thought that decisions regarding the organization structure of individual firms would simply revolve around questions concerning optimal production scale. If economics of scale were important, large corporations would evolve to minimize production costs. If economies of scale were slight to nonexistent, small and nimble corporations would evolve to exploit niche markets. Today, answering the question of how to achieve an optimal corporate design has become much more complicated. When economies of scope are relevant, it becomes attractive to offer customers bundles of related products and services, despite the fact that the returns to scale characteristic may be quite different for each individual product.

For example, there is an obvious complement-good relationship between soda and pizza products. Pepsi-Cola goes great with pizza. Still, business success does not require that both products be owned and distributed by the same company simply because they are consumed together. During 1997, Pepsico announced a plan to divest its Pizza Hut, KFC, and Taco Bell restaurant brands, now called Tricon Global Restaurants Inc., because it failed to realize the expected synergy from jointly owning and operating these soda and fast-food businesses. The fast-food business is mature in the United States and features both cutthroat pricing and razor-thin margins. This contrasts sharply with the soft drink industry, which remains one of the most profitable businesses in the world. Together, Coca-Cola and Pepsi-Cola dominate soft drinks, a business that features low capital investment requirements, generous profit margins, and above-average growth. However, rather than extending its advantages in the soft drink industry by controlling an important segment of the fast-food business, Pepsico found itself at a disadvantage when McDonald's and other non-Pepsico chains refused to serve Pepsi products lest they help a prime competitor in the fast-food business. Coca-Cola's licensing agreements with fast-food franchises proved superior to Pepsico's joint ownership of fast-food and soft drink businesses. Thus, Coca-Cola solidified its lead as the dominant soft drink bottler in the world, at least in part, because its organization structure was superior to that featured by Pepsico, a prime competitor.

organization structure
Vertical and horizontal relationships among the firm, its customers, and suppliers

vertical relation
Business connection between companies at different points along the production-distribution chain

horizontal relation
Business affiliation between companies at the same point along the production-distribution chain

Of course, the optimal boundaries and structure of the firm are not static; they are dynamic and responsive to the changing needs of the marketplace. Before the mid-nineteenth century, hierarchal organization structures were virtually nonexistent. Transportation and information technology had not yet progressed to the point where large-scale consolidation in business was possible. This changed radically when steamship and railroad transportation and the telegraph and telephone made for speedy transport and near-instantaneous communication. Suddenly, the means for coordination in large-scale enterprise became available. At the start of the twentieth century, company sizes grew rapidly to take advantage of economies of scale in production to better serve nations hungry for industrial and consumer products. This process of industrial consolidation flourished throughout the early post–World War II era.

The emerging information age of the twenty-first century promises to further refine corporate boundaries. Whereas the post–World War II corporate environment was designed for the efficient mass production of standardized industrial and consumer goods, present-day customers are more interested in unique combinations of goods and services to meet specialized needs. Just as the industrial revolution transformed the competitive landscape of the twentieth century, so too is the information revolution transforming corporate boundaries. Highly skilled managers no longer need to locate in New York, Chicago, or Los Angeles to find exciting career opportunities. Powerful desktop computers, the Internet, and low-cost satellite-based communications make it possible to work in Los Angeles while living on Catalina Island; in Sante Fe, New Mexico; or Durango, Colorado. Centralized authority supported by layers of managerial staff is being replaced by desktop computers and sophisticated software that make line personnel instantly accountable for bottom-line performance. Chief financial officers do not want detailed reports filed by cumbersome staffs of accounting and financial personnel; they want immediate access to the data with user-friendly software. Ramifications of this ongoing revolution in information technology for corporate organizations should not be underestimated. Invention of the airplane did not make it important to become a faster walker; it changed the nature of travel. Similarly, invention of the Internet did not just increase the importance of computer literacy in the workplace; it promises to fundamentally change the size, scope, and viability of organizations throughout the economy.

Before considering problems encountered in arriving at an optimal corporate design, it is worth considering briefly the very nature of the firm.

Transaction Costs and the Nature of Firms

Nobel laureate Ronald Coase is famous for his work on defining the nature of the firm. At its core, Coase saw the firm as a nexus or collection of contractual agreements among owners, managers, workers, suppliers, and customers. It has no physical presence; it exists only as a legal device.

From this perspective, the efficiency of firms depends upon the ability of participants to find effective means to minimize the **transactions costs** of coordinating productive activity. Important categories of transactions costs encountered within the firm include

transactions costs
Coordination expenses

- information costs
- decision costs
- enforcement costs

To appreciate the importance of transaction costs in defining the nature of firms it will prove useful to consider each category in some detail.

information costs
Search outlays

decision costs
Bargaining expenditures

Search or **information costs** encompass expenses encountered in discovering the type and quality of goods and services demanded by consumers. Information costs also include expenses encountered in securing necessary raw materials, attracting and training a skilled workforce, developing brand-name recognition, and so on. Bargaining or **decision costs** include expenditures involved with successfully negotiating production agreements. For example, labor bargaining is sometimes referred to as a continuously renegotiable agreement between management and labor. Even with a long-term union contract, the labor bargain is continuously renegotiable in the sense that the trade-off between pay and effort varies daily according to the level of effort expended. Reluctant workers do not work very hard. Policing or **enforcement costs** include charges necessary to make sure that all parties live up to their contractual commitments. Supervisory costs are an example of enforcement costs. Some transactions costs involve cash outlays for insurance, legal fees, and so on. However, many transaction costs involve implicit or opportunity costs. Necessary delays to facilitate consensus building, group meetings, and constant communication among team members are all manifestations of transaction costs.

enforcement costs
Charges tied to contractual commitments

In the early post–World War II period, notable transaction costs associated with coordinating large-scale production and distribution of industrial and consumer goods were more than offset by significant economies of scale in production. As a result, top firms in the industrial world reached gigantic size in terms of assets, employment, sales revenues, and profits. More recently, consumers have tended to prefer distinctive goods and services tailored to specific needs. Economies of scale in production tend to be much less important when production needs are specialized and are often nonexistent in the provision of services. At the same time, the costs of coordinating activity among increasingly specialized and highly educated professionals tend to be much higher than the costs of coordinating effort among less specialized workers. Therefore, it is not surprising to note the recent downsizing trend among giant corporations throughout the industrial world and the coincident growth in importance of entrepreneurship and small business.

Coase Theorem

According to Coase, firms exist as an economic force because they are an effective means of minimizing transaction costs. It would be prohibitively expensive for each of us to organize production of all goods and services that we desire. For example, most consumers are unprepared to deal with the complexity of building a home. As a result, most consumers contract with real estate developers, who contract with builders who, in turn, contract with carpenters, electricians, plumbers, landscapers, and so on. If sufficient ongoing demand exists, builders employ their own staff of professionals; they form a firm. If demand is sporadic, contracting will ensue prior to the start of each independent home building project. In deciding whether or not to retain their own staff of building professionals, builders compare the costs of negotiating for the completion of individual home projects with the costs of maintaining a less than fully utilized staff during slack periods. In the same way, law firms, medical practices, and professional consultants consider transaction costs in decisions concerning the scope and scale of professional enterprises.

Similarly, Coase sees firms as well-equipped to deal with traditional problems caused by negative externalities, such as pollution. Because individuals respond to economic incentives, they seek out and undertake mutually beneficial trades. For example, suppose a power plant reduced recreational opportunities by fouling a nearby river. Such a company might appease local residents by purchasing land for general recreation use upriver or by matching public tax spending to reduce or eliminate downriver pollution. The power plant might also be willing to pay some other local polluter, say, a municipal water treatment plant, to reduce its pollution, and hence the total amount of emissions, to an acceptable level. This latter alternative might prove especially attractive if the marginal cost of reducing pollution by the municipal water facility is much less than the marginal cost of reducing power plant emissions. In fact, some local jurisdictions award "pollution rights" that are traded among polluters who seek the lowest cost method for reducing total emissions. According to what is now referred to as the **Coase Theorem**, resource allocation will be efficient so long as transaction costs remain low and property rights can be freely assigned and exchanged.

Coase Theorem
Resource allocation is efficient if transaction costs are low and property rights are freely traded

Organization Design at GE

Home to over 313,000 employees, the General Electric Company (GE) is a diversified industrial giant producing a wide variety of products for the generation, transmission, distribution, control, and utilization of electricity. By 2005, GE sales revenue is expected to continue its steady 9 percent per year climb to $92 billion, while profits grow by 14 percent per year to $22.9 billion. Expectations of rising profit margins due to ferocious cost-cutting have made GE a stock-market darling. With a stock-market capitalization in excess of $400 billion, GE is one of the most valuable and revered corporations in the world.

Although GE is a gigantic business, it has crafted an organization design that allows the company to take advantage of its large size and yet still function like a number of much smaller and more nimble organizations. Like many large corporations, GE is divided into profit centers and operating units. Although each line of business is responsible for its own profit numbers, GE seeks synergy by having managers share management techniques that can work across functional areas. Stories of management success and failure are shared openly. Though GE has nine layers of management, its

legendary informality means that front-line managers and employees often "violate" the chain of command by communicating across layers of management. This is what many management theorists regard as being unique about GE. GE makes every executive, manager, and employee personally responsible for their own performance. Unexpected visits to plants and offices, surprise luncheons, and countless handwritten notes make everyone feel like an important part of a complex organization.

At GE, quality is an ongoing process of continuing improvement. With hundreds of specific projects, GE's quality initiative, dubbed Six Sigma, involves constant training of thousands of employees. In a real sense, GE is a learning and evolving organization. It is an organization designed to renew and reinvigorate itself. So far, it seems to be working for management employees, customers, and stockholders.

See: Rachel Emma and Ken Brown, "General Electric: Some Seek More Light on the Finances," *The Wall Street Journal Online*, January 23, 2002 (http://online.wsj.com).

The transaction cost concept is important in managerial economics because it provides the context necessary for considering the economic significance of organization structure. To understand the importance of organization structure in the ongoing success of firms, it is necessary to learn how organization structure is dictated by the nature of the firm's economic environment and competitive strategy. As a first step in this process, it is necessary to ask: Why are there economic conflicts within firms?

AGENCY PROBLEMS: SOURCES OF CONFLICT WITHIN FIRMS

Throughout corporate America, a familiar complaint is often heard: "Why can't we all just learn to work together?" Although manifestations of this difficulty are varied and complex, they often share a common root cause. In managerial economics, it is called the **agency problem**, or natural conflict between owners and managers.

agency problem
Natural conflict between owners and managers

What Is the Firm's Agency Problem?

Given their ownership position, stockholders are the principals of the firm. Managers and other employees without any ownership interest can be thought of as hired hands, or agents of the stockholders. An agency problem is present to the extent that unresolved material conflicts exist between the self-seeking goals of (agent) managers and the value maximization goal of (principal) stockholders. **Agency costs** are the explicit and implicit transaction costs necessary to overcome the natural divergence of interest between agent managers and principal stockholders. Agency costs incurred by stockholders are reflected in expenses for managerial monitoring, the overconsumption of perquisites by managers, and lost opportunities due to

agency costs
Expenditures necessary to overcome owner-manager conflicts

excessive risk avoidance. This characterization of the conflict problem within firms has a long history in managerial economics. Modern concern with the topic began in the 1930s when Adolf Berle and Gardiner Means predicted that managers with little direct ownership interest, and thus having "own" rather than stockholder interests in mind, would come to run the bulk of business enterprise by the latter part of the twentieth century. Before them, economists' concern with the "other people's money" problem dates from 1776 and Adam Smith, who noted that people tend to look after their own affairs with more care than they use in looking after the affairs of others.

Agency problems exist because of conflicts between the incentives and rewards that face owners and managers. Such conflicts commonly arise given owner-manager differences in

- risk exposure
- investment horizons
- familiarity with investment opportunities

Problems mount because differing economic incentives between owners and managers can cause predictable, but hard to correct, hurdles that must be overcome if the shareholder's value maximization objective is to be achieved.

Risk Management Problems

excessive risk-taking problem
Agent preference for value-reducing speculation

Significant differences in the risk exposure of managers and stockholders often leads to an **excessive risk-taking problem**. In 1995, for example, London's famous Barings Bank, a bank founded in 1762 that had helped fund Britain's war effort against Napoleon, was brought to its knees given excessive risk taking by a single individual. A trader by the name of Nick Leeson in Barings' Singapore branch had been charged with the responsibility of overseeing the branch's risk-free arbitrage business. In risk-free arbitrage, banks and other financial institutions seek to profit by taking advantage of price discrepancies in different markets. By instantaneously buying and selling the same security in different markets, arbitrage by banks and other financial institutions can result in small but risk-free profits. Unfortunately, when imperfect hedging led to losses rather than profits, Leeson began to engage in the far riskier business of foreign currency market speculation. Leeson guessed wrong and lost $1.4 billion of the bank's money. While Leeson ended up in jail, Barings was sold to ING, the large Dutch financial institution, for a mere £1.

"other people's money" problem
Tendency by agents to be careless with principal's resources

This Barings Bank episode is an obvious manifestation of the **"other people's money" problem**. It stemmed from the fact that Leeson was not speculating with his own resources; he was gambling with Barings Bank funds. Other related agency problems tied to differences between the investment horizons of stockholders and management can also emerge. Salary and bonus payments tied to short-term performance often constitute a large part of the annual total compensation package earned by management. Thus, managers typically have huge personal incentives to turn in favorable year-to-year growth in revenues, profits, and earnings per share. This can sometimes have the unfortunate effect of focusing managerial attention on near-term accounting performance to the detriment of long-term value maximization. To combat such myopic behavior, more and more companies are insisting that managerial compensation be directly tied to long-term performance. An efficient means for establishing this link is to demand that top management hold a significant stock position that cannot be sold until some time *after* retirement. When it was an independent entity, investment bank Salomon, Inc., established a compensation plan whereby managers were required to take a significant portion of total compensation in the form of common stock that could not be sold until 5 years after the employee left the bank. Over time, traders, managing directors, top management, and other employees at Salomon came to own roughly 35 percent of the company. Most impressively, this significant employee ownership was achieved through direct stock purchases in the open market; no outright grants of employee or executive stock options were involved. At Salomon, a giant boost to employee stock ownership was being accomplished in such a way as to preserve the ownership position of other stockholders. This contrasts with the much more common situation where generous grants of stock options to top management realize the desired end of aligning managerial and shareholder interests, but only at the significant cost of a material dilution in the ownership interest of outside shareholders.

Many credit the resurgence in Salomon's performance during the mid-1990s to its enlightened management compensation and stock ownership practices. Traveler's Group, Inc., chairman and CEO Sandy Weill was sufficiently impressed to buy Salomon, Inc., during late 1997. Interestingly, other investment banks, like Lehman Brothers Holdings, Inc., have also come to appreciate the advantages of encouraging top executives to make open market purchases of the firm's common stock. It is a trend that seems to be spreading.

Investment Horizon Problems

The typical CEO of a giant U.S. corporation is 55 to 60 years old, has been with the company 20 to 25 years, and looks forward to a term in office of 8 to 10 years. With this demographic background, most top executives can only expect to see the fruits of their actions at the top of the organization if such benefits accrue quickly as opposed to slowly. Similarly, many managers pin their hopes for promotion on the basis of results achieved during fairly short time frames. As a result, top executives and many other managers tend to have fairly short time horizons within which they and others within the corporation evaluate investment and operating decisions. This tendency toward focusing on short-term versus long-term results is both reflected in and reinforced by compensation plans that rely on near-term corporate performance.

During 2001, *Business Week* reported that the average CEO at a giant U.S. corporation pulled in a stupendous $13.1 million in total compensation. On average, more than 75 percent of this total is tied to near-term company and stock-price performance in the form of salary, bonus pay, and other compensation. Salary and other compensation (such as health and retirement benefits) are often tied to longevity; bonus pay, is typically tied to accounting performance as measured by the annual growth in earnings per share, profitability as captured by the annual rate of return on stockholders' equity, or other such annual measures of firm performance. Despite the obvious benefits of bonus plans and the incentive-based pay, short-term compensation plans can narrow the focus of top executives to near-term versus long-term corporate performance.

managerial myopia problem
Inefficient preference for stable or short-term performance

To combat the potential for shortsighted operating and investment decisions, sometimes referred to as the **managerial myopia problem**, most corporations now tie a significant portion of total compensation for top executives and other managers to the company's long-term stock-price performance. Stock options and other payments tied to stock-price appreciation now account for a significant portion of top executive pay. Similarly, a wide variety of employee stock ownership plans give managers and other employees strong incentives to consider the long-term implications of present-day decisions. Such plans work best if they consider stock-price gains over extended periods, say 10 years. To reflect the *marginal* contribution of a given top executive or managerial team, managers must only be rewarded for *above-average* stock-price appreciation.

board of directors
Group of people legally charged with the responsibility for governing a corporation

For example, most would agree that Roberto Goizueta did a superb job as head of soft drink juggernaut Coca-Cola. During the 1980s and 1990s, Goizueta set an enviable standard for CEO performance in terms of global brand development, market share expansion, profitable asset deployment, and market value creation. From when Goizueta took charge in 1981 until his death in 1998, Coca-Cola revenues grew at roughly 8 percent per year, earnings per share soared more than 16 percent per year, and its stock price skyrocketed a whopping 27 percent per year. In light of the company's outstanding performance, one can understand why the Coca-Cola **board of directors** awarded Goizueta generous salary, bonus, and stock awards totaling over $1 billion dollars during his tenure.

However, such executive rewards can only be justified if they reflect truly extraordinary performance. Because the average rate of appreciation for all common stocks is roughly 10 percent per year, it is difficult to credit Goizueta with the first 10 percent of Coca-Cola's annual stock-price appreciation. However, Goizueta's superior performance can be cited as an important contributor to Coca-Cola's above-market performance during his tenure. As such, his total compensation, like that of any top executive, should have reflected a share of above-market returns, not including the easy-to-achieve typical return of 10 percent per year.

end-of-game problem
Senior manager preference for value-reducing stable or short-term performance

Finally, given the advanced age of most top executives and many senior managers, firms must be on guard against what is sometimes referred to as the **end-of-game problem**. The end-of-game problem is the most serious manifestation of myopic decision making, or inefficient risk avoidance, and reflects the fact that it becomes difficult to discipline poorly performing managers at the end of their career. Young managers have lucrative future job opportunities both inside and outside the firm as an incentive for hard work and honest dealings with their current employer. Older managers enjoy no such future opportunities and face correspondingly weaker incentives for hard work and honest dealing. Like any such problem involving managerial myopia, most firms deal with the end-of-game problem by insisting that senior managers take a significant portion of total compensation in the form of pay tied to long-term stock-price appreciation.

Information Problems

information asymmetry problem
Disadvantage created by management's inherently superior access to information inside the firm

Yet another potential source of agency problems is tied to management's inherently superior access to information inside the firm, or the **information asymmetry problem**. When compared with outside shareholders, management inside the firm has access to more and better information concerning the firm's relative performance and investment opportunities. By definition, "insiders" know more than "outsiders" about the firm's performance, prospects, and opportunities. The problem is made more serious by the fact that, despite the conspicuous limitations of accounting earnings information, most indicators of firm and top executive performance typically rely upon accounting measures that are collected and reported by management. Because managers are themselves responsible for the collection and processing of accounting information, they control the reporting mechanism designed to monitor managerial and firm performance. Incentive pay plans linked to accounting performance offer more than just incentives for efficient operating and financial decisions. Such plans also give inducements for accounting earnings manipulation and bias.

Earnings manipulation and bias can occur when managers choose accounting methods that lead to income inflation, income smoothing, or both. Managers have incentives for income inflation when higher reported earnings boost managerial compensation, provide greater job security, or both. Incentives exist for income smoothing to the extent that spectacular short-run performance creates expectations that are difficult or impossible to satisfy and, therefore, leads to stockholder disappointment and sanctions. Incentives for income smoothing are also present if stockholder risk aversion leads to an asymmetry of managerial rewards and penalties following short-term earnings "success" versus "failure." Recent studies in managerial economics document the effects of executive incentive pay plans on the reporting strategy of top managers. Their results confirm that the compensation schemes chosen by shareholders and/or boards of directors have a direct influence on the degree of earnings manipulation and bias.

In the modern corporate environment, it is shortsighted to focus concern about poor firm performance on the tendency of inefficient managers to waste money on fancy offices, corporate aircraft, and other such perquisites. Knowledgeable critics of managerial inefficiency are much more troubled about the inherent difficulty of gauging excess compensation, unprofitable empire building, and other elements of managerial malfeasance when managers control the flow of information about firm and managerial performance.

ORGANIZATION DESIGN

organization design
Institutional framework

The value-maximizing **organization design** minimizes unproductive conflict within the firm. Such an optimal organization structure design involves a balanced consideration of how to allocate decision-making authority, how to monitor and evaluate performance, and how to reward productive behavior.

Resolving Unproductive Conflict Within Firms

Successful firms get close to the customer, efficiently identify customer needs and expectations, and then exceed those expectations. Such firms are effective production and distribution systems. Similarly, they are effective means for collecting and processing a vast array of sometimes conflicting information about customer demands, technology, input prices, raw material supplies, and so on. The information-processing function of firms is sometimes overlooked. Also neglected are the costs and benefits of effective information processing. However, these are vital concepts and key determinants of firm success.

Useful information has a price. It must be identified, combined with complementary information, and effectively communicated within the organization. This is made difficult by the fact that bits of useful information are typically dispersed among several different individuals on several different levels up and down the organization. For example, research scientists may encounter problems communicating with engineering staff about problems with the commercial applications of a given discovery. Scientists often share a common language, and it might conflict with the common language of engineers. In turn, both scientists and engineers may confront obstacles in communicating with accounting staff, who themselves share a language that is common to accountants, but foreign to many others. However, the problem is much more serious than just a failure to share a common vocabulary. It is not just that various specialists and subspecialists within the firm talk different languages; communication is made difficult by the fact that many "owners" of valuable information within the firm have conflicting incentives to hide useful details.

Constructive communication within the firm is essential if customer needs are to be met effectively. The design of the organization is appropriate if it facilitates the firm's function as an information-processing mechanism. In considering the design of any organization, basic needs must be met to facilitate worthwhile activity. As shown in Figure 16.1, three prime considerations are the needs to

- allocate decision authority
- monitor and evaluate performance
- reward productive behavior

decision authority
Control choice

Authority is simply the ability to command, control, or influence. An effective organization design is one that allocates **decision authority** to that person or team of persons best able to perform a given task or influence a particular outcome. Decision authority, or decision rights, allows individual employees to determine how and when to best deploy the productive resources and valuable information at their disposal.

With decision authority comes responsibility. It is thus imperative to monitor and evaluate performance. Managers and all employees must be held accountable for outcomes tied to individual decisions. Accountability can only be measured in terms of the tangible and intangible rewards derived from productive activity and in terms of the penalties or sanctions tied to unproductive behavior. Therefore, to minimize the costs of unproductive conflict with the firm, it is essential that the design of the organization effectively allocate decision-making authority, monitor and evaluate performance, and reward productive behavior.

FIGURE 16.1

Organization Design Must Facilitate Effective Decision Making and Efficient Performance
Constructive communication within the firm is essential.

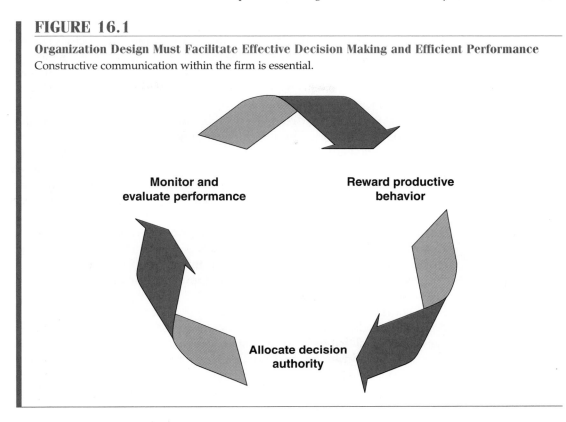

Centralization Versus Decentralization

centralized decision authority
"Top-down," management style

decentralized decision authority
"Close-to-the-customer" management style

A fundamental question facing management of all companies is the basic issue of when and how to centralize versus decentralize decision-making authority. With **centralized decision authority**, detailed judgments concerning how to best manage corporate resources, deal with suppliers and customers, and so on, are handled by top-line executives within the organization. Many corporations with a centralized, or "top-down," management style employ a significant central office staff. With **decentralized decision authority**, front-line employees, often those in direct communication with customers, are empowered to make fundamental judgments concerning how to best serve customer needs. Most companies that feature a decentralized, "bottom-up" or "flat," organization structure employ a minimal decision support staff in the central office. The decision to feature a centralized or decentralized management structure is often an evolutionary process. At some companies, when the size and scale of operation grow, effective resource management requires greater centralization of decision-making authority. At others, the need to remain nimble in responding to customer needs requires ongoing employee empowerment.

Decentralized decision authority works best when local managers or other employees working directly with customers have valuable up-to-the-minute information about the needs and price sensitivity of customers. Decentralized decision-making authority and local or customer-specific knowledge can be a powerful combination when seeking to quickly satisfy local customers. Centralized decision making that requires local managers to seek permission to change prices or reconfigure products takes time that can result in costly delay. Of course, e-mail and other such innovations in communications technology have greatly reduced the delay involved with telling customers "I'll get back to you with that information."

An important benefit of decentralized decision making is that it trains local managers and other employees to put the customer first and to accept personal responsibility for satisfying customer needs. On the other hand, decentralized decisions that fail to account for indirect or company-wide consequences can sometimes prove counterproductive. For example, a price cut in one region or for a single product line may divert sales from other regions or products. Local managers often ignore important interaction effects. Similarly, information about customer needs or product quality considerations may be more reliable and used more effectively when pooled from various local operations.

At most firms, strategic planning decisions are the responsibility of the chairman and board of directors, as supported by the chief executive officer and central office staff. At the same time, corporations that feature highly centralized strategic planning may emphasize significant decentralization and employee empowerment when it comes to operating decisions. Nowhere is this dichotomy more apparent than at extraordinarily successful Berkshire Hathaway, Inc. At $110 billion Berkshire, chairman and chief executive officer Warren Buffett and vice chairman Charles Munger make all decisions regarding capital allocation. Heads of operating subsidiaries make all operating decisions. Division heads have complete operating authority when it comes to Berkshire's diverse operations in insurance, manufacturing, and financial services. What is unusual about this division of responsibility is that Buffett and Munger, who live in California, run their empire from an office in Omaha, Nebraska, that features a staff of roughly a dozen employees!

In commenting on the situation, Buffett once replied to a Securities and Exchange Commission subpoena for Berkshire's "staff papers" concerning a pending multimillion-dollar merger proposal that there were no staff papers; in fact, there was no staff! After talking things over, Buffett and Munger had decided to go ahead on the basis of widely available public information. Buffett and Munger credit Berkshire's outstanding success to the fact that they are supported by an outstanding group of operating managers, but they alone are responsible for capital allocation decisions. Indeed, Berkshire's annual report to stockholders typically features an "advertisement" detailing acquisition criteria for "large purchases" up to $3 to $5 billion and emphasizes that the company is able to assess the level of its interest in a potential acquisition rather quickly—usually within 5 minutes!

Assigning Decision Rights

flat organization
One or few levels of decision-making authority

vertical organization
Multiple levels of decision-making authority

tasks
Assignments

jobs
Bundle of related tasks

The question of centralization versus decentralization focuses on defining the appropriate numbers of levels within the organization. A **flat organization** has few or a single level of decision-making authority; a **vertical organization** features multiple ascending levels of decision-making authority. Irrespective of which organizational form is appropriate, it becomes necessary to choose where in a given organization structure any given decision should be made. In all instances, the issue is one of making effective use of local or customer-specific knowledge, while at the same time maintaining an effective use of centralized information.

At its most basic level, the production process encompasses a sequence of related **tasks**, or assignments necessary to effectively meet customer needs. In turn, related tasks are bundled into **jobs**, when such packaging facilitates cost savings and a more productive use of firm resources. Complex jobs involve the completion of a large number or wide variety of tasks. Simple jobs involve only one elementary chore or a few related responsibilities. Both simple and complex jobs can feature a mix of decision authority. Management trainees may be assigned fairly simple jobs with little or no decision authority; senior management routinely take on complex jobs with complete decision authority. Thus, an appropriate organization design features a constructive mapping of individual skills with task assignments and a correct allotment of decision rights.

As in the case of deciding upon a centralized versus decentralized organization design, judgments regarding the correct bundling of tasks into jobs involve a trade-off between the costs and benefits of coordination and control. When the distribution of useful knowledge is broad and coordination costs are high, jobs tend to be complex and encompass significant authority to make important decisions about how to best serve customers. When the distribution of useful knowledge is narrow and coordination costs are modest, jobs tend to be simple and embody minimal decision authority. During the 1990s, the explosion of small business, especially small professional corporations, implies rapid growth in the number of complex jobs with significant decision authority. The sophisticated types of goods and services offered by small professional corporations typically involve levels of complexity and customer-specific knowledge that make large-scale coordination uneconomic, even in the face of impressive recent advances in communications technology, like e-mail. In terms of professional career opportunities, this increasing complexity places a high premium on motivated individuals capable of independent self-directed cognitive activity.

team
Worker groups given shared responsibility

Many larger organizations facing the need to successfully deal with increasingly complex tasks have turned to **team** concepts. Here the word *team* refers to worker groups given shared responsibility for making and distributing products, managing activity, or providing recommendations. Production teams are often given complete responsibility for managing product flow, setting work schedules, maintaining quality control, and so on. In many instances, production teams are an effective means of empowering and motivating front-line employees. The team concept has also proven successful in helping firms bring together input from a variety of functional areas. Teams are especially adept at sharing local or customer-specific information that is sufficiently complex or far reaching so as to be beyond the grasp of any single individual. Teams are less effective in dealing with problems where the process of consensus building is unduly slow, or where monitoring and motivating underperforming team members is prohibitively expensive. Because communication costs and shirking problems rise with team size, most effective teams involve just a handful of participants, often less than a dozen or so members. In all cases, an optimal team size is defined by the trade-offs involved between the marginal costs and marginal benefits of adding additional team members.

Decision Management and Control

decision management
Generating, choosing, and implementing management decisions

decision control
Manner of assessing the decision management process

Decision management is the vital process of generating, choosing, and implementing management decisions. **Decision control** is the essential process of assessing how well the decision management process functions. As illustrated in Figure 16.2, it is useful to characterize the decision management and control process as consisting of four distinct parts. To be successful, this process must effectively

FIGURE 16.2

The Decision Management and Control Process

The decision management and control process consists of four distinct parts.

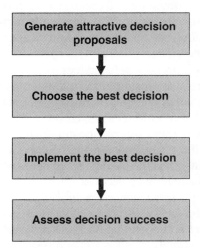

Company Information on the Internet

When looking for easy-to-use business data, news, or analysis, the best advice is to simply "Check the Internet." Company Web sites are a great place to start. The annual report to shareholders is where management tells about all of the good things they are doing for the company. Read financial statements carefully (especially the footnotes), but be skeptical about the commentary. Annual reports are notorious for overlooking shortcomings and glossing over problem areas. Quarterly 10Q and annual 10K reports to the Securities and Exchange Commission contain all necessary financial statements and include detailed information about competitive challenges and legal problems. In plain black and white, SEC reports give the unvarnished truth about company performance at http://www.sec.gov. Don't miss the proxy statement, called the 14 A report. The proxy statement is the annual meeting announcement and includes important information about legal matters brought up for shareholder vote.

From an investor's standpoint, the proxy statement is also interesting because it gives detailed information about compensation and share ownership for members of the board of directors and top management.

Any list of favorite Web sites for general business news and information on the Internet is apt to be long and getting longer. Some favorites are given here. Although the Web sites mentioned provide a good starting point for analysis, it is impossible to cite even a small fraction of the useful Web sites. The best advice is to simply log onto the Internet, type a keyword on Google (http://www.google.com) or your favorite search engine, sit back, and prepare to be amazed!

See: Associated Press, "SEC Creates Three Fake Web Sites to Encourage Savvy Online Investing," *The Wall Street Journal Online*, December 10, 2001 (http://online.wsj.com).

Name	Information	Internet address
Bloomberg.com	Financial news and analysis	http://www.bloomberg.com
The Wall Street Journal Online	Business news	http://public.wsj.com/home.html
Barron's Online	Business analysis	http://www.barrons.com
msn Money Central	Company and industry data	http://www.msn.com
Yahoo! Finance	Financial news, message boards	http://finance.yahoo.com

- generate attractive decision proposals
- choose the best decision
- implement the best decision
- assess decision success

A recurring problem in decision management and control is that it is often difficult to generate a large number of attractive choice alternatives. Managers and other employees from a given work environment tend to have similar perspectives based upon a common work experience or educational background. This makes "groupthink" and the inability to take a fresh look at problems from new perspectives a common problem. To avoid this, successful management teams often look for input from different functional areas within the firm or from individuals who base their proposals on unconventional underlying assumptions. If the decision process is to represent a legitimate search among desirable alternatives, choices must represent valid options with the reasonable potential to offer an attractive trade-off between marginal costs and benefits. If the best decision alternative is to be chosen, the decision process must settle on the option that offers the best marginal net benefit after all direct and indirect costs and benefits to the firm have been considered.

economic expectations
A reasonable before-the-fact forecast of monetary implications

Finally, constructive management demands an ongoing assessment of the decision-making process and the success, or lack thereof, of past decisions. It is important to remember that correct investment and operating decisions are made on the basis of **economic expectations**, or a reasonable before-the-fact forecast of monetary implications. Moreover, judging the wisdom of past

economic realizations
Financial monetary outcomes

decisions involves much more than a simple after-the-fact analysis of **economic realizations**, or financial outcomes.

For example, a decision to buy fire insurance is sound if the chance for material loss is present and insurance is obtained in a cost-effective manner. This is true whether or not a fire loss is actually incurred. Similarly, a given managerial decision is sound if expected profits yield a reasonable risk-adjusted return. Of course, if after-the-fact realizations consistently exceed or fall short of before-the-fact expectations, it becomes necessary to seek out and correct the biases or errors responsible for decision failures.

INCENTIVE COMPENSATION

incentive compensation
Performance-based pay

Incentive compensation has the potential to act as a powerful catalyst for a convergence of interests and effort between the management and owners of a corporation. To maximize effectiveness, such incentive compensation plans must be designed correctly and communicated effectively.

Match Worker Incentives with Managerial Motives

Years ago, overnight document delivery giant FedEx Corp. faced nagging delays in getting parcels sorted and processed at its main terminal in Memphis, Tennessee. All across the country, FedEx's red, white, and blue trucks pick up customer documents and parcels for delivery to homes and businesses within a 24-hour or 2-day time frame. Because of enormous economies of scale in sorting and distribution, all packages from across the United States are flown to Memphis, sorted, flown to regional airports, and then taken by courier truck to their eventual destinations. Even packages sent from Los Angeles to San Francisco have a stop in Memphis in between.

Both speed and accuracy are of paramount importance in this sorting process. Timing is critical. A slow sort in Memphis leads to costly delays, late shipments, and irate customers; a quick sort means cost efficiency, timely deliveries, and happy customers. The problem was, How do you motivate employees to quickly accomplish this vital function? When paid on an hourly basis, costly delays were a recurring management nightmare. Problems continued until someone came up with the idea of paying teams of employees by the job performed and not according to the number of hours taken in accomplishing it. Whenever the sort was completed, all employees were done and could go home. Until the sort was completed, the job was not finished, and nobody could go home. Not only were individual employees motivated to complete their tasks as quickly and efficiently as possible, but monitoring employee performance also became less of a management headache and more of a team responsibility. Costly delay became a thing of the past, and FedEx's business boomed as it gained a well-deserved reputation for efficient and timely deliveries. In a similar fashion, efficient mail delivery and garbage collection services can be provided when employees are paid for completing service along specific routes ("task completion") rather than by more conventional hourly compensation.

FedEx Corp. accomplished three important objectives when it revised its employee compensation methods at its Memphis distribution center. First, by switching from hourly compensation to a task completion compensation scheme, FedEx is better able to align employee incentives with managerial objectives for timely and accurate service. This greatly reduces management's need for monitoring. Second, by tying compensation to output generated rather than input hours, FedEx empowers front-line employees to design the method of task completion to suit worker needs preferences. By allocating important decision rights to front-line employees, these workers are better able to serve customers by quickly responding to unpredictable problems tied to weather, scheduling snafus, and so on. Finally, by empowering front-line workers, FedEx is able to attract and retain workers who seek jobs that demand and reward individual initiative.

Individual Pay for Performance

Many compensation plans fail to achieve desired ends because they focus on input-oriented measures rather than output-oriented criteria. In the case of FedEx, a hourly compensation plan not only failed to provide incentives for timely and accurate sorting of parcels and packages, but it actually rewarded employees if scheduling holdups resulted in delayed deliveries. In the regulation of public utilities, where utilities are typically promised a "fair" rate of return on necessary investment, charges of excessive investment and "gold-plated" service are often heard. Similarly, Department of Defense procurement policies that promise government contractors a price equal to cost plus a fixed profit percentage have led to significant cost overruns. In these and other cases, the obvious challenge is to base compensation on measures of productivity that are output oriented.

pay for performance
Compensation according to measurable indicators of productivity

Pay for performance simply means to adjust the level of compensation according to measurable indicators of worker productivity. When each worker is paid according to his or her marginal revenue product, the level of compensation is tied directly to the amount of economic value derived from employment. The economic value derived from employment is said to originate from two distinct sources. Productivity that stems from the worker's natural dexterity, intelligence, or general education is derived from the worker's **general human capital**, where human capital is the capitalized value of future productivity derived from worker skills. General human capital can be applied in a wide variety of work settings. Therefore, workers need not depend upon the availability of any specific job opportunity in order to earn a return on general human capital. General human capital can be contrasted with **specific human capital**, which is any special aptitude, education, or skill that gives rise to added productivity in a unique work setting. To realize the full benefits of specific human capital, workers must have access to specific job opportunities where such skills can be best applied.

general human capital
Capitalized value of future productivity derived from worker skills

specific human capital
Value derived from any special aptitude, education, or skill

Workers that seek jobs outside the firm are able to command a general labor market wage that offers a fair risk-adjusted rate of return on general human capital. Because the marginal revenue product derived from employment fairly reflects the beneficial effects of general human capital, the outside labor market will offer workers job opportunities that provide compensation that fairly reflects general human capital. The wage rate that could be obtained in any worker's next-best employment opportunity, sometimes called the **reservation wage** rate, is the opportunity cost of continuing to work for the worker's current employer. To attract valued employees, the wage rate inside the firm must at least equal the outside labor market opportunity cost, or reservation wage. To retain valued employees, the wage rate inside the firm must at least equal the reservation wage plus some percentage of the value derived from firm-specific human capital. Thus, firms can justify paying more than the price any competing employer would pay, so long as the wage premium offered to retain valued employees is a fair reflection of the added value generated by such employees.

reservation wage
Opportunity cost of continuing to work for the current employer

To illustrate the role of the outside labor market in setting lower bounds for worker compensation, consider the case of municipal police and fire workers in Madison, Wisconsin. Years ago, a controversy arose as to what level of pay would result in a "fair" rate of relative compensation for police and fire workers. Industrial psychologists retained by the city argued persuasively that the level of stress, responsibility, and demands placed upon fire workers were quite comparable with those placed upon law enforcement personnel. As a result, they recommended that comparable rates of pay be set for police and fire personnel. Others in the community contended that demands placed upon the police were far greater than those placed upon fire workers and that the police deserved a significant wage premium. This controversy was resolved in favor of a wage premium for the police when it was pointed out that at similar wages a significant shortage of qualified police recruits was being experienced, while an excessively large number of qualified fire worker applicants had applied for positions. The local labor market was telling the city that the police had the far tougher job and that it had to raise police wages to find sufficient qualified applicants. Conversely, fire workers were overpaid, at least on a relative basis.

At the other end of the wage scale, remember that the typical CEO of a giant U.S. corporation has been with the company 20 to 25 years. It is quite rare to find a successful top executive recruited from outside the firm because successful CEOs typically require a plethora of detailed knowledge about the firm, top employees, competitors, industry regulation, and so on. Louis Gerstner, former CEO of IBM, was recruited from IBM customer American Express and is a prominent exception to this rule. Much more typical is the case of Coca-Cola's former CEO Roberto Goizueta, who spent an entire business career of 45 years learning and exploiting the nuances of the soda business. It is therefore unsurprising that top executives of major U.S. corporations earn total compensation far in excess of what they might reasonably earn in some alternative employment. The typical top executive generates far more value for his or her current employer than in any other outside employment opportunity. Similarly, senior managers and other long-term employees are often able to use a wealth of firm-specific knowledge to the great net benefit of their employers, even after giving full consideration to their above-average compensation.

Divisional Pay for Performance

divisions
Independent subunits with decision-making authority, operating budgets, and performance evaluations

Organizations are often divided into subunits, or **divisions**, with independent decision-making authority, operating budgets, and performance evaluations. As in the case of deciding to empower employees with a team-based operating strategy, a divisional approach stems from the perception that transaction costs can be minimized when a group-based method of production or distribution is adopted. For maximum effectiveness, it is essential that divisional performance evaluation and reward systems be fashioned in a manner that is consistent with the decision authority granted. This is made difficult by the fact that outside monitoring of divisional performance suffers from many of the same informational disadvantages common to all "outsider" evaluations of group performance, plus some unique problems tied to divisional performance evaluations.

Performance evaluation and reward setting is relatively easy when a single individual has complete decision authority for completing a given task. After controlling for the influence of extraneous factors, if any, assessments of individual productivity can be tied directly to output-oriented performance criteria. On the other hand, assessments of the productivity of an entire firm are made on a daily basis in the stock market. For publicly-traded firms, a rise in stock price is consistent with an increase in the present value of future profits; a fall in stock price is compatible with a decline in prospects for future earnings. Because all stockholders share in the value created by a rise in stock prices, it is easy to see why many publicly-traded firms tie an enormous share of top executive and employee compensation to stock-price appreciation. However, although assessments can be quite straightforward in the case of individual and firm-wide performance evaluations, this is seldom the case with divisional performance evaluation. As in the case of any evaluation of group-based performance, monitoring costs are typically much higher in the case of divisional versus individual performance evaluation. Divisional performance evaluation suffers from the additional problem that there are few widely accepted benchmarks for judging divisional performance. There are no divisional stock-price performance measures.

The great variety of division types can also lead to performance evaluation difficulty. Cost centers, given responsibility for the cost-effective production of goods or services, are typically judged according to their ability to minimize costs for a target level of output, or proficiency in maximizing output for a given budget. Like cost centers, revenue centers have only partial responsibility for generating a profit. Marketing efforts organized into revenue centers are frequently given responsibility for maximizing revenues given a certain price or quantity of output. These efforts are consistent with overall profit maximization, provided correct pricing and output decisions are made at the firm level. Although cost centers are an effective means for organizing manufacturing units, other nonrevenue-producing services provided within the firm are typically organized as expense centers. Accounting, capital budgeting, human resources, investor relations, and legal services are all typical examples of expense centers. A proven way for controlling costs in expense centers is to adopt an internal market within the firm for expense-center services. In this approach, operating units are free to decide whether or not they wish to "purchase" services from the firm's own expense centers. Operating units can decide whether or not to employ internal legal services, for example, and will do so when the price-performance trade-off for internal legal services is more attractive than for services provided by outside law firms. Thus, under a "charge-back" system, the level of internally provided services is optimal when internal supply and demand conditions are in exact balance. Finally, some divisions are set up as independent profit centers. As in the case of investment project evaluation, profit centers must be careful to adjust accounting cost figures to allow for a clear assessment of incremental costs and benefits. Profit centers must also be cautious to properly account for goods and services transferred among divisions and to allow for any interdependence between divisional performance measures.

As described in Chapter 15, an increasingly popular method for judging the performance of divisional profit centers is called economic value-added (EVA©) analysis. At the divisional level, EVA© is measured by adjusted accounting earnings minus an appropriate charge for the cost of capital employed by the division. Before deducting capital costs, accounting earnings for the division are modified to account for intangible investments, interdivisional transfers, and any opportunity costs tied to noncash charges. The cost of capital employed by a division must be estimated because it is the corporation, not the division, that is typically responsible for obtaining long-term debt and equity financing. If special financing is obtained to fund division activity, and particularly if division assets are used to secure such financing, then the divisional cost of funds can be readily calculated based on such direct costs. More commonly, the divisional cost of financing must be estimated based upon an interest rate calculated as the firm's weighted average cost of capital. If the firm has a 60 percent/40 percent mix of equity and debt financing, with a 15 percent after-tax cost of equity and 10 percent cost of debt, the weighted-average cost of divisional financing would be 13 percent (= $0.6 \times 15\% + 0.4 \times 10\%$). This assumes, of course, that the risks of capital employed in the division correspond with the level of risk incurred throughout the corporation. If divisional risk exceeds corporate norms, a higher divisional cost of capital would be appropriate. If divisional risk is less than that typical throughout the corporation, a lower divisional cost of capital should be used. In any event, the aim is to charge each division an appropriate amount to encourage a wise use of assets throughout the corporation.

EVA© methodology is important not only because it encourages a prudent use of corporate assets, but it is also an essential part of setting suitable divisional performance standards for pay purposes. Because EVA© measures the value added to the enterprise through superior divisional

FIGURE 16.3

The Goal of Incentive Compensation Is to Match Worker Incentives with Managerial Motives
Pay for performance must reward productive individual and group effort.

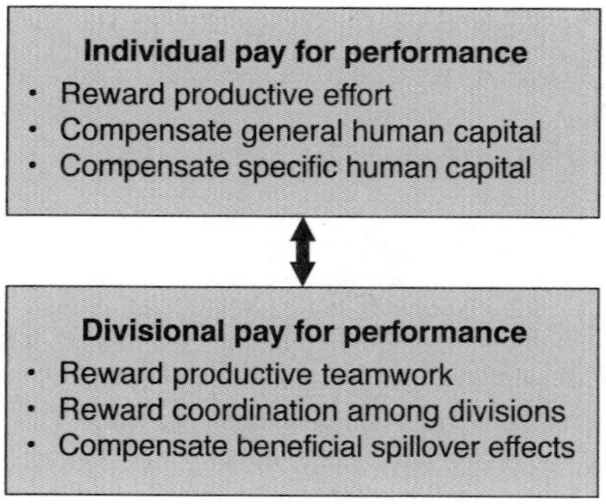

Individual pay for performance
- Reward productive effort
- Compensate general human capital
- Compensate specific human capital

Divisional pay for performance
- Reward productive teamwork
- Reward coordination among divisions
- Compensate beneficial spillover effects

Related Party Transactions

Companies with good corporate governance have able, independent members on the board of directors. To ensure board independence, legislation and generally accepted accounting principles require full disclosure of "related party transactions" between the company on which a board member sits, the board member, and/or entities controlled by the board member. Related party transactions are carefully monitored and reported to shareholders on an annual basis in the proxy statement. Only "arms length" transactions between a board member and the company, where the board member is treated like any other customer, need not be reported.

Company proxies are sometimes laden with disclosures about consulting contracts and business arrangements with "independent" directors. For example, in 2000

- Jerome York, CEO of one of Apple Computer's top customers, was a member of the computer maker's audit committee.

- Thomas Collins was on the audit committee of McLeodUSA even though he was a partner in a law firm that billed the telecom company more than $600,000.
- At Enron, side payments were a way of life. Lord John Wakeham was paid $72,000 for consulting, and John Mendelsohn was president of the University of Texas M.D. Anderson Cancer Center, which received almost $600,000 in donations from the company and its CEO, Kenneth Lay. Wendy Gramm was also director of the Mercatus Center at George Mason University, which received $50,000 in Enron contributions over 5 years.

Investors need to be on the lookout for companies with frequent related party transactions. An abundance of related party transactions often suggests material conflicts of interest.

See: Tom Hamburger, "Enron Lawyer Warned Officials About Partnerships in Late 2000," *The Wall Street Journal Online*, February 6, 2002 (http://online.wsj.com).

performance, it is a useful measure of the exceptional productivity of divisional employees. If the relative contribution of each divisional employee can be assessed independently, individual bonuses can be set to supplement base salaries. If it is difficult or impossible to measure the relative contribution of each employee separately, then superior divisional performance is derived from superior group or team performance, and members should share proportionately in a bonus pool based upon the amount of EVA© generated by the division.

Figure 16.3 shows the necessary link between effective individual and divisional pay for performance plans. In all instances, a suitable divisional pay for performance plan sets bonus payments based upon the relative productivity of individual employees or groups of employees as measured by their contribution to the amount of EVA© generated by the division. It is also important that the share of divisional EVA© paid out in the form of bonuses to divisional employees, versus the amount of divisional EVA© retained by the corporation, represent a valid risk-sharing arrangement with stockholders. If 100 percent of divisional EVA© were paid out in the form of divisional bonuses, stockholders would not benefit from superior performance and receive no compensation for taking on the risk associated with poor relative performance. On the other hand, if none of divisional EVA© is paid out in the form of divisional bonuses, division employees would have little incentive for superior performance. For any divisional pay for performance plan to be both fair and effective, the benefits of superior performance must be shared among the corporation's stockholders and divisional employees in a manner that adequately compensates both stockholders' risk-taking activity and exceptional worker productivity.

CORPORATE GOVERNANCE

corporate governance
Control system that helps corporations effectively manage, administer, and direct economic resources

Corporate governance is the system of controls that helps the corporation effectively manage, administer, and direct economic resources. If any corporation fails to effectively command its economic resources, this corporate failure can often be blamed on a similar failure of its corporate governance mechanisms.

Role Played by Boards of Directors

The most important and closely monitored corporate governance mechanism is the company board of directors. The board of directors is a group of people legally charged with the responsibility for governing a corporation. In a for-profit corporation, it is generally accepted that the board of directors is responsible to stockholders. Some adopt the broader perspective that the board is responsible to "corporate stakeholders"—that is, to everyone who is interested and/ or can be affected by the corporation. Corporate stakeholders include stockholders, customers, employees, the community at large, and so on. In a nonprofit corporation, the board generally reports to stakeholders, particularly the local communities in which the nonprofit serves. Boards of directors provide continuity for the organization by maintaining a legal existence. A primary responsibility is to select, appoint, and review the performance of a chief executive officer responsible for day-to-day decision making and administration of the organization.

Table 16.1 shows five important attributes of effective corporate boards of directors and corresponding limitations of ineffectual corporate boards.

The National Center for Nonprofit Boards, in their booklet *Ten Basic Responsibilities of Nonprofit Boards*, itemize 10 responsibilities for nonprofit boards:

- determine the organization's mission and purpose
- select the executive
- support the executive and review his or her performance

TABLE 16.1

Attributes of Effective and Ineffectual Boards of Directors

Attribute	Effective Board	Ineffectual Board
Integrity	Board members must take pains to ensure that words and actions are in the best long-term interests of large and small shareholders.	Board decisions and management compensation plans are sometimes structured to favor entrenched management at the expense of stockholders.
Competence	Training and business experience of board members must be up to the task of providing value-added oversight to managerial decisions.	Board members with little or no relevant training or business experience are too often encountered. Celebrities are great at cocktail parties, but make poor board members.
Independence	Through words and deeds, it must be clear that the board of directors effectively represents shareholder interests in its oversight of managerial decisions.	Cronies of top management, or cozy consulting arrangements between companies and board members, can compromise if not undermine board member independence.
Accountability	Clear lines of authority and responsibility must be drawn. Both the board and top management must be held accountable for corporate performance.	Some boards are too large by design. When the board of directors has more than a dozen members, it can quickly become impossible to wield effective decision-making power.
Transparency	Actions must be carefully and completely disclosed in timely shareholder reports and SEC filings.	Too many boards of directors allow management to hide subpar corporate performance through misleading corporate communications or endless restructuring.

- ensure effective organizational planning
- ensure adequate resources
- manage resources effectively
- determine and monitor the organization's programs and services
- enhance the organization's public image
- serve as a court of appeal
- assess its own performance

Though intended as a guide to nonprofit institutions, these responsibilities often apply to the boards of directors for profit-seeking corporations as well.

Corporate Governance Mechanisms Inside the Firm

Corporate control mechanisms inside the firm are useful means for helping ameliorate the potential divergence of interests between managers and stockholders. Organization design, including the degree of vertical integration and the horizontal scope of the corporation, are examples of essential corporate governance mechanisms inside the firm. When inputs can be reliably obtained from suppliers operating in perfectly competitive markets, it is seldom attractive to produce such components in-house. Simple market procurement tends to work better. Similarly, when important economies of scale in production are operative, it is preferable to obtain inputs from large specialized suppliers. A high degree of vertical integration only makes sense when input production is within the firm's core competency and supply is erratic or suppliers charge excessive markups. In such instances, vertical integration can result in better coordination of the production process and thereby protect the firm's tangible and intangible investments.

Vertical integration is sometimes seen as a useful means for deterring competitor entry into a company's primary market. Years ago, IBM made a huge strategic error in licensing Intel Corp. to manufacture key components for the personal computer. Intel started out as simply a microprocessor manufacturer supplying the "brains" to manufacturers of personal computers and other "smart" electronics. Today, Intel dominates that business with a market share approaching 90 percent, enjoys sky-high margins and an enviable rate of return on investment. To spur future growth, Intel is now branching out into the production of other PC components like modems, networking equipment, and so on. Soon, the famous trademark "Intel Inside" may have to be replaced with "Intel Inside and Outside." Meanwhile, IBM earns only anemic returns in the PC business. All manufacturers would do well to contemplate IBM's experience with Intel before licensing to others the production of key components.

Another useful means for controlling the flow of corporate resources is provided by internal markets established among divisions to better balance the supply and demand conditions for divisional goods and services. So, too, is incentive compensation perhaps the most obvious corporate governance mechanism inside the firm. In many circumstances, the proper design and implementation of a appropriate incentive pay plan is the most fundamental determinant of whether or not corporate resources will be administered effectively and equitably. Like any effective corporate governance mechanism inside the firm, such arrangements must further the objective of minimizing transaction costs by effectively joining decision authority with the system of performance evaluation and rewards.

Franchise Agreements

A wide variety of monitoring mechanisms outside the firm work together with mechanisms inside the firm to establish an optimal set of restrictions on firm activity. Interestingly, firms themselves often suggest such restrictions. Commercial bank loan covenants, financial audits by independent auditors, and performance scrutiny by independent security analysts are all common examples of outside monitoring mechanisms agreed to by firms.

franchise agreements
Formal contractual arrangement specifying a parent-subsidiary relationship

Franchise agreements are a prime example of voluntary contractual arrangements outside the firm that can be viewed as corporate governance mechanisms. Franchise agreements give local companies the limited right to offer goods or services developed or advertised on a national basis. Franchise agreements are especially popular in instances where personalized customer service is crucial to success and when the performance of local managers is hard to measure over short periods of time.

For example, McDonald's Corp. operates an extensive franchise system of fast-food restaurants throughout the world. Local franchise owners make a credible commitment to the company by paying for the construction of local restaurants and undergoing extensive training at "Hamburger University," as McDonald's likes to call its Oak Brook, Illinois, training facility. In turn, McDonald's makes a credible commitment by awarding local franchisees exclusive rights to market McDonald's food in a given trade area. In this way, McDonald's can be assured that local outlets will be run effectively, and local franchisees have the assurance that McDonald's will continue its aggressive advertising and franchise development programs. Both parties hold viable threats over the other. The valuable right to sell McDonald's food products can be taken away from local franchisees if food quality or store cleanliness falters. Local managers could choose to withhold their support for corporate marketing and pricing policies if they deem that insufficient support has been provided for local markets.

In addition to the fast-food business, franchise agreements are common in the automotive repair business. In automotive repair, performance is hard to measure because shoddy repair service shows up only over long periods of time. The quality assurance offered to repair service customers improves when local managers of auto service outlets have an owner's incentive to stand behind work quality. Similarly, franchise agreements give local managers and owners incentive to develop the economic potential of local markets. Like the local customers of gas and service stations, car buyers benefit from a network of new car dealers who promote and stand behind the quality of products produced by Ford, DaimlerChrysler, GM and other major automobile manufacturers. Without an owner's incentive to build and maintain customer loyalty, the new car business would suffer from many of the same image problems that have dogged the used-car business for decades.

Strategic Alliances

strategic alliances
Formal operating agreements among independent companies

Strategic alliances are formal operating agreements between independent companies that also can be viewed as corporate governance mechanisms. These combinations are increasingly used to improve foreign marketing. Cereal Partners Worldwide, a strategic alliance between General Mills, Inc., and Nestlè, is used to market breakfast cereal products. Snack Food Ventures Europe, a partnership between General Mills and Pepsico, markets snack foods in Belgium, France, Holland, Spain, Portugal, and Greece. Another proposed alliance between British Airways and American Airlines was abandoned after serious antitrust concerns were raised in Britain and the United States because such an arrangement has the potential to allow the companies to squeeze out competition and dominate the lucrative U.S.–London business and tourist travel market.

Cisco Systems, Inc., is one of the most aggressive proponents of corporate strategic alliances. At Cisco, strategic alliances are designed to help deliver a customer-centric, total solutions approach to solving problems. Cisco and its partners have found strategic alliances to be an effective means for exploiting business opportunities and creating sustainable competitive advantages for its customers. For example, IBM Global Services and Cisco Systems have a strategic alliance to drive development of the global Internet economy by combining their mutual strengths in the rapid deployment of networking applications and joint creation and delivery of end-to-end e-business solutions. The IBM–Cisco strategic alliance is helping businesses successfully migrate to an Internet infrastructure and thereby enabling higher levels of customer satisfaction. In another alliance, Hewlett-Packard and Cisco are collaborating to deliver end-to-end, network-enabled solutions that will allow new and joint customers to optimize and reduce the complexity of their networks.

Institutional Investors Are Corporate Activists

Institutional investors have ready access to detailed financial information about corporate performance and are quick to sell underperforming companies. Rising dissatisfaction among institutional shareholders can lead to a rapidly falling stock price or prompt support for an unfriendly takeover bid. As a result, corporate management and boards of directors are responsive to suggestions by institutional shareholders that control a meaningful percentage of company stock. They are also listening carefully to detailed operating and strategic advice from institutional shareholders.

The Council of Institutional Investors announces an annual list of companies it says have significant performance problems. The Council's Focus List highlights 20 companies in Standard & Poor's 500 that most underperform industry averages in 1-year, 3-year, and 5-year total shareholder returns. Separately, the California Public Employees Retirement System (CalPERS) gives companies letter grades on each board's performance in terms of corporate governance issues. As a means of applying pressure on individual members of boards of directors, CalPERS has gone so far as to publish lists naming those persons who have served most often on the boards of underperforming companies. Such pressure tactics appear to work. Shareholder wealth tends to increase for responsive firms that adopt CalPERS suggestions; shareholder wealth decreases for unresponsive firms that reject CalPERS recommendations.

A growing role for institutional investors in corporate governance is a worldwide phenomenon. Institutional investors in Canada show an increased willingness to take on subpar management. In France, institutional investors have recently expressed their ire at bylaw changes that reduce the possibility for unfriendly takeovers. In most Italian companies, there is a major shareholder, or coalition of shareholders, who exercises majority control on the firm and is thus able to choose and remove management. In New Zealand, Australia, and elsewhere, institutions are also becoming much more actively involved in corporate governance issues. All of this speaks well for the growing efficiency of corporate governance.

See: Pui-Wing Tam, "Institutional Investors Slowly Warm Up to the Proposed H-P, Compaq Merger," *The Wall Street Journal Online,* January 31, 2002 (http://online.wsj.com).

Strategic alliances also arise when participating companies enjoy complementary capabilities. For example, Oracle Corp. develops, manufactures, and distributes computer software that helps corporations manage and grow their businesses. Oracle software products can be categorized into two broad areas: systems software and Internet business applications software. Systems software is used to deploy applications on the Internet and corporate intranets. It includes database management software that allows users to create, retrieve, and modify the various types of data stored in a computer system. Internet business applications software allows users to access information or use applications through a simple Internet browser. In a collaborative alliance, Oracle and Cisco, a networking equipment supplier, have agreed to develop network-enhanced database technology and enterprise applications. Oracle and Cisco plan to deliver flexible and secure solutions to maximize customer advantage and satisfaction.

Another longtime proponent of strategic alliances is TRW Inc., a global manufacturing and services company focused on supplying advanced technology. The Cleveland, Ohio–based company uses strategic alliances to acquire technology, create synergy, extend its own manufacturing capabilities, enter new markets, and build existing customer relationships. TRW strategic alliances produce automotive occupant safety systems, chassis systems, electronics, and engine components for spacecraft and space communications, defense systems, telecommunications products, information technology, public safety systems, and other complex integrated systems.

Mandatory Corporate Governance Mechanisms Outside the Firm

Other outside monitoring mechanisms can be mandatory. Such compulsory mechanisms include the wide variety of federal, state, and local laws and regulations that govern corporate behavior. Indeed, the potential exploitation of stockholders, bondholders, and other residual claimants by opportunistic decision agents is often reflected in arguments leading to the establishment of broad regulatory initiatives, such as those stemming from establishment of the SEC.

Calculated or inadvertent violations of federal laws have the potential to impose significant costs on shareholders and other residual claimants. The pursuit of illegal short-term strategies can represent a form of self-dealing by managers who seek to reap short-term personal gain while escaping detection. Actual or suspected violations of federal laws have the potential to result in significant costs measured in terms of investigation expenditures, litigation expenses, fines and seizures, and lost reputational capital for the firm—all of which can measurably reduce future cash flows and current market values. Within this context, federal laws can be seen as part of the institutional framework that contributes to the range of control mechanisms that originate inside and outside the firm to comprise an effective system of corporate governance. Because short-term "hit and run" managers may possess incentives to "cut" legal and ethical corners, the design and administration of federal laws can be seen as a means of outside monitoring designed to ensure a coincidence of managerial incentives, stockholder interests, and broader social objectives.

OWNERSHIP STRUCTURE AS A CORPORATE GOVERNANCE MECHANISM

ownership structure
Divergent claims on the value of the firm

The field of finance has long placed great emphasis on the firm's debt versus equity financing decision. More recently, economists in general have become interested in the corporate governance implications of the **ownership structure** of the firm, or the complex array of divergent claims on the value of the firm.

Dimensions of Ownership Structure

In financial economics, the capital structure of the firm has been traditionally described in terms of the share of total financing obtained from equity investors versus lenders (debt). Today, interest has shifted from capital structure to ownership structure, as measured along a number of important dimensions, including inside equity, institutional equity, widely dispersed outside equity, bank debt, and widely dispersed outside debt. Among these, the percentage of inside equity financing receives the most attention. **Inside equity** is the share of stock closely held by the firm's CEO, other corporate insiders including top managers, and members of the board of directors. Employees are another important source of inside equity financing, perhaps as part of an employee stock ownership plan, or ESOP. The balance of equity financing is obtained from large single-party outside shareholders, mutual funds, insurance companies, pension funds, and the general public.

inside equity
Common stock closely held by management and employees

When the share of insider holdings is "large," a similarly substantial self-interest in the ongoing performance of the firm can be presumed. Managers with a significant ownership interest have an obvious incentive to run the firm in a value-maximizing manner. Similarly, when ownership is concentrated among a small group of large and vocal institutional shareholders, called **institutional equity**, managers often have strong incentives to maximize corporate performance. On the other hand, when the amount of closely held stock held is "small," and equity ownership is instead dispersed among a large number of small individual investors, that top management can sometimes become insulated from the threat of stockholder sanctions following poor operating performance.

institutional equity
Common stock held by mutual funds, pension plans, and other large investors

To get some direct insight on ownership structure among large firms, Table 16.2 shows insider and institutional stock ownership for a sample of large firms included in the Standard & Poor's 500 index. These companies have an average market capitalization of $23.3 billion. The chief executive officer, other members of top management, and members of the board of

TABLE 16.2

Insider and Institutional Stock Ownership Among S&P 500 Firms

Company Name	Industry	Market Capitalization ($ millions)	Insider Holdings (%)	Institutional Holdings (%)
A. High Market Capitalization Companies				
General Electric	Electrical equipment	442,805	1.0	51.0
Microsoft Corp.	Computer software and services	281,947	19.8	41.6
ExxonMobil Corp.	Petroleum (integrated)	281,571	4.0	49.9
Citigroup Inc.	Financial services	274,475	1.0	62.3
Pfizer, Inc.	Drug	266,954	1.0	60.0
Cisco Systems	Computer and peripherals	259,695	1.8	56.1
Wal-Mart Stores	Retail store	230,889	40.0	34.1
Intel Corp.	Semiconductor	222,090	3.7	49.8
American International Group	Financial services	200,296	6.7	57.3
Merck & Co.	Drug	191,840	1.0	54.3
Averages		265,256	8.0	51.6
B. High Inside Ownership Companies				
Nordstrom, Inc.	Retail store	2,478	57.1	38.8
Wal-Mart Stores	Retail store	230,889	40.0	34.1
Franklin Resources	Financial services	9,421	37.5	38.3
Qwest Communications	Telecom. services	75,664	36.9	40.9
Sapient Corp.	Internet	1,971	35.7	47.5
Broadcom Corp.	Telecom. services	16,805	35.0	35.3
Brown-Forman	Beverage (alcoholic)	2,358	32.0	46.5
Allied Waste	Environmental	2,940	31.9	58.6
Loews Corp.	Financial services	9,504	29.7	49.7
King Pharmaceuticals	Drug	6,890	13.8	5.7
Averages		35,892	35.0	39.5
C. High Institutional Ownership Companies				
Lockheed Martin	Aerospace/defense	14,547	1.0	97.7
Ambac Financial Group	Financial services	5,180	3.0	97.0
Calpine Corp.	Electric utility (west)	8,763	3.6	96.4
Federated Dept. Stores	Retail store	7,701	1.0	95.6
Sanmina Corp.	Electronics	11,521	2.5	95.5
Ceridian Corp.	Computer software and services	2,604	1.4	94.2
Bed Bath & Beyond	Retail (special lines)	6,536	6.7	93.3
Mercury Interactive	Computer software and services	5,642	6.7	93.2
Tenet Healthcare	Medical services	14,070	3.9	92.8
ALZA Corp.	Drug	9,231	1.8	92.6
Averages		8,579	3.2	94.8
Averages for S&P 500 companies		23,301	5.9	62.7
Medians for S&P 500 companies		8,209	2.8	63.4

Data source: *The Value Line Investment Survey for Windows,* (http://www.valueline.com).

directors together own an average 5.9 percent of the corporations they lead. Because insiders at the largest U.S. corporations typically own only a small percentage of the companies they lead, the median amount of inside ownership in the S&P 500 is only 2.8 percent. In addition to inside ownership, institutions own an average 62.7 percent of these companies. The median amount of institutional ownership among such firms is 63.4 percent. Inasmuch as insider holdings tend to be relatively large when institutional holdings are relatively small, and vice versa, the percentage of closely held shares, or insider plus institutional holdings, has a mean of 66.2 percent and a median of 67.3 percent. This implies that 32.7 percent of a typical S&P 500 company's common stock is widely dispersed among the general public.

Notice how the share of insider and institutional share ownership tends to vary according to firm size, even among corporate behemoths. Among true corporate giants like GE, Exxon, Citigroup, and Pfizer, for example, insiders own little stock in their employer when insider ownership is measured on a percentage basis. For them, insider ownership is much smaller than institutional ownership. Still, insider holdings of roughly 1 percent at GE, for example, represent an equity commitment of $4.4 billion—more than enough to provide top management with strong incentives to operate efficiently. Thus, even though the percentage of common stock held by insiders is relatively low among corporate giants, the dollar values involved can be more than sufficient to provide necessary incentives for value maximization.

Figure 16.4, panel A, depicts the percentage of insider and institutional holdings for the S&P 500. As illustrated in Figure 16.4, panel A, insider holdings are clearly skewed toward zero. The percentage of institutional holdings is more uniformly distributed.

Is Ownership Structure Endogenous?

Data described in Table 16.2 and in Figure 16.4 reflect the well-established trend toward replacement of small atomistic shareholders by large institutional investors. Because this trend towards institutional share ownership is relatively recent in the United States, the economic advantages it entails may be relatively unappreciated.

Clearly, the probability that outside investors will discover evidence of managerial inefficiency or malfeasance is increased when institutional ownership is substantial. Many institutional investors are forced to liquidate their holdings in the event of dividend omissions or bankruptcy filings. As a result, institutional investors are especially sensitive to such possibilities. Fiduciary responsibility also forces many institutional investors to tender their shares in the event of an above-market tender offer or takeover bid. At the same time, when institutional share ownership is high, the costs of proxy solicitations are reduced. Thus, managers of firms with high institutional ownership are relatively more susceptible to unfriendly takeover bids. Fiduciary responsibility and the dynamics of ownership concentration have the potential to make institutional stockholders especially effective in the managerial monitoring process.

Insider and institutional stock ownership represent alternative forms of ownership concentration that combine to form an effective method for monitoring managerial decisions. Remember, a relatively high concentration of insider plus institutional ownership is descriptive of the modern corporation.

Economists have identified four general forces affecting corporate ownership structure, including

- amenity potential
- regulatory potential
- quality control potential
- ownership control potential

amenity potential
Ownership value derived from the ability to control the type of output produced

Amenity potential is derived from the ability to influence the type of goods produced. Such benefits can be derived from ownership of mass media and professional sports teams, for

FIGURE 16.4

Insider and Institutional Stock Ownership Among Large U.S. Firms

Panel A shows that the percentage of insider holdings, or common stock held by persons associated with the company, is strongly skewed toward zero. In panel B, the percentage of institutional holdings is seen as somewhat more evenly distributed than insider holdings, although moderate skewness toward zero is again evident. When the percentage of insider holdings shares and institutional holdings are added together, as in panel C, the distribution of ownership concentration becomes nearly normal. This suggests a substitute-type relationship between each source of ownership concentration.

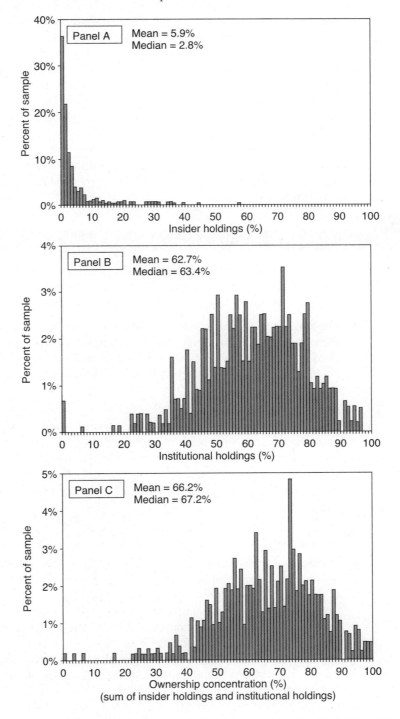

example, and explain why such endeavors tend to be tightly controlled by top management. On the other hand, the diffuse ownership structure of regulated utilities can be explained by extensive rate-of-return regulation, or **regulatory potential**, that limits the capacity of managers to influence firm performance. In the case of firms that produce easily identifiable products subject to economies of scale in production, a relatively diffuse ownership structure can be consistent with shareholder wealth maximization. In the case of firms that produce goods and services with the potential for high quality variation, or **quality control potential**, a more concentrated ownership structure may be required to give shareholders the amount of control necessary to mollify other suppliers and customers. Finally, the **ownership control potential** of the firm is the wealth gain achievable through more effective monitoring of managerial performance. For example, heavy advertisers or high-tech firms that depend on hard-to-monitor advertising or R&D activity for their success may require more concentrated ownership structure than would be true of low-tech firms that produce easily monitored goods and services. When the quality of output is hard to measure and production involves inputs with little collateral value, a high degree of ownership concentration gives outside investors, suppliers, and customers the confidence necessary for quality assurance.

In short, ownership structure appears to vary systematically across firm size classes and among industries in ways that are consistent with value maximization. It thus appears relevant to argue that observed differences in corporate ownership structure are an optimal reflection of economic forces.

regulatory potential
Limitation on ownership value due to government regulation or control

quality control potential
Ownership value derived from the ability to control the quality of output

ownership control potential
Ownership value achieved through more effective monitoring of managerial performance

SUMMARY

Questions of what and how to produce become equally important as organizations strive to better serve demanding customers. As a result, the design and control of effective organizations have become an integral part of managerial economics.

- **Organization structure** is described by the vertical and horizontal relationships among the firm, its customers, and suppliers. A **vertical relation** is a business connection between companies at *different* points along the production-distribution chain; a **horizontal relation** is a business affiliation between companies at the *same* point along the production-distribution chain.

- The efficiency of firms depends upon the ability of participants to find effective means to minimize the **transactions costs** of coordinating productive activity. Search or **information costs** encompass expenses encountered in discovering the type and quality of goods and services demanded by consumers. Bargaining or **decision costs** include expenditures involved with successfully negotiating production agreements. Policing or **enforcement costs** include charges necessary to make sure that all parties live up to their contractual commitments.

- According to the **Coase Theorem**, resource allocation will be efficient so long as transaction costs remain low and property rights can be freely assigned and exchanged.

- The **agency problem** is the natural conflict between owners and managers. **Agency costs** are the explicit and implicit transaction costs necessary to overcome the natural divergence of interest between agent managers and principal stockholders. Significant differences in the risk exposure of managers and stockholders often lead to an **excessive risk-taking problem**. This and other examples of the **"other people's money" problem** arise when decision makers control resources that they do not own. To combat shortsighted operating and investment decisions, the **managerial myopia problem**, most corporations tie a significant portion of total compensation for top management and the **board of directors** to long-term performance. The board of directors is a group of people legally charged with the responsibility for governing a corporation. To guard against the **end-of-game problem**, corporations also set long-term goals for senior managers. The **information asymmetry problem** is tied to management's inherently superior access to information inside the firm.

- The value-maximizing **organization design** minimizes unproductive conflict within the firm. An effective organization design is one that allocates **decision authority** to that person or team best able to perform a given task. With **centralized decision authority**, detailed judgments are handled by top-line executives. With **decentralized decision authority**, front-line employees are empowered to make fundamental judgments concerning how to best serve customers. A **flat organization** has only one or a very few levels of decision-making authority; a **vertical organization** features multiple ascending levels of decision-making authority.

- At its most basic level, the production process encompasses a sequence of related **tasks,** or assignments necessary to effectively meet customer needs. In turn, related tasks are bundled into **jobs,** when such packaging facilitates cost savings and a more productive use of firm resources. The word **team** refers to worker groups given shared responsibility for making and distributing products.

- **Decision management** is the vital process of generating, choosing, and implementing management decisions. **Decision control** is the essential process of assessing how well the decision management process functions. Decisions are made on the basis of **economic expectations**, or a reasonable before-the-fact forecast of monetary implications; judging past decisions involves more than a simple after-the-fact analysis of **economic realizations**, or financial outcomes.

- **Incentive compensation** has the potential to act as a powerful catalyst for a convergence of interests between owners and managers. **Pay for performance** simply means to adjust compensation according to productivity. Productivity that stems from the worker's natural dexterity, intelligence, or general education is derived from the worker's **general human capital**, where human capital is the capitalized value of future productivity derived from worker skills. **Specific human capital** is any special aptitude, education, or skill that gives rise to added productivity in a unique work setting. The wage rate that could be obtained in any worker's next-best employment opportunity, sometimes called the **reservation wage** rate, does not typically reflect the value of firm-specific human capital.

- Organizations are often divided into subunits, or **divisions**, with independent decision-making authority, operating budgets, and performance evaluations. Economic value-added (EVA©) analysis is an increasingly popular method for judging the performance of divisional profit centers.

- **Corporate governance** is the system of controls that helps the corporation effectively manage, administer, and direct economic resources. **Franchise agreements** are a prime example of voluntary contractual arrangements outside the firm that can be viewed as corporate governance mechanisms. **Strategic alliances** are formal operating agreements between independent companies that also can be viewed as corporate governance mechanisms.

- **Ownership structure** is the array of divergent claims on the value of the firm. **Inside equity** is the share of stock closely held by the firm's managers, directors, and employees. When ownership is concentrated among insiders or a small group of large and vocal institutional shareholders, called **institutional equity**, managers often have strong incentives to maximize corporate performance.

- The ownership structure of corporations is sensitive to economic influences like **amenity potential**, or the ability to influence the type of products produced. Such benefits explain why mass media and professional sports teams tend to be tightly controlled by top management. Diffuse ownership structures are common for utilities because their **regulatory potential** limits the capacity of managers to influence firm performance. In the case of firms that produce goods and services with the potential for high quality variation, or **quality control potential**, a more concentrated ownership structure may be required to give shareholders the amount of control necessary to mollify other suppliers and customers. Finally, the **ownership control potential** of the firm is the wealth gain achievable through more effective monitoring of managerial performance.

QUESTIONS

Q16.1 What is the difference between a vertical and a horizontal business relationship?

Q16.2 During the last few years, the desktop computer has evolved from a tool for computation to an Internet-centered communications device. Is this apt to change corporate structures by increasing the efficiency of smaller, more nimble corporations? Discuss.

Q16.3 Cite three important categories of transactions costs encountered within the firm, and give some examples.

Q16.4 What is the Coase Theorem, and why is it important in managerial economics?

Q16.5 In a typical corporation, who are the "principals" and who are the "agents"? What is the firm's agency problem?

Q16.6 Executive stock options are often seen as a simple and effective solution to the "other people's money" problem that can occur when managers with little ownership interest mismanage firm investment opportunities. Can you foresee any advantages and/or potential pitfalls to the use of executive stock options for this purpose?

Q16.7 What are agency costs? Describe some.

Q16.8 Describe three basic needs that must be met in the design of any organization.

Q16.9 Discuss important differences between centralized and decentralized allocations of decision authority within an organization. Are these methods of decision authority allocation mutually exclusive?

Q16.10 Describe four essential components of an effective decision management and control system.

SELF-TEST PROBLEMS AND SOLUTIONS

ST16.1 Agency Problem. In the 1930s, economists Adolf A. Berle and Gardiner C. Means expressed concern that managers with relatively little ownership interest might demonstrate a suboptimal focus on transitory short-term profits rather than durable long-run value. Berle and Means also voiced concern for value-reducing risk avoidance on the part of management-controlled firms.

   A. In general, describe the "agency problem" referred to by Berle and Means. Then, specifically describe how inefficient risk avoidance by top managers could be a problem.

   B. What corporate governance mechanisms are commonly employed to combat the agency problems feared by Berle and Means?

ST16.1 Solution

   A. So-called agency problems stem from the natural conflict that exists between owners and managers. Given their ownership position, stockholders are the principals of the firm. Managers and other employees without any ownership interest can be thought of as hired hands, or agents of the stockholders. An agency problem is present to the extent that unresolved material conflicts exist between the self-seeking goals of (agent) managers and the value maximization goal of (principal) stockholders. Agency costs are the explicit and implicit transaction costs necessary to overcome the natural divergence of interest between agent managers and principal stockholders. Agency costs incurred by stockholders are reflected in expenses for managerial monitoring, the overconsumption of perquisites by managers, lost opportunities due to excessive risk avoidance, and so on.

Managers have incentives for risk avoidance to the extent that spectacular short-run performance creates expectations that are difficult or impossible to satisfy and, therefore, leads to stockholder disappointment and sanctions. Incentives for managerial risk avoidance are also present if stockholder risk aversion leads to an asymmetry of managerial rewards and penalties following short-term "success" versus "failure."

B. Although the potential for such a managerial risk-avoidance problem clearly exists, long-term performance plans are employed on a widespread basis to force a convergence between managerial and stockholder interests. Some of these plans tie executive and employee pay to well-defined accounting performance measures, like the accounting return on equity, or return on assets over extended periods. Others tie managerial rewards to long-term stock performance over, say, 5- to 10-year time intervals. Finally, executive stock option or stock ownership plans are an effective means of tying managerial incentives to the shareholder's preferred value maximization objective.

ST16.2 Ownership Structure. Both General Electric and Microsoft Corp. feature charismatic and highly effective chief executive officers, display enviable records of serving growing markets with remarkable efficiency, and enjoy sterling accounting returns and stock-market valuations. GE and Microsoft are also huge organizations that rank near the top in stock-market valuation among U.S. companies. Interestingly, both feature significant institutional ownership, but are starkly different in terms of the amount of common stock held by insiders. At GE, insider holdings total a mere 1%, about average among industrial giants. At Microsoft, insiders hold an astounding 19.8% of the company.

A. What economic differences in the products produced by GE and Microsoft could be used to explain such stark differences in ownership structure?

B. Legend has it that IBM turned down a chance to buy 50% of Microsoft for $50 million in the early 1980s. Was this a mistake on IBM's part?

ST16.2 Solution

A. GE is a widely diversified manufacturer that produces a extensive variety of products in a broad array of industries. Many of GE's products are well-known by long-satisfied customers and produced at standard production facilities in the United States. GE's operating facilities have good loan collateral value, and the company uses extensive financial leverage. Many outside investors find it easy to assess the financial performance and prospects of GE and have been eager to supply outside equity financing. As a result, it is easy to see why GE has been able to flourish despite having little of its huge capital needs supplied by insiders.

In contrast, Microsoft produces PC software and services that are hard to fathom for most customers, lenders, and outside suppliers of equity. Microsoft uses little in the way of traditional capital resources; most of the capital employed by Microsoft is human capital, not physical plant and equipment. When intangible assets such as patents, copyrights, and trademarks form the preponderance of firm resources, outside investors tend to be reluctant to supply the bulk of firm financing. Without clear loan collateral value, lenders back away from extending significant amounts of credit. Because the value of patents, copyrights, and trademarks is often closely tied to managerial efficiency, outside investors can also be reluctant to supply equity financing. Because Microsoft's success depends upon the efficiency with which its human capital is exploited, both lenders and outside suppliers of equity demand that the company feature a significant amount of inside equity financing so that insiders have a strong incentive to maximize the value of the firm.

B. With 20/20 hindsight, it is easy to say that IBM blew it by not purchasing 50% of Microsoft for $50 million in the early 1980s. After all, with a total market capitalization in excess of $200 billion for Microsoft today, IBM would have achieved an enormous windfall from such an investment. (While we are on the subject, you and I also blew it by not buying MSFT stock when it first became publicly traded in 1982.)

However, it is not appropriate to evaluate this decision with the benefits of 20/20 hindsight. Back in 1980, for example, it was not clear that bringing the graphical user interface of the Apple Computer to IBM-compatible PCs would be such an amazing success story. Before the fact, much of the unrealized value potential of Microsoft was tied up in the dreams and imagination of Bill Gates, Paul Allen, and a cadre of hardworking computer "geeks." If IBM had purchased 50% of Microsoft, would they all have worked as hard to make Microsoft a success? Maybe, but perhaps not. In the case of Microsoft, Coca-Cola, Intel, and other companies with significant intangible assets, investors and lenders require high levels of inside equity financing as a signal of the credible commitment by insiders to maximize the value of the firm.

PROBLEMS

P16.1 **Organization Structure.** Determine whether each of the following statements is true or false. Explain why.

  A. A vertical relation is a business connection between companies at the same point along the production-distribution chain.

  B. A work slowdown due to an unexpected strike by unionized workers is a type of decision cost.

  C. A merger between rival retailers Wal-Mart and Target would be horizontal in nature.

  D. When a corporation files for bankruptcy, it is an admission that the organization was unable to minimize transactions costs.

  E. Because the Internet allows customers to lower information costs, it will have the obvious long-run effect of reducing costs and boosting corporate profits.

P16.2 **Agency Costs.** Indicate whether each of the following transaction costs is explicit or implicit, and describe how it is a manifestation of a particular type of agency problem.

  A. A trader at an investment banking firm loses millions of corporate dollars through unsuccessful rank speculation.

  B. A manager fails to achieve optimum efficiency by letting past-due accounts languish unpaid.

  C. Senior executives decline value-increasing investment projects in order to make cash flow targets during the last year of employment.

  D. Value-increasing product development projects are postponed in order to boost near-term accounting performance.

  E. Executives manipulate accounting data to boost managerial compensation by placing dismal operating performance in a better light.

P16.3 **Ownership Structure.** Describe each of the following factors as being responsible for increasing, decreasing, or having no effect on the amount of concentrated inside equity. Explain why.

  A. High research and development expenditure requirements

  B. A corporate history of poor operating performance

  C. High levels of brand-name recognition

  D. Intense news coverage of corporate activities

  E. Imposition of rate of return regulation

P16.4 **"Other Peoples' Money Problem."** In February, 2002, Congress began a week full of hearings into the collapse of Houston-based energy giant Enron Corp., aiming to discover how to protect against similar disasters. The spectacular implosion of Enron led to the largest corporate bankruptcy in U.S. history, and billions of dollars in losses for investors in the company's debt and equity securities. According to a 217–page report from a panel of Enron's independent directors, Enron's former chief financial officer Andrew Fastow and former chief executive Jeffrey Skilling devised a complex scheme involving limited partnership arrangements that allowed some of the company's top executives to take millions of dollars "they should never have received." The document also revealed that Enron's former chief executive and chairman Kenneth Lay personally approved partnership arrangements that led to enormous liabilities being kept off of Enron's balance sheet, thereby misleading investors as to the company's financial soundness. Enron's collapse was not only scrutinized by more than a dozen Congressional committees, it became the subject of a criminal investigation by the U. S. Department of Justice.

A. Explain how the Enron fiasco can be seen as a manifestation of the "other peoples' money" problem.

B. How could it have been avoided?

P16.5 **Coase Theorem.** According to the Coase Theorem, resource allocation will be efficient so long as transaction costs remain low and property rights can be freely assigned and exchanged.

A. Does the Coase Theorem imply that government has little if any role to play in the market economy? Explain.

B. If the Coase Theorem holds, are efficient and equitable economic outcomes assured? Explain.

P16.6 **Decision Authority.** At the end of World War II, goods production and services provision were each responsible for roughly one-half of economic activity and total employment in the United States. Today, the provision of services is responsible for roughly two-thirds of employment and three-quarters of total employment.

A. Can you explain the decline of centralized decision authority, and the emergence of the "flat" organization style, as a natural result of these trends in aggregate economic activity and employment?

B. Is the emerging use of personal computers as Internet-centered communications devices apt to favor flat organization? Why or why not?

P16.7 **Specific Human Capital.** Ralph S. Larsen is chairman of the board of directors and chief executive officer of top-performing Johnson & Johnson. Larsen was elected to the board of directors in 1987 and appointed to the executive committee in 1986. He assumed his current responsibilities in 1989. He joined the company in 1962 as a manufacturing trainee with Johnson & Johnson Products, Inc., and was named vice president of marketing for the McNeil Consumer Products Company in 1980. He left Johnson & Johnson for 2 years to serve as president of Becton Dickinson's Consumer Products Division and returned to Johnson & Johnson as president of its Chicopee subsidiary in 1983. Larsen was appointed company group chairman in 1986 before being appointed vice chairman of the executive committee and chairman of a sector operating committee later in 1986. Larsen is justly famous for his skill at maintaining the standout performance of this health-care products powerhouse. In his tenure as chairman and CEO of Johnson & Johnson, Larsen has aptly demonstrated a keen intellect, deft leadership skills, and a commanding knowledge of the health-care products business. All have been important contributors to Larsen's and the company's recent success.

A. Use the specific human capital concept to explain why Larsen, like almost all successful CEOs, was promoted from within the ranks of the company itself, rather than hired from some other organization.

B. Assume that much of Larsen's success is in fact due to the careful exploitation of his specific human capital tied to the Johnson & Johnson organization. Would this result in Larsen's marginal revenue product being higher or lower than his reservation wage? Explain.

P16.8 **Information Asymmetry Problem.** Shareholders face a daunting information asymmetry problem when it comes to measuring the performance of the CEO. As head of the corporation, the CEO is in charge of the firm's management information system. Accounting methods always leave room for managerial interpretation, and this flexibility can and has been used to understate expenses and inflate reported earnings. When CEO compensation is tied to various accounting performance targets, it is a bit like asking students to fill out their own final grade report. At a minimum, shareholders should not be surprised when accounting data places firm and managerial performance in a favorable light. More seriously, shareholders must take steps to guard against significant manipulation of accounting standards and/or accounting bias that results in a meaningful distortion of accounting performance.

A. What pitfalls are faced by independent auditors and boards of directors in their efforts to maintain the firm's accounting statements as independent and unbiased indicators of firm and managerial performance?

B. What corporate governance mechanisms might be used to guard against the manipulation of the firm's accounting statements?

P16.9 **Executive Stock Options.** Warren Buffett, chairman and CEO of Berkshire Hathaway, Inc., is an outspoken critic of executive stock-option plans, at least as they are commonly employed. In a typical stock-option plan, top executives are given the right to buy company stock at the current price for a period of up to 10 years in length. Such options have obvious economic value given the 10%+ long-run rate of return on common stocks. Nevertheless, the costs of executive stock-option–based compensation are typically not reflected in the company's income statement.

A. Explain how the failure to include stock-option–based compensation costs in the firm's income statement could lead to a type of information asymmetry problem.

B. How could the potential for such a problem be avoided? In other words, how would you design an effective executive stock-option–based compensation plan?

P16.10 **Institutional Stock Ownership.** During the amazing bull market of the 1990s, an investment strategy of simply mimicking Standard & Poor's 500 Index became popular. The S&P 500 is a value-weighted market index of 500 common stocks thought to measure overall movement in the aggregate stock market. Under this investment strategy, the amount invested in each stock is proportionate to each component's share of the total market valuation of all 500 companies. If the largest component, GE, accounts for roughly 4.1% of the index, and the second largest component, Microsoft, accounts for roughly 2.6%, index followers simply invest 4.1% of their portfolio in GE, 2.6% in Microsoft, and so on.

A. Explain how the stock market's ability to discipline the managers of underperforming firms could be reduced if all investors simply purchased index funds that mimicked the S&P 500.

B. Explain how institutional investors, even those with index funds, actually discipline the managers of underperforming firms in practice.

CASE STUDY

Do Boards of Directors Make Good Corporate Watchdogs?

Is the large publicly traded corporation in eclipse? Some say yes. Harvard financial economist Michael Jensen, for example, argues that the experience of the past 2 decades indicates that corporate internal control systems have failed to deal effectively with economic changes, especially slow growth and the requirement for exit from declining industries. In some parts of the economy, new and smaller organizations are emerging to take the place of giant corporations. Although corporate in form, these agile organizations eschew public shareholders. Their major source of capital is public and private debt rather than publicly traded equity. In analyzing the late 1980s trend toward leveraged buyouts (LBOs), Jensen observed that LBOs

CASE STUDY (continued)

differ from publicly held conglomerates in at least four important respects: management incentives are closely tied to performance, decentralization is common, a heavy reliance on leverage is typical, and obligations to creditors and residual claimants are clearly specified. In suggesting ways for public corporations to "heal" themselves, Jensen advised that public companies should become more like LBOs by decentralizing, borrowing to repurchase stock or pay large dividends, or increasing equity ownership among corporate directors, managers, and other employees.

Of course, given recent experience it is quite valid to express concern with respect to the adaptive capability of some large corporations. Still, pronouncements concerning the "death" of the modern corporation may be premature. The corporate form has endured because it is a useful and effective means for gathering and deploying economic resources. Questions about corporate effectiveness are ultimately questions about what is referred to as "corporate governance." Corporate governance is the system of controls that helps the corporation effectively manage, administer, and direct economic resources.

Problems in corporate governance exist to the extent that unresolved material conflicts endure between the self-seeking goals of (agent) managers and the value maximization goal of (principal) stockholders. "Agency costs" incurred by stockholders are reflected in expenses for managerial monitoring, the overconsumption of perquisites by managers, and lost opportunities due to excessive risk avoidance. Although this agency cost characterization of the corporate governance issue is fairly recent, modern concern with the topic began more than 60 years ago when Berle and Means predicted that managers with little direct ownership interest, and thus having "own" rather than stockholder interests in mind, would come to run the bulk of U.S. business enterprise. Interestingly, economists' concern with this "other people's money" problem dates from 1776 and the work of Adam Smith. One of the most important corporate governance mechanisms is a board of directors that is focused and motivated to further shareholder interests. Within this context, a relevant question is, Do company boards of directors make good corporate watchdogs? Perhaps the best way to answer this question is to look at some evidence.

Hiring the right chief executive officer is widely viewed as a board of director's most difficult task. However, firing a deficient CEO can be even more important because board negligence can leave a company permanently impaired. Dismissing an underperforming CEO is tough because it constitutes an implicit concession that the board failed to hire an executive that was up to the task. Indeed, researchers have found that turnover among directors after the dismissal of a CEO is higher than after a normal CEO succession. Still, faced with rapidly deteriorating corporate performance, boards sometime have no alternative but to seek new leadership.

For example, in July 2000, database software maker Informix Corp. fired CEO Jean-Yves Dexmier, replacing him with board member Peter Gyenes. The change came little more than a week after Informix surprised investors with weaker-than-expected second quarter operating results. A spokeswoman for the Informix board simply reported that the board had met and decided that "a change was in order." Dexmier had only held the job for little more than a year; Gyenes was CEO at Ardent Software Inc., which Informix had bought out earlier. Rick Thoman, who presided over an unsuccessful restructuring at Xerox Corp., was ousted as CEO in May 2000. After a rocky tenure of only 13 months, Thoman was sacked following earnings disappointments and a sharp fall in the company's stock price. Although the Xerox board is to be applauded for moving quickly to stem a growing management crisis, replacing the CEO is seldom easy and never cheap. Thoman received an annual retirement benefit of $800,000, another $375,000 as a prorated 2000 bonus, and $200,000 in lieu of continued life-insurance benefits.

In a poorly concealed and drawn termination process, Lucent Technologies fired CEO Rich McGinn during late October 2000. After three consecutive quarters of earnings warnings, the board of directors decided that it would be best to find a CEO with "a different set of skills." Although Lucent shareholders were justifiably pleased with McGinn's removal, they were gratified to learn that Lucent's management and business model remain sound. At the time of

CASE STUDY (continued)

TABLE 16.3

10 of the Best and 10 of the Worst Boards of Directors

10 Top Boards of Directors		10 of the Worst Boards of Directors	
Company	**Details**	**Company**	**Details**
Campbell Soup	Board ties pay with performance for top management and the board itself	Archer Daniels Midland	Company has the dubious distinction of consistently failing to heed shareholder interests; nepotism and cronyism run rampant here
Cisco Systems	A small and nimble board represents shareholder interests effectively in a rapidly changing industry	Bank of America	Big mergers have created a board that is too big and too unwieldy to effectively look after shareholder interests
General Electric Co.	Board reads like a business hall of fame; both inside and outside directors hold millions of dollars in GE stock	Cendant	Board has been too willing to trust management expertise; lack of oversight led to huge merger snafu
Home Depot	Board members are required to get out and "kick the tires" as they visit the stores	Dillards Department Stores	Dillard family rules the roost and has stood idly by while the fox ravaged the chicken coop
IBM	Blue chip board gets high marks for independence and accountability	Enron Corp.	Board looked the other way while management self-dealing led to largest U.S. bankruptcy
Intel	A business savvy and independent board boosts shareholder interests	Fruit of the Loom	Board stood by while the company slid from prominence to bankruptcy
Johnson & Johnson	Board members are widely recognized for business expertise; company sets the standard for board independence and accountability	General Motors	The board has sat idly by while management focuses on financial engineering rather than on designing high-quality cars that customers like to drive
Lucent Technologies	Strong board has dealt decisively with industry turmoil; nobody here is afraid of making tough decisions	Rite Aid	Lax oversight paved the way for a downward spiral in corporate performance
Merck	Outsiders dominate this action-oriented board	The Walt Disney Co.	Board reads like a who's who of Hollywood celebrities; too bad so few have the business expertise to ensure shareholder-motivated decision making
Texas Instruments	Industry smarts, mandated TI shareholding, and independence make for a shareholder-motivated board	Waste Management	Insider trading questions hampered the company's "roll-up" merger strategy

McGinn's ouster, leading analysts pointed out that Lucent did not have three bad quarters. Rather, it kept having the same bad quarter over and over. The company had simply refused to take its medicine and flush its financial system of bad debts and questionable accounting practices. So long as reported profits and revenues were growing, there was little pressure to reform. However, Lucent's practice of giving generous credit terms to shaky customers was bound to create problems during a downturn in the economy, and it did. McGinn's termina-

CASE STUDY (continued)

tion stemmed from the fact that he failed to effectively manage the company's financial resources and product cycle. Worse yet, presented with an erroneous corporate strategy, McGinn failed to quickly and decisively make it right. Faced with similar problems, the heads of Oracle, Corning, and Nortel did the right thing, and survived a sharp industry downturn. McGinn did not, and got canned.

In many other instances, shareholder-led boardroom revolts have led to dramatically improved performance for trimmed down and refocused corporate giants. After such stunning success in improving management strategy and operating performance, stockholders and stockholder groups have finally gotten the attention they deserve from refocused and energized corporate boards of directors. As shown in Table 16.3, some of the best corporate boards have clearly gotten the message; some of the worst corporate boards still have much to learn.

A. Does incompetence by top management and corporate boards of directors invalidate the value-maximization theory of the firm?

B. Many shareholder groups prefer to split the chairman and CEO posts, and install an outsider as chairman of the board of directors. From the shareholder viewpoint, discuss some of the advantages and disadvantages of an "outside" chairman.

C. Shareholders often want change when corporate performance is poor, top executive pay is excessive, and/or management is unresponsive. However, removing corporate directors by shareholder vote remains almost impossible. In annual proxy contests, shareholders are generally offered only one slate of candidates, and they can express their dissatisfaction only by withholding votes from would-be board members. Does this mean that the current shareholder voting process is an ineffectual means of corporate control? How might this process be improved?

D. In addition to casting their vote in annual proxy contests, shareholders "vote with their feet" when they sell the stock of poorly performing companies. How is this likely to influence inferior performance by top management and the board of directors?

SELECTED REFERENCES

Asiedu, Elizabeth, and Hadi Salehi Esfahani. "Ownership Structure in Foreign Direct Investment Projects." *Review of Economics and Statistics* 83 (November 2001): 647–663.

Athey, Susan, and John Roberts. "Organizational Design: Decision Rights and Incentive Contracts." *American Economic Review* 91 (May 2001): 200–205.

Baker, George P., and Thomas N. Hubbard. "Empirical Strategies in Contract Economics: Information and the Boundary of the Firm." *American Economic Review* 91 (May 2001): 189–194.

Bushman, Robert M., and Abbie J. Smith. "Financial Accounting Information and Corporate Governance." *Journal of Accounting and Economics* 32 (December 2001): 237–333.

Caroli, Eve, and John Van Reenen. "Skill-Biased Organizational Change? Evidence from a Panel of British and French Establishments." *Quarterly Journal of Economics* 116 (November 2001): 1449–1492.

Filatotchev, Igor, Rostislav Kapelyushnikov, Natalya Dyomina, and Sergey Aukutsionek. "The Effects of Ownership Concentration on Investment and Performance in Privatized Firms in Russia." *Managerial & Decision Economics* 22 (September 2001): 299–313.

Grossman, Herschel I. "The Creation of Effective Property Rights." *American Economic Review* 91 (May 2001): 347–352.

Huson, Mark R., Robert Parrino, and Laura T. Starks. "Internal Monitoring Mechanisms and CEO Turnover: A Long-Term Perspective." *Journal of Finance* 56 (December 2001): 2265–2298.

Jenkinson, Tim, and Alexander Ljungqvist. "The Role of Hostile Stakes in German Corporate Governance." *Journal of Corporate Finance* 7 (December 2001): 397–446.

Kaplan, Steven N., and Per Ströömberg. "Venture Capitalists as Principals: Contracting, Screening, and Monitoring." *American Economic Review* 91 (May 2001): 426–430.

Mak, Y. T., and Yuan Li. "Determinants of Corporate Ownership and Board Structure: Evidence from Singapore." *Journal of Corporate Finance* 7 (September 2001): 235–256.

Mullainathan, Sendhil, and David Scharfstein. "Do Firm Boundaries Matter?" *American Economic Review* 91 (May 2001): 195–199.

Rajan, Raghuram G., and Luigi Zingales. "The Influence of the Financial Revolution on the Nature of Firms." *American Economic Review* 91 (May 2001): 206–211.

Whinston, Michael D. "Assessing the Property Rights and Transaction-Cost Theories of Firm Scope." *American Economic Review* 91 (May 2001): 184–188.

Woidtke, Tracie. "Agents Watching Agents? Evidence from Pension Fund Ownership and Firm Value." *Journal of Financial Economics* 63 (January 2002): 99–131.

CHAPTER SEVENTEEN

Public Management

The information age has revolutionized the competitive environment and led to gut-wrenching corporate change. Instant awareness and accountability now demand the same level of dramatic, structural change in government. Rising demands for a balanced federal budget mark a fundamental shift in taxpayer attitudes toward the public management of economic resources. No longer is government seen as the clear and easy solution to all economic and social problems. Instead, it is sometimes viewed as an unnecessary impediment to lower taxes, lower interest rates, and more growth in a freer and more vibrant economy.[1] Like corporate executives who must justify investment decisions to increasingly wary stockholders, public-sector managers often find themselves before restive taxpayers defending basic duties and responsibilities that had long been taken for granted.

This chapter focuses on how national, state, and local governments can pursue wise public policies that have the potential to improve economic performance. Such policies have the capacity to lay a better foundation for economic growth, a healthy environment, and the necessary balance between the private and public sectors. A balanced view is presented that recognizes limitations of public policy without precluding the possibility that well-articulated policy can be immensely helpful. From this perspective, the methodology of managerial economics provides a practical framework for effectively comparing the relative costs and benefits of social programs and public-sector investment decisions. As such, managerial economics can help improve both the efficiency and equity of the public-sector decision-making process.

---

1 See Mary Anastasia O'Grady, "Should U.S. Taxpayers Subsidize More Bad Government in Argentina?" *The Wall Street Journal Online*, February 1, 2002 (http://online.wsj.com).

RATIONALE FOR PUBLIC MANAGEMENT

Managers in the public and not-for-profit sectors must optimize resource use under a variety of operating constraints. When issues of economic efficiency are encountered, the decision tools and criteria discussed throughout managerial economics can be applied across the entire spectrum of the economy. As issues of economic equity or fairness are addressed, economic theory and methodology can be used to understand and improve the public decision-making process.

Public Versus Private Goods

Government regulation and antitrust policy are often used to protect consumers, workers, and the environment; to discourage and regulate monopoly; and to overcome problems posed by externalities such as pollution. Another important function of government is to provide goods and services that cannot be provided and allocated in optimal quantities by the private sector.

> **public good**
> Products or services in which consumption by one individual does not reduce the amount available for others

If the consumption of a product by one individual does not reduce the amount available for others, the product is a **public good**. Once public goods are provided for a single consumer, they become available to all consumers at no additional marginal cost. Classic examples of public goods include national defense and police and fire protection. Over-the-air radio and TV broadcasts are typical examples of public goods provided by the private sector in the United States, even though radio and TV programming is provided by the public sector in many foreign countries. By way of contrast, a **private good** is one where consumption by one individual precludes or limits consumption by others. Food, clothing, and shelter are all private goods because the number of potential consumers of a fixed amount is strictly limited. The distinguishing characteristic of public goods is that they share the attribute of **nonrival consumption**. In the case of public goods, use by certain individuals does not reduce availability for others. For example, when an individual watches a network broadcast of a popular TV program such as *The Simpsons*, this does not interfere with the enjoyment of that same TV program by others. In contrast, if an individual consumes a 12-ounce can of Diet Coke, this same can of soda is not available for others to consume.

> **private good**
> Products or services in which consumption by one individual precludes or limits consumption by others

> **nonrival consumption**
> When use by certain individuals does not reduce availability for others

> **nonexclusion concept**
> When it is impossible or prohibitively expensive to confine the benefits of consumption to paying customers

The concept of nonrival consumption must be distinguished from the **nonexclusion concept**. A good or service is characterized as nonexclusionary if it is impossible or prohibitively expensive to confine the benefits of consumption to paying customers. Although nonrival consumption and nonexclusion often go hand-in-hand, theory defines public goods only in terms of the nonrival consumption concept. Because national defense and network TV broadcasts can be enjoyed equally by more than one consumer at the same point in time, they are both public goods. National defense also exhibits the characteristic of nonexclusion because when it is provided for by taxpayers, nontax-paying citizens cannot be excluded from also enjoying the benefits of a strong national defense. On the other hand, the enjoyment of TV broadcasts can be made exclusive by restricting viewership, as is true with cable TV customers. Public goods that are nonrival in consumption would not be provided in the optimal amount by the private sector.

Because public goods can be enjoyed by more than one consumer at the same point in time, the aggregate or total demand for a public good is determined through the vertical summation of the demand curves of all consuming individuals. As shown in Figure 17.1, D_A is the demand curve of consumer A, and D_B is the demand curve of consumer B for public good Y. If consumers A and B are the only two individuals in the market, the aggregate demand curve for public good Y, D_T is obtained by the vertical summation of D_A and D_B. This contrasts with the market demand curve for any private good, which is determined by the horizontal summation of individual demand curves. Given market supply curve S_Y for public good Y in Figure 17.1, the optimal amount of Y is Q_Y units per time period given by the intersection of D_T and S_Y at point T. At point T, the sum of marginal benefits enjoyed by both consumers equals the marginal social cost of producing Q_Y units of the public good. That is, $P_T = P_A + P_B = MC_Y$.

FIGURE 17.1

Optimal Amount of a Public Good

Aggregate demand curve D_T for public good Y is obtained by the *vertical* summation of individual demand curves D_A and D_B. The reason for this is that each unit of public good Y can be consumed by both individuals at the same time. Given market supply curve S_Y, the optimal amount of Y is Q_Y units per time period (indicated by the intersection of D_T and S_Y). At Q_Y, the sum of the individual's marginal benefits equals the marginal social costs (i.e., $P_T = P_A + P_B = MSC_Y$).

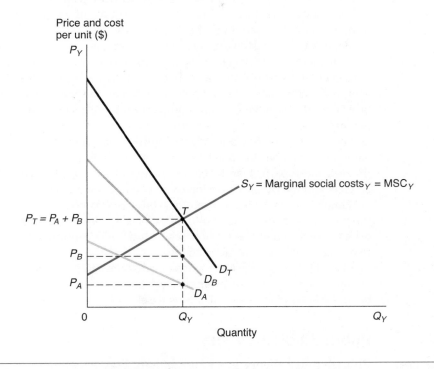

Although the optimal quantity is Q_Y units in Figure 17.1, there are two related reasons why less than this amount is likely to be supplied by the private sector. First, because individuals not paying for public good Y cannot be excluded from consumption, there is a tendency for consumers to avoid payment responsibility. A **free-rider problem** emerges because each consumer believes that the public good will be provided irrespective of his or her contribution toward covering its costs. When several people share the cost of providing public goods, consumers often believe that their individual failure to provide financial support will have no effect on the provision of the good. When many individuals behave this way, however, less than the optimal amount of the public good will be provided. This problem is generally overcome when the government initiates a tax on the general public to pay for the provision of important public goods, like national defense. In the private sector, free-rider problems are sometimes resolved through group consensus to support local zoning covenants, charitable associations, and so on.

free-rider problem
Tendency of consumers to avoid making any contribution toward covering the costs of public goods

A **hidden preferences problem** also emerges in the provision of public goods because individuals have no economic incentive to accurately reveal their true demand. Consumers are reluctant to reveal high demand for public goods because they fear similarly high payment demands. With private goods, the price that consumers are willing to pay provides a credible signal to producers regarding the quantity and quality that should be produced. No such pricing signals are available in the case of public goods and services. As a result, it is difficult to determine the optimal amount that should be provided.

hidden preferences problem
Difficulty of determining true desires for public goods

Of course, many goods and services do not fit neatly within the categories of pure private goods and pure public goods. Examples of goods and services with some but not all of the characteristics of public goods include airports, basic research programs, day-care centers, highways, hospital facilities, immunization programs, the judicial system, parks, primary and secondary education, and trash collection. Given the many difficulties involved with accurately determining the demand for these and other quasi-public goods, it is necessary to be cautious when using the power of government to tax or otherwise compel popular support. Public policy must focus narrowly on the source of any perceived private-market imperfections and address these impediments directly.

For example, trash collection involves elements of a public good because the timely removal of trash and other debris limits the propagation of insects and rodents and, therefore, the spread of infectious diseases. Moreover, there are immense economies of density in trash collection. It is far more efficient for a monopoly trash hauler to service an entire neighborhood on a weekly basis than it is to have multiple competitors serve a single area. In recognition of the potential for problems with unregulated private-market trash collection, some local governments regulate private suppliers while others pay for this service out of general tax revenues. In theory, either approach has the potential to result in better trash collection services. In practice, regulation is seldom perfect, and local governments often find it difficult to maintain a high level of efficiency in the public provision of trash collection services.

Finally, it must be recognized that some goods and services provided by the public and not-for-profit sectors are designed to meet social goals of equity or fairness, rather than efficiency-oriented objectives. These purposes include redistributing income by giving assistance to the poor, sick, and uneducated; stabilizing economic growth; and providing for the national defense. However, efficiency considerations remain important even when these alternative objectives are important concerns of a government-sponsored or regulated program. Government has an obligation to use public funds wisely.

Public Choice Theory

public choice theory
Philosophy of how government decisions are made and implemented

Public choice theory is a philosophy of how government decisions are made and implemented. Public choice theory considers how government and the political process actually work, rather than how they should work. It explicitly recognizes the possibility of **government failure**, or circumstances where public policies reflect narrow private interests, rather than the public interest. Just because unregulated market activity does not always work perfectly does not mean that government policies will improve the situation. It is possible that government intervention will make a bad situation worse. Similarly, the fact that government policies are inefficient does not necessarily mean that private markets can do better. For example, substantial waste in government defense expenditures does not necessarily mean that the provision of national defense should be left to private interests.

government failure
Circumstances in which public policies reflect narrow private interests, rather than the general public interest

Like the capture theory of regulation discussed in Chapter 13, the theory of public choice is based on the premise that individuals attempt to further personal interests in the political arena just as they seek to further private economic interests in the marketplace. Economists have long recognized that when an individual pursues private economic interests in the marketplace, that person is moved by an "invisible hand" to also promote the welfare of society as whole. The study of public choice theory seeks to learn whether such an invisible hand mechanism is also at work in the political system. In other words, when individuals attempt to further personal interests through political activity, is the welfare of society also promoted?

voters
Persons who elect public officials

Public choice theory examines how government decisions are made and implemented by analyzing the behavior of four broad groups of participants in the political system. **Voters** in the political process are the counterpart of consumers in the marketplace. Instead of purchasing goods and services in the marketplace, voters elect government representatives who make and enforce government policies. Other things being equal, voters support candidates who favor policies that further their personal economic interests. According to public choice theory, however, voters are less informed about political decisions than about market decisions due to their **rational ignorance**. Because elected officials act for the community as a whole, there is less of a need for individual voters to be fully informed about public choices. It is also generally more expensive for individuals to gather information about public choices than about market choices. Moreover, as a voter, each individual has relatively little ability to directly influence public choices. For all of these reasons, voters find it sensible to remain relatively uninformed about public policy decisions.

rational ignorance
Tendency to remain relatively uninformed about public policy decisions

Politicians are the political-system counterpart of entrepreneurs and managers in the private market system. Although the entrepreneur or manager of a private firm seeks to maximize the value of the firm, politicians seek to maximize chances for reelection. In doing so, politicians must respond to the desires of well-organized, well-informed, and well-funded special-interest groups. Examples of such interest groups in the United States include associations of primary and secondary school teachers, farmers, medical doctors, and many others. Faced with the rational ignorance of the majority of voters, politicians often support policies that greatly benefit special-interest groups who contribute heavily to reelection campaigns at the expense of the mostly silent and uninformed majority.

politicians
Elected representatives or leaders

Perhaps the most maligned and misunderstood groups participating in the political process are **special-interest groups**. Organized lobbyists actively support the passage of laws and regulations that further narrow economic interests. For example, the National Education Association has successfully blocked the advance of innovative voucher systems of public school financing and maintained a public school monopoly on public financing of primary and secondary education. The American Medical Association has succeeded in limiting admissions to medical schools, thereby reducing the supply of medical doctors and increasing doctors' incomes. Grain and dairy farmers have successfully lobbied the government to provide billions of dollars in subsidies each year, while poultry and pork producers fail to share in such benefits. Restrictions on auto and truck imports from Japan and other countries benefit General Motors and Ford, while consumers pay higher than necessary prices. The success of special-interest groups is explained by the fact that such bodies provide millions of dollars in financial support to politicians who advocate their cause. Although special-interest groups play a valuable role in the democratic process, problems are often obvious. Unfortunately, when large economic benefits for special interests are weighed against individually small but collectively huge social costs, it is the economic interest of special-interest groups that often prevails.

special-interest groups
Organized lobbyists that actively support the passage of laws and regulations that further their own narrow economic interests

Bureaus are government agencies that carry out policies enacted by Congress and other legislative bodies. According to public choice theory, public employees, or **bureaucrats**, are not passive executors of adopted policies; they actively seek to influence policies to further personal interests. They do so by seeking to increase the magnitude and scope of bureau activity and funding. This stems from the fact that the income, power, and prestige of top bureaucrats are directly related to the employment size and growth of the bureau. Bureaucrats can become a separate special-interest group within government.

bureaucrats
Appointed government employees and civil servants

Policy Implications of Public Choice Theory

The characterization of the political process by public choice theorists is sometimes viewed as cynical. Many voters are well informed and unselfish in their political beliefs. Politicians also sometimes refuse to compromise basic principles simply to maximize chances for reelection. Collectively important public interests prevail more often than one might expect; powerful special-interest groups are sometimes defeated. Government bureaucracies are often staffed by well-intentioned and committed public servants. For example, a majority of high-income voters

Global Political Corruption

Nobel Laureate Gary S. Becker, who teaches at the University of Chicago, believes that the best way to reduce undesirable business influence over the political process is to discard regulations that serve as tollgates for graft. In support of this argument, Becker cites major scandals that involve corruption by prominent politicians and businessmen. Despite fundamental differences in political and business systems around the globe, Becker argues that corruption is a common denominator whenever big government infiltrates all facets of economic life.

Bribery and illegal favor-seeking do considerable damage. They always divert resources away from the production of useful goods and services. Such activities also promote policies that distort economic efficiency. Criminals are sometimes able to wrest monopoly prices through bribes and intimidation. Roads are sometimes badly built or diverted to less useful routes to reward builders and landowners with undue influence. Loans from government banks and agencies sometimes go to companies with political clout rather than where they can be invested most fruitfully.

In several countries, politicians caught with their hands in the till have been ousted. Evidence of political corruption has been highlighted by scandals in the Clinton Administration, as well as in several Spanish-speaking and African countries. Public corruption is often seen as rampant in Cameroon, Paraguay, Honduras, Nigeria, and Tanzania. In these and other emerging markets, political corruption is a significant drag on economic growth. By contrast, Denmark, Finland, Sweden, New Zealand, and Canada benefit from having what are widely regarded as the cleanest political systems.

One way to discourage corruption is to vote out crooked politicians and punish people in business who illegally influence the political process. Becker argues that the only way to permanently reduce undesirable business influence over the political process is to simplify and standardize needed regulations. The temptation to bribe public officials is weakened considerably when they lack the power to "bend" the rules.

See: Timothy Mapes and Tom Wright, "Foreign Investors in Indonesia Battle Lawsuits and Corruption," *The Wall Street Journal Online*, April 9, 2002 (http://online.wsj.com).

---

consistently support social welfare programs that involve a redistribution of income to poor people. During the 1990s, large cuts in defense spending occurred despite the best efforts of the military-industrial complex; the tobacco lobby has suffered one defeat after another. The American Medical Association is no longer able to restrict admissions to medical schools; milk and grain price supports are under attack. Even the Civil Aeronautics Board, a large and influential agency of the federal government, proposed its own elimination following airline deregulation and was abolished.

Nevertheless, these contradictions do not invalidate the theory of public choice. Although public policy can improve the economic system in the presence of market failures, the public policy process itself is subject to systematic influences that can lead to government failure. The theory of public choice can be used to suggest institutional changes that can lead to improvements in public-sector performance.

One method that public choice theory suggests for improving public-sector performance is to subject government bureaus and agencies to private-market competition whenever possible. For example, families could be provided with vouchers to finance primary and secondary education at public or private institutions. This would stimulate competition among private and public schools, just like student-specific federal support for higher education stimulates competition among private and public colleges and universities. Still another means for increasing government efficiency is to encourage interagency competition. Although streamlining government eliminates some duplication and waste, it also eliminates competition and incentives for efficient operation. For example, the cost effectiveness of the Department of Defense might actually have declined following the consolidation of the three branches of the armed forces to a single department.

Public choice theory also proposes at least two ways for reducing the leverage of special-interest groups. One is to rely more on referenda to decide important political issues. When important decisions are subject to popular referendum, special-interest groups must focus their energy on influencing the general public rather than on currying favor with important politicians. Another method for reducing the influence of special-interest groups is to specify the total amount of public funds budgeted for the year and encourage different groups to compete for government funding and support. When the total amount of public expenditures is fixed, one group can gain only at the expense of others. Each group is then likely to present its best case for funding while exposing the weakness in competitor funding requests.

BENEFIT-COST ANALYSIS

As the trustees of valuable public resources, public-sector managers must administer economic resources in a responsible manner. This task is made difficult by problems involved with assessing the true level of public demand for government-provided or government-administered goods and services. A variety of nonmarket-based mechanisms have evolved that can be used to effectively administer government programs and investment expenditures. The most prevalent of these methods compares relative costs and benefits.

Benefit-Cost Analysis Theory

Many public programs are promoted on the premise that all citizens will benefit. If investment in a public project makes at least one individual better off and no one worse off, then the project is described as **Pareto satisfactory**, after the noted Italian economist Vilfredo Pareto. When all such projects have been undertaken, the situation is deemed **Pareto optimal**. In practice, most public expenditures increase the welfare of some individuals while reducing the welfare of others. As a result, it is often regarded as too stringent to require that all public works fit the Pareto satisfactory criterion. Instead, it is often required that they meet the criteria of a **potential Pareto improvement**, where there are positive *net* benefits. In other words, a government program or project is deemed attractive under the potential Pareto improvement criterion when beneficiaries could fully compensate losers and still receive positive net benefit.

The potential Pareto improvement criterion provides the rationale for benefit-cost analysis: Public programs and projects are desirable from a social standpoint so long as benefits exceed costs. Whether beneficiaries actually compensate losers is immaterial. The allocation of benefits and costs among various individuals is a separate equity issue. Much like the distribution of tax burdens, the allocation of costs and benefits from public programs and projects is thought to depend upon popular notions of fairness, rather than upon efficiency considerations.

In theory, any public good or service should be supplied up to the amount that equates marginal social costs and marginal social benefits. This principle is similar to the profit-maximizing standard that output should increase to the point where marginal revenue equals marginal cost. For purposes of public-sector analysis, social benefits play the role of revenue and social costs play the role of production expenditures. As in the process of profit maximization, benefit-cost analysis presumes that all relevant pluses and minuses associated with public programs and projects can be measured in present-day dollar terms.

The **marginal social costs** of any good or service equal the marginal cost of production plus any **marginal external costs**, such as pollution (discussed in Chapter 13), that are not directly borne by producers or their customers. Production costs borne by producers and their customers represent private economic costs; external costs include the value of foregone

Pareto satisfactory
If investment in a public project makes at least one individual better off and no one worse off

Pareto optimal
When all Pareto satisfactory programs and investment projects have been undertaken

potential Pareto improvement
When an anticipated program or project involves positive *net* benefits

marginal social costs
Added private and public expenses

marginal external costs
Expenses that are not directly borne by producers or their customers

marginal private
costs
Production expenses
borne by producers
and their customers

marginal social
benefits
Added private and
public advantages

marginal private
benefits
Value enjoyed by those
who directly pay for
any good or service

marginal external
benefits
Value enjoyed by non-
purchasers and not
reflected in market
prices

alternative goods and services. In the absence of marginal external costs, **marginal private costs** and marginal social costs are equal at all levels of output. **Marginal social benefits** are the sum of **marginal private benefits** plus **marginal external benefits**. Marginal private benefits are enjoyed by those who directly pay for any good or service; marginal external benefits are enjoyed by purchasers and nonpurchasers alike and are not reflected in market prices. When no externalities are present, marginal social benefits equal marginal private benefits.

The optimal allocation of social resources is shown in Figure 17.2 where the marginal social cost curve intersects the marginal social benefit curve at Q^*. Marginal social cost and marginal social benefit curves show that for all levels of output greater than Q^*, additional social costs exceed additional social benefits. For output levels less than Q^*, the marginal *net* benefit to society is positive. For output levels greater than Q^*, the marginal *net* benefit to society is negative.

The optimal production of public-sector goods and services follows the same rules as optimal private-sector production. For example, consider the simplified case of two government programs or public-sector investment projects, project X and project Y. Optimal relative amounts of X and Y are made available to consumers so long as the ratio of marginal social benefits equals the ratio of marginal social costs for both projects:

(17.1)

$$\frac{\text{Marginal Social Benefit}_X}{\text{Marginal Social Benefit}_Y} = \frac{\text{Marginal Social Cost}_X}{\text{Marginal Social Cost}_Y}$$

When the ratio of marginal social benefits is equal to the ratio of marginal social costs across all government programs and public-sector investment projects, each respective program

FIGURE 17.2

Maximization of Social Benefits from Government Programs and Public-Sector Investments
Social benefits are maximized from government programs and public-sector investments when the marginal social cost equals marginal social benefits. Output level Q^* maximizes society's net benefits.

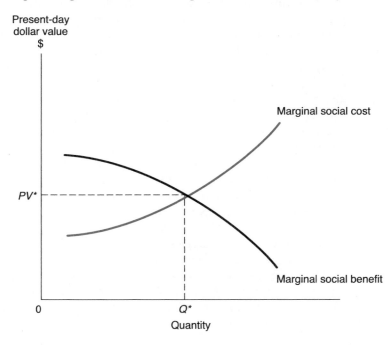

and/or project represents an equally effective use of taxpayer funds in that it results in an identical payoff per dollar of marginal social cost.

Alternatively, optimal relative amounts of *X* and *Y* are made available to consumers so long as the marginal social benefit to marginal social cost ratio is equal for each respective program or public-sector investment project:

(17.2)
$$\frac{\text{Marginal Social Benefit}_X}{\text{Marginal Social Cost}_X} = \frac{\text{Marginal Social Benefit}_Y}{\text{Marginal Social Cost}_Y}$$

Notice that each side of Equation 17.2 shows the dollar amount of marginal social benefit relative to the dollar amount of marginal social cost for each project. When the *MSB/MSC* ratio is equal across all government programs and public-sector investment projects, each respective program and/or project represents an equally effective use of taxpayer funds and results in an identical payoff per dollar of marginal social cost. When the ratio *MSB/MSC* > 1, the value of marginal social benefits exceeds the value of marginal social costs. When the ratio *MSB/MSC* < 1, then the value of marginal social benefits is less than the value of marginal social costs. If the ratio *MSB/MSC* = 1, the value of marginal social benefits exactly equals the value of marginal social costs.

When *MSB/MSC* = 1, a dollar's worth of social benefit is received for each additional dollar spent on government programs and public-investment projects. This relationship implies an important decision rule, assuming that marginal social benefits fall and marginal social costs rise with an increase in the number of government programs and public-sector investment projects. If resources are fully employed throughout the economy, society's net benefit will be maximized when *MSB/MSC* = 1 for the last or *marginal* government program or public-sector investment project. Further net marginal benefits to society are possible through an expansion in the public sector when *MSB/MSC* > 1 for the marginal public-sector project; resources are being squandered in the public sector when *MSB/MSC* < 1 for the marginal public-sector project. Only when *MSB/MSC* = 1 for the marginal public-sector project and private-sector project are resources effectively allocated between the public and private sectors.

Benefit-Cost Analysis Methodology

Benefit-cost analysis is often used when the economic consequences of a project or a policy change are apt to extend beyond 1 year. When compared to the capital budgeting process employed by a private firm, benefit-cost analysis is more complex because it seeks to measure both direct and indirect effects of government programs and public-sector investment projects. Although the activities of both private firms and public agencies produce externalities, private firms do not typically consider external effects because they are not able to charge for them. Because public agencies seek to maximize social benefits, they must measure both direct and indirect benefits and costs.

The guiding principle of benefit-cost analysis is economic efficiency in a global sense. Resources are allocated efficiently when they lead to the maximization of total social benefits. The purpose of benefit-cost analysis is to determine if a given public expenditure would produce greater benefits than if such funds were invested in an alternative public program, or if they were instead left in the private sector. The method has been used to determine whether a public-sector program should be undertaken or expanded and the funding level at which such programs should be supported. Although benefit-cost analysis was first applied in France in the 1840s, it was not until the early part of the twentieth century that it was used extensively in the United States to evaluate river and harbor projects. It has also been applied to projects involving defense, hydroelectric power, water supply availability, recreational facilities, transportation systems, urban renewal projects, educational systems, health, and job creation programs.

All benefit-cost analyses consist of five major elements: (1) statement of objectives, (2) discussion of alternatives, (3) quantification of related costs and benefits, (4) selection of a criterion for acceptable project determination, and (5) specification of an appropriate social discount rate. Benefit-cost analysis objectives must be stated clearly. Objectives should specify a target group, problem, or condition and the nature of the change expected as a result of implementing the program. For example, reducing the nighttime crime rate is not a clear enough objective for effective police department management. A clear objective would be to reduce burglaries by 20 percent and car thefts by 10 percent, following an increase in nighttime patrol hours by 50 percent. The discussion of project alternatives may consist of a choice between one project and no project, or among several public projects differing in purpose, scope, location, and size. If no public project is chosen, the implicit decision is to leave resources in the private sector. A common criticism of benefit-cost analysis is that sophisticated models are applied to poorly chosen alternatives. Because the goal of benefit-cost analysis is the efficient use of social resources, it is necessary to include all realistic alternatives.

Social Rate of Discount

social rate of discount
The interest-rate cost of public funds

Because the benefits and costs of most government programs and public-sector investment projects extend beyond 1 year, it is necessary to convert these benefits and costs into present-day dollars to accurately compare decision alternatives. Determining the appropriate **social rate of discount**, or interest-rate cost of public funds, is critical to the selection of appropriate alternatives. A low rate favors long-term investments with substantial future benefits; a higher rate favors short-term projects with benefits that accrue soon after the initial investment.

A common approach is to discount the benefits and costs associated with public projects based on the government's cost of borrowed funds. Because government loans are considered risk-free, the government's cost of borrowing is much lower than the private cost of borrowing. An important disadvantage of these low public-sector rates is that they fail to recognize the opportunity cost of funds transferred from the private sector to the public sector. Competition between public-sector and private-sector projects for resources is essential to the efficient allocation of investment capital. Most economists argue that because private-sector resources are used to fund public-sector projects, the marginal private-sector opportunity cost of funds of roughly 10 percent is the appropriate social rate of discount. The opportunity cost of funds transferred from private investment to the public sector is computed from the average pretax rate of return on private corporate investments. This rate includes a risk premium for the uncertainty about the returns accruing as a result of allocating funds for a given venture. The pretax rate of return for private investments must be used because returns from public-sector projects are not taxed.

The average pretax rate of return on government securities is a very conservative estimate of the opportunity cost of private-sector consumption that is diverted to public use. This is a conservative basis because the interest rate on government securities does not embody any default risk premium, as would be true of long-term corporate bonds. The average pretax rate of return on private-sector investment is a similarly useful estimate of the opportunity cost of funds diverted from private investment. In both cases, the pretax rate of return is used because personal and corporate income taxes simply represent a redistribution of income from the private to the public sector. Because funds for public investments are likely to come from both private consumption and private investments, the weighted average of the opportunity cost of funds coming from these two components of the private sector should be used to compute the social rate of discount.

During recent years, a typical pretax rate of return on long-term government bonds is 7.5 percent, a standard after-tax return on investment in the private sector is 10 percent, the marginal corporate and individual tax rate is roughly 40 percent, and consumption averages 94 percent of total income. Using the assumptions provided, an appropriate average social rate of discount of 8 percent is calculated as follows:

$$\text{Social rate} \atop \text{of discount} = \begin{pmatrix} \text{Percentage of} \\ \text{funds diverted} \\ \text{from private-sector} \\ \text{consumption} \end{pmatrix} \times \begin{pmatrix} \text{Before-tax} \\ \text{opportunity} \\ \text{cost of} \\ \text{private-sector} \\ \text{consumption} \\ \text{(govt. bond rate)} \end{pmatrix}$$

(17.3)

$$+ \begin{pmatrix} \text{Percentage of} \\ \text{funds diverted} \\ \text{from private-sector} \\ \text{investment} \end{pmatrix} \times \begin{pmatrix} \text{After-tax} \\ \text{opportunity} \\ \text{cost of} \\ \text{private-sector} \\ \dfrac{\text{investment}}{(1 - \text{tax rate})} \end{pmatrix}$$

$$= (94\%) \times (7.5\%) + (6\%) \times \left(\frac{10\%}{(1 - 40\%)} \right)$$

$$= 8\%$$

Social Net Present-Value Analysis

If adequate public funds are available for all decision alternatives, the appropriate decision criterion must rank-order decision alternatives so that net social benefits are maximized. If public funds are inadequate to fund all desirable decision alternatives, the appropriate decision criterion must rank-order decision alternatives so that marginal social benefits are maximized per dollar of marginal social cost.

social net present value
Present-value difference between marginal social benefits and marginal social costs

Under the **social net present-value** (SNPV) criterion, marginal social benefits and marginal social costs are discounted back to the present using an appropriate social discount rate. Individual government programs and public-sector investment projects are acceptable if the present value of marginal social benefits is greater than or equal to the present value of marginal social costs. In other words, public-sector projects are desirable when the *difference* between the present value of direct and indirect benefits and the present value of direct and indirect costs is greater than or equal to zero. Like net present-value analysis in private-sector project evaluation, the social net present-value criterion establishes a rank-order of acceptable projects according to the magnitude of the net present value of resulting benefits. Whereas all projects with $SNPV > 0$ represent a productive use of public-sector resources, the highest-value projects are those with the highest SNPV.

In equation form, the social net present value of an individual government program or public-sector investment project can be written as

(17.4)
$$V_i = \sum_{t=1}^{n} \frac{\text{Marginal Social Benefits}_{it}}{(1 + k_i)^t} - \sum_{t=1}^{n} \frac{\text{Marginal Social Costs}_{it}}{(1 + k_i)^t}$$

where $SNPV_i$ is the social net present value of the ith project, Marginal Social Benefits$_{it}$ represent the expected direct and indirect social benefits of the ith project in the tth year, k_i is the appropriate risk-adjusted social discount rate applicable to the ith public-sector project, and Marginal Social Cost$_i$ is the government program's or public-sector investment project's cost or initial cash outflow.

As with the profitability index method described in Chapter 15, the social net present-value criterion employs an appropriate interest-rate discount factor. In the social net present-value approach, the appropriate interest-rate discount factor is the social rate of discount. This rate is comprised of a risk-free component to compensate taxpayers for the economic cost of waiting, plus a risk premium that reflects the level of uncertainty surrounding the realization of program benefits. In equation form, the social rate of discount factor is

(17.5) $$\text{Social rate of discount } (k_i) = \frac{\text{Risk-free rate}}{\text{of return } (R_F)} + \frac{\text{Risk Premium}}{(R_p)}$$

To illustrate the SNPV method, consider the data contained in Table 17.1 for three hypothetical 20-year government programs. Dollar values of marginal social benefits are shown for each year over the projected 20-year life of each program. For simplicity, assume that these values are net of all ongoing costs for program administration; they can be thought of as net marginal social benefits per year. The present values of marginal social costs for each program are comprised of the initial cash outlay required. Notice that program A and program C have an identical investment requirement of $5 million, whereas program B has a somewhat smaller initial outlay of $3 million. Marginal social benefits in nominal terms, or before discounting, total $8.65 million for program A, $10 million for program B, and $24 million for program C. Marginal social benefits

TABLE 17.1

Hypothetical Benefit-Cost Ratio Analysis for Three Government Programs

	Years	\multicolumn{3}{c}{Annual Dollar Value of Marginal Social Benefit}
		A	B	C
		($5,000,000)	($3,000,000)	($5,000,000)
	1	575,000	500,000	250,000
	2	560,000	500,000	350,000
	3	545,000	500,000	450,000
	4	530,000	500,000	550,000
	5	515,000	500,000	650,000
	6	500,000	500,000	750,000
	7	485,000	500,000	850,000
	8	470,000	500,000	950,000
	9	455,000	500,000	1,050,000
	10	440,000	500,000	1,150,000
	11	425,000	500,000	1,250,000
	12	410,000	500,000	1,350,000
	13	395,000	500,000	1,450,000
	14	380,000	500,000	1,550,000
	15	365,000	500,000	1,650,000
	16	350,000	500,000	1,750,000
	17	335,000	500,000	1,850,000
	18	320,000	500,000	1,950,000
	19	305,000	500,000	2,050,000
	20	290,000	500,000	2,150,000
Marginal social benefits (in nominal terms)		$8,650,000	$10,000,000	$24,000,000
Present value of marginal social cost (PV of MSC)		$5,000,000	$3,000,000	$5,000,000
Social rate of discount (interest rate)		8%	10%	12%
Present value of marginal social benefits (PV of MSB)		$4,609,087.90	$4,256,781.86	$6,364,117.84
Social net present value (= PV of MSB – PV of MSC)		($390,912.10)	$1,256,781.86	$1,364,117.84
Benefit-cost ratio (= (PV of MSB)/(PV of MSC))		0.92	1.42	1.27

before discounting are a misleading measure of the attractiveness of each project because they do not reflect differences in the time frame over which program benefits and costs are generated.

A relevant measure of the attractiveness of each respective program is the social net present value of each program, where each dollar of marginal social benefits and marginal social costs is converted into a common current-dollar basis. The social rate of discount used to convert nominal dollar values into present-value terms is 8 percent for program A, 10 percent for program B, and 12 percent for program C. Each respective social discount rate plays the role of a present-value interest factor that can be used to convert nominal dollar costs and benefits to a common present-value basis. If a 5 percent yield to maturity on short-term Treasury bills is taken as a proxy for the risk-free rate, program A involves a 3 percent risk premium, program B entails a 5 percent risk premium, and program C employs a 7 percent risk premium.

Because social benefits received in the future are worth less than social costs incurred at the beginning of the program, the SNPV for any public program tends to be much less than the nominal dollar amount of social benefits. Using a program-specific social rate of discount, the present value of marginal social benefits is $4,609,087.90 for program A, $4,256,781.86 for program B, and $6,364,117.84 for program C. After considering the present value of marginal social cost for each program, the SNPV for program A is $SNPV_A = -\$390,912.10$, calculated as follows:

$$
\begin{aligned}
SNPV_A &= PV \text{ of } MSB - PV \text{ of } MSC \\
&= \$4,609,087.90 - \$5,000,000 \\
&= -\$390,912.10
\end{aligned}
$$

(17.6)

The $SNPV_A = -\$390,912.10$ means that the present value of marginal social costs for this program exceeds the present value of marginal social benefits. Funding program A would represent an unwise use of public resources. Whenever $SNPV < 0$, program funding is unwise on an economic basis. A judicious use of social resources requires that $SNPV > 0$ for every public program or public investment project.

Again using an appropriate program-specific social rate of discount, the present value of marginal social benefits is $4,256,781.86 for program B and $6,364,117.84 for program C. After considering the present value of marginal social cost for each program, the SNPV for program B is $1,256,781.86 and for program C is $1,364,117.84. Both programs B and C represent a wise use of public resources because $SNPV_B > 0$ and $SNPV_C > 0$. If public funding is sufficient to fund both projects at the same time, both should be underwritten. If public funding is scarce and both programs cannot be funded, program C is preferred to program B since $SNPV_C > SNPV_B$.

As discussed in Chapter 15, large projects tend to be favored through the use of net present-value criterion because large net present values usually require the commitment of significant capital resources. In a similar fashion, the SNPV can result in a bias toward larger projects because a large social net present value typically requires the commitment of significant marginal social costs. This has the potential to result in a bias toward larger as opposed to smaller social programs and public-sector investment projects when the SNPV criterion is employed. To avoid such a bias, it becomes necessary to introduce two additional public-sector capital budgeting decision rules.

benefit-cost (B/C) ratio analysis
Present value of marginal social benefits per dollar of marginal social cost

Benefit-Cost Ratio Analysis

A variant of SNPV analysis that is often used in complex capital budgeting situations is called **benefit-cost (B/C) ratio analysis**. The benefit-cost ratio is calculated as follows:

(17.7)

$$
B/C \text{ ratio}_i = \frac{PV \text{ of } MSB_i}{PV \text{ of } MSC_i} = \frac{\sum_{t=1}^{n} [MSB_{it}/(1 + k_i)^t]}{\sum_{t=1}^{n} [MSC_{it}/(1 + k_i)^t]}
$$

The B/C ratio shows the *relative* attractiveness of any social program or public-sector investment project, or the present value of marginal social benefits per dollar of marginal social cost.

In Table 17.1, $SNPV > 0$ implies a desirable investment program and B/C ratio > 1. For example, the benefit-cost ratio for program B is

$$B/C \text{ ratio} = \frac{PV \text{ of } MSB}{PV \text{ of } MSC}$$

$$= \frac{\$4,256,781.86}{\$3,000,000}$$

$$= 1.42$$

This means that program B returns $1.42 in marginal social benefits for each dollar of marginal social costs, when both figures are expressed in present-value terms. On the other hand, program A returns only 92¢ in marginal social benefits for each dollar of marginal social costs, whereas program C returns $1.27 in marginal social benefits for each dollar of marginal social cost.

In B/C ratio analysis, any social program with B/C ratio > 1 should be accepted; any program with B/C ratio < 1 should be rejected. Programs will be accepted provided that they return more than a dollar of discounted benefits for each dollar of cost. The B/C ratio and SNPV methods always indicate the same accept/reject decisions for independent programs, because B/C ratio > 1 implies $SNPV > 0$ and B/C ratio < 1 implies $SNPV < 0$. However, for alternative programs of unequal size, B/C ratio and SNPV criteria can give different program rankings.

social internal rate of return
Interest or discount rate that equates the present value of the future benefits to the initial cost or outlay

Internal Rate of Return Analysis

The **social internal rate of return** (SIRR) is the interest or discount rate that equates the present value of future receipts to the initial cost or outlay. The equation for calculating the social internal rate of return is simply the SNPV formula set equal to zero:

(17.8)
$$SNPV_i = 0 = \sum_{t=1}^{n} \frac{MSB_{it}}{(1 + k_i^*)^t} - \sum_{t=1}^{n} \frac{MSC_{it}}{(1 + k_i^*)^t}$$

This equation is solved for the discount rate, k_i^*, that produces a zero net present value by setting discounted future marginal social benefits equal to marginal social costs. That discount rate is the social internal rate of return earned by the program, that is, $SIRR_i = k_i^*$.

Because the social net present-value equation is complex, it is difficult to solve for the actual social internal rate of return on an investment without a computer spreadsheet. For this reason, trial and error is sometimes employed. One begins by arbitrarily selecting a social discount rate, such as 10 percent. If it yields a positive SNPV, the social internal rate of return must be greater than the 10 percent interest or discount rate used, and another higher rate is tried. If the chosen rate yields a negative SNPV, the internal rate of return on the program is lower than the 10 percent social discount rate, and the SNPV calculation must be repeated using a lower social discount rate. This process of changing the social discount rate and recalculating the net present value continues until the discounted present value of future marginal social benefits equals the present value of marginal social costs. The interest rate that brings about this equality is the yield, or social internal rate of return on the program.

Using trial and error, an electronic financial calculator, or a spreadsheet software program, the internal rate of return for program A is $SIRR_A = 6.79\%$. Similarly, $SIRR_B = 15.78\%$ and $SIRR_C = 14.81\%$. Because $SIRR_B$ and $SIRR_C$ exceed the cost of capital, program B and program C are attractive and should be undertaken. Because $SIRR_A$ is less than the cost of capital, program A is unattractive and should not be undertaken. In general, social internal rate of return analysis suggests that programs should be accepted when the $SIRR > k$ and rejected when the $SIRR < k$.

Global Competition Policy

One of the most striking economic differences between the United States and Canada and the rest of the world is the extreme lack of competition in many local markets. U.S. and Canadian consumers have a plethora of department stores, specialty outlets, and discount retailers to choose among, while Asian consumers, for example, typically face severely limited shopping alternatives. Whereas U.S. and Canadian shoppers have access to a wide variety of domestic and imported goods and services, Asian consumers typically have only Asian–made products at their disposal. In fact, the typical Asian consumer is completely unaware of how the lack of competition in Asian retail trade restricts purchase options and raises prices. As a result, Asian consumers have never lobbied government trade officials for greater retail competition and for access to large retail stores that offer bargain prices.

Thanks to relentless pressure by foreign trade representatives, government officials in Japan and other countries have moved to free up anticompetitive trade laws. Before recent changes, mom-and-pop retail stores in Japan were able to delay the opening of any large chain or retail store for as long as 10 years. Since trade reforms instituted

in the early 1990s, stores like U.S. retail giant Toys "R" Us are opening at a quicker pace.

Well-designed public policies have the effect of reducing barriers to competition and facilitating economic growth. Among the most important lessons learned during recent years are

- Stable money policies promote low inflation and modest interest rates.

- Low tax rates provide positive incentives for savings, investment, and economic growth.

- Open markets facilitate trade and the growth of both foreign and domestic markets.

Poorly designed policies stifle competition and delay economic betterment. The increasingly competitive global economy has already conferred significant benefits on consumers, but policy initiatives must be designed to maintain that momentum. Competitive markets work best when public policy creates an environment that allows efficient firms to win and lets inefficient firms lose.

See: Michael Williams, "Japan Will Muddle Through...Again," *The Wall Street Journal Online*, January 29, 2002 (http://online.wsj.com).

When the *SIRR* > *k*, the marginal rate of return exceeds the marginal cost of capital. As in the case of programs with an *SNPV* > 0 and *B/C* ratio > 1, the acceptance of all investment programs with *SIRR* > *k* will lead public-sector managers to maximize net social benefits. In instances in which capital is scarce and only a limited number of desirable programs can be undertaken at one point in time, the *SIRR* can be used to derive a rank-ordering of programs from most desirable to least desirable. Like a rank-ordering of all *SNPV* > 0 programs from highest to lowest B/C ratios, a rank-ordering of potential investment programs from highest to lowest SIRRs allows public-sector managers to effectively employ scarce public funds.

Limitations of Benefit-Cost Analysis

Although the benefit-cost analysis is conceptually appealing, it has several limitations that must be considered. Primary among these is the fact that existing measurement techniques are sometimes inadequate for comparing diverse public programs. Without competitive markets for public goods and services, it is difficult to ascertain the social value placed on public programs. How much is it worth to society to provide food stamps and other financial support to poor parents and their children? Is this value reduced when the poor refuse minimum-wage employment opportunities or when government funds are used for unintended purposes (e.g., to buy alcohol, cigarettes, or illegal drugs)? How do you measure the social value of sophisticated new defense weapons, and how do you compare this value to the value of social programs? What is the social value of the agricultural milk-price support program?

Benefit-cost analysis requires public-sector managers to quantify all relevant factors in dollar terms. Where dollar-value estimation is not possible, qualitative factors must still be considered to prevent the omission of important indirect and intangible impacts. However, the inclusion of qualitative factors makes benefit-cost analysis more complex and its conclusions more ambiguous. At times, analytical results cannot be summarized in a single comparable ratio. Evaluation problems also occur when a nonefficiency objective, such as reducing the level of highway noise pollution around a schoolyard, must be considered alongside an efficiency objective, such as increasing business activity along a new highway corridor.

Despite these and other obvious problems, benefit-cost analysis enjoys well-documented success as a vital tool for public-sector decision making. At a minimum, benefit-cost analysis forces the itemization and computation of costs and benefits in a manner that is far more precise and useful than many other methods of public-sector decision making. As a result, benefit-cost analysis allows for a more thorough analysis of public policy alternatives than other more limited techniques.

 ## ADDITIONAL METHODS FOR IMPROVING PUBLIC MANAGEMENT

Whereas benefit-cost studies attempt to measure all relevant factors in dollar terms, measurement problems sometimes preclude this possibility. In such situations, alternative means for assessing the effectiveness of decision alternatives must be explored. The most popular of such methods allow public-sector managers to focus attention on narrowly monitoring the results of existing programs.

Cost-Effectiveness Analysis

cost-effectiveness analysis
Method used to determine how to best employ resources in a given social program or public-sector investment project

Another technique commonly used to improve public-sector performance is **cost-effectiveness analysis**. The purpose of cost-effectiveness analysis is to determine how to best employ resources in a given social program or public-sector investment project. One common approach is to hold output or service levels constant and then evaluate cost differences resulting from alternative program strategies. For example, a local school board might be interested in evaluating alternative special education programs and their respective costs. The cost-effectiveness analysis approach might compare mainstreaming, separate classrooms, or itinerant teaching in terms of their effectiveness in meeting important special education goals. The most cost-effective method is the decision alternative that meets specific educational goals at minimum cost.

Cost-effectiveness analysis is useful for evaluating the effectiveness of social programs and public-sector investment projects where output can be identified and measured in qualitative terms but is difficult to express in monetary terms. For example, cost-effectiveness analysis can be used to evaluate the success of alternative transportation programs such as taxis or social service vehicles for the handicapped but cannot be used to determine if providing transportation for the handicapped is worthwhile from a resource allocation standpoint. Cost-effectiveness studies are also useful in situations where significant externalities or other intangibles exist that cannot be easily measured in dollar terms. In such cases, negative impacts of social programs can be dealt with by excluding from consideration all decision alternatives that generate negative impacts beyond a certain level. The selection of a preferred alternative is made on the basis of differences in tangible performance measures.

Privatization

privatization
Transfer of public-sector resources to the private sector

During the 1980s, a **privatization** movement began and accelerated in Europe, the former Soviet Union, and former Eastern Bloc countries. With privatization, public-sector resources are transferred to the private sector in the hope that the profit motive might spur higher product quality, better customer service, and lower costs. The privatization movement gained momentum during the 1990s in response to growing dissatisfaction with the low quality of many government services and increasing dissatisfaction with cost overruns at the federal, state, and local levels of government.

In the United States, the privatization movement has thus far failed to generate the type of enthusiasm seen in many foreign countries. Nevertheless, local municipalities across the United States are increasing the amount of private-sector contracting for snow removal, garbage collection, and transit services. Since the late 1980s, a majority of state and local governments have greatly increased the amount of public goods and services contracted out to private providers. At the federal level, the U.S. Postal Service, now a quasi-private monopoly, has long used private carriers for rural deliveries. Similarly, the Department of Health and Human Services uses private contractors to process Medicare claims. The privatization movement has clearly made dramatic inroads in countries throughout Europe and Latin America, where government control over the economy has traditionally been comprehensive. During the 1990s, European and Latin American governments greatly increased the pace at which previously nationalized companies have been returned to the private sector. Prominent examples include electrical utilities, railroads, telecommunications businesses, and steel companies.

The economic justification for privatization is that cheaper and better goods and services result as the profit motive entices firms to improve quality and cut costs. Public agencies and government employees that face competition from the private sector also display an encouraging tendency to improve performance and operating efficiency. In Chicago, for example, competitive bidding between private contractors and city cleanup and repair crews creates incentives for public employees and public managers to become more effective. In a similar situation, the city of Phoenix Public Works Department won back a number of garbage collection districts previously lost to private bidders after instituting innovations that lowered operating costs below that of private competitors. Several city and county administrators have reported similar cost savings as a result of privatizing public services. In Milwaukee, school vouchers are given to low-income children to select the private school of their choice. Although parental satisfaction with Milwaukee's school voucher program is high, it is too early to tell whether educational quality has risen for both private and public schoolchildren.

Opponents of privatization argue that the transfer of government programs to the private sector does not necessarily lead to smaller government and fewer budget deficits. Profit-seeking firms who become dependent on public financing lobby for an expansion of public-sector spending with as much vigor as public-sector employees. Evaluating the success of private firms in providing public goods is also made difficult by inadequate performance measures and lax performance monitoring. For example, after the federal government relinquished direct control for job training, under the Job Training Partnership Act, measures used to evaluate program quality appeared to show the program was a success. Fully two-thirds of adult trainees found jobs. These performance measures were biased, however, because training contractors boosted their measured performance by only selecting the most promising job applicants. Similarly, in 1963, the federal government gave millions of dollars to private firms to build and staff mental health centers without developing a process to track results. By the 1980s, many of these centers were converted to for-profit status and served only those able to pay, leaving the poor and indigent without adequate mental healthcare.

A final argument against privatization is that the goal of public services is not just to achieve a high level of efficiency but to provide benefits that private markets cannot or do not provide. A private firm may, for example, find it unprofitable to educate unruly children from single-parent homes with little commitment to education. For-profit hospitals may find it prohibitively expensive to offer emergency room care to violent teens from inner-city neighborhoods. As a result, questions of what and how much to privatize must focus on those instances where privatization can work best. Successful privatization also requires specific goals and measurement criteria that clearly define the public interest. Finally, successful privatization efforts depend upon a direct link between the achievement of recognized goals and the compensation of public-sector and private-sector managers.

MACROECONOMIC GROWTH AND STABILIZATION POLICY

Macroeconomic policies shape the environment within which households and businesses make decisions. These policies are also important tools used to pursue the goals of economic growth, full employment, and stable purchasing power for the national currency. Economic growth increases social welfare because it leads to improved living standards. Such progress is fostered by an economic environment that includes fee markets, well-designed and efficient regulation where necessary, and legal protection of property rights.

Business Cycles and Long-Term Economic Performance

business cycle
Fluctuations of output around a long-term trend, or recessions followed by recoveries and expansions

The **business cycle** refers to fluctuations of output around a long-term trend, or recessions followed by recoveries and expansions. However, there is nothing regular about the timing and magnitude of these fluctuations. The relative economic stability of the post–World War II era reflects fewer or less severe economic disturbances. During the 1990s, many leaders from business and the public sector began to speak about a "New Economy" that features rapid economic growth, low unemployment, and moderate inflation (see Figure 17.3). Such virtuous economic performance is undoubtably nourished by the quickening pace of innovation, better worker education and training, and growing capital investment.

stabilization policy
Strategy designed to offset temporary economic disruptions

Superior economic performance has also been helped by the development of **stabilization policy** designed to offset temporary economic disruptions. Stabilization policy is particularly important in light of the fact that the costs of recessions are not shared evenly across the population. For most families, incomes remain roughly the same or continue to grow during a recession; the economic and social costs of recessions fall disproportionately on those who

FIGURE 17.3

High GDP Growth, Coupled with Low Unemployment and Inflation, Made for a Vibrant "New Economy" in the 1990s

The 1990s featured an extraordinary expansion, falling unemployment, and dropping inflation.

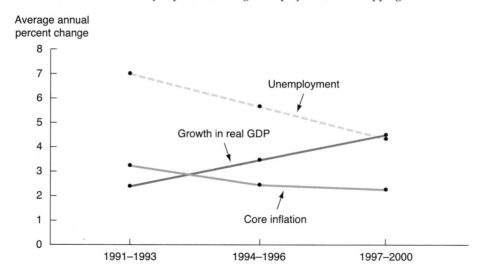

Note: Real GDP growth (chained 1996 dollars) and inflation (measured by the CPI-U-RS) are average annual rates from the end of the preceding year through the end of the period. Unemployment rates are monthly averages. Data for 2000 are through the third quarter for real GDP and through November for unemployment and inflation.

Sources: Department of Commerce (Bureau of Economic Analysis) and Department of Labor (Bureau of Labor Statistics).

experience unemployment. Although carefully chosen stabilization policies cannot eliminate recessions, they have the potential to reduce the frequency and severity of economic downturns. As seen in Figure 17.4, the benign economic environment of the late 1990s featured faster and more equally distributed income growth than was experienced during the previous 20 years.

To understand the limitations of policy, factors that contribute to recessions must be taken into account. A sharp reduction in national defense expenditures, for example, gives rise to structural adjustments in production and employment. Such reductions followed World War II, the Korean, and Vietnam wars and are now taking place in response to the end of the Cold War. Although society as a whole is obviously better off when conflict ends and the resources devoted to national defense can be put to better use, large decreases in military spending disrupt employment as production patterns adjust to meet changing demands. External shocks in the form of large and sudden oil price increases have also been an important factor in several recent recessions. The partial embargo on oil exports by the Organization of Petroleum Exporting Countries in 1973 tripled world oil prices. Because oil is an important input in production, oil price shocks forced many industries to change production methods. Moreover, because the United States is a net oil importer, oil price shocks transfer income and wealth to oil exporting countries and thereby reduce the overall demand for domestic output. It is important to recognize that even if no policy mistakes are made, structural adjustments and external shocks may cause occasional periods of declining output. It is unrealistic to expect that well-chosen public policies can compensate completely for all types of economic disturbances.

FIGURE 17.4

Growth in Real Household Income by Quintile, 1973–1993 and 1993–1999
Growth in household income since 1993 has been stronger and more equally distributed than it was during the previous 20 years.

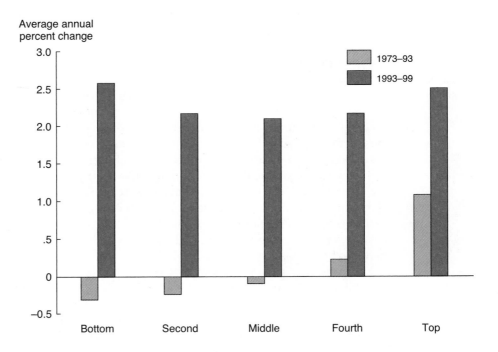

Source: Department of Commerce (Bureau of the Census).

Monetary Policy

monetary policy
Actions taken by the Federal Reserve that influence bank reserves, the money stock, and interest rates

Monetary policy refers to actions taken by the Federal Reserve (the Fed) that influence bank reserves, the money stock, and interest rates. An expansionary monetary policy lowers short-term interest rates by increasing the availability of money and credit. Lower interest rates encourage spending, particularly on investment projects. If the economy is operating well below capacity, increased spending is likely to lead to increased output. Once the economy is at or near capacity, however, rapid monetary expansion leads to inflation (a sustained increase in prices) rather than output growth. Conversely, tight monetary policy reduces the growth rate of the money stock, increases short-term interest rates, and eventually lowers inflation. In the short run, the Fed can use monetary policy to increase the availability of credit and to lower interest rates. In the long run, an excessively expansionary monetary policy leads to inflation and higher nominal interest rates. Although interest rates, monetary aggregates, and other indicators help the Fed assess the effects of its actions, no set of indicators provides a reliable forecast of the future consequences of current monetary policy choices.

The goal of using monetary policy to increase output without increasing inflation is inherently difficult to achieve. When the Fed increases or decreases bank reserves, the path from reserve changes to interest rates to output and prices is often unpredictable. In recent years, a number of factors have further complicated the task of setting monetary policy. The weakening in the relation among the money supply, interest rates, and nominal GDP has decreased the reliability of monetary aggregates as indicators of policy. Transitory problems in financial markets and structural changes in the global economy have also altered the response of the U.S. economy to Fed policy. As such, the use of monetary policy to fine-tune the U.S. economy has become increasingly problematic.

Fiscal Policy

fiscal policy
Spending and taxing policies of the government

Fiscal policy refers to the spending and taxing policies of the federal government. Fiscal policy can influence total demand in the economy by changing taxes and government spending. Expansionary fiscal policy, for example, implements tax cuts, increases government spending, or both, to increase economic activity during business downturns. Fiscal policy can also affect incentives to work, save, invest, and innovate. Changes in taxes on capital, for example, affect the after-tax return on investment in physical assets and thus the incentive for capital accumulation.

automatic stabilizers
Buffers designed to smooth the pace of economic activity

Automatic stabilizers act as buffers when the economy weakens by automatically reducing taxes and increasing government spending. Mandatory spending for programs such as unemployment insurance, food stamps, welfare programs, and Medicaid increases when the economy slows down because benefit criteria depend upon income or employment status. These transfer payments help consumers maintain spending. The tax system as a whole also acts as an automatic stabilizer. In an economic slump, personal income and corporate profits are lower, so tax payments fall, thus helping to reduce the decline in after-tax incomes that might otherwise occur. Government revenues from excise and other sales-based taxes also fall when purchases decline. In fact, taxes typically change by a larger proportion than GDP, primarily because average income tax rates fall with income levels. This feature of the tax system makes after-tax income more stable than pretax income, which helps insulate consumption spending from changes in income.

discretionary policy
Unrestricted changes in spending and taxes

Discretionary policy refers to new changes in spending and taxes. Classic examples of discretionary fiscal policy include the 2001 tax cut intended to stimulate spending and economic expansion, and the income tax surcharge of 1968 designed to curb rising inflation. Because the change in total expenditures determines whether policy has been expansionary or contractionary, it is difficult to attribute expansionary fiscal policy to specific acts of spending. For example, increased highway spending is expansionary only if it is not offset by a decline in some other appropriation. Nevertheless, net changes in discretionary spending by federal, state, and local governments can have significant effects on the overall economy.

Discretionary fiscal policy can also have a dramatic influence on the economy through its effects on the federal deficit. As shown in Figure 17.5, long-term budget balance projections differ widely under various policy assumptions. For example, if discretionary federal spending grows with GDP, projected surpluses will gradually diminish and be eliminated by 2059. Projected surpluses will be eliminated more quickly with tax cuts, like that passed in 2001, or with more rapid spending increases.

Limits of Monetary and Fiscal Policy

Support for activist economic policy was weakened considerably by the historical experience of the 1960s and 1970s. Output grew rapidly in the 1960s, but inflation, as measured by the rate of change in the consumer price index, rose from 0.7 percent during 1961 to 6.20 percent during 1969. In the 1970s, the economy experienced simultaneous increases in inflation and unemployment. This contradicted the idea of a stable trade-off between inflation and unemployment and led to a rethinking of the efficacy of fine-tuning. Given recent failures in fine-tuning the U.S. economy, some have taken the position that there is no predictable benefit to countercyclical policies. This argument is based on the belief that policy changes increase costly uncertainty among private-sector decision makers.

economic expectations
Anticipated financial considerations

To be sure, changes in **economic expectations** place severe limits on the effectiveness of fiscal and monetary stabilization policy. People's actions depend not only on their current situation but also on their expectations for the future. For example, when the government introduces a temporary investment tax credit, businesses have an incentive to shift investment

FIGURE 17.5

Long-Term Budget Balance Projections Differ Widely Under Various Policy Assumptions
Decisions to increase spending or cut taxes can undermine the outlook for continued surpluses.

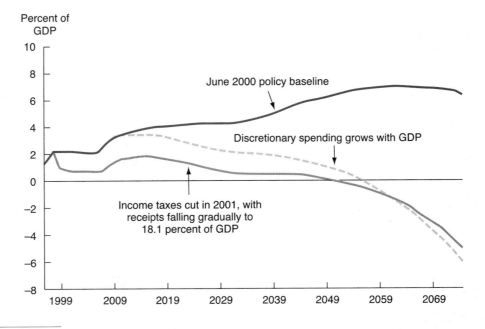

Note: Data are for fiscal years. Projections are based on policy and economic assumptions from the June 2000 Mid-session review updated for actual economic performance through the third quarter of 2000.

Source: Office of Management and Budget.

MANAGERIAL APPLICATION   17.3

Free Trade Helps Everyone

In the early 1990s, backers of the North American Free Trade Agreement (NAFTA) argued that free trade would open Mexico's economy, causing a surge in exports from the United States and Canada. It was also argued that NAFTA would reduce illegal immigration by raising the standard of living for Mexican workers. The case against NAFTA was most forcefully carried by the former head of Electronic Data Systems, ex-presidential candidate Ross Perot. It was Perot's suggestion of "a giant sucking sound" that fueled the debate. That's the sound one would supposedly hear as, in one great whoosh, the United States lost millions of jobs to low-wage Mexicans. Happily, the economic facts are more positive than the political rhetoric.

When NAFTA went into effect on January 1, 1994, the United States and Canada already had a free trade agreement. NAFTA merely extended that agreement to include Mexico and permit duty-free and quota-free movement of goods across all of North America. Perhaps the most glaring irony of the NAFTA debate is that much of the job opportunity loss feared by Perot and other critics failed to materialize. When productivity differences are considered, Mexican labor is no cheaper than higher-priced but more efficient labor from the United States and Canada.

The economic facts are obvious. Free trade is enormously beneficial to all Americans, whether they be from Canada, Mexico, or the United States. Before NAFTA, the tariff imposed by the United States on Mexican goods averaged about 4 percent, while the tariff imposed by Mexico on U.S. goods averaged about 11 percent. With NAFTA, Mexican, U.S., and Canadian export industries and their workers benefit enormously from the increased access across national boundaries that follows from the abolition of all such tariffs. To extend the many benefits of free and open trade, Congress is now considering bills that would extend NAFTA privileges to Caribbean nations. Such a pact would make way for broad trade agreements that might encompass the southern hemisphere and eventually our European and Asian trade partners as well.

With free trade, economic activity flows to where business is most efficient in producing the high-quality goods and services that customers demand. It is a fact that every business day, talented and well-educated U.S. workers compete effectively with low-wage competitors.

See: Damian Milverton, "U.S. Says NAFTA Partners Agree to Accelerate Tariff Cuts," *The Wall Street Journal Online*, January 9, 2002 (http://online.wsj.com).

---

expenditures to the period in which the credit applies. However, if they merely shift capital spending from one period to another rather than increase the overall amount of investment, the positive effect on economic growth will be limited.

Changes in government purchases may also have limited effects on total spending. For example, if an appropriation for the construction of a new highway system is not accompanied by a corresponding increase in tax revenues, the budget deficit and government borrowing will increase. Such an increase in government borrowing can put upward pressure on interest rates and discourage investment spending, thus offsetting at least part of the increase in total demand resulting from the construction project. The reduction in private and consumption investment associated with an increase in government spending is known as the **crowding out** phenomenon. Given the already enormous public-sector budgets of the 1990s, further increases in government spending can create tighter conditions in credit markets and exacerbate the crowding out problem.

crowding out
Reduction in private investment associated with an increase in government spending

ECONOMIC GROWTH POLICY

Americans enjoy a remarkably high average standard of living. Retirees today enjoy roughly three times the level of real personal consumption expenditures typical when they were born. At this same rate of growth, our current standard of living will rise by 50 percent in less than 25 years and double in roughly 40 years. Such is the power of economic growth.

Public and Private Benefits of Growth

Productive investments in institutions, technology, education, and physical capital all contribute to growth. A prime contributor to economic growth has been rising labor productivity made possible by a better trained and better educated workforce.

Figure 17.6 shows that both labor productivity growth and total factor productivity growth was higher in the United States than in other leading developed countries during the late 1990s. Notice the close relationship between labor productivity growth and total factor productivity growth. Clearly, private- and public-sector investments in education and other "human capital" have paid off in terms of economic betterment.

Economic betterment also stems from rising capital investment. Resources for investment are obtained when people save and invest. Growth can be accomplished by encouraging current generations to sacrifice so that future generations may be better off. Conversely, growth can be reduced when the capital stock is run down or when governments borrow from future generations to increase consumption today.

Some argue that because future generations are not represented in the political process, government actions that reduce their well-being are inherently unfair. The national debt, a liability passed on to the future, is sometimes cited as indicative of a government financial policy that is unjust in this sense. Future generations, however, inherit stocks of private and public capital, technology, knowledge, and institutions. Government-sponsored public schools and financial aid to college and university students represent transfers from older to younger generations.

FIGURE 17.6

Recent Global Changes in Labor Productivity and Total Factor Productivity (1990–1995 to 1996–1999)

Productivity growth has been higher in the United States than in other leading countries.

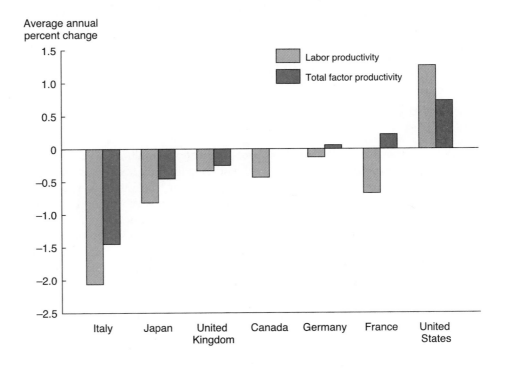

Source: Board of Governors of the Federal Reserve System.

Government-sponsored scientific research also provides benefits to both current and future generations. With a constantly growing stock of productive assets, consumers on average are likely to be better off in the future than they are today. Some argue that given rising income, it is proper for the government to redistribute income from future generations to the current generation, much like any income redistribution from the rich to the poor. Others seek to increase the ability of future generations to raise living standards, as have past generations.

Few people, however, would argue that ever-higher economic growth rates are worthwhile regardless of cost. Even if such increases were desirable, current sacrifice alone does not ensure rapid growth. For example, the former Soviet Union directed massive amounts of resources away from consumption and into investment, but such investments were so poorly managed that this sacrifice went largely unrewarded. The collapse of communism in Eastern Europe and the former Soviet Union is in large part the result of the failure of that economic system to raise living standards.

Economic Growth and the Environment

Properly understood, economic growth means not just "more" but "better." Living standards rise not just because people consume more goods and services, but because the quality of those goods and services improves. This includes the services of a sound environment. As the United States has grown economically, it has also devoted an increasing share of national income to environmental protection.

To ensure economic progress consistent with environmental concerns, some have advocated the concept of "sustainable development." To some, sustainable development means that each generation should pass on to future generations an undiminished stock of natural resources. However, such a definition fails to take into account the fact that a reduction in the stock of one resource can be worthwhile for present and future generations if it generates more valuable increases in another resource. For example, future generations could benefit if part of a forest is harvested to build a school, yet they might be harmed if the school were built with the last remaining ancient forest. A better definition of sustainable development is growth in which every generation passes on a stock of "net resources" no lower in per-capita value than the stock it received. Net resources include natural and environmental resources as well as knowledge, technology, and physical capital.

Limits to Growth?

Some believe that economic growth is severely constrained by finite natural resources. This view traces its roots at least as far back as Thomas Malthus, who wrote in the eighteenth century that the population has a natural tendency to grow faster than food production and hence is constrained by starvation, pestilence, and war. The "limits-to-growth" view, however, neglects the fact that competitive markets adjust to scarcity. When goods, services, or raw materials become scarce, prices rise, and both consumers and producers are motivated to find more efficient ways of obtaining and using them. Rising energy prices encourage conservation; rising land prices encourage improvements in agricultural techniques that increase food output. Contrary to the Malthusian view, world cereal production has actually grown faster than global population for nearly 200 years.

Nevertheless, when markets do not operate well, valuable resources can be consumed too rapidly or be exhausted. Inadequate property rights in water or forest resources, for example, can result in their future value being neglected. In such cases, establishing reliable property rights or, where markets are seriously deficient, establishing appropriate fees or regulations constitute the economically sensible approach.

Public policies designed to enhance the skills and productivity of the labor force are critical to ensuring that the rising living standards made possible by economic growth are spread throughout the economy. Increased funding for Head Start, a program aimed at developing learning skills at an early age; promoting school choice for elementary and secondary education; better access to higher education; and improved job training all have the potential to spur economic growth. Sound policies to protect the environment and manage natural resources can also strengthen the framework for growth. The current income tax system can also be reformed to eliminate aspects that inhibit growth. Among these modifications are cutting the tax rate on savings and entrepreneurship, depreciation reform, and eliminating the double taxation of corporate dividends.

TRADE POLICY

international trade
Voluntary exchange of goods and services across national boundaries

International trade, or the voluntary exchange of goods and services across national boundaries, increases the well-being of all participants by promoting economic efficiency in a variety of ways. International trade allows each country to concentrate on its most productive activities. Trade also gives firms access to the large international market, allowing them to increase output and lower average costs by taking advantage of scale economies. Access to world markets for raw materials, capital goods, and technology also improves productivity. Foreign competition forces domestic monopolies or oligopolies to lower prices, and imported goods provide consumers with greater choice. Finally, a liberal trade environment can provide a better climate for investment and innovation, thus raising the rate of economic growth.

Public Benefits of Free Trade

International trade has grown much faster than world production during recent years. The rapid recent increase in world trade is, in part, the result of the General Agreement on Tariffs and Trade (GATT), which was created after World War II to reduce tariffs and remove other nontariff barriers to international trade. Expanding opportunities for international trade have effects similar to those of technological improvements: For the same amount of input, more output will be produced.

In the United States, expanding world trade has created new employment opportunities in high-wage industries. As shown in Figure 17.7, trade in capital goods industries grew especially fast during the late 1990s. Open trade is also beneficial to developing economies that have less competitive markets and need modern capital goods. By creating new competition, providing domestic producers with access to large international markets, and improving the environment for investment, international trade can make a vital contribution to global economic development.

An important counterpart to an integrated global trade system is a well-functioning international financial system. The international financial system serves several important functions. It provides traders with access to foreign exchange and credit, thereby expanding the scope for commercial transactions. It also allows nations to finance trade imbalances through private capital flows, government borrowing and lending, or changes in reserves. The international financial system also encourages capital to move to countries where it is more productive. Capital inflows can finance domestic investment and thereby enable a country to invest more than it saves. Finally, international finance allows investors to diversify investment portfolios and reduce the risk of loss due to poor economic performance or political upheaval in any single country.

Eurodollar market
Market in which banks outside the United States accept deposits and make loans denominated in dollars

The growth in international finance is the result not only of the increase in international trade but also of improvements in technology, financial innovations, and changes in regulation. As an important example, the removal of external capital restrictions in Europe contributed to the creation in the 1950s and 1960s of **Eurodollar markets**, in which banks outside the United States accept deposits and make loans denominated in dollars. More recently, Eurodollar markets have

FIGURE 17.7

Average Annual Percent Change in Imports and Exports by End-Use Category (1996–2000)

Trade in capital goods has grown especially fast during recent years.

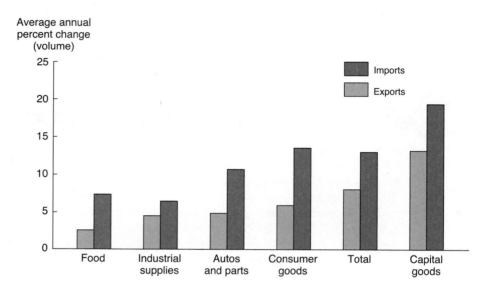

Note: Total includes "other," which is not shown. Estimates for 2000 are based on data for the first three quarters.
Source: Department of Commerce (Bureau of the Census).

Eurocurrency markets
Markets in which bank transactions are denominated in a variety of currencies

developed into **Eurocurrency markets** with transactions in a variety of currencies in addition to dollars and have expanded throughout much of the globe. Both markets play an important role in taking deposits from countries running trade surpluses and lending those funds to nations needing funds to pay for trade deficits.

North American Free Trade Agreement (NAFTA)

In 1992, the United States, Canada, and Mexico reached an agreement to create a free-trade area with more than 360 million consumers and over $6 trillion in annual output. The so-called NAFTA accord will stimulate growth, promote investment in North America, enhance the ability of North American producers to compete, and raise the standard of living of all three countries. NAFTA will also speed technological progress and provide innovating companies with a larger market. Many economic studies show that NAFTA will lead to higher wages, lower prices, and higher economic growth.

NAFTA is an important recent example of the worldwide move to open trade among countries. NAFTA eliminates most barriers to trade among Canada, Mexico, and the United States; opens markets in banking, insurance, and telecommunications; ensures nondiscriminatory treatment for global investors; protects intellectual property rights; and provides dispute settlement mechanisms. Like any free-trade agreement, NAFTA reinforces the market-based economic reforms underway in Mexico. As the Mexican economy grows, it will provide the United States with a valuable and growing market for exports. Benefits derived from NAFTA, and lessons learned in its negotiation, will help in the twenty-first century as the global community struggles to define the relationship between trade and competition policy, a code of conduct for government support of high-technology industries, and the clarification of trade and environmental issues.

MANAGERIAL APPLICATION   17.4

Global Price Controls for Pharmaceutical Drugs

In the United States, Medicare, Medicaid, and state-run health-care cost reimbursement plans funnel federal and state dollars to help share the burden of exploding health-care costs. What is not generally understood is that such programs in the United States and abroad can contribute to higher health-care prices.

Consider the market for pharmaceuticals. If the market for prescription drugs was a typical free market, demand would be limited by the extent to which consumers are willing to pay for innovative therapies. However, if each dollar of consumer demand is matched by federal or state funds, the demand for prescription drugs skyrockets. Suppose a given prescription costs $15, but that 80 percent of this cost is borne by the government. Most consumers focus on the $3 cost that they must pay, rather than the overall cost of $15. As government health-care benefits rise, it is the matching share paid by consumers that constrains industry demand. Rather than cut the cost to consumers of high-priced drugs, government matching schemes allow drug companies and other health-care providers to raise prices. In the United States,

the eruption in prescription drug prices and other health-care costs coincides with the growth of government-sponsored cost-sharing plans. It is perhaps ironic that government-sponsored plans designed to help consumers with sky-high drug prices actually contribute to higher drug prices.

Now, global governments are getting tight-fisted. In the United States, cost containment measures are sure to pinch profit margins for prescription drugs. European governments go one step further and demand stiff discounts from drug prices prevalent in the United States. For example, French price controls set prices at only 42 percent of the U.S. average for prescription drugs. In Japan, allowed prices are based upon a weighted average of prices in other markets. Clearly, global governments are using their buying power to reduce the industry's pricing flexibility. Stay tuned. It looks like price controls might give the industry a headache.

See: Stephen Pollard, "Big Pharmaceuticals Take the Gloves Off," *The Wall Street Journal Online*, December 17, 2001 (http://online.wsj.com).

PUBLIC MANAGEMENT OF HEALTH CARE

Americans are living longer, healthier lives. Since 1960, average life expectancy has increased by more than 5 years. American physicians have access to the best technology in the world, and more than one-half of the world's medical research is funded by private and public sources in the United States. At the same time, the share of national income devoted to health care has been growing rapidly. Concern about rising expenditures and reduced access to insurance has led to the development of a variety of proposals for health-care reform, from market-based managed care to calls for a government-run national health insurance program. Economic analysis is very helpful in understanding the potential of these alternative approaches.

Economics of Health Care

Two features of health-care services have significant economic implications. First, it is difficult for consumers to independently evaluate the quality of health-care services. Consumers typically rely on the advice of service providers in deciding what to buy. Although the lack of independent information is not unique to the health-care market (car owners often rely on mechanics), it can lead to the purchase of poor quality, unnecessary, or high-cost services. Second, to protect consumers from unscrupulous or incompetent providers, licensing boards in every state regulate those who work in the health-care field. Such licensing procedures can increase the cost of health-care services by limiting price and product quality competition.

Physicians have much more information about treating particular illnesses than do patients. Patients often find it difficult to evaluate the efficacy of their treatment. Even if they get better, they may not be able to tell whether they have enjoyed a natural recovery or have benefited from especially effective treatment. Lack of service quality information also makes it difficult for people to make rational decisions about purchasing health-care services. Without an accurate way to measure quality, health-care plans, hospitals, and providers have a difficult time competing on the basis of the price of services they offer. To address this problem, insurers and employers have recently been working together to develop systems for measuring the quality of health-care provided.

In some instances, health-care costs have risen because of restrictive government regulations. Industry costs typically rise when skilled personnel and materials are in short supply. In most cases, short-term shortages cause wages to rise, attracting new supplies of skilled workers. As a result, extreme personnel shortages and the high wages that they produce are not likely to persist. Historically, high physician incomes did not lead to an increased supply of doctors because the medical profession limited the number of new physicians receiving licenses. For many years, professional associations also controlled advertising and the types of fee arrangements that doctors could accept. These problems are less serious today. With new and more enlightened government regulation, the number of practicing doctors and price competition have increased greatly.

moral hazard problem
Changes in incentives that results from the purchase of insurance

A further problem stems from the fact that all medical insurance, whether privately or publicly provided, affects the incentives of the insured. Because they are protected against the full cost of a serious illness or injury, insureds have less incentive to take steps to limit the losses associated with such events. The change in incentives that results from the purchase of insurance is known as the **moral hazard problem**, or the difficulty encountered when the full costs of economic activity are not directly borne by the consumer. This term carries no connotation of dishonesty; it simply refers to the typical reduction in the economic incentive to avoid undesirable events. For example, people insured against car theft may leave their doors unlocked, increasing the chance that their cars may be stolen. Although people with health insurance may be careful about avoiding health risks, they are prone to go to the doctor often and choose complex medical procedures. Among health economists, the term *moral hazard* has come to explain why insurance provides incentives for the overconsumption of health-care services.

Market-Based Health-Care Reform

Uncontrolled increases in health-care expenditures and a growing number of uninsured, especially among the poor (see Figure 17.8), have led to a proliferation of proposals for U.S. health-care reform. Although most of these plans seek to alleviate the symptoms of trouble in the health-care market, relatively few address underlying causes of health-care cost increases and gaps in insurance coverage. Because the health-care sector is flexible and responsive, health reforms that address underlying economic problems and provide sound incentives can be effective. Reforms that ignore the economics of health care are likely to lead to unexpected and undesirable results. Table 17.2 summarizes general features of four well-known proposals for health-care reform.

Among the most promising health-care reform proposals is a market-based reform plan designed to expand access to health insurance and to improve the private markets for health-care services. The market-based plan would provide low-income Americans with a transferable tax credit for purchasing health insurance. Those who do not file tax returns would receive the credit in the form of a transferable health insurance certificate. Because low-income Americans would be able to purchase basic health insurance using tax credits, they would no longer have to rely on the public hospital safety net. At the same time, the fixed-dollar nature of the credit or deduction would discourage overconsumption of health insurance.

The market-based plan would expand health insurance coverage by promoting the use of health insurance networks to act as group purchasing agents for smaller employers, thus obtaining more favorable premiums and reducing administrative costs. The plan would incorporate health risk pools that spread the cost of serious health problems among all those

FIGURE 17.8

Health Insurance Coverage of Those Under Age 65, by Insurance Type and Income, 1999

Higher income people generally receive health insurance through employers. Lower income people tend to receive it through government programs, or not at all.

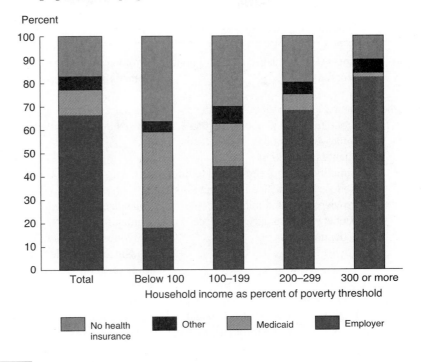

Source: Department of Commerce (Bureau of the Census).

purchasing health insurance. Low- and middle-income people with chronic health problems would have greatly improved access to health care through this combination of tax credits and health risk pools. Under the market-based plan, everyone would not be required to purchase health insurance. Those eligible for only a partial credit or deduction could decide not to purchase health insurance and continue to pay their own expenses or rely on the existing health-care safety net.

In any such market-based system, the role played by health maintenance organizations (HMOs) would continue to grow. During the 1990s, HMOs became a vital part of our health-care system by helping stem the rate of cost inflation. As shown in Figure 17.9, growth in health-care expenditures tends to slow with rising HMO enrollments.

Public Management of Health-Care Reform

In an evolving plan for comprehensive health-care reform, the Clinton Administration proposed an alternative "managed competition" approach. Although managed competition has some market-oriented features, it would greatly increase the role of government in the health-care system and limit the range of health insurance options available. The concept of managed competition is built around the "accountable health partnership," an organization similar to an HMO that would provide both health benefits and consumer information. Each accountable health partnership would be registered with a national health board that would define "uniform effective health benefits" that each partnership would be required to provide. All insurers, both private and public, would be required to offer the same basic benefit plan.

TABLE 17.2

Side-by-Side Comparison of Health-Care Reform Proposals

Issue	Market-Based Proposal	Managed Competition Proposal	Pay-or-Play	National Health Insurance
Moral hazard	Encourages managed care for public programs	Promotes use of basic benefit package	—	—
Cost containment	Increases competition in small group market and public programs Improves availability of health-care quality information Simplifies recordkeeping and billing Reduces malpractice litigation costs	Increases competition in small group markets	Provider and hospital fee schedule	Global budgets Physician and hospital fee schedule
Access to poor	Provides low- and middle-income people with insurance certificate/deduction	Mandates coverage through employers Provides subsidies to low-income people who are not employed and to part-time workers	Requires employers to offer insurance or pay into public plan	Universal coverage
Access for those in ill health	Implements health risk adjusters for high-risk people in individual and small group health insurance markets	Provides age-adjusted community-rated coverage in individual and small group health insurance markets	Covers employed persons in ill health	Universal coverage

Source: *Economic Report of the President*, 1993, p. 155.

The mechanism for cost containment under this plan is competition among accountable health partnerships over the price of a minimum benefit package. Although taxpayers could choose any minimum benefits insurance package offered by any participating accountable health partnership, they would not be able to deduct from taxable income more than the cost of the minimum benefit package offered by the cheapest accountable health partnership. Theoretically, this tax subsidy limit would encourage taxpayers to choose less comprehensive health insurance and efficiently run insurance plans. With managed competition, the government would take an active role in selecting the basic benefit package and in defining the type of insurance that most people would be able to purchase.

Outlook for Health-Care Reform

It is speculative to project that the U.S. health-care system will evolve along the lines of market-based proposals, managed competition plans, or by more traditional "play-or-pay" or national health insurance proposals. Pay-or-play plans require firms to provide basic health insurance to employees and their dependents ("play") or pay a payroll tax to cover enrollment in a public health-care plan ("pay"). Proposals for national health insurance envision replacing the private health insurance market with a single national health insurer. National health insurance would be funded through taxes and care would be free (as in Canada) or provided at a low cost-sharing level.

FIGURE 17.9

Health Expenditures and Enrollment in Health Maintenance Organizations
Growth in health expenditures slowed in the 1990s while HMO enrollments rose.

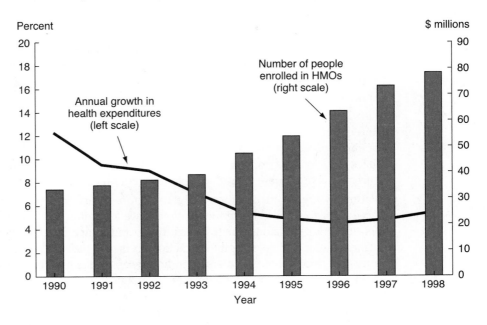

Sources: Department of Health and Human Services (Health Care Financing Administration) and Employee Benefits Research Institute.

Clearly, no plan for health-care reform is without its pluses and minuses, costs and benefits. Although managed competition would encourage rivalry among health insurers providing a basic benefit package, the government would become responsible for defining the benefits that most Americans would receive. On the other hand, play-or-pay proposals would improve access to insurance by mandating employer coverage, but they do not address the problem of rising medical costs and may cause firms to lay off low-wage workers. National health insurance proposals would provide insurance for all Americans but could lead to a cost explosion. Reforms that give consumers, insurers, and providers appropriate incentives are likely to be most effective in controlling costs, improving access, and giving consumers the quality of health care that they want.

SUMMARY

Public and not-for-profit organizations face many of the same problems that challenge companies in the for-profit sector. Competing demands on public funds and not-for-profit organization budgets force responsible managers to consider the marginal social benefits and marginal social costs of each alternative program and investment project. Like managers of companies in the for-profit sector, government officials and managers of not-for-profit organizations must optimize resource use under a variety of operating constraints.

- A traditional rationale for public management of economic resources is the perception of private market failures to efficiently provide and equitably allocate economic goods and services. If the consumption of a product by one individual does not reduce the amount available for others, the product is referred to as a **public good**. A **private good** is one where consumption by one individual precludes or limits consumption by others. The distinguishing characteristic of public goods is the concept of **nonrival consumption**. In the case of public goods, use by certain individuals does not reduce availability for others. A good or service is characterized by the **nonexclusion concept** if it is impossible or prohibitively expensive to confine the benefits of consumption to paying customers.

- A **free-rider problem** often materializes in the case of public goods because each consumer believes that the public good will be provided irrespective of his or her contribution toward covering its costs. A **hidden preferences problem** also emerges in the provision of public goods because individuals have no economic incentive to accurately reveal their true demand for public goods.

- **Public choice theory** is the philosophy of how government decisions are made and implemented. The study of public choice theory considers how government and the political process actually work, rather than how they should work. It explicitly recognizes the possibility of **government failure**, or circumstances where public policies reflect narrow private interests, rather than the general public interest.

- **Voters** in the political process are the counterpart of consumers in the marketplace. According to public choice theory, voters are less informed about political decisions than about market decisions due to their **rational ignorance**. Because elected officials act for the community as a whole, high information costs and each individual's low ability to directly influence public choices, voters often find it sensible to remain relatively uninformed about public policy decisions. **Politicians** are the political system counterpart of entrepreneurs and managers in the private market system. **Special-interest groups** are organized lobbyists that actively support the passage of laws and regulations that further their own narrow economic interests. According to public choice theory, public employees, or **bureaucrats**, are not passive executors of adopted policies; they actively seek to influence these policies to further personal interests.

- If investment in a public project makes at least one individual better off and no one worse off, then the project is described as **Pareto satisfactory**. When all such government programs and investment projects have been undertaken, the situation is deemed to be **Pareto optimal**. In practice, it is often deemed adequate when public programs and projects meet the criteria of a **potential Pareto improvement**, in which there are positive *net* benefits.

- The **marginal social costs** of any good or service equal the marginal cost of production plus any **marginal external costs** that are not directly borne by producers or their customers. Production costs that are borne by producers and their customers represent private economic costs; external costs include the value of foregone alternative goods and services. In the absence of marginal external costs, **marginal private costs** and marginal social costs are equal at all levels of output. **Marginal social benefits** are the sum of **marginal private benefits** plus **marginal external benefits**. Marginal private benefits are enjoyed by those who directly pay for any good or service; marginal external benefits are enjoyed by purchasers and nonpurchasers alike and are not reflected in market prices. When no externalities are present, marginal social benefits equal marginal private benefits.

- The **social rate of discount** is the interest-rate cost of public funds. According to the **social net present-value** (SNPV) criterion, social programs and public-sector investment projects are acceptable if the present value of marginal social benefits is greater than or equal to the present value of marginal social costs. **Benefit-cost (B-C) ratio analysis** shows the relative attractiveness of any social program or public-sector investment project, or the present value of marginal social benefits per dollar of marginal social cost. The **social internal rate of return** (SIRR) is the interest or discount rate that equates the present value of the future receipts of a program to the initial cost or outlay.

- Once the resource allocation decision has been made, the purpose of **cost-effectiveness analysis** is to determine how to best employ resources in a given social program or public-sector investment project. With **privatization**, public-sector resources are sold or otherwise transferred to the private sector in the hope that the profit motive might spur higher product quality, better customer service, and lower costs for production and distribution.

- **Monetary policy** refers to actions taken by the Federal Reserve (the Fed) that influence bank reserves, the money stock, and interest rates. **Fiscal policy** refers to the spending and taxing policies of the federal government. The **business cycle** refers to fluctuations of output around a long-term trend, or recessions followed by recoveries and expansions. Recent reductions in the volatility of economic activity may be due to the development of **stabilization policy** designed to offset temporary economic disruptions. **Automatic stabilizers** act as buffers when the economy weakens by automatically reducing taxes and increasing government spending. **Discretionary policy** refers to new changes in spending and taxes.

- **International trade**, or the voluntary exchange of goods and services across national boundaries, increases the well-being of all participants by promoting economic efficiency in a variety of ways. The **Eurodollar market** is a market in which banks outside the United States accept deposits and make loans denominated in dollars. Eurodollar markets have developed into **Eurocurrency markets** with transactions in a variety of currencies in addition to dollars.

- Although sometimes effective, changes in **economic expectations** and certain indirect effects of government actions place severe limits on the effectiveness of fiscal and monetary stabilization policy. The reduction in private investment associated with an increase in government spending is known as the **crowding out** phenomenon. Change in incentives that results from the purchase of insurance is known as the **moral hazard problem**, or the difficulty encountered when the full costs of economic activity are not directly borne by the consumer.

During the 1990s, microeconomic and macroeconomic policies were employed by all levels of government as a means for improving upon private-sector price and output decisions. At the same time, government agencies and not-for-profit organizations found themselves besieged by competing demands for scarce goods and services. This chapter illustrates how the tools and techniques of managerial economics can be employed to improve decision making in the not-for-profit sector and refine the management of scarce public resources.

QUESTIONS

Q17.1 Describe the traditional rationale for public management of economic resources. Is this rationale viable when government deficit spending is substantial?

Q17.2 What is the essential difference between public and private goods? Give some examples of each and some examples of goods and services that involve elements of both.

Q17.3 Does the fact that public decisions are sometimes made by self-interested politicians and bureaucrats undermine the basic premise of public choice theory?

Q17.4 List some potential causes of the Great Depression and the range of factors that influence the timing and magnitude of economic fluctuations in general.

Q17.5 One of the most vexing issues to complicate the health-care debate is the problem that there is no simple link between general health and well-being and the amount spent on health care. Briefly describe why the connection between health care and health is not a simple one. Does the weakness of the link between health and health care have any implications for mandatory universal coverage proposals?

Q17.6 What features of the health-care services market can lead to the purchase of poor quality, unnecessary, or high-cost services?

Q17.7 Among health economists, the term *moral hazard* has come to explain why insurance provides incentives for the overconsumption of health-care services. Describe this idea and its economic implications.

Q17.8 Is government policy that increases the well-being of one generation at the expense of another just in the ethical sense?

Q17.9 "Economic growth is ultimately constrained by finite natural resources. In a capitalist system, the population has a natural tendency to grow faster than food production and hence is only constrained by starvation, pestilence, and war. It is the proper role of government to own and manage natural resources so that the limits to growth are managed in a humane manner." Discuss this statement.

Q17.10 Describe some of the social benefits of international trade.

SELF-TEST PROBLEMS AND SOLUTIONS

ST17.1 Benefit-Cost Analysis Methodology. The benefit-cost approach is not new: The concept first surfaced in France in 1844. In this century, benefit-cost analysis has been widely used in the evaluation of river and harbor projects since as early as 1902. In the United States, the 1936 Flood Control Act authorized federal assistance in developing flood-control programs "if the benefits to whomsoever they may accrue are in excess of the estimated costs." By 1950, federal agency practice required the consideration of both direct and indirect benefits and costs and that unmeasured intangible influences be listed. Despite this long history of widespread use, it has only been since 1970 that public-sector managers have sought to broadly apply the principles of benefit-cost analysis to the evaluation of agricultural programs, rapid transit projects, highway construction, urban renewal projects, recreation facility construction, job training programs, health-care reform, education, research and development projects, and defense policies.

A. Briefly describe major similarities and differences between public-sector benefit-cost analysis and the private-sector capital budgeting process.

B. What major questions must be answered before meaningful benefit-cost analysis is possible?

C. Although the maximization of society's wealth is the primary objective of benefit-cost analysis, it is important to recognize that constraints often limit government's ability to achieve certain objectives. Enumerate some of the common economic, political, and social constraints faced in public-sector benefit-cost analysis.

D. In light of these constraints, discuss some of the pluses and minuses associated with the use of benefit-cost analysis as the foundation for a general approach to the allocation of government-entrusted resources.

ST17.1 Solution

A. Benefit-cost analysis is a method for assessing the desirability of social programs and public-sector investment projects when it is necessary to take a long view of the public and private repercussions of such expenditures. As in the case of private-sector capital budgeting, benefit-cost analysis is frequently used in cases where the economic consequences of a program or project are likely to extend beyond 1 year in time. Unlike capital budgeting, however, benefit-cost analysis seeks to measure both direct private effects and indirect social implications of public-sector investment decisions and policy changes.

B. Before meaningful benefit-cost analysis is possible, a number of important policy questions must be answered. Among these policy questions are

- What is the social objective function that is to be maximized?
- What constraints are placed on the decision-making process?

- What marginal social benefits and marginal social costs are to be included, and how are they to be measured?
- What social investment criterion should be used?
- What is the appropriate social rate of discount?

C. A number of constraints impinge upon society's ability to maximize the social benefits derived from public expenditures. Among these constraints are

- *Physical constraints.* Program alternatives are limited by the available state of technology and by current production possibilities. For example, it is not yet possible to cure AIDS. Therefore, major emphasis for public policy in this area must be directed toward prevention, early detection and treatment, and research.
- *Legal constraints.* Domestic laws and international agreements place limits on property rights, the right of eminent domain, due process, constitutional limits on a particular agency's activities, and so on. These legal constraints often play an important role in shaping the realm of public policy.
- *Administrative constraints.* Effective programs require competent management and execution. Qualified individuals must be available to carry out social objectives. Even the best-conceived program is doomed to failure unless managers and workers with the proper mix of technical and administrative skill are available.
- *Distributional constraints.* Social programs and public-sector investment projects affect different groups in different ways. The "gainers" are seldom the same as "losers." When distributional impacts of public policy are of paramount concern, the objective of benefit-cost analysis might maximize subject to the constraint that equity considerations be met.
- *Political constraints.* That which is optimal may not be feasible because of slowness and inefficiency in the political process. Often what is best is tempered by what is possible, given the existence of strong competing special-interest groups.
- *Budget constraints.* Public agencies often work within the bounds of a predetermined budget. As a result, virtually all social programs and public-sector investment projects have some absolute financial ceiling above which the program cannot be expanded, irrespective of social benefits.
- *Social or religious constraints.* Social or religious constraints may limit the range of feasible program alternatives. It is futile to attempt to combat teen pregnancy with public support for family planning if religious constraints prohibit the use of modern birth control methods.

D. An important potential use of benefit-cost analysis is as the structure for a general philosophy of government resource allocation. As such, the results of benefit-cost studies have the potential to serve as a guide for resource-allocation decisions within and among government programs and investment projects in agriculture, defense, education, health care, welfare, and other areas. The objective of such a comprehensive benefit-cost approach to government would be to maximize the net present value of the difference between the marginal social benefits and the marginal social costs derived from all social programs and public-sector investment projects.

Although a benefit-cost approach to evaluating all levels and forms of government is conceptually appealing on an efficiency basis, it suffers from a number of serious practical limitations. Perhaps most importantly, the measurement of marginal social benefits and marginal social costs for goods and services that are not or cannot be provided by the private sector is often primitive, at best. Measurement systems have not been sufficiently refined or standardized to permit meaningful comparisons among the social net present value of "Star Wars" defense systems, the guaranteed student loan program for college students, funding for AIDS research, Medicare, and Medicaid. A further problem arises because benefit-cost analysis is largely restricted to a consideration of the efficiency objective;

equity-related considerations are seldom accorded full treatment in benefit-cost analysis. In addition, as discussed previously, a number of important economic, political, and social constraints limit the effectiveness of benefit-cost analysis. As a result, significant problems arise when a given social program or public-sector investment project is designed to meet efficiency and equity-related objectives.

For these reasons, benefit-cost analysis is traditionally viewed within the narrow context of a decision technique that is helpful in focusing interest on the economic consequences of proposed social programs and public-sector investment projects. Its greatest use is in comparing programs and projects that are designed to achieve the same or similar objectives and as a tool for focusing resources on the best use of resources intended to meet a given social objective.

ST17.2 Trade Policy. In 1992, the United States, Canada, and Mexico reached an agreement to create a free-trade area with more than 360 million consumers and over $6 trillion in annual output. This so-called North American Free Trade Agreement (NAFTA) accord links the United States with its first- and third-largest trading partners.

A. Summarize the main economic features of NAFTA.

B. In the years prior to NAFTA, Mexico had opened its markets and implemented sweeping economic reforms. Briefly describe some of the economic and political benefits derived from these reforms.

C. In light of this experience, what economic and political benefits do you project as a result of NAFTA?

ST17.2 Solution

A. According to NAFTA, existing duties on most goods and services will be either eliminated or phased out. NAFTA will also eliminate quotas along with import licenses unless they are essential for such purposes as protecting human health. In addition to dismantling trade barriers in industrial goods, NAFTA includes agreements in services, investment, intellectual property rights, agriculture, and the strengthening of trade rules. There are also side agreements on labor provisions and protection of the environment.

Under NAFTA, the three countries extend most-favored-nation treatment in services to each other. Each NAFTA country must treat service providers from other NAFTA countries no less favorably than it treats its own service providers and no less favorably than it treats service providers from non-NAFTA countries. In addition, a NAFTA country may not require that a service provider of another NAFTA country establish or maintain a residence as a condition for providing the service.

B. In recent years, Mexico has opened its markets and implemented sweeping economic reforms. In 1986, Mexico joined the General Agreement on Tariffs and Trade (GATT) and began to unilaterally lower its tariffs and other trade barriers. Mexico's reforms have raised its economic growth rate and helped make it an important export market for the United States. As an added economic benefit, as economic opportunities in Mexico improve, Mexican workers will have fewer incentives to migrate to the United States. Thus, a stable and prosperous Mexico is important from both an economic and a political standpoint.

C. NAFTA will stimulate growth, promote investment in North America, enhance the ability of North American producers to compete, and raise the standard of living of all three countries. NAFTA will also speed technological progress and provide innovating companies with a larger market. Many economic studies show that NAFTA will lead to higher wages, lower prices, and higher economic growth rates. NAFTA will also reinforce market reforms already underway in Mexico.

Perhaps most importantly, passage of NAFTA strengthens peaceful ties among the United States, Canada, and Mexico. As important partners in mutually beneficial trade, these three countries have a common interest in maintaining a strong peaceful coexistence.

PROBLEMS

P17.1 **Public Versus Private Goods.** Publicly funded lighthouses provide a valuable service along coastal waterways and in the Great Lakes Region. Through visual light-beam signals, lighthouses mark the route of safe passage for cargo ships and pleasure craft 24 hours per day, 365 days per year. The service provided by such lighthouses is an often-cited classic example of a public good. Once a lighthouse is built, it can send signals to additional cargo ships and pleasure craft at practically zero marginal cost. Thus, lighthouse signals are said to be an excellent example of a government-provided service that is nonrival in consumption. As such, proponents of government funding for lighthouses argue that such services would not be provided by the private sector.

  A. Briefly describe and contrast the nonrival consumption and nonexclusion concepts.

  B. Do lighthouse services display both nonrival consumption and nonexclusion characteristics?

  C. Explain how private-sector providers of public goods can operate profitably when such goods and services do not embody the nonexclusion concept.

P17.2 **Goal Setting in Public Management.** The objectives of social programs are set by the public through their support for various political representatives. In the election process, policy alternatives are enumerated, explored, and revised in light of popular preferences and operative constraints. These alternatives are then evaluated by comparing the present-value size of marginal social benefits and marginal social costs. According to the social net present-value criterion, any social program or public-sector investment project is desirable so long as the present value of marginal social benefits exceeds the present value of marginal social costs.

  A. Explain how the social net present-value criterion is related to the Pareto satisfactory concept.

  B. Do you see any problems with the adoption of the Pareto satisfactory criterion?

  C. Is there any straightforward method for overcoming the limitations of the Pareto satisfactory criterion?

P17.3 **Social Rate of Discount.** Because resources for social programs and public-sector investment projects come from private-sector consumption and/or investment, economists typically advocate the use of a social rate of discount that reflects this private-sector opportunity cost. A good estimate of the opportunity cost of funds diverted from private consumption is the rate of return on government securities that is available to individual investors. Similarly, the average rate of return on private investments can be taken as the opportunity cost of private-sector investment funds.

  A. Should pretax or after-tax rates of return be used to estimate the opportunity cost of resources diverted from the private sector to fund social programs or public-sector investment projects? Why?

  B. Assume that the rate of return on long-term government bonds is 8%, a typical after-tax return on investment in the private sector is 10%, the marginal corporate and individual tax rate is 30%, and consumption averages 95% of total income. Based on the information provided, calculate an economically appropriate social rate of discount.

P17.4 **Equity and Efficiency in Benefit-Cost Analysis.** In benefit-cost analysis, public-sector managers seek to learn if society as a whole will be better off by the adoption of a specific social program or public-sector investment project. Rather than seeking to maximize profits or the value of the firm, public-sector managers use benefit-cost analysis to maximize, or at least move toward a maximization of, the excess of marginal social benefits over marginal social costs. With this goal in mind, from an efficiency perspective, the distribution of any social net present value is of no importance. For example, when the city of Denver sponsors a new Denver International Airport at an initial cost of $3.5 billion, it makes no difference whether the city pays the entire cost or whether the city, the state of Colorado, and the federal government split these costs. Similarly, if the city of Denver is motivated by the desire to lure business and tourist traffic from Chicago or Los Angeles, the benefits of increased economic activity in Denver that has merely shifted from other transportation centers should not be counted. In both instances, the proper concern is the increase in aggregate social wealth, not aggregate local wealth.

A. Assume that the city of Denver and local airline customers must pay only 10% of the costs of Denver International Airport, with the federal government picking up the other 90% of the tab. Describe how a local benefit-cost analysis of the airport project might be distorted by this cost-sharing arrangement.

B. Under the federal revenue sharing program, the federal government collects tax revenues that are then returned to states and other local units of government to support a wide variety of social programs. Can you see any problems for an efficient allocation of public expenditures when the spending and taxing authority of government is divided in this manner?

C. As a practical matter, can the equity and efficiency implications of social programs and public-sector investment projects be completely separated?

P17.5 Benefit-Cost Analysis. According to the National Highway Traffic Safety Administration (NHTSA), 41,800 people were killed in highway crashes in 2000, up from 41,611 in 1999, a 0.5% increase. The fatality rate per 100 million vehicle miles was 1.6, which means that 1.6 people were killed for every 100 million miles traveled. This figure is up from a record low fatality rate of 1.5 in 1999. "These statistics underscore the challenges facing this country in highway safety," said U.S. Transportation Secretary Norman Mineta. "Safety is an individual as well as government responsibility, and we must work together to improve it."

As a practical matter, it is important to recognize that almost all of the tens of thousands of highway fatalities per year are preventable. Using current technology, highway fatalities could be substantially reduced or eliminated by draconian public policy measures such as a strictly enforced nationwide 20 mph speed limit. Needless to say, popular opposition would be intense for any such proposal. Speed limits as high as 75 mph on major highways are widely popular because consumers derive significant economic and social benefits from speedy automobile transportation. However, by failing to sharply reduce or eliminate highway fatalities, speed limit policy places a finite and measurable value on human life.

A. From an economic standpoint, explain how practical public policy sets a dollar value on human life. Is it efficient to do so?

B. Are there equity considerations one must weigh in judging the fairness of dollar estimates of the value of human life?

P17.6 Privatization. In Massachusetts, a state education law authorized the establishment of up to 25 so-called charter schools. Charter schools are public schools that receive state funding as well as some measure of autonomy from local school boards and the rules that govern conventional schools. As a result, students and educators in Boston face the ready prospect of classrooms with politicians as lecturers, academic instruction aided by yoga, school doors open from dawn to dusk, and public schools run on a for-profit basis.

Charter schools already are operating in Minnesota and California, and five other states promise to join the trend with recently enacted charter-school legislation. Advocates of such schools argue that they provide badly needed competition for existing public schools. Under the charter-school concept, anyone with a good education idea gets access to government funding, so long as they can attract and effectively train students.

A. Explain how breaking the public-school monopoly on access to public funding could help improve the quality of public- and private-school primary education.

B. Explain why primary-school privatization might not create such benefits.

P17.7 Growth Implications of the Federal Deficit. The amount of federal debt held by the public is the sum total of all previous deficits minus any surpluses. Federal debt held by the public equals the value of outstanding Treasury bills, notes, bonds, U.S. savings bonds, and other financial obligations of the federal government that the Treasury sells to the public. Debt held by the public does not include debt held in government trust funds. This debt is owed by the government to itself, so economists generally use the debt held by the public as the economically meaningful measure of the national debt. In 2001, government debt held by the public was roughly $5.8 trillion, or roughly $20,606 for every man, woman, and child in the United States.

Of the many government activities that may affect future living standards, considerable attention has focused on the federal debt and the large and persistent federal budget deficits.

A. Explain how government debt and deficits can affect intergenerational equity and, under certain conditions, adversely affect the economy's productive capacity.

B. Explain why government debt and deficits may not affect intergenerational equity and adversely affect the economy's productive capacity.

C. Illustrate how balancing the budget might actually harm the economy, and why zero deficits are not a prerequisite to reducing the debt-to-GDP ratio.

P17.8 Trade Policy. The past half-century has been marked by a number of experiments with different international exchange-rate arrangements. Under the Bretton Woods system, designed at the end of World War II, currencies of participating nations were pegged to the dollar and only occasionally adjusted. Since that system was abandoned in the early 1970s, exchange rates of major industrialized countries have generally "floated" against each other in response to market forces. However, a number of European countries revived the pegged exchange-rate system when they created the European Monetary System (EMS) in 1979.

In the Maastricht Treaty of 1991, members of the European Community agreed to replace their national currencies with a single currency by the year 2000, thereby superseding the current system of pegged exchange rates under the EMS and permanently ruling out exchange-rate changes. Ironically, events in 1992, including the temporary withdrawal of a number of countries from the EMS exchange-rate mechanism, underscored the shortcomings of a pegged exchange-rate system in the face of economic disturbances.

A. Explain why progress toward a single European currency might be viewed as complementary to the increasing integration of the European market for goods and services.

B. Contrast the economic benefits of a single European currency with the economic benefits of an elimination of European trade barriers. Is a single European currency necessary for a complete integration of the European market?

P17.9 The Economics of Health Care. The United States spends more per person on health care than any other country in the world. Still, recent studies show that the United States ranks relatively low in the overall quality of health care provided. France is often described as providing its citizens with the globe's best health care. Japan wins the distinction as having the world's healthiest people. Although good at expensive care, like open-heart surgery, the U.S. health-care delivery system is often described as poor for low-cost preventive care. Measuring how long people live in good health, and not just how long they live, the Japanese beat Americans by 4.5 years. Yet it is surprising that Japan spends just $1,750 per person on health care, and France spends $2,100. Both figures are far below the standard set in the United States, where health-care spending was a whopping $3,724 per person in 2001.

A. Why is health-care demand different from the demand for many other services?

B. Consumers buy health care to improve their health and well-being, but research suggests only a weak connection between health-care spending and health. Explain why there might be only a weak link between health-care expenditures and health.

C. Why is health-care spending rising rapidly on a worldwide basis? Is robust growth in health-care spending likely to continue?

P17.10 Health-Care Reform. Representative Tom Allen (D-ME) introduced the Prescription Drug Fairness for Seniors Act (H.R. 664) on February 10, 1999, and quickly amassed over 100 sponsors. If made law, the bill would force prescription drug manufacturers to sell their products to retail pharmacies at the lowest price paid by any agency or department of the U.S. government, or the manufacturer's best price for outpatient drugs, whichever is lower. Critics contend that such prescription drug price regulation would not lower patient costs but instead result in higher prices and reduced availability of new prescription drugs.

A. With respect to the demand for prescription drugs, explain how price controls might have the unintended effect of actually increasing prices.

B. Explain how price controls might affect the supply of new and innovative drugs.

CASE STUDY

Oh, Lord, Won't You Buy Me a Mercedes-Benz (Factory)?[2]

On October 1, 1993, Alabama emerged victorious as the site of Mercedes-Benz AG's first U.S. car plant. States like Alabama are vying more desperately than ever to lure new industrial jobs and hold on to those they have. To start with, they give away millions of dollars in free land. After that come fat checks for site clearance, training, even employee salaries. Both foreign and domestic companies are finding ingenious ways to cash in.

Mercedes initially had so little interest in Alabama that Andreas Renschler, who headed Mercedes's site-selection team and is expected to run the new factory, says he did not even plan to visit. Of more than 20 states that Mercedes looked at seriously, it initially leaned toward North Carolina, where Mercedes's parent, Daimler-Benz AG, already builds Freightliner trucks. North Carolina officials say Governor Jim Hunt pursued Mercedes harder than he ever had pursued a potential investor. Mercedes officials were reportedly surprised at the various states' ardor, but they quickly cashed in on it. Mercedes would get offers for certain things from certain states, put it on their ideal contract proposal, and then come back to the other states and ask if they would be willing to do the same. For example, Mercedes persuaded all the main competitors to offer $5 million for a welcome center next to the factory, where customers could pick up cars, have them serviced, and visit an auto museum. It got commitments for free 18-month employee-training programs. It also got state governments and utilities to promise to buy large quantities of the four-wheel-drive recreational vehicles that the new factory will produce. Perhaps the biggest bombshell, Mercedes officials even asked the states to pick up the salaries of its 1,500 workers for their first year or so on the job, at a cost of $45 million. The workers would be in a training program and would not be producing anything, Mercedes explained. Although North Carolina and other state officials said no, Alabama said yes, even to the salary request. "The Mercedes project simply was worth more to us than it was to any other state," says Billy Joe Camp, Alabama's economic development director.

When Mercedes found North Carolina proposing to build a $35 million training center at the company's plant, the German automaker enticed Alabama to more than match the North Carolina offer. To outbid the competition, the Alabama governor hurriedly won legislative approval for special, lavish tax concessions—dubbed Alabama's Mercedes Law—and offered to spend tens of millions of dollars buying more than 2,500 Mercedes vehicles for state use. In the bargain, Mercedes says it agreed to limit itself to using just $42.6 million per year in income and payroll tax credits; Alabama officials say that was all Mercedes expected to be

---

2. Rick Brooks, "How Big Incentives Won Alabama a Piece of the Auto Industry," *The Wall Street Journal*, April 3, 2002, A1, A24.

able to use, based on profit projections. It also will be allowed, however, to escape more than $9 million a year in property taxes and other fees, as permitted under existing law. Although South Carolina offered $80 million in tax credits over a period of 20 years, Alabama granted Mercedes a more attractive tax credit, available in advance in the form of an interest-free loan. Mercedes officials also say Alabama's promised education spending was double any other state's promise. Alabama officials even agreed to place Mercedes's distinctive emblem atop a local scoreboard in time for the big, televised Alabama-Tennessee football game. The price? Why, free, of course.

In all, Alabama wound up promising Mercedes over $300 million in incentives, which economic development experts call a record package for a foreign company. How has it worked out in the long run? Very well, say supporters of the Alabama program. On August 30, 2000, DaimlerChrysler announced it will invest another $1 billion in a major expansion at its Tuscaloosa, Alabama, site to double production for the next generation Mercedes-Benz M-class sport utility vehicle. The expansion is expected to double production capacity from 80,000 units to roughly 160,000 units at the Tuscaloosa facility and generate up to 2,000 new jobs. In announcing the expansion, company officials stressed that their success would not have been possible without the great partnership they had formed with the state of Alabama and the strong workforce that they found there. With the new expansion, DaimlerChrysler could become the fifth largest employer in Alabama, with more than 7,000 employees between its Chrysler electronics plant in Huntsville, Alabama, and the Tuscaloosa Mercedes-Benz factory. The total capital investment made by DaimlerChrysler since 1994 in Alabama is expect to rise to more than $2.5 billion, once the expansion is complete

A. With $300 million in state aid to attract 1,500 new jobs, the initial marginal social cost to Alabama taxpayers of attracting the Mercedes plant was $200,000 per job. Estimate the minimum marginal social benefit required to make this a reasonable expenditure from the perspective of Alabama taxpayers. Do the facts of this case lead you to believe that it is more likely that Alabama underbid or overbid for this project? Explain.

B. Does the fact that the bidding process for the Mercedes plant took place at the state and local level of government have any implications for the amount of inducements offered? Would these numbers change dramatically if only the federal government could offer tax breaks for industrial development? Explain.

C. In 1993, Ypsilanti, Michigan, lost a court battle to reverse General Motors Corp.'s 1991 decision to close a plant. Local authorities had just given it a $13 million tax credit in a vain attempt to keep the plant open. In its ruling, the Michigan Court of Appeals said, "It has never been held that . . . an abatement carries a promise of continued employment." Explain how such risks could be accounted for in a benefit-cost analysis of the Alabama Mercedes project.

D. Explain how a benefit-cost analysis of the Alabama Mercedes project could account for any potential erosion of the local tax base at the state and local level.

SELECTED REFERENCES

Athanasoulis, Stefano G., and Eric Van Wincoop. "Risk Sharing Within the United States: What Do Financial Markets and Fiscal Federalism Accomplish?" *Review of Economics and Statistics* 83 (November 2001): 688–698.

Davis, Donald R., and David E. Weinstein. "An Account of Global Factor Trade." *American Economic Review* 91 (December 2001): 1423–1453.

Dornisch, David. "Competitive Dynamics in Polish Telecommunications, 1990–2000: Growth, Regulation, and Privatization of an Infrastructural Multinetwork." *Telecommunications Policy* 25 (July 2001): 381–407.

Ederington, Josh. "International Coordination of Trade and Domestic Policies." *American Economic Review* 91 (December 2001): 1580–1593.

Ellingsen, Tore, and Ulf Sööderströöm. "Monetary Policy and Market Interest Rates." *American Economic Review* 91 (December 2001): 1594–1607.

Hanushek, Eric A. "Black-White Achievement Differences and Governmental Interventions." *American Economic Review* 91 (May 2001): 24–28.

Henriksson, Lennart E. "Gambling in Canada: Some Insights for Cost-Benefit Analysis." *Managerial & Decision Economics* 22 (January–May 2001): 113–123.

Hoxby, Caroline M. "All School Finance Equalizations Are Not Created Equal." *Quarterly Journal of Economics* 116 (November 2001): 1189–1231.

Jaksch, John, Mark Weimar, Joan Young, et al. "Privatization: The Use of Risk, Economic, and Finance Models to Ensure Its Success." *Journal of Project Finance* 6 (Winter 2001): 37–48.

Littlechild, Stephen. "Privatization, Restructuring, and Regulation of Network Utilities: The Walras-Pareto Lectures." *Economic Journal* 111 (November 2001): F753–F755.

Matsuyama, Kiminori. "Comparative Politics and Public Finance." *Journal of Political Economy* 108 (December 2000): 1121–1161.

Persky, Joseph. "Retrospectives: Cost-Benefit Analysis and the Classical Creed." *Journal of Economic Perspectives* 15 (Fall 2001): 199–208.

Sappington, David E. M. "You Don't Always Get What You Pay For: The Economics of Privatization." *Journal of Economic Literature* 39 (June 2001): 601–603.

Uddin, Shahzad, and Trevor A. Hopper. "Bangladesh Soap Opera: Privatization, Accounting, and Regimes of Control in a Less Developed Country." *Accounting, Organizations & Society* 26 (October/November 2001): 643–672.

Wolfson, Adam. "The Costs and Benefits of Cost-Benefit Analysis." *Public Interest* 145 (Fall 2001): 93–99.

Compounding and the Time Value of Money

The concepts of compound growth and the time value of money are widely used in all aspects of business and economics. Compounding is the principle that underlies growth, whether it is growth in value, growth in sales, or growth in assets. The time value of money—the fact that a dollar received in the future is worth less than a dollar in hand today—also plays an important role in managerial economics. Cash flows occurring in different periods must be adjusted to their value at a common point in time to be analyzed and compared. Because of the importance of these concepts in economic analysis, thorough understanding of the material on future (compound) and present values in the appendix is important for the study of managerial economics.

FUTURE VALUE (OR COMPOUND VALUE)

Suppose that you deposit $100 in a bank savings account that pays 5% interest compounded annually. How much will you have at the end of one year? Let us define terms as follows:

PV = Present value of your account, or the beginning amount, $100

i = Interest rate the bank pays you = 5% per year, or, expressed in decimal terms, 0.05

I = Dollars of interest earned during the year

FV_n = Future value, or ending amount, of your account at the end of n years. Whereas PV is the value now, at the present time, FV_n is the value n years into the future, after compound interest has been earned. Note also that FV_0 is the future value zero years into the future, which is the present, so $FV_0 = PV$.

In our example, $n = 1$, so $FV_n = FV_1$, and it is calculated as follows:

(A.1)

$$\begin{aligned} FV_1 &= PV + I \\ &= PV + PV \times i \\ &= PV(1 + i) \end{aligned}$$

We can now use Equation A.1 to find how much the account is worth at the end of 1 year:

$$FV_1 = \$100(1 + 0.05) = \$100(1.05) = \$105$$

Your account earned $5 of interest (I = $5), so you have $105 at the end of the year.

Now suppose that you leave your funds on deposit for 5 years; how much will you have at the end of the fifth year? The answer is $127.63; this value is worked out in Table A.1.

Notice that the Table A.1 value for FV_2, the value of the account at the end of year 2, is equal to

$$FV_2 = FV_1(1 + i) = PV(1 + i)(1 + i) = PV(1 + i)^2$$

FV_3, the balance after 3 years, is

$$FV_3 = FV_2(1 + i) = PV(1 + i)^3$$

In general, FV_n, the future value at the end of n years, is found as

(A.2)
$$FV_n = PV(1 + i)^n$$

Applying Equation A.2 in the case of a 5-year account that earns 5% per year gives

$$
\begin{aligned}
PV_5 &= \$100(1.05)^5 \\
&= \$100(1.2763) \\
&= \$127.63
\end{aligned}
$$

which is the same as the value in Table A.1.

If an electronic calculator is handy, it is easy enough to calculate $(1 + i)^n$ directly.[1] However, tables have been constructed for values of $(1 + i)^n$ for wide ranges of i and n, as Table A.2 illustrates. Table B.1 in Appendix B contains a more complete set of compound value interest factors. Interest compounding can occur over periods of time different from 1 year. Thus, although compounding is often on an annual basis, it can be quarterly, semiannually, monthly, or for any other period.

TABLE A.1

Compound Interest Calculations

Year	Beginning Amount, PV	×	(1 + i)	=	Ending Amount, FV_n
1	$100.00		1.05		$105.00
2	105.00		1.05		110.25
3	110.25		1.05		115.76
4	115.76		1.05		121.55
5	121.55		1.05		127.63

---

1   For example, to calculate $(1 + i)^n$ for $i = 5\% = 0.05$ and $n = 5$ years, simply multiply $(1 + i) = (1.05)$ times (1.05); multiply this product by (1.05); and so on:

$$(1 + i)^n = (1.05)(1.05)(1.05)(1.05)(1.05) = (1.05)^5 = 1.2763$$

TABLE A.2

Future Value of $1 at the End of *n* Periods: $FVIF_{i,n} = (1 + i)^n$

Period (n)	1%	2%	3%	4%	5%	6%	7%	8%	9%	10%
0	1.0000	1.0000	1.0000	1.0000	1.0000	1.0000	1.0000	1.0000	1.0000	1.0000
1	1.0100	1.0200	1.0300	1.0400	1.0500	1.0600	1.0700	1.0800	1.0900	1.1000
2	1.0201	1.0404	1.0609	1.0816	1.1025	1.1236	1.1449	1.1664	1.1881	1.2100
3	1.0303	1.0612	1.0927	1.1249	1.1576	1.1910	1.2250	1.2597	1.2950	1.3310
4	1.0406	1.0824	1.1255	1.1699	1.2155	1.2625	1.3108	1.3605	1.4116	1.4641
5	1.0510	1.1041	1.1593	1.2167	1.2763	1.3382	1.4026	1.4693	1.5386	1.6105
6	1.0615	1.1262	1.1941	1.2653	1.3401	1.4185	1.5007	1.5869	1.6771	1.7716
7	1.0721	1.1487	1.2299	1.3159	1.4071	1.5036	1.6058	1.7138	1.8280	1.9487
8	1.0829	1.1717	1.2668	1.3686	1.4775	1.5938	1.7182	1.8509	1.9926	2.1436
9	1.0937	1.1951	1.3048	1.4233	1.5513	1.6895	1.8385	1.9990	2.1719	2.3579
10	1.1046	1.2190	1.3439	1.4802	1.6289	1.7908	1.9672	2.1589	2.3674	2.5937
11	1.1157	1.2434	1.3842	1.5395	1.7103	1.8983	2.1049	2.3316	2.5804	2.8531
12	1.1268	1.2682	1.4258	1.6010	1.7959	2.0122	2.2522	2.5182	2.8127	3.1384
13	1.1381	1.2936	1.4685	1.6651	1.8856	2.1329	2.4098	2.7196	3.0658	3.4523
14	1.1495	1.3195	1.5126	1.7317	1.9799	2.2609	2.5785	2.9372	3.3417	3.7975
15	1.1610	1.3459	1.5580	1.8009	2.0789	2.3966	2.7590	3.1722	3.6425	4.1772

The term *future value interest factor* ($FVIF_{i,n}$) equals $(1 + i)^n$. Therefore, Equation A.2 may be written as $FV_n = PV(FVIF_{i,n})$. One need only to go to an appropriate interest table to find the proper interest factor. For example, the correct interest factor for our 5-year, 5% illustration can be found in Table A.2. Simply look down the Period column to 5, then across this row to the 5% column to find the interest factor, 1.2763. Then, using this interest factor, we find the value of $100 after 5 years as $FV_n = PV(FVIF_{i,n}) = \$100(1.2763) = \$127.63$, which is identical to the value obtained by the long method in Table A.1.

Graphic View of the Compounding Process: Growth

Figure A.1 shows how $1 (or any other initial quantity) grows over time at various rates of interest. The higher the rate of interest, the faster the rate of growth. The interest rate is, in fact, the growth rate: If a sum is deposited and earns 5%, then the funds on deposit grow at the rate of 5% per period. Similarly, the sales of a firm or the gross domestic product (GDP) of a country might be expected to grow at a constant rate. Projections of future sales or GDP could be obtained using the compound value method.

Future value curves could be drawn for any interest rate, including fractional rates. In Figure A.1, we have plotted curves for 0%, 5%, and 10%, using the data from Table A.2.

PRESENT VALUE

Suppose that you are offered the alternative of receiving either $127.63 at the end of 5 years or *X* dollars today. There is no question that the $127.63 will be paid in full (perhaps the payer is the U.S. government). Having no current need for the money, you would deposit it in a bank account that pays 5% interest. (Five percent is your *opportunity cost*, or the rate of interest you

FIGURE A.1

Relations Among Future Value Interest Factors, Interest Rates, and Time

The future value interest factor rises with increases in the interest rate and in the number of periods for interest compounding.

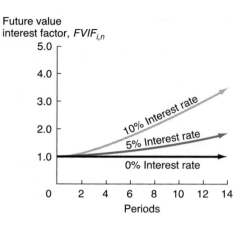

could earn on alternative investments of equal risk.) What value of X will make you indifferent between X dollars today or the promise of $127.63 5 years hence?

Table A.1 shows that the initial amount of $100 growing at 5% a year yields $127.63 at the end of 5 years. Thus, you should be indifferent in your choice between $100 today and $127.63 at the end of 5 years. The $100 is the present value, or PV, of $127.63 due in 5 years when the applicable interest rate is 5%. Therefore, if X is anything less than $100, you would prefer the promise of $127.63 in 5 years to X dollars today.

In general, the present value of a sum due n years in the future is the amount that, if it were invested today, would grow to equal the future sum over a period of n years. Because $100 would grow to $127.63 in 5 years at a 5% interest rate, $100 is the present value of $127.63 due 5 years in the future when the appropriate interest rate is 5%.

Finding present values (or *discounting*, as it is commonly called) is simply the reverse of compounding, and Equation A.2 can readily be transformed into a present value formula:

$$FV_n = PV(1 + i)^n$$

which, when solved for PV, gives

(A.3)
$$PV = \frac{FV_n}{(1 + i)^n} = FV_n \left[\frac{1}{(1 + i)^n}\right]$$

Tables have been constructed for the term in brackets for various values of i and n; Table A.3 is an example. For a more complete table, see Table B.2 in Appendix B. For the case being considered, look down the 5% column in Table A.3 to the fifth row. The figure shown there, 0.7835, is the *present value interest factor* ($PVIF_{i,n}$) used to determine the present value of $127.63 payable in 5 years, discounted at 5%:

$$PV = FV_5 (PVIF_{i,n})$$
$$= \$127.63(0.7835)$$
$$= \$100$$

Graphic View of the Discounting Process

Figure A.2 shows how the interest factors for discounting decrease as the discounting period increases. The curves in the figure were plotted with data taken from Table A.3; they show that the present value of a sum to be received at some future date decreases (1) as the payment date is extended further into the future and (2) as the discount rate increases. If relatively high discount rates apply, funds due in the future are worth very little today. Even at relatively low

FIGURE A.2

Relations Among Present Value Interest Factors, Interest Rates, and Time

The present value interest factor falls with increases in the interest rate and in the number of periods prior to payment.

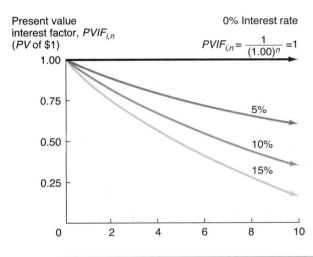

TABLE A.3

Present Values of $1 Due at the End of *n* Periods

$$PVIF_{i,n} = \frac{1}{(1 + i)^n} = \left[\frac{1}{(1 + i)}\right]^n$$

Period (n)	1%	2%	3%	4%	5%	6%	7%	8%	9%	10%	12%	14%	15%
1	.9901	.9804	.9709	.9615	.9524	.9434	.9346	.9259	.9174	.9091	.8929	.8772	.8696
2	.9803	.9612	.9426	.9246	.9070	.8900	.8734	.8573	.8417	.8264	.7972	.7695	.7561
3	.9706	.9423	.9151	.8890	.8638	.8396	.8163	.7938	.7722	.7513	.7118	.6750	.6575
4	.9610	.9238	.8885	.8548	.8227	.7921	.7629	.7350	.7084	.6830	.6355	.5921	.5718
5	.9515	.9057	.8626	.8219	.7835	.7473	.7130	.6806	.6499	.6209	.5674	.5194	.4972
6	.9420	.8880	.8375	.7903	.7462	.7050	.6663	.6302	.5963	.5645	.5066	.4556	.4323
7	.9327	.8706	.8131	.7599	.7107	.6651	.6227	.5835	.5470	.5132	.4523	.3996	.3759
8	.9235	.8535	.7894	.7307	.6768	.6274	.5820	.5403	.5019	.4665	.4039	.3506	.3269
9	.9143	.8368	.7664	.7026	.6446	.5919	.5439	.5002	.4604	.4241	.3606	.3075	.2843
10	.9053	.8203	.7441	.6756	.6139	.5584	.5083	.4632	.4224	.3855	.3220	.2697	.2472

discount rates, the present values of funds due in the distant future are quite small. For example, $1 due in 10 years is worth about 61¢ today if the discount rate is 5%. It is worth only 25¢ today at a 15% discount rate. Similarly, $1 due in 5 years at 10% is worth 62¢ today, but at the same discount rate, $1 due in 10 years is worth only 39¢ today.

FUTURE VALUE VERSUS PRESENT VALUE

Notice that Equation A.2, the basic equation for compounding, was developed from the logical sequence set forth in Table A.1; the equation merely presents in mathematical form the steps outlined in the table. The present value interest factor ($PVIF_{i,n}$) in Equation A.3, the basic equation for discounting or finding present values, was found as the *reciprocal* of the future value interest factor ($FVIF_{i,n}$) for the same i, n combination:

$$PVIF_{i,n} = \frac{1}{FVIF_{i,n}}$$

For example, the *future value interest factor* for 5% over 5 years is seen in Table A.2 to be 1.2763. The *present value interest factor* for 5% over 5 years must be the reciprocal of 1.2763:

$$PVIF_{5\%,\,5\,years} = \frac{1}{1.2763} = 0.7835$$

The $PVIF_{i,n}$ found in this manner does, of course, correspond with the $PVIF_{i,n}$ shown in Table A.3.

The reciprocal relation between present value and future value permits us to find present values in two ways—by multiplying or by dividing. Thus, the present value of $1,000 due in 5 years and discounted at 5% may be found as

$$PV = FV_n \left[\frac{1}{1 + i}\right]^n = FV_n(PVIF_{i,n}) = \$1,000(0.7835) = \$783.50$$

or as

$$PV = \frac{FV_n}{(1 + i)^n} = \frac{FV_n}{FVIF_{i,n}} = \frac{\$1,000}{1.2763} = \$783.50$$

To conclude this comparison of present and future values, compare Figures A.1 and A.2.[2]

FUTURE VALUE OF AN ANNUITY

An annuity is defined as a series of payments of a fixed amount for a specified number of periods. Each payment occurs at the end of the period.[3] For example, a promise to pay $1,000 a year for 3 years is a 3-year annuity. If you were to receive such an annuity and were to deposit each annual payment in a savings account paying 4% interest, how much would you have at the end of 3 years? The answer is shown graphically as a *time line* in Figure A.3. The first payment is made at the end of year 1, the second at the end of year 2, and the third at the end of year

---

2   Notice that Figure A.2 is not a mirror image of Figure A.1. The curves in Figure A.1 approach ∞ as n increases; in Figure A.2 the curves approach zero, not −∞.

3   Had the payment been made at the beginning of the period, each receipt would simply have been shifted back 1 year. The annuity would have been called an *annuity due*; the one in the present discussion, with payments made at the end of each period, is called a *regular annuity* or, sometimes, a *deferred annuity*.

FIGURE A.3

Time Line for an Annuity: Future Value ($i = 4\%$)

When the interest rate is 4%, the future value of $1,000 annuity to be paid over 3 years is $3,121.60.

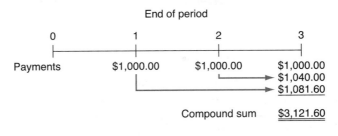

3. The last payment is not compounded at all, the second payment is compounded for 1 year, and the first is compounded for 2 years. When the future values of each of the payments are added, their total is the sum of the annuity. In the example, this total is $3,121.60.

Expressed algebraically, with S_N defined as the future value, R as the periodic receipt, n as the length of the annuity, and $FVIFA_{i,n}$ as the future value interest factor for an annuity, the formula for S_n is

(A.4)

$$
\begin{aligned}
S_n &= R(1 + i)^{n-1} + R(1 + i)^{n-2} + \ldots + R(1 + i)^1 + R(1 + i)^0 \\
&= R[(1 + i)^{n-1} + (1 + i)^{n-2} + \ldots + (1 + i)^1 + (1 + i)^0] \\
&= R\sum_{t=1}^{n}(1 + i)^{n-t} \text{ or } = R\sum_{t=1}^{n}(1 + i)^{t-1} \\
&= R(FVIFA_{i,n})
\end{aligned}
$$

The expression in parentheses, $FVIFA_{i,n}$, has been calculated for various combinations of i and n.[4] An illustrative set of these annuity interest factors is given in Table A.4.[5] To find the answer to the 3-year, $1,000 annuity problem, simply refer to Table A.4, look down the 4% column to the row of the third period, and multiply the factor 3.1216 by $1,000. The answer is the same as the one derived by the long method illustrated in Figure A.3:

$$
\begin{aligned}
S_n &= R(FVIFA_{i,n}) \\
S_3 &= \$1,000(3.1216) = \$3,121.60
\end{aligned}
$$

Notice that for all positive interest rates, the $FVIFA_{i,n}$ for the sum of an annuity is always equal to or greater than the number of periods the annuity runs.[6]

---

4 The third equation is simply a shorthand expression in which sigma (Σ) signifies *sum up* or add the values of n factors. The symbol $\sum_{t=1}^{n}$ simply says, "Go through the following process: Let $t = 1$ and find the first factor. Then let $t = 2$ and find the second factor. Continue until each individual factor has been found, and then add these individual factors to find the value of the annuity."

5 The equation given in Table A.4 recognizes that the *FVIFA* factor is the sum of a geometric progression. The proof of this equation is given in most algebra texts. Notice that it is easy to use the equation to develop annuity factors. This is especially useful if you need the *FVIFA* for some interest rate not given in the tables (for example, 6.5%).

6 It is worth noting that the entry for each period t in Table A.4 equals the sum of the entries in Table A.2 up to the period $n - 1$. For example, the entry for Period 3 under the 4% column in Table A.4 is equal to 1.000 + 1.0400 + 1.0816 = 3.1216.

Also, had the annuity been an *annuity due*, with payments received at the beginning rather than at the end of each period, the three payments would have occurred at $t = 0$, $t = 1$, and $t = 2$. To find the future value of an annuity due, look up the $FVIFA_{i,n}$ for $n + 1$ years, then subtract 1.0 from the amount to get the $FVIFA_{i,n}$ for the annuity due. In the example, the annuity due $FVIFA_{i,n}$ is 4.2465 – 1.0 = 3.2465, versus 3.1216 for a regular annuity. Because payments on an annuity due come earlier, it is a little more valuable than a regular annuity.

TABLE A.4

Future Value of an Annuity of $1 per Period for *n* Periods

$$FVIFA_{i,n} = \sum_{t=1}^{n} (1 + i)^{t-1}$$

$$= \frac{(1 + i)^n - 1}{i}$$

Number of Periods	1%	2%	3%	4%	5%	6%	7%	8%
1	1.0000	1.0000	1.0000	1.0000	1.0000	1.0000	1.0000	1.0000
2	2.0100	2.0200	2.0300	2.0400	2.0500	2.0600	2.0700	2.0800
3	3.0301	3.0604	3.0909	3.1216	3.1525	3.1836	3.2149	3.2464
4	4.0604	4.1216	4.1836	4.2465	4.3101	4.3746	4.4399	4.5061
5	5.1010	5.2040	5.3091	5.4163	5.5256	5.6371	5.7507	5.8666
6	6.1520	6.3081	6.4684	6.6330	6.8019	6.9753	7.1533	7.3359
7	7.2135	7.4343	7.6625	7.8983	8.1420	8.3938	8.6540	8.9228
8	8.2857	8.5830	8.8923	9.2142	9.5491	9.8975	10.2598	10.6366
9	9.3685	9.7546	10.1591	10.5828	11.0266	11.4913	11.9780	12.4876
10	10.4622	10.9497	11.4639	12.0061	12.5779	13.1808	13.8164	14.4866

PRESENT VALUE OF AN ANNUITY

Suppose that you were offered the following alternatives: a 3-year annuity of $1,000 per year or a lump-sum payment today. You have no need for the money during the next 3 years, so if you accept the annuity, you would simply deposit the receipts in a savings account paying 4% interest. How large must the lump-sum payment be to make it equivalent to the annuity? The time line shown in Figure A.4 will help explain the problem.

The present value of the first receipt is $R[1/(1 + i)]$, the second is $R[1/(1 + i)]^2$, and so on. Designating the present value of an annuity of *n* years as A_n and the present value interest factor for an annuity as $PVIFA_{i,n}$, we may write the following equation:

(A.5)
$$A_n = R\left(\frac{1}{1 + i}\right)^1 + R\left(\frac{1}{1 + i}\right)^2 + \ldots + R\left(\frac{1}{1 + i}\right)^n$$

$$= R\left(\frac{1}{(1 + i)^1} + \frac{1}{(1 + i)^2} + \ldots + \frac{1}{(1 + i)^n}\right)$$

$$= R\sum_{t=1}^{n} \frac{1}{(1 + i)^t}$$

$$= R(PVIFA_{i,n})$$

Again, tables have been worked out for $PVIFA_{i,n}$, the term in parentheses in Equation A.5, as Table A.5 illustrates; a more complete listing is found in Table B.4 in Appendix B. From Table A.5, the $PVIFA_{i,n}$ for a 3-year, 4% annuity is found to be 2.7751. Multiplying this factor by the $1,000 annual receipt gives $2,775.10, the present value of the annuity. This figure is identical to the long-method answer shown in Figure A.4:

FIGURE A.4

Time Line for an Annuity: Present Value ($i = 4\%$)

When the interest rate is 4%, the present value of a $1,000 annuity to be paid over 3 years is $2,775.10.

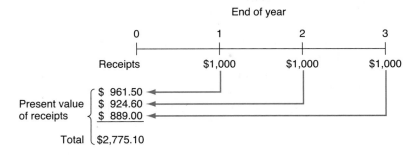

End of year

| 0 | 1 | 2 | 3 |

Receipts $1,000 $1,000 $1,000

Present value $ 961.50
of receipts $ 924.60
                  $ 889.00

Total $2,775.10

TABLE A.5

Present Value of an Annuity of $1 per Period for n Periods

$$PVIFA_{i,n} = \sum_{t=1}^{n} \frac{1}{(1 + i)^t} = \frac{1 - \dfrac{1}{(1 + i)^n}}{i}$$

Period	1%	2%	3%	4%	5%	6%	7%	8%	9%	10%
1	0.9901	0.9804	0.9709	0.9615	0.9524	0.9434	0.9346	0.9259	0.9174	0.9091
2	1.9704	1.9416	1.9135	1.8861	1.8594	1.8334	1.8080	1.7833	1.7591	1.7355
3	2.9410	2.8839	2.8286	2.7751	2.7232	2.6730	2.6243	2.5771	2.5313	2.4869
4	3.9020	3.8077	3.7171	3.6299	3.5460	3.4651	3.3872	3.3121	3.2397	3.1699
5	4.8534	4.7135	4.5797	4.4518	4.3295	4.2124	4.1002	3.9927	3.8897	3.7908
6	5.7955	5.6014	5.4172	5.2421	5.0757	4.9173	4.7665	4.6229	4.4859	4.3553
7	6.7282	6.4720	6.2303	6.0021	5.7864	5.5824	5.3893	5.2064	5.0330	4.8684
8	7.6517	7.3255	7.0197	6.7327	6.4632	6.2098	5.9713	5.7466	5.5348	5.3349
9	8.5660	8.1622	7.7861	7.4353	7.1078	6.8017	6.5152	6.2469	5.9952	5.7590
10	9.4713	8.9826	8.5302	8.1109	7.7217	7.3601	7.0236	6.7101	6.4177	6.1446

$$A_n = R(PVIFA_{i,n})$$
$$A_3 = \$1,000(2.7751)$$
$$= \$2,775.10$$

Notice that the entry for each period n in Table A.5 is equal to the sum of the entries in Table A.3 up to and including period n. For example, the *PVIFA* for 4%, three periods as shown in Table A.5, could have been calculated by summing values from Table A.3:

$$0.9615 + 0.9246 + 0.8890 = 2.7751$$

Notice also that for all positive interest rates, $PVIFA_{i,n}$ for the *present value* of an annuity is always less than the number of periods.[7]

---

7   To find the $PVIFA_{i,n}$ for an *annuity due,* look up the $PVIFA_{i,n}$ for $n - 1$ periods, then add 1.0 to this amount to obtain the $PVIFA_{i,n}$ for the annuity due. In the example, the $PVIFA_{i,n}$ for a 4%, 3-year annuity due is 1.8861 + 1.0 = 2.8861.

PRESENT VALUE OF AN UNEVEN SERIES OF RECEIPTS

The definition of an annuity includes the words *fixed amount*—in other words, annuities involve situations in which cash flows are *identical* in every period. Although many managerial decisions involve constant cash flows, some important decisions are concerned with uneven cash flows. Consequently, it is necessary to deal with varying payment streams.

The *PV* of an uneven stream of future income is found as the sum of the *PV*s of the individual components of the stream. For example, suppose that we are trying to find the *PV* of the stream of receipts shown in Table A.6, discounted at 6%. As shown in the table, we multiply each receipt by the appropriate $PVIF_{i,n}$, then sum these products to obtain the *PV* of the stream, $1,413.24. Figure A.5 gives a graphic view of the cash-flow stream.

The *PV* of the receipts shown in Table A.6 and Figure A.5 can also be found by using the annuity equation; the steps in this alternative solution process are as follows:

- *Step 1:* Find *PV* of $100 due in 1 year:

$$\$100(0.9434) = \$94.34$$

- *Step 2:* Recognize that a $200 annuity will be received during years 2 through 5. Thus, we can determine the value of a 5-year annuity, subtract from it the value of a 1-year annuity, and have remaining the value of a 4-year annuity whose first payment is due in 2 years. This result is achieved by subtracting the *PVIFA* for a 1-year, 6% annuity from the *PVIFA* for a 5-year annuity and then multiplying the difference by $200:

$$
\begin{aligned}
PV \text{ of the Annuity} &= (PVIFA_{6\%,\,5\text{ yrs.}} - PVIFA_{6\%,\,1\text{ yr.}})(\$200) \\
&= (4.2124 - 0.9434)(\$200) \\
&= \$653.80
\end{aligned}
$$

Thus, the present value of the annuity component of the uneven stream is $653.80.

- *Step 3:* Find the *PV* of the $1,000 due in year 7:

$$\$1,000(0.6651) = \$665.10$$

- *Step 4:* Sum the components:

$$\$94.34 + \$653.80 + \$665.10 = \$1,413.24$$

TABLE A.6

Present Value of an Uneven Stream of Receipts (i = 6%)

Year	Stream of Receipts	×	$PVIF_{i,n}$	=	PV of Individual Receipts
1	$ 100		0.9434		$ 94.34
2	200		0.8900		178.00
3	200		0.8396		167.92
4	200		0.7921		158.42
5	200		0.7473		149.46
6	0		0.7050		0
7	1,000		0.6651		665.10
				PV = Sum =	$1,413.24

FIGURE A.5

Time Line for an Uneven Cash Flow Stream (i = 6%)

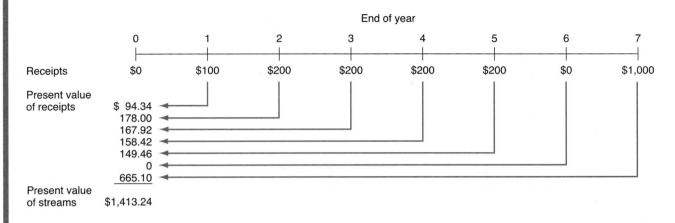

Either of the two methods can be used to solve problems of this type. However, the alternative (annuity) solution is easier if the annuity component runs for many years. For example, the alternative solution would be clearly superior for finding the PV of a stream consisting of $100 in year 1, $200 in Years 2 through 29, and $1,000 in year 30.

ANNUAL PAYMENTS FOR ACCUMULATION OF A FUTURE SUM

Suppose that you want to know the amount of money that must be deposited at 5% for each of the next 5 years in order to have $10,000 available to pay off a debt at the end of the fifth year. Dividing both sides of Equation A.4 by *FVIFA* obtains:

(A.6)
$$R = \frac{S_n}{FVIFA_{i,n}}$$

Looking up the future value of an annuity interest factor for 5 years at 5% in Table A.4 and dividing this figure into $10,000 gives:

$$R = \frac{\$10,000}{5.5256} = \$1,810$$

Thus, if $1,810 is deposited each year in an account paying 5% interest, at the end of 5 years the account will have accumulated to $10,000.

ANNUAL RECEIPTS FROM AN ANNUITY

Suppose that on September 1, 1994, you received an inheritance of $7,500. The money is to be used for your education and is to be spent during the academic years beginning September 1995, 1996, and 1997. If you place the money in a bank account paying 6% annual interest and make three equal withdrawals at each of the specified dates, how large can each withdrawal be so as to leave you with exactly a zero balance after the last one has been made?

The solution requires application of the present value of an annuity formula, Equation A.5. Here, however, we know that the present value of the annuity is $7,500, and the problem is to find the three equal annual payments when the interest rate is 6%. This calls for dividing both sides of Equation A.5 by $PVIFA_{i,n}$ to derive Equation A.7:

(A.7)
$$R = \frac{A_n}{PVIFA_{i,n}}$$

The interest factor is found in Table A.5 to be 2.6730, and substituting this value into Equation A.7, the three annual withdrawals are calculated to be $2,806:

$$R = \frac{\$7,500}{2.6730} = \$2,806$$

This particular calculation is used frequently to set up insurance and pension-plan benefit schedules and to find the periodic payments necessary to retire a loan within a specified period. For example, if you want to retire in three equal annual payments a $7,500 bank loan accruing interest at 6% on the unpaid balance, each payment would be $2,806. In this case, the bank is acquiring an annuity with a present value of $7,500.

DETERMINING INTEREST RATES

We can use the basic equations developed earlier to determine the interest rates implicit in financial contracts.

Example 1. A bank offers to lend you $1,000 if you sign a note to repay $1,610.50 at the end of 5 years. What rate of interest are you paying? To solve the problem, recognize that $1,000 is the *PV* of $1,610.50 due in 5 years, and solve Equation A.3 for the present value interest factor ($PVIF_{i,n}$).

$$PV = FV_n \left[\frac{1}{(1 + i)^n} \right] = FV_n(PVIF_{i,n})$$

(A.3)
$$\$1,000 = \$1,610.50(PVIF_{i,n} \text{ for 5 years})$$

$$\$1,000/\$1,610.50 = 0.6209 = PVIF_{i,5 \text{ years}}$$

Now, go to Table A.3 and look across the row for year 5 until you find 0.6209. It is in the 10% column, so you would be paying a 10% rate of interest.

Example 2. A bank offers to lend you $100,000 to buy a house. You must sign a mortgage calling for payments of $8,882.73 at the end of each of the next 30 years, equivalent to roughly $740.23 per month. What interest rate is the bank charging you?

1. Recognize that $100,000 is the *PV* of a 30-year, $8,882.73 annuity:

$$\$100,000 = PV = \sum_{t=1}^{30} \$8,882.73 \left[\frac{1}{(1 + i)^t} \right] = \$8,882.73(PVIFA_{i,30 \text{ yrs}})$$

2. Solve for $PVIFA_{i,30 \text{ yrs}}$:

$$PVIFA_{i,30 \text{ yrs}} = \$100,000/\$8,882.73 = 11.2578$$

3. Turn to Table B.4 in Appendix B, because Table A.5 does not cover a 30-year period. Looking across the row for 30 periods, find 11.2578 under the column for 8%. Therefore, the rate of interest on this mortgage is 8%.

SEMIANNUAL AND OTHER COMPOUNDING PERIODS

All of the examples thus far have assumed that returns were received once a year, or annually. Suppose, however, that you put your $1,000 in a bank that offers to pay 6% interest compounded *semiannually*. How much will you have at the end of 1 year? Semiannual compounding means that interest is actually paid every 6 months, a fact taken into account in the tabular calculations in Table A.7. Here the annual interest rate is divided by two, but twice as many compounding periods are used because interest is paid twice a year. Comparing the amount on hand at the end of the second 6-month period, $1,060.90, with what would have been on hand under annual compounding, $1,060, shows that semiannual compounding is better from the standpoint of the saver. This result occurs because you earn interest on interest more frequently.

Throughout the economy, different types of investments use different compounding periods. For example, bank and savings and loan accounts generally pay interest quarterly, some bonds pay interest semiannually, and other bonds pay interest annually. Thus, if we are to compare securities with different compounding periods, we need to put them on a common basis. This need has led to the development of the terms *nominal*, or *stated*, *interest rate* and *effective annual*, or *annual percentage rate (APR)*. The stated, or nominal, rate is the quoted rate; thus, in our example the nominal rate is 6%. The annual percentage rate is the rate that would have produced the final compound value, $1,060.90, under annual rather than semiannual compounding. In this case, the effective annual rate is 6.09%:

$$\$1,000(1 + i) = \$1,060.90$$

$$i = \frac{\$1,060.90}{\$1,000} - 1 = 0.0609 = 6.09\%$$

Thus, if one bank offered 6% with semiannual compounding, whereas another offered 6.09% with annual compounding, they would both be paying the same effective rate of interest. In general, we can determine the effective annual rate of interest, given the nominal rate, as follows:

- *Step 1:* Find the *FV* of $1 at the end of 1 year, using the equation

$$FV = 1\left(1 + \frac{i_n}{M}\right)^M$$

Here i_n is the nominal rate, and M is the number of compounding periods per year.

- *Step 2:* Subtract 1.0 from the result in step 1; then multiply by 100. The final result is the effective annual rate.

Example. Find the effective annual rate if the nominal rate is 6%, compounded semiannually:

$$\text{Effective Annual Rate} = \left(1 + \frac{0.06}{2}\right)^2 - 1.0$$

TABLE A.7

Compound Interest Calculations with Semiannual Compounding

	Beginning Amount (*PV*)	×	(1 + *i*/2)	=	Ending Amount, *FV*$_n$
Period 1	$1,000.00		(1.03)		$1,030.00
Period 2	$1,030.00		(1.03)		$1,060.90

$$= (1.03)^2 - 1.0$$
$$= 1.0609 - 1.0$$
$$= 0.0609$$
$$= 6.09\%$$

The points made about semiannual compounding can be generalized as follows. When compounding periods are more frequent than once a year, use a modified version of Equation A.2:

(A.2)
$$FV_n = PV(1 + i)^n$$

(A.2a)
$$FV_n = PV\left(1 + \frac{i}{M}\right)^{Mn}$$

Here M is the number of times per year compounding occurs. When banks compute daily interest, the value of M is set at 365, and Equation A.2a is applied.

The interest tables can be used when compounding occurs more than once a year. Simply divide the nominal, or stated, interest rate by the number of times compounding occurs, and multiply the years by the number of compounding periods per year. For example, to find the amount to which $1,000 will grow after 6 years with semiannual compounding and a stated 8% interest rate, divide 8% by 2 and multiply the 6 years by 2. Then look in Table A.2 under the 4% column and in the row for Period 12. You will find an interest factor of 1.6010. Multiplying this by the initial $1,000 gives a value of $1,601, the amount to which $1,000 will grow in 6 years at 8% compounded semiannually. This compares with $1,586.90 for annual compounding.

The same procedure applies in all of the cases covered—compounding, discounting, single payments, and annuities. To illustrate semiannual discounting in finding the present value of an annuity, consider the case described in the section "Present Value of an Annuity"—$1,000 a year for 3 years, discounted at 4%. With annual discounting, the interest factor is 2.7751, and the present value of the annuity is $2,775.10. For semiannual discounting, look under the 2% column and in the Period 6 row of Table A.5 to find an interest factor of 5.6014. This is now multiplied by half of $1,000, or the $500 received each 6 months, to get the present value of the annuity, $2,800.70. The payments come a little more rapidly—the first $500 is paid after only 6 months (similarly with other payments)—so the annuity is a little more valuable if payments are received semiannually rather than annually.

SUMMARY

Managerial decisions often require determining the present value of a stream of future cash flows. Also, we often need to know the amount to which an initial quantity will grow during a specified time period, and at other times we must calculate the interest rate built into a financial contract. The basic concepts involved in these processes are called compounding and the time value of money.

The key procedures covered in this appendix are summarized here:

- *Future Value:* $FV_n = PV(1 + i)^n$, where FV_n is the future value of an initial amount, PV, compounded at the rate of i percent for n periods. The term $(1 + i)^n$ is the future value interest factor, $FVIF_{i,n}$. Values for $FVIF$ are contained in tables.

- *Present Value:* $PV = FV_n[1/(1 + i)]^n$. This equation is simply a transformation of the future value equation. The term $[1/(1 + i)]^n$ is the present value interest factor, $PVIF_{i,n}$.

- *Future Value of an Annuity:* An annuity is defined as a series of constant or equal payments of R dollars per period. The sum, or future value of an annuity, is given the symbol S_n, and it is found as follows: $S_n = R\left[\sum_{t=1}^{n} (1 + i)^{t-1}\right]$. The term $\left[\sum_{t=1}^{n} (1 + i)^{t-1}\right]$ is the future value interest factor for an annuity, $FVIFA_{i,n}$.

- *Present Value of an Annuity:* The present value of an annuity is identified by the symbol A_n, and it is found as follows: $A_n = R\left[\sum_{t=1}^{n} (1/1 + i)^t\right]$. The term $\left[\sum_{t=1}^{n} (1/1 + i)^t\right] = PVIFA_{i,n}$ is the present value interest factor for an annuity.

Interest Factor Tables

TABLE B.1

Future Value of \$1: $FVIF_{i,n} = (1 + i)^n$

Period	1%	2%	3%	4%	5%	6%	7%	8%	9%	10%
1	1.0100	1.0200	1.0300	1.0400	1.0500	1.0600	1.0700	1.0800	1.0900	1.1000
2	1.0201	1.0404	1.0609	1.0816	1.1025	1.1236	1.1449	1.1664	1.1881	1.2100
3	1.0303	1.0612	1.0927	1.1249	1.1576	1.1910	1.2250	1.2597	1.2950	1.3310
4	1.0406	1.0824	1.1255	1.1699	1.2155	1.2625	1.3108	1.3605	1.4116	1.4641
5	1.0510	1.1041	1.1593	1.2167	1.2763	1.3382	1.4026	1.4693	1.5386	1.6105
6	1.0615	1.1262	1.1941	1.2653	1.3401	1.4185	1.5007	1.5869	1.6771	1.7716
7	1.0721	1.1487	1.2299	1.3159	1.4071	1.5036	1.6058	1.7138	1.8280	1.9487
8	1.0829	1.1717	1.2668	1.3686	1.4775	1.5938	1.7182	1.8509	1.9926	2.1436
9	1.0937	1.1951	1.3048	1.4233	1.5513	1.6895	1.8385	1.9990	2.1719	2.3579
10	1.1046	1.2190	1.3439	1.4802	1.6289	1.7908	1.9672	2.1589	2.3674	2.5937
11	1.1157	1.2434	1.3842	1.5395	1.7103	1.8983	2.1049	2.3316	2.5804	2.8531
12	1.1268	1.2682	1.4258	1.6010	1.7959	2.1022	2.2522	2.5182	2.8127	3.1384
13	1.1381	1.2936	1.4685	1.6651	1.8856	2.1329	2.4098	2.7196	3.0658	3.4523
14	1.1495	1.3195	1.5126	1.7317	1.9799	2.2609	2.5785	2.9372	3.3417	3.7975
15	1.1610	1.3459	1.5580	1.8009	2.0789	2.3966	2.7590	3.1722	3.6425	4.1772
16	1.1726	1.3728	1.6047	1.8730	2.1829	2.5404	2.9522	3.4259	3.9703	4.5950
17	1.1843	1.4002	1.6528	1.9479	2.2920	2.6928	3.1588	3.7000	4.3276	5.0545
18	1.1961	1.4282	1.7024	2.0258	2.4066	2.8543	3.3799	3.9960	4.7171	5.5599
19	1.2081	1.4568	1.7535	2.1068	2.5270	3.0256	3.6165	4.3157	5.1417	6.1159
20	1.2202	1.4859	1.8061	2.1911	2.6533	3.2071	3.8697	4.6610	5.6044	6.7275
21	1.2324	1.5157	1.8603	2.2788	2.7860	3.3996	4.1406	5.0338	6.1088	7.4002
22	1.2447	1.5460	1.9161	2.3699	2.9253	3.6035	4.4304	5.4365	6.6586	8.1403
23	1.2572	1.5769	1.9736	2.4647	3.0715	3.8197	4.7405	5.8715	7.2579	8.9543
24	1.2697	1.6084	2.0328	2.5633	3.2251	4.0489	5.0724	6.3412	7.9111	9.8497
25	1.2824	1.6406	2.0938	2.6658	3.3864	4.2919	5.4274	6.8485	8.6231	10.834
26	1.2953	1.6734	2.1566	2.7725	3.5557	4.5494	5.8074	7.3964	9.3992	11.918
27	1.3082	1.7069	2.2213	2.8834	3.7335	4.8223	6.2139	7.9881	10.245	13.110
28	1.3213	1.7410	2.2879	2.9987	3.9201	5.1117	6.6488	8.6271	11.167	14.421
29	1.3345	1.7758	2.3566	3.1187	4.1161	5.4184	7.1143	9.3173	12.172	15.863
30	1.3478	1.8114	2.4273	3.2434	4.3219	5.7435	7.6123	10.062	13.267	17.449
40	1.4889	2.2080	3.2620	4.8010	7.0400	10.285	14.974	21.724	31.409	45.259
50	1.6446	2.6916	4.3839	7.1067	11.467	18.420	29.457	46.901	74.357	117.39
60	1.8167	3.2810	5.8916	10.519	18.679	32.987	57.946	101.25	176.03	304.48

TABLE B.1 *(continued)*

Future Value of $1: $FVIF_{i,n} = (1 + i)^n$

Period	12%	14%	15%	16%	18%	20%	24%	28%	32%	36%
1	1.1200	1.1400	1.1500	1.1600	1.1800	1.2000	1.2400	1.2800	1.3200	1.3600
2	1.2544	1.2996	1.3225	1.3456	1.3924	1.4400	1.5376	1.6384	1.7424	1.8496
3	1.4049	1.4815	1.5209	1.5609	1.6430	1.7280	1.9066	2.0972	2.3000	2.5155
4	1.5735	1.6890	1.7490	1.8106	1.9388	2.0736	2.3642	2.6844	3.0360	3.4210
5	1.7623	1.9254	2.0114	2.1003	2.2878	2.4883	2.9316	3.4360	4.0075	4.6526
6	1.9738	2.1950	2.3131	2.4364	2.6996	2.9860	3.6352	4.3980	5.2899	6.3275
7	2.2107	2.5023	2.6600	2.8262	3.1855	3.5832	4.5077	5.6295	6.9826	8.6054
8	2.4760	2.8526	3.0590	3.2784	3.7589	4.2998	5.5895	7.2058	9.2170	11.703
9	2.7731	3.2519	3.5179	3.8030	4.4355	5.1598	6.9310	9.2234	12.166	15.916
10	3.1058	3.7072	4.0456	4.4114	5.2338	6.1917	8.5944	11.805	16.059	21.646
11	3.4785	4.2262	4.6524	5.1173	6.1759	7.4301	10.657	15.111	21.198	29.439
12	3.8960	4.8179	5.3502	5.9360	7.2876	8.9161	13.214	19.342	27.982	40.037
13	4.3635	5.4924	6.1528	6.8858	8.5994	10.699	16.386	24.758	36.937	54.451
14	4.8871	6.2613	7.0757	7.9875	10.147	12.839	20.319	31.691	48.756	74.053
15	5.4736	7.1379	8.1371	9.2655	11.973	15.407	25.195	40.564	64.358	100.71
16	6.1304	8.1372	9.3576	10.748	14.129	18.488	31.242	51.923	84.953	136.96
17	6.8660	9.2765	10.761	12.467	16.672	22.186	38.740	66.461	112.13	186.27
18	7.6900	10.575	12.375	14.462	19.673	26.623	48.038	85.070	148.02	253.33
19	8.6128	12.055	14.231	16.776	23.214	31.948	59.567	108.89	195.39	344.53
20	9.6463	13.743	16.366	19.460	27.393	38.337	73.864	139.37	257.91	468.57
21	10.803	15.667	18.821	22.574	32.323	46.005	91.591	178.40	340.44	637.26
22	12.100	17.861	21.644	26.186	38.142	55.206	113.57	228.35	449.39	866.67
23	13.552	20.361	24.891	30.376	45.007	66.247	140.83	292.30	593.19	1178.6
24	15.178	23.212	28.625	35.236	53.108	79.496	174.63	374.14	783.02	1602.9
25	17.000	26.461	32.918	40.874	62.668	95.396	216.54	478.90	1033.5	2180.0
26	19.040	30.166	37.856	47.414	73.948	114.47	268.51	612.99	1364.3	2964.9
27	21.324	34.389	43.535	55.000	87.259	137.37	332.95	784.63	1800.9	4032.2
28	23.883	39.204	50.065	63.800	102.96	164.84	412.86	1004.3	2377.2	5483.8
29	26.749	44.693	57.575	74.008	121.50	197.81	511.95	1285.5	3137.9	7458.0
30	29.959	50.950	66.211	85.849	143.37	237.37	634.81	1645.5	4142.0	10143.
40	93.050	188.88	267.86	378.72	750.37	1469.7	5455.9	19426.	66520.	*
50	289.00	700.23	1083.6	1670.7	3927.3	9100.4	46890.	*	*	*
60	897.59	2595.9	4383.9	7370.1	20555.	56347.	*	*	*	*

*$FVIF$ > 99,999.

TABLE B.2

Present Value of $1: $PVIF_{i,n} = 1/(1 + i)^n = 1/FVIF_{i,n}$

Period	1%	2%	3%	4%	5%	6%	7%	8%	9%	10%
1	.9901	.9804	.9709	.9615	.9524	.9434	.9346	.9259	.9174	.9091
2	.9803	.9612	.9426	.9246	.9070	.8900	.8734	.8573	.8417	.8264
3	.9706	.9423	.9151	.8890	.8638	.8396	.8163	.7938	.7722	.7513
4	.9610	.9238	.8885	.8548	.8227	.7921	.7629	.7350	.7084	.6830
5	.9515	.9057	.8626	.8219	.7835	.7473	.7130	.6806	.6499	.6209
6	.9420	.8880	.8375	.7903	.7462	.7050	.6663	.6302	.5963	.5645
7	.9327	.8706	.8131	.7599	.7107	.6651	.6227	.5835	.5470	.5132
8	.9235	.8535	.7894	.7307	.6768	.6274	.5820	.5403	.5019	.4665
9	.9143	.8368	.7664	.7026	.6446	.5919	.5439	.5002	.4604	.4241
10	.9053	.8203	.7441	.6756	.6139	.5584	.5083	.4632	.4224	.3855
11	.8963	.8043	.7224	.6496	.5847	.5268	.4751	.4289	.3875	.3505
12	.8874	.7885	.7014	.6246	.5568	.4970	.4440	.3971	.3555	.3186
13	.8787	.7730	.6810	.6006	.5303	.4688	.4150	.3677	.3262	.2897
14	.8700	.7579	.6611	.5775	.5051	.4423	.3878	.3405	.2992	.2633
15	.8613	.7430	.6419	.5553	.4810	.4173	.3624	.3152	.2745	.2394
16	.8528	.7284	.6232	.5339	.4581	.3936	.3387	.2919	.2519	.2176
17	.8444	.7142	.6050	.5134	.4363	.3714	.3166	.2703	.2311	.1978
18	.8360	.7002	.5874	.4936	.4155	.3503	.2959	.2502	.2120	.1799
19	.8277	.6854	.5703	.4746	.3957	.3305	.2765	.2317	.1945	.1635
20	.8195	.6730	.5537	.4564	.3769	.3118	.2584	.2145	.1784	.1486
21	.8114	.6598	.5375	.4388	.3589	.2942	.2415	.1987	.1637	.1351
22	.8034	.6468	.5219	.4220	.3418	.2775	.2257	.1839	.1502	.1228
23	.7954	.6342	.5067	.4057	.3256	.2618	.2109	.1703	.1378	.1117
24	.7876	.6217	.4919	.3901	.3101	.2470	.1971	.1577	.1264	.1015
25	.7798	.6095	.4776	.3751	.2953	.2330	.1842	.1460	.1160	.0923
26	.7720	.5976	.4637	.3607	.2812	.2198	.1722	.1352	.1064	.0839
27	.7644	.5859	.4502	.3468	.2678	.2074	.1609	.1252	.0976	.0763
28	.7568	.5744	.4371	.3335	.2551	.1956	.1504	.1159	.0895	.0693
29	.7493	.5631	.4243	.3207	.2429	.1846	.1406	.1073	.0822	.0630
30	.7419	.5521	.4120	.3083	.2314	.1741	.1314	.0994	.0754	.0573
35	.7059	.5000	.3554	.2534	.1813	.1301	.0937	.0676	.0490	.0356
40	.6717	.4529	.3066	.2083	.1420	.0972	.0668	.0460	.0318	.0221
45	.6391	.4102	.2644	.1712	.1113	.0727	.0476	.0313	.0207	.0137
50	.6080	.3715	.2281	.1407	.0872	.0543	.0339	.0213	.0134	.0085
55	.5785	.3365	.1968	.1157	.0683	.0406	.0242	.0145	.0087	.0053

TABLE B.2 *(continued)*

Present Value of $1: $PVIF_{i,n} = 1/(1 + i)^n = 1/FVIF_{i,n}$

Period	12%	14%	15%	16%	18%	20%	24%	28%	32%	36%
1	.8929	.8772	.8969	.8621	.8475	.8333	.8065	.7813	.7576	.7353
2	.7972	.7695	.7561	.7432	.7182	.6944	.6504	.6104	.5739	.5407
3	.7118	.6750	.6575	.6407	.6086	.5787	.5245	.4768	.4348	.3975
4	.6355	.5921	.5718	.5523	.5158	.4823	.4230	.3725	.3294	.2923
5	.5674	.5194	.4972	.4761	.4371	.4091	.3411	.2910	.2495	.2149
6	.5066	.4556	.4323	.4104	.3704	.3349	.2751	.2274	.1890	.1580
7	.4523	.3996	.3759	.3538	.3139	.2791	.2218	.1776	.1432	.1162
8	.4039	.3506	.3269	.3050	.2660	.2326	.1789	.1388	.1085	.0854
9	.3606	.3075	.2843	.2630	.2255	.1938	.1443	.1084	.0822	.0628
10	.3220	.2697	.2472	.2267	.1911	.1615	.1164	.0847	.0623	.0462
11	.2875	.2366	.2149	.1954	.1619	.1346	.0938	.0662	.0472	.0340
12	.2567	.2076	.1869	.1685	.1372	.1122	.0757	.0517	.0357	.0250
13	.2292	.1821	.1625	.1452	.1163	.0935	.0610	.0404	.0271	.0184
14	.2046	.1597	.1413	.1252	.0985	.0779	.0492	.0316	.0205	.0135
15	.1827	.1401	.1229	.1079	.0835	.0649	.0397	.0247	.0155	.0099
16	.1631	.1229	.1069	.0930	.0708	.0541	.0320	.0193	.0118	.0073
17	.1456	.1078	.0929	.0802	.0600	.0451	.0258	.0150	.0089	.0054
18	.1300	.0946	.0808	.0691	.0508	.0376	.0208	.0118	.0068	.0039
19	.1161	.0829	.0703	.0596	.0431	.0313	.0168	.0092	.0051	.0029
20	.1037	.0728	.0611	.0514	.0365	.0261	.0135	.0072	.0039	.0021
21	.0926	.0638	.0531	.0443	.0309	.0217	.0109	.0056	.0029	.0016
22	.0826	.0560	.0462	.0382	.0262	.0181	.0088	.0044	.0022	.0012
23	.0738	.0491	.0402	.0329	.0222	.0151	.0071	.0034	.0017	.0008
24	.0659	.0431	.0349	.0284	.0188	.0126	.0057	.0027	.0013	.0006
25	.0588	.0378	.0304	.0245	.0160	.0105	.0046	.0021	.0010	.0005
26	.0525	.0331	.0264	.0211	.0135	.0087	.0037	.0016	.0007	.0003
27	.0469	.0291	.0230	.0182	.0115	.0073	.0030	.0013	.0006	.0002
28	.0419	.0255	.0200	.0157	.0097	.0061	.0024	.0010	.0004	.0002
29	.0374	.0224	.0174	.0135	.0082	.0051	.0020	.0008	.0003	.0001
30	.0334	.0196	.0151	.0116	.0070	.0042	.0016	.0006	.0002	.0001
35	.0189	.0102	.0075	.0055	.0030	.0017	.0005	.0002	.0001	*
40	.0107	.0053	.0037	.0026	.0013	.0007	.0002	.0001	*	*
45	.0061	.0027	.0019	.0013	.0006	.0003	.0001	*	*	*
50	.0035	.0014	.0009	.0006	.0003	.0001	*	*	*	*
55	.0020	.0007	.0005	.0003	.0001	*	*	*	*	*

*The factor is zero to four decimal places.

TABLE B.3

Future Value of an Annuity of $1 for *n* Periods

$$FVIFA_{i,n} = \sum_{t=1}^{n} (1 + i)^{t-1}$$

$$= \frac{(1 + i)^n - 1}{i}$$

Number of Periods	1%	2%	3%	4%	5%	6%	7%	8%	9%	10%
1	1.0000	1.0000	1.0000	1.0000	1.0000	1.0000	1.0000	1.0000	1.0000	1.0000
2	2.0100	2.0200	2.0300	2.0400	2.0500	2.0600	2.0700	2.0800	2.0900	2.1000
3	3.0301	3.0604	3.0909	3.1216	3.1525	3.1836	3.2149	3.2465	3.2781	3.3100
4	4.0604	4.1216	4.1836	4.2465	4.3101	4.3746	4.4399	4.5061	4.5731	4.6410
5	5.1010	5.2040	5.3091	5.4163	5.5256	5.6371	5.7507	5.8666	5.9847	6.1051
6	6.1520	6.3081	6.4684	6.6330	6.8019	6.9753	7.1533	7.3359	7.5233	7.7156
7	7.2135	7.4343	7.6625	7.8983	8.1420	8.3938	8.6540	8.9228	9.2004	9.4872
8	8.2857	8.5830	8.8923	9.2142	9.5491	9.8975	10.259	10.636	11.028	11.435
9	9.3685	9.7546	10.159	10.582	11.026	11.491	11.978	12.487	13.021	13.579
10	10.462	10.949	11.463	12.006	12.577	13.180	13.816	14.486	15.192	15.937
11	11.566	12.168	12.807	13.486	14.206	14.971	15.783	16.645	17.560	18.531
12	12.682	13.412	14.192	15.025	15.917	16.869	17.888	18.977	20.140	21.384
13	13.809	14.680	15.617	16.626	17.713	18.882	20.140	21.495	22.953	24.522
14	14.947	15.973	17.086	18.291	19.598	21.015	22.550	24.214	26.019	27.975
15	16.096	17.293	18.598	20.023	21.578	23.276	25.129	27.152	29.360	31.772
16	17.257	18.639	20.156	21.824	23.657	25.672	27.888	30.324	33.003	35.949
17	18.430	20.012	21.761	23.697	25.840	28.212	30.840	33.750	36.973	40.544
18	19.614	21.412	23.414	25.645	28.132	30.905	33.999	37.450	41.301	45.599
19	20.810	22.840	25.116	27.671	30.539	33.760	37.379	41.446	46.018	51.159
20	22.019	24.297	26.870	29.778	33.066	36.785	40.995	45.762	51.160	57.275
21	23.239	25.783	28.676	31.969	35.719	39.992	44.865	50.422	56.764	64.002
22	24.471	27.299	30.536	34.248	38.505	43.392	49.005	55.456	62.873	71.402
23	25.716	28.845	32.452	36.617	41.430	46.995	53.436	60.893	69.531	79.543
24	26.973	30.421	34.426	39.082	44.502	50.815	58.176	66.764	76.789	88.497
25	28.243	32.030	36.459	41.645	47.727	54.864	63.249	73.105	84.700	98.347
26	29.525	33.670	38.553	44.311	51.113	59.156	68.676	79.954	93.323	109.18
27	30.820	35.344	40.709	47.084	54.669	63.705	74.483	87.350	102.72	121.09
28	32.129	37.051	42.930	49.967	58.402	68.528	80.697	95.338	112.96	134.20
29	33.450	38.792	45.218	52.966	62.322	73.639	87.346	103.96	124.13	148.63
30	34.784	40.568	47.575	56.084	66.438	79.058	94.460	113.28	136.30	164.49
40	48.886	60.402	75.401	95.025	120.79	154.76	199.63	259.05	337.88	442.59
50	64.463	84.579	112.79	152.66	209.34	290.33	406.52	573.76	815.08	1163.9
60	81.669	114.05	163.05	237.99	353.58	533.12	813.52	1253.2	1944.7	3034.8

TABLE B.3 *(continued)*

Future Value of an Annuity of $1 for *n* Periods

$$FVIFA_{i,n} = \sum_{t=1}^{n} (1 + i)^{t-1}$$

$$= \frac{(1 + i)^n - 1}{i}$$

Number of Periods	12%	14%	15%	16%	18%	20%	24%	28%	32%	36%
1	1.0000	1.0000	1.0000	1.0000	1.0000	1.0000	1.0000	1.0000	1.0000	1.0000
2	2.1200	2.1400	2.1500	2.1600	2.1800	2.2000	2.2400	2.2800	2.3200	2.3600
3	3.3744	3.4396	3.4725	3.5056	3.5724	3.6400	3.7776	3.9184	4.0624	4.2096
4	4.7793	4.9211	4.9934	5.0665	5.2154	5.3680	5.6842	6.0156	6.3624	6.7251
5	6.3528	6.6101	6.7424	6.8771	7.1542	7.4416	8.0484	8.6999	9.3983	10.146
6	8.1152	8.5355	8.7537	8.9775	9.4420	9.9299	10.980	12.135	13.405	14.798
7	10.089	10.730	11.066	11.413	12.141	12.915	14.615	16.533	18.695	21.126
8	12.299	13.232	13.726	14.240	15.327	16.499	19.122	22.163	25.678	29.731
9	14.775	16.085	16.785	17.518	19.085	20.798	24.712	29.369	34.895	41.435
10	17.548	19.337	20.303	21.321	23.521	25.958	31.643	38.592	47.061	57.351
11	20.654	23.044	24.349	25.732	28.755	32.150	40.237	50.398	63.121	78.998
12	24.133	27.270	29.001	30.850	34.931	39.580	50.894	65.510	84.320	108.43
13	28.029	32.088	34.351	36.786	42.218	48.496	64.109	84.852	112.30	148.47
14	32.392	37.581	40.504	43.672	50.818	59.195	80.496	109.61	149.23	202.92
15	37.279	43.842	47.580	51.659	60.965	72.035	100.81	141.30	197.99	276.97
16	42.753	50.980	55.717	60.925	72.939	87.442	126.01	181.86	262.35	377.69
17	48.883	59.117	65.075	71.673	87.068	105.93	157.25	233.79	347.30	514.66
18	55.749	68.394	75.836	84.140	103.74	128.11	195.99	300.25	459.44	700.93
19	63.439	78.969	88.211	98.603	123.41	154.74	244.03	385.32	607.47	954.27
20	72.052	91.024	102.44	115.37	146.62	186.68	303.60	494.21	802.86	1298.8
21	81.698	104.76	118.81	134.84	174.02	225.02	377.46	633.59	1060.7	1767.3
22	92.502	120.43	137.63	157.41	206.34	271.03	469.05	811.99	1401.2	2404.6
23	104.60	138.29	159.27	183.60	244.48	326.23	582.62	1040.3	1850.6	3271.3
24	118.15	158.65	184.16	213.97	289.49	392.48	723.46	1332.6	2443.8	4449.9
25	133.33	181.87	212.79	249.21	342.60	471.98	898.09	1706.8	3226.8	6052.9
26	150.33	208.33	245.71	290.08	405.27	567.37	1114.6	2185.7	4260.4	8233.0
27	169.37	238.49	283.56	337.50	479.22	681.85	1383.1	2798.7	5624.7	11197.9
28	190.69	272.88	327.10	392.50	566.48	819.22	1716.0	3583.3	7425.6	15230.2
29	214.58	312.09	377.16	456.30	669.44	984.06	2128.9	4587.6	9802.9	20714.1
30	241.33	356.78	434.74	530.31	790.94	1181.8	2640.9	5873.2	12940.	28172.2
40	767.09	1342.0	1779.0	2360.7	4163.2	7343.8	22728.	69377.	*	*
50	2400.0	4994.5	7217.7	10435.	21813.	45497.	*	*	*	*
60	7471.6	18535.	29219.	46057.	*	*	*	*	*	*

*FVIVA > 99,999.

TABLE B.4

Present Value of an Annuity of $1 for *n* Periods

$$PVIFA_{i,n} = \sum_{t=1}^{n} \frac{1}{(1 + i)^t} = \frac{1 - \dfrac{1}{(1 + i)^n}}{i}$$

Number of Payments	1%	2%	3%	4%	5%	6%	7%	8%	9%
1	0.9901	0.9804	0.9709	0.9615	0.9524	0.9434	0.9346	0.9259	0.9174
2	1.09704	1.9416	1.9135	1.8861	1.8594	1.8334	1.8080	1.7833	1.7591
3	2.9410	2.8839	2.8286	2.7751	2.7232	2.6730	2.6243	2.5771	2.5313
4	3.9020	3.8077	3.7171	3.6299	3.5460	3.4651	3.3872	3.3121	3.2397
5	4.8534	4.7135	4.5797	4.4518	4.3295	4.2124	4.1002	3.9927	3.8897
6	5.7955	5.6014	5.4172	5.2421	5.0757	4.9173	4.7665	4.6229	4.4859
7	6.7282	6.4720	6.2303	6.0021	5.7864	5.5824	5.3893	5.2064	5.0330
8	7.6517	7.3255	7.0197	6.7327	6.4632	6.2098	5.9713	5.7466	5.5348
9	8.5660	8.1622	7.7861	7.4353	7.1078	6.8017	6.5152	6.2469	5.9952
10	9.4713	8.9826	8.5302	8.1109	7.7217	7.3601	7.0236	6.7101	6.4177
11	10.3676	9.7868	9.2526	8.7605	8.3064	7.8869	7.4987	7.1390	6.8052
12	11.2551	10.5753	9.9540	9.3851	8.8633	8.3838	7.9427	7.5361	7.1607
13	12.1337	11.3484	10.6350	9.9856	9.3936	8.8527	8.3577	7.9038	7.4869
14	13.0037	12.1062	11.2961	10.5631	9.8986	9.2950	8.7455	8.2442	7.7862
15	13.8651	12.8493	11.9379	11.1184	10.3797	9.7122	9.1079	8.5595	8.0607
16	14.7179	13.5777	12.5611	11.6523	10.8378	10.1059	9.4466	8.8514	8.3126
17	15.5623	14.2919	13.1661	12.1657	11.2741	10.4773	9.7632	9.1216	8.5436
18	16.3983	14.9920	13.7535	12.6593	11.6896	10.8276	10.0591	9.3719	8.7556
19	17.2260	15.6785	14.3238	13.1339	12.0853	11.1581	10.3356	9.6036	8.9501
20	18.0456	16.3514	14.8775	13.5903	12.4622	11.4699	10.5940	9.8181	9.1285
21	18.8570	17.0112	15.4150	14.0292	12.8212	11.7641	10.8355	10.0168	9.2922
22	19.6604	17.6580	15.9369	14.4511	13.1630	12.0416	11.0612	10.2007	9.4424
23	20.4558	18.2922	16.4436	14.8568	13.4886	12.3034	11.2722	10.3711	9.5802
24	21.2434	18.9139	16.9355	15.2470	13.7986	12.5504	11.4693	10.5288	9.7066
25	22.0232	19.5235	17.4131	15.6221	14.0939	12.7834	11.6536	10.6748	9.8226
26	22.7952	20.1210	17.8768	15.9828	14.3752	13.0032	11.8258	10.8100	9.9290
27	23.5596	20.7069	18.3270	16.3296	14.6430	13.2105	11.9867	10.9352	10.0266
28	24.3164	21.2813	18.7641	16.6631	14.8981	13.4062	12.1371	11.0511	10.1161
29	25.0658	21.8444	19.1885	16.9837	15.1411	13.5907	12.2777	11.1584	10.1983
30	25.8077	22.3965	19.6004	17.2920	15.3725	13.7648	12.4090	11.2578	10.2737
35	29.4086	24.9986	21.4872	18.6646	16.3742	14.4982	12.9477	11.6546	10.5668
40	32.8347	27.3555	23.1148	19.7928	17.1591	15.0463	13.3317	11.9246	10.7574
45	36.0945	29.4902	24.5187	20.7200	17.7741	15.4558	13.6055	12.1084	10.8812
50	39.1961	31.4236	25.7298	21.4822	18.2559	15.7619	13.8007	12.2335	10.9617
55	42.1472	33.1748	26.7744	22.1086	18.6335	15.9905	13.9399	12.3186	11.0140

TABLE B.4 *(continued)*

Present Value of an Annuity of $1 for *n* Periods

$$PVIFA_{i,n} = \sum_{t=1}^{n} \frac{1}{(1 + i)^t} = \frac{1 - \dfrac{1}{(1 + i)^n}}{i}$$

Number of Payments	10%	12%	14%	15%	16%	18%	20%	24%	28%	32%
1	0.9091	0.8929	0.8772	0.8696	0.8621	0.8475	0.8333	0.8065	0.7813	0.7576
2	1.7355	1.6901	1.6467	1.6257	1.6052	1.5656	1.5278	1.4568	1.3916	1.3315
3	2.4869	2.4018	2.3216	2.2832	2.2459	2.1743	2.1065	1.9813	1.8684	1.7663
4	3.1699	3.0373	2.9137	2.8550	2.7982	2.6901	2.5887	2.4043	2.2410	2.0957
5	3.7908	3.6048	3.4331	3.3522	3.2743	3.1272	2.9906	2.7454	2.5320	2.3452
6	4.3553	4.1114	3.8887	3.7845	3.6847	3.4976	3.3255	3.0205	2.7594	2.5342
7	4.8684	4.5638	4.2883	4.1604	4.0386	3.8115	3.6046	3.2423	2.9370	2.6775
8	5.3349	4.9676	4.6389	4.4873	4.3436	4.0776	3.8372	3.4212	3.0758	2.7860
9	5.7590	5.3282	4.9464	4.7716	4.6065	4.3030	4.0310	3.5655	3.1842	2.8681
10	6.1446	5.6502	5.2161	5.0188	4.8332	4.4941	4.1925	3.6819	3.2689	2.9304
11	6.4951	5.9377	5.4527	5.2337	5.0286	4.6560	4.3271	3.7757	3.3351	2.9776
12	6.8137	6.1944	5.6603	5.4206	5.1971	4.7932	4.4392	3.8514	3.3868	3.0133
13	7.1034	6.4235	5.8424	5.5831	5.3423	4.9095	4.5327	3.9124	3.4272	3.0404
14	7.3667	6.6282	6.0021	5.7245	5.4675	5.0081	4.6106	3.9616	3.4587	3.0609
15	7.6061	6.8109	6.1422	5.8474	5.5755	5.0916	4.6755	4.0013	3.4834	3.0764
16	7.8237	6.9740	6.2651	5.9542	5.6685	5.1624	4.7296	4.0333	3.5026	3.0882
17	8.0216	7.1196	6.3729	6.0472	5.7487	5.2223	4.7746	4.0591	3.5177	3.0971
18	8.2014	7.2497	6.4674	6.1280	5.8178	5.2732	4.8122	4.0799	3.5294	3.1039
19	8.3649	7.3658	6.5504	6.1982	5.8775	5.3162	4.8435	4.0967	3.5386	3.1090
20	8.5136	7.4694	6.6231	6.2593	5.9288	5.3527	4.8696	4.1103	3.5458	3.1129
21	8.6487	7.5620	6.6870	6.3125	5.9731	5.3837	4.8913	4.1212	3.5514	3.1158
22	8.7715	7.6446	6.7429	6.3587	6.0113	5.4099	4.9094	4.1300	3.5558	3.1180
23	8.8832	7.7184	6.7921	6.3988	6.0442	5.4321	4.9245	4.1371	3.5592	3.1197
24	8.9847	7.7843	6.8351	6.4338	6.0726	5.4510	4.9371	4.1428	3.5619	3.1210
25	9.0770	7.8431	6.8729	6.4642	6.0971	5.4669	4.9476	4.1474	3.5640	3.1220
26	9.1609	7.8957	6.9061	6.4906	6.1182	5.4804	4.9563	4.1511	3.5656	3.1227
27	9.2372	7.9426	6.9352	6.5135	6.1364	5.4919	4.9636	4.1542	3.5669	3.1233
28	9.3066	7.9844	6.9607	6.5335	6.1520	6.5016	4.9697	4.1566	3.5679	3.1237
29	9.3696	8.0218	6.9830	6.5509	6.1656	5.5098	4.9747	4.1585	3.5687	3.1240
30	9.4269	8.0552	7.0027	6.5660	6.1772	5.5168	4.9789	4.1601	3.5693	3.1242
35	9.6442	8.1755	7.0700	6.6166	6.2153	5.5386	4.9915	4.1644	3.5708	3.1248
40	9.7791	8.2438	7.1050	6.6418	6.2335	5.5482	4.9966	4.1659	3.5712	3.1250
45	9.8628	8.2825	7.1232	6.6543	6.2421	5.5523	4.9986	4.1664	3.5714	3.1250
50	9.9148	8.3045	7.1327	6.6605	6.2463	5.5541	4.9995	4.1666	3.5714	3.1250
55	9.9471	8.3170	7.1376	6.6636	6.2482	5.5549	4.9998	4.1666	3.5714	3.1250

APPENDIX C

Statistical Tables

TABLE C.1

Distribution of a Variable z (Percent of Total Area Under the Normal Curve Between x and μ)

z^1	0.00	0.01	0.02	0.03	0.04	0.05	0.06	0.07	0.08	0.09
0.0	.0000	.0040	.0080	.0120	.0160	.0199	.0239	.0279	.0319	.0359
0.1	.0398	.0438	.0478	.0517	.0557	.0596	.0636	.0675	.0714	.0753
0.2	.0793	.0832	.0871	.0910	.0948	.0987	.1026	.1064	.1103	.1141
0.3	.1179	.1217	.1255	.1293	.1331	.1368	.1406	.1443	.1480	.1517
0.4	.1554	.1591	.1628	.1664	.1700	.1736	.1772	.1808	.1844	.1879
0.5	.1915	.1950	.1985	.2019	.2054	.2088	.2123	.2157	.2190	.2224
0.6	.2257	.2291	.2324	.2357	.2389	.2422	.2454	.2486	.2517	.2549
0.7	.2580	.2611	.2642	.2673	.2704	.2734	.2764	.2794	.2823	.2852
0.8	.2881	.2910	.2939	.2967	.2995	.3023	.3051	.3078	.3106	.3133
0.9	.3159	.3186	.3212	.3238	.3264	.3289	.3315	.3340	.3365	.3389
1.0	.3413	.3438	.3461	.3485	.3508	.3531	.3554	.3577	.3599	.3621
1.1	.3643	.3665	.3686	.3708	.3729	.3749	.3770	.3790	.3810	.3830
1.2	.3849	.3869	.3888	.3907	.3925	.3944	.3962	.3980	.3997	.4015
1.3	.4032	.4049	.4066	.4082	.4099	.4115	.4131	.4147	.4162	.4177
1.4	.4192	.4207	.4222	.4236	.4251	.4265	.4279	.4292	.4306	.4319
1.5	.4332	.4345	.4357	.4370	.4382	.4394	.4406	.4418	.4429	.4441
1.6	.4452	.4463	.4474	.4484	.4495	.4505	.4515	.4525	.4535	.4545
1.7	.4554	.4564	.4573	.4582	.4591	.4599	.4608	.4616	.4625	.4633
1.8	.4641	.4649	.4656	.4664	.4671	.4678	.4686	.4693	.4699	.4706
1.9	.4713	.4719	.4726	.4732	.4738	.4744	.4750	.4756	.4761	.4767
2.0	.4773	.4778	.4783	.4788	.4793	.4798	.4803	.4808	.4812	.4817
2.1	.4821	.4826	.4830	.4834	.4838	.4842	.4846	.4850	.4854	.4857
2.2	.4861	.4864	.4868	.4871	.4875	.4878	.4881	.4884	.4887	.4890
2.3	.4893	.4896	.4898	.4901	.4904	.4906	.4909	.4911	.4913	.4916
2.4	.4918	.4920	.4922	.4925	.4927	.4929	.4931	.4932	.4934	.4936
2.5	.4938	.4940	.4941	.4943	.4945	.4946	.4948	.4949	.4951	.4952
2.6	.4953	.4955	.4956	.4957	.4959	.4960	.4961	.4962	.4963	.4964
2.7	.4965	.4966	.4967	.4968	.4969	.4970	.4971	.4972	.4973	.4974
2.8	.4974	.4975	.4976	.4977	.4977	.4978	.4979	.4979	.4980	.4981
2.9	.4981	.4982	.4982	.4982	.4894	.4984	.4985	.4985	.4986	.4986
3.0	.4987	.4987	.4987	.4988	.4988	.4989	.4989	.4989	.4990	.4990

[1] z is the standardized variable, where $z = x - \mu/\sigma$ and x is the point of interest, μ is the mean, and σ is the standard deviation of a distribution. Thus, z measures the number of standard deviations between a point of interest x and the mean of a given distribution. In the table above, we indicate the percentage of the total area under the normal curve between x and μ. Thus, .3413 or 34.13% of the area under the normal curve lies between a point of interest and the mean when $z = 1.0$.

TABLE C.2

Critical *F* Values at the 90 Percent Confidence Level (α = .10)[1]

Degrees of Freedom in the Numerator $(df = k - 1)$

$df = n - k$	1	2	3	4	5	6	7	8	9	10	12	15	20	24	30	40	60	120	∞
1	39.86	49.50	53.59	55.83	57.24	58.20	58.91	59.44	59.86	60.19	60.71	61.22	61.74	62.00	62.26	62.53	62.79	63.06	63.33
2	8.53	9.00	9.16	9.24	9.29	9.33	9.35	9.37	9.38	9.39	9.41	9.42	9.44	9.45	9.46	9.47	9.47	9.48	9.49
3	5.54	5.46	5.39	5.34	5.31	5.28	5.27	5.25	5.24	5.23	5.22	5.20	5.18	5.18	5.17	5.16	5.15	5.14	5.13
4	4.54	4.32	4.19	4.11	4.05	4.01	3.98	3.95	3.94	3.92	3.90	3.87	3.84	3.83	3.82	3.80	3.79	3.78	3.76
5	4.06	3.78	3.62	3.52	3.45	3.40	3.37	3.34	3.32	3.30	3.27	3.24	3.21	3.19	3.17	3.16	3.14	3.12	3.10
6	3.78	3.46	3.29	3.18	3.11	3.05	3.01	2.98	2.96	2.94	2.90	2.87	2.84	2.82	2.80	2.78	2.76	2.74	2.72
7	3.59	3.26	3.07	2.96	2.88	2.83	2.78	2.75	2.72	2.70	2.67	2.63	2.59	2.58	2.56	2.54	2.51	2.49	2.47
8	3.46	3.11	2.92	2.81	2.73	2.67	2.62	2.59	2.56	2.54	2.50	2.46	2.42	2.40	2.38	2.36	2.34	2.32	2.29
9	3.36	3.01	2.81	2.69	2.61	2.55	2.51	2.47	2.44	2.42	2.38	2.34	2.30	2.28	2.25	2.23	2.21	2.18	2.16
10	3.29	2.92	2.73	2.61	2.52	2.46	2.41	2.38	2.35	2.32	2.28	2.24	2.20	2.18	2.16	2.13	2.11	2.08	2.06
11	3.23	2.86	2.66	2.54	2.45	2.39	2.34	2.30	2.27	2.25	2.21	2.17	2.12	2.10	2.08	2.05	2.03	2.00	1.97
12	3.18	2.81	2.61	2.48	2.39	2.33	2.28	2.24	2.21	2.19	2.15	2.10	2.06	2.04	2.01	1.99	1.96	1.93	1.90
13	3.14	2.76	2.56	2.43	2.35	2.28	2.23	2.20	2.16	2.14	2.10	2.05	2.01	1.98	1.96	1.93	1.90	1.88	1.85
14	3.10	2.73	2.52	2.39	2.31	2.24	2.19	2.15	2.12	2.10	2.05	2.01	1.96	1.94	1.91	1.89	1.86	1.83	1.80
15	3.07	2.70	2.49	2.36	2.27	2.21	2.16	2.12	2.09	2.06	2.02	1.97	1.92	1.90	1.87	1.85	1.82	1.79	1.76
16	3.05	2.67	2.46	2.33	2.24	2.18	2.13	2.09	2.06	2.03	1.99	1.94	1.89	1.87	1.84	1.81	1.78	1.75	1.72
17	3.03	2.64	2.44	2.31	2.22	2.15	2.10	2.06	2.03	2.00	1.96	1.91	1.86	1.84	1.81	1.78	1.75	1.72	1.69
18	3.01	2.62	2.42	2.29	2.20	2.13	2.08	2.04	2.00	1.98	1.93	1.89	1.84	1.81	1.78	1.75	1.72	1.69	1.66
19	2.99	2.61	2.40	2.27	2.18	2.11	2.06	2.02	1.98	1.96	1.91	1.86	1.81	1.79	1.76	1.73	1.70	1.67	1.63
20	2.97	2.59	2.38	2.25	2.16	2.09	2.04	2.00	1.96	1.94	1.89	1.84	1.79	1.77	1.74	1.71	1.68	1.64	1.61
21	2.96	2.57	2.36	2.23	2.14	2.08	2.02	1.98	1.95	1.92	1.87	1.83	1.78	1.75	1.72	1.69	1.66	1.62	1.59
22	2.95	2.56	2.35	2.22	2.13	2.06	2.01	1.97	1.93	1.90	1.86	1.81	1.76	1.73	1.70	1.67	1.64	1.60	1.57
23	2.94	2.55	2.34	2.21	2.11	2.05	1.99	1.95	1.92	1.89	1.84	1.80	1.74	1.72	1.69	1.66	1.62	1.59	1.55
24	2.93	2.54	2.33	2.19	2.10	2.04	1.98	1.94	1.91	1.88	1.83	1.78	1.73	1.70	1.67	1.64	1.61	1.57	1.53
25	2.92	2.53	2.32	2.18	2.09	2.02	1.97	1.93	1.89	1.87	1.82	1.77	1.72	1.69	1.66	1.63	1.59	1.56	1.52
26	2.91	2.52	2.31	2.17	2.08	2.01	1.96	1.92	1.88	1.86	1.81	1.76	1.71	1.68	1.65	1.61	1.58	1.54	1.50
27	2.90	2.51	2.30	2.17	2.07	2.00	1.95	1.91	1.87	1.85	1.80	1.75	1.70	1.67	1.64	1.60	1.57	1.53	1.49
28	2.89	2.50	2.29	2.16	2.06	2.00	1.94	1.90	1.87	1.84	1.79	1.74	1.69	1.66	1.63	1.59	1.56	1.52	1.48
29	2.89	2.50	2.28	2.15	2.06	1.99	1.93	1.89	1.86	1.83	1.78	1.73	1.68	1.65	1.62	1.58	1.55	1.51	1.47
30	2.88	2.49	2.28	2.14	2.05	1.98	1.93	1.88	1.85	1.82	1.77	1.72	1.67	1.64	1.61	1.57	1.54	1.50	1.46
40	2.84	2.44	2.23	2.09	2.00	1.93	1.87	1.83	1.79	1.76	1.71	1.66	1.61	1.57	1.54	1.51	1.47	1.42	1.38
60	2.79	2.39	2.18	2.04	1.95	1.87	1.82	1.77	1.74	1.71	1.66	1.60	1.54	1.51	1.48	1.44	1.40	1.35	1.29
120	2.75	2.35	2.13	1.99	1.90	1.82	1.77	1.72	1.68	1.65	1.60	1.55	1.48	1.45	1.41	1.37	1.32	1.26	1.19
∞	2.71	2.30	2.08	1.94	1.85	1.77	1.72	1.67	1.63	1.60	1.55	1.49	1.42	1.38	1.34	1.30	1.24	1.17	1.00

Degrees of Freedom in the Denominator $(df = n - k)$

[1] The F statistic provides evidence on whether or not a statistically significant proportion of the total variation in the dependent variable Y has been explained. The F statistic can be calculated in terms of the coefficient of determination as: $F_{k-1, n-k} = R^2/(k-1) \div (1 - R^2)/n - k$, where R^2 is the coefficient of determination, k is the number of estimated coefficients in the regression model (including the intercept), and n is the number of data observations. When the critical F value is exceeded, we can conclude with a given level of confidence (e.g., α = 0.01 or 90 percent confidence) that the regression equation, taken as a whole, significantly explains the variation in Y.

TABLE C.2 (continued)

Critical *F* Values at the 95 Percent Confidence Level ($\alpha = .05$)

Degrees of Freedom in the Numerator ($df = k - 1$)

$df = n - k$	1	2	3	4	5	6	7	8	9	10	12	15	20	24	30	40	60	120	∞
1	161.4	199.5	215.7	224.6	230.2	234.0	236.8	238.9	240.5	241.9	243.9	245.9	248.0	249.1	250.1	251.1	252.2	253.3	254.3
2	18.51	19.00	19.16	19.25	19.30	19.33	19.35	19.37	19.38	19.40	19.41	19.43	19.45	19.45	19.46	19.47	19.48	19.49	19.50
3	10.13	9.55	9.28	9.12	9.01	8.94	8.89	8.85	8.81	8.79	8.74	8.70	8.66	8.64	8.62	8.59	8.57	8.55	8.53
4	7.71	6.94	6.59	6.39	6.26	6.16	6.09	6.04	6.00	5.96	5.91	5.86	5.80	5.77	5.75	5.72	5.69	5.66	5.63
5	6.61	5.79	5.41	5.19	5.05	4.95	4.88	4.82	4.77	4.74	4.68	4.62	4.56	4.53	4.50	4.46	4.43	4.40	4.36
6	5.99	5.14	4.76	4.53	4.39	4.28	4.21	4.15	4.10	4.06	4.00	3.94	3.87	3.84	3.81	3.77	3.74	3.70	3.67
7	5.59	4.74	4.35	4.12	3.97	3.87	3.79	3.73	3.68	3.64	3.57	3.51	3.44	3.41	3.38	3.34	3.30	3.27	3.23
8	5.32	4.46	4.07	3.84	3.69	3.58	3.50	3.44	3.39	3.35	3.28	3.22	3.15	3.12	3.08	3.04	.301	2.97	2.93
9	5.12	4.26	3.86	3.63	3.48	3.37	3.29	3.23	3.18	3.14	3.07	3.01	2.94	2.90	2.86	2.83	2.79	2.75	2.71
10	4.96	4.10	3.71	3.48	3.33	3.22	3.14	3.07	3.02	2.98	2.91	2.85	2.77	2.74	2.70	2.66	2.62	2.58	2.54
11	4.84	3.98	3.59	3.36	3.20	3.09	3.01	2.95	2.90	2.85	2.79	2.72	2.65	2.61	2.57	2.53	2.49	2.45	2.40
12	4.75	3.89	3.49	3.26	3.11	3.00	2.91	2.85	2.80	2.75	2.69	2.62	2.54	2.51	2.47	2.43	2.38	2.34	2.30
13	4.67	3.81	3.41	3.18	3.03	2.92	2.83	2.77	2.71	2.67	2.60	2.53	2.46	2.42	2.38	2.34	2.30	2.25	2.21
14	4.60	3.74	3.34	3.11	2.96	2.85	2.76	2.70	2.65	2.60	2.53	2.46	2.39	2.35	2.31	2.27	2.22	2.18	2.13
15	4.54	3.68	3.29	3.06	2.90	2.79	2.71	2.64	2.59	2.54	2.48	2.40	2.33	2.29	2.25	2.20	2.16	2.11	2.07
16	4.49	3.63	3.24	3.01	2.85	2.74	2.66	2.59	2.54	2.49	2.42	2.35	2.28	2.24	2.19	2.15	2.11	2.06	2.01
17	4.45	3.59	3.20	2.96	2.81	2.70	2.61	2.55	2.49	2.45	2.38	2.31	2.23	2.19	2.15	2.10	2.06	2.01	1.96
18	4.41	3.55	3.16	2.93	2.77	2.66	2.58	2.51	2.46	2.41	2.34	2.27	2.19	2.15	2.11	2.06	2.02	1.97	1.92
19	4.38	3.52	3.13	2.90	2.74	2.63	2.54	2.48	2.42	2.38	2.31	2.23	2.16	2.11	2.07	2.03	1.98	1.93	1.88
20	4.35	3.49	3.10	2.87	2.71	2.60	2.51	2.45	2.39	2.35	2.28	2.20	2.12	2.08	2.04	1.99	1.95	1.90	1.84
21	4.32	3.47	3.07	2.84	2.68	2.57	2.49	2.42	2.37	2.32	2.25	2.18	2.10	2.05	2.01	1.96	1.92	1.87	1.81
22	4.30	3.44	3.05	2.82	2.66	2.55	2.46	2.40	2.34	2.30	2.23	2.15	2.07	2.03	1.98	1.94	1.89	1.84	1.78
23	4.28	3.42	3.03	2.80	2.64	2.53	2.44	2.37	2.32	2.27	2.20	2.13	2.05	2.01	1.96	1.91	1.86	1.81	1.76
24	4.26	3.40	3.01	2.78	2.62	2.51	2.42	2.36	2.30	2.25	2.18	2.11	2.03	1.98	1.94	1.89	1.84	1.79	1.73
25	4.24	3.39	2.99	2.76	2.60	2.49	2.40	2.34	2.28	2.24	2.16	2.09	2.01	1.96	1.92	1.87	1.82	1.77	1.71
26	4.23	3.37	2.98	2.74	2.59	2.47	2.39	2.32	2.27	2.22	2.15	2.07	1.99	1.95	1.90	1.85	1.80	1.75	1.69
27	4.21	3.35	2.96	2.73	2.57	2.46	2.37	2.31	2.25	2.20	2.13	2.06	1.97	1.93	1.88	1.84	1.79	1.73	1.67
28	4.20	3.34	2.95	2.71	2.56	2.45	2.36	2.29	2.24	2.19	2.12	2.04	1.96	1.91	1.87	1.82	1.77	1.71	1.65
29	4.18	3.33	2.93	2.70	2.55	2.43	2.35	2.28	2.22	2.18	2.10	2.03	1.94	1.90	1.85	1.81	1.75	1.70	1.64
30	4.17	3.32	2.92	2.69	2.53	2.42	2.33	2.27	2.21	2.16	2.09	2.01	1.93	1.89	1.84	1.79	1.74	1.68	1.62
40	4.08	3.23	2.84	2.61	2.45	2.34	2.25	2.18	2.12	2.08	2.00	1.92	1.84	1.79	1.74	1.69	1.64	1.58	1.51
60	4.00	3.15	2.76	2.53	2.37	2.25	2.17	2.10	2.04	1.99	1.92	1.84	1.75	1.70	1.65	1.59	1.53	1.47	1.39
120	3.92	3.07	2.68	2.45	2.29	2.17	2.09	2.02	1.96	1.91	1.83	1.75	1.66	1.61	1.55	1.50	1.43	1.35	1.25
∞	3.84	3.00	2.60	2.37	2.21	2.10	2.01	1.94	1.88	1.83	1.75	1.67	1.57	1.52	1.46	1.39	1.32	1.22	1.00

Degrees of Freedom in the Denominator ($df = n - k$)

TABLE C.2 (continued)

Critical *F* Values at the 99 Percent Confidence Level ($\alpha = .01$)

Denom. df ($df = n - k$)																			
	1	**2**	**3**	**4**	**5**	**6**	**7**	**8**	**9**	**10**	**12**	**15**	**20**	**24**	**30**	**40**	**60**	**120**	**∞**
1	4052	4999.5	5403	5625	5764	5859	5928	5982	6022	6056	6106	6157	6209	6235	6261	6287	6313	6339	6336
2	98.50	99.00	99.17	99.25	99.30	99.33	99.36	99.37	99.39	99.40	99.42	99.43	99.45	99.46	99.47	99.47	99.48	99.49	99.50
3	34.12	30.82	29.46	28.71	28.24	27.91	27.67	27.49	27.35	27.23	27.05	26.87	26.69	26.60	26.50	26.41	26.32	26.22	26.13
4	21.20	18.00	16.69	15.98	15.52	15.21	14.98	14.80	14.66	14.55	14.37	14.20	14.02	13.93	13.84	13.75	13.65	13.56	13.46
5	16.26	13.27	12.06	11.39	10.97	10.67	10.46	10.29	10.16	10.05	9.89	9.72	9.55	9.47	9.38	9.29	9.20	9.11	9.02
6	13.75	10.92	9.78	9.15	8.75	8.47	8.26	8.10	7.98	7.87	7.72	7.56	7.40	7.31	7.23	7.14	7.06	6.97	6.88
7	12.25	9.55	8.45	7.85	7.46	7.19	6.99	6.84	6.72	6.62	6.47	6.31	6.16	6.07	5.99	5.91	5.82	5.74	5.65
8	11.26	8.65	7.59	7.01	6.63	6.37	6.18	6.03	5.91	5.81	5.67	5.52	5.36	5.28	5.20	5.12	5.03	4.95	4.86
9	10.56	8.02	6.99	6.42	6.06	5.80	5.61	5.47	5.35	5.26	5.11	4.96	4.81	4.73	4.65	4.57	4.48	4.40	4.31
10	10.04	7.56	6.55	5.99	5.64	5.39	5.20	5.06	4.94	4.85	4.71	4.56	4.41	4.33	4.25	4.17	4.08	4.00	3.91
11	9.65	7.21	6.22	5.67	5.32	5.07	4.89	4.74	4.63	4.54	4.40	4.25	4.10	4.02	3.94	3.86	3.78	3.69	3.60
12	9.33	6.93	5.95	5.41	5.06	4.82	4.64	4.50	4.39	4.30	4.16	4.01	3.86	3.78	3.70	3.62	3.54	3.45	3.36
13	9.07	6.70	5.74	5.21	4.86	4.62	4.44	4.30	4.19	4.10	3.96	3.82	3.66	3.59	3.51	3.43	3.34	3.25	3.17
14	8.86	6.51	5.56	5.04	4.69	4.46	4.28	4.14	4.03	3.94	3.80	3.66	3.51	3.43	3.35	3.27	3.18	3.09	3.00
15	8.68	6.36	5.42	4.89	4.56	4.32	4.14	4.00	3.89	3.80	3.67	3.52	3.37	3.29	3.21	3.13	3.05	2.96	2.87
16	8.53	6.23	5.29	4.77	4.44	4.20	4.03	3.89	3.78	3.69	3.55	3.41	3.26	3.18	3.10	3.02	2.93	2.84	2.75
17	8.40	6.11	5.18	4.67	4.34	4.10	3.93	3.79	3.68	3.59	3.46	3.31	3.16	3.08	3.00	2.92	2.83	2.75	2.65
18	8.29	6.01	5.09	4.58	4.25	4.01	3.84	3.71	3.60	3.51	3.37	3.23	3.08	3.00	2.92	2.84	2.75	2.66	2.57
19	8.18	5.93	5.01	4.50	4.17	3.94	3.77	3.63	3.52	3.43	3.30	3.15	3.00	2.92	2.84	2.76	2.67	2.58	2.49
20	8.10	5.85	4.94	4.43	4.10	3.87	3.70	3.56	3.46	3.37	3.23	3.09	2.94	2.86	2.78	2.69	2.61	2.52	2.42
21	8.02	5.78	4.87	4.37	4.04	3.81	3.64	3.51	3.40	3.31	3.17	3.03	2.88	2.80	2.72	2.64	2.55	2.46	2.36
22	7.95	5.72	4.82	4.31	3.99	3.76	3.59	3.45	3.35	3.26	3.12	2.98	2.83	2.75	2.67	2.58	2.50	2.40	2.31
23	7.88	5.66	4.76	4.26	3.94	3.71	3.54	3.41	3.30	3.21	3.07	2.93	2.78	2.70	2.62	2.54	2.45	2.35	2.26
24	7.82	5.61	4.72	4.22	3.90	3.67	3.50	3.36	3.26	3.17	3.03	2.89	2.74	2.66	2.58	2.49	2.40	2.31	2.21
25	7.77	5.57	4.68	4.18	3.85	3.63	3.46	3.32	3.22	3.13	2.99	2.85	2.70	2.62	2.54	2.45	2.36	2.27	2.17
26	7.72	5.53	4.64	4.14	3.82	3.59	3.42	3.29	3.18	3.09	2.96	2.81	2.66	2.58	2.50	2.42	2.33	2.23	2.13
27	7.68	5.49	4.60	4.11	3.78	3.56	3.39	3.26	3.15	3.06	2.93	2.78	2.63	2.55	2.47	2.38	2.29	2.20	2.10
28	7.64	5.45	4.57	4.07	3.75	3.53	3.36	3.23	3.12	3.03	2.90	2.75	2.60	2.52	2.44	2.35	2.26	2.17	2.06
29	7.60	5.42	4.54	4.04	3.73	3.50	3.33	3.20	3.09	3.00	2.87	2.73	2.57	2.49	2.41	2.33	2.23	2.14	2.03
30	7.56	5.39	4.51	4.02	3.70	3.47	3.30	3.17	3.07	2.98	2.84	2.70	2.55	2.47	2.39	2.30	2.21	2.11	2.01
40	7.31	5.18	4.31	3.83	3.51	3.29	3.12	2.99	2.89	2.80	2.66	2.52	2.37	2.29	2.20	2.11	2.02	1.92	1.80
60	7.08	4.98	4.13	3.65	3.34	3.12	2.95	2.82	2.72	2.63	2.50	2.35	2.20	2.12	2.03	1.94	1.84	1.73	1.60
120	6.85	4.79	3.95	3.48	3.17	2.96	2.79	2.66	2.56	2.47	2.34	2.19	2.03	1.95	1.86	1.76	1.66	1.53	1.38
∞	6.63	4.61	3.78	3.32	3.02	2.80	2.64	2.51	2.41	2.32	2.18	2.04	1.88	1.79	1.70	1.59	1.47	1.32	1.00

Degrees of Freedom in the Numerator ($df = k - 1$)

Degrees of Freedom in the Denominator ($df = n - k$)

TABLE C.3

Students' *T* Distribution[1]

Degrees of Freedom	Area in the Rejection Region (Two-Tail Test)												
	0.9	0.8	0.7	0.6	0.5	0.4	0.3	0.2	0.1	0.05	0.02	0.01	0.001
1	0.158	0.325	0.510	0.727	1.000	1.376	1.963	3.078	**6.314**	**12.706**	31.821	**63.657**	636.619
2	0.142	0.289	0.445	0.617	0.816	1.061	1.386	1.886	**2.920**	**4.303**	6.965	**9.925**	31.598
3	0.137	0.277	0.424	0.584	0.765	0.978	1.250	1.638	**2.353**	**3.182**	4.541	**5.841**	12.924
4	0.134	0.271	0.414	0.569	0.741	0.941	1.190	1.533	**2.132**	**2.776**	3.747	**4.604**	8.610
5	0.132	0.267	0.408	0.559	0.727	0.920	1.156	1.476	**2.015**	**2.571**	3.365	**4.032**	6.869
6	0.131	0.265	0.404	0.553	0.718	0.906	1.134	1.440	**1.943**	**2.447**	3.143	**3.707**	5.959
7	0.130	0.263	0.402	0.549	0.711	0.896	1.119	1.415	**1.895**	**2.365**	2.998	**3.499**	5.408
8	0.130	0.262	0.399	0.546	0.706	0.889	1.108	1.397	**1.860**	**2.306**	2.896	**3.355**	5.041
9	0.129	0.261	0.398	0.543	0.703	0.883	1.100	1.383	**1.833**	**2.262**	2.821	**3.250**	4.781
10	0.129	0.260	0.397	0.542	0.700	0.879	1.093	1.372	**1.812**	**2.228**	2.764	**3.169**	4.587
11	0.129	0.260	0.396	0.540	0.697	0.876	1.088	1.363	**1.796**	**2.201**	2.718	**3.106**	4.437
12	0.128	0.259	0.395	0.539	0.695	0.873	1.083	1.356	**1.782**	**2.179**	2.681	**3.055**	4.318
13	0.128	0.259	0.394	0.538	0.694	0.870	1.079	1.350	**1.771**	**2.160**	2.650	**3.012**	4.221
14	0.128	0.258	0.393	0.537	0.692	0.868	1.076	1.345	**1.761**	**2.145**	2.624	**2.977**	4.140
15	0.128	0.258	0.393	0.536	0.691	0.866	1.074	1.341	**1.753**	**2.131**	2.602	**2.947**	4.073
16	0.128	0.258	0.392	0.535	0.690	0.865	1.071	1.337	**1.746**	**2.120**	2.583	**2.921**	4.015
17	0.128	0.257	0.392	0.534	0.689	0.863	1.069	1.333	**1.740**	**2.110**	2.567	**2.898**	3.965
18	0.127	0.257	0.392	0.534	0.688	0.862	1.067	1.330	**1.734**	**2.101**	2.552	**2.878**	3.922
19	0.127	0.257	0.391	0.533	0.688	0.861	1.066	1.328	**1.729**	**2.093**	2.539	**2.861**	3.883
20	0.127	0.257	0.391	0.533	0.687	0.860	1.064	1.325	**1.725**	**2.086**	2.528	**2.845**	3.850
21	0.127	0.257	0.391	0.532	0.686	0.859	1.063	1.323	**1.721**	**2.080**	2.518	**2.831**	3.819
22	0.127	0.256	0.390	0.532	0.686	0.858	1.061	1.321	**1.717**	**2.074**	2.508	**2.819**	3.792
23	0.127	0.256	0.390	0.532	0.685	0.858	1.060	1.319	**1.714**	**2.069**	2.500	**2.807**	3.767
24	0.127	0.256	0.390	0.531	0.685	0.857	1.059	1.318	**1.711**	**2.064**	2.492	**2.797**	3.745
25	0.127	0.256	0.390	0.531	0.684	0.856	1.058	1.316	**1.708**	**2.060**	2.485	**2.787**	3.725
26	0.127	0.256	0.390	0.531	0.684	0.856	1.058	1.315	**1.706**	**2.056**	2.479	**2.779**	3.707
27	0.127	0.256	0.389	0.531	0.684	0.855	1.057	1.314	**1.703**	**2.052**	2.473	**2.771**	3.690
28	0.127	0.256	0.389	0.530	0.683	0.855	1.056	1.313	**1.701**	**2.048**	2.467	**2.763**	3.674
29	0.127	0.256	0.389	0.530	0.683	0.854	1.055	1.311	**1.699**	**2.045**	2.462	**2.756**	3.659
30	0.127	0.256	0.389	0.530	0.683	0.854	1.055	1.310	**1.697**	**2.042**	2.457	**2.750**	3.646
40	0.126	0.255	0.388	0.529	0.681	0.851	1.050	1.303	**1.684**	**2.021**	2.423	**2.704**	3.551
60	0.126	0.254	0.387	0.527	0.679	0.848	1.046	1.296	**1.671**	**2.000**	2.390	**2.660**	3.460
120	0.126	0.254	0.386	0.526	0.677	0.845	1.041	1.289	**1.658**	**1.980**	2.358	**2.617**	3.373
∞	0.126	0.253	0.385	0.524	0.674	0.842	1.036	1.282	**1.645**	**1.960**	2.326	**2.576**	3.291

[1] Columns in bold-face type indicate critical *t* values for popular levels of significance for two-tail hypothesis testing. Thus, critical *t* values for $\alpha = 0.1$ (90 percent confidence), $\alpha = 0.05$ (95 percent confidence), and $\alpha = 0.01$ (99 percent confidence) are highlighted. When the calculated *t* statistic $= b/\sigma_b$ exceeds the relevant critical *t* value, we can reject the hypothesis that there is no relationship between the dependent variable *Y* and a given independent variable *X*. For simple *t* tests, the relevant number of degrees of freedom (column row) is found as follows: $df = n - k$, where *n* is the number of data observations and *k* is the number of estimated coefficients (including the intercept).

Selected Check Figures for End-of-Chapter Problems

2.1
B. $Q = 5$

2.2
B. $Q = 5$
C. $Q = 8$

2.4
B. $ME = 5, NH = 3, VT = 2$
C. Commission income = $4,000

2.5
B. $I = 3$
C. $I = 4$

2.6
A. $Q = 8,000$
B. $\pi = \$50,000$

2.7
A. $Q = 25,000$
B. $\pi = \$625,000, MGN = 3.3\%$

2.8
A. $Q = 4,000$, Surplus = $500,000
B. $Q = 3,800$, Surplus = $110,000
C. $Q = 4,000$, Surplus = $100,000

2.9
A. $Q = 500, P = \$500, \pi = \$150,000$
B. $Q = 450, P = \$550, \pi = \$152,500$

2.10
A. $Q = 55,000, MC = \$1,240, AC = \$1,240,$
   $P = \$1,470, \pi = \$12,650,000$
B. $Q = 50,000, MC = \$1,200, AC = \$1,242,$
   $P = \$1,500, \pi = \$12,900,000$

3.2
A. $P = \$10$
B. $P = \$1$
C. $P = \$4, Q = 300,000$

3.5
A. $Q = 15,000$
B. $Q = 22,500$

3.6
B. $Q = 20,000, TR = \$2,000,000$

3.7
B. $P = \$50, Q = 0$
   $P = \$60, Q = 5,000,000$
   $P = \$70, Q = 10,000,000$
C. $Q = 4,000,000, P = \$58$
   $Q = 6,000,000, P = \$62$
   $Q = 8,000,000, P = \$66$

3.8
B. $P = \$325, Q_O = 0, Q_P = 875,000$
   $P = \$350, Q_O = 0, Q_P = 1,000,000$
   $P = \$375, Q_O = 500,000, Q_P = 1,125,000$

3.9
B. $P = \$8, Q_C = 0, Q_P = 0$
   $P = \$10, Q_C = 0, Q_P = 250$
   $P = \$12, Q_C = 500, Q_P = 500$

3.10
B. $P = \$1.50$, Shortage = 50,000,000
   $P = \$2$, Surplus = Shortage = 0
   $P = \$2.50$, Surplus = 50,000,000
C. $P = \$2, Q = 50,000,000$

4.1
C. $G = 2$

4.2
B. $S = 4$
C. $G = 4$
D. $G = 2$, $S = 4$

4.3
B. 20¢ per util
C. $P = \$10$, $G = 1$
$P = \$8$, $G = 2$
$P = \$6$, $G = 3$
$P = \$4$, $G = 4$
$P = \$2$, $G = 5$

4.5
A. $Q = 600$
B. $P = \$3$
C. $P = \$7.50$
D. $Q = 1,500$
E. $\epsilon_P = -2$

4.6
A. $\epsilon_P = -4$
B. $P = \$14,500$

4.7
A. $E_P = -2$
B. $E_{PX} = -2.67$

4.8
A. $E_I = 6$
B. $E_P = -8$

4.9
A. $E_{PX} = 1.5$
B. $E_P = -3$
C. $\Delta P = -\$20$

4.10
A. $E_P = -2$
B. $\Delta P = -\$2$
C. $E_A = 1$

5.3
A. $Q = 250,000 - 25P$

5.4
A. Demand: $P = \$20 - \$0.005Q_D + \$10T$
Supply: $P = \$10 + \$0.005Q_S$

5.5
C. $\epsilon_A = 1$
D. $Pr = 50\%$

6.1
A. $g = 3.1\%$
B. $g = 3.0\%$

6.2
B. $g = 7.23\%$
C. $g = 7.4\%$

6.3
A. $g = 10\%$
B. $S_5 = \$104,715,000$, $S_{10} = \$168,610,000$

6.4
A. $g = 7.4\%$
B. $t = 2$ years

6.5
B. $A_t = 80$

6.6
B. $S_{t+1} = \$295,000$

6.7
B. $D_{t+1} = 375$

6.8
B. $S_{t+1} = 12,500$

6.9
B. Regular price: $TR = \$6,400$
Special price: $TR = \$12,450$
C. Regular price: $\pi = \$2,645$
Special price: $\pi = \$6,247.50$

6.10
$I = \$1,800$ billion
$GDP = \$11,000$ billion
$C = \$7,530$ billion
$T = \$1,760$ billion
$Y = \$9,240$ billion

7.1
C. $Y = 3$

7.5
A. Doyle = 3.75%, Moon = 4.5%,
M. Crane = 4%, N. Crane = 3.33%
B. Doyle = \$8,000, Moon = \$5,000,
M. Crane = \$4,500, N. Crane = \$3,750

7.6
B. Inquiries = 4,000

7.7
B. Attendants = 3
C. Wage = \$140

7.8
C. Advertising = 50

7.9
A. $MRP_P = \$156,250$, $MRP_A = \$87,500$

7.10
A. $\Delta Q/Q = -1.12\%$
B. $\Delta Q/Q = -2.88\%$

8.1
A. $X = 0$ to $X = 2$
B. $X = 3$
C. Minimum $AC = \$1.25$
D. $MC = \$1.25$

8.4
A. $\pi = \$175,000$

8.5
C. $Q_{BE} = 15,000$

8.6
A. $\Delta Q = 20,000$
B. $E_P = -3$

8.7
A. $Q_{BE} = 1,000$
B. $\epsilon_C = 0.82$

8.8
A. $Q_M = 60,000$
   $Q_N = 55,000$
   $Q_D = 47,500$

8.9
A. $TC = \$450,000$, $AC = \$112.50$
B. Learning = $-\$5.50$, or 5%

8.10
A. $\Delta Q_{BE} = 250,000$
B. $\Delta DOL = 0.4$
C. $\Delta \pi = \$1,000,000$

9.2
A. $L = 4$, $K = 400$, $Q = 1$
   $L = 16$, $K = 1,600$, $Q = 4$
B. $\Delta MP_L = -0.0625$, $\Delta MP_K = -0.000625$
C. $Q = 1,000$
D. $MP_L = 0.25$, $MP_K = 0$

9.3
C. $\pi = \$2,350$

9.4
B. $A = 1$, $B = 4$, $L_F = 4$, $L_R = 0$, $L_{FC} = 0$,
   $C = \$240,000$
C. $\Delta TC = -\$32,000$
D. $\Delta C_A > \$120,000$

9.5
B. $C = \$50,000,000$, $P = \$50,000,000$,
   $S_D = \$0$, $S_B = \$100,000,000$,
   $S_C = \$25,000,000$, $S_A = \$0$, $\pi = \$1,750,000$

9.6
B. $I = 0.75$, $J = 0.25$, $L_I = 0$, $L_J = 0.05$,
   $L_L = 0$, $i = 0.0975$
C. $\Delta R_J > -3\%$
D. Maximum cash = 20%

9.7
B. $E = 30$, $W = 40$, $S_H = 0$, $S_S = 0.15$,
   $S_P = 0$, $C = \$2,500$
C. $\Delta P_W = \$12.50$

9.8
B. $I = 120$, $C = 40$, $S_A = 0$, $S_B = 80$,
   $S_S = 0$, $\pi = \$18,000$
C. $\pi = \$1,900$
D. $\pi = \$5,500$
E. $L_I = L_C = 0$, $V_A = \$50$, $V_B = \$0$,
   $V_S = \$50$, $\pi^* = \$18,000$

9.9
B. $Q_1 = 5$, $Q_2 = 3$, $S_D = 0$, $S_A = 5$,
   $S_{AR} = 0$, $R = \$21,000$
   $L_1 = L_2 = 0$, $V_D = \$125$, $V_A = \$0$,
   $V_{AR} = \$250$, $R^* = \$21,000$

9.10
B. $Q_A = 0$, $Q_B = 2$, $Q_C = 2$, $S_L = S_P = 0$, $Q = 4$
   $L_A = 0.625$, $L_B = L_C = 0$, $V_L = 0.125$,
   $V_P = 0.375$, $Q^* = 4$

10.2
B. $P = MC = \$50$
C. $P = \$75$, $Q = 3$
   $P = \$100$, $Q = 6$

10.3
B. $P = \$6.25$, $Q = 50$
C. Excess supply = 18

10.4

A. $Q = 5,000$, $P = \$400$
$Q = 10,000$, $P = \$600$
$Q = 15,000$, $P = \$800$

B. $P = \$200$, $Q = 0$
$P = \$500$, $Q = 7,500$
$P = \$1,000$, $Q = 20,000$

10.5

C. $Q_S = 31,250,000$

10.6

A. $Q = 200,000$, $\pi = \$3,000,000$
B. $Q = 50,000$, $\pi = -\$750,000$
C. $Q = 100,000$, $P = \$40$, $\pi = \$0$

10.7

A. $P = \$200$, $Q = 100,000$
B. $\pi = \$5,000,000$, $MGN = 25\%$

10.8

A. $Q = 1,000,000$, $P = \$10$, $\pi = \$5,000,000$
B. $P = MC = \$5$, $\pi = 0$

10.9

A. $Q = 100,000$, $P = \$5,000$, $\pi = \$50,000,000$
B. $Q = 200,000$, $P = \$4,500$, $\pi = \$0$

10.10

A $Q = 150,000$, $P = \$3.50$, $\pi = \$287,500$
B. $Q = 100,000$, $P = \$1.50$, $\pi = \$0$

11.3

B. $Q = 6,000,000$, $P = \$14$, $\pi = \$0$
C. $Q = 9,000,000$, $P = \$11$, $\pi = \$0$
D. $Q = 3,000,000$, $P = \$17$, $\pi = \$9,000,000$

11.4

A. $Q = 12$, $P = \$36$ million, $\pi = \$88$ million,
$\epsilon_P = -2$
B. High-price/low-output:
$Q = 10$, $P = \$31$ million, $\pi = \$0$
Low-price/high-output:
$Q = 20$, $P = \$26$ million, $\pi = 0$
C. $Q_2 = 16.2$, high-price/low-output
$Q_2 = 23.4$, low-price/high-output

11.6

A. $P = \$2$, $Q = 40,000$
B. $P = \$3.60$, $Q = 24,000$

11.7

C. $P = \$50$, $Q = 10(000)$, $\pi = \$150(000)$

11.8

A. $P_A > \$250$, $P_B > \$200$

11.9

A. $P = \$4.50$, $Q = 7,000$
B. $P = \$4.65$, $Q = 8,375$

11.10

C. $Q_L = 40,000$, $P_L = \$23$
D. $P = \$23$, $Q_M = 6,000$, $Q_N = 4,000$

12.3

A. $\epsilon_P = -5$
B. $P = \$150$

12.4

A. $E_P = -3.5$
B. Optimal markup on cost = 40%,
$P = \$11.99$

12.5

A. $P = \$2,875,000 + \epsilon$
B. $P = \$2,701,000 + \epsilon$

12.6

A. $\pi_1 = \$112,000$, $\pi_2 = \$104,000$

12.7

A. $Q_W = 500$, $P_W = \$12,500$, $Q_R = 1,000$,
$P_R = \$30,000$, $\pi = \$21,250,000$
B. $\epsilon_{WP} = -5$, $\epsilon_{RP} = -1.5$

12.8

A. $P = \$45$, $Q = 10$, $\pi = \$400$, $CS = \$200$
B. $P = \$5$, $Q = 20$, Membership = $800,
$\pi = \$800$
C. $\pi = \$300,000$

12.9

A. $Q_S = Q_L = 20,000$, $P_S = \$10.40$, $P_L = \$0.30$
B. $Q_S = 150,000$, $P_S = \$32.50$, $Q_L = 40,000$,
$P_L = 20¢$

12.10

A. $Q = 10,000$, $P = \$850$, $\pi = \$500,000$
B. $P_T = \$600$
C. $Q_{NA} = 8,500$, $P_{NA} = \$872.50$, $Q_E = 6,000$,
$P_E = \$645$, $\pi = \$635,000$

13.5

A. $HHI_A = 2,850$, $\Delta HHI_A = 150$
$HHI_B = 1,602$, $\Delta HHI_B = 120$
$HHI_C = 840$, $\Delta HHI_C = 128$,
$HHI_D = 3,334$, $\Delta HHI_D = 40$

13.6

A. $Q_L = 400$, $P_L = \$10,000$, $Q_H = 2,500$,
$P_H = \$7,500$, $\pi = \$3,250,000$
B. $Q_L = 360$, $P_L = \$10,500$, $Q_H = 2,000$,
$P_H = \$8,000$, $\pi = \$620,000$
C. $\epsilon_{PL} = -2$, $\epsilon_{PH} = -3$

13.7

A. $Q = 100,000$, $\pi = \$0$

B. $Q = 100,000$, $\pi = \$0$

C. $Q = 75,000$, $\pi = -\$437,500$ (a loss)

13.8

A. $Q = 10,000$, $P = \$11,500$, $\pi = \$8,000,000$

B. $Q = 9,000$, $P = \$11,730$, $\pi = \$3,630,000$

13.9

A. $Q = 1,600$, $P_M = \$24$, $P_A = \$288$, $i = 12.5\%$

B. $Q = 1,800$, $i = 12.25\%$

C. $Q = 2,000$, $P_M = \$20$

13.10

A. $Q = 10,000$, $P = \$4,500$, $D = 1,000,000$,
   $\pi = \$2,000,000$

B. $Q = 9,500$, $P = \$4,575$, $D = 950,000$,
   $\pi = \$50,000$

C. $Q = 7,600$, $P = \$4,860$, $D = 0$,
   $\pi = -\$3,560,000$ (a loss)

14.3

A. $E(NC) = \$125$

14.4

A. $E(\pi_{MA}) = \$1,000,000$, $E(\pi_{PS}) = \$750,000$

14.5

A. $E(\pi_1) = \$500,000$, $E(\pi_2) = \$375,000$

C. $\sigma_1 = \$300,000$, $\sigma_2 = \$125,000$

D. $E(u_1) = 1,172$, $E(u_2) = 1,162.50$

14.6

A. $E(CF_1) = \$10,000$, $E(CF_2) = \$10,000$

B. $\sigma_1 = \$3,000$, $\sigma_2 = \$1,000$

C. $NPV_1 = \$5,000$, $NPV_2 = \$7,500$

14.7

A. $E(\pi_A) = \$150,000$, $\sigma_A = \$50,000$,
   $V_A = 0.33$, $E(\pi_{SF}) = \$200,000$,
   $\sigma_{SF} = \$140,000$, $V_{SF} = 0.7$

B. $\alpha_A = 0.8$, $\alpha_{SF} = 0.85$

14.8

A. $Pr = 40\%$

14.9

A. $Pr = 50\%$

B. $P = \$23.29$

C. $Pr = 93.32\%$

15.5

A. $NPV_{LB} = \$500,000$, $NPV_{SD} = \$600,000$

B. $PI_{LB} = 1.25$, $PI_{SD} = 1.2$

15.6

A. $E(CF_1) = \$1,000,000$, $\sigma_1 = \$200,000$,
   $V_1 = 0.2$, $E(CF_2) = \$900,000$,
   $\sigma_2 = \$360,000$, $V_2 = 0.4$

B. $NPV_1 = \$1,192,500$, $NPV_2 = -\$362,640$
   (a loss)

C. $PI_1 = 1.40$, $PI_2 = 0.88$

15.7

A. $E(CF_{A1}) = \$50,000$, $\sigma_{A1} = \$30,000$, $V_{A1} = 0.6$
   $E(CF_{A2}) = \$50,000$, $\sigma_{A2} = \$20,000$, $V_{A2} = 0.4$
   $E(CF_{B1}) = \$100,000$, $\sigma_{B1} = \$100,000$, $V_{B1} = 1$
   $E(CF_{B2}) = \$100,000$, $\sigma_{B2} = \$50,000$, $V_{B2} = 0.5$

B. $NPV_A = \$9,505$, $NPV_B = \$12,570$

C. $PI_A = 1.13$, $PI_B = 1.08$

D. $IRR_A = IRR_B = 21.6\%$

15.8

A. $CF = \$8,000$

15.9

A. Net cash inflow:
   $A = \$1,576,667$, $B = \$1,603,333$,
   $C = \$1,323,333$

B. $NPV_A = \$1,131,132$, $NPV_B = \$1,034,830$,
   $NPV_C = \$1,146,003$

15.10

A. $k_e = 20\%$

B. $k = 16.95\%$

17.7

B. Social rate of discount = 8.3%

Index